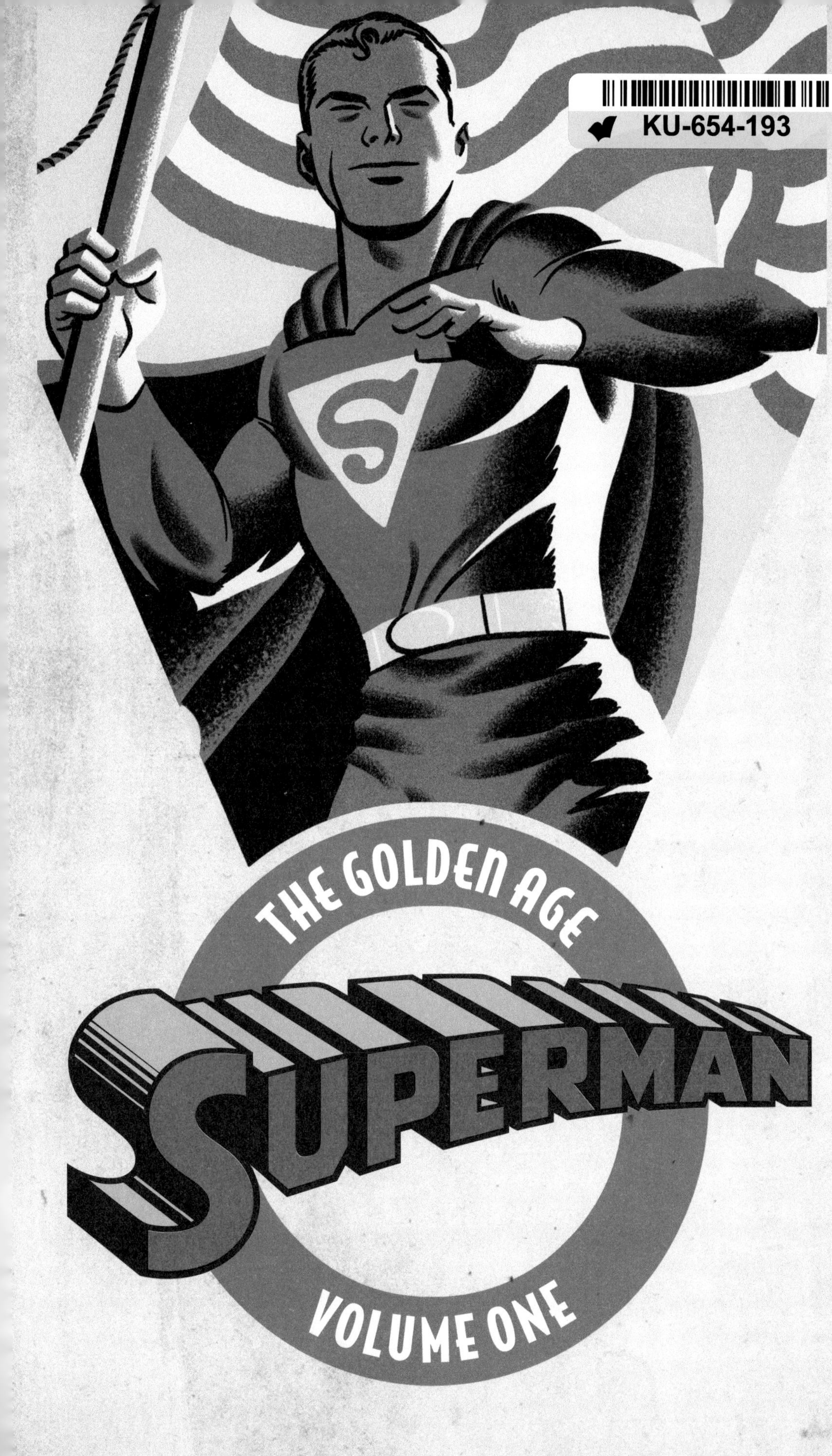

THE GOLDEN AGE SUPERMAN

VOLUME ONE

JERRY SIEGEL
WRITER

JOE SHUSTER
ARTIST

MICHAEL CHO
COVER ARTIST

SUPERMAN created by JERRY SIEGEL and JOE SHUSTER.
By special arrangement with the Jerry Siegel family.

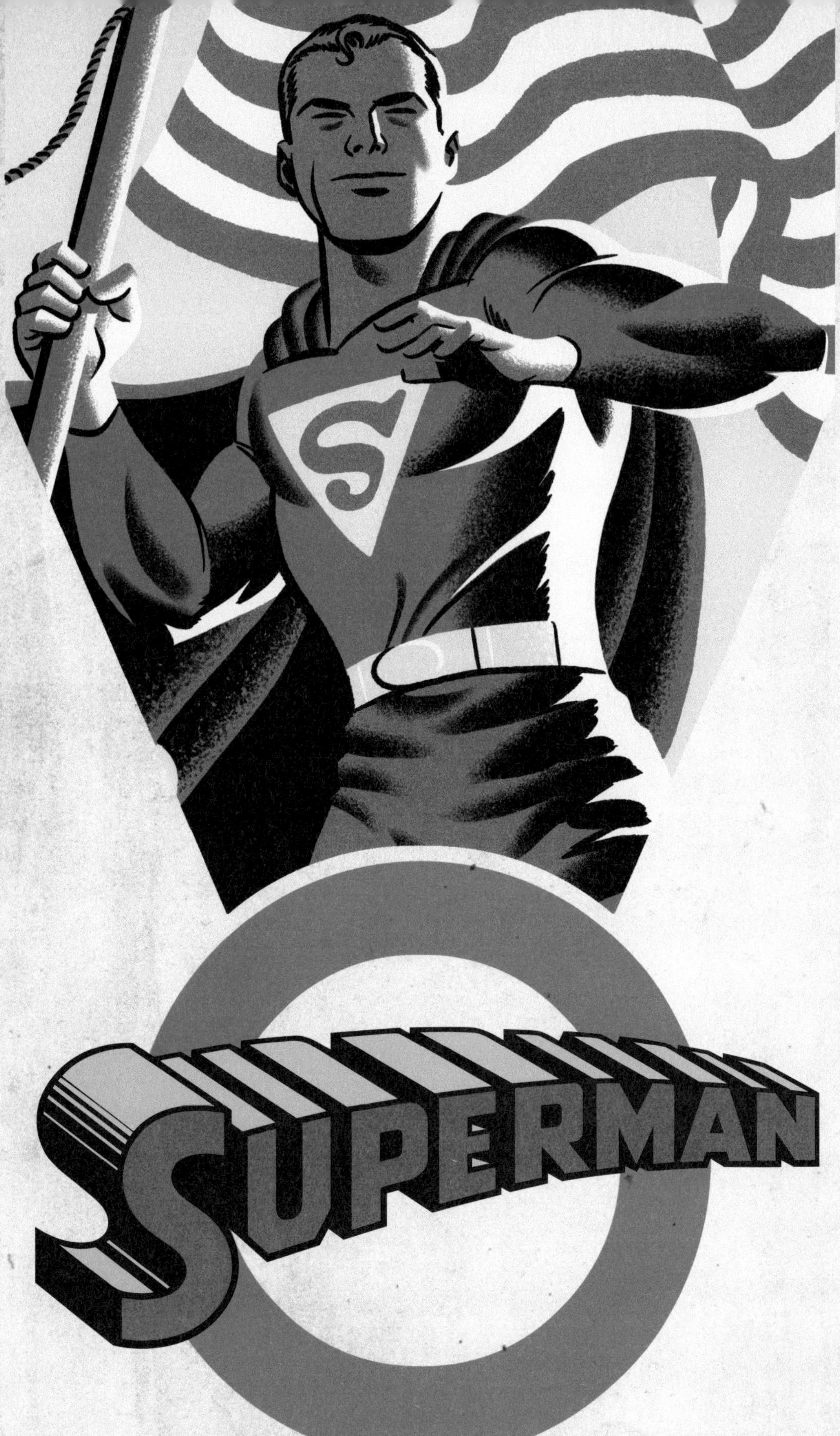
SUPERMAN

VINCENT SULLIVAN, WHITNEY ELLSWORTH Editors – Original Series
JEB WOODARD Group Editor – Collected Editions   PAUL SANTOS Editor – Collected Edition
STEVE COOK Design Director – Books   LOUIS PRANDI Publication Design

BOB HARRAS Senior VP – Editor-in-Chief, DC Comics

President DIANE NELSON
Co-Publishers DAN DIDIO and JIM LEE
Chief Creative Officer GEOFF JOHNS
Senior VP – Marketing & Global Franchise Management AMIT DESAI
Senior VP – Finance NAIRI GARDINER
VP – Digital Marketing SAM ADES
VP – Talent Development BOBBIE CHASE
Senior VP – Art, Design & Collected Editions MARK CHIARELLO
VP – Content Strategy JOHN CUNNINGHAM
VP – Strategy Planning & Reporting ANNE DEPIES
VP – Manufacturing Operations DON FALLETTI
VP – Editorial Administration & Talent Relations LAWRENCE GANEM

ALISON GILL Senior VP – Manufacturing & Operations
HANK KANALZ Senior VP – Editorial Strategy & Administration
JAY KOGAN VP – Legal Affairs
DEREK MADDALENA Senior VP – Sales & Business Development
JACK MAHAN VP – Business Affairs
DAN MIRON VP – Sales Planning & Trade Development
NICK NAPOLITANO VP – Manufacturing Administration
CAROL ROEDER VP – Marketing
EDDIE SCANNELL VP – Mass Account & Digital Sales
COURTNEY SIMMONS Senior VP – Publicity & Communications
JIM (SKI) SOKOLOWSKI VP – Comic Book Specialty & Newsstand Sales
SANDY YI Senior VP – Global Franchise Management

SUPERMAN: THE GOLDEN AGE VOLUME 1

DC Comics, 2900 West Alameda Ave., Burbank, CA 91505
Printed by RR Donnelley, Salem, VA, USA. 2/12/16. First Printing.
ISBN: 978-1-4012-6109-2

Library of Congress Cataloging-in-Publication Data is Available.

MIX
Paper from
responsible sources
FSC
www.fsc.org
FSC® C101537

All stories by **JERRY SIEGEL** and all art by **JOE SHUSTER**.

*These titles were originally untitled and are titled here for reader convenience.

DC strives to be as thorough as possible in its effort to determine creators' identities from all available sources.
This process is not perfect, and as a result, some attributions may be incomplete or wrongly assigned.

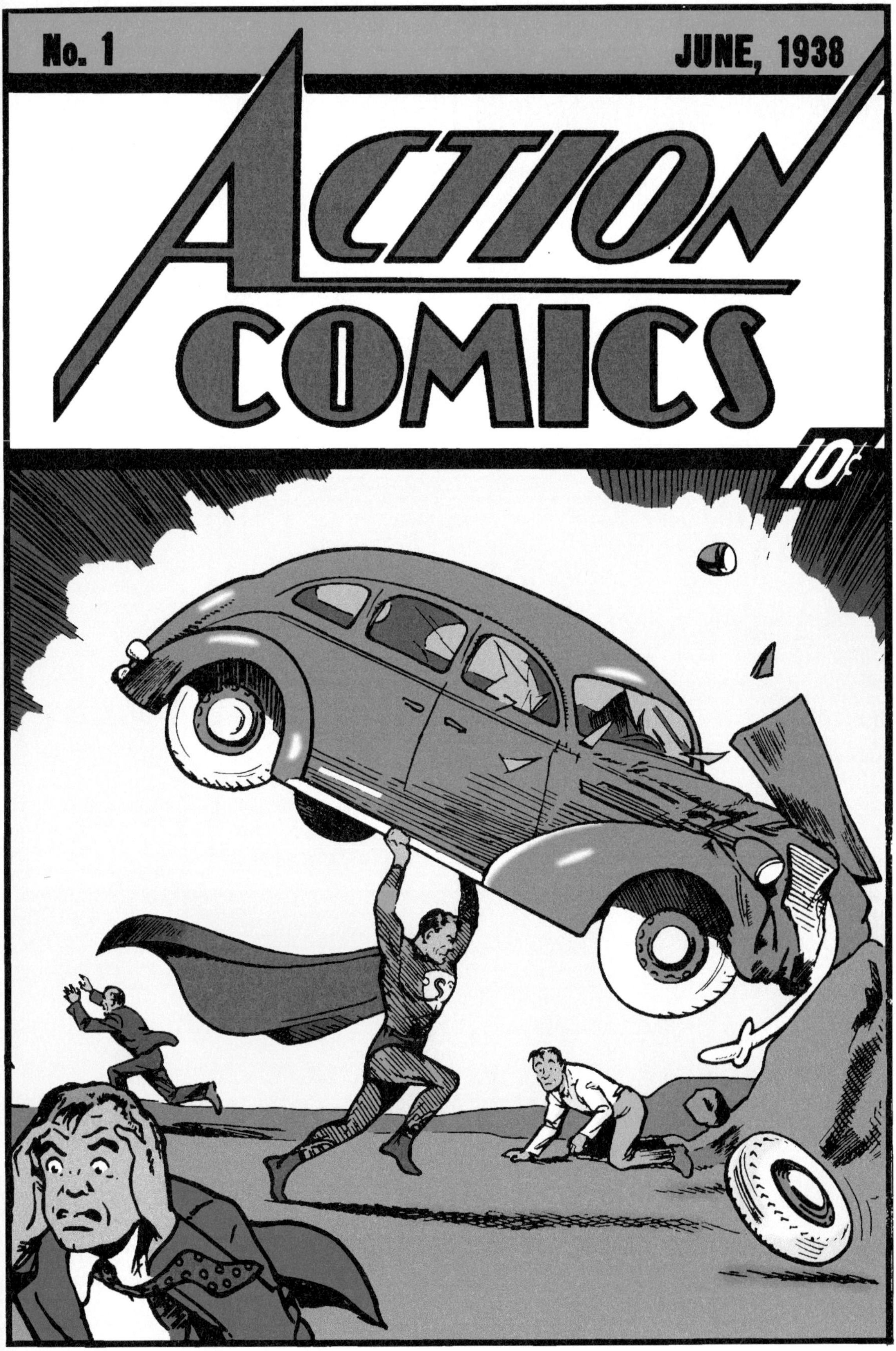
No. 1
JUNE, 1938
ACTION
COMICS
10¢

SUPERMAN

JEROME SIEGEL # JOE SHUSTER

As a distant planet was destroyed by old age, a scientist placed his infant son within a hastily devised space-ship, launching it toward Earth!

When the vehicle landed on Earth, a passing motorist, discovering the sleeping babe within, turned the child over to an orphanage

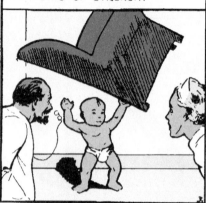

Attendants, unaware the child's physical structure was millions of years advanced of their own, were astounded at his feats of strength

When maturity was reached, he discovered he could easily:

Leap ⅛th of a mile; hurdle a twenty-story building...

Raise tremendous weights...

...Run faster than an express train...

...And that nothing less than a bursting shell could penetrate his skin!

Early, Clark decided he must turn his titanic strength into channels that would benefit mankind

And so was created...

SUPERMAN!

Champion of the oppressed, the physical marvel who had sworn to devote his existence to helping those in need!

A SCIENTIFIC EXPLANATION OF CLARK KENT'S AMAZING STRENGTH

Kent had come from a planet whose inhabitants' physical structure was millions of years advanced of our own. Upon reaching maturity, the people of his race became gifted with titanic strength!

--Incredible? No! For even today on our world exist creatures with super-strength!

The lowly ant can support weights hundreds of times its own

The grasshopper leaps what to man would be the space of several city blocks

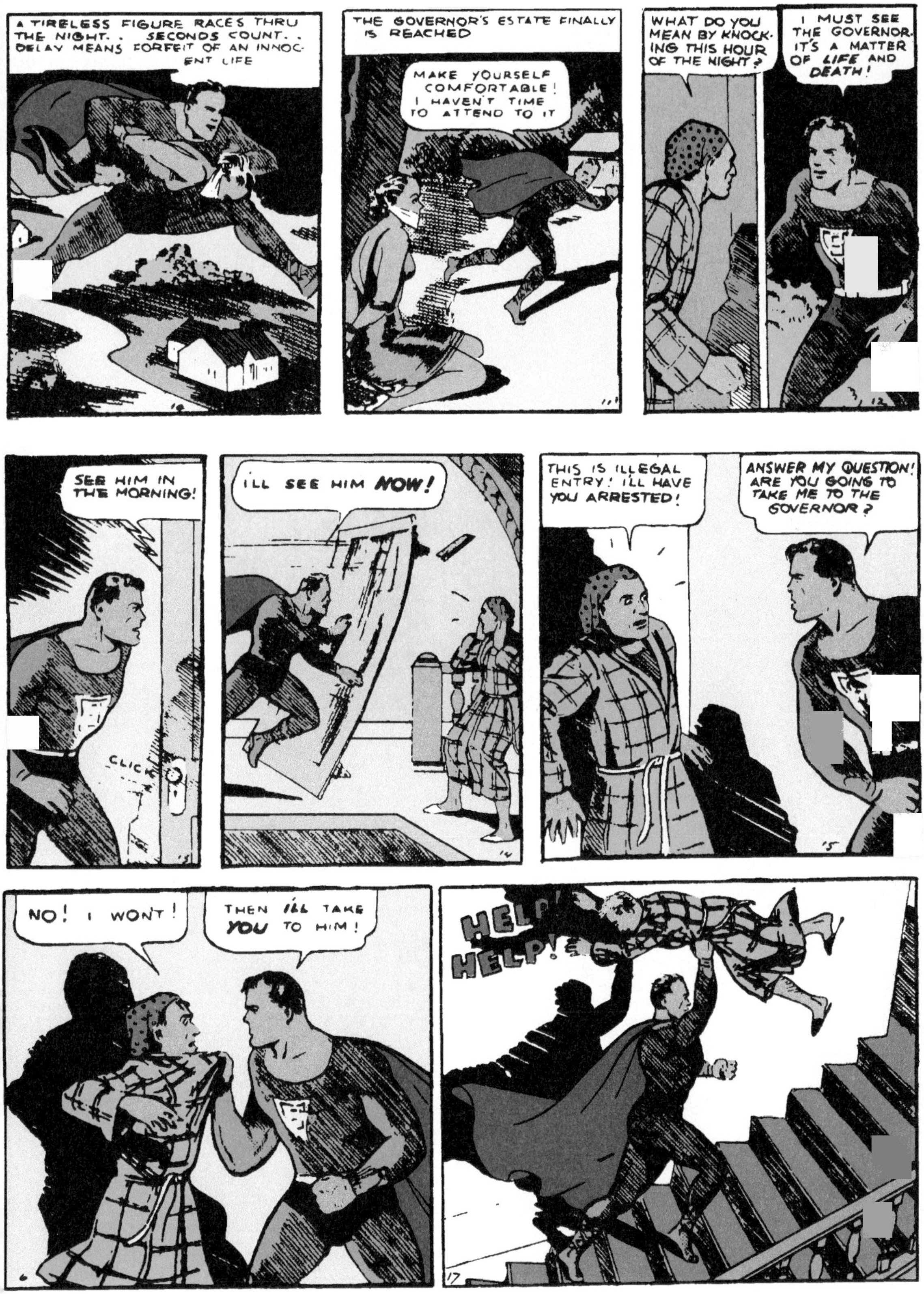
A TIRELESS FIGURE RACES THRU THE NIGHT. . SECONDS COUNT. . DELAY MEANS FORFEIT OF AN INNOCENT LIFE
THE GOVERNOR'S ESTATE FINALLY IS REACHED
MAKE YOURSELF COMFORTABLE! I HAVEN'T TIME TO ATTEND TO IT
WHAT DO YOU MEAN BY KNOCKING THIS HOUR OF THE NIGHT?
I MUST SEE THE GOVERNOR. IT'S A MATTER OF LIFE AND DEATH!
SEE HIM IN THE MORNING!
CLICK
I'LL SEE HIM NOW!
THIS IS ILLEGAL ENTRY! I'LL HAVE YOU ARRESTED!
ANSWER MY QUESTION! ARE YOU GOING TO TAKE ME TO THE GOVERNOR?
NO! I WON'T!
THEN I'LL TAKE YOU TO HIM!
HELP! HELP!

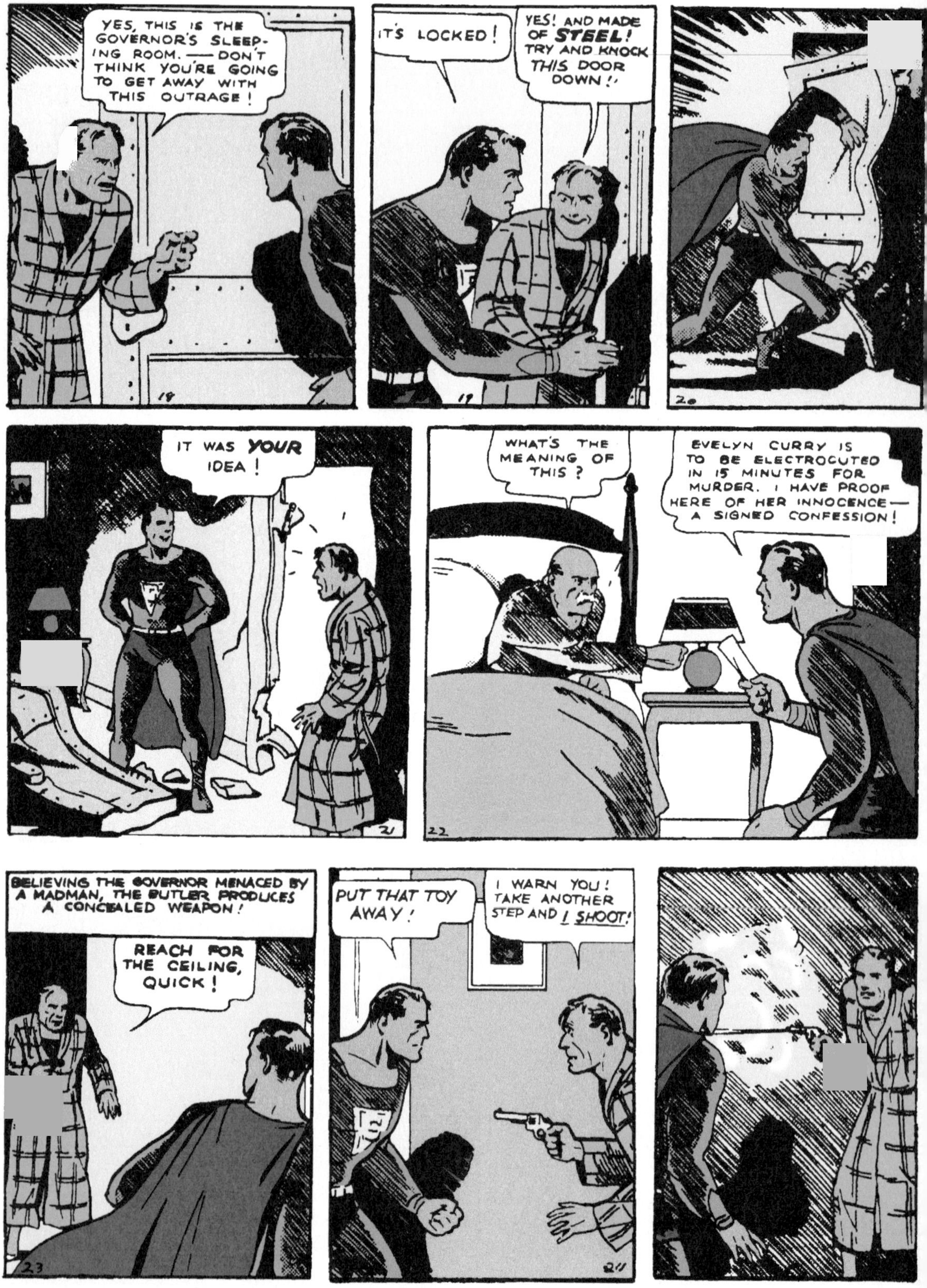
YES, THIS IS THE GOVERNOR'S SLEEPING ROOM. — DON'T THINK YOU'RE GOING TO GET AWAY WITH THIS OUTRAGE!
IT'S LOCKED!
YES! AND MADE OF STEEL! TRY AND KNOCK THIS DOOR DOWN!
IT WAS YOUR IDEA!
WHAT'S THE MEANING OF THIS?
EVELYN CURRY IS TO BE ELECTROCUTED IN 15 MINUTES FOR MURDER. I HAVE PROOF HERE OF HER INNOCENCE — A SIGNED CONFESSION!
BELIEVING THE GOVERNOR MENACED BY A MADMAN, THE BUTLER PRODUCES A CONCEALED WEAPON!
REACH FOR THE CEILING, QUICK!
PUT THAT TOY AWAY!
I WARN YOU! TAKE ANOTHER STEP AND I SHOOT!

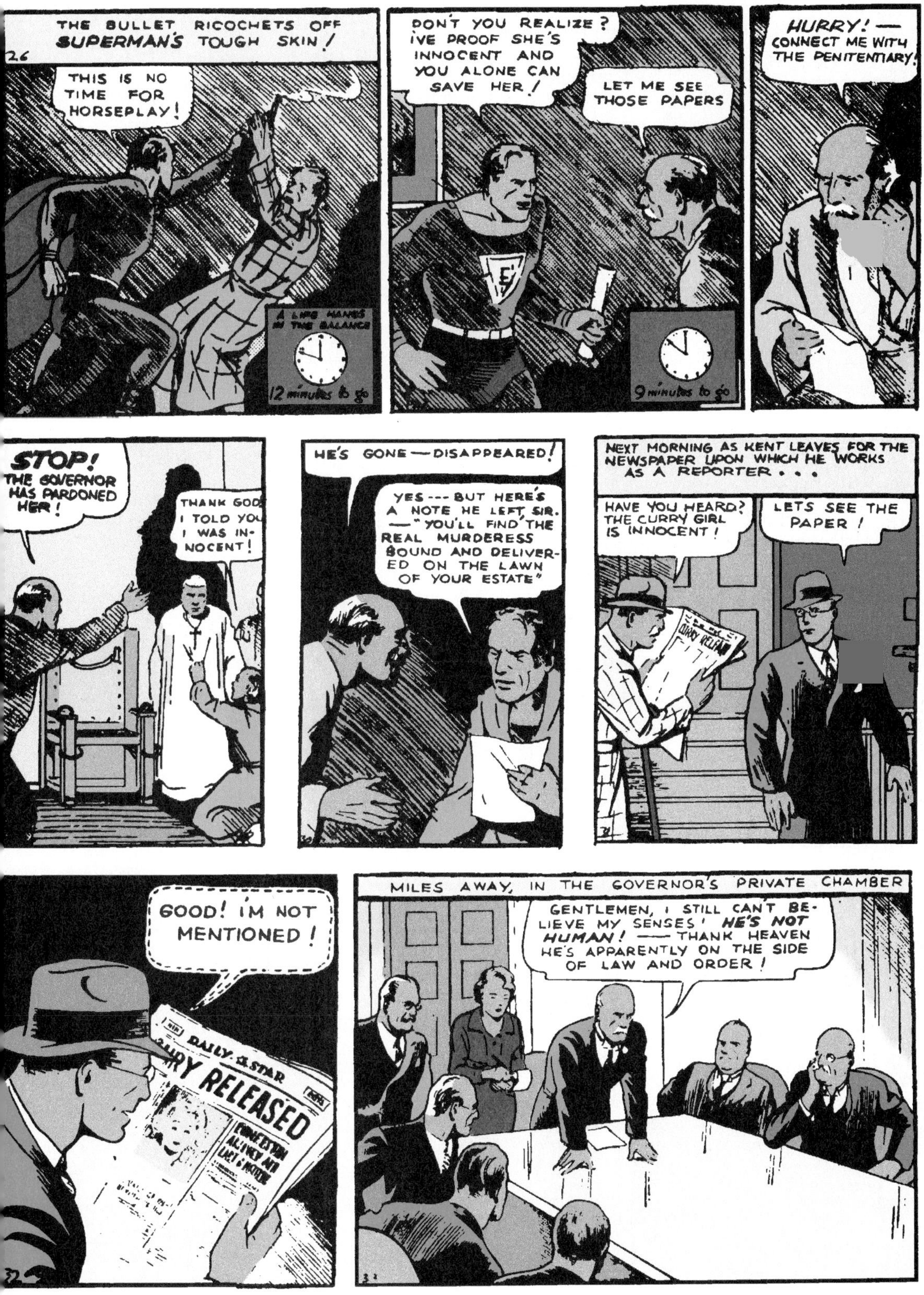
THE BULLET RICOCHETS OFF SUPERMAN'S TOUGH SKIN!
THIS IS NO TIME FOR HORSEPLAY!
A LIFE HANGS IN THE BALANCE
12 minutes to go
DON'T YOU REALIZE? I'VE PROOF SHE'S INNOCENT AND YOU ALONE CAN SAVE HER!
LET ME SEE THOSE PAPERS
9 minutes to go
HURRY! — CONNECT ME WITH THE PENITENTIARY!
STOP! THE GOVERNOR HAS PARDONED HER!
THANK GOD! I TOLD YOU I WAS INNOCENT!
HE'S GONE — DISAPPEARED!
YES --- BUT HERE'S A NOTE HE LEFT SIR. — "YOU'LL FIND THE REAL MURDERESS BOUND AND DELIVERED ON THE LAWN OF YOUR ESTATE"
NEXT MORNING AS KENT LEAVES FOR THE NEWSPAPER UPON WHICH HE WORKS AS A REPORTER . . .
HAVE YOU HEARD? THE CURRY GIRL IS INNOCENT!
LETS SEE THE PAPER!
GOOD! I'M NOT MENTIONED!
DAILY STAR
RELEASED
MILES AWAY, IN THE GOVERNOR'S PRIVATE CHAMBER
GENTLEMEN, I STILL CAN'T BELIEVE MY SENSES! HE'S NOT HUMAN! —— THANK HEAVEN HE'S APPARENTLY ON THE SIDE OF LAW AND ORDER!

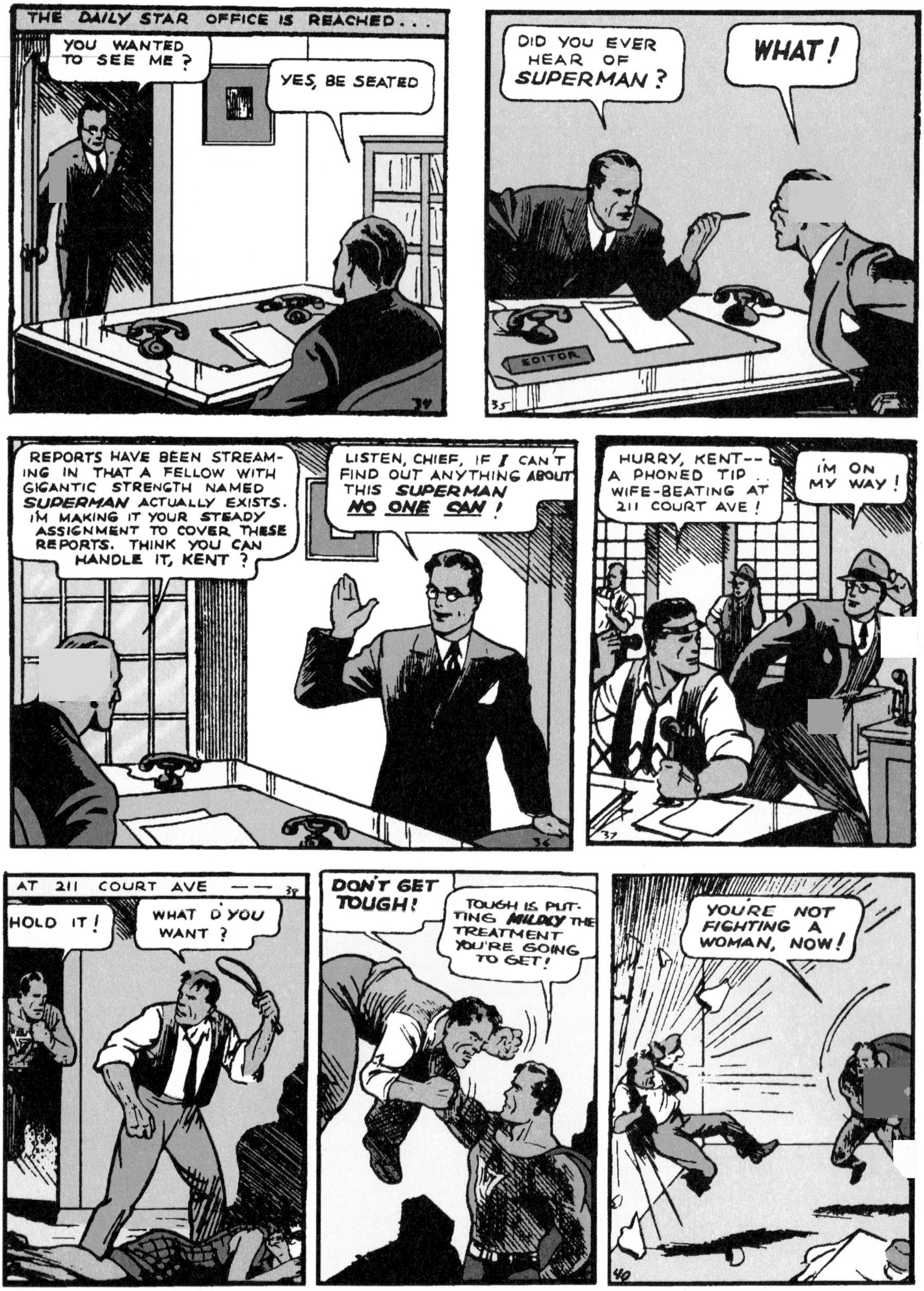
THE DAILY STAR OFFICE IS REACHED...
YOU WANTED TO SEE ME ?
YES, BE SEATED
DID YOU EVER HEAR OF SUPERMAN ?
WHAT !
EDITOR
REPORTS HAVE BEEN STREAMING IN THAT A FELLOW WITH GIGANTIC STRENGTH NAMED SUPERMAN ACTUALLY EXISTS. I'M MAKING IT YOUR STEADY ASSIGNMENT TO COVER THESE REPORTS. THINK YOU CAN HANDLE IT, KENT ?
LISTEN, CHIEF, IF I CAN'T FIND OUT ANYTHING ABOUT THIS SUPERMAN NO ONE CAN !
HURRY, KENT-- A PHONED TIP .. WIFE-BEATING AT 211 COURT AVE !
I'M ON MY WAY !
AT 211 COURT AVE ——
HOLD IT !
WHAT D'YOU WANT ?
DON'T GET TOUGH !
TOUGH IS PUTTING MILDLY THE TREATMENT YOU'RE GOING TO GET !
YOU'RE NOT FIGHTING A WOMAN, NOW !

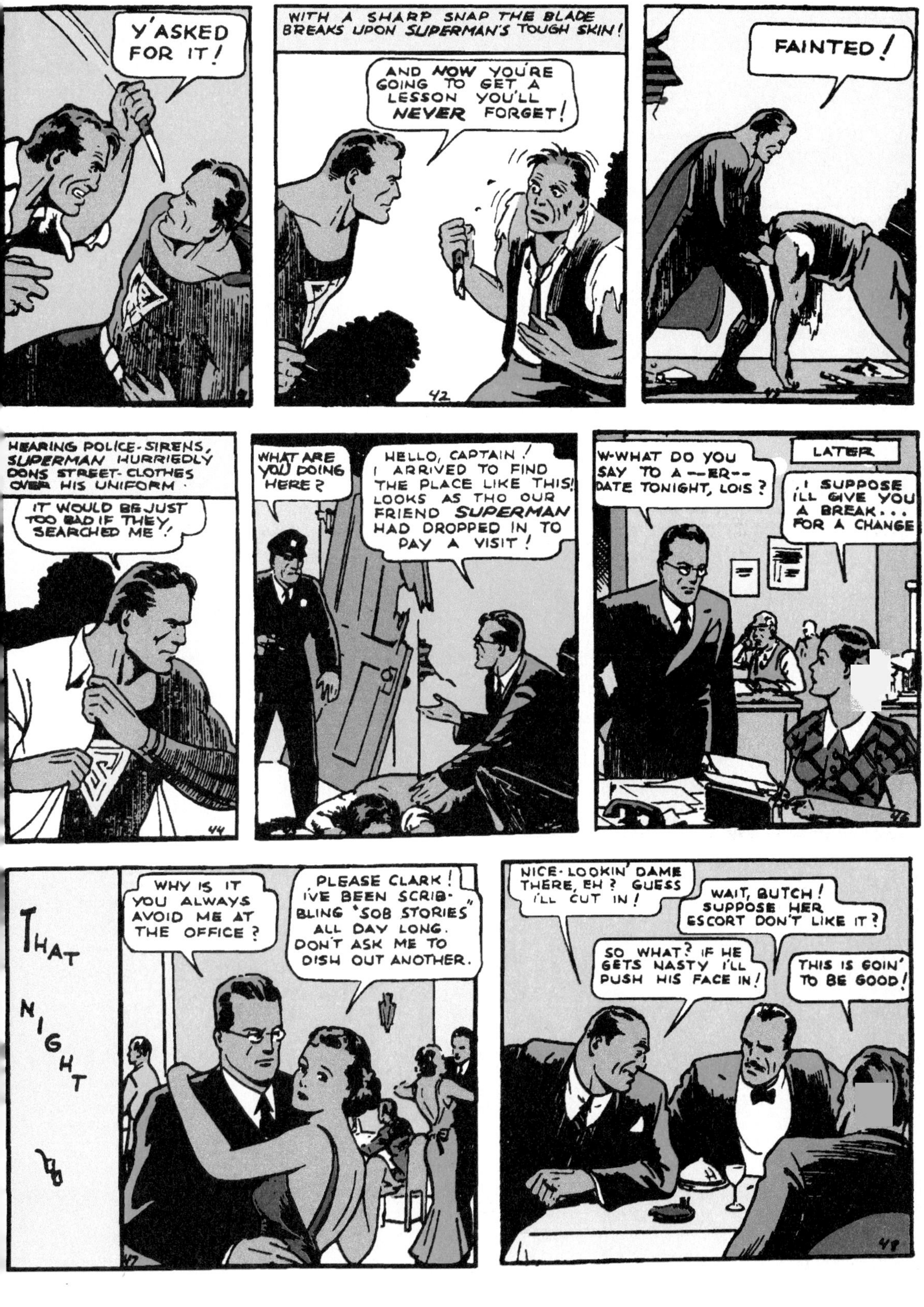

Y'ASKED FOR IT!
WITH A SHARP SNAP THE BLADE BREAKS UPON SUPERMAN'S TOUGH SKIN!
AND NOW YOU'RE GOING TO GET A LESSON YOU'LL NEVER FORGET!
FAINTED!
HEARING POLICE-SIRENS, SUPERMAN HURRIEDLY DONS STREET-CLOTHES OVER HIS UNIFORM.
IT WOULD BE JUST TOO BAD IF THEY SEARCHED ME!
WHAT ARE YOU DOING HERE?
HELLO, CAPTAIN! I ARRIVED TO FIND THE PLACE LIKE THIS! LOOKS AS THO OUR FRIEND SUPERMAN HAD DROPPED IN TO PAY A VISIT!
LATER
W-WHAT DO YOU SAY TO A --ER-- DATE TONIGHT, LOIS?
I SUPPOSE I'LL GIVE YOU A BREAK... FOR A CHANGE
THAT NIGHT
WHY IS IT YOU ALWAYS AVOID ME AT THE OFFICE?
PLEASE CLARK! I'VE BEEN SCRIBBLING "SOB STORIES" ALL DAY LONG. DON'T ASK ME TO DISH OUT ANOTHER.
NICE-LOOKIN' DAME THERE, EH? GUESS I'LL CUT IN!
WAIT, BUTCH! SUPPOSE HER ESCORT DON'T LIKE IT?
SO WHAT? IF HE GETS NASTY I'LL PUSH HIS FACE IN!
THIS IS GOIN' TO BE GOOD!

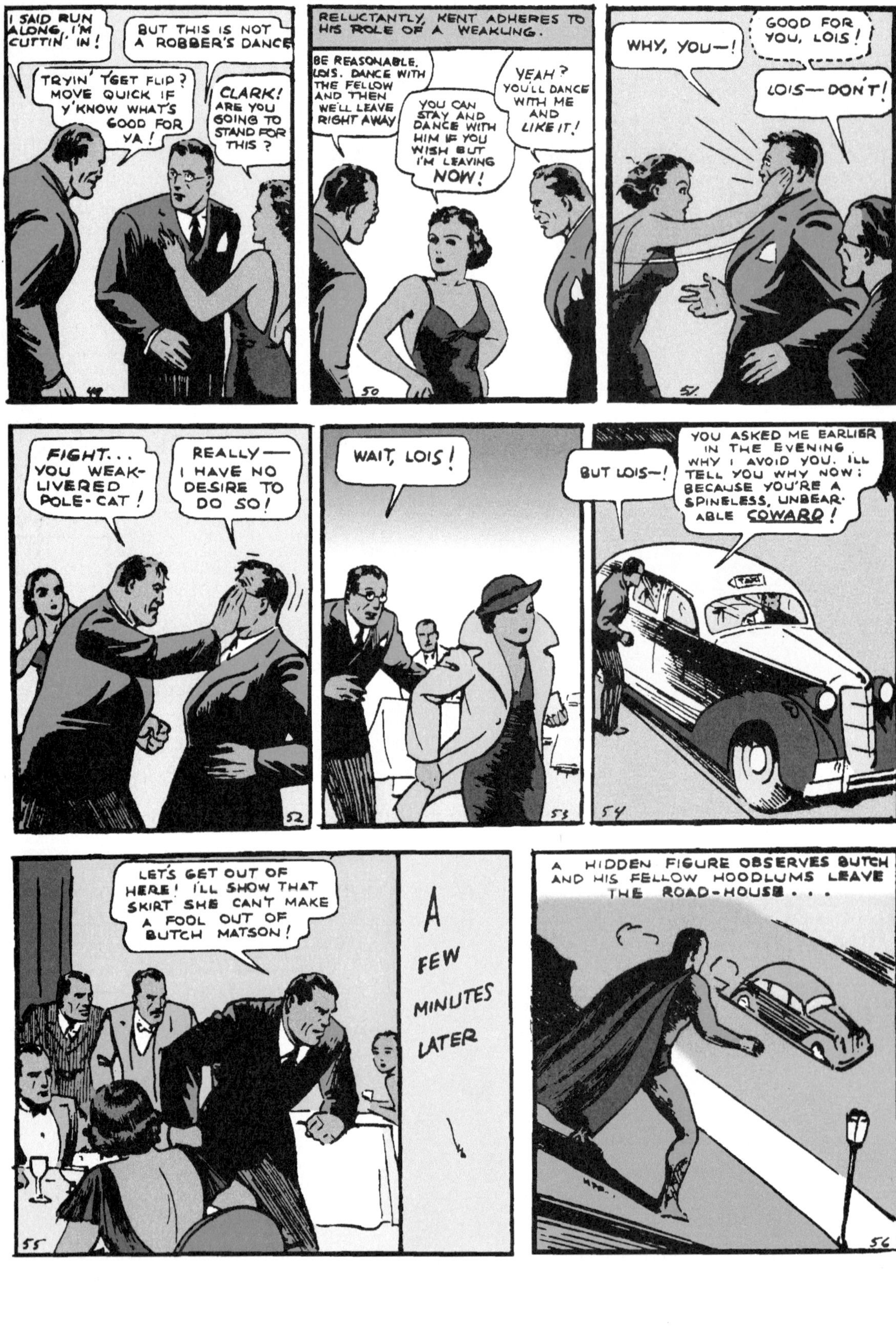
I SAID RUN ALONG, I'M CUTTIN' IN!
BUT THIS IS NOT A ROBBER'S DANCE
TRYIN' T'GET FLIP? MOVE QUICK IF Y'KNOW WHAT'S GOOD FOR YA!
CLARK! ARE YOU GOING TO STAND FOR THIS?
49
RELUCTANTLY, KENT ADHERES TO HIS ROLE OF A WEAKLING.
BE REASONABLE, LOIS. DANCE WITH THE FELLOW AND THEN WE'LL LEAVE RIGHT AWAY
YOU CAN STAY AND DANCE WITH HIM IF YOU WISH BUT I'M LEAVING NOW!
YEAH? YOU'LL DANCE WITH ME AND LIKE IT!
50
WHY, YOU—!
GOOD FOR YOU, LOIS!
LOIS—DON'T!
51
FIGHT... YOU WEAK-LIVERED POLE-CAT!
REALLY— I HAVE NO DESIRE TO DO SO!
52
WAIT, LOIS!
53
BUT LOIS—!
YOU ASKED ME EARLIER IN THE EVENING WHY I AVOID YOU. I'LL TELL YOU WHY NOW: BECAUSE YOU'RE A SPINELESS, UNBEARABLE COWARD!
TAXI
54
LET'S GET OUT OF HERE! I'LL SHOW THAT SKIRT SHE CAN'T MAKE A FOOL OUT OF BUTCH MATSON!
55
A FEW MINUTES LATER
A HIDDEN FIGURE OBSERVES BUTCH AND HIS FELLOW HOODLUMS LEAVE THE ROAD-HOUSE...
56

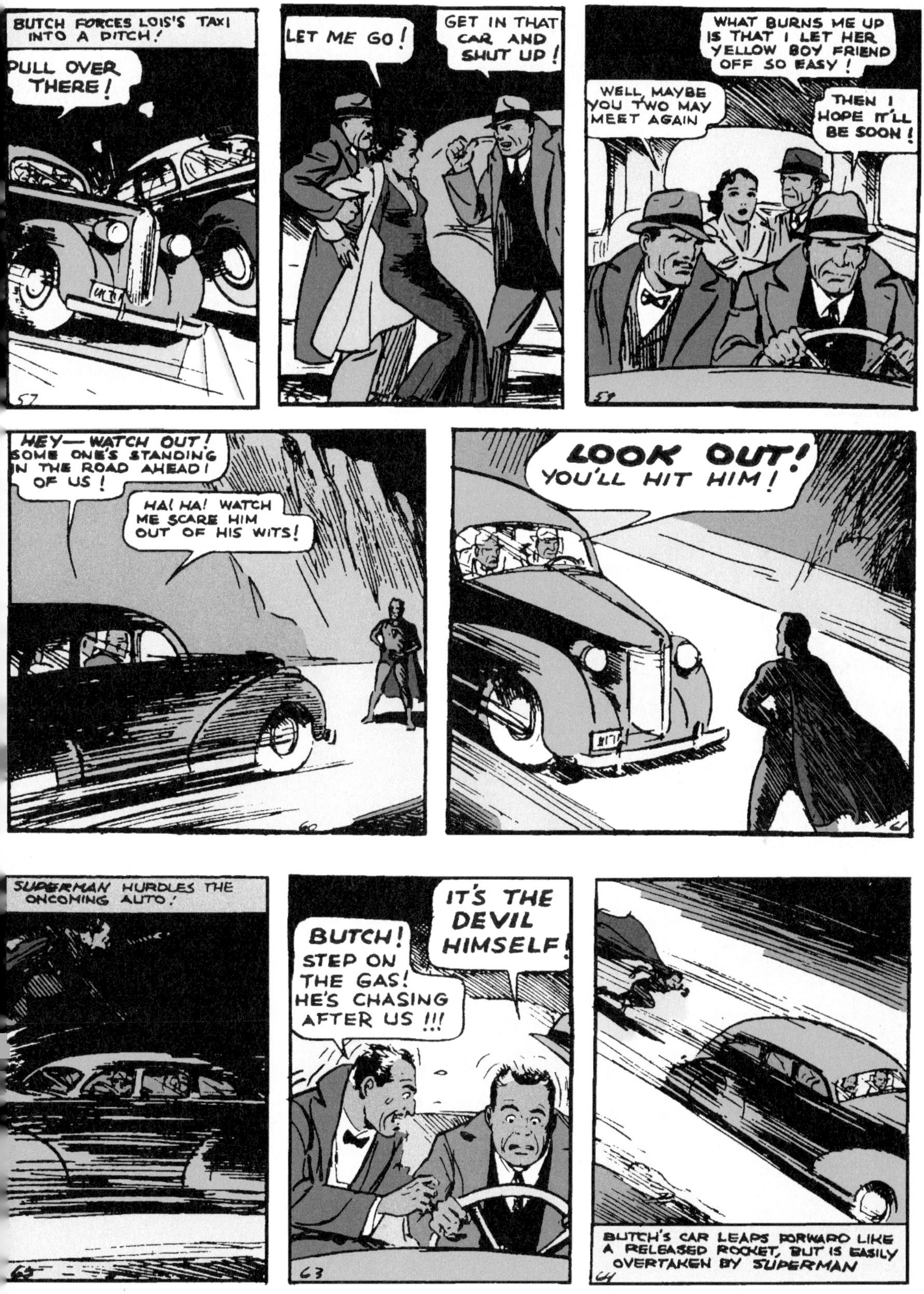
BUTCH FORCES LOIS'S TAXI INTO A DITCH!
PULL OVER THERE!
LET ME GO!
GET IN THAT CAR AND SHUT UP!
WHAT BURNS ME UP IS THAT I LET HER YELLOW BOY FRIEND OFF SO EASY!
WELL, MAYBE YOU TWO MAY MEET AGAIN
THEN I HOPE IT'LL BE SOON!
HEY—WATCH OUT! SOME ONE'S STANDING IN THE ROAD AHEAD OF US!
HA! HA! WATCH ME SCARE HIM OUT OF HIS WITS!
LOOK OUT! YOU'LL HIT HIM!
SUPERMAN HURDLES THE ONCOMING AUTO!
IT'S THE DEVIL HIMSELF!
BUTCH! STEP ON THE GAS! HE'S CHASING AFTER US!!!
BUTCH'S CAR LEAPS FORWARD LIKE A RELEASED ROCKET, BUT IS EASILY OVERTAKEN BY SUPERMAN

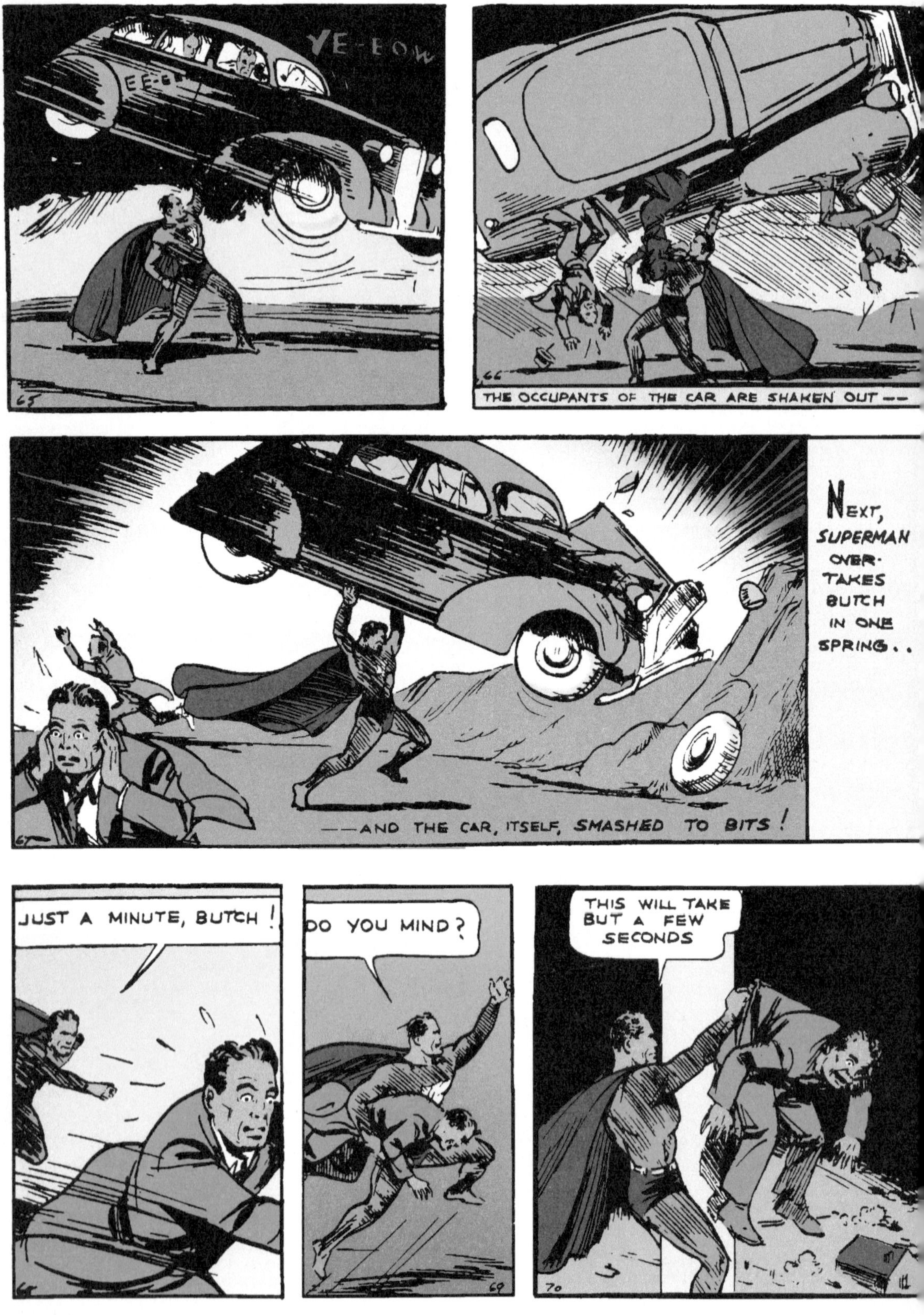
YE-E-OW
EE-E
THE OCCUPANTS OF THE CAR ARE SHAKEN OUT --
--AND THE CAR, ITSELF, SMASHED TO BITS !
NEXT, SUPERMAN OVER-TAKES BUTCH IN ONE SPRING . .
JUST A MINUTE, BUTCH !
DO YOU MIND ?
THIS WILL TAKE BUT A FEW SECONDS

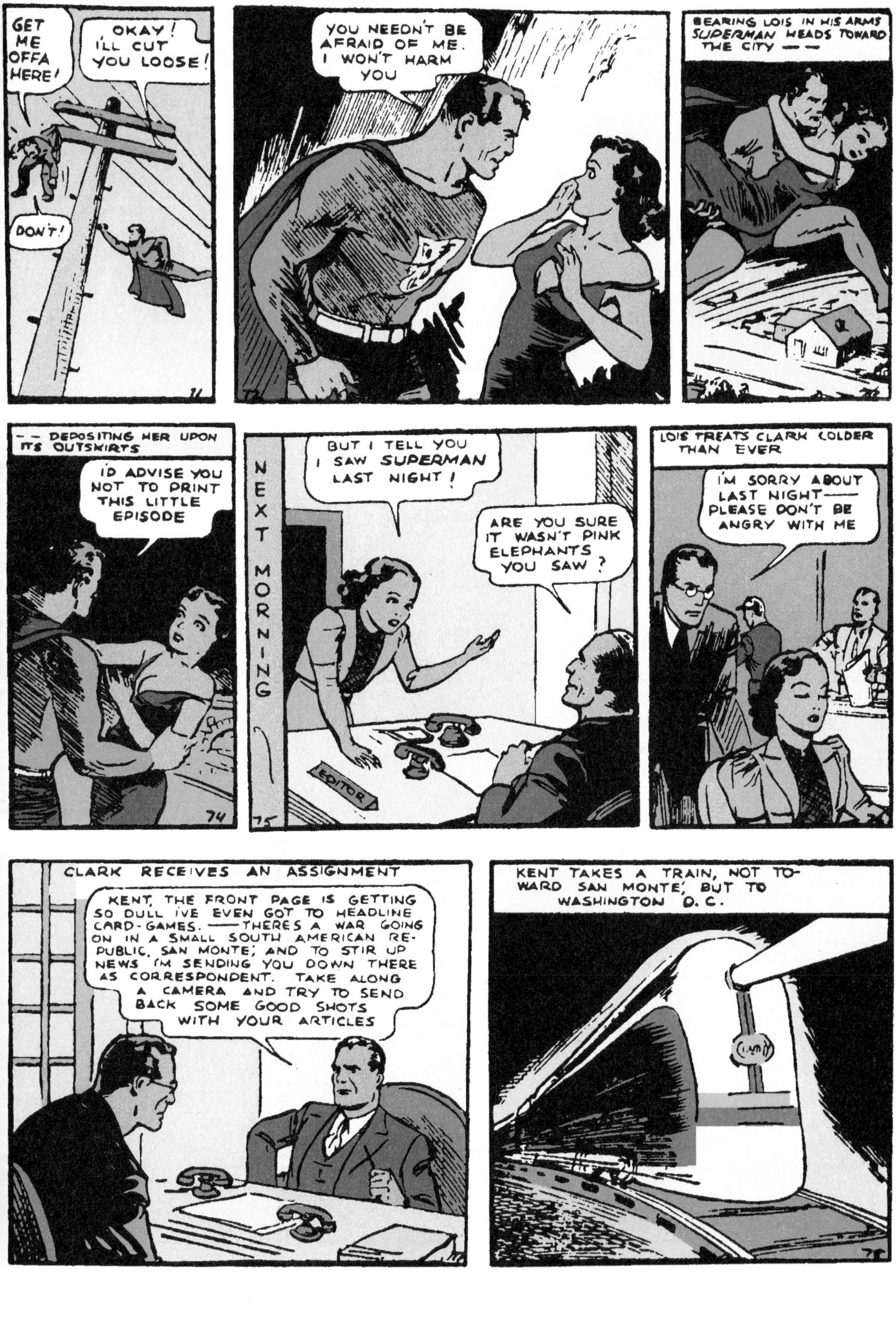
GET ME OFFA HERE!
OKAY! I'LL CUT YOU LOOSE!
DON'T!
YOU NEEDN'T BE AFRAID OF ME. I WON'T HARM YOU
BEARING LOIS IN HIS ARMS SUPERMAN HEADS TOWARD THE CITY — —
— — DEPOSITING HER UPON ITS OUTSKIRTS
I'D ADVISE YOU NOT TO PRINT THIS LITTLE EPISODE
NEXT MORNING
BUT I TELL YOU I SAW SUPERMAN LAST NIGHT!
ARE YOU SURE IT WASN'T PINK ELEPHANTS YOU SAW?
EDITOR
LOIS TREATS CLARK COLDER THAN EVER
I'M SORRY ABOUT LAST NIGHT—— PLEASE DON'T BE ANGRY WITH ME
CLARK RECEIVES AN ASSIGNMENT
KENT, THE FRONT PAGE IS GETTING SO DULL I'VE EVEN GOT TO HEADLINE CARD-GAMES. ——THERES A WAR GOING ON IN A SMALL SOUTH AMERICAN REPUBLIC, SAN MONTE; AND TO STIR UP NEWS I'M SENDING YOU DOWN THERE AS CORRESPONDENT. TAKE ALONG A CAMERA AND TRY TO SEND BACK SOME GOOD SHOTS WITH YOUR ARTICLES
KENT TAKES A TRAIN, NOT TOWARD SAN MONTE, BUT TO WASHINGTON D.C.

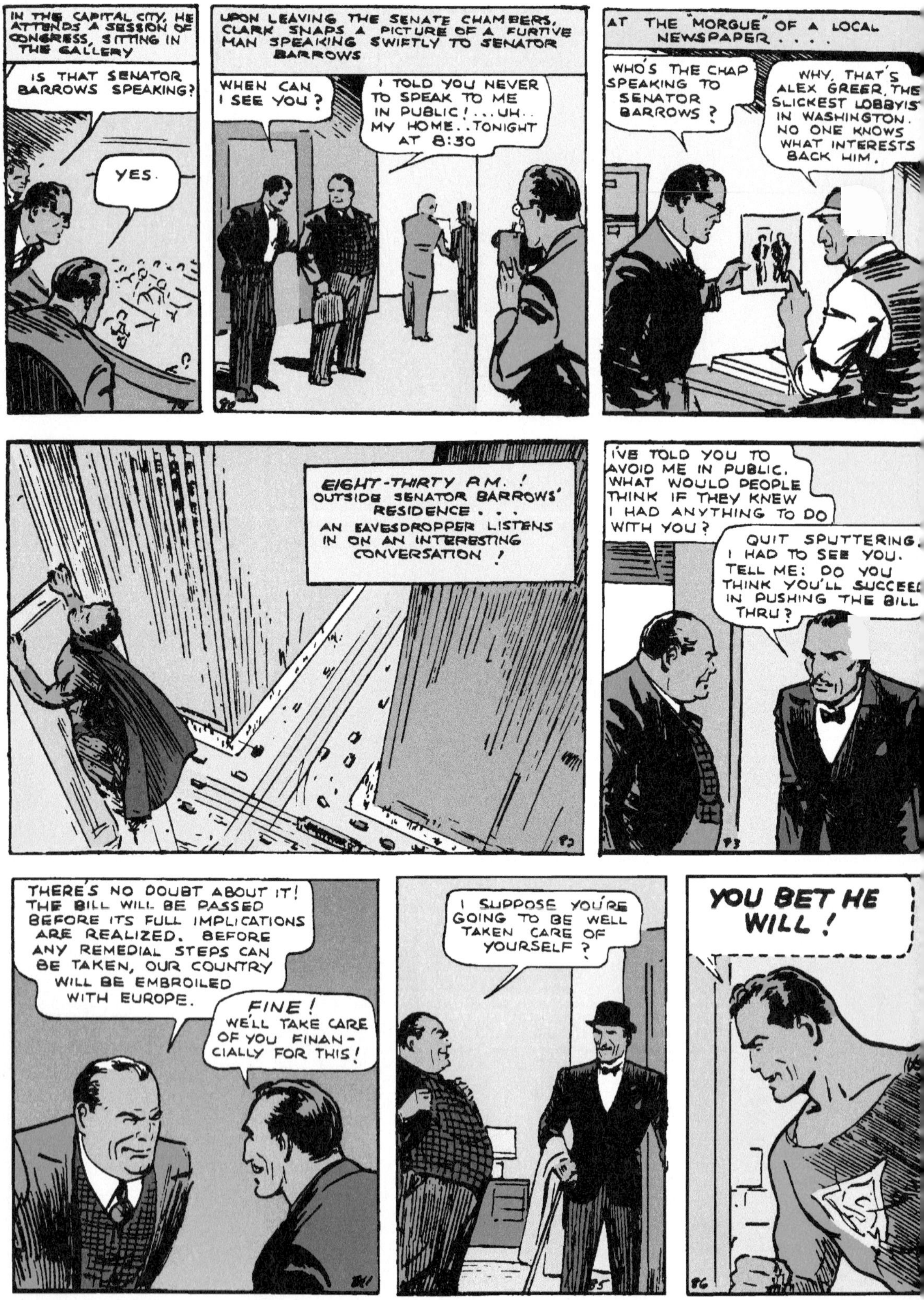

IN THE CAPITAL CITY, HE ATTENDS A SESSION OF CONGRESS, SITTING IN THE GALLERY
IS THAT SENATOR BARROWS SPEAKING?
YES.
UPON LEAVING THE SENATE CHAMBERS, CLARK SNAPS A PICTURE OF A FURTIVE MAN SPEAKING SWIFTLY TO SENATOR BARROWS
WHEN CAN I SEE YOU?
I TOLD YOU NEVER TO SPEAK TO ME IN PUBLIC!...UH.. MY HOME..TONIGHT AT 8:30
AT THE "MORGUE" OF A LOCAL NEWSPAPER....
WHO'S THE CHAP SPEAKING TO SENATOR BARROWS?
WHY, THAT'S ALEX GREER, THE SLICKEST LOBBYIST IN WASHINGTON. NO ONE KNOWS WHAT INTERESTS BACK HIM.
EIGHT-THIRTY P.M.! OUTSIDE SENATOR BARROWS' RESIDENCE... AN EAVESDROPPER LISTENS IN ON AN INTERESTING CONVERSATION!
I'VE TOLD YOU TO AVOID ME IN PUBLIC. WHAT WOULD PEOPLE THINK IF THEY KNEW I HAD ANYTHING TO DO WITH YOU?
QUIT SPUTTERING. I HAD TO SEE YOU. TELL ME: DO YOU THINK YOU'LL SUCCEED IN PUSHING THE BILL THRU?
THERE'S NO DOUBT ABOUT IT! THE BILL WILL BE PASSED BEFORE ITS FULL IMPLICATIONS ARE REALIZED. BEFORE ANY REMEDIAL STEPS CAN BE TAKEN, OUR COUNTRY WILL BE EMBROILED WITH EUROPE.
FINE! WE'LL TAKE CARE OF YOU FINANCIALLY FOR THIS!
I SUPPOSE YOU'RE GOING TO BE WELL TAKEN CARE OF YOURSELF?
YOU BET HE WILL!

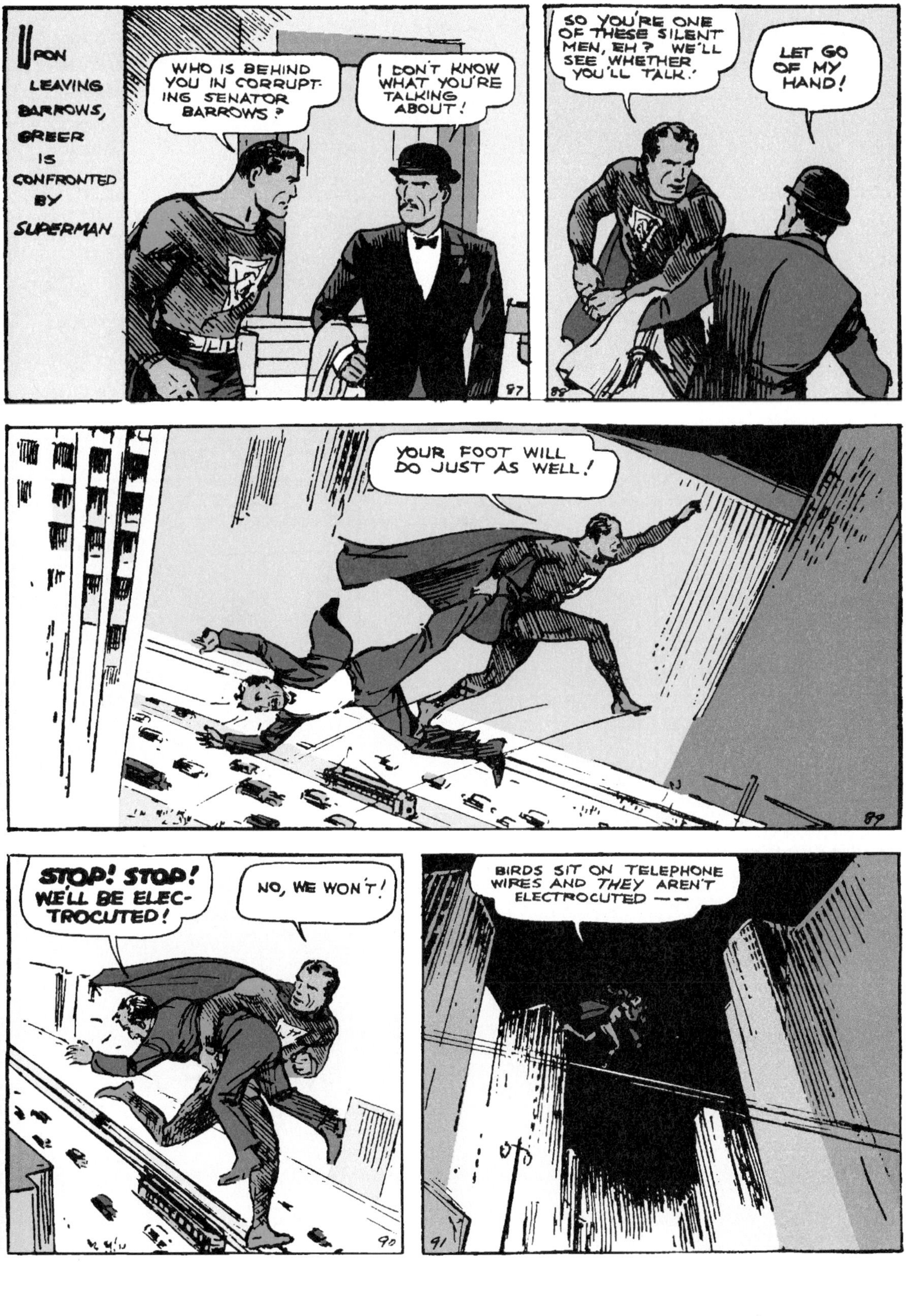
UPON LEAVING BARROWS, GREER IS CONFRONTED BY SUPERMAN
WHO IS BEHIND YOU IN CORRUPTING SENATOR BARROWS?
I DON'T KNOW WHAT YOU'RE TALKING ABOUT!
87
SO YOU'RE ONE OF THESE SILENT MEN, EH? WE'LL SEE WHETHER YOU'LL TALK!
LET GO OF MY HAND!
88
YOUR FOOT WILL DO JUST AS WELL!
89
STOP! STOP! WE'LL BE ELECTROCUTED!
NO, WE WON'T!
90
BIRDS SIT ON TELEPHONE WIRES AND THEY AREN'T ELECTROCUTED --
91

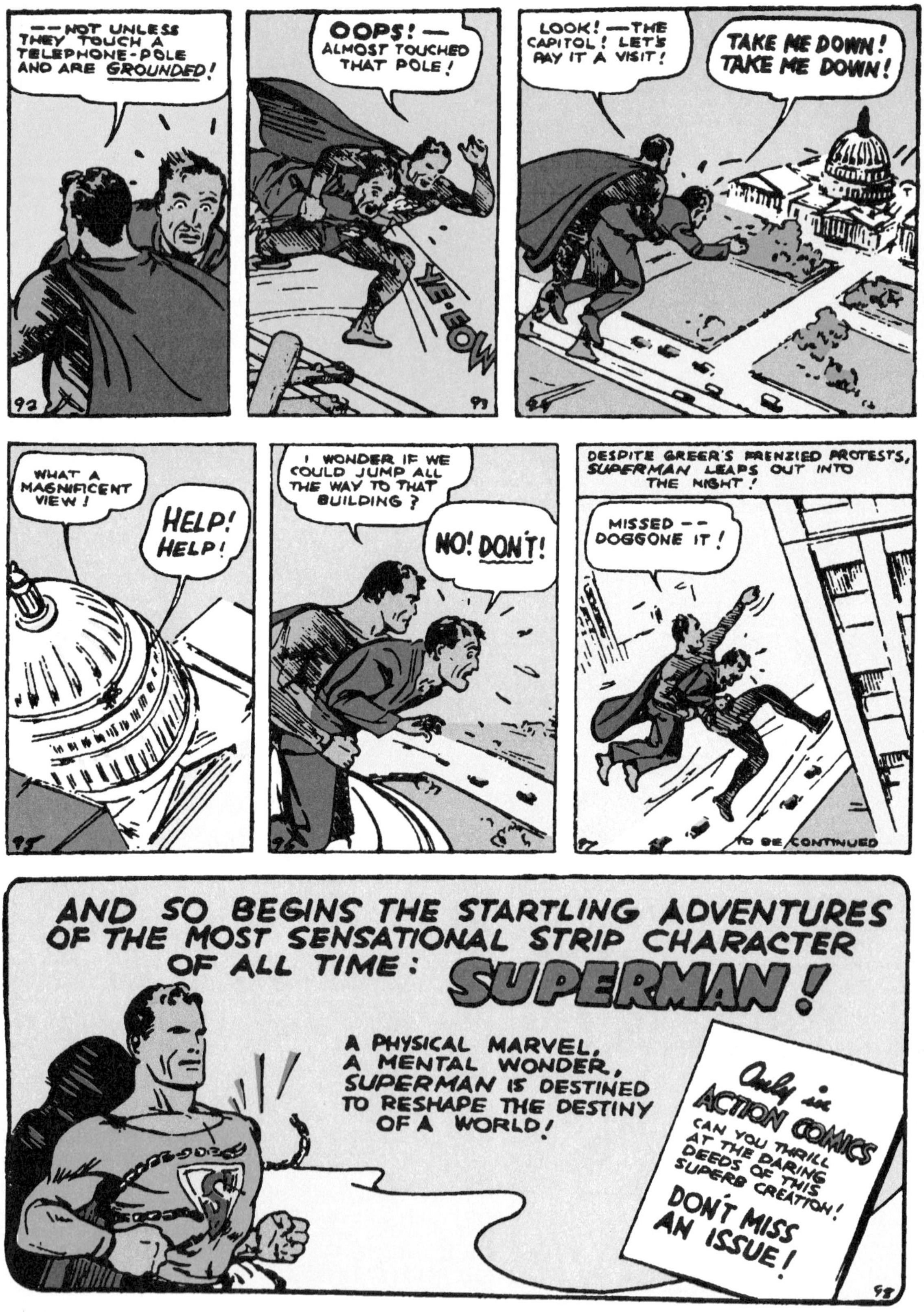

--NOT UNLESS THEY TOUCH A TELEPHONE-POLE AND ARE GROUNDED!
92
OOPS!— ALMOST TOUCHED THAT POLE!
YE-EOW
93
LOOK!—THE CAPITOL! LET'S PAY IT A VISIT!
TAKE ME DOWN! TAKE ME DOWN!
94
WHAT A MAGNIFICENT VIEW!
HELP! HELP!
95
I WONDER IF WE COULD JUMP ALL THE WAY TO THAT BUILDING?
NO! DON'T!
96
DESPITE GREER'S FRENZIED PROTESTS, SUPERMAN LEAPS OUT INTO THE NIGHT!
MISSED -- DOGGONE IT!
97
TO BE CONTINUED
AND SO BEGINS THE STARTLING ADVENTURES OF THE MOST SENSATIONAL STRIP CHARACTER OF ALL TIME: SUPERMAN!
A PHYSICAL MARVEL, A MENTAL WONDER, SUPERMAN IS DESTINED TO RESHAPE THE DESTINY OF A WORLD!
Only in ACTION COMICS CAN YOU THRILL AT THE DARING DEEDS OF THIS SUPERB CREATION!
DON'T MISS AN ISSUE!
98

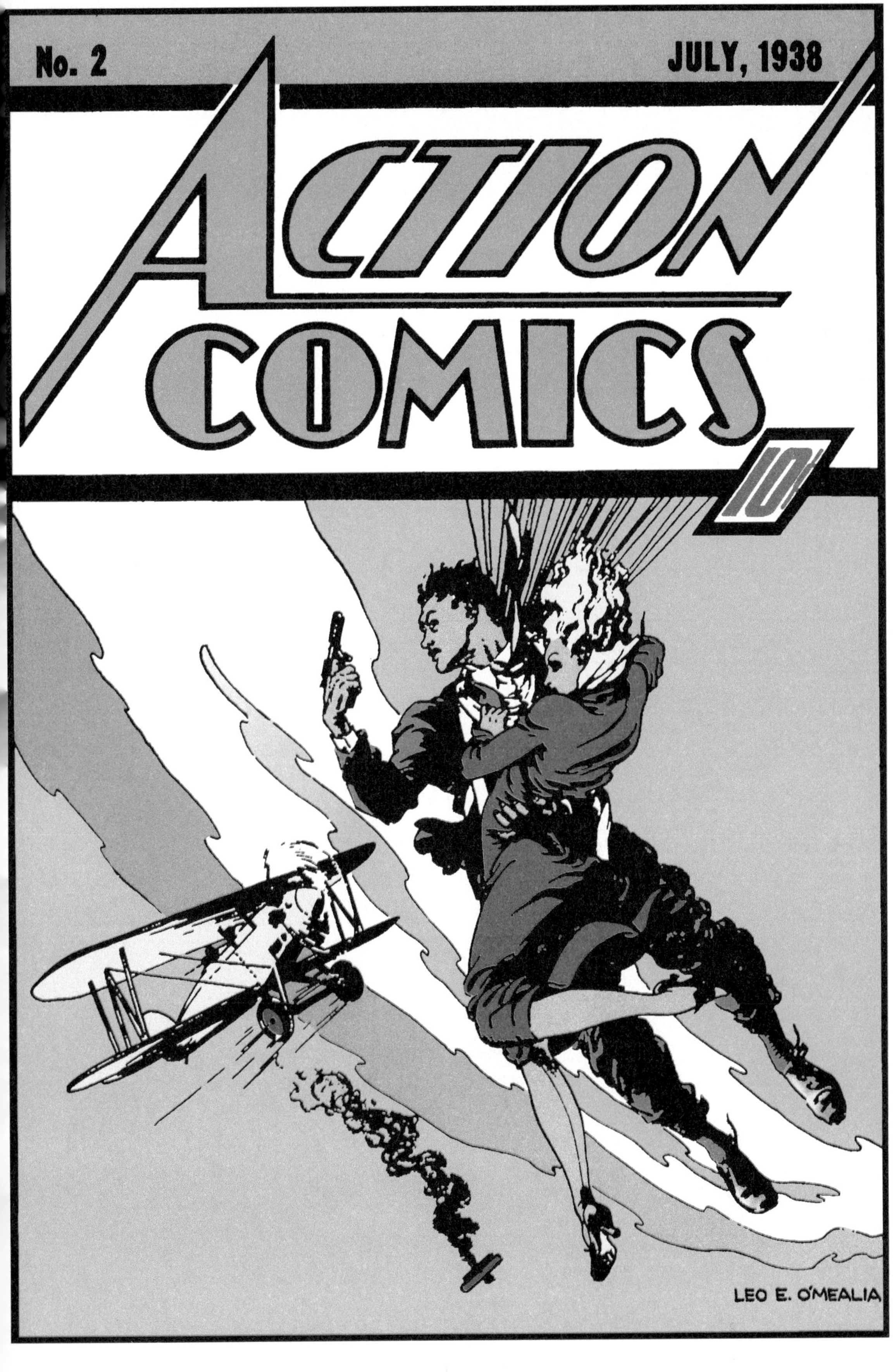
No. 2
JULY, 1938
ACTION COMICS
10¢
LEO E. O'MEALIA

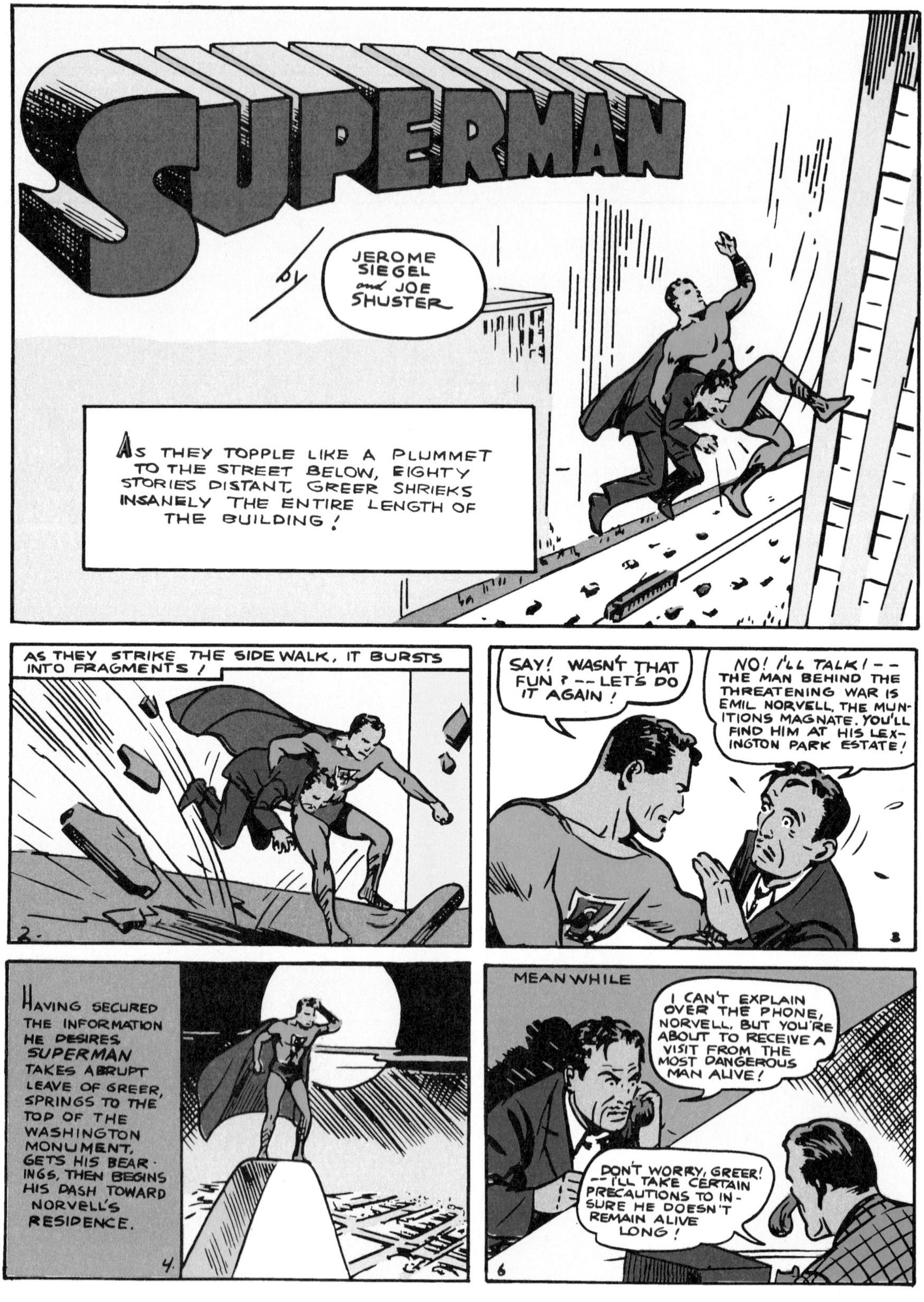
SUPERMAN
BY JEROME SIEGEL and JOE SHUSTER
AS THEY TOPPLE LIKE A PLUMMET TO THE STREET BELOW, EIGHTY STORIES DISTANT, GREER SHRIEKS INSANELY THE ENTIRE LENGTH OF THE BUILDING!
AS THEY STRIKE THE SIDEWALK, IT BURSTS INTO FRAGMENTS!
SAY! WASN'T THAT FUN? -- LET'S DO IT AGAIN!
NO! I'LL TALK! -- THE MAN BEHIND THE THREATENING WAR IS EMIL NORVELL, THE MUNITIONS MAGNATE. YOU'LL FIND HIM AT HIS LEXINGTON PARK ESTATE!
HAVING SECURED THE INFORMATION HE DESIRES, SUPERMAN TAKES ABRUPT LEAVE OF GREER, SPRINGS TO THE TOP OF THE WASHINGTON MONUMENT, GETS HIS BEARINGS, THEN BEGINS HIS DASH TOWARD NORVELL'S RESIDENCE.
MEANWHILE
I CAN'T EXPLAIN OVER THE PHONE, NORVELL, BUT YOU'RE ABOUT TO RECEIVE A VISIT FROM THE MOST DANGEROUS MAN ALIVE!
DON'T WORRY, GREER! -- I'LL TAKE CERTAIN PRECAUTIONS TO INSURE HE DOESN'T REMAIN ALIVE LONG!

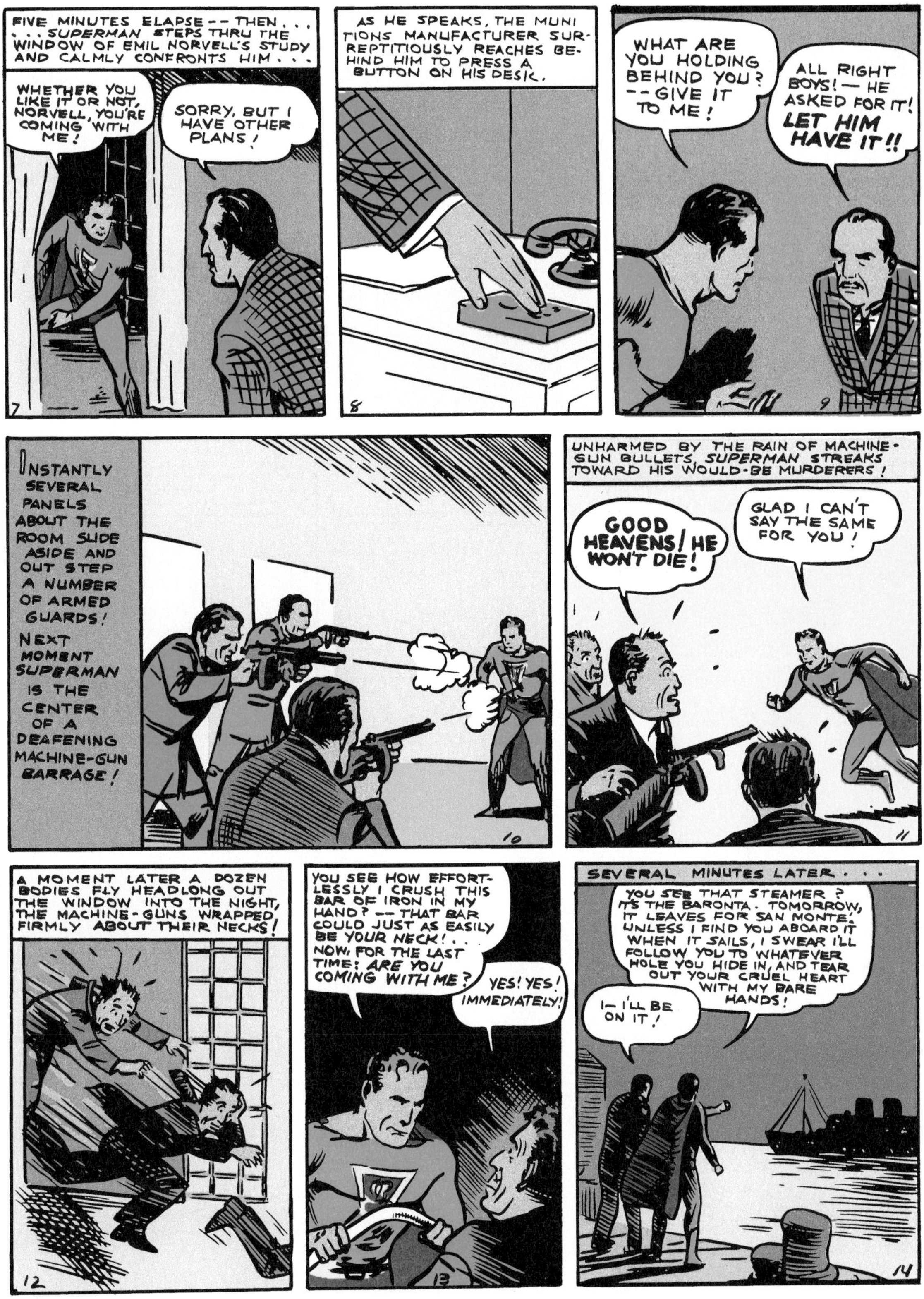
FIVE MINUTES ELAPSE -- THEN . . . . . . SUPERMAN STEPS THRU THE WINDOW OF EMIL NORVELL'S STUDY AND CALMLY CONFRONTS HIM . . .
WHETHER YOU LIKE IT OR NOT, NORVELL, YOU'RE COMING WITH ME!
SORRY, BUT I HAVE OTHER PLANS!
AS HE SPEAKS, THE MUNITIONS MANUFACTURER SURREPTITIOUSLY REACHES BEHIND HIM TO PRESS A BUTTON ON HIS DESK.
WHAT ARE YOU HOLDING BEHIND YOU? -- GIVE IT TO ME!
ALL RIGHT BOYS! — HE ASKED FOR IT! LET HIM HAVE IT!!
INSTANTLY SEVERAL PANELS ABOUT THE ROOM SLIDE ASIDE AND OUT STEP A NUMBER OF ARMED GUARDS! NEXT MOMENT SUPERMAN IS THE CENTER OF A DEAFENING MACHINE-GUN BARRAGE!
UNHARMED BY THE RAIN OF MACHINE-GUN BULLETS, SUPERMAN STREAKS TOWARD HIS WOULD-BE MURDERERS!
GOOD HEAVENS! HE WON'T DIE!
GLAD I CAN'T SAY THE SAME FOR YOU!
A MOMENT LATER A DOZEN BODIES FLY HEADLONG OUT THE WINDOW INTO THE NIGHT, THE MACHINE-GUNS WRAPPED FIRMLY ABOUT THEIR NECKS!
YOU SEE HOW EFFORTLESSLY I CRUSH THIS BAR OF IRON IN MY HAND? -- THAT BAR COULD JUST AS EASILY BE YOUR NECK! . . NOW, FOR THE LAST TIME: ARE YOU COMING WITH ME?
YES! YES! IMMEDIATELY!
SEVERAL MINUTES LATER . . .
YOU SEE THAT STEAMER? IT'S THE BARONTA. TOMORROW, IT LEAVES FOR SAN MONTE! UNLESS I FIND YOU ABOARD IT WHEN IT SAILS, I SWEAR I'LL FOLLOW YOU TO WHATEVER HOLE YOU HIDE IN, AND TEAR OUT YOUR CRUEL HEART WITH MY BARE HANDS!
I— I'LL BE ON IT!

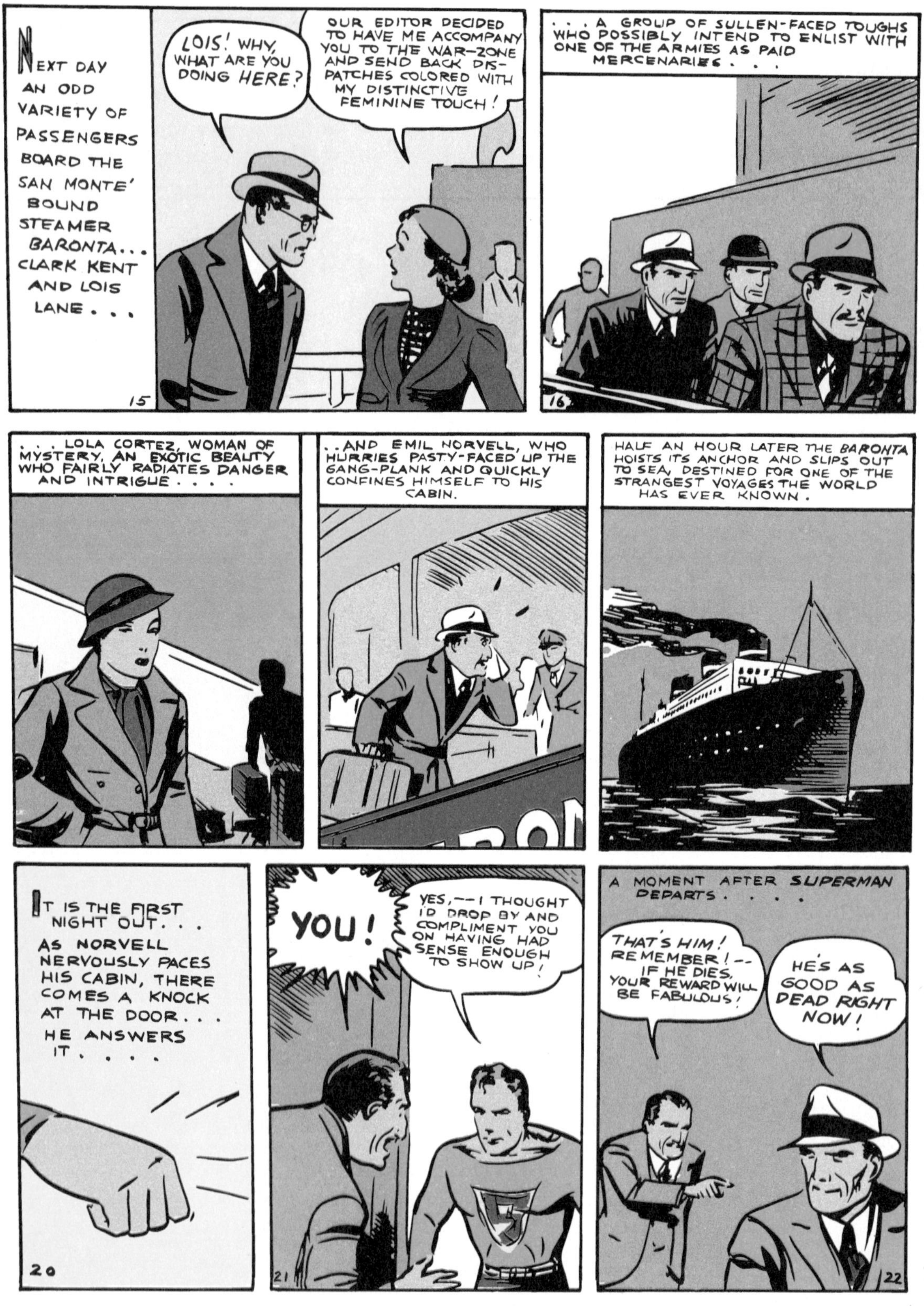
NEXT DAY AN ODD VARIETY OF PASSENGERS BOARD THE SAN MONTE' BOUND STEAMER BARONTA... CLARK KENT AND LOIS LANE . . .
LOIS! WHY, WHAT ARE YOU DOING HERE?
OUR EDITOR DECIDED TO HAVE ME ACCOMPANY YOU TO THE WAR-ZONE AND SEND BACK DISPATCHES COLORED WITH MY DISTINCTIVE FEMININE TOUCH!
15
. . . A GROUP OF SULLEN-FACED TOUGHS WHO POSSIBLY INTEND TO ENLIST WITH ONE OF THE ARMIES AS PAID MERCENARIES . . .
16
. . . LOLA CORTEZ, WOMAN OF MYSTERY, AN EXOTIC BEAUTY WHO FAIRLY RADIATES DANGER AND INTRIGUE . . .
..AND EMIL NORVELL, WHO HURRIES PASTY-FACED UP THE GANG-PLANK AND QUICKLY CONFINES HIMSELF TO HIS CABIN.
HALF AN HOUR LATER THE BARONTA HOISTS ITS ANCHOR AND SLIPS OUT TO SEA, DESTINED FOR ONE OF THE STRANGEST VOYAGES THE WORLD HAS EVER KNOWN.
IT IS THE FIRST NIGHT OUT. . . AS NORVELL NERVOUSLY PACES HIS CABIN, THERE COMES A KNOCK AT THE DOOR . . . HE ANSWERS IT . . . .
20
YOU!
YES,--I THOUGHT I'D DROP BY AND COMPLIMENT YOU ON HAVING HAD SENSE ENOUGH TO SHOW UP!
21
A MOMENT AFTER SUPERMAN DEPARTS . . .
THAT'S HIM! REMEMBER!-- IF HE DIES, YOUR REWARD WILL BE FABULOUS!
HE'S AS GOOD AS DEAD RIGHT NOW!
22

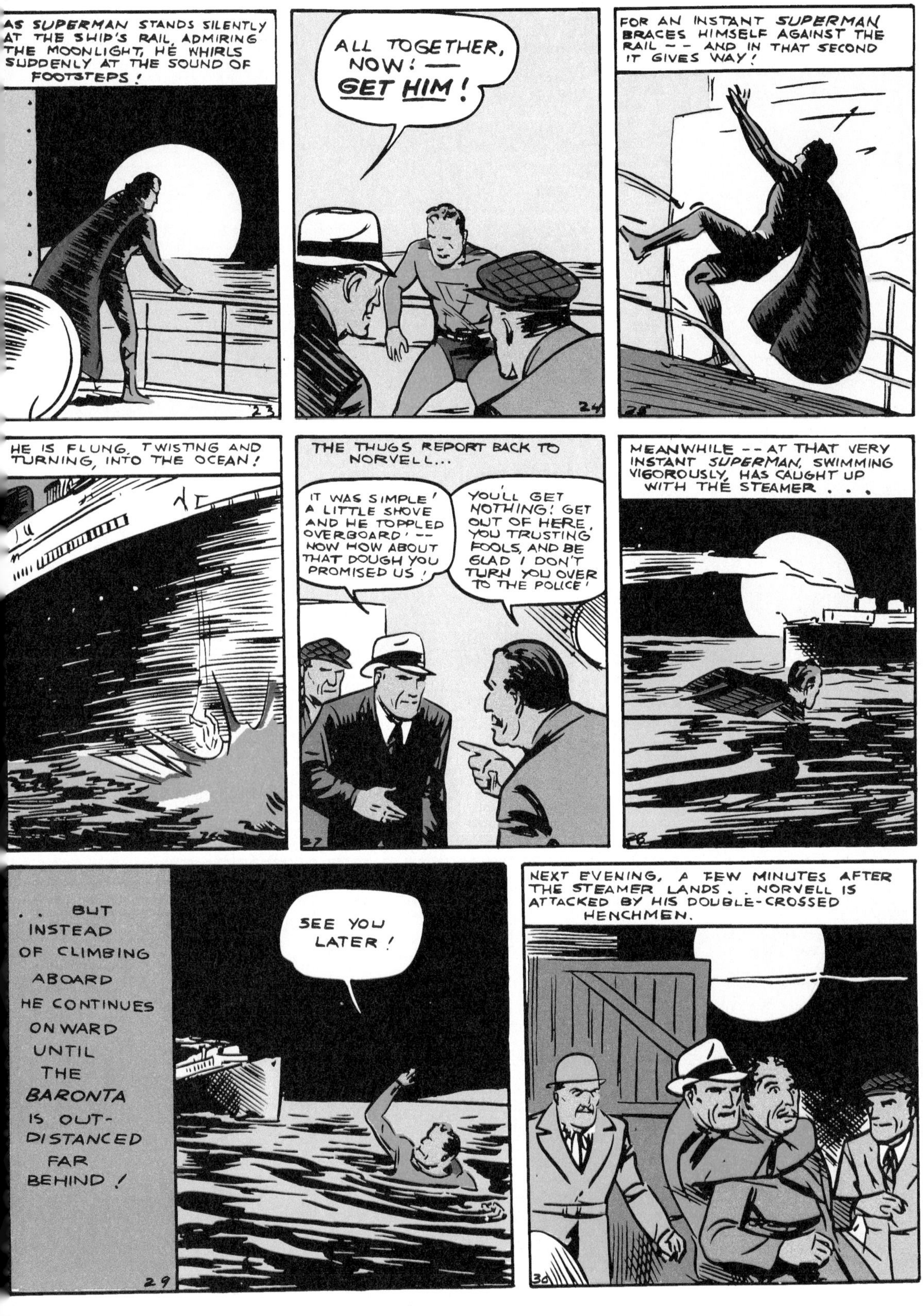
AS SUPERMAN STANDS SILENTLY AT THE SHIP'S RAIL, ADMIRING THE MOONLIGHT, HE WHIRLS SUDDENLY AT THE SOUND OF FOOTSTEPS!
ALL TOGETHER, NOW! — GET HIM!
FOR AN INSTANT SUPERMAN BRACES HIMSELF AGAINST THE RAIL -- AND IN THAT SECOND IT GIVES WAY!
HE IS FLUNG, TWISTING AND TURNING, INTO THE OCEAN!
THE THUGS REPORT BACK TO NORVELL...
IT WAS SIMPLE! A LITTLE SHOVE AND HE TOPPLED OVERBOARD! -- NOW HOW ABOUT THAT DOUGH YOU PROMISED US!
YOU'LL GET NOTHING! GET OUT OF HERE, YOU TRUSTING FOOLS, AND BE GLAD I DON'T TURN YOU OVER TO THE POLICE!
MEANWHILE -- AT THAT VERY INSTANT SUPERMAN, SWIMMING VIGOROUSLY, HAS CAUGHT UP WITH THE STEAMER . . .
. . BUT INSTEAD OF CLIMBING ABOARD HE CONTINUES ONWARD UNTIL THE BARONTA IS OUT-DISTANCED FAR BEHIND!
SEE YOU LATER!
NEXT EVENING, A FEW MINUTES AFTER THE STEAMER LANDS . . NORVELL IS ATTACKED BY HIS DOUBLE-CROSSED HENCHMEN.

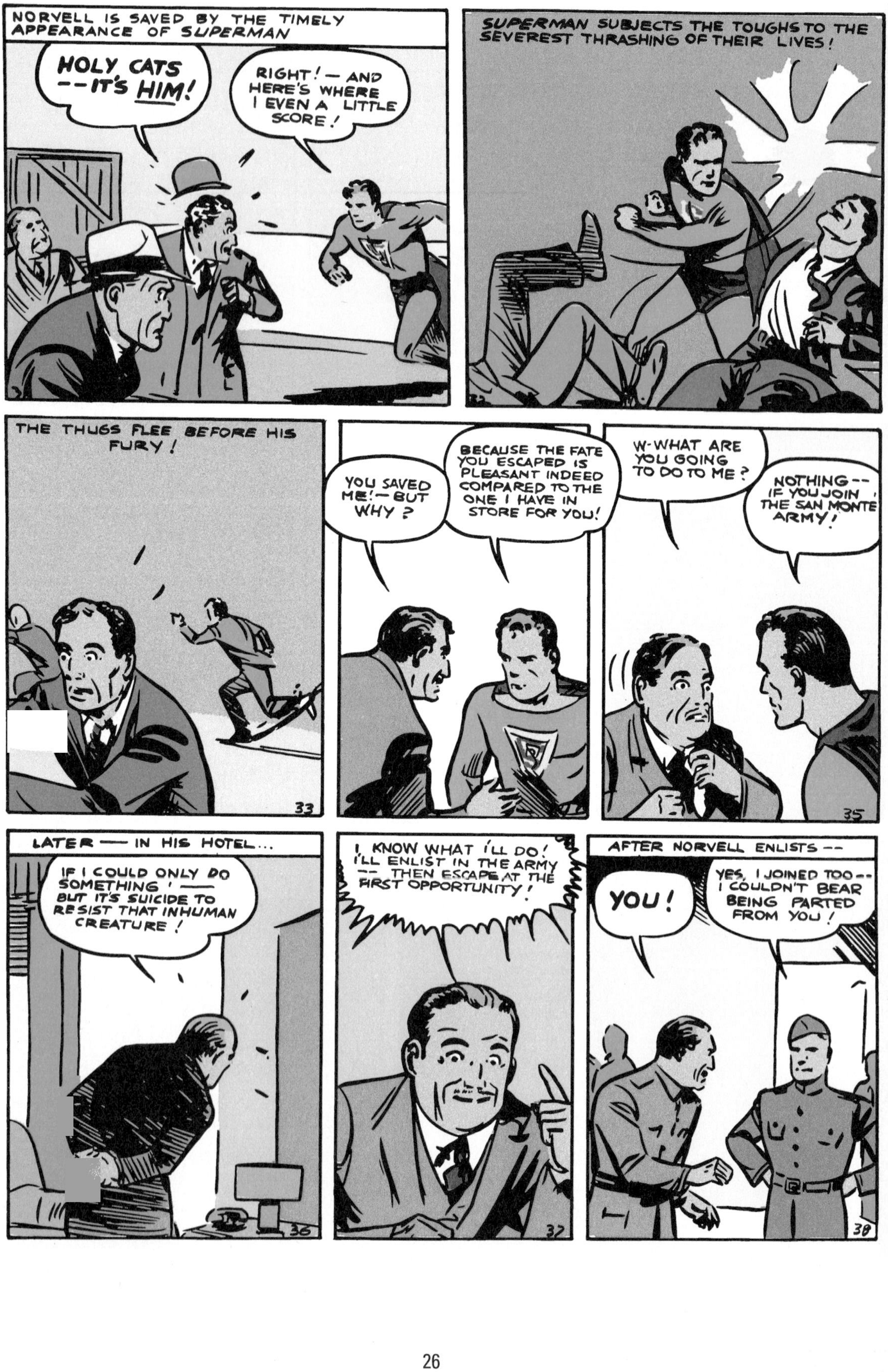
NORVELL IS SAVED BY THE TIMELY APPEARANCE OF SUPERMAN
HOLY CATS --IT'S HIM!
RIGHT! — AND HERE'S WHERE I EVEN A LITTLE SCORE!
SUPERMAN SUBJECTS THE TOUGHS TO THE SEVEREST THRASHING OF THEIR LIVES!
THE THUGS FLEE BEFORE HIS FURY!
YOU SAVED ME! — BUT WHY?
BECAUSE THE FATE YOU ESCAPED IS PLEASANT INDEED COMPARED TO THE ONE I HAVE IN STORE FOR YOU!
W-WHAT ARE YOU GOING TO DO TO ME?
NOTHING -- IF YOU JOIN THE SAN MONTE ARMY!
LATER — IN HIS HOTEL...
IF I COULD ONLY DO SOMETHING! — BUT IT'S SUICIDE TO RESIST THAT INHUMAN CREATURE!
I KNOW WHAT I'LL DO! I'LL ENLIST IN THE ARMY -- THEN ESCAPE AT THE FIRST OPPORTUNITY!
AFTER NORVELL ENLISTS --
YOU!
YES, I JOINED TOO -- I COULDN'T BEAR BEING PARTED FROM YOU!

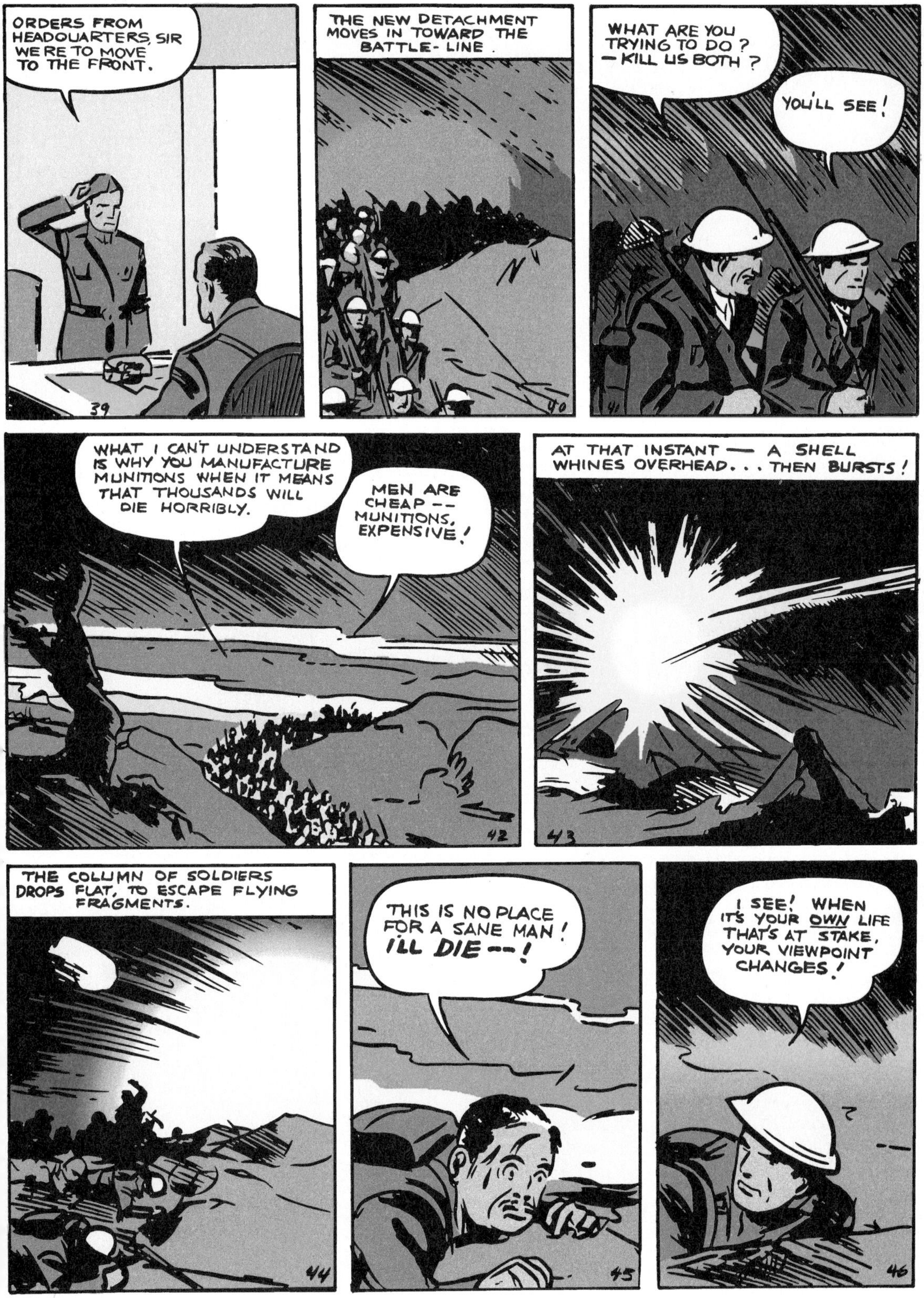
ORDERS FROM HEADQUARTERS, SIR WE'RE TO MOVE TO THE FRONT.
THE NEW DETACHMENT MOVES IN TOWARD THE BATTLE-LINE.
WHAT ARE YOU TRYING TO DO? —KILL US BOTH?
YOU'LL SEE!
WHAT I CAN'T UNDERSTAND IS WHY YOU MANUFACTURE MUNITIONS WHEN IT MEANS THAT THOUSANDS WILL DIE HORRIBLY.
MEN ARE CHEAP -- MUNITIONS, EXPENSIVE!
AT THAT INSTANT — A SHELL WHINES OVERHEAD. . . THEN BURSTS!
THE COLUMN OF SOLDIERS DROPS FLAT, TO ESCAPE FLYING FRAGMENTS.
THIS IS NO PLACE FOR A SANE MAN! I'LL DIE --!
I SEE! WHEN IT'S YOUR OWN LIFE THAT'S AT STAKE, YOUR VIEWPOINT CHANGES!

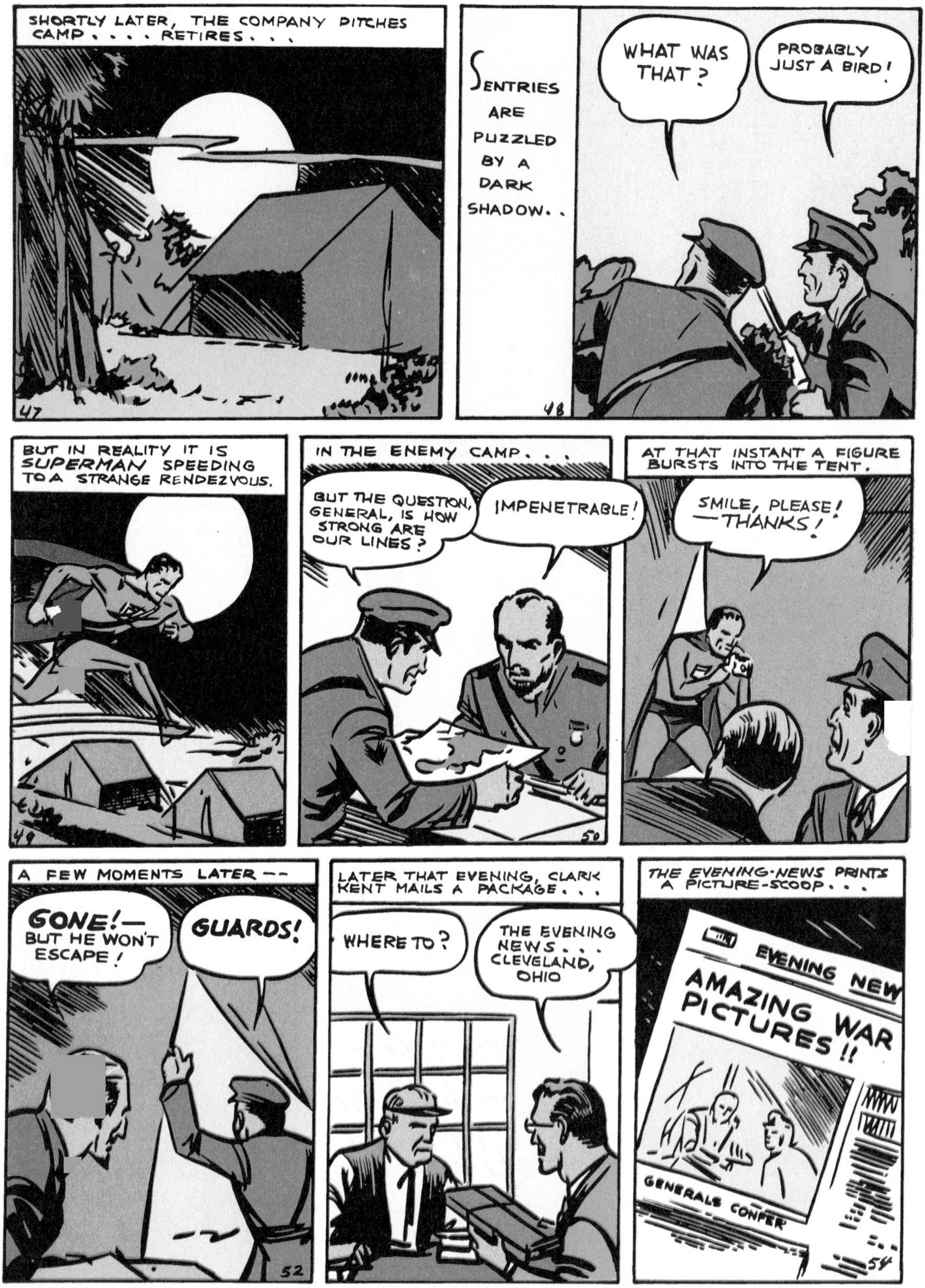
SHORTLY LATER, THE COMPANY PITCHES CAMP. . . . RETIRES. . .
SENTRIES ARE PUZZLED BY A DARK SHADOW. .
WHAT WAS THAT?
PROBABLY JUST A BIRD!
BUT IN REALITY IT IS SUPERMAN SPEEDING TO A STRANGE RENDEZVOUS.
IN THE ENEMY CAMP. . .
BUT THE QUESTION, GENERAL, IS HOW STRONG ARE OUR LINES?
IMPENETRABLE!
AT THAT INSTANT A FIGURE BURSTS INTO THE TENT.
SMILE, PLEASE! —THANKS!
A FEW MOMENTS LATER --
GONE!— BUT HE WON'T ESCAPE!
GUARDS!
LATER THAT EVENING, CLARK KENT MAILS A PACKAGE. . .
WHERE TO?
THE EVENING NEWS. . . CLEVELAND, OHIO
THE EVENING-NEWS PRINTS A PICTURE-SCOOP. . .
EVENING NEW
AMAZING WAR PICTURES!!
GENERALS CONFER

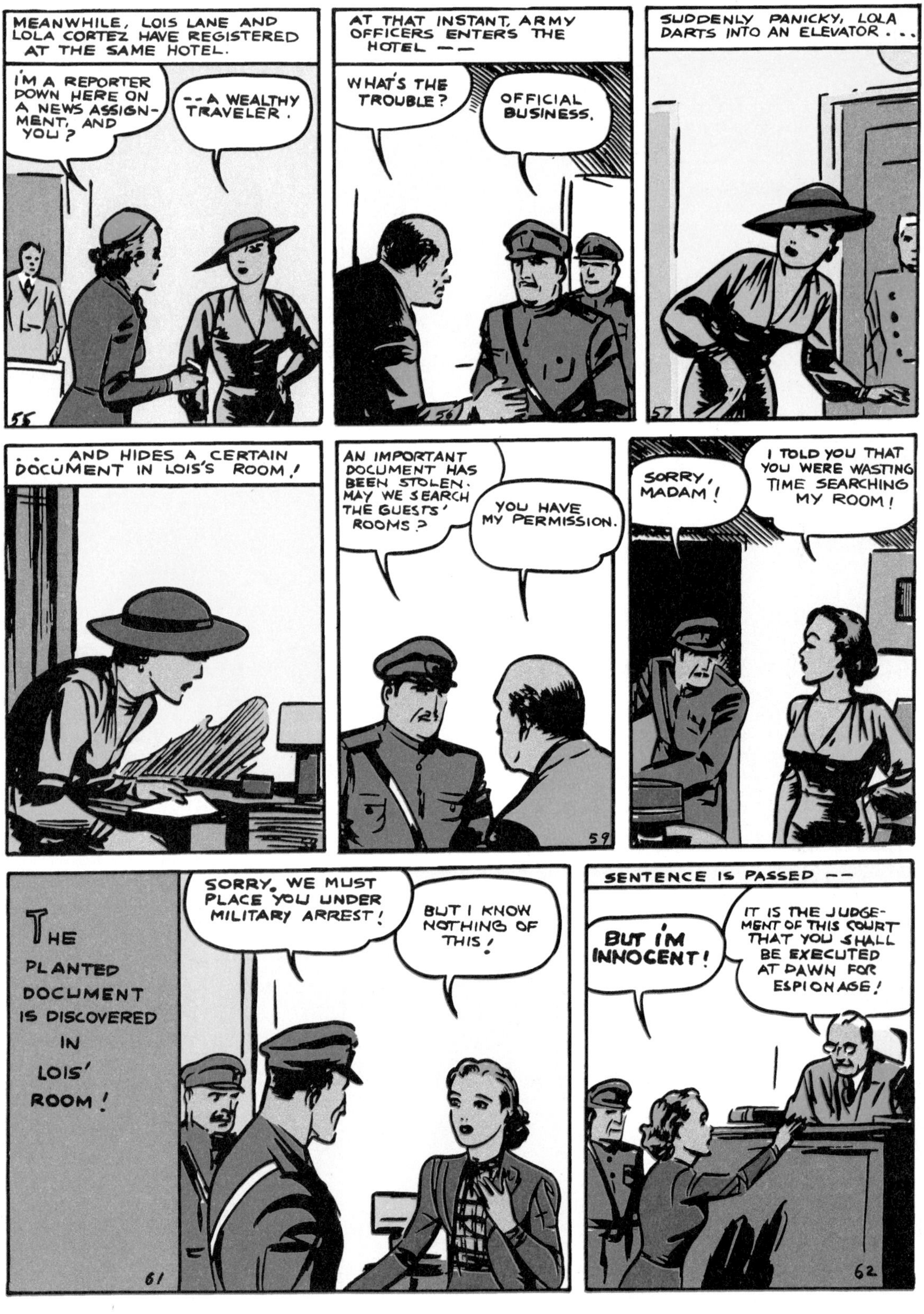
MEANWHILE, LOIS LANE AND LOLA CORTEZ HAVE REGISTERED AT THE SAME HOTEL.
I'M A REPORTER DOWN HERE ON A NEWS ASSIGNMENT, AND YOU?
--A WEALTHY TRAVELER.
AT THAT INSTANT, ARMY OFFICERS ENTERS THE HOTEL --
WHAT'S THE TROUBLE?
OFFICIAL BUSINESS.
SUDDENLY PANICKY, LOLA DARTS INTO AN ELEVATOR . . .
. . . AND HIDES A CERTAIN DOCUMENT IN LOIS'S ROOM!
AN IMPORTANT DOCUMENT HAS BEEN STOLEN. MAY WE SEARCH THE GUESTS' ROOMS?
YOU HAVE MY PERMISSION.
SORRY, MADAM!
I TOLD YOU THAT YOU WERE WASTING TIME SEARCHING MY ROOM!
THE PLANTED DOCUMENT IS DISCOVERED IN LOIS' ROOM!
SORRY, WE MUST PLACE YOU UNDER MILITARY ARREST!
BUT I KNOW NOTHING OF THIS!
SENTENCE IS PASSED --
BUT I'M INNOCENT!
IT IS THE JUDGEMENT OF THIS COURT THAT YOU SHALL BE EXECUTED AT DAWN FOR ESPIONAGE!

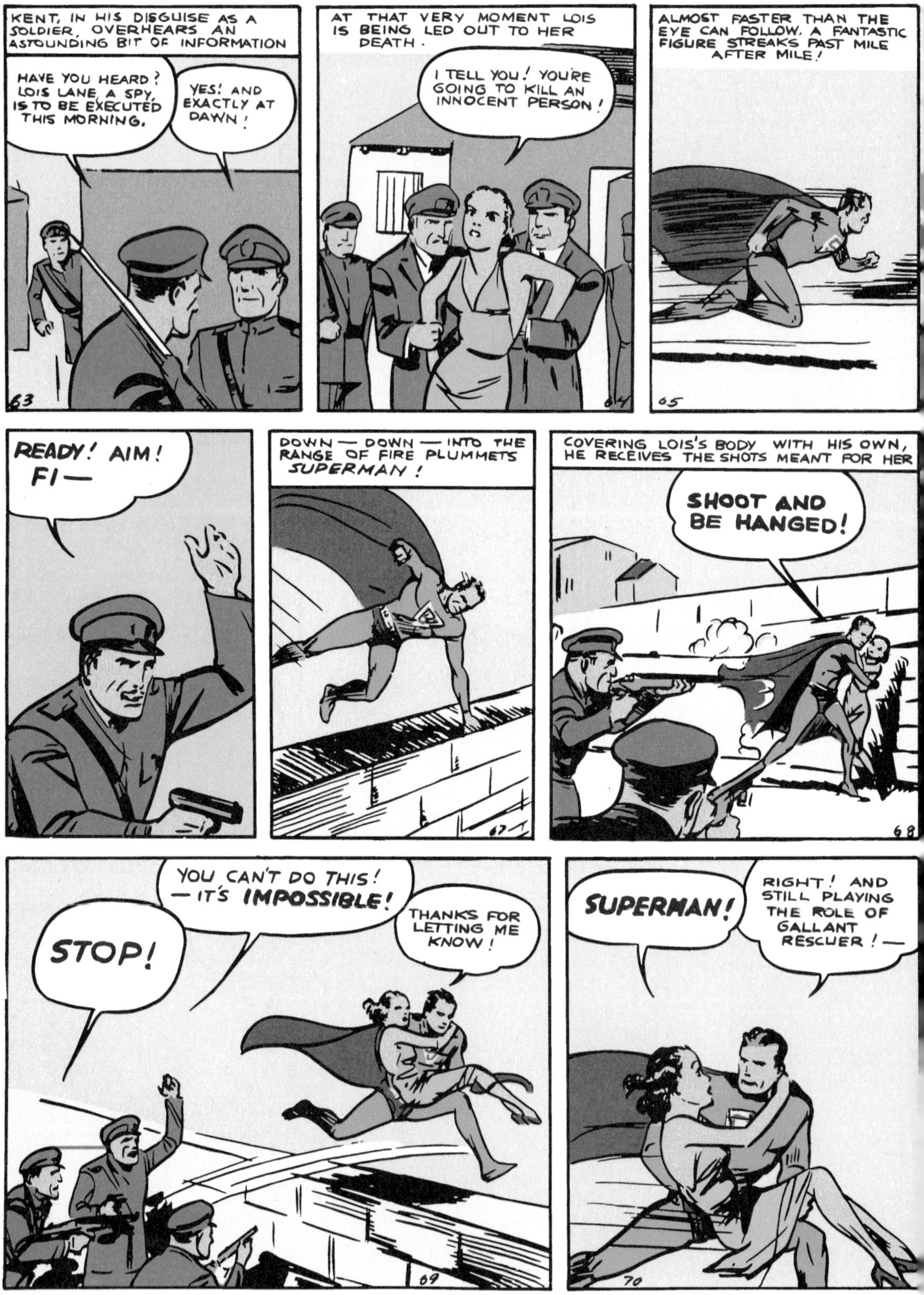

KENT, IN HIS DISGUISE AS A SOLDIER, OVERHEARS AN ASTOUNDING BIT OF INFORMATION
HAVE YOU HEARD? LOIS LANE, A SPY, IS TO BE EXECUTED THIS MORNING.
YES! AND EXACTLY AT DAWN!
AT THAT VERY MOMENT LOIS IS BEING LED OUT TO HER DEATH.
I TELL YOU! YOU'RE GOING TO KILL AN INNOCENT PERSON!
ALMOST FASTER THAN THE EYE CAN FOLLOW, A FANTASTIC FIGURE STREAKS PAST MILE AFTER MILE!
READY! AIM! FI—
DOWN — DOWN — INTO THE RANGE OF FIRE PLUMMETS SUPERMAN!
COVERING LOIS'S BODY WITH HIS OWN, HE RECEIVES THE SHOTS MEANT FOR HER
SHOOT AND BE HANGED!
STOP!
YOU CAN'T DO THIS! — IT'S IMPOSSIBLE!
THANKS FOR LETTING ME KNOW!
SUPERMAN!
RIGHT! AND STILL PLAYING THE ROLE OF GALLANT RESCUER! —

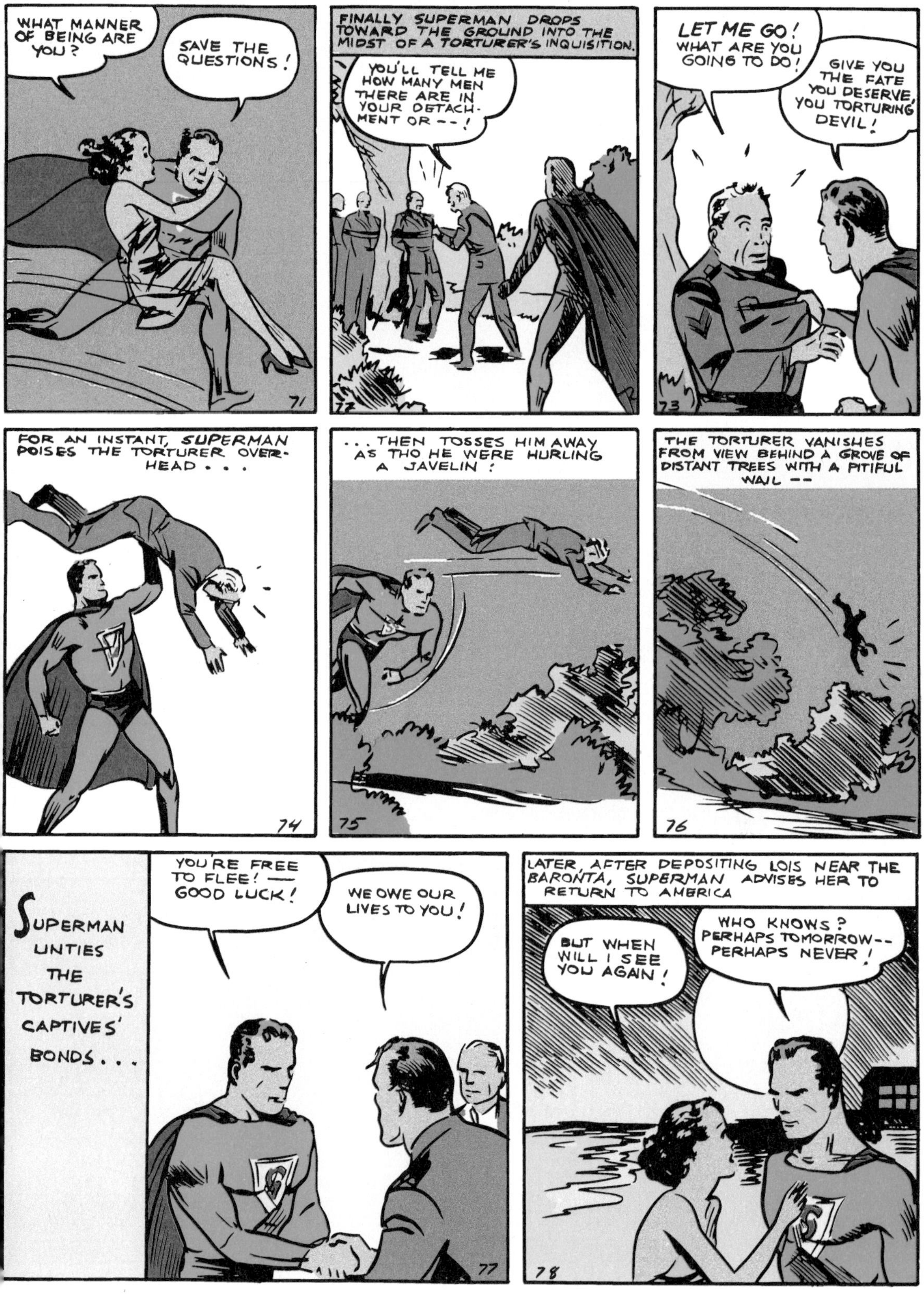
WHAT MANNER OF BEING ARE YOU?
SAVE THE QUESTIONS!
71
FINALLY SUPERMAN DROPS TOWARD THE GROUND INTO THE MIDST OF A TORTURER'S INQUISITION.
YOU'LL TELL ME HOW MANY MEN THERE ARE IN YOUR DETACHMENT OR --!
72
LET ME GO! WHAT ARE YOU GOING TO DO!
GIVE YOU THE FATE YOU DESERVE, YOU TORTURING DEVIL!
73
FOR AN INSTANT, SUPERMAN POISES THE TORTURER OVERHEAD . . .
74
. . . THEN TOSSES HIM AWAY AS THO HE WERE HURLING A JAVELIN!
75
THE TORTURER VANISHES FROM VIEW BEHIND A GROVE OF DISTANT TREES WITH A PITIFUL WAIL --
76
SUPERMAN UNTIES THE TORTURER'S CAPTIVES' BONDS . . .
YOU'RE FREE TO FLEE! — GOOD LUCK!
WE OWE OUR LIVES TO YOU!
77
LATER, AFTER DEPOSITING LOIS NEAR THE BARONTA, SUPERMAN ADVISES HER TO RETURN TO AMERICA
BUT WHEN WILL I SEE YOU AGAIN!
WHO KNOWS? PERHAPS TOMORROW-- PERHAPS NEVER!
78

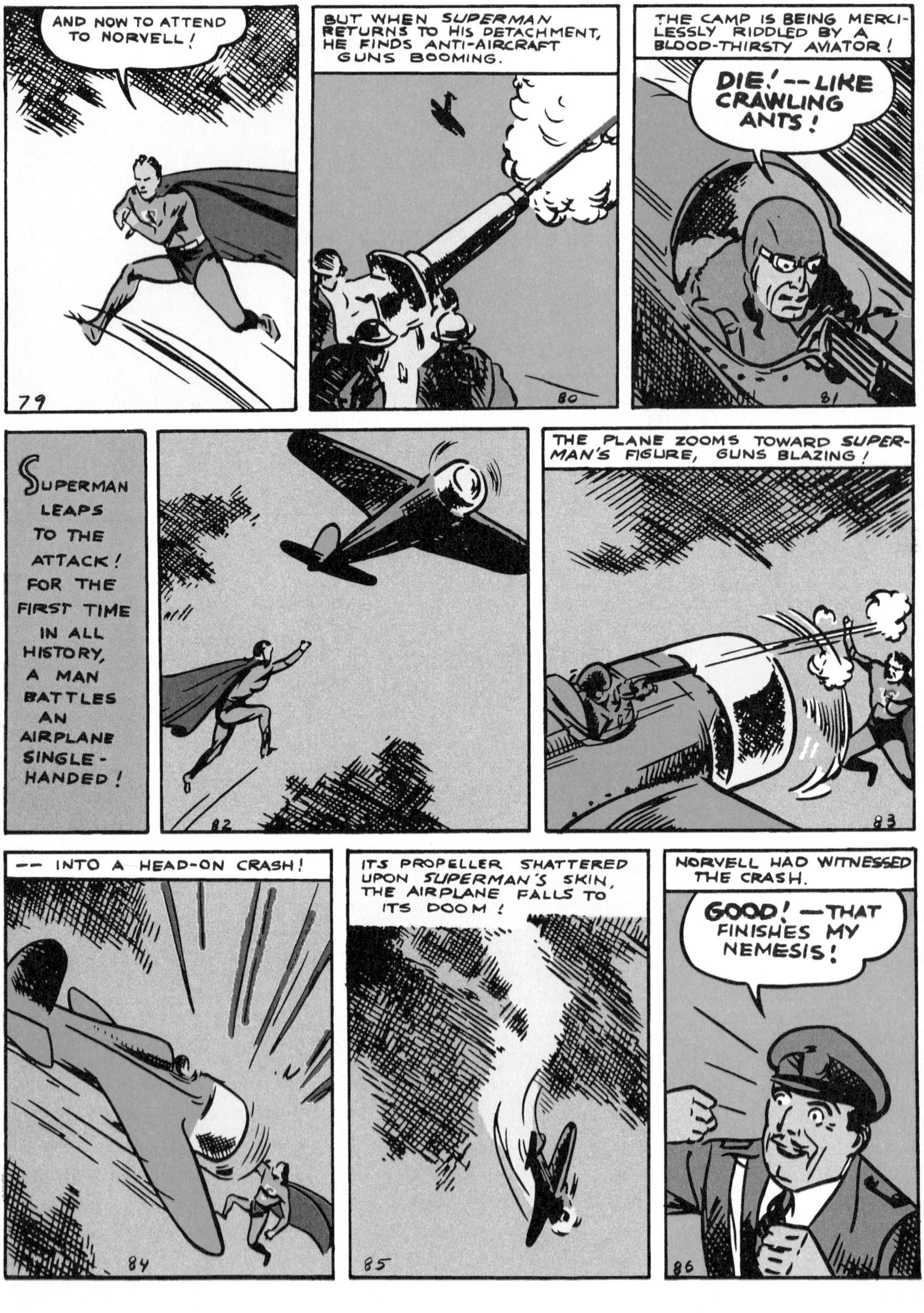
AND NOW TO ATTEND TO NORVELL!
79
BUT WHEN SUPERMAN RETURNS TO HIS DETACHMENT, HE FINDS ANTI-AIRCRAFT GUNS BOOMING.
80
THE CAMP IS BEING MERCILESSLY RIDDLED BY A BLOOD-THIRSTY AVIATOR!
DIE! --LIKE CRAWLING ANTS!
81
SUPERMAN LEAPS TO THE ATTACK! FOR THE FIRST TIME IN ALL HISTORY, A MAN BATTLES AN AIRPLANE SINGLE-HANDED!
82
THE PLANE ZOOMS TOWARD SUPERMAN'S FIGURE, GUNS BLAZING!
83
-- INTO A HEAD-ON CRASH!
84
ITS PROPELLER SHATTERED UPON SUPERMAN'S SKIN, THE AIRPLANE FALLS TO ITS DOOM!
85
NORVELL HAD WITNESSED THE CRASH.
GOOD! —THAT FINISHES MY NEMESIS!
86

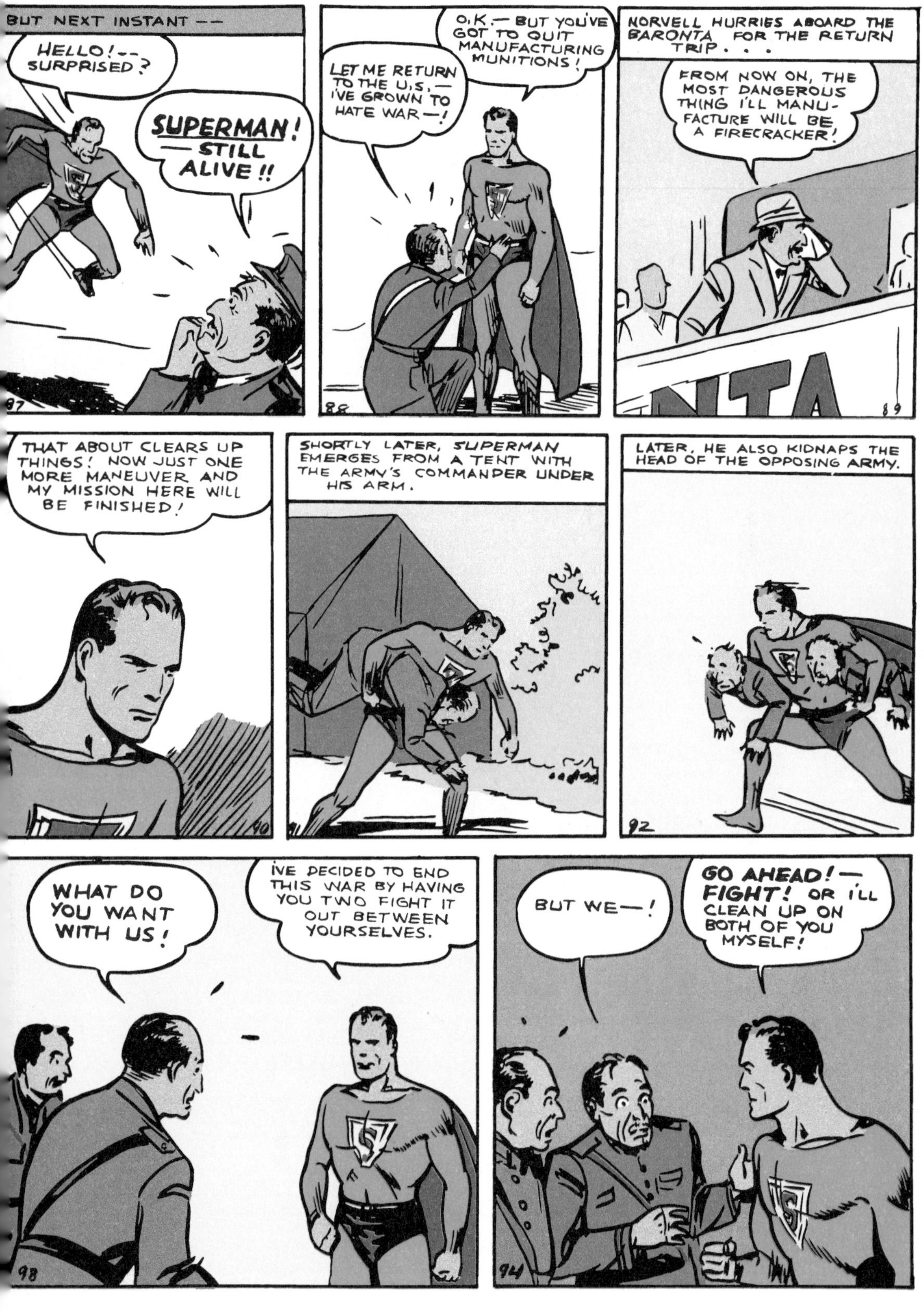
BUT NEXT INSTANT --
HELLO!-- SURPRISED?
SUPERMAN! — STILL ALIVE!!
O.K.— BUT YOU'VE GOT TO QUIT MANUFACTURING MUNITIONS!
LET ME RETURN TO THE U.S.— I'VE GROWN TO HATE WAR—!
NORVELL HURRIES ABOARD THE BARONTA FOR THE RETURN TRIP . . .
FROM NOW ON, THE MOST DANGEROUS THING I'LL MANUFACTURE WILL BE A FIRECRACKER!
NTA
THAT ABOUT CLEARS UP THINGS! NOW JUST ONE MORE MANEUVER AND MY MISSION HERE WILL BE FINISHED!
SHORTLY LATER, SUPERMAN EMERGES FROM A TENT WITH THE ARMY'S COMMANDER UNDER HIS ARM.
LATER, HE ALSO KIDNAPS THE HEAD OF THE OPPOSING ARMY.
WHAT DO YOU WANT WITH US!
I'VE DECIDED TO END THIS WAR BY HAVING YOU TWO FIGHT IT OUT BETWEEN YOURSELVES.
BUT WE—!
GO AHEAD!— FIGHT! OR I'LL CLEAN UP ON BOTH OF YOU MYSELF!

BUT WHY SHOULD WE FIGHT?
WE'RE NOT ANGRY AT EACH OTHER!
THEN WHY ARE YOUR ARMIES BATTLING?
I DON'T KNOW! CAN YOU TELL ME?
NO. CAN YOU?
GENTLEMEN, IT'S OBVIOUS YOU'VE BEEN FIGHTING ONLY TO PROMOTE THE SALE OF MUNITIONS! — WHY NOT SHAKE HANDS AND MAKE UP?
AND SO, DUE TO THE CONCILIATORY EFFORTS OF SUPERMAN, THE WAR IS HALTED.
WHEN KENT REPORTS BACK TO HIS EDITOR . .
SINCE YOU'VE BEEN GONE, THERE'S BEEN NO SUPERMAN NEWS. MAYBE HE'S RETIRED FOR GOOD!
SOMEHOW, CHIEF, I'VE A HUNCH HE'LL MAKE HIS APPEARANCE AGAIN--SOON!
THE END

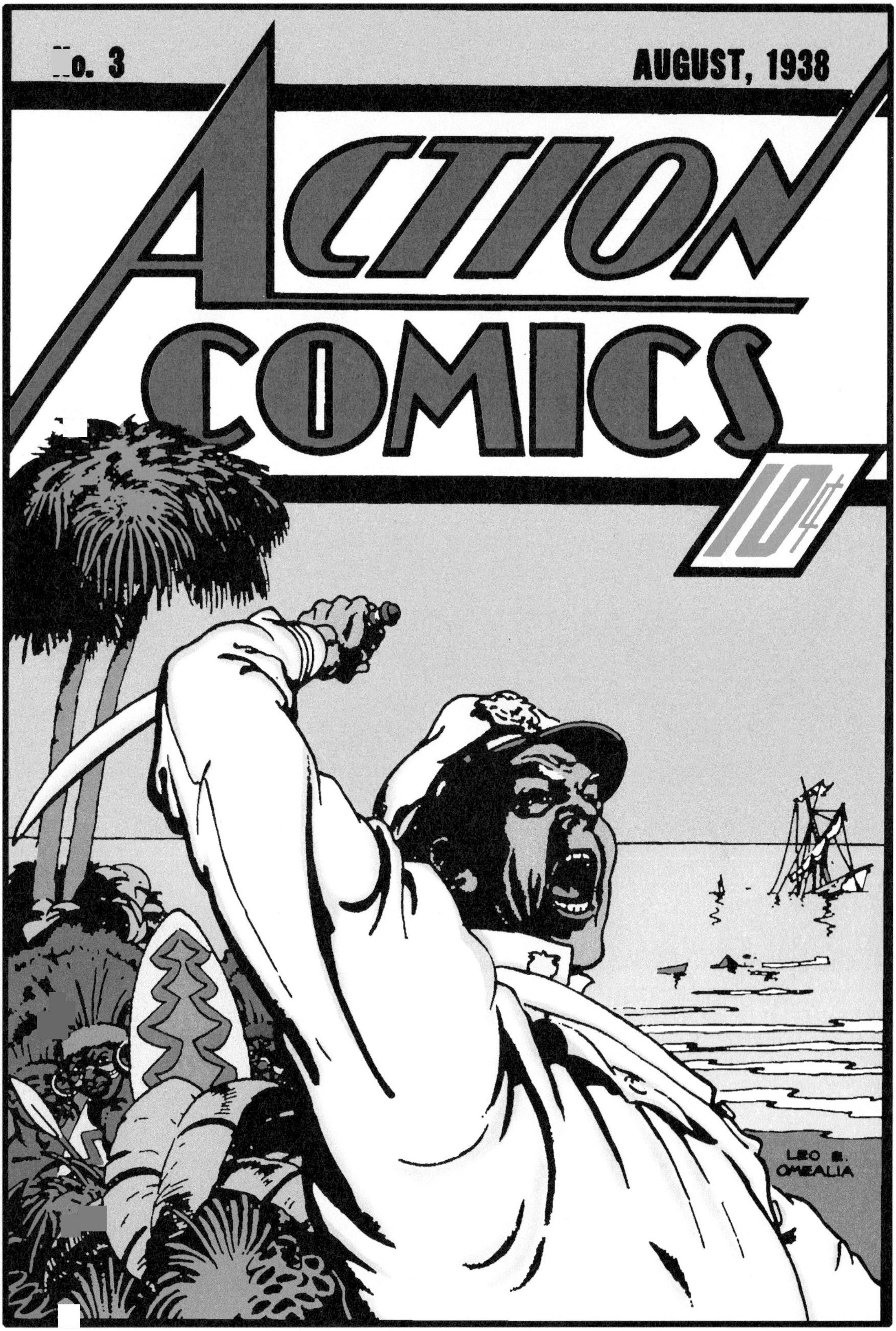
AUGUST, 1938
ACTION COMICS
10¢
LEO E. OMEALIA

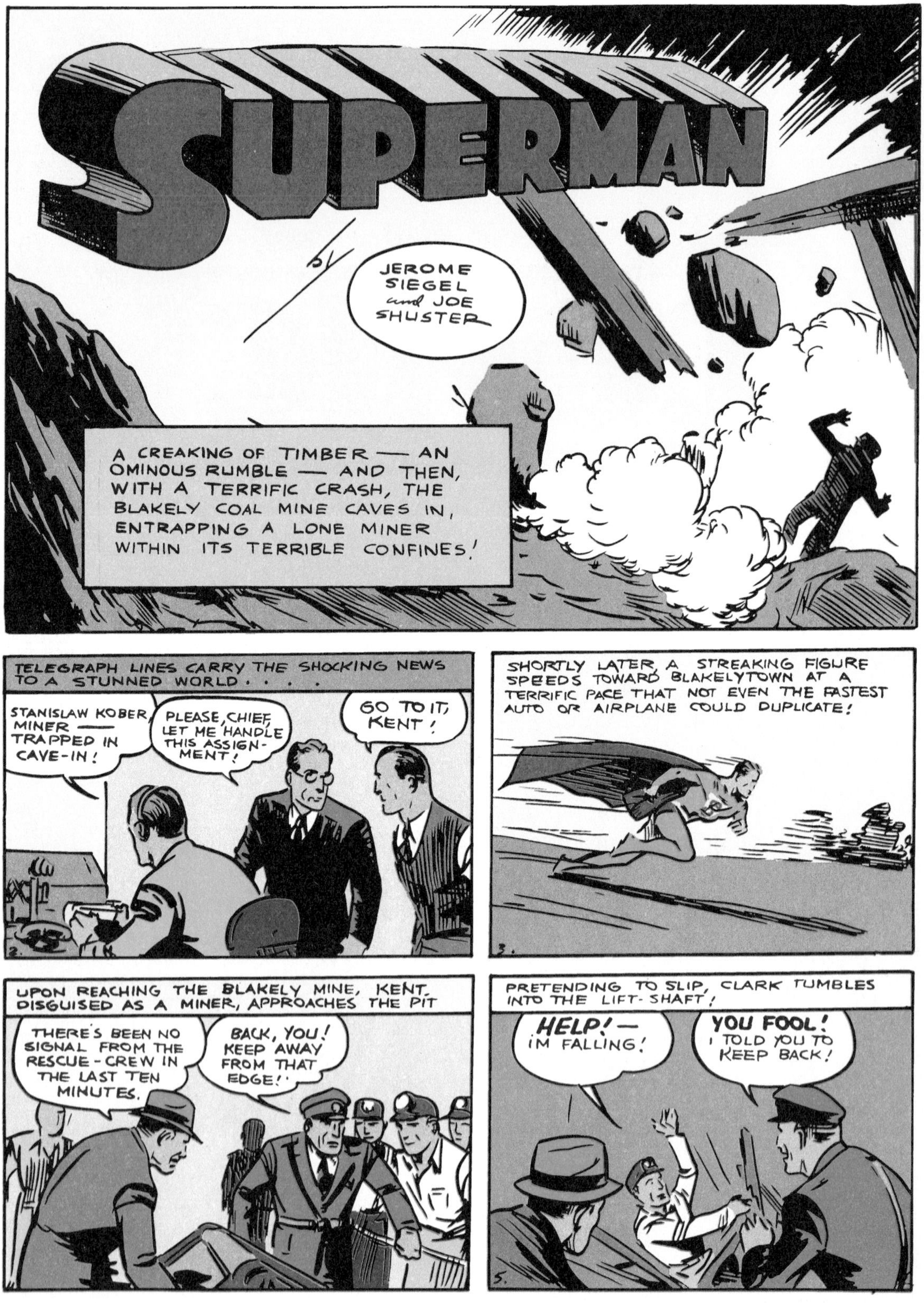
SUPERMAN
by
JEROME SIEGEL and JOE SHUSTER
A CREAKING OF TIMBER — AN OMINOUS RUMBLE — AND THEN, WITH A TERRIFIC CRASH, THE BLAKELY COAL MINE CAVES IN, ENTRAPPING A LONE MINER WITHIN ITS TERRIBLE CONFINES!
TELEGRAPH LINES CARRY THE SHOCKING NEWS TO A STUNNED WORLD. . . .
STANISLAW KOBER, MINER — TRAPPED IN CAVE-IN!
PLEASE, CHIEF, LET ME HANDLE THIS ASSIGNMENT!
GO TO IT, KENT!
2.
SHORTLY LATER, A STREAKING FIGURE SPEEDS TOWARD BLAKELYTOWN AT A TERRIFIC PACE THAT NOT EVEN THE FASTEST AUTO OR AIRPLANE COULD DUPLICATE!
3.
UPON REACHING THE BLAKELY MINE, KENT, DISGUISED AS A MINER, APPROACHES THE PIT
THERE'S BEEN NO SIGNAL FROM THE RESCUE-CREW IN THE LAST TEN MINUTES.
BACK, YOU! KEEP AWAY FROM THAT EDGE!
PRETENDING TO SLIP, CLARK TUMBLES INTO THE LIFT-SHAFT!
HELP! — IM FALLING!
YOU FOOL! I TOLD YOU TO KEEP BACK!
5.

DOWN PLUNGES *SUPERMAN* IN A FALL WHICH WOULD HAVE MEANT DEATH FOR AN ORDINARY MAN *!*

6.

AS *SUPERMAN* STRIKES THE BOTTOM OF THE SHAFT, HE DETECTS ——

GAS! — POISON GAS !

7.

HIS PHYSICAL STRUCTURE UNAFFECTED BY THE GAS, *SUPERMAN* CONTINUES ALONG THE MINE'S BOTTOM --

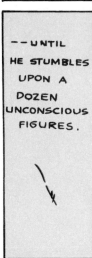

——UNTIL HE STUMBLES UPON A DOZEN UNCONSCIOUS FIGURES.

THE RESCUE-PARTY! I'D BETTER GET THEM OUT OF HERE *BEFORE* THE GAS FINISHES ITS DEADLY WORK!

10.

A TRIFLE UNCEREMONIOUS —— BUT THE OCCASION DEMANDS IT !

11.

PLACING THE MEN ON THE LIFT, *SUPERMAN* JERKS THE SIGNAL CORD, AND THE ELEVATOR BEGINS ITS UPWARD JOURNEY.

12.

THAT'S THAT ! — AND NOW TO *REALLY* GET TO WORK !

13.

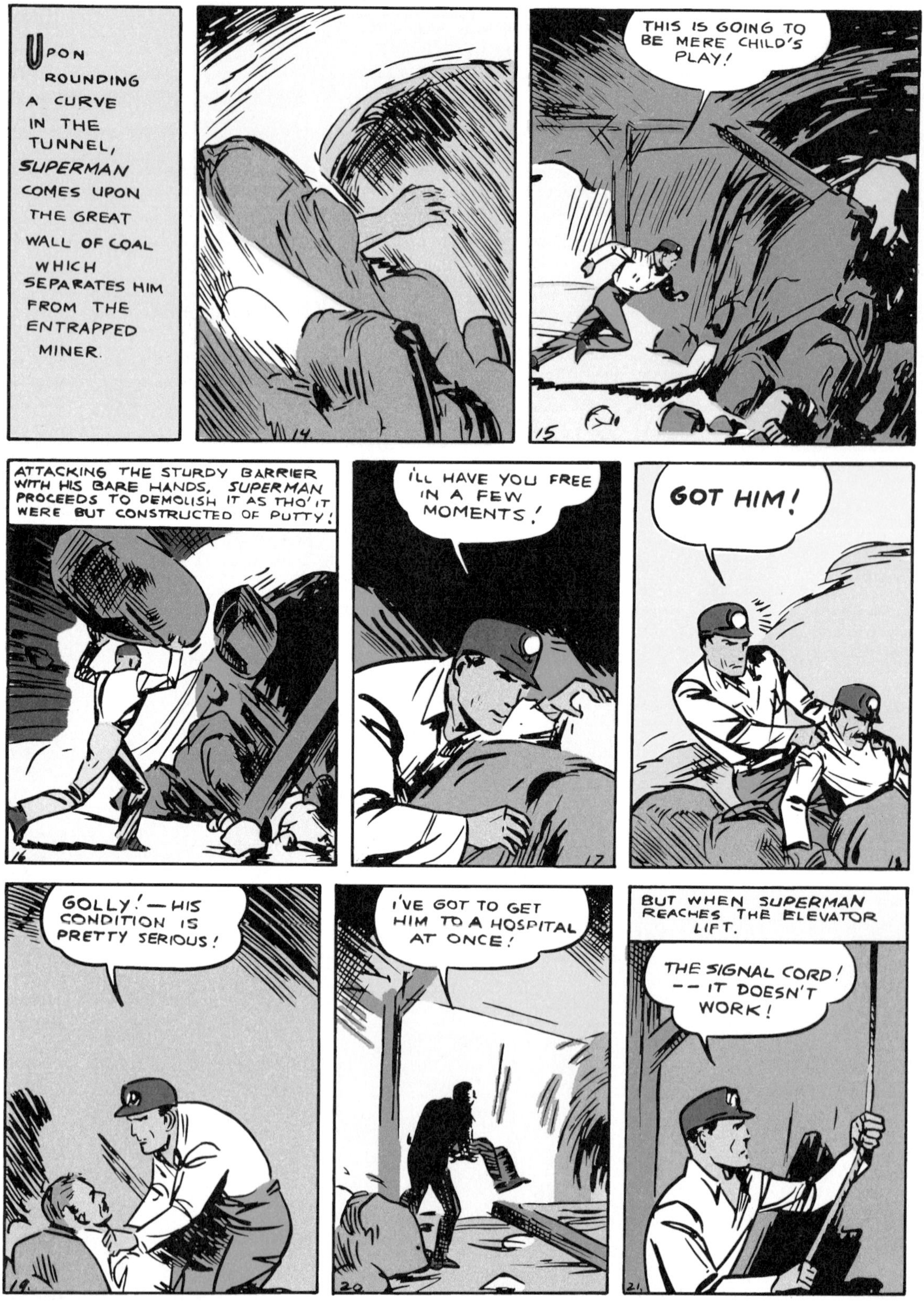
UPON ROUNDING A CURVE IN THE TUNNEL, SUPERMAN COMES UPON THE GREAT WALL OF COAL WHICH SEPARATES HIM FROM THE ENTRAPPED MINER.
THIS IS GOING TO BE MERE CHILD'S PLAY!
ATTACKING THE STURDY BARRIER WITH HIS BARE HANDS, SUPERMAN PROCEEDS TO DEMOLISH IT AS THO' IT WERE BUT CONSTRUCTED OF PUTTY!
I'LL HAVE YOU FREE IN A FEW MOMENTS!
GOT HIM!
GOLLY!—HIS CONDITION IS PRETTY SERIOUS!
I'VE GOT TO GET HIM TO A HOSPITAL AT ONCE!
BUT WHEN SUPERMAN REACHES THE ELEVATOR LIFT.
THE SIGNAL CORD! -- IT DOESN'T WORK!

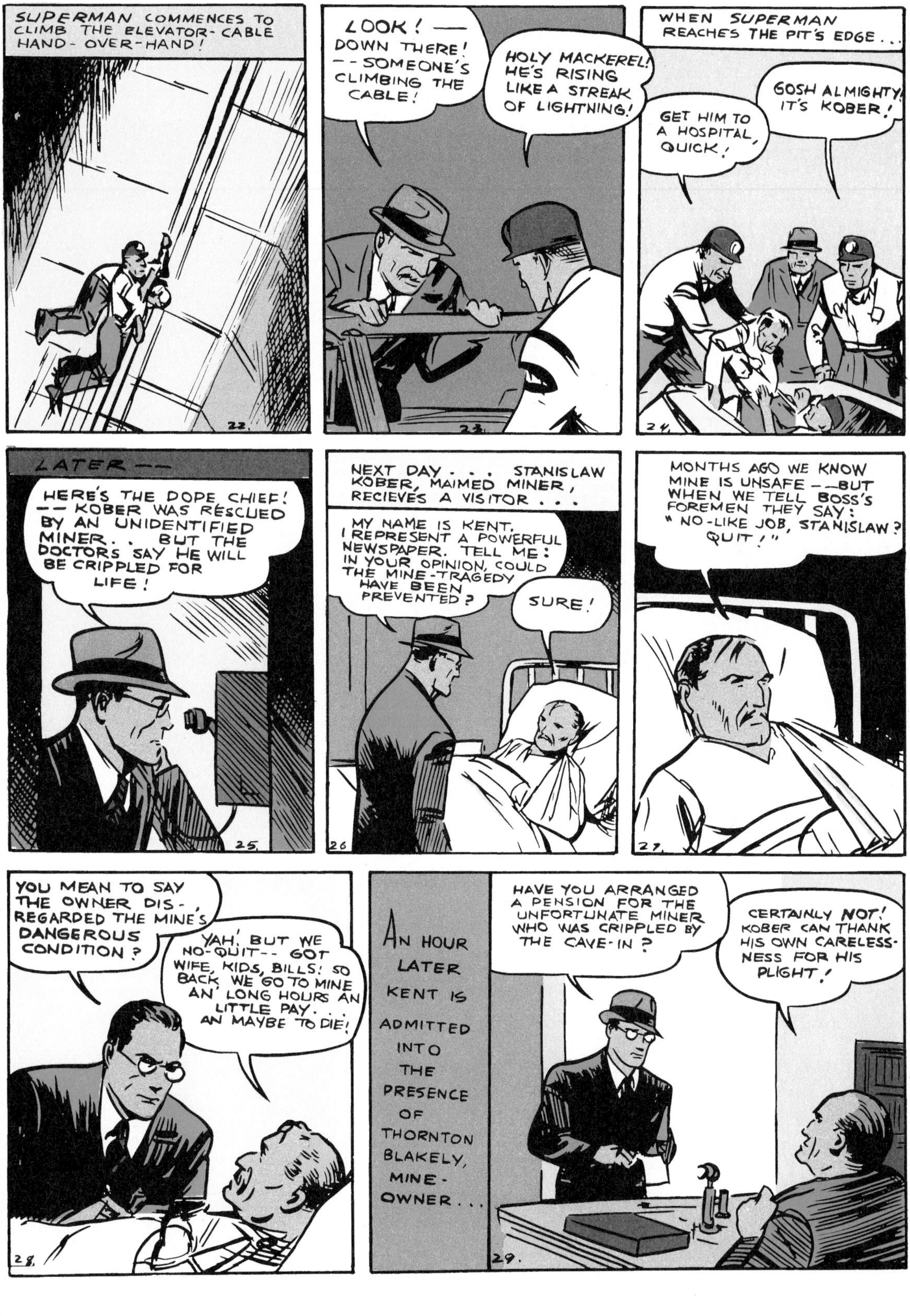
SUPERMAN COMMENCES TO CLIMB THE ELEVATOR-CABLE HAND-OVER-HAND!
22.
LOOK! — DOWN THERE! --SOMEONE'S CLIMBING THE CABLE!
HOLY MACKEREL! HE'S RISING LIKE A STREAK OF LIGHTNING!
23.
WHEN SUPERMAN REACHES THE PIT'S EDGE...
GOSH ALMIGHTY! IT'S KOBER!
GET HIM TO A HOSPITAL, QUICK!
24.
LATER --
HERE'S THE DOPE CHIEF! -- KOBER WAS RESCUED BY AN UNIDENTIFIED MINER.. BUT THE DOCTORS SAY HE WILL BE CRIPPLED FOR LIFE!
25.
NEXT DAY... STANISLAW KOBER, MAIMED MINER, RECIEVES A VISITOR...
MY NAME IS KENT. I REPRESENT A POWERFUL NEWSPAPER. TELL ME: IN YOUR OPINION, COULD THE MINE-TRAGEDY HAVE BEEN PREVENTED?
SURE!
26
MONTHS AGO WE KNOW MINE IS UNSAFE --BUT WHEN WE TELL BOSS'S FOREMEN THEY SAY: "NO-LIKE JOB, STANISLAW? QUIT!"
27.
YOU MEAN TO SAY THE OWNER DIS-REGARDED THE MINE'S DANGEROUS CONDITION?
YAH! BUT WE NO-QUIT-- GOT WIFE, KIDS, BILLS! SO BACK WE GO TO MINE AN' LONG HOURS AN LITTLE PAY... AN MAYBE TO DIE!
28.
AN HOUR LATER KENT IS ADMITTED INTO THE PRESENCE OF THORNTON BLAKELY, MINE-OWNER...
HAVE YOU ARRANGED A PENSION FOR THE UNFORTUNATE MINER WHO WAS CRIPPLED BY THE CAVE-IN?
CERTAINLY NOT! KOBER CAN THANK HIS OWN CARELESS-NESS FOR HIS PLIGHT!
29.

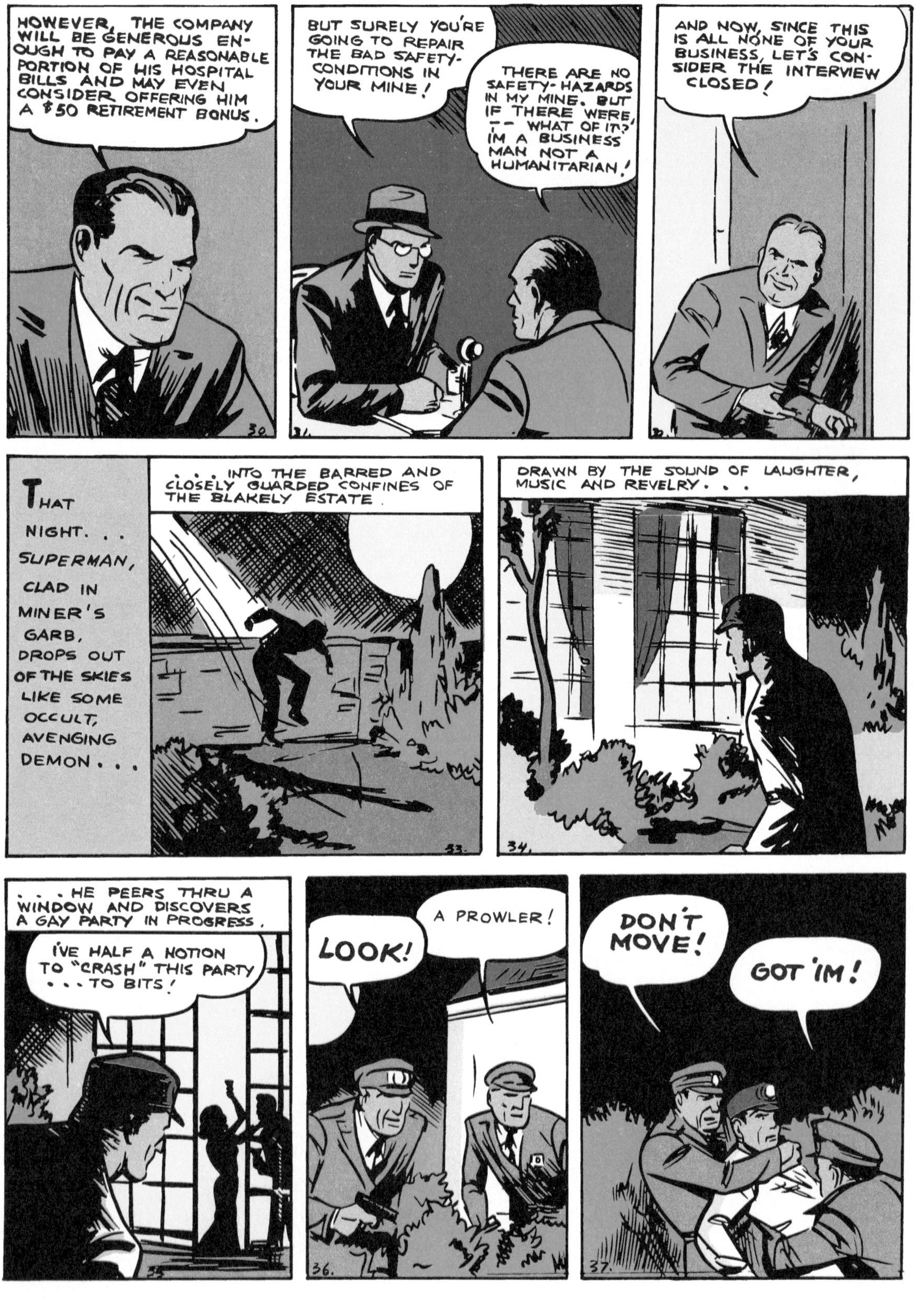
HOWEVER, THE COMPANY WILL BE GENEROUS ENOUGH TO PAY A REASONABLE PORTION OF HIS HOSPITAL BILLS AND MAY EVEN CONSIDER OFFERING HIM A $50 RETIREMENT BONUS.
BUT SURELY YOU'RE GOING TO REPAIR THE BAD SAFETY-CONDITIONS IN YOUR MINE!
THERE ARE NO SAFETY-HAZARDS IN MY MINE. BUT IF THERE WERE, -- WHAT OF IT? I'M A BUSINESS MAN NOT A HUMANITARIAN!
AND NOW, SINCE THIS IS ALL NONE OF YOUR BUSINESS, LET'S CONSIDER THE INTERVIEW CLOSED!
THAT NIGHT... SUPERMAN, CLAD IN MINER'S GARB, DROPS OUT OF THE SKIES LIKE SOME OCCULT, AVENGING DEMON...
...INTO THE BARRED AND CLOSELY GUARDED CONFINES OF THE BLAKELY ESTATE.
DRAWN BY THE SOUND OF LAUGHTER, MUSIC AND REVELRY...
...HE PEERS THRU A WINDOW AND DISCOVERS A GAY PARTY IN PROGRESS.
I'VE HALF A NOTION TO "CRASH" THIS PARTY ...TO BITS!
LOOK!
A PROWLER!
DON'T MOVE!
GOT 'IM!

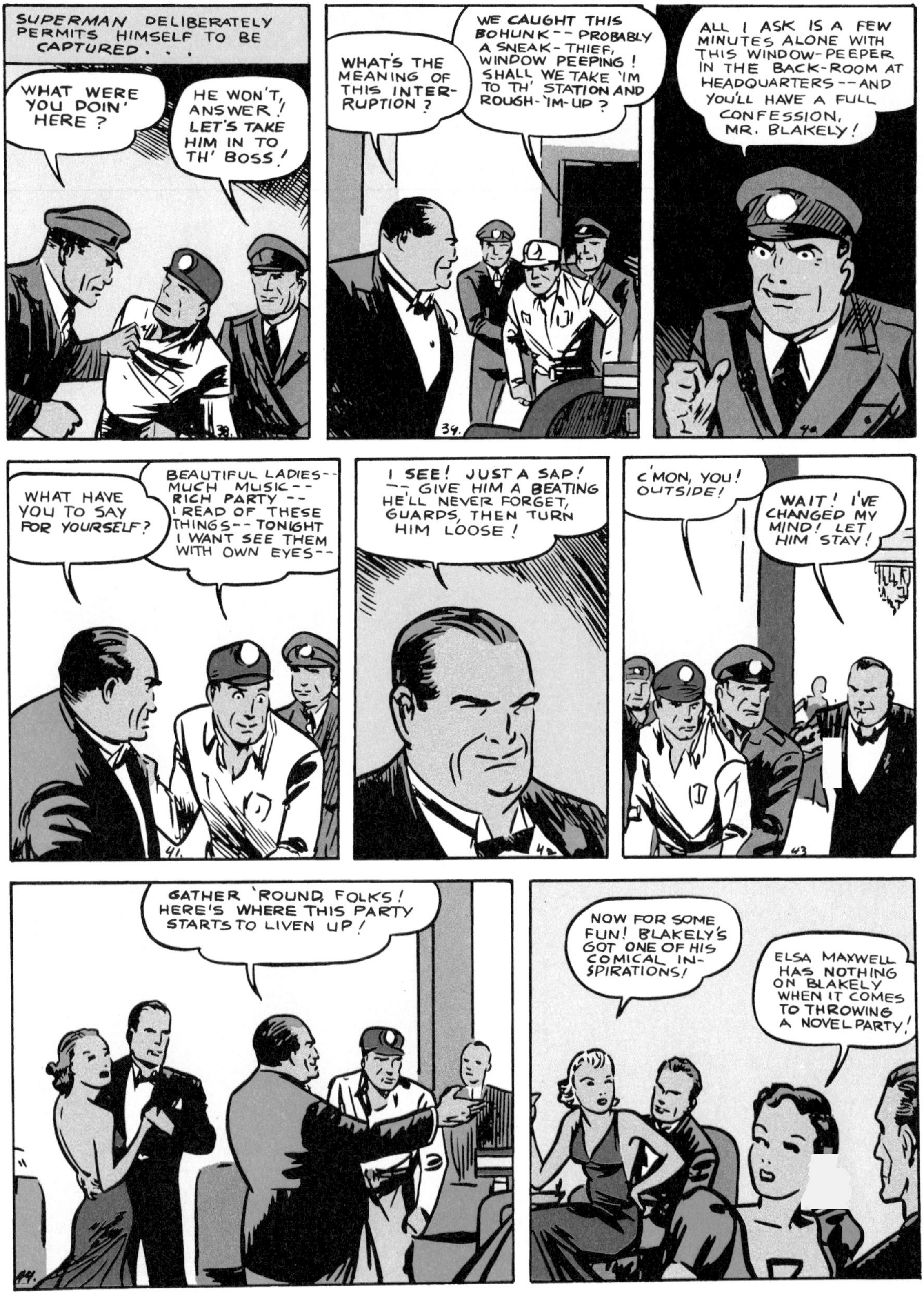
SUPERMAN DELIBERATELY PERMITS HIMSELF TO BE CAPTURED . . .
WHAT WERE YOU DOIN' HERE ?
HE WON'T ANSWER ! LET'S TAKE HIM IN TO TH' BOSS !
38.
WHAT'S THE MEANING OF THIS INTERRUPTION ?
WE CAUGHT THIS BOHUNK -- PROBABLY A SNEAK-THIEF, WINDOW PEEPING ! SHALL WE TAKE 'IM TO TH' STATION AND ROUGH-'IM-UP ?
39.
ALL I ASK IS A FEW MINUTES ALONE WITH THIS WINDOW-PEEPER IN THE BACK-ROOM AT HEADQUARTERS -- AND YOU'LL HAVE A FULL CONFESSION, MR. BLAKELY !
40
WHAT HAVE YOU TO SAY FOR YOURSELF ?
BEAUTIFUL LADIES -- MUCH MUSIC -- RICH PARTY -- I READ OF THESE THINGS -- TONIGHT I WANT SEE THEM WITH OWN EYES --
41.
I SEE ! JUST A SAP ! -- GIVE HIM A BEATING HE'LL NEVER FORGET, GUARDS, THEN TURN HIM LOOSE !
42
C'MON, YOU ! OUTSIDE !
WAIT ! I'VE CHANGED MY MIND ! LET HIM STAY !
43
GATHER 'ROUND, FOLKS ! HERE'S WHERE THIS PARTY STARTS TO LIVEN UP !
44.
NOW FOR SOME FUN ! BLAKELY'S GOT ONE OF HIS COMICAL IN-SPIRATIONS !
ELSA MAXWELL HAS NOTHING ON BLAKELY WHEN IT COMES TO THROWING A NOVEL PARTY !

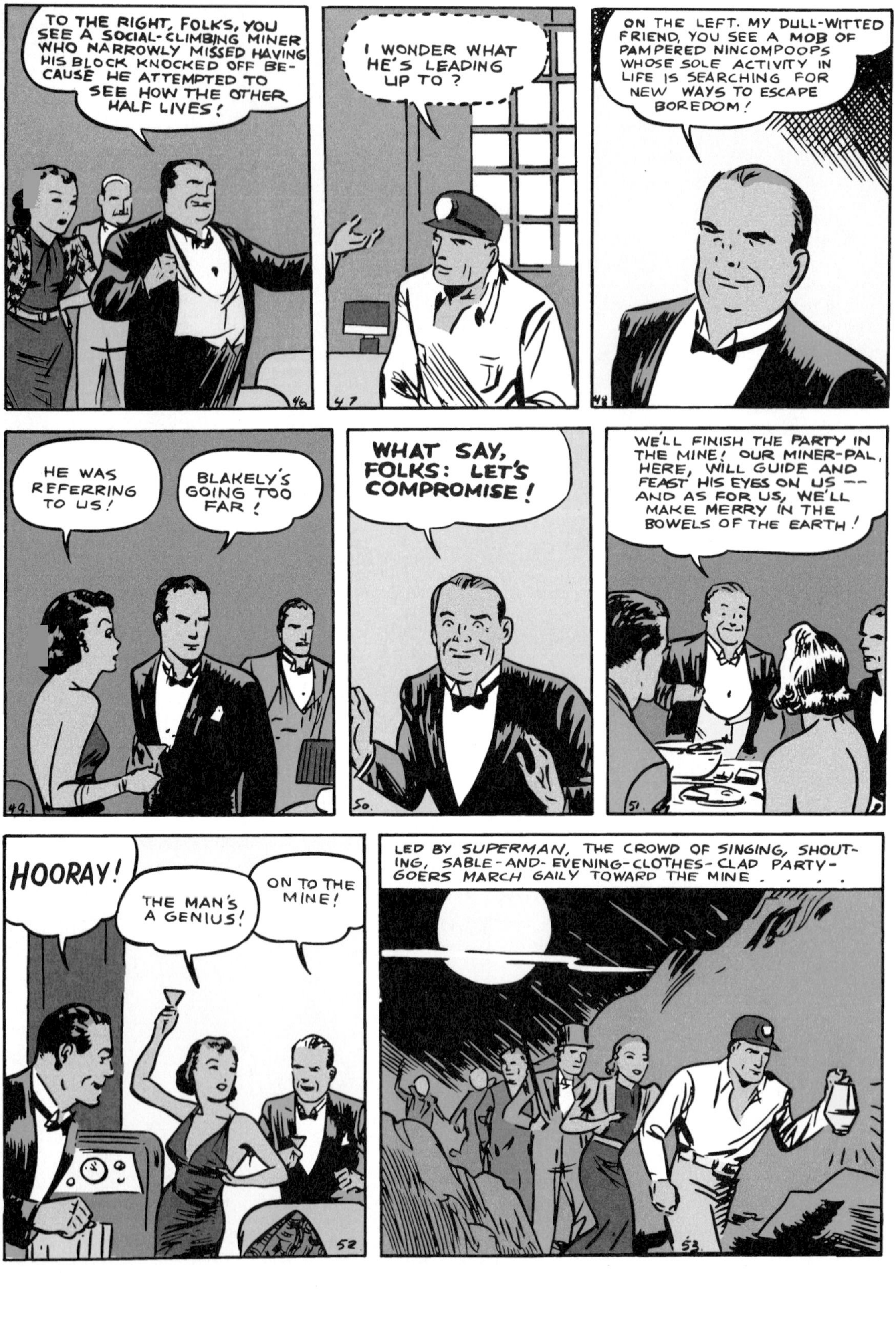
TO THE RIGHT, FOLKS, YOU SEE A SOCIAL-CLIMBING MINER WHO NARROWLY MISSED HAVING HIS BLOCK KNOCKED OFF BECAUSE HE ATTEMPTED TO SEE HOW THE OTHER HALF LIVES!
I WONDER WHAT HE'S LEADING UP TO?
ON THE LEFT. MY DULL-WITTED FRIEND, YOU SEE A MOB OF PAMPERED NINCOMPOOPS WHOSE SOLE ACTIVITY IN LIFE IS SEARCHING FOR NEW WAYS TO ESCAPE BOREDOM!
HE WAS REFERRING TO US!
BLAKELY'S GOING TOO FAR!
WHAT SAY, FOLKS: LET'S COMPROMISE!
WE'LL FINISH THE PARTY IN THE MINE! OUR MINER-PAL, HERE, WILL GUIDE AND FEAST HIS EYES ON US -- AND AS FOR US, WE'LL MAKE MERRY IN THE BOWELS OF THE EARTH!
HOORAY!
THE MAN'S A GENIUS!
ON TO THE MINE!
LED BY SUPERMAN, THE CROWD OF SINGING, SHOUTING, SABLE-AND-EVENING-CLOTHES-CLAD PARTY-GOERS MARCH GAILY TOWARD THE MINE . . . .

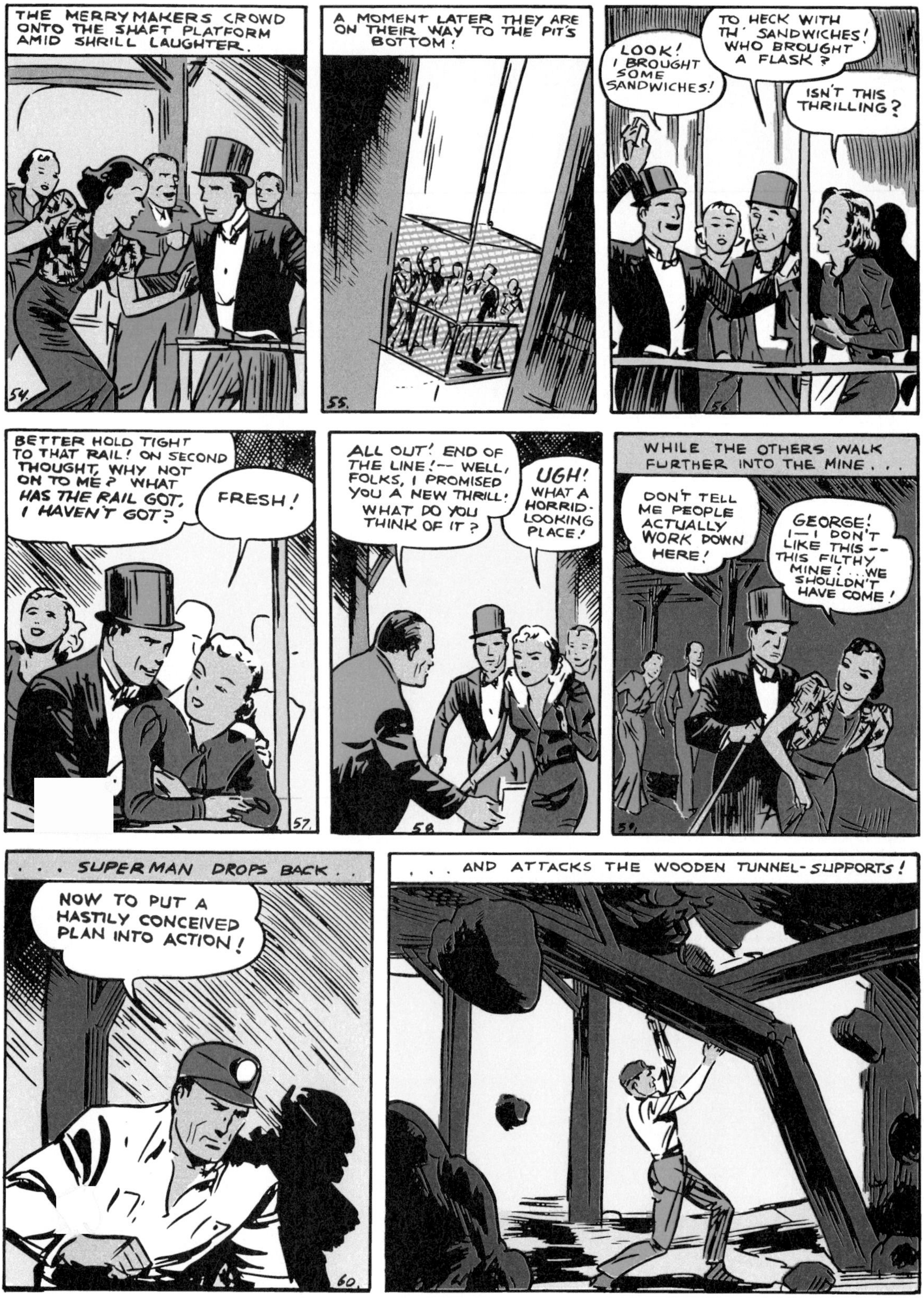
THE MERRYMAKERS CROWD ONTO THE SHAFT PLATFORM AMID SHRILL LAUGHTER.
A MOMENT LATER THEY ARE ON THEIR WAY TO THE PIT'S BOTTOM!
LOOK! I BROUGHT SOME SANDWICHES!
TO HECK WITH TH' SANDWICHES! WHO BROUGHT A FLASK?
ISN'T THIS THRILLING?
BETTER HOLD TIGHT TO THAT RAIL! ON SECOND THOUGHT, WHY NOT ON TO ME? WHAT HAS THE RAIL GOT, I HAVEN'T GOT?
FRESH!
ALL OUT! END OF THE LINE!-- WELL, FOLKS, I PROMISED YOU A NEW THRILL! WHAT DO YOU THINK OF IT?
UGH! WHAT A HORRID-LOOKING PLACE!
WHILE THE OTHERS WALK FURTHER INTO THE MINE . . .
DON'T TELL ME PEOPLE ACTUALLY WORK DOWN HERE!
GEORGE! I--I DON'T LIKE THIS -- THIS FILTHY MINE! . . WE SHOULDN'T HAVE COME!
. . . SUPERMAN DROPS BACK . .
NOW TO PUT A HASTILY CONCEIVED PLAN INTO ACTION!
. . . AND ATTACKS THE WOODEN TUNNEL-SUPPORTS!

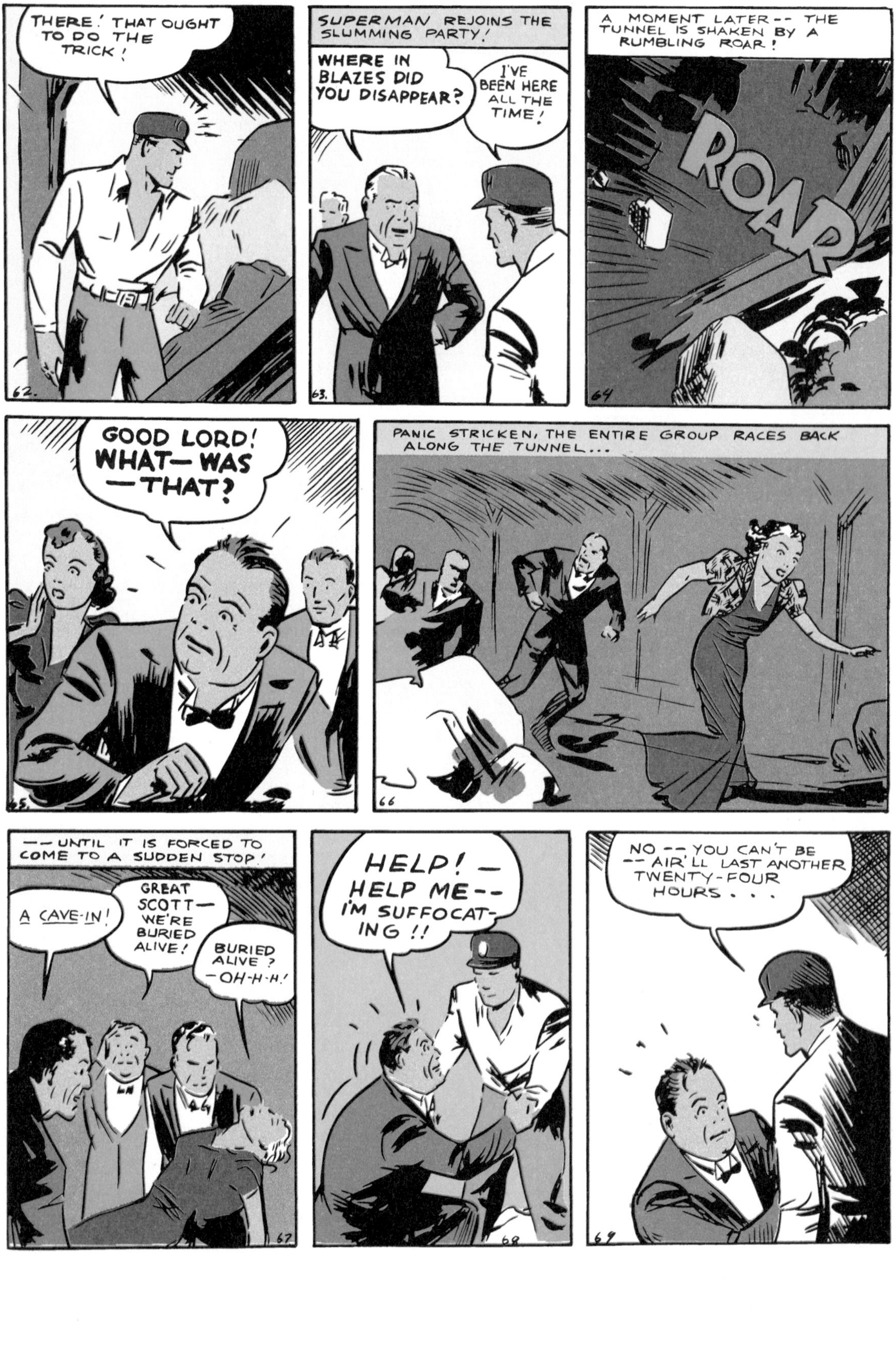

THERE! THAT OUGHT TO DO THE TRICK!
SUPERMAN REJOINS THE SLUMMING PARTY!
WHERE IN BLAZES DID YOU DISAPPEAR?
I'VE BEEN HERE ALL THE TIME!
A MOMENT LATER -- THE TUNNEL IS SHAKEN BY A RUMBLING ROAR!
ROAR
GOOD LORD! WHAT—WAS —THAT?
PANIC STRICKEN, THE ENTIRE GROUP RACES BACK ALONG THE TUNNEL...
-- UNTIL IT IS FORCED TO COME TO A SUDDEN STOP!
A CAVE-IN!
GREAT SCOTT— WE'RE BURIED ALIVE!
BURIED ALIVE? —OH-H-H!
HELP! — HELP ME-- I'M SUFFOCATING!!
NO -- YOU CAN'T BE -- AIR'LL LAST ANOTHER TWENTY-FOUR HOURS . . .

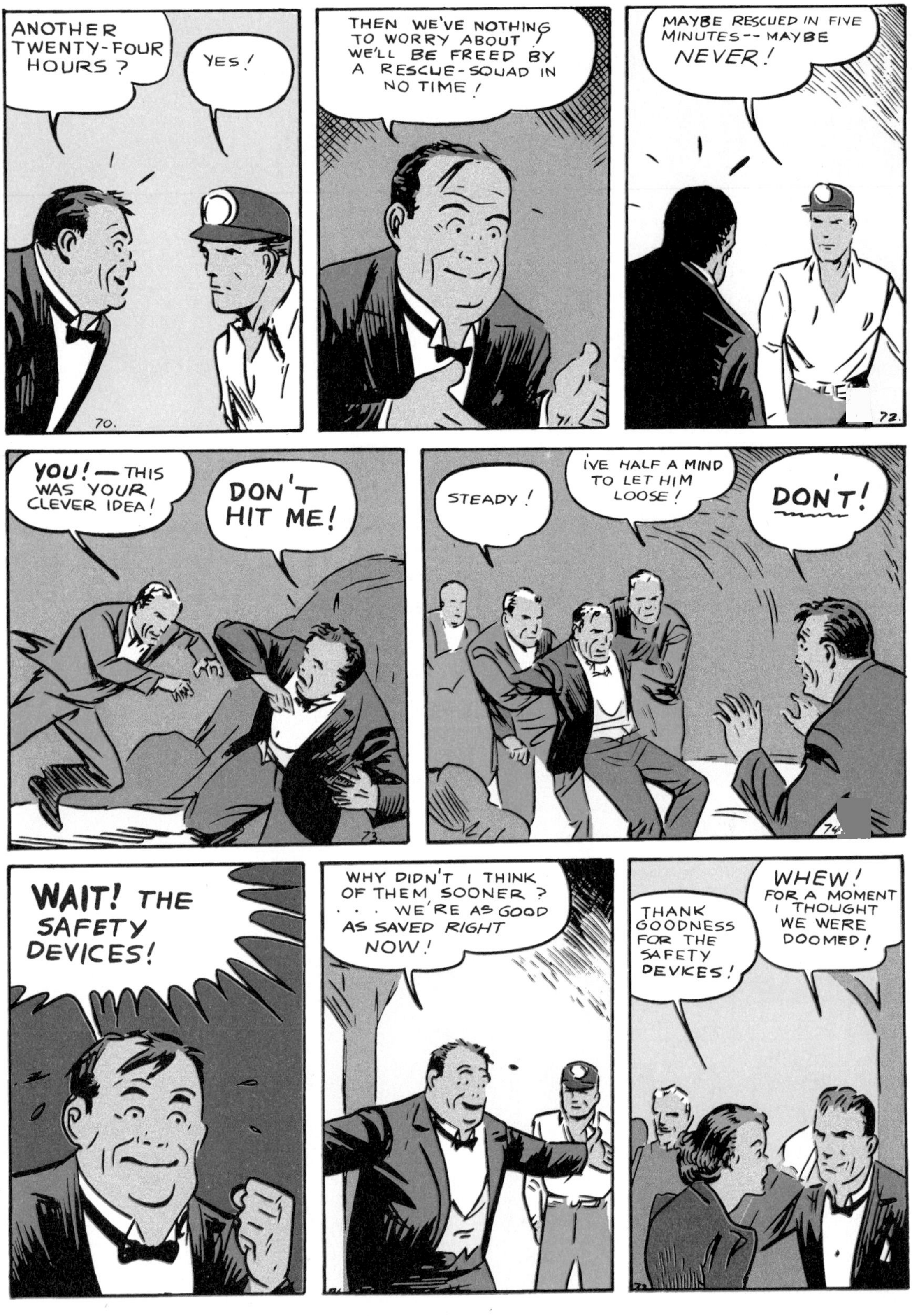

ANOTHER TWENTY-FOUR HOURS?
YES!
THEN WE'VE NOTHING TO WORRY ABOUT! WE'LL BE FREED BY A RESCUE-SQUAD IN NO TIME!
MAYBE RESCUED IN FIVE MINUTES-- MAYBE NEVER!
YOU!—THIS WAS YOUR CLEVER IDEA!
DON'T HIT ME!
STEADY!
I'VE HALF A MIND TO LET HIM LOOSE!
DON'T!
WAIT! THE SAFETY DEVICES!
WHY DIDN'T I THINK OF THEM SOONER? . . . WE'RE AS GOOD AS SAVED RIGHT NOW!
THANK GOODNESS FOR THE SAFETY DEVICES!
WHEW! FOR A MOMENT I THOUGHT WE WERE DOOMED!

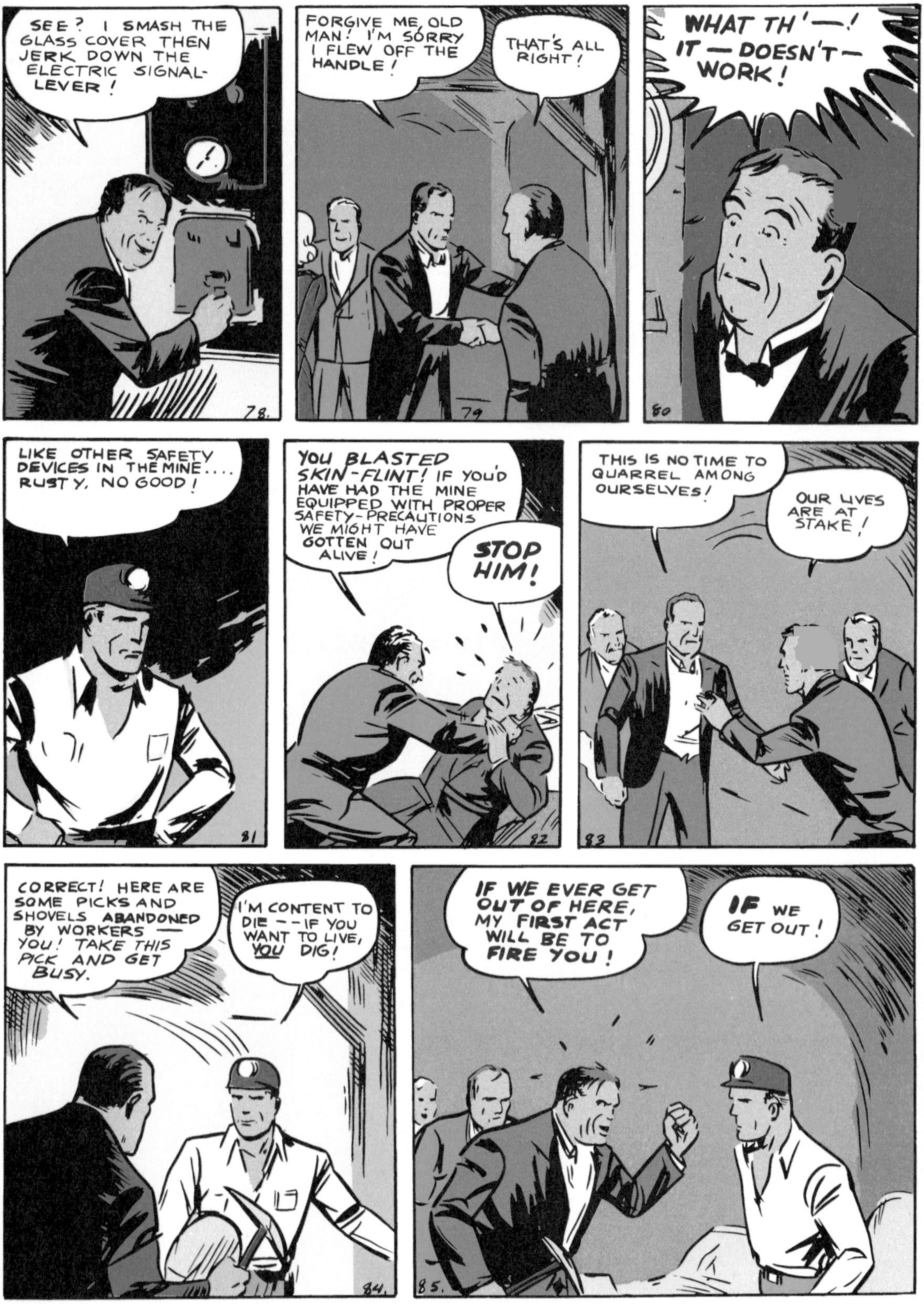
SEE? I SMASH THE GLASS COVER THEN JERK DOWN THE ELECTRIC SIGNAL-LEVER!
78.
FORGIVE ME, OLD MAN! I'M SORRY I FLEW OFF THE HANDLE!
THAT'S ALL RIGHT!
79
WHAT TH'—! IT—DOESN'T—WORK!
80
LIKE OTHER SAFETY DEVICES IN THE MINE.... RUSTY, NO GOOD!
81
YOU BLASTED SKIN-FLINT! IF YOU'D HAVE HAD THE MINE EQUIPPED WITH PROPER SAFETY-PRECAUTIONS WE MIGHT HAVE GOTTEN OUT ALIVE!
STOP HIM!
82
THIS IS NO TIME TO QUARREL AMONG OURSELVES!
OUR LIVES ARE AT STAKE!
83
CORRECT! HERE ARE SOME PICKS AND SHOVELS ABANDONED BY WORKERS — YOU! TAKE THIS PICK AND GET BUSY.
I'M CONTENT TO DIE -- IF YOU WANT TO LIVE, YOU DIG!
84.
IF WE EVER GET OUT OF HERE, MY FIRST ACT WILL BE TO FIRE YOU!
IF WE GET OUT!
85.

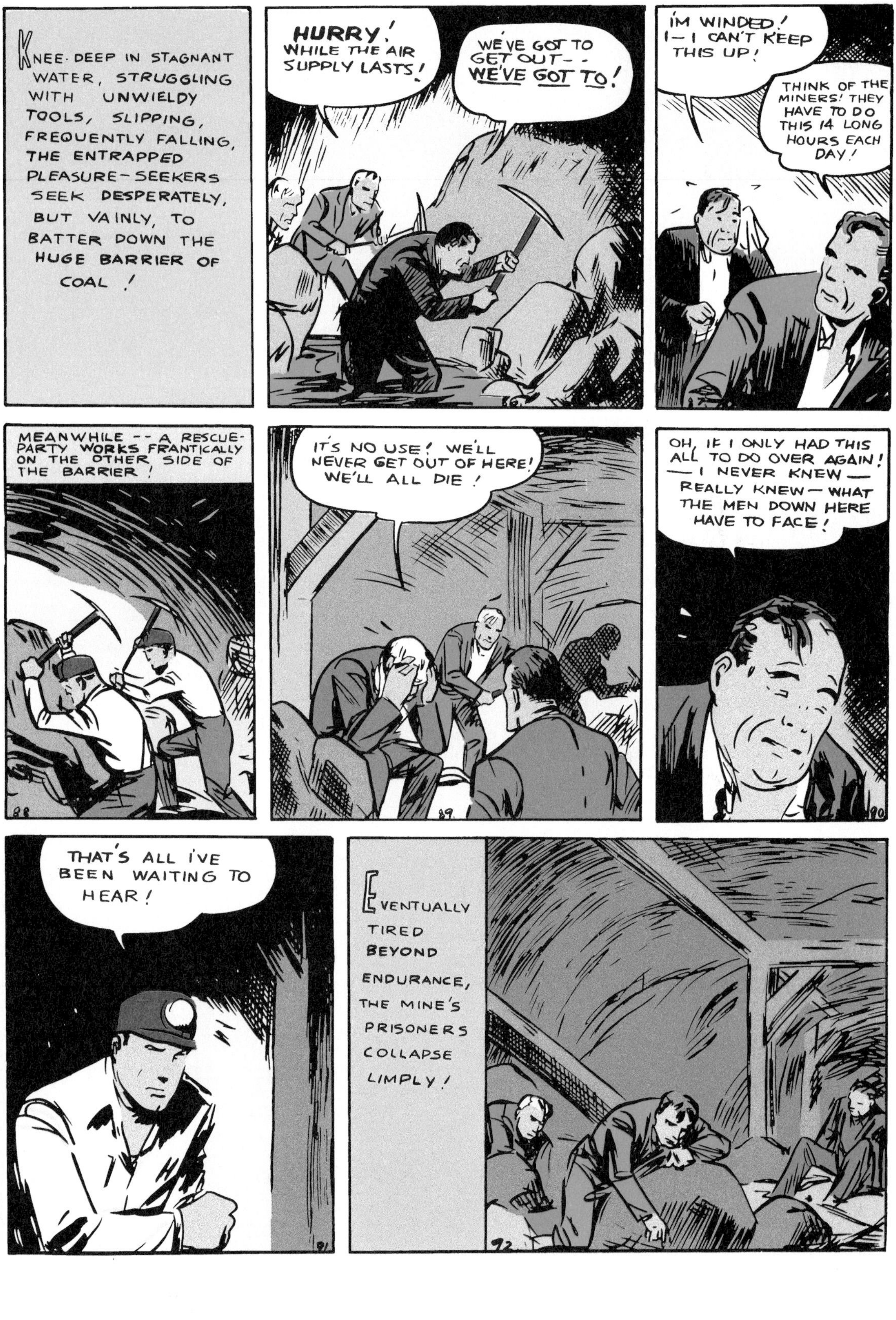
Knee-deep in stagnant water, struggling with unwieldy tools, slipping, frequently falling, the entrapped pleasure-seekers seek desperately, but vainly, to batter down the huge barrier of coal!
HURRY! While the air supply lasts!
We've got to get out-- we've got to!
I'm winded! I-- I can't keep this up!
Think of the miners! They have to do this 14 long hours each day!
Meanwhile -- a rescue-party works frantically on the other side of the barrier!
It's no use! We'll never get out of here! We'll all die!
Oh, if I only had this all to do over again! -- I never knew -- really knew -- what the men down here have to face!
That's all I've been waiting to hear!
Eventually tired beyond endurance, the mine's prisoners collapse limply!
88
89
90
91
92

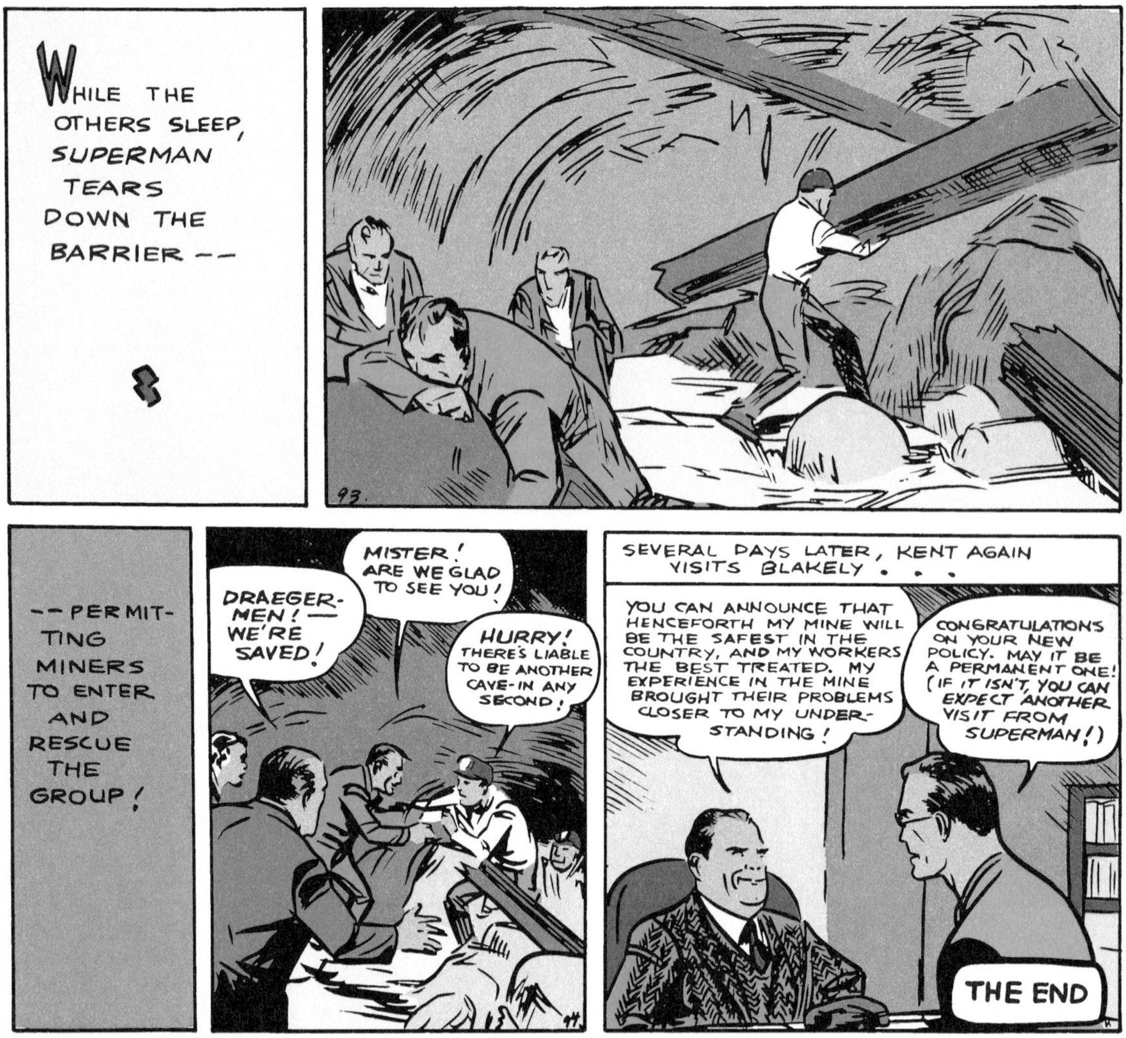
WHILE THE OTHERS SLEEP, SUPERMAN TEARS DOWN THE BARRIER --
93.
-- PERMITTING MINERS TO ENTER AND RESCUE THE GROUP!
DRAEGER-MEN! — WE'RE SAVED!
MISTER! ARE WE GLAD TO SEE YOU!
HURRY! THERE'S LIABLE TO BE ANOTHER CAVE-IN ANY SECOND!
94.
SEVERAL DAYS LATER, KENT AGAIN VISITS BLAKELY . . .
YOU CAN ANNOUNCE THAT HENCEFORTH MY MINE WILL BE THE SAFEST IN THE COUNTRY, AND MY WORKERS THE BEST TREATED. MY EXPERIENCE IN THE MINE BROUGHT THEIR PROBLEMS CLOSER TO MY UNDER-STANDING!
CONGRATULATIONS ON YOUR NEW POLICY. MAY IT BE A PERMANENT ONE! (IF IT ISN'T, YOU CAN EXPECT ANOTHER VISIT FROM SUPERMAN!)
THE END

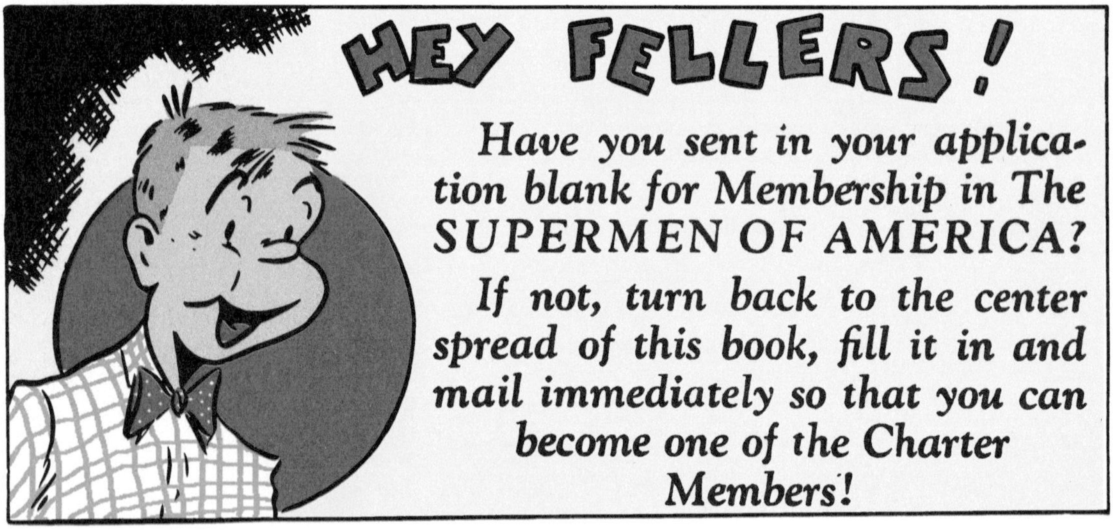
HEY FELLERS!
Have you sent in your application blank for Membership in The SUPERMEN OF AMERICA?
If not, turn back to the center spread of this book, fill it in and mail immediately so that you can become one of the Charter Members!

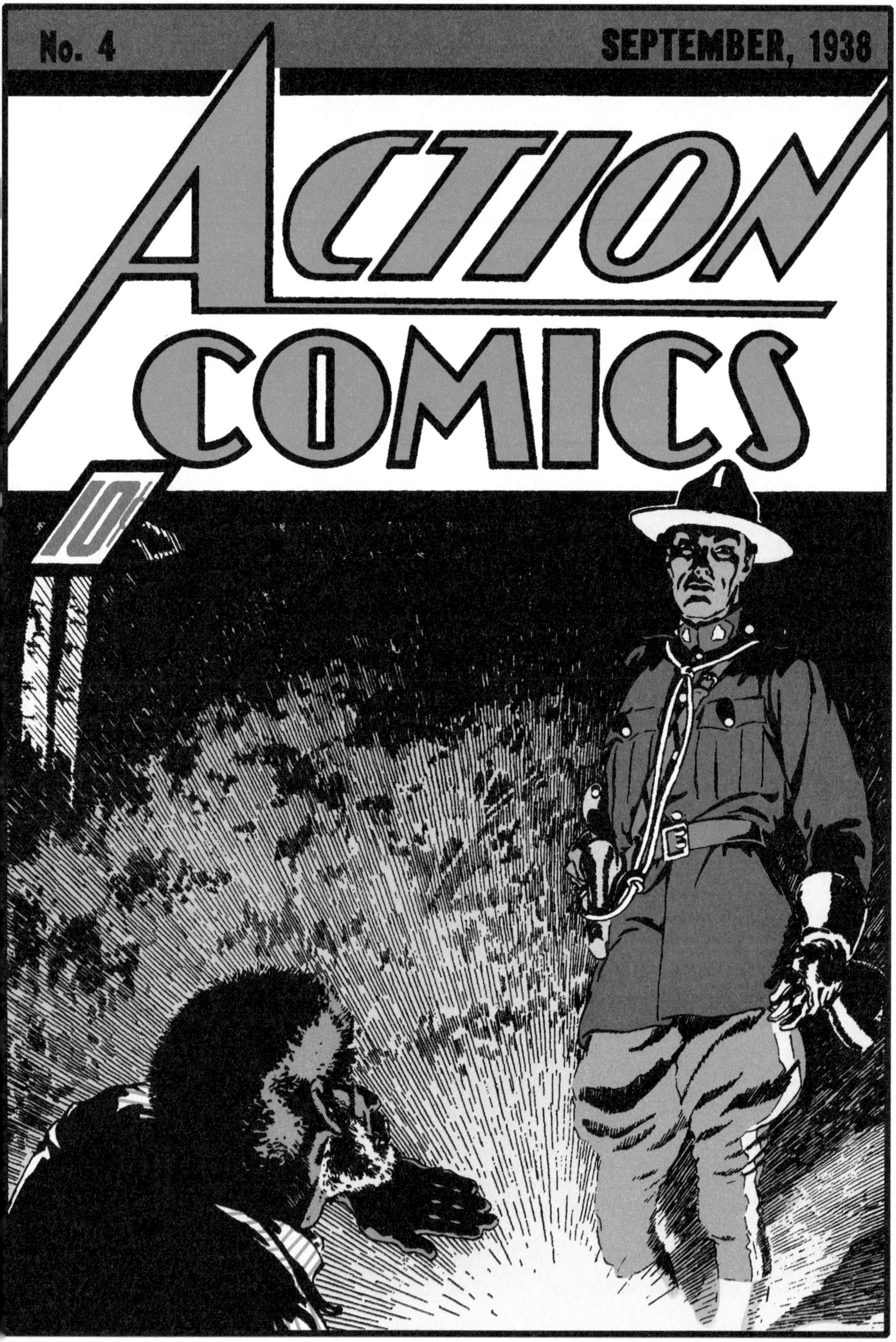
No. 4
SEPTEMBER, 1938
ACTION COMICS
10¢

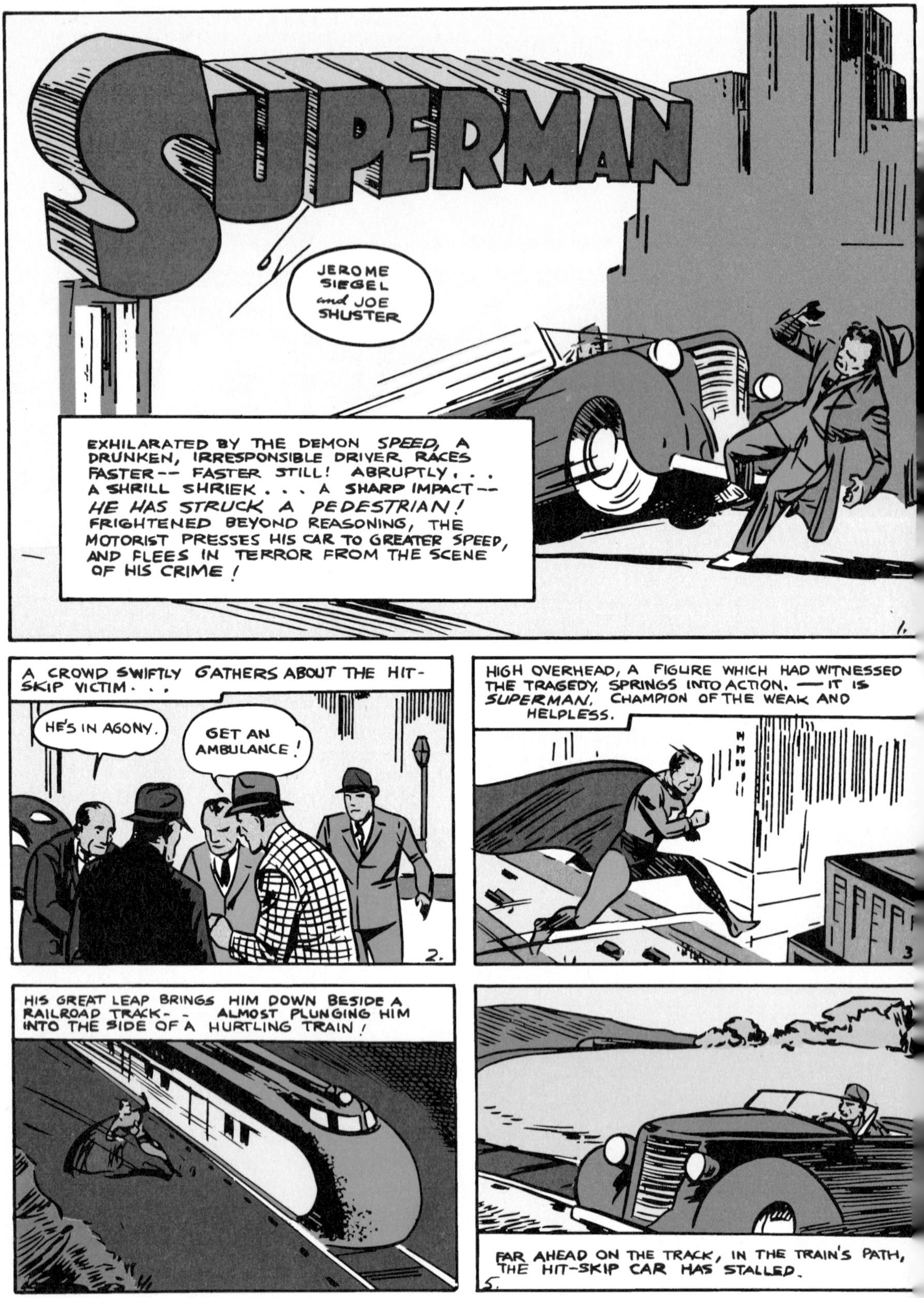
SUPERMAN
by
JEROME SIEGEL and JOE SHUSTER
EXHILARATED BY THE DEMON SPEED, A DRUNKEN, IRRESPONSIBLE DRIVER RACES FASTER-- FASTER STILL! ABRUPTLY. . . A SHRILL SHRIEK . . . A SHARP IMPACT-- HE HAS STRUCK A PEDESTRIAN! FRIGHTENED BEYOND REASONING, THE MOTORIST PRESSES HIS CAR TO GREATER SPEED, AND FLEES IN TERROR FROM THE SCENE OF HIS CRIME!
1.
A CROWD SWIFTLY GATHERS ABOUT THE HIT-SKIP VICTIM. . .
HE'S IN AGONY.
GET AN AMBULANCE!
2.
HIGH OVERHEAD, A FIGURE WHICH HAD WITNESSED THE TRAGEDY, SPRINGS INTO ACTION. —IT IS SUPERMAN, CHAMPION OF THE WEAK AND HELPLESS.
3
HIS GREAT LEAP BRINGS HIM DOWN BESIDE A RAILROAD TRACK-- ALMOST PLUNGING HIM INTO THE SIDE OF A HURTLING TRAIN!
FAR AHEAD ON THE TRACK, IN THE TRAIN'S PATH, THE HIT-SKIP CAR HAS STALLED.
5.

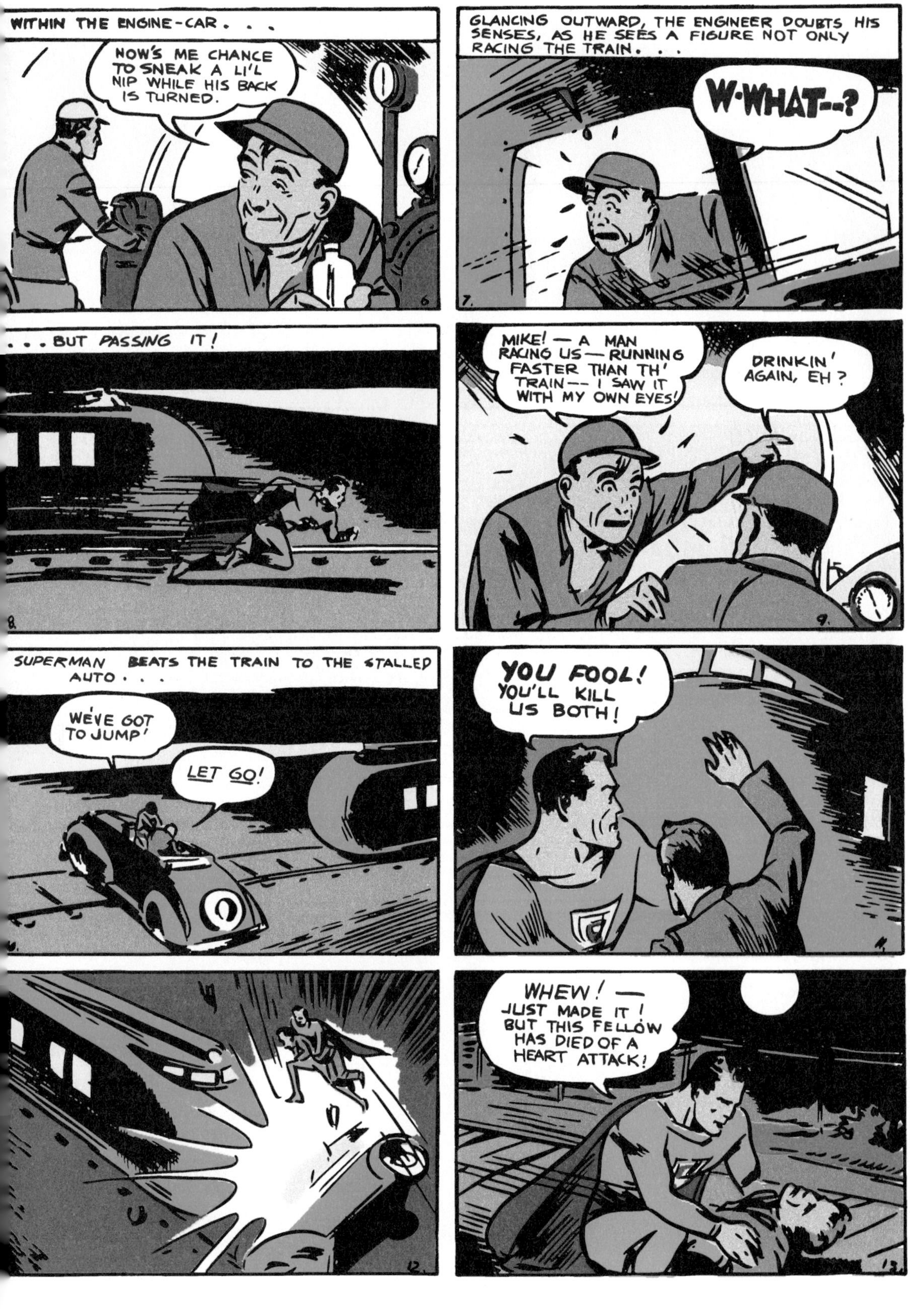

WITHIN THE ENGINE-CAR . . .
NOW'S ME CHANCE TO SNEAK A LI'L NIP WHILE HIS BACK IS TURNED.
GLANCING OUTWARD, THE ENGINEER DOUBTS HIS SENSES, AS HE SEES A FIGURE NOT ONLY RACING THE TRAIN . . .
W-WHAT--?
. . . BUT PASSING IT!
MIKE! — A MAN RACING US — RUNNING FASTER THAN TH' TRAIN-- I SAW IT WITH MY OWN EYES!
DRINKIN' AGAIN, EH?
SUPERMAN BEATS THE TRAIN TO THE STALLED AUTO . . .
WE'VE GOT TO JUMP'
LET GO!
YOU FOOL! YOU'LL KILL US BOTH!
WHEW! — JUST MADE IT! BUT THIS FELLOW HAS DIED OF A HEART ATTACK!

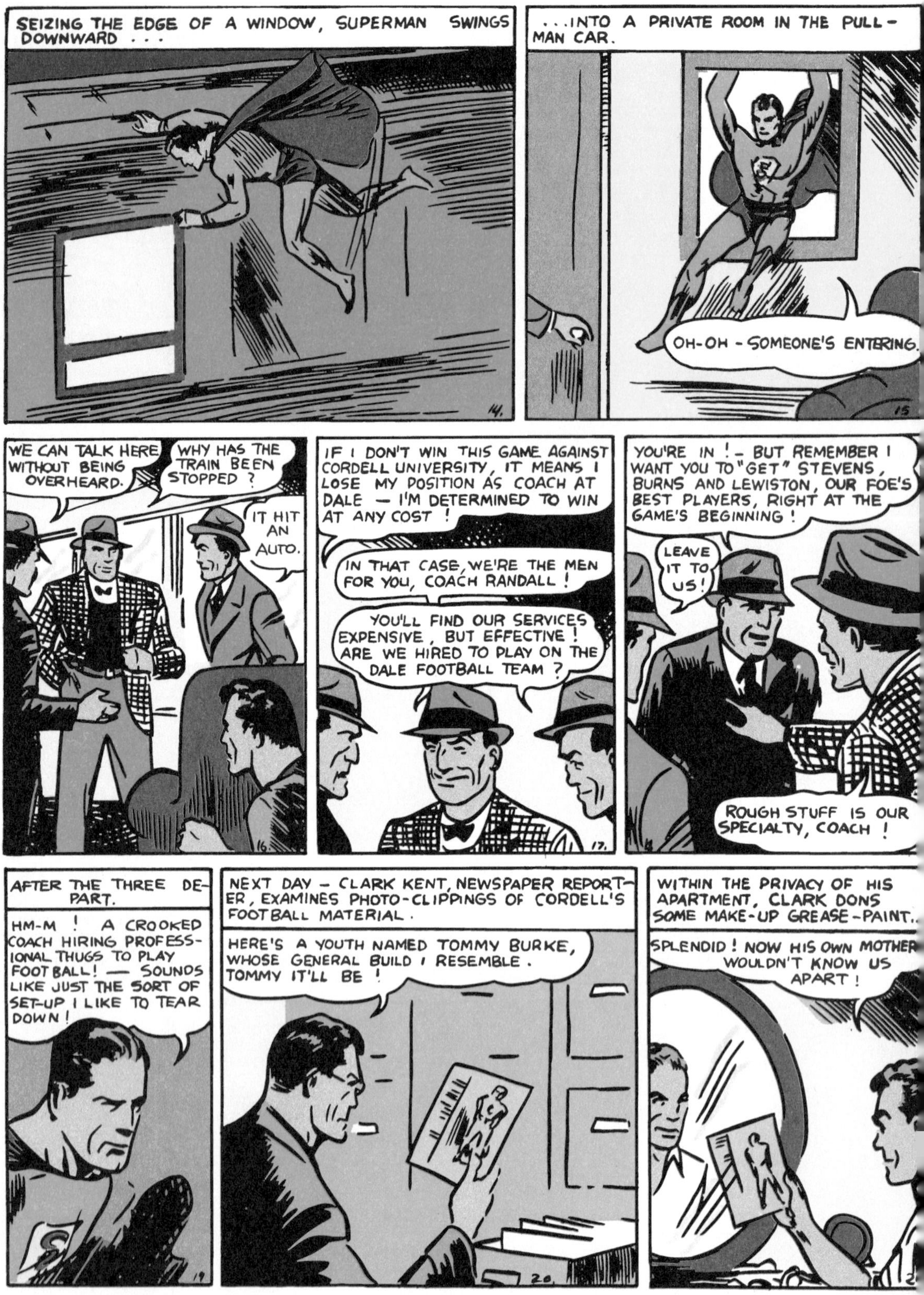
SEIZING THE EDGE OF A WINDOW, SUPERMAN SWINGS DOWNWARD . . .
. . . INTO A PRIVATE ROOM IN THE PULL-MAN CAR.
OH-OH - SOMEONE'S ENTERING.
WE CAN TALK HERE WITHOUT BEING OVERHEARD.
WHY HAS THE TRAIN BEEN STOPPED ?
IT HIT AN AUTO.
IF I DON'T WIN THIS GAME AGAINST CORDELL UNIVERSITY, IT MEANS I LOSE MY POSITION AS COACH AT DALE — I'M DETERMINED TO WIN AT ANY COST !
IN THAT CASE, WE'RE THE MEN FOR YOU, COACH RANDALL !
YOU'LL FIND OUR SERVICES EXPENSIVE, BUT EFFECTIVE ! ARE WE HIRED TO PLAY ON THE DALE FOOTBALL TEAM ?
YOU'RE IN ! - BUT REMEMBER I WANT YOU TO "GET" STEVENS, BURNS AND LEWISTON, OUR FOE'S BEST PLAYERS, RIGHT AT THE GAME'S BEGINNING !
LEAVE IT TO US !
ROUGH STUFF IS OUR SPECIALTY, COACH !
AFTER THE THREE DE-PART.
HM-M ! A CROOKED COACH HIRING PROFESS-IONAL THUGS TO PLAY FOOTBALL! — SOUNDS LIKE JUST THE SORT OF SET-UP I LIKE TO TEAR DOWN !
NEXT DAY - CLARK KENT, NEWSPAPER REPORT-ER, EXAMINES PHOTO-CLIPPINGS OF CORDELL'S FOOTBALL MATERIAL.
HERE'S A YOUTH NAMED TOMMY BURKE, WHOSE GENERAL BUILD I RESEMBLE. TOMMY IT'LL BE !
WITHIN THE PRIVACY OF HIS APARTMENT, CLARK DONS SOME MAKE-UP GREASE-PAINT.
SPLENDID ! NOW HIS OWN MOTHER WOULDN'T KNOW US APART !

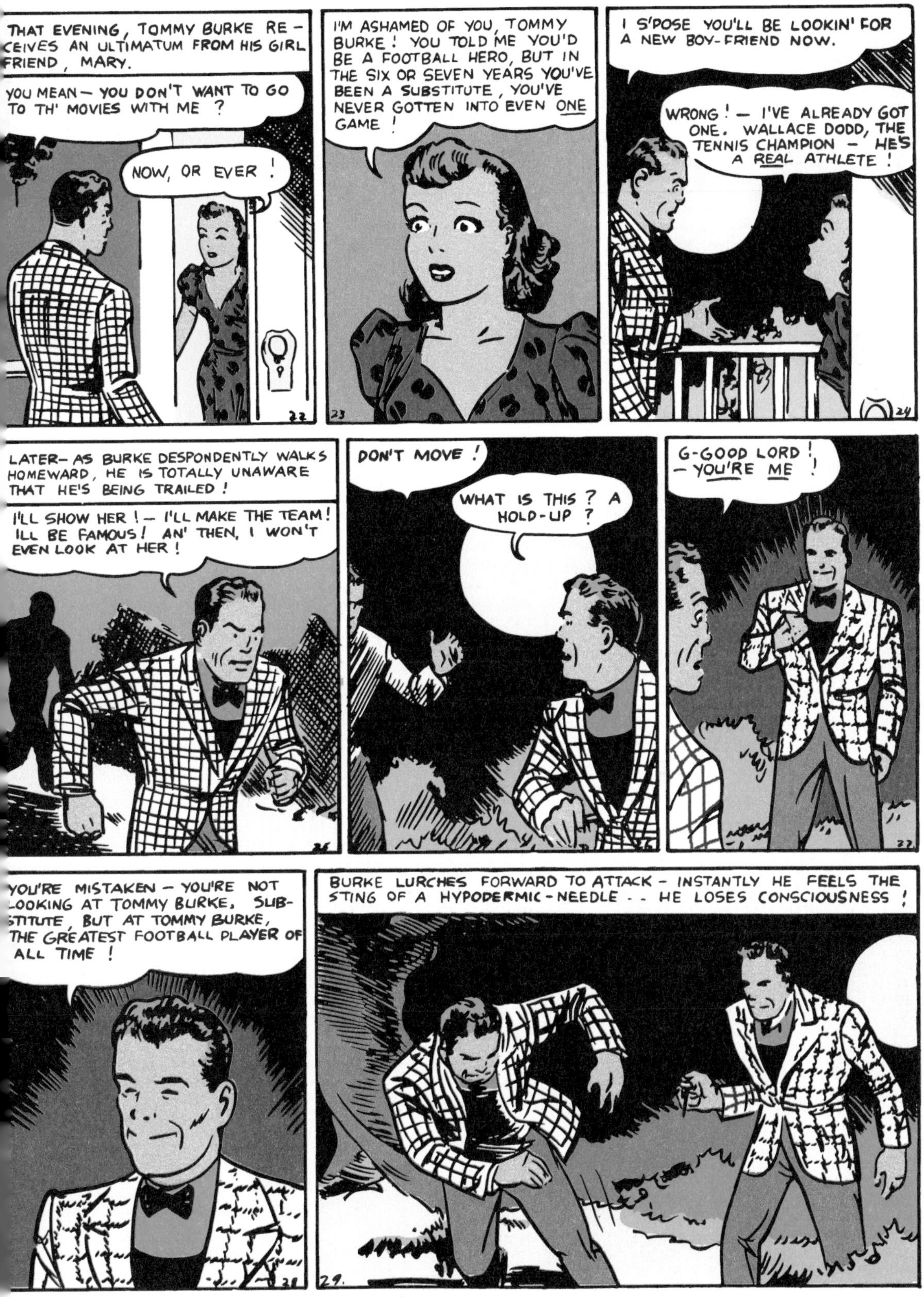
THAT EVENING, TOMMY BURKE RECEIVES AN ULTIMATUM FROM HIS GIRL FRIEND, MARY.
YOU MEAN— YOU DON'T WANT TO GO TO TH' MOVIES WITH ME ?
NOW, OR EVER !
I'M ASHAMED OF YOU, TOMMY BURKE! YOU TOLD ME YOU'D BE A FOOTBALL HERO, BUT IN THE SIX OR SEVEN YEARS YOU'VE BEEN A SUBSTITUTE, YOU'VE NEVER GOTTEN INTO EVEN ONE GAME !
I S'POSE YOU'LL BE LOOKIN' FOR A NEW BOY-FRIEND NOW.
WRONG ! — I'VE ALREADY GOT ONE. WALLACE DODD, THE TENNIS CHAMPION — HE'S A REAL ATHLETE !
LATER— AS BURKE DESPONDENTLY WALKS HOMEWARD, HE IS TOTALLY UNAWARE THAT HE'S BEING TRAILED !
I'LL SHOW HER ! — I'LL MAKE THE TEAM! I'LL BE FAMOUS! AN' THEN, I WON'T EVEN LOOK AT HER !
DON'T MOVE !
WHAT IS THIS ? A HOLD-UP ?
G-GOOD LORD ! — YOU'RE ME !
YOU'RE MISTAKEN — YOU'RE NOT LOOKING AT TOMMY BURKE, SUBSTITUTE, BUT AT TOMMY BURKE, THE GREATEST FOOTBALL PLAYER OF ALL TIME !
BURKE LURCHES FORWARD TO ATTACK — INSTANTLY HE FEELS THE STING OF A HYPODERMIC-NEEDLE - - HE LOSES CONSCIOUSNESS !

BURKE REGAINS CONSCIOUSNESS TO DISCOVER HIMSELF A PRISONER IN HIS OWN APARTMENT.

W- WHAT HAVE YOU DONE TO ME ? I CAN'T MOVE !

YOU NEEDN'T WORRY YOU'RE JUST RENDERED PASSIVE BY A DRUG.

BUT WHAT'S TH' BIG IDEA ?

MERELY THIS: I'M GOING TO TAKE YOUR PLACE IN LIFE FOR A FEW DAYS — SO LONG, FOR NOW !

DISGUISED AS BURKE, SUPERMAN REPORTS TO THE LOCKER-ROOM OF CORDELL UNIVERSITY, PREPARATORY TO FOOTBALL PRACTICE.

WELL, HERE GOES ! — WONDER IF I'LL GET AWAY WITH IT ?

LOCKER ROOM

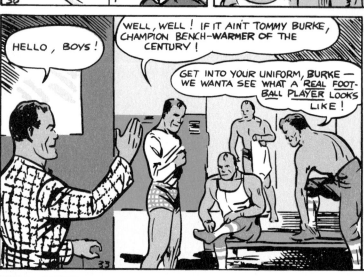

HELLO, BOYS !

WELL, WELL ! IF IT AIN'T TOMMY BURKE, CHAMPION BENCH-WARMER OF THE CENTURY !

GET INTO YOUR UNIFORM, BURKE — WE WANTA SEE WHAT A REAL FOOTBALL PLAYER LOOKS LIKE !

I DON'T KNOW IN WHICH LOCKER BURKE KEEPS HIS STUFF — I'LL JUST CHOOSE ONE AT RANDOM ... THIS ONE WILL DO.

SAY ! — WHAT TH' BLAZES YOU DOIN' IN MY LOCKER ?

SORRY-- MY MISTAKE.

I'LL GIVE YOU SOMETHING TO BE REALLY SORRY ABOUT !

DON'T STAND THERE GRINNING ! PUT UP YOUR HANDS AND FIGHT !

BUT IT'S MORE FUN TO SIMPLY WATCH !

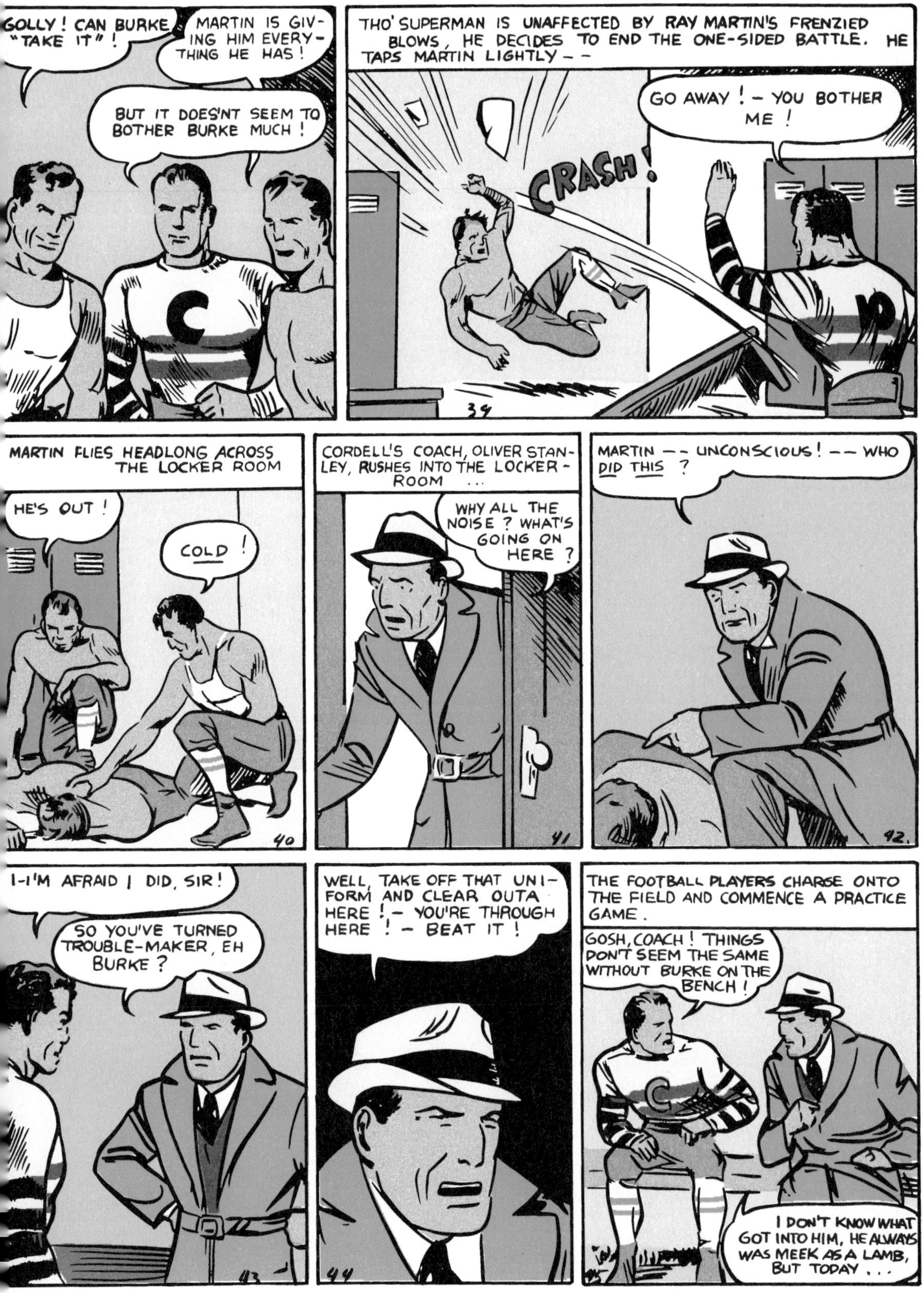
GOLLY! CAN BURKE "TAKE IT"!
MARTIN IS GIVING HIM EVERYTHING HE HAS!
BUT IT DOESN'T SEEM TO BOTHER BURKE MUCH!
THO' SUPERMAN IS UNAFFECTED BY RAY MARTIN'S FRENZIED BLOWS, HE DECIDES TO END THE ONE-SIDED BATTLE. HE TAPS MARTIN LIGHTLY – –
GO AWAY! – YOU BOTHER ME!
CRASH!
39
MARTIN FLIES HEADLONG ACROSS THE LOCKER ROOM
HE'S OUT!
COLD!
40
CORDELL'S COACH, OLIVER STANLEY, RUSHES INTO THE LOCKER-ROOM ...
WHY ALL THE NOISE? WHAT'S GOING ON HERE?
41
MARTIN – – UNCONSCIOUS! – – WHO DID THIS?
42.
I-I'M AFRAID I DID, SIR!
SO YOU'VE TURNED TROUBLE-MAKER, EH BURKE?
43
WELL, TAKE OFF THAT UNIFORM AND CLEAR OUTA HERE! – YOU'RE THROUGH HERE! – BEAT IT!
44
THE FOOTBALL PLAYERS CHARGE ONTO THE FIELD AND COMMENCE A PRACTICE GAME.
GOSH, COACH! THINGS DON'T SEEM THE SAME WITHOUT BURKE ON THE BENCH!
I DON'T KNOW WHAT GOT INTO HIM, HE ALWAYS WAS MEEK AS A LAMB, BUT TODAY ...
45

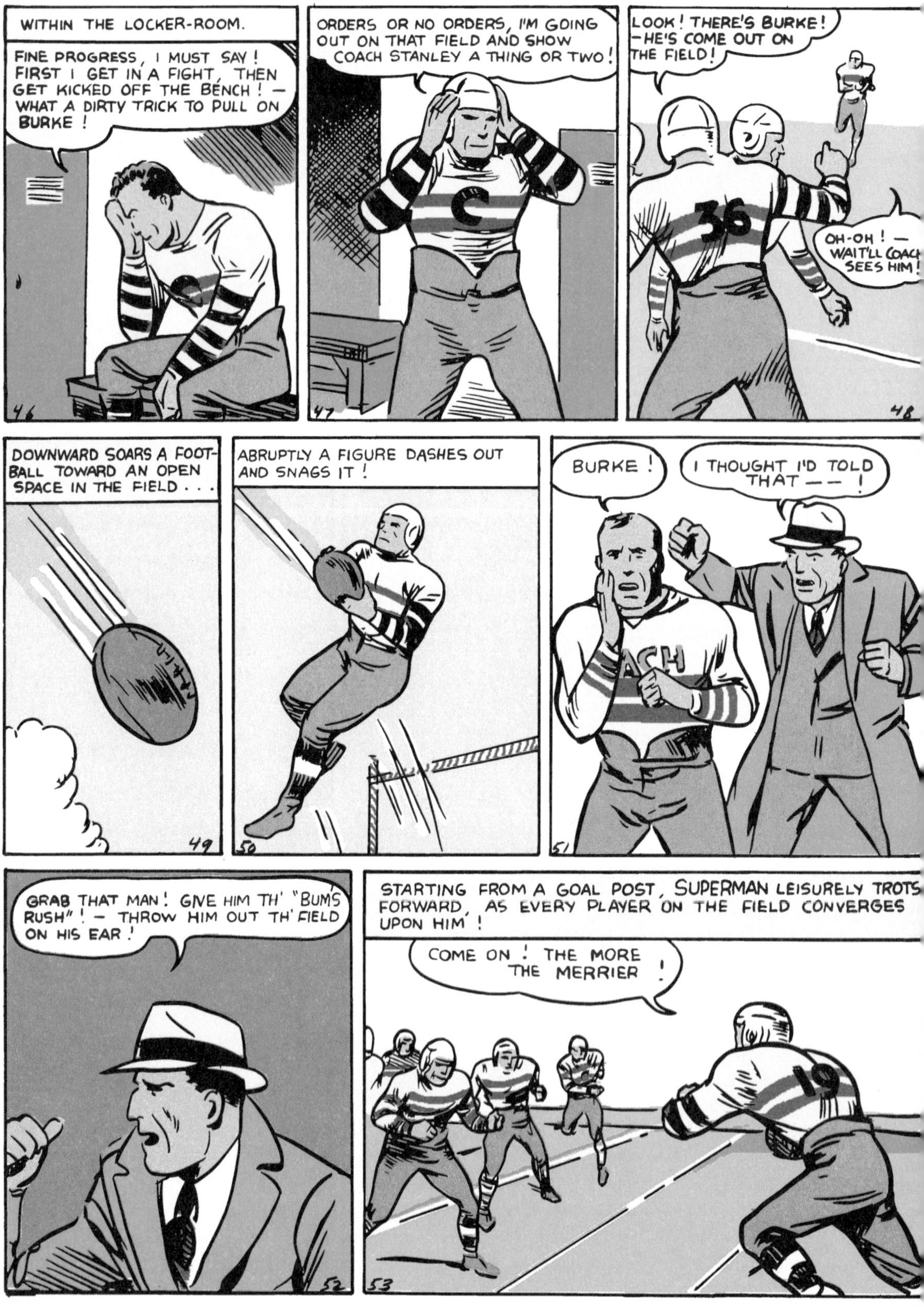
WITHIN THE LOCKER-ROOM.
FINE PROGRESS, I MUST SAY! FIRST I GET IN A FIGHT, THEN GET KICKED OFF THE BENCH! — WHAT A DIRTY TRICK TO PULL ON BURKE!
ORDERS OR NO ORDERS, I'M GOING OUT ON THAT FIELD AND SHOW COACH STANLEY A THING OR TWO!
LOOK! THERE'S BURKE! —HE'S COME OUT ON THE FIELD!
36
OH-OH! — WAIT'LL COACH SEES HIM!
DOWNWARD SOARS A FOOTBALL TOWARD AN OPEN SPACE IN THE FIELD . . .
ABRUPTLY A FIGURE DASHES OUT AND SNAGS IT!
BURKE!
I THOUGHT I'D TOLD THAT — — !
GRAB THAT MAN! GIVE HIM TH' "BUM'S RUSH"! — THROW HIM OUT TH' FIELD ON HIS EAR!
STARTING FROM A GOAL POST, SUPERMAN LEISURELY TROTS FORWARD, AS EVERY PLAYER ON THE FIELD CONVERGES UPON HIM!
COME ON! THE MORE THE MERRIER!
19

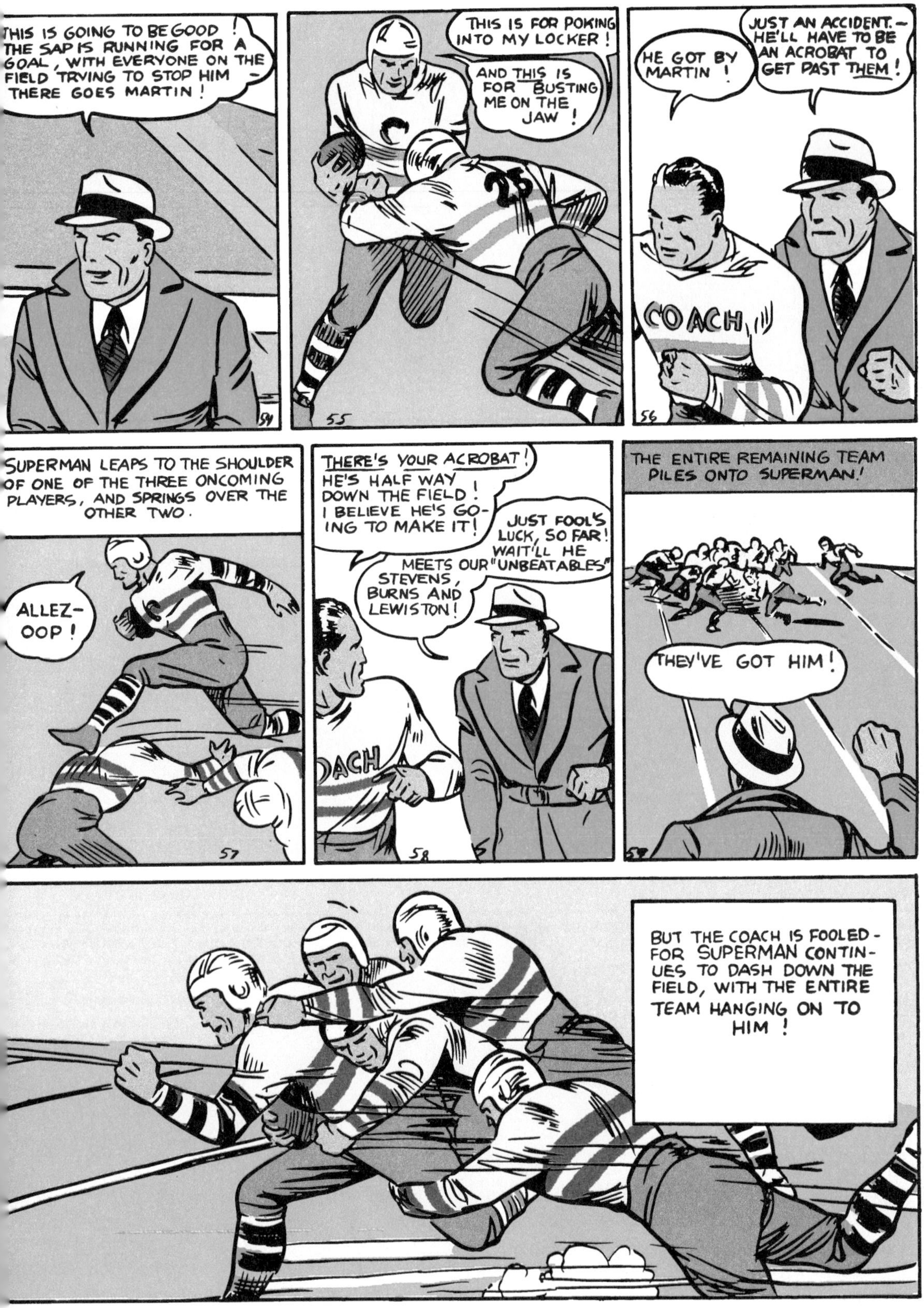
THIS IS GOING TO BE GOOD! THE SAP IS RUNNING FOR A GOAL, WITH EVERYONE ON THE FIELD TRYING TO STOP HIM — THERE GOES MARTIN!
THIS IS FOR POKING INTO MY LOCKER!
AND THIS IS FOR BUSTING ME ON THE JAW!
HE GOT BY MARTIN!
JUST AN ACCIDENT.— HE'LL HAVE TO BE AN ACROBAT TO GET PAST THEM!
SUPERMAN LEAPS TO THE SHOULDER OF ONE OF THE THREE ONCOMING PLAYERS, AND SPRINGS OVER THE OTHER TWO.
ALLEZ-OOP!
THERE'S YOUR ACROBAT! HE'S HALF WAY DOWN THE FIELD! I BELIEVE HE'S GOING TO MAKE IT!
JUST FOOL'S LUCK, SO FAR! WAIT'LL HE MEETS OUR "UNBEATABLES" STEVENS, BURNS AND LEWISTON!
THE ENTIRE REMAINING TEAM PILES ONTO SUPERMAN!
THEY'VE GOT HIM!
BUT THE COACH IS FOOLED - FOR SUPERMAN CONTINUES TO DASH DOWN THE FIELD, WITH THE ENTIRE TEAM HANGING ON TO HIM!

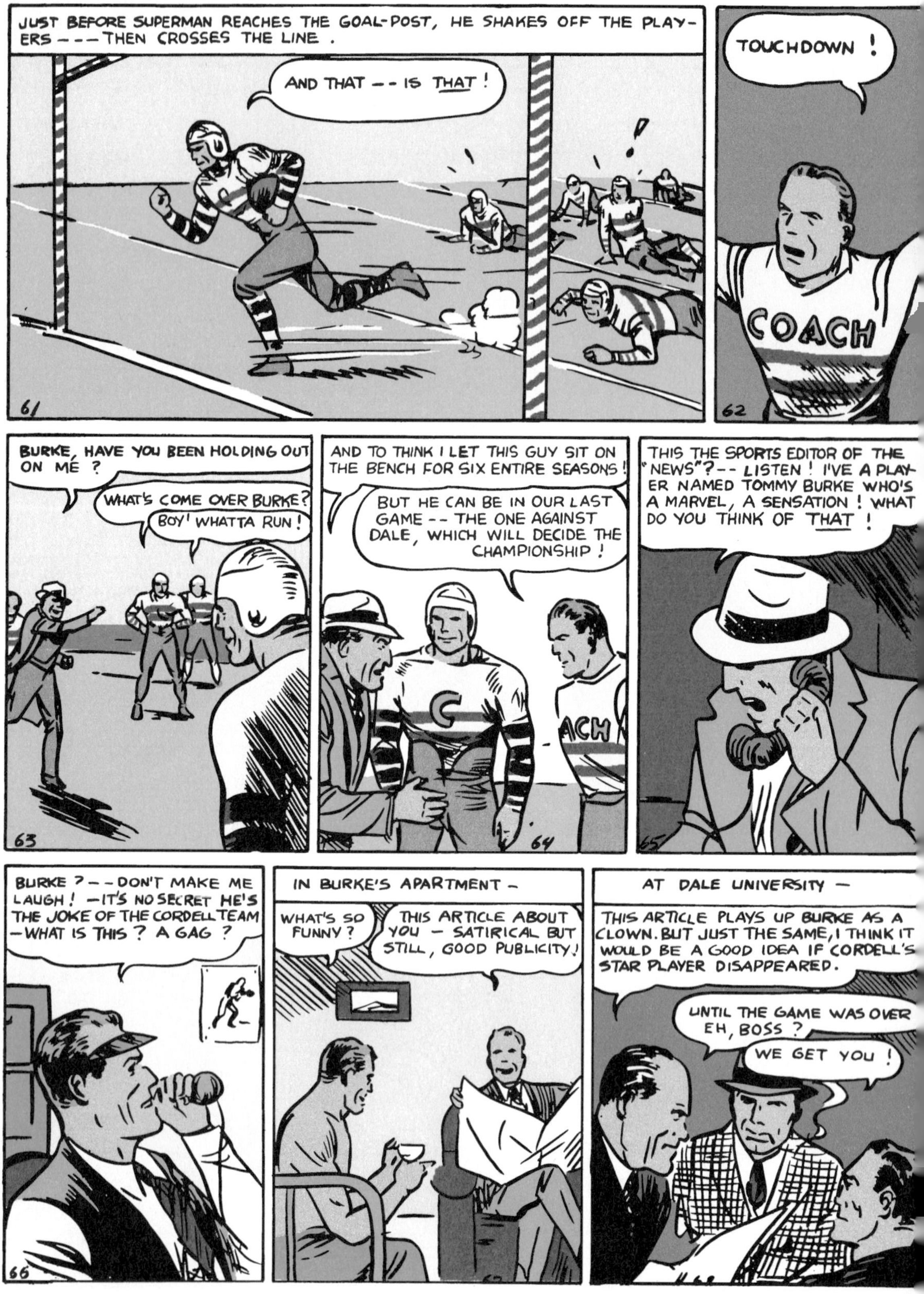

JUST BEFORE SUPERMAN REACHES THE GOAL-POST, HE SHAKES OFF THE PLAYERS --- THEN CROSSES THE LINE.
AND THAT -- IS THAT!
61
TOUCHDOWN!
COACH
62
BURKE, HAVE YOU BEEN HOLDING OUT ON ME?
WHAT'S COME OVER BURKE?
BOY! WHATTA RUN!
63
AND TO THINK I LET THIS GUY SIT ON THE BENCH FOR SIX ENTIRE SEASONS!
BUT HE CAN BE IN OUR LAST GAME -- THE ONE AGAINST DALE, WHICH WILL DECIDE THE CHAMPIONSHIP!
64
THIS THE SPORTS EDITOR OF THE "NEWS"? -- LISTEN! I'VE A PLAYER NAMED TOMMY BURKE WHO'S A MARVEL, A SENSATION! WHAT DO YOU THINK OF THAT!
65
BURKE? -- DON'T MAKE ME LAUGH! -IT'S NO SECRET HE'S THE JOKE OF THE CORDELL TEAM -WHAT IS THIS? A GAG?
66
IN BURKE'S APARTMENT -
WHAT'S SO FUNNY?
THIS ARTICLE ABOUT YOU - SATIRICAL BUT STILL, GOOD PUBLICITY!
AT DALE UNIVERSITY -
THIS ARTICLE PLAYS UP BURKE AS A CLOWN. BUT JUST THE SAME, I THINK IT WOULD BE A GOOD IDEA IF CORDELL'S STAR PLAYER DISAPPEARED.
UNTIL THE GAME WAS OVER EH, BOSS?
WE GET YOU!

DURING THE FOLLOWING DAYS, THE CORDELL TEAM PRACTICES STEADILY FOR THE BIG GAME.

I STILL DON'T GET IT! –HOW IN THE WORLD CAN A PLAYER BECOME SO GOOD OVERNIGHT?

IF YOU KNEW, YOU'D BE THE GREATEST COACH IN THE WORLD!

TOMORROW'S THE GAME WITH DALE! NOW REMEMBER –– EARLY TO BED, NO SMOKING, NO DRINKING! – PLEASANT DREAMS!

THAT EVENING ––

BURKE IS ASLEEP IN THAT A- PARTMENT, – YOU KNOW WHAT TO DO.

LATER –

HE'S COMPLETELY TIED!

STRANGE HE DIDN'T STRUGGLE AT ALL!

THE TWO THUGS ARE UNAWARE BURKE IS UNDER THE INFLUENCE OF A SLEEP-INDUCING DRUG OR THAT SUPERMAN IS OB- SERVING THEM FROM THE MOLD- ING OVERHEAD!

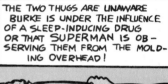

WHEN THE KIDNAPPERS DRIVE OFF, SUPERMAN RACES IN PURSUIT, EASILY KEEPING THEIR AUTO IN SIGHT!

BURKE IS BROUGHT INTO A DESERTED HOUSE!

W–WHERE AM I?

WHERE YOU WON'T BE ABLE TO GET INTO TOMORROW'S GAME.

BUT YOU DON'T WANT ME – I'M JUST A' SUB- STITUTE AND BESIDES–

ARE YOU TOMMY BURKE?

YES, BUT IT ISN'T ME WHO– –

THAT'S ALL WE WANTA KNOW - THIS GAG'LL QUIET YOU DOWN.

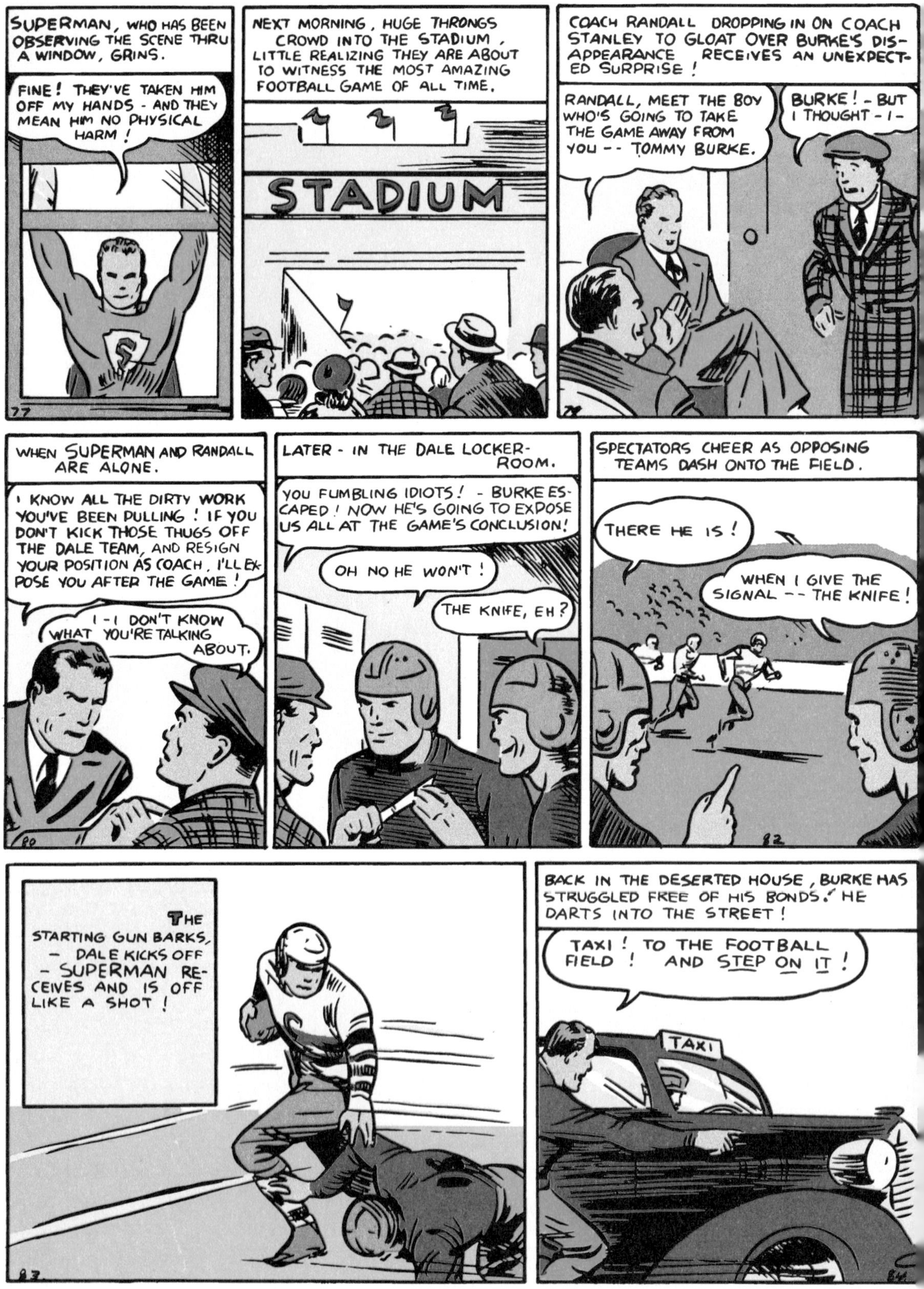
SUPERMAN, WHO HAS BEEN OBSERVING THE SCENE THRU A WINDOW, GRINS.
FINE! THEY'VE TAKEN HIM OFF MY HANDS - AND THEY MEAN HIM NO PHYSICAL HARM!
NEXT MORNING, HUGE THRONGS CROWD INTO THE STADIUM, LITTLE REALIZING THEY ARE ABOUT TO WITNESS THE MOST AMAZING FOOTBALL GAME OF ALL TIME.
STADIUM
COACH RANDALL DROPPING IN ON COACH STANLEY TO GLOAT OVER BURKE'S DISAPPEARANCE RECEIVES AN UNEXPECTED SURPRISE!
RANDALL, MEET THE BOY WHO'S GOING TO TAKE THE GAME AWAY FROM YOU -- TOMMY BURKE.
BURKE! - BUT I THOUGHT - I -
WHEN SUPERMAN AND RANDALL ARE ALONE.
I KNOW ALL THE DIRTY WORK YOU'VE BEEN PULLING! IF YOU DON'T KICK THOSE THUGS OFF THE DALE TEAM, AND RESIGN YOUR POSITION AS COACH, I'LL EXPOSE YOU AFTER THE GAME!
I - I DON'T KNOW WHAT YOU'RE TALKING ABOUT.
LATER - IN THE DALE LOCKER-ROOM.
YOU FUMBLING IDIOTS! - BURKE ESCAPED! NOW HE'S GOING TO EXPOSE US ALL AT THE GAME'S CONCLUSION!
OH NO HE WON'T!
THE KNIFE, EH?
SPECTATORS CHEER AS OPPOSING TEAMS DASH ONTO THE FIELD.
THERE HE IS!
WHEN I GIVE THE SIGNAL -- THE KNIFE!
THE STARTING GUN BARKS, - DALE KICKS OFF - SUPERMAN RECEIVES AND IS OFF LIKE A SHOT!
BACK IN THE DESERTED HOUSE, BURKE HAS STRUGGLED FREE OF HIS BONDS! HE DARTS INTO THE STREET!
TAXI! TO THE FOOTBALL FIELD! AND STEP ON IT!
TAXI

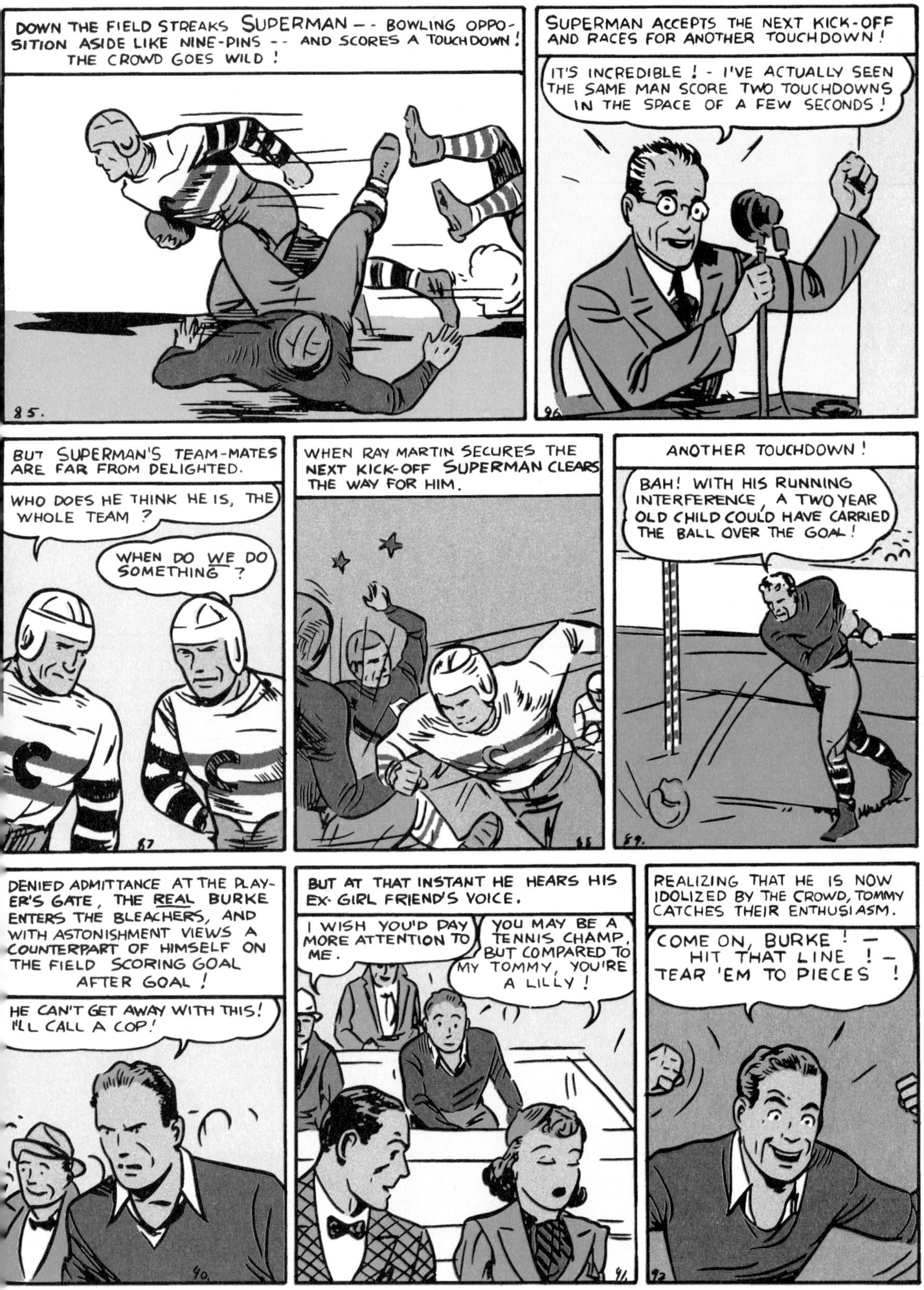
DOWN THE FIELD STREAKS SUPERMAN -- BOWLING OPPOSITION ASIDE LIKE NINE-PINS -- AND SCORES A TOUCHDOWN! THE CROWD GOES WILD!
SUPERMAN ACCEPTS THE NEXT KICK-OFF AND RACES FOR ANOTHER TOUCHDOWN!
IT'S INCREDIBLE! - I'VE ACTUALLY SEEN THE SAME MAN SCORE TWO TOUCHDOWNS IN THE SPACE OF A FEW SECONDS!
BUT SUPERMAN'S TEAM-MATES ARE FAR FROM DELIGHTED.
WHO DOES HE THINK HE IS, THE WHOLE TEAM?
WHEN DO WE DO SOMETHING?
WHEN RAY MARTIN SECURES THE NEXT KICK-OFF SUPERMAN CLEARS THE WAY FOR HIM.
ANOTHER TOUCHDOWN!
BAH! WITH HIS RUNNING INTERFERENCE, A TWO YEAR OLD CHILD COULD HAVE CARRIED THE BALL OVER THE GOAL!
DENIED ADMITTANCE AT THE PLAYER'S GATE, THE REAL BURKE ENTERS THE BLEACHERS, AND WITH ASTONISHMENT VIEWS A COUNTERPART OF HIMSELF ON THE FIELD SCORING GOAL AFTER GOAL!
HE CAN'T GET AWAY WITH THIS! I'LL CALL A COP!
BUT AT THAT INSTANT HE HEARS HIS EX-GIRL FRIEND'S VOICE.
I WISH YOU'D PAY MORE ATTENTION TO ME.
YOU MAY BE A TENNIS CHAMP, BUT COMPARED TO MY TOMMY, YOU'RE A LILLY!
REALIZING THAT HE IS NOW IDOLIZED BY THE CROWD, TOMMY CATCHES THEIR ENTHUSIASM.
COME ON, BURKE! — HIT THAT LINE! — TEAR 'EM TO PIECES!

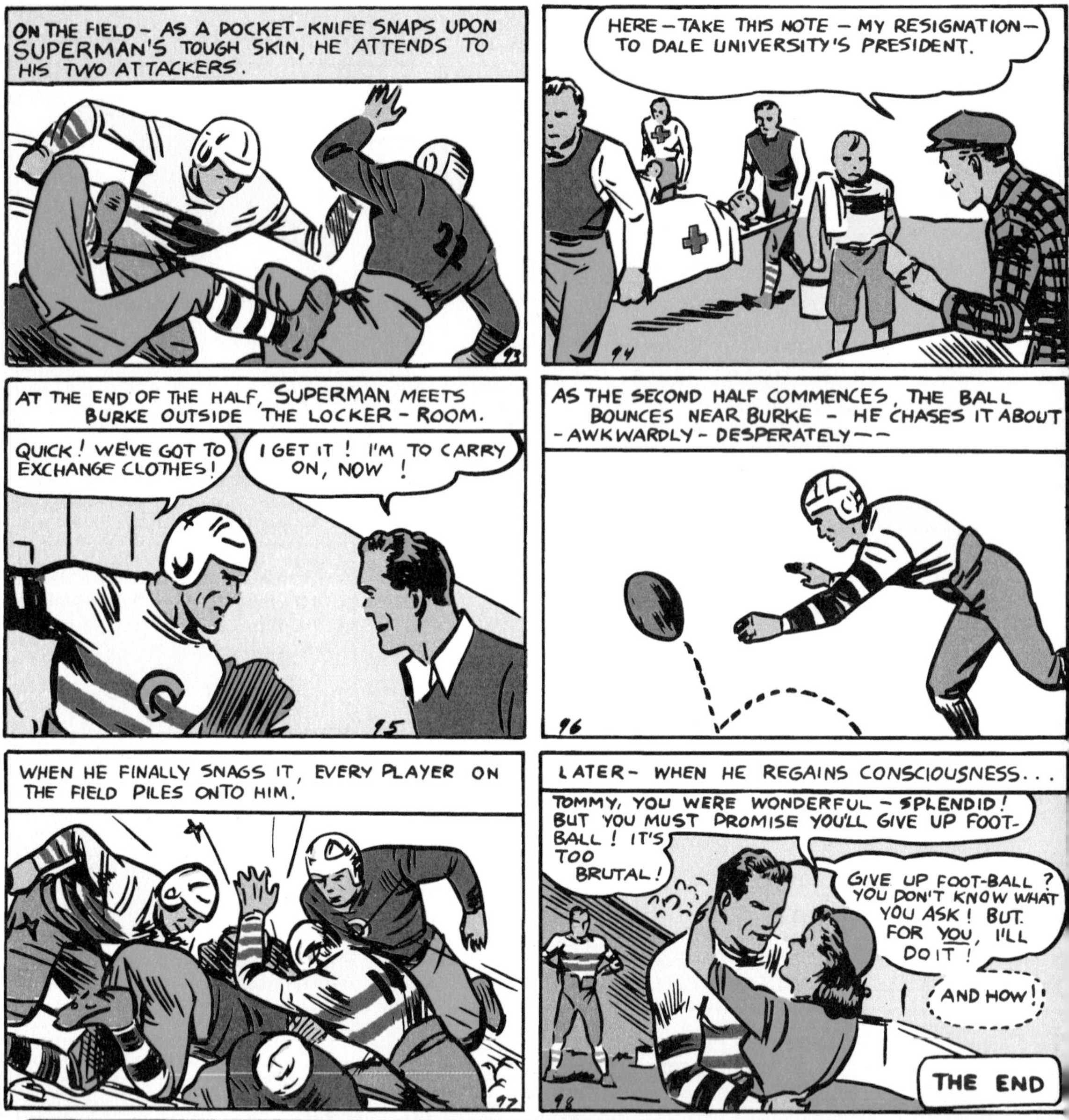
ON THE FIELD - AS A POCKET-KNIFE SNAPS UPON SUPERMAN'S TOUGH SKIN, HE ATTENDS TO HIS TWO ATTACKERS.
HERE - TAKE THIS NOTE - MY RESIGNATION - TO DALE UNIVERSITY'S PRESIDENT.
AT THE END OF THE HALF, SUPERMAN MEETS BURKE OUTSIDE THE LOCKER-ROOM.
QUICK! WE'VE GOT TO EXCHANGE CLOTHES!
I GET IT! I'M TO CARRY ON, NOW!
AS THE SECOND HALF COMMENCES, THE BALL BOUNCES NEAR BURKE - HE CHASES IT ABOUT - AWKWARDLY - DESPERATELY--
WHEN HE FINALLY SNAGS IT, EVERY PLAYER ON THE FIELD PILES ONTO HIM.
LATER- WHEN HE REGAINS CONSCIOUSNESS...
TOMMY, YOU WERE WONDERFUL - SPLENDID! BUT YOU MUST PROMISE YOU'LL GIVE UP FOOT-BALL! IT'S TOO BRUTAL!
GIVE UP FOOT-BALL? YOU DON'T KNOW WHAT YOU ASK! BUT FOR YOU, I'LL DO IT!
AND HOW!
THE END

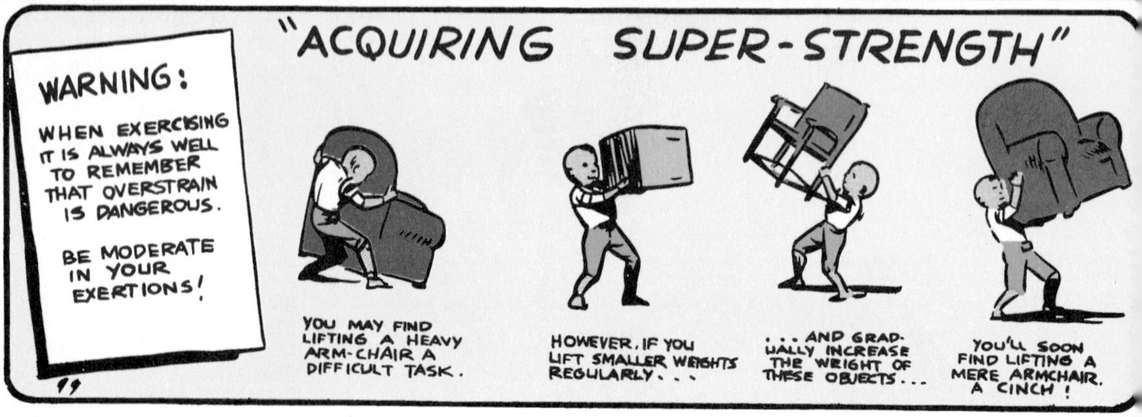
"ACQUIRING SUPER-STRENGTH"
WARNING:
WHEN EXERCISING IT IS ALWAYS WELL TO REMEMBER THAT OVERSTRAIN IS DANGEROUS.
BE MODERATE IN YOUR EXERTIONS!
YOU MAY FIND LIFTING A HEAVY ARM-CHAIR A DIFFICULT TASK.
HOWEVER, IF YOU LIFT SMALLER WEIGHTS REGULARLY...
...AND GRADUALLY INCREASE THE WEIGHT OF THESE OBJECTS...
YOU'LL SOON FIND LIFTING A MERE ARMCHAIR A CINCH!

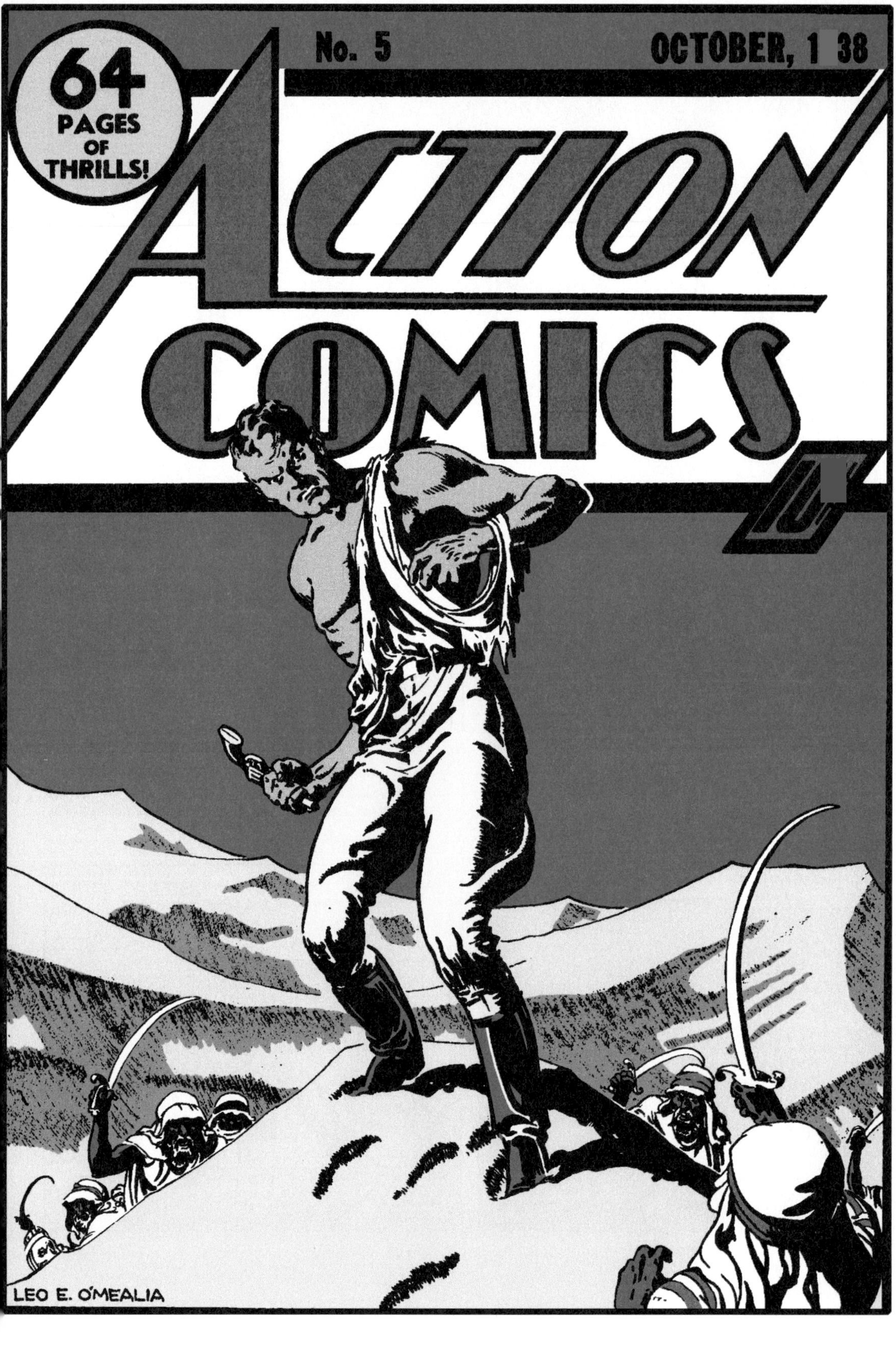
64
PAGES
OF
THRILLS!
No. 5
OCTOBER, 1 38
ACTION
COMICS
LEO E. O'MEALIA

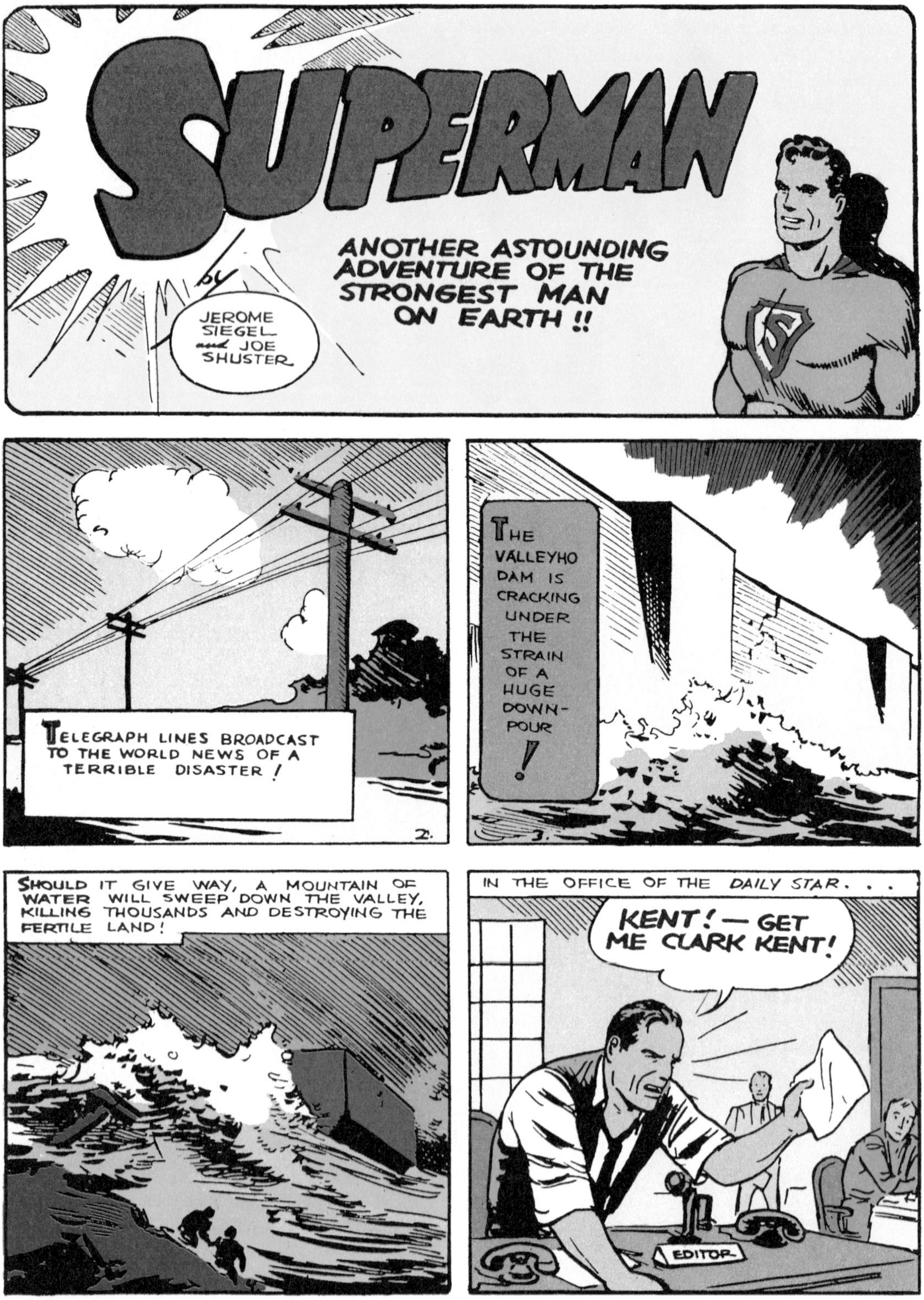
SUPERMAN
by
JEROME SIEGEL and JOE SHUSTER
ANOTHER ASTOUNDING ADVENTURE OF THE STRONGEST MAN ON EARTH !!
TELEGRAPH LINES BROADCAST TO THE WORLD NEWS OF A TERRIBLE DISASTER !
2.
THE VALLEYHO DAM IS CRACKING UNDER THE STRAIN OF A HUGE DOWN-POUR !
3.
SHOULD IT GIVE WAY, A MOUNTAIN OF WATER WILL SWEEP DOWN THE VALLEY, KILLING THOUSANDS AND DESTROYING THE FERTILE LAND !
IN THE OFFICE OF THE DAILY STAR . . .
KENT ! — GET ME CLARK KENT !
EDITOR

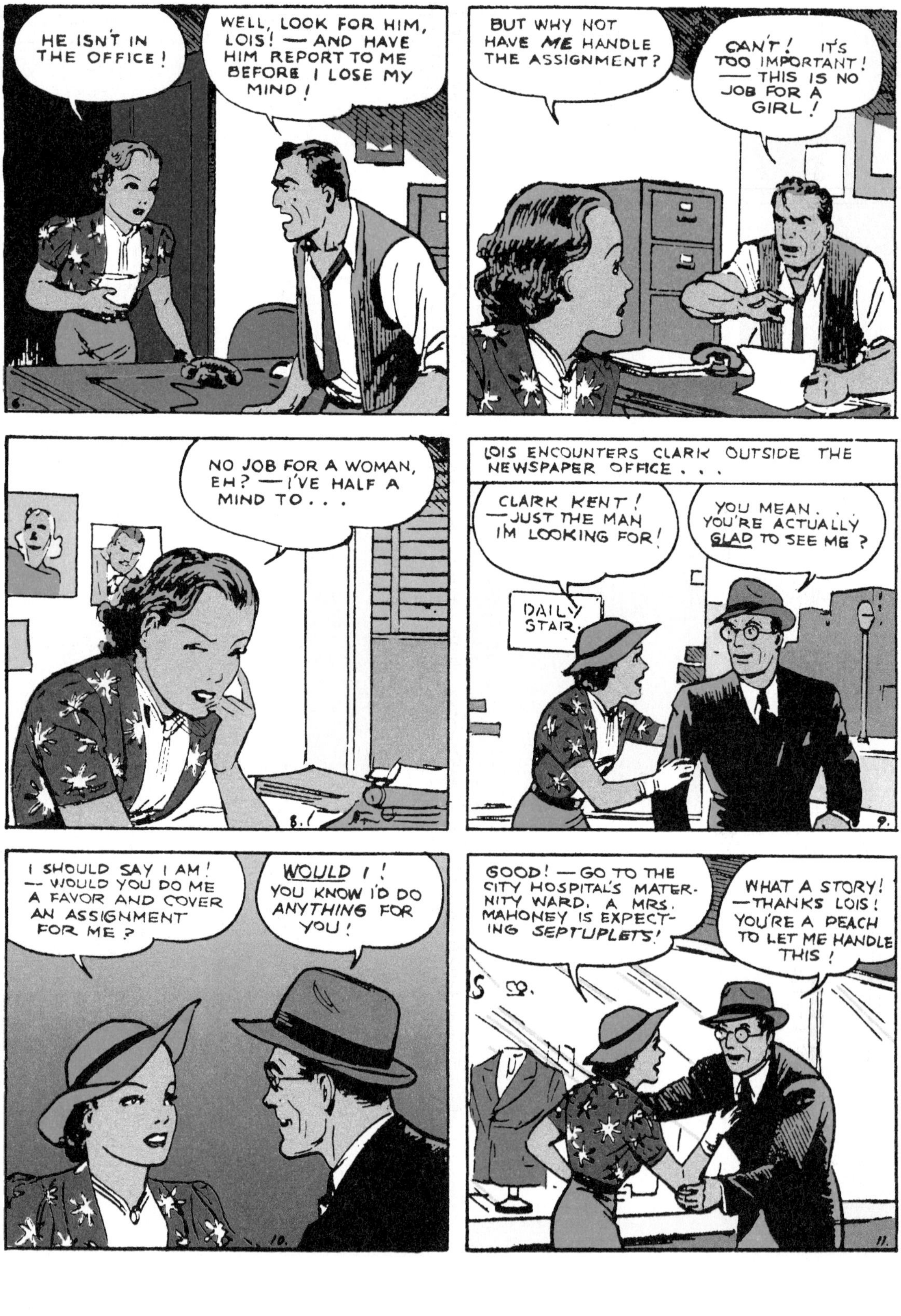
HE ISN'T IN THE OFFICE!
WELL, LOOK FOR HIM, LOIS! — AND HAVE HIM REPORT TO ME BEFORE I LOSE MY MIND!
BUT WHY NOT HAVE *ME* HANDLE THE ASSIGNMENT?
CAN'T! IT'S TOO IMPORTANT! — THIS IS NO JOB FOR A GIRL!
NO JOB FOR A WOMAN, EH? — I'VE HALF A MIND TO . . .
LOIS ENCOUNTERS CLARK OUTSIDE THE NEWSPAPER OFFICE . . .
CLARK KENT! — JUST THE MAN I'M LOOKING FOR!
YOU MEAN . . . YOU'RE ACTUALLY GLAD TO SEE ME?
DAILY STAR
I SHOULD SAY I AM! -- WOULD YOU DO ME A FAVOR AND COVER AN ASSIGNMENT FOR ME?
WOULD I! YOU KNOW I'D DO *ANYTHING* FOR YOU!
GOOD! — GO TO THE CITY HOSPITAL'S MATERNITY WARD. A MRS. MAHONEY IS EXPECTING *SEPTUPLETS*!
WHAT A STORY! — THANKS LOIS! YOU'RE A PEACH TO LET ME HANDLE THIS!

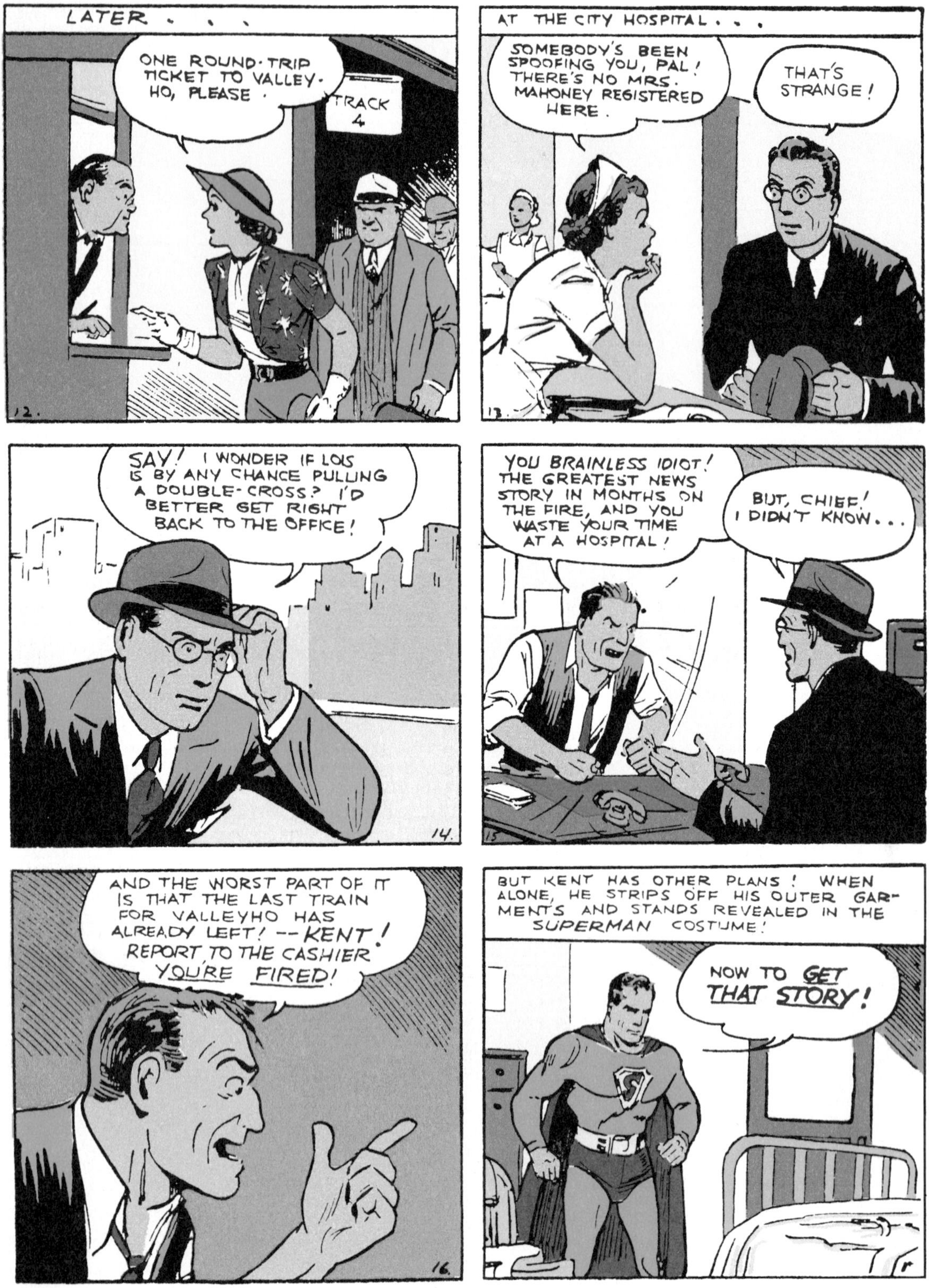
LATER . . .
ONE ROUND-TRIP TICKET TO VALLEY-HO, PLEASE.
TRACK 4
AT THE CITY HOSPITAL . . .
SOMEBODY'S BEEN SPOOFING YOU, PAL! THERE'S NO MRS. MAHONEY REGISTERED HERE.
THAT'S STRANGE!
SAY! I WONDER IF LOIS IS BY ANY CHANCE PULLING A DOUBLE-CROSS? I'D BETTER GET RIGHT BACK TO THE OFFICE!
YOU BRAINLESS IDIOT! THE GREATEST NEWS STORY IN MONTHS ON THE FIRE, AND YOU WASTE YOUR TIME AT A HOSPITAL!
BUT, CHIEF! I DIDN'T KNOW . . .
AND THE WORST PART OF IT IS THAT THE LAST TRAIN FOR VALLEYHO HAS ALREADY LEFT! --KENT! REPORT TO THE CASHIER YOU'RE FIRED!
BUT KENT HAS OTHER PLANS! WHEN ALONE, HE STRIPS OFF HIS OUTER GARMENTS AND STANDS REVEALED IN THE SUPERMAN COSTUME!
NOW TO GET THAT STORY!

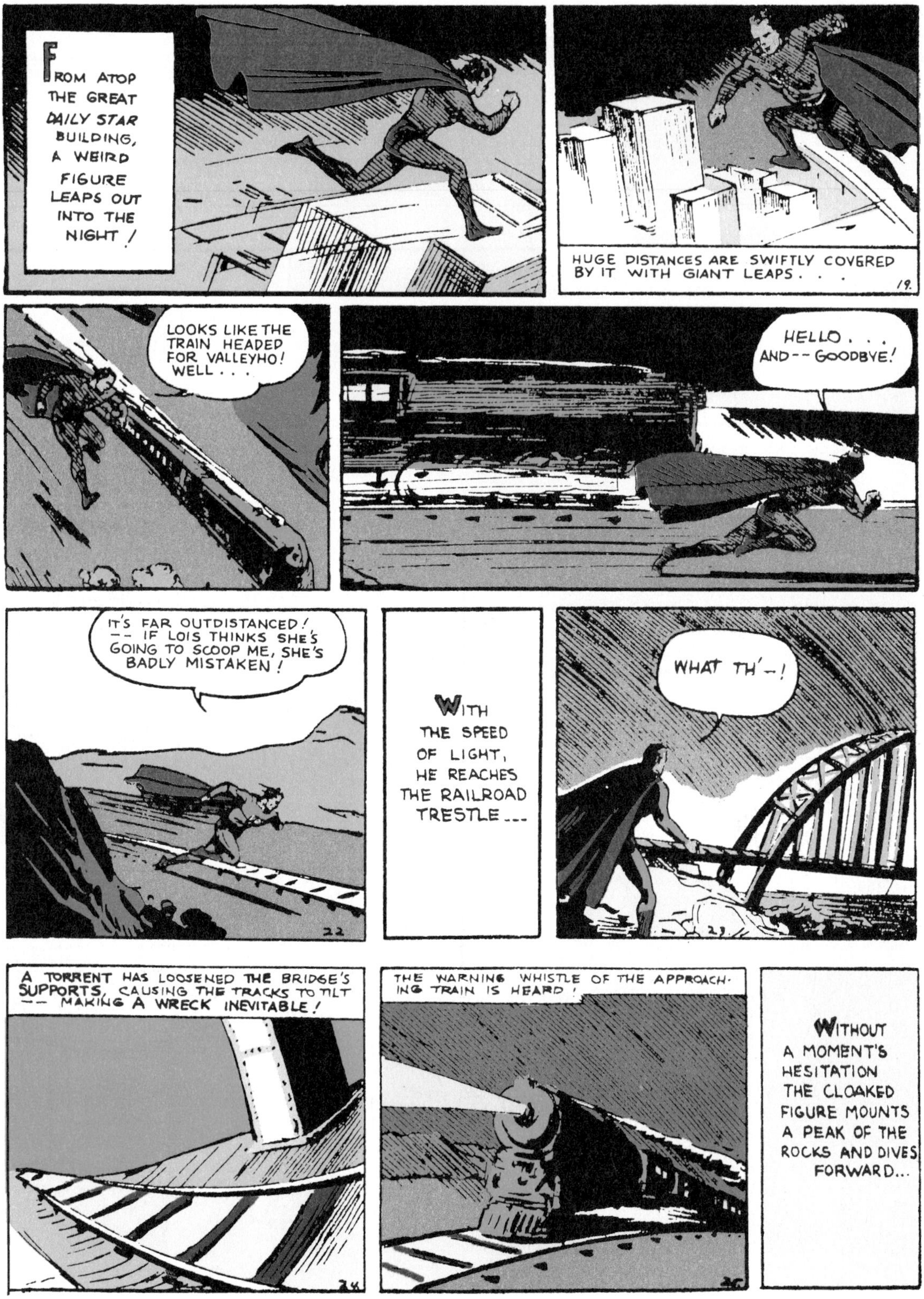
FROM ATOP THE GREAT *DAILY STAR* BUILDING, A WEIRD FIGURE LEAPS OUT INTO THE NIGHT!
HUGE DISTANCES ARE SWIFTLY COVERED BY IT WITH GIANT LEAPS . . .
LOOKS LIKE THE TRAIN HEADED FOR VALLEYHO! WELL . . .
HELLO . . . AND -- GOODBYE!
IT'S FAR OUTDISTANCED! -- IF LOIS THINKS SHE'S GOING TO SCOOP ME, SHE'S BADLY MISTAKEN!
WITH THE SPEED OF LIGHT, HE REACHES THE RAILROAD TRESTLE...
WHAT TH'--!
A TORRENT HAS LOOSENED THE BRIDGE'S SUPPORTS, CAUSING THE TRACKS TO TILT -- MAKING A WRECK INEVITABLE!
THE WARNING WHISTLE OF THE APPROACHING TRAIN IS HEARD!
WITHOUT A MOMENT'S HESITATION THE CLOAKED FIGURE MOUNTS A PEAK OF THE ROCKS AND DIVES FORWARD...

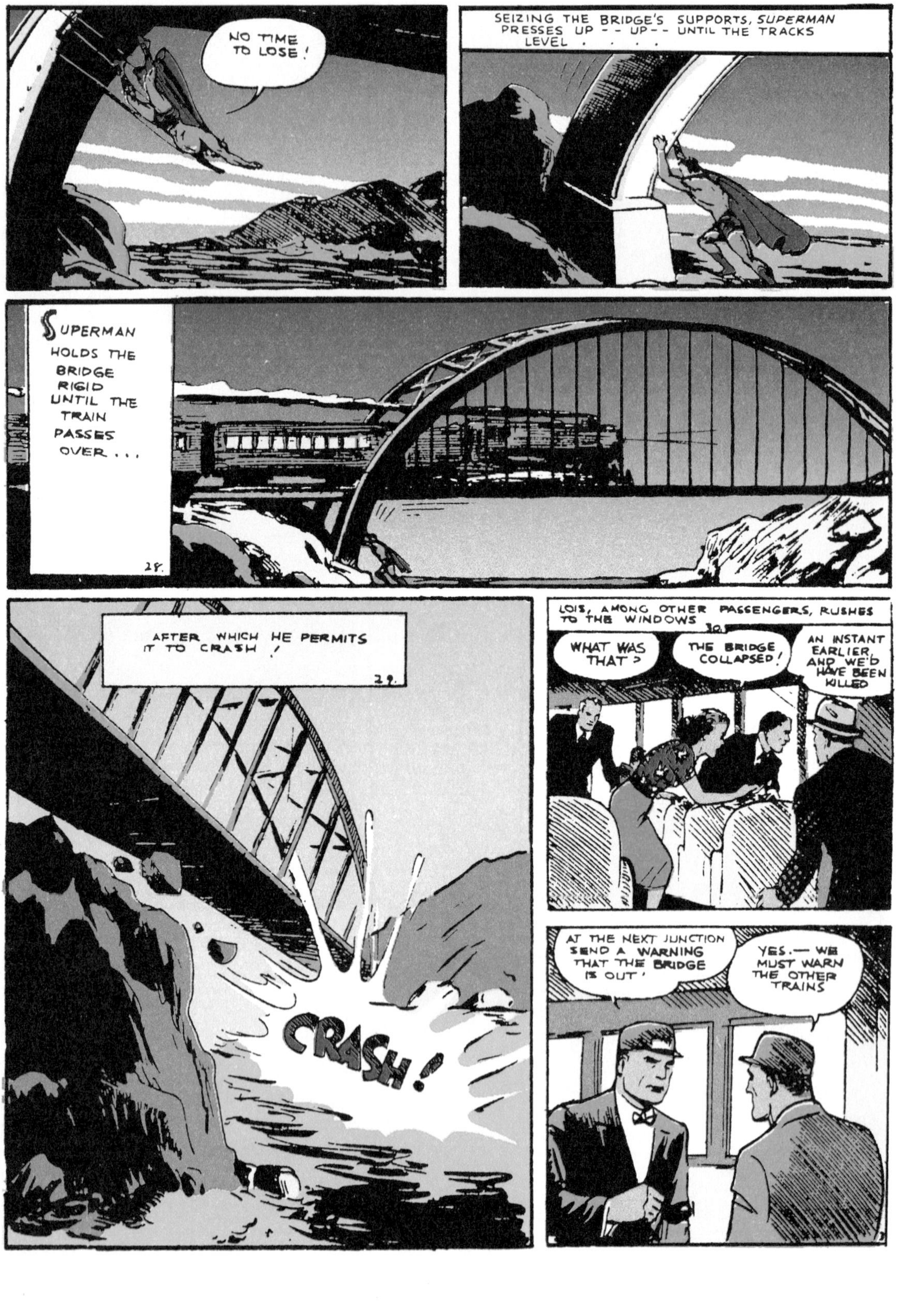

NO TIME TO LOSE!
SEIZING THE BRIDGE'S SUPPORTS, SUPERMAN PRESSES UP -- UP -- UNTIL THE TRACKS LEVEL . . . .
SUPERMAN HOLDS THE BRIDGE RIGID UNTIL THE TRAIN PASSES OVER . . .
28.
AFTER WHICH HE PERMITS IT TO CRASH!
29.
CRASH!
LOIS, AMONG OTHER PASSENGERS, RUSHES TO THE WINDOWS
30.
WHAT WAS THAT?
THE BRIDGE COLLAPSED!
AN INSTANT EARLIER, AND WE'D HAVE BEEN KILLED
AT THE NEXT JUNCTION SEND A WARNING THAT THE BRIDGE IS OUT!
YES.— WE MUST WARN THE OTHER TRAINS

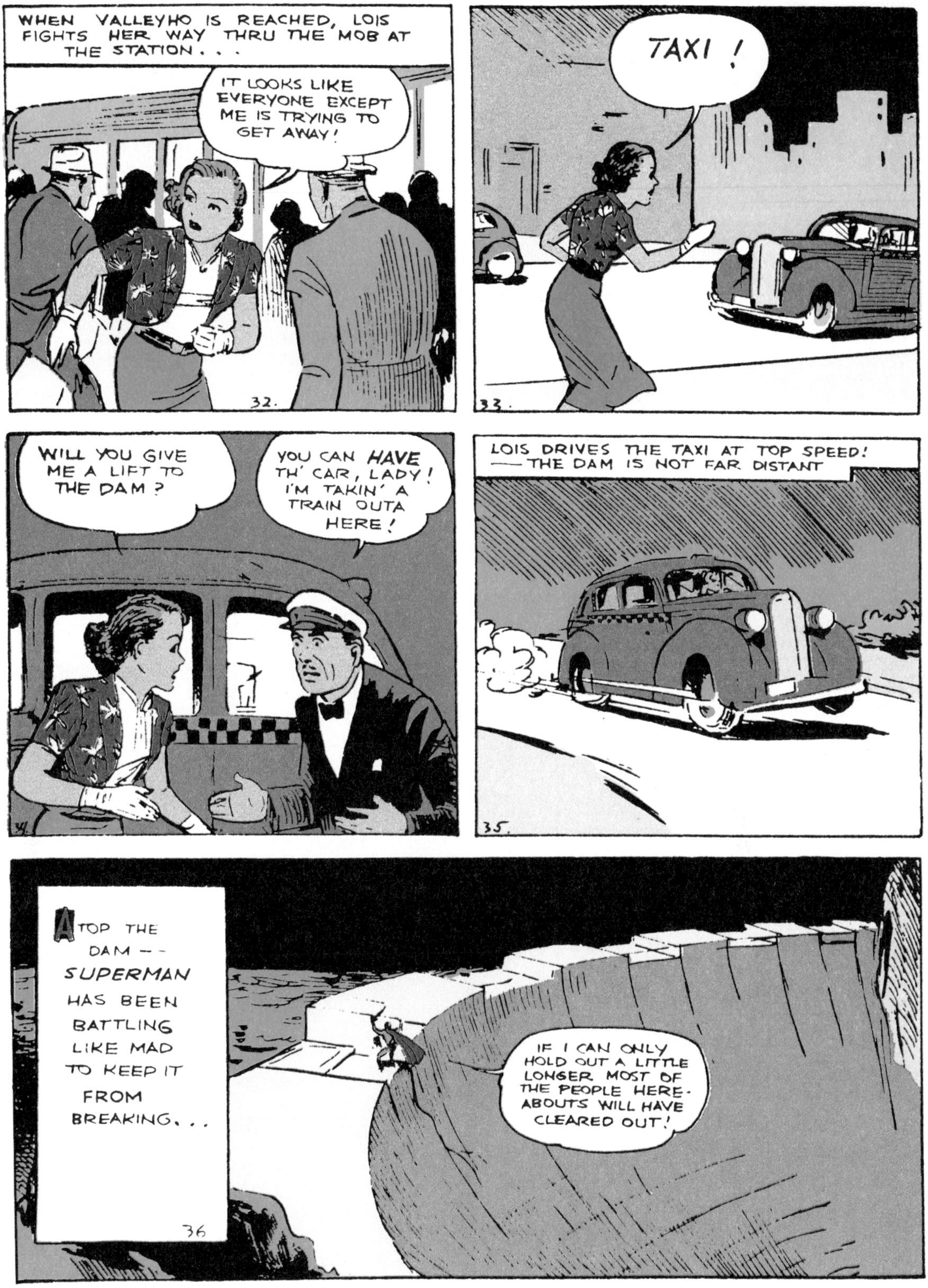
WHEN VALLEYHO IS REACHED, LOIS FIGHTS HER WAY THRU THE MOB AT THE STATION . . .
IT LOOKS LIKE EVERYONE EXCEPT ME IS TRYING TO GET AWAY!
32.
TAXI !
33.
WILL YOU GIVE ME A LIFT TO THE DAM ?
YOU CAN HAVE TH' CAR, LADY! I'M TAKIN' A TRAIN OUTA HERE!
34.
LOIS DRIVES THE TAXI AT TOP SPEED! —THE DAM IS NOT FAR DISTANT
35.
ATOP THE DAM -- SUPERMAN HAS BEEN BATTLING LIKE MAD TO KEEP IT FROM BREAKING. . .
IF I CAN ONLY HOLD OUT A LITTLE LONGER MOST OF THE PEOPLE HEREABOUTS WILL HAVE CLEARED OUT!
36

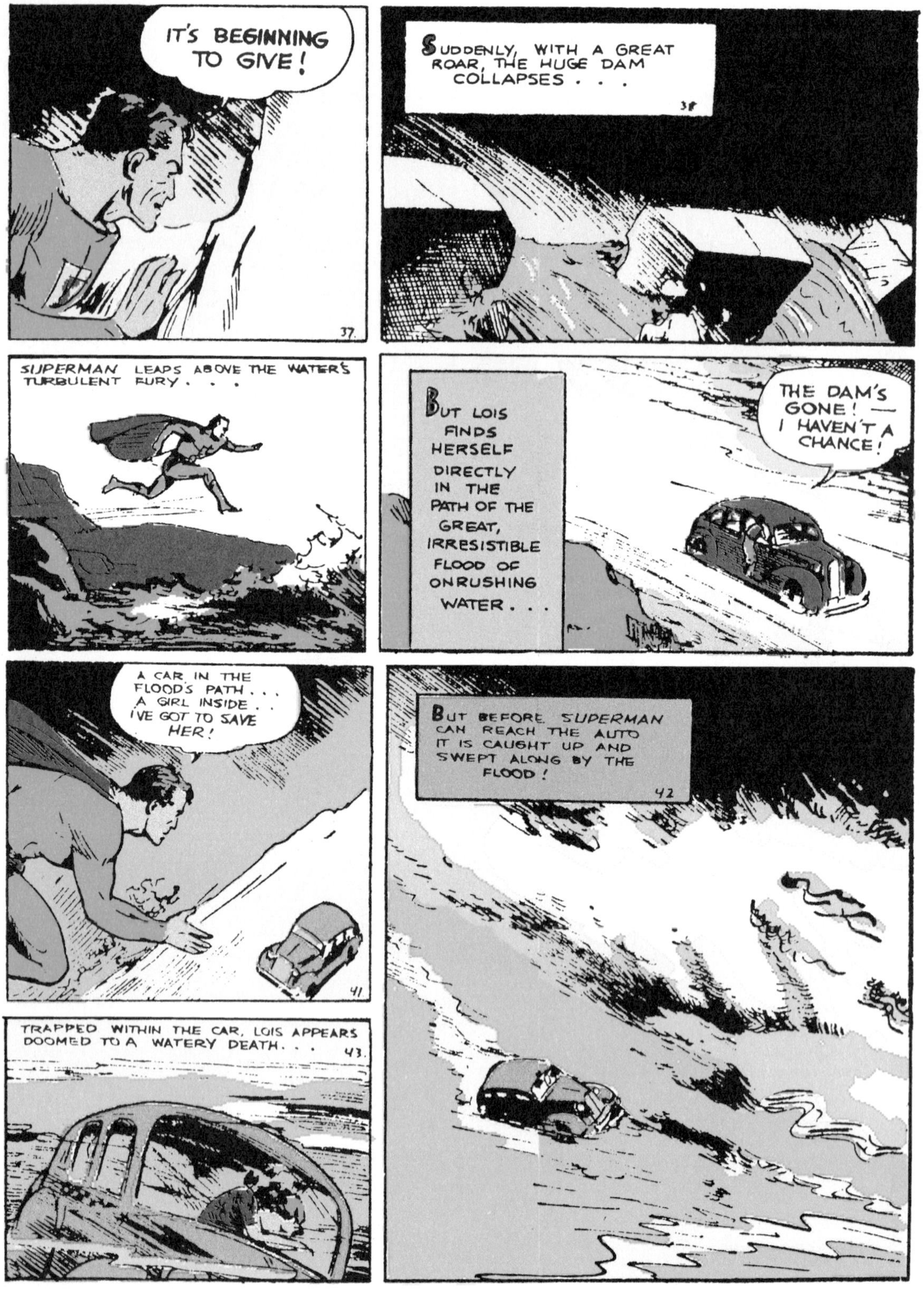
IT'S BEGINNING TO GIVE!
37.
SUDDENLY, WITH A GREAT ROAR, THE HUGE DAM COLLAPSES . . .
38
SUPERMAN LEAPS ABOVE THE WATER'S TURBULENT FURY . . .
BUT LOIS FINDS HERSELF DIRECTLY IN THE PATH OF THE GREAT, IRRESISTIBLE FLOOD OF ONRUSHING WATER . . .
THE DAM'S GONE! — I HAVEN'T A CHANCE!
A CAR IN THE FLOOD'S PATH . . . A GIRL INSIDE . . I'VE GOT TO SAVE HER!
41.
BUT BEFORE SUPERMAN CAN REACH THE AUTO IT IS CAUGHT UP AND SWEPT ALONG BY THE FLOOD!
42
TRAPPED WITHIN THE CAR, LOIS APPEARS DOOMED TO A WATERY DEATH . . .
43.

. . . UNTIL SUPERMAN. UPON REACHING IT, TEARS THE AUTO APART AND RISES WITH LOIS IN HIS ARMS TOWARD THE WATER'S SURFACE!

POWERFUL STROKES BRING THEM TO SHORE . . .

INSTANTLY SUPERMAN IS OFF LIKE A SHOT, RACING THE FLOOD!

HE CATCHES UP WITH ITS BEGINNING . . . . . .

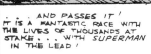

. . . AND PASSES IT! IT IS A FANTASTIC RACE WITH THE LIVES OF THOUSANDS AT STAKE . . . WITH SUPERMAN IN THE LEAD!

AHEAD OF THE RAGING, RUSHING TORRENT, HE SPRINGS TO A HIGH PINNACLE . . . .

. . . THEN PITS HIS TREMENDOUS STRENGTH AGAINST A GREAT PROJECTION OF ROCK!

BEFORE SUPERMAN'S MIGHT, THE HUGE MOUNTAIN PEAK CRACKS . . . . AND CASCADES DOWNWARD IN THE FACE OF THE FLOOD! THE AVALANCHE OF ROCK CRAMS SHUT THE MOUNTAIN-GAP BELOW — CUTTING OFF, DIVERTING THE FLOOD TO ANOTHER DIRECTION, AWAY FROM VALLEYHO TOWN!

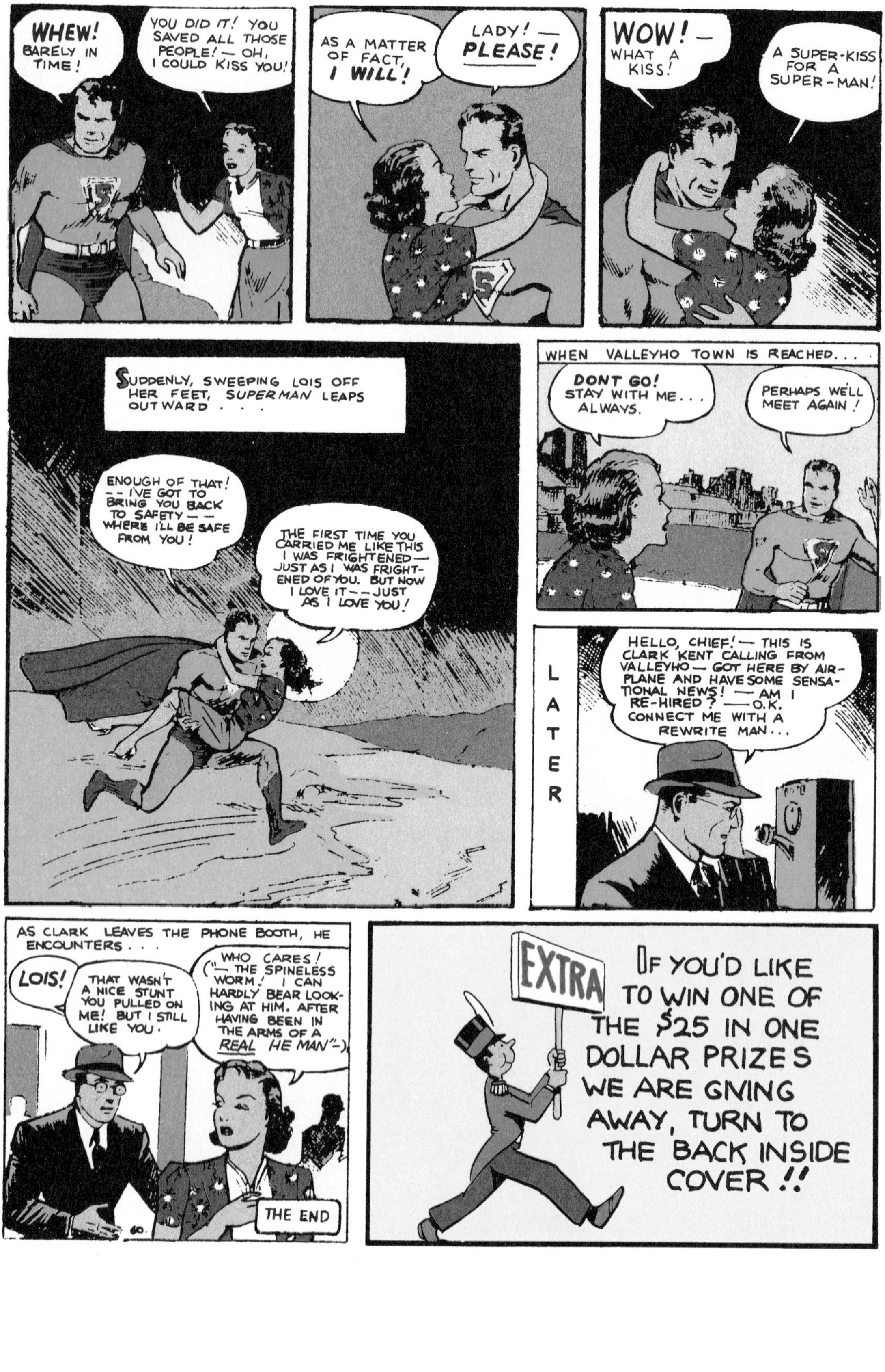
WHEW! BARELY IN TIME!
YOU DID IT! YOU SAVED ALL THOSE PEOPLE! — OH, I COULD KISS YOU!
AS A MATTER OF FACT, I WILL!
LADY! — PLEASE!
WOW! — WHAT A KISS!
A SUPER-KISS FOR A SUPER-MAN!
SUDDENLY, SWEEPING LOIS OFF HER FEET, SUPERMAN LEAPS OUTWARD . . .
ENOUGH OF THAT! -- I'VE GOT TO BRING YOU BACK TO SAFETY -- WHERE I'LL BE SAFE FROM YOU!
THE FIRST TIME YOU CARRIED ME LIKE THIS I WAS FRIGHTENED— JUST AS I WAS FRIGHTENED OF YOU. BUT NOW I LOVE IT -- JUST AS I LOVE YOU!
WHEN VALLEYHO TOWN IS REACHED . . .
DONT GO! STAY WITH ME . . . ALWAYS.
PERHAPS WE'LL MEET AGAIN!
LATER
HELLO, CHIEF! — THIS IS CLARK KENT CALLING FROM VALLEYHO — GOT HERE BY AIRPLANE AND HAVE SOME SENSATIONAL NEWS! — AM I RE-HIRED? — O.K. CONNECT ME WITH A REWRITE MAN . . .
AS CLARK LEAVES THE PHONE BOOTH, HE ENCOUNTERS . . .
LOIS!
THAT WASN'T A NICE STUNT YOU PULLED ON ME! BUT I STILL LIKE YOU.
WHO CARES! ("— THE SPINELESS WORM! I CAN HARDLY BEAR LOOKING AT HIM. AFTER HAVING BEEN IN THE ARMS OF A REAL HE MAN"—)
THE END
EXTRA
IF YOU'D LIKE TO WIN ONE OF THE $25 IN ONE DOLLAR PRIZES WE ARE GIVING AWAY, TURN TO THE BACK INSIDE COVER !!

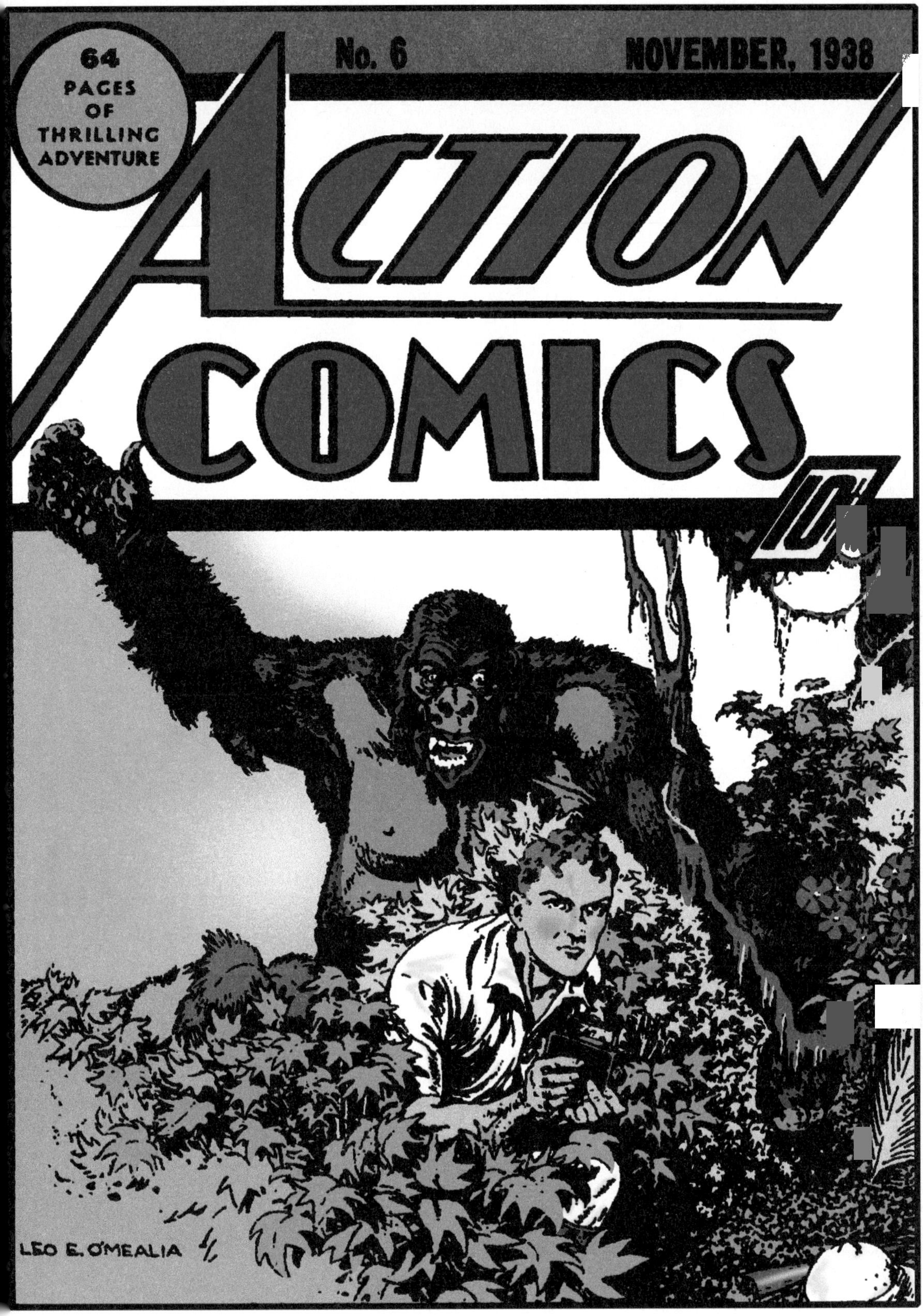
64 PAGES OF THRILLING ADVENTURE
No. 6
NOVEMBER, 1938
ACTION COMICS
10¢
LEO E. O'MEALIA

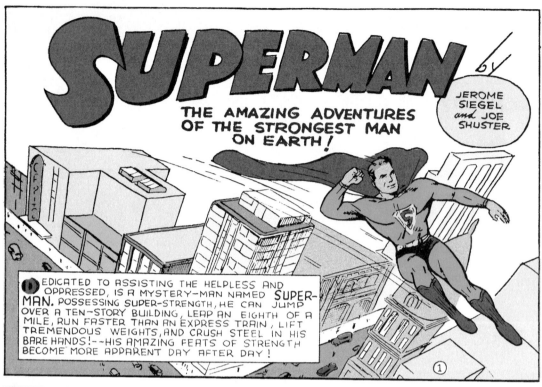

SUPERMAN

by JEROME SIEGEL and JOE SHUSTER

THE AMAZING ADVENTURES OF THE STRONGEST MAN ON EARTH!

DEDICATED TO ASSISTING THE HELPLESS AND OPPRESSED, IS A MYSTERY-MAN NAMED SUPER-MAN. POSSESSING SUPER-STRENGTH, HE CAN JUMP OVER A TEN-STORY BUILDING, LEAP AN EIGHTH OF A MILE, RUN FASTER THAN AN EXPRESS TRAIN, LIFT TREMENDOUS WEIGHTS, AND CRUSH STEEL IN HIS BARE HANDS!--HIS AMAZING FEATS OF STRENGTH BECOME MORE APPARENT DAY AFTER DAY!

NEWSPAPERS HEADLINE HIS ACTIVITIES WITH EVER-INCREASING REGULARITY!

MORNING SUPERMAN SMASHES MUNITIONS-RING

EVENING SUPERMAN WARS ON INJUSTICES

DAILY STAR MYSTERY MAN OF STEEL RE-APPEARS

ORLD HERALD ENTIRE TOWN SAVED BY SUPERMAN

ESPECIALLY ASSIGNED TO TRACK DOWN ALL SUPERMAN NEWS, IS CLARK KENT, MEEK ACE-REPORTER OF THE DAILY STAR.

ONE DAY, CLARK RECEIVES ASTONISHING NEWS WHEN SUMMONED BEFORE HIS EDITOR ...

KENT, MEET NICK WILLIAMS, SUPERMAN'S PERSONAL MANAGER.

WHAT!

KENT'S HAND HAD BEEN TOYING WITH AN ASH-TRAY. UNDER HIS STARTLED, IN-CREASED GRASP, IT TWISTS INTO A SHAPE-LESS PULP. --AMAZING? NOT AT ALL! ...FOR IN REALITY, CLARK KENT IS SUPERMAN!

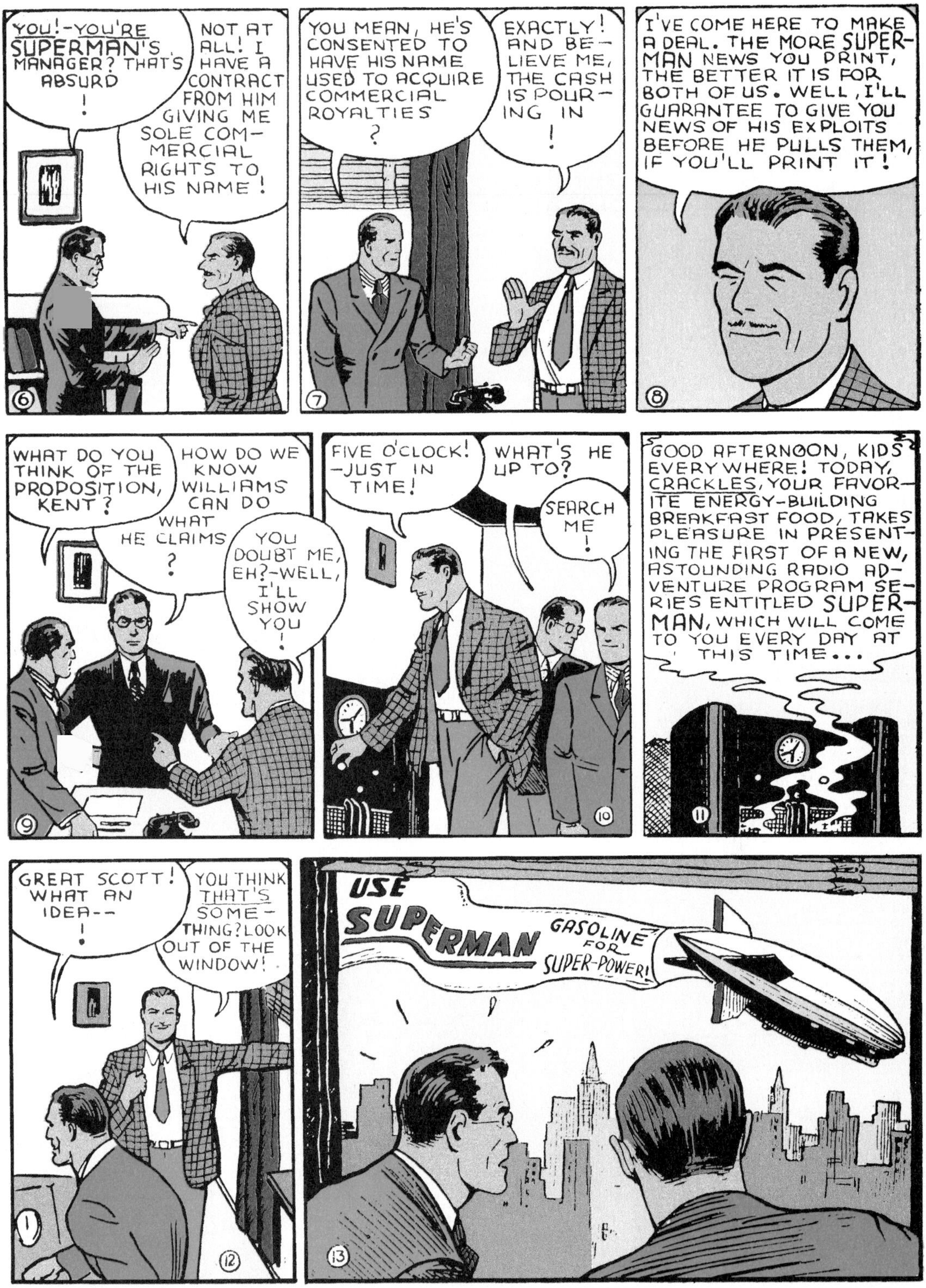
YOU!-YOU'RE SUPERMAN'S MANAGER? THAT'S ABSURD!
NOT AT ALL! I HAVE A CONTRACT FROM HIM GIVING ME SOLE COMMERCIAL RIGHTS TO HIS NAME!
YOU MEAN, HE'S CONSENTED TO HAVE HIS NAME USED TO ACQUIRE COMMERCIAL ROYALTIES?
EXACTLY! AND BELIEVE ME, THE CASH IS POURING IN!
I'VE COME HERE TO MAKE A DEAL. THE MORE SUPERMAN NEWS YOU PRINT, THE BETTER IT IS FOR BOTH OF US. WELL, I'LL GUARANTEE TO GIVE YOU NEWS OF HIS EXPLOITS BEFORE HE PULLS THEM, IF YOU'LL PRINT IT!
WHAT DO YOU THINK OF THE PROPOSITION, KENT?
HOW DO WE KNOW WILLIAMS CAN DO WHAT HE CLAIMS?
YOU DOUBT ME, EH?-WELL, I'LL SHOW YOU!
FIVE O'CLOCK! -JUST IN TIME!
WHAT'S HE UP TO?
SEARCH ME!
GOOD AFTERNOON, KIDS EVERYWHERE! TODAY, CRACKLES, YOUR FAVORITE ENERGY-BUILDING BREAKFAST FOOD, TAKES PLEASURE IN PRESENTING THE FIRST OF A NEW, ASTOUNDING RADIO ADVENTURE PROGRAM SERIES ENTITLED SUPERMAN, WHICH WILL COME TO YOU EVERY DAY AT THIS TIME...
GREAT SCOTT! WHAT AN IDEA--!
YOU THINK THAT'S SOMETHING? LOOK OUT OF THE WINDOW!
USE SUPERMAN GASOLINE FOR SUPER-POWER!

GOOD LORD! —WHAT NEXT?

TAKE A GANDER AT THAT BILLBOARD OVER YONDER!

The *SUPERMAN* Streamline-Special

AMERICA'S FAVORITE AUTOMOBILE

⑮

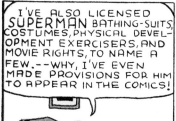

I'VE ALSO LICENSED *SUPERMAN* BATHING-SUITS, COSTUMES, PHYSICAL DEVELOPMENT EXERCISERS, AND MOVIE RIGHTS, TO NAME A FEW.-- WHY, I'VE EVEN MADE PROVISIONS FOR HIM TO APPEAR IN THE COMICS!

⑯

ALL VERY INTERESTING! BUT HOW DID *SUPERMAN* CONTACT YOU?

HE DROPPED IN ON ME AND SPRUNG THE PROPOSITION. I LIKED THE IDEA, AND WE EVOLVED A PARTNERSHIP.

⑰

VERY INTERESTING --IF TRUE!

YOU DOUBT ME? VERY WELL THEN! WOULD A *PERSONAL INTERVIEW* WITH *SUPERMAN* INTEREST YOU?

⑱

I SHOULD SAY IT WOULD! --IN FACT, I'D LIKE TO MEET HIM VERY MUCH!

FINE! COME TO MY OFFICE TONIGHT, AND I'LL ARRANGE YOUR FIRST INTERVIEW WITH THE STRONGEST MAN ON EARTH!

⑲

GOSH!

⑳

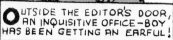

OUTSIDE THE EDITOR'S DOOR, AN INQUISITIVE OFFICE-BOY HAS BEEN GETTING AN EARFUL!

CAN Y'IMAGINE THAT, LOIS? CLARK KENT IS GOING TO SEE *SUPERMAN* TONIGHT, IN PERSON!

HE IS! --THEN SO WILL I!

㉑

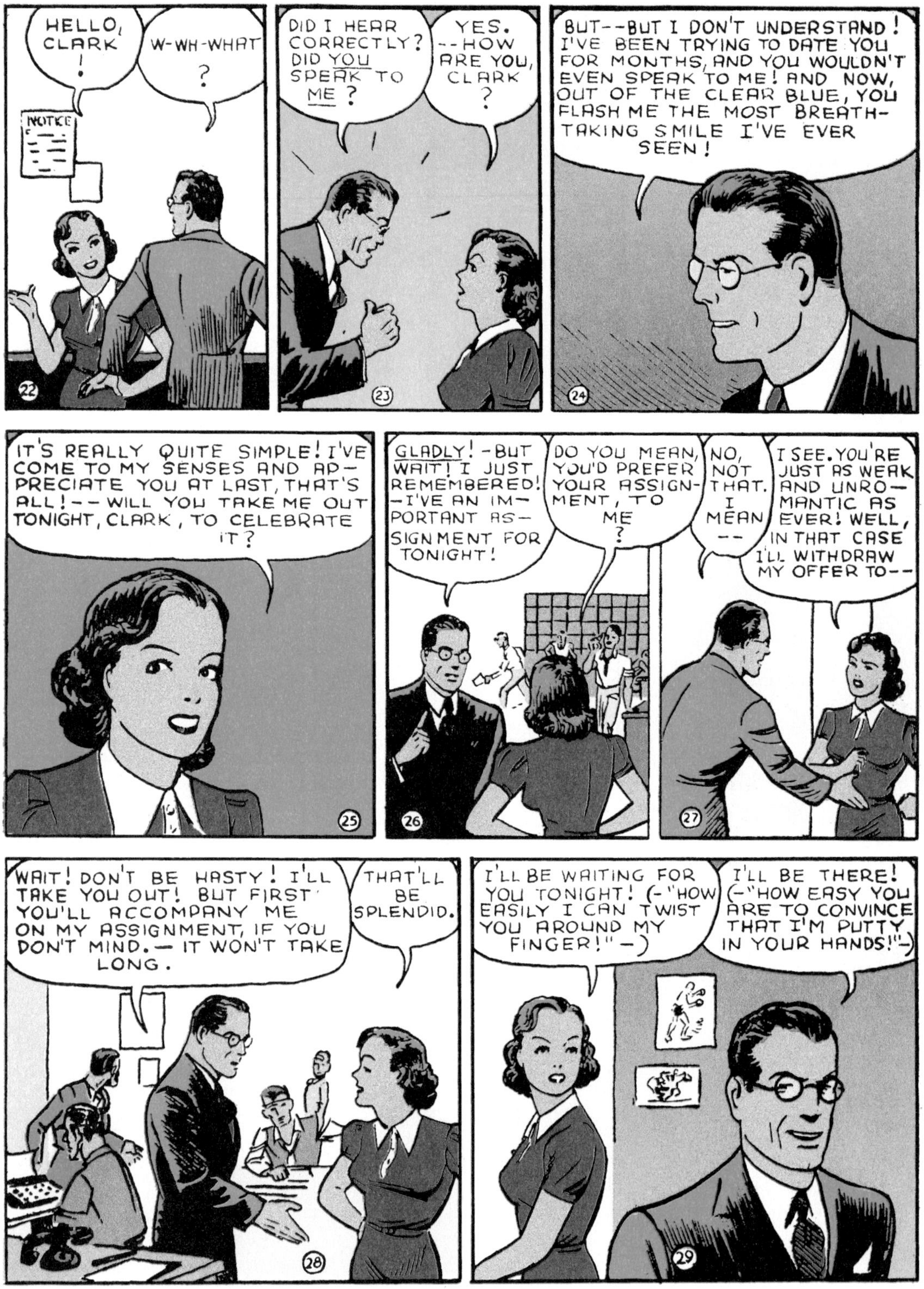
HELLO, CLARK!
W-WH-WHAT?
NOTICE
DID I HEAR CORRECTLY? DID YOU SPEAK TO ME?
YES. --HOW ARE YOU, CLARK?
BUT--BUT I DON'T UNDERSTAND! I'VE BEEN TRYING TO DATE YOU FOR MONTHS, AND YOU WOULDN'T EVEN SPEAK TO ME! AND NOW, OUT OF THE CLEAR BLUE, YOU FLASH ME THE MOST BREATH-TAKING SMILE I'VE EVER SEEN!
IT'S REALLY QUITE SIMPLE! I'VE COME TO MY SENSES AND APPRECIATE YOU AT LAST, THAT'S ALL!-- WILL YOU TAKE ME OUT TONIGHT, CLARK, TO CELEBRATE IT?
GLADLY! -BUT WAIT! I JUST REMEMBERED! -I'VE AN IMPORTANT ASSIGNMENT FOR TONIGHT!
DO YOU MEAN, YOU'D PREFER YOUR ASSIGNMENT, TO ME?
NO, NOT THAT. I MEAN --
I SEE. YOU'RE JUST AS WEAK AND UNROMANTIC AS EVER! WELL, IN THAT CASE I'LL WITHDRAW MY OFFER TO--
WAIT! DON'T BE HASTY! I'LL TAKE YOU OUT! BUT FIRST YOU'LL ACCOMPANY ME ON MY ASSIGNMENT, IF YOU DON'T MIND.— IT WON'T TAKE LONG.
THAT'LL BE SPLENDID.
I'LL BE WAITING FOR YOU TONIGHT! (-"HOW EASILY I CAN TWIST YOU AROUND MY FINGER!"-)
I'LL BE THERE! (-"HOW EASY YOU ARE TO CONVINCE THAT I'M PUTTY IN YOUR HANDS!"-)

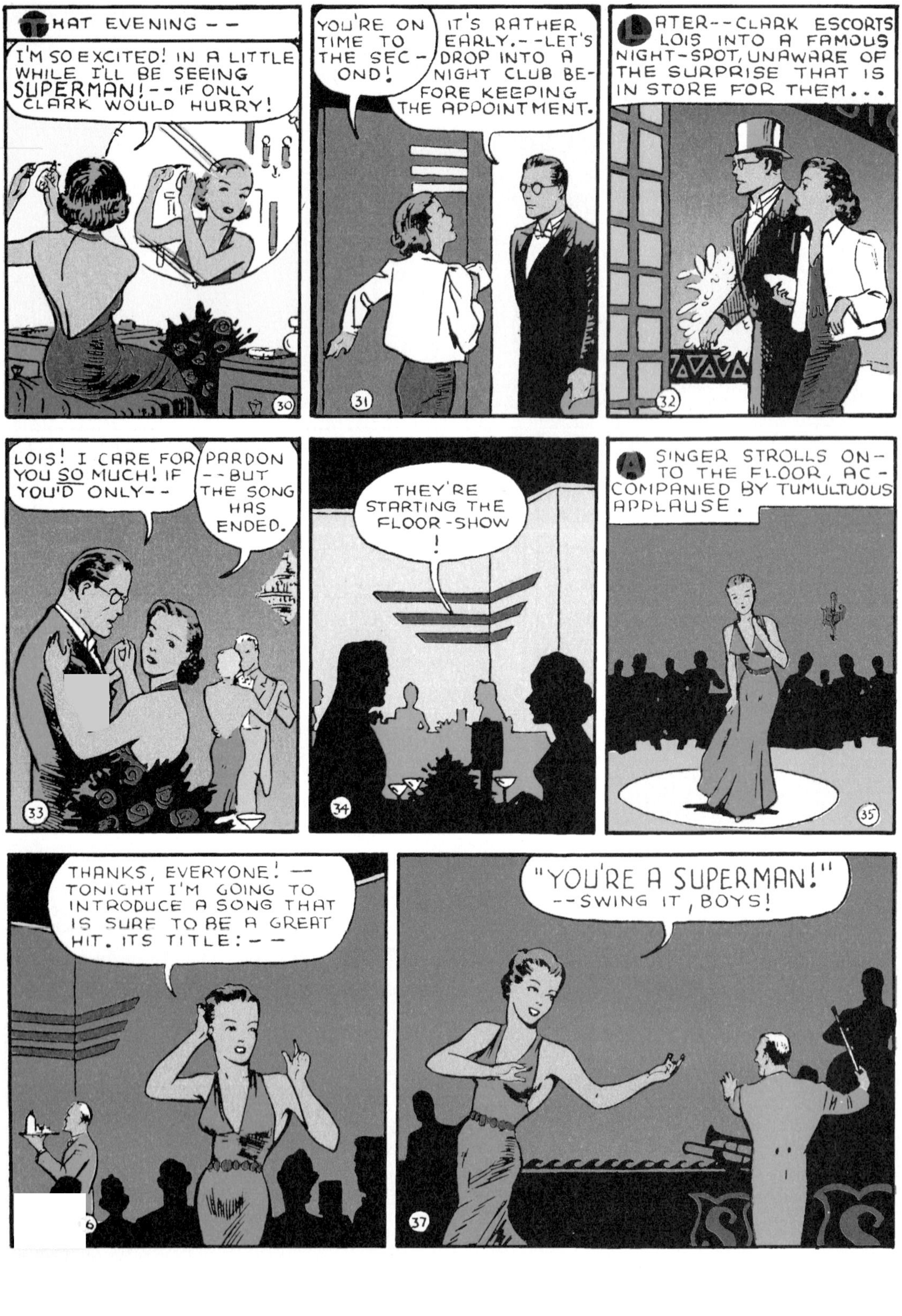
THAT EVENING --
I'M SO EXCITED! IN A LITTLE WHILE I'LL BE SEEING SUPERMAN! -- IF ONLY CLARK WOULD HURRY!
30
YOU'RE ON TIME TO THE SECOND!
IT'S RATHER EARLY. -- LET'S DROP INTO A NIGHT CLUB BEFORE KEEPING THE APPOINTMENT.
31
LATER -- CLARK ESCORTS LOIS INTO A FAMOUS NIGHT-SPOT, UNAWARE OF THE SURPRISE THAT IS IN STORE FOR THEM...
32
LOIS! I CARE FOR YOU SO MUCH! IF YOU'D ONLY--
PARDON -- BUT THE SONG HAS ENDED.
33
THEY'RE STARTING THE FLOOR-SHOW!
34
A SINGER STROLLS ONTO THE FLOOR, ACCOMPANIED BY TUMULTUOUS APPLAUSE.
35
THANKS, EVERYONE! — TONIGHT I'M GOING TO INTRODUCE A SONG THAT IS SURE TO BE A GREAT HIT. ITS TITLE: --
"YOU'RE A SUPERMAN!" -- SWING IT, BOYS!
37

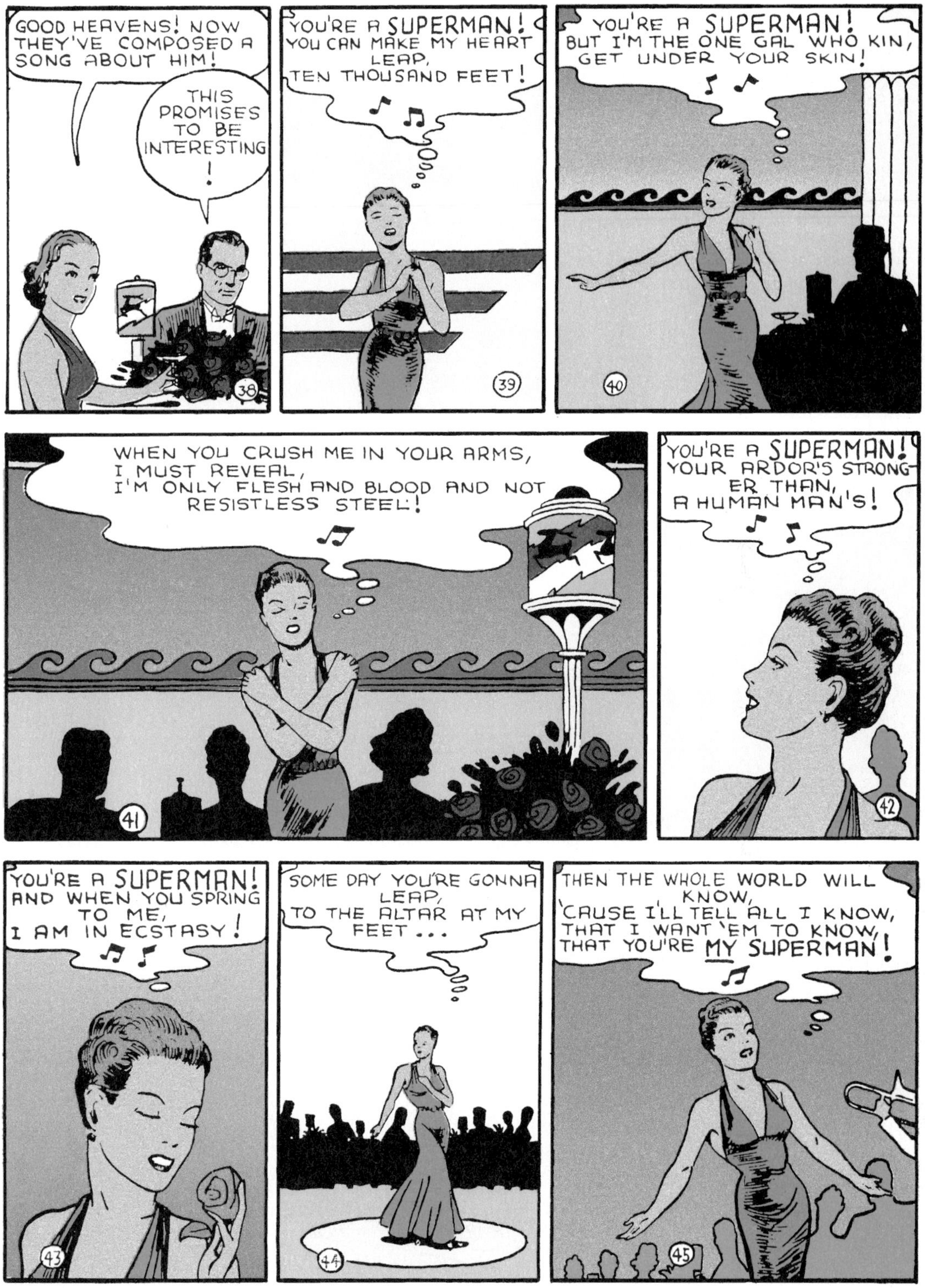
GOOD HEAVENS! NOW THEY'VE COMPOSED A SONG ABOUT HIM!
THIS PROMISES TO BE INTERESTING!
YOU'RE A SUPERMAN! YOU CAN MAKE MY HEART LEAP, TEN THOUSAND FEET!
YOU'RE A SUPERMAN! BUT I'M THE ONE GAL WHO KIN, GET UNDER YOUR SKIN!
WHEN YOU CRUSH ME IN YOUR ARMS, I MUST REVEAL, I'M ONLY FLESH AND BLOOD AND NOT RESISTLESS STEEL!
YOU'RE A SUPERMAN! YOUR ARDOR'S STRONGER THAN, A HUMAN MAN'S!
YOU'RE A SUPERMAN! AND WHEN YOU SPRING TO ME, I AM IN ECSTASY!
SOME DAY YOU'RE GONNA LEAP, TO THE ALTAR AT MY FEET...
THEN THE WHOLE WORLD WILL KNOW, 'CAUSE I'LL TELL ALL I KNOW, THAT I WANT 'EM TO KNOW, THAT YOU'RE MY SUPERMAN!

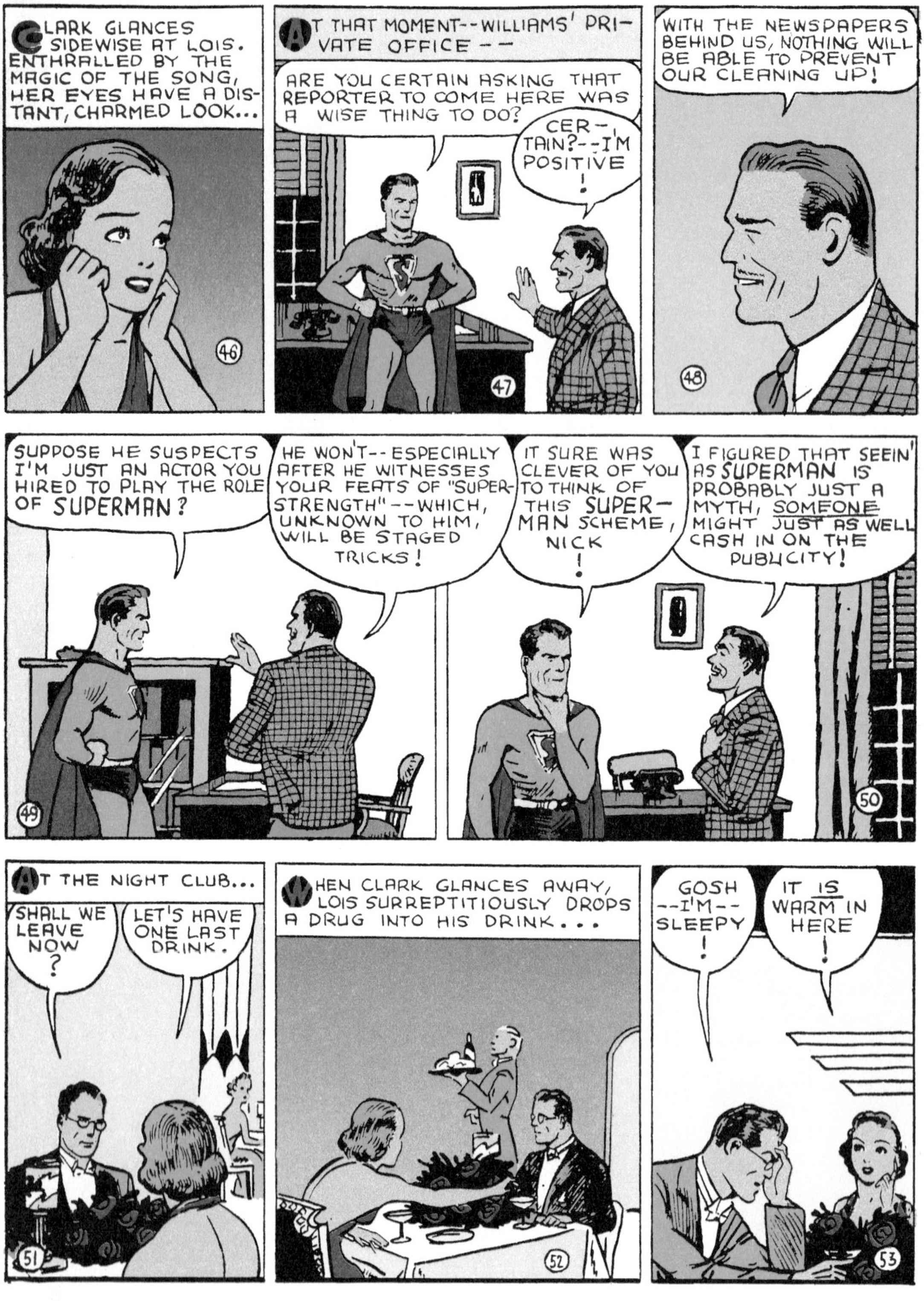
CLARK GLANCES SIDEWISE AT LOIS. ENTHRALLED BY THE MAGIC OF THE SONG, HER EYES HAVE A DISTANT, CHARMED LOOK...
46
AT THAT MOMENT--WILLIAMS' PRIVATE OFFICE --
ARE YOU CERTAIN ASKING THAT REPORTER TO COME HERE WAS A WISE THING TO DO?
CERTAIN?--I'M POSITIVE!
47
WITH THE NEWSPAPERS BEHIND US, NOTHING WILL BE ABLE TO PREVENT OUR CLEANING UP!
48
SUPPOSE HE SUSPECTS I'M JUST AN ACTOR YOU HIRED TO PLAY THE ROLE OF SUPERMAN?
HE WON'T--ESPECIALLY AFTER HE WITNESSES YOUR FEATS OF "SUPER-STRENGTH"--WHICH, UNKNOWN TO HIM, WILL BE STAGED TRICKS!
49
IT SURE WAS CLEVER OF YOU TO THINK OF THIS SUPERMAN SCHEME, NICK!
I FIGURED THAT SEEIN' AS SUPERMAN IS PROBABLY JUST A MYTH, SOMEONE MIGHT JUST AS WELL CASH IN ON THE PUBLICITY!
50
AT THE NIGHT CLUB...
SHALL WE LEAVE NOW?
LET'S HAVE ONE LAST DRINK.
51
WHEN CLARK GLANCES AWAY, LOIS SURREPTITIOUSLY DROPS A DRUG INTO HIS DRINK...
52
GOSH --I'M-- SLEEPY!
IT IS WARM IN HERE!
53

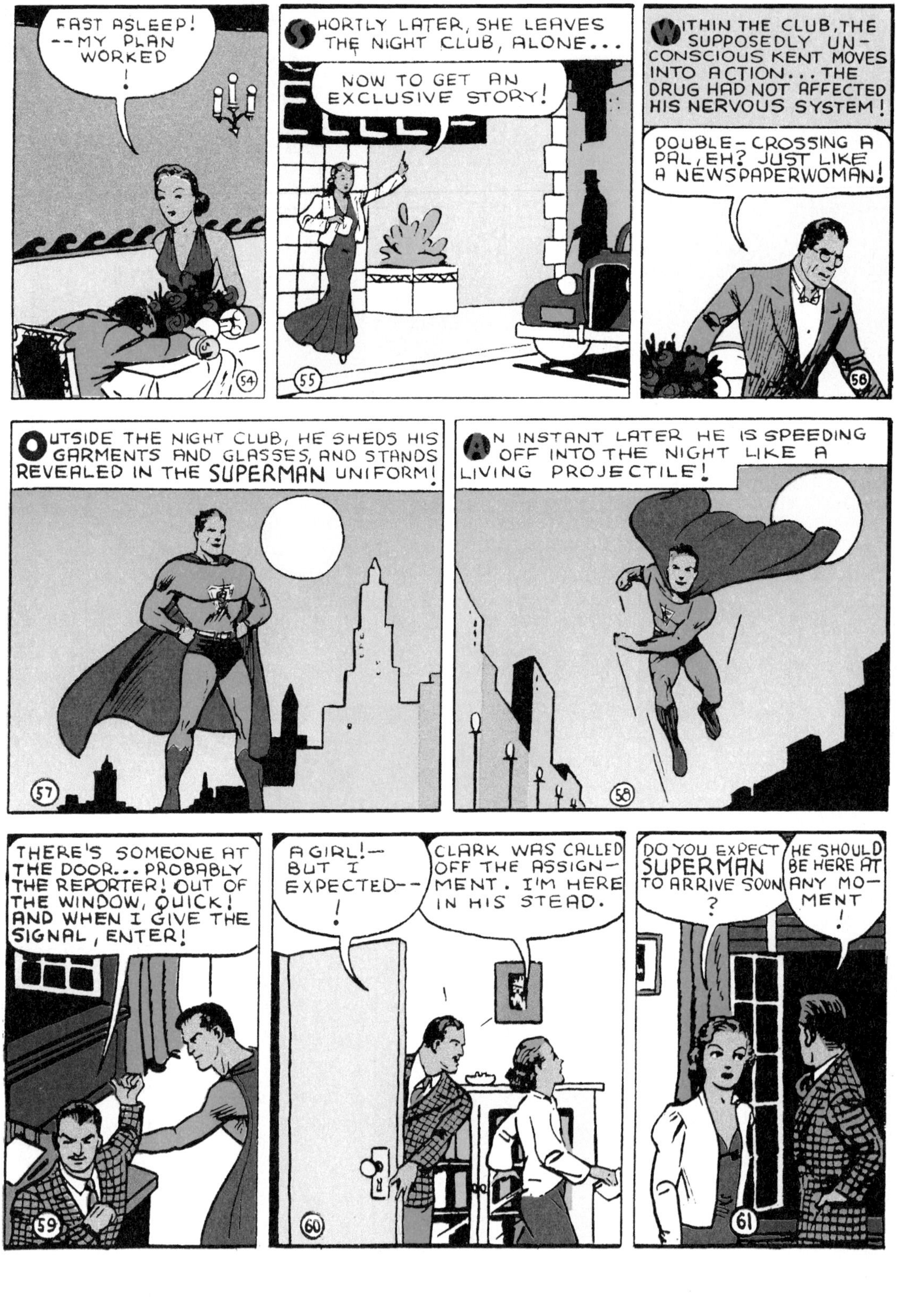
FAST ASLEEP! --MY PLAN WORKED!
SHORTLY LATER, SHE LEAVES THE NIGHT CLUB, ALONE...
NOW TO GET AN EXCLUSIVE STORY!
WITHIN THE CLUB, THE SUPPOSEDLY UN-CONSCIOUS KENT MOVES INTO ACTION... THE DRUG HAD NOT AFFECTED HIS NERVOUS SYSTEM!
DOUBLE-CROSSING A PAL, EH? JUST LIKE A NEWSPAPERWOMAN!
OUTSIDE THE NIGHT CLUB, HE SHEDS HIS GARMENTS AND GLASSES, AND STANDS REVEALED IN THE SUPERMAN UNIFORM!
AN INSTANT LATER HE IS SPEEDING OFF INTO THE NIGHT LIKE A LIVING PROJECTILE!
THERE'S SOMEONE AT THE DOOR... PROBABLY THE REPORTER! OUT OF THE WINDOW, QUICK! AND WHEN I GIVE THE SIGNAL, ENTER!
A GIRL!— BUT I EXPECTED——!
CLARK WAS CALLED OFF THE ASSIGN-MENT. I'M HERE IN HIS STEAD.
DO YOU EXPECT SUPERMAN TO ARRIVE SOON?
HE SHOULD BE HERE AT ANY MO-MENT!

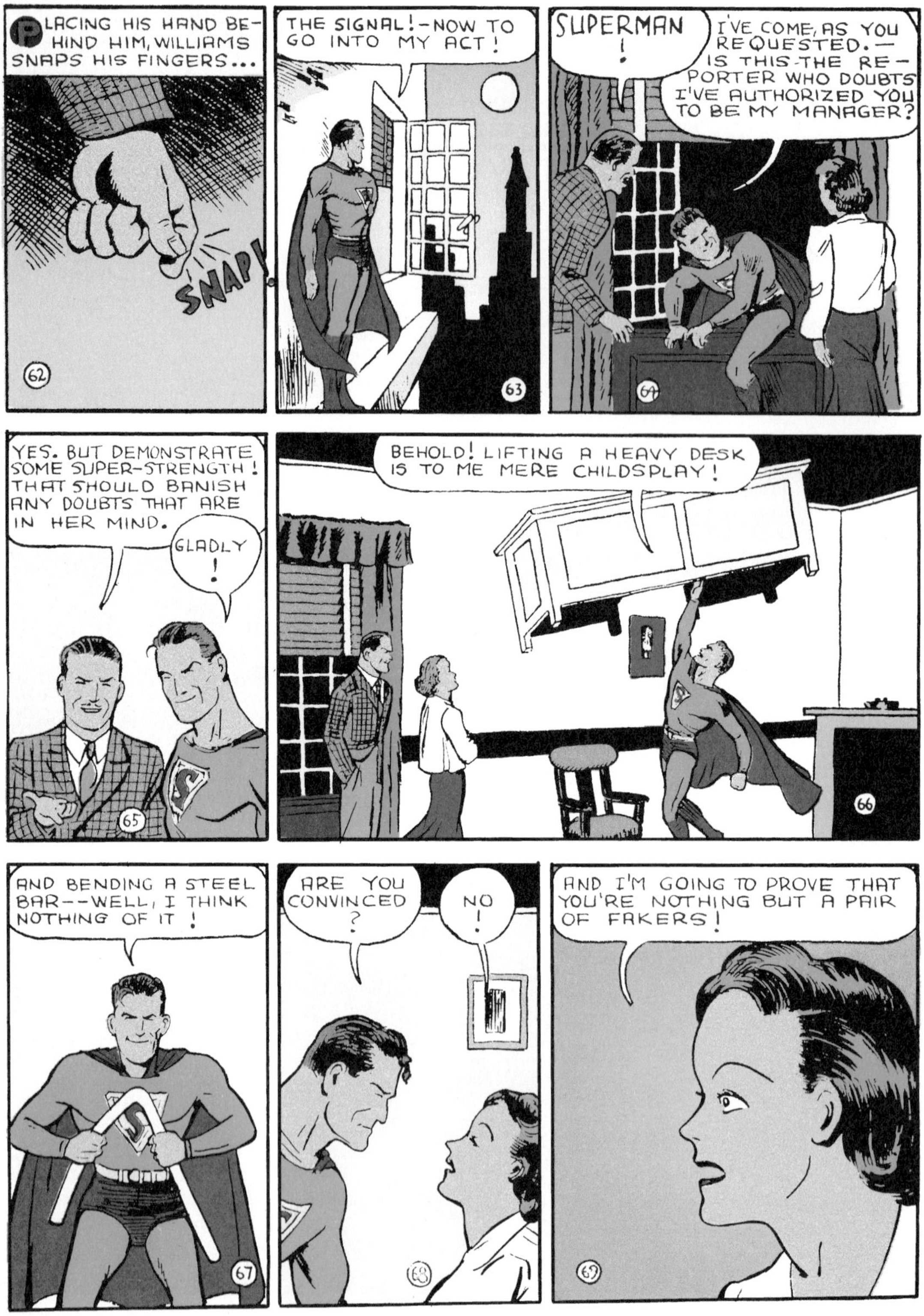

PLACING HIS HAND BEHIND HIM, WILLIAMS SNAPS HIS FINGERS...
SNAP!
62
THE SIGNAL! -NOW TO GO INTO MY ACT!
63
SUPERMAN!
I'VE COME, AS YOU REQUESTED. -IS THIS THE REPORTER WHO DOUBTS I'VE AUTHORIZED YOU TO BE MY MANAGER?
64
YES. BUT DEMONSTRATE SOME SUPER-STRENGTH! THAT SHOULD BANISH ANY DOUBTS THAT ARE IN HER MIND.
GLADLY!
65
BEHOLD! LIFTING A HEAVY DESK IS TO ME MERE CHILDSPLAY!
66
AND BENDING A STEEL BAR--WELL, I THINK NOTHING OF IT!
67
ARE YOU CONVINCED?
NO!
68
AND I'M GOING TO PROVE THAT YOU'RE NOTHING BUT A PAIR OF FAKERS!
69

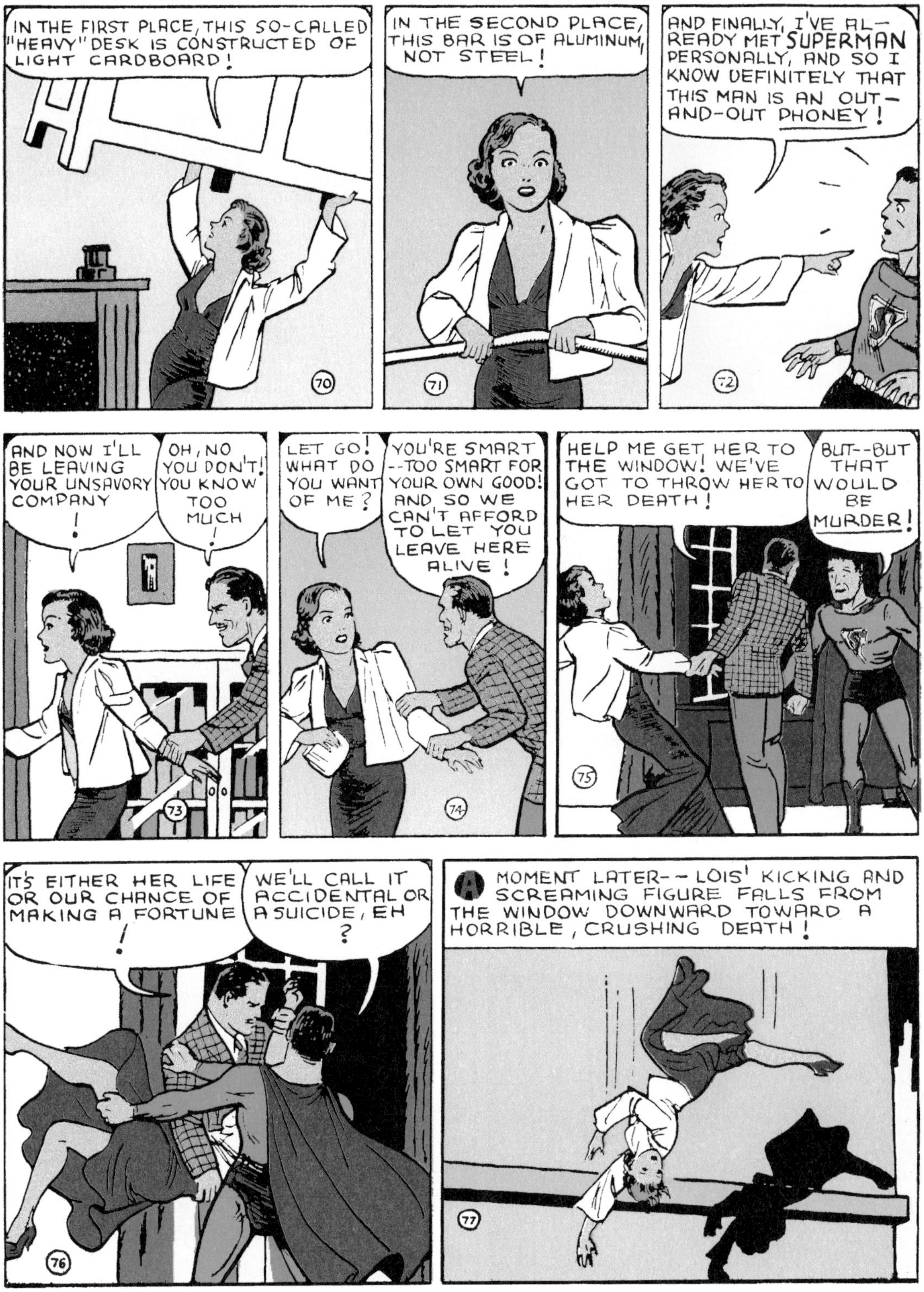
IN THE FIRST PLACE, THIS SO-CALLED "HEAVY" DESK IS CONSTRUCTED OF LIGHT CARDBOARD!
70
IN THE SECOND PLACE, THIS BAR IS OF ALUMINUM, NOT STEEL!
71
AND FINALLY, I'VE ALREADY MET SUPERMAN PERSONALLY, AND SO I KNOW DEFINITELY THAT THIS MAN IS AN OUT-AND-OUT PHONEY!
72
AND NOW I'LL BE LEAVING YOUR UNSAVORY COMPANY!
OH, NO YOU DON'T! YOU KNOW TOO MUCH!
73
LET GO! WHAT DO YOU WANT OF ME?
YOU'RE SMART --TOO SMART FOR YOUR OWN GOOD! AND SO WE CAN'T AFFORD TO LET YOU LEAVE HERE ALIVE!
74
HELP ME GET HER TO THE WINDOW! WE'VE GOT TO THROW HER TO HER DEATH!
BUT--BUT THAT WOULD BE MURDER!
75
IT'S EITHER HER LIFE OR OUR CHANCE OF MAKING A FORTUNE!
WE'LL CALL IT ACCIDENTAL OR A SUICIDE, EH?
76
A MOMENT LATER-- LOIS' KICKING AND SCREAMING FIGURE FALLS FROM THE WINDOW DOWNWARD TOWARD A HORRIBLE, CRUSHING DEATH!
77

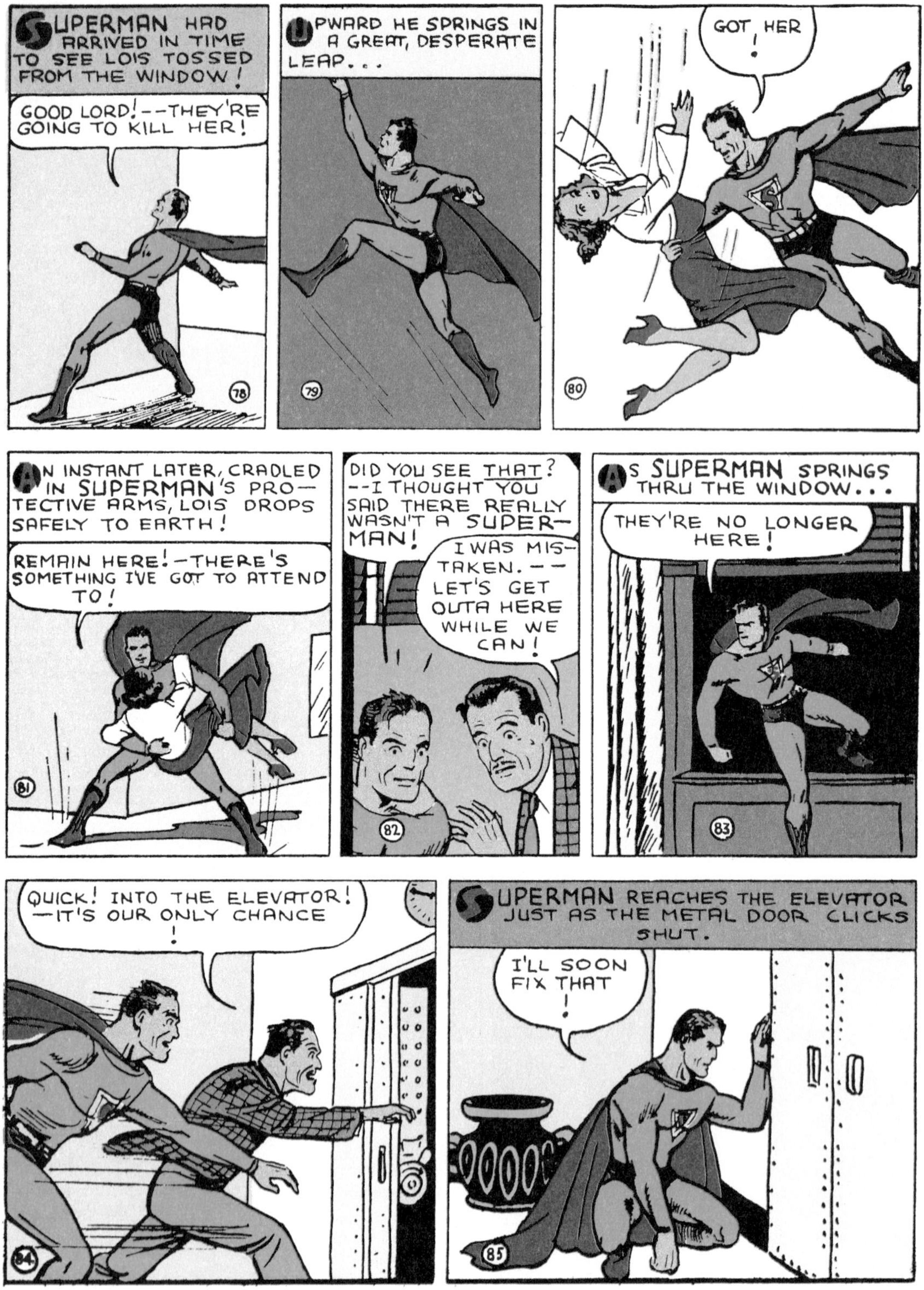
SUPERMAN HAD ARRIVED IN TIME TO SEE LOIS TOSSED FROM THE WINDOW!
GOOD LORD!--THEY'RE GOING TO KILL HER!
78
UPWARD HE SPRINGS IN A GREAT, DESPERATE LEAP...
79
GOT HER!
80
AN INSTANT LATER, CRADLED IN SUPERMAN'S PROTECTIVE ARMS, LOIS DROPS SAFELY TO EARTH!
REMAIN HERE!—THERE'S SOMETHING I'VE GOT TO ATTEND TO!
81
DID YOU SEE THAT? --I THOUGHT YOU SAID THERE REALLY WASN'T A SUPERMAN!
I WAS MISTAKEN.-- LET'S GET OUTA HERE WHILE WE CAN!
82
AS SUPERMAN SPRINGS THRU THE WINDOW...
THEY'RE NO LONGER HERE!
83
QUICK! INTO THE ELEVATOR! —IT'S OUR ONLY CHANCE!
84
SUPERMAN REACHES THE ELEVATOR JUST AS THE METAL DOOR CLICKS SHUT.
I'LL SOON FIX THAT!
85

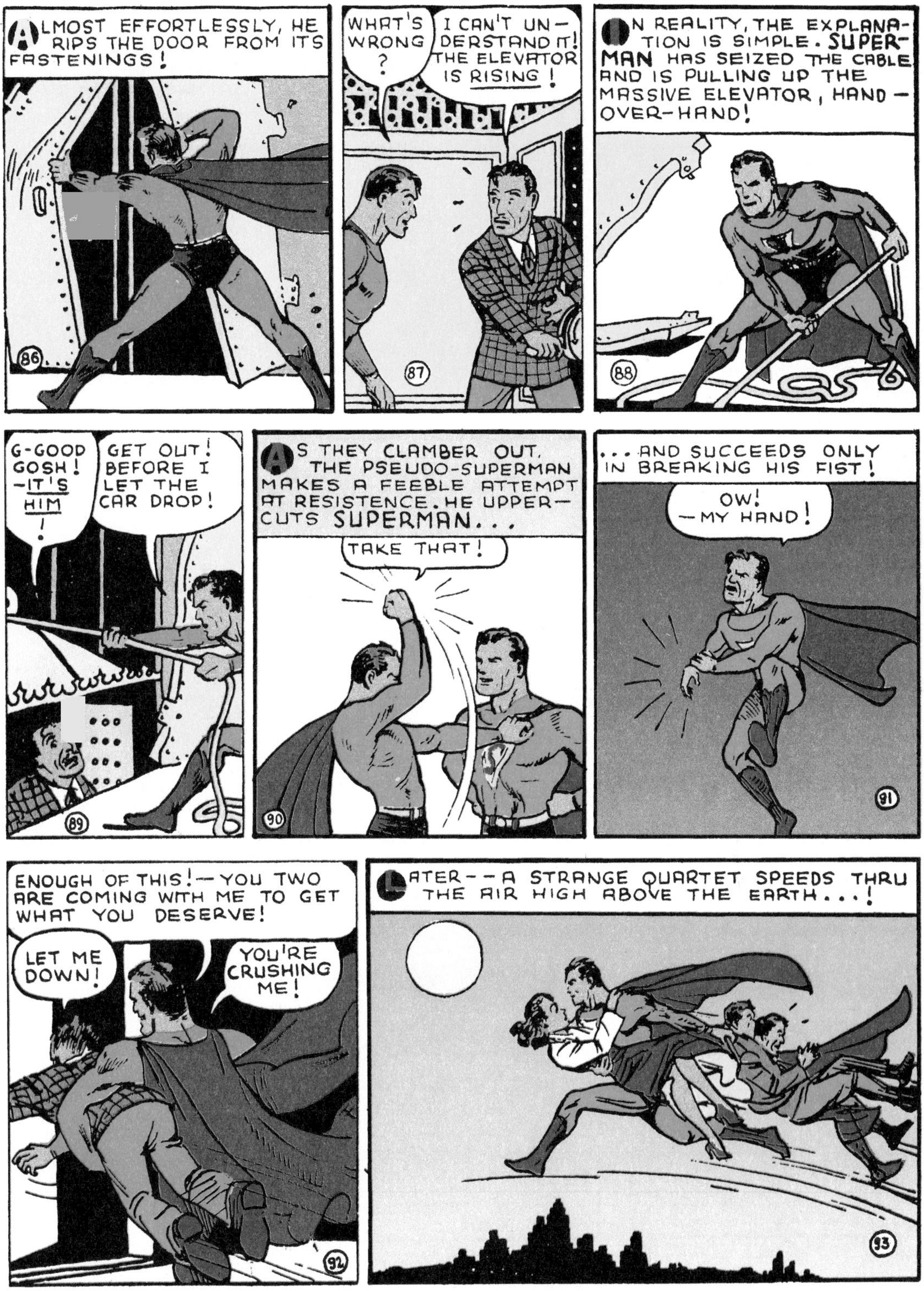
ALMOST EFFORTLESSLY, HE RIPS THE DOOR FROM ITS FASTENINGS!
86
WHAT'S WRONG ?
I CAN'T UNDERSTAND IT! THE ELEVATOR IS RISING!
87
IN REALITY, THE EXPLANATION IS SIMPLE. SUPERMAN HAS SEIZED THE CABLE AND IS PULLING UP THE MASSIVE ELEVATOR, HAND-OVER-HAND!
88
G-GOOD GOSH! -IT'S HIM !
GET OUT! BEFORE I LET THE CAR DROP!
89
AS THEY CLAMBER OUT, THE PSEUDO-SUPERMAN MAKES A FEEBLE ATTEMPT AT RESISTENCE. HE UPPER-CUTS SUPERMAN...
TAKE THAT!
90
...AND SUCCEEDS ONLY IN BREAKING HIS FIST!
OW! -MY HAND!
91
ENOUGH OF THIS!—YOU TWO ARE COMING WITH ME TO GET WHAT YOU DESERVE!
LET ME DOWN!
YOU'RE CRUSHING ME!
92
LATER--A STRANGE QUARTET SPEEDS THRU THE AIR HIGH ABOVE THE EARTH...!
93

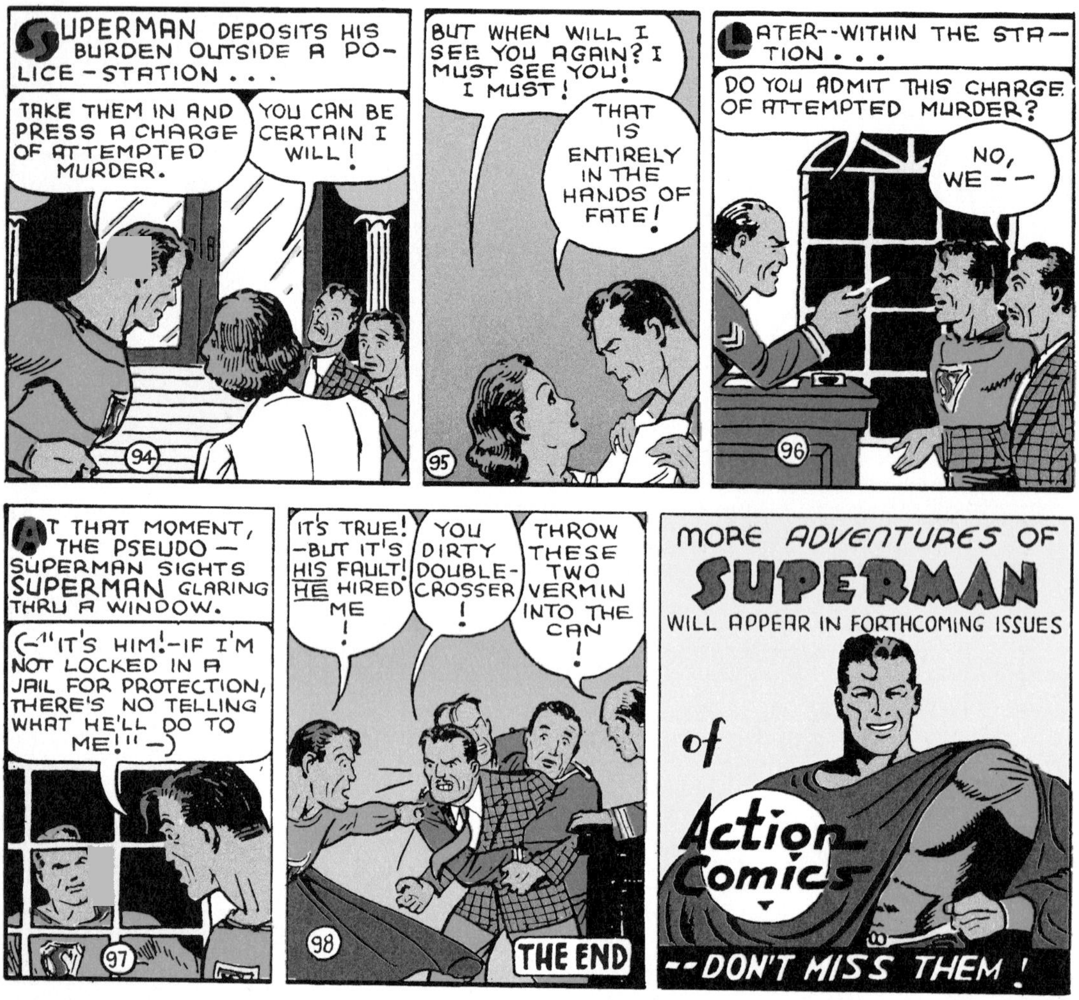
SUPERMAN DEPOSITS HIS BURDEN OUTSIDE A POLICE-STATION . . .
TAKE THEM IN AND PRESS A CHARGE OF ATTEMPTED MURDER.
YOU CAN BE CERTAIN I WILL!
94
BUT WHEN WILL I SEE YOU AGAIN? I MUST SEE YOU! I MUST!
THAT IS ENTIRELY IN THE HANDS OF FATE!
95
LATER--WITHIN THE STATION . . .
DO YOU ADMIT THIS CHARGE OF ATTEMPTED MURDER?
NO, WE--
96
AT THAT MOMENT, THE PSEUDO-SUPERMAN SIGHTS SUPERMAN GLARING THRU A WINDOW.
(-"IT'S HIM!-IF I'M NOT LOCKED IN A JAIL FOR PROTECTION, THERE'S NO TELLING WHAT HE'LL DO TO ME!"-)
97
IT'S TRUE! -BUT IT'S HIS FAULT! HE HIRED ME!
YOU DIRTY DOUBLE-CROSSER!
THROW THESE TWO VERMIN INTO THE CAN!
98
THE END
MORE ADVENTURES OF SUPERMAN WILL APPEAR IN FORTHCOMING ISSUES
of Action Comics
--DON'T MISS THEM!

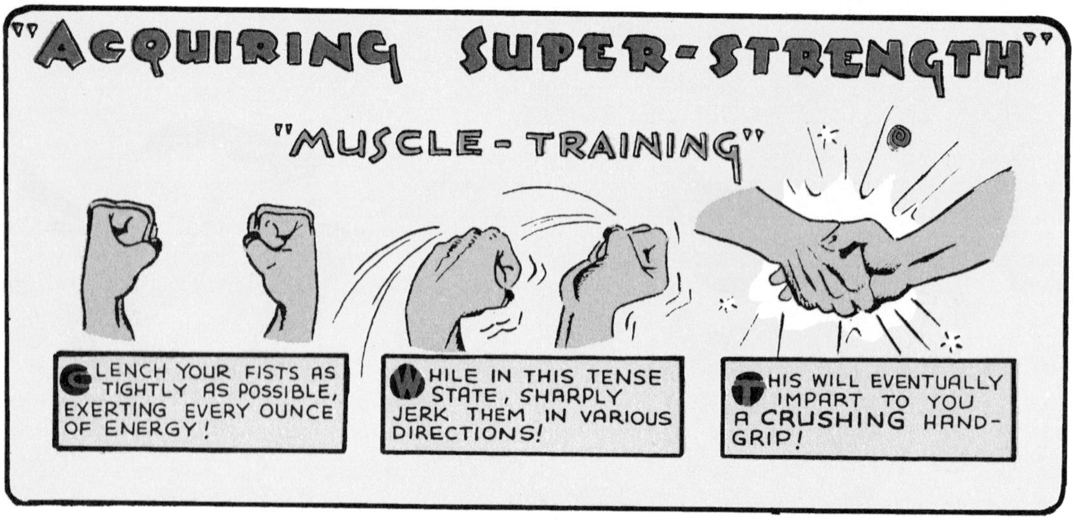
"ACQUIRING SUPER-STRENGTH"
"MUSCLE-TRAINING"
CLENCH YOUR FISTS AS TIGHTLY AS POSSIBLE, EXERTING EVERY OUNCE OF ENERGY!
WHILE IN THIS TENSE STATE, SHARPLY JERK THEM IN VARIOUS DIRECTIONS!
THIS WILL EVENTUALLY IMPART TO YOU A CRUSHING HAND-GRIP!

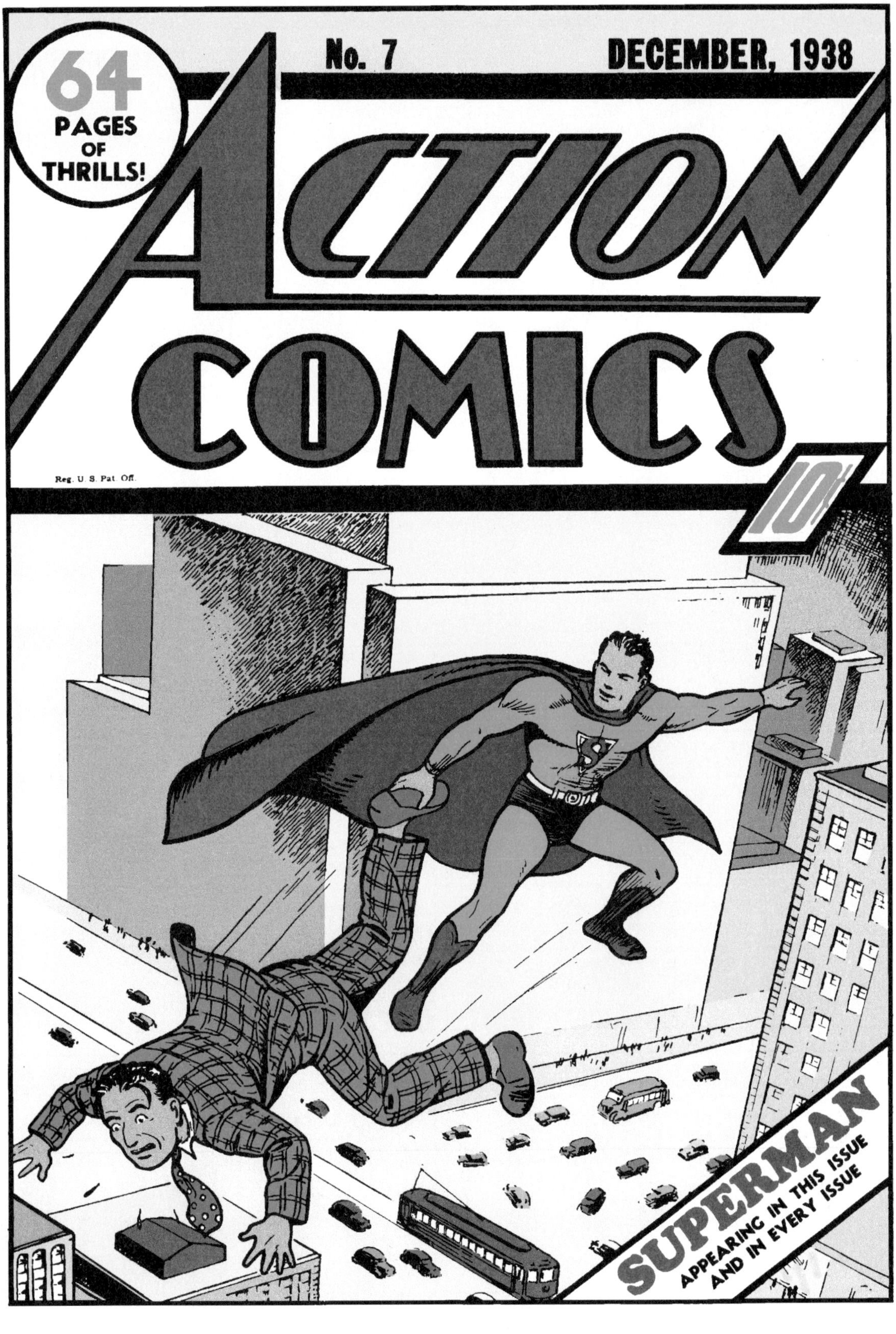
No. 7
DECEMBER, 1938
64 PAGES OF THRILLS!
ACTION COMICS
Reg. U. S. Pat. Off.
10¢
SUPERMAN
APPEARING IN THIS ISSUE
AND IN EVERY ISSUE

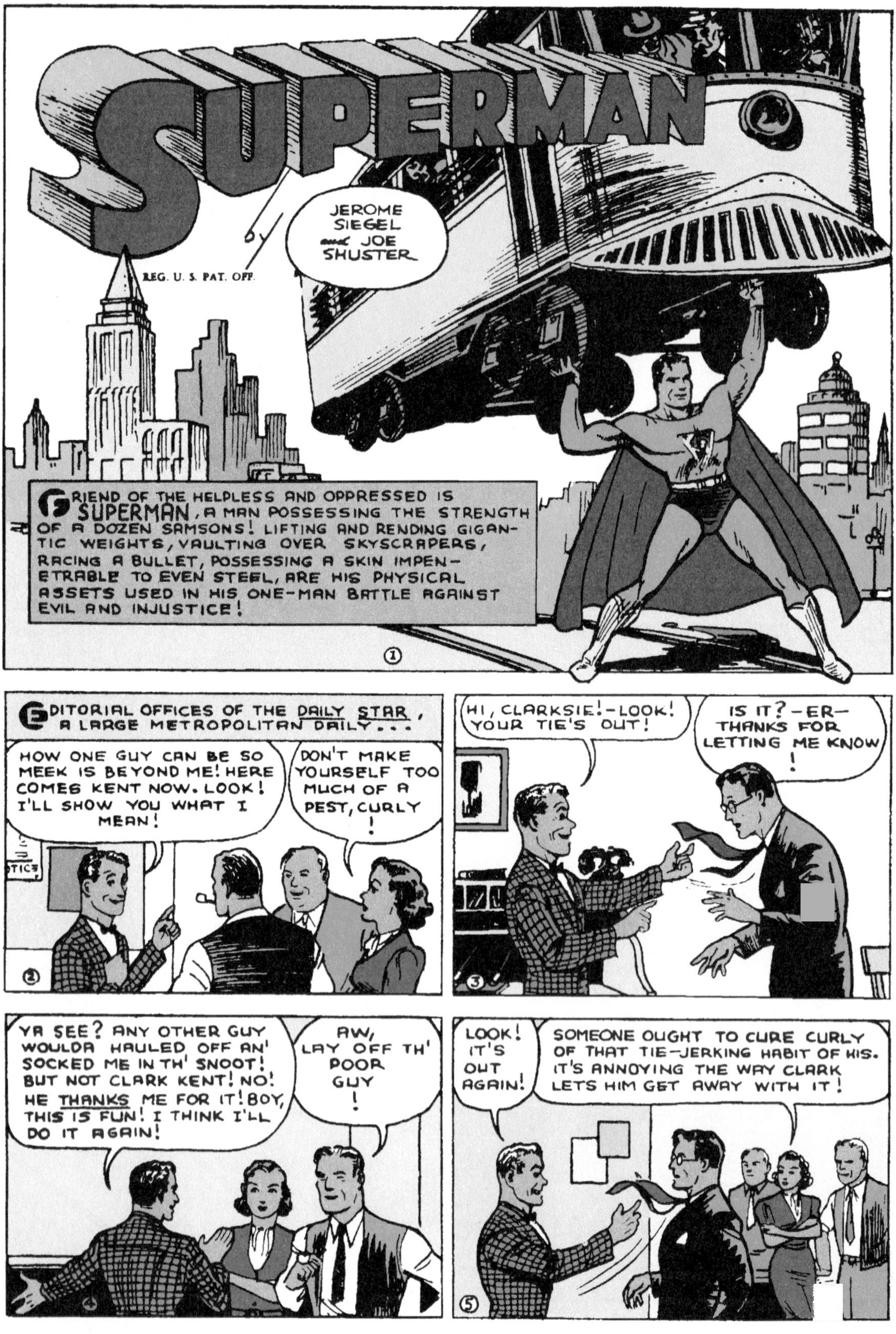
SUPERMAN
by
JEROME SIEGEL and JOE SHUSTER
REG. U. S. PAT. OFF.
FRIEND OF THE HELPLESS AND OPPRESSED IS SUPERMAN, A MAN POSSESSING THE STRENGTH OF A DOZEN SAMSONS! LIFTING AND RENDING GIGANTIC WEIGHTS, VAULTING OVER SKYSCRAPERS, RACING A BULLET, POSSESSING A SKIN IMPENETRABLE TO EVEN STEEL, ARE HIS PHYSICAL ASSETS USED IN HIS ONE-MAN BATTLE AGAINST EVIL AND INJUSTICE!
EDITORIAL OFFICES OF THE DAILY STAR, A LARGE METROPOLITAN DAILY...
HOW ONE GUY CAN BE SO MEEK IS BEYOND ME! HERE COMES KENT NOW. LOOK! I'LL SHOW YOU WHAT I MEAN!
DON'T MAKE YOURSELF TOO MUCH OF A PEST, CURLY!
HI, CLARKSIE!-LOOK! YOUR TIE'S OUT!
IS IT?-ER-THANKS FOR LETTING ME KNOW!
YA SEE? ANY OTHER GUY WOULDA HAULED OFF AN' SOCKED ME IN TH' SNOOT! BUT NOT CLARK KENT! NO! HE THANKS ME FOR IT! BOY, THIS IS FUN! I THINK I'LL DO IT AGAIN!
AW, LAY OFF TH' POOR GUY!
LOOK! IT'S OUT AGAIN!
SOMEONE OUGHT TO CURE CURLY OF THAT TIE-JERKING HABIT OF HIS. IT'S ANNOYING THE WAY CLARK LETS HIM GET AWAY WITH IT!

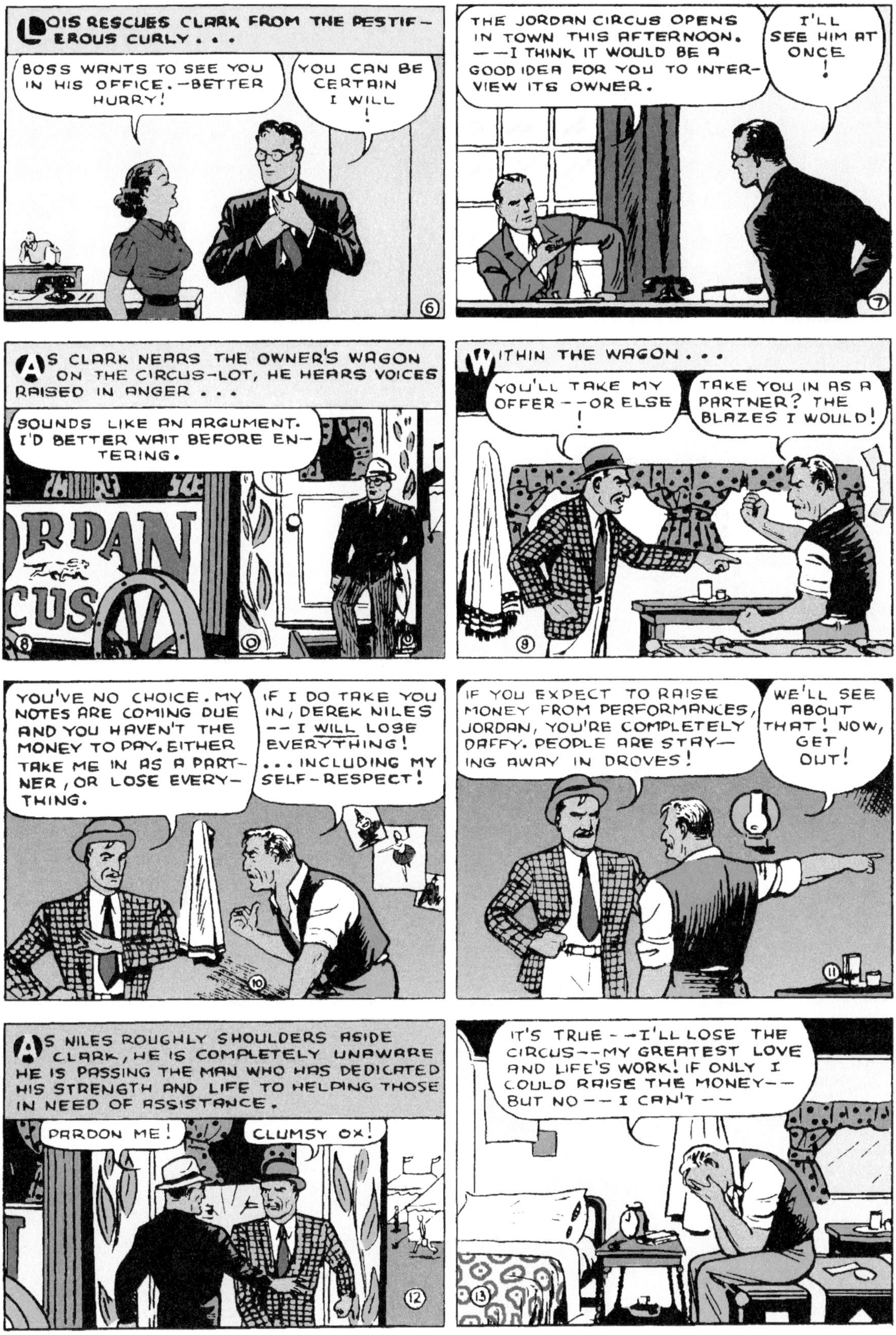
LOIS RESCUES CLARK FROM THE PESTIF-EROUS CURLY . . .
BOSS WANTS TO SEE YOU IN HIS OFFICE.—BETTER HURRY!
YOU CAN BE CERTAIN I WILL!
THE JORDAN CIRCUS OPENS IN TOWN THIS AFTERNOON. ——I THINK IT WOULD BE A GOOD IDEA FOR YOU TO INTER-VIEW ITS OWNER.
I'LL SEE HIM AT ONCE!
AS CLARK NEARS THE OWNER'S WAGON ON THE CIRCUS-LOT, HE HEARS VOICES RAISED IN ANGER . . .
SOUNDS LIKE AN ARGUMENT. I'D BETTER WAIT BEFORE EN-TERING.
WITHIN THE WAGON . . .
YOU'LL TAKE MY OFFER ——OR ELSE!
TAKE YOU IN AS A PARTNER? THE BLAZES I WOULD!
YOU'VE NO CHOICE. MY NOTES ARE COMING DUE AND YOU HAVEN'T THE MONEY TO PAY. EITHER TAKE ME IN AS A PART-NER, OR LOSE EVERY-THING.
IF I DO TAKE YOU IN, DEREK NILES —— I WILL LOSE EVERYTHING! . . . INCLUDING MY SELF-RESPECT!
IF YOU EXPECT TO RAISE MONEY FROM PERFORMANCES, JORDAN, YOU'RE COMPLETELY DAFFY. PEOPLE ARE STAY-ING AWAY IN DROVES!
WE'LL SEE ABOUT THAT! NOW, GET OUT!
AS NILES ROUGHLY SHOULDERS ASIDE CLARK, HE IS COMPLETELY UNAWARE HE IS PASSING THE MAN WHO HAS DEDICATED HIS STRENGTH AND LIFE TO HELPING THOSE IN NEED OF ASSISTANCE.
PARDON ME!
CLUMSY OX!
IT'S TRUE ——I'LL LOSE THE CIRCUS——MY GREATEST LOVE AND LIFE'S WORK! IF ONLY I COULD RAISE THE MONEY—— BUT NO —— I CAN'T ——

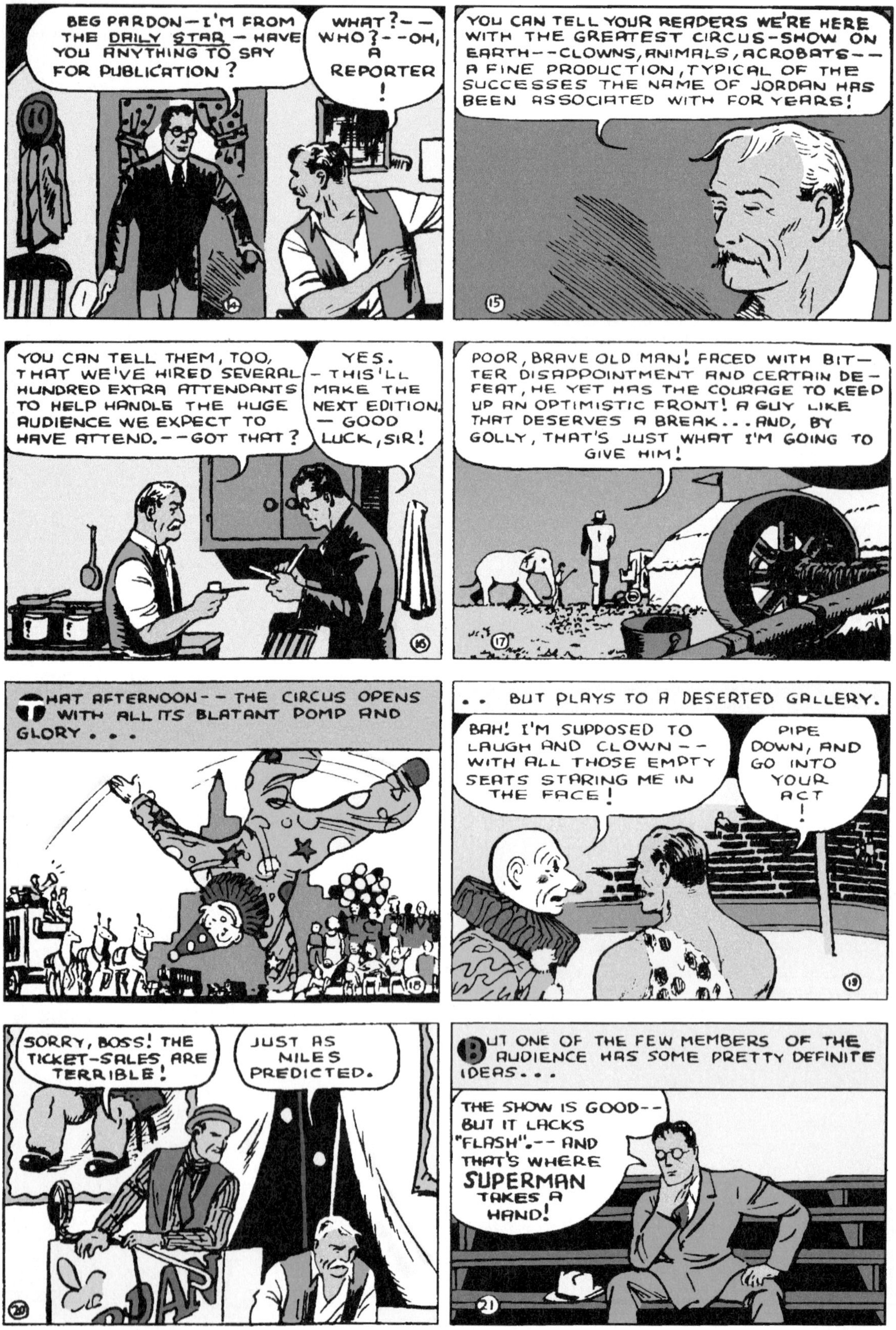
BEG PARDON—I'M FROM THE DAILY STAR — HAVE YOU ANYTHING TO SAY FOR PUBLICATION?
WHAT?— — WHO?— —OH, A REPORTER!
YOU CAN TELL YOUR READERS WE'RE HERE WITH THE GREATEST CIRCUS-SHOW ON EARTH— —CLOWNS, ANIMALS, ACROBATS— — A FINE PRODUCTION, TYPICAL OF THE SUCCESSES THE NAME OF JORDAN HAS BEEN ASSOCIATED WITH FOR YEARS!
YOU CAN TELL THEM, TOO, THAT WE'VE HIRED SEVERAL HUNDRED EXTRA ATTENDANTS TO HELP HANDLE THE HUGE AUDIENCE WE EXPECT TO HAVE ATTEND.— —GOT THAT?
YES. — THIS'LL MAKE THE NEXT EDITION. — GOOD LUCK, SIR!
POOR, BRAVE OLD MAN! FACED WITH BITTER DISAPPOINTMENT AND CERTAIN DEFEAT, HE YET HAS THE COURAGE TO KEEP UP AN OPTIMISTIC FRONT! A GUY LIKE THAT DESERVES A BREAK . . . AND, BY GOLLY, THAT'S JUST WHAT I'M GOING TO GIVE HIM!
THAT AFTERNOON— — THE CIRCUS OPENS WITH ALL ITS BLATANT POMP AND GLORY . . .
. . BUT PLAYS TO A DESERTED GALLERY.
BAH! I'M SUPPOSED TO LAUGH AND CLOWN— — WITH ALL THOSE EMPTY SEATS STARING ME IN THE FACE!
PIPE DOWN, AND GO INTO YOUR ACT!
SORRY, BOSS! THE TICKET-SALES ARE TERRIBLE!
JUST AS NILES PREDICTED.
BUT ONE OF THE FEW MEMBERS OF THE AUDIENCE HAS SOME PRETTY DEFINITE IDEAS . . .
THE SHOW IS GOOD— — BUT IT LACKS "FLASH".— — AND THAT'S WHERE SUPERMAN TAKES A HAND!

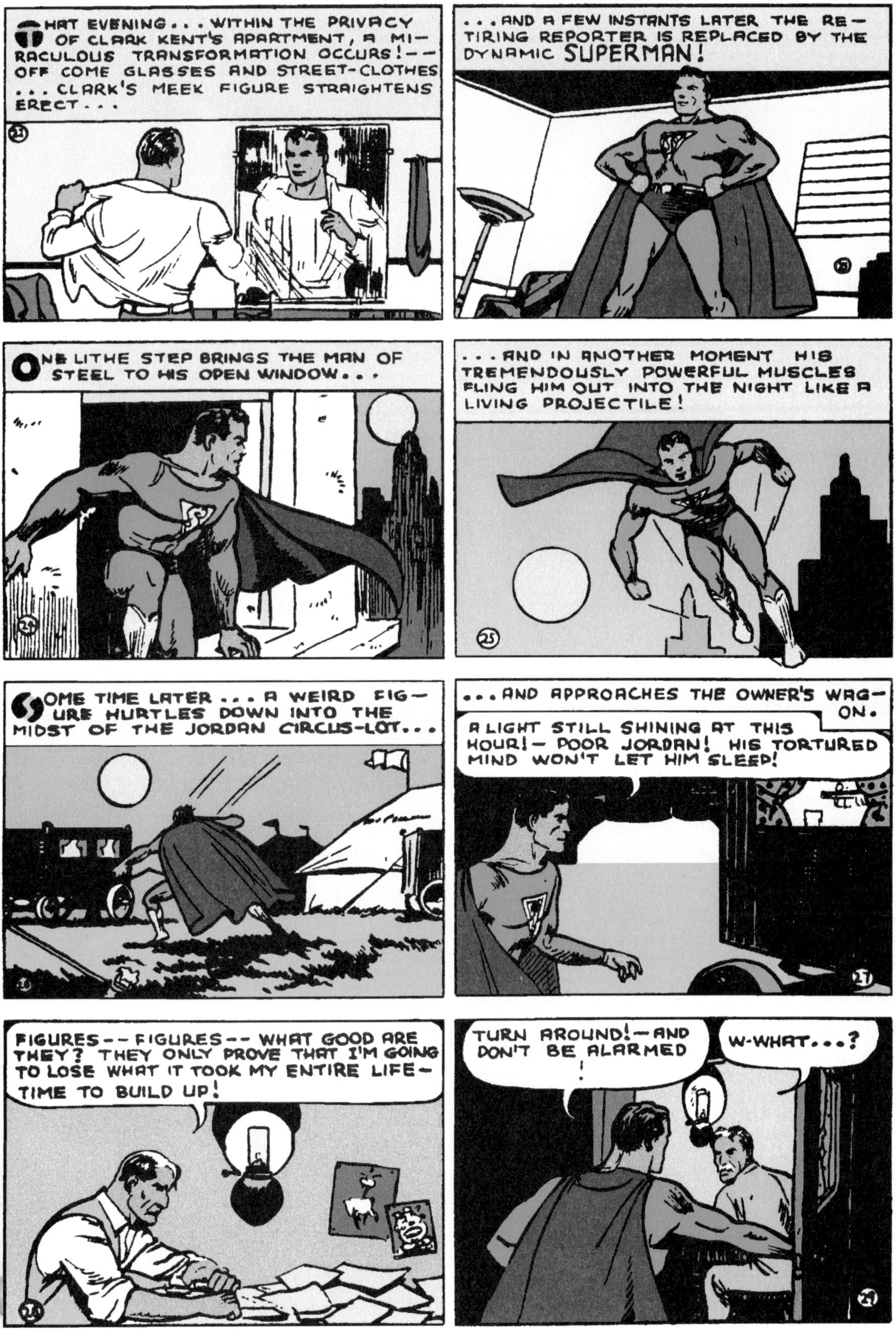
THAT EVENING . . . WITHIN THE PRIVACY OF CLARK KENT'S APARTMENT, A MIRACULOUS TRANSFORMATION OCCURS!-- OFF COME GLASSES AND STREET-CLOTHES . . . CLARK'S MEEK FIGURE STRAIGHTENS ERECT . . .
. . . AND A FEW INSTANTS LATER THE RETIRING REPORTER IS REPLACED BY THE DYNAMIC SUPERMAN!
ONE LITHE STEP BRINGS THE MAN OF STEEL TO HIS OPEN WINDOW . . .
. . . AND IN ANOTHER MOMENT HIS TREMENDOUSLY POWERFUL MUSCLES FLING HIM OUT INTO THE NIGHT LIKE A LIVING PROJECTILE!
SOME TIME LATER . . . A WEIRD FIGURE HURTLES DOWN INTO THE MIDST OF THE JORDAN CIRCUS-LOT . . .
. . . AND APPROACHES THE OWNER'S WAGON.
A LIGHT STILL SHINING AT THIS HOUR! — POOR JORDAN! HIS TORTURED MIND WON'T LET HIM SLEEP!
FIGURES -- FIGURES -- WHAT GOOD ARE THEY? THEY ONLY PROVE THAT I'M GOING TO LOSE WHAT IT TOOK MY ENTIRE LIFE-TIME TO BUILD UP!
TURN AROUND! — AND DON'T BE ALARMED!
W-WHAT . . . ?

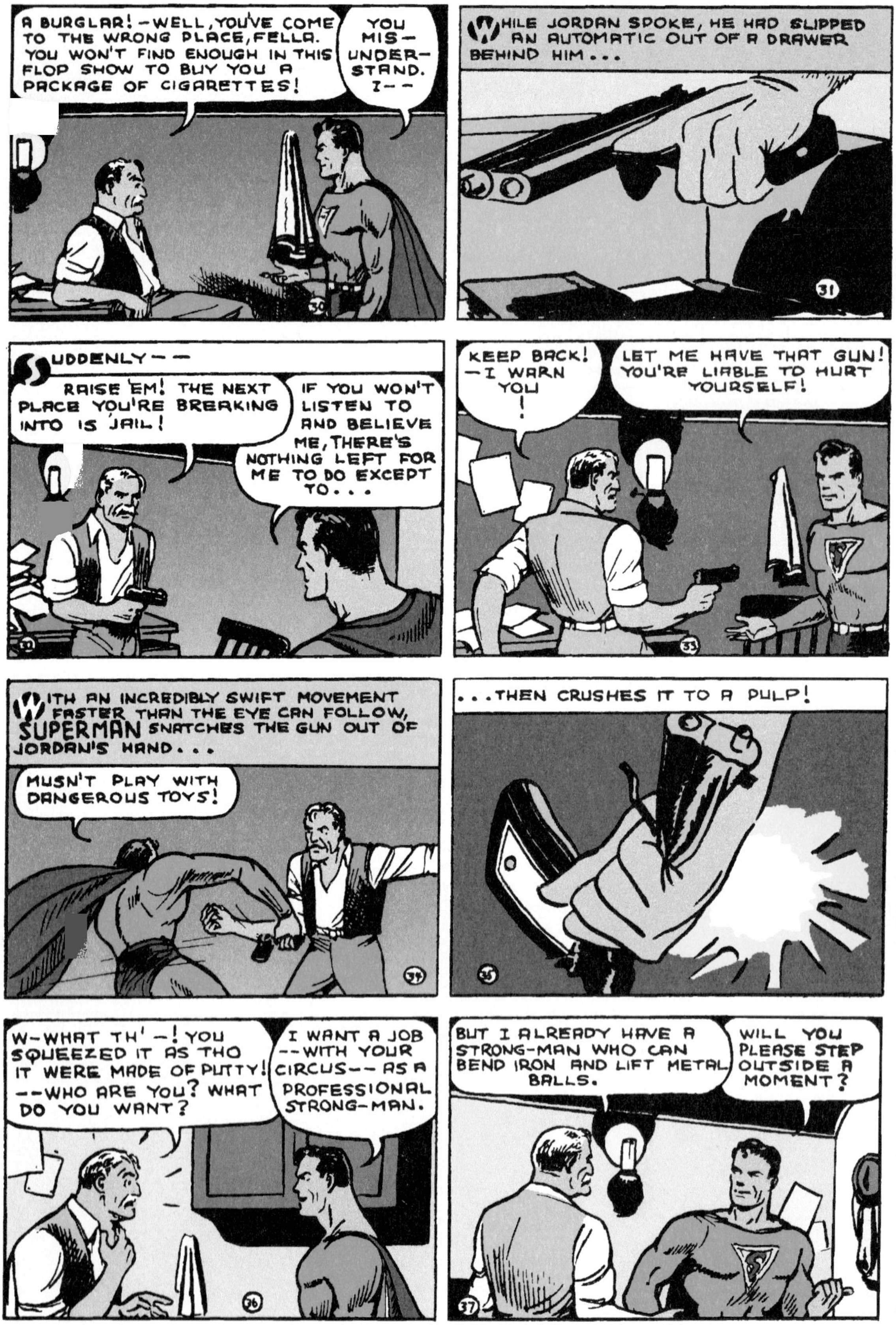
A BURGLAR! —WELL, YOU'VE COME TO THE WRONG PLACE, FELLA. YOU WON'T FIND ENOUGH IN THIS FLOP SHOW TO BUY YOU A PACKAGE OF CIGARETTES!
YOU MIS-UNDER-STAND. I— —
WHILE JORDAN SPOKE, HE HAD SLIPPED AN AUTOMATIC OUT OF A DRAWER BEHIND HIM . . .
SUDDENLY— —
RAISE 'EM! THE NEXT PLACE YOU'RE BREAKING INTO IS JAIL!
IF YOU WON'T LISTEN TO AND BELIEVE ME, THERE'S NOTHING LEFT FOR ME TO DO EXCEPT TO . . .
KEEP BACK! —I WARN YOU!
LET ME HAVE THAT GUN! YOU'RE LIABLE TO HURT YOURSELF!
WITH AN INCREDIBLY SWIFT MOVEMENT FASTER THAN THE EYE CAN FOLLOW, SUPERMAN SNATCHES THE GUN OUT OF JORDAN'S HAND . . .
MUSN'T PLAY WITH DANGEROUS TOYS!
. . . THEN CRUSHES IT TO A PULP!
W-WHAT TH' —! YOU SQUEEZED IT AS THO IT WERE MADE OF PUTTY! — —WHO ARE YOU? WHAT DO YOU WANT?
I WANT A JOB — —WITH YOUR CIRCUS— — AS A PROFESSIONAL STRONG-MAN.
BUT I ALREADY HAVE A STRONG-MAN WHO CAN BEND IRON AND LIFT METAL BALLS.
WILL YOU PLEASE STEP OUTSIDE A MOMENT?

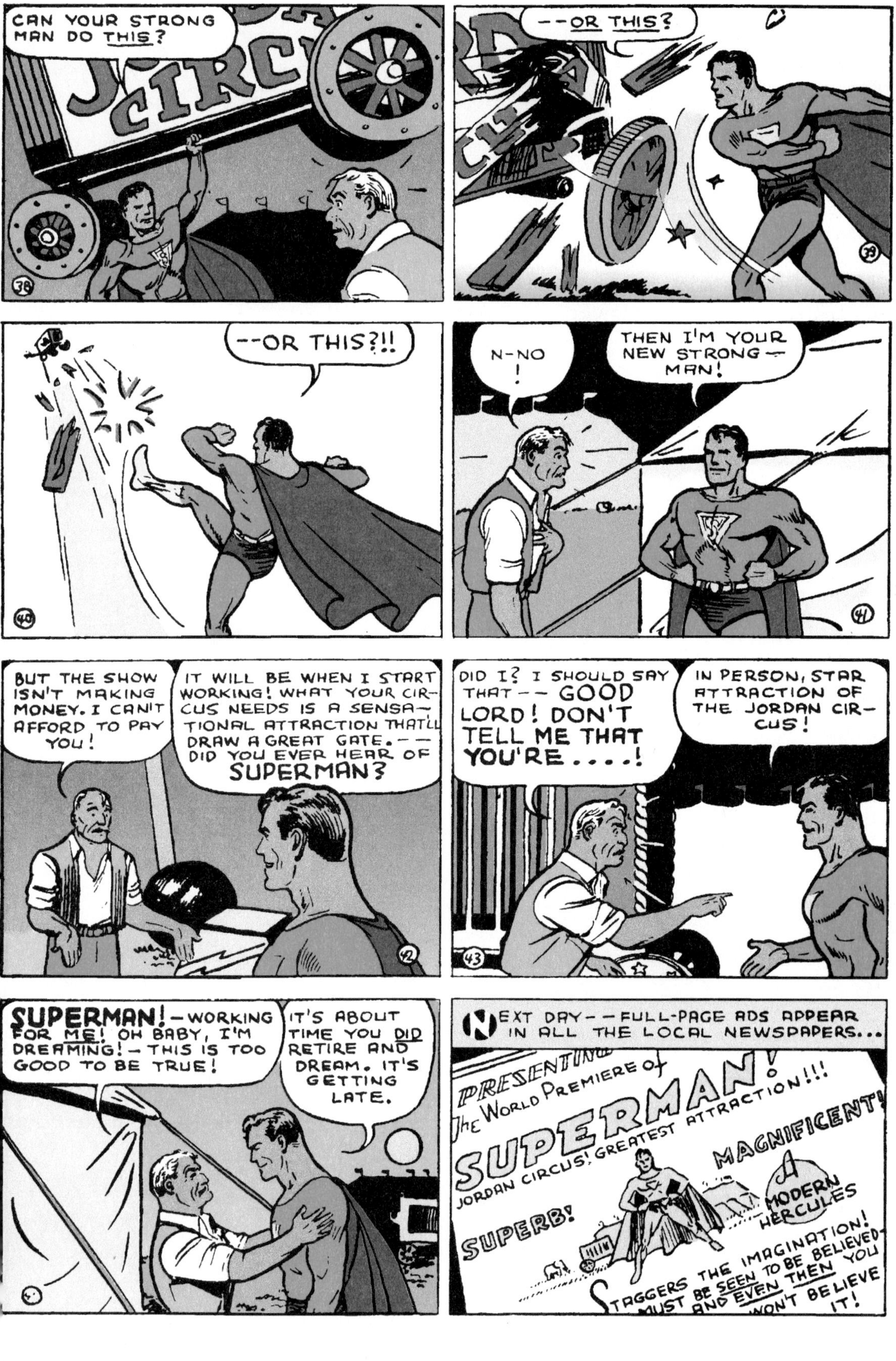
CAN YOUR STRONG MAN DO THIS?
--OR THIS?
--OR THIS?!!
N-NO!
THEN I'M YOUR NEW STRONG-MAN!
BUT THE SHOW ISN'T MAKING MONEY. I CAN'T AFFORD TO PAY YOU!
IT WILL BE WHEN I START WORKING! WHAT YOUR CIRCUS NEEDS IS A SENSATIONAL ATTRACTION THAT'LL DRAW A GREAT GATE.-- DID YOU EVER HEAR OF SUPERMAN?
DID I? I SHOULD SAY THAT-- GOOD LORD! DON'T TELL ME THAT YOU'RE....!
IN PERSON, STAR ATTRACTION OF THE JORDAN CIRCUS!
SUPERMAN!-WORKING FOR ME! OH BABY, I'M DREAMING!-THIS IS TOO GOOD TO BE TRUE!
IT'S ABOUT TIME YOU DID RETIRE AND DREAM. IT'S GETTING LATE.
NEXT DAY--FULL-PAGE ADS APPEAR IN ALL THE LOCAL NEWSPAPERS...
PRESENTING
The WORLD PREMIERE of
SUPERMAN!
JORDAN CIRCUS! GREATEST ATTRACTION!!!
MAGNIFICENT!
SUPERB!
MODERN HERCULES
STAGGERS THE IMAGINATION!
MUST BE SEEN TO BE BELIEVED-
AND EVEN THEN YOU WON'T BELIEVE IT!

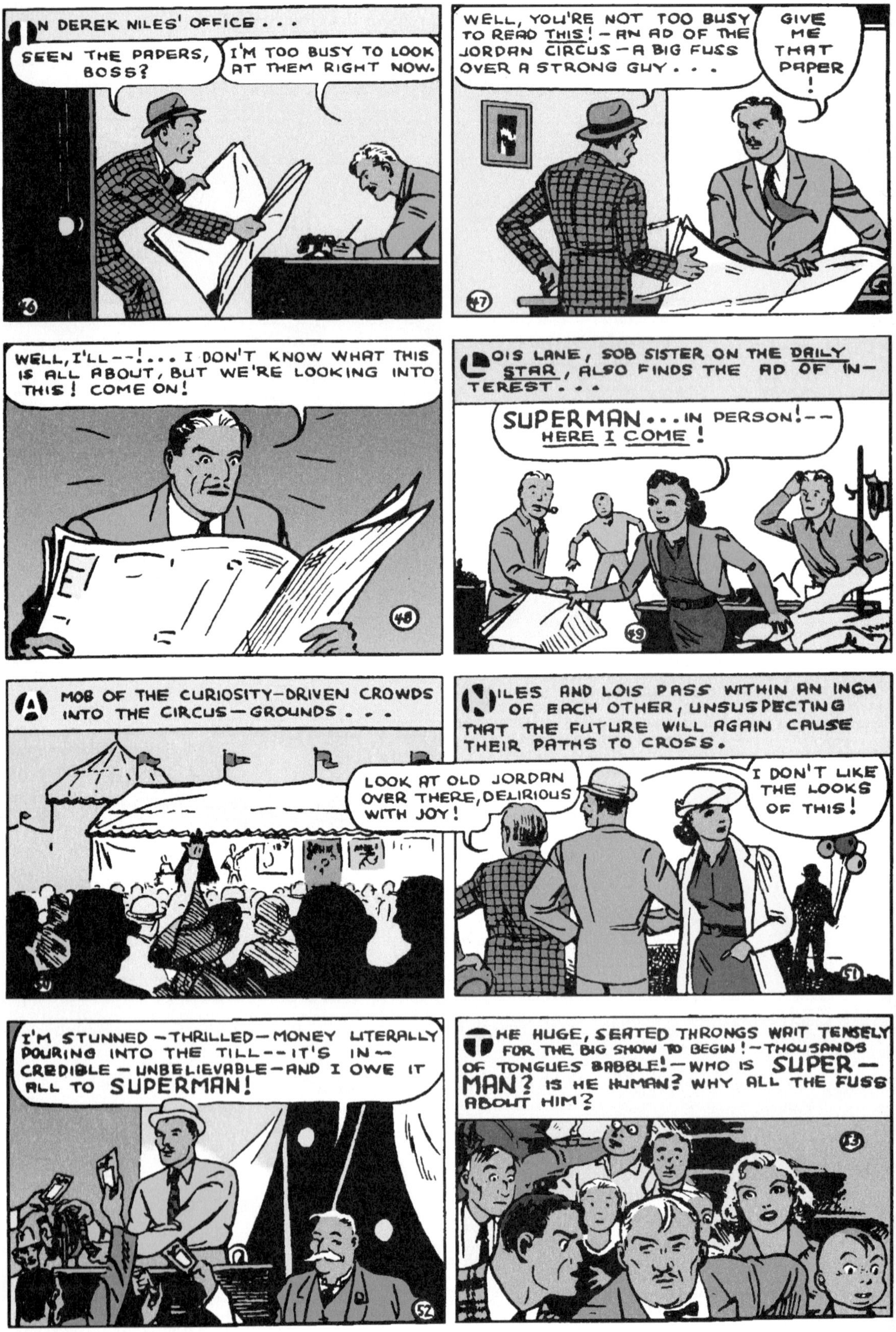
IN DEREK NILES' OFFICE . . .
SEEN THE PAPERS, BOSS?
I'M TOO BUSY TO LOOK AT THEM RIGHT NOW.
WELL, YOU'RE NOT TOO BUSY TO READ THIS! — AN AD OF THE JORDAN CIRCUS — A BIG FUSS OVER A STRONG GUY . . .
GIVE ME THAT PAPER!
WELL, I'LL --! . . . I DON'T KNOW WHAT THIS IS ALL ABOUT, BUT WE'RE LOOKING INTO THIS! COME ON!
LOIS LANE, SOB SISTER ON THE DAILY STAR, ALSO FINDS THE AD OF INTEREST . . .
SUPERMAN . . . IN PERSON! -- HERE I COME!
A MOB OF THE CURIOSITY-DRIVEN CROWDS INTO THE CIRCUS-GROUNDS . . .
NILES AND LOIS PASS WITHIN AN INCH OF EACH OTHER, UNSUSPECTING THAT THE FUTURE WILL AGAIN CAUSE THEIR PATHS TO CROSS.
LOOK AT OLD JORDAN OVER THERE, DELIRIOUS WITH JOY!
I DON'T LIKE THE LOOKS OF THIS!
I'M STUNNED — THRILLED — MONEY LITERALLY POURING INTO THE TILL -- IT'S IN-CREDIBLE — UNBELIEVABLE — AND I OWE IT ALL TO SUPERMAN!
THE HUGE, SEATED THRONGS WAIT TENSELY FOR THE BIG SHOW TO BEGIN! — THOUSANDS OF TONGUES BABBLE! — WHO IS SUPER-MAN? IS HE HUMAN? WHY ALL THE FUSS ABOUT HIM?

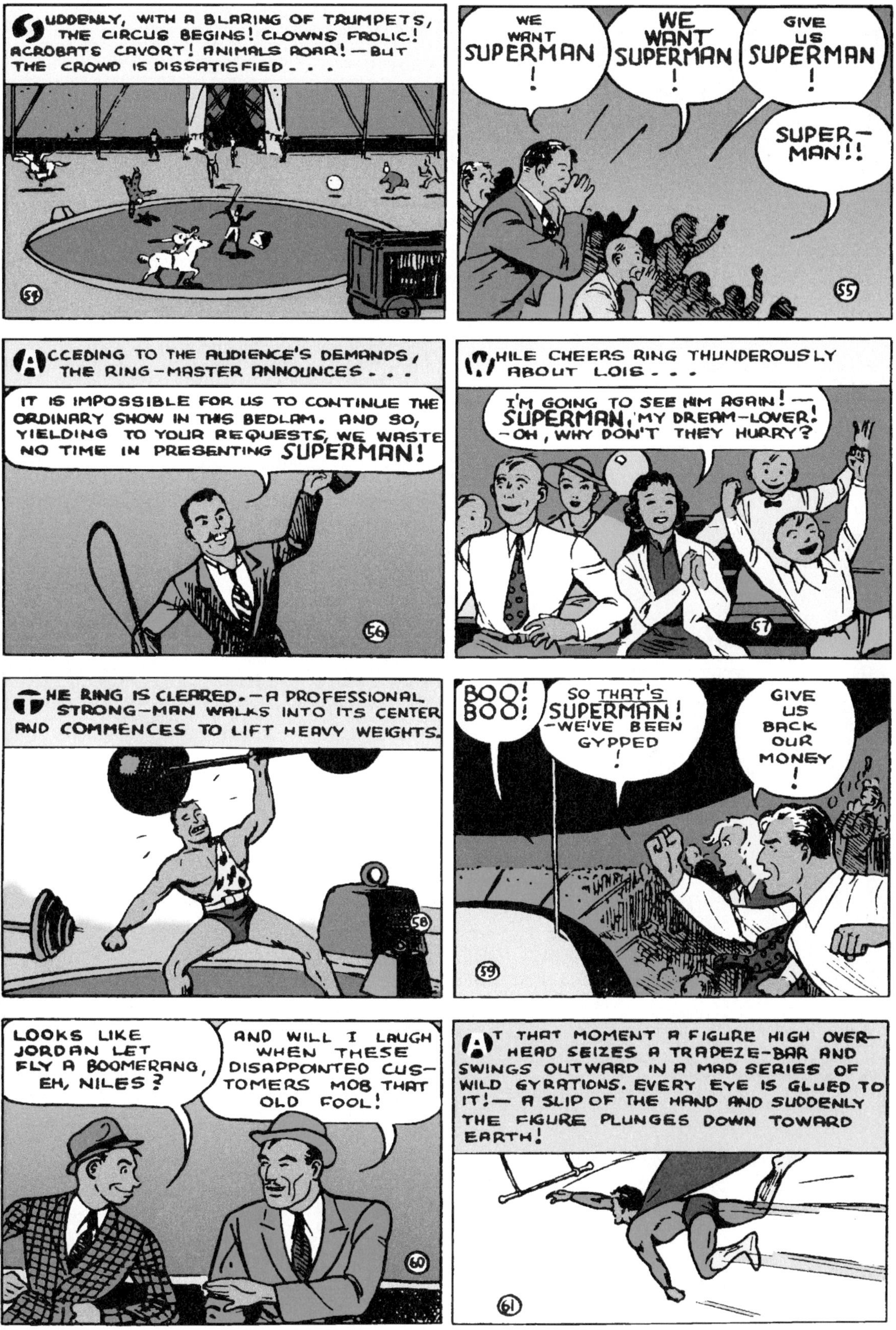
SUDDENLY, WITH A BLARING OF TRUMPETS, THE CIRCUS BEGINS! CLOWNS FROLIC! ACROBATS CAVORT! ANIMALS ROAR!—BUT THE CROWD IS DISSATISFIED . . .
WE WANT SUPERMAN!
WE WANT SUPERMAN!
GIVE US SUPERMAN!
SUPER-MAN!!
ACCEDING TO THE AUDIENCE'S DEMANDS, THE RING-MASTER ANNOUNCES . . .
IT IS IMPOSSIBLE FOR US TO CONTINUE THE ORDINARY SHOW IN THIS BEDLAM. AND SO, YIELDING TO YOUR REQUESTS, WE WASTE NO TIME IN PRESENTING SUPERMAN!
WHILE CHEERS RING THUNDEROUSLY ABOUT LOIS . . .
I'M GOING TO SEE HIM AGAIN!—SUPERMAN, MY DREAM-LOVER! —OH, WHY DON'T THEY HURRY?
THE RING IS CLEARED.—A PROFESSIONAL STRONG-MAN WALKS INTO ITS CENTER AND COMMENCES TO LIFT HEAVY WEIGHTS.
BOO! BOO!
SO THAT'S SUPERMAN! —WE'VE BEEN GYPPED!
GIVE US BACK OUR MONEY!
LOOKS LIKE JORDAN LET FLY A BOOMERANG, EH, NILES?
AND WILL I LAUGH WHEN THESE DISAPPOINTED CUSTOMERS MOB THAT OLD FOOL!
AT THAT MOMENT A FIGURE HIGH OVERHEAD SEIZES A TRAPEZE-BAR AND SWINGS OUTWARD IN A MAD SERIES OF WILD GYRATIONS. EVERY EYE IS GLUED TO IT!— A SLIP OF THE HAND AND SUDDENLY THE FIGURE PLUNGES DOWN TOWARD EARTH!

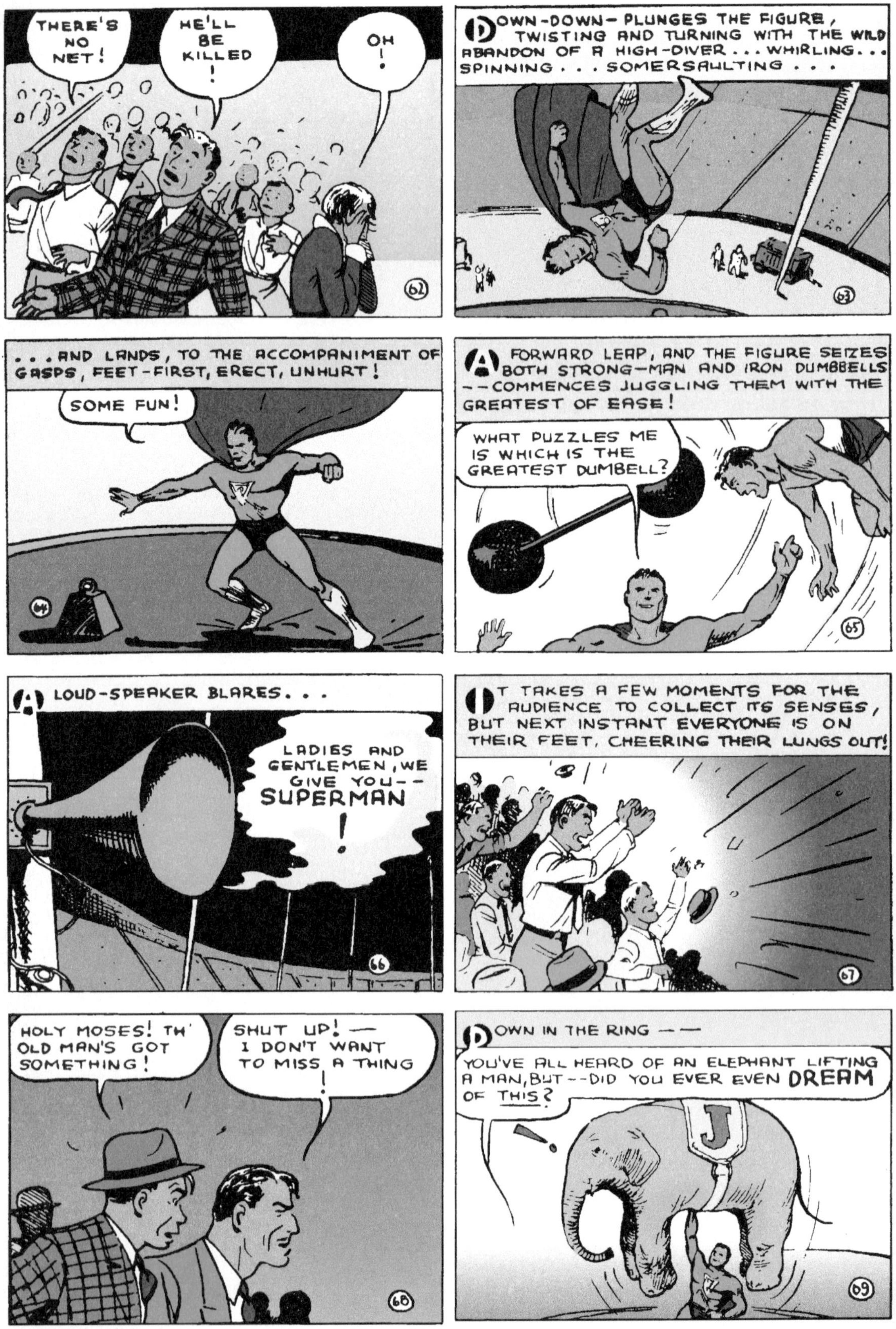
THERE'S NO NET!
HE'LL BE KILLED!
OH!
DOWN-DOWN- PLUNGES THE FIGURE, TWISTING AND TURNING WITH THE WILD ABANDON OF A HIGH-DIVER . . . WHIRLING . . . SPINNING . . . SOMERSAULTING . . .
. . . AND LANDS, TO THE ACCOMPANIMENT OF GASPS, FEET-FIRST, ERECT, UNHURT!
SOME FUN!
A FORWARD LEAP, AND THE FIGURE SEIZES BOTH STRONG-MAN AND IRON DUMBBELLS --COMMENCES JUGGLING THEM WITH THE GREATEST OF EASE!
WHAT PUZZLES ME IS WHICH IS THE GREATEST DUMBELL?
A LOUD-SPEAKER BLARES . . .
LADIES AND GENTLEMEN, WE GIVE YOU-- SUPERMAN!
IT TAKES A FEW MOMENTS FOR THE AUDIENCE TO COLLECT ITS SENSES, BUT NEXT INSTANT EVERYONE IS ON THEIR FEET, CHEERING THEIR LUNGS OUT!
HOLY MOSES! TH' OLD MAN'S GOT SOMETHING!
SHUT UP! — I DON'T WANT TO MISS A THING!
DOWN IN THE RING ——
YOU'VE ALL HEARD OF AN ELEPHANT LIFTING A MAN, BUT --DID YOU EVER EVEN DREAM OF THIS?
J

A DRUNK IN THE AUDIENCE TAKES ONE LOOK AT **SUPERMAN** LIFTING THE ELEPHANT AND PROCLAIMS TO THE AMUSE-MENT OF THOSE ABOUT HIM . . .

I DON'T MIND SEEING PINK ELEPHANTS, BUT (—HIC—) THIS IS <u>TOO</u> MUCH!

LET'S GET OUTTA HERE! I GOTTA GET WHERE I CAN THINK——<u>THINK</u>!

THIS CALLS FOR A CONFERENCE!

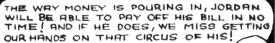

THE WAY MONEY IS POURING IN, JORDAN WILL BE ABLE TO PAY OFF HIS BILL IN NO TIME! AND IF HE DOES, WE MISS GETTING OUR HANDS ON THAT CIRCUS OF HIS!

GOT ANY IDEAS?

YES, IF <u>ACCIDENTS</u> STARTED TO HAPPEN ABOUT THE CIRCUS LOT, IF SEVERAL CUSTOMERS AND PERFORMERS WERE TO BE INJURED——BY ACCIDENT, OF COURSE——THAT WOULD BE TOO BAD, WOULDN'T IT? THE CIRCUS WOULD BE CALLED JINXED AND AVOIDED BY THE PUBLIC!

I GET YOU!—NILES, I'VE GOT TO HAND IT TO YOU! YOU'VE GOT <u>BRAINS</u>!

W HEN LOIS SEEKS TO SEE **SUPERMAN,** AFTER THE PERFORMANCE, WITH OTHER REPORTERS . . .

"DRESSING ROOM"

SORRY. **SUPERMAN** AIN'T SEEIN' NO ONE! — <u>GET MOVIN'</u>!

B UT LOIS ISN'T THE TYPE TO GIVE UP EASILY ONCE SHE'S MADE UP HER MIND.

IF I WERE TO CONCEAL MYSELF IN HIS DRESSING-ROOM TONIGHT, I'D CATCH HIM WHEN HE REPORTED TO WORK IN THE MORNING!

T HAT EVENING . . . LOIS BREAKS INTO THE DESERTED "BIG-TENT" BY CRAWLING UNDER THE EDGE OF A CANVAS-FLAP. . .

HAVEN'T DONE THIS SINCE I WAS A KID!

B UT ONCE WITHIN THE TENT, SHE HALTS WITH A QUICK INTAKE OF BREATH AS SHE SIGHTS A SHADOWY FIGURE AHEAD...

A PROWLER!

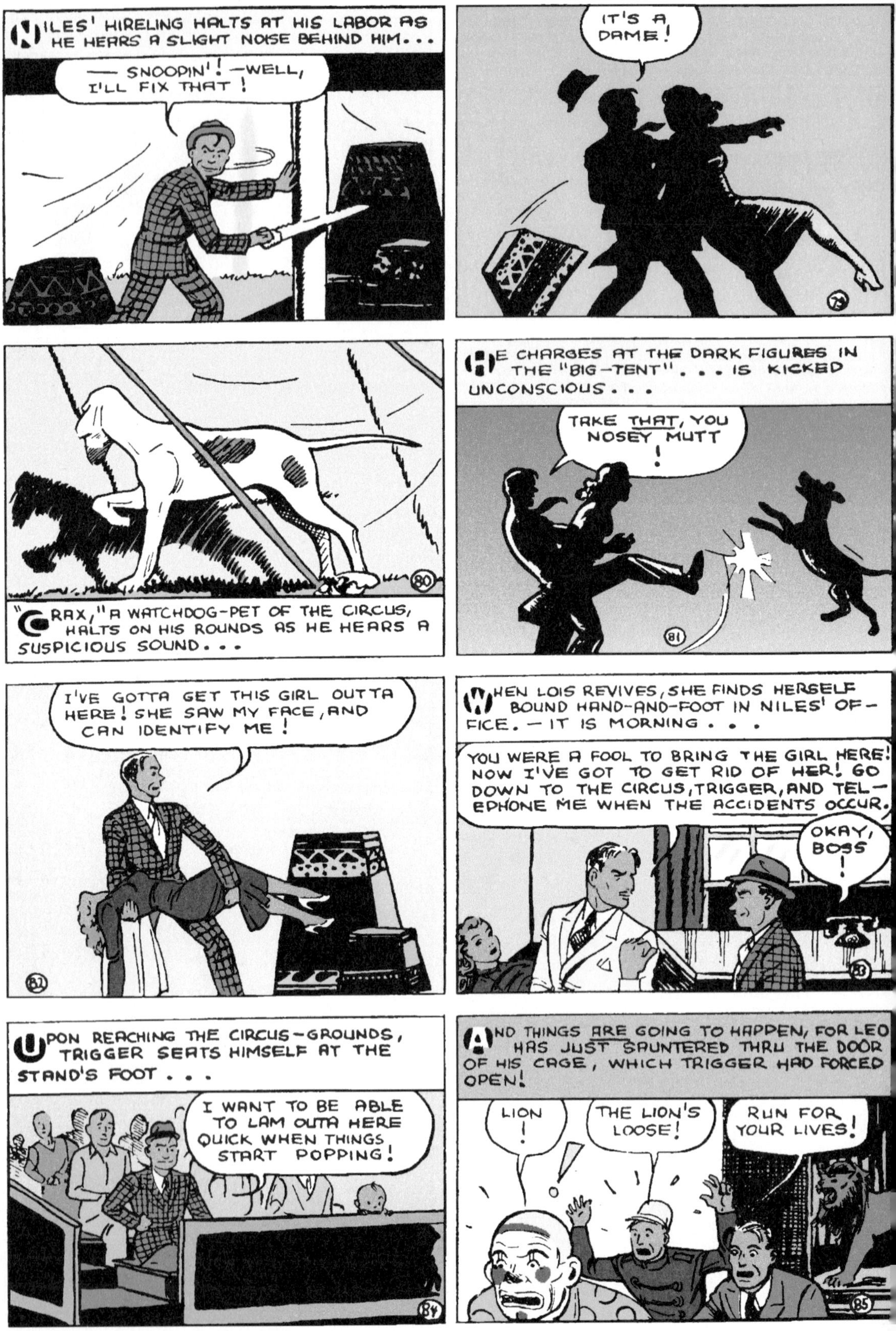
NILES' HIRELING HALTS AT HIS LABOR AS HE HEARS A SLIGHT NOISE BEHIND HIM...
— SNOOPIN'! —WELL, I'LL FIX THAT!
IT'S A DAME!
79
80
"GRAX," A WATCHDOG-PET OF THE CIRCUS, HALTS ON HIS ROUNDS AS HE HEARS A SUSPICIOUS SOUND...
HE CHARGES AT THE DARK FIGURES IN THE "BIG-TENT"... IS KICKED UNCONSCIOUS...
TAKE THAT, YOU NOSEY MUTT!
81
I'VE GOTTA GET THIS GIRL OUTTA HERE! SHE SAW MY FACE, AND CAN IDENTIFY ME!
82
WHEN LOIS REVIVES, SHE FINDS HERSELF BOUND HAND-AND-FOOT IN NILES' OFFICE. — IT IS MORNING...
YOU WERE A FOOL TO BRING THE GIRL HERE! NOW I'VE GOT TO GET RID OF HER! GO DOWN TO THE CIRCUS, TRIGGER, AND TELEPHONE ME WHEN THE ACCIDENTS OCCUR.
OKAY, BOSS!
83
UPON REACHING THE CIRCUS-GROUNDS, TRIGGER SEATS HIMSELF AT THE STAND'S FOOT...
I WANT TO BE ABLE TO LAM OUTA HERE QUICK WHEN THINGS START POPPING!
84
AND THINGS ARE GOING TO HAPPEN, FOR LEO HAS JUST SAUNTERED THRU THE DOOR OF HIS CAGE, WHICH TRIGGER HAD FORCED OPEN!
LION!
THE LION'S LOOSE!
RUN FOR YOUR LIVES!
85

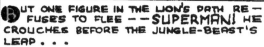

BUT ONE FIGURE IN THE LION'S PATH RE-FUSES TO FLEE -- SUPERMAN! HE CROUCHES BEFORE THE JUNGLE-BEAST'S LEAP...

COME AN' GET IT!

WITH AN INCREDIBLY AGILE MOVEMENT, HE TWISTS ASIDE, SEIZES LEO BY THE SCRUFF OF HIS NECK...

WANTA PLAY, HUH?

...AND CARRIES THE FEROCIOUS CARNI-VORE BACK TO ITS CAGE, AS THOUGH IT WERE A HARMLESS KITTEN!

DON'T YOU KNOW IT'S NAUGHTY TO PLAY HOOKY FROM YOUR CAGE?

THE AUDIENCE SINKS BACK INTO ITS SEATS WITH SIGHS OF RELIEF. BUT NEXT INSTANT THEY SHRIEK ALOUD AS A TRAPEZE PERFORMER'S TAMPERED BAR SHATTERS, AND SHE PLUNGES TOWARD EARTH!

EE-EE-EE!

SPRINGING ALOFT, SUPERMAN CATCHES HER IN MID-AIR, AND BRINGS HER DOWN TO SAFETY!

THERE'S SOMETHING DEFINITELY CROOKED GOING ON. I WONDER IF...

A MOMENT LATER, THE HUGE POLE WHICH HOLDS UP THE ENTIRE "BIG-TENT," CUNNINGLY SAWED BY TRIGGER, SWAYS PRE-PARATORY TO CRASHING...!

AND NOW, THIS!

SEIZING THE HUGE POLE WITH A POWERFUL GRIP, SUPERMAN HOLDS IT RIGID WHILE ATTENDANTS COMPLETE REPAIRS...

"CRAX" SURE IS BARKING AT THAT GUY TRYING TO LEAVE!

I WONDER IF THAT HAS ANYTHING TO DO WITH THESE ACCIDENTS AND "CRAX" HAVING BEEN FOUND UNCONSCIOUS THIS MORNING?

SUDDENLY SUSPICIOUS, SUPERMAN GRIPS TRIGGER...

WHAT DO YOU KNOW ABOUT THESE DELIBERATE ATTEMPTS TO RUIN THE CIRCUS?

NOTHIN'! LET ME GO!

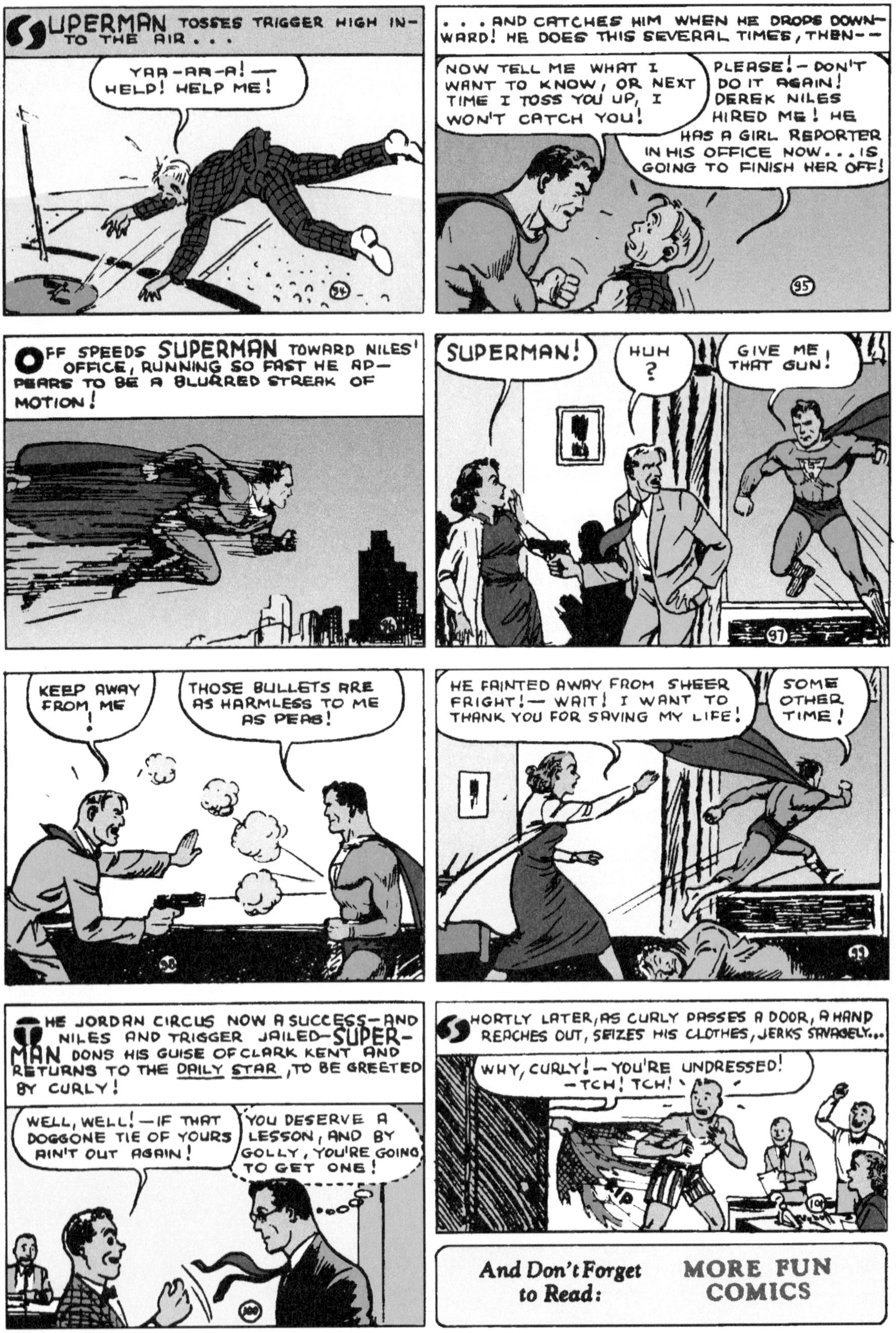
SUPERMAN TOSSES TRIGGER HIGH INTO THE AIR . . .
YAA-AA-A! — HELP! HELP ME!
. . . AND CATCHES HIM WHEN HE DROPS DOWNWARD! HE DOES THIS SEVERAL TIMES, THEN--
NOW TELL ME WHAT I WANT TO KNOW, OR NEXT TIME I TOSS YOU UP, I WON'T CATCH YOU!
PLEASE! — DON'T DO IT AGAIN! DEREK NILES HIRED ME! HE HAS A GIRL REPORTER IN HIS OFFICE NOW . . . IS GOING TO FINISH HER OFF!
OFF SPEEDS SUPERMAN TOWARD NILES' OFFICE, RUNNING SO FAST HE APPEARS TO BE A BLURRED STREAK OF MOTION!
SUPERMAN!
HUH ?
GIVE ME THAT GUN!
KEEP AWAY FROM ME !
THOSE BULLETS ARE AS HARMLESS TO ME AS PEAS!
HE FAINTED AWAY FROM SHEER FRIGHT! — WAIT! I WANT TO THANK YOU FOR SAVING MY LIFE!
SOME OTHER TIME!
THE JORDAN CIRCUS NOW A SUCCESS—AND NILES AND TRIGGER JAILED—SUPERMAN DONS HIS GUISE OF CLARK KENT AND RETURNS TO THE DAILY STAR, TO BE GREETED BY CURLY!
WELL, WELL! — IF THAT DOGGONE TIE OF YOURS AIN'T OUT AGAIN!
YOU DESERVE A LESSON, AND BY GOLLY, YOU'RE GOING TO GET ONE!
SHORTLY LATER, AS CURLY PASSES A DOOR, A HAND REACHES OUT, SEIZES HIS CLOTHES, JERKS SAVAGELY...
WHY, CURLY! — YOU'RE UNDRESSED! — TCH! TCH!
RIP
And Don't Forget to Read: MORE FUN COMICS

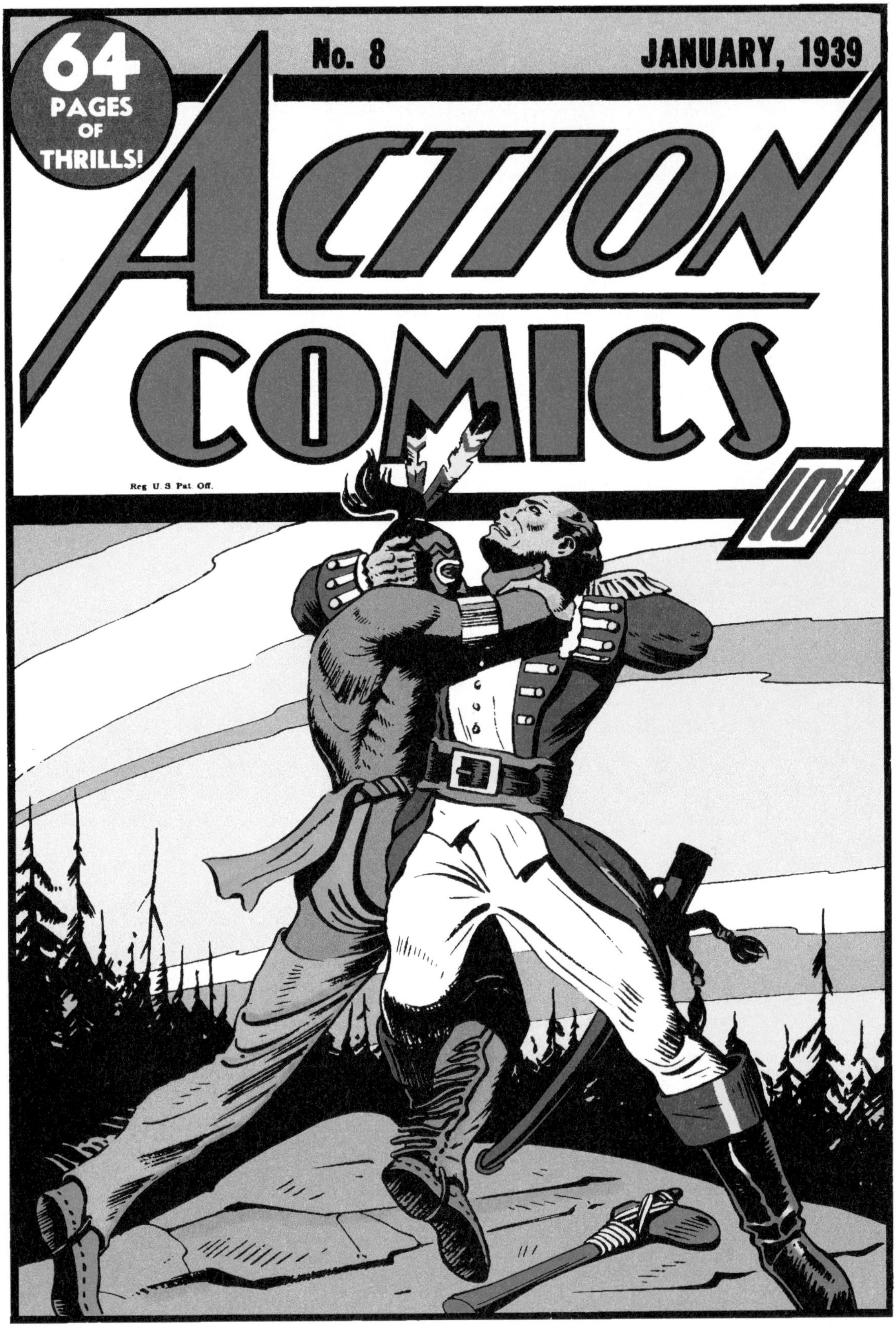
64 PAGES OF THRILLS!
No. 8
JANUARY, 1939
ACTION COMICS
Reg. U. S. Pat. Off.
10¢

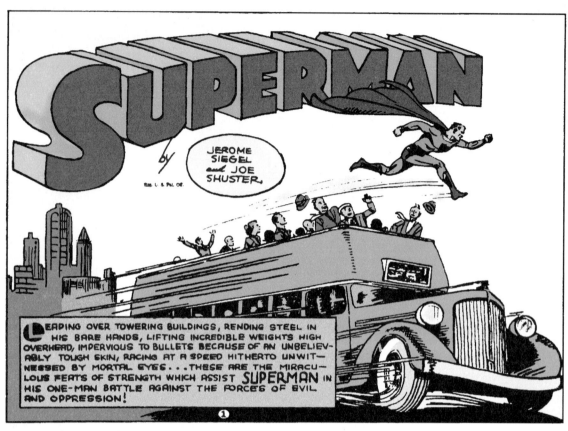

SUPERMAN

by JEROME SIEGEL and JOE SHUSTER.

Reg. U. S. Pat. Off.

1. LEAPING OVER TOWERING BUILDINGS, RENDING STEEL IN HIS BARE HANDS, LIFTING INCREDIBLE WEIGHTS HIGH OVERHEAD, IMPERVIOUS TO BULLETS BECAUSE OF AN UNBELIEVABLY TOUGH SKIN, RACING AT A SPEED HITHERTO UNWITNESSED BY MORTAL EYES... THESE ARE THE MIRACULOUS FEATS OF STRENGTH WHICH ASSIST **SUPERMAN** IN HIS ONE-MAN BATTLE AGAINST THE FORCES OF EVIL AND OPPRESSION!

2. A SESSION OF JUVENILE-COURT...

FRANKIE MARELLO... YOU ARE CHARGED WITH ASSAULT AND BATTERY. WHAT HAVE YOU TO SAY IN YOUR DEFENSE?

NOT'IN--'CEPT IF HE HAD HANDED OVER HIS DOUGH WIT' OUT SQUAWKIN' I WOULDN'TA HIT 'IM SO HARD.

3. YOU SPEAK LIKE A HARDENED CRIMINAL. IN THAT CASE, I HAVE NO COURSE BUT TO--

WAIT! WAIT, YOUR HONOR!

4. OF COURSE HE TALKS TOUGH--WHAT'S MORE HE IS TOUGH, YOUR HONOR--BUT HE'S ONLY LIKE ALL THE OTHER BOYS IN OUR NEIGHBORHOOD... HARD, RESENTFUL, UNDERPRIVILEGED. HE'S MY ONLY SON, SIR HE MIGHT HAVE BEEN A GOOD BOY EXCEPT FOR HIS ENVIRONMENT. HE STILL MIGHT BE-- IF YOU'LL BE MERCIFUL!

5. AMONG THE SPECTATORS IN THE COURT-ROOM IS CLARK KENT, ACE NEWSPAPER REPORTER... HE LISTENS INTENTLY, COMPLETELY ENGROSSED...

THE MOTHER'S RIGHT! BUT IF I KNOW THE COURT OF LAW... HER PLEA HASN'T A CHANCE!

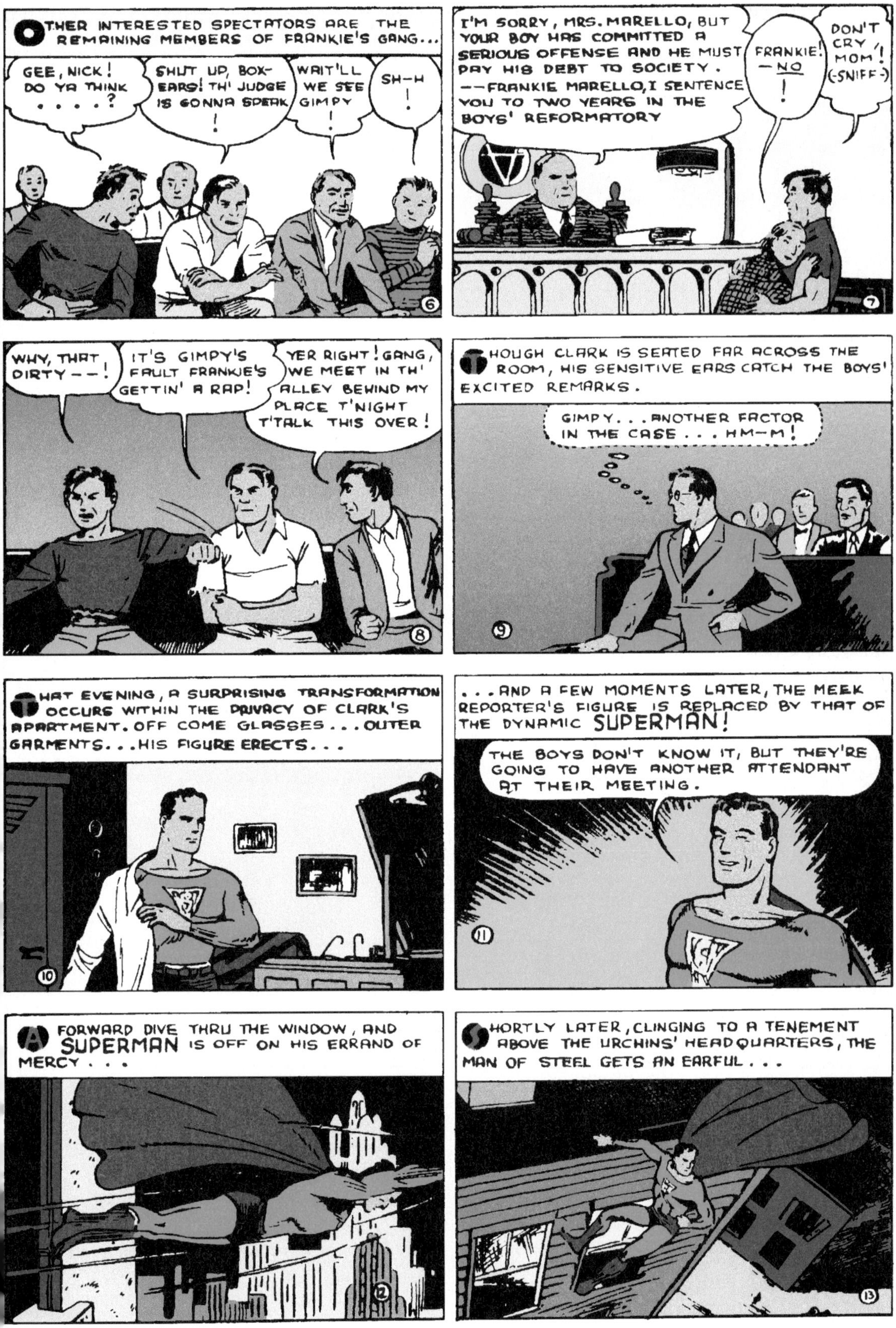
OTHER INTERESTED SPECTATORS ARE THE REMAINING MEMBERS OF FRANKIE'S GANG...
GEE, NICK! DO YA THINK ....?
SHUT UP, BOX-EARS! TH' JUDGE IS GONNA SPEAK!
WAIT'LL WE SEE GIMPY!
SH-H!
I'M SORRY, MRS. MARELLO, BUT YOUR BOY HAS COMMITTED A SERIOUS OFFENSE AND HE MUST PAY HIS DEBT TO SOCIETY. --FRANKIE MARELLO, I SENTENCE YOU TO TWO YEARS IN THE BOYS' REFORMATORY
FRANKIE! —NO!
DON'T CRY, MOM! (-SNIFF-)
WHY, THAT DIRTY--!
IT'S GIMPY'S FAULT FRANKIE'S GETTIN' A RAP!
YER RIGHT! GANG, WE MEET IN TH' ALLEY BEHIND MY PLACE T'NIGHT T'TALK THIS OVER!
THOUGH CLARK IS SEATED FAR ACROSS THE ROOM, HIS SENSITIVE EARS CATCH THE BOYS' EXCITED REMARKS.
GIMPY... ANOTHER FACTOR IN THE CASE... HM-M!
THAT EVENING, A SURPRISING TRANSFORMATION OCCURS WITHIN THE PRIVACY OF CLARK'S APARTMENT. OFF COME GLASSES... OUTER GARMENTS... HIS FIGURE ERECTS...
...AND A FEW MOMENTS LATER, THE MEEK REPORTER'S FIGURE IS REPLACED BY THAT OF THE DYNAMIC SUPERMAN!
THE BOYS DON'T KNOW IT, BUT THEY'RE GOING TO HAVE ANOTHER ATTENDANT AT THEIR MEETING.
A FORWARD DIVE THRU THE WINDOW, AND SUPERMAN IS OFF ON HIS ERRAND OF MERCY...
SHORTLY LATER, CLINGING TO A TENEMENT ABOVE THE URCHINS' HEADQUARTERS, THE MAN OF STEEL GETS AN EARFUL...

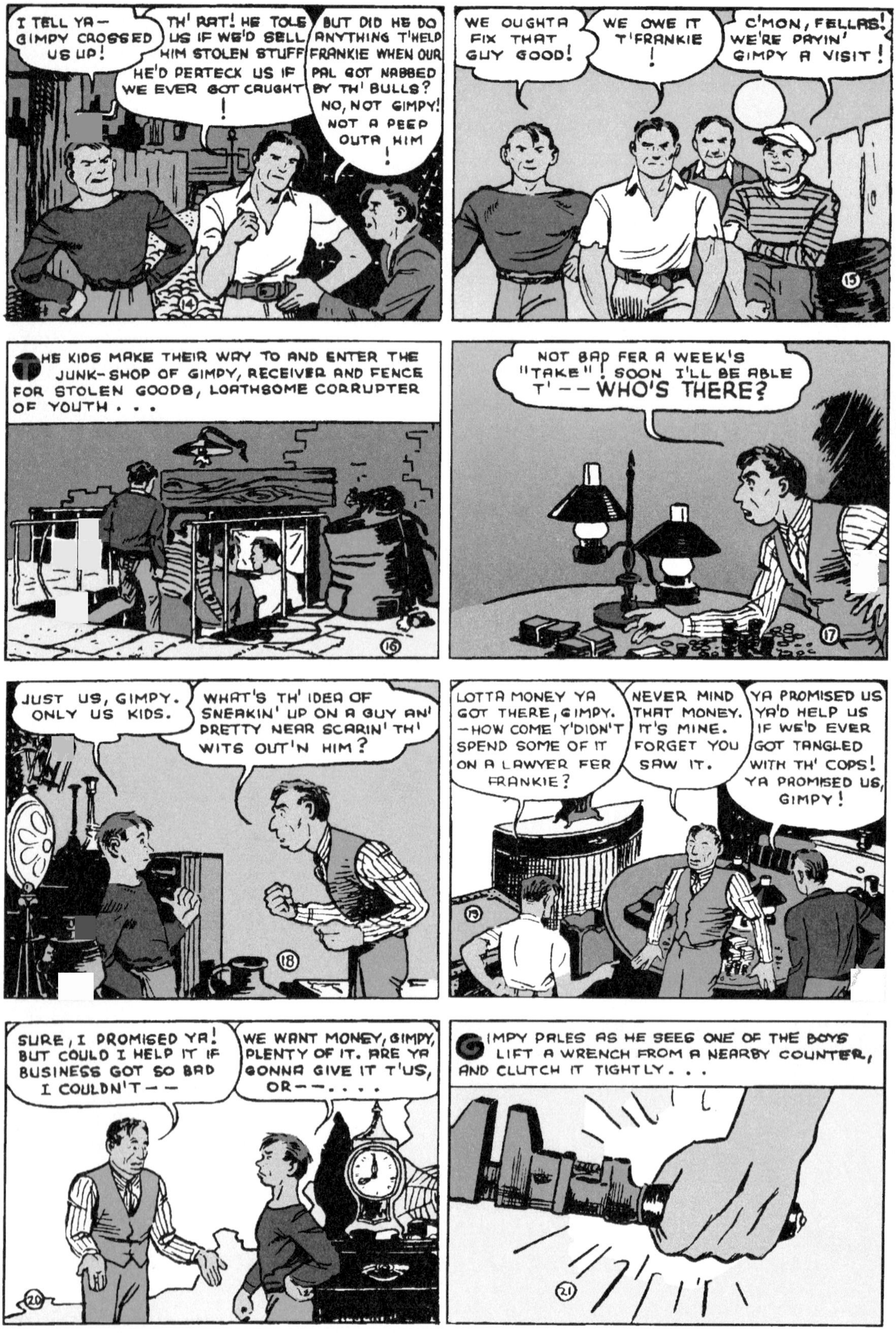
I TELL YA— GIMPY CROSSED US UP!
TH' RAT! HE TOLE US IF WE'D SELL HIM STOLEN STUFF HE'D PERTECK US IF WE EVER GOT CAUGHT!
BUT DID HE DO ANYTHING T'HELP FRANKIE WHEN OUR PAL GOT NABBED BY TH' BULLS? NO, NOT GIMPY! NOT A PEEP OUTA HIM!
WE OUGHTA FIX THAT GUY GOOD!
WE OWE IT T'FRANKIE!
C'MON, FELLAS! WE'RE PAYIN' GIMPY A VISIT!
THE KIDS MAKE THEIR WAY TO AND ENTER THE JUNK-SHOP OF GIMPY, RECEIVER AND FENCE FOR STOLEN GOODS, LOATHSOME CORRUPTER OF YOUTH . . .
NOT BAD FER A WEEK'S "TAKE"! SOON I'LL BE ABLE T' — — WHO'S THERE?
JUST US, GIMPY. ONLY US KIDS.
WHAT'S TH' IDEA OF SNEAKIN' UP ON A GUY AN' PRETTY NEAR SCARIN' TH' WITS OUT'N HIM?
LOTTA MONEY YA GOT THERE, GIMPY. —HOW COME Y'DIDN'T SPEND SOME OF IT ON A LAWYER FER FRANKIE?
NEVER MIND THAT MONEY. IT'S MINE. FORGET YOU SAW IT.
YA PROMISED US YA'D HELP US IF WE'D EVER GOT TANGLED WITH TH' COPS! YA PROMISED US, GIMPY!
SURE, I PROMISED YA! BUT COULD I HELP IT IF BUSINESS GOT SO BAD I COULDN'T — —
WE WANT MONEY, GIMPY, PLENTY OF IT. ARE YA GONNA GIVE IT T'US, OR — — . . . .
GIMPY PALES AS HE SEES ONE OF THE BOYS LIFT A WRENCH FROM A NEARBY COUNTER, AND CLUTCH IT TIGHTLY . . .

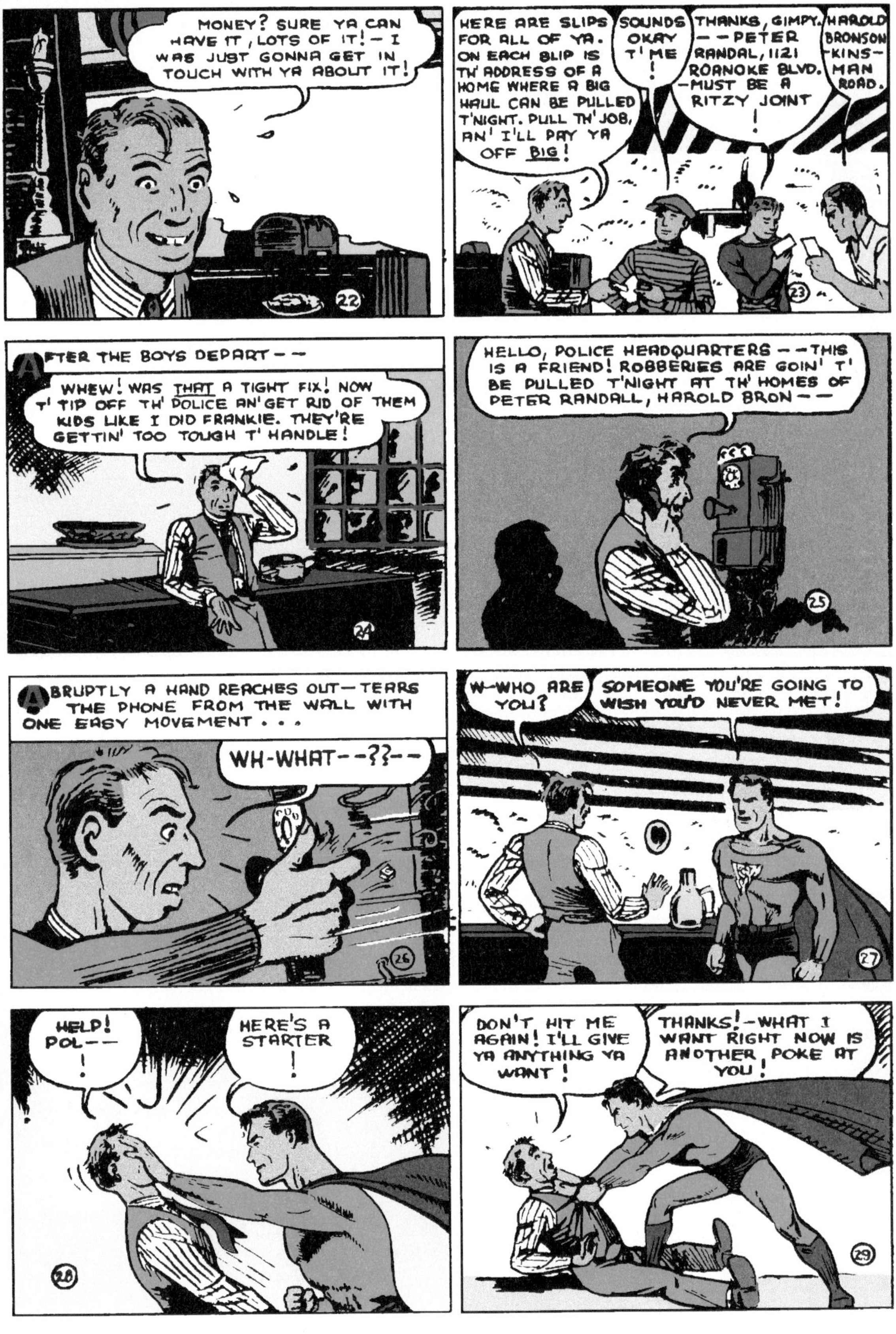
MONEY? SURE YA CAN HAVE IT, LOTS OF IT! — I WAS JUST GONNA GET IN TOUCH WITH YA ABOUT IT!
HERE ARE SLIPS FOR ALL OF YA. ON EACH SLIP IS TH' ADDRESS OF A HOME WHERE A BIG HAUL CAN BE PULLED T'NIGHT. PULL TH' JOB, AN' I'LL PAY YA OFF BIG!
SOUNDS OKAY T' ME!
THANKS, GIMPY. — — PETER RANDAL, 1121 ROANOKE BLVD. —MUST BE A RITZY JOINT!
HAROLD BRONSON — KINSMAN ROAD.
AFTER THE BOYS DEPART — —
WHEW! WAS THAT A TIGHT FIX! NOW T' TIP OFF TH' POLICE AN' GET RID OF THEM KIDS LIKE I DID FRANKIE. THEY'RE GETTIN' TOO TOUGH T' HANDLE!
HELLO, POLICE HEADQUARTERS — — THIS IS A FRIEND! ROBBERIES ARE GOIN' T' BE PULLED T'NIGHT AT TH' HOMES OF PETER RANDALL, HAROLD BRON — —
ABRUPTLY A HAND REACHES OUT — TEARS THE PHONE FROM THE WALL WITH ONE EASY MOVEMENT . . .
WH-WHAT — — ?? — —
W-WHO ARE YOU?
SOMEONE YOU'RE GOING TO WISH YOU'D NEVER MET!
HELP! POL — — !
HERE'S A STARTER!
DON'T HIT ME AGAIN! I'LL GIVE YA ANYTHING YA WANT!
THANKS! — WHAT I WANT RIGHT NOW IS ANOTHER POKE AT YOU!

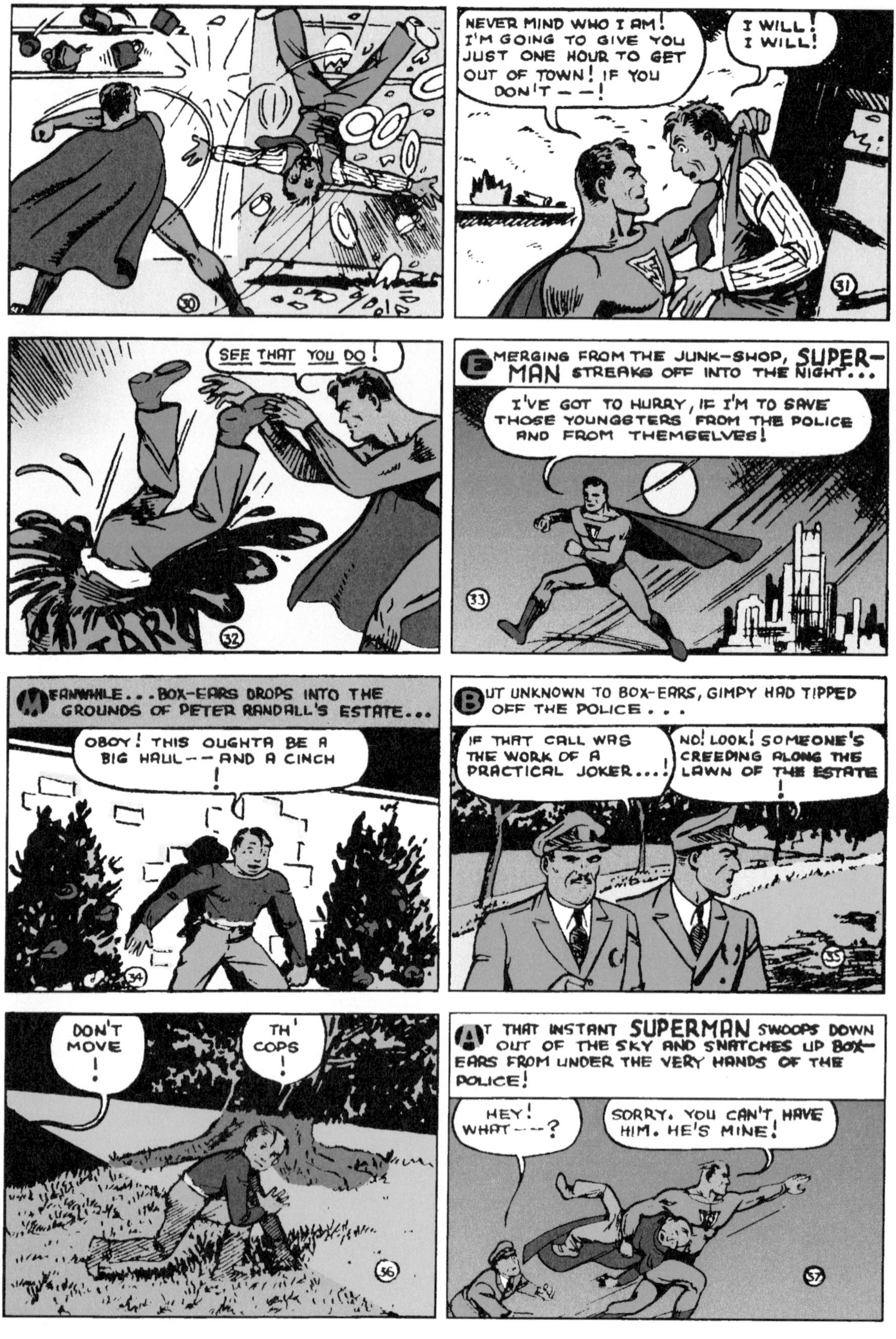
30
NEVER MIND WHO I AM! I'M GOING TO GIVE YOU JUST ONE HOUR TO GET OUT OF TOWN! IF YOU DON'T --!
I WILL! I WILL!
31
SEE THAT YOU DO!
32
EMERGING FROM THE JUNK-SHOP, SUPERMAN STREAKS OFF INTO THE NIGHT...
I'VE GOT TO HURRY, IF I'M TO SAVE THOSE YOUNGSTERS FROM THE POLICE AND FROM THEMSELVES!
33
MEANWHILE...BOX-EARS DROPS INTO THE GROUNDS OF PETER RANDALL'S ESTATE...
OBOY! THIS OUGHTA BE A BIG HAUL--AND A CINCH!
34
BUT UNKNOWN TO BOX-EARS, GIMPY HAD TIPPED OFF THE POLICE . . .
IF THAT CALL WAS THE WORK OF A PRACTICAL JOKER...!
NO! LOOK! SOMEONE'S CREEPING ALONG THE LAWN OF THE ESTATE!
35
DON'T MOVE!
TH' COPS!
36
AT THAT INSTANT SUPERMAN SWOOPS DOWN OUT OF THE SKY AND SNATCHES UP BOX-EARS FROM UNDER THE VERY HANDS OF THE POLICE!
HEY! WHAT---?
SORRY. YOU CAN'T HAVE HIM. HE'S MINE!
37

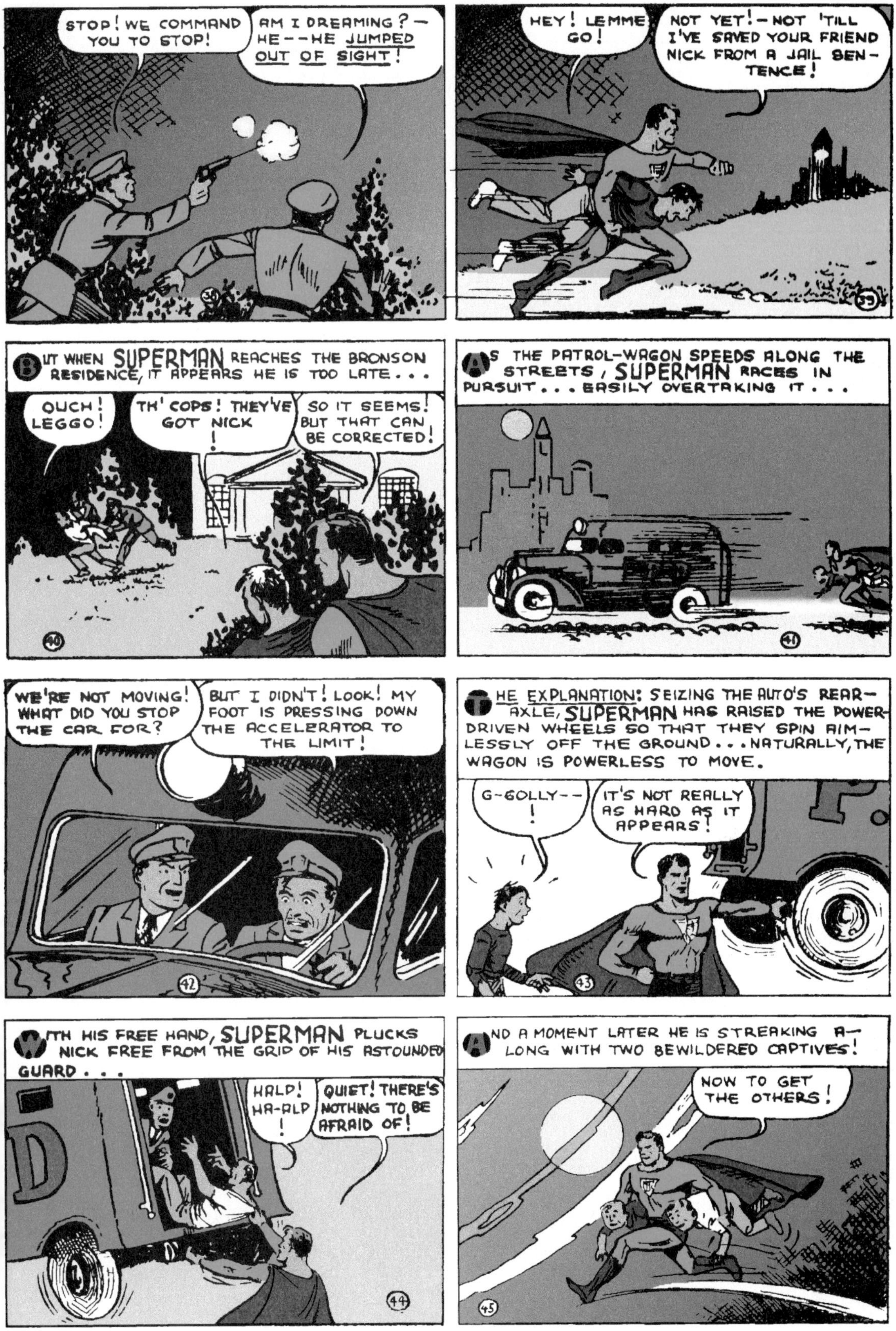
STOP! WE COMMAND YOU TO STOP!
AM I DREAMING? — HE — — HE JUMPED OUT OF SIGHT!
HEY! LEMME GO!
NOT YET! — NOT 'TILL I'VE SAVED YOUR FRIEND NICK FROM A JAIL SENTENCE!
BUT WHEN SUPERMAN REACHES THE BRONSON RESIDENCE, IT APPEARS HE IS TOO LATE . . .
OUCH! LEGGO!
TH' COPS! THEY'VE GOT NICK!
SO IT SEEMS! BUT THAT CAN BE CORRECTED!
AS THE PATROL-WAGON SPEEDS ALONG THE STREETS, SUPERMAN RACES IN PURSUIT . . . EASILY OVERTAKING IT . . .
WE'RE NOT MOVING! WHAT DID YOU STOP THE CAR FOR?
BUT I DIDN'T! LOOK! MY FOOT IS PRESSING DOWN THE ACCELERATOR TO THE LIMIT!
THE EXPLANATION: SEIZING THE AUTO'S REAR-AXLE, SUPERMAN HAS RAISED THE POWER-DRIVEN WHEELS SO THAT THEY SPIN AIMLESSLY OFF THE GROUND . . . NATURALLY, THE WAGON IS POWERLESS TO MOVE.
G-GOLLY — — !
IT'S NOT REALLY AS HARD AS IT APPEARS!
WITH HIS FREE HAND, SUPERMAN PLUCKS NICK FREE FROM THE GRIP OF HIS ASTOUNDED GUARD . . .
HALP! HA-ALP!
QUIET! THERE'S NOTHING TO BE AFRAID OF!
AND A MOMENT LATER HE IS STREAKING ALONG WITH TWO BEWILDERED CAPTIVES!
NOW TO GET THE OTHERS!

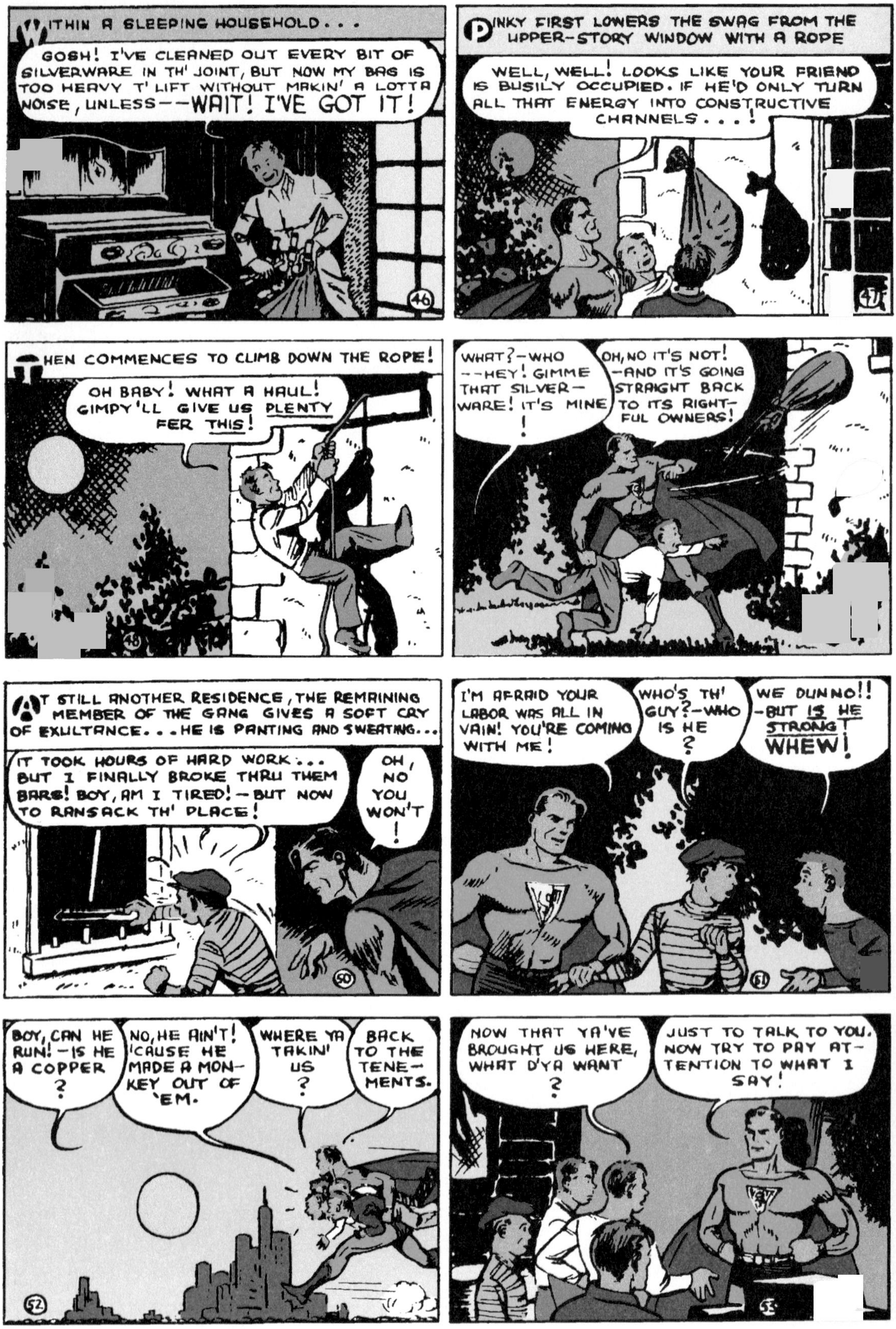
WITHIN A SLEEPING HOUSEHOLD . . .
GOSH! I'VE CLEANED OUT EVERY BIT OF SILVERWARE IN TH' JOINT, BUT NOW MY BAG IS TOO HEAVY T' LIFT WITHOUT MAKIN' A LOTTA NOISE, UNLESS--WAIT! I'VE GOT IT!
46
PINKY FIRST LOWERS THE SWAG FROM THE UPPER-STORY WINDOW WITH A ROPE
WELL, WELL! LOOKS LIKE YOUR FRIEND IS BUSILY OCCUPIED. IF HE'D ONLY TURN ALL THAT ENERGY INTO CONSTRUCTIVE CHANNELS . . . !
47
THEN COMMENCES TO CLIMB DOWN THE ROPE!
OH BABY! WHAT A HAUL! GIMPY'LL GIVE US PLENTY FER THIS!
48
WHAT?-WHO --HEY! GIMME THAT SILVER-WARE! IT'S MINE!
OH, NO IT'S NOT! -AND IT'S GOING STRAIGHT BACK TO ITS RIGHT-FUL OWNERS!
AT STILL ANOTHER RESIDENCE, THE REMAINING MEMBER OF THE GANG GIVES A SOFT CRY OF EXULTANCE . . . HE IS PANTING AND SWEATING . . .
IT TOOK HOURS OF HARD WORK . . . BUT I FINALLY BROKE THRU THEM BARS! BOY, AM I TIRED! -BUT NOW TO RANSACK TH' PLACE!
OH, NO YOU WON'T!
50
I'M AFRAID YOUR LABOR WAS ALL IN VAIN! YOU'RE COMING WITH ME!
WHO'S TH' GUY?-WHO IS HE?
WE DUNNO!! -BUT IS HE STRONG! WHEW!
51
BOY, CAN HE RUN! -IS HE A COPPER?
NO, HE AIN'T! 'CAUSE HE MADE A MON-KEY OUT OF 'EM.
WHERE YA TAKIN' US?
BACK TO THE TENE-MENTS.
52
NOW THAT YA'VE BROUGHT US HERE, WHAT D'YA WANT?
JUST TO TALK TO YOU. NOW TRY TO PAY AT-TENTION TO WHAT I SAY!
53

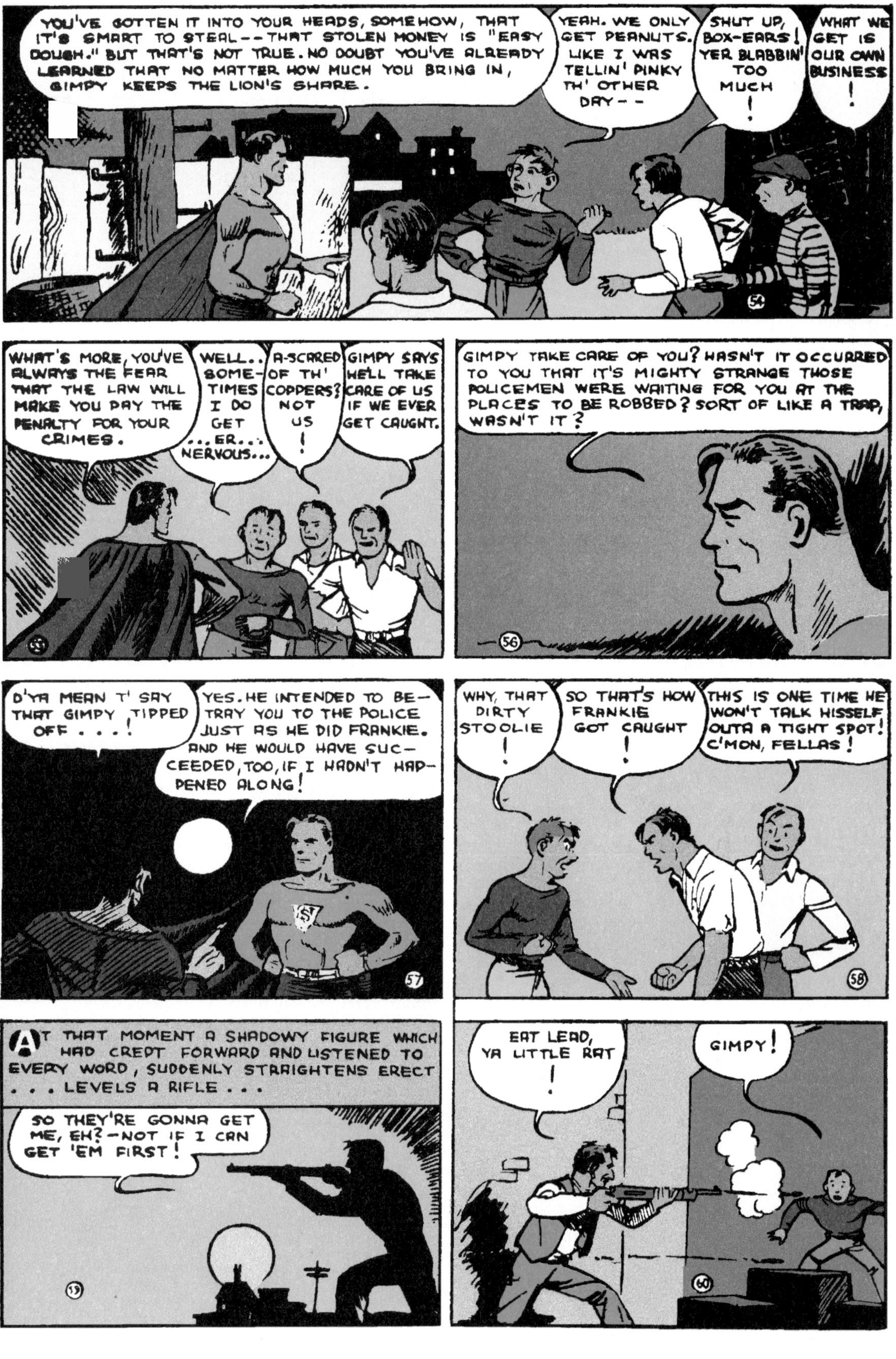
YOU'VE GOTTEN IT INTO YOUR HEADS, SOMEHOW, THAT IT'S SMART TO STEAL--THAT STOLEN MONEY IS "EASY DOUGH." BUT THAT'S NOT TRUE. NO DOUBT YOU'VE ALREADY LEARNED THAT NO MATTER HOW MUCH YOU BRING IN, GIMPY KEEPS THE LION'S SHARE.
YEAH. WE ONLY GET PEANUTS. LIKE I WAS TELLIN' PINKY TH' OTHER DAY--
SHUT UP, BOX-EARS! YER BLABBIN' TOO MUCH!
WHAT WE GET IS OUR OWN BUSINESS!
WHAT'S MORE, YOU'VE ALWAYS THE FEAR THAT THE LAW WILL MAKE YOU PAY THE PENALTY FOR YOUR CRIMES.
WELL.. SOME-TIMES I DO GET ...ER... NERVOUS...
A-SCARED OF TH' COPPERS? NOT US!
GIMPY SAYS HE'LL TAKE CARE OF US IF WE EVER GET CAUGHT.
GIMPY TAKE CARE OF YOU? HASN'T IT OCCURRED TO YOU THAT IT'S MIGHTY STRANGE THOSE POLICEMEN WERE WAITING FOR YOU AT THE PLACES TO BE ROBBED? SORT OF LIKE A TRAP, WASN'T IT?
D'YA MEAN T' SAY THAT GIMPY TIPPED OFF...!
YES. HE INTENDED TO BE-TRAY YOU TO THE POLICE JUST AS HE DID FRANKIE. AND HE WOULD HAVE SUC-CEEDED, TOO, IF I HADN'T HAP-PENED ALONG!
WHY, THAT DIRTY STOOLIE!
SO THAT'S HOW FRANKIE GOT CAUGHT!
THIS IS ONE TIME HE WON'T TALK HISSELF OUTA A TIGHT SPOT! C'MON, FELLAS!
AT THAT MOMENT A SHADOWY FIGURE WHICH HAD CREPT FORWARD AND LISTENED TO EVERY WORD, SUDDENLY STRAIGHTENS ERECT ... LEVELS A RIFLE ...
SO THEY'RE GONNA GET ME, EH?—NOT IF I CAN GET 'EM FIRST!
EAT LEAD, YA LITTLE RAT!
GIMPY!

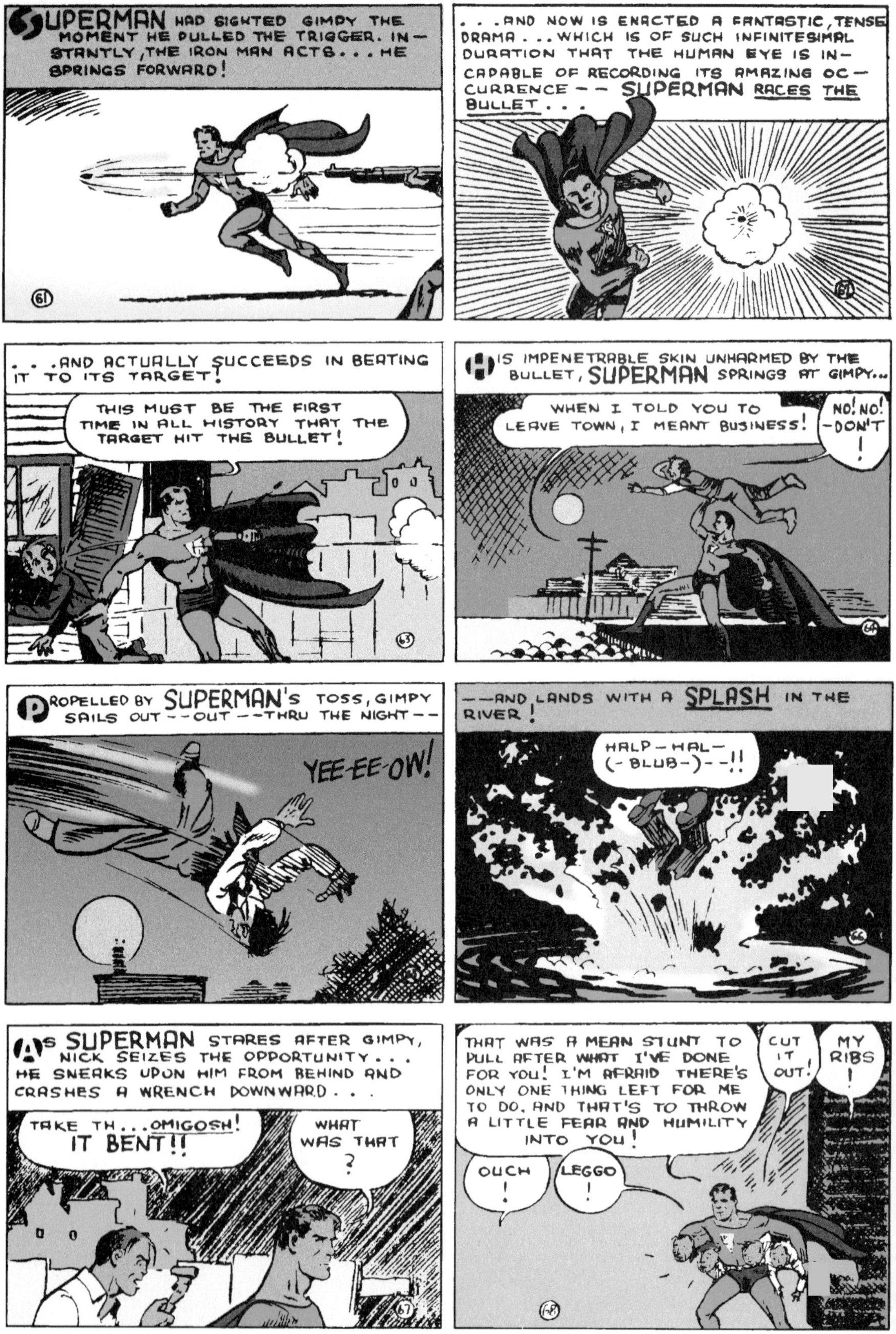
SUPERMAN HAD SIGHTED GIMPY THE MOMENT HE PULLED THE TRIGGER. INSTANTLY, THE IRON MAN ACTS... HE SPRINGS FORWARD!
...AND NOW IS ENACTED A FANTASTIC, TENSE DRAMA...WHICH IS OF SUCH INFINITESIMAL DURATION THAT THE HUMAN EYE IS INCAPABLE OF RECORDING ITS AMAZING OCCURRENCE -- SUPERMAN RACES THE BULLET...
...AND ACTUALLY SUCCEEDS IN BEATING IT TO ITS TARGET!
THIS MUST BE THE FIRST TIME IN ALL HISTORY THAT THE TARGET HIT THE BULLET!
HIS IMPENETRABLE SKIN UNHARMED BY THE BULLET, SUPERMAN SPRINGS AT GIMPY...
WHEN I TOLD YOU TO LEAVE TOWN, I MEANT BUSINESS!
NO! NO! -DON'T!
PROPELLED BY SUPERMAN'S TOSS, GIMPY SAILS OUT--OUT--THRU THE NIGHT--
YEE-EE-OW!
--AND LANDS WITH A SPLASH IN THE RIVER!
HALP-HAL-(-BLUB-)--!!
AS SUPERMAN STARES AFTER GIMPY, NICK SEIZES THE OPPORTUNITY... HE SNEAKS UPON HIM FROM BEHIND AND CRASHES A WRENCH DOWNWARD...
TAKE TH...OMIGOSH! IT BENT!!
WHAT WAS THAT?
THAT WAS A MEAN STUNT TO PULL AFTER WHAT I'VE DONE FOR YOU! I'M AFRAID THERE'S ONLY ONE THING LEFT FOR ME TO DO, AND THAT'S TO THROW A LITTLE FEAR AND HUMILITY INTO YOU!
CUT IT OUT!
MY RIBS!
OUCH!
LEGGO!

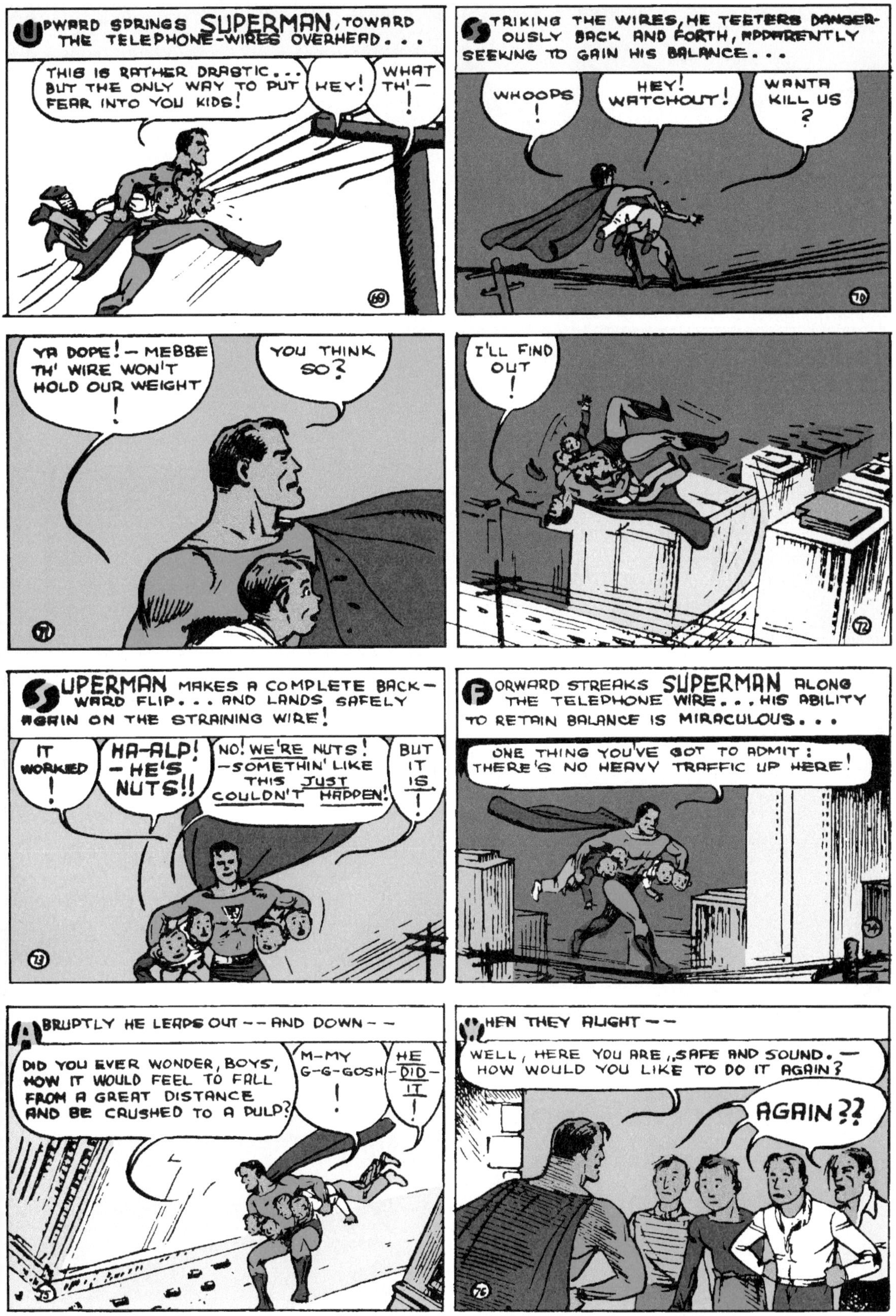
UPWARD SPRINGS SUPERMAN, TOWARD THE TELEPHONE-WIRES OVERHEAD...
THIS IS RATHER DRASTIC... BUT THE ONLY WAY TO PUT FEAR INTO YOU KIDS!
HEY!
WHAT TH'—!
STRIKING THE WIRES, HE TEETERS DANGEROUSLY BACK AND FORTH, APPARENTLY SEEKING TO GAIN HIS BALANCE...
WHOOPS!
HEY! WATCHOUT!
WANTA KILL US?
YA DOPE!—MEBBE TH' WIRE WON'T HOLD OUR WEIGHT!
YOU THINK SO?
I'LL FIND OUT!
SUPERMAN MAKES A COMPLETE BACK-WARD FLIP... AND LANDS SAFELY AGAIN ON THE STRAINING WIRE!
IT WORKED!
HA-ALP! —HE'S NUTS!!
NO! WE'RE NUTS! —SOMETHIN' LIKE THIS JUST COULDN'T HAPPEN!
BUT IT IS!
FORWARD STREAKS SUPERMAN ALONG THE TELEPHONE WIRE... HIS ABILITY TO RETAIN BALANCE IS MIRACULOUS...
ONE THING YOU'VE GOT TO ADMIT: THERE'S NO HEAVY TRAFFIC UP HERE!
ABRUPTLY HE LEAPS OUT -- AND DOWN --
DID YOU EVER WONDER, BOYS, HOW IT WOULD FEEL TO FALL FROM A GREAT DISTANCE AND BE CRUSHED TO A PULP?
M-MY G-G-GOSH!
HE DID IT!
WHEN THEY ALIGHT --
WELL, HERE YOU ARE, SAFE AND SOUND. —HOW WOULD YOU LIKE TO DO IT AGAIN?
AGAIN??

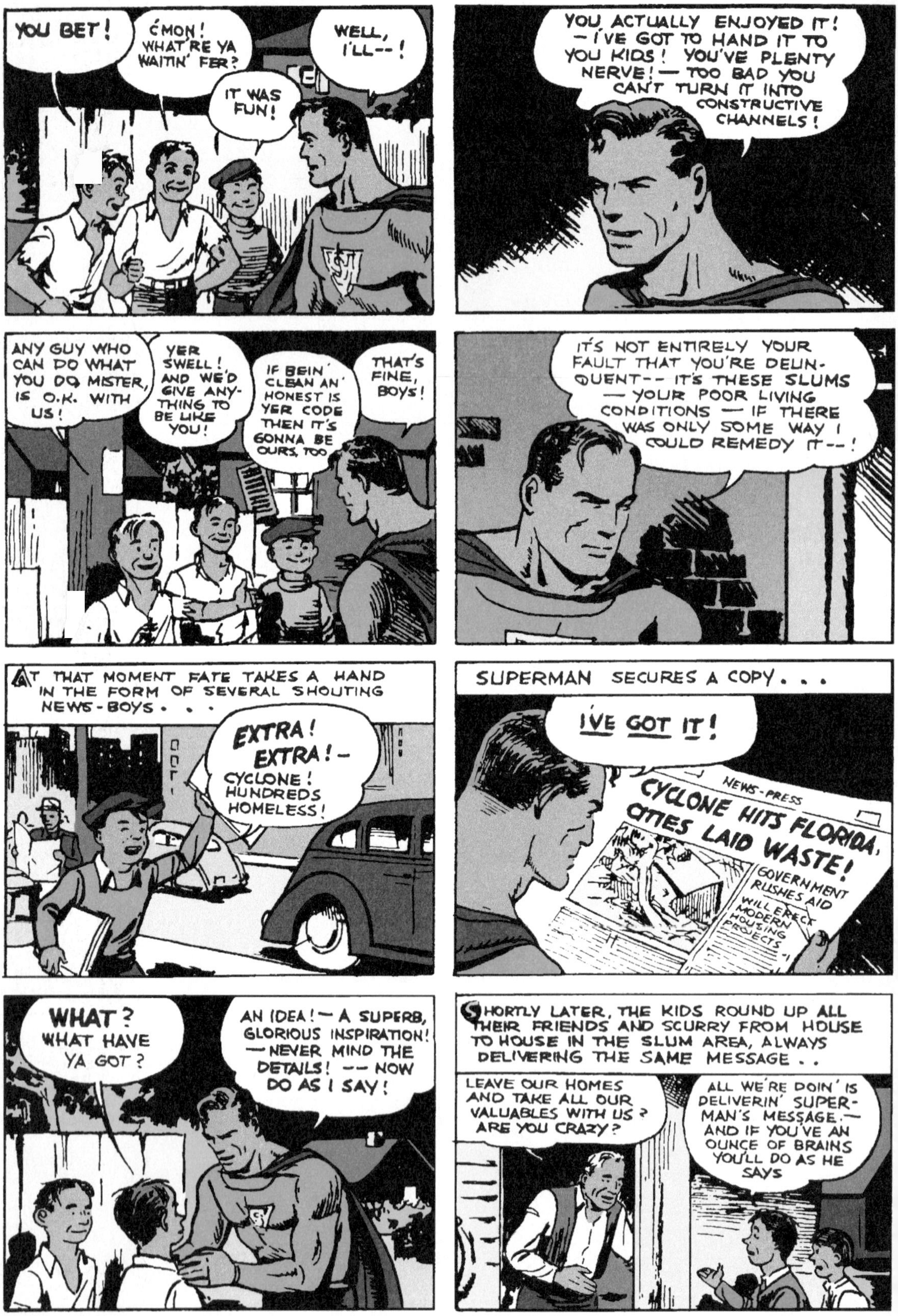
YOU BET!
C'MON! WHAT'RE YA WAITIN' FER?
IT WAS FUN!
WELL, I'LL--!
YOU ACTUALLY ENJOYED IT! —I'VE GOT TO HAND IT TO YOU KIDS! YOU'VE PLENTY NERVE!— TOO BAD YOU CAN'T TURN IT INTO CONSTRUCTIVE CHANNELS!
ANY GUY WHO CAN DO WHAT YOU DO MISTER, IS O.K. WITH US!
YER SWELL! AND WE'D GIVE ANYTHING TO BE LIKE YOU!
IF BEIN' CLEAN AN' HONEST IS YER CODE THEN IT'S GONNA BE OURS, TOO
THAT'S FINE, BOYS!
IT'S NOT ENTIRELY YOUR FAULT THAT YOU'RE DELINQUENT-- IT'S THESE SLUMS — YOUR POOR LIVING CONDITIONS — IF THERE WAS ONLY SOME WAY I COULD REMEDY IT--!
AT THAT MOMENT FATE TAKES A HAND IN THE FORM OF SEVERAL SHOUTING NEWS-BOYS . . .
EXTRA! EXTRA!— CYCLONE! HUNDREDS HOMELESS!
SUPERMAN SECURES A COPY . . .
I'VE GOT IT!
NEWS-PRESS
CYCLONE HITS FLORIDA, CITIES LAID WASTE!
GOVERNMENT RUSHES AID
WILL ERECT MODERN HOUSING PROJECTS
WHAT? WHAT HAVE YA GOT?
AN IDEA!— A SUPERB, GLORIOUS INSPIRATION! —NEVER MIND THE DETAILS! -- NOW DO AS I SAY!
SHORTLY LATER, THE KIDS ROUND UP ALL THEIR FRIENDS AND SCURRY FROM HOUSE TO HOUSE IN THE SLUM AREA, ALWAYS DELIVERING THE SAME MESSAGE . .
LEAVE OUR HOMES AND TAKE ALL OUR VALUABLES WITH US? ARE YOU CRAZY?
ALL WE'RE DOIN' IS DELIVERIN' SUPERMAN'S MESSAGE.— AND IF YOU'VE AN OUNCE OF BRAINS YOU'LL DO AS HE SAYS

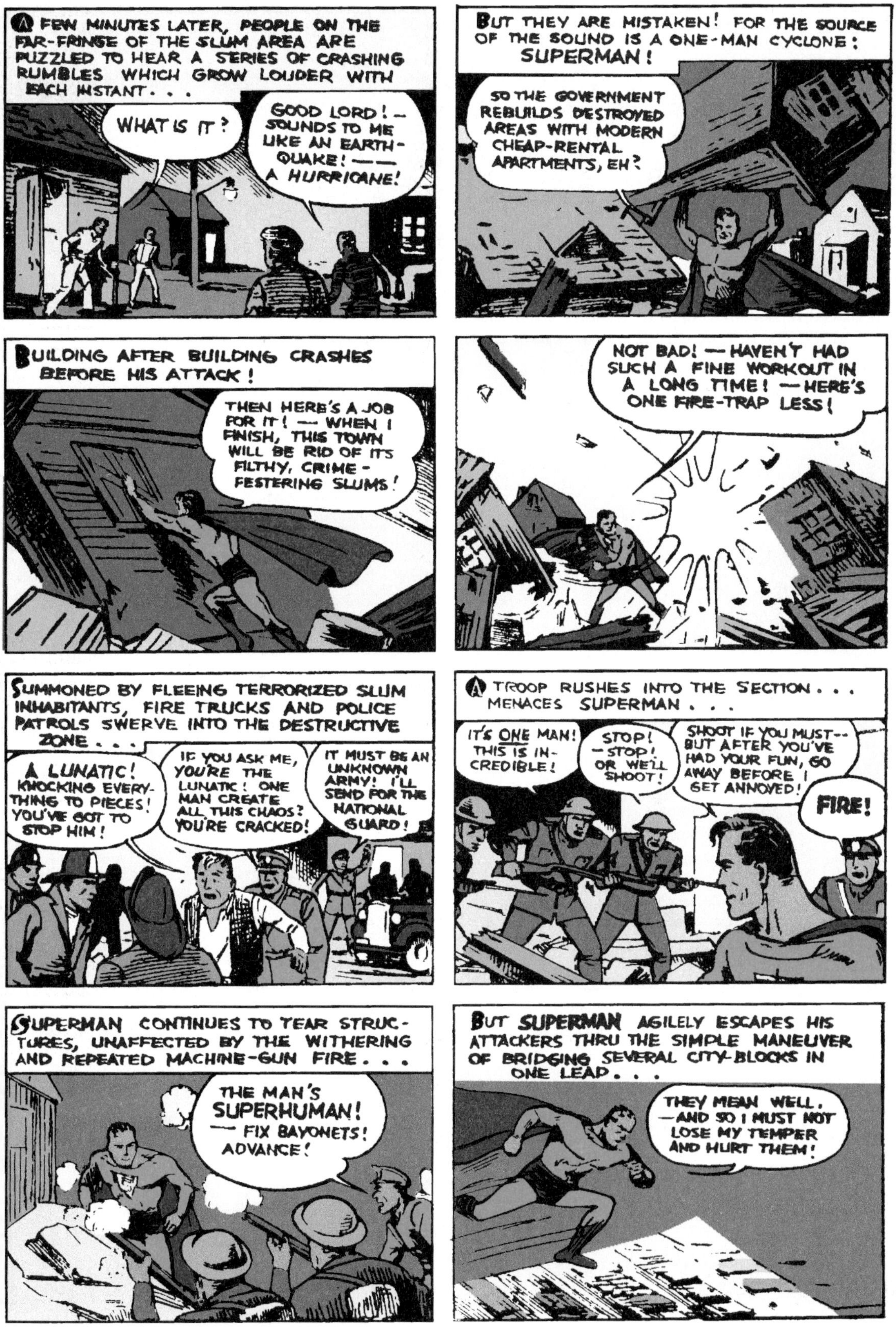
A FEW MINUTES LATER, PEOPLE ON THE FAR-FRINGE OF THE SLUM AREA ARE PUZZLED TO HEAR A SERIES OF CRASHING RUMBLES WHICH GROW LOUDER WITH EACH INSTANT. . .
WHAT IS IT?
GOOD LORD! — SOUNDS TO ME LIKE AN EARTH-QUAKE! —— A HURRICANE!
BUT THEY ARE MISTAKEN! FOR THE SOURCE OF THE SOUND IS A ONE-MAN CYCLONE: SUPERMAN!
SO THE GOVERNMENT REBUILDS DESTROYED AREAS WITH MODERN CHEAP-RENTAL APARTMENTS, EH?
BUILDING AFTER BUILDING CRASHES BEFORE HIS ATTACK!
THEN HERE'S A JOB FOR IT! — WHEN I FINISH, THIS TOWN WILL BE RID OF ITS FILTHY, CRIME-FESTERING SLUMS!
NOT BAD! — HAVEN'T HAD SUCH A FINE WORKOUT IN A LONG TIME! — HERE'S ONE FIRE-TRAP LESS!
SUMMONED BY FLEEING TERRORIZED SLUM INHABITANTS, FIRE TRUCKS AND POLICE PATROLS SWERVE INTO THE DESTRUCTIVE ZONE. . .
A LUNATIC! KNOCKING EVERY-THING TO PIECES! YOU'VE GOT TO STOP HIM!
IF YOU ASK ME, YOU'RE THE LUNATIC! ONE MAN CREATE ALL THIS CHAOS? YOU'RE CRACKED!
IT MUST BE AN UNKNOWN ARMY! I'LL SEND FOR THE NATIONAL GUARD!
A TROOP RUSHES INTO THE SECTION. . . MENACES SUPERMAN. . .
IT'S ONE MAN! THIS IS IN-CREDIBLE!
STOP! —STOP! OR WE'LL SHOOT!
SHOOT IF YOU MUST-- BUT AFTER YOU'VE HAD YOUR FUN, GO AWAY BEFORE I GET ANNOYED!
FIRE!
SUPERMAN CONTINUES TO TEAR STRUC-TURES, UNAFFECTED BY THE WITHERING AND REPEATED MACHINE-GUN FIRE. . .
THE MAN'S SUPERHUMAN! — FIX BAYONETS! ADVANCE!
BUT SUPERMAN AGILELY ESCAPES HIS ATTACKERS THRU THE SIMPLE MANEUVER OF BRIDGING SEVERAL CITY-BLOCKS IN ONE LEAP. . .
THEY MEAN WELL. —AND SO I MUST NOT LOSE MY TEMPER AND HURT THEM!

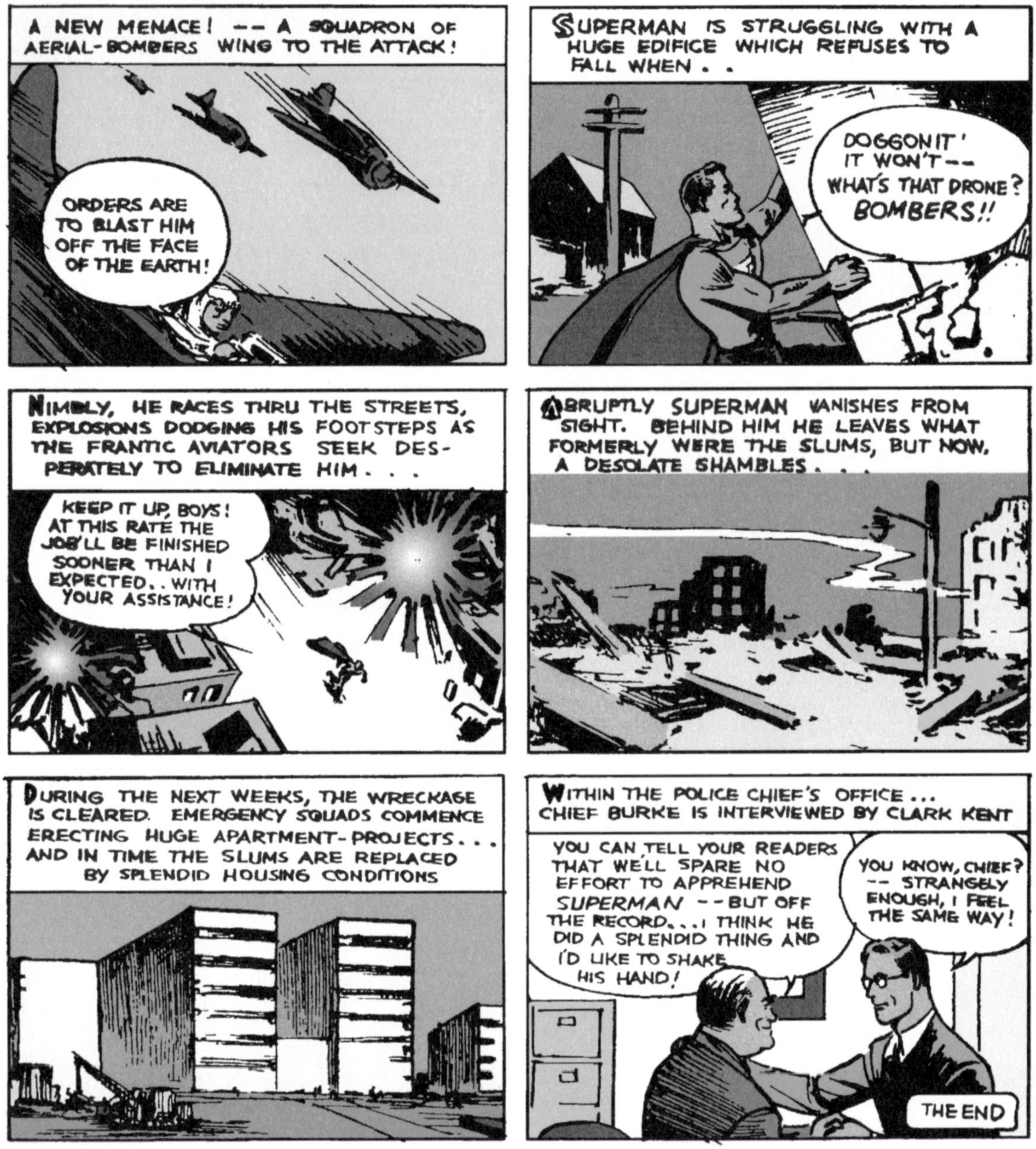
A NEW MENACE! -- A SQUADRON OF AERIAL-BOMBERS WING TO THE ATTACK!
ORDERS ARE TO BLAST HIM OFF THE FACE OF THE EARTH!
SUPERMAN IS STRUGGLING WITH A HUGE EDIFICE WHICH REFUSES TO FALL WHEN . .
DOGGONIT' IT WON'T -- WHAT'S THAT DRONE? BOMBERS!!
NIMBLY, HE RACES THRU THE STREETS, EXPLOSIONS DODGING HIS FOOTSTEPS AS THE FRANTIC AVIATORS SEEK DESPERATELY TO ELIMINATE HIM . . .
KEEP IT UP, BOYS! AT THIS RATE THE JOB'LL BE FINISHED SOONER THAN I EXPECTED.. WITH YOUR ASSISTANCE!
ABRUPTLY SUPERMAN VANISHES FROM SIGHT. BEHIND HIM HE LEAVES WHAT FORMERLY WERE THE SLUMS, BUT NOW, A DESOLATE SHAMBLES . . .
DURING THE NEXT WEEKS, THE WRECKAGE IS CLEARED. EMERGENCY SQUADS COMMENCE ERECTING HUGE APARTMENT-PROJECTS . . . AND IN TIME THE SLUMS ARE REPLACED BY SPLENDID HOUSING CONDITIONS
WITHIN THE POLICE CHIEF'S OFFICE ... CHIEF BURKE IS INTERVIEWED BY CLARK KENT
YOU CAN TELL YOUR READERS THAT WE'LL SPARE NO EFFORT TO APPREHEND SUPERMAN -- BUT OFF THE RECORD... I THINK HE DID A SPLENDID THING AND I'D LIKE TO SHAKE HIS HAND!
YOU KNOW, CHIEF? -- STRANGELY ENOUGH, I FEEL THE SAME WAY!
THE END

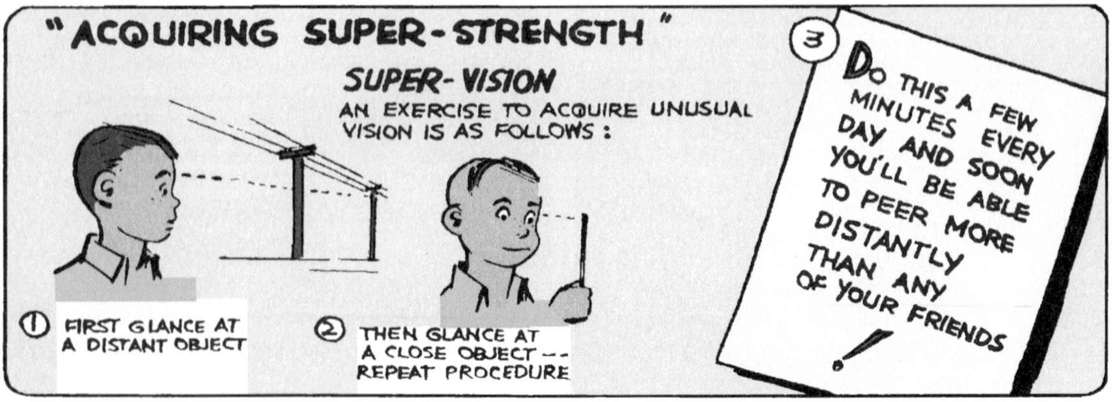
"ACQUIRING SUPER-STRENGTH"
SUPER-VISION
AN EXERCISE TO ACQUIRE UNUSUAL VISION IS AS FOLLOWS:
① FIRST GLANCE AT A DISTANT OBJECT
② THEN GLANCE AT A CLOSE OBJECT -- REPEAT PROCEDURE
③ DO THIS A FEW MINUTES EVERY DAY AND SOON YOU'LL BE ABLE TO PEER MORE DISTANTLY THAN ANY OF YOUR FRIENDS!

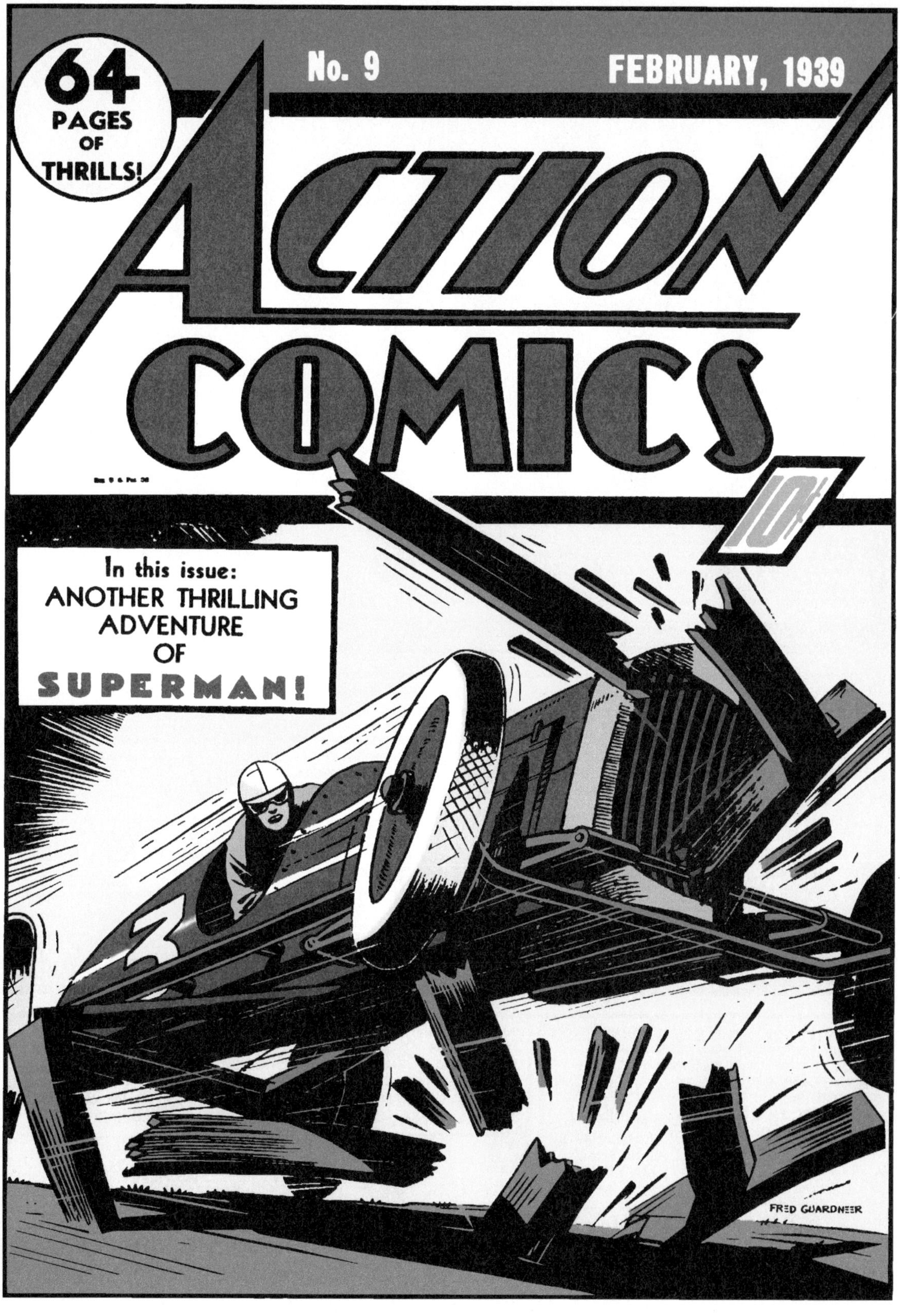
64 PAGES OF THRILLS!
No. 9
FEBRUARY, 1939
ACTION COMICS
10¢
In this issue:
ANOTHER THRILLING
ADVENTURE
OF
SUPERMAN!
FRED GUARDNEER

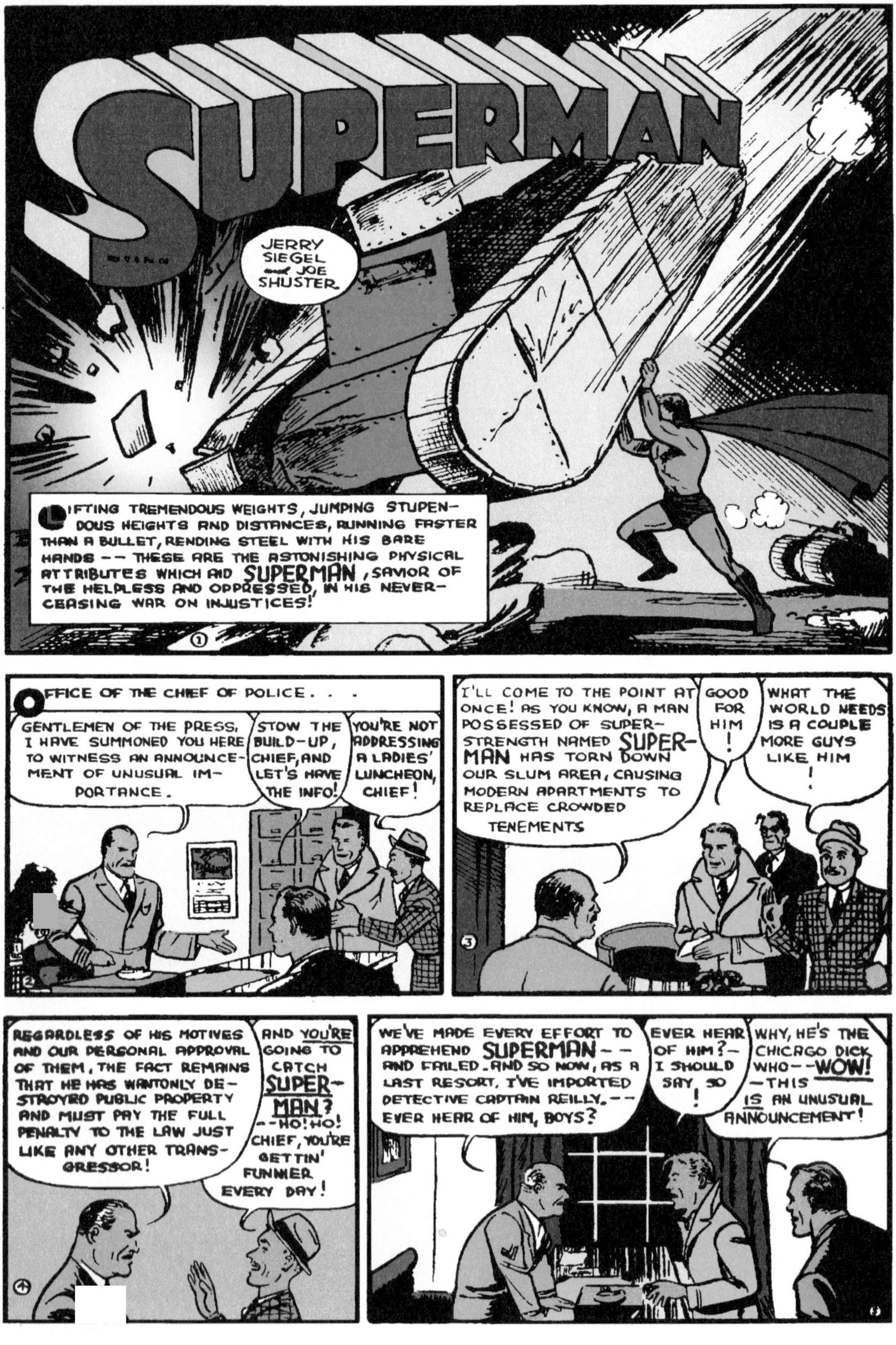
SUPERMAN
JERRY SIEGEL and JOE SHUSTER
LIFTING TREMENDOUS WEIGHTS, JUMPING STUPENDOUS HEIGHTS AND DISTANCES, RUNNING FASTER THAN A BULLET, RENDING STEEL WITH HIS BARE HANDS -- THESE ARE THE ASTONISHING PHYSICAL ATTRIBUTES WHICH AID SUPERMAN, SAVIOR OF THE HELPLESS AND OPPRESSED, IN HIS NEVER-CEASING WAR ON INJUSTICES!
OFFICE OF THE CHIEF OF POLICE . . .
GENTLEMEN OF THE PRESS, I HAVE SUMMONED YOU HERE TO WITNESS AN ANNOUNCEMENT OF UNUSUAL IMPORTANCE.
STOW THE BUILD-UP, CHIEF, AND LET'S HAVE THE INFO!
YOU'RE NOT ADDRESSING A LADIES' LUNCHEON, CHIEF!
I'LL COME TO THE POINT AT ONCE! AS YOU KNOW, A MAN POSSESSED OF SUPER-STRENGTH NAMED SUPERMAN HAS TORN DOWN OUR SLUM AREA, CAUSING MODERN APARTMENTS TO REPLACE CROWDED TENEMENTS
GOOD FOR HIM!
WHAT THE WORLD NEEDS IS A COUPLE MORE GUYS LIKE HIM!
REGARDLESS OF HIS MOTIVES AND OUR PERSONAL APPROVAL OF THEM, THE FACT REMAINS THAT HE HAS WANTONLY DESTROYED PUBLIC PROPERTY AND MUST PAY THE FULL PENALTY TO THE LAW JUST LIKE ANY OTHER TRANSGRESSOR!
AND YOU'RE GOING TO CATCH SUPERMAN? --HO! HO! CHIEF, YOU'RE GETTIN' FUNNIER EVERY DAY!
WE'VE MADE EVERY EFFORT TO APPREHEND SUPERMAN-- AND FAILED. AND SO NOW, AS A LAST RESORT, I'VE IMPORTED DETECTIVE CAPTAIN REILLY.-- EVER HEAR OF HIM, BOYS?
EVER HEAR OF HIM?-- I SHOULD SAY SO!
WHY, HE'S THE CHICAGO DICK WHO--WOW! --THIS IS AN UNUSUAL ANNOUNCEMENT!

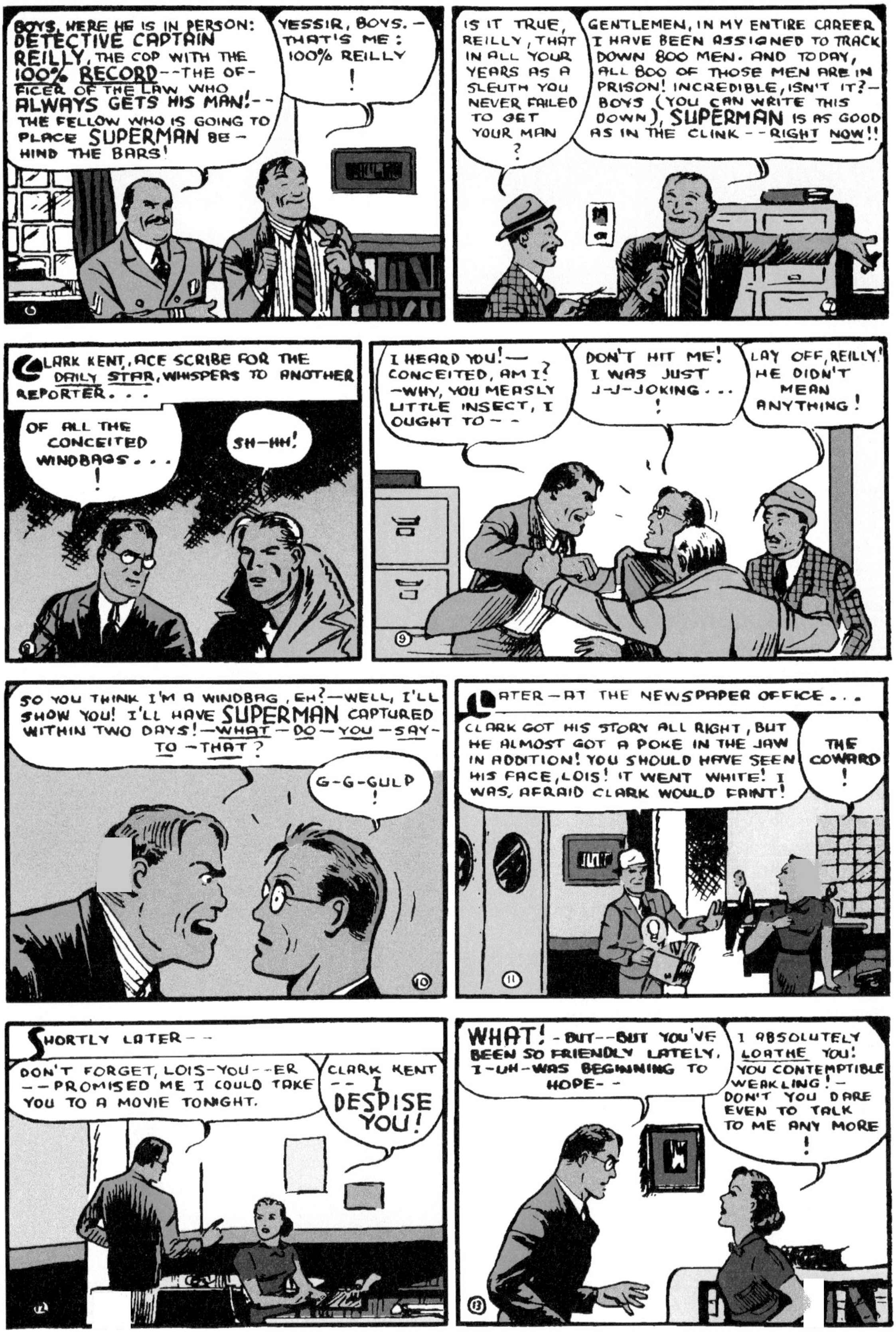
BOYS, HERE HE IS IN PERSON: DETECTIVE CAPTAIN REILLY, THE COP WITH THE 100% RECORD--THE OFFICER OF THE LAW WHO ALWAYS GETS HIS MAN!--THE FELLOW WHO IS GOING TO PLACE SUPERMAN BEHIND THE BARS!
YESSIR, BOYS.—THAT'S ME: 100% REILLY!
IS IT TRUE, REILLY, THAT IN ALL YOUR YEARS AS A SLEUTH YOU NEVER FAILED TO GET YOUR MAN?
GENTLEMEN, IN MY ENTIRE CAREER I HAVE BEEN ASSIGNED TO TRACK DOWN 800 MEN. AND TODAY, ALL 800 OF THOSE MEN ARE IN PRISON! INCREDIBLE, ISN'T IT?—BOYS (YOU CAN WRITE THIS DOWN), SUPERMAN IS AS GOOD AS IN THE CLINK--RIGHT NOW!!
CLARK KENT, ACE SCRIBE FOR THE DAILY STAR, WHISPERS TO ANOTHER REPORTER...
OF ALL THE CONCEITED WINDBAGS...!
SH-HH!
I HEARD YOU!—CONCEITED, AM I? —WHY, YOU MEASLY LITTLE INSECT, I OUGHT TO--
DON'T HIT ME! I WAS JUST J-J-JOKING...!
LAY OFF, REILLY! HE DIDN'T MEAN ANYTHING!
SO YOU THINK I'M A WINDBAG, EH?—WELL, I'LL SHOW YOU! I'LL HAVE SUPERMAN CAPTURED WITHIN TWO DAYS!—WHAT—DO—YOU—SAY—TO—THAT?
G-G-GULP!
LATER—AT THE NEWSPAPER OFFICE...
CLARK GOT HIS STORY ALL RIGHT, BUT HE ALMOST GOT A POKE IN THE JAW IN ADDITION! YOU SHOULD HAVE SEEN HIS FACE, LOIS! IT WENT WHITE! I WAS AFRAID CLARK WOULD FAINT!
THE COWARD!
SHORTLY LATER--
DON'T FORGET, LOIS-YOU--ER--PROMISED ME I COULD TAKE YOU TO A MOVIE TONIGHT.
CLARK KENT--I DESPISE YOU!
WHAT!-BUT--BUT YOU'VE BEEN SO FRIENDLY LATELY. I-UH-WAS BEGINNING TO HOPE--
I ABSOLUTELY LOATHE YOU! YOU CONTEMPTIBLE WEAKLING!—DON'T YOU DARE EVEN TO TALK TO ME ANY MORE!

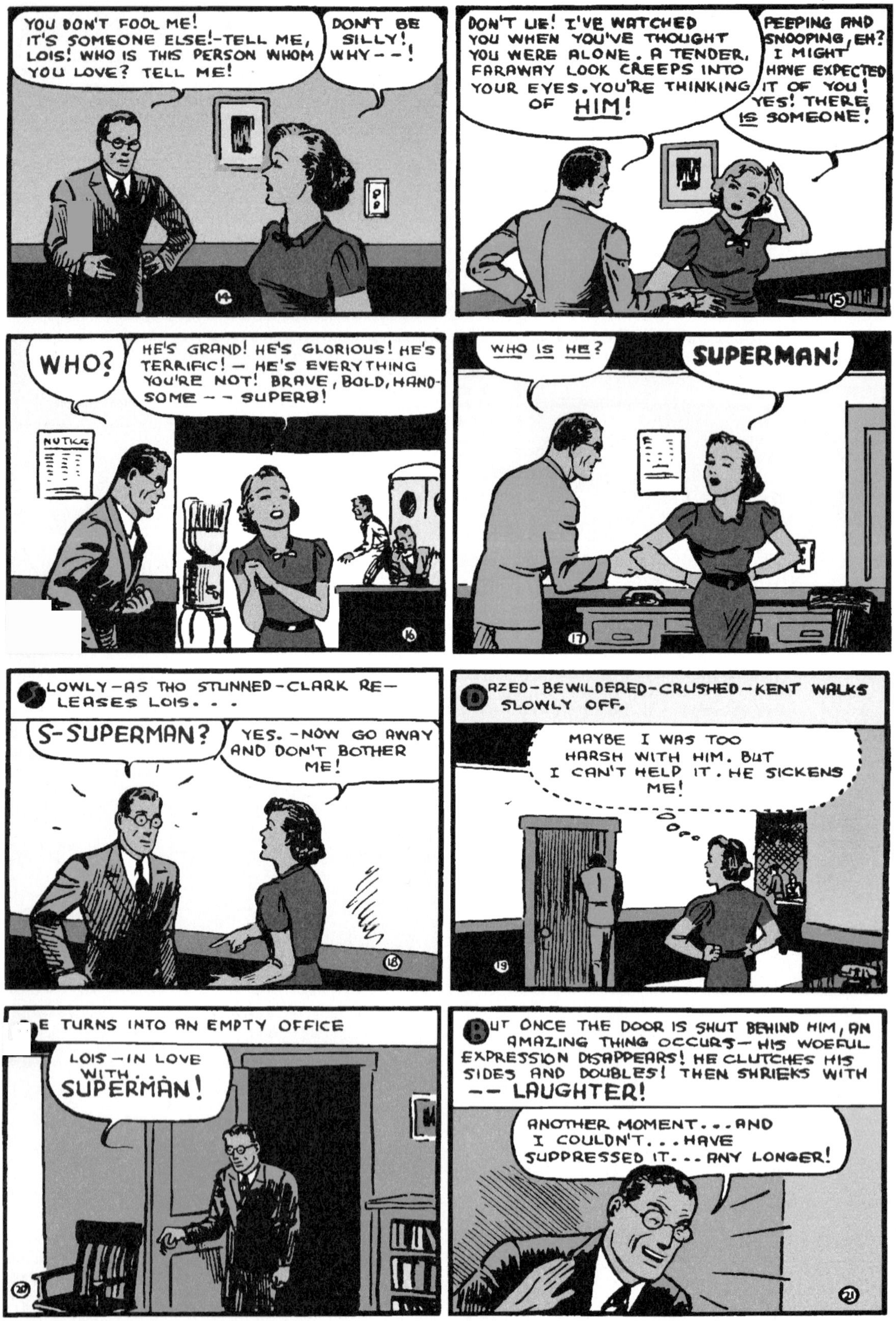
YOU DON'T FOOL ME! IT'S SOMEONE ELSE!-TELL ME, LOIS! WHO IS THIS PERSON WHOM YOU LOVE? TELL ME!
DON'T BE SILLY! WHY--!
DON'T LIE! I'VE WATCHED YOU WHEN YOU'VE THOUGHT YOU WERE ALONE. A TENDER, FARAWAY LOOK CREEPS INTO YOUR EYES. YOU'RE THINKING OF HIM!
PEEPING AND SNOOPING, EH? I MIGHT HAVE EXPECTED IT OF YOU! YES! THERE IS SOMEONE!
WHO?
HE'S GRAND! HE'S GLORIOUS! HE'S TERRIFIC! — HE'S EVERYTHING YOU'RE NOT! BRAVE, BOLD, HANDSOME -- SUPERB!
NOTICE
WHO IS HE?
SUPERMAN!
SLOWLY-AS THO STUNNED-CLARK RELEASES LOIS...
S-SUPERMAN?
YES. -NOW GO AWAY AND DON'T BOTHER ME!
DAZED-BEWILDERED-CRUSHED-KENT WALKS SLOWLY OFF.
MAYBE I WAS TOO HARSH WITH HIM. BUT I CAN'T HELP IT. HE SICKENS ME!
HE TURNS INTO AN EMPTY OFFICE
LOIS-IN LOVE WITH... SUPERMAN!
BUT ONCE THE DOOR IS SHUT BEHIND HIM, AN AMAZING THING OCCURS-HIS WOEFUL EXPRESSION DISAPPEARS! HE CLUTCHES HIS SIDES AND DOUBLES! THEN SHRIEKS WITH -- LAUGHTER!
ANOTHER MOMENT...AND I COULDN'T...HAVE SUPPRESSED IT...ANY LONGER!

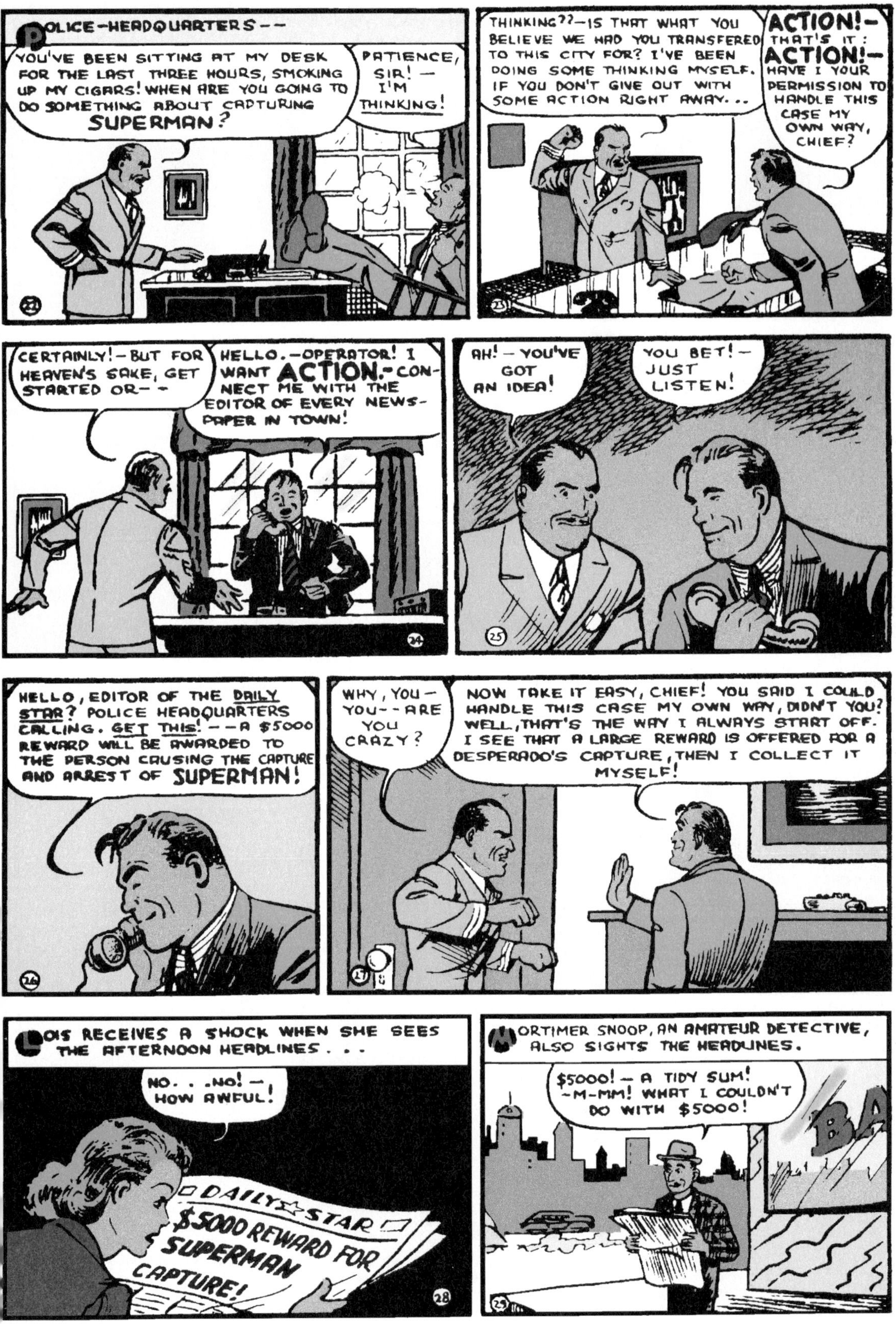
POLICE-HEADQUARTERS--
YOU'VE BEEN SITTING AT MY DESK FOR THE LAST THREE HOURS, SMOKING UP MY CIGARS! WHEN ARE YOU GOING TO DO SOMETHING ABOUT CAPTURING SUPERMAN?
PATIENCE, SIR! — I'M THINKING!
THINKING??—IS THAT WHAT YOU BELIEVE WE HAD YOU TRANSFERED TO THIS CITY FOR? I'VE BEEN DOING SOME THINKING MYSELF. IF YOU DON'T GIVE OUT WITH SOME ACTION RIGHT AWAY...
ACTION!— THAT'S IT: ACTION!— HAVE I YOUR PERMISSION TO HANDLE THIS CASE MY OWN WAY, CHIEF?
CERTAINLY!—BUT FOR HEAVEN'S SAKE, GET STARTED OR--
HELLO.—OPERATOR! I WANT ACTION.—CONNECT ME WITH THE EDITOR OF EVERY NEWSPAPER IN TOWN!
AH!—YOU'VE GOT AN IDEA!
YOU BET!— JUST LISTEN!
HELLO, EDITOR OF THE DAILY STAR? POLICE HEADQUARTERS CALLING. GET THIS!--A $5000 REWARD WILL BE AWARDED TO THE PERSON CAUSING THE CAPTURE AND ARREST OF SUPERMAN!
WHY, YOU— YOU--ARE YOU CRAZY?
NOW TAKE IT EASY, CHIEF! YOU SAID I COULD HANDLE THIS CASE MY OWN WAY, DIDN'T YOU? WELL, THAT'S THE WAY I ALWAYS START OFF. I SEE THAT A LARGE REWARD IS OFFERED FOR A DESPERADO'S CAPTURE, THEN I COLLECT IT MYSELF!
LOIS RECEIVES A SHOCK WHEN SHE SEES THE AFTERNOON HEADLINES...
NO..NO!— HOW AWFUL!
DAILY STAR
$5000 REWARD FOR SUPERMAN CAPTURE!
MORTIMER SNOOP, AN AMATEUR DETECTIVE, ALSO SIGHTS THE HEADLINES.
$5000!—A TIDY SUM! -M-MM! WHAT I COULDN'T DO WITH $5000!

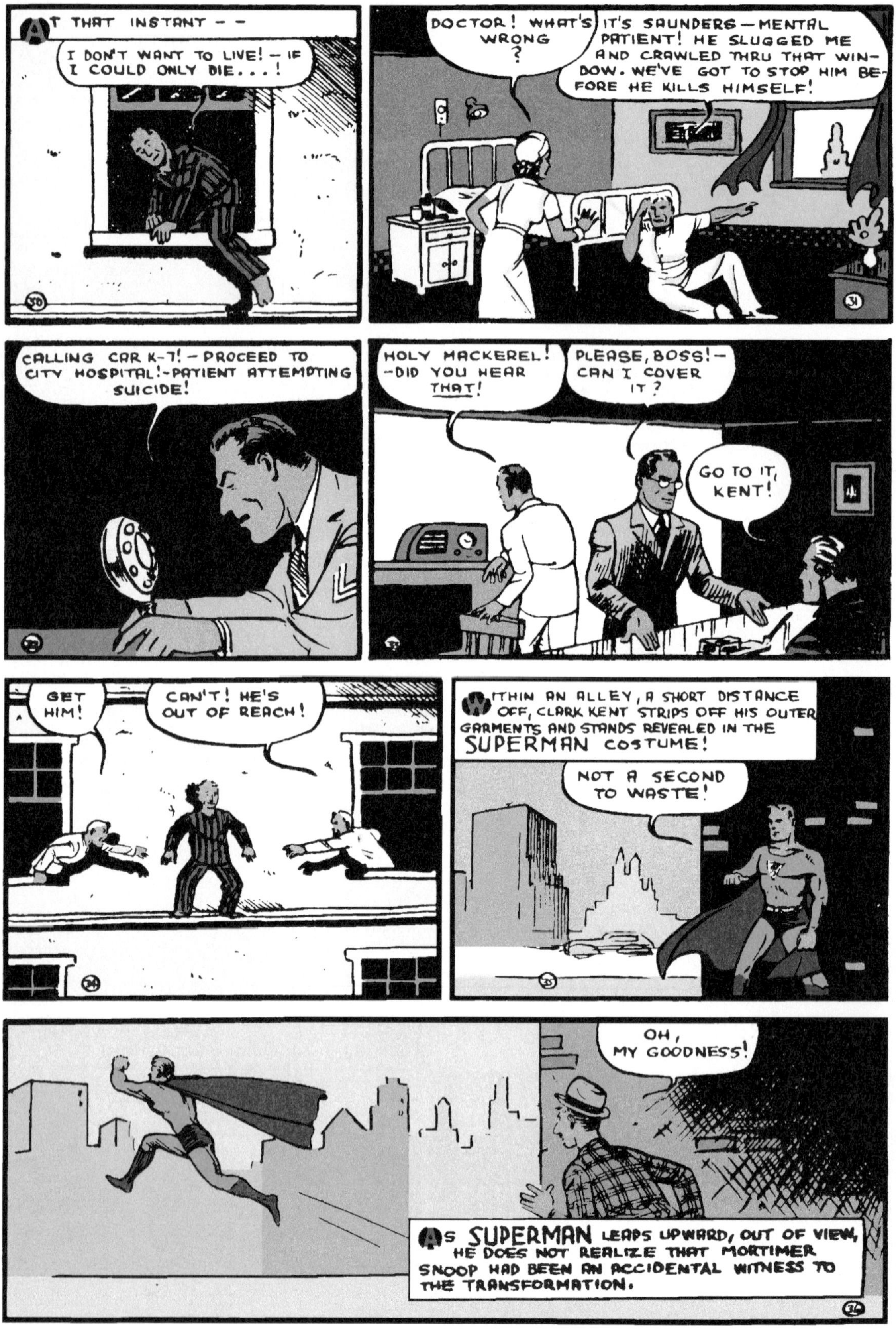
AT THAT INSTANT - -
I DON'T WANT TO LIVE! — IF I COULD ONLY DIE. . . !
DOCTOR! WHAT'S WRONG ?
IT'S SAUNDERS — MENTAL PATIENT! HE SLUGGED ME AND CRAWLED THRU THAT WINDOW. WE'VE GOT TO STOP HIM BEFORE HE KILLS HIMSELF!
CALLING CAR K-7! — PROCEED TO CITY HOSPITAL! - PATIENT ATTEMPTING SUICIDE!
HOLY MACKEREL! - DID YOU HEAR THAT!
PLEASE, BOSS! — CAN I COVER IT ?
GO TO IT, KENT!
GET HIM!
CAN'T! HE'S OUT OF REACH!
WITHIN AN ALLEY, A SHORT DISTANCE OFF, CLARK KENT STRIPS OFF HIS OUTER GARMENTS AND STANDS REVEALED IN THE SUPERMAN COSTUME!
NOT A SECOND TO WASTE!
OH, MY GOODNESS!
AS SUPERMAN LEAPS UPWARD, OUT OF VIEW, HE DOES NOT REALIZE THAT MORTIMER SNOOP HAD BEEN AN ACCIDENTAL WITNESS TO THE TRANSFORMATION.

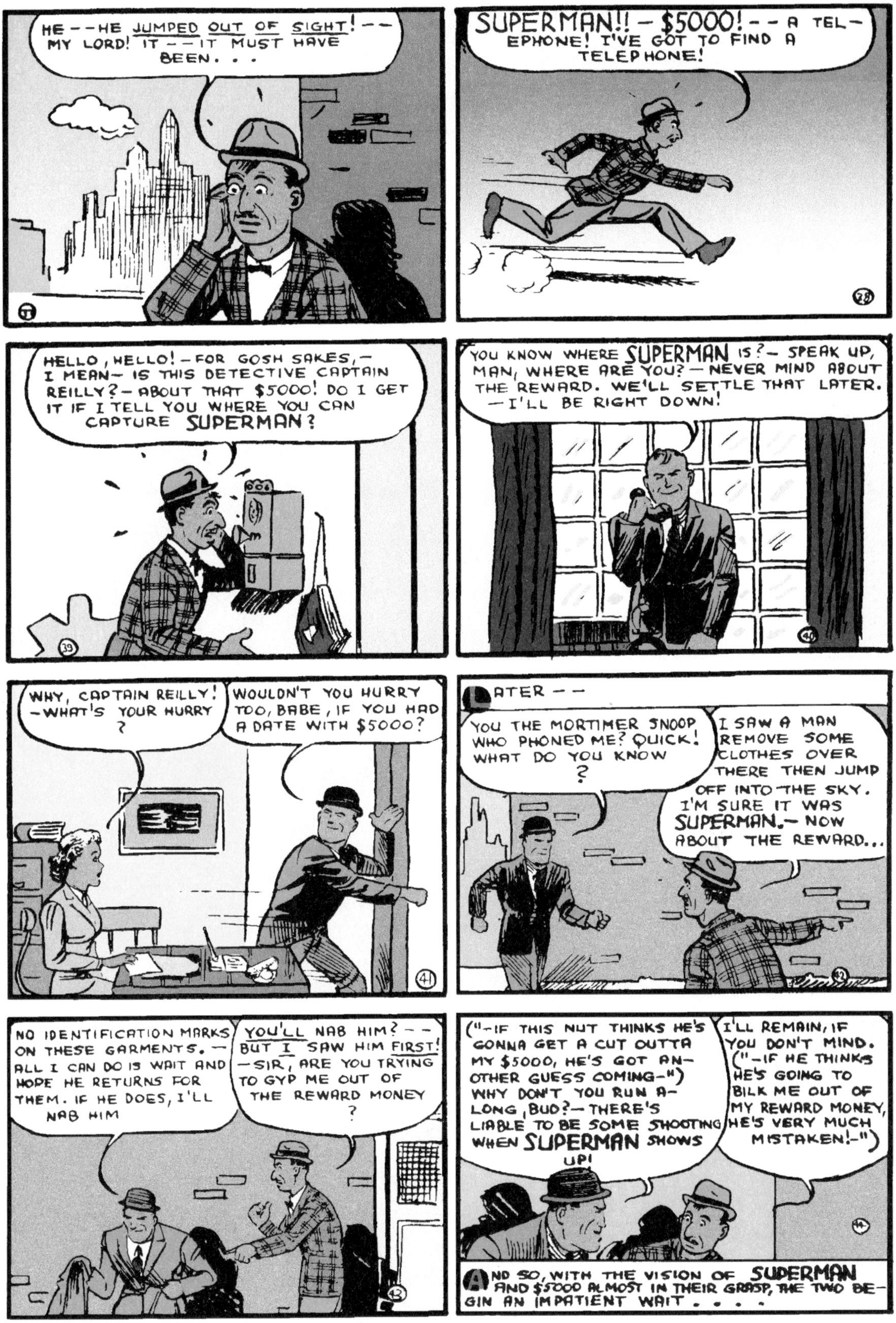
HE--HE JUMPED OUT OF SIGHT!-- MY LORD! IT--IT MUST HAVE BEEN. . .
SUPERMAN!! - $5000! -- A TELEPHONE! I'VE GOT TO FIND A TELEPHONE!
HELLO, HELLO! - FOR GOSH SAKES, - I MEAN - IS THIS DETECTIVE CAPTAIN REILLY? - ABOUT THAT $5000! DO I GET IT IF I TELL YOU WHERE YOU CAN CAPTURE SUPERMAN?
YOU KNOW WHERE SUPERMAN IS? - SPEAK UP, MAN, WHERE ARE YOU? - NEVER MIND ABOUT THE REWARD. WE'LL SETTLE THAT LATER. - I'LL BE RIGHT DOWN!
WHY, CAPTAIN REILLY! - WHAT'S YOUR HURRY?
WOULDN'T YOU HURRY TOO, BABE, IF YOU HAD A DATE WITH $5000?
LATER --
YOU THE MORTIMER SNOOP WHO PHONED ME? QUICK! WHAT DO YOU KNOW?
I SAW A MAN REMOVE SOME CLOTHES OVER THERE THEN JUMP OFF INTO THE SKY. I'M SURE IT WAS SUPERMAN. - NOW ABOUT THE REWARD...
NO IDENTIFICATION MARKS ON THESE GARMENTS. - ALL I CAN DO IS WAIT AND HOPE HE RETURNS FOR THEM. IF HE DOES, I'LL NAB HIM
YOU'LL NAB HIM? -- BUT I SAW HIM FIRST! - SIR, ARE YOU TRYING TO GYP ME OUT OF THE REWARD MONEY?
("-IF THIS NUT THINKS HE'S GONNA GET A CUT OUTTA MY $5000, HE'S GOT ANOTHER GUESS COMING-") WHY DON'T YOU RUN ALONG, BUD? - THERE'S LIABLE TO BE SOME SHOOTING WHEN SUPERMAN SHOWS UP!
I'LL REMAIN, IF YOU DON'T MIND. ("-IF HE THINKS HE'S GOING TO BILK ME OUT OF MY REWARD MONEY, HE'S VERY MUCH MISTAKEN!-")
AND SO, WITH THE VISION OF SUPERMAN AND $5000 ALMOST IN THEIR GRASP, THE TWO BEGIN AN IMPATIENT WAIT . . .

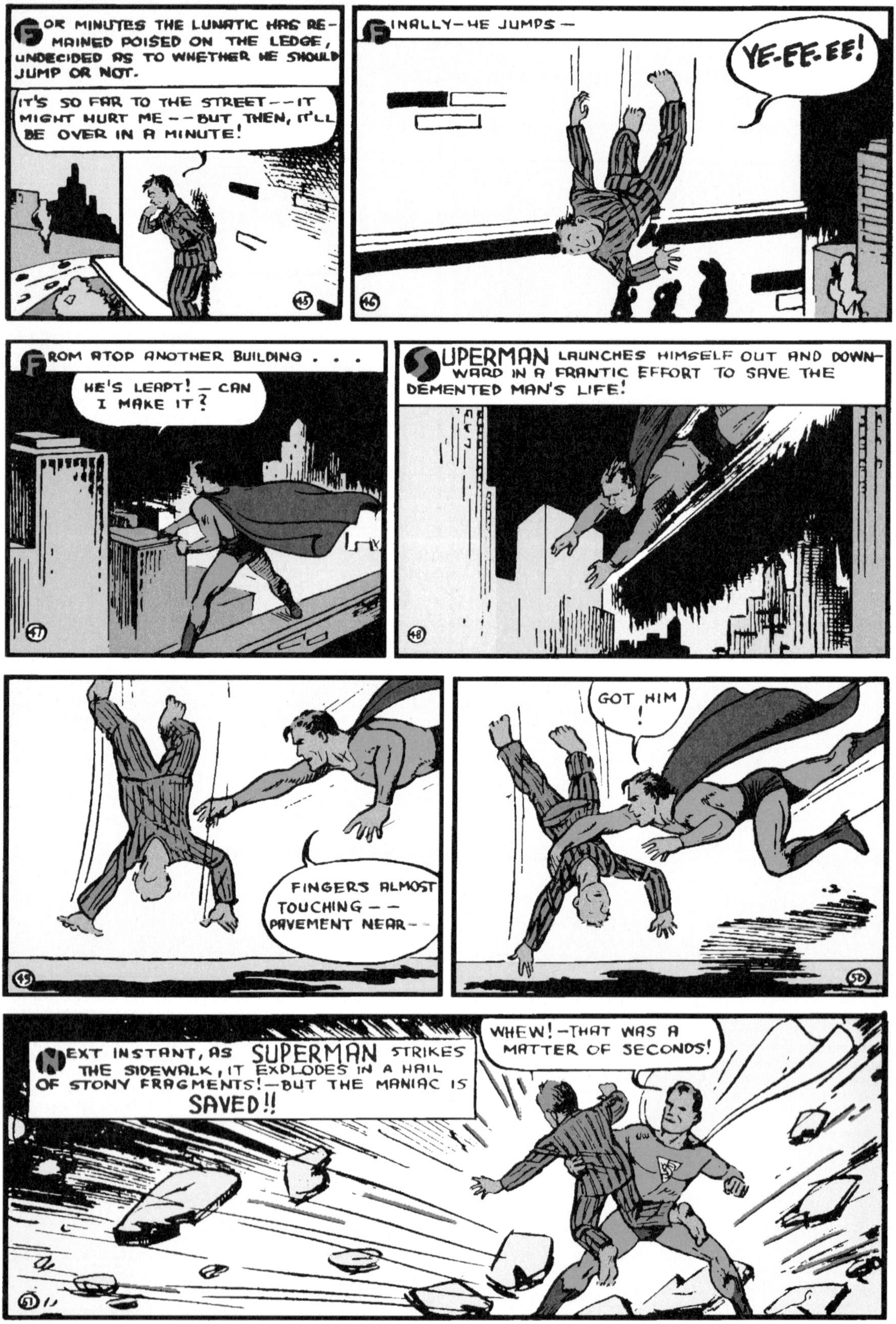
FOR MINUTES THE LUNATIC HAS RE-MAINED POISED ON THE LEDGE, UNDECIDED AS TO WHETHER HE SHOULD JUMP OR NOT.
IT'S SO FAR TO THE STREET--IT MIGHT HURT ME--BUT THEN, IT'LL BE OVER IN A MINUTE!
FINALLY—HE JUMPS—
YE-EE-EE!
FROM ATOP ANOTHER BUILDING . . .
HE'S LEAPT! — CAN I MAKE IT?
SUPERMAN LAUNCHES HIMSELF OUT AND DOWN-WARD IN A FRANTIC EFFORT TO SAVE THE DEMENTED MAN'S LIFE!
FINGERS ALMOST TOUCHING-- PAVEMENT NEAR--
GOT HIM!
NEXT INSTANT, AS SUPERMAN STRIKES THE SIDEWALK, IT EXPLODES IN A HAIL OF STONY FRAGMENTS!—BUT THE MANIAC IS SAVED!!
WHEW!—THAT WAS A MATTER OF SECONDS!

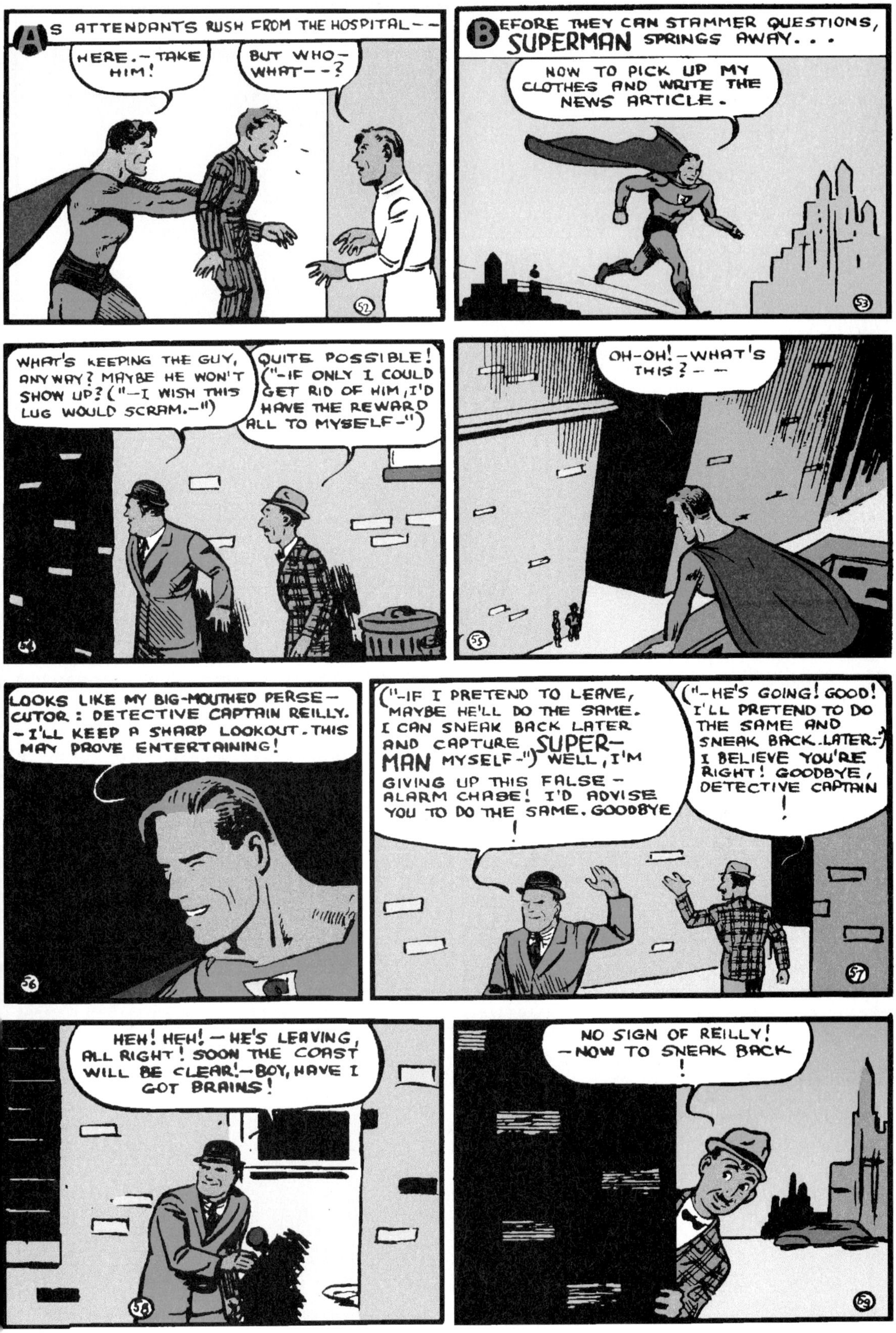
AS ATTENDANTS RUSH FROM THE HOSPITAL--
HERE.-TAKE HIM!
BUT WHO-WHAT--?
BEFORE THEY CAN STAMMER QUESTIONS, SUPERMAN SPRINGS AWAY...
NOW TO PICK UP MY CLOTHES AND WRITE THE NEWS ARTICLE.
WHAT'S KEEPING THE GUY, ANYWAY? MAYBE HE WON'T SHOW UP? ("-I WISH THIS LUG WOULD SCRAM.-")
QUITE POSSIBLE! ("-IF ONLY I COULD GET RID OF HIM, I'D HAVE THE REWARD ALL TO MYSELF-")
OH-OH!-WHAT'S THIS?--
LOOKS LIKE MY BIG-MOUTHED PERSE-CUTOR: DETECTIVE CAPTAIN REILLY. -I'LL KEEP A SHARP LOOKOUT. THIS MAY PROVE ENTERTAINING!
("-IF I PRETEND TO LEAVE, MAYBE HE'LL DO THE SAME. I CAN SNEAK BACK LATER AND CAPTURE SUPERMAN MYSELF-") WELL, I'M GIVING UP THIS FALSE-ALARM CHASE! I'D ADVISE YOU TO DO THE SAME. GOODBYE!
("-HE'S GOING! GOOD! I'LL PRETEND TO DO THE SAME AND SNEAK BACK LATER-") I BELIEVE YOU'RE RIGHT! GOODBYE, DETECTIVE CAPTAIN!
HEH! HEH!-HE'S LEAVING, ALL RIGHT! SOON THE COAST WILL BE CLEAR!-BOY, HAVE I GOT BRAINS!
NO SIGN OF REILLY! -NOW TO SNEAK BACK!

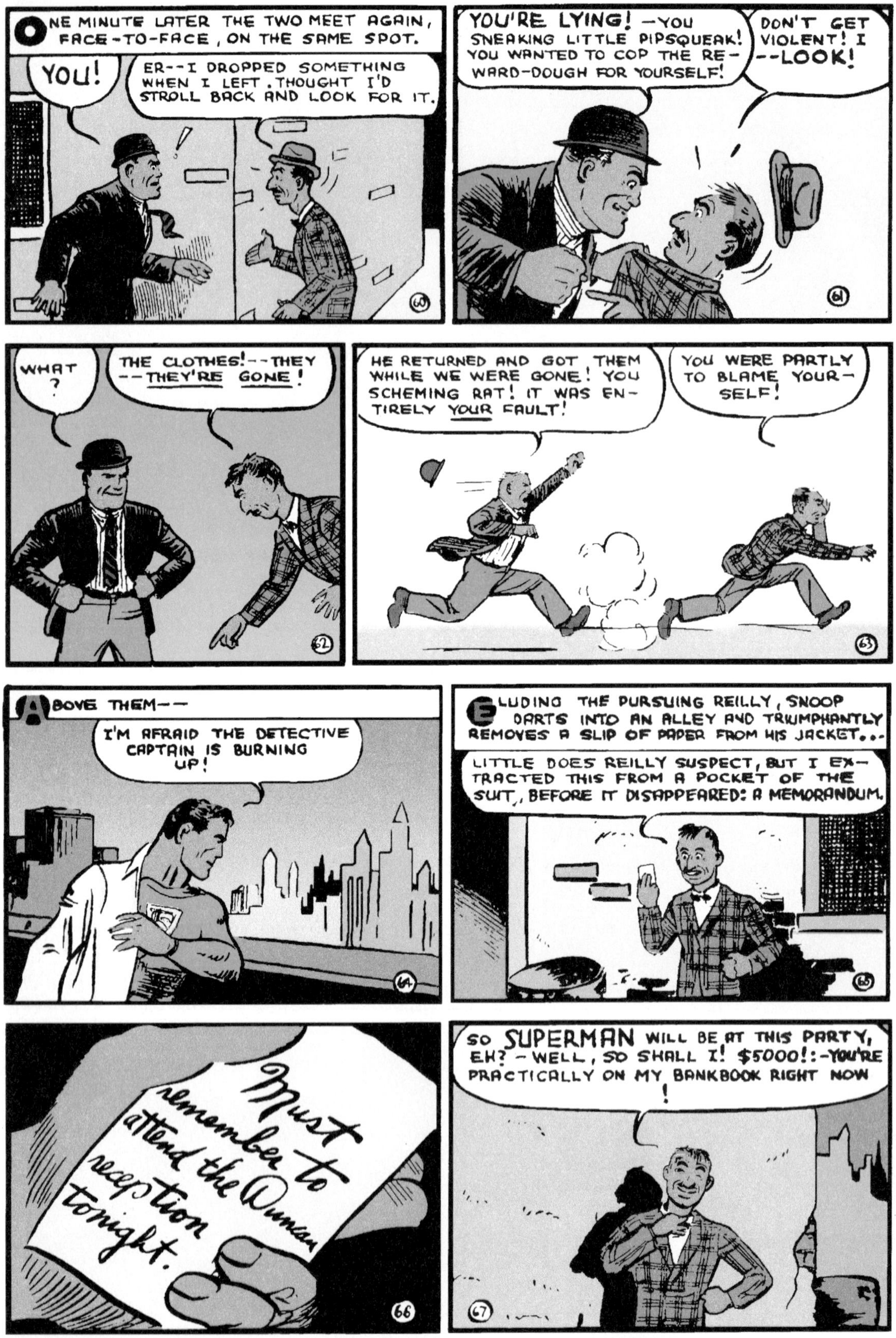
ONE MINUTE LATER THE TWO MEET AGAIN, FACE-TO-FACE, ON THE SAME SPOT.
YOU!
ER--I DROPPED SOMETHING WHEN I LEFT. THOUGHT I'D STROLL BACK AND LOOK FOR IT.
!
YOU'RE LYING! --YOU SNEAKING LITTLE PIPSQUEAK! YOU WANTED TO COP THE REWARD-DOUGH FOR YOURSELF!
DON'T GET VIOLENT! I --LOOK!
WHAT ?
THE CLOTHES!--THEY --THEY'RE GONE!
HE RETURNED AND GOT THEM WHILE WE WERE GONE! YOU SCHEMING RAT! IT WAS ENTIRELY YOUR FAULT!
YOU WERE PARTLY TO BLAME YOURSELF!
ABOVE THEM--
I'M AFRAID THE DETECTIVE CAPTAIN IS BURNING UP!
ELUDING THE PURSUING REILLY, SNOOP DARTS INTO AN ALLEY AND TRIUMPHANTLY REMOVES A SLIP OF PAPER FROM HIS JACKET...
LITTLE DOES REILLY SUSPECT, BUT I EXTRACTED THIS FROM A POCKET OF THE SUIT, BEFORE IT DISAPPEARED: A MEMORANDUM.
Must remember to attend the Dunsan reception tonight.
SO SUPERMAN WILL BE AT THIS PARTY, EH? --WELL, SO SHALL I! $5000!:--YOU'RE PRACTICALLY ON MY BANKBOOK RIGHT NOW!

THAT EVENING, SNOOP PRESENTS HIMSELF AT THE DUNCAN HOME, BUT RECEIVES AN UNEXPECTED REBUFF...

BUT, I TELL YOU! IT'S IMPORTANT I ENTER!

SORRY, SIR! NO ONE CAN ENTER WITH-OUT AN INVITATION!

I CAN'T MUFF THIS OPPORTUNITY! — I'VE GOT TO DO SOMETHING! — WAIT! I'VE GOT IT!

HELLO, DAILY STAR? MAY I SPEAK TO THE SOCIETY EDITOR?

LOIS, WORKING OVERTIME, ANSWERS THE PHONE...

SHE ISN'T IN, BUT CAN I TAKE THE MESSAGE?

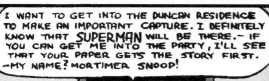

I WANT TO GET INTO THE DUNCAN RESIDENCE TO MAKE AN IMPORTANT CAPTURE. I DEFINITELY KNOW THAT SUPERMAN WILL BE THERE. — IF YOU CAN GET ME INTO THE PARTY, I'LL SEE THAT YOUR PAPER GETS THE STORY FIRST. — MY NAME? MORTIMER SNOOP!

("—I MUST GET TO THE PARTY FIRST, AND WARN SUPERMAN.—") — I BELIEVE I CAN HELP YOU. MEET ME IN FRONT OF THE DUNCAN RESIDENCE.

LATER --

HERE SHE IS. SHE'LL TELL YOU TO LET ME IN

GOOD EVENING, MISS LANE. — SHALL I ADMIT THIS "PERSON" WHO PERSISTS HE KNOWS YOU?

I DON'T KNOW HIM, AND I DON'T CARE TO

THAT MEANS YOU EXIT! — NOW GET GOING BEFORE I CALL THE POLICE!

I'VE BEEN DOUBLE-CROSSED! SHE WANTS THE REWARD MONEY FOR HERSELF!

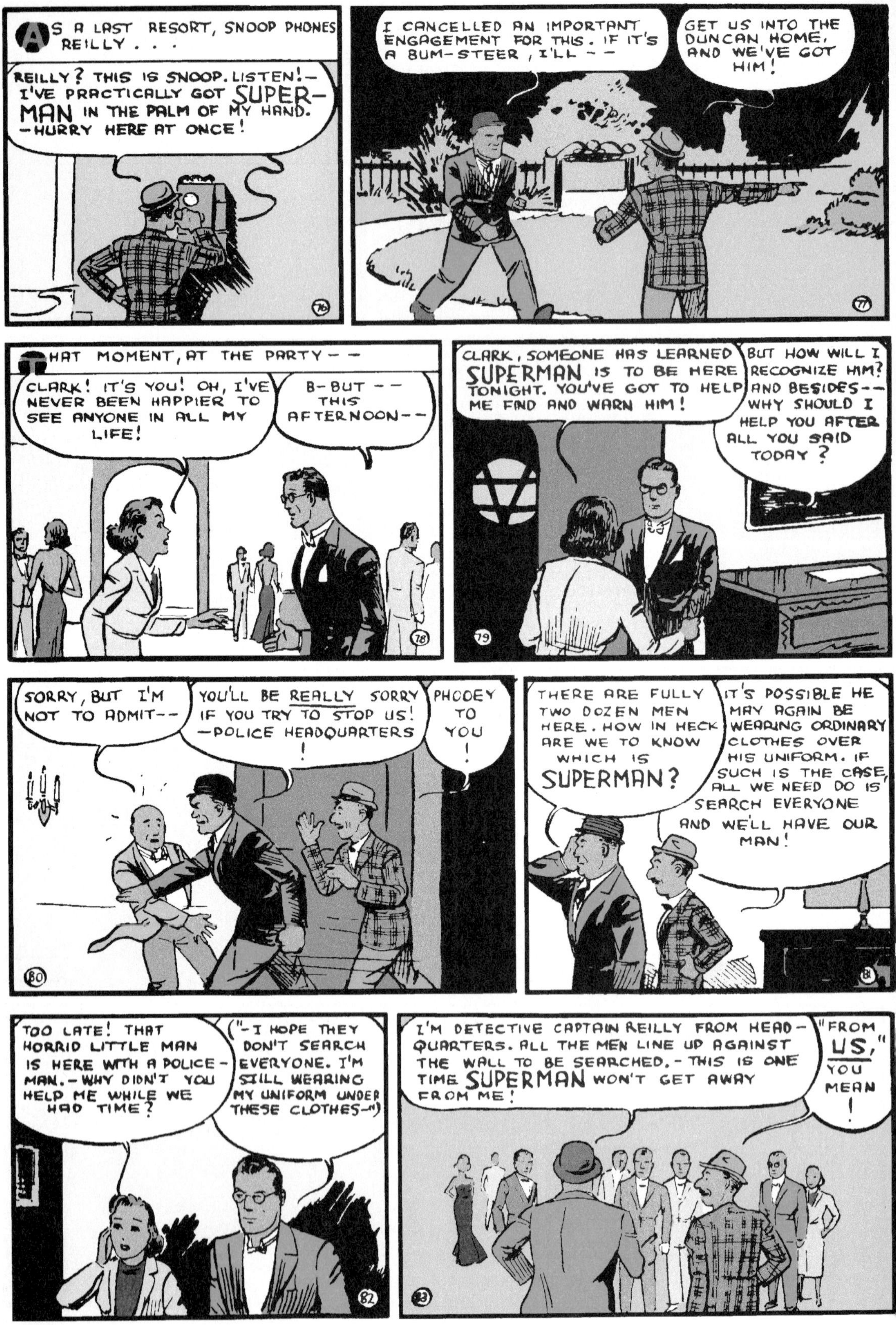
AS A LAST RESORT, SNOOP PHONES REILLY . . .
REILLY? THIS IS SNOOP. LISTEN!—I'VE PRACTICALLY GOT SUPERMAN IN THE PALM OF MY HAND.—HURRY HERE AT ONCE!
I CANCELLED AN IMPORTANT ENGAGEMENT FOR THIS. IF IT'S A BUM-STEER, I'LL --
GET US INTO THE DUNCAN HOME, AND WE'VE GOT HIM!
THAT MOMENT, AT THE PARTY--
CLARK! IT'S YOU! OH, I'VE NEVER BEEN HAPPIER TO SEE ANYONE IN ALL MY LIFE!
B-BUT -- THIS AFTERNOON--
CLARK, SOMEONE HAS LEARNED SUPERMAN IS TO BE HERE TONIGHT. YOU'VE GOT TO HELP ME FIND AND WARN HIM!
BUT HOW WILL I RECOGNIZE HIM? AND BESIDES--WHY SHOULD I HELP YOU AFTER ALL YOU SAID TODAY?
SORRY, BUT I'M NOT TO ADMIT--
YOU'LL BE REALLY SORRY IF YOU TRY TO STOP US! —POLICE HEADQUARTERS!
PHOOEY TO YOU!
THERE ARE FULLY TWO DOZEN MEN HERE. HOW IN HECK ARE WE TO KNOW WHICH IS SUPERMAN?
IT'S POSSIBLE HE MAY AGAIN BE WEARING ORDINARY CLOTHES OVER HIS UNIFORM. IF SUCH IS THE CASE, ALL WE NEED DO IS SEARCH EVERYONE AND WE'LL HAVE OUR MAN!
TOO LATE! THAT HORRID LITTLE MAN IS HERE WITH A POLICEMAN.—WHY DIDN'T YOU HELP ME WHILE WE HAD TIME?
("—I HOPE THEY DON'T SEARCH EVERYONE. I'M STILL WEARING MY UNIFORM UNDER THESE CLOTHES—")
I'M DETECTIVE CAPTAIN REILLY FROM HEADQUARTERS. ALL THE MEN LINE UP AGAINST THE WALL TO BE SEARCHED.—THIS IS ONE TIME SUPERMAN WON'T GET AWAY FROM ME!
"FROM US," YOU MEAN!

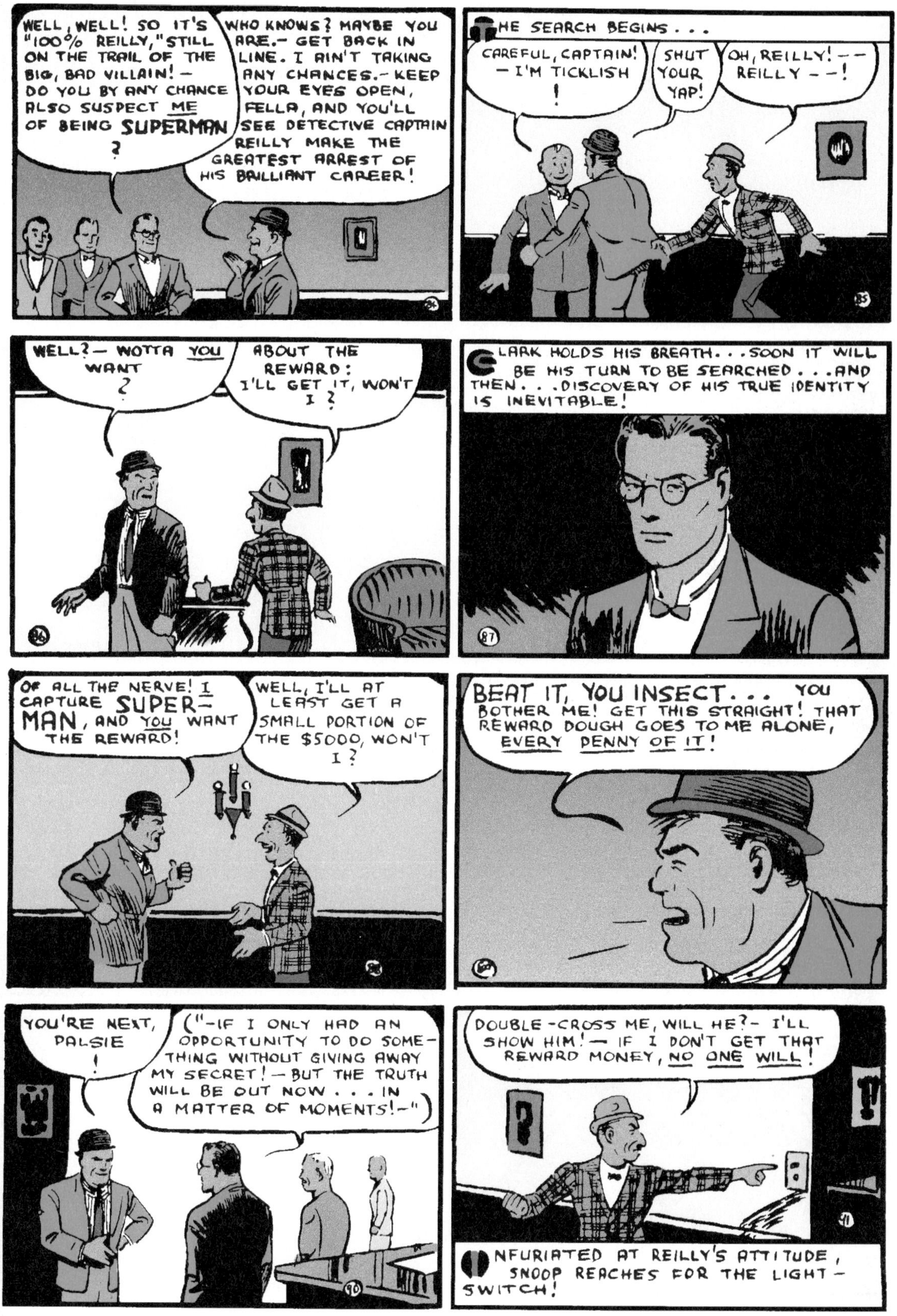
WELL, WELL! SO IT'S "100% REILLY," STILL ON THE TRAIL OF THE BIG, BAD VILLAIN! — DO YOU BY ANY CHANCE ALSO SUSPECT ME OF BEING SUPERMAN ?
WHO KNOWS? MAYBE YOU ARE.— GET BACK IN LINE. I AIN'T TAKING ANY CHANCES.— KEEP YOUR EYES OPEN, FELLA, AND YOU'LL SEE DETECTIVE CAPTAIN REILLY MAKE THE GREATEST ARREST OF HIS BRILLIANT CAREER!
THE SEARCH BEGINS . . .
CAREFUL, CAPTAIN! — I'M TICKLISH !
SHUT YOUR YAP!
OH, REILLY! — — REILLY — —!
WELL? — WOTTA YOU WANT ?
ABOUT THE REWARD: I'LL GET IT, WON'T I ?
CLARK HOLDS HIS BREATH . . . SOON IT WILL BE HIS TURN TO BE SEARCHED . . . AND THEN . . . DISCOVERY OF HIS TRUE IDENTITY IS INEVITABLE!
OF ALL THE NERVE! I CAPTURE SUPER-MAN, AND YOU WANT THE REWARD!
WELL, I'LL AT LEAST GET A SMALL PORTION OF THE $5000, WON'T I ?
BEAT IT, YOU INSECT . . . YOU BOTHER ME! GET THIS STRAIGHT! THAT REWARD DOUGH GOES TO ME ALONE, EVERY PENNY OF IT!
YOU'RE NEXT, PALSIE !
("—IF I ONLY HAD AN OPPORTUNITY TO DO SOME-THING WITHOUT GIVING AWAY MY SECRET! — BUT THE TRUTH WILL BE OUT NOW . . . IN A MATTER OF MOMENTS!—")
DOUBLE-CROSS ME, WILL HE?— I'LL SHOW HIM! — IF I DON'T GET THAT REWARD MONEY, NO ONE WILL!
INFURIATED AT REILLY'S ATTITUDE, SNOOP REACHES FOR THE LIGHT-SWITCH!

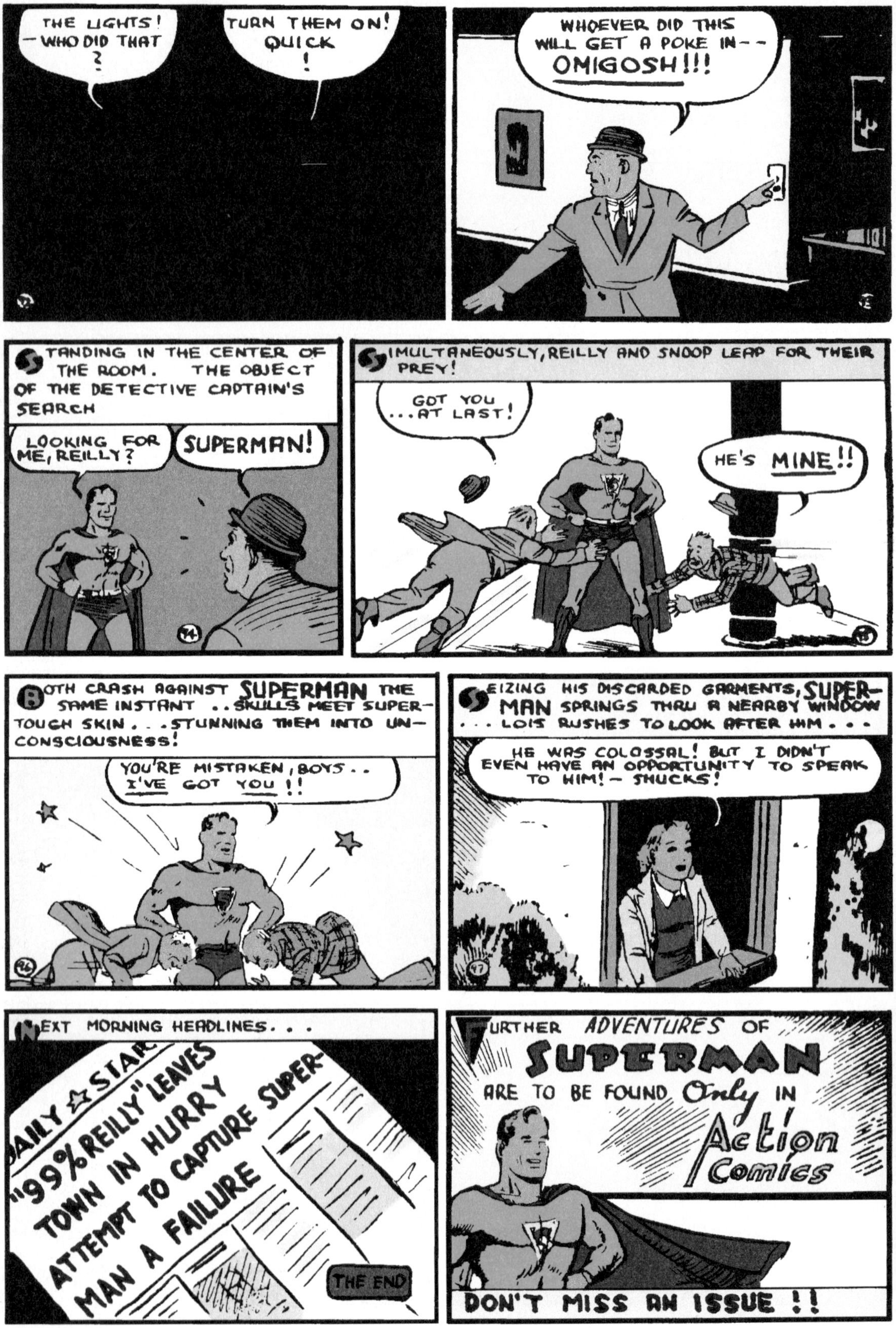
THE LIGHTS! —WHO DID THAT ?
TURN THEM ON! QUICK !
WHOEVER DID THIS WILL GET A POKE IN— — OMIGOSH!!!
STANDING IN THE CENTER OF THE ROOM. THE OBJECT OF THE DETECTIVE CAPTAIN'S SEARCH
LOOKING FOR ME, REILLY?
SUPERMAN!
SIMULTANEOUSLY, REILLY AND SNOOP LEAP FOR THEIR PREY!
GOT YOU ...AT LAST!
HE'S MINE!!
BOTH CRASH AGAINST SUPERMAN THE SAME INSTANT ..SKULLS MEET SUPER-TOUGH SKIN...STUNNING THEM INTO UN-CONSCIOUSNESS!
YOU'RE MISTAKEN, BOYS.. I'VE GOT YOU!!
SEIZING HIS DISCARDED GARMENTS, SUPER-MAN SPRINGS THRU A NEARBY WINDOW ...LOIS RUSHES TO LOOK AFTER HIM...
HE WAS COLOSSAL! BUT I DIDN'T EVEN HAVE AN OPPORTUNITY TO SPEAK TO HIM!—SHUCKS!
NEXT MORNING HEADLINES...
DAILY STAR
"99% REILLY" LEAVES TOWN IN HURRY
ATTEMPT TO CAPTURE SUPER-MAN A FAILURE
THE END
FURTHER ADVENTURES OF SUPERMAN ARE TO BE FOUND Only IN Action Comics
DON'T MISS AN ISSUE !!

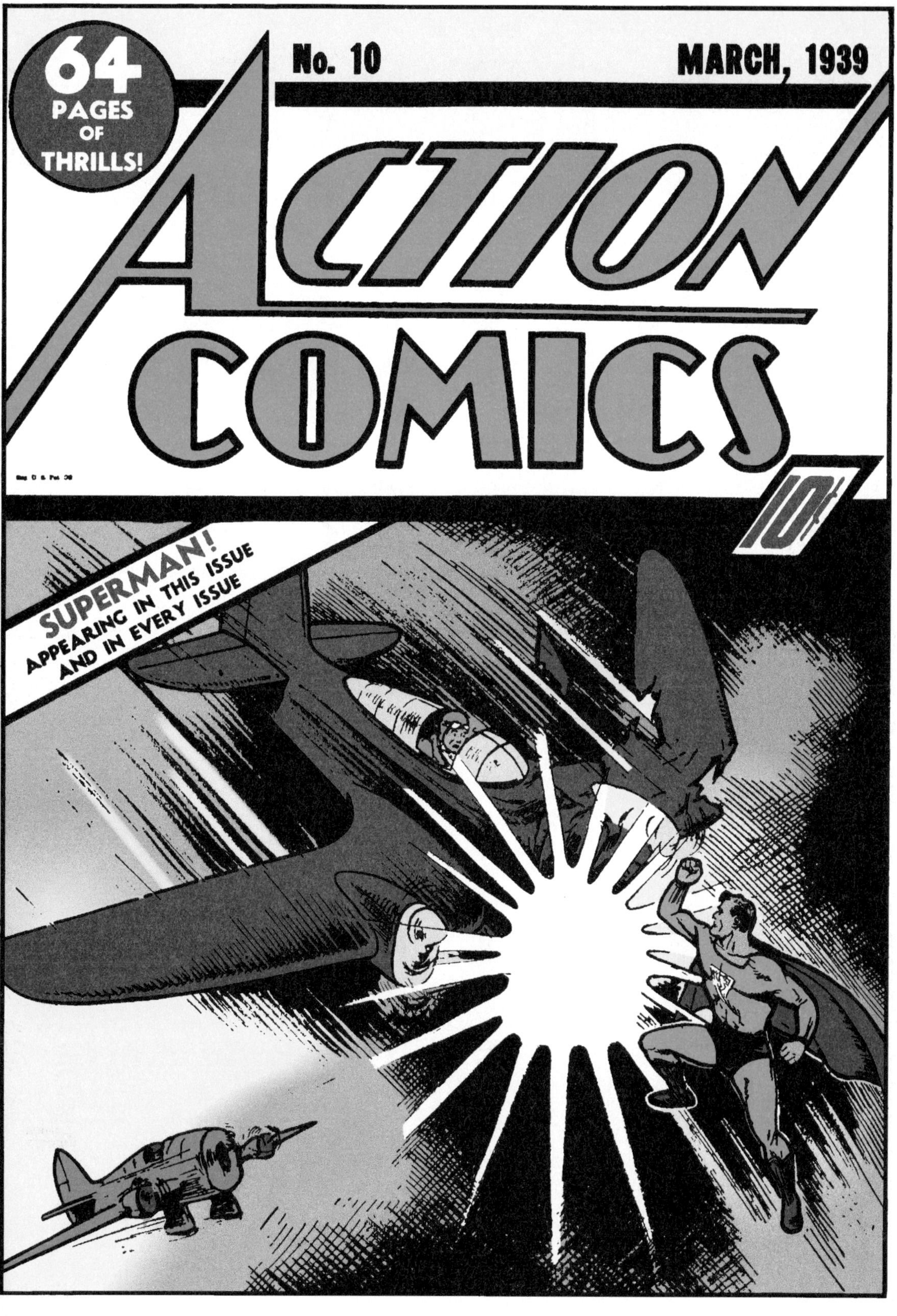
64 PAGES OF THRILLS!
No. 10
MARCH, 1939
ACTION COMICS
10¢
SUPERMAN! APPEARING IN THIS ISSUE AND IN EVERY ISSUE

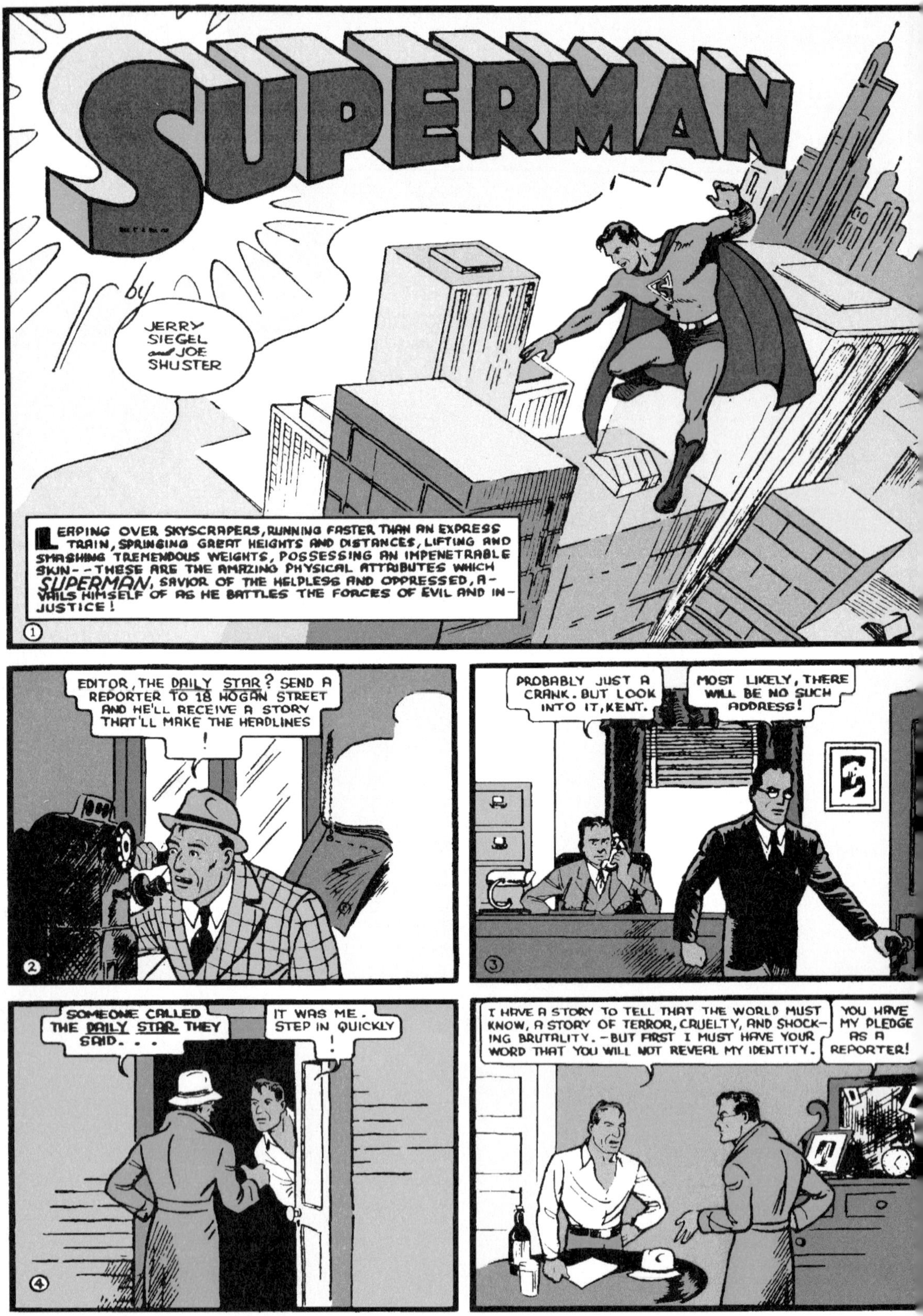
SUPERMAN
by
JERRY SIEGEL and JOE SHUSTER
LEAPING OVER SKYSCRAPERS, RUNNING FASTER THAN AN EXPRESS TRAIN, SPRINGING GREAT HEIGHTS AND DISTANCES, LIFTING AND SMASHING TREMENDOUS WEIGHTS, POSSESSING AN IMPENETRABLE SKIN--THESE ARE THE AMAZING PHYSICAL ATTRIBUTES WHICH SUPERMAN, SAVIOR OF THE HELPLESS AND OPPRESSED, AVAILS HIMSELF OF AS HE BATTLES THE FORCES OF EVIL AND INJUSTICE!
1
EDITOR, THE DAILY STAR? SEND A REPORTER TO 18 HOGAN STREET AND HE'LL RECEIVE A STORY THAT'LL MAKE THE HEADLINES!
2
PROBABLY JUST A CRANK. BUT LOOK INTO IT, KENT.
MOST LIKELY, THERE WILL BE NO SUCH ADDRESS!
3
SOMEONE CALLED THE DAILY STAR. THEY SAID. . .
IT WAS ME. STEP IN QUICKLY!
4
I HAVE A STORY TO TELL THAT THE WORLD MUST KNOW, A STORY OF TERROR, CRUELTY, AND SHOCKING BRUTALITY.-BUT FIRST I MUST HAVE YOUR WORD THAT YOU WILL NOT REVEAL MY IDENTITY.
YOU HAVE MY PLEDGE AS A REPORTER!

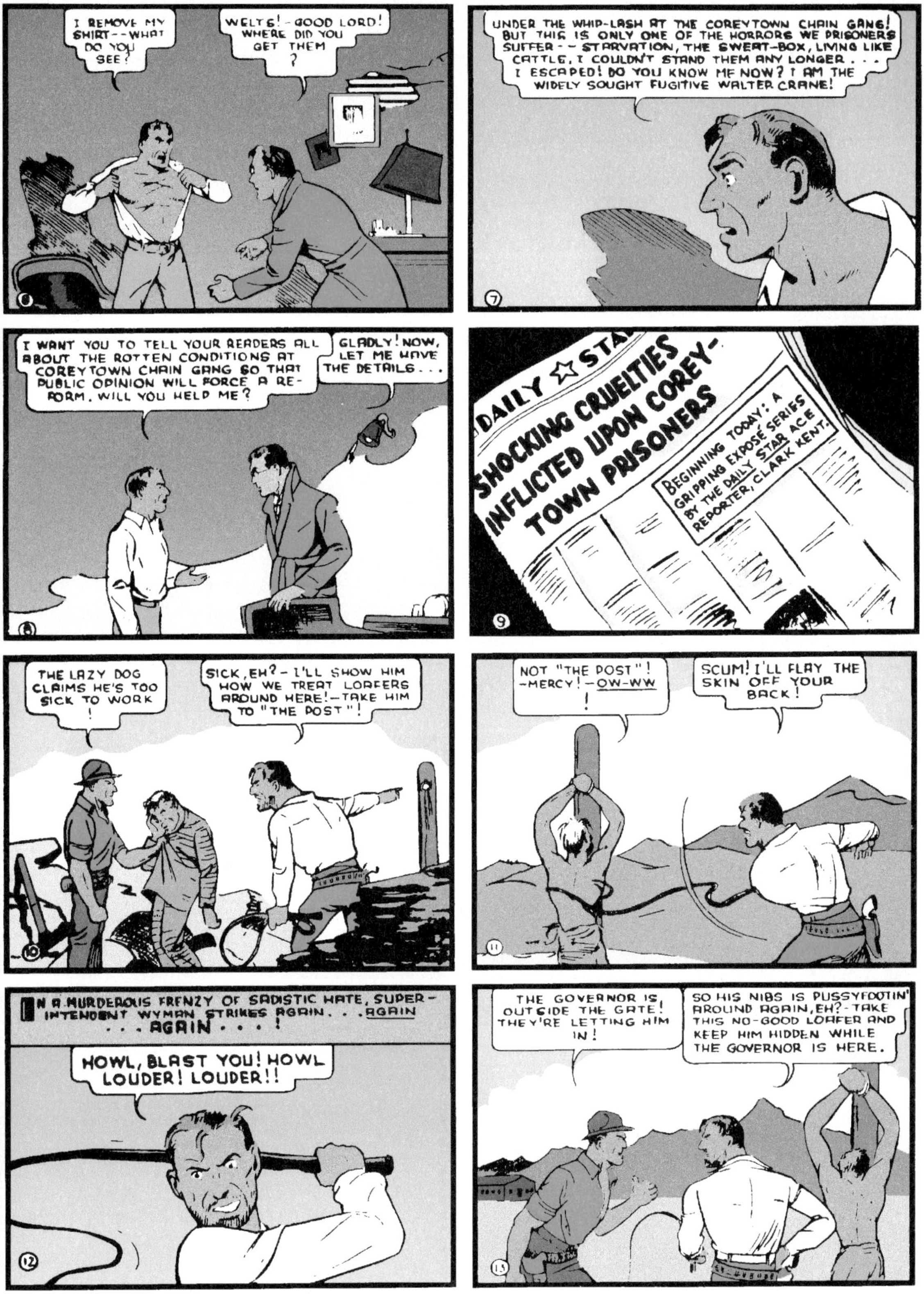
I REMOVE MY SHIRT--WHAT DO YOU SEE?
WELTS!-GOOD LORD! WHERE DID YOU GET THEM ?
UNDER THE WHIP-LASH AT THE COREYTOWN CHAIN GANG! BUT THIS IS ONLY ONE OF THE HORRORS WE PRISONERS SUFFER--STARVATION, THE SWEAT-BOX, LIVING LIKE CATTLE. I COULDN'T STAND THEM ANY LONGER... I ESCAPED! DO YOU KNOW ME NOW? I AM THE WIDELY SOUGHT FUGITIVE WALTER CRANE!
I WANT YOU TO TELL YOUR READERS ALL ABOUT THE ROTTEN CONDITIONS AT COREYTOWN CHAIN GANG SO THAT PUBLIC OPINION WILL FORCE A RE-FORM. WILL YOU HELP ME?
GLADLY! NOW, LET ME HAVE THE DETAILS...
DAILY
SHOCKING CRUELTIES INFLICTED UPON COREY-TOWN PRISONERS
BEGINNING TODAY: A GRIPPING EXPOSÉ SERIES BY THE DAILY STAR ACE REPORTER, CLARK KENT.
THE LAZY DOG CLAIMS HE'S TOO SICK TO WORK !
SICK, EH?-I'LL SHOW HIM HOW WE TREAT LOAFERS AROUND HERE!-TAKE HIM TO "THE POST"!
NOT "THE POST"! -MERCY!-OW-WW !
SCUM! I'LL FLAY THE SKIN OFF YOUR BACK!
IN A MURDEROUS FRENZY OF SADISTIC HATE, SUPER-INTENDENT WYMAN STRIKES AGAIN...AGAIN...AGAIN...!
HOWL, BLAST YOU! HOWL LOUDER! LOUDER!!
THE GOVERNOR IS OUTSIDE THE GATE! THEY'RE LETTING HIM IN!
SO HIS NIBS IS PUSSYFOOTIN' AROUND AGAIN, EH?-TAKE THIS NO-GOOD LOAFER AND KEEP HIM HIDDEN WHILE THE GOVERNOR IS HERE.

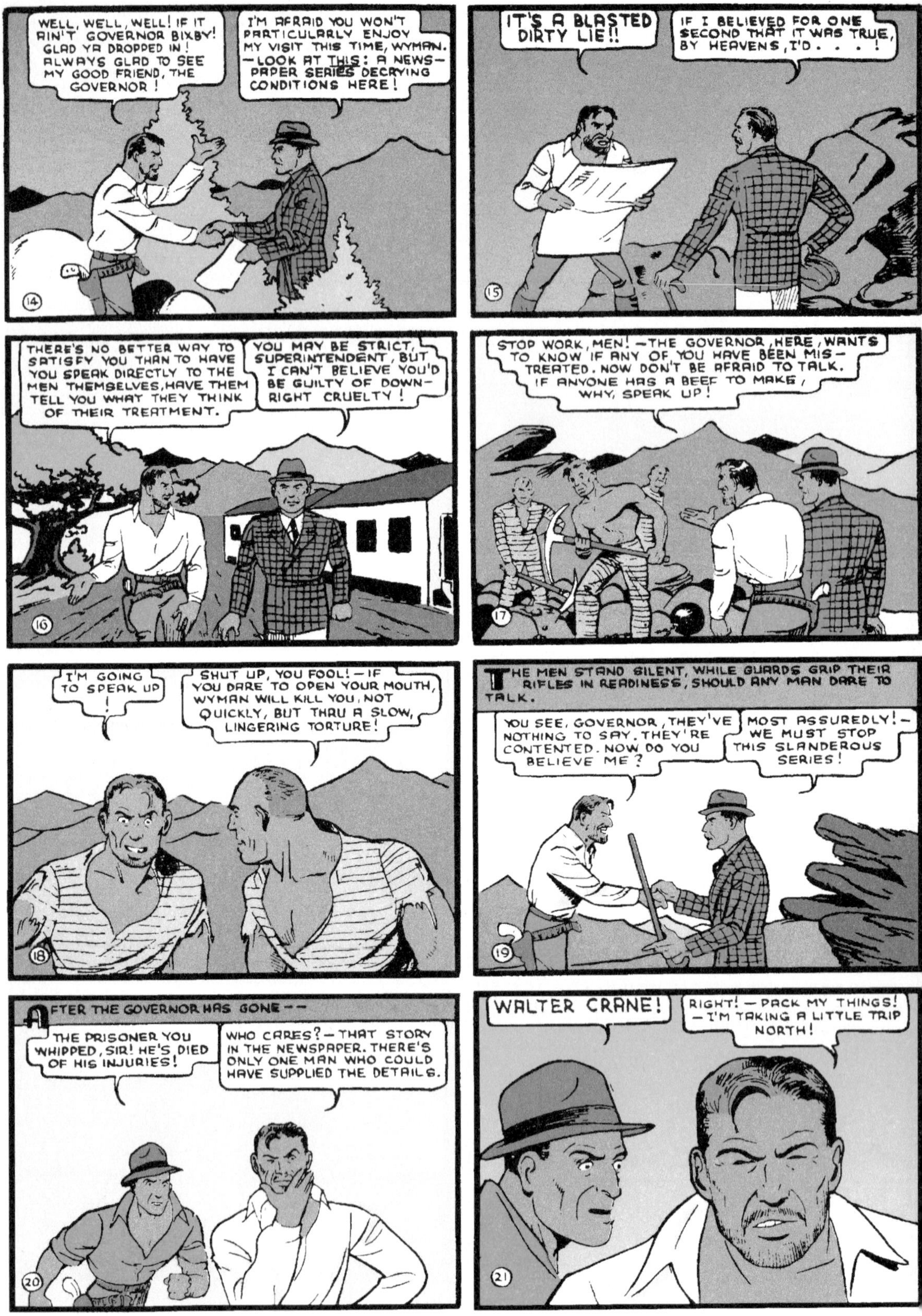
WELL, WELL, WELL! IF IT AIN'T GOVERNOR BIXBY! GLAD YA DROPPED IN! ALWAYS GLAD TO SEE MY GOOD FRIEND, THE GOVERNOR!
I'M AFRAID YOU WON'T PARTICULARLY ENJOY MY VISIT THIS TIME, WYMAN. —LOOK AT THIS: A NEWSPAPER SERIES DECRYING CONDITIONS HERE!
14
IT'S A BLASTED DIRTY LIE!!
IF I BELIEVED FOR ONE SECOND THAT IT WAS TRUE, BY HEAVENS, I'D . . . !
15
THERE'S NO BETTER WAY TO SATISFY YOU THAN TO HAVE YOU SPEAK DIRECTLY TO THE MEN THEMSELVES, HAVE THEM TELL YOU WHAT THEY THINK OF THEIR TREATMENT.
YOU MAY BE STRICT, SUPERINTENDENT, BUT I CAN'T BELIEVE YOU'D BE GUILTY OF DOWNRIGHT CRUELTY!
16
STOP WORK, MEN! —THE GOVERNOR, HERE, WANTS TO KNOW IF ANY OF YOU HAVE BEEN MISTREATED. NOW DON'T BE AFRAID TO TALK. IF ANYONE HAS A BEEF TO MAKE, WHY, SPEAK UP!
17
I'M GOING TO SPEAK UP!
SHUT UP, YOU FOOL! —IF YOU DARE TO OPEN YOUR MOUTH, WYMAN WILL KILL YOU, NOT QUICKLY, BUT THRU A SLOW, LINGERING TORTURE!
18
THE MEN STAND SILENT, WHILE GUARDS GRIP THEIR RIFLES IN READINESS, SHOULD ANY MAN DARE TO TALK.
YOU SEE, GOVERNOR, THEY'VE NOTHING TO SAY. THEY'RE CONTENTED. NOW DO YOU BELIEVE ME?
MOST ASSUREDLY! —WE MUST STOP THIS SLANDEROUS SERIES!
19
AFTER THE GOVERNOR HAS GONE——
THE PRISONER YOU WHIPPED, SIR! HE'S DIED OF HIS INJURIES!
WHO CARES? —THAT STORY IN THE NEWSPAPER. THERE'S ONLY ONE MAN WHO COULD HAVE SUPPLIED THE DETAILS.
20
WALTER CRANE!
RIGHT! —PACK MY THINGS! —I'M TAKING A LITTLE TRIP NORTH!
21

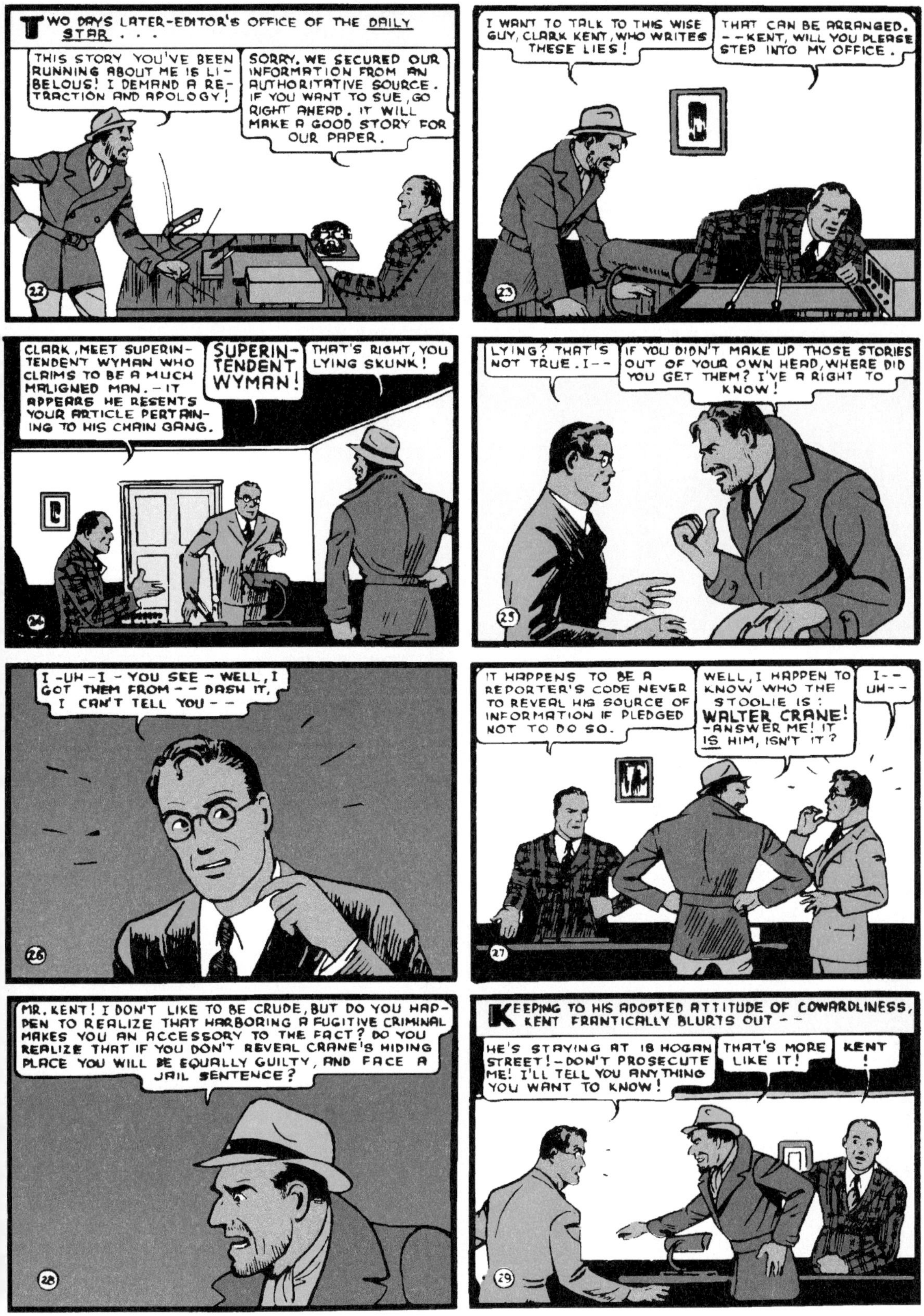
TWO DAYS LATER-EDITOR'S OFFICE OF THE DAILY STAR . . .
THIS STORY YOU'VE BEEN RUNNING ABOUT ME IS LI-BELOUS! I DEMAND A RE-TRACTION AND APOLOGY!
SORRY. WE SECURED OUR INFORMATION FROM AN AUTHORITATIVE SOURCE. IF YOU WANT TO SUE, GO RIGHT AHEAD. IT WILL MAKE A GOOD STORY FOR OUR PAPER.
I WANT TO TALK TO THIS WISE GUY, CLARK KENT, WHO WRITES THESE LIES!
THAT CAN BE ARRANGED. --KENT, WILL YOU PLEASE STEP INTO MY OFFICE.
CLARK, MEET SUPERIN-TENDENT WYMAN WHO CLAIMS TO BE A MUCH MALIGNED MAN.—IT APPEARS HE RESENTS YOUR ARTICLE PERTAIN-ING TO HIS CHAIN GANG.
SUPERIN-TENDENT WYMAN!
THAT'S RIGHT, YOU LYING SKUNK!
LYING? THAT'S NOT TRUE. I--
IF YOU DIDN'T MAKE UP THOSE STORIES OUT OF YOUR OWN HEAD, WHERE DID YOU GET THEM? I'VE A RIGHT TO KNOW!
I-UH-I - YOU SEE - WELL, I GOT THEM FROM -- DASH IT, I CAN'T TELL YOU --
IT HAPPENS TO BE A REPORTER'S CODE NEVER TO REVEAL HIS SOURCE OF INFORMATION IF PLEDGED NOT TO DO SO.
WELL, I HAPPEN TO KNOW WHO THE STOOLIE IS: WALTER CRANE! -ANSWER ME! IT IS HIM, ISN'T IT?
I--UH--
MR. KENT! I DON'T LIKE TO BE CRUDE, BUT DO YOU HAP-PEN TO REALIZE THAT HARBORING A FUGITIVE CRIMINAL MAKES YOU AN ACCESSORY TO THE FACT? DO YOU REALIZE THAT IF YOU DON'T REVEAL CRANE'S HIDING PLACE YOU WILL BE EQUALLY GUILTY, AND FACE A JAIL SENTENCE?
KEEPING TO HIS ADOPTED ATTITUDE OF COWARDLINESS, KENT FRANTICALLY BLURTS OUT --
HE'S STAYING AT 18 HOGAN STREET! - DON'T PROSECUTE ME! I'LL TELL YOU ANYTHING YOU WANT TO KNOW!
THAT'S MORE LIKE IT!
KENT!

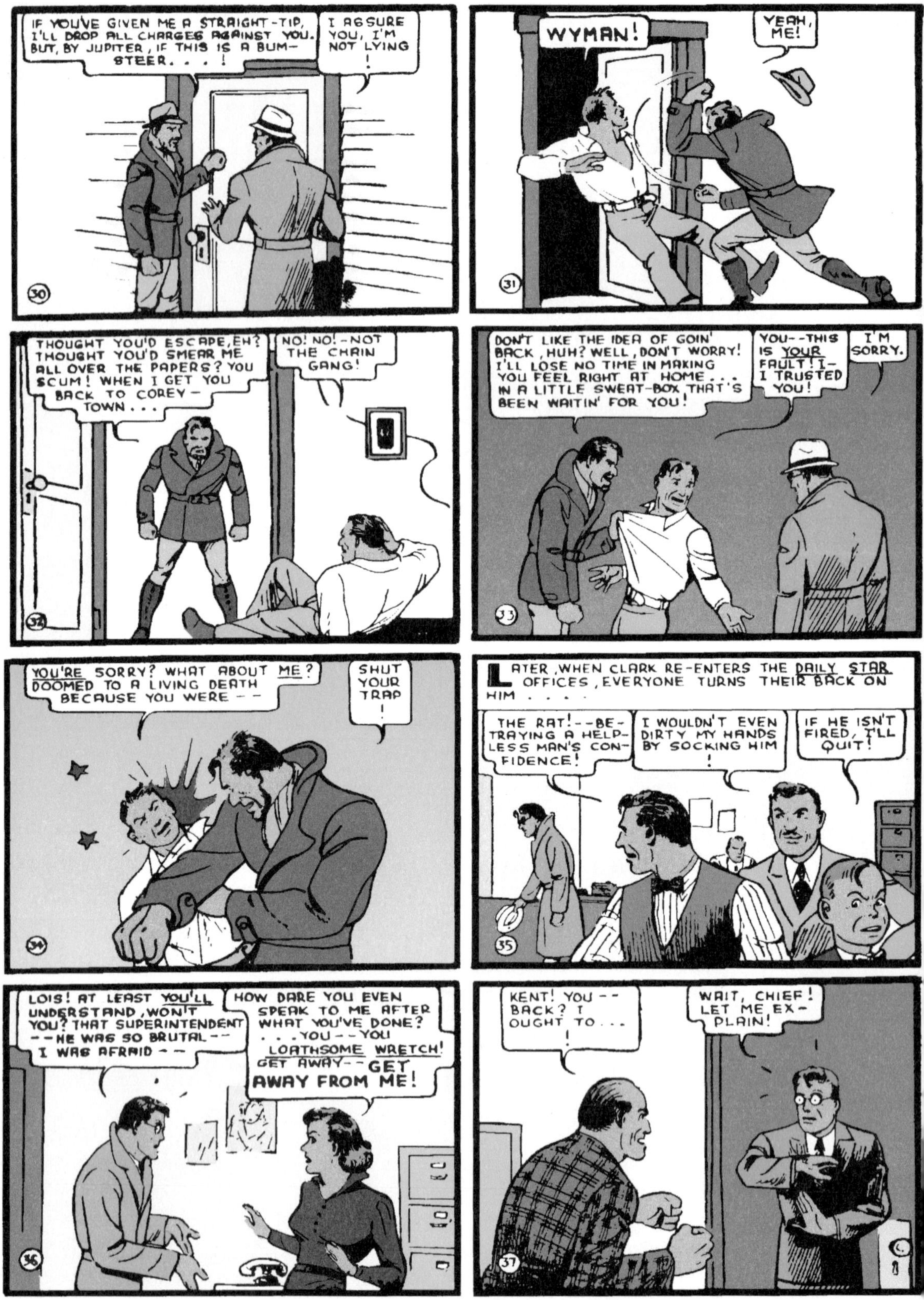
IF YOU'VE GIVEN ME A STRAIGHT-TIP, I'LL DROP ALL CHARGES AGAINST YOU. BUT, BY JUPITER, IF THIS IS A BUM-STEER. . . !
I ASSURE YOU, I'M NOT LYING!
WYMAN!
YEAH, ME!
THOUGHT YOU'D ESCAPE, EH? THOUGHT YOU'D SMEAR ME ALL OVER THE PAPERS? YOU SCUM! WHEN I GET YOU BACK TO COREY-TOWN . . .
NO! NO! -- NOT THE CHAIN GANG!
DON'T LIKE THE IDEA OF GOIN' BACK, HUH? WELL, DON'T WORRY! I'LL LOSE NO TIME IN MAKING YOU FEEL RIGHT AT HOME . . . IN A LITTLE SWEAT-BOX THAT'S BEEN WAITIN' FOR YOU!
YOU--THIS IS YOUR FAULT! I-I TRUSTED YOU!
I'M SORRY.
YOU'RE SORRY? WHAT ABOUT ME? DOOMED TO A LIVING DEATH BECAUSE YOU WERE --
SHUT YOUR TRAP!
LATER, WHEN CLARK RE-ENTERS THE DAILY STAR OFFICES, EVERYONE TURNS THEIR BACK ON HIM . . . .
THE RAT! -- BE-TRAYING A HELP-LESS MAN'S CON-FIDENCE!
I WOULDN'T EVEN DIRTY MY HANDS BY SOCKING HIM!
IF HE ISN'T FIRED, I'LL QUIT!
LOIS! AT LEAST YOU'LL UNDERSTAND, WON'T YOU? THAT SUPERINTENDENT -- HE WAS SO BRUTAL -- I WAS AFRAID --
HOW DARE YOU EVEN SPEAK TO ME AFTER WHAT YOU'VE DONE? . . . YOU -- YOU LOATHSOME WRETCH! GET AWAY -- GET AWAY FROM ME!
KENT! YOU -- BACK? I OUGHT TO . . . !
WAIT, CHIEF! LET ME EX-PLAIN!

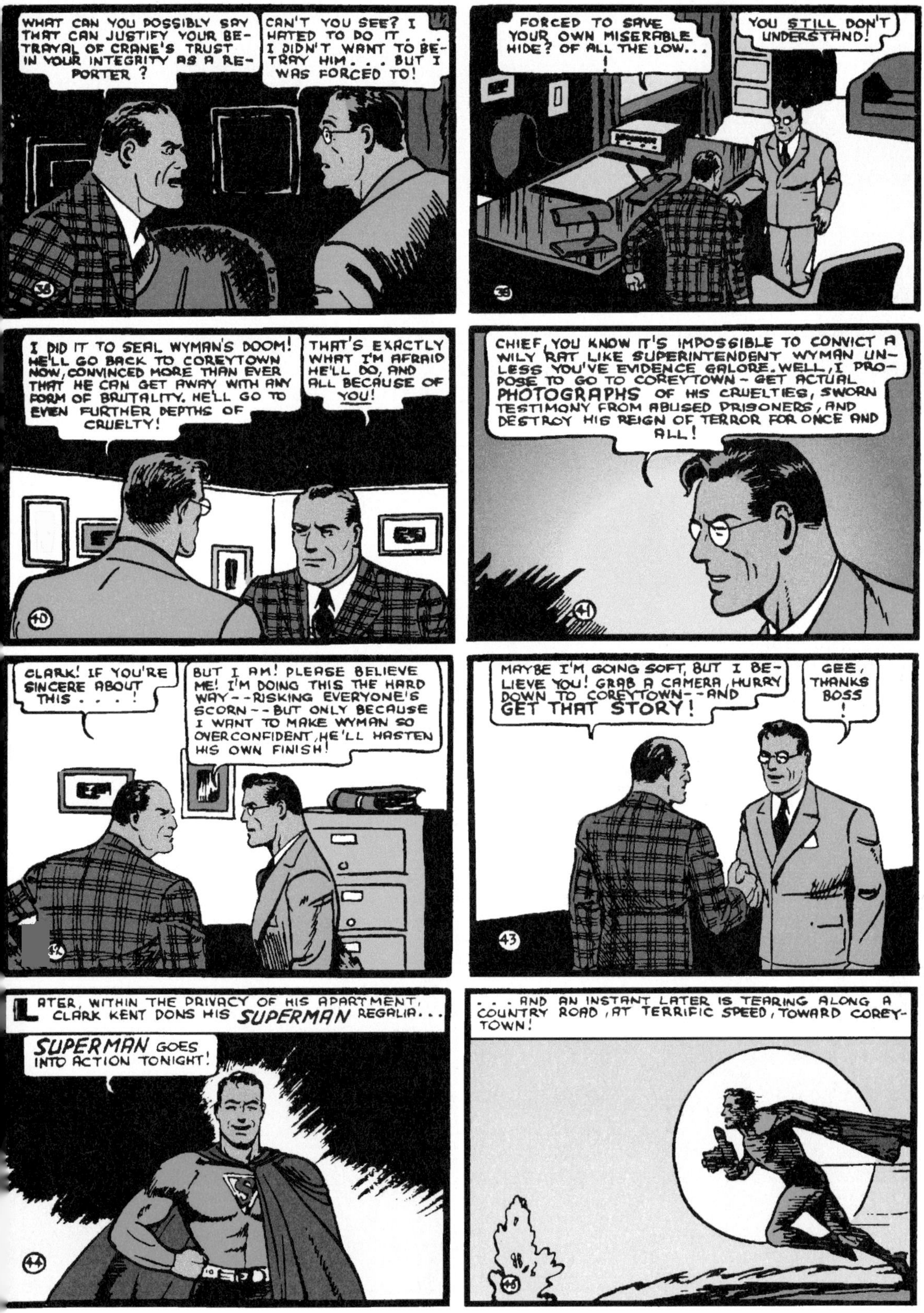
WHAT CAN YOU POSSIBLY SAY THAT CAN JUSTIFY YOUR BETRAYAL OF CRANE'S TRUST IN YOUR INTEGRITY AS A REPORTER?
CAN'T YOU SEE? I HATED TO DO IT... I DIDN'T WANT TO BETRAY HIM... BUT I WAS FORCED TO!
FORCED TO SAVE YOUR OWN MISERABLE HIDE? OF ALL THE LOW...!
YOU STILL DON'T UNDERSTAND!
I DID IT TO SEAL WYMAN'S DOOM! HE'LL GO BACK TO COREYTOWN NOW, CONVINCED MORE THAN EVER THAT HE CAN GET AWAY WITH ANY FORM OF BRUTALITY. HE'LL GO TO EVEN FURTHER DEPTHS OF CRUELTY!
THAT'S EXACTLY WHAT I'M AFRAID HE'LL DO, AND ALL BECAUSE OF YOU!
CHIEF, YOU KNOW IT'S IMPOSSIBLE TO CONVICT A WILY RAT LIKE SUPERINTENDENT WYMAN UNLESS YOU'VE EVIDENCE GALORE. WELL, I PROPOSE TO GO TO COREYTOWN - GET ACTUAL PHOTOGRAPHS OF HIS CRUELTIES, SWORN TESTIMONY FROM ABUSED PRISONERS, AND DESTROY HIS REIGN OF TERROR FOR ONCE AND ALL!
CLARK! IF YOU'RE SINCERE ABOUT THIS...!
BUT I AM! PLEASE BELIEVE ME! I'M DOING THIS THE HARD WAY--RISKING EVERYONE'S SCORN--BUT ONLY BECAUSE I WANT TO MAKE WYMAN SO OVERCONFIDENT, HE'LL HASTEN HIS OWN FINISH!
MAYBE I'M GOING SOFT, BUT I BELIEVE YOU! GRAB A CAMERA, HURRY DOWN TO COREYTOWN--AND GET THAT STORY!
GEE, THANKS BOSS!
LATER, WITHIN THE PRIVACY OF HIS APARTMENT, CLARK KENT DONS HIS SUPERMAN REGALIA...
SUPERMAN GOES INTO ACTION TONIGHT!
...AND AN INSTANT LATER IS TEARING ALONG A COUNTRY ROAD, AT TERRIFIC SPEED, TOWARD COREYTOWN!

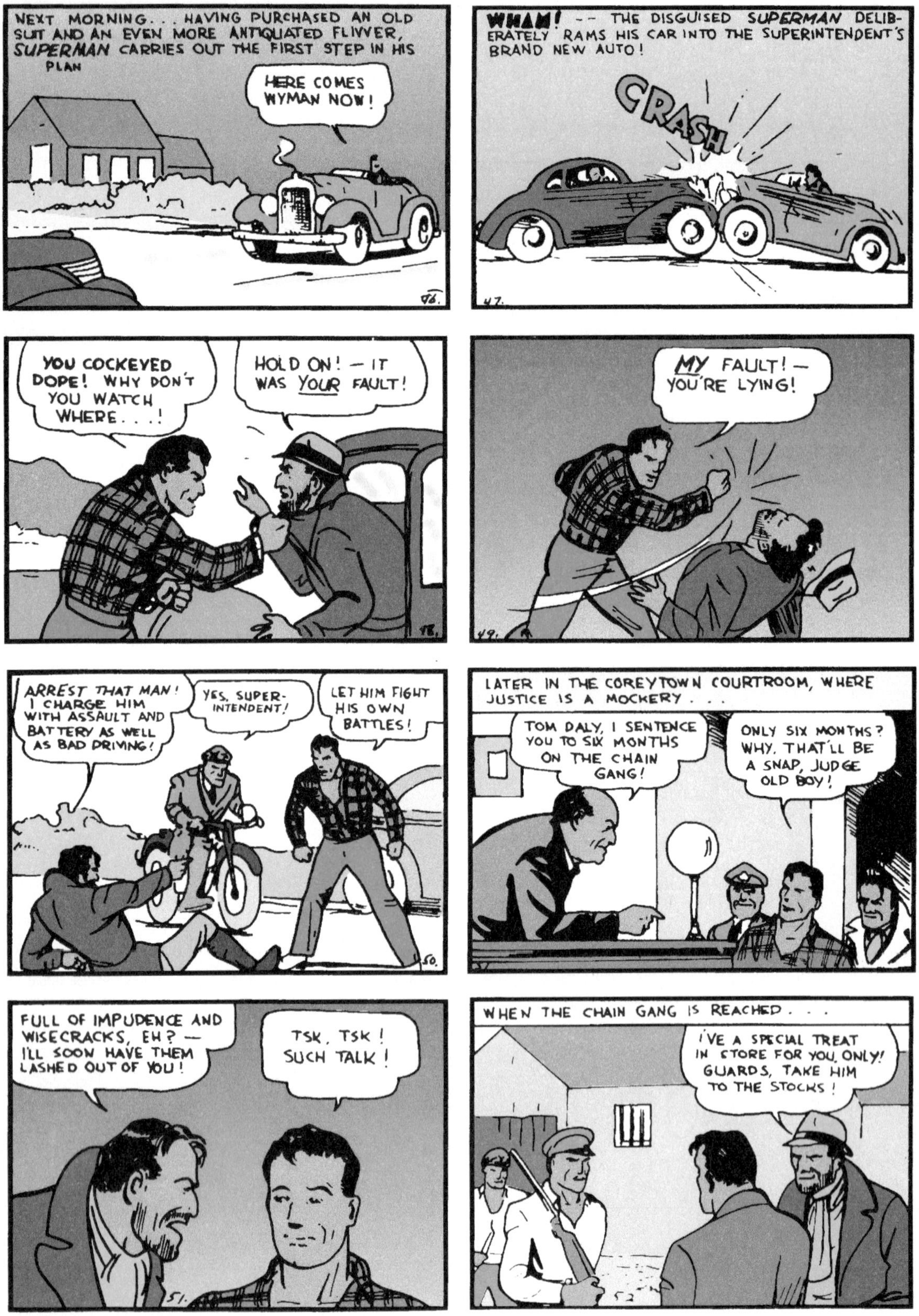
NEXT MORNING... HAVING PURCHASED AN OLD SUIT AND AN EVEN MORE ANTIQUATED FLIVVER, SUPERMAN CARRIES OUT THE FIRST STEP IN HIS PLAN
HERE COMES WYMAN NOW!
WHAM! -- THE DISGUISED SUPERMAN DELIBERATELY RAMS HIS CAR INTO THE SUPERINTENDENT'S BRAND NEW AUTO!
CRASH
YOU COCKEYED DOPE! WHY DON'T YOU WATCH WHERE...!
HOLD ON! — IT WAS YOUR FAULT!
MY FAULT! — YOU'RE LYING!
ARREST THAT MAN! I CHARGE HIM WITH ASSAULT AND BATTERY AS WELL AS BAD DRIVING!
YES, SUPER-INTENDENT!
LET HIM FIGHT HIS OWN BATTLES!
LATER IN THE COREYTOWN COURTROOM, WHERE JUSTICE IS A MOCKERY...
TOM DALY, I SENTENCE YOU TO SIX MONTHS ON THE CHAIN GANG!
ONLY SIX MONTHS? WHY, THAT'LL BE A SNAP, JUDGE OLD BOY!
FULL OF IMPUDENCE AND WISECRACKS, EH? — I'LL SOON HAVE THEM LASHED OUT OF YOU!
TSK, TSK! SUCH TALK!
WHEN THE CHAIN GANG IS REACHED...
I'VE A SPECIAL TREAT IN STORE FOR YOU, ONLY! GUARDS, TAKE HIM TO THE STOCKS!

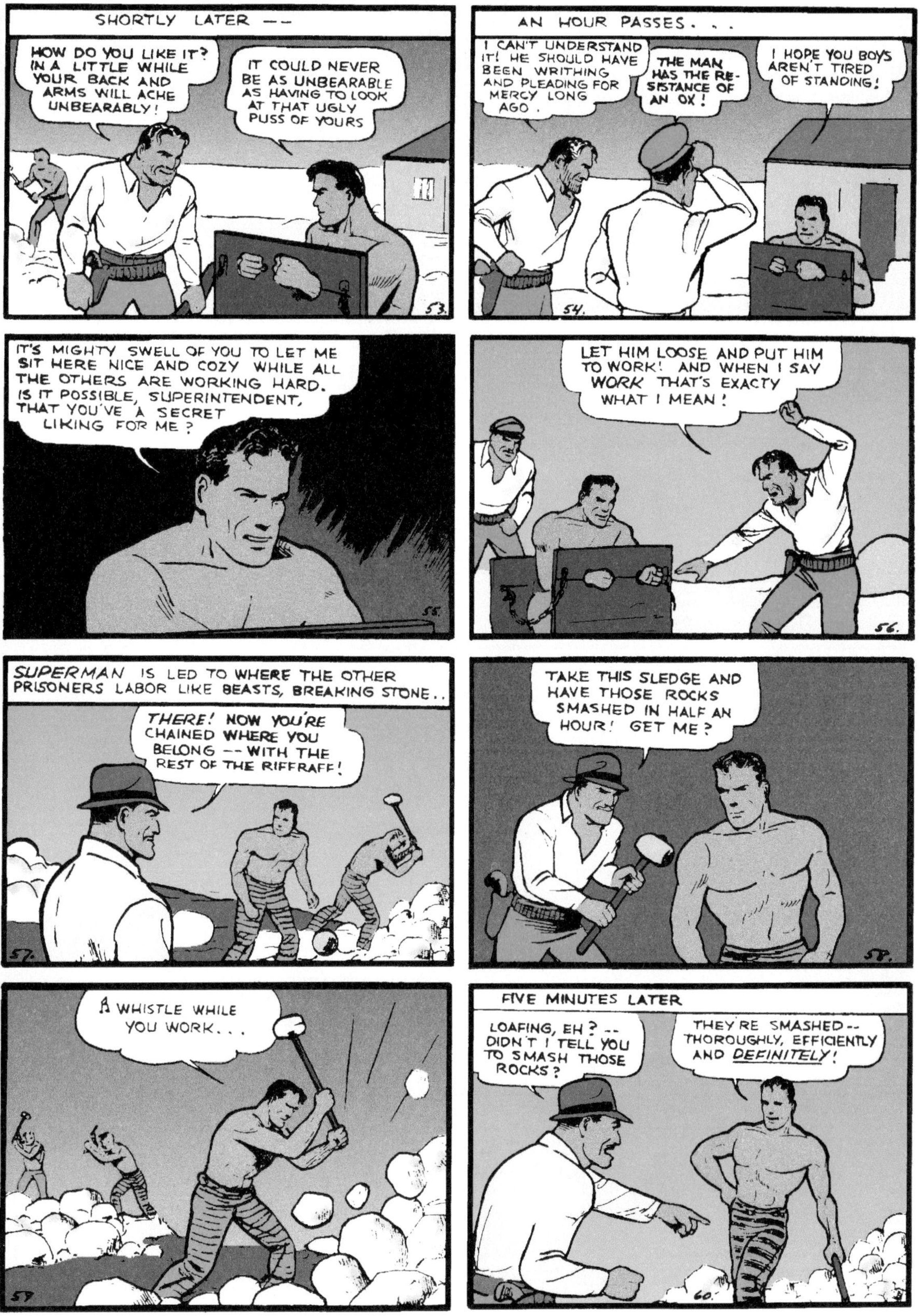
SHORTLY LATER --
HOW DO YOU LIKE IT? IN A LITTLE WHILE YOUR BACK AND ARMS WILL ACHE UNBEARABLY!
IT COULD NEVER BE AS UNBEARABLE AS HAVING TO LOOK AT THAT UGLY PUSS OF YOURS
AN HOUR PASSES. . .
I CAN'T UNDERSTAND IT! HE SHOULD HAVE BEEN WRITHING AND PLEADING FOR MERCY LONG AGO.
THE MAN HAS THE RE-SISTANCE OF AN OX!
I HOPE YOU BOYS AREN'T TIRED OF STANDING!
IT'S MIGHTY SWELL OF YOU TO LET ME SIT HERE NICE AND COZY WHILE ALL THE OTHERS ARE WORKING HARD. IS IT POSSIBLE, SUPERINTENDENT, THAT YOU'VE A SECRET LIKING FOR ME?
LET HIM LOOSE AND PUT HIM TO WORK! AND WHEN I SAY WORK THAT'S EXACTY WHAT I MEAN!
SUPERMAN IS LED TO WHERE THE OTHER PRISONERS LABOR LIKE BEASTS, BREAKING STONE..
THERE! NOW YOU'RE CHAINED WHERE YOU BELONG -- WITH THE REST OF THE RIFFRAFF!
TAKE THIS SLEDGE AND HAVE THOSE ROCKS SMASHED IN HALF AN HOUR! GET ME?
♫ WHISTLE WHILE YOU WORK...
FIVE MINUTES LATER
LOAFING, EH? -- DIDN'T I TELL YOU TO SMASH THOSE ROCKS?
THEY'RE SMASHED -- THOROUGHLY, EFFICIENTLY AND DEFINITELY!

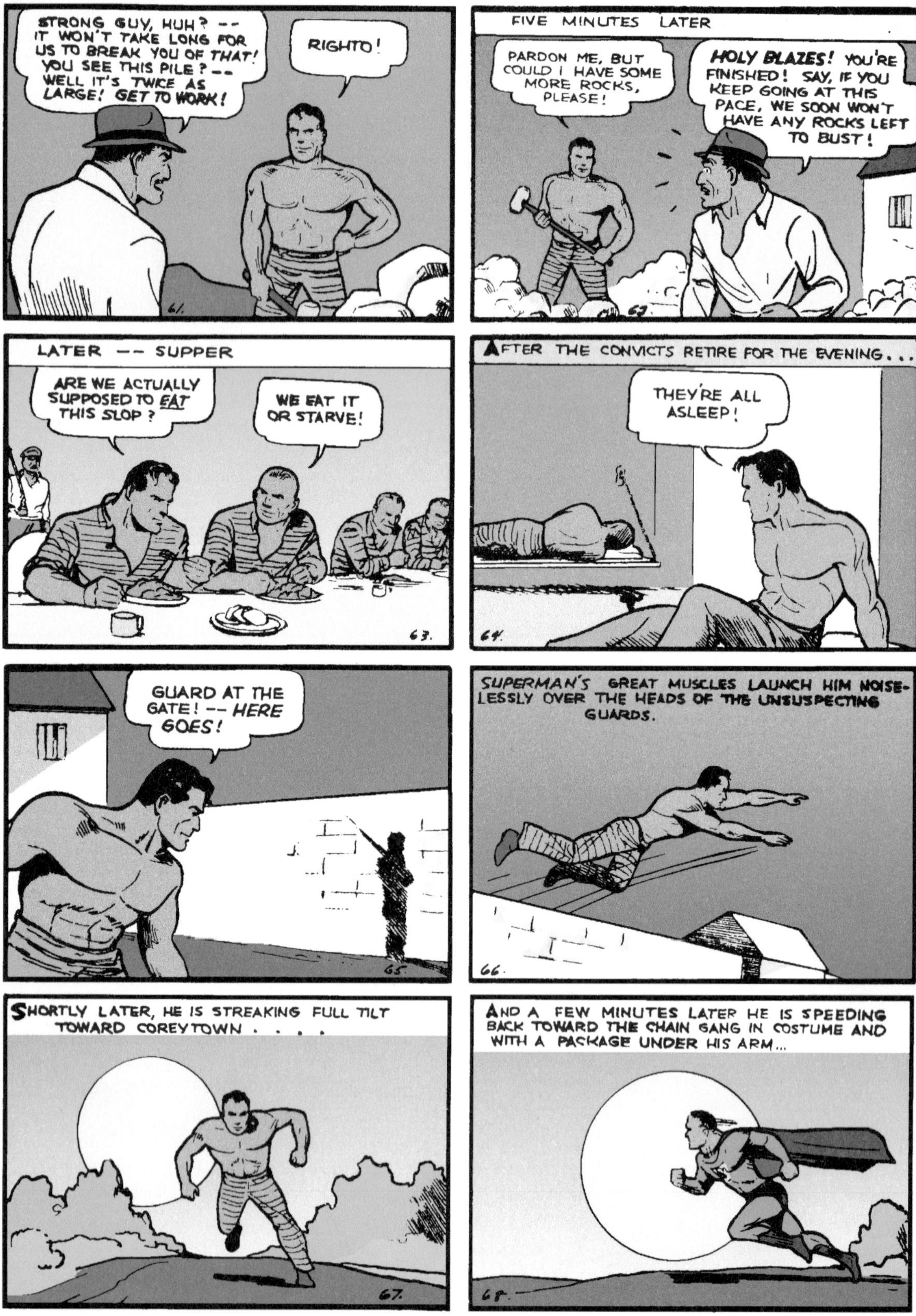
STRONG GUY, HUH? -- IT WON'T TAKE LONG FOR US TO BREAK YOU OF THAT! YOU SEE THIS PILE? -- WELL IT'S TWICE AS LARGE! GET TO WORK!
RIGHTO!
61.
FIVE MINUTES LATER
PARDON ME, BUT COULD I HAVE SOME MORE ROCKS, PLEASE!
HOLY BLAZES! YOU'RE FINISHED! SAY, IF YOU KEEP GOING AT THIS PACE, WE SOON WON'T HAVE ANY ROCKS LEFT TO BUST!
62.
LATER -- SUPPER
ARE WE ACTUALLY SUPPOSED TO EAT THIS SLOP?
WE EAT IT OR STARVE!
63.
AFTER THE CONVICTS RETIRE FOR THE EVENING...
THEY'RE ALL ASLEEP!
64.
GUARD AT THE GATE! -- HERE GOES!
65.
SUPERMAN'S GREAT MUSCLES LAUNCH HIM NOISELESSLY OVER THE HEADS OF THE UNSUSPECTING GUARDS.
66.
SHORTLY LATER, HE IS STREAKING FULL TILT TOWARD COREYTOWN....
67.
AND A FEW MINUTES LATER HE IS SPEEDING BACK TOWARD THE CHAIN GANG IN COSTUME AND WITH A PACKAGE UNDER HIS ARM...
68.

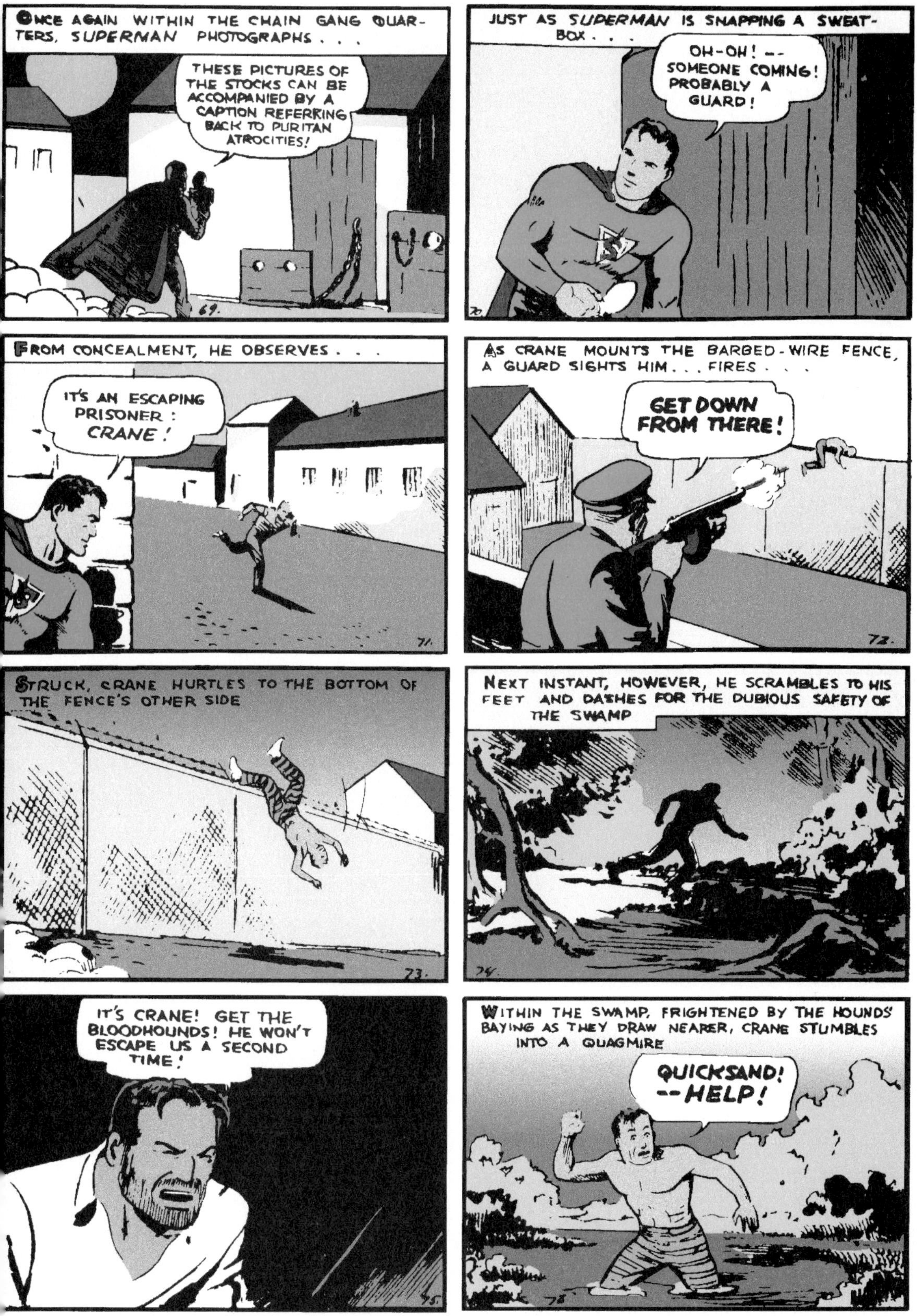
ONCE AGAIN WITHIN THE CHAIN GANG QUARTERS, SUPERMAN PHOTOGRAPHS . . .
THESE PICTURES OF THE STOCKS CAN BE ACCOMPANIED BY A CAPTION REFERRING BACK TO PURITAN ATROCITIES!
69.
JUST AS SUPERMAN IS SNAPPING A SWEAT-BOX . . .
OH-OH! -- SOMEONE COMING! PROBABLY A GUARD!
70.
FROM CONCEALMENT, HE OBSERVES . . .
IT'S AN ESCAPING PRISONER: CRANE!
71.
AS CRANE MOUNTS THE BARBED-WIRE FENCE, A GUARD SIGHTS HIM . . . FIRES . . .
GET DOWN FROM THERE!
72.
STRUCK, CRANE HURTLES TO THE BOTTOM OF THE FENCE'S OTHER SIDE
73.
NEXT INSTANT, HOWEVER, HE SCRAMBLES TO HIS FEET AND DASHES FOR THE DUBIOUS SAFETY OF THE SWAMP
74.
IT'S CRANE! GET THE BLOODHOUNDS! HE WON'T ESCAPE US A SECOND TIME!
75.
WITHIN THE SWAMP, FRIGHTENED BY THE HOUNDS' BAYING AS THEY DRAW NEARER, CRANE STUMBLES INTO A QUAGMIRE
QUICKSAND! --HELP!
76.

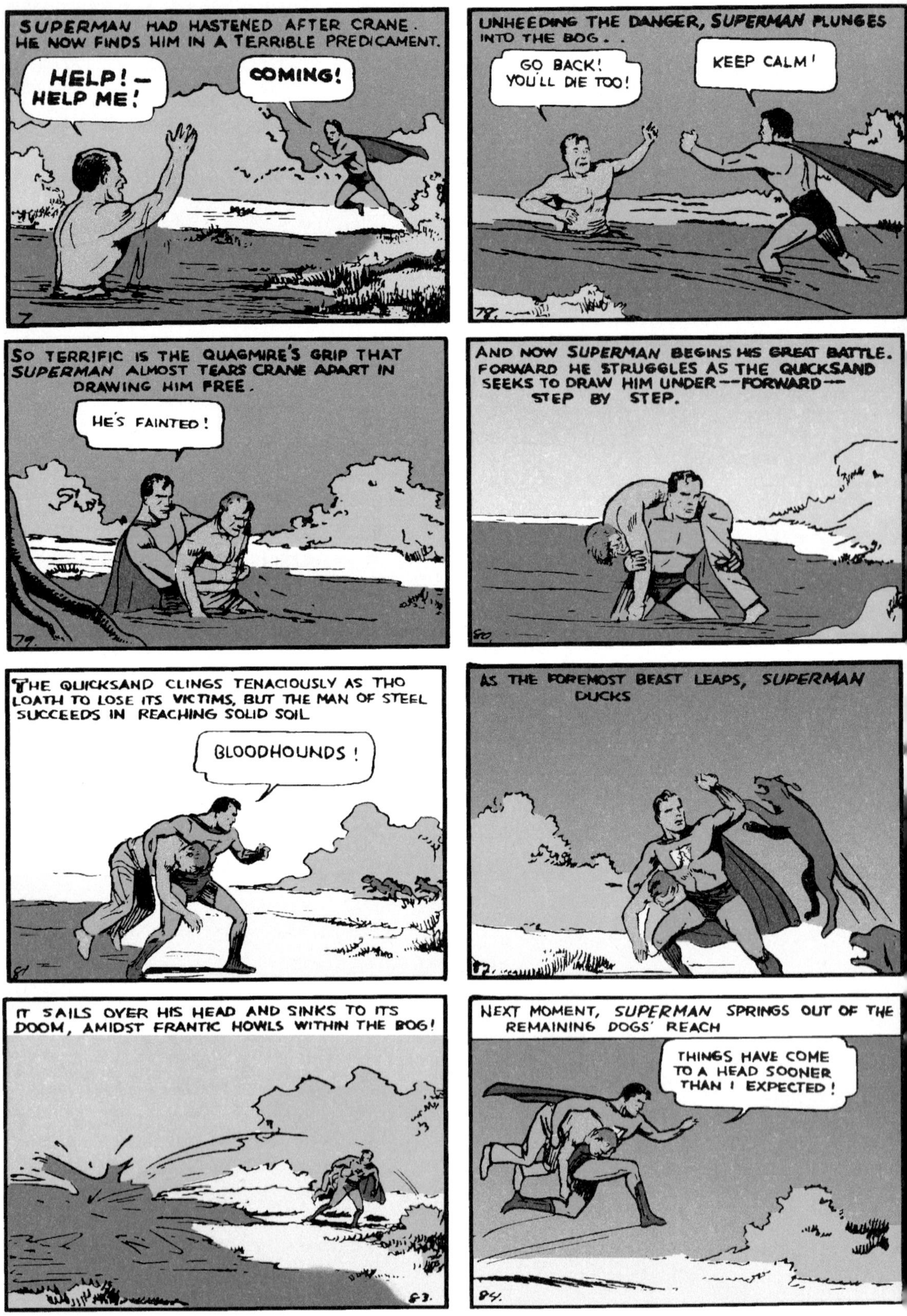
SUPERMAN HAD HASTENED AFTER CRANE. HE NOW FINDS HIM IN A TERRIBLE PREDICAMENT.
HELP! — HELP ME!
COMING!
UNHEEDING THE DANGER, SUPERMAN PLUNGES INTO THE BOG . .
GO BACK! YOU'LL DIE TOO!
KEEP CALM!
SO TERRIFIC IS THE QUAGMIRE'S GRIP THAT SUPERMAN ALMOST TEARS CRANE APART IN DRAWING HIM FREE.
HE'S FAINTED!
AND NOW SUPERMAN BEGINS HIS GREAT BATTLE. FORWARD HE STRUGGLES AS THE QUICKSAND SEEKS TO DRAW HIM UNDER — FORWARD — STEP BY STEP.
THE QUICKSAND CLINGS TENACIOUSLY AS THO LOATH TO LOSE ITS VICTIMS, BUT THE MAN OF STEEL SUCCEEDS IN REACHING SOLID SOIL
BLOODHOUNDS!
AS THE FOREMOST BEAST LEAPS, SUPERMAN DUCKS
IT SAILS OVER HIS HEAD AND SINKS TO ITS DOOM, AMIDST FRANTIC HOWLS WITHIN THE BOG!
NEXT MOMENT, SUPERMAN SPRINGS OUT OF THE REMAINING DOGS' REACH
THINGS HAVE COME TO A HEAD SOONER THAN I EXPECTED!

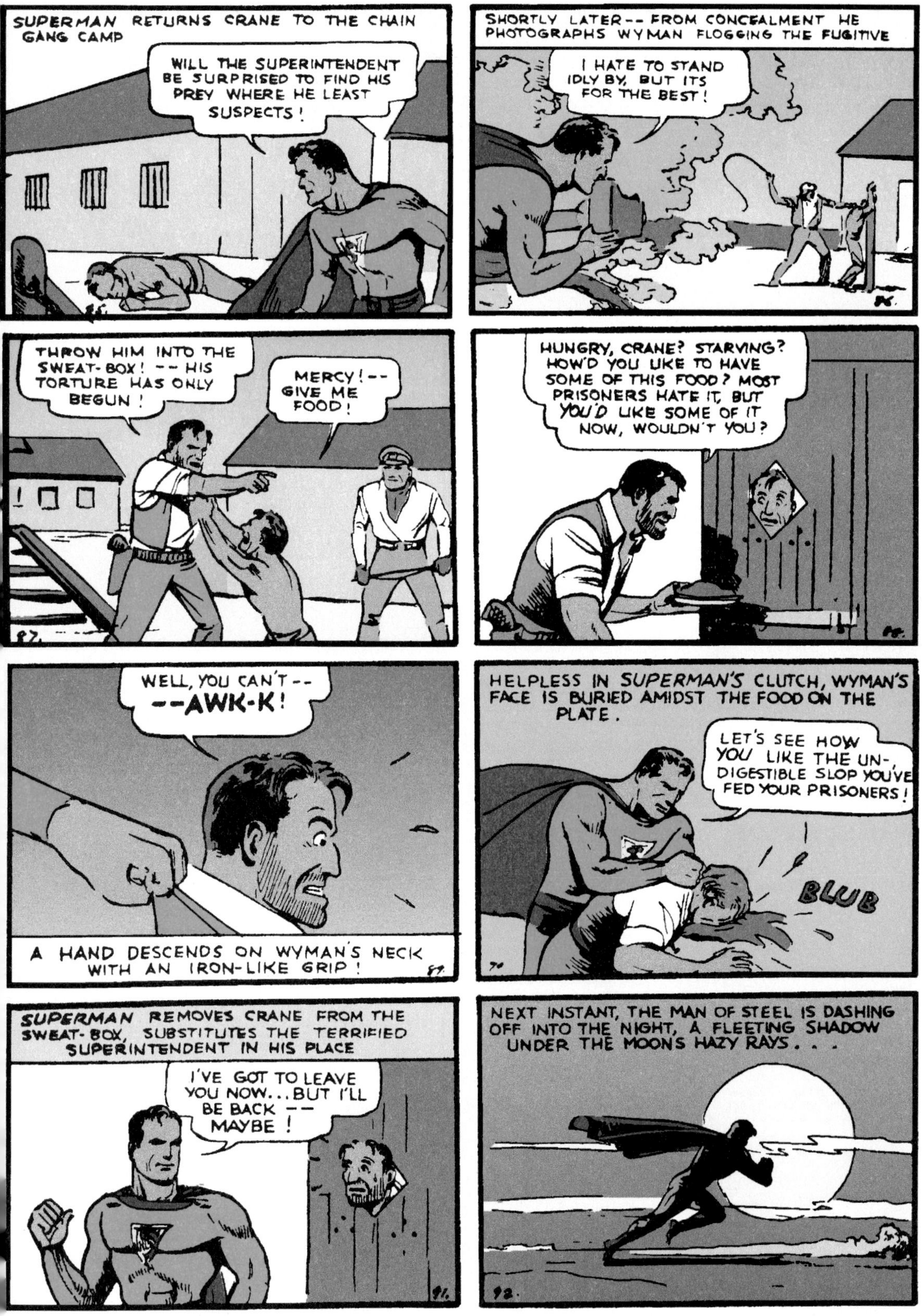
SUPERMAN RETURNS CRANE TO THE CHAIN GANG CAMP
WILL THE SUPERINTENDENT BE SURPRISED TO FIND HIS PREY WHERE HE LEAST SUSPECTS!
SHORTLY LATER -- FROM CONCEALMENT HE PHOTOGRAPHS WYMAN FLOGGING THE FUGITIVE
I HATE TO STAND IDLY BY, BUT ITS FOR THE BEST!
THROW HIM INTO THE SWEAT-BOX! -- HIS TORTURE HAS ONLY BEGUN!
MERCY! -- GIVE ME FOOD!
HUNGRY, CRANE? STARVING? HOW'D YOU LIKE TO HAVE SOME OF THIS FOOD? MOST PRISONERS HATE IT, BUT YOU'D LIKE SOME OF IT NOW, WOULDN'T YOU?
WELL, YOU CAN'T -- --AWK-K!
A HAND DESCENDS ON WYMAN'S NECK WITH AN IRON-LIKE GRIP!
HELPLESS IN SUPERMAN'S CLUTCH, WYMAN'S FACE IS BURIED AMIDST THE FOOD ON THE PLATE.
LET'S SEE HOW YOU LIKE THE UN-DIGESTIBLE SLOP YOU'VE FED YOUR PRISONERS!
BLUB
SUPERMAN REMOVES CRANE FROM THE SWEAT-BOX, SUBSTITUTES THE TERRIFIED SUPERINTENDENT IN HIS PLACE
I'VE GOT TO LEAVE YOU NOW... BUT I'LL BE BACK -- MAYBE!
NEXT INSTANT, THE MAN OF STEEL IS DASHING OFF INTO THE NIGHT, A FLEETING SHADOW UNDER THE MOONS HAZY RAYS . . .

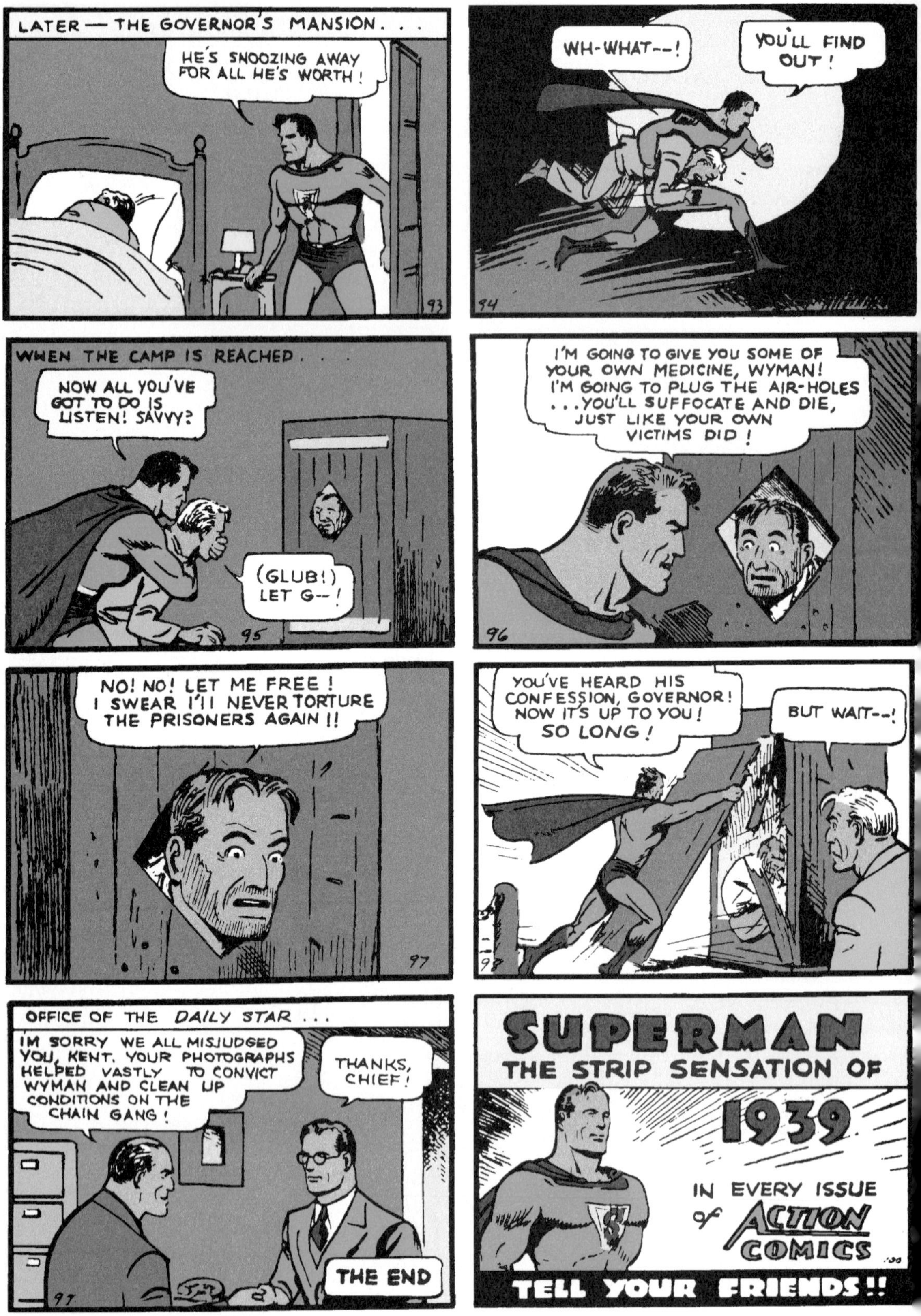

LATER — THE GOVERNOR'S MANSION . . .
HE'S SNOOZING AWAY FOR ALL HE'S WORTH!
WH-WHAT--!
YOU'LL FIND OUT!
WHEN THE CAMP IS REACHED . . .
NOW ALL YOU'VE GOT TO DO IS LISTEN! SAVVY?
(GLUB!) LET G--!
I'M GOING TO GIVE YOU SOME OF YOUR OWN MEDICINE, WYMAN! I'M GOING TO PLUG THE AIR-HOLES . . . YOU'LL SUFFOCATE AND DIE, JUST LIKE YOUR OWN VICTIMS DID!
NO! NO! LET ME FREE! I SWEAR I'LL NEVER TORTURE THE PRISONERS AGAIN!!
YOU'VE HEARD HIS CONFESSION, GOVERNOR! NOW IT'S UP TO YOU! SO LONG!
BUT WAIT--!
OFFICE OF THE DAILY STAR . . .
I'M SORRY WE ALL MISJUDGED YOU, KENT. YOUR PHOTOGRAPHS HELPED VASTLY TO CONVICT WYMAN AND CLEAN UP CONDITIONS ON THE CHAIN GANG!
THANKS, CHIEF!
THE END
SUPERMAN
THE STRIP SENSATION OF
1939
IN EVERY ISSUE of ACTION COMICS
TELL YOUR FRIENDS!!

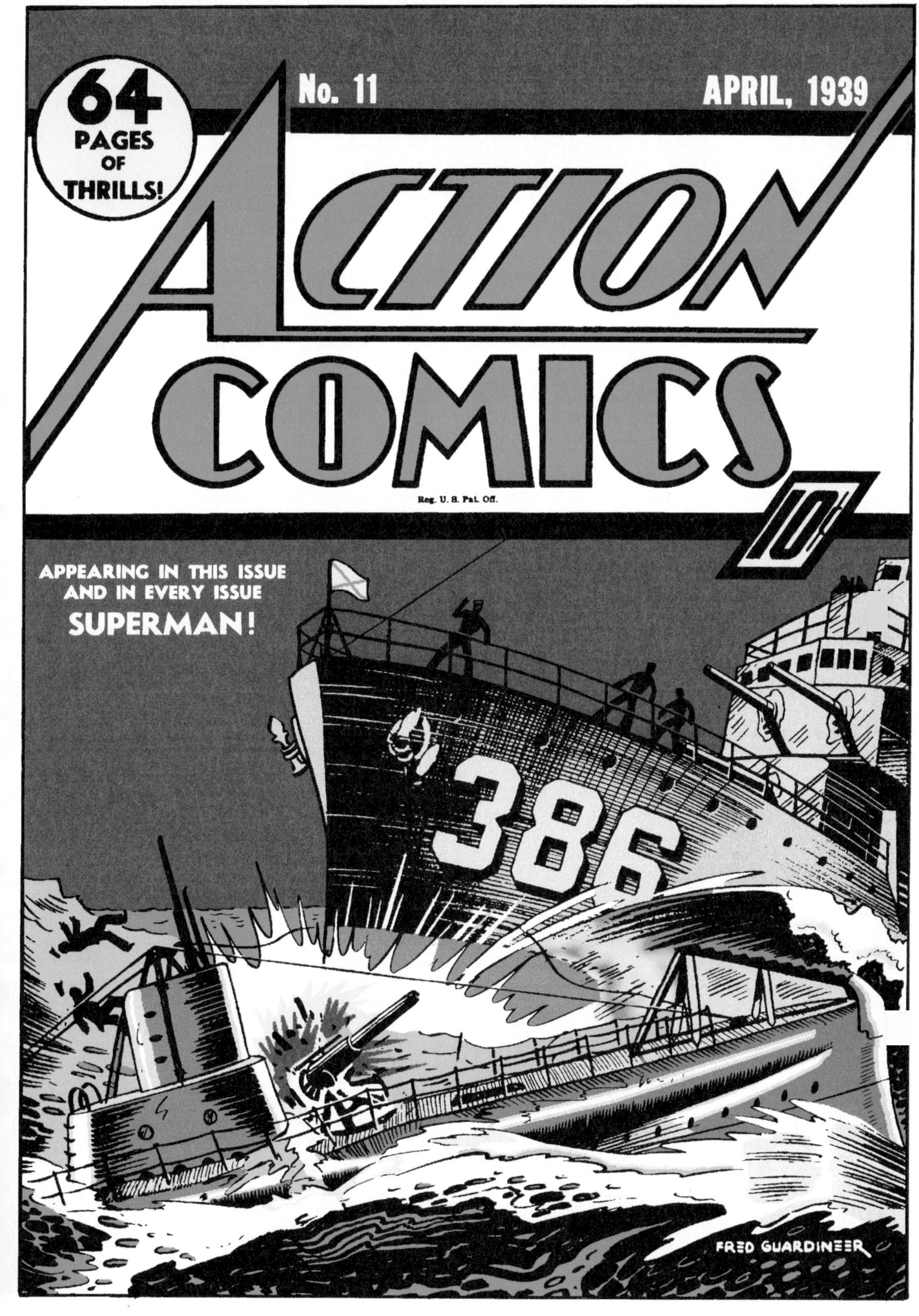

64 PAGES OF THRILLS!
No. 11
APRIL, 1939
ACTION COMICS
Reg. U. S. Pat. Off.
10¢
APPEARING IN THIS ISSUE AND IN EVERY ISSUE SUPERMAN!
386
FRED GUARDINEER

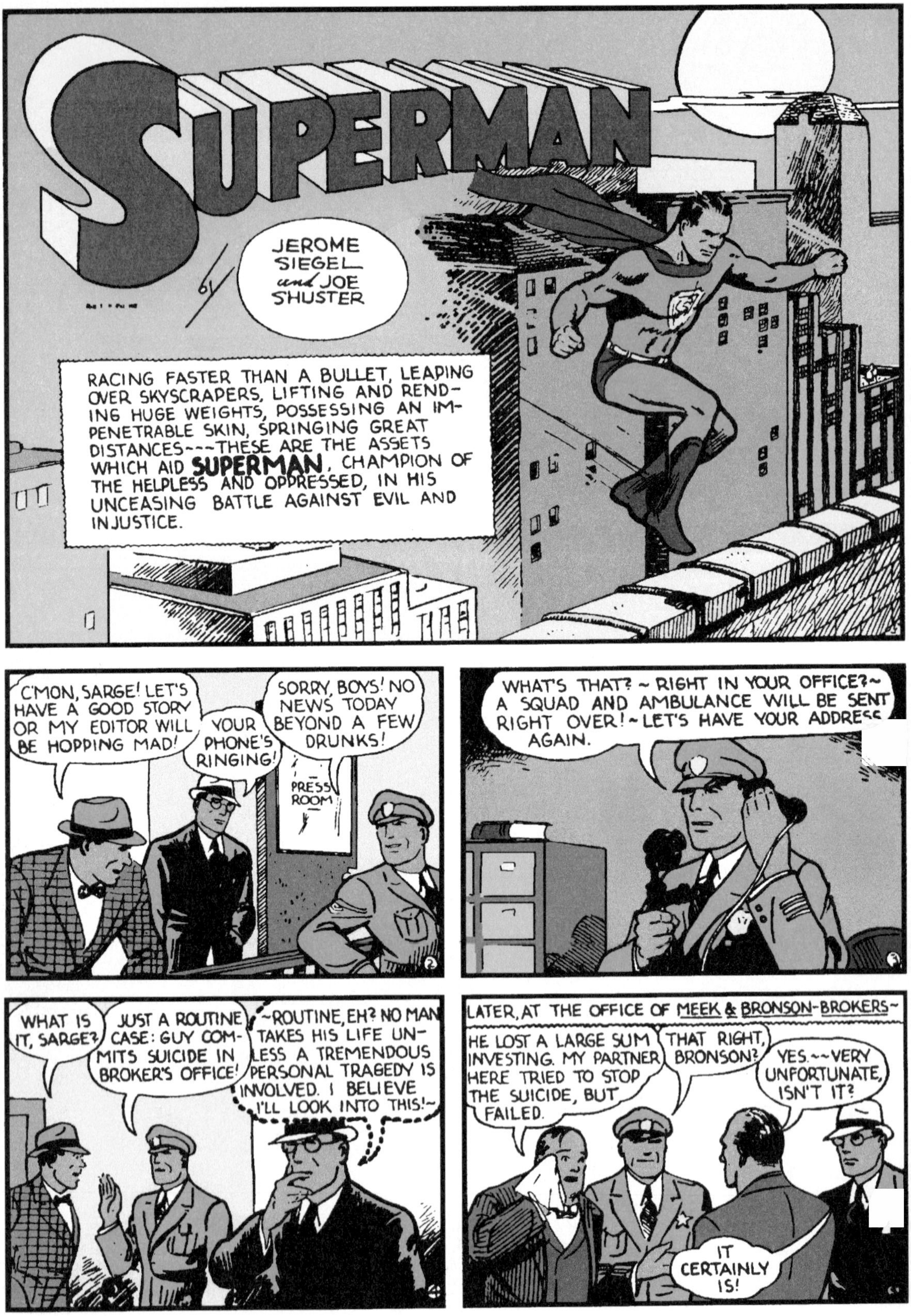
SUPERMAN
by
JEROME SIEGEL and JOE SHUSTER
RACING FASTER THAN A BULLET, LEAPING OVER SKYSCRAPERS, LIFTING AND RENDING HUGE WEIGHTS, POSSESSING AN IMPENETRABLE SKIN, SPRINGING GREAT DISTANCES---THESE ARE THE ASSETS WHICH AID SUPERMAN, CHAMPION OF THE HELPLESS AND OPPRESSED, IN HIS UNCEASING BATTLE AGAINST EVIL AND INJUSTICE.
C'MON, SARGE! LET'S HAVE A GOOD STORY OR MY EDITOR WILL BE HOPPING MAD!
SORRY, BOYS! NO NEWS TODAY BEYOND A FEW DRUNKS!
YOUR PHONE'S RINGING!
PRESS ROOM
WHAT'S THAT? ~ RIGHT IN YOUR OFFICE?~ A SQUAD AND AMBULANCE WILL BE SENT RIGHT OVER! ~ LET'S HAVE YOUR ADDRESS AGAIN.
WHAT IS IT, SARGE?
JUST A ROUTINE CASE: GUY COMMITS SUICIDE IN BROKER'S OFFICE!
~ROUTINE, EH? NO MAN TAKES HIS LIFE UNLESS A TREMENDOUS PERSONAL TRAGEDY IS INVOLVED. I BELIEVE I'LL LOOK INTO THIS!~
LATER, AT THE OFFICE OF MEEK & BRONSON-BROKERS~
HE LOST A LARGE SUM INVESTING. MY PARTNER HERE TRIED TO STOP THE SUICIDE, BUT FAILED.
THAT RIGHT, BRONSON?
YES.~~VERY UNFORTUNATE, ISN'T IT?
IT CERTAINLY IS!

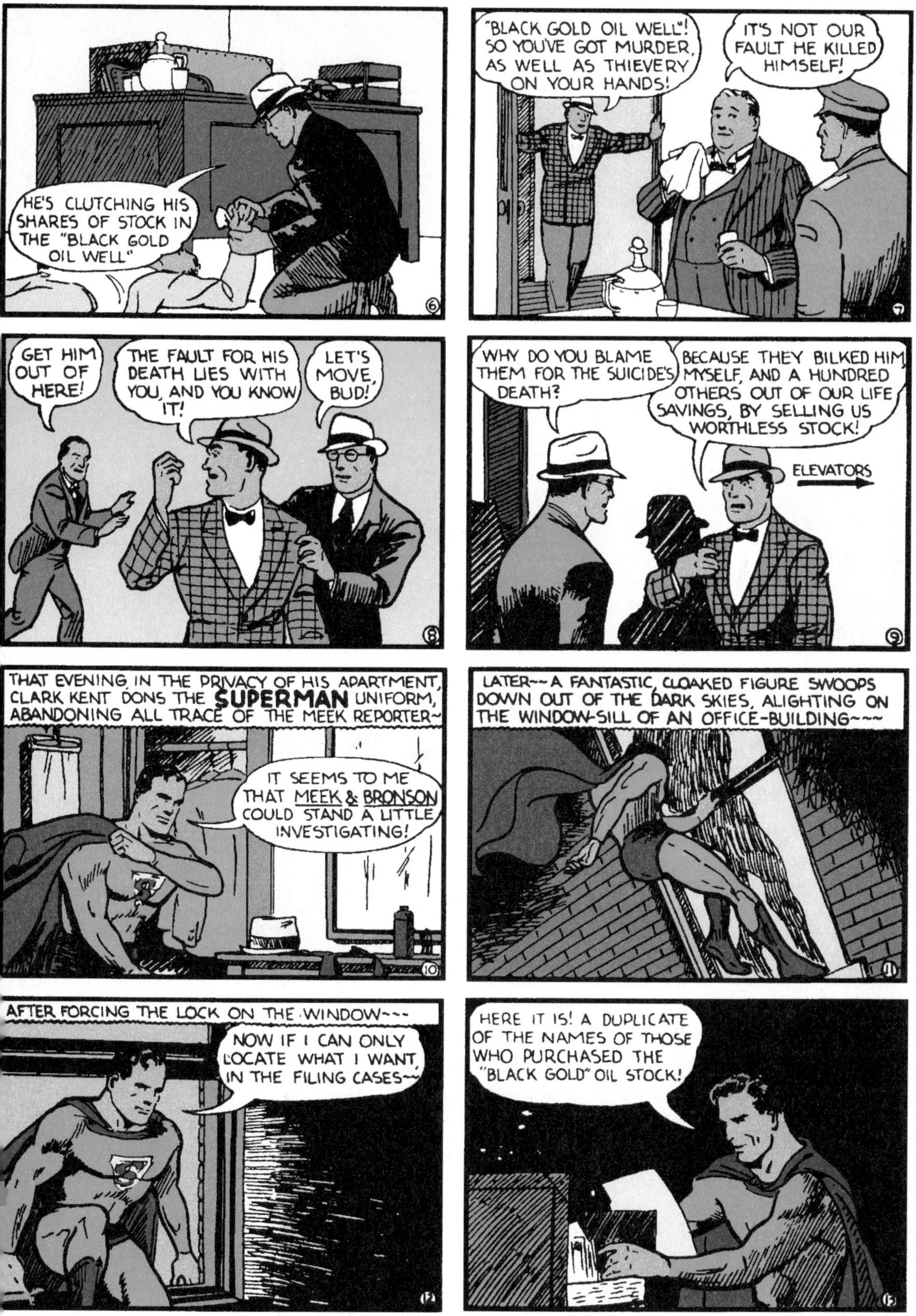
HE'S CLUTCHING HIS SHARES OF STOCK IN THE "BLACK GOLD OIL WELL"
"BLACK GOLD OIL WELL"! SO YOU'VE GOT MURDER, AS WELL AS THIEVERY ON YOUR HANDS!
IT'S NOT OUR FAULT HE KILLED HIMSELF!
GET HIM OUT OF HERE!
THE FAULT FOR HIS DEATH LIES WITH YOU, AND YOU KNOW IT!
LET'S MOVE, BUD!
WHY DO YOU BLAME THEM FOR THE SUICIDE'S DEATH?
BECAUSE THEY BILKED HIM, MYSELF, AND A HUNDRED OTHERS OUT OF OUR LIFE SAVINGS, BY SELLING US WORTHLESS STOCK!
ELEVATORS
THAT EVENING, IN THE PRIVACY OF HIS APARTMENT, CLARK KENT DONS THE SUPERMAN UNIFORM, ABANDONING ALL TRACE OF THE MEEK REPORTER~
IT SEEMS TO ME THAT MEEK & BRONSON COULD STAND A LITTLE INVESTIGATING!
LATER-- A FANTASTIC, CLOAKED FIGURE SWOOPS DOWN OUT OF THE DARK SKIES, ALIGHTING ON THE WINDOW-SILL OF AN OFFICE-BUILDING---
AFTER FORCING THE LOCK ON THE WINDOW---
NOW IF I CAN ONLY LOCATE WHAT I WANT, IN THE FILING CASES--
HERE IT IS! A DUPLICATE OF THE NAMES OF THOSE WHO PURCHASED THE "BLACK GOLD" OIL STOCK!

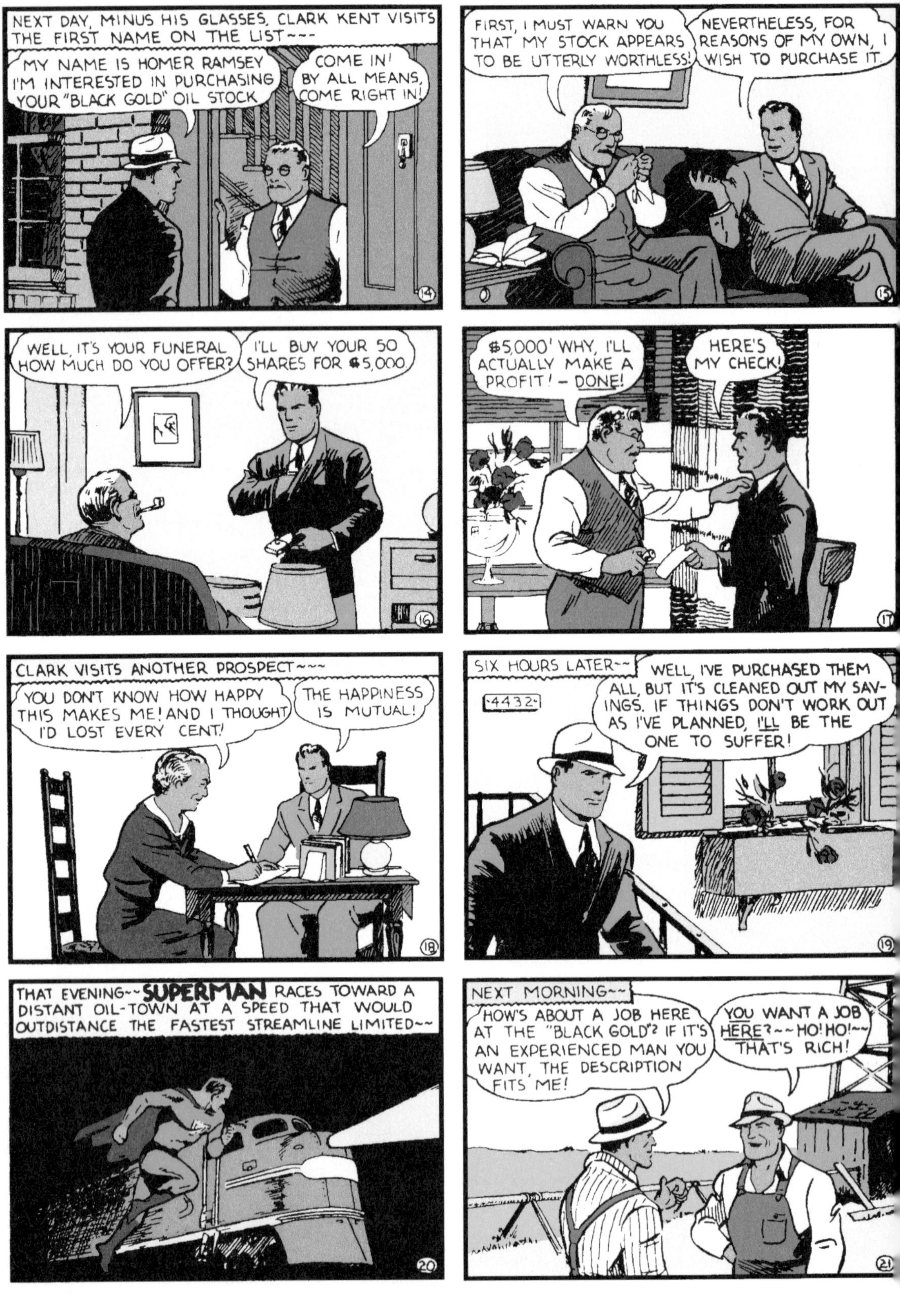
NEXT DAY, MINUS HIS GLASSES, CLARK KENT VISITS THE FIRST NAME ON THE LIST---
MY NAME IS HOMER RAMSEY I'M INTERESTED IN PURCHASING YOUR "BLACK GOLD" OIL STOCK
COME IN! BY ALL MEANS, COME RIGHT IN!
FIRST, I MUST WARN YOU THAT MY STOCK APPEARS TO BE UTTERLY WORTHLESS!
NEVERTHELESS, FOR REASONS OF MY OWN, I WISH TO PURCHASE IT.
WELL, IT'S YOUR FUNERAL HOW MUCH DO YOU OFFER?
I'LL BUY YOUR 50 SHARES FOR $5,000
$5,000! WHY, I'LL ACTUALLY MAKE A PROFIT! - DONE!
HERE'S MY CHECK!
CLARK VISITS ANOTHER PROSPECT---
YOU DON'T KNOW HOW HAPPY THIS MAKES ME! AND I THOUGHT I'D LOST EVERY CENT!
THE HAPPINESS IS MUTUAL!
SIX HOURS LATER--
4432
WELL, I'VE PURCHASED THEM ALL, BUT IT'S CLEANED OUT MY SAVINGS. IF THINGS DON'T WORK OUT AS I'VE PLANNED, I'LL BE THE ONE TO SUFFER!
THAT EVENING--SUPERMAN RACES TOWARD A DISTANT OIL-TOWN AT A SPEED THAT WOULD OUTDISTANCE THE FASTEST STREAMLINE LIMITED--
NEXT MORNING--
HOW'S ABOUT A JOB HERE AT THE "BLACK GOLD"? IF IT'S AN EXPERIENCED MAN YOU WANT, THE DESCRIPTION FITS ME!
YOU WANT A JOB HERE?--HO! HO!--THAT'S RICH!

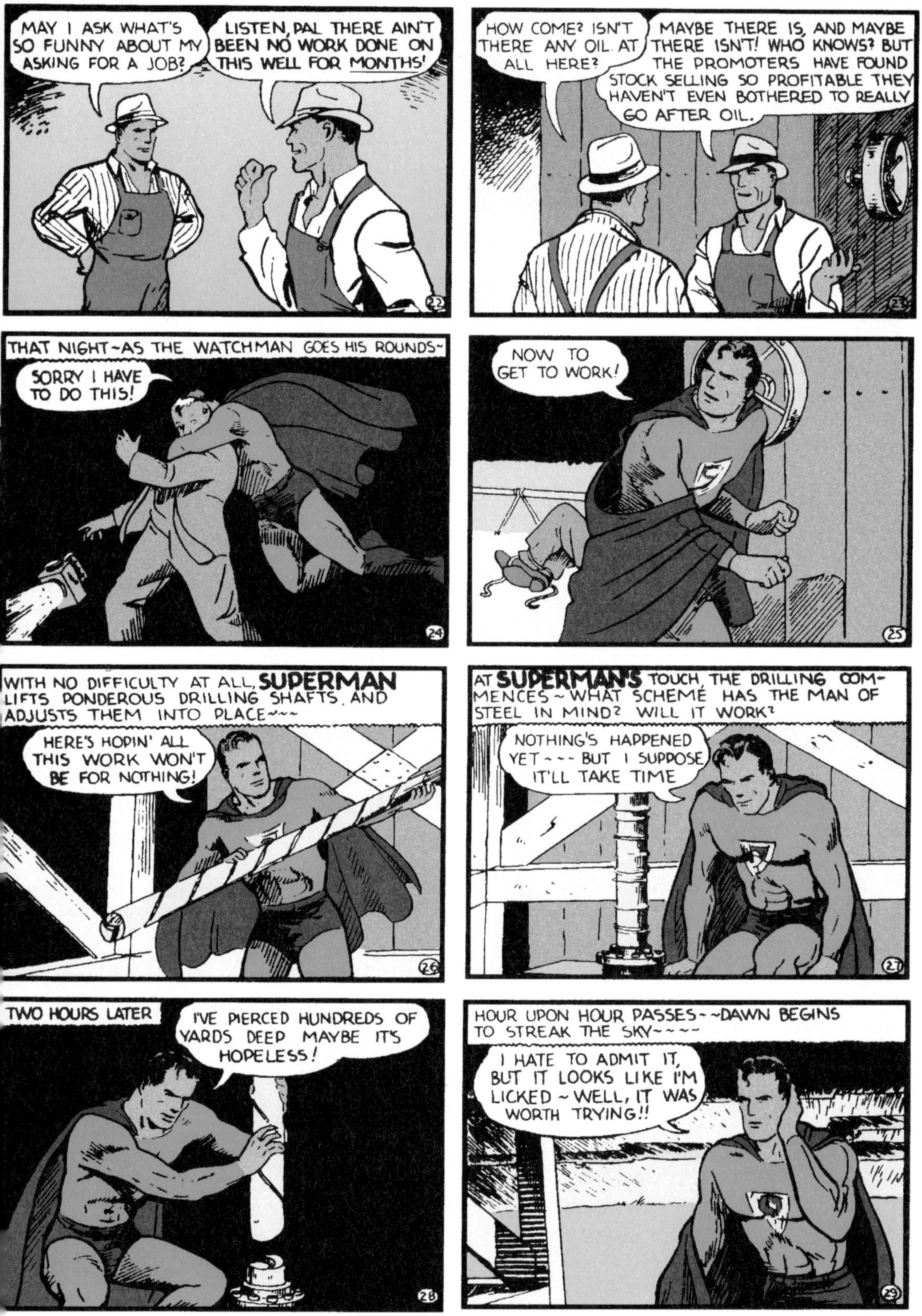
MAY I ASK WHAT'S SO FUNNY ABOUT MY ASKING FOR A JOB?
LISTEN, PAL THERE AIN'T BEEN NO WORK DONE ON THIS WELL FOR MONTHS!
22
HOW COME? ISN'T THERE ANY OIL AT ALL HERE?
MAYBE THERE IS, AND MAYBE THERE ISN'T! WHO KNOWS? BUT THE PROMOTERS HAVE FOUND STOCK SELLING SO PROFITABLE THEY HAVEN'T EVEN BOTHERED TO REALLY GO AFTER OIL.
23
THAT NIGHT~AS THE WATCHMAN GOES HIS ROUNDS~
SORRY I HAVE TO DO THIS!
24
NOW TO GET TO WORK!
25
WITH NO DIFFICULTY AT ALL, SUPERMAN LIFTS PONDEROUS DRILLING SHAFTS, AND ADJUSTS THEM INTO PLACE~~~
HERE'S HOPIN' ALL THIS WORK WON'T BE FOR NOTHING!
26
AT SUPERMAN'S TOUCH, THE DRILLING COMMENCES~WHAT SCHEME HAS THE MAN OF STEEL IN MIND? WILL IT WORK?
NOTHING'S HAPPENED YET~~~BUT I SUPPOSE IT'LL TAKE TIME
27
TWO HOURS LATER
I'VE PIERCED HUNDREDS OF YARDS DEEP MAYBE IT'S HOPELESS!
28
HOUR UPON HOUR PASSES~~DAWN BEGINS TO STREAK THE SKY~~~~
I HATE TO ADMIT IT, BUT IT LOOKS LIKE I'M LICKED~WELL, IT WAS WORTH TRYING!!
29

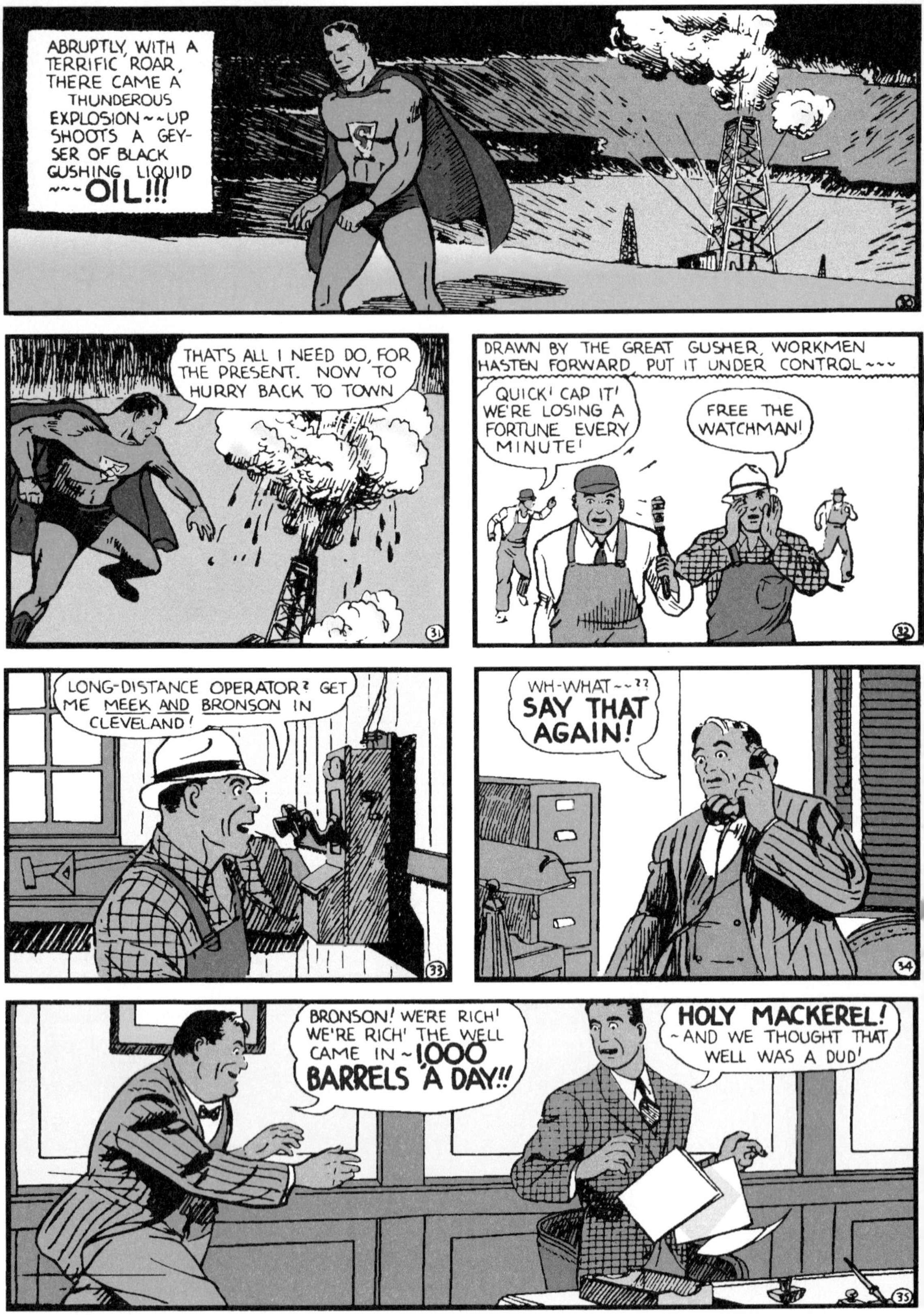
ABRUPTLY, WITH A TERRIFIC ROAR, THERE CAME A THUNDEROUS EXPLOSION~~UP SHOOTS A GEYSER OF BLACK GUSHING LIQUID ~~~OIL!!!
THAT'S ALL I NEED DO, FOR THE PRESENT. NOW TO HURRY BACK TO TOWN
DRAWN BY THE GREAT GUSHER, WORKMEN HASTEN FORWARD, PUT IT UNDER CONTROL~~~
QUICK! CAP IT! WE'RE LOSING A FORTUNE EVERY MINUTE!
FREE THE WATCHMAN!
LONG-DISTANCE OPERATOR? GET ME MEEK AND BRONSON IN CLEVELAND!
WH-WHAT~~?? SAY THAT AGAIN!
BRONSON! WE'RE RICH! WE'RE RICH! THE WELL CAME IN ~1000 BARRELS A DAY!!
HOLY MACKEREL! ~AND WE THOUGHT THAT WELL WAS A DUD!

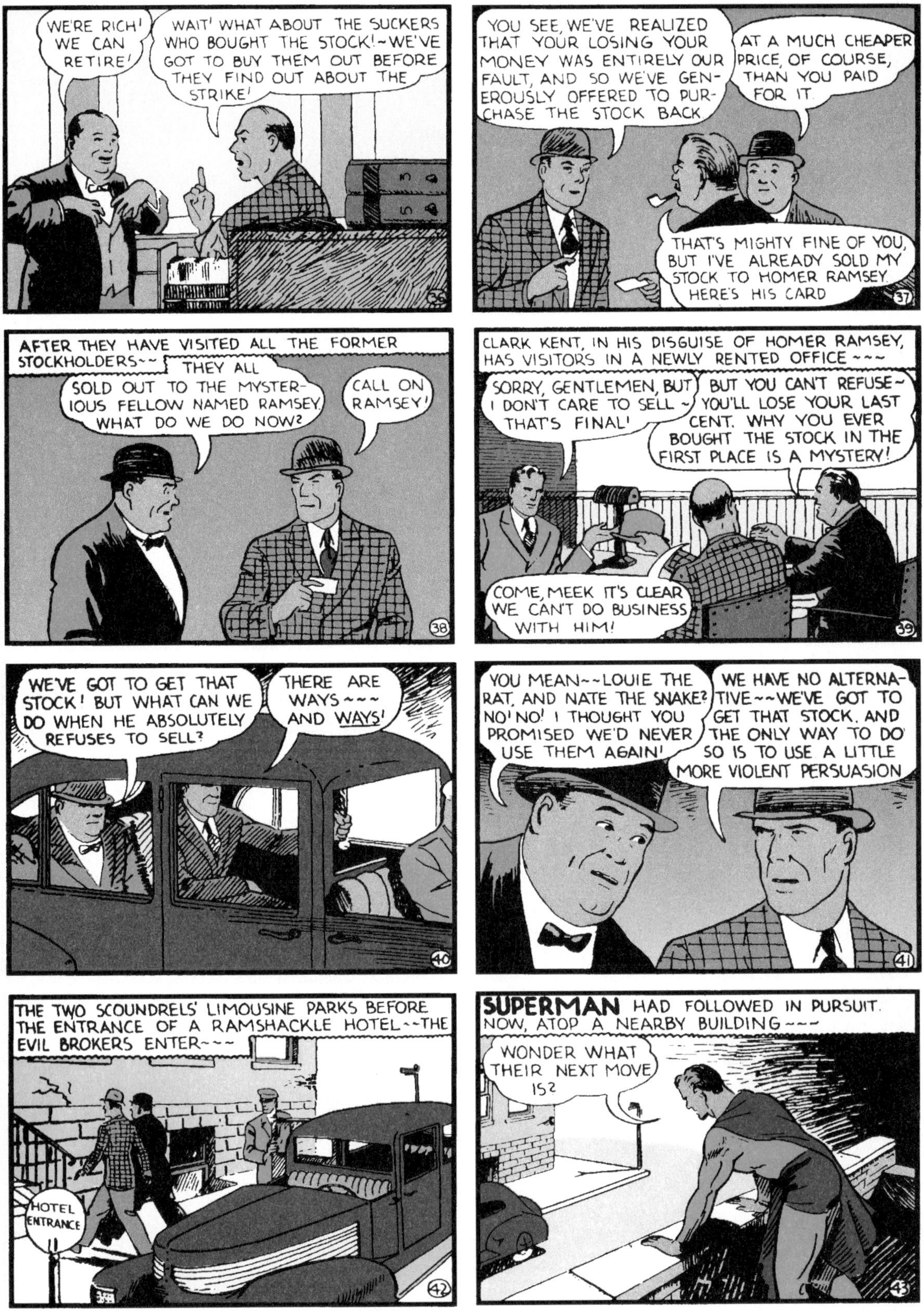
WE'RE RICH! WE CAN RETIRE!
WAIT! WHAT ABOUT THE SUCKERS WHO BOUGHT THE STOCK!~WE'VE GOT TO BUY THEM OUT BEFORE THEY FIND OUT ABOUT THE STRIKE!
YOU SEE, WE'VE REALIZED THAT YOUR LOSING YOUR MONEY WAS ENTIRELY OUR FAULT, AND SO WE'VE GENEROUSLY OFFERED TO PURCHASE THE STOCK BACK
AT A MUCH CHEAPER PRICE, OF COURSE, THAN YOU PAID FOR IT.
THAT'S MIGHTY FINE OF YOU, BUT I'VE ALREADY SOLD MY STOCK TO HOMER RAMSEY. HERE'S HIS CARD
AFTER THEY HAVE VISITED ALL THE FORMER STOCKHOLDERS~~
THEY ALL SOLD OUT TO THE MYSTERIOUS FELLOW NAMED RAMSEY. WHAT DO WE DO NOW?
CALL ON RAMSEY!
CLARK KENT, IN HIS DISGUISE OF HOMER RAMSEY, HAS VISITORS IN A NEWLY RENTED OFFICE ~~~
SORRY, GENTLEMEN, BUT I DON'T CARE TO SELL ~ THAT'S FINAL!
BUT YOU CAN'T REFUSE~ YOU'LL LOSE YOUR LAST CENT. WHY YOU EVER BOUGHT THE STOCK IN THE FIRST PLACE IS A MYSTERY!
COME, MEEK IT'S CLEAR WE CAN'T DO BUSINESS WITH HIM!
WE'VE GOT TO GET THAT STOCK! BUT WHAT CAN WE DO WHEN HE ABSOLUTELY REFUSES TO SELL?
THERE ARE WAYS~~~ AND WAYS!
YOU MEAN~~LOUIE THE RAT, AND NATE THE SNAKE? NO! NO! I THOUGHT YOU PROMISED WE'D NEVER USE THEM AGAIN!
WE HAVE NO ALTERNATIVE~~WE'VE GOT TO GET THAT STOCK. AND THE ONLY WAY TO DO SO IS TO USE A LITTLE MORE VIOLENT PERSUASION
THE TWO SCOUNDRELS' LIMOUSINE PARKS BEFORE THE ENTRANCE OF A RAMSHACKLE HOTEL~~THE EVIL BROKERS ENTER~~~
HOTEL ENTRANCE
SUPERMAN HAD FOLLOWED IN PURSUIT. NOW, ATOP A NEARBY BUILDING~~~
WONDER WHAT THEIR NEXT MOVE IS?

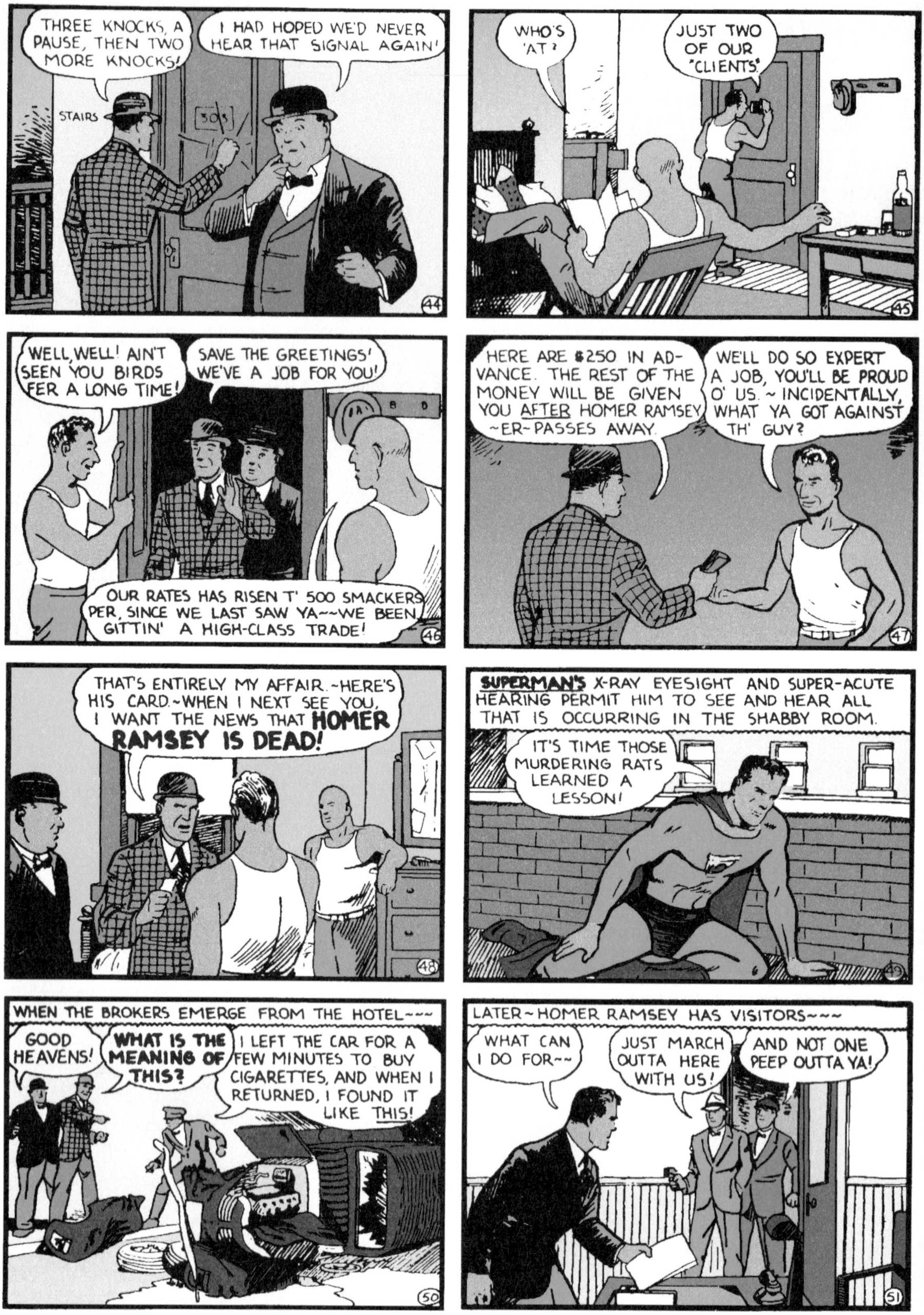
THREE KNOCKS, A PAUSE, THEN TWO MORE KNOCKS!
I HAD HOPED WE'D NEVER HEAR THAT SIGNAL AGAIN!
STAIRS
44
WHO'S 'AT?
JUST TWO OF OUR "CLIENTS"
45
WELL, WELL! AIN'T SEEN YOU BIRDS FER A LONG TIME!
SAVE THE GREETINGS! WE'VE A JOB FOR YOU!
OUR RATES HAS RISEN T' 500 SMACKERS PER, SINCE WE LAST SAW YA~~WE BEEN GITTIN' A HIGH-CLASS TRADE!
46
HERE ARE $250 IN ADVANCE. THE REST OF THE MONEY WILL BE GIVEN YOU AFTER HOMER RAMSEY ~ER~ PASSES AWAY.
WE'LL DO SO EXPERT A JOB, YOU'LL BE PROUD O' US. ~ INCIDENTALLY, WHAT YA GOT AGAINST TH' GUY?
47
THAT'S ENTIRELY MY AFFAIR.~HERE'S HIS CARD.~WHEN I NEXT SEE YOU, I WANT THE NEWS THAT HOMER RAMSEY IS DEAD!
48
SUPERMAN'S X-RAY EYESIGHT AND SUPER-ACUTE HEARING PERMIT HIM TO SEE AND HEAR ALL THAT IS OCCURRING IN THE SHABBY ROOM.
IT'S TIME THOSE MURDERING RATS LEARNED A LESSON!
49
WHEN THE BROKERS EMERGE FROM THE HOTEL~~~
GOOD HEAVENS!
WHAT IS THE MEANING OF THIS?
I LEFT THE CAR FOR A FEW MINUTES TO BUY CIGARETTES, AND WHEN I RETURNED, I FOUND IT LIKE THIS!
50
LATER~HOMER RAMSEY HAS VISITORS~~~
WHAT CAN I DO FOR~~
JUST MARCH OUTTA HERE WITH US!
AND NOT ONE PEEP OUTTA YA!
51

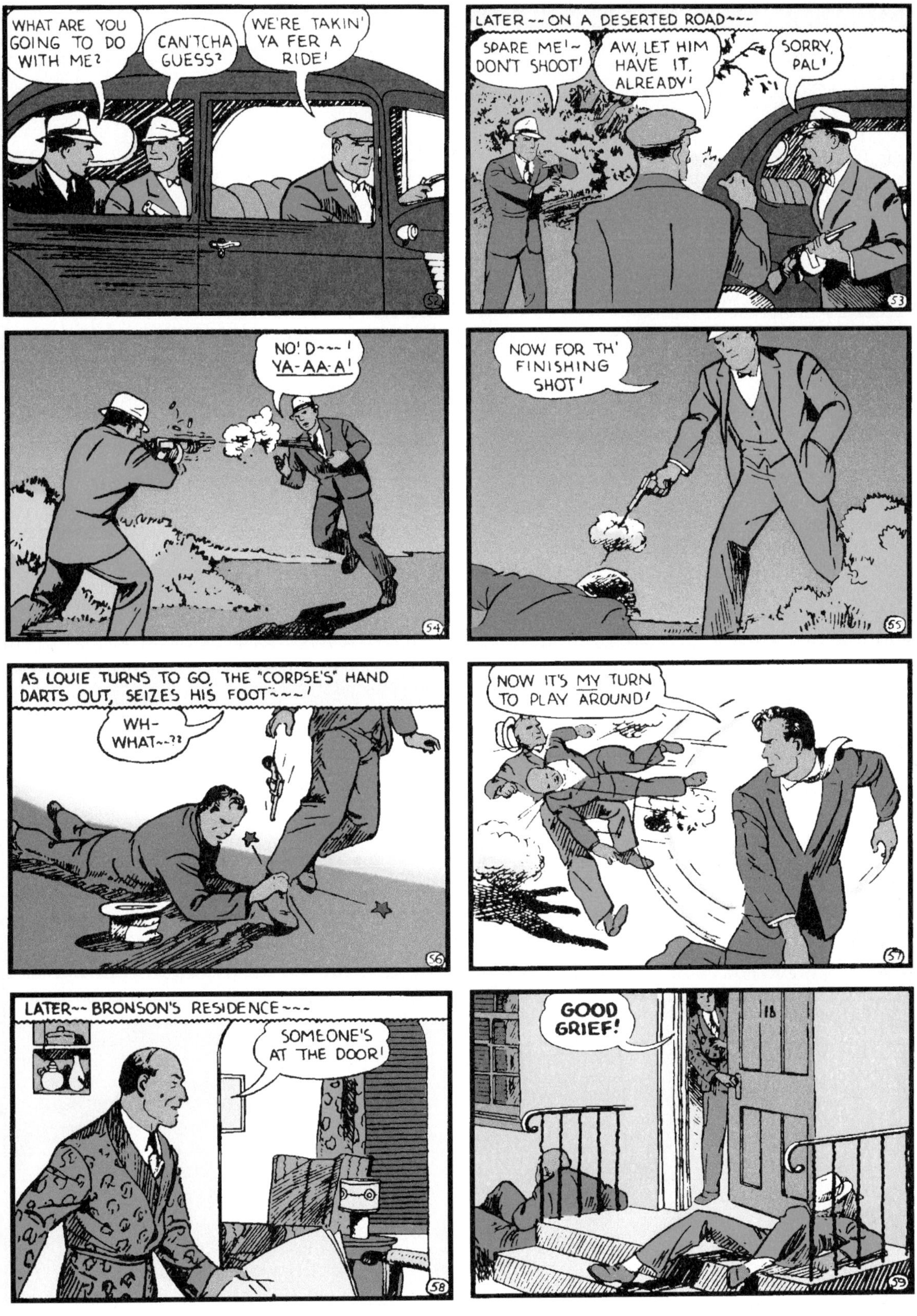
WHAT ARE YOU GOING TO DO WITH ME?
CAN'TCHA GUESS?
WE'RE TAKIN' YA FER A RIDE!
LATER--ON A DESERTED ROAD---
SPARE ME!-DON'T SHOOT!
AW, LET HIM HAVE IT, ALREADY!
SORRY, PAL!
NO! D---! YA-AA-A!
NOW FOR TH' FINISHING SHOT!
AS LOUIE TURNS TO GO, THE "CORPSE'S" HAND DARTS OUT, SEIZES HIS FOOT---!
WH-WHAT--??
NOW IT'S MY TURN TO PLAY AROUND!
LATER--BRONSON'S RESIDENCE---
SOMEONE'S AT THE DOOR!
GOOD GRIEF!

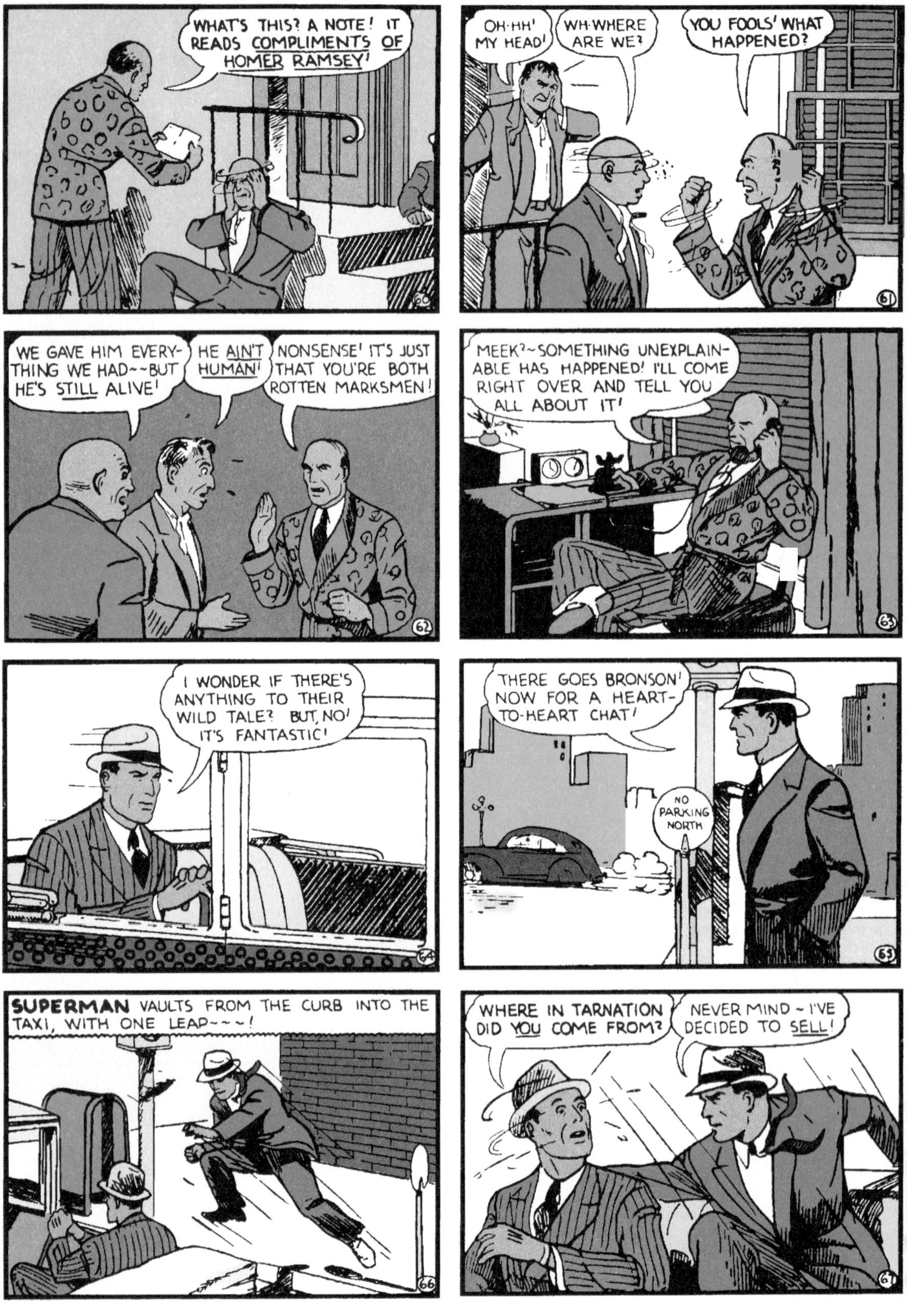
WHAT'S THIS? A NOTE! IT READS COMPLIMENTS OF HOMER RAMSEY!
OH-HH! MY HEAD!
WH-WHERE ARE WE?
YOU FOOLS! WHAT HAPPENED?
WE GAVE HIM EVERYTHING WE HAD--BUT HE'S STILL ALIVE!
HE AIN'T HUMAN!
NONSENSE! IT'S JUST THAT YOU'RE BOTH ROTTEN MARKSMEN!
MEEK?~SOMETHING UNEXPLAINABLE HAS HAPPENED! I'LL COME RIGHT OVER AND TELL YOU ALL ABOUT IT!
I WONDER IF THERE'S ANYTHING TO THEIR WILD TALE? BUT, NO! IT'S FANTASTIC!
THERE GOES BRONSON! NOW FOR A HEART-TO-HEART CHAT!
NO PARKING NORTH
SUPERMAN VAULTS FROM THE CURB INTO THE TAXI, WITH ONE LEAP~~~!
WHERE IN TARNATION DID YOU COME FROM?
NEVER MIND ~ I'VE DECIDED TO SELL!

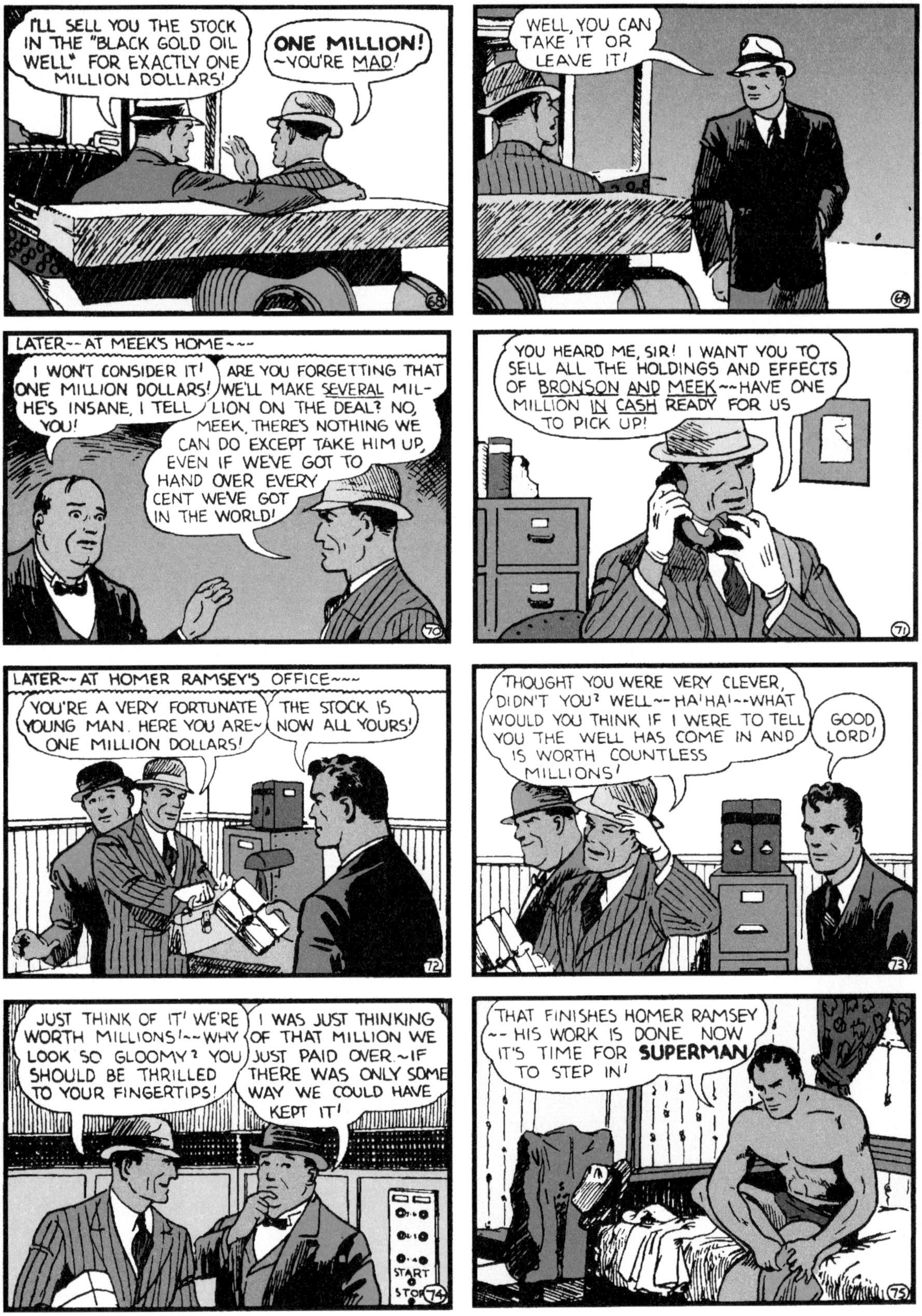
I'LL SELL YOU THE STOCK IN THE "BLACK GOLD OIL WELL" FOR EXACTLY ONE MILLION DOLLARS!
ONE MILLION! ~YOU'RE MAD!
WELL, YOU CAN TAKE IT OR LEAVE IT!
LATER--AT MEEK'S HOME---
I WON'T CONSIDER IT! ONE MILLION DOLLARS! HE'S INSANE, I TELL YOU!
ARE YOU FORGETTING THAT WE'LL MAKE SEVERAL MILLION ON THE DEAL? NO, MEEK, THERE'S NOTHING WE CAN DO EXCEPT TAKE HIM UP, EVEN IF WE'VE GOT TO HAND OVER EVERY CENT WE'VE GOT IN THE WORLD!
YOU HEARD ME, SIR! I WANT YOU TO SELL ALL THE HOLDINGS AND EFFECTS OF BRONSON AND MEEK--HAVE ONE MILLION IN CASH READY FOR US TO PICK UP!
LATER--AT HOMER RAMSEY'S OFFICE---
YOU'RE A VERY FORTUNATE YOUNG MAN. HERE YOU ARE~ ONE MILLION DOLLARS!
THE STOCK IS NOW ALL YOURS!
THOUGHT YOU WERE VERY CLEVER, DIDN'T YOU? WELL--HA!HA!--WHAT WOULD YOU THINK IF I WERE TO TELL YOU THE WELL HAS COME IN AND IS WORTH COUNTLESS MILLIONS!
GOOD LORD!
JUST THINK OF IT! WE'RE WORTH MILLIONS!--WHY LOOK SO GLOOMY? YOU SHOULD BE THRILLED TO YOUR FINGERTIPS!
I WAS JUST THINKING OF THAT MILLION WE JUST PAID OVER~IF THERE WAS ONLY SOME WAY WE COULD HAVE KEPT IT!
START
STOP
THAT FINISHES HOMER RAMSEY--HIS WORK IS DONE. NOW IT'S TIME FOR SUPERMAN TO STEP IN!

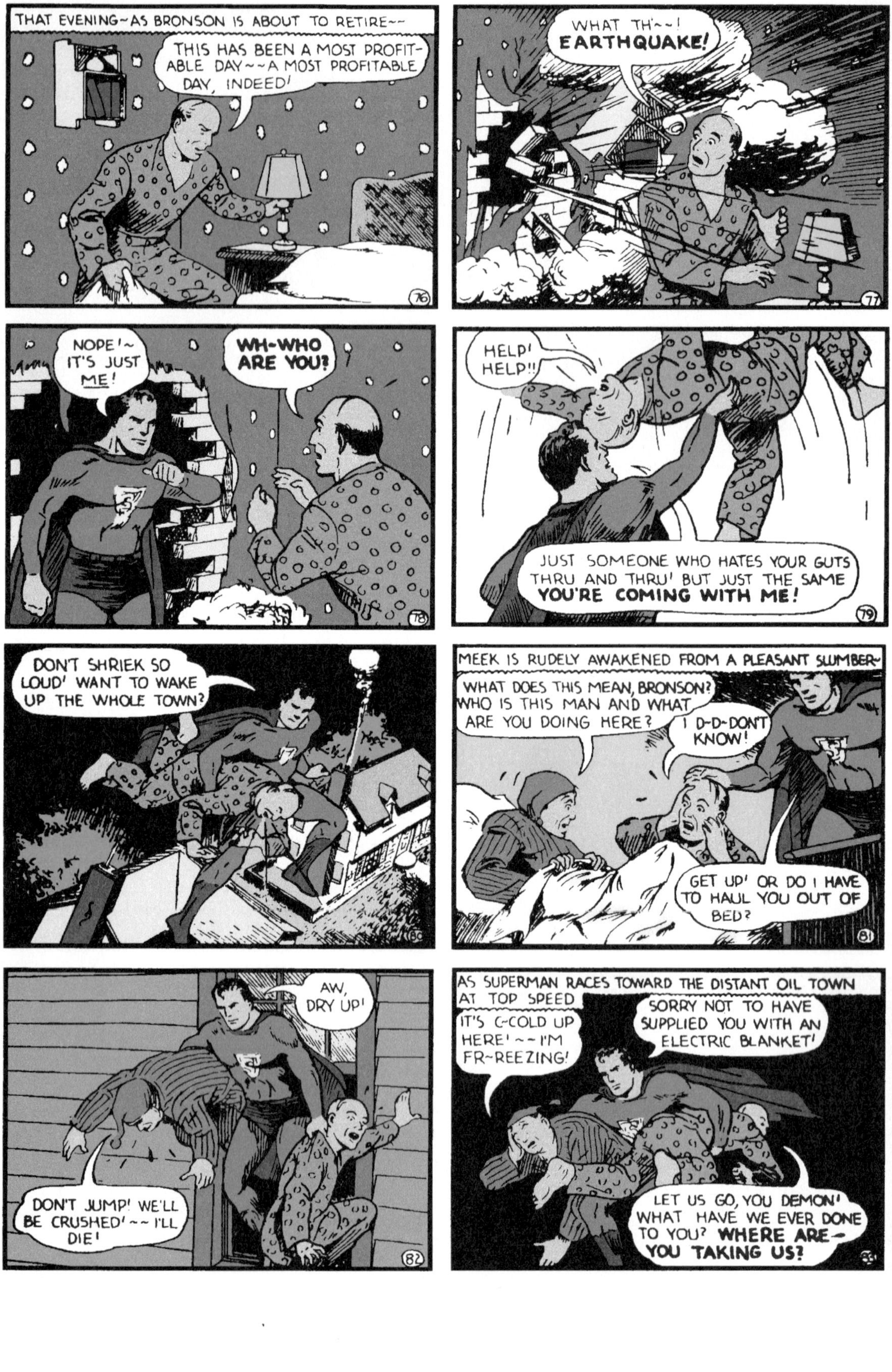

THAT EVENING~AS BRONSON IS ABOUT TO RETIRE~~
THIS HAS BEEN A MOST PROFITABLE DAY~~A MOST PROFITABLE DAY, INDEED!
76
WHAT TH'~~! EARTHQUAKE!
77
NOPE!~ IT'S JUST ME!
WH-WHO ARE YOU?
78
HELP! HELP!!
JUST SOMEONE WHO HATES YOUR GUTS THRU AND THRU! BUT JUST THE SAME YOU'RE COMING WITH ME!
79
DON'T SHRIEK SO LOUD! WANT TO WAKE UP THE WHOLE TOWN?
80
MEEK IS RUDELY AWAKENED FROM A PLEASANT SLUMBER~
WHAT DOES THIS MEAN, BRONSON? WHO IS THIS MAN AND WHAT ARE YOU DOING HERE?
I D-D-DON'T KNOW!
GET UP! OR DO I HAVE TO HAUL YOU OUT OF BED?
81
AW, DRY UP!
DON'T JUMP! WE'LL BE CRUSHED!~~I'LL DIE!
82
AS SUPERMAN RACES TOWARD THE DISTANT OIL TOWN AT TOP SPEED
IT'S C-COLD UP HERE!~~I'M FR~REEZING!
SORRY NOT TO HAVE SUPPLIED YOU WITH AN ELECTRIC BLANKET!
LET US GO, YOU DEMON! WHAT HAVE WE EVER DONE TO YOU? WHERE ARE YOU TAKING US?

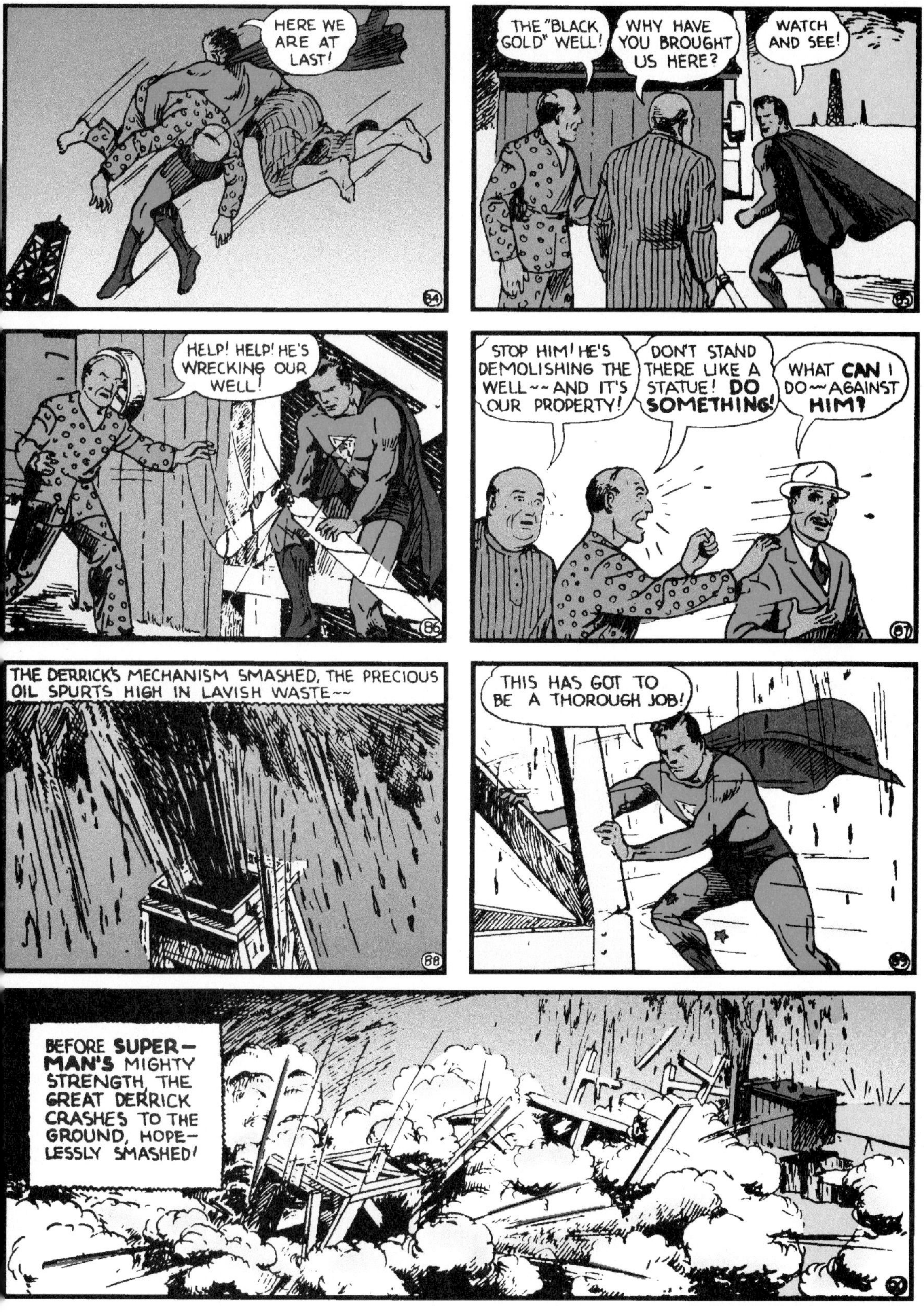
HERE WE ARE AT LAST!
THE "BLACK GOLD" WELL!
WHY HAVE YOU BROUGHT US HERE?
WATCH AND SEE!
HELP! HELP! HE'S WRECKING OUR WELL!
STOP HIM! HE'S DEMOLISHING THE WELL-- AND IT'S OUR PROPERTY!
DON'T STAND THERE LIKE A STATUE! **DO SOMETHING!**
WHAT **CAN** I DO--AGAINST **HIM?**
THE DERRICK'S MECHANISM SMASHED, THE PRECIOUS OIL SPURTS HIGH IN LAVISH WASTE--
THIS HAS GOT TO BE A THOROUGH JOB!
BEFORE **SUPERMAN'S** MIGHTY STRENGTH, THE **GREAT DERRICK** CRASHES TO THE GROUND, HOPELESSLY SMASHED!

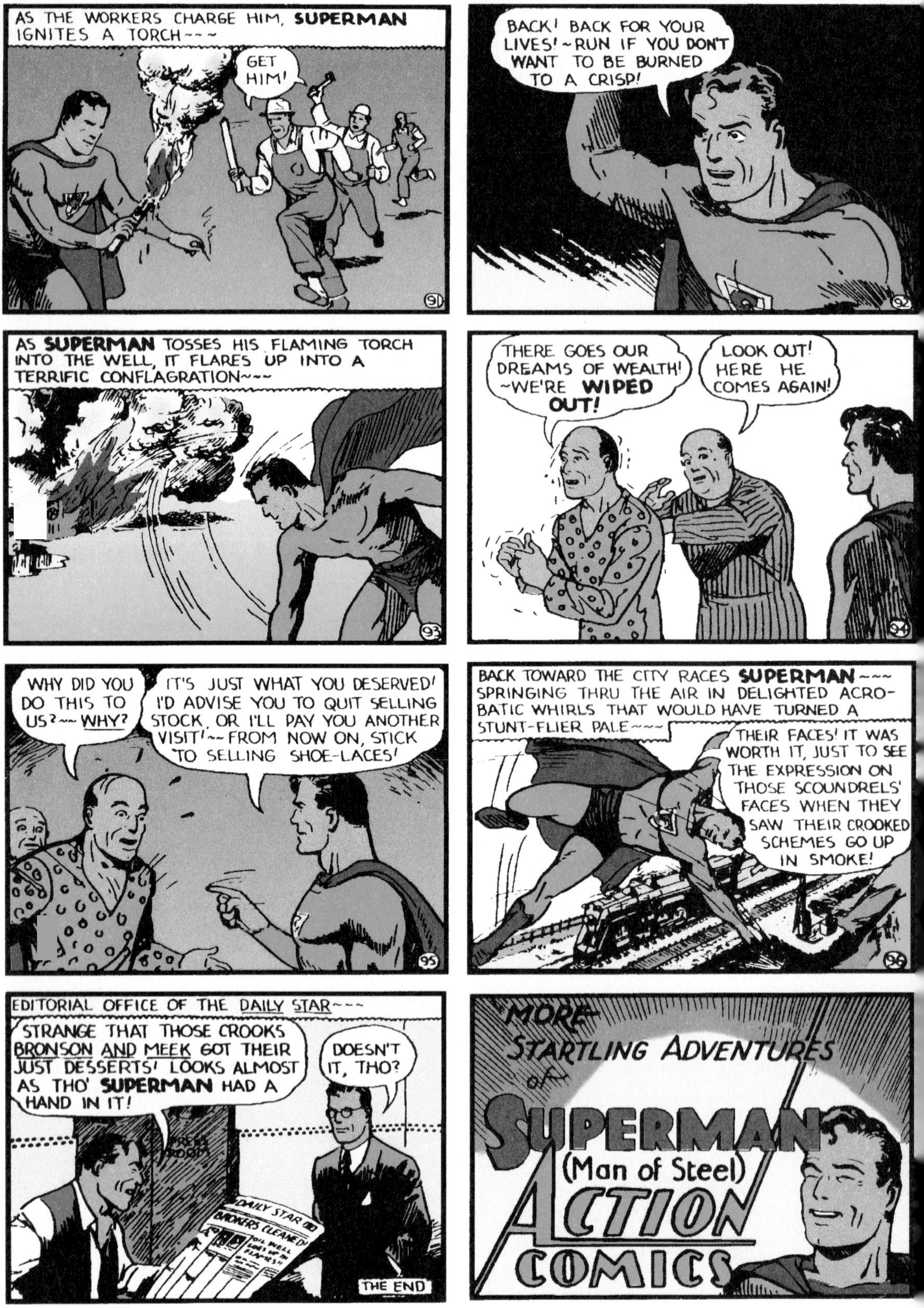
AS THE WORKERS CHARGE HIM, SUPERMAN IGNITES A TORCH---
GET HIM!
BACK! BACK FOR YOUR LIVES! ~RUN IF YOU DON'T WANT TO BE BURNED TO A CRISP!
AS SUPERMAN TOSSES HIS FLAMING TORCH INTO THE WELL, IT FLARES UP INTO A TERRIFIC CONFLAGRATION---
THERE GOES OUR DREAMS OF WEALTH! ~WE'RE WIPED OUT!
LOOK OUT! HERE HE COMES AGAIN!
WHY DID YOU DO THIS TO US? ~~ WHY?
IT'S JUST WHAT YOU DESERVED! I'D ADVISE YOU TO QUIT SELLING STOCK, OR I'LL PAY YOU ANOTHER VISIT! ~~ FROM NOW ON, STICK TO SELLING SHOE-LACES!
BACK TOWARD THE CITY RACES SUPERMAN--- SPRINGING THRU THE AIR IN DELIGHTED ACRO-BATIC WHIRLS THAT WOULD HAVE TURNED A STUNT-FLIER PALE---
THEIR FACES! IT WAS WORTH IT, JUST TO SEE THE EXPRESSION ON THOSE SCOUNDRELS' FACES WHEN THEY SAW THEIR CROOKED SCHEMES GO UP IN SMOKE!
EDITORIAL OFFICE OF THE DAILY STAR---
STRANGE THAT THOSE CROOKS BRONSON AND MEEK GOT THEIR JUST DESSERTS! LOOKS ALMOST AS THO' SUPERMAN HAD A HAND IN IT!
DOESN'T IT, THO?
DAILY STAR
BROKERS CLEANED
THE END
MORE STARTLING ADVENTURES of
SUPERMAN
(Man of Steel)
ACTION COMICS

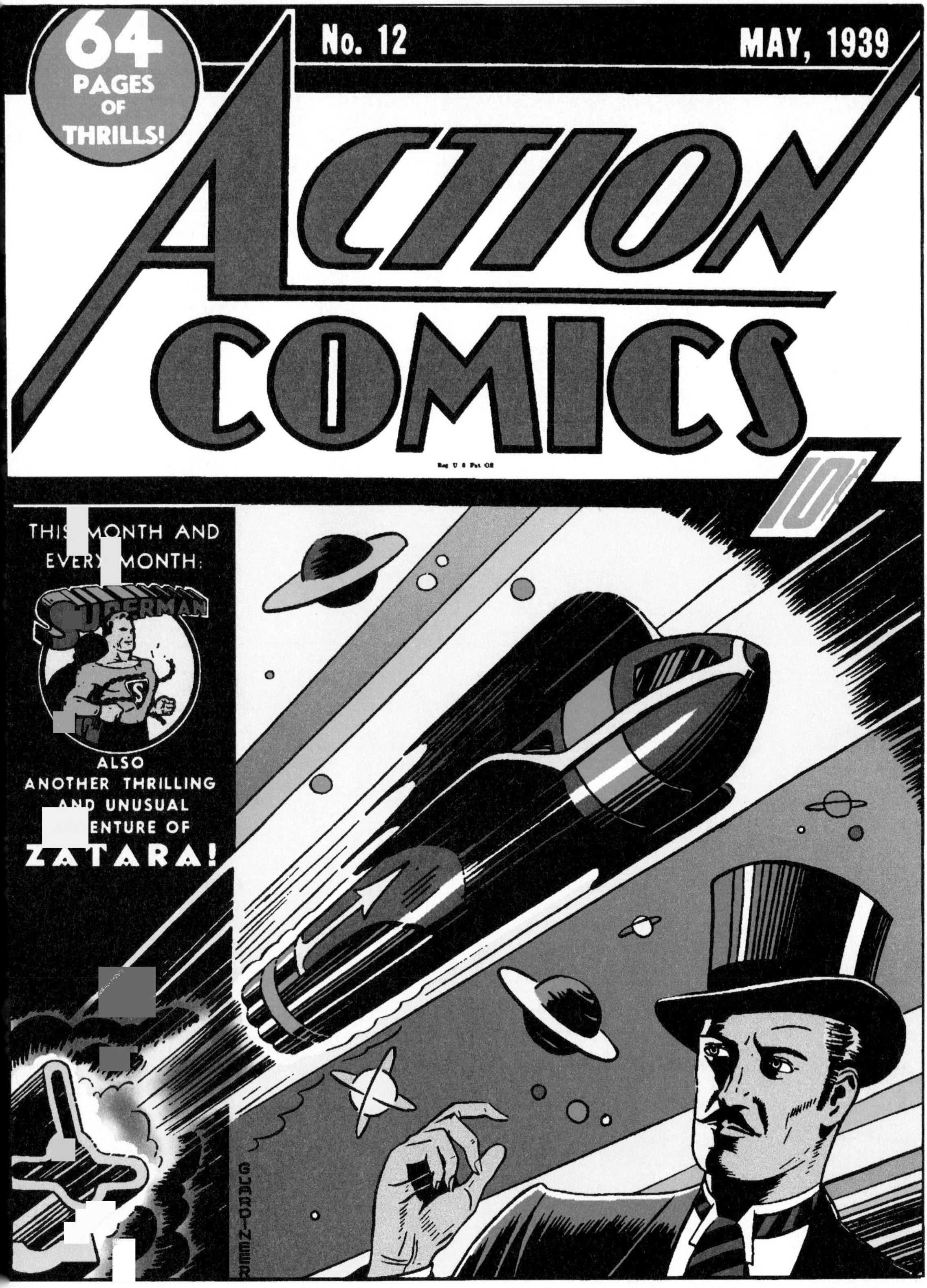

64 PAGES OF THRILLS!
No. 12
MAY, 1939
ACTION COMICS
10¢
THIS MONTH AND EVERY MONTH:
SUPERMAN
ALSO ANOTHER THRILLING AND UNUSUAL ENTURE OF
ZATARA!
GUARDINEER

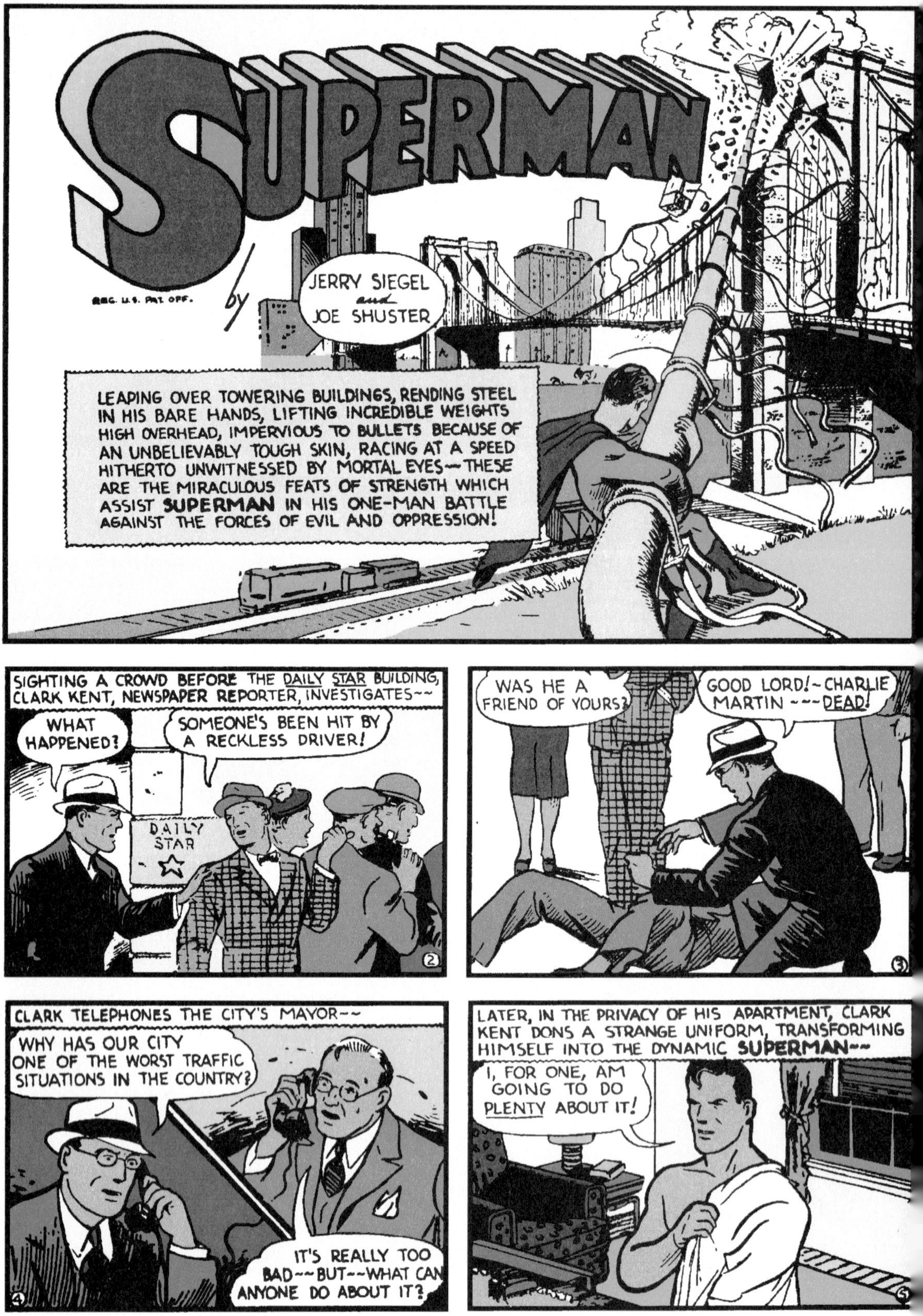
SUPERMAN
REG. U.S. PAT. OFF.
by
JERRY SIEGEL and JOE SHUSTER
LEAPING OVER TOWERING BUILDINGS, RENDING STEEL IN HIS BARE HANDS, LIFTING INCREDIBLE WEIGHTS HIGH OVERHEAD, IMPERVIOUS TO BULLETS BECAUSE OF AN UNBELIEVABLY TOUGH SKIN, RACING AT A SPEED HITHERTO UNWITNESSED BY MORTAL EYES -- THESE ARE THE MIRACULOUS FEATS OF STRENGTH WHICH ASSIST SUPERMAN IN HIS ONE-MAN BATTLE AGAINST THE FORCES OF EVIL AND OPPRESSION!
SIGHTING A CROWD BEFORE THE DAILY STAR BUILDING, CLARK KENT, NEWSPAPER REPORTER, INVESTIGATES--
WHAT HAPPENED?
SOMEONE'S BEEN HIT BY A RECKLESS DRIVER!
DAILY STAR
2
WAS HE A FRIEND OF YOURS?
GOOD LORD!-- CHARLIE MARTIN ---DEAD!
3
CLARK TELEPHONES THE CITY'S MAYOR--
WHY HAS OUR CITY ONE OF THE WORST TRAFFIC SITUATIONS IN THE COUNTRY?
IT'S REALLY TOO BAD--BUT--WHAT CAN ANYONE DO ABOUT IT?
4
LATER, IN THE PRIVACY OF HIS APARTMENT, CLARK KENT DONS A STRANGE UNIFORM, TRANSFORMING HIMSELF INTO THE DYNAMIC SUPERMAN--
I, FOR ONE, AM GOING TO DO PLENTY ABOUT IT!
5

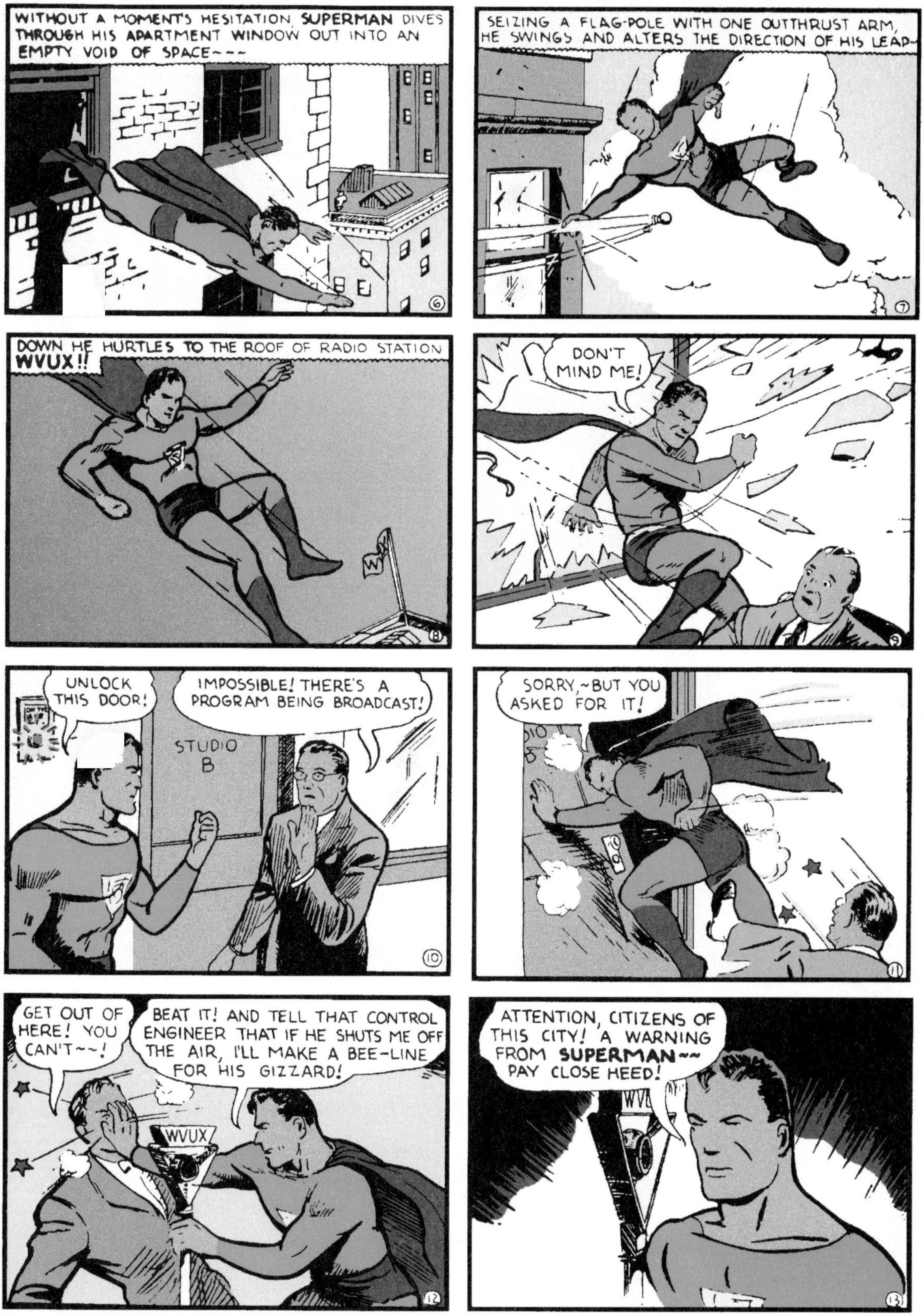
WITHOUT A MOMENT'S HESITATION, SUPERMAN DIVES THROUGH HIS APARTMENT WINDOW OUT INTO AN EMPTY VOID OF SPACE---
SEIZING A FLAG-POLE WITH ONE OUTTHRUST ARM, HE SWINGS AND ALTERS THE DIRECTION OF HIS LEAP--
DOWN HE HURTLES TO THE ROOF OF RADIO STATION WVUX!!
DON'T MIND ME!
UNLOCK THIS DOOR!
IMPOSSIBLE! THERE'S A PROGRAM BEING BROADCAST!
STUDIO B
SORRY,~BUT YOU ASKED FOR IT!
GET OUT OF HERE! YOU CAN'T~~!
BEAT IT! AND TELL THAT CONTROL ENGINEER THAT IF HE SHUTS ME OFF THE AIR, I'LL MAKE A BEE-LINE FOR HIS GIZZARD!
WVUX
ATTENTION, CITIZENS OF THIS CITY! A WARNING FROM SUPERMAN~~ PAY CLOSE HEED!

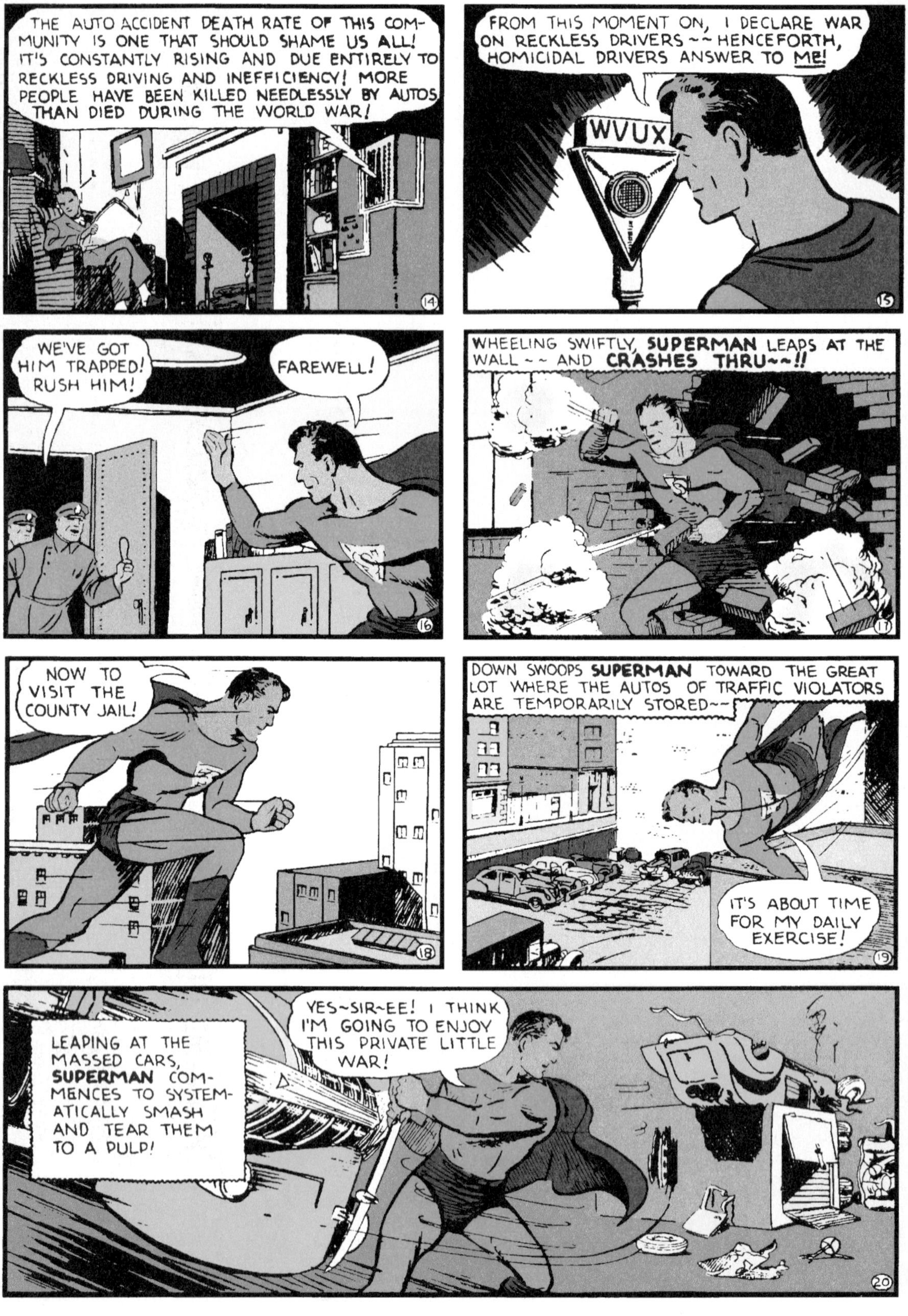
THE AUTO ACCIDENT DEATH RATE OF THIS COMMUNITY IS ONE THAT SHOULD SHAME US ALL! IT'S CONSTANTLY RISING AND DUE ENTIRELY TO RECKLESS DRIVING AND INEFFICIENCY! MORE PEOPLE HAVE BEEN KILLED NEEDLESSLY BY AUTOS THAN DIED DURING THE WORLD WAR!
FROM THIS MOMENT ON, I DECLARE WAR ON RECKLESS DRIVERS ~~ HENCEFORTH, HOMICIDAL DRIVERS ANSWER TO ME!
WVUX
WE'VE GOT HIM TRAPPED! RUSH HIM!
FAREWELL!
WHEELING SWIFTLY, SUPERMAN LEAPS AT THE WALL ~~ AND CRASHES THRU~~!!
NOW TO VISIT THE COUNTY JAIL!
DOWN SWOOPS SUPERMAN TOWARD THE GREAT LOT WHERE THE AUTOS OF TRAFFIC VIOLATORS ARE TEMPORARILY STORED~~
IT'S ABOUT TIME FOR MY DAILY EXERCISE!
LEAPING AT THE MASSED CARS, SUPERMAN COMMENCES TO SYSTEMATICALLY SMASH AND TEAR THEM TO A PULP!
YES~SIR~EE! I THINK I'M GOING TO ENJOY THIS PRIVATE LITTLE WAR!

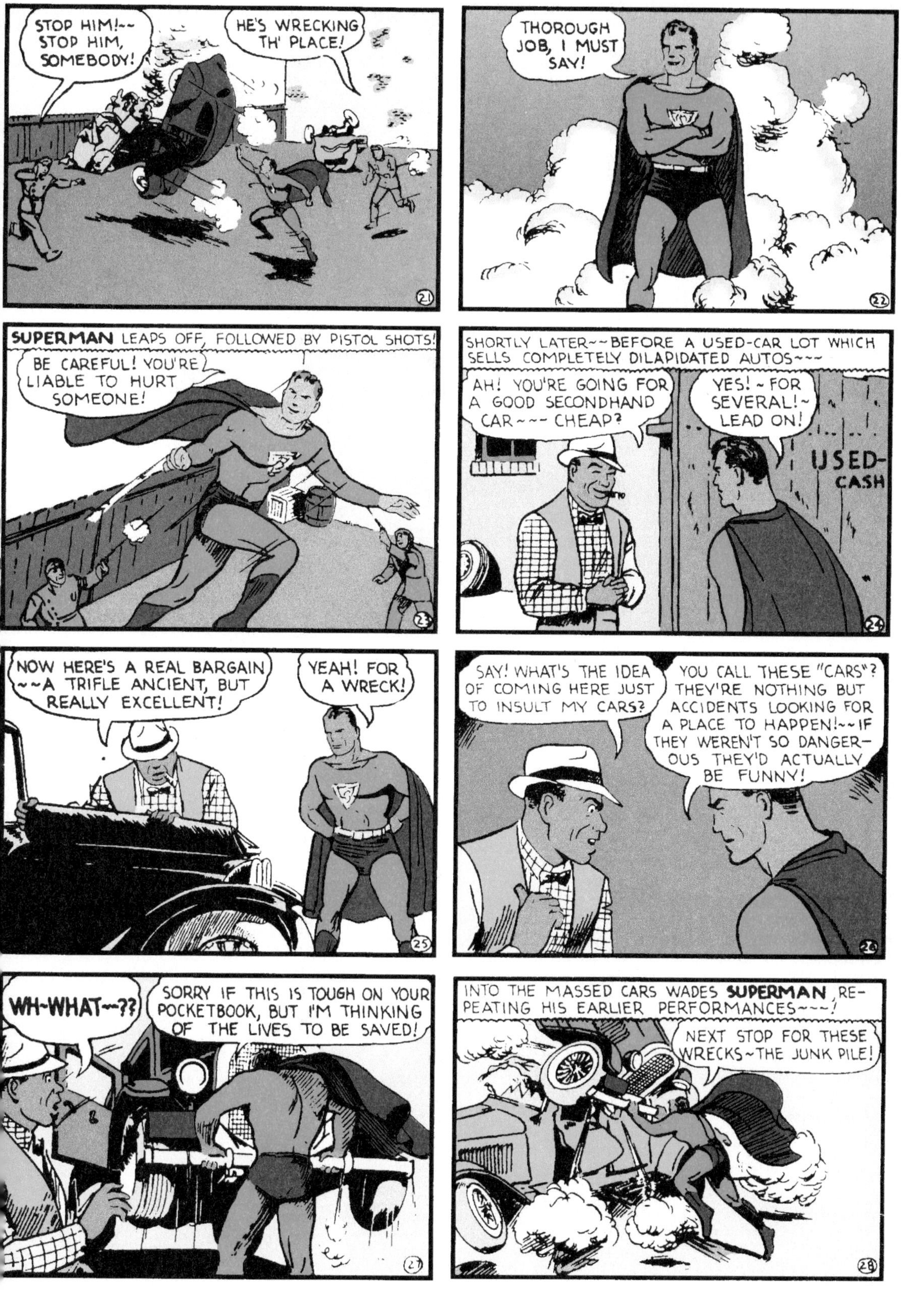
STOP HIM!-- STOP HIM, SOMEBODY!
HE'S WRECKING TH' PLACE!
THOROUGH JOB, I MUST SAY!
SUPERMAN LEAPS OFF, FOLLOWED BY PISTOL SHOTS!
BE CAREFUL! YOU'RE LIABLE TO HURT SOMEONE!
SHORTLY LATER--BEFORE A USED-CAR LOT WHICH SELLS COMPLETELY DILAPIDATED AUTOS---
AH! YOU'RE GOING FOR A GOOD SECONDHAND CAR--- CHEAP?
YES! - FOR SEVERAL!- LEAD ON!
USED- CASH
NOW HERE'S A REAL BARGAIN --A TRIFLE ANCIENT, BUT REALLY EXCELLENT!
YEAH! FOR A WRECK!
SAY! WHAT'S THE IDEA OF COMING HERE JUST TO INSULT MY CARS?
YOU CALL THESE "CARS"? THEY'RE NOTHING BUT ACCIDENTS LOOKING FOR A PLACE TO HAPPEN!--IF THEY WEREN'T SO DANGEROUS THEY'D ACTUALLY BE FUNNY!
WH-WHAT--??
SORRY IF THIS IS TOUGH ON YOUR POCKETBOOK, BUT I'M THINKING OF THE LIVES TO BE SAVED!
INTO THE MASSED CARS WADES SUPERMAN, REPEATING HIS EARLIER PERFORMANCES---!
NEXT STOP FOR THESE WRECKS-THE JUNK PILE!

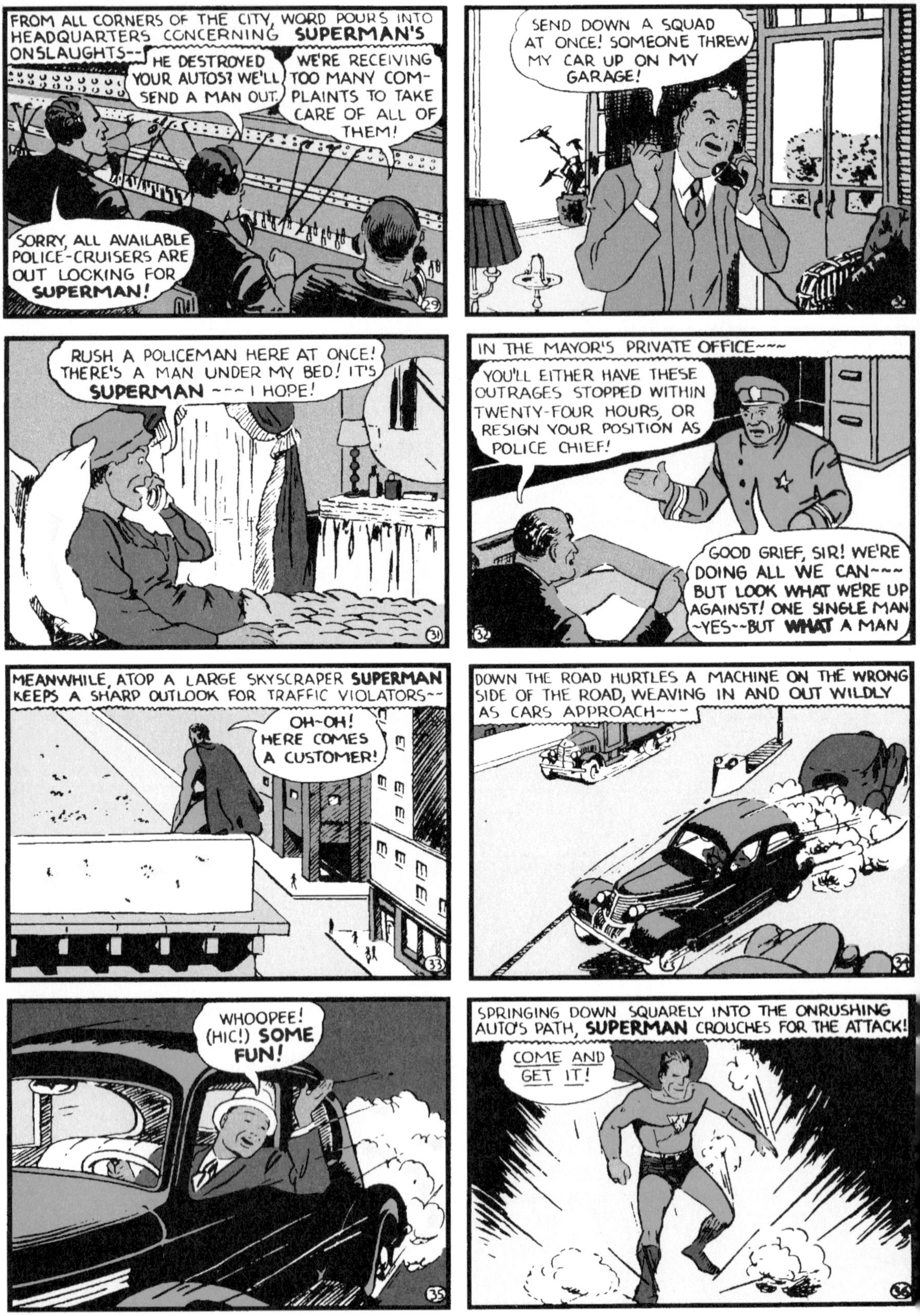
FROM ALL CORNERS OF THE CITY, WORD POURS INTO HEADQUARTERS CONCERNING SUPERMAN'S ONSLAUGHTS--
HE DESTROYED YOUR AUTOS? WE'LL SEND A MAN OUT.
WE'RE RECEIVING TOO MANY COM-PLAINTS TO TAKE CARE OF ALL OF THEM!
SORRY, ALL AVAILABLE POLICE-CRUISERS ARE OUT LOOKING FOR SUPERMAN!
SEND DOWN A SQUAD AT ONCE! SOMEONE THREW MY CAR UP ON MY GARAGE!
RUSH A POLICEMAN HERE AT ONCE! THERE'S A MAN UNDER MY BED! IT'S SUPERMAN --- I HOPE!
IN THE MAYOR'S PRIVATE OFFICE---
YOU'LL EITHER HAVE THESE OUTRAGES STOPPED WITHIN TWENTY-FOUR HOURS, OR RESIGN YOUR POSITION AS POLICE CHIEF!
GOOD GRIEF, SIR! WE'RE DOING ALL WE CAN--- BUT LOOK WHAT WE'RE UP AGAINST! ONE SINGLE MAN ~YES--BUT WHAT A MAN
MEANWHILE, ATOP A LARGE SKYSCRAPER SUPERMAN KEEPS A SHARP OUTLOOK FOR TRAFFIC VIOLATORS--
OH-OH! HERE COMES A CUSTOMER!
DOWN THE ROAD HURTLES A MACHINE ON THE WRONG SIDE OF THE ROAD, WEAVING IN AND OUT WILDLY AS CARS APPROACH---
WHOOPEE! (HIC!) SOME FUN!
SPRINGING DOWN SQUARELY INTO THE ONRUSHING AUTO'S PATH, SUPERMAN CROUCHES FOR THE ATTACK!
COME AND GET IT!

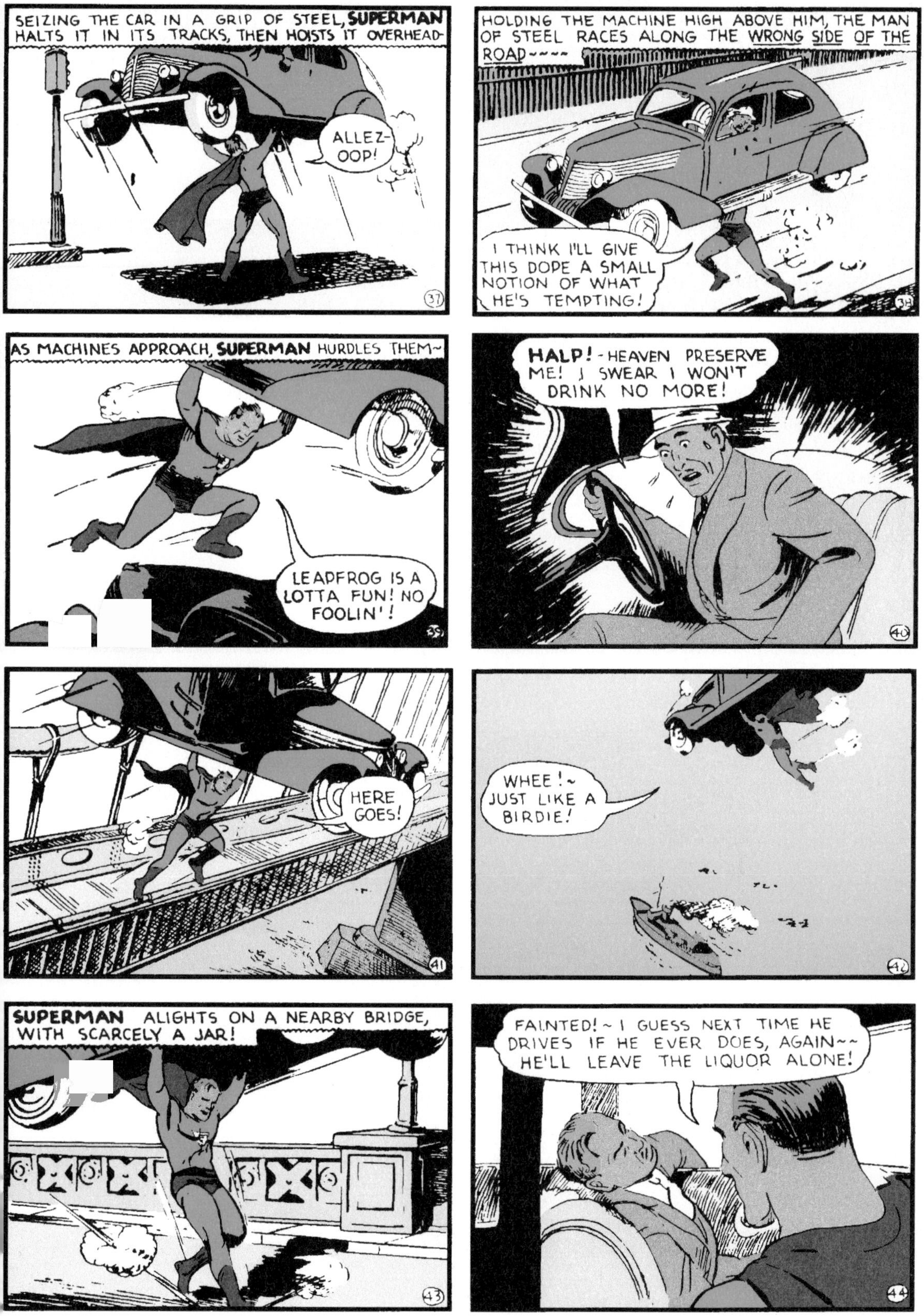
SEIZING THE CAR IN A GRIP OF STEEL, SUPERMAN HALTS IT IN ITS TRACKS, THEN HOISTS IT OVERHEAD-
ALLEZ-OOP!
HOLDING THE MACHINE HIGH ABOVE HIM, THE MAN OF STEEL RACES ALONG THE WRONG SIDE OF THE ROAD~~~~
I THINK I'LL GIVE THIS DOPE A SMALL NOTION OF WHAT HE'S TEMPTING!
AS MACHINES APPROACH, SUPERMAN HURDLES THEM~
LEAPFROG IS A LOTTA FUN! NO FOOLIN'!
HALP! - HEAVEN PRESERVE ME! I SWEAR I WON'T DRINK NO MORE!
HERE GOES!
WHEE!~ JUST LIKE A BIRDIE!
SUPERMAN ALIGHTS ON A NEARBY BRIDGE, WITH SCARCELY A JAR!
FAINTED! ~ I GUESS NEXT TIME HE DRIVES IF HE EVER DOES, AGAIN~~ HE'LL LEAVE THE LIQUOR ALONE!

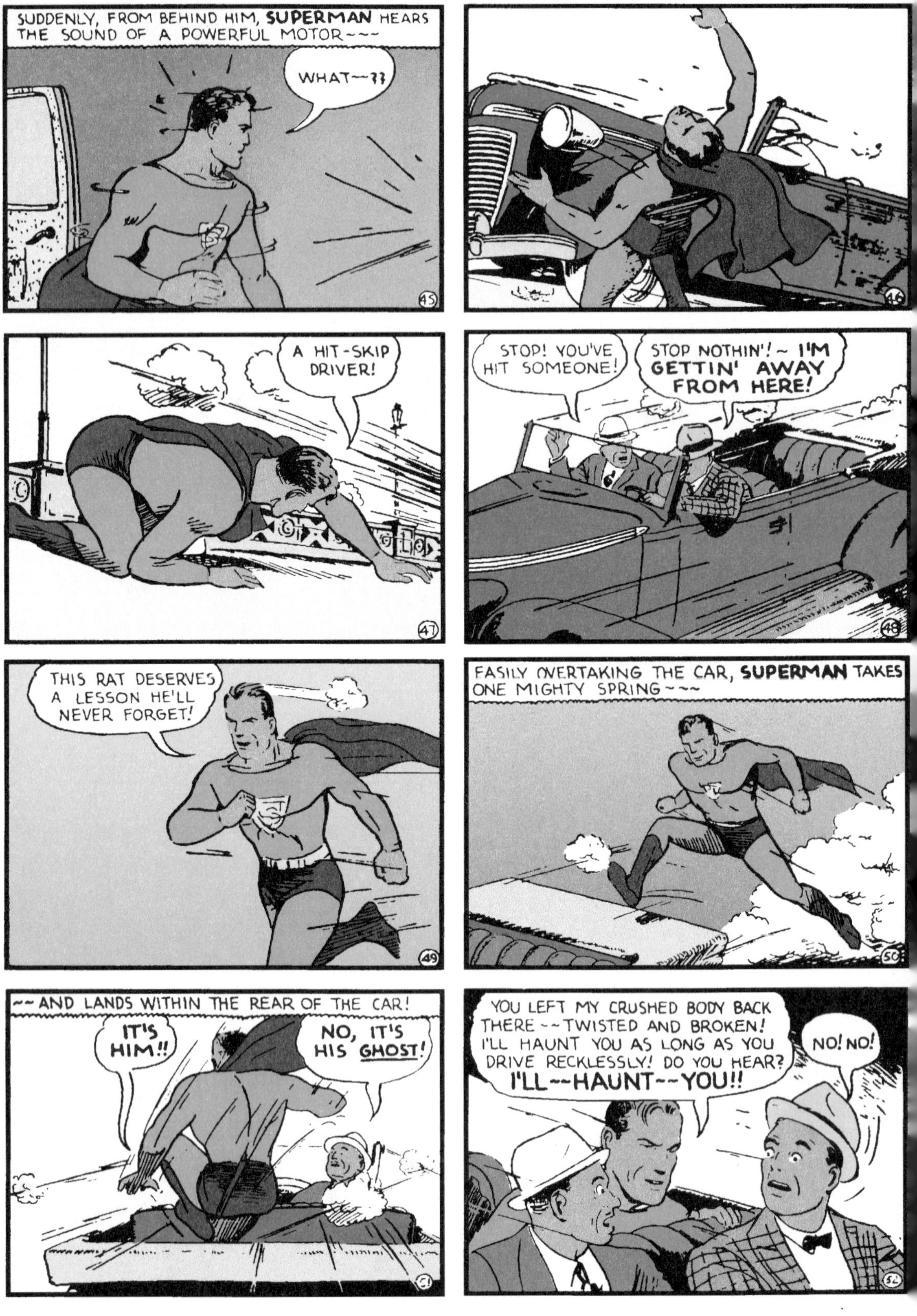

SUDDENLY, FROM BEHIND HIM, **SUPERMAN** HEARS THE SOUND OF A POWERFUL MOTOR---
WHAT--??
A HIT-SKIP DRIVER!
STOP! YOU'VE HIT SOMEONE!
STOP NOTHIN'!~ **I'M GETTIN' AWAY FROM HERE!**
THIS RAT DESERVES A LESSON HE'LL NEVER FORGET!
EASILY OVERTAKING THE CAR, **SUPERMAN** TAKES ONE MIGHTY SPRING---
--AND LANDS WITHIN THE REAR OF THE CAR!
IT'S HIM!!
NO, IT'S HIS GHOST!
YOU LEFT MY CRUSHED BODY BACK THERE--TWISTED AND BROKEN! I'LL HAUNT YOU AS LONG AS YOU DRIVE RECKLESSLY! DO YOU HEAR? **I'LL--HAUNT--YOU!!**
NO! NO!

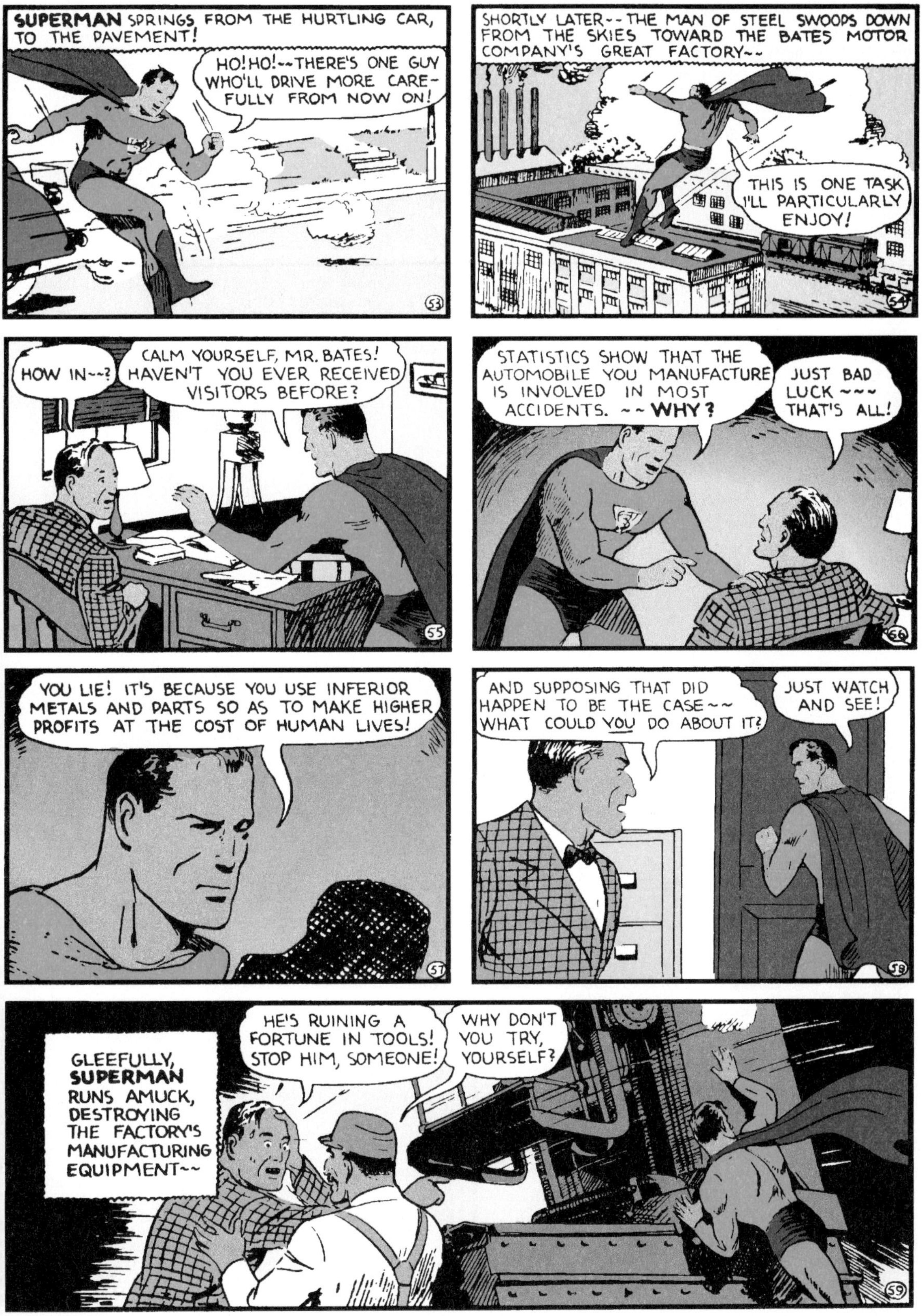
SUPERMAN SPRINGS FROM THE HURTLING CAR, TO THE PAVEMENT!
HO! HO!--THERE'S ONE GUY WHO'LL DRIVE MORE CAREFULLY FROM NOW ON!
SHORTLY LATER--THE MAN OF STEEL SWOOPS DOWN FROM THE SKIES TOWARD THE BATES MOTOR COMPANY'S GREAT FACTORY--
THIS IS ONE TASK I'LL PARTICULARLY ENJOY!
HOW IN--?
CALM YOURSELF, MR. BATES! HAVEN'T YOU EVER RECEIVED VISITORS BEFORE?
STATISTICS SHOW THAT THE AUTOMOBILE YOU MANUFACTURE IS INVOLVED IN MOST ACCIDENTS. --WHY?
JUST BAD LUCK --- THAT'S ALL!
YOU LIE! IT'S BECAUSE YOU USE INFERIOR METALS AND PARTS SO AS TO MAKE HIGHER PROFITS AT THE COST OF HUMAN LIVES!
AND SUPPOSING THAT DID HAPPEN TO BE THE CASE-- WHAT COULD YOU DO ABOUT IT?
JUST WATCH AND SEE!
GLEEFULLY, SUPERMAN RUNS AMUCK, DESTROYING THE FACTORY'S MANUFACTURING EQUIPMENT--
HE'S RUINING A FORTUNE IN TOOLS! STOP HIM, SOMEONE!
WHY DON'T YOU TRY, YOURSELF?

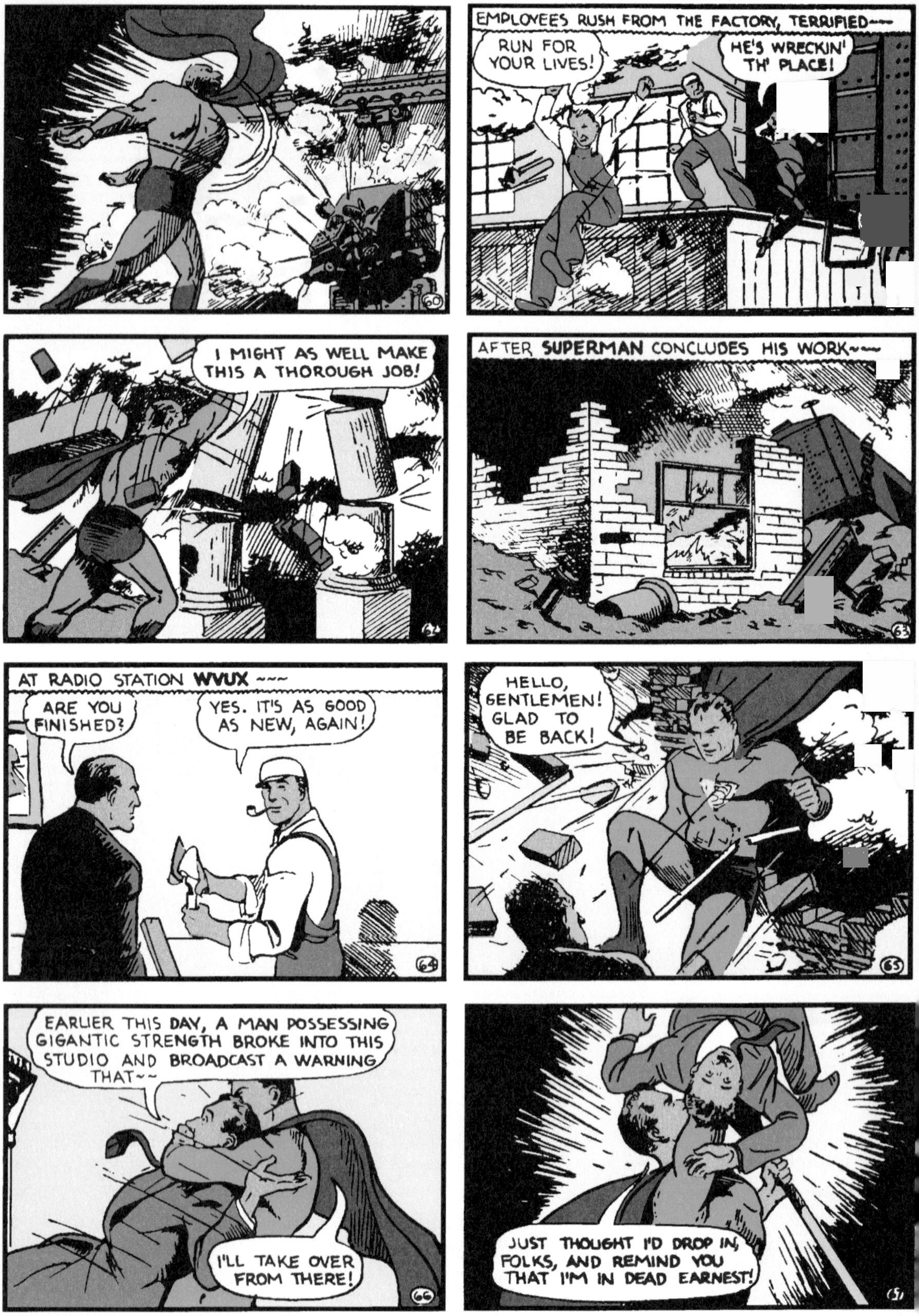
EMPLOYEES RUSH FROM THE FACTORY, TERRIFIED~~~
RUN FOR YOUR LIVES!
HE'S WRECKIN' TH' PLACE!
I MIGHT AS WELL MAKE THIS A THOROUGH JOB!
AFTER SUPERMAN CONCLUDES HIS WORK~~~
AT RADIO STATION WVUX ~~~
ARE YOU FINISHED?
YES. IT'S AS GOOD AS NEW, AGAIN!
HELLO, GENTLEMEN! GLAD TO BE BACK!
EARLIER THIS DAY, A MAN POSSESSING GIGANTIC STRENGTH BROKE INTO THIS STUDIO AND BROADCAST A WARNING THAT~~
I'LL TAKE OVER FROM THERE!
JUST THOUGHT I'D DROP IN, FOLKS, AND REMIND YOU THAT I'M IN DEAD EARNEST!

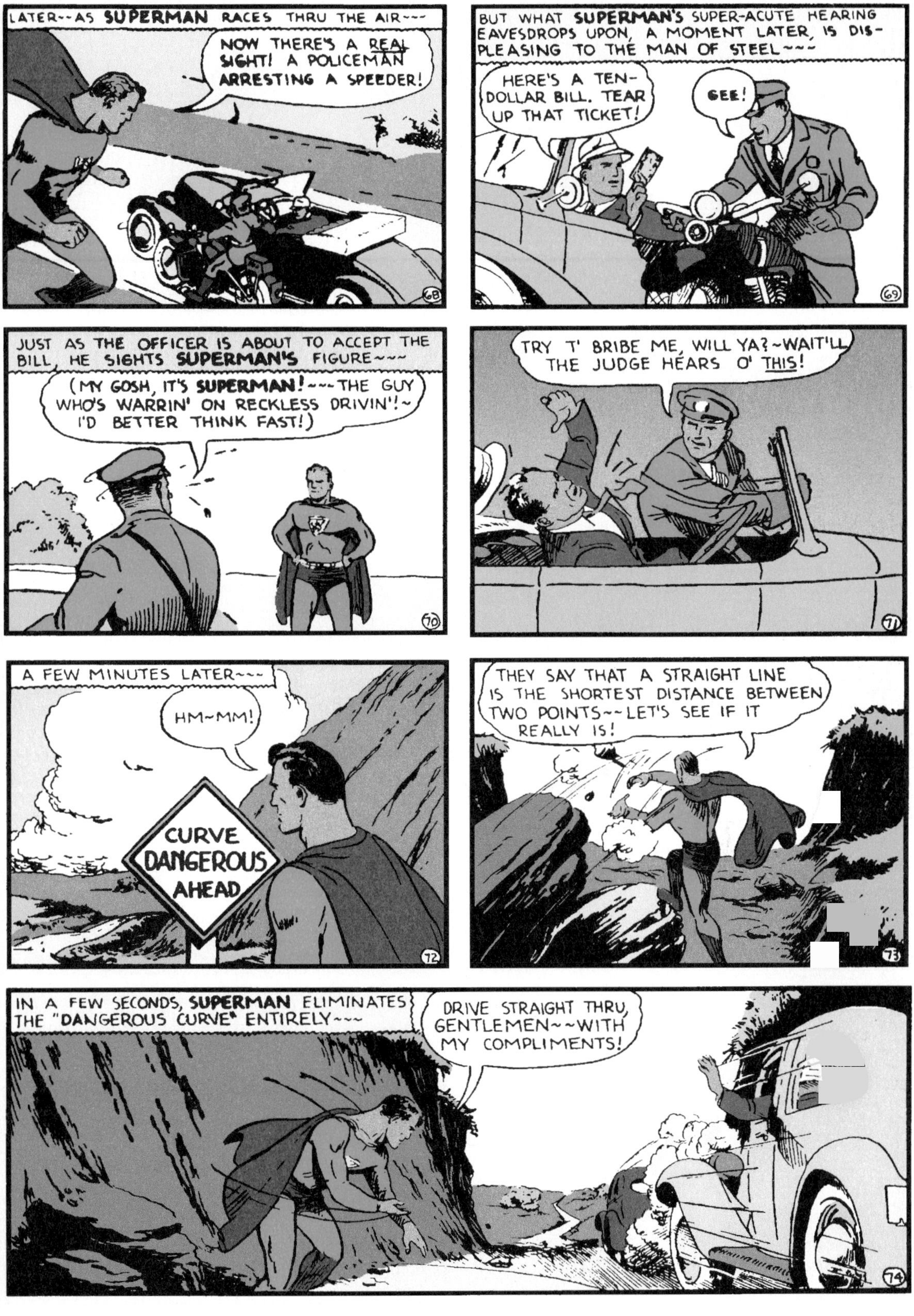
LATER--AS SUPERMAN RACES THRU THE AIR---
NOW THERE'S A REAL SIGHT! A POLICEMAN ARRESTING A SPEEDER!
BUT WHAT SUPERMAN'S SUPER-ACUTE HEARING EAVESDROPS UPON, A MOMENT LATER, IS DISPLEASING TO THE MAN OF STEEL---
HERE'S A TEN-DOLLAR BILL. TEAR UP THAT TICKET!
GEE!
JUST AS THE OFFICER IS ABOUT TO ACCEPT THE BILL, HE SIGHTS SUPERMAN'S FIGURE---
(MY GOSH, IT'S SUPERMAN!---THE GUY WHO'S WARRIN' ON RECKLESS DRIVIN'!~ I'D BETTER THINK FAST!)
TRY T' BRIBE ME, WILL YA?~WAIT'LL THE JUDGE HEARS O' THIS!
A FEW MINUTES LATER---
HM~MM!
CURVE DANGEROUS AHEAD
THEY SAY THAT A STRAIGHT LINE IS THE SHORTEST DISTANCE BETWEEN TWO POINTS~~LET'S SEE IF IT REALLY IS!
IN A FEW SECONDS, SUPERMAN ELIMINATES THE "DANGEROUS CURVE" ENTIRELY---
DRIVE STRAIGHT THRU, GENTLEMEN~~WITH MY COMPLIMENTS!

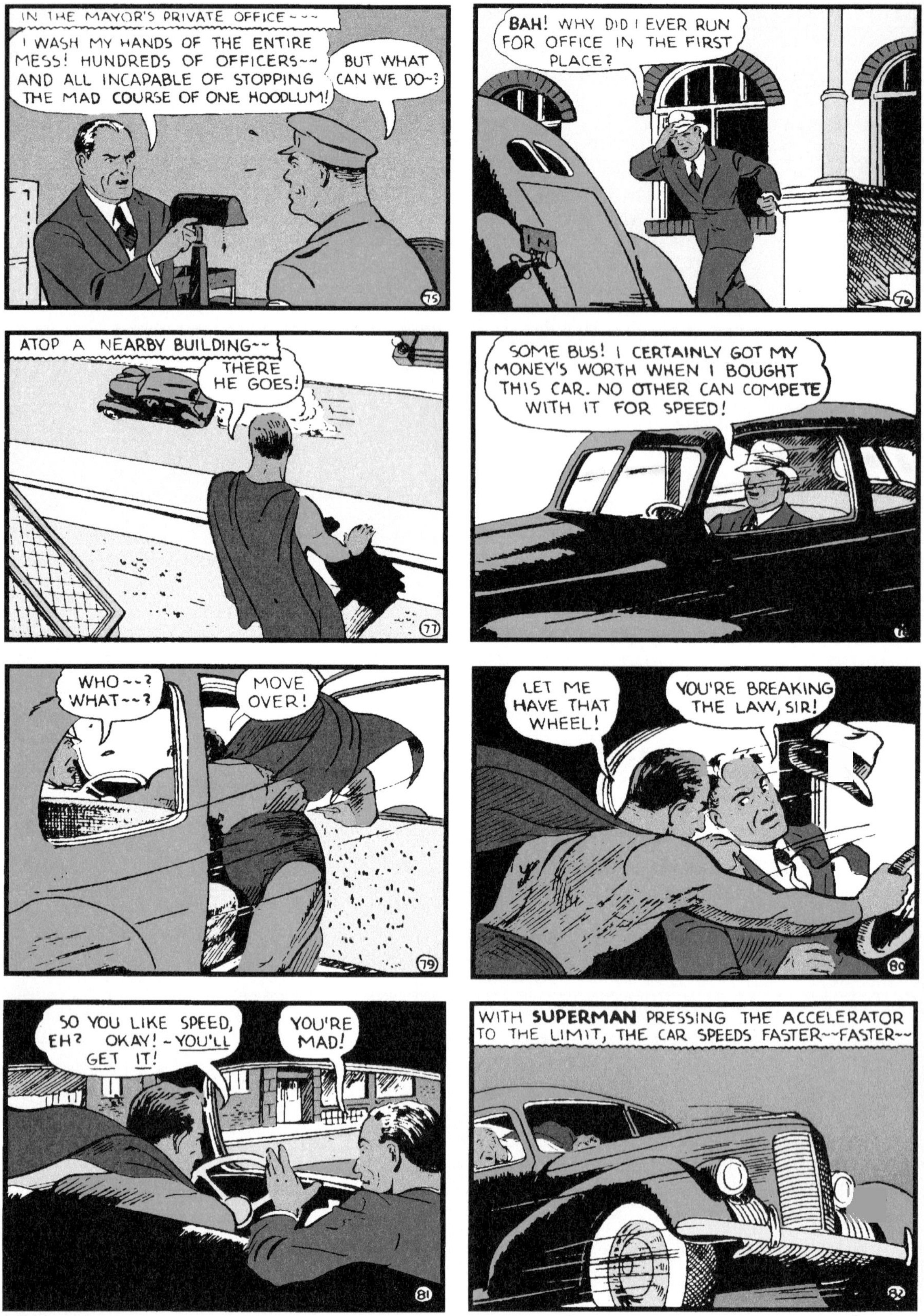

IN THE MAYOR'S PRIVATE OFFICE---
I WASH MY HANDS OF THE ENTIRE MESS! HUNDREDS OF OFFICERS-- AND ALL INCAPABLE OF STOPPING THE MAD COURSE OF ONE HOODLUM!
BUT WHAT CAN WE DO-?
75
BAH! WHY DID I EVER RUN FOR OFFICE IN THE FIRST PLACE?
76
ATOP A NEARBY BUILDING--
THERE HE GOES!
77
SOME BUS! I CERTAINLY GOT MY MONEY'S WORTH WHEN I BOUGHT THIS CAR. NO OTHER CAN COMPETE WITH IT FOR SPEED!
WHO--? WHAT--?
MOVE OVER!
79
LET ME HAVE THAT WHEEL!
YOU'RE BREAKING THE LAW, SIR!
80
SO YOU LIKE SPEED, EH? OKAY! ~YOU'LL GET IT!
YOU'RE MAD!
81
WITH SUPERMAN PRESSING THE ACCELERATOR TO THE LIMIT, THE CAR SPEEDS FASTER--FASTER--
82

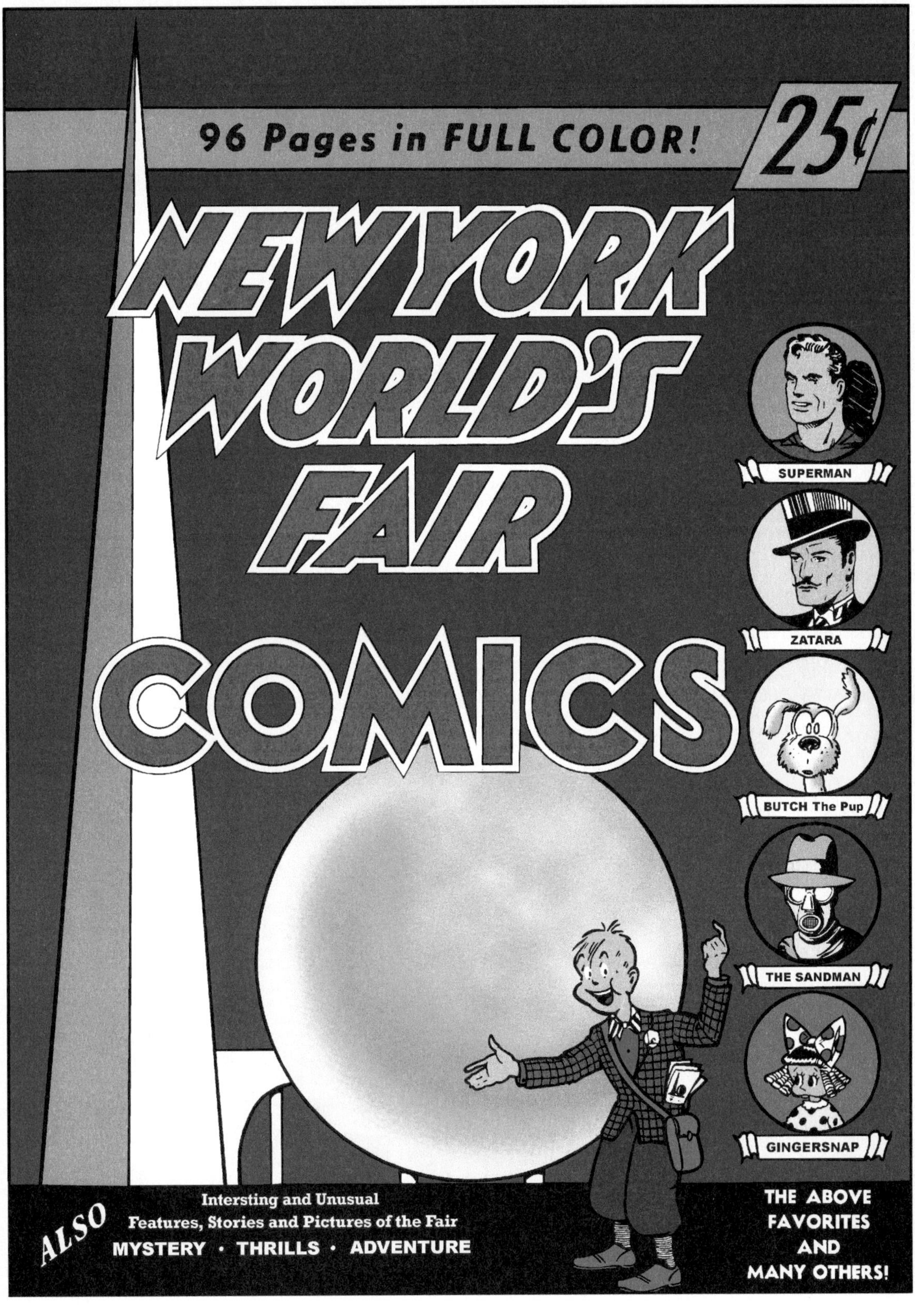
96 Pages in FULL COLOR!
25¢
NEW YORK WORLD'S FAIR
COMICS
SUPERMAN
ZATARA
BUTCH The Pup
THE SANDMAN
GINGERSNAP
ALSO
Intersting and Unusual
Features, Stories and Pictures of the Fair
MYSTERY · THRILLS · ADVENTURE
THE ABOVE FAVORITES AND MANY OTHERS!

SUPERMAN
at the
WORLD'S FAIR

by JERRY SIEGEL and JOE SHUSTER

FRIEND OF THE HELPLESS AND OPPRESSED IS SUPERMAN, A MAN POSSESSING THE STRENGTH OF A DOZEN SAMSONS! LIFTING AND RENDING GIGANTIC WEIGHTS, VAULTING OVER SKYSCRAPERS, RACING A BULLET, POSSESSING A SKIN IMPENETRABLE EVEN TO STEEL, ARE HIS PHYSICAL ASSETS USED IN HIS ONE-MAN BATTLE AGAINST EVIL AND INJUSTICE!

AW, COME ON!

LET US IN!

WE'LL PUT YOUR NAME IN THE ARTICLE!

NOTHING DOING, BOYS! WHEN THE COMMITTEE IS READY TO ANNOUNCE WHO THEY'RE NOMINATING AS CANDIDATE FOR GOVERNOR, YOU'LL GET IN~ ~BUT NOT A MOMENT BEFORE!

ONE OF THE REPORTERS, CLARK KENT OF THE DAILY STAR UNOBTRUSIVELY SLIPS AWAY~~~

THIS CALLS FOR SPECIAL TACTICS!

LATER, IN AN ALLEY BESIDE THE BUILDING, THE MEEK SCRIBE REMOVES HIS OUTER GARMENTS AND STANDS REVEALED IN SUPERMAN GARB~~~

HERE GOES!

UPWARD LEAPS THE MAN OF STEEL~~ NOT INCHES, OR MERELY FEET, BUT YARDS~~~INTO THE AIR!

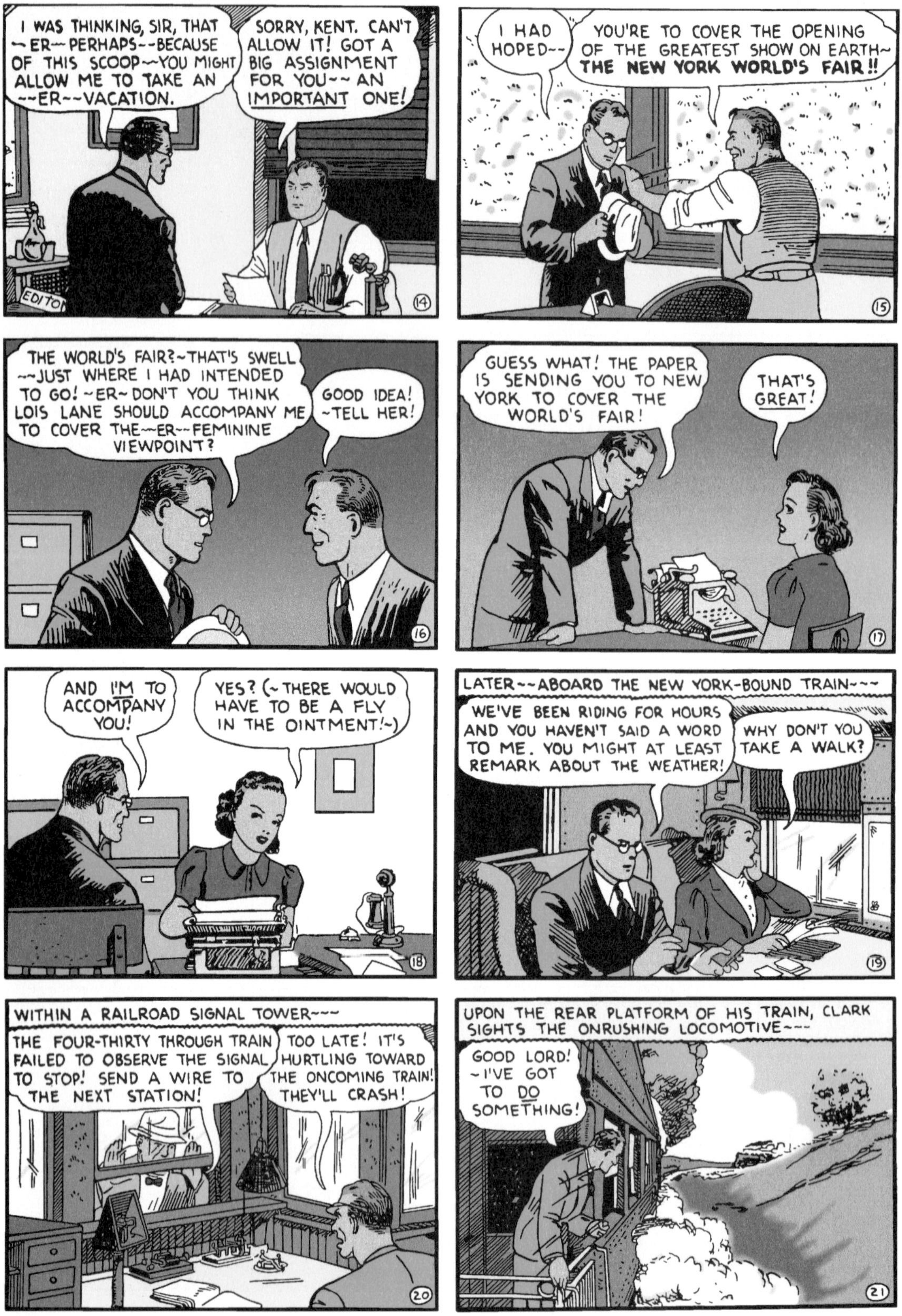

I WAS THINKING, SIR, THAT ~ER~ PERHAPS--BECAUSE OF THIS SCOOP~~YOU MIGHT ALLOW ME TO TAKE AN --ER--VACATION.
SORRY, KENT. CAN'T ALLOW IT! GOT A BIG ASSIGNMENT FOR YOU~~ AN IMPORTANT ONE!
EDITO
14
I HAD HOPED--
YOU'RE TO COVER THE OPENING OF THE GREATEST SHOW ON EARTH~ THE NEW YORK WORLD'S FAIR!!
15
THE WORLD'S FAIR?~THAT'S SWELL ~~JUST WHERE I HAD INTENDED TO GO! ~ER~ DON'T YOU THINK LOIS LANE SHOULD ACCOMPANY ME TO COVER THE~~ER--FEMININE VIEWPOINT?
GOOD IDEA! ~TELL HER!
16
GUESS WHAT! THE PAPER IS SENDING YOU TO NEW YORK TO COVER THE WORLD'S FAIR!
THAT'S GREAT!
17
AND I'M TO ACCOMPANY YOU!
YES? (~THERE WOULD HAVE TO BE A FLY IN THE OINTMENT!~)
18
LATER--ABOARD THE NEW YORK-BOUND TRAIN---
WE'VE BEEN RIDING FOR HOURS AND YOU HAVEN'T SAID A WORD TO ME. YOU MIGHT AT LEAST REMARK ABOUT THE WEATHER!
WHY DON'T YOU TAKE A WALK?
19
WITHIN A RAILROAD SIGNAL TOWER---
THE FOUR-THIRTY THROUGH TRAIN FAILED TO OBSERVE THE SIGNAL TO STOP! SEND A WIRE TO THE NEXT STATION!
TOO LATE! IT'S HURTLING TOWARD THE ONCOMING TRAIN! THEY'LL CRASH!
20
UPON THE REAR PLATFORM OF HIS TRAIN, CLARK SIGHTS THE ONRUSHING LOCOMOTIVE---
GOOD LORD! ~I'VE GOT TO DO SOMETHING!
21

A GREAT LEAP CARRIES **SUPERMAN** OVER THE LENGTH OF THE TRAIN ~~~

~~LANDING HIM ATOP THE ENGINE!

THE BRAKES! ~ BUT WE'LL NEVER STOP IN TIME!

DOWN BEFORE THE TRAIN SPRINGS **SUPERMAN** ~~ AS ITS SCREECHING BRAKES ARE APPLIED ~~~!

PITTING HIS MIGHTY STRENGTH AGAINST THE GREAT STEED OF IRON, **SUPERMAN** FORCES IT TO SLOW ~~~MOVE SLOWER YET~~~!

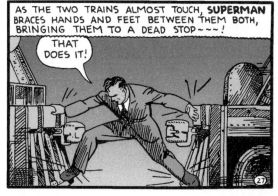

AS THE TWO TRAINS ALMOST TOUCH, **SUPERMAN** BRACES HANDS AND FEET BETWEEN THEM BOTH, BRINGING THEM TO A DEAD STOP~~~!

THAT DOES IT!

I SAW HIM! A MAN~~ HOLDING THE TWO TRAINS APART!

I SAW HIM, TOO! IT'S A MIRACLE WE DIDN'T CRASH!

BUT~~~ HE'S GONE!

HAVE YOU HEARD? **SUPERMAN** JUST AVERTED A TRAIN WRECK! WE OWE OUR LIVES TO HIM!

Y-YOU MEAN I ALMOST WAS KILLED! ~GULP!~ I DIDN'T EVEN KNOW!

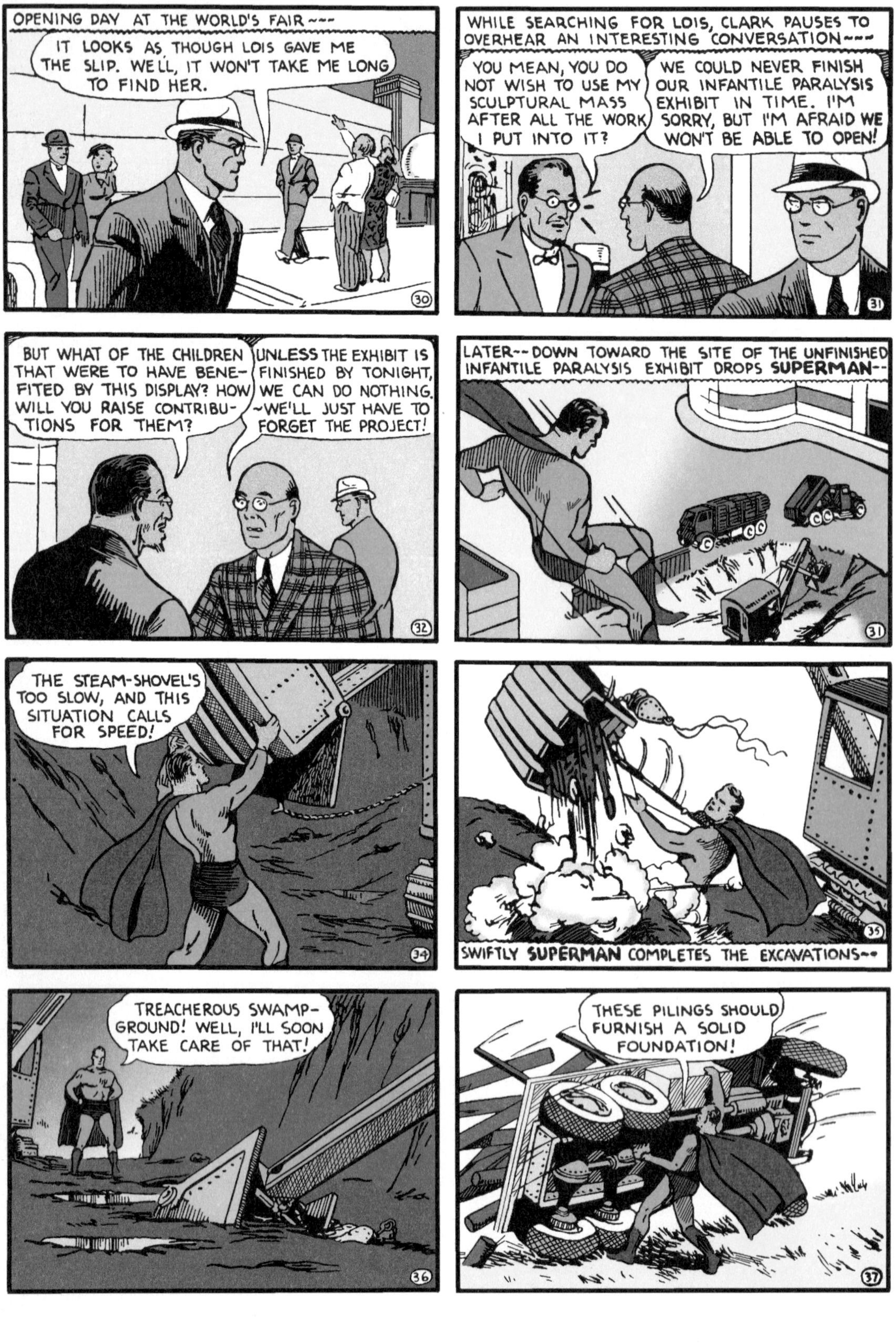
OPENING DAY AT THE WORLD'S FAIR---
IT LOOKS AS THOUGH LOIS GAVE ME THE SLIP. WELL, IT WON'T TAKE ME LONG TO FIND HER.
WHILE SEARCHING FOR LOIS, CLARK PAUSES TO OVERHEAR AN INTERESTING CONVERSATION---
YOU MEAN, YOU DO NOT WISH TO USE MY SCULPTURAL MASS AFTER ALL THE WORK I PUT INTO IT?
WE COULD NEVER FINISH OUR INFANTILE PARALYSIS EXHIBIT IN TIME. I'M SORRY, BUT I'M AFRAID WE WON'T BE ABLE TO OPEN!
BUT WHAT OF THE CHILDREN THAT WERE TO HAVE BENE-FITED BY THIS DISPLAY? HOW WILL YOU RAISE CONTRIBU-TIONS FOR THEM?
UNLESS THE EXHIBIT IS FINISHED BY TONIGHT, WE CAN DO NOTHING. --WE'LL JUST HAVE TO FORGET THE PROJECT!
LATER--DOWN TOWARD THE SITE OF THE UNFINISHED INFANTILE PARALYSIS EXHIBIT DROPS SUPERMAN--
THE STEAM-SHOVEL'S TOO SLOW, AND THIS SITUATION CALLS FOR SPEED!
SWIFTLY SUPERMAN COMPLETES THE EXCAVATIONS--
TREACHEROUS SWAMP-GROUND! WELL, I'LL SOON TAKE CARE OF THAT!
THESE PILINGS SHOULD FURNISH A SOLID FOUNDATION!

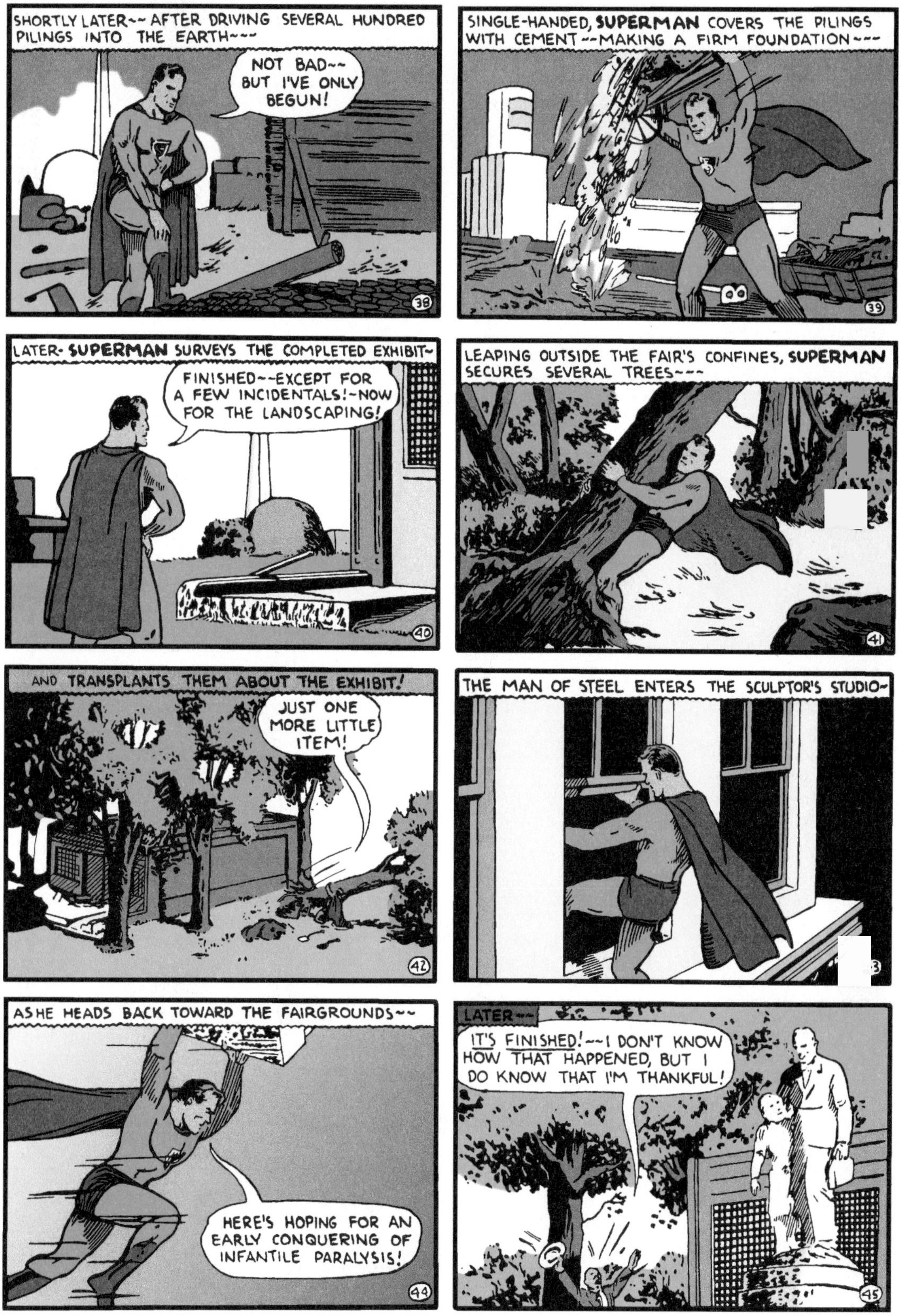
SHORTLY LATER-- AFTER DRIVING SEVERAL HUNDRED PILINGS INTO THE EARTH---
NOT BAD-- BUT I'VE ONLY BEGUN!
SINGLE-HANDED, SUPERMAN COVERS THE PILINGS WITH CEMENT--MAKING A FIRM FOUNDATION---
LATER- SUPERMAN SURVEYS THE COMPLETED EXHIBIT-
FINISHED--EXCEPT FOR A FEW INCIDENTALS!-NOW FOR THE LANDSCAPING!
LEAPING OUTSIDE THE FAIR'S CONFINES, SUPERMAN SECURES SEVERAL TREES---
AND TRANSPLANTS THEM ABOUT THE EXHIBIT!
JUST ONE MORE LITTLE ITEM!
THE MAN OF STEEL ENTERS THE SCULPTOR'S STUDIO-
AS HE HEADS BACK TOWARD THE FAIRGROUNDS--
HERE'S HOPING FOR AN EARLY CONQUERING OF INFANTILE PARALYSIS!
LATER--
IT'S FINISHED!--I DON'T KNOW HOW THAT HAPPENED, BUT I DO KNOW THAT I'M THANKFUL!

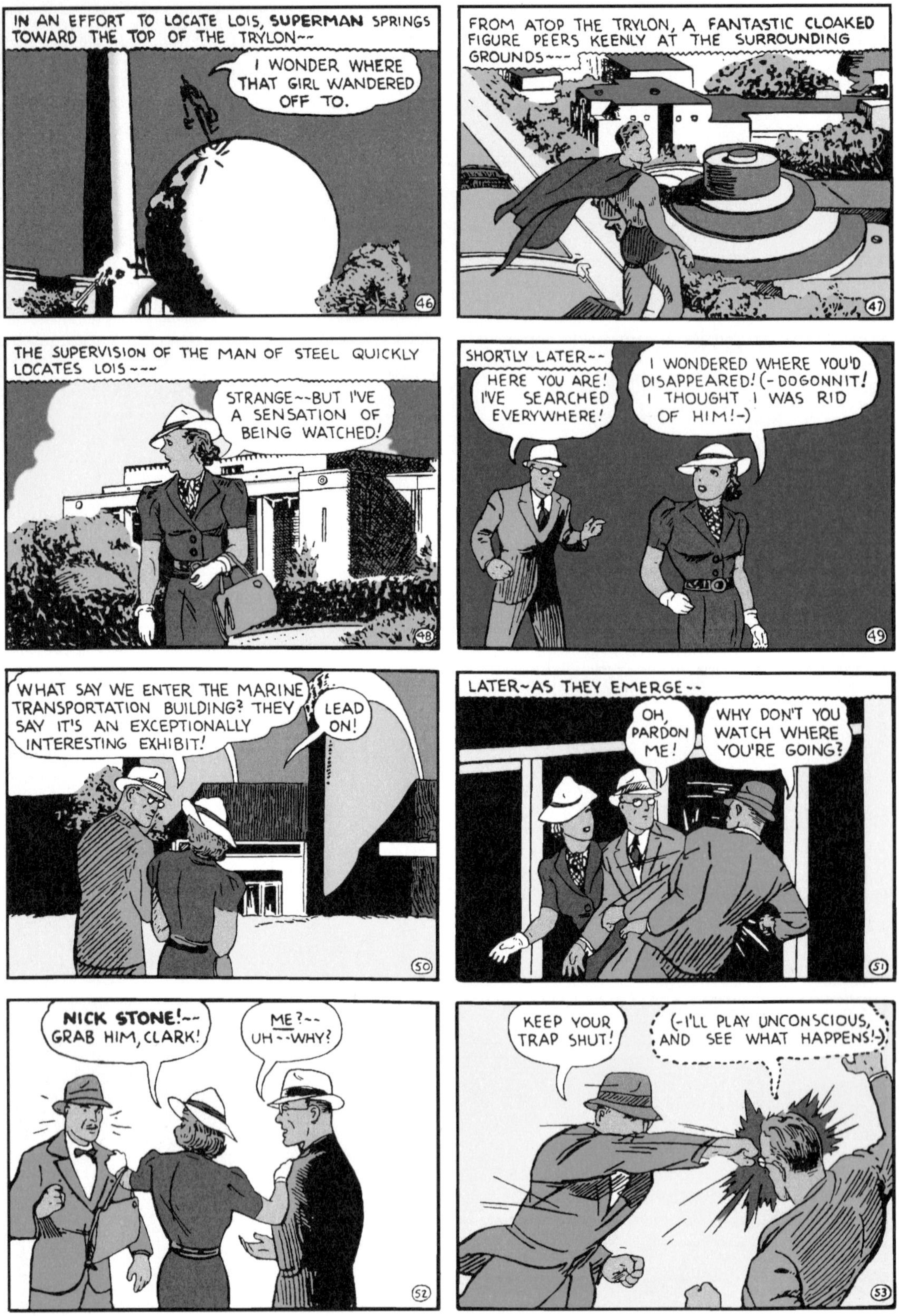

IN AN EFFORT TO LOCATE LOIS, SUPERMAN SPRINGS TOWARD THE TOP OF THE TRYLON--
I WONDER WHERE THAT GIRL WANDERED OFF TO.
46
FROM ATOP THE TRYLON, A FANTASTIC CLOAKED FIGURE PEERS KEENLY AT THE SURROUNDING GROUNDS---
47
THE SUPERVISION OF THE MAN OF STEEL QUICKLY LOCATES LOIS---
STRANGE--BUT I'VE A SENSATION OF BEING WATCHED!
48
SHORTLY LATER--
HERE YOU ARE! I'VE SEARCHED EVERYWHERE!
I WONDERED WHERE YOU'D DISAPPEARED! (-DOGONNIT! I THOUGHT I WAS RID OF HIM!-)
49
WHAT SAY WE ENTER THE MARINE TRANSPORTATION BUILDING? THEY SAY IT'S AN EXCEPTIONALLY INTERESTING EXHIBIT!
LEAD ON!
50
LATER-AS THEY EMERGE--
OH, PARDON ME!
WHY DON'T YOU WATCH WHERE YOU'RE GOING?
51
NICK STONE!-- GRAB HIM, CLARK!
ME?-- UH--WHY?
52
KEEP YOUR TRAP SHUT!
(-I'LL PLAY UNCONSCIOUS, AND SEE WHAT HAPPENS!-)
53

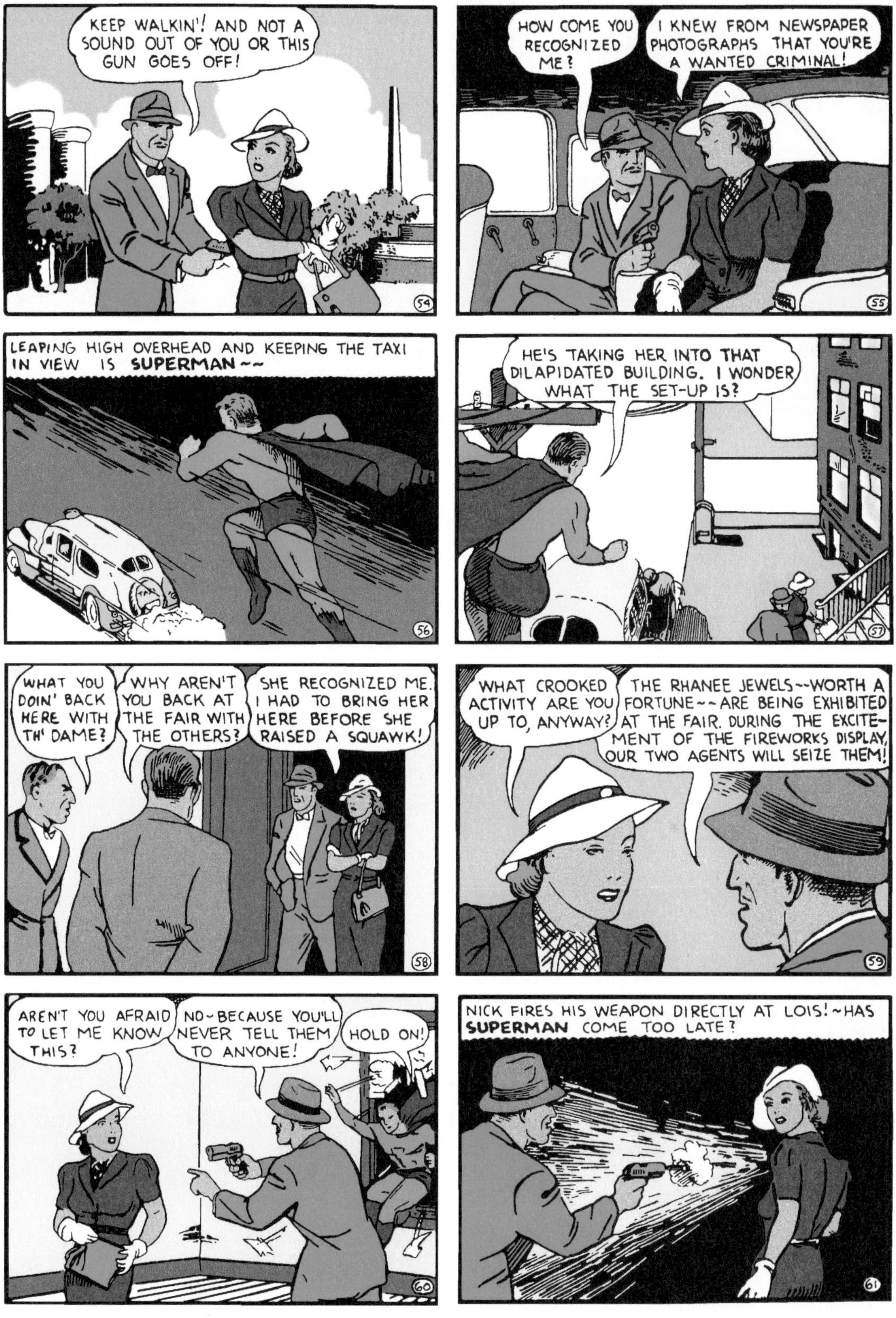
KEEP WALKIN'! AND NOT A SOUND OUT OF YOU OR THIS GUN GOES OFF!
HOW COME YOU RECOGNIZED ME?
I KNEW FROM NEWSPAPER PHOTOGRAPHS THAT YOU'RE A WANTED CRIMINAL!
LEAPING HIGH OVERHEAD AND KEEPING THE TAXI IN VIEW IS SUPERMAN~~
HE'S TAKING HER INTO THAT DILAPIDATED BUILDING. I WONDER WHAT THE SET-UP IS?
WHAT YOU DOIN' BACK HERE WITH TH' DAME?
WHY AREN'T YOU BACK AT THE FAIR WITH THE OTHERS?
SHE RECOGNIZED ME. I HAD TO BRING HER HERE BEFORE SHE RAISED A SQUAWK!
WHAT CROOKED ACTIVITY ARE YOU UP TO, ANYWAY?
THE RHANEE JEWELS--WORTH A FORTUNE--ARE BEING EXHIBITED AT THE FAIR. DURING THE EXCITEMENT OF THE FIREWORKS DISPLAY, OUR TWO AGENTS WILL SEIZE THEM!
AREN'T YOU AFRAID TO LET ME KNOW THIS?
NO~BECAUSE YOU'LL NEVER TELL THEM TO ANYONE!
HOLD ON!
NICK FIRES HIS WEAPON DIRECTLY AT LOIS!~HAS SUPERMAN COME TOO LATE?

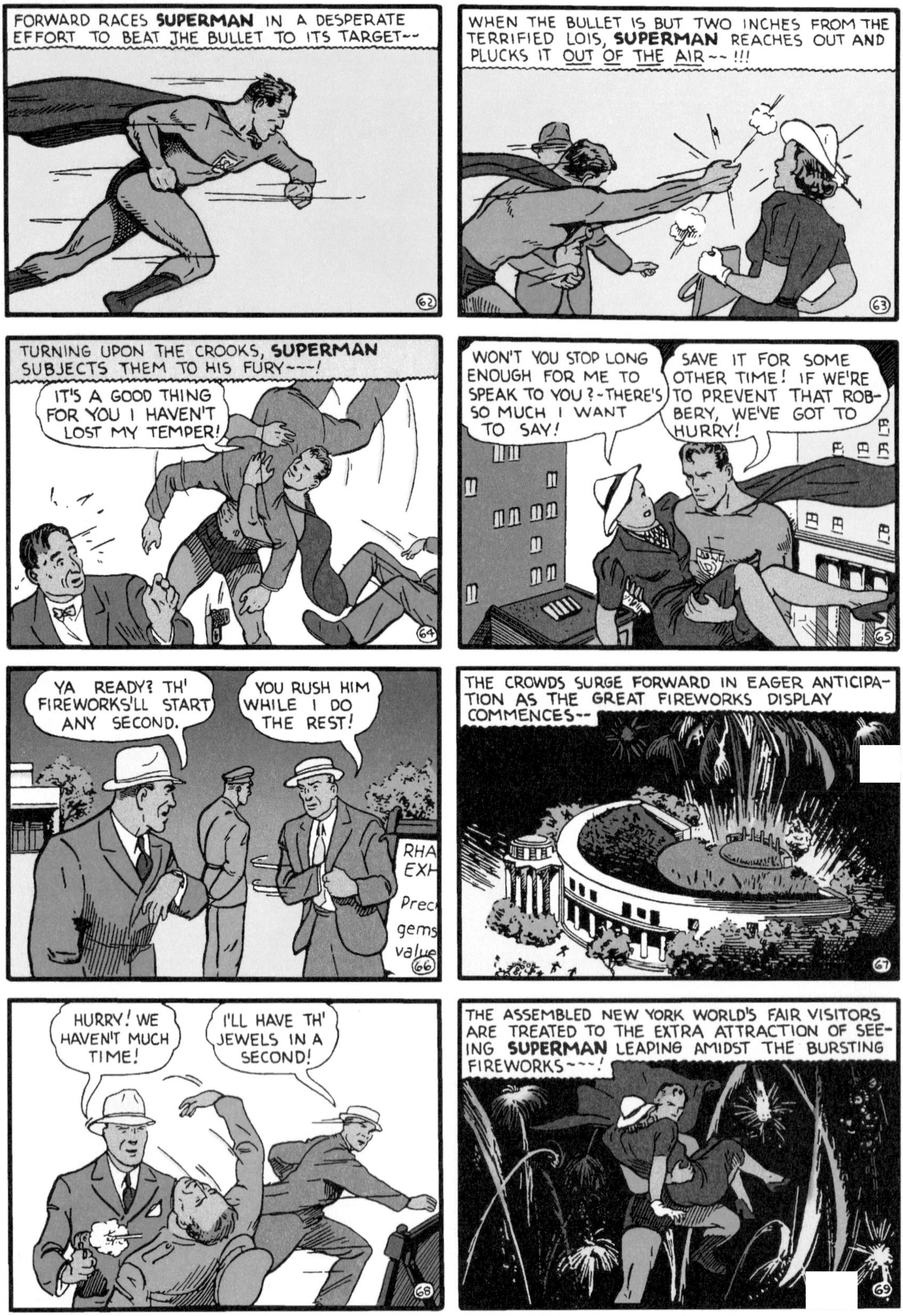

FORWARD RACES SUPERMAN IN A DESPERATE EFFORT TO BEAT THE BULLET TO ITS TARGET--
62
WHEN THE BULLET IS BUT TWO INCHES FROM THE TERRIFIED LOIS, SUPERMAN REACHES OUT AND PLUCKS IT OUT OF THE AIR -- !!!
63
TURNING UPON THE CROOKS, SUPERMAN SUBJECTS THEM TO HIS FURY---!
IT'S A GOOD THING FOR YOU I HAVEN'T LOST MY TEMPER!
64
WON'T YOU STOP LONG ENOUGH FOR ME TO SPEAK TO YOU? - THERE'S SO MUCH I WANT TO SAY!
SAVE IT FOR SOME OTHER TIME! IF WE'RE TO PREVENT THAT ROBBERY, WE'VE GOT TO HURRY!
65
YA READY? TH' FIREWORKS'LL START ANY SECOND.
YOU RUSH HIM WHILE I DO THE REST!
RHA
EXH
Prec
gems
value
66
THE CROWDS SURGE FORWARD IN EAGER ANTICIPATION AS THE GREAT FIREWORKS DISPLAY COMMENCES--
67
HURRY! WE HAVEN'T MUCH TIME!
I'LL HAVE TH' JEWELS IN A SECOND!
68
THE ASSEMBLED NEW YORK WORLD'S FAIR VISITORS ARE TREATED TO THE EXTRA ATTRACTION OF SEEING SUPERMAN LEAPING AMIDST THE BURSTING FIREWORKS---!
69

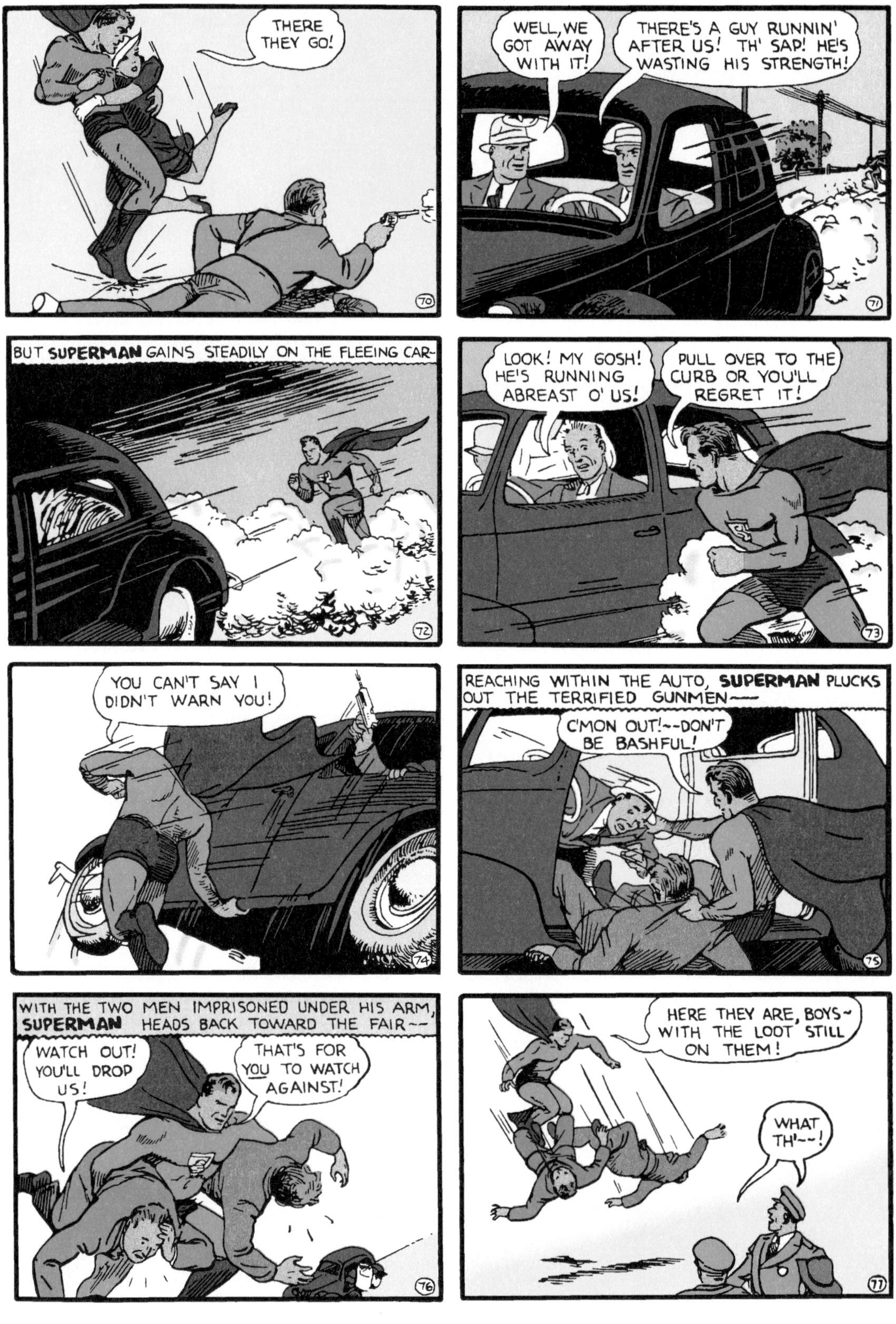
THERE THEY GO!
WELL, WE GOT AWAY WITH IT!
THERE'S A GUY RUNNIN' AFTER US! TH' SAP! HE'S WASTING HIS STRENGTH!
BUT SUPERMAN GAINS STEADILY ON THE FLEEING CAR--
LOOK! MY GOSH! HE'S RUNNING ABREAST O' US!
PULL OVER TO THE CURB OR YOU'LL REGRET IT!
YOU CAN'T SAY I DIDN'T WARN YOU!
REACHING WITHIN THE AUTO, SUPERMAN PLUCKS OUT THE TERRIFIED GUNMEN---
C'MON OUT!--DON'T BE BASHFUL!
WITH THE TWO MEN IMPRISONED UNDER HIS ARM, SUPERMAN HEADS BACK TOWARD THE FAIR--
WATCH OUT! YOU'LL DROP US!
THAT'S FOR YOU TO WATCH AGAINST!
HERE THEY ARE, BOYS-- WITH THE LOOT STILL ON THEM!
WHAT TH'--!

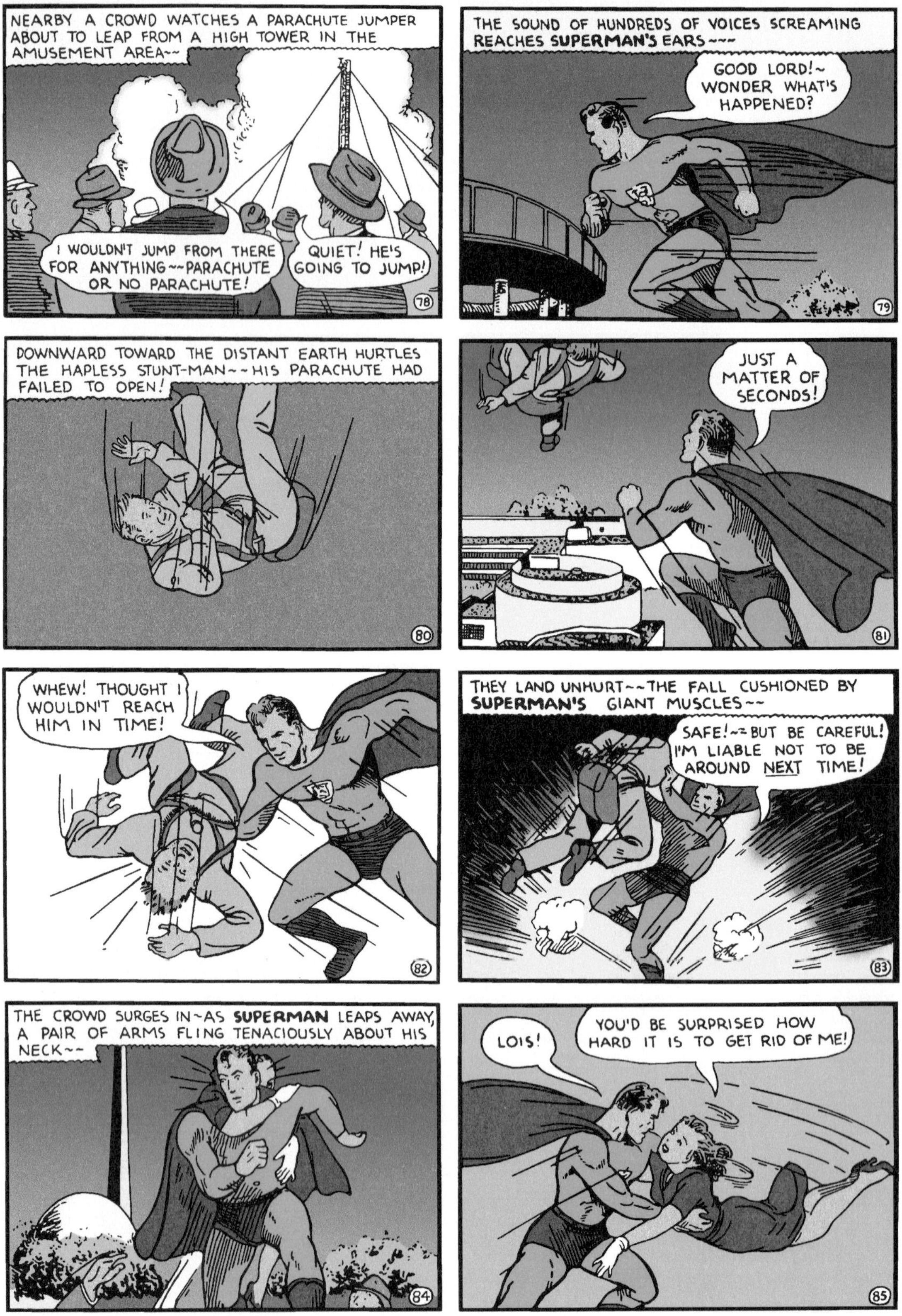

NEARBY A CROWD WATCHES A PARACHUTE JUMPER ABOUT TO LEAP FROM A HIGH TOWER IN THE AMUSEMENT AREA~~
I WOULDN'T JUMP FROM THERE FOR ANYTHING~~PARACHUTE OR NO PARACHUTE!
QUIET! HE'S GOING TO JUMP!
78
THE SOUND OF HUNDREDS OF VOICES SCREAMING REACHES SUPERMAN'S EARS~~~
GOOD LORD!~ WONDER WHAT'S HAPPENED?
79
DOWNWARD TOWARD THE DISTANT EARTH HURTLES THE HAPLESS STUNT-MAN~~HIS PARACHUTE HAD FAILED TO OPEN!
80
JUST A MATTER OF SECONDS!
81
WHEW! THOUGHT I WOULDN'T REACH HIM IN TIME!
82
THEY LAND UNHURT~~THE FALL CUSHIONED BY SUPERMAN'S GIANT MUSCLES~~
SAFE!~~BUT BE CAREFUL! I'M LIABLE NOT TO BE AROUND NEXT TIME!
83
THE CROWD SURGES IN~AS SUPERMAN LEAPS AWAY, A PAIR OF ARMS FLING TENACIOUSLY ABOUT HIS NECK~~
84
LOIS!
YOU'D BE SURPRISED HOW HARD IT IS TO GET RID OF ME!
85

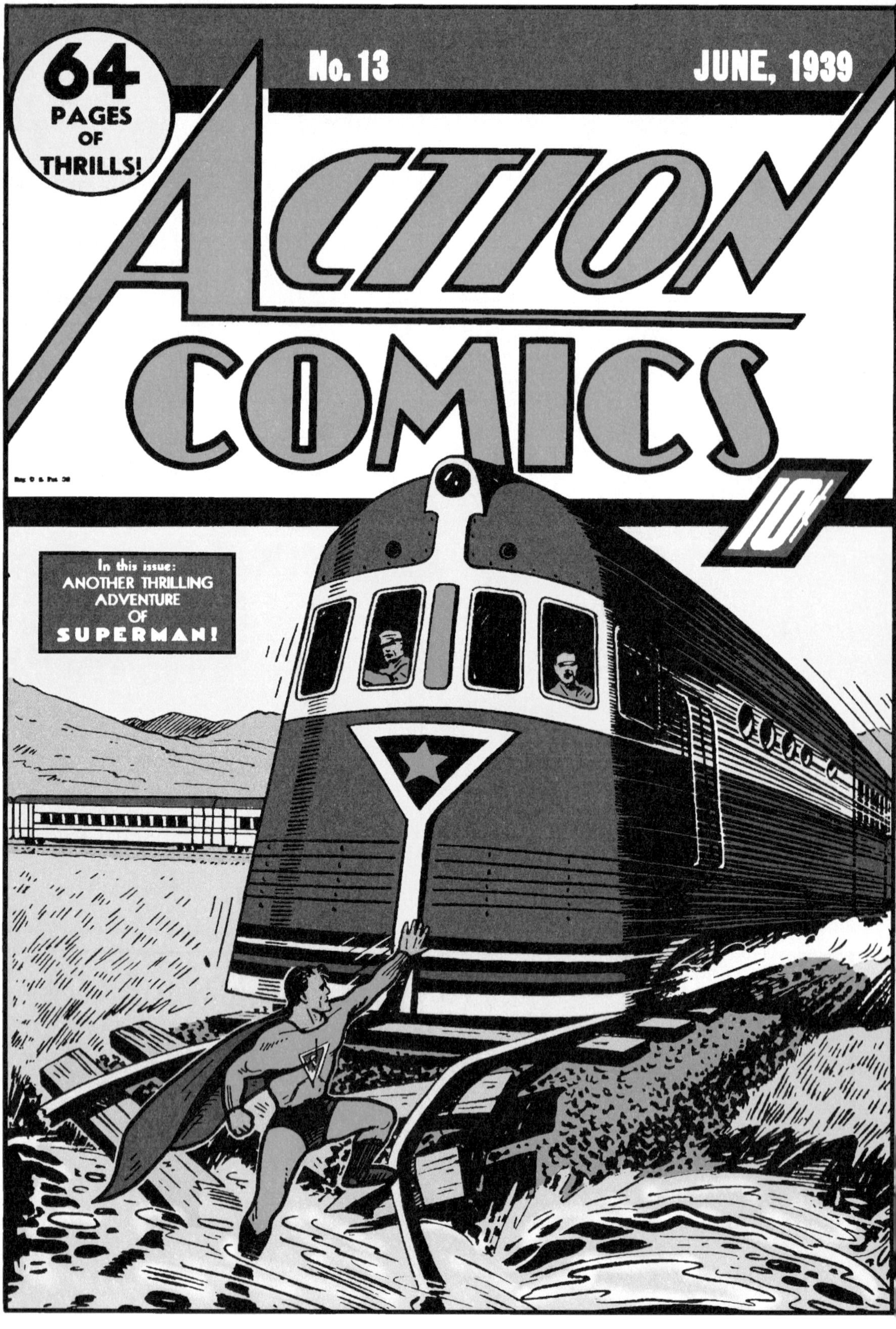
64 PAGES OF THRILLS!
No. 13
JUNE, 1939
ACTION COMICS
10¢
In this issue:
ANOTHER THRILLING ADVENTURE OF SUPERMAN!

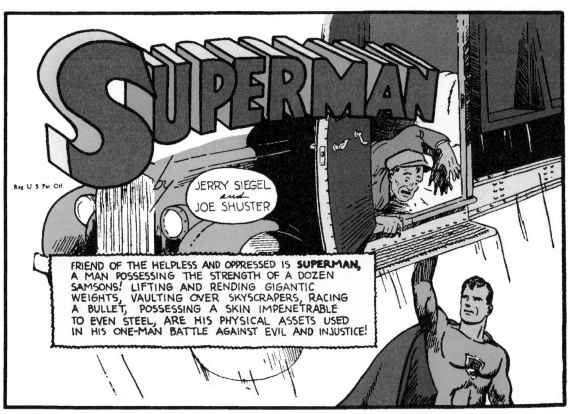

SUPERMAN

Reg U.S. Pat. Off.

by JERRY SIEGEL and JOE SHUSTER

FRIEND OF THE HELPLESS AND OPPRESSED IS **SUPERMAN**, A MAN POSSESSING THE STRENGTH OF A DOZEN SAMSONS! LIFTING AND RENDING GIGANTIC WEIGHTS, VAULTING OVER SKYSCRAPERS, RACING A BULLET, POSSESSING A SKIN IMPENETRABLE TO EVEN STEEL, ARE HIS PHYSICAL ASSETS USED IN HIS ONE-MAN BATTLE AGAINST EVIL AND INJUSTICE!

THE CAB IN WHICH CLARK KENT, ACE REPORTER OF THE <u>DAILY STAR</u>, IS DRIVING TO WORK, IS DELIBERATELY RAMMED BY ANOTHER CAB!

WATCH OUT!

YOU DID THAT ON PURPOSE!

PROVE IT!

THAT WAS NO ACCIDENT! HE DELIBERATELY RAN INTO US! ~WHY?

HE BELONGS TO THE <u>CAB PROTECTIVE LEAGUE</u>, AN ORGANIZATION THAT IS TRYING TO VICTIMIZE THE INDEPENDENT COMPANIES!

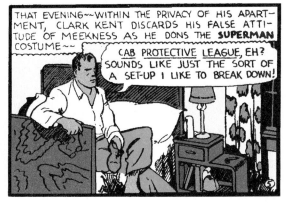

THAT EVENING~~WITHIN THE PRIVACY OF HIS APARTMENT, CLARK KENT DISCARDS HIS FALSE ATTITUDE OF MEEKNESS AS HE DONS THE **SUPERMAN** COSTUME~~

<u>CAB PROTECTIVE LEAGUE</u>, EH? SOUNDS LIKE JUST THE SORT OF A SET-UP I LIKE TO BREAK DOWN!

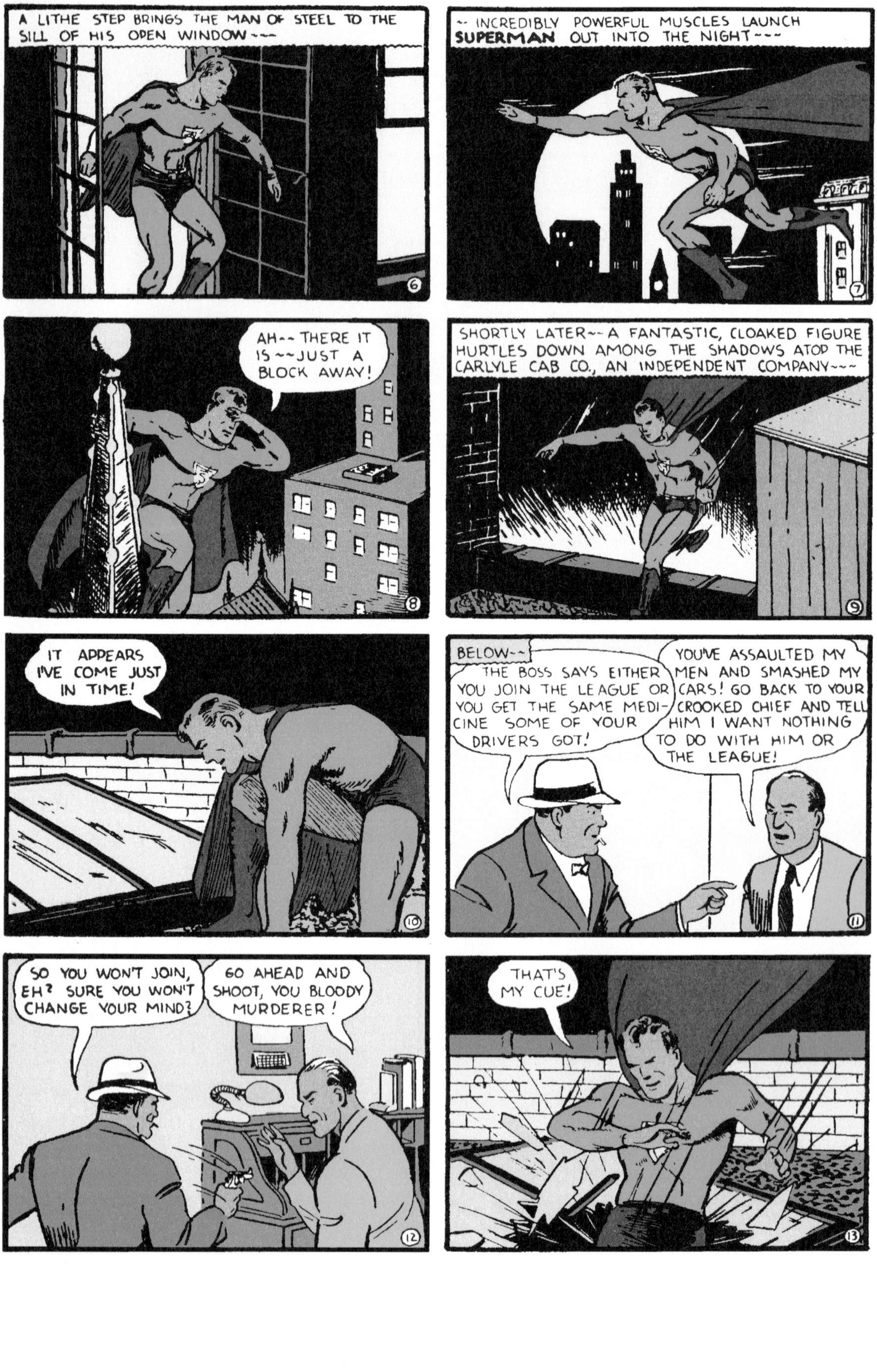
A LITHE STEP BRINGS THE MAN OF STEEL TO THE SILL OF HIS OPEN WINDOW---
-- INCREDIBLY POWERFUL MUSCLES LAUNCH SUPERMAN OUT INTO THE NIGHT---
AH-- THERE IT IS --JUST A BLOCK AWAY!
SHORTLY LATER-- A FANTASTIC, CLOAKED FIGURE HURTLES DOWN AMONG THE SHADOWS ATOP THE CARLYLE CAB CO., AN INDEPENDENT COMPANY---
IT APPEARS I'VE COME JUST IN TIME!
BELOW--
THE BOSS SAYS EITHER YOU JOIN THE LEAGUE OR YOU GET THE SAME MEDI-
CINE SOME OF YOUR DRIVERS GOT!
YOU'VE ASSAULTED MY MEN AND SMASHED MY CARS! GO BACK TO YOUR CROOKED CHIEF AND TELL HIM I WANT NOTHING TO DO WITH HIM OR THE LEAGUE!
SO YOU WON'T JOIN, EH? SURE YOU WON'T CHANGE YOUR MIND?
GO AHEAD AND SHOOT, YOU BLOODY MURDERER!
THAT'S MY CUE!

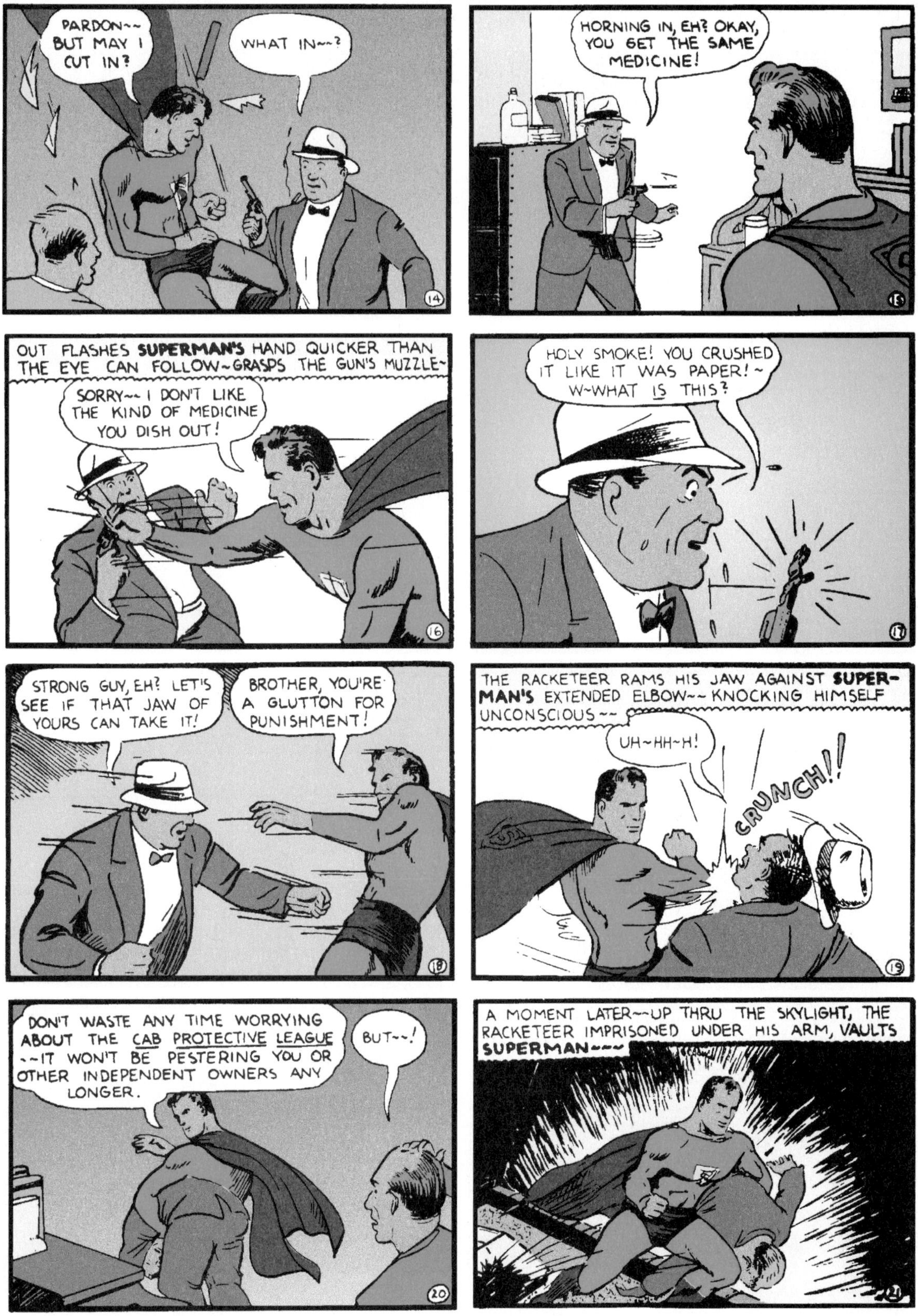
PARDON-- BUT MAY I CUT IN?
WHAT IN--?
HORNING IN, EH? OKAY, YOU GET THE SAME MEDICINE!
OUT FLASHES SUPERMAN'S HAND QUICKER THAN THE EYE CAN FOLLOW~GRASPS THE GUN'S MUZZLE~
SORRY-- I DON'T LIKE THE KIND OF MEDICINE YOU DISH OUT!
HOLY SMOKE! YOU CRUSHED IT LIKE IT WAS PAPER! ~ W~WHAT IS THIS?
STRONG GUY, EH? LET'S SEE IF THAT JAW OF YOURS CAN TAKE IT!
BROTHER, YOU'RE A GLUTTON FOR PUNISHMENT!
THE RACKETEER RAMS HIS JAW AGAINST SUPERMAN'S EXTENDED ELBOW-- KNOCKING HIMSELF UNCONSCIOUS--
UH~HH~H!
CRUNCH!!
DON'T WASTE ANY TIME WORRYING ABOUT THE CAB PROTECTIVE LEAGUE --IT WON'T BE PESTERING YOU OR OTHER INDEPENDENT OWNERS ANY LONGER.
BUT--!
A MOMENT LATER--UP THRU THE SKYLIGHT, THE RACKETEER IMPRISONED UNDER HIS ARM, VAULTS SUPERMAN---

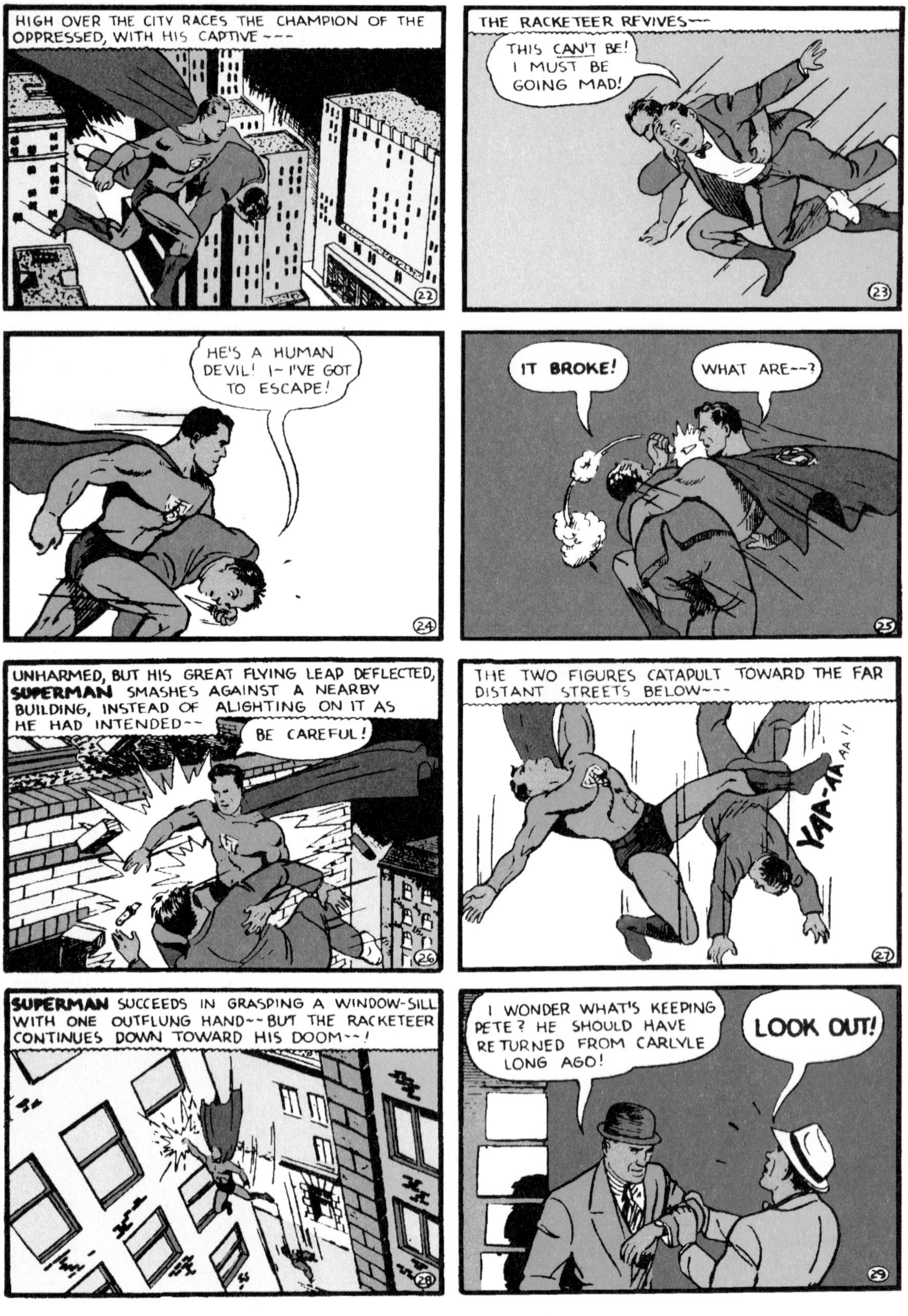
HIGH OVER THE CITY RACES THE CHAMPION OF THE OPPRESSED, WITH HIS CAPTIVE---
22
THE RACKETEER REVIVES---
THIS CAN'T BE! I MUST BE GOING MAD!
23
HE'S A HUMAN DEVIL! I-- I'VE GOT TO ESCAPE!
24
IT BROKE!
WHAT ARE--?
25
UNHARMED, BUT HIS GREAT FLYING LEAP DEFLECTED, SUPERMAN SMASHES AGAINST A NEARBY BUILDING, INSTEAD OF ALIGHTING ON IT AS HE HAD INTENDED--
BE CAREFUL!
26
THE TWO FIGURES CATAPULT TOWARD THE FAR DISTANT STREETS BELOW---
YAA-AAAA!!
27
SUPERMAN SUCCEEDS IN GRASPING A WINDOW-SILL WITH ONE OUTFLUNG HAND--BUT THE RACKETEER CONTINUES DOWN TOWARD HIS DOOM--!
28
I WONDER WHAT'S KEEPING PETE? HE SHOULD HAVE RETURNED FROM CARLYLE LONG AGO!
LOOK OUT!
29

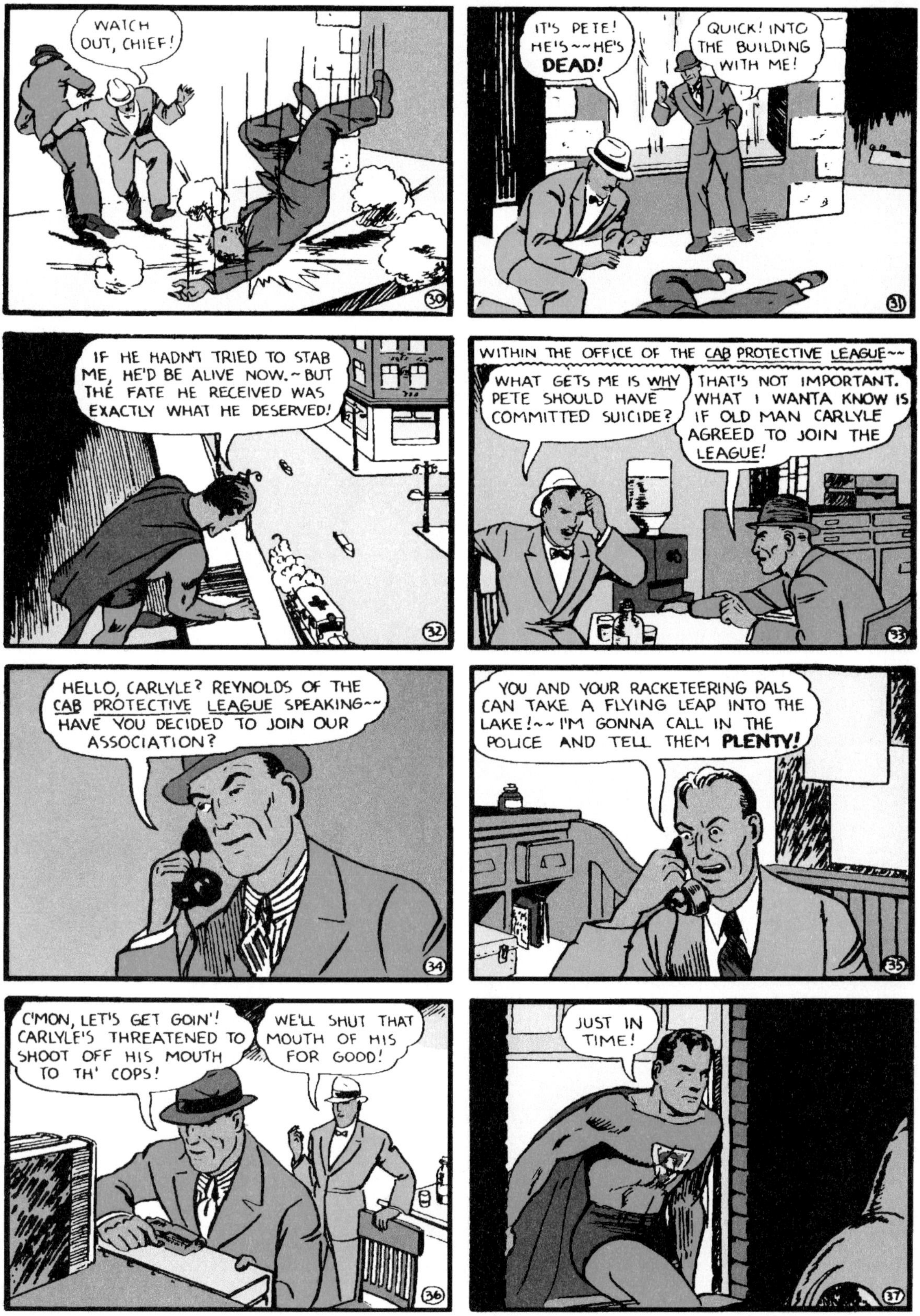
WATCH OUT, CHIEF!
IT'S PETE! HE'S~~HE'S **DEAD!**
QUICK! INTO THE BUILDING WITH ME!
IF HE HADN'T TRIED TO STAB ME, HE'D BE ALIVE NOW.~BUT THE FATE HE RECEIVED WAS EXACTLY WHAT HE DESERVED!
WITHIN THE OFFICE OF THE CAB PROTECTIVE LEAGUE~~
WHAT GETS ME IS WHY PETE SHOULD HAVE COMMITTED SUICIDE?
THAT'S NOT IMPORTANT. WHAT I WANTA KNOW IS IF OLD MAN CARLYLE AGREED TO JOIN THE LEAGUE!
HELLO, CARLYLE? REYNOLDS OF THE CAB PROTECTIVE LEAGUE SPEAKING~~ HAVE YOU DECIDED TO JOIN OUR ASSOCIATION?
YOU AND YOUR RACKETEERING PALS CAN TAKE A FLYING LEAP INTO THE LAKE!~~I'M GONNA CALL IN THE POLICE AND TELL THEM **PLENTY!**
C'MON, LET'S GET GOIN'! CARLYLE'S THREATENED TO SHOOT OFF HIS MOUTH TO TH' COPS!
WE'LL SHUT THAT MOUTH OF HIS FOR GOOD!
JUST IN TIME!

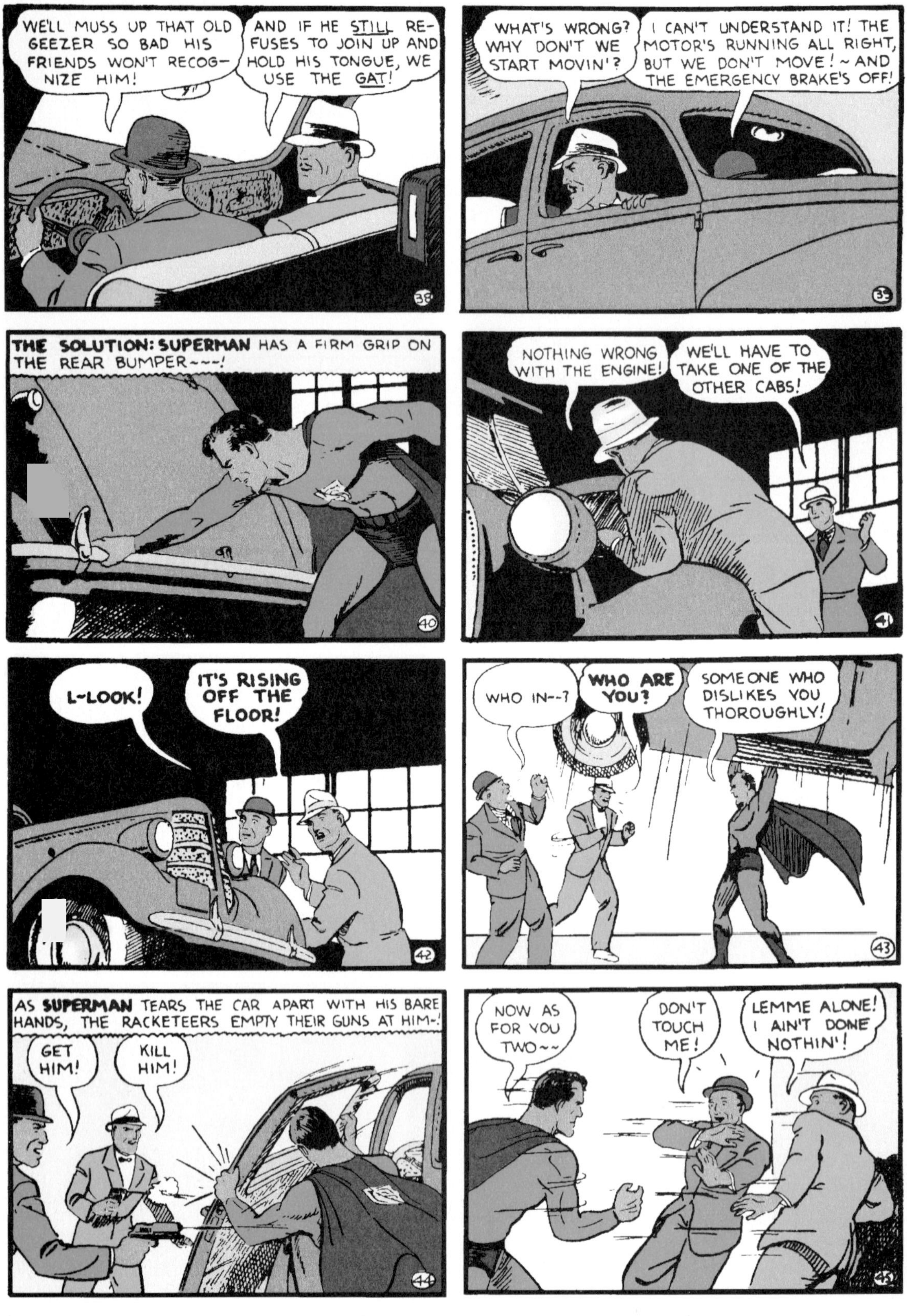
WE'LL MUSS UP THAT OLD GEEZER SO BAD HIS FRIENDS WON'T RECOG-NIZE HIM!
AND IF HE STILL RE-FUSES TO JOIN UP AND HOLD HIS TONGUE, WE USE THE GAT!
WHAT'S WRONG? WHY DON'T WE START MOVIN'?
I CAN'T UNDERSTAND IT! THE MOTOR'S RUNNING ALL RIGHT, BUT WE DON'T MOVE! ~ AND THE EMERGENCY BRAKE'S OFF!
THE SOLUTION: SUPERMAN HAS A FIRM GRIP ON THE REAR BUMPER~~~!
NOTHING WRONG WITH THE ENGINE!
WE'LL HAVE TO TAKE ONE OF THE OTHER CABS!
L~LOOK!
IT'S RISING OFF THE FLOOR!
WHO IN--?
WHO ARE YOU?
SOMEONE WHO DISLIKES YOU THOROUGHLY!
AS SUPERMAN TEARS THE CAR APART WITH HIS BARE HANDS, THE RACKETEERS EMPTY THEIR GUNS AT HIM-!
GET HIM!
KILL HIM!
NOW AS FOR YOU TWO~~
DON'T TOUCH ME!
LEMME ALONE! I AIN'T DONE NOTHIN'!

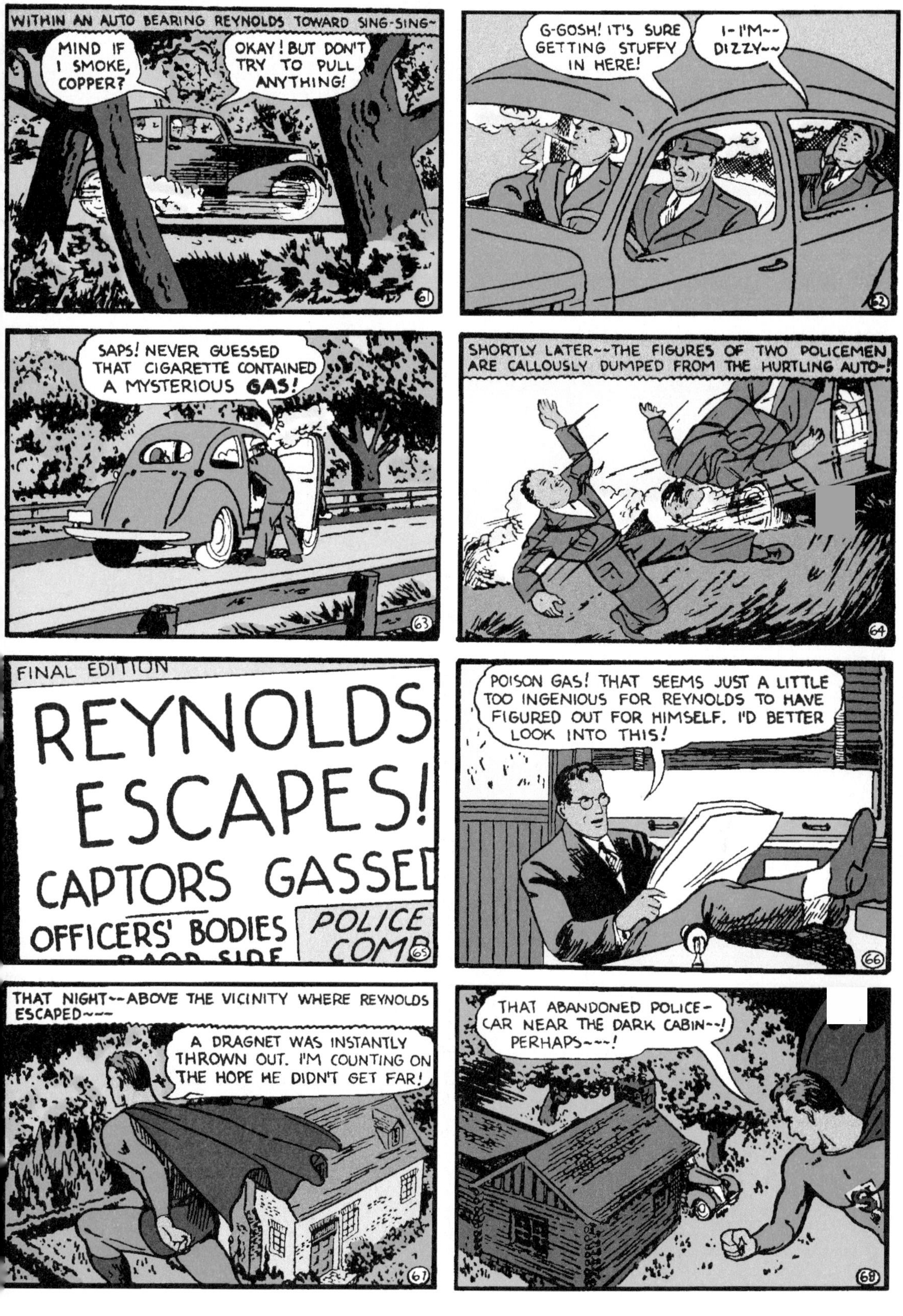

WITHIN AN AUTO BEARING REYNOLDS TOWARD SING-SING~
MIND IF I SMOKE, COPPER?
OKAY! BUT DON'T TRY TO PULL ANYTHING!
G-GOSH! IT'S SURE GETTING STUFFY IN HERE!
I-I'M~~ DIZZY~~
SAPS! NEVER GUESSED THAT CIGARETTE CONTAINED A MYSTERIOUS GAS!
SHORTLY LATER~~THE FIGURES OF TWO POLICEMEN ARE CALLOUSLY DUMPED FROM THE HURTLING AUTO~!
FINAL EDITION
REYNOLDS ESCAPES!
CAPTORS GASSED
OFFICERS' BODIES
POLICE COMB
POISON GAS! THAT SEEMS JUST A LITTLE TOO INGENIOUS FOR REYNOLDS TO HAVE FIGURED OUT FOR HIMSELF. I'D BETTER LOOK INTO THIS!
THAT NIGHT~~ABOVE THE VICINITY WHERE REYNOLDS ESCAPED~~~
A DRAGNET WAS INSTANTLY THROWN OUT. I'M COUNTING ON THE HOPE HE DIDN'T GET FAR!
THAT ABANDONED POLICE-CAR NEAR THE DARK CABIN~~! PERHAPS~~~!

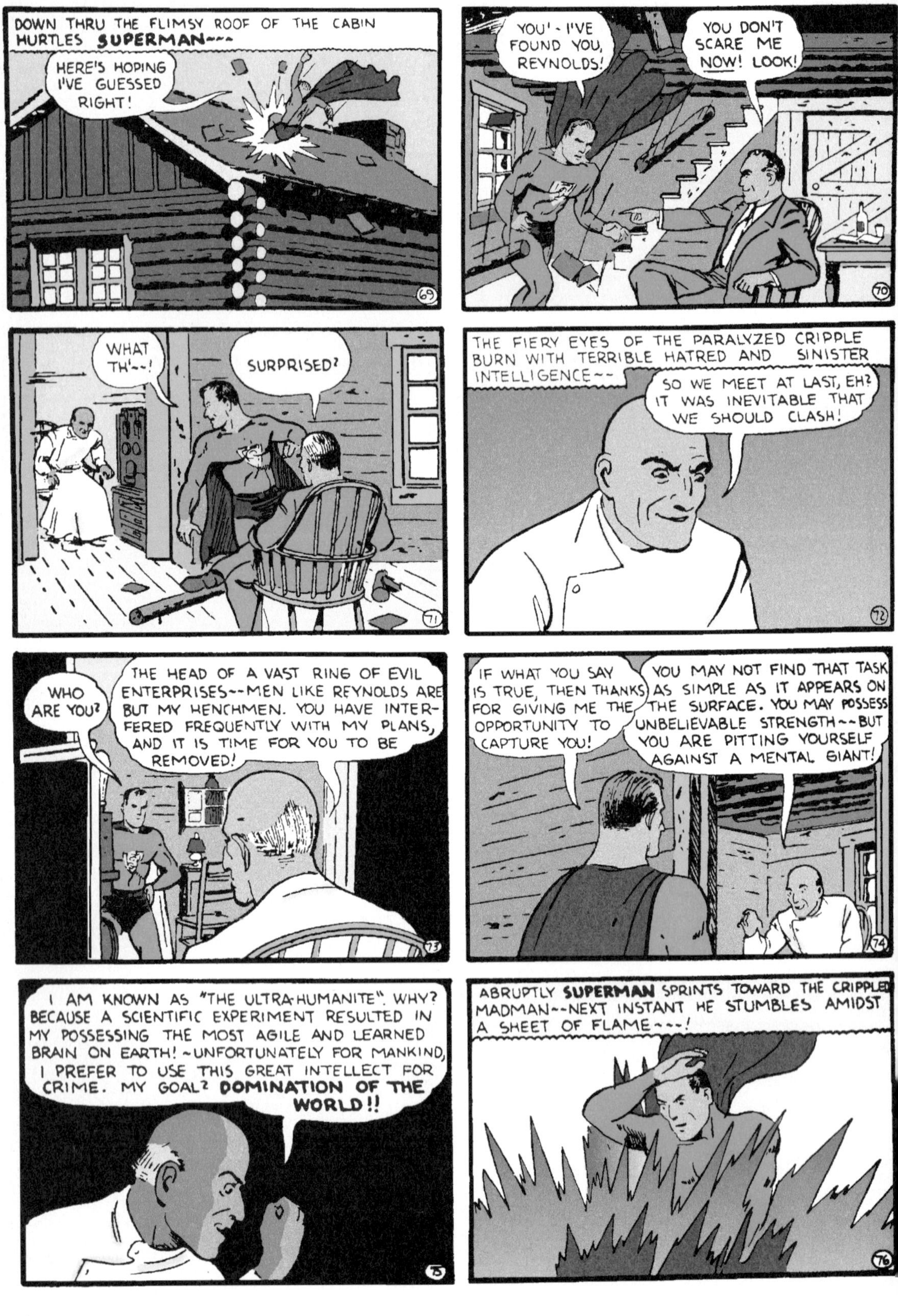
DOWN THRU THE FLIMSY ROOF OF THE CABIN HURTLES SUPERMAN---
HERE'S HOPING I'VE GUESSED RIGHT!
YOU! - I'VE FOUND YOU, REYNOLDS!
YOU DON'T SCARE ME NOW! LOOK!
WHAT TH'--!
SURPRISED?
THE FIERY EYES OF THE PARALYZED CRIPPLE BURN WITH TERRIBLE HATRED AND SINISTER INTELLIGENCE--
SO WE MEET AT LAST, EH? IT WAS INEVITABLE THAT WE SHOULD CLASH!
WHO ARE YOU?
THE HEAD OF A VAST RING OF EVIL ENTERPRISES--MEN LIKE REYNOLDS ARE BUT MY HENCHMEN. YOU HAVE INTERFERED FREQUENTLY WITH MY PLANS, AND IT IS TIME FOR YOU TO BE REMOVED!
IF WHAT YOU SAY IS TRUE, THEN THANKS FOR GIVING ME THE OPPORTUNITY TO CAPTURE YOU!
YOU MAY NOT FIND THAT TASK AS SIMPLE AS IT APPEARS ON THE SURFACE. YOU MAY POSSESS UNBELIEVABLE STRENGTH--BUT YOU ARE PITTING YOURSELF AGAINST A MENTAL GIANT!
I AM KNOWN AS "THE ULTRA-HUMANITE". WHY? BECAUSE A SCIENTIFIC EXPERIMENT RESULTED IN MY POSSESSING THE MOST AGILE AND LEARNED BRAIN ON EARTH! - UNFORTUNATELY FOR MANKIND, I PREFER TO USE THIS GREAT INTELLECT FOR CRIME. MY GOAL? DOMINATION OF THE WORLD!!
ABRUPTLY SUPERMAN SPRINTS TOWARD THE CRIPPLED MADMAN--NEXT INSTANT HE STUMBLES AMIDST A SHEET OF FLAME---!

195

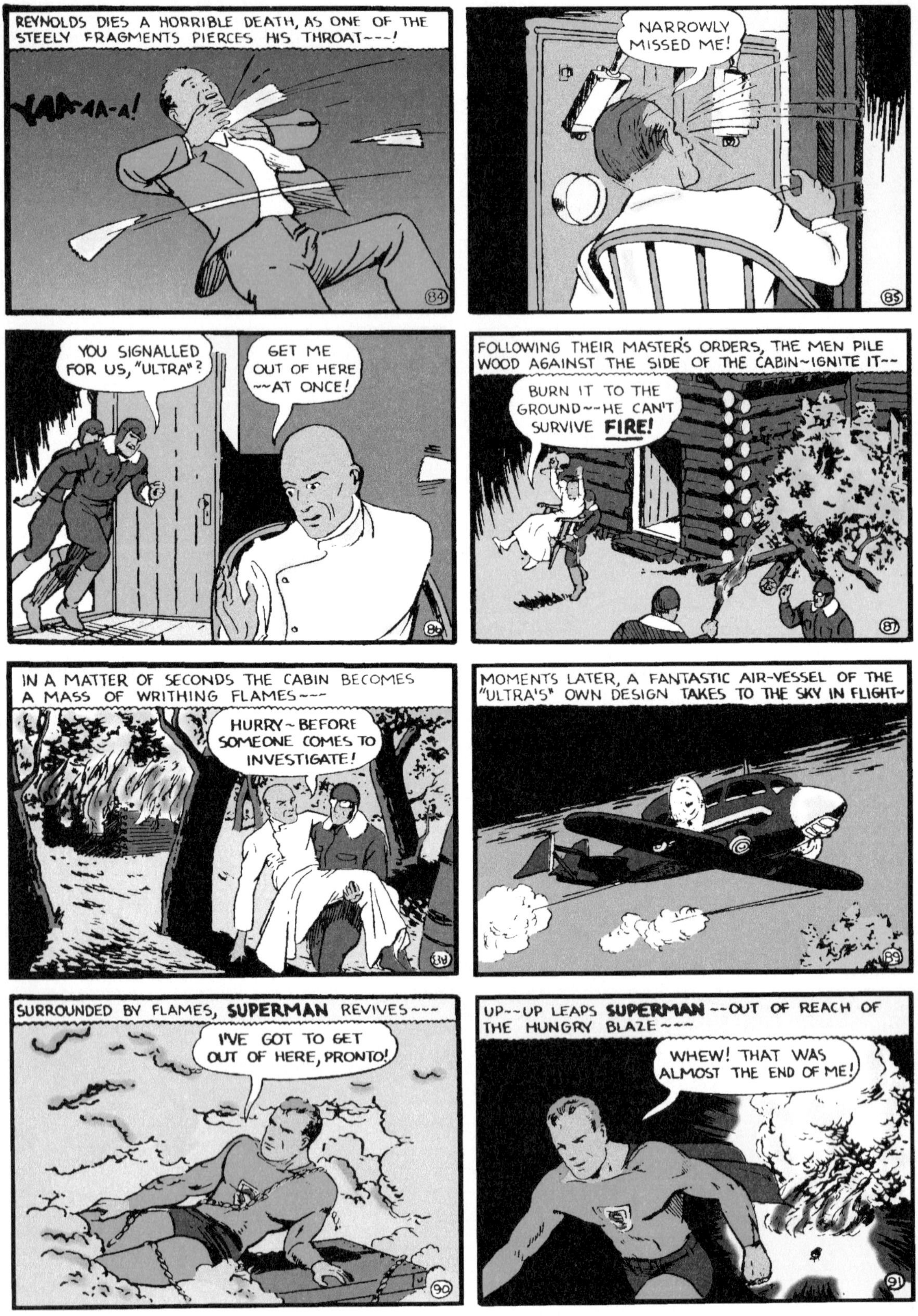
REYNOLDS DIES A HORRIBLE DEATH, AS ONE OF THE STEELY FRAGMENTS PIERCES HIS THROAT---!
YAAAA-A!
NARROWLY MISSED ME!
YOU SIGNALLED FOR US, "ULTRA"?
GET ME OUT OF HERE --AT ONCE!
FOLLOWING THEIR MASTER'S ORDERS, THE MEN PILE WOOD AGAINST THE SIDE OF THE CABIN~IGNITE IT--
BURN IT TO THE GROUND--HE CAN'T SURVIVE FIRE!
IN A MATTER OF SECONDS THE CABIN BECOMES A MASS OF WRITHING FLAMES---
HURRY~BEFORE SOMEONE COMES TO INVESTIGATE!
MOMENTS LATER, A FANTASTIC AIR-VESSEL OF THE "ULTRA'S" OWN DESIGN TAKES TO THE SKY IN FLIGHT~
SURROUNDED BY FLAMES, SUPERMAN REVIVES---
I'VE GOT TO GET OUT OF HERE, PRONTO!
UP--UP LEAPS SUPERMAN --OUT OF REACH OF THE HUNGRY BLAZE---
WHEW! THAT WAS ALMOST THE END OF ME!

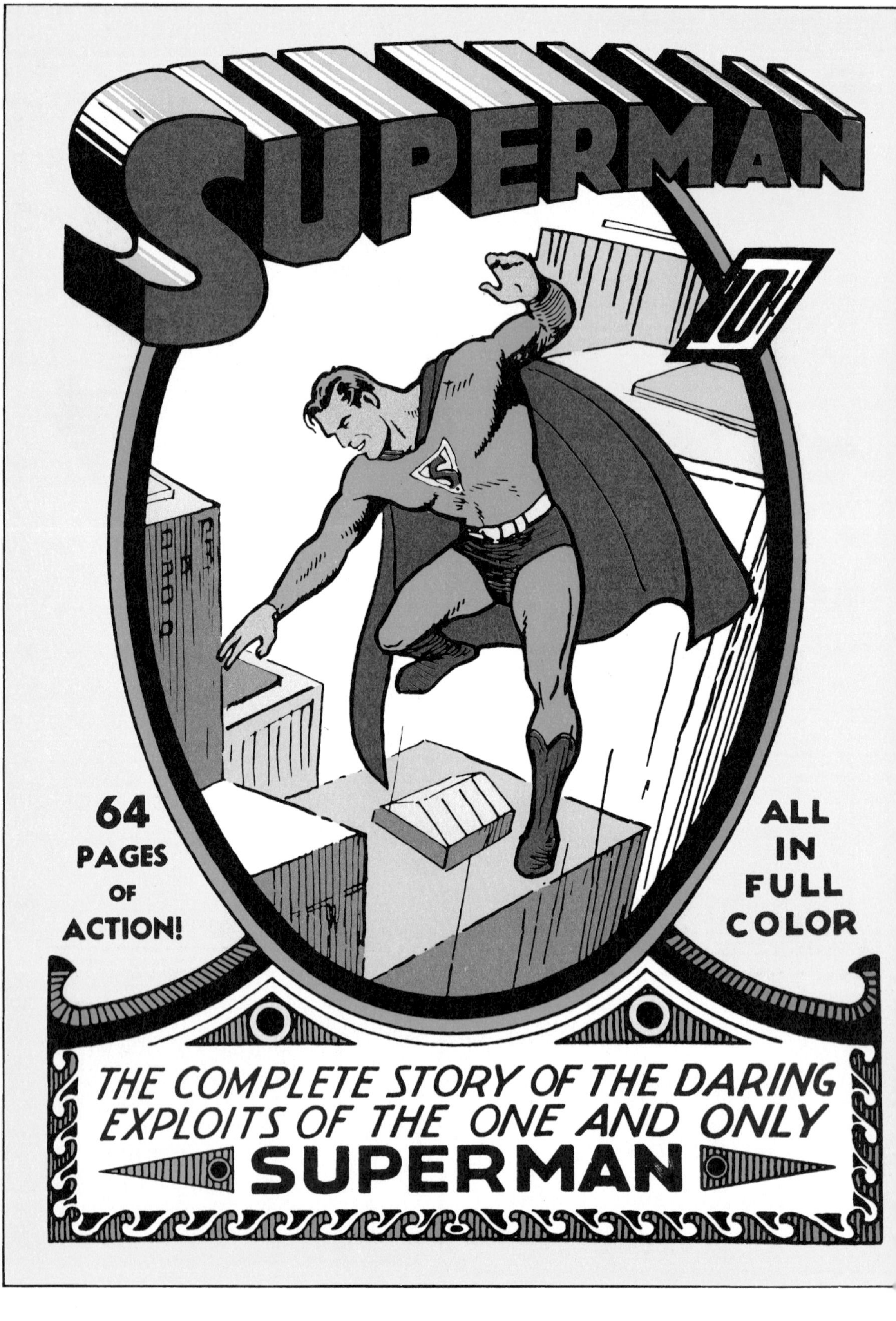
SUPERMAN
10¢
64 PAGES OF ACTION!
ALL IN FULL COLOR
THE COMPLETE STORY OF THE DARING EXPLOITS OF THE ONE AND ONLY
SUPERMAN

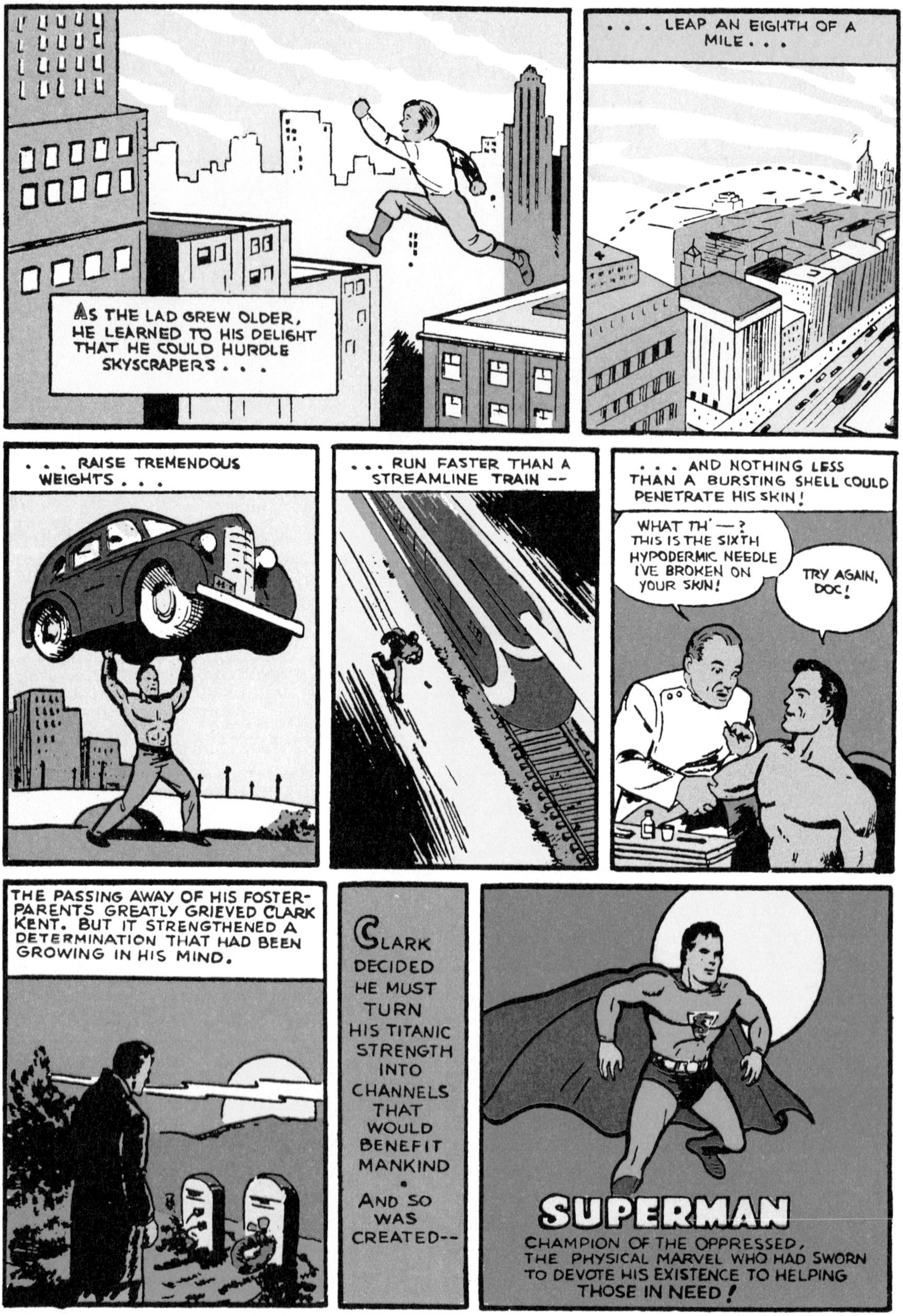
AS THE LAD GREW OLDER, HE LEARNED TO HIS DELIGHT THAT HE COULD HURDLE SKYSCRAPERS . . .
. . . LEAP AN EIGHTH OF A MILE . . .
. . . RAISE TREMENDOUS WEIGHTS . . .
. . . RUN FASTER THAN A STREAMLINE TRAIN --
. . . AND NOTHING LESS THAN A BURSTING SHELL COULD PENETRATE HIS SKIN!
WHAT TH'—? THIS IS THE SIXTH HYPODERMIC NEEDLE I'VE BROKEN ON YOUR SKIN!
TRY AGAIN, DOC!
THE PASSING AWAY OF HIS FOSTER-PARENTS GREATLY GRIEVED CLARK KENT. BUT IT STRENGTHENED A DETERMINATION THAT HAD BEEN GROWING IN HIS MIND.
CLARK DECIDED HE MUST TURN HIS TITANIC STRENGTH INTO CHANNELS THAT WOULD BENEFIT MANKIND • AND SO WAS CREATED--
SUPERMAN
CHAMPION OF THE OPPRESSED, THE PHYSICAL MARVEL WHO HAD SWORN TO DEVOTE HIS EXISTENCE TO HELPING THOSE IN NEED!

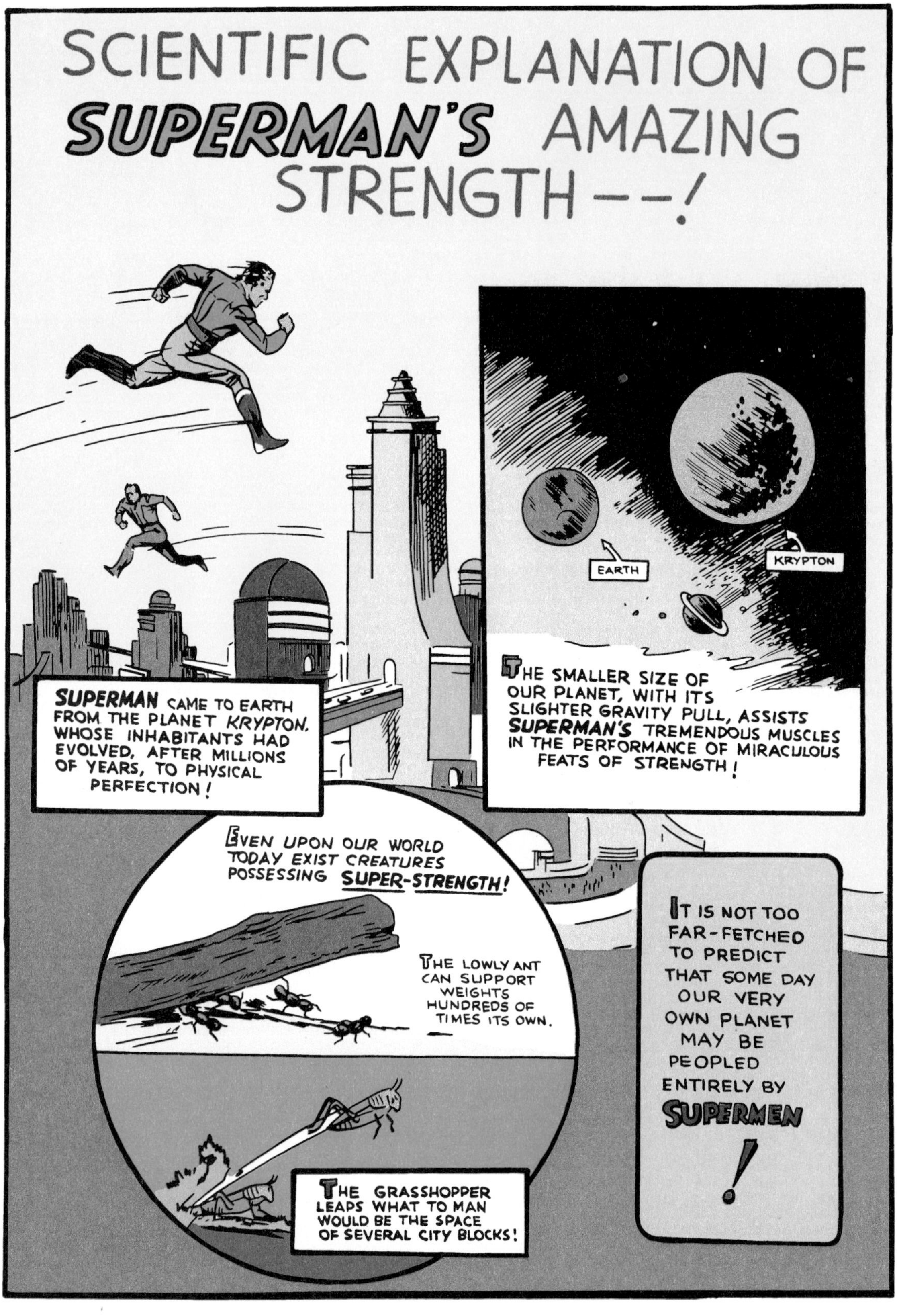
SCIENTIFIC EXPLANATION OF SUPERMAN'S AMAZING STRENGTH--!
SUPERMAN CAME TO EARTH FROM THE PLANET KRYPTON, WHOSE INHABITANTS HAD EVOLVED, AFTER MILLIONS OF YEARS, TO PHYSICAL PERFECTION!
EARTH
KRYPTON
THE SMALLER SIZE OF OUR PLANET, WITH ITS SLIGHTER GRAVITY PULL, ASSISTS SUPERMAN'S TREMENDOUS MUSCLES IN THE PERFORMANCE OF MIRACULOUS FEATS OF STRENGTH!
EVEN UPON OUR WORLD TODAY EXIST CREATURES POSSESSING SUPER-STRENGTH!
THE LOWLY ANT CAN SUPPORT WEIGHTS HUNDREDS OF TIMES ITS OWN.
THE GRASSHOPPER LEAPS WHAT TO MAN WOULD BE THE SPACE OF SEVERAL CITY BLOCKS!
IT IS NOT TOO FAR-FETCHED TO PREDICT THAT SOME DAY OUR VERY OWN PLANET MAY BE PEOPLED ENTIRELY BY SUPERMEN!

SUPERMAN

by JERRY SIEGEL AND JOE SHUSTER

SMASHED desks, overturned filing cabinets, strewn plaster, gaping holes in the walls, shining steel fixtures drooping in sad caricature of their former modernistic splendor, greeted the startled Detective Sergeant's eyes, as he swung open the office door to the firm *Harvey Brown, Patent Attorney*

A quivering wreck of a man arose from the floor, stridently shrieked, "He can't do this to me! Get him! Arrest him!"

Sergeant Blake surveyed the fellow's torn clothing, mussed hair, and blackened eyes, then once again speechlessly regarded the carnage in the room. "What in blazes has happened here?" he roared, finding his voice at last, "A cyclone?"

"Cyclone, nothing!" exclaimed the trembling man. "Worse! I've just had a visit from SUPERMAN!"

"SUPERMAN!" The word burst from Blake's lips with the force of an explosion.

"Yes! He claimed I've stolen my clients' inventions. After he wrecked the place, he warned me that if I didn't go out of business, he'd come back and finish the job! I demand . . . " Brown halted his tirade. The Detective Sergeant was no longer in the room.

The remaining members of the riot squad were taken aback to see their superior officer come hurtling out into the hall at full tilt.

"Quick!" shouted Blake. "Seen anyone since I charged into the room?"

"No one," volunteered a puzzled officer. "That is, no one except a guy wearing a strange costume who asked what the trouble was, then stepped into the elevator."

A howl of baffled rage left the Sergeant as he sprang to the wall and desperately jabbed the elevator button. "Fools!" he roared. "That was SUPERMAN!"

Concerted cries left the policemen. "SUPERMAN! . . . and he's in that elevator! . . . What'll we do?"

Blake seized the hand of one of his men, and shoved it against the button. "Keep that pressed down for a full three minutes, Mooney—or I'll have your badge.—You others, come with me!"

Toward the nearby stairway dashed Blake, followed by his men. As they clattered down at top speed, he explained, "Fortunately, the elevator is automatically operated by the push-buttons on the various floors. As long as Mooney presses the button, SUPERMAN is trapped. And when the three minutes are up, and the Man of Steel gets off at the bottom floor, we'll be ready for him!"

Two minutes later found the policemen ranged before the first floor entrance to the elevator, guns out, all eyes strained on the indicator which showed that the car was stalled somewhere between the second and the first floor. Triumph blazed in Sergeant Blake's eyes. Visions of a pat on the back from the Commissioner, a promotion in rank, and a boost in salary, dangled tantalizingly in his mind.

"Careful, men!" he warned the officers grouped about him. "We've prayed for this break for months, and now that it's come, we don't want to muff it. He was seen going into that elevator . . . and he's bound to come out of that door any moment!"

"And *that's* what bothers me," muttered someone, "What'll we do when he *does* emerge?"

Said another "Our guns are useless against him!"

"Nonsense!" retorted Sergeant Blake. "All we've got to do is keep cool, and we've got him!"

But his glib comeback didn't satisfy even the Detective Sergeant himself. There were some very wild tales being circulated about this fellow who called himself SUPERMAN. He was said to be a modern Robin Hood . . . a person who had dedicated his existence to assisting the weak and oppressed. It was whispered that he possessed super-strength, could lift tremendous weights, smash steel with his bare hands, jump over buildings, and that nothing could penetrate his amazingly super-tough skin. But, of course, pondered the Sergeant, these were mere rumors, fantastic fairy tales. Probably SUPERMAN was just an ordinary person whose better than average strength had been immensely exaggerated Without a doubt!

Nevertheless, the hardboiled cop couldn't prevent an apprehensive shiver from creeping up his spine!

Suddenly, the arrow on the indicator began to move. The three minutes were up! Mooney had released the button, and the elevator was descending!

With a clash of metal the door to the elevator swung open. Fingers tensed on gun-triggers . . . Then . . .

A hesitant, alarmed voice broke the electric silence: "My word! Put down those guns!"

Out of the elevator stepped a slim, nervous figure. Meek eyes blinked fearfully behind thick-rimmed glasses. No SUPERMAN, this! Rather, a very much frightened young man.

From somewhere behind him, the dumbfounded Detective Sergeant heard a smothered titter. His face reddened. "Where's SUPERMAN?" he shouted at the mouse-like young man who stood before him. "What in all that's holy are *you* doing in that elevator?"

"I was just—er—descending to the lobby, when something apparently went wrong with the mechanism. "I'll admit I was terrified for a few moments, but . . . "

"Answer me!" thundered Blake. "Did you see a man in a strange uniform in that elevator?"

"No one at all . . . that is, except myself. I'm afraid there must be some mistake, Sergeant. I'm Clark Kent, reporter on the *Daily Star.*"

"But SUPERMAN was seen to enter the elevator by one of my men How do you explain that?"

Clark shrugged. "It's beyond me," he said. "Possibly your man was high-strung, or had an over-active imagination"

A loud laugh went up at this. The Detective Sergeant whirled to face his men, his features registering keen disappointment. "I guess it was just a false alarm, at that! Let's head back for headquarters, to turn in a report."

"I say, that's odd!" interrupted Kent. "I was just about to go to Police Headquarters myself, in search of a story. Do you mind if I accompany you?"

Later, as they sped through the streets with the squad car, Clark learned that people adjoining Brown's office had telephoned for a police car, complaining of a terrific rumpus going on in the Patent Attorney's office . . . and how Blake had expected SUPERMAN to emerge from the elevator.

"Very amusing," chuckled Clark. "It'll make a good feature article for the *Daily Star*."

"Hold on!" bellowed Blake in protest. "You can't print that. It would make me look like a sap!—Don't print it! And maybe some day I'll return the favor!"

The reporter shrugged. "Well, if you feel that strongly about it, I'll forget the yarn . . . temporarily."

The conversation was cut short as they parked before the police station. As they emerged from the car, an officer rushed up and exclaimed to Blake. "Have you heard? 'Biff' Dugan has just been captured!"

A happy grin quickly chased the glum expression from the Detective Sergeant's face. "Biff" was a long-sought murderer who had been eluding the law for months. "I knew we'd catch up with that rat," Blake chuckled.

Swift strides hurried Blake and Kent into the station. A few moments later the prisoner, an ugly hulking brute who sullenly refused to talk, stood before them.

"Thought you could evade the law, did you?" demanded the Sergeant. "Well, maybe you know better now!"

Clark tugged at Blake's sleeve. "Remember, Sergeant? You offered to do me a favor. I'd like to take you up, now!"

Suspiciously, Blake inquired: "What?"

"Allow me to interview the prisoner in private."

"And what," asked Blake, "is wrong with interviewing him right here in front of me?"

"You can see he's in no mood to talk. Perhaps if I could speak to him alone . . . "

"Are you looney? It's against regulations. It's . . . "

Clark smiled tauntingly. "If I can't have this interview, I'll have to write up a certain other story One about a dumb Detective Sergeant who had his men surround an elevator in the hope . . . "

"Wait!" cried Blake. "You can have that interview!" He added ominously. "But if anything happens to the prisoner, you'll be held personally responsible."

Shortly later, within an adjoining room, Clark was occupied with the task of prying replies from a glum prisoner when there came a knocking at the room's door.

Bart turned from the prisoner. Opened the door slightly.

It was Blake. He demanded: "Is the prisoner still there?"

"Naturally," replied Clark, exasperated. "See for yours . . . " Abruptly Kent's words were choked off in a gasp of astonishment. Alarmed, the Sergeant burst into the room. In one glance he saw the reporter's hand pointing toward an open window . . . and no sight of Dugan anywhere.

"He's escaped!" exclaimed Clark.

Sergeant Blake roared with rage, seized the frail reporter, and shook him angrily. "You—!" he choked. "It's *your* fault! This makes you an accessory to the fact!"

The Detective Sergeant will never completely remember what happened just then. One moment he was shaking a fear-struck reporter, and the next instant he was whirling up into the air, as though caught in the grip of a hurricane. Next instant he struck the wall, uttered a groan, and lapsed into unconsciousness.

Clark Kent looked at the Sergeant's recumbent figure, mutteerd, "Sorry, but I haven't time to use

kid gloves," then, with amazing rapidity he stripped off his glasses and outer garments, revealing himself clad in a weird close-fitting costume, and flaring cape. In this apparel, it was apparent that he really possessed a fine physique of breathtaking symmetry.

One lithe leap brought him to the window-sill. There he poised momentarily, while his keen telescopic vision surveyed the vicinity. And then, as he sighted the figure of "Biff" scrambling into a parked auto, he dived out into space.

Out—out—sped the fantastic figure . . . its mighty muscles launching it across an incredible distance. The auto was a full three hundred yards away, but SUPERMAN smashed down into the gravel before it, just as the car's gears clashed and it leapt ahead.

Within the car, Dugan snarled. This solitary figure which had hurtled down from nowhere . . . it alone stood between him and escape. He pressed the accelerator down to the limit, with the intention of smashing into the body, crushing it beneath his auto's wheels.

He struck the figure with a *crash!* But then, the impossible happened! Instead of being flung beneath the wheels, SUPERMAN held his ground . . . actually kept the roaring machine from moving!

Astounded by this miracle, "Biff" threw the clutch into reverse, but again he was treated to an exhibition of super-strength. Having seized the front bumper, the Man of Steel prevented the automobile from backing up!

A shriek of sheer horror tore from Dugan's throat. Frenziedly, he flung open the door of the automobile, sprang out . . . and looked up to find himself faced by SUPERMAN'S grim figure!

Half mad with fright he leapt at the Man of Tomorrow, seeking to fight his way past. But it was like bucking against a stone wall. His fists encountered flesh as hard as metal, fracturing his knuckles!

Suddenly "Biff" was possessed with but one desire. To flee . . . to get away from this indestructible demon of wrath! He whirled, raced off with all his might, screeching at the top of his lungs. Next instant, arms of steel encircled him from behind. There was a pressure at the back of his neck. Then . . . unconsciousness. . .

SERGEANT Blake revived to find Clark Kent kneeling beside him. He felt his forehead groggily, then suddenly remembering what had occurred, seized the reporter. "You're under arrest!" he shouted.

"What for?" inquired Kent.

"For aiding 'Biff' Dugan to escape, that's why! And . . . "

Clark pointed to a figure huddled on the floor nearby. "Before you say any more, look over there!"

Blake looked, blinked uncomprehendingly, then exclaimed: "Dugan!—But how . . . ?"

"All I know," replied Clark, "is that a man wearing a strange costume jumped to the window-sill, tossed 'Biff' in, then leapt away."

The Detective Sergeant sprang erect. "Do you realize who that must have been! SUPERMAN!"

Clark's eyes widened. "Gosh! I guess you're right!"

"You know," grudgingly admitted Sergeant Blake. "sometimes I think SUPERMAN isn't such a bad guy, at that. But," he hastily amended, "don't think that doesn't mean I won't arrest him the minute I get my hands on him!"

"Let's hope you get within reaching distance," said Clark Kent.

Detective Sergeant Blake cast a quick suspicious glance at the reporter. For a moment he'd fancied he had detected a trace of mockery in Kent's voice. But Clark's visage was completely solemn.

THE END

Boys and Girls: Meet the creators of the one and only SUPERMAN—America's Greatest Adventure Strip!

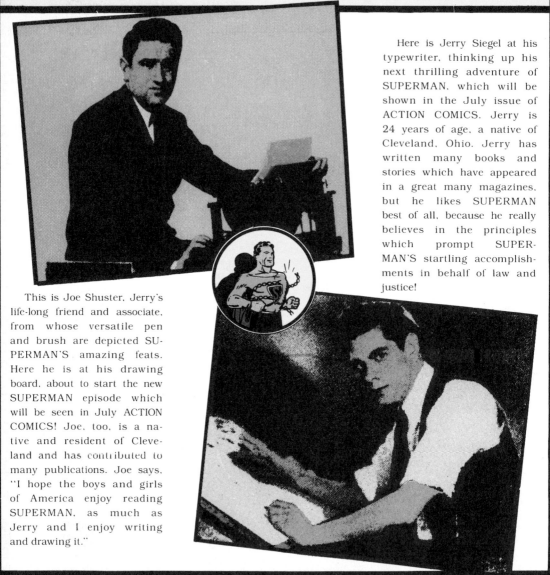

Here is Jerry Siegel at his typewriter, thinking up his next thrilling adventure of SUPERMAN, which will be shown in the July issue of ACTION COMICS. Jerry is 24 years of age, a native of Cleveland, Ohio. Jerry has written many books and stories which have appeared in a great many magazines, but he likes SUPERMAN best of all, because he really believes in the principles which prompt SUPERMAN'S startling accomplishments in behalf of law and justice!

This is Joe Shuster, Jerry's life-long friend and associate, from whose versatile pen and brush are depicted SUPERMAN'S amazing feats. Here he is at his drawing board, about to start the new SUPERMAN episode which will be seen in July ACTION COMICS! Joe, too, is a native and resident of Cleveland and has contributed to many publications. Joe says, "I hope the boys and girls of America enjoy reading SUPERMAN, as much as Jerry and I enjoy writing and drawing it."

JERRY SIEGEL and JOE SHUSTER are also the creators of "Slam Bradley" and "Spy" which appear in DETECTIVE COMICS; "Radio Squad" which appears in MORE FUN COMICS; and "Federal Men" which appears monthly in ADVENTURE COMICS.

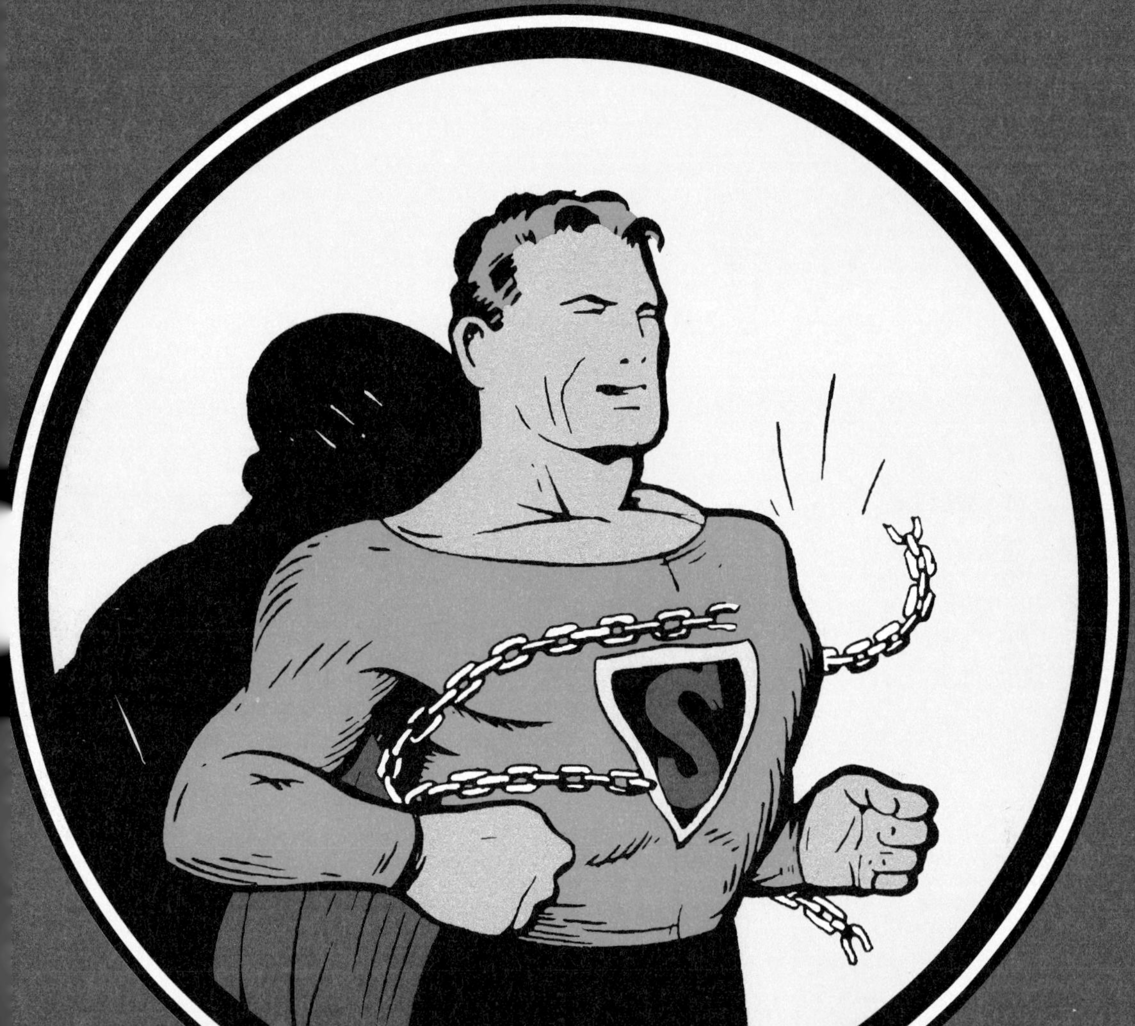

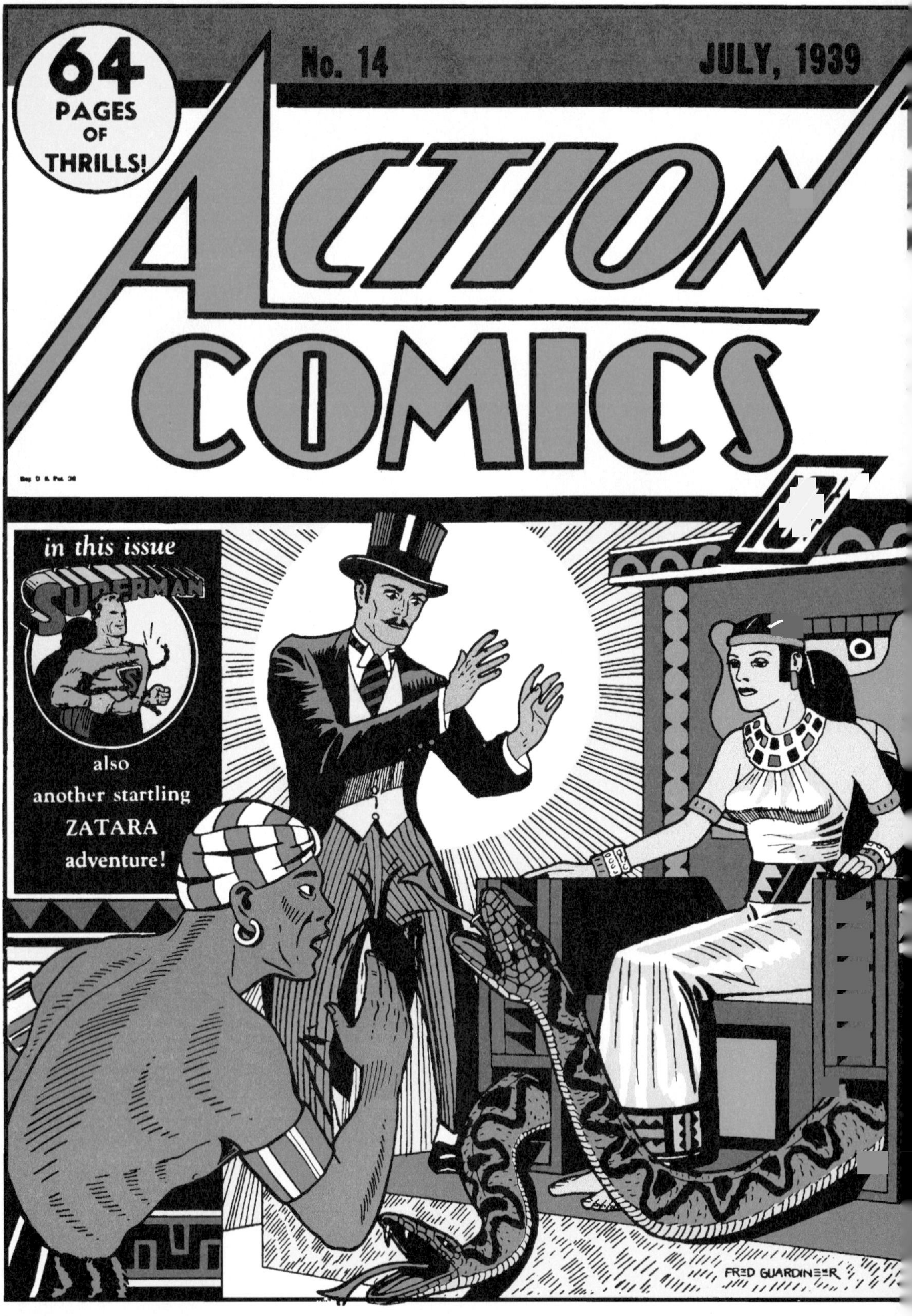
64 PAGES OF THRILLS!
No. 14
JULY, 1939
ACTION COMICS
in this issue
SUPERMAN
also
another startling
ZATARA
adventure!
FRED GUARDINEER

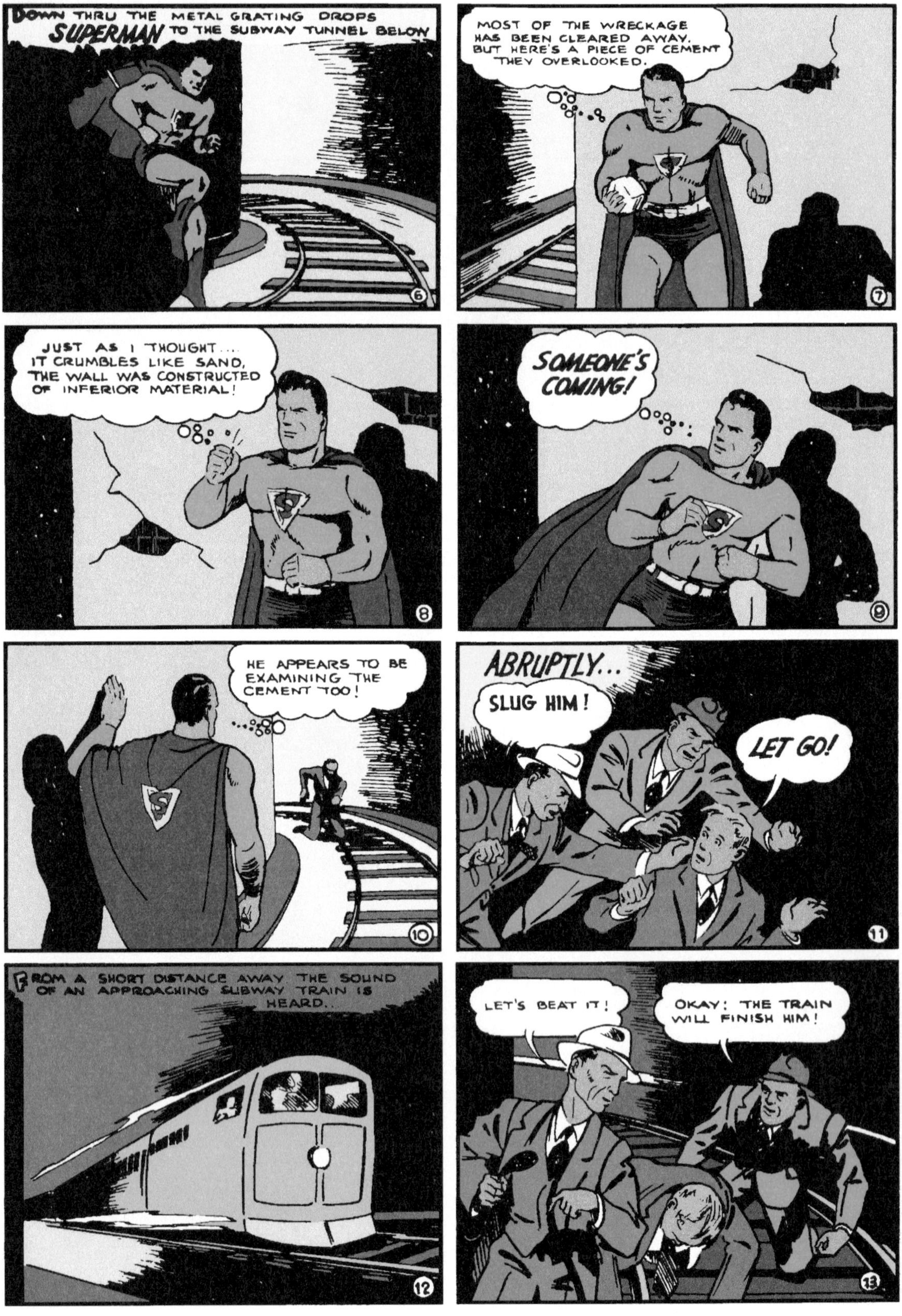
DOWN THRU THE METAL GRATING DROPS SUPERMAN TO THE SUBWAY TUNNEL BELOW
MOST OF THE WRECKAGE HAS BEEN CLEARED AWAY. BUT HERE'S A PIECE OF CEMENT THEY OVERLOOKED.
JUST AS I THOUGHT.... IT CRUMBLES LIKE SAND, THE WALL WAS CONSTRUCTED OF INFERIOR MATERIAL!
SOMEONE'S COMING!
HE APPEARS TO BE EXAMINING THE CEMENT TOO!
ABRUPTLY...
SLUG HIM!
LET GO!
FROM A SHORT DISTANCE AWAY THE SOUND OF AN APPROACHING SUBWAY TRAIN IS HEARD...
LET'S BEAT IT!
OKAY: THE TRAIN WILL FINISH HIM!

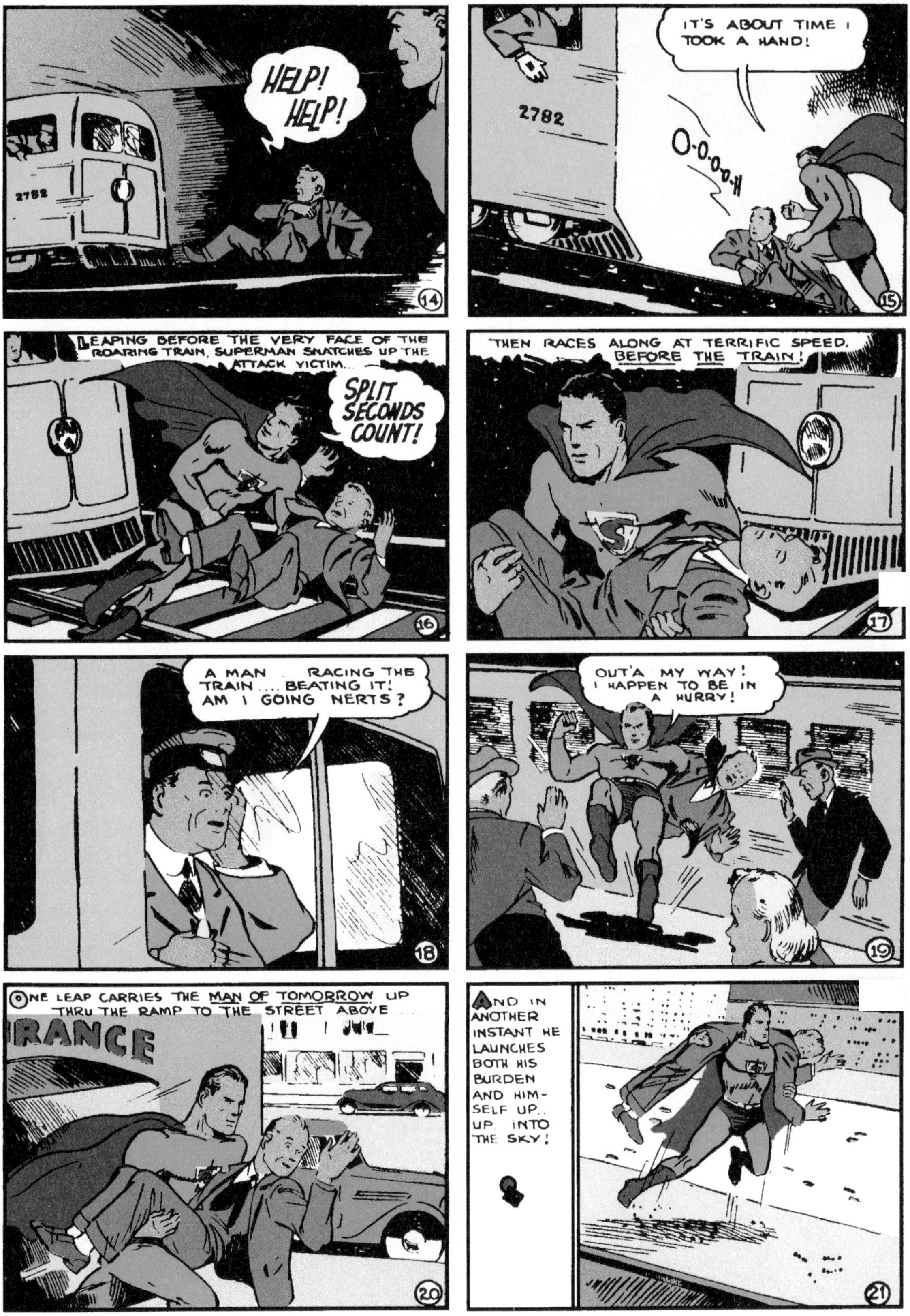
HELP! HELP!
2782
IT'S ABOUT TIME I TOOK A HAND!
2782
O-O-O-O-H
LEAPING BEFORE THE VERY FACE OF THE ROARING TRAIN, SUPERMAN SNATCHES UP THE ATTACK VICTIM...
SPLIT SECONDS COUNT!
THEN RACES ALONG AT TERRIFIC SPEED, BEFORE THE TRAIN!
A MAN ... RACING THE TRAIN ... BEATING IT! AM I GOING NERTS?
OUT'A MY WAY! I HAPPEN TO BE IN A HURRY!
ONE LEAP CARRIES THE MAN OF TOMORROW UP THRU THE RAMP TO THE STREET ABOVE ...
RANCE
AND IN ANOTHER INSTANT HE LAUNCHES BOTH HIS BURDEN AND HIMSELF UP.. UP. INTO THE SKY!

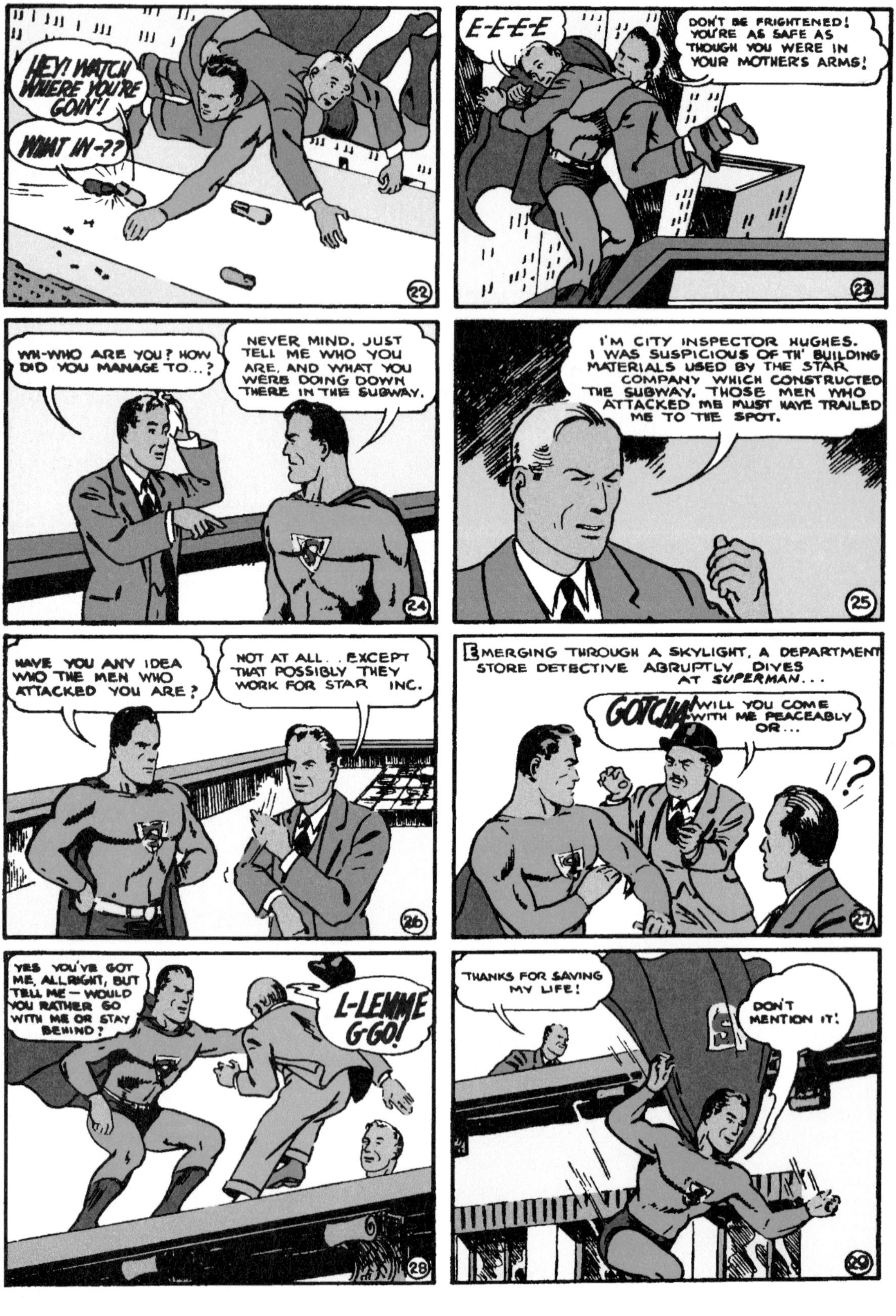
HEY! WATCH WHERE YOU'RE GOIN'!
WHAT IN-??
E-E-E-E
DON'T BE FRIGHTENED! YOU'RE AS SAFE AS THOUGH YOU WERE IN YOUR MOTHER'S ARMS!
WH-WHO ARE YOU? HOW DID YOU MANAGE TO...?
NEVER MIND. JUST TELL ME WHO YOU ARE, AND WHAT YOU WERE DOING DOWN THERE IN THE SUBWAY.
I'M CITY INSPECTOR HUGHES. I WAS SUSPICIOUS OF TH' BUILDING MATERIALS USED BY THE STAR COMPANY WHICH CONSTRUCTED THE SUBWAY. THOSE MEN WHO ATTACKED ME MUST HAVE TRAILED ME TO THE SPOT.
HAVE YOU ANY IDEA WHO THE MEN WHO ATTACKED YOU ARE?
NOT AT ALL.. EXCEPT THAT POSSIBLY THEY WORK FOR STAR INC.
EMERGING THROUGH A SKYLIGHT, A DEPARTMENT STORE DETECTIVE ABRUPTLY DIVES AT SUPERMAN...
GOTCHA! WILL YOU COME WITH ME PEACEABLY OR...
?
YES YOU'VE GOT ME, ALLRIGHT, BUT TELL ME — WOULD YOU RATHER GO WITH ME OR STAY BEHIND?
L-LEMME G-GO!
THANKS FOR SAVING MY LIFE!
DON'T MENTION IT!

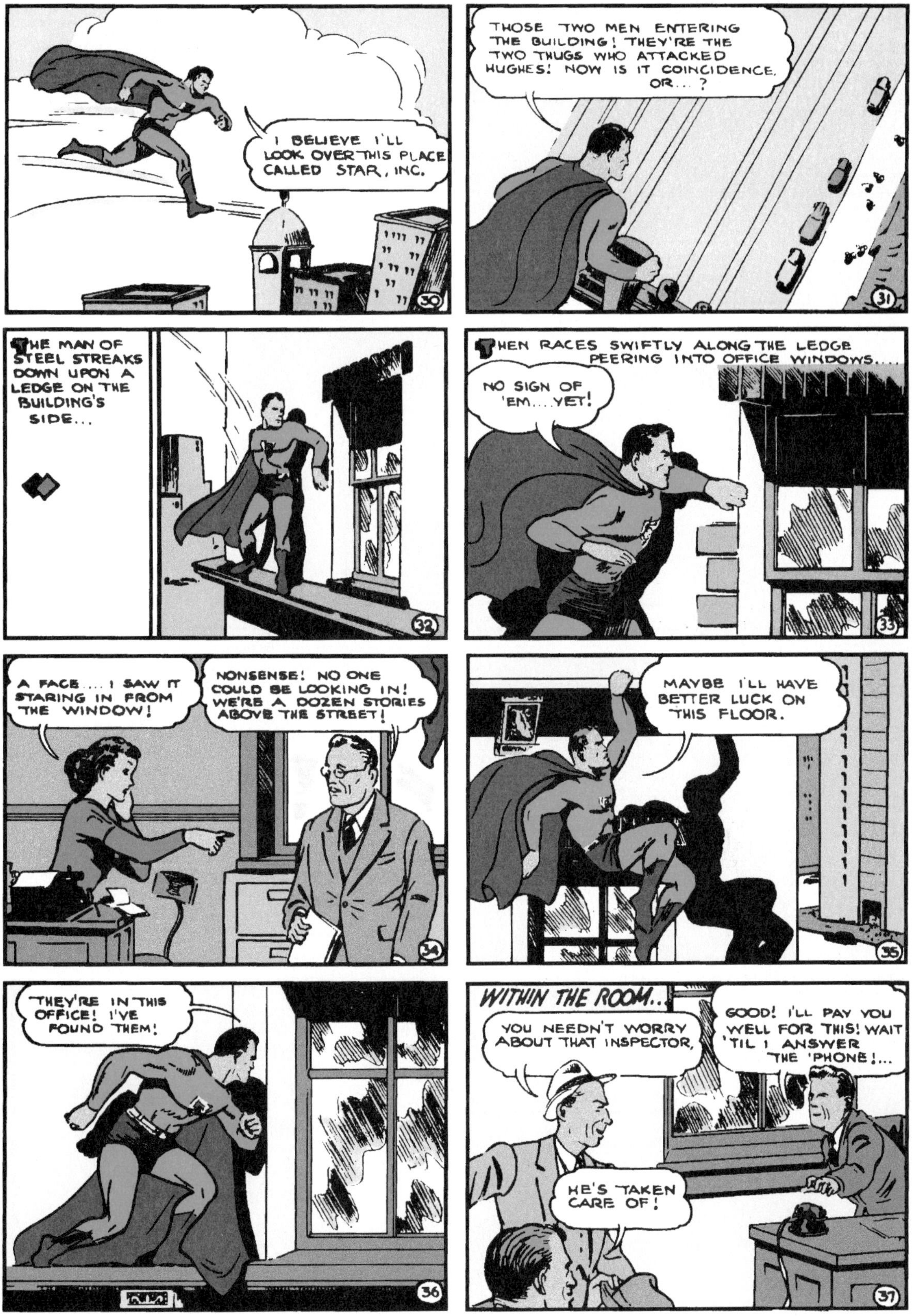
I BELIEVE I'LL LOOK OVER THIS PLACE CALLED STAR, INC.
30
THOSE TWO MEN ENTERING THE BUILDING! THEY'RE THE TWO THUGS WHO ATTACKED HUGHES! NOW IS IT COINCIDENCE, OR...?
31
THE MAN OF STEEL STREAKS DOWN UPON A LEDGE ON THE BUILDING'S SIDE...
32
THEN RACES SWIFTLY ALONG THE LEDGE PEERING INTO OFFICE WINDOWS...
NO SIGN OF 'EM....YET!
33
A FACE.... I SAW IT STARING IN FROM THE WINDOW!
NONSENSE! NO ONE COULD BE LOOKING IN! WE'RE A DOZEN STORIES ABOVE THE STREET!
34
MAYBE I'LL HAVE BETTER LUCK ON THIS FLOOR.
35
THEY'RE IN THIS OFFICE! I'VE FOUND THEM!
36
WITHIN THE ROOM...
YOU NEEDN'T WORRY ABOUT THAT INSPECTOR,
HE'S TAKEN CARE OF!
GOOD! I'LL PAY YOU WELL FOR THIS! WAIT 'TIL I ANSWER THE 'PHONE!...
37

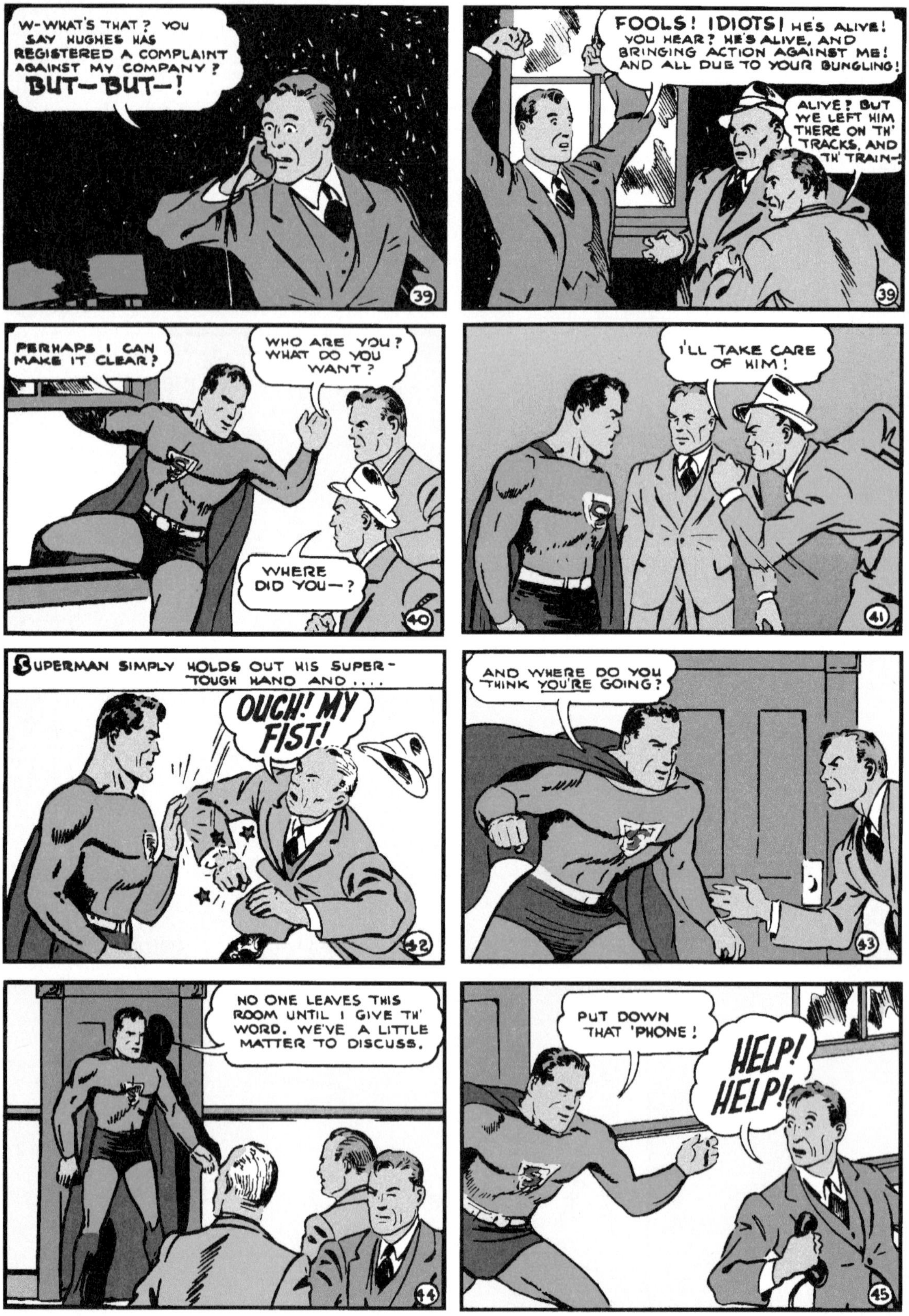
W-WHAT'S THAT? YOU SAY HUGHES HAS REGISTERED A COMPLAINT AGAINST MY COMPANY? BUT—BUT—!
39
FOOLS! IDIOTS! HE'S ALIVE! YOU HEAR? HE'S ALIVE, AND BRINGING ACTION AGAINST ME! AND ALL DUE TO YOUR BUNGLING!
ALIVE? BUT WE LEFT HIM THERE ON TH' TRACKS, AND TH' TRAIN—!
39
PERHAPS I CAN MAKE IT CLEAR?
WHO ARE YOU? WHAT DO YOU WANT?
WHERE DID YOU—?
40
I'LL TAKE CARE OF HIM!
41
SUPERMAN SIMPLY HOLDS OUT HIS SUPER-TOUGH HAND AND....
OUCH! MY FIST!
42
AND WHERE DO YOU THINK YOU'RE GOING?
43
NO ONE LEAVES THIS ROOM UNTIL I GIVE TH' WORD. WE'VE A LITTLE MATTER TO DISCUSS.
44
PUT DOWN THAT 'PHONE!
HELP! HELP!
45

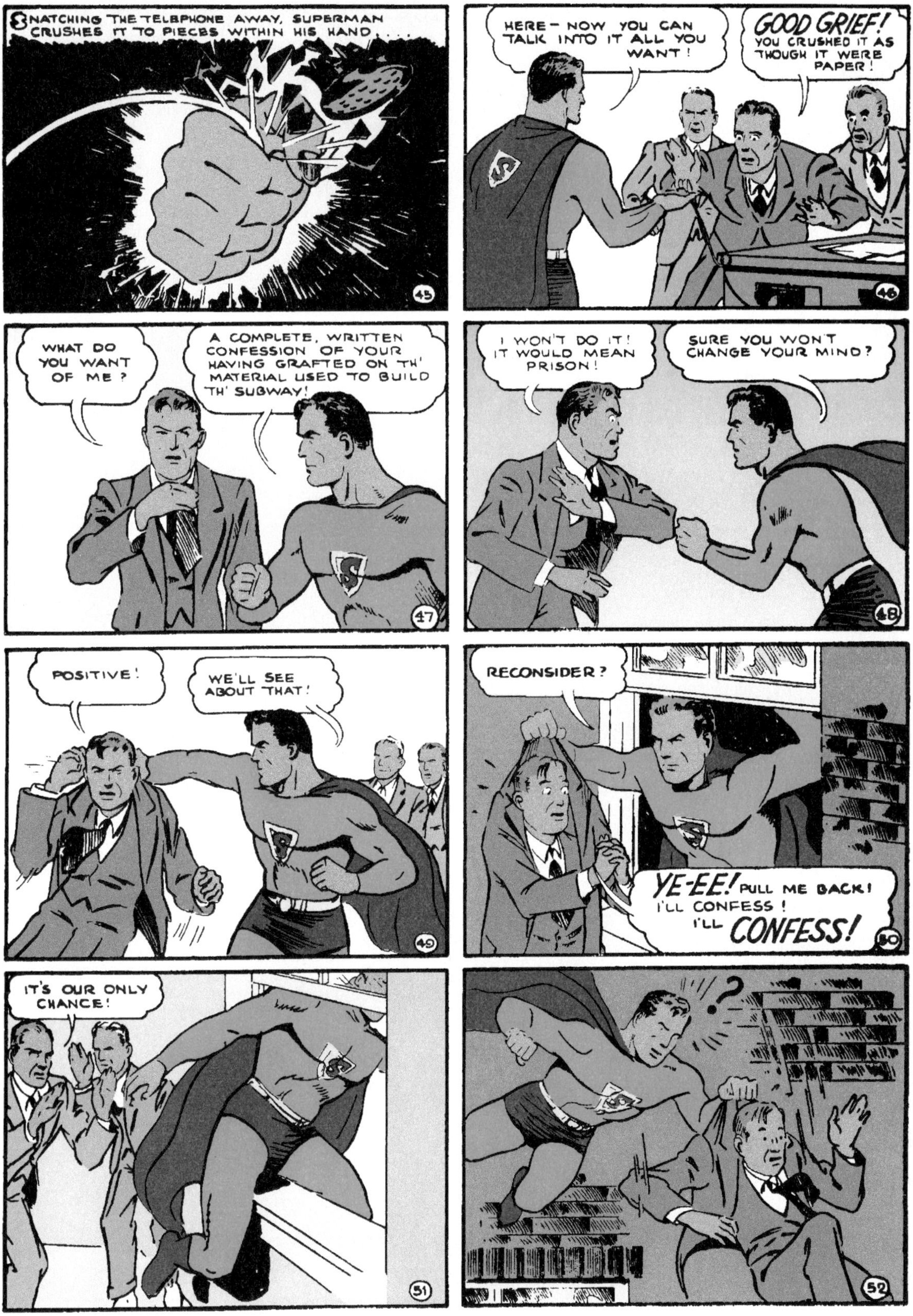
SNATCHING THE TELEPHONE AWAY, SUPERMAN CRUSHES IT TO PIECES WITHIN HIS HAND. . . .
45
HERE — NOW YOU CAN TALK INTO IT ALL YOU WANT!
GOOD GRIEF! YOU CRUSHED IT AS THOUGH IT WERE PAPER!
46
WHAT DO YOU WANT OF ME?
A COMPLETE, WRITTEN CONFESSION OF YOUR HAVING GRAFTED ON TH' MATERIAL USED TO BUILD TH' SUBWAY!
47
I WON'T DO IT! IT WOULD MEAN PRISON!
SURE YOU WON'T CHANGE YOUR MIND?
48
POSITIVE!
WE'LL SEE ABOUT THAT!
49
RECONSIDER?
YE-EE! PULL ME BACK! I'LL CONFESS! I'LL CONFESS!
50
IT'S OUR ONLY CHANCE!
51
?
52

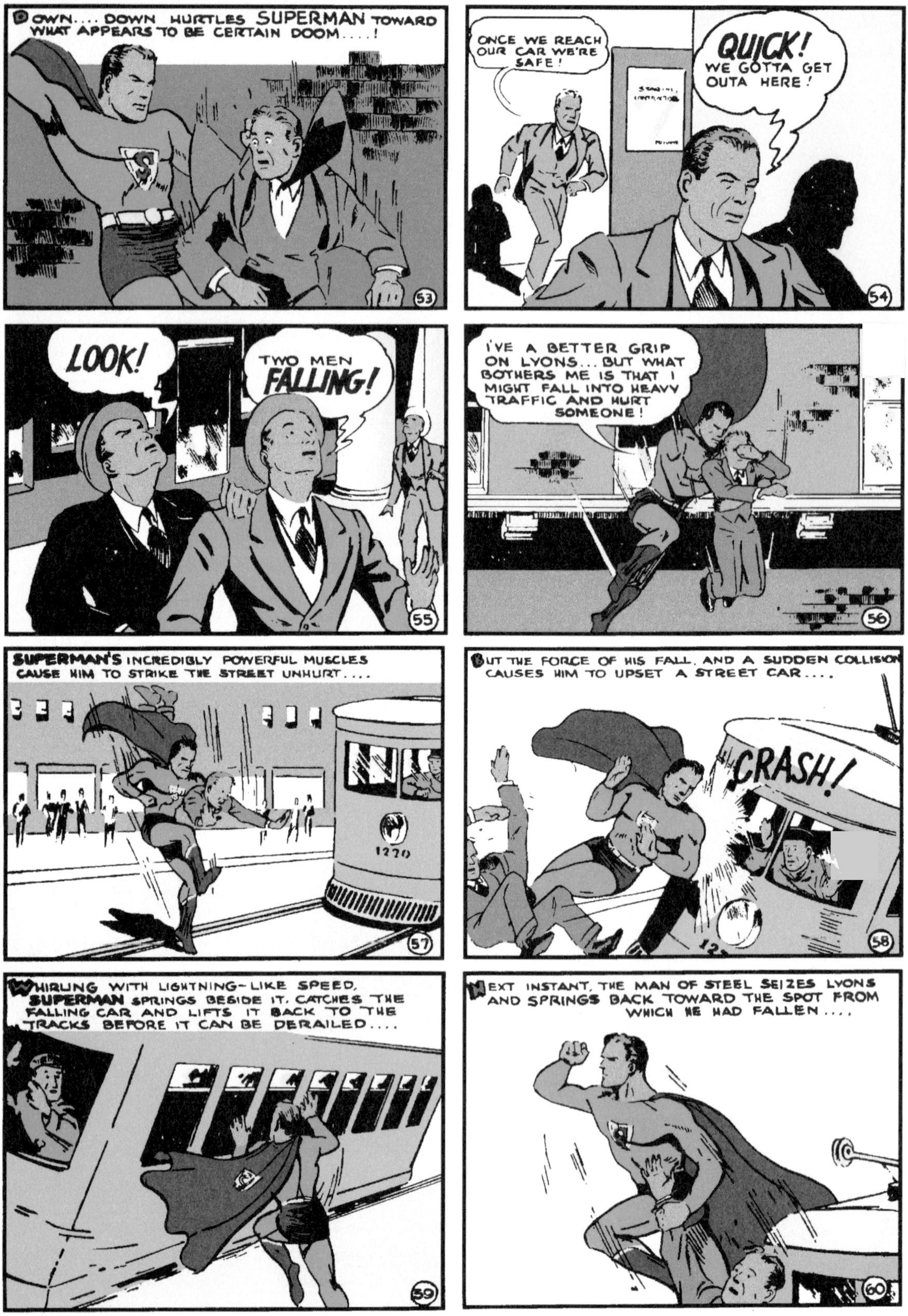
DOWN.... DOWN HURTLES SUPERMAN TOWARD WHAT APPEARS TO BE CERTAIN DOOM....!
53
ONCE WE REACH OUR CAR WE'RE SAFE!
QUICK! WE GOTTA GET OUTA HERE!
54
LOOK!
TWO MEN FALLING!
55
I'VE A BETTER GRIP ON LYONS... BUT WHAT BOTHERS ME IS THAT I MIGHT FALL INTO HEAVY TRAFFIC AND HURT SOMEONE!
56
SUPERMAN'S INCREDIBLY POWERFUL MUSCLES CAUSE HIM TO STRIKE THE STREET UNHURT....
1220
57
BUT THE FORCE OF HIS FALL, AND A SUDDEN COLLISION CAUSES HIM TO UPSET A STREET CAR....
CRASH!
58
WHIRLING WITH LIGHTNING-LIKE SPEED, SUPERMAN SPRINGS BESIDE IT, CATCHES THE FALLING CAR AND LIFTS IT BACK TO THE TRACKS BEFORE IT CAN BE DERAILED....
59
NEXT INSTANT, THE MAN OF STEEL SEIZES LYONS AND SPRINGS BACK TOWARD THE SPOT FROM WHICH HE HAD FALLEN....
60

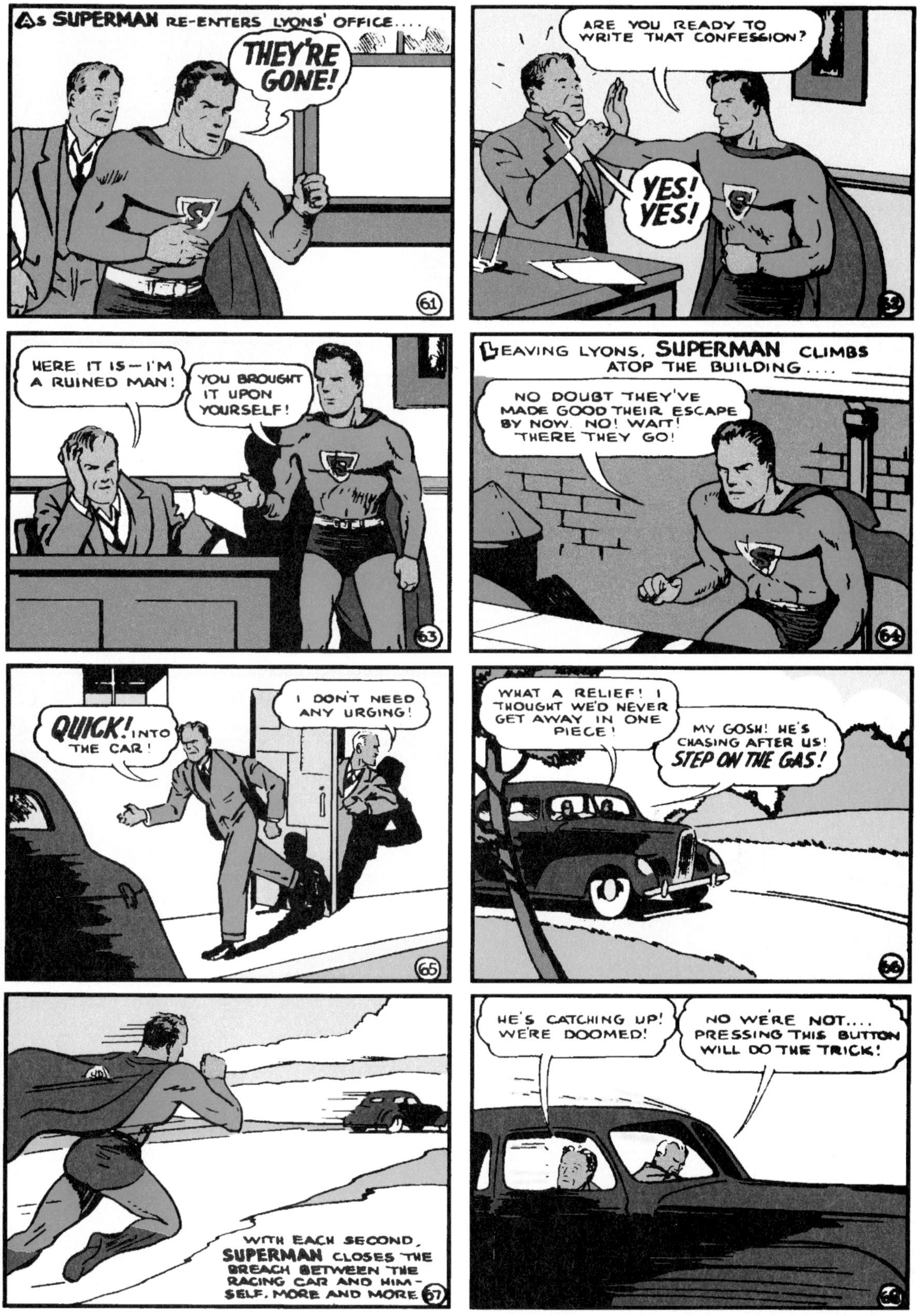
AS SUPERMAN RE-ENTERS LYONS' OFFICE....
THEY'RE GONE!
61
ARE YOU READY TO WRITE THAT CONFESSION?
YES! YES!
HERE IT IS—I'M A RUINED MAN!
YOU BROUGHT IT UPON YOURSELF!
63
LEAVING LYONS, SUPERMAN CLIMBS ATOP THE BUILDING....
NO DOUBT THEY'VE MADE GOOD THEIR ESCAPE BY NOW. NO! WAIT! THERE THEY GO!
64
QUICK! INTO THE CAR!
I DON'T NEED ANY URGING!
65
WHAT A RELIEF! I THOUGHT WE'D NEVER GET AWAY IN ONE PIECE!
MY GOSH! HE'S CHASING AFTER US! STEP ON THE GAS!
WITH EACH SECOND, SUPERMAN CLOSES THE BREACH BETWEEN THE RACING CAR AND HIMSELF, MORE AND MORE
67
HE'S CATCHING UP! WE'RE DOOMED!
NO WE'RE NOT.... PRESSING THIS BUTTON WILL DO THE TRICK!

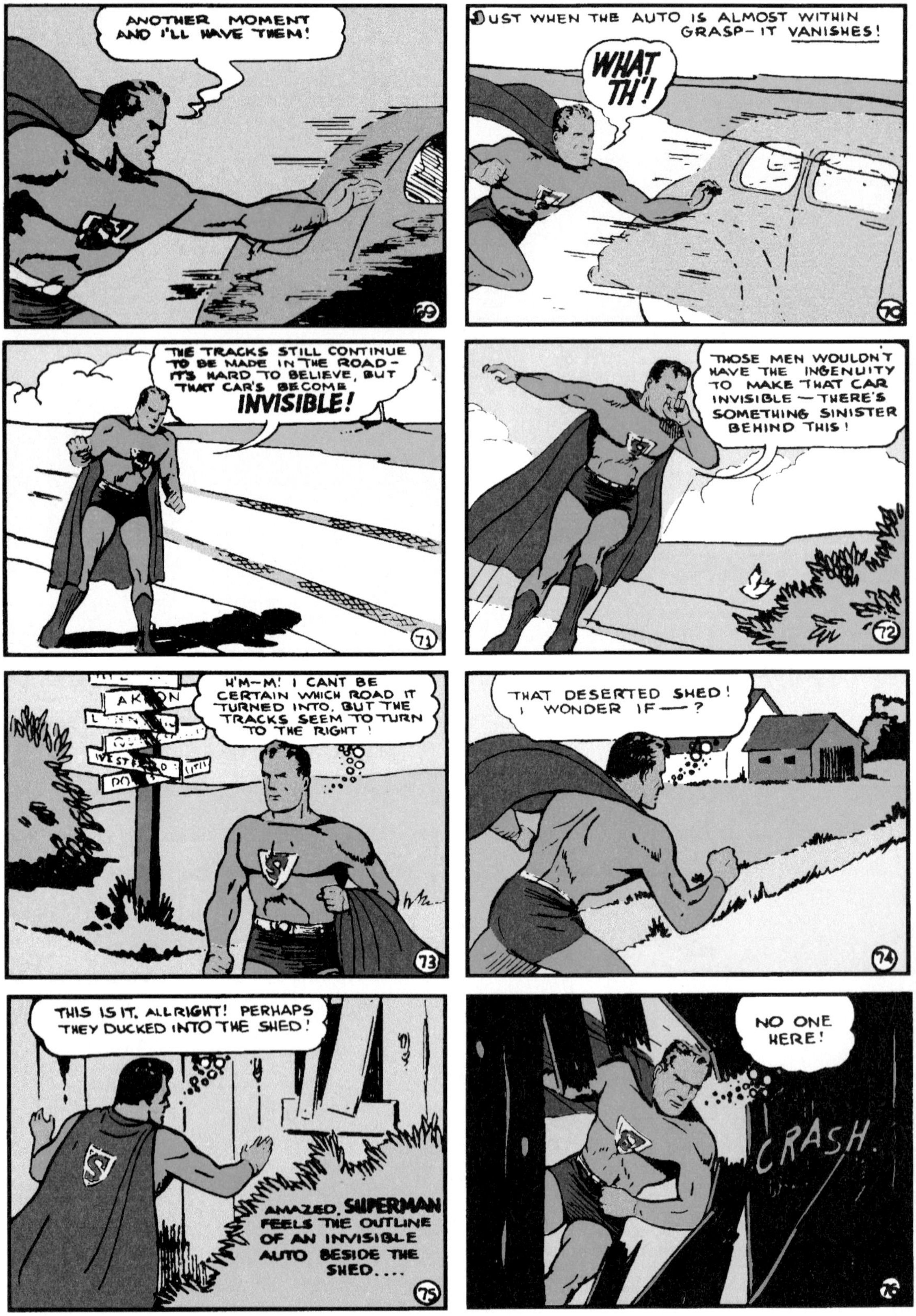
ANOTHER MOMENT AND I'LL HAVE THEM!
JUST WHEN THE AUTO IS ALMOST WITHIN GRASP– IT VANISHES!
WHAT TH'!
THE TRACKS STILL CONTINUE TO BE MADE IN THE ROAD– IT'S HARD TO BELIEVE, BUT THAT CAR'S BECOME INVISIBLE!
THOSE MEN WOULDN'T HAVE THE INGENUITY TO MAKE THAT CAR INVISIBLE — THERE'S SOMETHING SINISTER BEHIND THIS!
H'M–M! I CANT BE CERTAIN WHICH ROAD IT TURNED INTO, BUT THE TRACKS SEEM TO TURN TO THE RIGHT!
THAT DESERTED SHED! I WONDER IF—?
THIS IS IT, ALLRIGHT! PERHAPS THEY DUCKED INTO THE SHED!
AMAZED, SUPERMAN FEELS THE OUTLINE OF AN INVISIBLE AUTO BESIDE THE SHED....
NO ONE HERE!
CRASH

ABRUPTLY...

WHIR-R-R

WHAM!

As SUPERMAN FALLS INTO THE TANK, IT AUTOMATICALLY SEALS ITSELF. MOTORS HUM, ELECTRIC BOLTS FLASH!

YOU'RE TH' ONLY MAN ON EARTH WHO COULD'VE DONE IT!

AND THAT IS THE END OF SUPERMAN!

THE TWO THUGS WHEEL THE CRIPPLED "ULTRA-HUMANITE" INTO THE ROOM.....

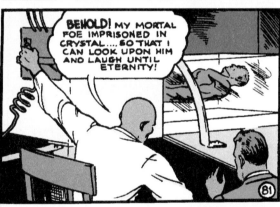

BEHOLD! MY MORTAL FOE IMPRISONED IN CRYSTAL.... SO THAT I CAN LOOK UPON HIM AND LAUGH UNTIL ETERNITY!

WHEN HE DESTROYED MY PLANE, HE THOUGHT I, TOO, HAD BEEN ELIMINATED! BUT UNKNOWN TO SUPERMAN, I ESCAPED WITH A PARACHUTE!

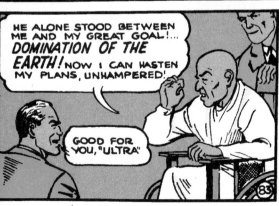

HE ALONE STOOD BETWEEN ME AND MY GREAT GOAL!... DOMINATION OF THE EARTH! NOW I CAN HASTEN MY PLANS, UNHAMPERED!

GOOD FOR YOU, "ULTRA"

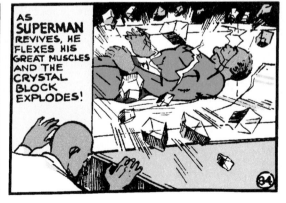

AS SUPERMAN REVIVES, HE FLEXES HIS GREAT MUSCLES AND THE CRYSTAL BLOCK EXPLODES!

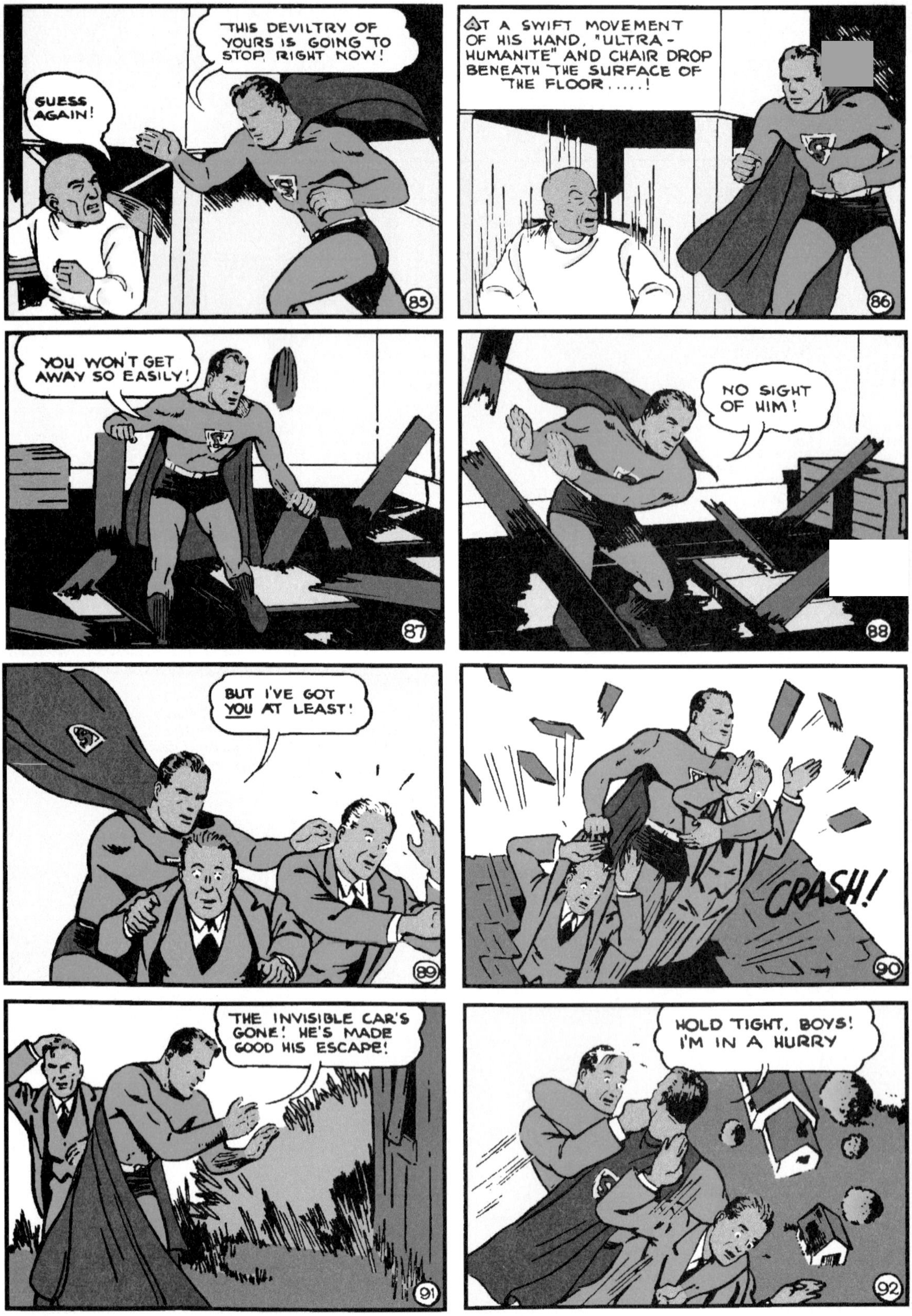
THIS DEVILTRY OF YOURS IS GOING TO STOP RIGHT NOW!
GUESS AGAIN!
AT A SWIFT MOVEMENT OF HIS HAND, "ULTRA-HUMANITE" AND CHAIR DROP BENEATH THE SURFACE OF THE FLOOR.....!
YOU WON'T GET AWAY SO EASILY!
NO SIGHT OF HIM!
BUT I'VE GOT YOU AT LEAST!
CRASH!
THE INVISIBLE CAR'S GONE! HE'S MADE GOOD HIS ESCAPE!
HOLD TIGHT, BOYS! I'M IN A HURRY

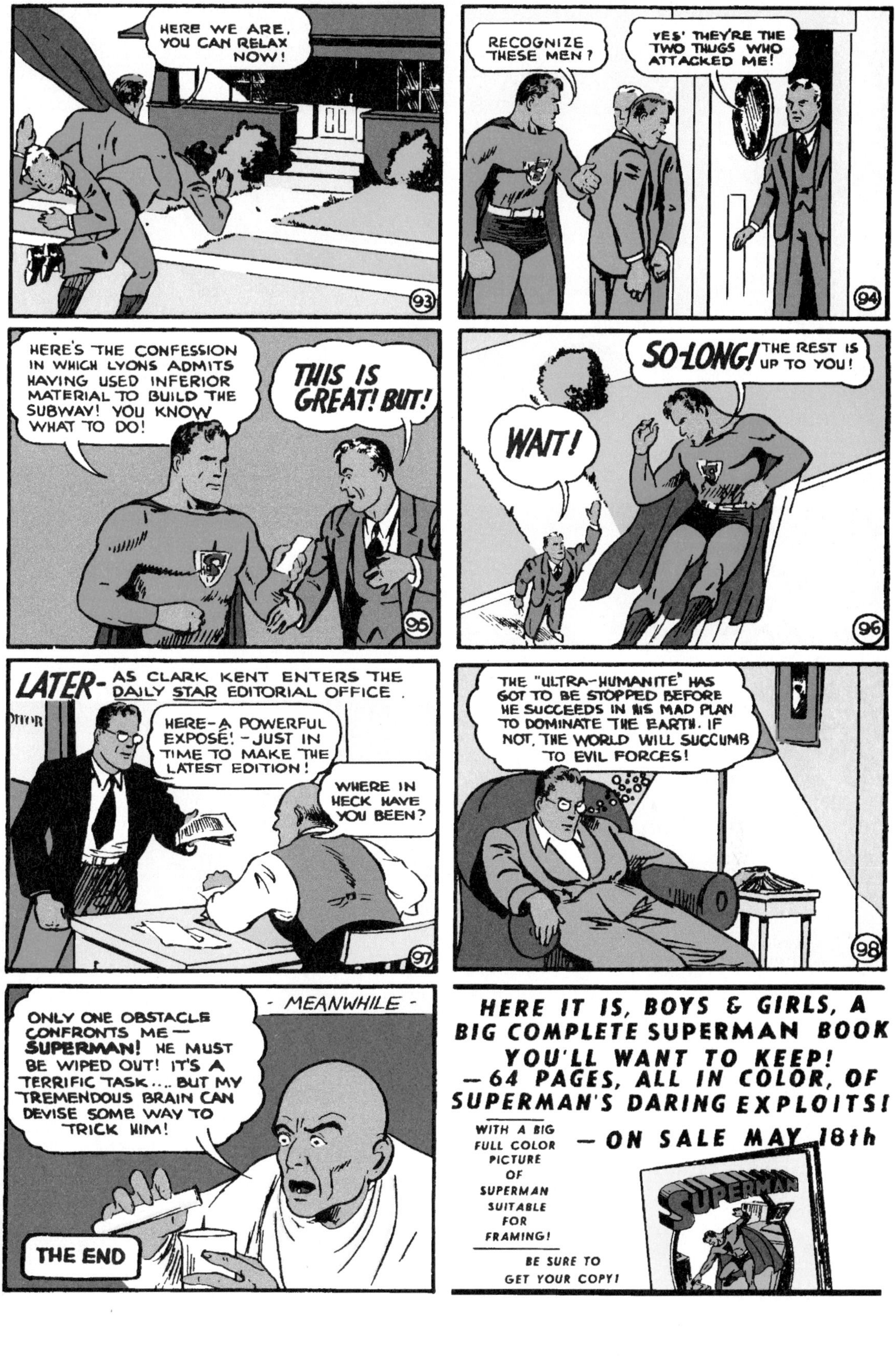

HERE WE ARE. YOU CAN RELAX NOW!
RECOGNIZE THESE MEN?
YES' THEY'RE THE TWO THUGS WHO ATTACKED ME!
HERE'S THE CONFESSION IN WHICH LYONS ADMITS HAVING USED INFERIOR MATERIAL TO BUILD THE SUBWAY! YOU KNOW WHAT TO DO!
THIS IS GREAT! BUT!
SO-LONG! THE REST IS UP TO YOU!
WAIT!
LATER- AS CLARK KENT ENTERS THE DAILY STAR EDITORIAL OFFICE.
HERE-A POWERFUL EXPOSÉ! -JUST IN TIME TO MAKE THE LATEST EDITION!
WHERE IN HECK HAVE YOU BEEN?
THE "ULTRA-HUMANITE" HAS GOT TO BE STOPPED BEFORE HE SUCCEEDS IN HIS MAD PLAN TO DOMINATE THE EARTH. IF NOT, THE WORLD WILL SUCCUMB TO EVIL FORCES!
- MEANWHILE -
ONLY ONE OBSTACLE CONFRONTS ME— SUPERMAN! HE MUST BE WIPED OUT! IT'S A TERRIFIC TASK.... BUT MY TREMENDOUS BRAIN CAN DEVISE SOME WAY TO TRICK HIM!
THE END
HERE IT IS, BOYS & GIRLS, A BIG COMPLETE SUPERMAN BOOK YOU'LL WANT TO KEEP! —64 PAGES, ALL IN COLOR, OF SUPERMAN'S DARING EXPLOITS!
WITH A BIG FULL COLOR PICTURE OF SUPERMAN SUITABLE FOR FRAMING!
—ON SALE MAY 18th
SUPERMAN
BE SURE TO GET YOUR COPY!

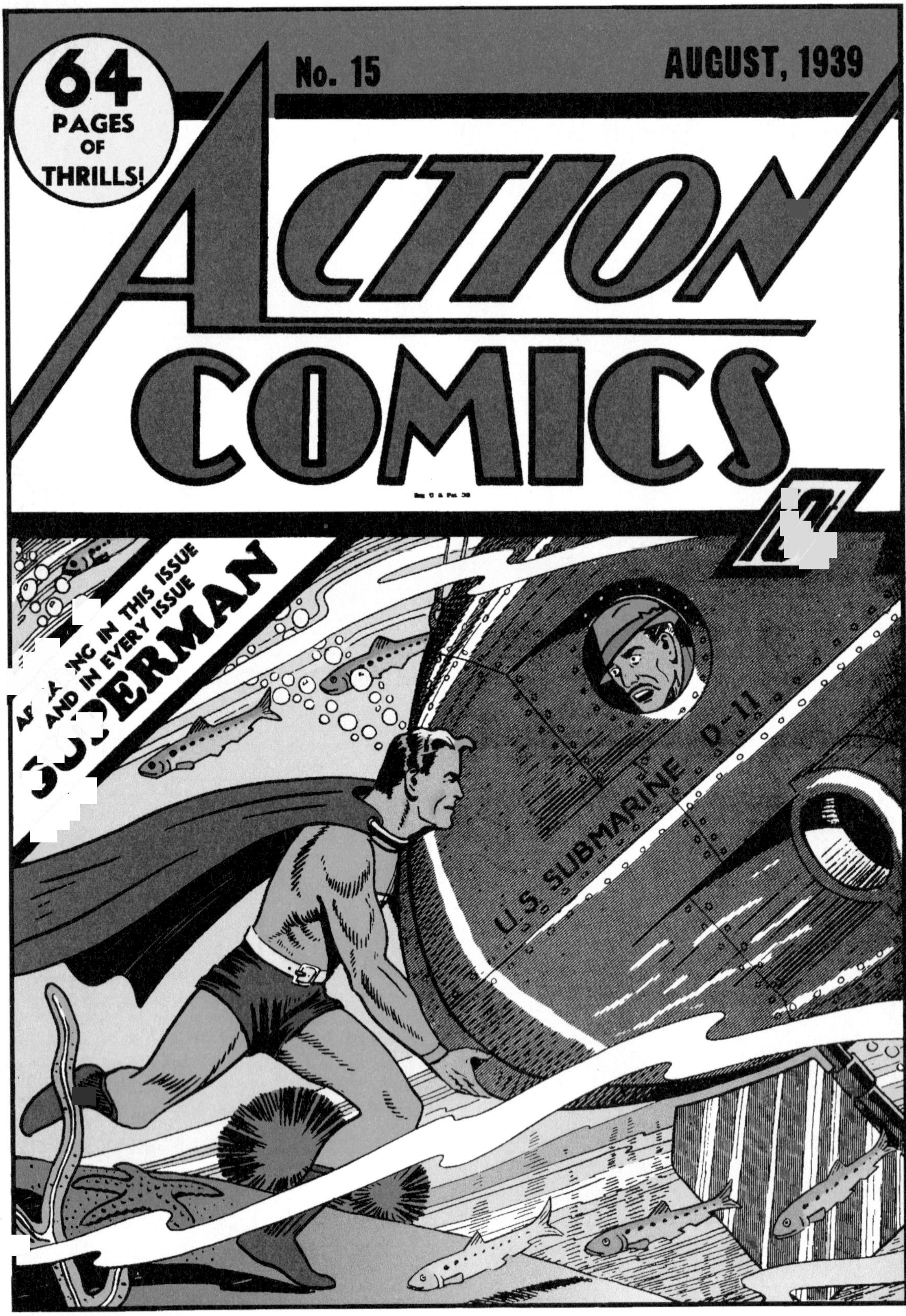
64 PAGES OF THRILLS!
No. 15
AUGUST, 1939
ACTION COMICS
IN THIS ISSUE
AND IN EVERY ISSUE
U.S. SUBMARINE D-11

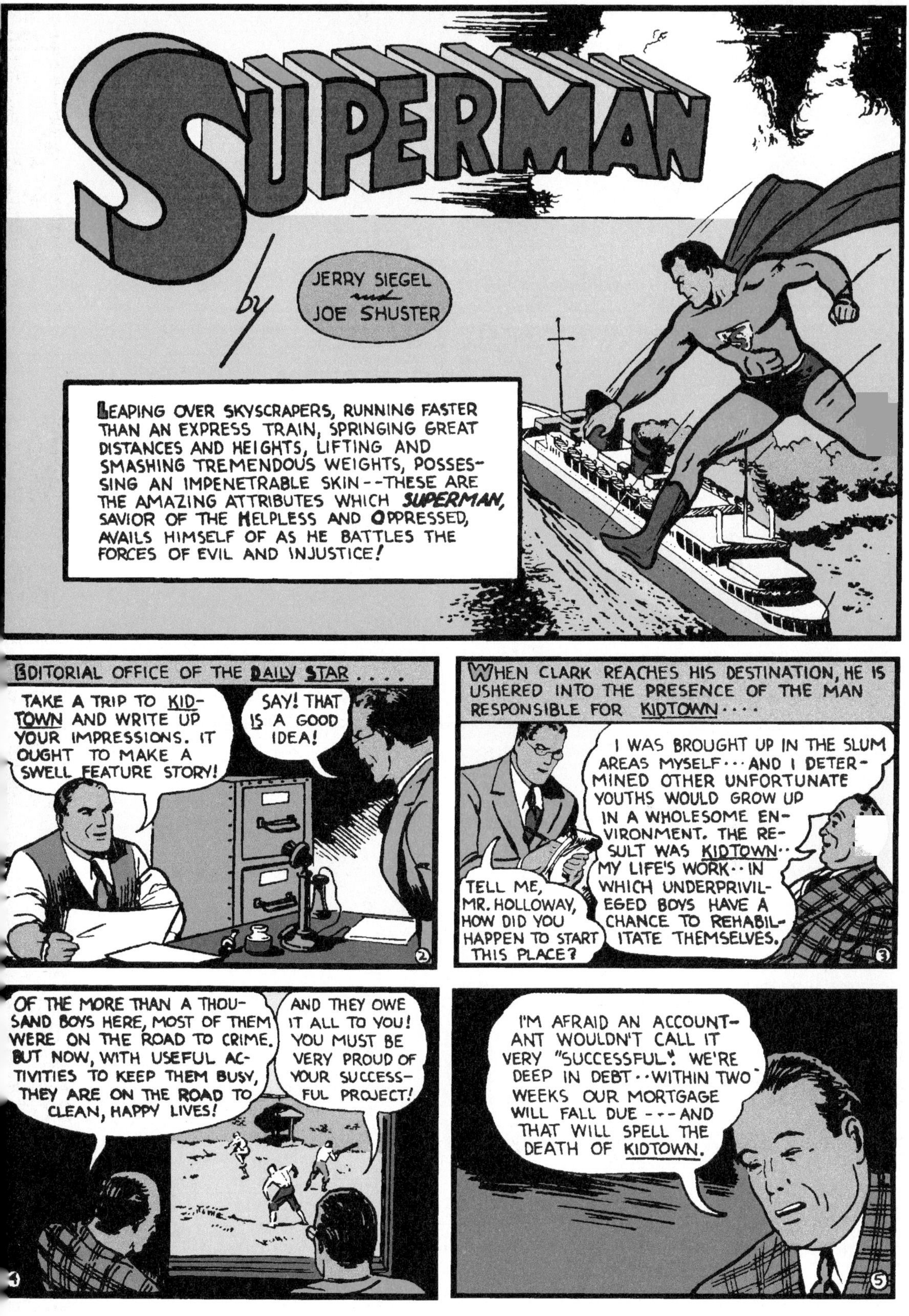
SUPERMAN
by JERRY SIEGEL and JOE SHUSTER
LEAPING OVER SKYSCRAPERS, RUNNING FASTER THAN AN EXPRESS TRAIN, SPRINGING GREAT DISTANCES AND HEIGHTS, LIFTING AND SMASHING TREMENDOUS WEIGHTS, POSSESSING AN IMPENETRABLE SKIN--THESE ARE THE AMAZING ATTRIBUTES WHICH SUPERMAN, SAVIOR OF THE HELPLESS AND OPPRESSED, AVAILS HIMSELF OF AS HE BATTLES THE FORCES OF EVIL AND INJUSTICE!
EDITORIAL OFFICE OF THE DAILY STAR....
TAKE A TRIP TO KIDTOWN AND WRITE UP YOUR IMPRESSIONS. IT OUGHT TO MAKE A SWELL FEATURE STORY!
SAY! THAT IS A GOOD IDEA!
2
WHEN CLARK REACHES HIS DESTINATION, HE IS USHERED INTO THE PRESENCE OF THE MAN RESPONSIBLE FOR KIDTOWN....
TELL ME, MR. HOLLOWAY, HOW DID YOU HAPPEN TO START THIS PLACE?
I WAS BROUGHT UP IN THE SLUM AREAS MYSELF...AND I DETERMINED OTHER UNFORTUNATE YOUTHS WOULD GROW UP IN A WHOLESOME ENVIRONMENT. THE RESULT WAS KIDTOWN.. MY LIFE'S WORK..IN WHICH UNDERPRIVILEGED BOYS HAVE A CHANCE TO REHABILITATE THEMSELVES.
3
OF THE MORE THAN A THOUSAND BOYS HERE, MOST OF THEM WERE ON THE ROAD TO CRIME. BUT NOW, WITH USEFUL ACTIVITIES TO KEEP THEM BUSY, THEY ARE ON THE ROAD TO CLEAN, HAPPY LIVES!
AND THEY OWE IT ALL TO YOU! YOU MUST BE VERY PROUD OF YOUR SUCCESSFUL PROJECT!
4
I'M AFRAID AN ACCOUNTANT WOULDN'T CALL IT VERY "SUCCESSFUL". WE'RE DEEP IN DEBT..WITHIN TWO WEEKS OUR MORTGAGE WILL FALL DUE ---AND THAT WILL SPELL THE DEATH OF KIDTOWN.
5

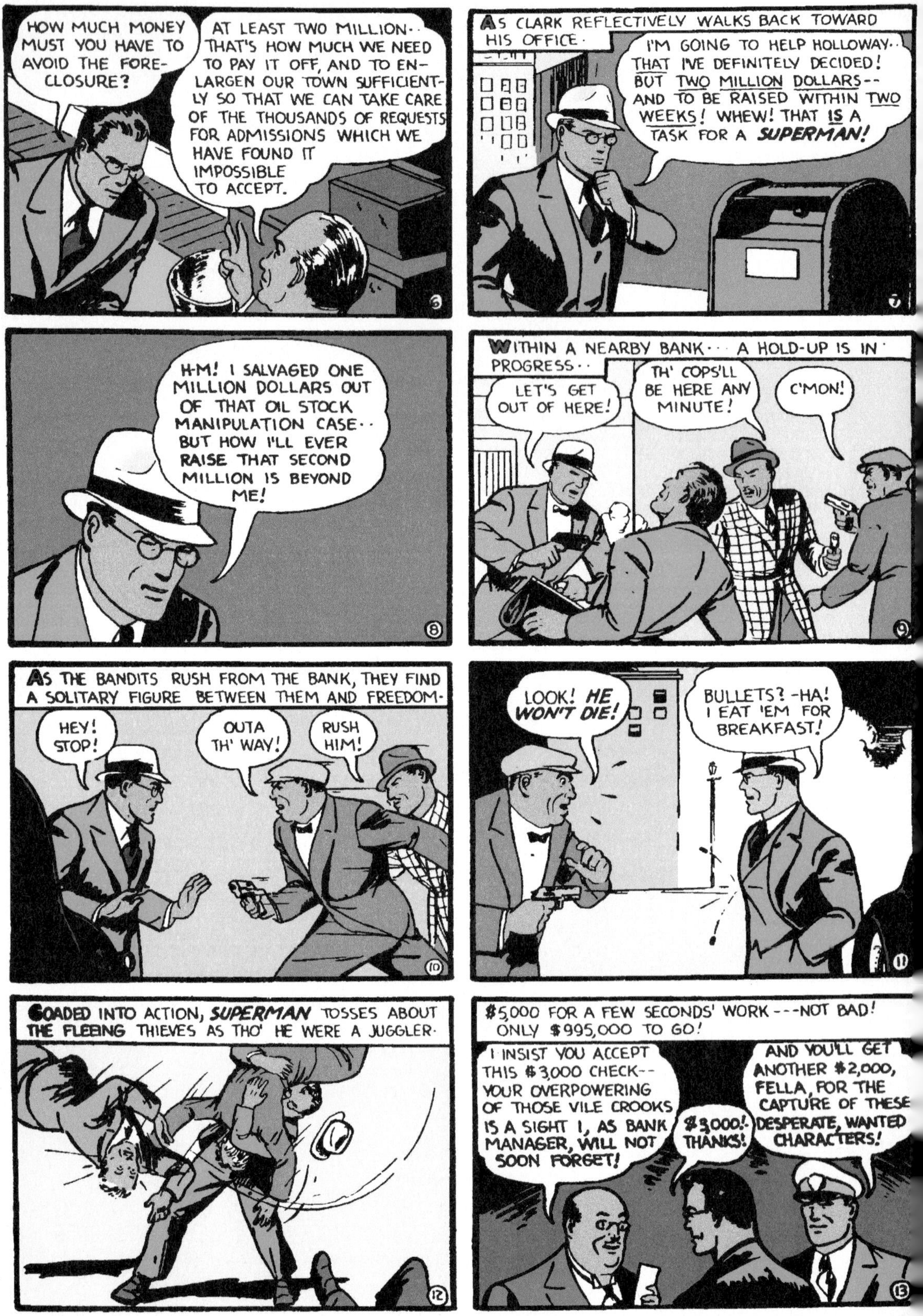
HOW MUCH MONEY MUST YOU HAVE TO AVOID THE FORE-CLOSURE?
AT LEAST TWO MILLION·· THAT'S HOW MUCH WE NEED TO PAY IT OFF, AND TO EN-LARGEN OUR TOWN SUFFICIENT-LY SO THAT WE CAN TAKE CARE OF THE THOUSANDS OF REQUESTS FOR ADMISSIONS WHICH WE HAVE FOUND IT IMPOSSIBLE TO ACCEPT.
AS CLARK REFLECTIVELY WALKS BACK TOWARD HIS OFFICE·
I'M GOING TO HELP HOLLOWAY·· THAT I'VE DEFINITELY DECIDED! BUT TWO MILLION DOLLARS-- AND TO BE RAISED WITHIN TWO WEEKS! WHEW! THAT IS A TASK FOR A SUPERMAN!
H-M! I SALVAGED ONE MILLION DOLLARS OUT OF THAT OIL STOCK MANIPULATION CASE·· BUT HOW I'LL EVER RAISE THAT SECOND MILLION IS BEYOND ME!
WITHIN A NEARBY BANK··· A HOLD-UP IS IN PROGRESS··
LET'S GET OUT OF HERE!
TH' COPS'LL BE HERE ANY MINUTE!
C'MON!
AS THE BANDITS RUSH FROM THE BANK, THEY FIND A SOLITARY FIGURE BETWEEN THEM AND FREEDOM·
HEY! STOP!
OUTA TH' WAY!
RUSH HIM!
LOOK! HE WON'T DIE!
BULLETS? -HA! I EAT 'EM FOR BREAKFAST!
GOADED INTO ACTION, SUPERMAN TOSSES ABOUT THE FLEEING THIEVES AS THO' HE WERE A JUGGLER·
$5,000 FOR A FEW SECONDS' WORK---NOT BAD! ONLY $995,000 TO GO!
I INSIST YOU ACCEPT THIS $3,000 CHECK-- YOUR OVERPOWERING OF THOSE VILE CROOKS IS A SIGHT I, AS BANK MANAGER, WILL NOT SOON FORGET!
$3,000! THANKS!
AND YOU'LL GET ANOTHER $2,000, FELLA, FOR THE CAPTURE OF THESE DESPERATE, WANTED CHARACTERS!

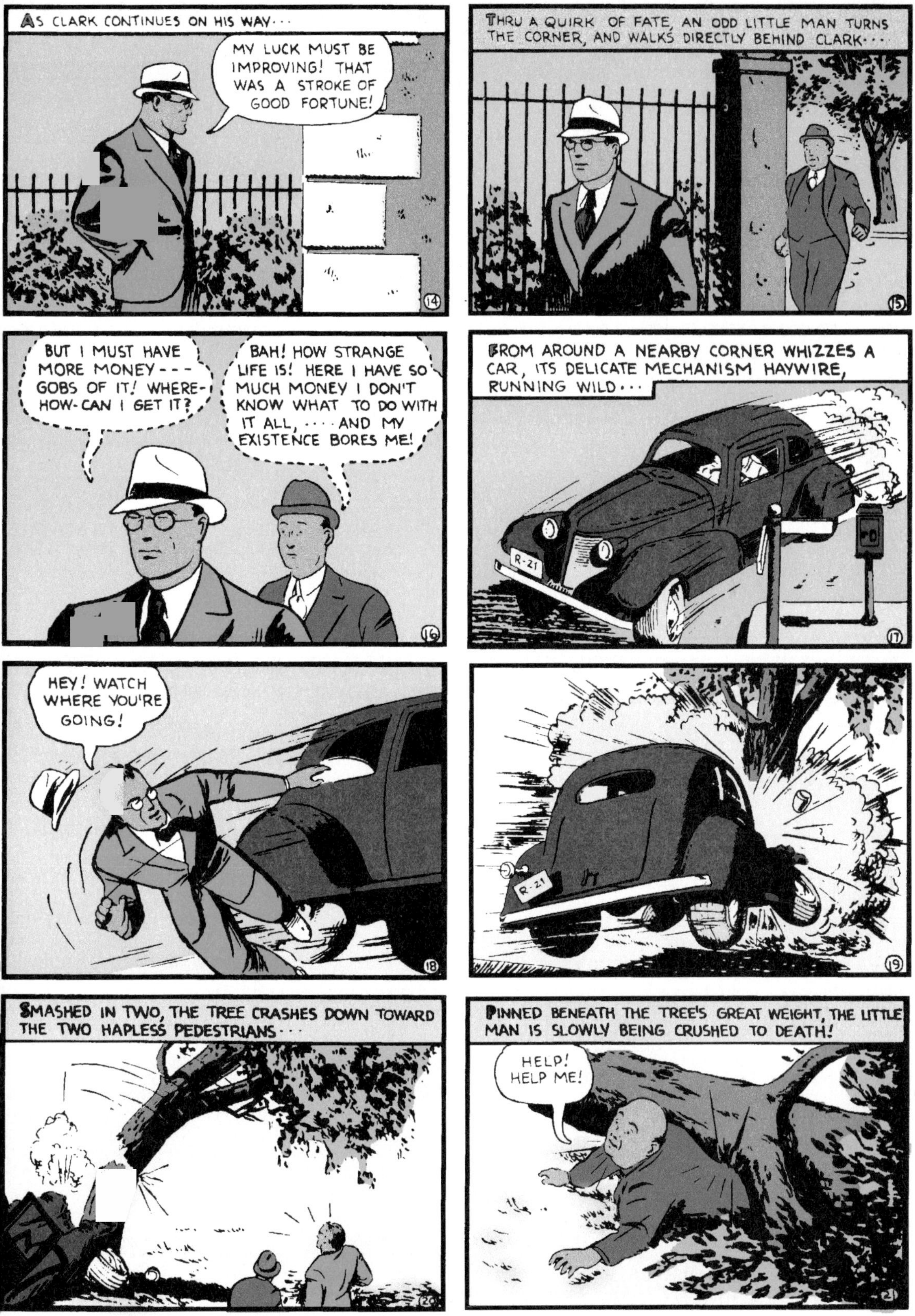
AS CLARK CONTINUES ON HIS WAY···
MY LUCK MUST BE IMPROVING! THAT WAS A STROKE OF GOOD FORTUNE!
THRU A QUIRK OF FATE, AN ODD LITTLE MAN TURNS THE CORNER, AND WALKS DIRECTLY BEHIND CLARK···
BUT I MUST HAVE MORE MONEY--- GOBS OF IT! WHERE- HOW- CAN I GET IT?
BAH! HOW STRANGE LIFE IS! HERE I HAVE SO MUCH MONEY I DON'T KNOW WHAT TO DO WITH IT ALL, ····AND MY EXISTENCE BORES ME!
FROM AROUND A NEARBY CORNER WHIZZES A CAR, ITS DELICATE MECHANISM HAYWIRE, RUNNING WILD···
R-21
HEY! WATCH WHERE YOU'RE GOING!
R-21
SMASHED IN TWO, THE TREE CRASHES DOWN TOWARD THE TWO HAPLESS PEDESTRIANS···
PINNED BENEATH THE TREE'S GREAT WEIGHT, THE LITTLE MAN IS SLOWLY BEING CRUSHED TO DEATH!
HELP! HELP ME!

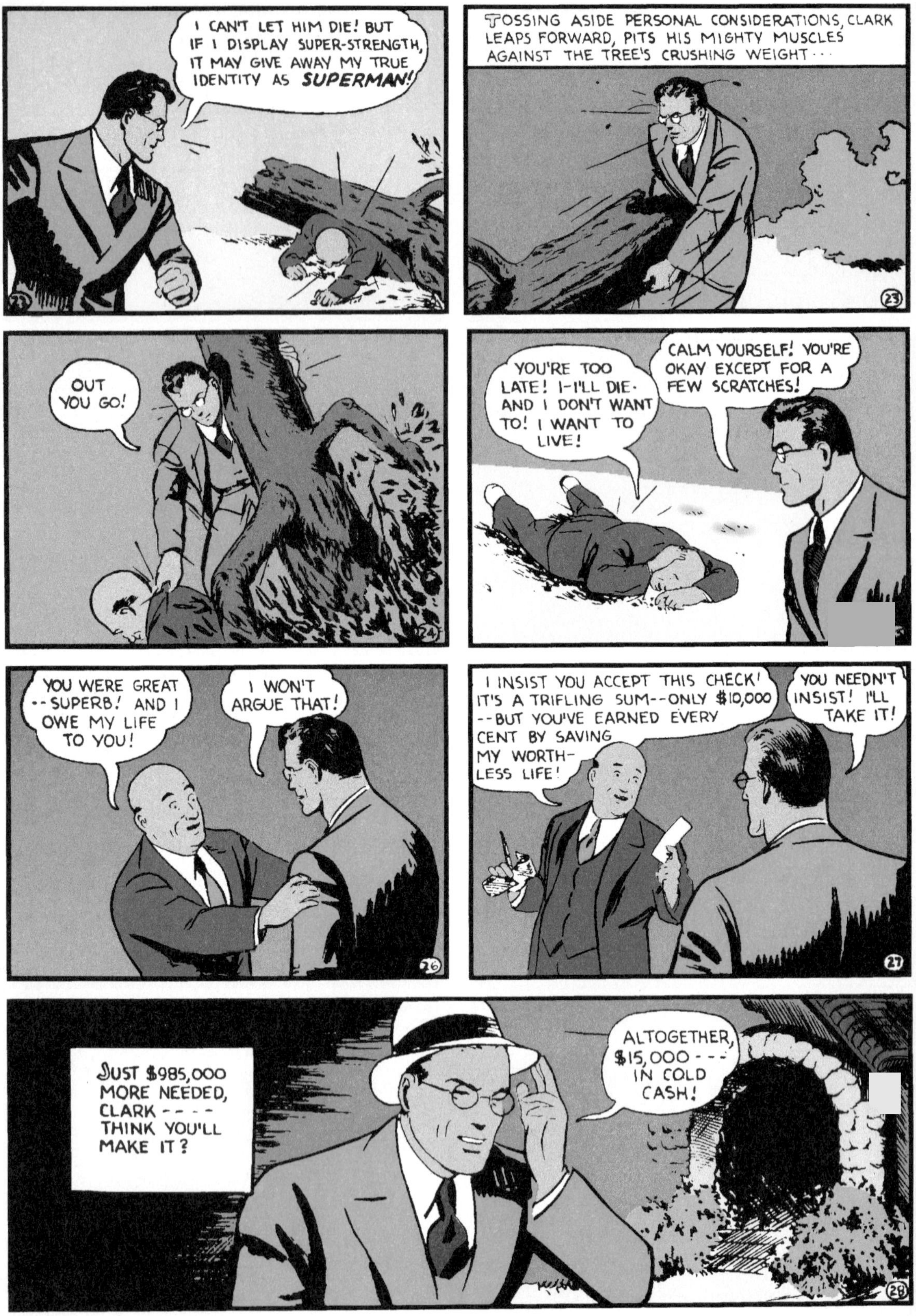
I CAN'T LET HIM DIE! BUT IF I DISPLAY SUPER-STRENGTH, IT MAY GIVE AWAY MY TRUE IDENTITY AS SUPERMAN!
TOSSING ASIDE PERSONAL CONSIDERATIONS, CLARK LEAPS FORWARD, PITS HIS MIGHTY MUSCLES AGAINST THE TREE'S CRUSHING WEIGHT...
OUT YOU GO!
YOU'RE TOO LATE! I-I'LL DIE-AND I DON'T WANT TO! I WANT TO LIVE!
CALM YOURSELF! YOU'RE OKAY EXCEPT FOR A FEW SCRATCHES!
YOU WERE GREAT --SUPERB! AND I OWE MY LIFE TO YOU!
I WON'T ARGUE THAT!
I INSIST YOU ACCEPT THIS CHECK! IT'S A TRIFLING SUM--ONLY $10,000 --BUT YOU'VE EARNED EVERY CENT BY SAVING MY WORTHLESS LIFE!
YOU NEEDN'T INSIST! I'LL TAKE IT!
JUST $985,000 MORE NEEDED, CLARK ---- THINK YOU'LL MAKE IT?
ALTOGETHER, $15,000 --- IN COLD CASH!

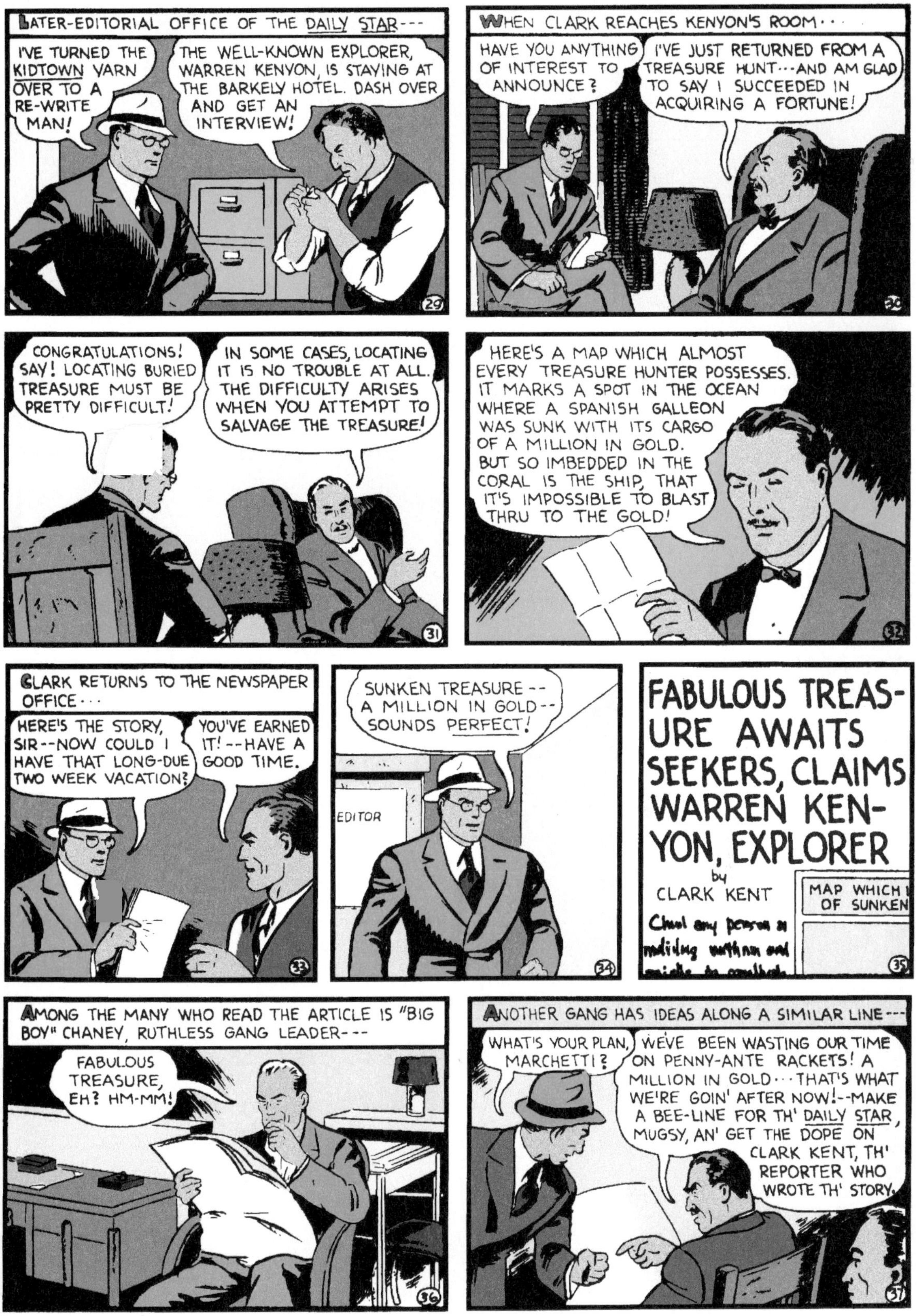
LATER-EDITORIAL OFFICE OF THE DAILY STAR---
I'VE TURNED THE KIDTOWN YARN OVER TO A RE-WRITE MAN!
THE WELL-KNOWN EXPLORER, WARREN KENYON, IS STAYING AT THE BARKELY HOTEL. DASH OVER AND GET AN INTERVIEW!
WHEN CLARK REACHES KENYON'S ROOM···
HAVE YOU ANYTHING OF INTEREST TO ANNOUNCE?
I'VE JUST RETURNED FROM A TREASURE HUNT···AND AM GLAD TO SAY I SUCCEEDED IN ACQUIRING A FORTUNE!
CONGRATULATIONS! SAY! LOCATING BURIED TREASURE MUST BE PRETTY DIFFICULT!
IN SOME CASES, LOCATING IT IS NO TROUBLE AT ALL. THE DIFFICULTY ARISES WHEN YOU ATTEMPT TO SALVAGE THE TREASURE!
HERE'S A MAP WHICH ALMOST EVERY TREASURE HUNTER POSSESSES. IT MARKS A SPOT IN THE OCEAN WHERE A SPANISH GALLEON WAS SUNK WITH ITS CARGO OF A MILLION IN GOLD. BUT SO IMBEDDED IN THE CORAL IS THE SHIP, THAT IT'S IMPOSSIBLE TO BLAST THRU TO THE GOLD!
CLARK RETURNS TO THE NEWSPAPER OFFICE···
HERE'S THE STORY, SIR--NOW COULD I HAVE THAT LONG-DUE TWO WEEK VACATION?
YOU'VE EARNED IT!--HAVE A GOOD TIME.
SUNKEN TREASURE-- A MILLION IN GOLD-- SOUNDS PERFECT!
EDITOR
FABULOUS TREASURE AWAITS SEEKERS, CLAIMS WARREN KENYON, EXPLORER
by CLARK KENT
MAP WHICH OF SUNKEN
AMONG THE MANY WHO READ THE ARTICLE IS "BIG BOY" CHANEY, RUTHLESS GANG LEADER---
FABULOUS TREASURE, EH? HM-MM!
ANOTHER GANG HAS IDEAS ALONG A SIMILAR LINE---
WHAT'S YOUR PLAN, MARCHETTI?
WE'VE BEEN WASTING OUR TIME ON PENNY-ANTE RACKETS! A MILLION IN GOLD··· THAT'S WHAT WE'RE GOIN' AFTER NOW!--MAKE A BEE-LINE FOR TH' DAILY STAR, MUGSY, AN' GET THE DOPE ON CLARK KENT, TH' REPORTER WHO WROTE TH' STORY.

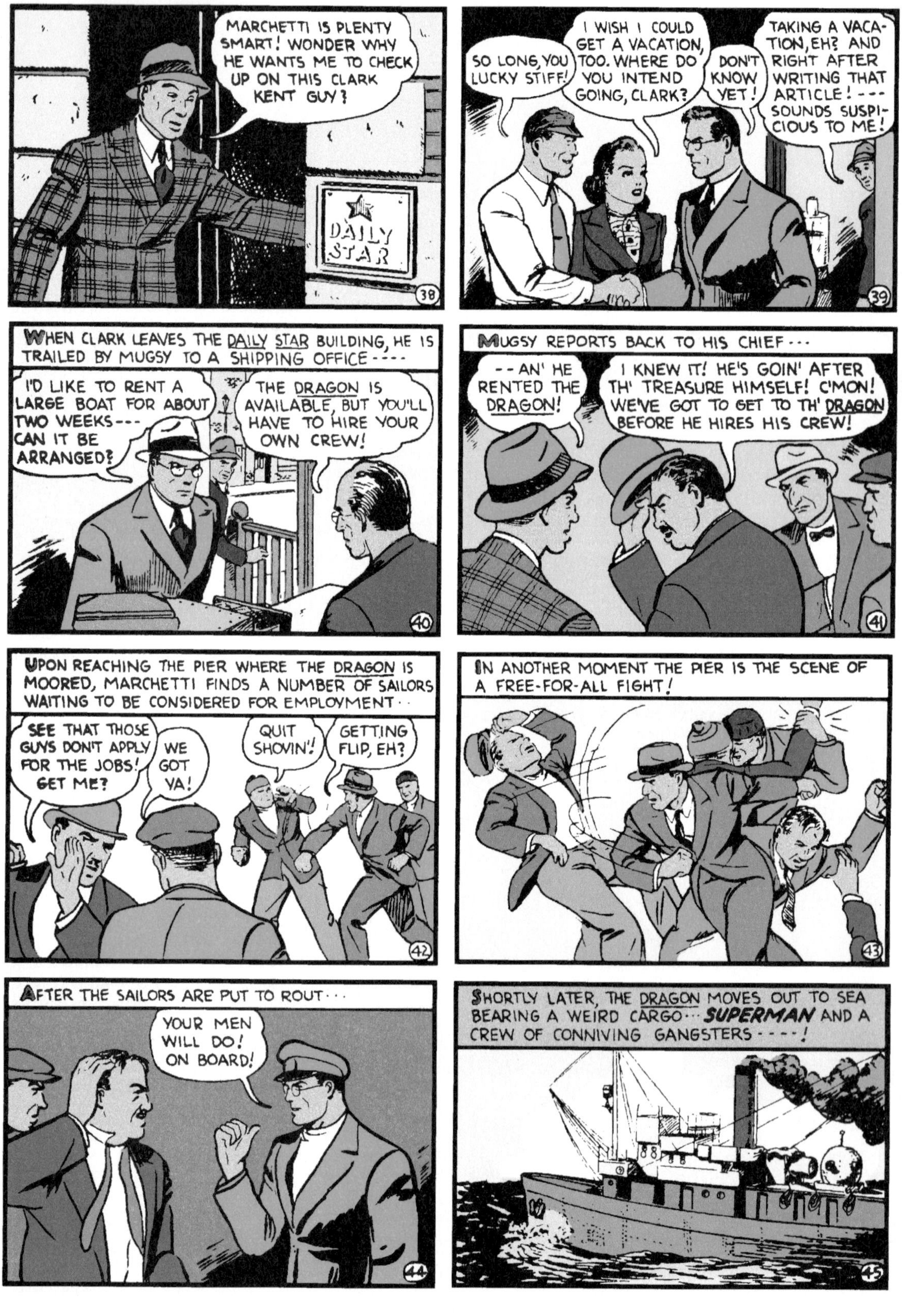
MARCHETTI IS PLENTY SMART! WONDER WHY HE WANTS ME TO CHECK UP ON THIS CLARK KENT GUY?
DAILY STAR
SO LONG, YOU LUCKY STIFF!
I WISH I COULD GET A VACATION, TOO. WHERE DO YOU INTEND GOING, CLARK?
DON'T KNOW YET!
TAKING A VACATION, EH? AND RIGHT AFTER WRITING THAT ARTICLE! --- SOUNDS SUSPICIOUS TO ME!
WHEN CLARK LEAVES THE DAILY STAR BUILDING, HE IS TRAILED BY MUGSY TO A SHIPPING OFFICE ----
I'D LIKE TO RENT A LARGE BOAT FOR ABOUT TWO WEEKS--- CAN IT BE ARRANGED?
THE DRAGON IS AVAILABLE, BUT YOU'LL HAVE TO HIRE YOUR OWN CREW!
MUGSY REPORTS BACK TO HIS CHIEF ---
-- AN' HE RENTED THE DRAGON!
I KNEW IT! HE'S GOIN' AFTER TH' TREASURE HIMSELF! C'MON! WE'VE GOT TO GET TO TH' DRAGON BEFORE HE HIRES HIS CREW!
UPON REACHING THE PIER WHERE THE DRAGON IS MOORED, MARCHETTI FINDS A NUMBER OF SAILORS WAITING TO BE CONSIDERED FOR EMPLOYMENT ..
SEE THAT THOSE GUYS DON'T APPLY FOR THE JOBS! GET ME?
WE GOT YA!
QUIT SHOVIN'!
GETTING FLIP, EH?
IN ANOTHER MOMENT THE PIER IS THE SCENE OF A FREE-FOR-ALL FIGHT!
AFTER THE SAILORS ARE PUT TO ROUT ...
YOUR MEN WILL DO! ON BOARD!
SHORTLY LATER, THE DRAGON MOVES OUT TO SEA BEARING A WEIRD CARGO... SUPERMAN AND A CREW OF CONNIVING GANGSTERS ----!

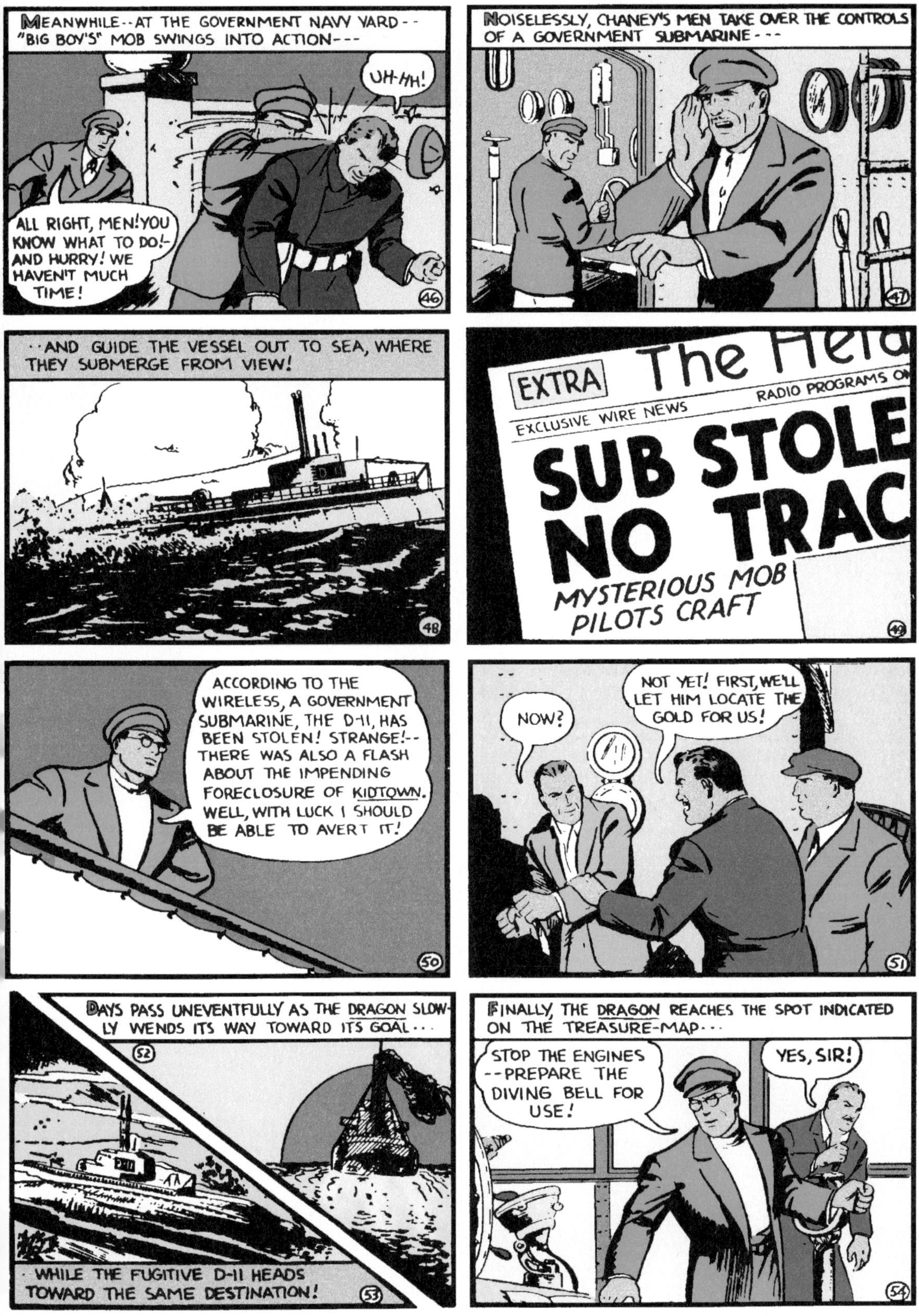
MEANWHILE--AT THE GOVERNMENT NAVY YARD--
"BIG BOY'S" MOB SWINGS INTO ACTION---
UH-HH!
ALL RIGHT, MEN! YOU KNOW WHAT TO DO!-- AND HURRY! WE HAVEN'T MUCH TIME!
46
NOISELESSLY, CHANEY'S MEN TAKE OVER THE CONTROLS OF A GOVERNMENT SUBMARINE---
47
··AND GUIDE THE VESSEL OUT TO SEA, WHERE THEY SUBMERGE FROM VIEW!
48
EXTRA
The Hera
RADIO PROGRAMS ON
EXCLUSIVE WIRE NEWS
SUB STOLE
NO TRAC
MYSTERIOUS MOB PILOTS CRAFT
49
ACCORDING TO THE WIRELESS, A GOVERNMENT SUBMARINE, THE D-11, HAS BEEN STOLEN! STRANGE!-- THERE WAS ALSO A FLASH ABOUT THE IMPENDING FORECLOSURE OF KIDTOWN. WELL, WITH LUCK I SHOULD BE ABLE TO AVERT IT!
50
NOW?
NOT YET! FIRST, WE'LL LET HIM LOCATE THE GOLD FOR US!
51
DAYS PASS UNEVENTFULLY AS THE DRAGON SLOWLY WENDS ITS WAY TOWARD ITS GOAL···
52
·WHILE THE FUGITIVE D-11 HEADS TOWARD THE SAME DESTINATION!
53
FINALLY, THE DRAGON REACHES THE SPOT INDICATED ON THE TREASURE-MAP···
STOP THE ENGINES --PREPARE THE DIVING BELL FOR USE!
YES, SIR!
54

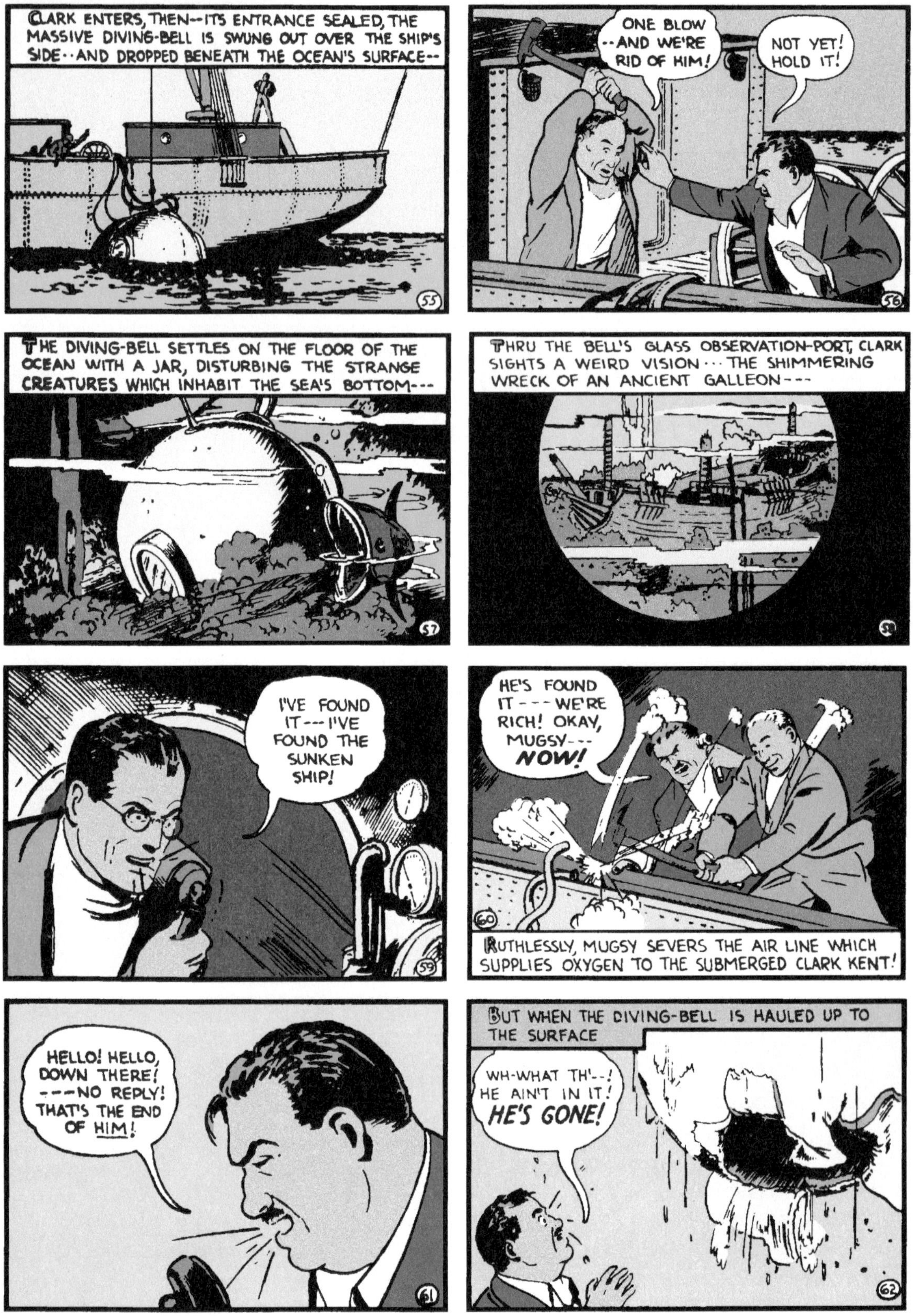
CLARK ENTERS, THEN--ITS ENTRANCE SEALED, THE MASSIVE DIVING-BELL IS SWUNG OUT OVER THE SHIP'S SIDE--AND DROPPED BENEATH THE OCEAN'S SURFACE--
ONE BLOW --AND WE'RE RID OF HIM!
NOT YET! HOLD IT!
THE DIVING-BELL SETTLES ON THE FLOOR OF THE OCEAN WITH A JAR, DISTURBING THE STRANGE CREATURES WHICH INHABIT THE SEA'S BOTTOM---
THRU THE BELL'S GLASS OBSERVATION-PORT, CLARK SIGHTS A WEIRD VISION--- THE SHIMMERING WRECK OF AN ANCIENT GALLEON---
I'VE FOUND IT---I'VE FOUND THE SUNKEN SHIP!
HE'S FOUND IT---WE'RE RICH! OKAY, MUGSY--- NOW!
RUTHLESSLY, MUGSY SEVERS THE AIR LINE WHICH SUPPLIES OXYGEN TO THE SUBMERGED CLARK KENT!
HELLO! HELLO, DOWN THERE! ---NO REPLY! THAT'S THE END OF HIM!
BUT WHEN THE DIVING-BELL IS HAULED UP TO THE SURFACE
WH-WHAT TH'--! HE AIN'T IN IT! HE'S GONE!

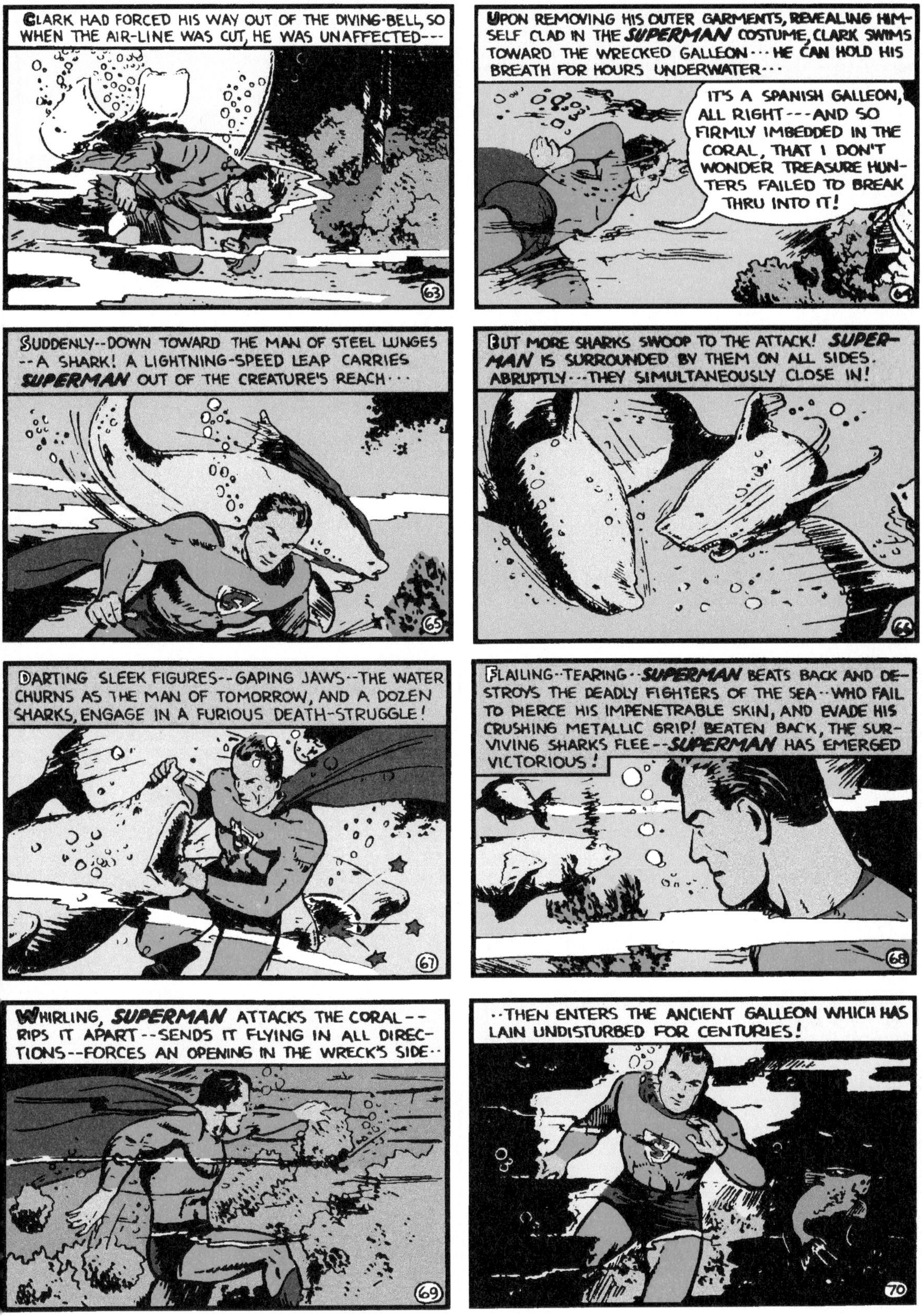
CLARK HAD FORCED HIS WAY OUT OF THE DIVING-BELL, SO WHEN THE AIR-LINE WAS CUT, HE WAS UNAFFECTED---
63
UPON REMOVING HIS OUTER GARMENTS, REVEALING HIMSELF CLAD IN THE SUPERMAN COSTUME, CLARK SWIMS TOWARD THE WRECKED GALLEON --- HE CAN HOLD HIS BREATH FOR HOURS UNDERWATER ---
IT'S A SPANISH GALLEON, ALL RIGHT---AND SO FIRMLY IMBEDDED IN THE CORAL, THAT I DON'T WONDER TREASURE HUNTERS FAILED TO BREAK THRU INTO IT!
64
SUDDENLY--DOWN TOWARD THE MAN OF STEEL LUNGES --A SHARK! A LIGHTNING-SPEED LEAP CARRIES SUPERMAN OUT OF THE CREATURE'S REACH ---
65
BUT MORE SHARKS SWOOP TO THE ATTACK! SUPERMAN IS SURROUNDED BY THEM ON ALL SIDES. ABRUPTLY---THEY SIMULTANEOUSLY CLOSE IN!
66
DARTING SLEEK FIGURES--GAPING JAWS--THE WATER CHURNS AS THE MAN OF TOMORROW, AND A DOZEN SHARKS, ENGAGE IN A FURIOUS DEATH-STRUGGLE!
67
FLAILING--TEARING--SUPERMAN BEATS BACK AND DESTROYS THE DEADLY FIGHTERS OF THE SEA--WHO FAIL TO PIERCE HIS IMPENETRABLE SKIN, AND EVADE HIS CRUSHING METALLIC GRIP! BEATEN BACK, THE SURVIVING SHARKS FLEE--SUPERMAN HAS EMERGED VICTORIOUS!
68
WHIRLING, SUPERMAN ATTACKS THE CORAL--RIPS IT APART--SENDS IT FLYING IN ALL DIRECTIONS--FORCES AN OPENING IN THE WRECK'S SIDE--
69
--THEN ENTERS THE ANCIENT GALLEON WHICH HAS LAIN UNDISTURBED FOR CENTURIES!
70

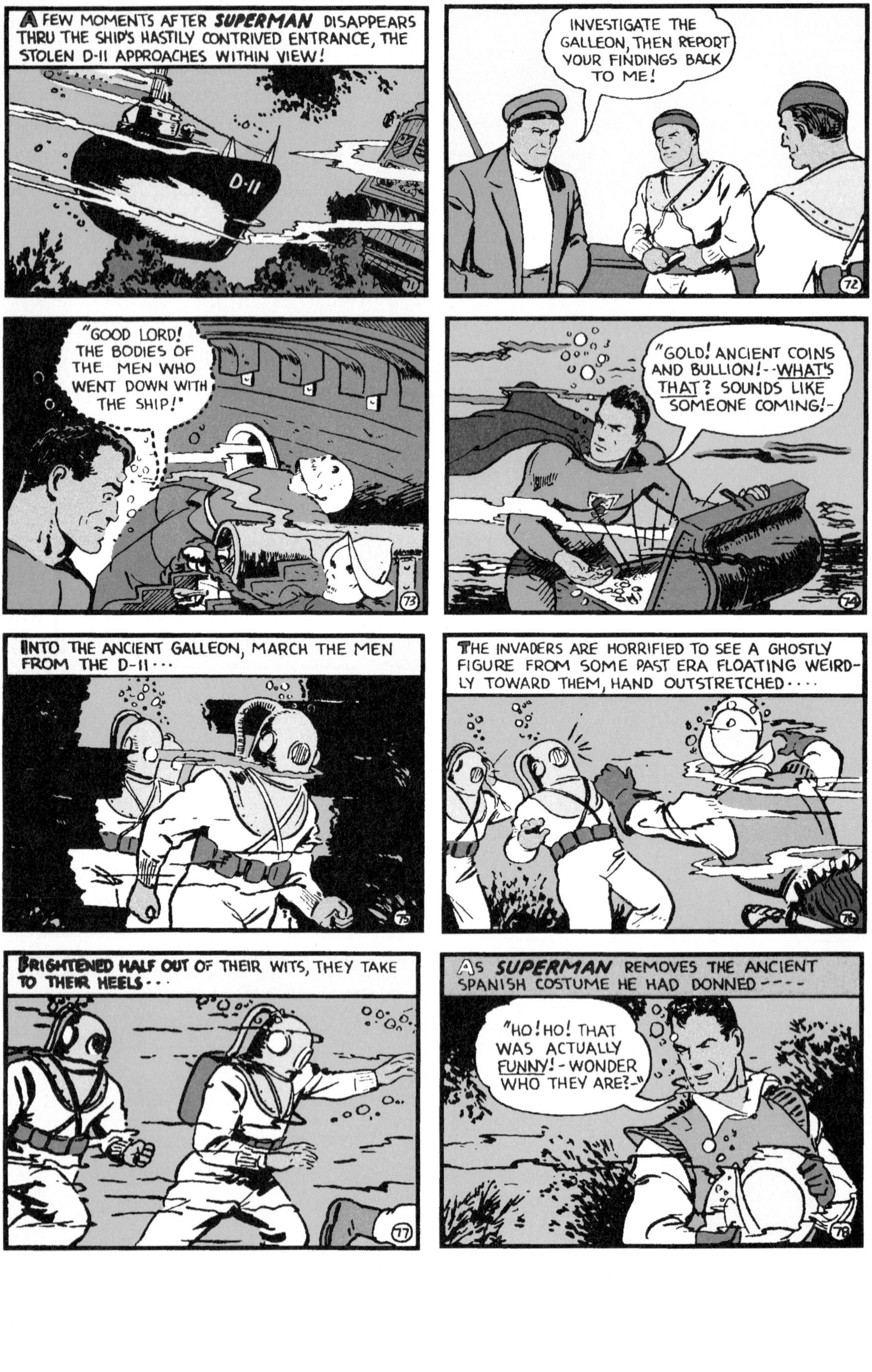
A FEW MOMENTS AFTER SUPERMAN DISAPPEARS THRU THE SHIP'S HASTILY CONTRIVED ENTRANCE, THE STOLEN D-11 APPROACHES WITHIN VIEW!
D-11
INVESTIGATE THE GALLEON, THEN REPORT YOUR FINDINGS BACK TO ME!
"GOOD LORD! THE BODIES OF THE MEN WHO WENT DOWN WITH THE SHIP!"
"GOLD! ANCIENT COINS AND BULLION!--WHAT'S THAT? SOUNDS LIKE SOMEONE COMING!-
INTO THE ANCIENT GALLEON, MARCH THE MEN FROM THE D-11...
THE INVADERS ARE HORRIFIED TO SEE A GHOSTLY FIGURE FROM SOME PAST ERA FLOATING WEIRDLY TOWARD THEM, HAND OUTSTRETCHED....
FRIGHTENED HALF OUT OF THEIR WITS, THEY TAKE TO THEIR HEELS...
AS SUPERMAN REMOVES THE ANCIENT SPANISH COSTUME HE HAD DONNED----
"HO! HO! THAT WAS ACTUALLY FUNNY!-WONDER WHO THEY ARE?-"

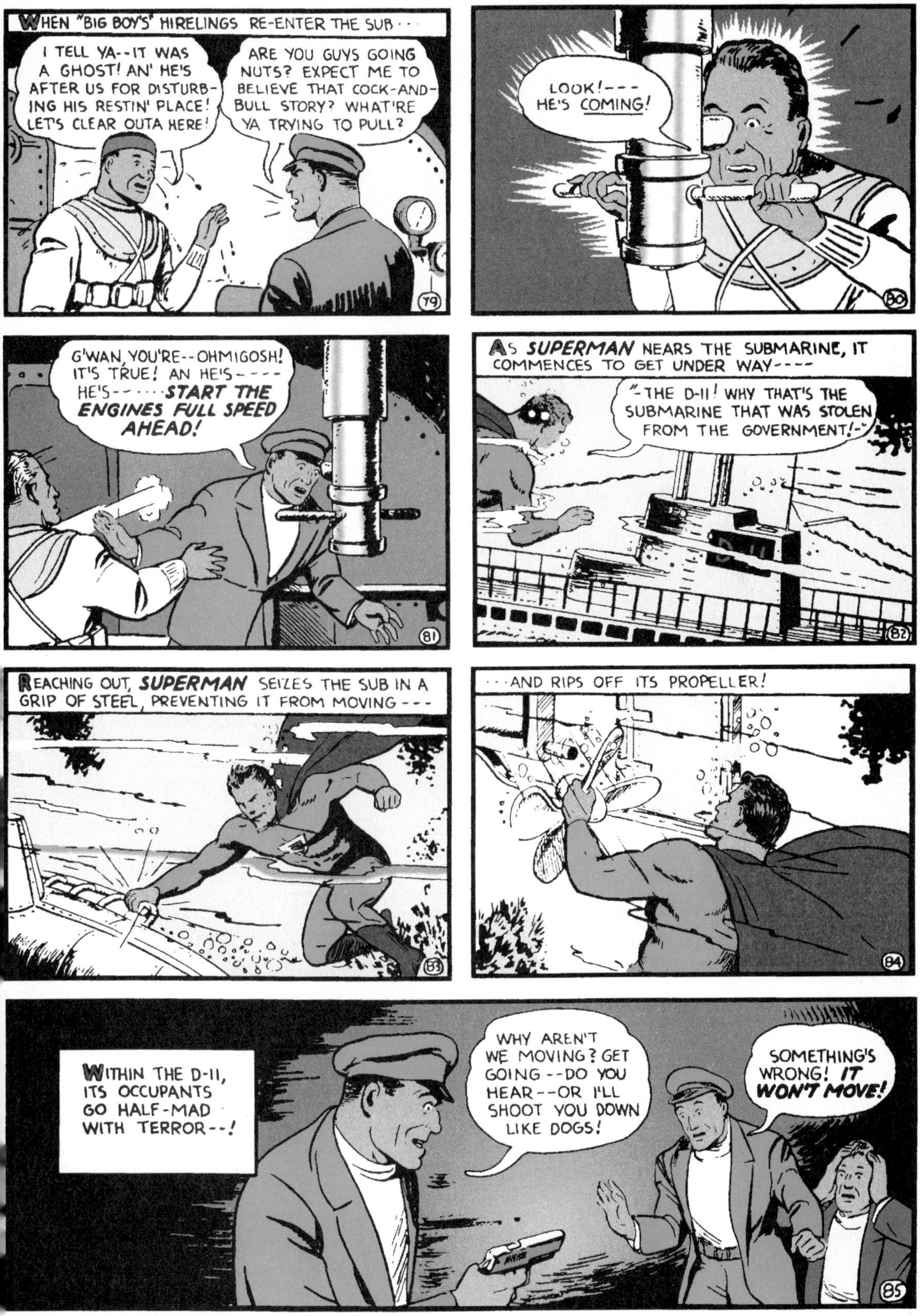
WHEN "BIG BOY'S" HIRELINGS RE-ENTER THE SUB · · ·
I TELL YA--IT WAS A GHOST! AN' HE'S AFTER US FOR DISTURB-ING HIS RESTIN' PLACE! LET'S CLEAR OUTA HERE!
ARE YOU GUYS GOING NUTS? EXPECT ME TO BELIEVE THAT COCK-AND-BULL STORY? WHAT'RE YA TRYING TO PULL?
79
LOOK!--- HE'S COMING!
80
G'WAN, YOU'RE--OHMIGOSH! IT'S TRUE! AN HE'S---- HE'S--···START THE ENGINES FULL SPEED AHEAD!
81
AS SUPERMAN NEARS THE SUBMARINE, IT COMMENCES TO GET UNDER WAY----
"-THE D-II! WHY THAT'S THE SUBMARINE THAT WAS STOLEN FROM THE GOVERNMENT!-"
82
REACHING OUT, SUPERMAN SEIZES THE SUB IN A GRIP OF STEEL, PREVENTING IT FROM MOVING---
83
···AND RIPS OFF ITS PROPELLER!
84
WITHIN THE D-II, ITS OCCUPANTS GO HALF-MAD WITH TERROR--!
WHY AREN'T WE MOVING? GET GOING--DO YOU HEAR--OR I'LL SHOOT YOU DOWN LIKE DOGS!
SOMETHING'S WRONG! IT WON'T MOVE!
85

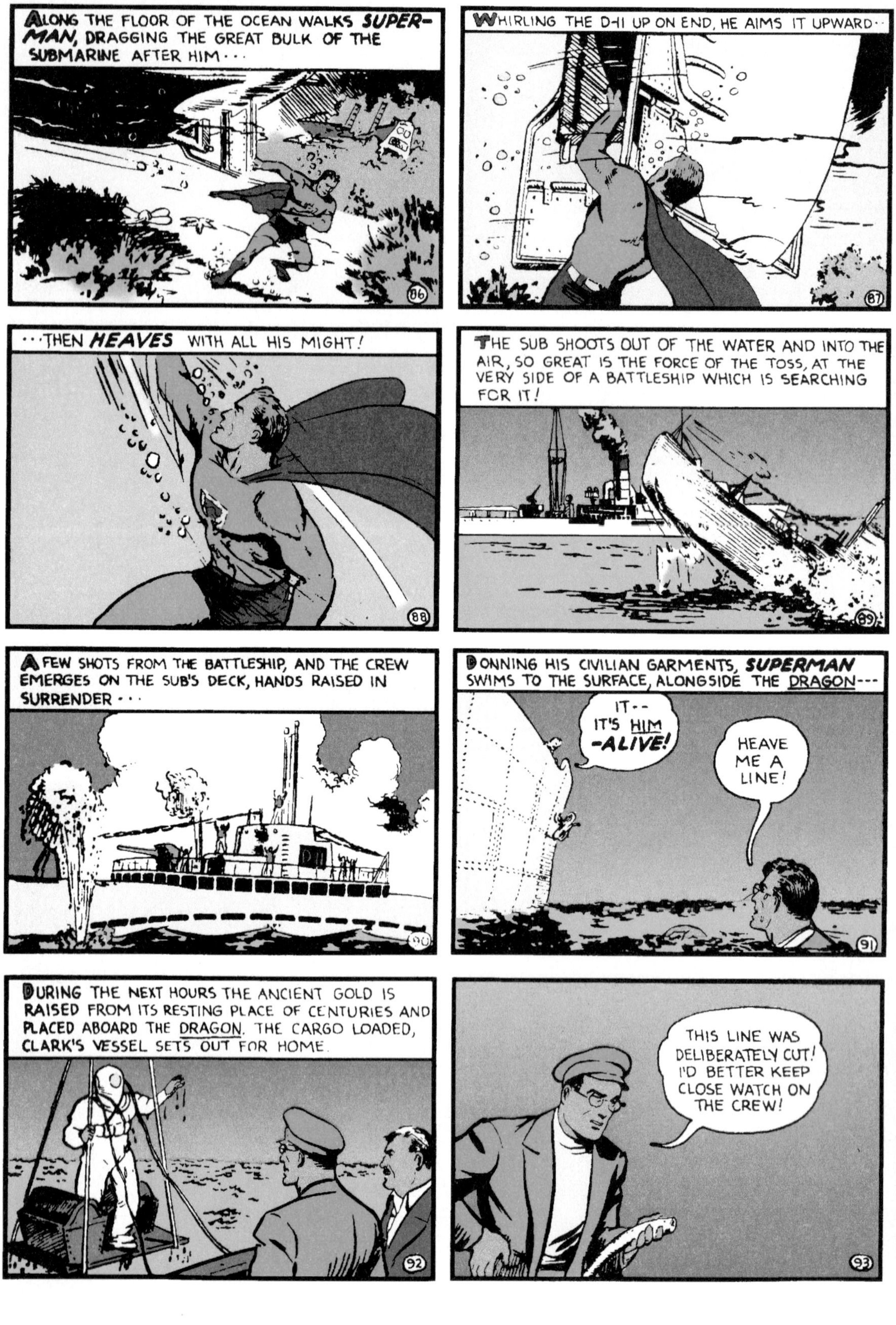
ALONG THE FLOOR OF THE OCEAN WALKS SUPERMAN, DRAGGING THE GREAT BULK OF THE SUBMARINE AFTER HIM . . .
86
WHIRLING THE D-11 UP ON END, HE AIMS IT UPWARD . .
87
. . . THEN HEAVES WITH ALL HIS MIGHT!
88
THE SUB SHOOTS OUT OF THE WATER AND INTO THE AIR, SO GREAT IS THE FORCE OF THE TOSS, AT THE VERY SIDE OF A BATTLESHIP WHICH IS SEARCHING FOR IT!
89
A FEW SHOTS FROM THE BATTLESHIP, AND THE CREW EMERGES ON THE SUB'S DECK, HANDS RAISED IN SURRENDER . . .
90
DONNING HIS CIVILIAN GARMENTS, SUPERMAN SWIMS TO THE SURFACE, ALONGSIDE THE DRAGON---
IT-- IT'S HIM -ALIVE!
HEAVE ME A LINE!
91
DURING THE NEXT HOURS THE ANCIENT GOLD IS RAISED FROM ITS RESTING PLACE OF CENTURIES AND PLACED ABOARD THE DRAGON. THE CARGO LOADED, CLARK'S VESSEL SETS OUT FOR HOME.
92
THIS LINE WAS DELIBERATELY CUT! I'D BETTER KEEP CLOSE WATCH ON THE CREW!
93

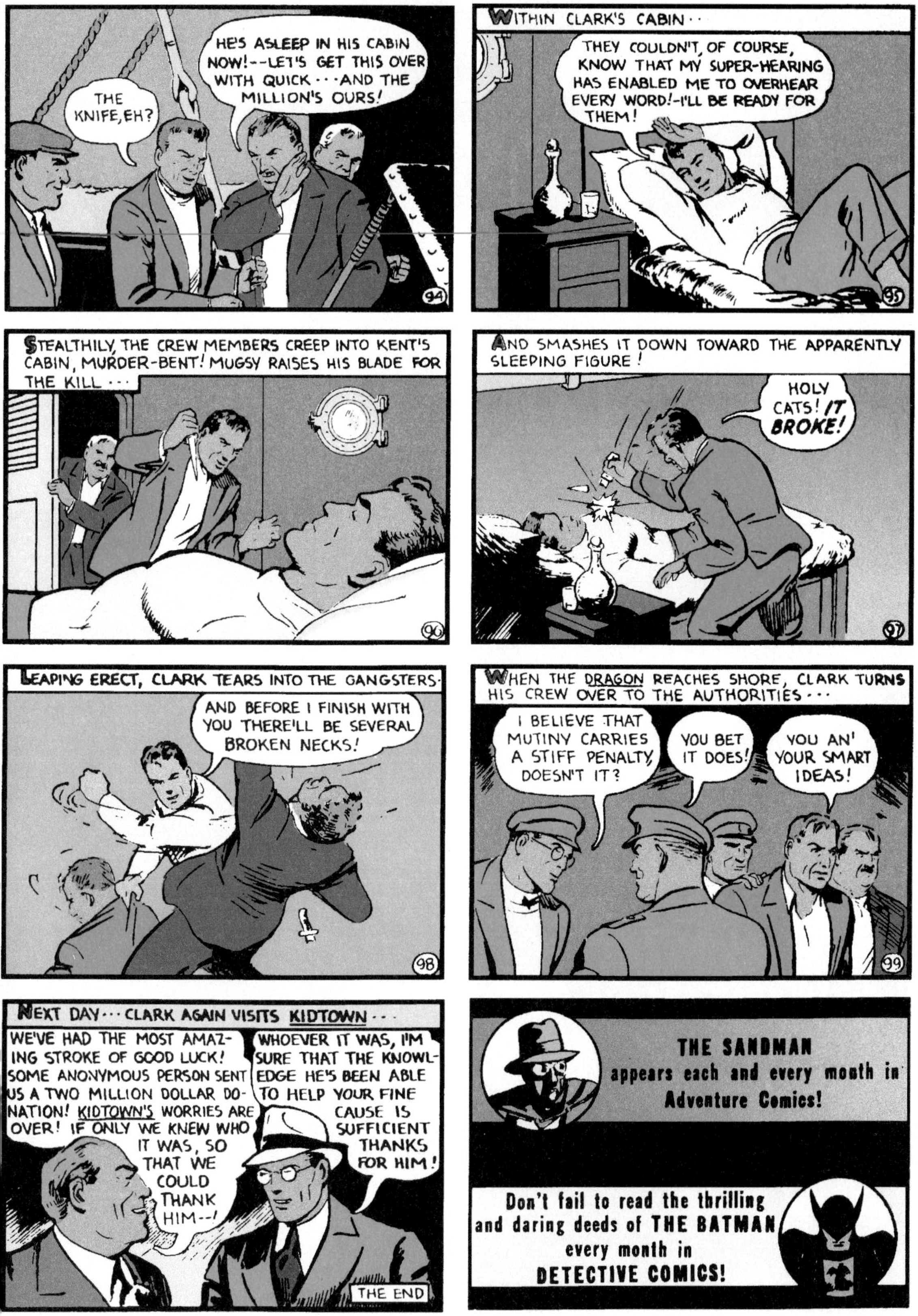
THE KNIFE, EH?
HE'S ASLEEP IN HIS CABIN NOW!--LET'S GET THIS OVER WITH QUICK···AND THE MILLION'S OURS!
WITHIN CLARK'S CABIN··
THEY COULDN'T, OF COURSE, KNOW THAT MY SUPER-HEARING HAS ENABLED ME TO OVERHEAR EVERY WORD!-I'LL BE READY FOR THEM!
STEALTHILY, THE CREW MEMBERS CREEP INTO KENT'S CABIN, MURDER-BENT! MUGSY RAISES HIS BLADE FOR THE KILL···
AND SMASHES IT DOWN TOWARD THE APPARENTLY SLEEPING FIGURE!
HOLY CATS! IT BROKE!
LEAPING ERECT, CLARK TEARS INTO THE GANGSTERS·
AND BEFORE I FINISH WITH YOU THERE'LL BE SEVERAL BROKEN NECKS!
WHEN THE DRAGON REACHES SHORE, CLARK TURNS HIS CREW OVER TO THE AUTHORITIES···
I BELIEVE THAT MUTINY CARRIES A STIFF PENALTY, DOESN'T IT?
YOU BET IT DOES!
YOU AN' YOUR SMART IDEAS!
NEXT DAY··· CLARK AGAIN VISITS KIDTOWN···
WE'VE HAD THE MOST AMAZING STROKE OF GOOD LUCK! SOME ANONYMOUS PERSON SENT US A TWO MILLION DOLLAR DONATION! KIDTOWN'S WORRIES ARE OVER! IF ONLY WE KNEW WHO IT WAS, SO THAT WE COULD THANK HIM--!
WHOEVER IT WAS, I'M SURE THAT THE KNOWLEDGE HE'S BEEN ABLE TO HELP YOUR FINE CAUSE IS SUFFICIENT THANKS FOR HIM!
THE END
THE SANDMAN appears each and every month in Adventure Comics!
Don't fail to read the thrilling and daring deeds of THE BATMAN every month in DETECTIVE COMICS!

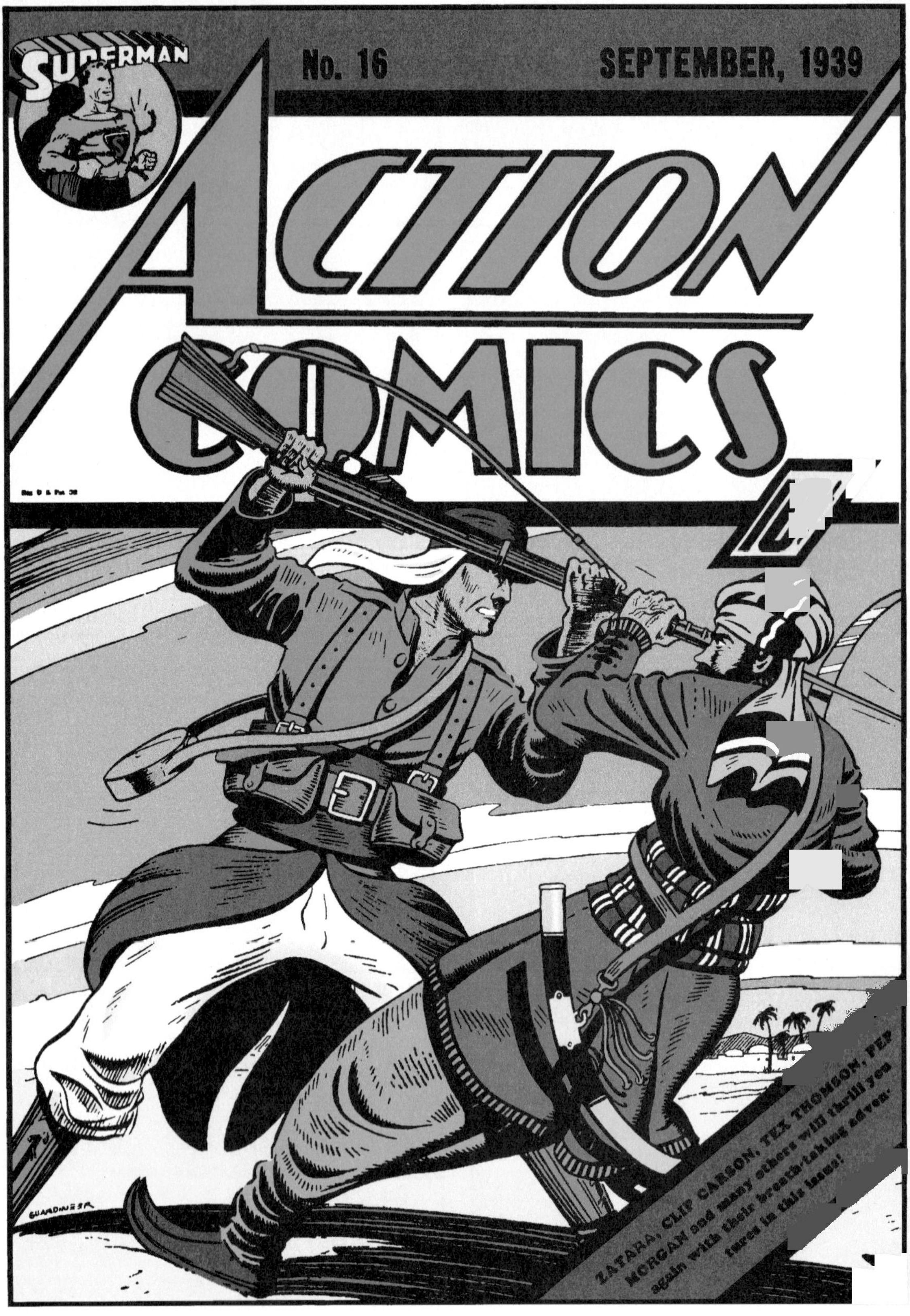

SUPERMAN
No. 16
SEPTEMBER, 1939
ACTION COMICS
ZATARA, CLIP CARSON, TEX THOMSON, PEP MORGAN and many others will thrill you again with their breath-taking adventures in this issue!
GUARDINEER

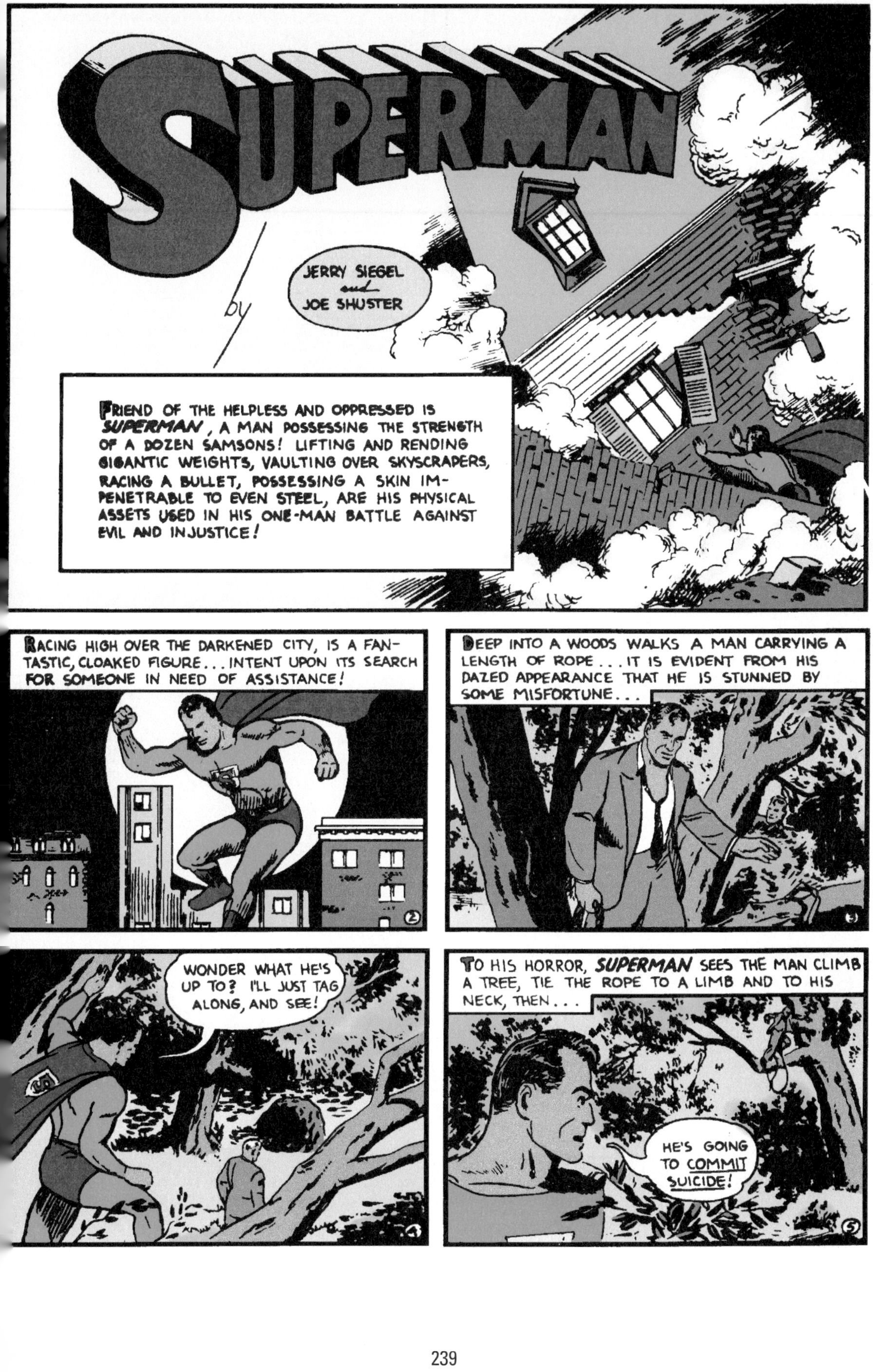
SUPERMAN
by
JERRY SIEGEL and JOE SHUSTER
FRIEND OF THE HELPLESS AND OPPRESSED IS SUPERMAN, A MAN POSSESSING THE STRENGTH OF A DOZEN SAMSONS! LIFTING AND RENDING GIGANTIC WEIGHTS, VAULTING OVER SKYSCRAPERS, RACING A BULLET, POSSESSING A SKIN IMPENETRABLE TO EVEN STEEL, ARE HIS PHYSICAL ASSETS USED IN HIS ONE-MAN BATTLE AGAINST EVIL AND INJUSTICE!
RACING HIGH OVER THE DARKENED CITY, IS A FANTASTIC, CLOAKED FIGURE... INTENT UPON ITS SEARCH FOR SOMEONE IN NEED OF ASSISTANCE!
DEEP INTO A WOODS WALKS A MAN CARRYING A LENGTH OF ROPE... IT IS EVIDENT FROM HIS DAZED APPEARANCE THAT HE IS STUNNED BY SOME MISFORTUNE...
WONDER WHAT HE'S UP TO? I'LL JUST TAG ALONG, AND SEE!
TO HIS HORROR, SUPERMAN SEES THE MAN CLIMB A TREE, TIE THE ROPE TO A LIMB AND TO HIS NECK, THEN...
HE'S GOING TO COMMIT SUICIDE!

OUTWARD FROM THE LIMB LEAPS THE MAN, IN A SUICIDE PLUNGE!

⑥

FAST AS LIGHT, *SUPERMAN* STREAKS FORWARD....

I'VE GOT TO SAVE HIM..

⑦

...WHETHER HE WANTS ME TO OR NOT!

⑧

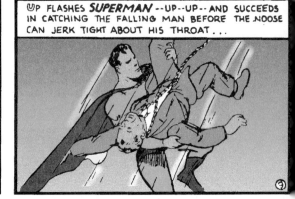

UP FLASHES *SUPERMAN* --UP--UP-- AND SUCCEEDS IN CATCHING THE FALLING MAN BEFORE THE NOOSE CAN JERK TIGHT ABOUT HIS THROAT...

⑨

SO GREAT IS THE FORCE OF *SUPERMAN'S* LEAP THAT THE HURTLING FIGURES CONTINUE UPWARD.. THE MAN OF STEEL'S HAND ENCOUNTERS THE LIMB, DRAWING THEM UP TO SAFETY...

⑩

REMOVING THE NOOSE FROM THE RESCUED MAN'S THROAT, *SUPERMAN* LEAPS TO EARTH...

⑪

IN HEAVEN'S NAME *WHO..WHAT.* ARE YOU?

SOMEONE WHO THINKS LIFE IS TOO PRECIOUS TO BE DESTROYED! WHAT MADE YOU DO IT?

⑫

YOU SHOULDN'T HAVE STOPPED ME FROM DESTROYING MY WORTHLESS LIFE. I'M A THIEF.. I'VE STOLEN MONEY FROM MY TRUSTING EMPLOYER!

⑬

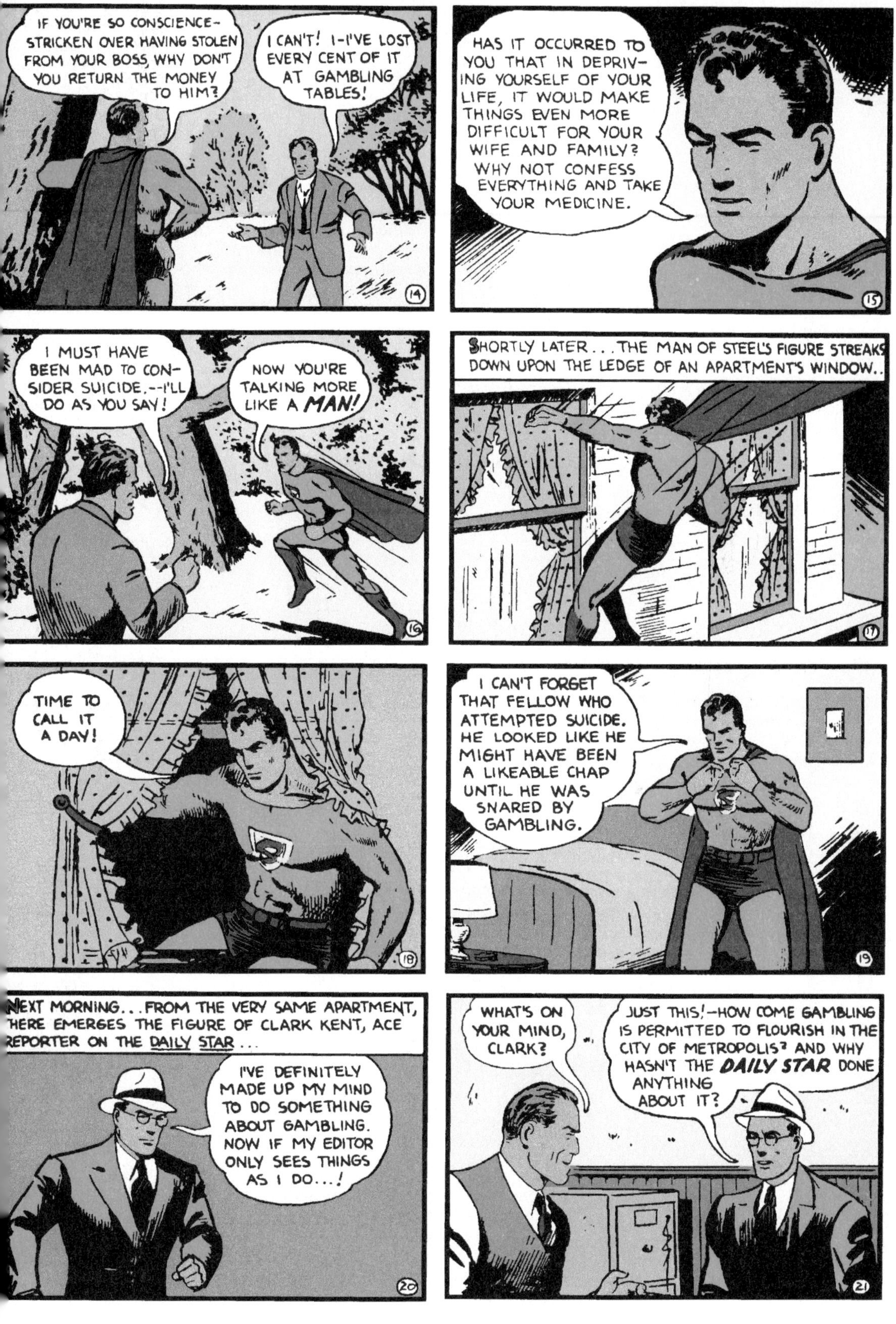
IF YOU'RE SO CONSCIENCE-STRICKEN OVER HAVING STOLEN FROM YOUR BOSS, WHY DON'T YOU RETURN THE MONEY TO HIM?
I CAN'T! I-I'VE LOST EVERY CENT OF IT AT GAMBLING TABLES!
14
HAS IT OCCURRED TO YOU THAT IN DEPRIVING YOURSELF OF YOUR LIFE, IT WOULD MAKE THINGS EVEN MORE DIFFICULT FOR YOUR WIFE AND FAMILY? WHY NOT CONFESS EVERYTHING AND TAKE YOUR MEDICINE.
15
I MUST HAVE BEEN MAD TO CONSIDER SUICIDE.--I'LL DO AS YOU SAY!
NOW YOU'RE TALKING MORE LIKE A MAN!
16
SHORTLY LATER... THE MAN OF STEEL'S FIGURE STREAKS DOWN UPON THE LEDGE OF AN APARTMENT'S WINDOW..
17
TIME TO CALL IT A DAY!
18
I CAN'T FORGET THAT FELLOW WHO ATTEMPTED SUICIDE. HE LOOKED LIKE HE MIGHT HAVE BEEN A LIKEABLE CHAP UNTIL HE WAS SNARED BY GAMBLING.
19
NEXT MORNING... FROM THE VERY SAME APARTMENT, THERE EMERGES THE FIGURE OF CLARK KENT, ACE REPORTER ON THE DAILY STAR...
I'VE DEFINITELY MADE UP MY MIND TO DO SOMETHING ABOUT GAMBLING. NOW IF MY EDITOR ONLY SEES THINGS AS I DO...!
20
WHAT'S ON YOUR MIND, CLARK?
JUST THIS!—HOW COME GAMBLING IS PERMITTED TO FLOURISH IN THE CITY OF METROPOLIS? AND WHY HASN'T THE DAILY STAR DONE ANYTHING ABOUT IT?
21

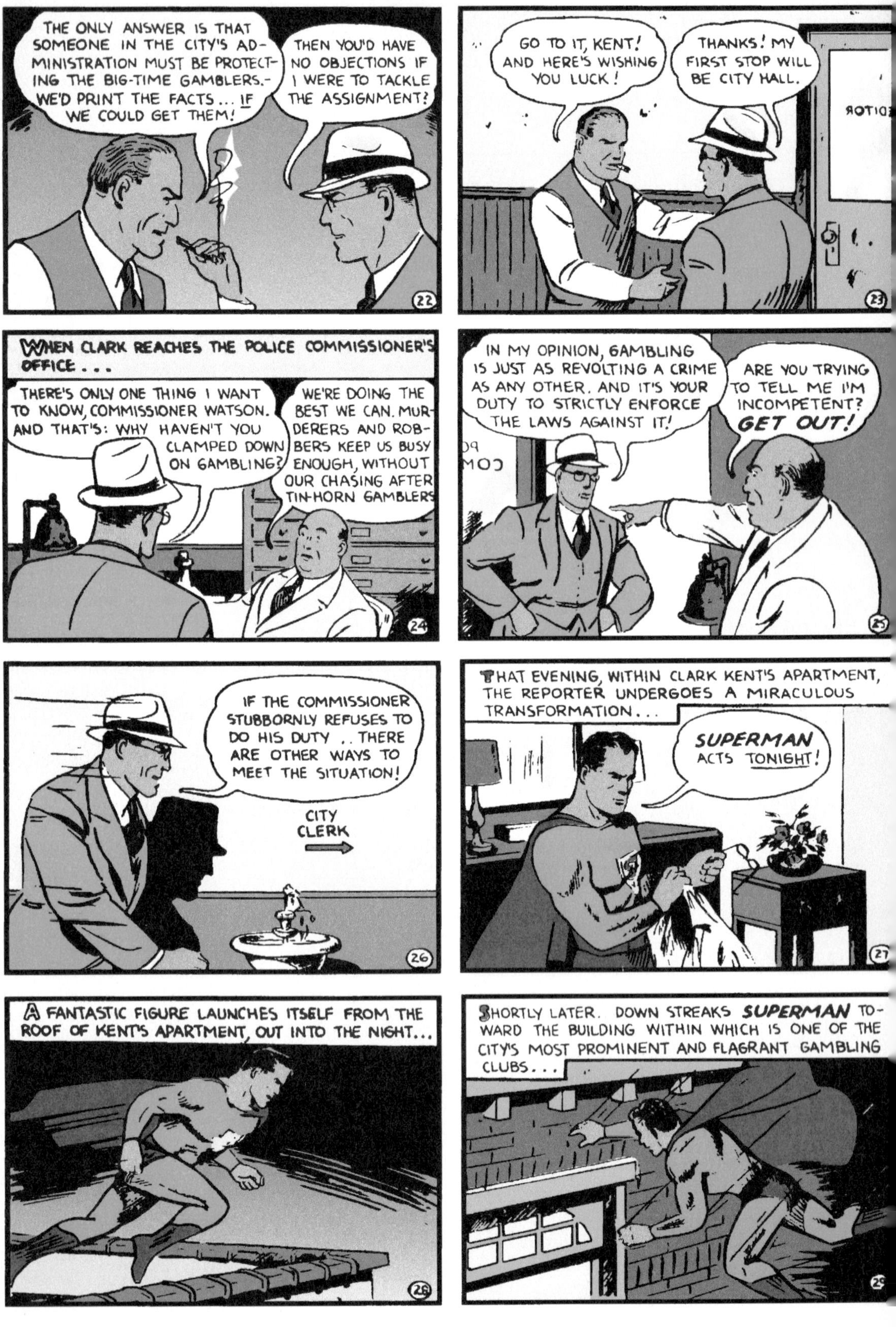
THE ONLY ANSWER IS THAT SOMEONE IN THE CITY'S ADMINISTRATION MUST BE PROTECTING THE BIG-TIME GAMBLERS.- WE'D PRINT THE FACTS... IF WE COULD GET THEM!
THEN YOU'D HAVE NO OBJECTIONS IF I WERE TO TACKLE THE ASSIGNMENT?
22
GO TO IT, KENT! AND HERE'S WISHING YOU LUCK!
THANKS! MY FIRST STOP WILL BE CITY HALL.
23
WHEN CLARK REACHES THE POLICE COMMISSIONER'S OFFICE...
THERE'S ONLY ONE THING I WANT TO KNOW, COMMISSIONER WATSON. AND THAT'S: WHY HAVEN'T YOU CLAMPED DOWN ON GAMBLING?
WE'RE DOING THE BEST WE CAN. MURDERERS AND ROBBERS KEEP US BUSY ENOUGH, WITHOUT OUR CHASING AFTER TIN-HORN GAMBLERS
24
IN MY OPINION, GAMBLING IS JUST AS REVOLTING A CRIME AS ANY OTHER. AND IT'S YOUR DUTY TO STRICTLY ENFORCE THE LAWS AGAINST IT!
ARE YOU TRYING TO TELL ME I'M INCOMPETENT? GET OUT!
25
IF THE COMMISSIONER STUBBORNLY REFUSES TO DO HIS DUTY .. THERE ARE OTHER WAYS TO MEET THE SITUATION!
CITY CLERK
26
THAT EVENING, WITHIN CLARK KENT'S APARTMENT, THE REPORTER UNDERGOES A MIRACULOUS TRANSFORMATION...
SUPERMAN ACTS TONIGHT!
27
A FANTASTIC FIGURE LAUNCHES ITSELF FROM THE ROOF OF KENT'S APARTMENT, OUT INTO THE NIGHT...
28
SHORTLY LATER. DOWN STREAKS SUPERMAN TOWARD THE BUILDING WITHIN WHICH IS ONE OF THE CITY'S MOST PROMINENT AND FLAGRANT GAMBLING CLUBS...

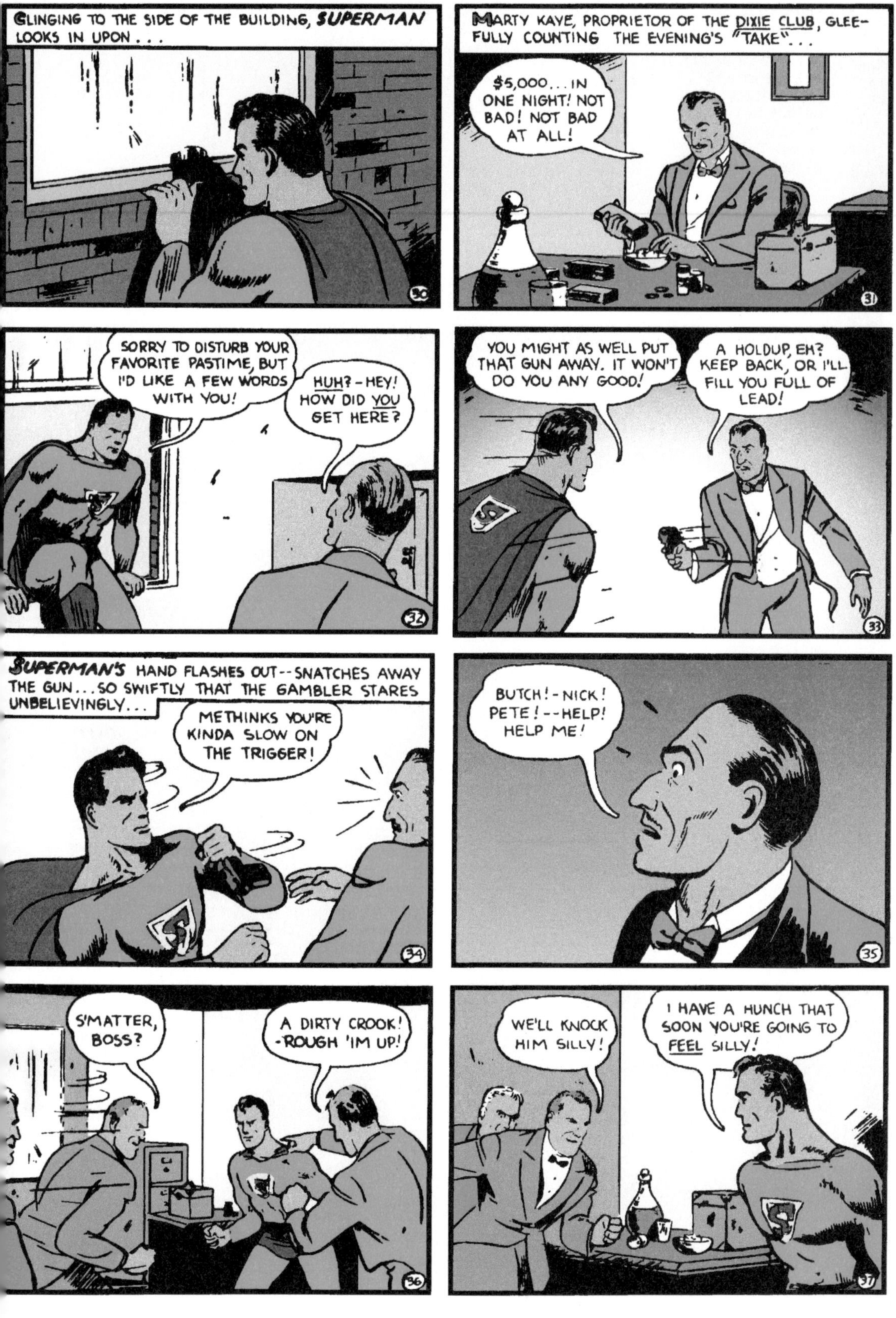
CLINGING TO THE SIDE OF THE BUILDING, SUPERMAN LOOKS IN UPON . . .
MARTY KAYE, PROPRIETOR OF THE DIXIE CLUB, GLEEFULLY COUNTING THE EVENING'S "TAKE". . .
$5,000... IN ONE NIGHT! NOT BAD! NOT BAD AT ALL!
SORRY TO DISTURB YOUR FAVORITE PASTIME, BUT I'D LIKE A FEW WORDS WITH YOU!
HUH? - HEY! HOW DID YOU GET HERE?
YOU MIGHT AS WELL PUT THAT GUN AWAY. IT WON'T DO YOU ANY GOOD!
A HOLDUP, EH? KEEP BACK, OR I'LL FILL YOU FULL OF LEAD!
SUPERMAN'S HAND FLASHES OUT--SNATCHES AWAY THE GUN...SO SWIFTLY THAT THE GAMBLER STARES UNBELIEVINGLY...
METHINKS YOU'RE KINDA SLOW ON THE TRIGGER!
BUTCH! - NICK! PETE! --HELP! HELP ME!
S'MATTER, BOSS?
A DIRTY CROOK! -ROUGH 'IM UP!
WE'LL KNOCK HIM SILLY!
I HAVE A HUNCH THAT SOON YOU'RE GOING TO FEEL SILLY!

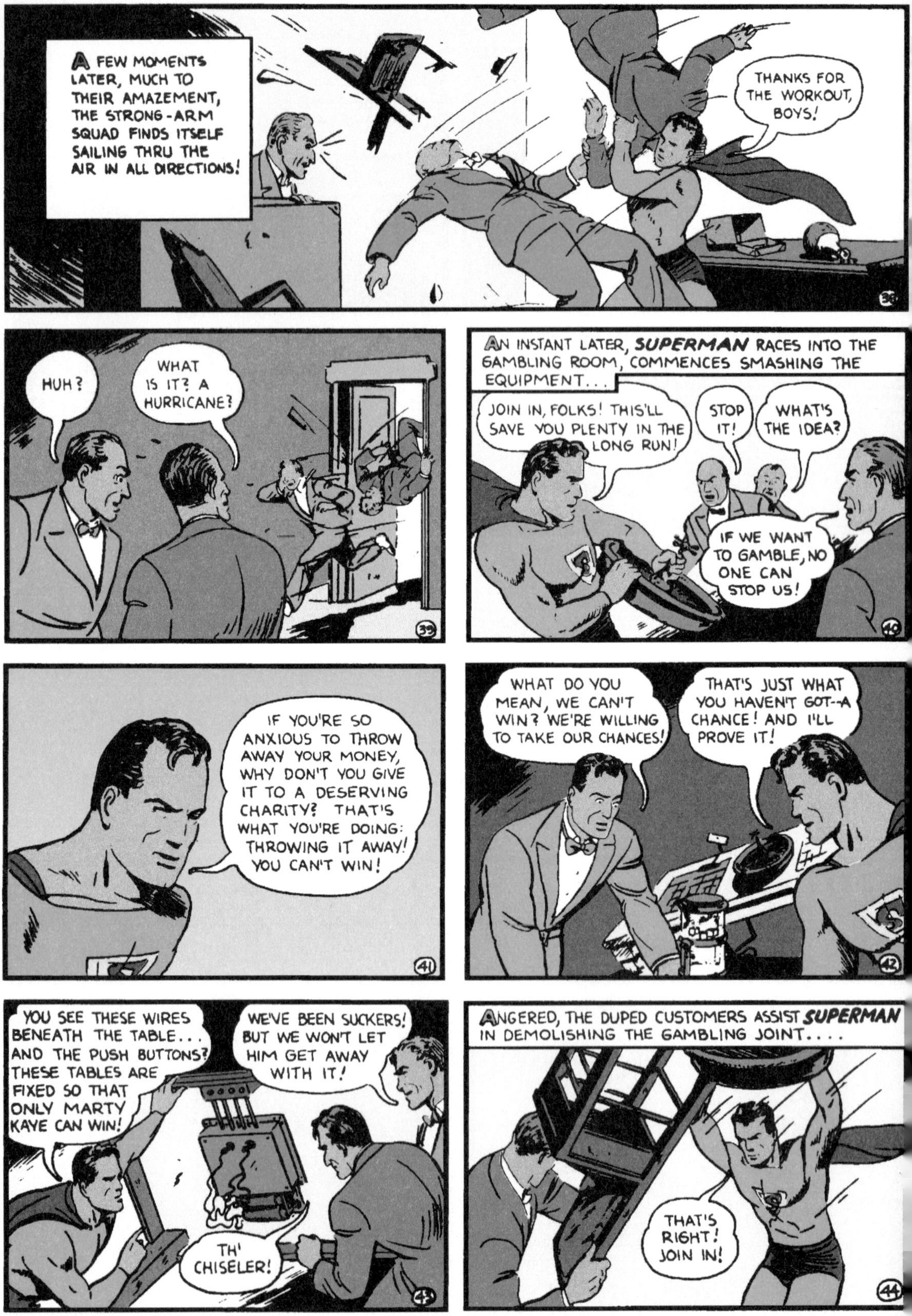
A FEW MOMENTS LATER, MUCH TO THEIR AMAZEMENT, THE STRONG-ARM SQUAD FINDS ITSELF SAILING THRU THE AIR IN ALL DIRECTIONS!
THANKS FOR THE WORKOUT, BOYS!
HUH?
WHAT IS IT? A HURRICANE?
AN INSTANT LATER, SUPERMAN RACES INTO THE GAMBLING ROOM, COMMENCES SMASHING THE EQUIPMENT...
JOIN IN, FOLKS! THIS'LL SAVE YOU PLENTY IN THE LONG RUN!
STOP IT!
WHAT'S THE IDEA?
IF WE WANT TO GAMBLE, NO ONE CAN STOP US!
IF YOU'RE SO ANXIOUS TO THROW AWAY YOUR MONEY, WHY DON'T YOU GIVE IT TO A DESERVING CHARITY? THAT'S WHAT YOU'RE DOING: THROWING IT AWAY! YOU CAN'T WIN!
WHAT DO YOU MEAN, WE CAN'T WIN? WE'RE WILLING TO TAKE OUR CHANCES!
THAT'S JUST WHAT YOU HAVEN'T GOT--A CHANCE! AND I'LL PROVE IT!
YOU SEE THESE WIRES BENEATH THE TABLE... AND THE PUSH BUTTONS? THESE TABLES ARE FIXED SO THAT ONLY MARTY KAYE CAN WIN!
WE'VE BEEN SUCKERS! BUT WE WON'T LET HIM GET AWAY WITH IT!
TH' CHISELER!
ANGERED, THE DUPED CUSTOMERS ASSIST SUPERMAN IN DEMOLISHING THE GAMBLING JOINT....
THAT'S RIGHT! JOIN IN!

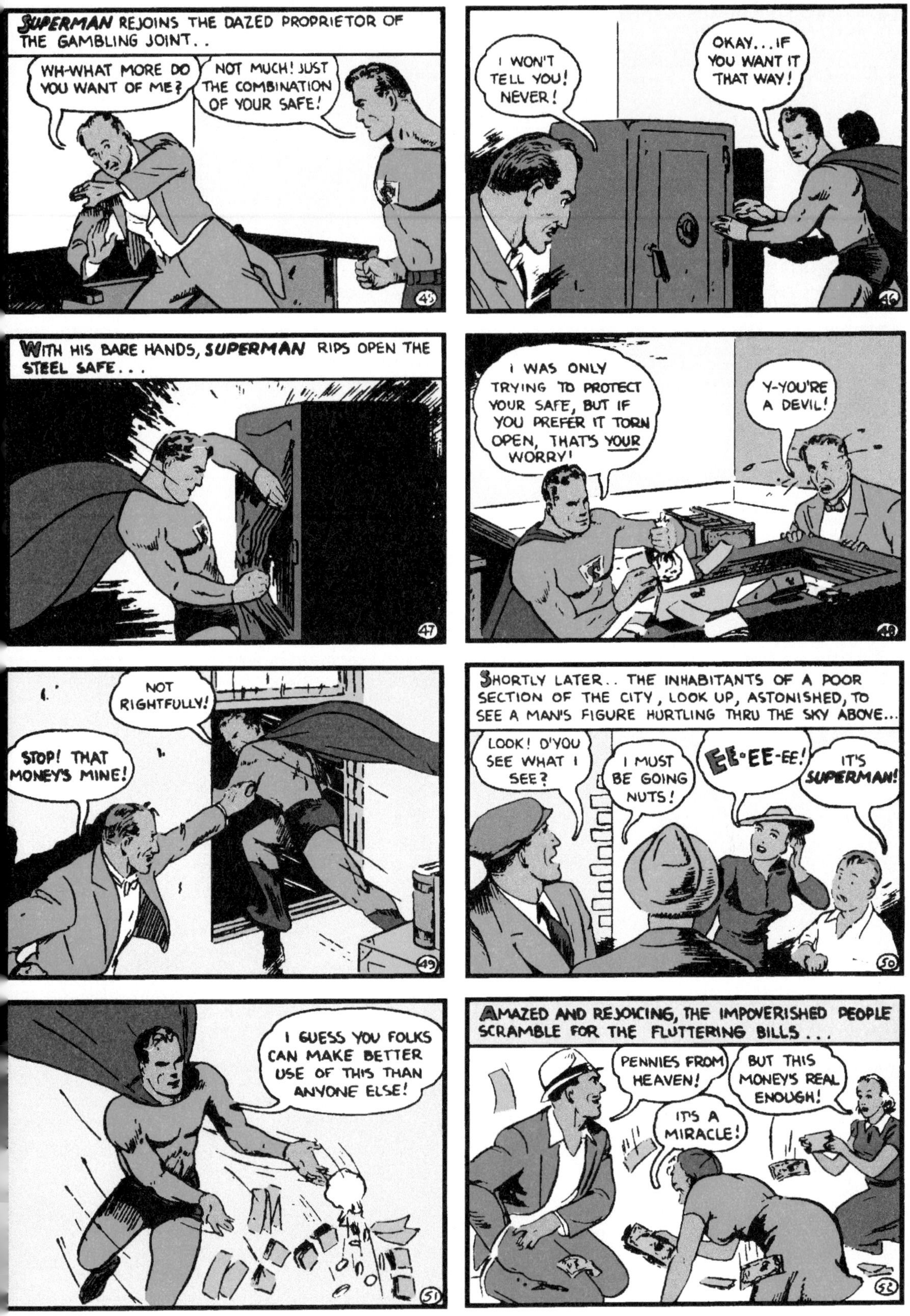
SUPERMAN REJOINS THE DAZED PROPRIETOR OF THE GAMBLING JOINT..
WH-WHAT MORE DO YOU WANT OF ME?
NOT MUCH! JUST THE COMBINATION OF YOUR SAFE!
45
I WON'T TELL YOU! NEVER!
OKAY...IF YOU WANT IT THAT WAY!
46
WITH HIS BARE HANDS, SUPERMAN RIPS OPEN THE STEEL SAFE...
47
I WAS ONLY TRYING TO PROTECT YOUR SAFE, BUT IF YOU PREFER IT TORN OPEN, THAT'S YOUR WORRY!
Y-YOU'RE A DEVIL!
48
STOP! THAT MONEY'S MINE!
NOT RIGHTFULLY!
49
SHORTLY LATER.. THE INHABITANTS OF A POOR SECTION OF THE CITY, LOOK UP, ASTONISHED, TO SEE A MAN'S FIGURE HURTLING THRU THE SKY ABOVE...
LOOK! D'YOU SEE WHAT I SEE?
I MUST BE GOING NUTS!
EE-EE-EE!
IT'S SUPERMAN!
50
I GUESS YOU FOLKS CAN MAKE BETTER USE OF THIS THAN ANYONE ELSE!
51
AMAZED AND REJOICING, THE IMPOVERISHED PEOPLE SCRAMBLE FOR THE FLUTTERING BILLS...
PENNIES FROM HEAVEN!
BUT THIS MONEY'S REAL ENOUGH!
IT'S A MIRACLE!
52

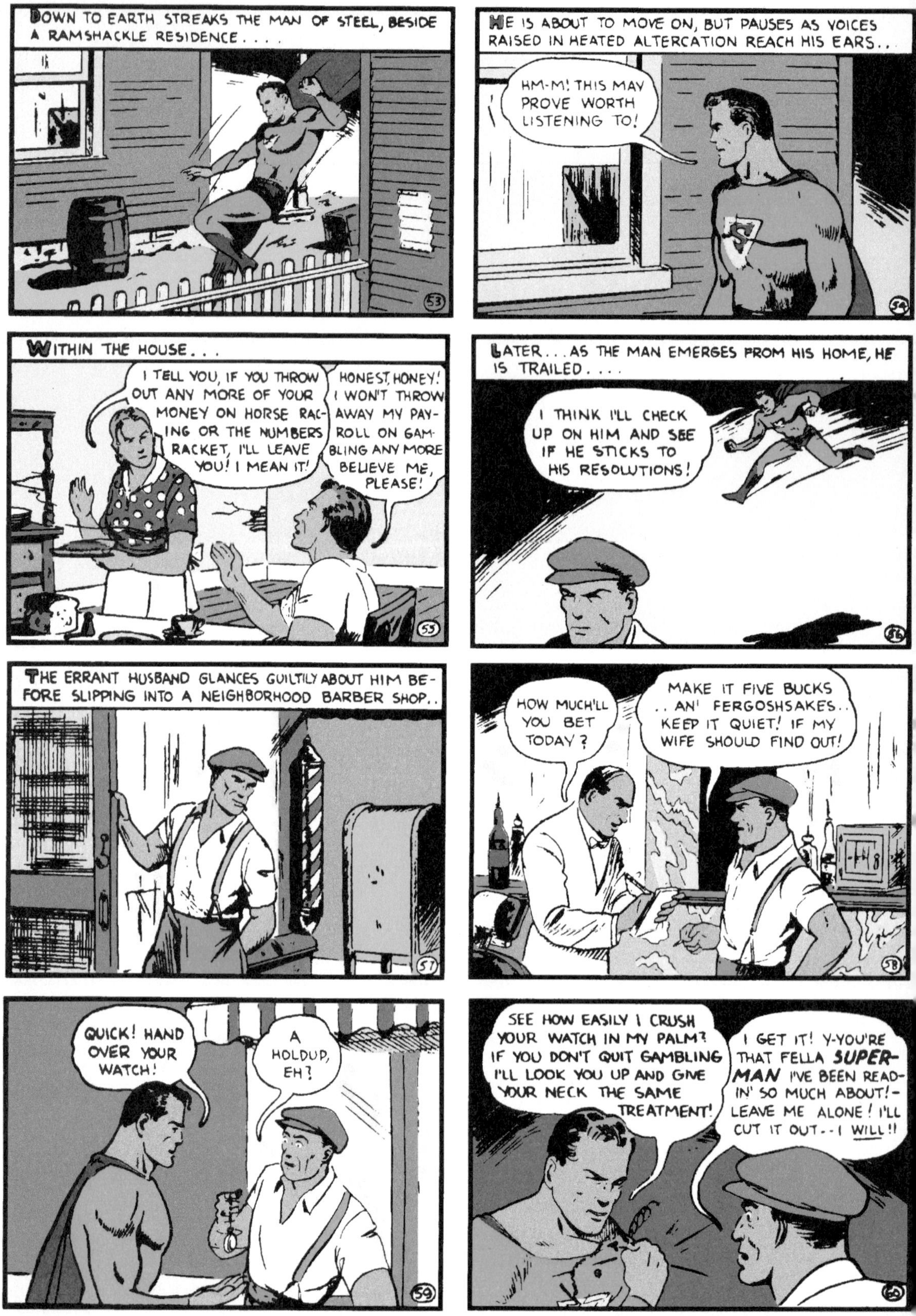
DOWN TO EARTH STREAKS THE MAN OF STEEL, BESIDE A RAMSHACKLE RESIDENCE . . . .
53
HE IS ABOUT TO MOVE ON, BUT PAUSES AS VOICES RAISED IN HEATED ALTERCATION REACH HIS EARS . .
HM-M! THIS MAY PROVE WORTH LISTENING TO!
54
WITHIN THE HOUSE . . .
I TELL YOU, IF YOU THROW OUT ANY MORE OF YOUR MONEY ON HORSE RACING OR THE NUMBERS RACKET, I'LL LEAVE YOU! I MEAN IT!
HONEST, HONEY! I WON'T THROW AWAY MY PAYROLL ON GAMBLING ANY MORE BELIEVE ME, PLEASE!
55
LATER . . . AS THE MAN EMERGES FROM HIS HOME, HE IS TRAILED . . . .
I THINK I'LL CHECK UP ON HIM AND SEE IF HE STICKS TO HIS RESOLUTIONS!
56
THE ERRANT HUSBAND GLANCES GUILTILY ABOUT HIM BEFORE SLIPPING INTO A NEIGHBORHOOD BARBER SHOP . .
57
HOW MUCH'LL YOU BET TODAY?
MAKE IT FIVE BUCKS . . AN' FERGOSHSAKES . . KEEP IT QUIET! IF MY WIFE SHOULD FIND OUT!
58
QUICK! HAND OVER YOUR WATCH!
A HOLDUP, EH?
59
SEE HOW EASILY I CRUSH YOUR WATCH IN MY PALM? IF YOU DON'T QUIT GAMBLING I'LL LOOK YOU UP AND GIVE YOUR NECK THE SAME TREATMENT!
I GET IT! Y-YOU'RE THAT FELLA SUPERMAN I'VE BEEN READIN' SO MUCH ABOUT! - LEAVE ME ALONE! I'LL CUT IT OUT - - I WILL!!
60

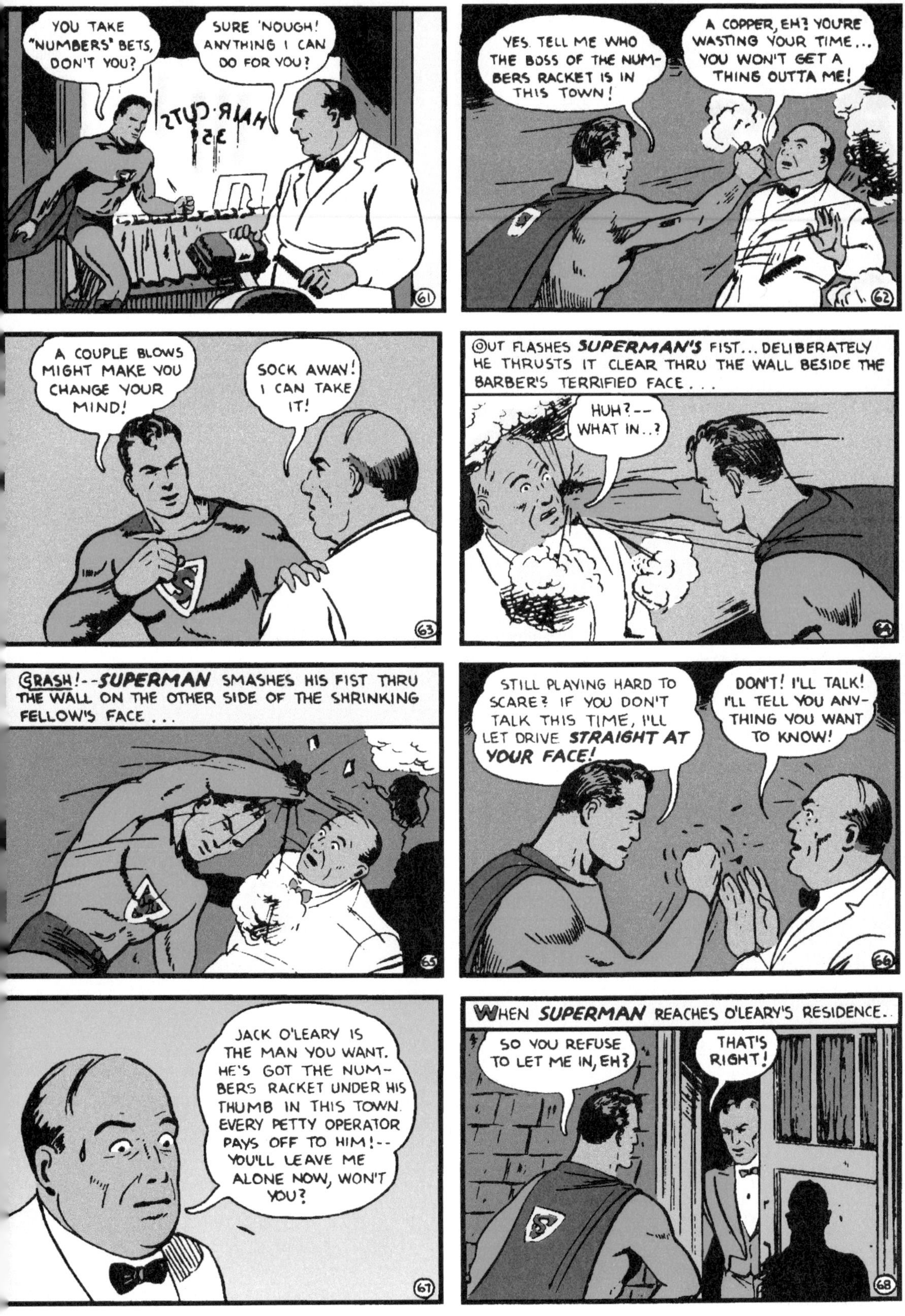
YOU TAKE "NUMBERS" BETS, DON'T YOU?
SURE 'NOUGH! ANYTHING I CAN DO FOR YOU?
HAIR CUTS 35¢
YES. TELL ME WHO THE BOSS OF THE NUMBERS RACKET IS IN THIS TOWN!
A COPPER, EH? YOU'RE WASTING YOUR TIME... YOU WON'T GET A THING OUTTA ME!
A COUPLE BLOWS MIGHT MAKE YOU CHANGE YOUR MIND!
SOCK AWAY! I CAN TAKE IT!
OUT FLASHES SUPERMAN'S FIST... DELIBERATELY HE THRUSTS IT CLEAR THRU THE WALL BESIDE THE BARBER'S TERRIFIED FACE...
HUH?-- WHAT IN..?
CRASH!--SUPERMAN SMASHES HIS FIST THRU THE WALL ON THE OTHER SIDE OF THE SHRINKING FELLOW'S FACE...
STILL PLAYING HARD TO SCARE? IF YOU DON'T TALK THIS TIME, I'LL LET DRIVE STRAIGHT AT YOUR FACE!
DON'T! I'LL TALK! I'LL TELL YOU ANYTHING YOU WANT TO KNOW!
JACK O'LEARY IS THE MAN YOU WANT. HE'S GOT THE NUMBERS RACKET UNDER HIS THUMB IN THIS TOWN. EVERY PETTY OPERATOR PAYS OFF TO HIM!--YOU'LL LEAVE ME ALONE NOW, WON'T YOU?
WHEN SUPERMAN REACHES O'LEARY'S RESIDENCE..
SO YOU REFUSE TO LET ME IN, EH?
THAT'S RIGHT!

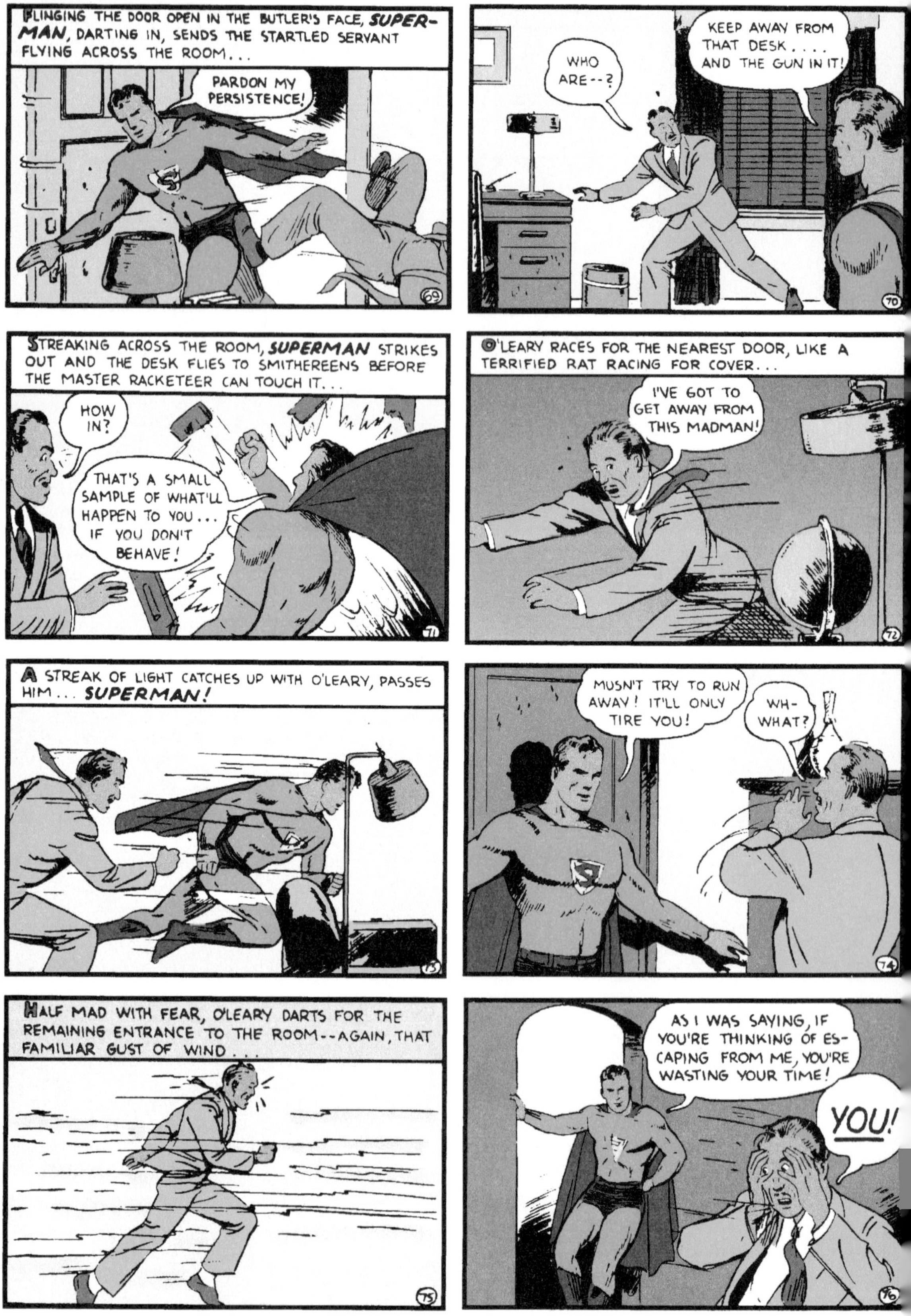
FLINGING THE DOOR OPEN IN THE BUTLER'S FACE, SUPERMAN, DARTING IN, SENDS THE STARTLED SERVANT FLYING ACROSS THE ROOM...
PARDON MY PERSISTENCE!
69
WHO ARE--?
KEEP AWAY FROM THAT DESK.... AND THE GUN IN IT!
70
STREAKING ACROSS THE ROOM, SUPERMAN STRIKES OUT AND THE DESK FLIES TO SMITHEREENS BEFORE THE MASTER RACKETEER CAN TOUCH IT...
HOW IN?
THAT'S A SMALL SAMPLE OF WHAT'LL HAPPEN TO YOU... IF YOU DON'T BEHAVE!
71
O'LEARY RACES FOR THE NEAREST DOOR, LIKE A TERRIFIED RAT RACING FOR COVER...
I'VE GOT TO GET AWAY FROM THIS MADMAN!
72
A STREAK OF LIGHT CATCHES UP WITH O'LEARY, PASSES HIM... SUPERMAN!
73
MUSN'T TRY TO RUN AWAY! IT'LL ONLY TIRE YOU!
WH-WHAT?
74
HALF MAD WITH FEAR, O'LEARY DARTS FOR THE REMAINING ENTRANCE TO THE ROOM--AGAIN, THAT FAMILIAR GUST OF WIND...
75
AS I WAS SAYING, IF YOU'RE THINKING OF ESCAPING FROM ME, YOU'RE WASTING YOUR TIME!
YOU!
76

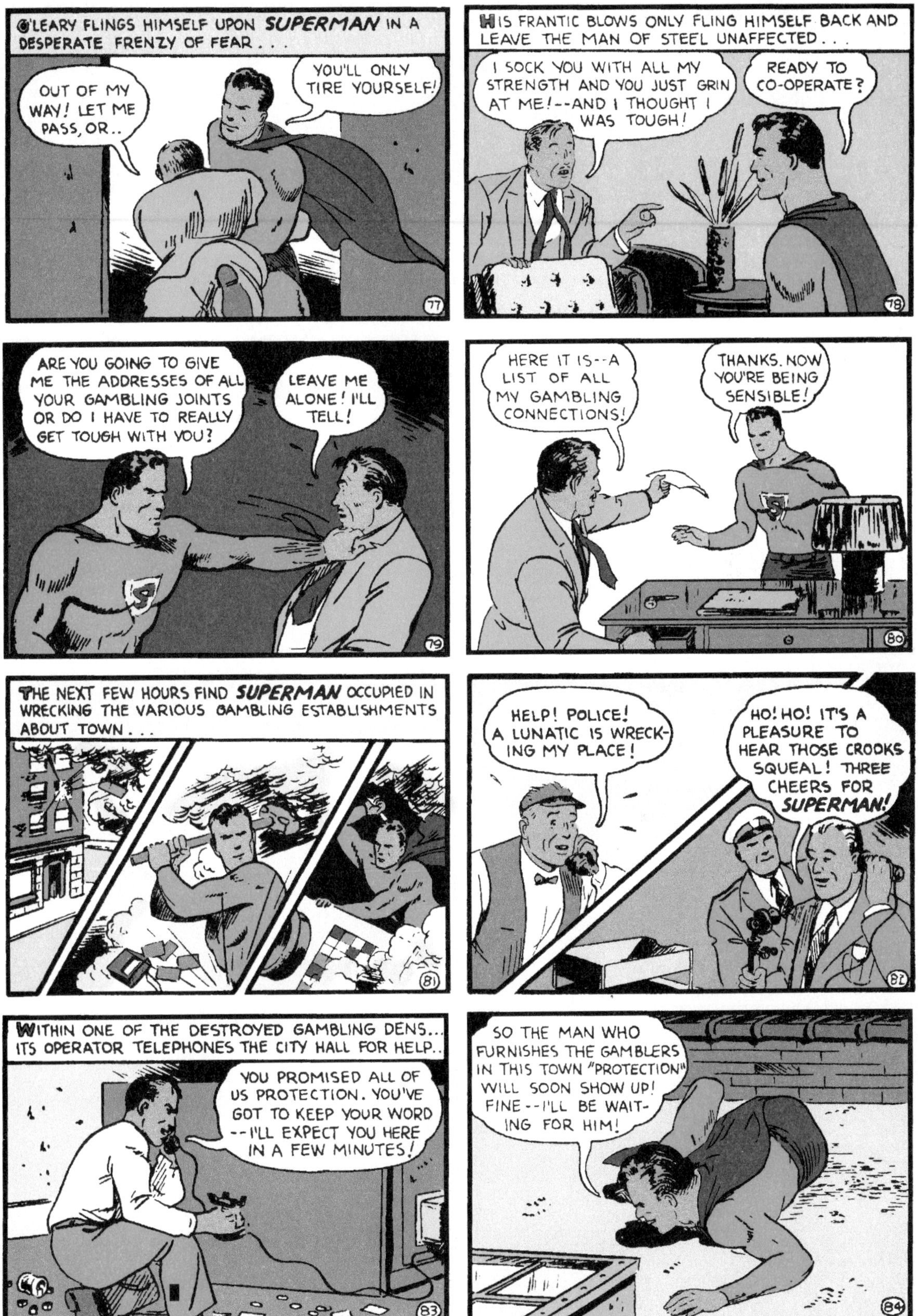
O'LEARY FLINGS HIMSELF UPON SUPERMAN IN A DESPERATE FRENZY OF FEAR . . .
OUT OF MY WAY! LET ME PASS, OR..
YOU'LL ONLY TIRE YOURSELF!
77
HIS FRANTIC BLOWS ONLY FLING HIMSELF BACK AND LEAVE THE MAN OF STEEL UNAFFECTED . . .
I SOCK YOU WITH ALL MY STRENGTH AND YOU JUST GRIN AT ME!--AND I THOUGHT I WAS TOUGH!
READY TO CO-OPERATE?
78
ARE YOU GOING TO GIVE ME THE ADDRESSES OF ALL YOUR GAMBLING JOINTS OR DO I HAVE TO REALLY GET TOUGH WITH YOU?
LEAVE ME ALONE! I'LL TELL!
79
HERE IT IS--A LIST OF ALL MY GAMBLING CONNECTIONS!
THANKS. NOW YOU'RE BEING SENSIBLE!
80
THE NEXT FEW HOURS FIND SUPERMAN OCCUPIED IN WRECKING THE VARIOUS GAMBLING ESTABLISHMENTS ABOUT TOWN . . .
81
HELP! POLICE! A LUNATIC IS WRECKING MY PLACE!
HO! HO! IT'S A PLEASURE TO HEAR THOSE CROOKS SQUEAL! THREE CHEERS FOR SUPERMAN!
82
WITHIN ONE OF THE DESTROYED GAMBLING DENS... ITS OPERATOR TELEPHONES THE CITY HALL FOR HELP..
YOU PROMISED ALL OF US PROTECTION. YOU'VE GOT TO KEEP YOUR WORD --I'LL EXPECT YOU HERE IN A FEW MINUTES!
83
SO THE MAN WHO FURNISHES THE GAMBLERS IN THIS TOWN "PROTECTION" WILL SOON SHOW UP! FINE--I'LL BE WAITING FOR HIM!
84

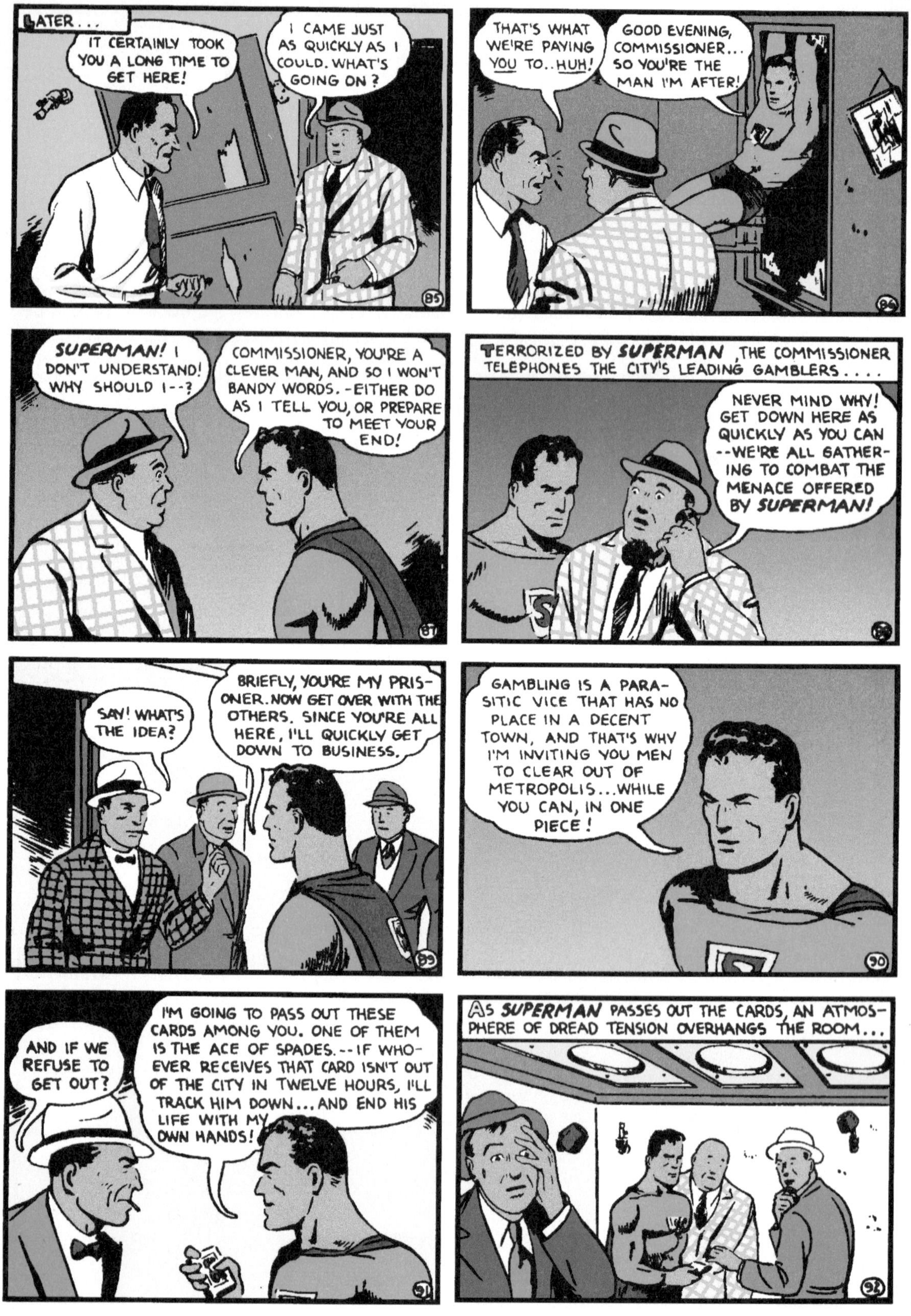
LATER...
IT CERTAINLY TOOK YOU A LONG TIME TO GET HERE!
I CAME JUST AS QUICKLY AS I COULD. WHAT'S GOING ON?
THAT'S WHAT WE'RE PAYING YOU TO.. HUH!
GOOD EVENING, COMMISSIONER... SO YOU'RE THE MAN I'M AFTER!
SUPERMAN! I DON'T UNDERSTAND! WHY SHOULD I--?
COMMISSIONER, YOU'RE A CLEVER MAN, AND SO I WON'T BANDY WORDS. -EITHER DO AS I TELL YOU, OR PREPARE TO MEET YOUR END!
TERRORIZED BY SUPERMAN, THE COMMISSIONER TELEPHONES THE CITY'S LEADING GAMBLERS....
NEVER MIND WHY! GET DOWN HERE AS QUICKLY AS YOU CAN --WE'RE ALL GATHERING TO COMBAT THE MENACE OFFERED BY SUPERMAN!
SAY! WHAT'S THE IDEA?
BRIEFLY, YOU'RE MY PRISONER. NOW GET OVER WITH THE OTHERS. SINCE YOU'RE ALL HERE, I'LL QUICKLY GET DOWN TO BUSINESS.
GAMBLING IS A PARASITIC VICE THAT HAS NO PLACE IN A DECENT TOWN, AND THAT'S WHY I'M INVITING YOU MEN TO CLEAR OUT OF METROPOLIS...WHILE YOU CAN, IN ONE PIECE!
AND IF WE REFUSE TO GET OUT?
I'M GOING TO PASS OUT THESE CARDS AMONG YOU. ONE OF THEM IS THE ACE OF SPADES.--IF WHOEVER RECEIVES THAT CARD ISN'T OUT OF THE CITY IN TWELVE HOURS, I'LL TRACK HIM DOWN...AND END HIS LIFE WITH MY OWN HANDS!
AS SUPERMAN PASSES OUT THE CARDS, AN ATMOSPHERE OF DREAD TENSION OVERHANGS THE ROOM...

FACES WHITEN WITH TERROR AS CARDS ARE HANDED TO THE GAMBLERS... WILL THEIR CHOICE BE THE DREAD ACE OF SPADES...?

WHEN *SUPERMAN* COLLECTS THE CARDS...

REMEMBER-TWELVE HOURS...NO MORE! AND NOW I LEAVE THE REST TO YOU!

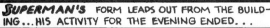
SUPERMAN'S FORM LEAPS OUT FROM THE BUILDING...HIS ACTIVITY FOR THE EVENING ENDED...

NEWS SECTION

PAGE 2.

COMMISSION RESIGNS—

by CLARK KENT

SUBMITS IT

NO DOUBT AS A RESULT OF *SUPERMAN'S* ACTIVITIES THE CITY WAS RID OF ITS GAMBLERS TODAY, AS THEY DEPARTED IN A MAD RUSH FOR PARTS UNKNOWN!

YOU COVERED THAT GAMBLING YARN VERY WELL.--BUT I WONDER HOW *SUPERMAN* GOT ALL THOSE CROOKS TO VACATE SO QUICKLY?

I DON'T KNOW.-- BUT I BET IT WOULD MAKE A GOOD STORY!

REPLACE ALL CLIPPINGS

LATER..:WHEN CLARK IS ALONE, HE REMOVES A DECK OF CARDS FROM HIS POCKET...

ALL OF THEM...THE ACE OF SPADES! THE IRONY OF IT! TRICKING A BUNCH OF EXPERIENCED GAMBLERS WITH A "FIXED DECK"!

THE END

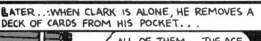

SUPERMAN
AT THE NEW YORK WORLD'S FAIR!

YOU CAN READ THIS THRILLING EPISODE OF **SUPERMAN** IN THE **NEW YORK WORLD'S FAIR COMICS!**

THE BACK INSIDE COVER OF THIS MAGAZINE WILL TELL YOU HOW TO GET YOUR COPY OF THIS DANDY BOOK! DON'T MISS IT!

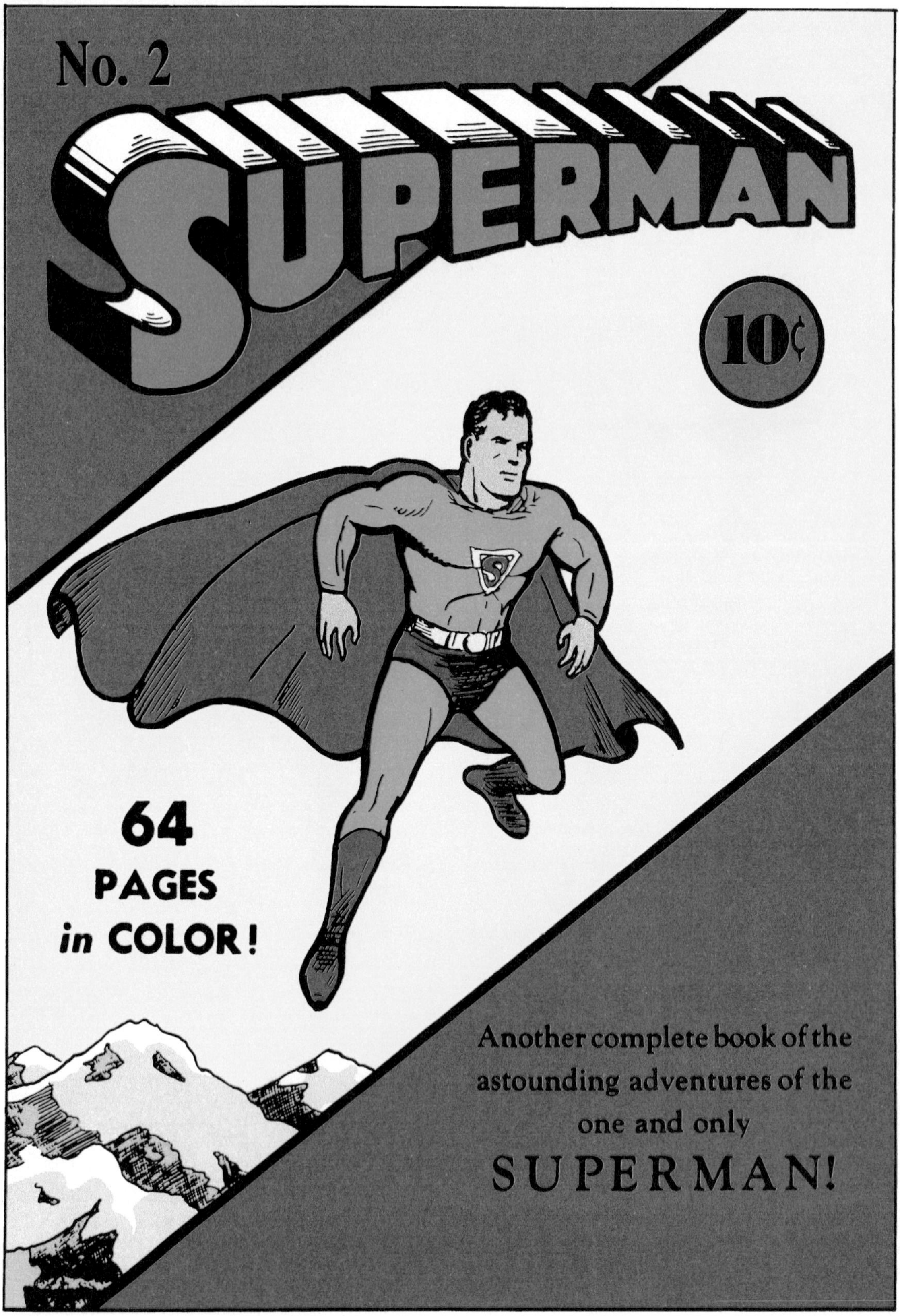
No. 2
SUPERMAN
10¢
64
PAGES
in COLOR!
Another complete book of the
astounding adventures of the
one and only
SUPERMAN!

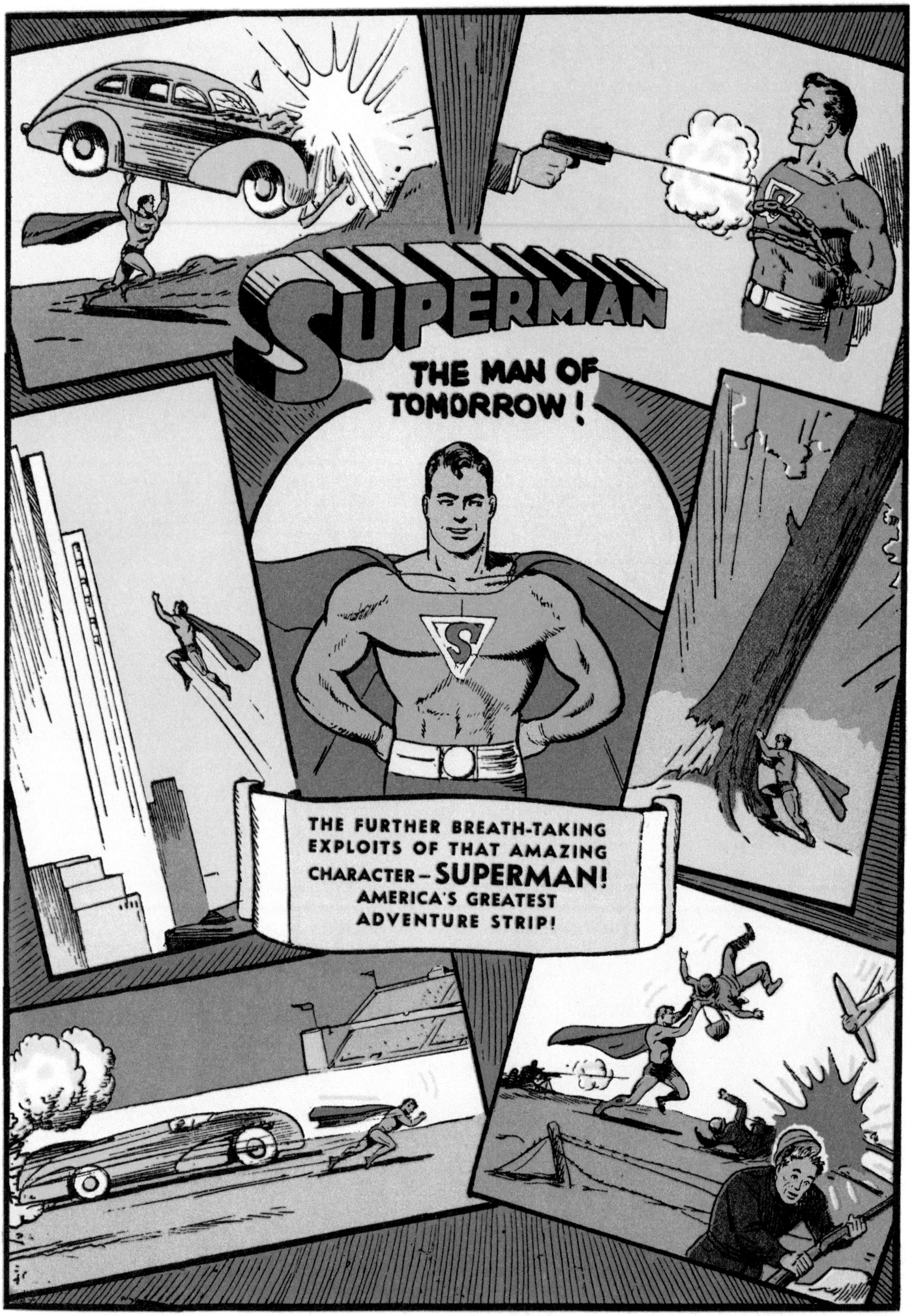
SUPERMAN
THE MAN OF TOMORROW!
THE FURTHER BREATH-TAKING EXPLOITS OF THAT AMAZING CHARACTER–SUPERMAN!
AMERICA'S GREATEST ADVENTURE STRIP!

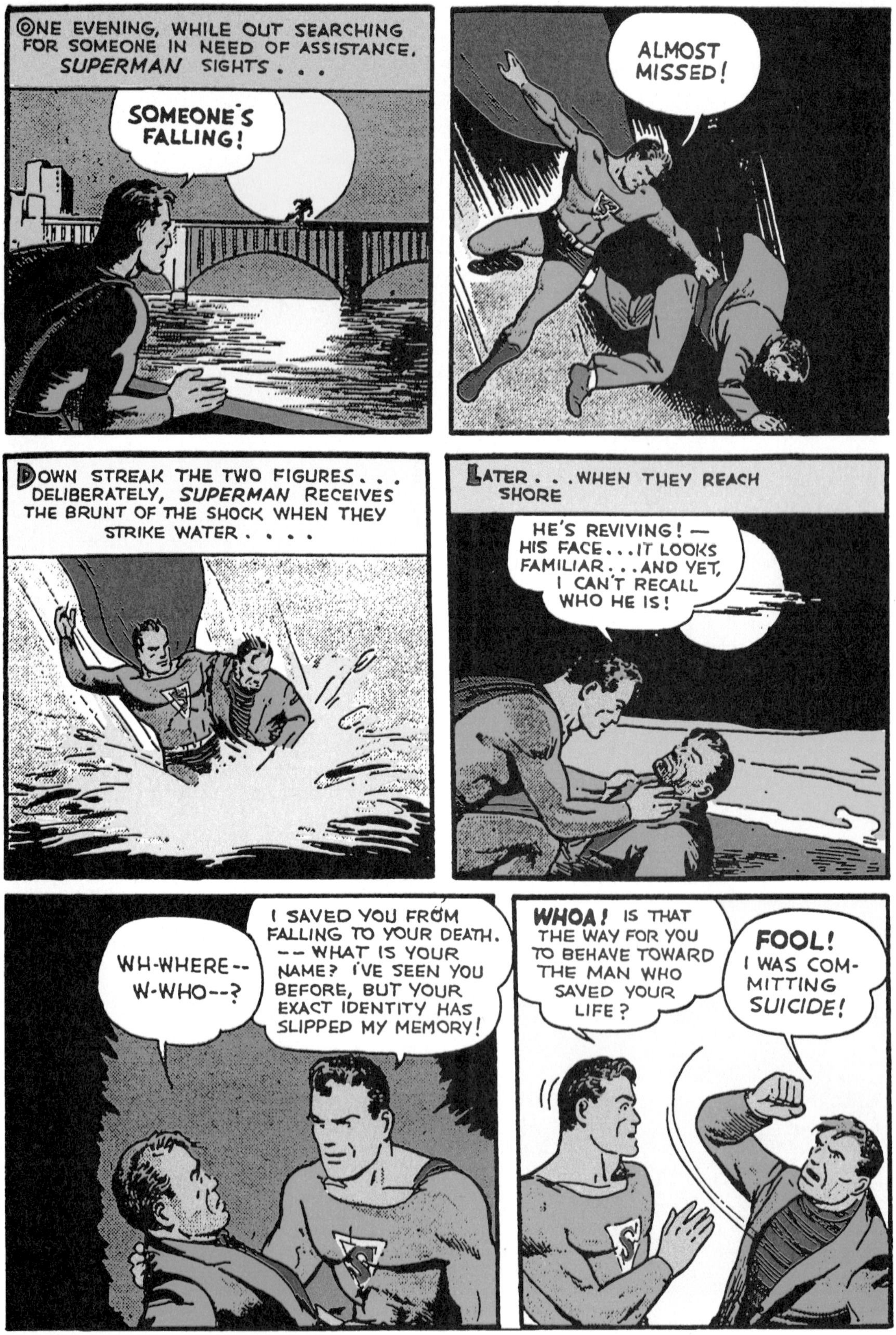
ONE EVENING, WHILE OUT SEARCHING FOR SOMEONE IN NEED OF ASSISTANCE, SUPERMAN SIGHTS . . .
SOMEONE'S FALLING!
ALMOST MISSED!
DOWN STREAK THE TWO FIGURES . . . DELIBERATELY, SUPERMAN RECEIVES THE BRUNT OF THE SHOCK WHEN THEY STRIKE WATER . . . .
LATER . . . WHEN THEY REACH SHORE
HE'S REVIVING! — HIS FACE . . . IT LOOKS FAMILIAR . . . AND YET, I CAN'T RECALL WHO HE IS!
WH-WHERE-- W-WHO--?
I SAVED YOU FROM FALLING TO YOUR DEATH. -- WHAT IS YOUR NAME? I'VE SEEN YOU BEFORE, BUT YOUR EXACT IDENTITY HAS SLIPPED MY MEMORY!
WHOA! IS THAT THE WAY FOR YOU TO BEHAVE TOWARD THE MAN WHO SAVED YOUR LIFE?
FOOL! I WAS COMMITTING SUICIDE!

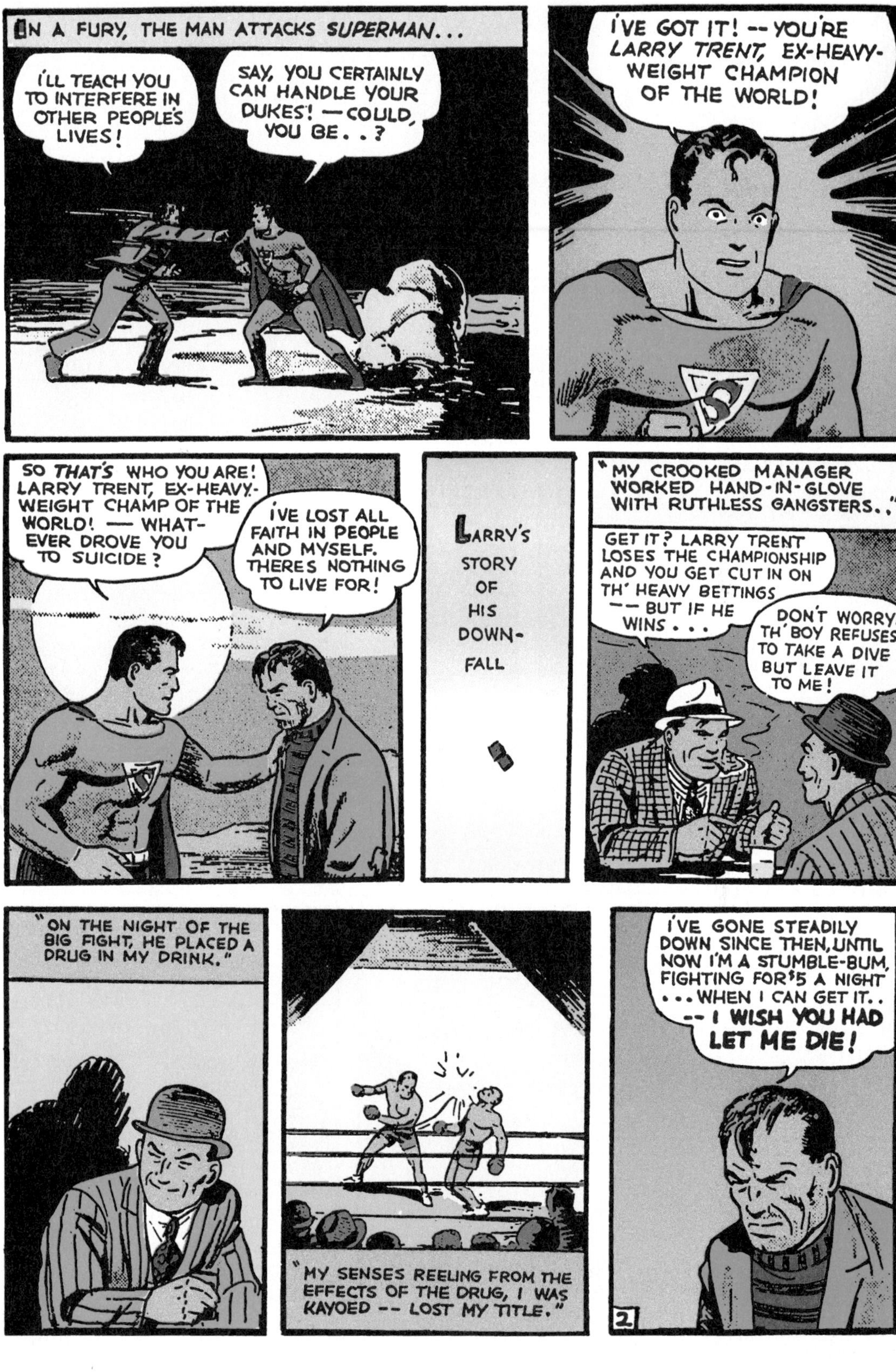

IN A FURY, THE MAN ATTACKS SUPERMAN...
I'LL TEACH YOU TO INTERFERE IN OTHER PEOPLE'S LIVES!
SAY, YOU CERTAINLY CAN HANDLE YOUR DUKES! — COULD, YOU BE..?
I'VE GOT IT! -- YOU'RE LARRY TRENT, EX-HEAVY-WEIGHT CHAMPION OF THE WORLD!
SO THAT'S WHO YOU ARE! LARRY TRENT, EX-HEAVY-WEIGHT CHAMP OF THE WORLD! — WHAT-EVER DROVE YOU TO SUICIDE?
I'VE LOST ALL FAITH IN PEOPLE AND MYSELF. THERES NOTHING TO LIVE FOR!
LARRY'S STORY OF HIS DOWN-FALL
"MY CROOKED MANAGER WORKED HAND-IN-GLOVE WITH RUTHLESS GANGSTERS.."
GET IT? LARRY TRENT LOSES THE CHAMPIONSHIP AND YOU GET CUT IN ON TH' HEAVY BETTINGS -- BUT IF HE WINS...
DON'T WORRY. TH' BOY REFUSES TO TAKE A DIVE BUT LEAVE IT TO ME!
"ON THE NIGHT OF THE BIG FIGHT, HE PLACED A DRUG IN MY DRINK."
"MY SENSES REELING FROM THE EFFECTS OF THE DRUG, I WAS KAYOED -- LOST MY TITLE."
I'VE GONE STEADILY DOWN SINCE THEN, UNTIL NOW I'M A STUMBLE-BUM, FIGHTING FOR $5 A NIGHT ...WHEN I CAN GET IT.. -- I WISH YOU HAD LET ME DIE!
2

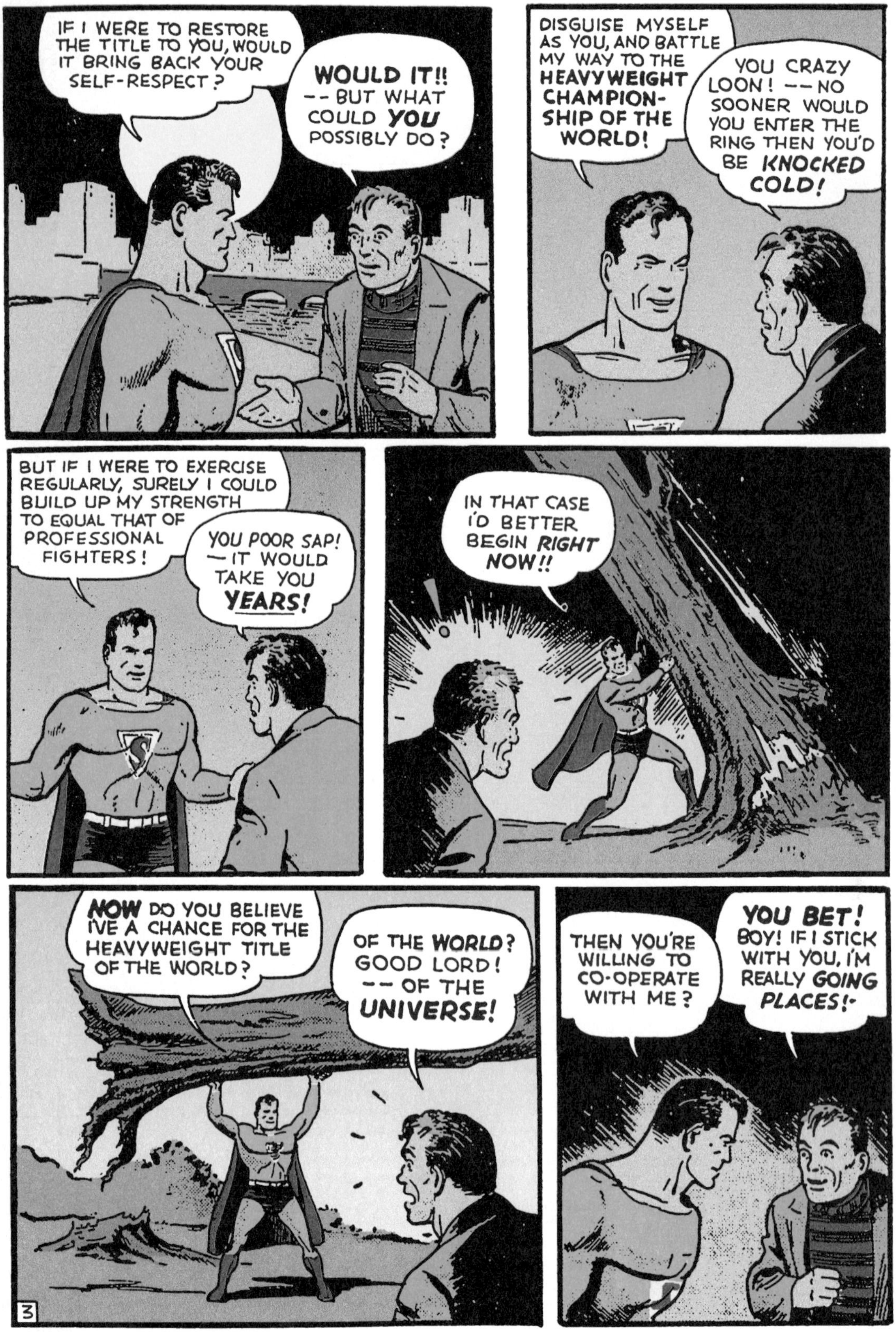
IF I WERE TO RESTORE THE TITLE TO YOU, WOULD IT BRING BACK YOUR SELF-RESPECT?
WOULD IT!! -- BUT WHAT COULD YOU POSSIBLY DO?
DISGUISE MYSELF AS YOU, AND BATTLE MY WAY TO THE HEAVYWEIGHT CHAMPIONSHIP OF THE WORLD!
YOU CRAZY LOON! -- NO SOONER WOULD YOU ENTER THE RING THEN YOU'D BE KNOCKED COLD!
BUT IF I WERE TO EXERCISE REGULARLY, SURELY I COULD BUILD UP MY STRENGTH TO EQUAL THAT OF PROFESSIONAL FIGHTERS!
YOU POOR SAP! — IT WOULD TAKE YOU YEARS!
IN THAT CASE I'D BETTER BEGIN RIGHT NOW!!
NOW DO YOU BELIEVE I'VE A CHANCE FOR THE HEAVYWEIGHT TITLE OF THE WORLD?
OF THE WORLD? GOOD LORD! -- OF THE UNIVERSE!
3
THEN YOU'RE WILLING TO CO-OPERATE WITH ME?
YOU BET! BOY! IF I STICK WITH YOU, I'M REALLY GOING PLACES!-

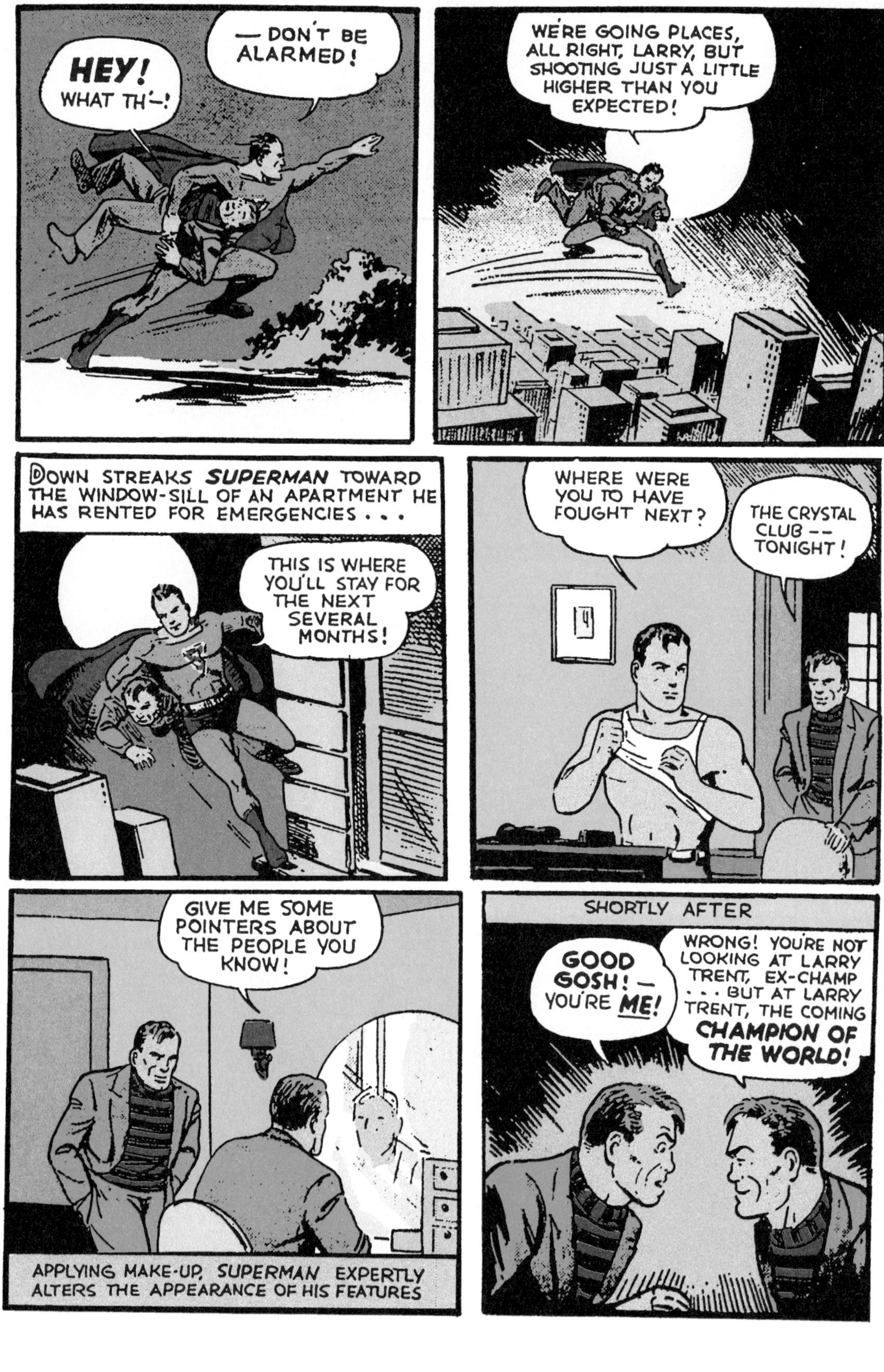
HEY! WHAT TH'—!
— DON'T BE ALARMED!
WE'RE GOING PLACES, ALL RIGHT, LARRY, BUT SHOOTING JUST A LITTLE HIGHER THAN YOU EXPECTED!
DOWN STREAKS SUPERMAN TOWARD THE WINDOW-SILL OF AN APARTMENT HE HAS RENTED FOR EMERGENCIES . . .
THIS IS WHERE YOU'LL STAY FOR THE NEXT SEVERAL MONTHS!
WHERE WERE YOU TO HAVE FOUGHT NEXT?
THE CRYSTAL CLUB -- TONIGHT!
GIVE ME SOME POINTERS ABOUT THE PEOPLE YOU KNOW!
APPLYING MAKE-UP, SUPERMAN EXPERTLY ALTERS THE APPEARANCE OF HIS FEATURES
SHORTLY AFTER
GOOD GOSH! — YOU'RE ME!
WRONG! YOU'RE NOT LOOKING AT LARRY TRENT, EX-CHAMP . . . BUT AT LARRY TRENT, THE COMING CHAMPION OF THE WORLD!

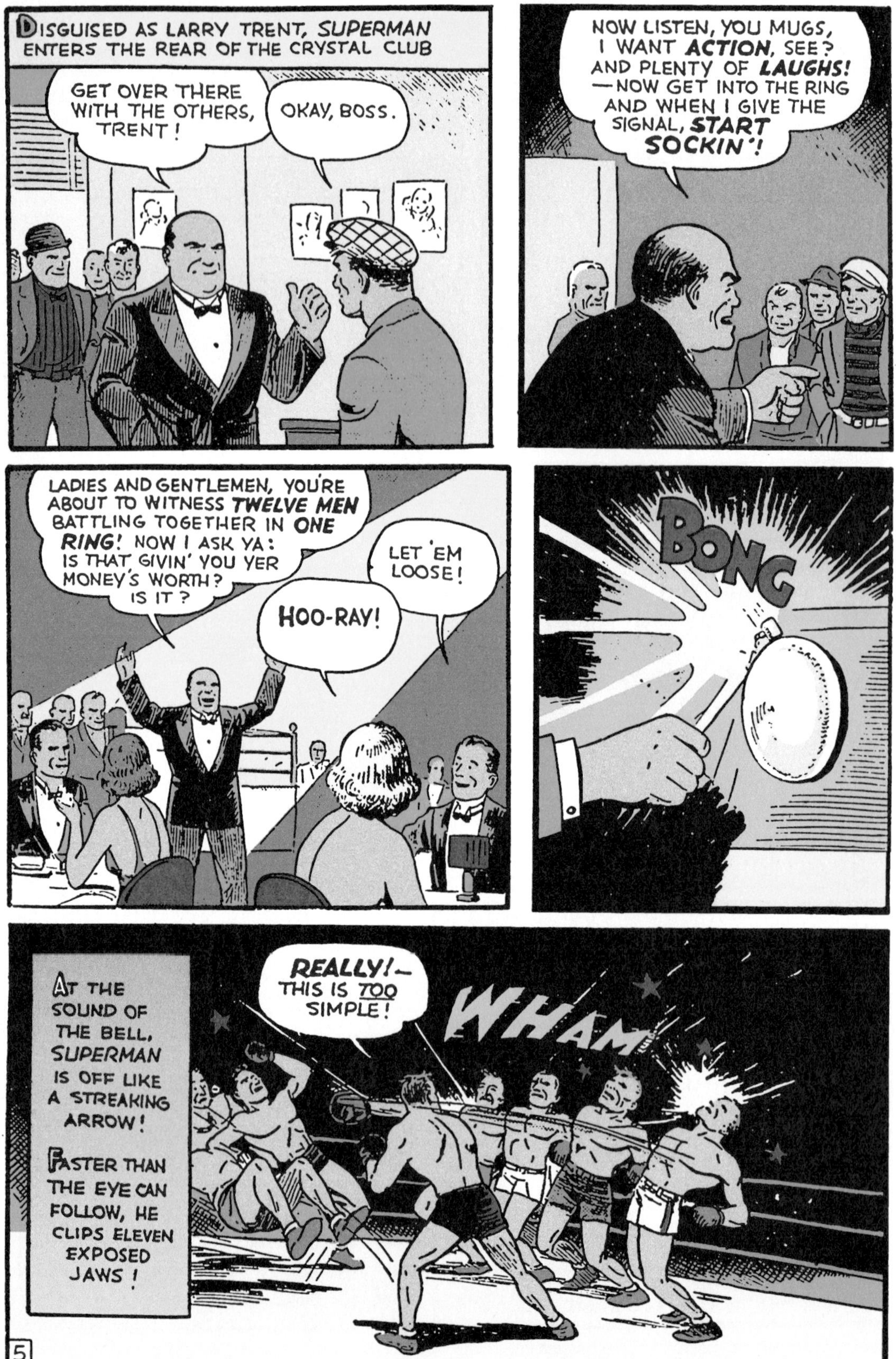

DISGUISED AS LARRY TRENT, SUPERMAN ENTERS THE REAR OF THE CRYSTAL CLUB
GET OVER THERE WITH THE OTHERS, TRENT!
OKAY, BOSS.
NOW LISTEN, YOU MUGS, I WANT ACTION, SEE? AND PLENTY OF LAUGHS! —NOW GET INTO THE RING AND WHEN I GIVE THE SIGNAL, START SOCKIN'!
LADIES AND GENTLEMEN, YOU'RE ABOUT TO WITNESS TWELVE MEN BATTLING TOGETHER IN ONE RING! NOW I ASK YA: IS THAT GIVIN' YOU YER MONEY'S WORTH? IS IT?
LET 'EM LOOSE!
HOO-RAY!
BONG
AT THE SOUND OF THE BELL, SUPERMAN IS OFF LIKE A STREAKING ARROW!
FASTER THAN THE EYE CAN FOLLOW, HE CLIPS ELEVEN EXPOSED JAWS!
REALLY! — THIS IS TOO SIMPLE!
WHAM
5

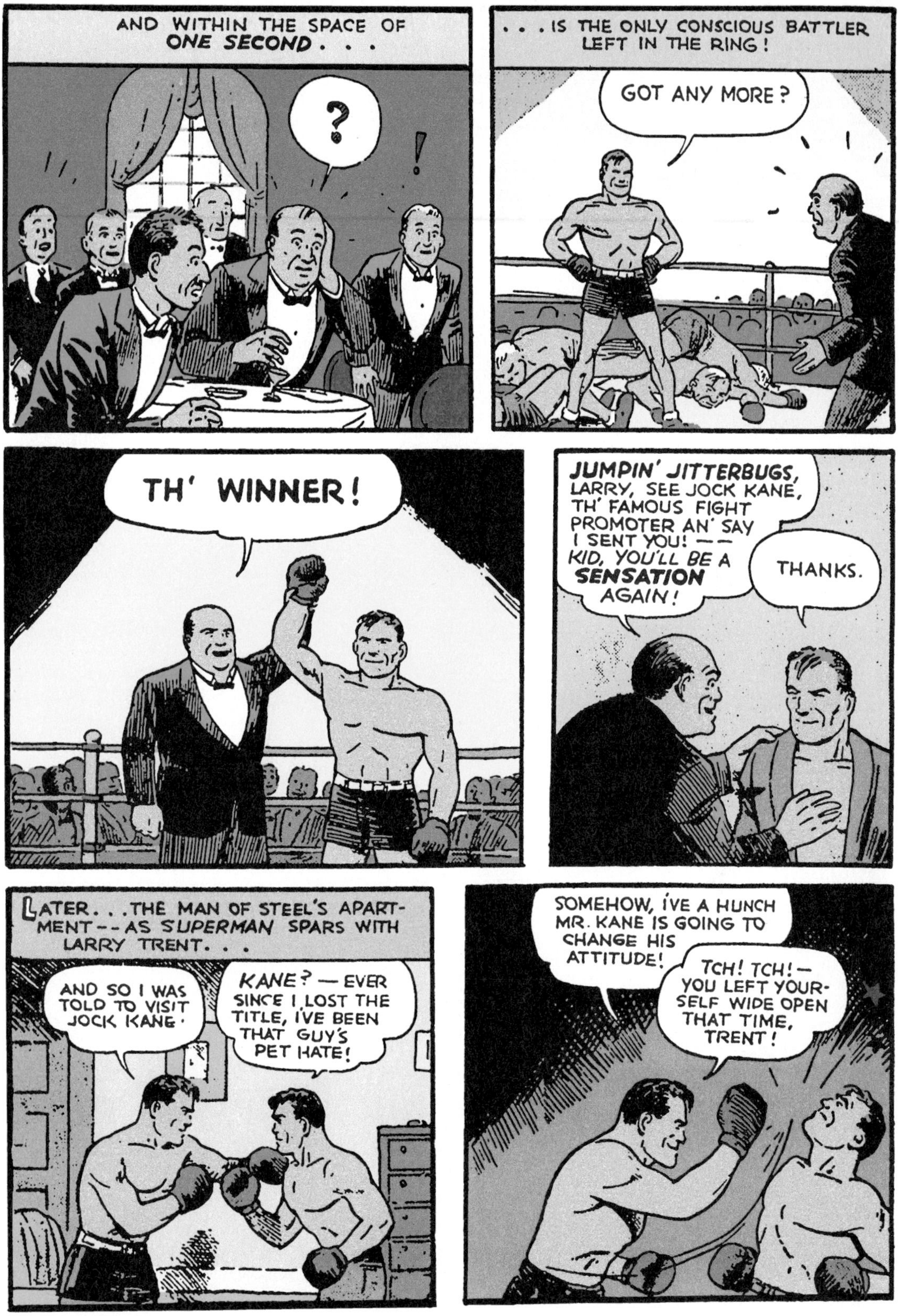
AND WITHIN THE SPACE OF ONE SECOND . . .
?
!
. . . IS THE ONLY CONSCIOUS BATTLER LEFT IN THE RING!
GOT ANY MORE?
TH' WINNER!
JUMPIN' JITTERBUGS, LARRY, SEE JOCK KANE, TH' FAMOUS FIGHT PROMOTER AN' SAY I SENT YOU! -- KID, YOU'LL BE A SENSATION AGAIN!
THANKS.
LATER. . . THE MAN OF STEEL'S APARTMENT--AS SUPERMAN SPARS WITH LARRY TRENT. . .
AND SO I WAS TOLD TO VISIT JOCK KANE.
KANE? — EVER SINCE I LOST THE TITLE, I'VE BEEN THAT GUY'S PET HATE!
SOMEHOW, I'VE A HUNCH MR. KANE IS GOING TO CHANGE HIS ATTITUDE!
TCH! TCH! — YOU LEFT YOURSELF WIDE OPEN THAT TIME, TRENT!

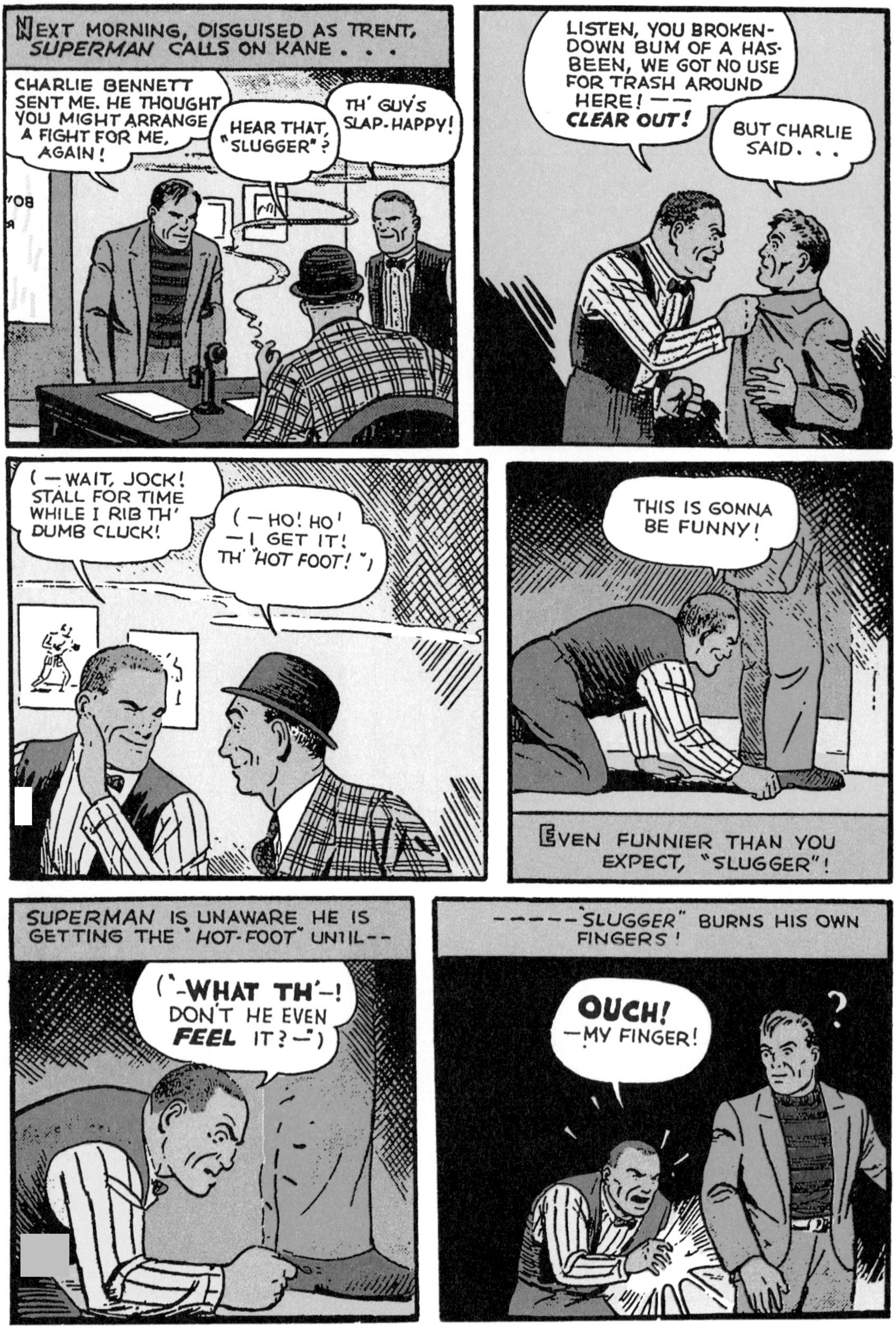
NEXT MORNING, DISGUISED AS TRENT, SUPERMAN CALLS ON KANE . . .
CHARLIE BENNETT SENT ME. HE THOUGHT YOU MIGHT ARRANGE A FIGHT FOR ME, AGAIN!
HEAR THAT, "SLUGGER"?
TH' GUY'S SLAP-HAPPY!
LISTEN, YOU BROKEN-DOWN BUM OF A HAS-BEEN, WE GOT NO USE FOR TRASH AROUND HERE! -- CLEAR OUT!
BUT CHARLIE SAID . . .
(-- WAIT, JOCK! STALL FOR TIME WHILE I RIB TH' DUMB CLUCK!
(-- HO! HO! -- I GET IT! TH' "HOT FOOT!")
THIS IS GONNA BE FUNNY!
EVEN FUNNIER THAN YOU EXPECT, "SLUGGER"!
SUPERMAN IS UNAWARE HE IS GETTING THE "HOT-FOOT" UNTIL--
("-WHAT TH'-! DON'T HE EVEN FEEL IT?-")
-----"SLUGGER" BURNS HIS OWN FINGERS!
OUCH! -MY FINGER!
?

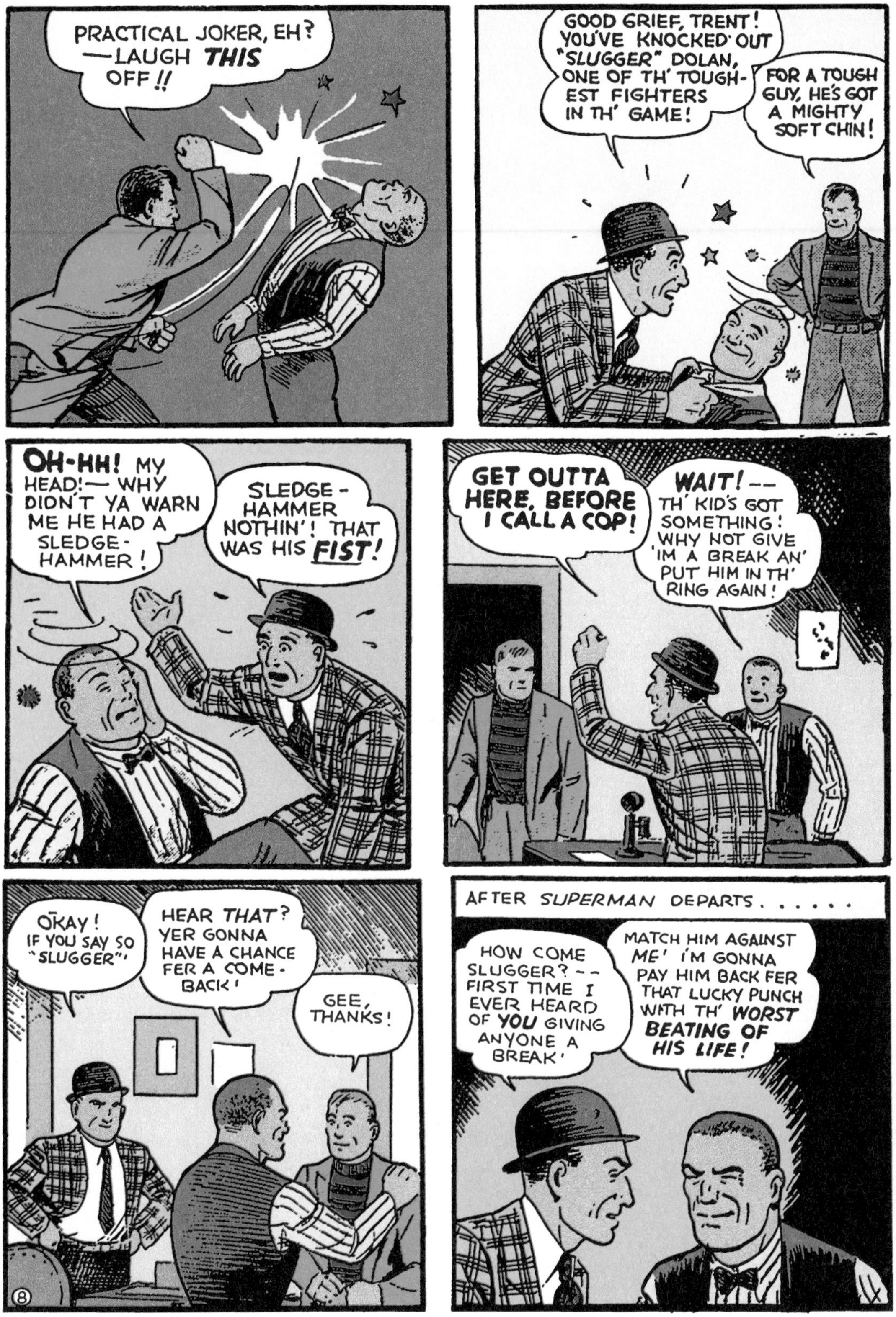
PRACTICAL JOKER, EH? —LAUGH THIS OFF!!
GOOD GRIEF, TRENT! YOU'VE KNOCKED OUT "SLUGGER" DOLAN, ONE OF TH' TOUGHEST FIGHTERS IN TH' GAME!
FOR A TOUGH GUY, HE'S GOT A MIGHTY SOFT CHIN!
OH-HH! MY HEAD!— WHY DIDN'T YA WARN ME HE HAD A SLEDGE-HAMMER!
SLEDGE-HAMMER NOTHIN'! THAT WAS HIS FIST!
GET OUTTA HERE, BEFORE I CALL A COP!
WAIT!-- TH' KID'S GOT SOMETHING! WHY NOT GIVE 'IM A BREAK AN' PUT HIM IN TH' RING AGAIN!
OKAY! IF YOU SAY SO "SLUGGER"!
HEAR THAT? YER GONNA HAVE A CHANCE FER A COME-BACK!
GEE, THANKS!
8
AFTER SUPERMAN DEPARTS . . . . .
HOW COME SLUGGER? -- FIRST TIME I EVER HEARD OF YOU GIVING ANYONE A BREAK!
MATCH HIM AGAINST ME! I'M GONNA PAY HIM BACK FER THAT LUCKY PUNCH WITH TH' WORST BEATING OF HIS LIFE!

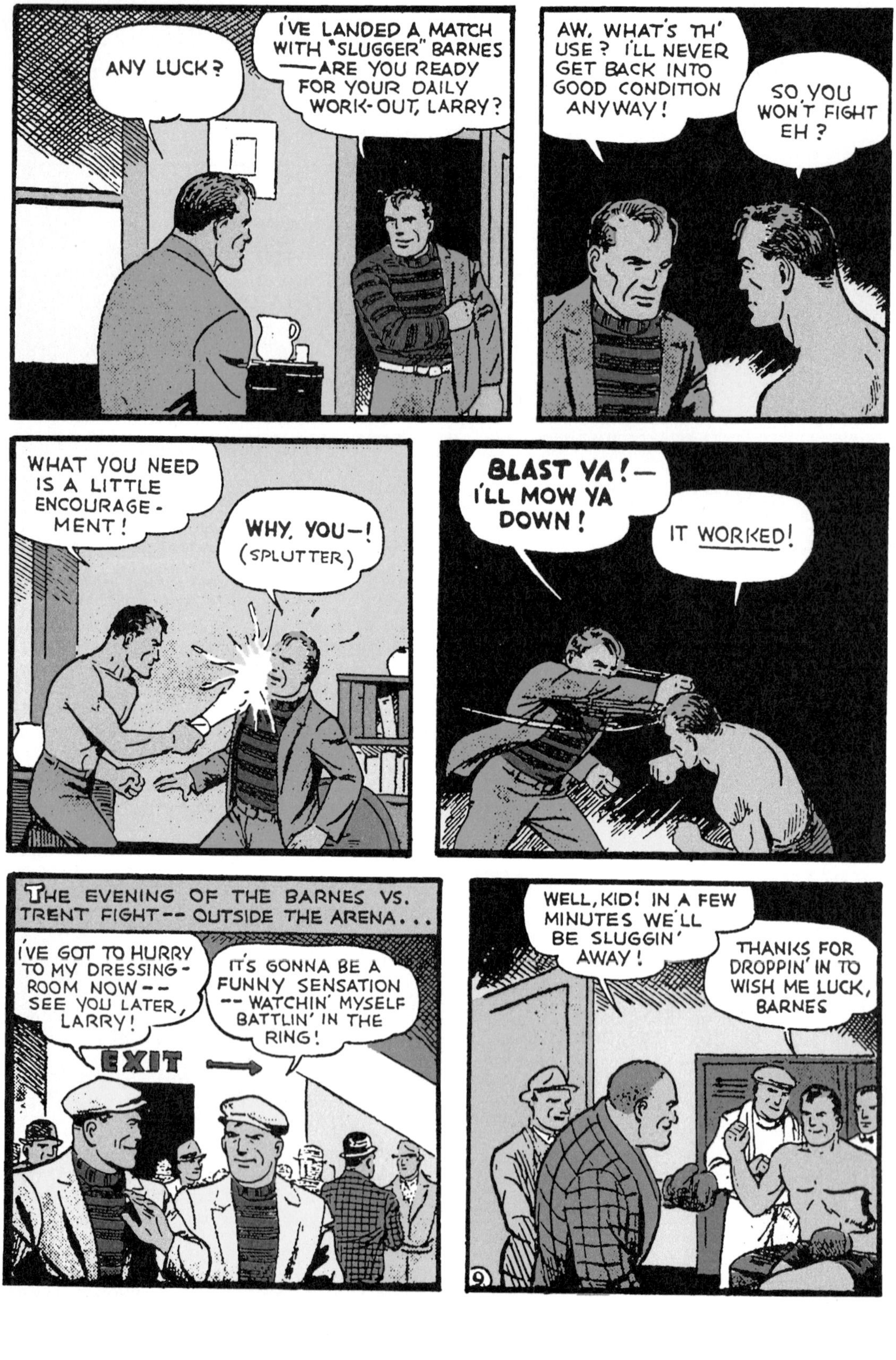
ANY LUCK?
I'VE LANDED A MATCH WITH "SLUGGER" BARNES —ARE YOU READY FOR YOUR DAILY WORK-OUT, LARRY?
AW, WHAT'S TH' USE? I'LL NEVER GET BACK INTO GOOD CONDITION ANYWAY!
SO, YOU WON'T FIGHT EH?
WHAT YOU NEED IS A LITTLE ENCOURAGE-MENT!
WHY, YOU—! (SPLUTTER)
BLAST YA!— I'LL MOW YA DOWN!
IT WORKED!
THE EVENING OF THE BARNES VS. TRENT FIGHT-- OUTSIDE THE ARENA...
I'VE GOT TO HURRY TO MY DRESSING-ROOM NOW-- SEE YOU LATER, LARRY!
IT'S GONNA BE A FUNNY SENSATION -- WATCHIN' MYSELF BATTLIN' IN THE RING!
EXIT
WELL, KID! IN A FEW MINUTES WE'LL BE SLUGGIN' AWAY!
THANKS FOR DROPPIN' IN TO WISH ME LUCK, BARNES
9

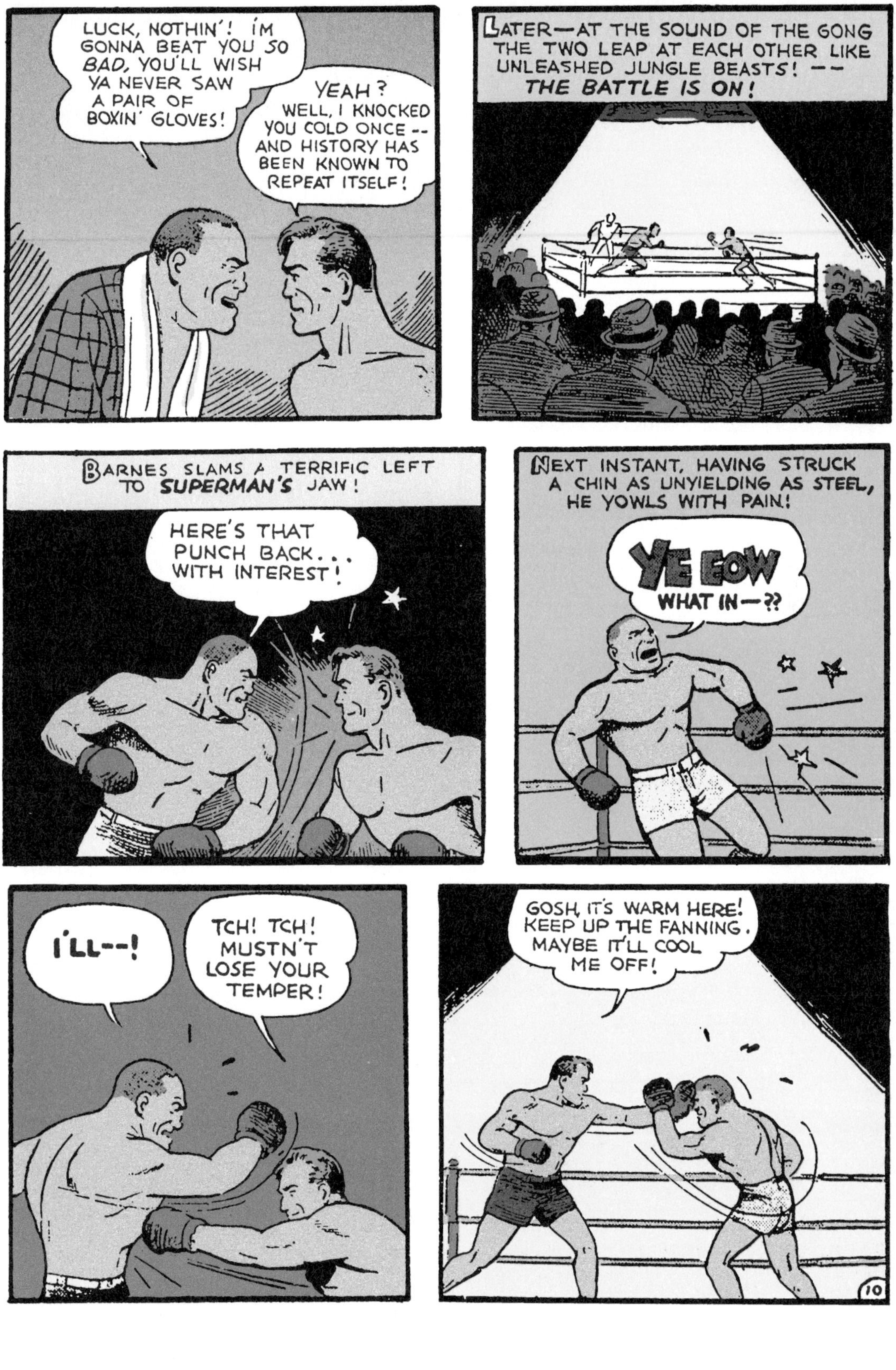
LUCK, NOTHIN'! I'M GONNA BEAT YOU SO BAD, YOU'LL WISH YA NEVER SAW A PAIR OF BOXIN' GLOVES!
YEAH? WELL, I KNOCKED YOU COLD ONCE -- AND HISTORY HAS BEEN KNOWN TO REPEAT ITSELF!
LATER—AT THE SOUND OF THE GONG THE TWO LEAP AT EACH OTHER LIKE UNLEASHED JUNGLE BEASTS! -- THE BATTLE IS ON!
BARNES SLAMS A TERRIFIC LEFT TO SUPERMAN'S JAW!
HERE'S THAT PUNCH BACK... WITH INTEREST!
NEXT INSTANT, HAVING STRUCK A CHIN AS UNYIELDING AS STEEL, HE YOWLS WITH PAIN!
YE EOW
WHAT IN—??
I'LL--!
TCH! TCH! MUSTN'T LOSE YOUR TEMPER!
GOSH, IT'S WARM HERE! KEEP UP THE FANNING. MAYBE IT'LL COOL ME OFF!
10

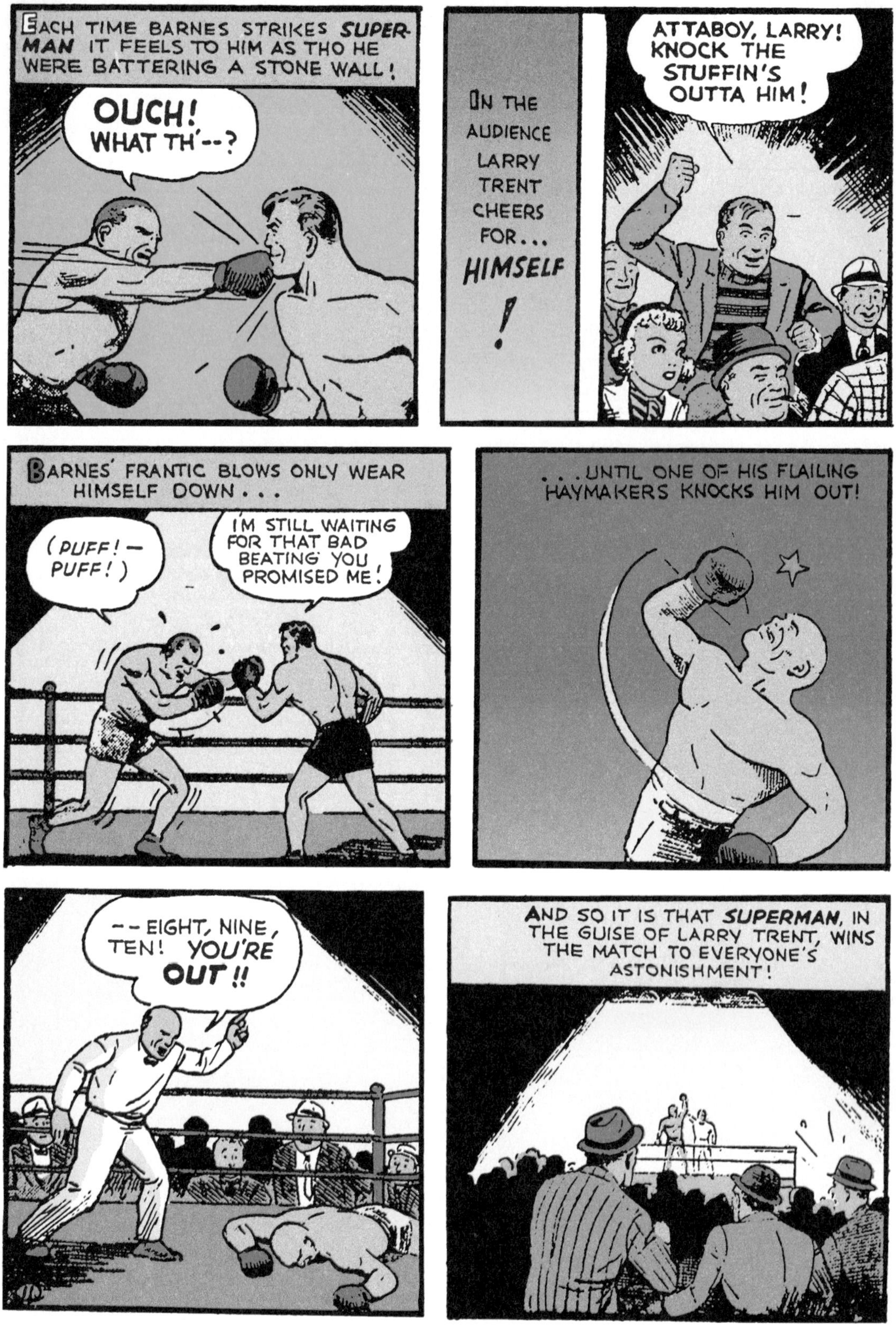
EACH TIME BARNES STRIKES SUPERMAN IT FEELS TO HIM AS THO HE WERE BATTERING A STONE WALL!
OUCH! WHAT TH'--?
IN THE AUDIENCE LARRY TRENT CHEERS FOR... HIMSELF!
ATTABOY, LARRY! KNOCK THE STUFFIN'S OUTTA HIM!
BARNES' FRANTIC BLOWS ONLY WEAR HIMSELF DOWN...
(PUFF!— PUFF!)
I'M STILL WAITING FOR THAT BAD BEATING YOU PROMISED ME!
...UNTIL ONE OF HIS FLAILING HAYMAKERS KNOCKS HIM OUT!
--EIGHT, NINE, TEN! YOU'RE OUT!!
AND SO IT IS THAT SUPERMAN, IN THE GUISE OF LARRY TRENT, WINS THE MATCH TO EVERYONE'S ASTONISHMENT!

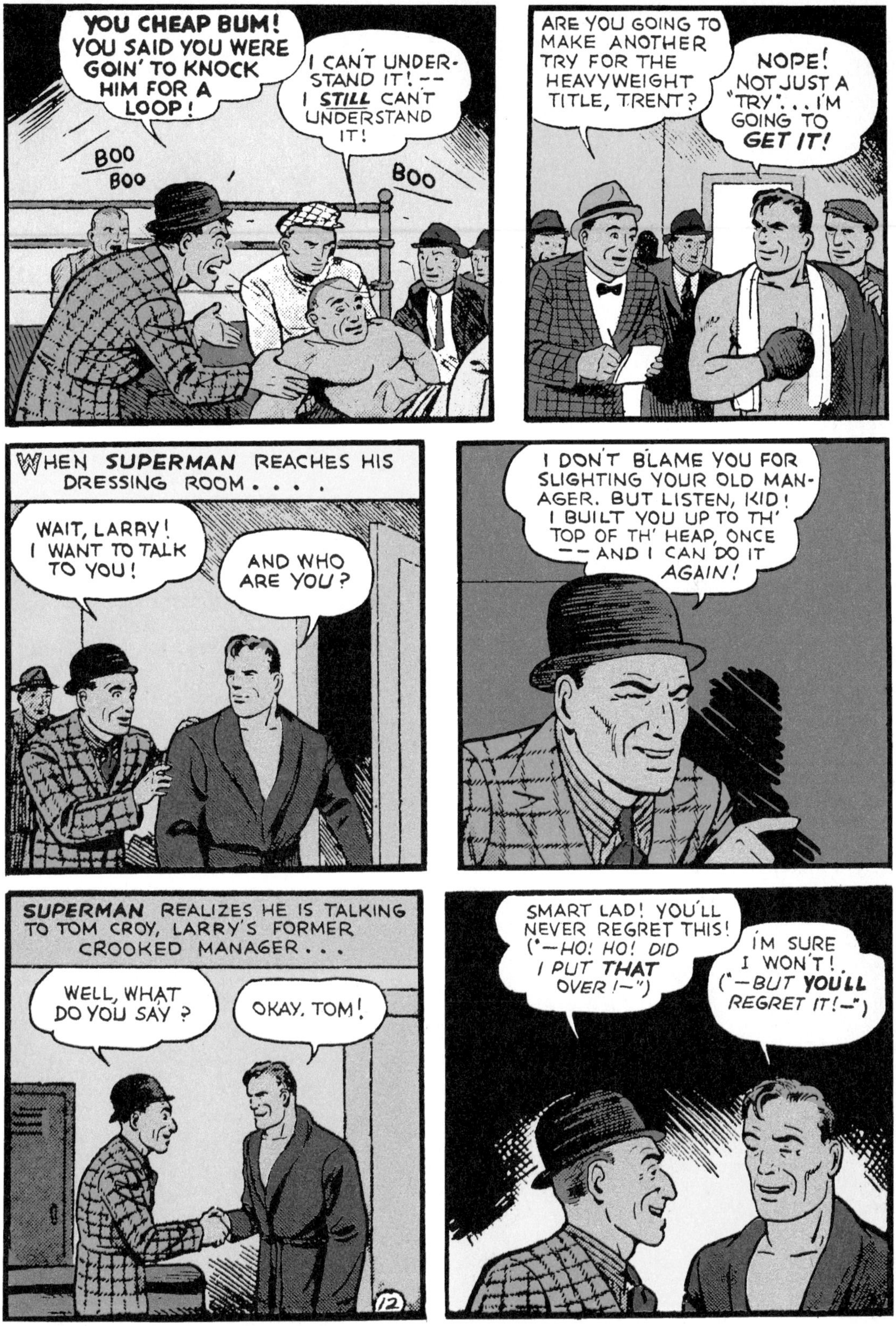
YOU CHEAP BUM! YOU SAID YOU WERE GOIN' TO KNOCK HIM FOR A LOOP!
I CAN'T UNDERSTAND IT! -- I STILL CAN'T UNDERSTAND IT!
BOO
BOO
BOO
ARE YOU GOING TO MAKE ANOTHER TRY FOR THE HEAVYWEIGHT TITLE, TRENT?
NOPE! NOT JUST A "TRY"... I'M GOING TO GET IT!
WHEN SUPERMAN REACHES HIS DRESSING ROOM....
WAIT, LARRY! I WANT TO TALK TO YOU!
AND WHO ARE YOU?
I DON'T BLAME YOU FOR SLIGHTING YOUR OLD MANAGER. BUT LISTEN, KID! I BUILT YOU UP TO TH' TOP OF TH' HEAP, ONCE -- AND I CAN DO IT AGAIN!
SUPERMAN REALIZES HE IS TALKING TO TOM CROY, LARRY'S FORMER CROOKED MANAGER...
WELL, WHAT DO YOU SAY?
OKAY, TOM!
12
SMART LAD! YOU'LL NEVER REGRET THIS! ("—HO! HO! DID I PUT THAT OVER!—")
I'M SURE I WON'T! ("—BUT YOU'LL REGRET IT!—")

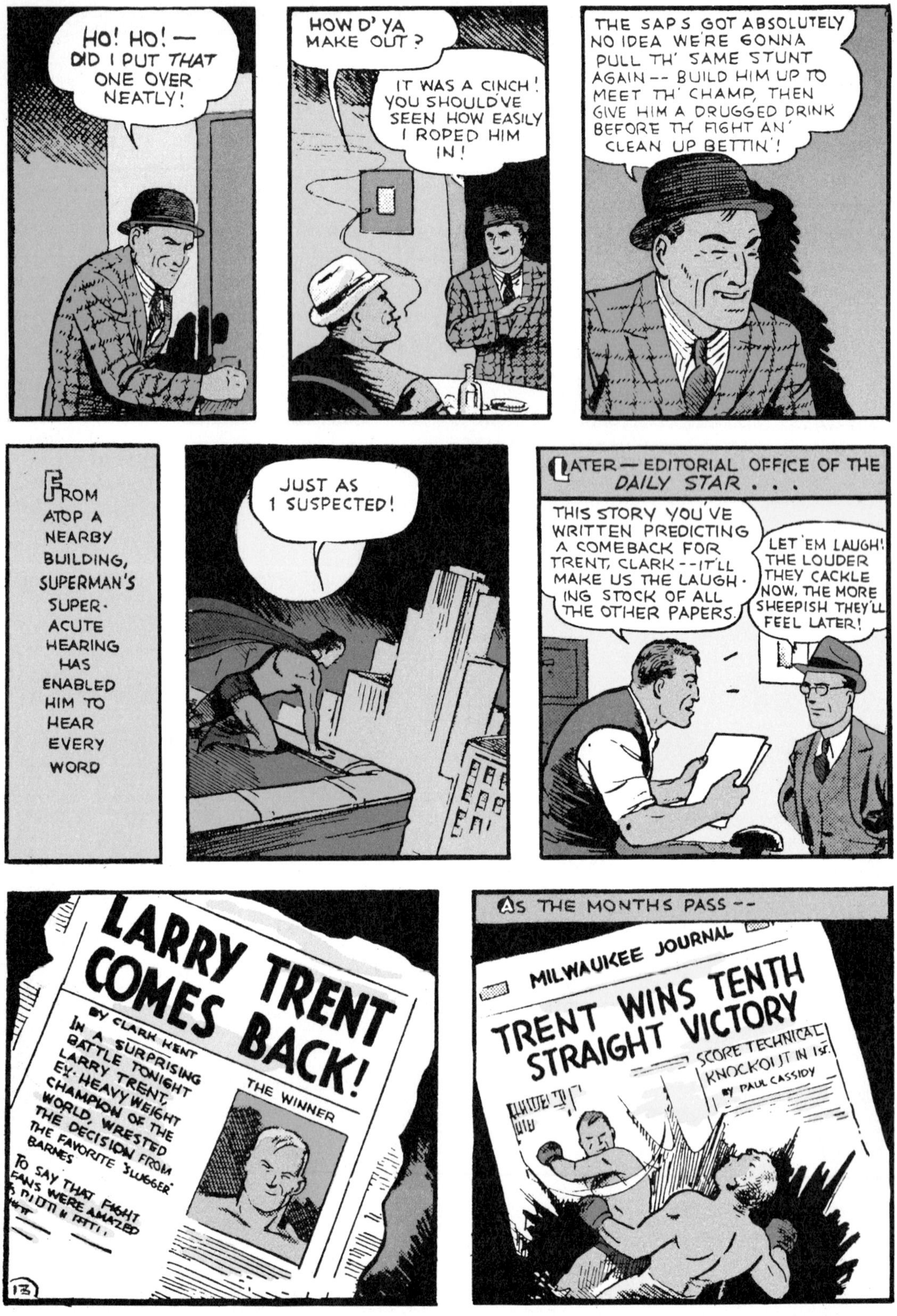
HO! HO! — DID I PUT *THAT* ONE OVER NEATLY!
HOW D'YA MAKE OUT?
IT WAS A CINCH! YOU SHOULD'VE SEEN HOW EASILY I ROPED HIM IN!
THE SAP'S GOT ABSOLUTELY NO IDEA WE'RE GONNA PULL TH' SAME STUNT AGAIN -- BUILD HIM UP TO MEET TH' CHAMP, THEN GIVE HIM A DRUGGED DRINK BEFORE TH' FIGHT AN' CLEAN UP BETTIN'!
FROM ATOP A NEARBY BUILDING, SUPERMAN'S SUPER-ACUTE HEARING HAS ENABLED HIM TO HEAR EVERY WORD
JUST AS I SUSPECTED!
LATER — EDITORIAL OFFICE OF THE *DAILY STAR* . . .
THIS STORY YOU'VE WRITTEN PREDICTING A COMEBACK FOR TRENT, CLARK -- IT'LL MAKE US THE LAUGHING STOCK OF ALL THE OTHER PAPERS.
LET 'EM LAUGH! THE LOUDER THEY CACKLE NOW, THE MORE SHEEPISH THEY'LL FEEL LATER!
LARRY TRENT COMES BACK!
BY CLARK KENT
IN A SURPRISING BATTLE TONIGHT LARRY TRENT, EX-HEAVYWEIGHT CHAMPION OF THE WORLD, WRESTED THE DECISION FROM THE FAVORITE 'SLUGGER' BARNES
TO SAY THAT FIGHT FANS WERE AMAZED
THE WINNER
13
AS THE MONTHS PASS --
MILWAUKEE JOURNAL
TRENT WINS TENTH STRAIGHT VICTORY
SCORE TECHNICAL KNOCKOUT IN 1st.
BY PAUL CASSIDY

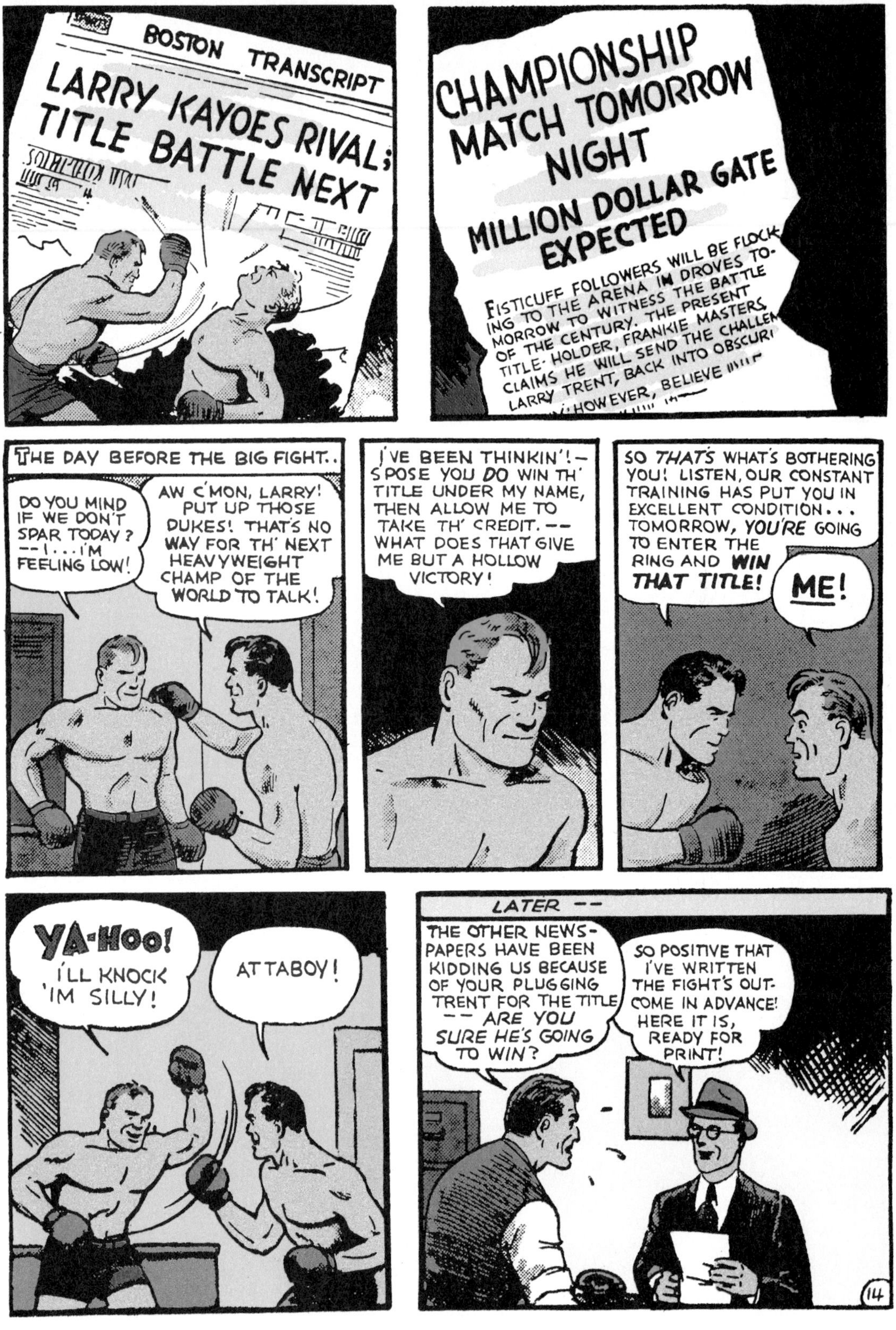
BOSTON TRANSCRIPT
LARRY KAYOES RIVAL; TITLE BATTLE NEXT
CHAMPIONSHIP MATCH TOMORROW NIGHT
MILLION DOLLAR GATE EXPECTED
FISTICUFF FOLLOWERS WILL BE FLOCK-
ING TO THE ARENA IN DROVES TO-
MORROW TO WITNESS THE BATTLE
OF THE CENTURY. THE PRESENT
TITLE-HOLDER, FRANKIE MASTERS,
CLAIMS HE WILL SEND THE CHALLEN
LARRY TRENT, BACK INTO OBSCURI
HOWEVER, BELIEVE
THE DAY BEFORE THE BIG FIGHT..
DO YOU MIND IF WE DON'T SPAR TODAY? --I...I'M FEELING LOW!
AW C'MON, LARRY! PUT UP THOSE DUKES! THAT'S NO WAY FOR TH' NEXT HEAVYWEIGHT CHAMP OF THE WORLD TO TALK!
I'VE BEEN THINKIN'!-- S'POSE YOU DO WIN TH' TITLE UNDER MY NAME, THEN ALLOW ME TO TAKE TH' CREDIT.-- WHAT DOES THAT GIVE ME BUT A HOLLOW VICTORY!
SO THAT'S WHAT'S BOTHERING YOU! LISTEN, OUR CONSTANT TRAINING HAS PUT YOU IN EXCELLENT CONDITION... TOMORROW, YOU'RE GOING TO ENTER THE RING AND WIN THAT TITLE!
ME!
YA-HOO! I'LL KNOCK 'IM SILLY!
ATTABOY!
LATER --
THE OTHER NEWS-PAPERS HAVE BEEN KIDDING US BECAUSE OF YOUR PLUGGING TRENT FOR THE TITLE -- ARE YOU SURE HE'S GOING TO WIN?
SO POSITIVE THAT I'VE WRITTEN THE FIGHT'S OUT-COME IN ADVANCE! HERE IT IS, READY FOR PRINT!
14

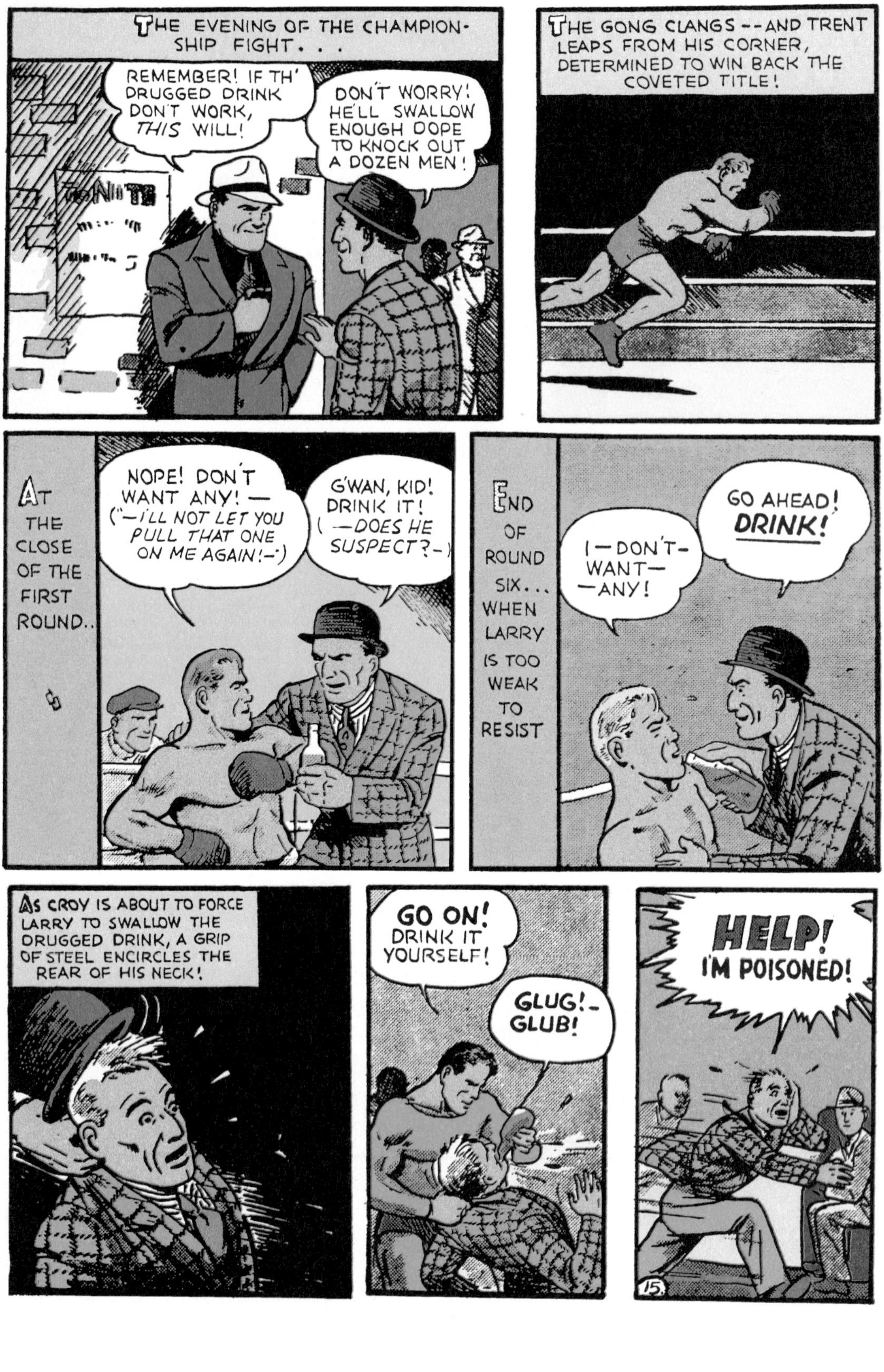
THE EVENING OF THE CHAMPIONSHIP FIGHT . . .
REMEMBER! IF TH' DRUGGED DRINK DON'T WORK, THIS WILL!
DON'T WORRY! HE'LL SWALLOW ENOUGH DOPE TO KNOCK OUT A DOZEN MEN!
THE GONG CLANGS -- AND TRENT LEAPS FROM HIS CORNER, DETERMINED TO WIN BACK THE COVETED TITLE!
AT THE CLOSE OF THE FIRST ROUND..
NOPE! DON'T WANT ANY! — ("—I'LL NOT LET YOU PULL THAT ONE ON ME AGAIN!—")
G'WAN, KID! DRINK IT! (—DOES HE SUSPECT?—)
END OF ROUND SIX... WHEN LARRY IS TOO WEAK TO RESIST
I—DON'T—WANT— —ANY!
GO AHEAD! DRINK!
AS CROY IS ABOUT TO FORCE LARRY TO SWALLOW THE DRUGGED DRINK, A GRIP OF STEEL ENCIRCLES THE REAR OF HIS NECK!
GO ON! DRINK IT YOURSELF!
GLUG!- GLUB!
HELP! I'M POISONED!
15

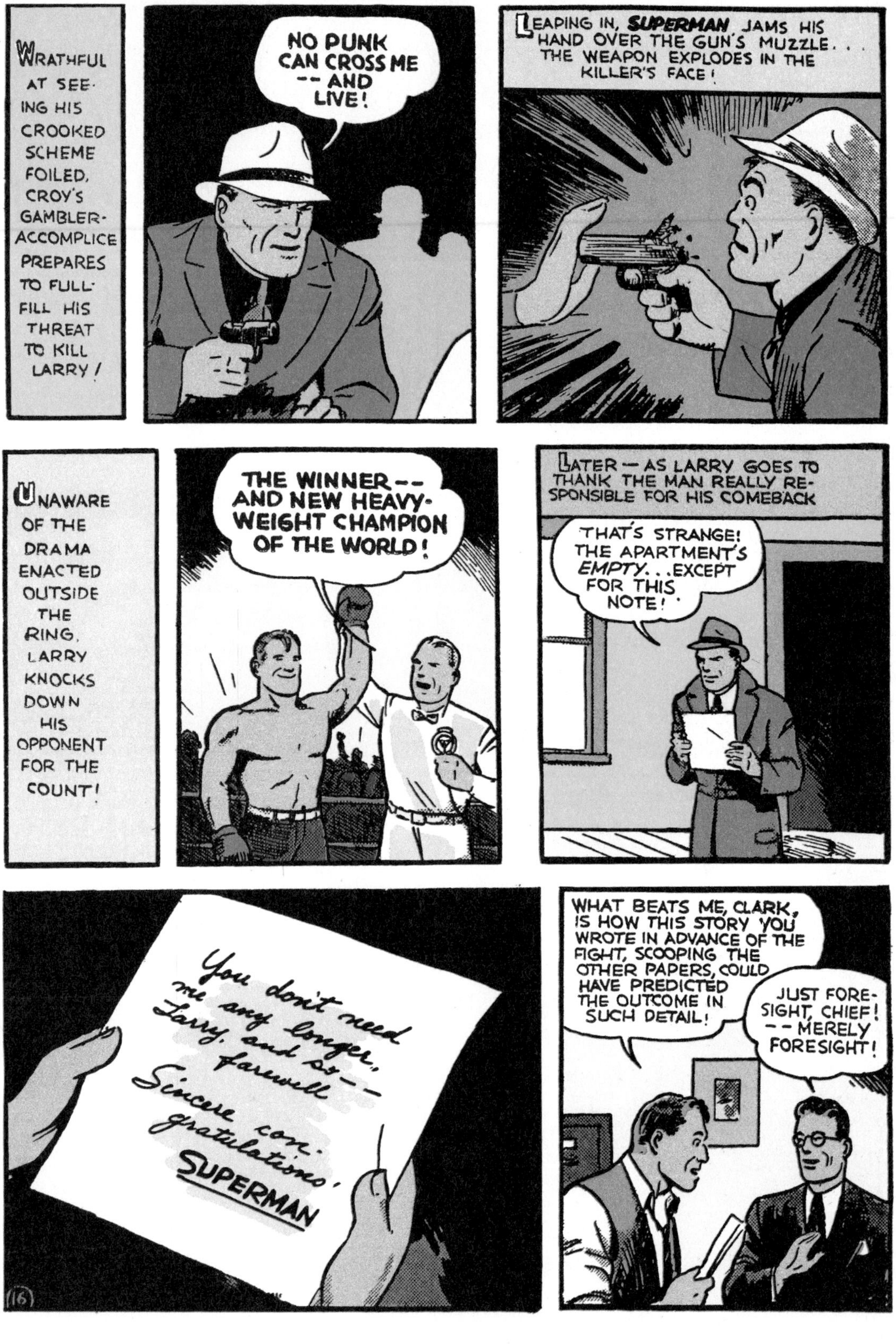

WRATHFUL AT SEEING HIS CROOKED SCHEME FOILED, CROY'S GAMBLER-ACCOMPLICE PREPARES TO FULLFILL HIS THREAT TO KILL LARRY!
NO PUNK CAN CROSS ME -- AND LIVE!
LEAPING IN, SUPERMAN JAMS HIS HAND OVER THE GUN'S MUZZLE . . . THE WEAPON EXPLODES IN THE KILLER'S FACE!
UNAWARE OF THE DRAMA ENACTED OUTSIDE THE RING, LARRY KNOCKS DOWN HIS OPPONENT FOR THE COUNT!
THE WINNER -- AND NEW HEAVY-WEIGHT CHAMPION OF THE WORLD!
LATER — AS LARRY GOES TO THANK THE MAN REALLY RESPONSIBLE FOR HIS COMEBACK
THAT'S STRANGE! THE APARTMENT'S EMPTY. . .EXCEPT FOR THIS NOTE!
You don't need me any longer, Larry, and so-- farewell
Sincere congratulations!
SUPERMAN
(16)
WHAT BEATS ME, CLARK, IS HOW THIS STORY YOU WROTE IN ADVANCE OF THE FIGHT, SCOOPING THE OTHER PAPERS, COULD HAVE PREDICTED THE OUTCOME IN SUCH DETAIL!
JUST FORESIGHT, CHIEF! -- MERELY FORESIGHT!

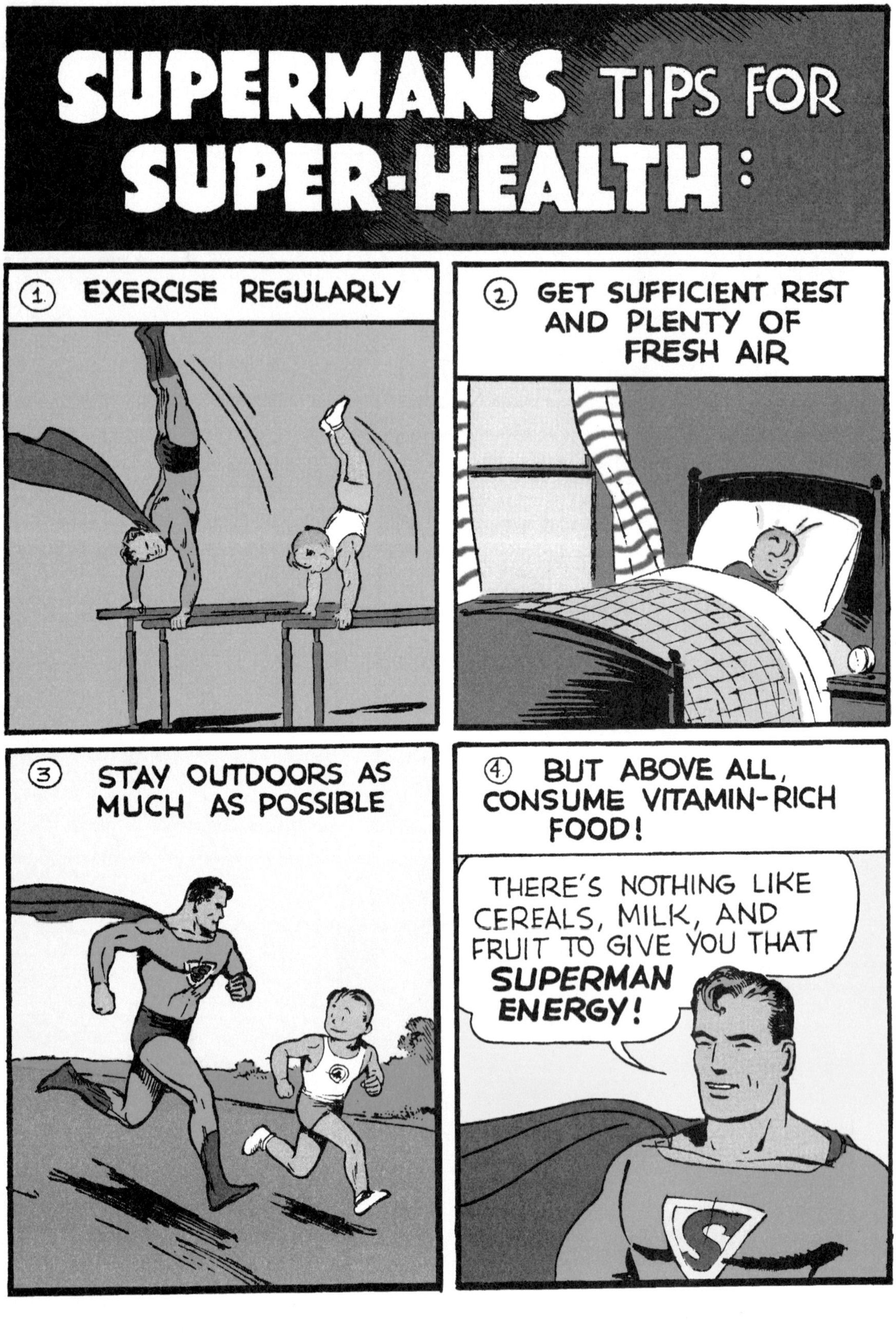
SUPERMAN S TIPS FOR SUPER-HEALTH:
1. EXERCISE REGULARLY
2. GET SUFFICIENT REST AND PLENTY OF FRESH AIR
3 STAY OUTDOORS AS MUCH AS POSSIBLE
4. BUT ABOVE ALL, CONSUME VITAMIN-RICH FOOD!
THERE'S NOTHING LIKE CEREALS, MILK, AND FRUIT TO GIVE YOU THAT SUPERMAN ENERGY!

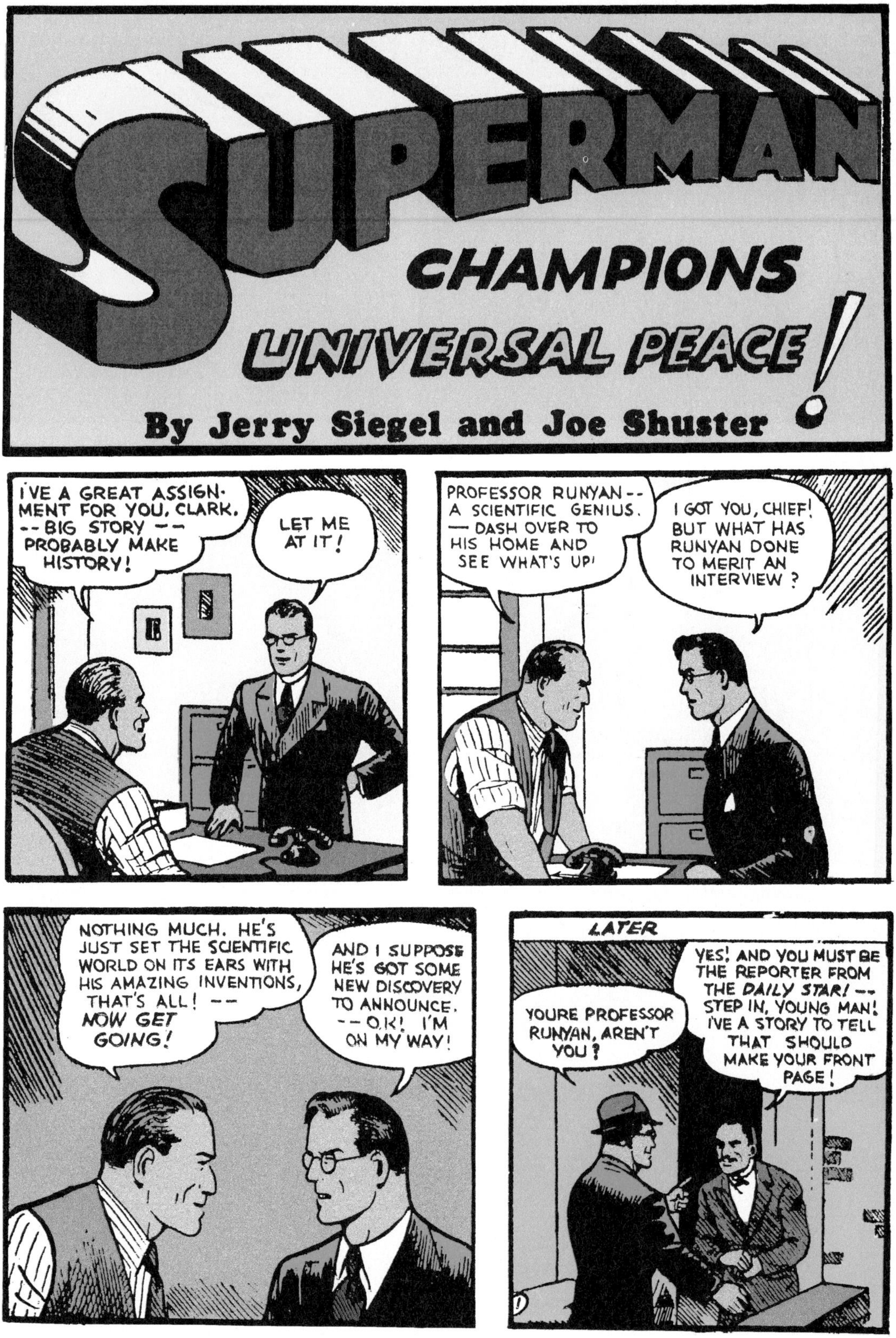
SUPERMAN
CHAMPIONS
UNIVERSAL PEACE!
By Jerry Siegel and Joe Shuster
I'VE A GREAT ASSIGN-MENT FOR YOU, CLARK. -- BIG STORY -- PROBABLY MAKE HISTORY!
LET ME AT IT!
PROFESSOR RUNYAN -- A SCIENTIFIC GENIUS. — DASH OVER TO HIS HOME AND SEE WHAT'S UP!
I GOT YOU, CHIEF! BUT WHAT HAS RUNYAN DONE TO MERIT AN INTERVIEW ?
NOTHING MUCH. HE'S JUST SET THE SCIENTIFIC WORLD ON ITS EARS WITH HIS AMAZING INVENTIONS, THAT'S ALL! -- NOW GET GOING!
AND I SUPPOSE HE'S GOT SOME NEW DISCOVERY TO ANNOUNCE. -- O.K! I'M ON MY WAY!
LATER
YOURE PROFESSOR RUNYAN, AREN'T YOU ?
YES! AND YOU MUST BE THE REPORTER FROM THE DAILY STAR! -- STEP IN, YOUNG MAN! I'VE A STORY TO TELL THAT SHOULD MAKE YOUR FRONT PAGE!

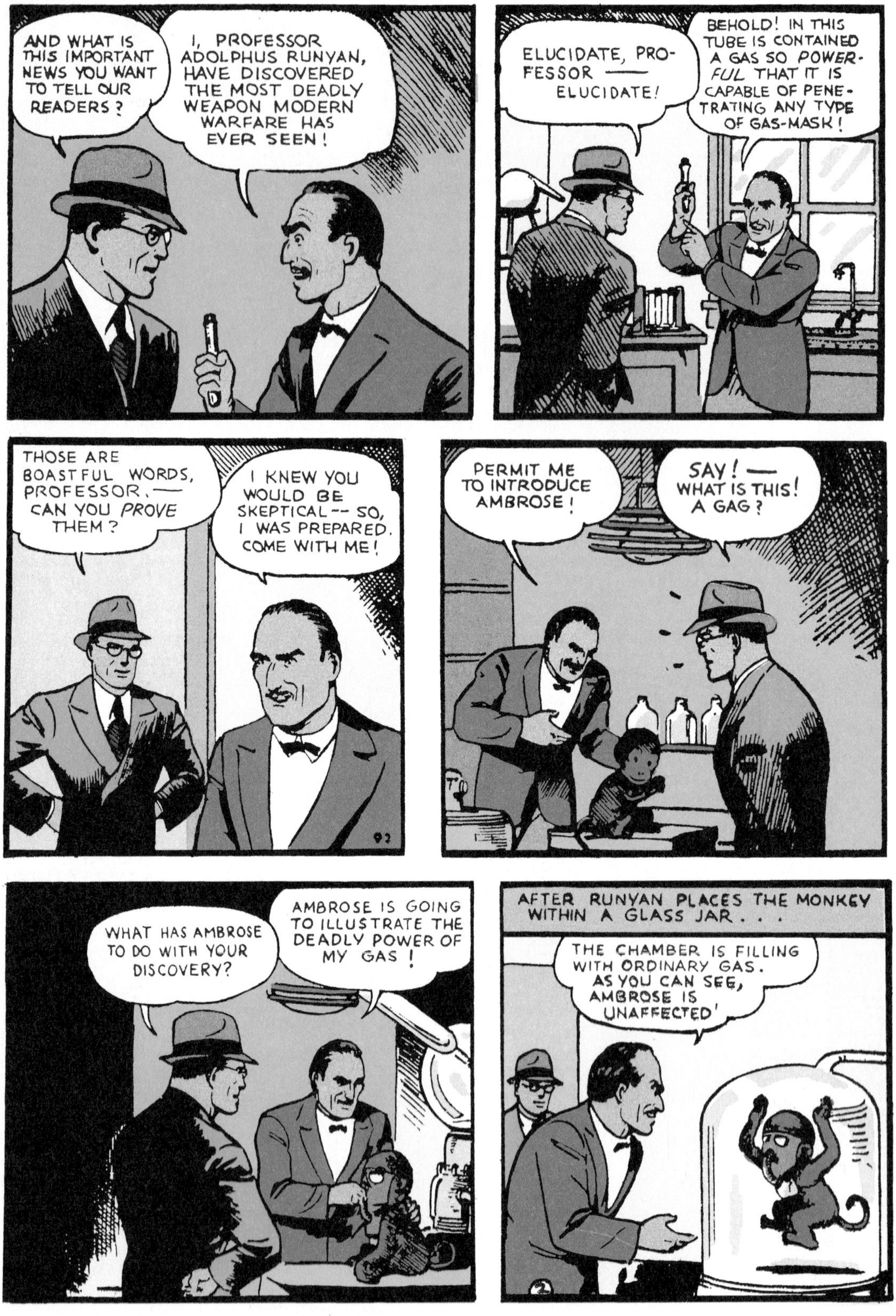
AND WHAT IS THIS IMPORTANT NEWS YOU WANT TO TELL OUR READERS?
I, PROFESSOR ADOLPHUS RUNYAN, HAVE DISCOVERED THE MOST DEADLY WEAPON MODERN WARFARE HAS EVER SEEN!
ELUCIDATE, PROFESSOR —— ELUCIDATE!
BEHOLD! IN THIS TUBE IS CONTAINED A GAS SO *POWERFUL* THAT IT IS CAPABLE OF PENETRATING ANY TYPE OF GAS-MASK!
THOSE ARE BOASTFUL WORDS, PROFESSOR.— CAN YOU *PROVE* THEM?
I KNEW YOU WOULD BE SKEPTICAL -- SO, I WAS PREPARED. COME WITH ME!
PERMIT ME TO INTRODUCE AMBROSE!
SAY! — WHAT IS THIS! A GAG?
WHAT HAS AMBROSE TO DO WITH YOUR DISCOVERY?
AMBROSE IS GOING TO ILLUSTRATE THE DEADLY POWER OF MY GAS!
AFTER RUNYAN PLACES THE MONKEY WITHIN A GLASS JAR . . .
THE CHAMBER IS FILLING WITH ORDINARY GAS. AS YOU CAN SEE, AMBROSE IS UNAFFECTED!

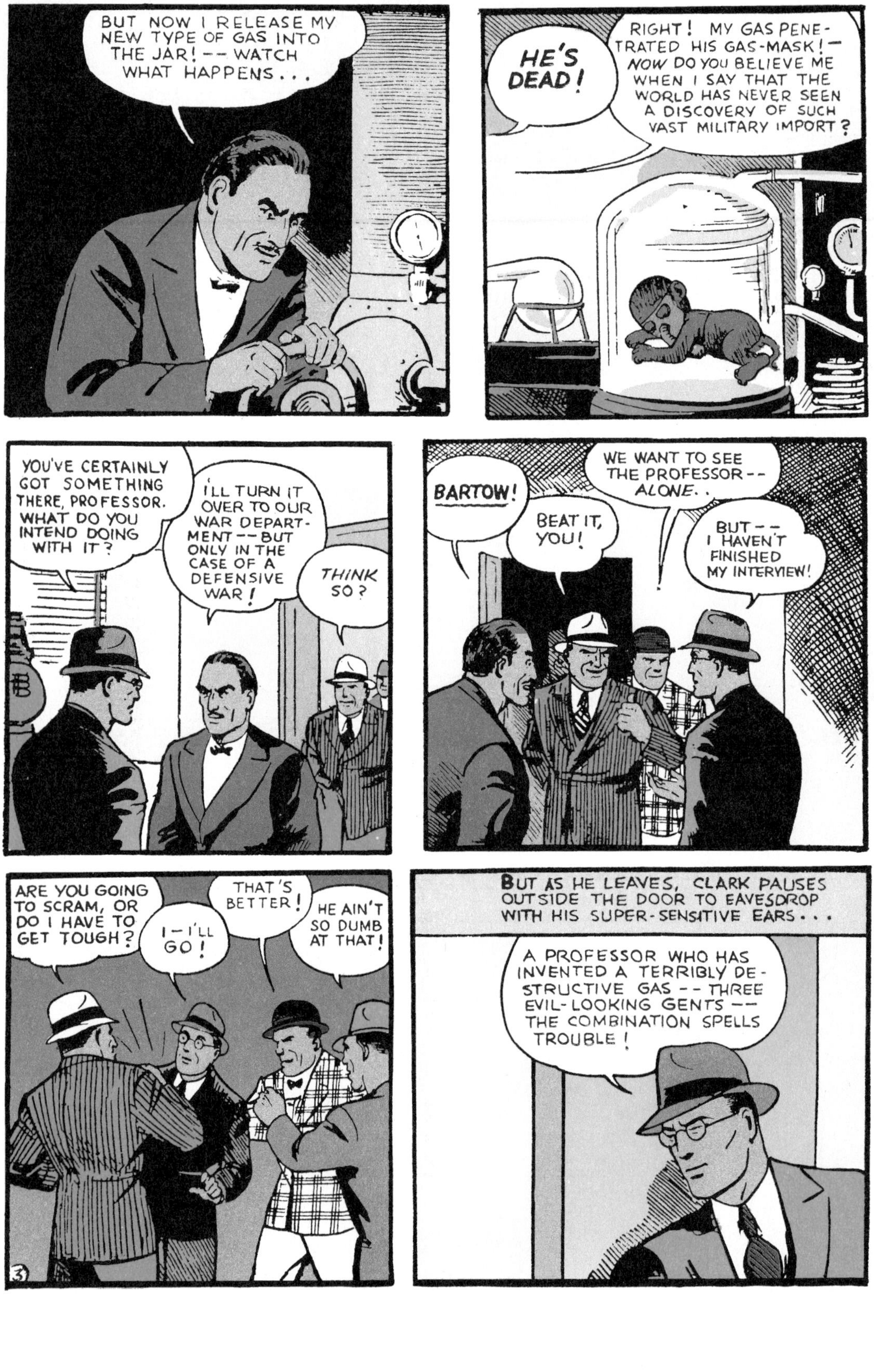

BUT NOW I RELEASE MY NEW TYPE OF GAS INTO THE JAR! -- WATCH WHAT HAPPENS . . .
HE'S DEAD!
RIGHT! MY GAS PENETRATED HIS GAS-MASK! — NOW DO YOU BELIEVE ME WHEN I SAY THAT THE WORLD HAS NEVER SEEN A DISCOVERY OF SUCH VAST MILITARY IMPORT?
YOU'VE CERTAINLY GOT SOMETHING THERE, PROFESSOR. WHAT DO YOU INTEND DOING WITH IT?
I'LL TURN IT OVER TO OUR WAR DEPARTMENT -- BUT ONLY IN THE CASE OF A DEFENSIVE WAR!
THINK SO?
BARTOW!
BEAT IT, YOU!
WE WANT TO SEE THE PROFESSOR -- ALONE. .
BUT -- I HAVEN'T FINISHED MY INTERVIEW!
ARE YOU GOING TO SCRAM, OR DO I HAVE TO GET TOUGH?
I — I'LL GO!
THAT'S BETTER!
HE AIN'T SO DUMB AT THAT!
3
BUT AS HE LEAVES, CLARK PAUSES OUTSIDE THE DOOR TO EAVESDROP WITH HIS SUPER-SENSITIVE EARS . . .
A PROFESSOR WHO HAS INVENTED A TERRIBLY DESTRUCTIVE GAS -- THREE EVIL-LOOKING GENTS — THE COMBINATION SPELLS TROUBLE!

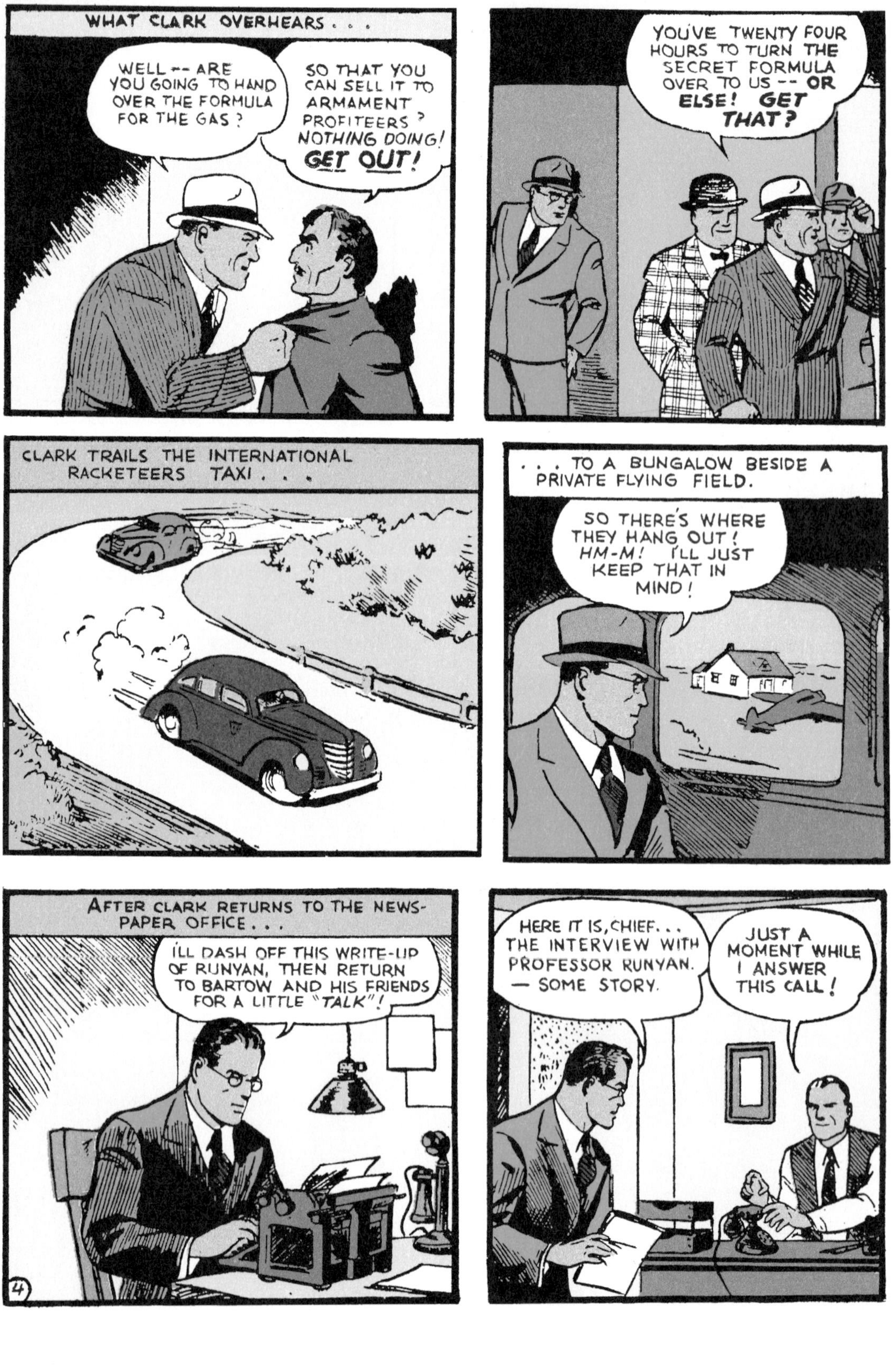
WHAT CLARK OVERHEARS . . .
WELL -- ARE YOU GOING TO HAND OVER THE FORMULA FOR THE GAS?
SO THAT YOU CAN SELL IT TO ARMAMENT PROFITEERS? NOTHING DOING! GET OUT!
YOU'VE TWENTY FOUR HOURS TO TURN THE SECRET FORMULA OVER TO US -- OR ELSE! GET THAT?
CLARK TRAILS THE INTERNATIONAL RACKETEERS TAXI . . .
. . . TO A BUNGALOW BESIDE A PRIVATE FLYING FIELD.
SO THERE'S WHERE THEY HANG OUT! HM-M! I'LL JUST KEEP THAT IN MIND!
AFTER CLARK RETURNS TO THE NEWS-PAPER OFFICE . . .
I'LL DASH OFF THIS WRITE-UP OF RUNYAN, THEN RETURN TO BARTOW AND HIS FRIENDS FOR A LITTLE "TALK"!
4
HERE IT IS, CHIEF. . . THE INTERVIEW WITH PROFESSOR RUNYAN. — SOME STORY.
JUST A MOMENT WHILE I ANSWER THIS CALL!

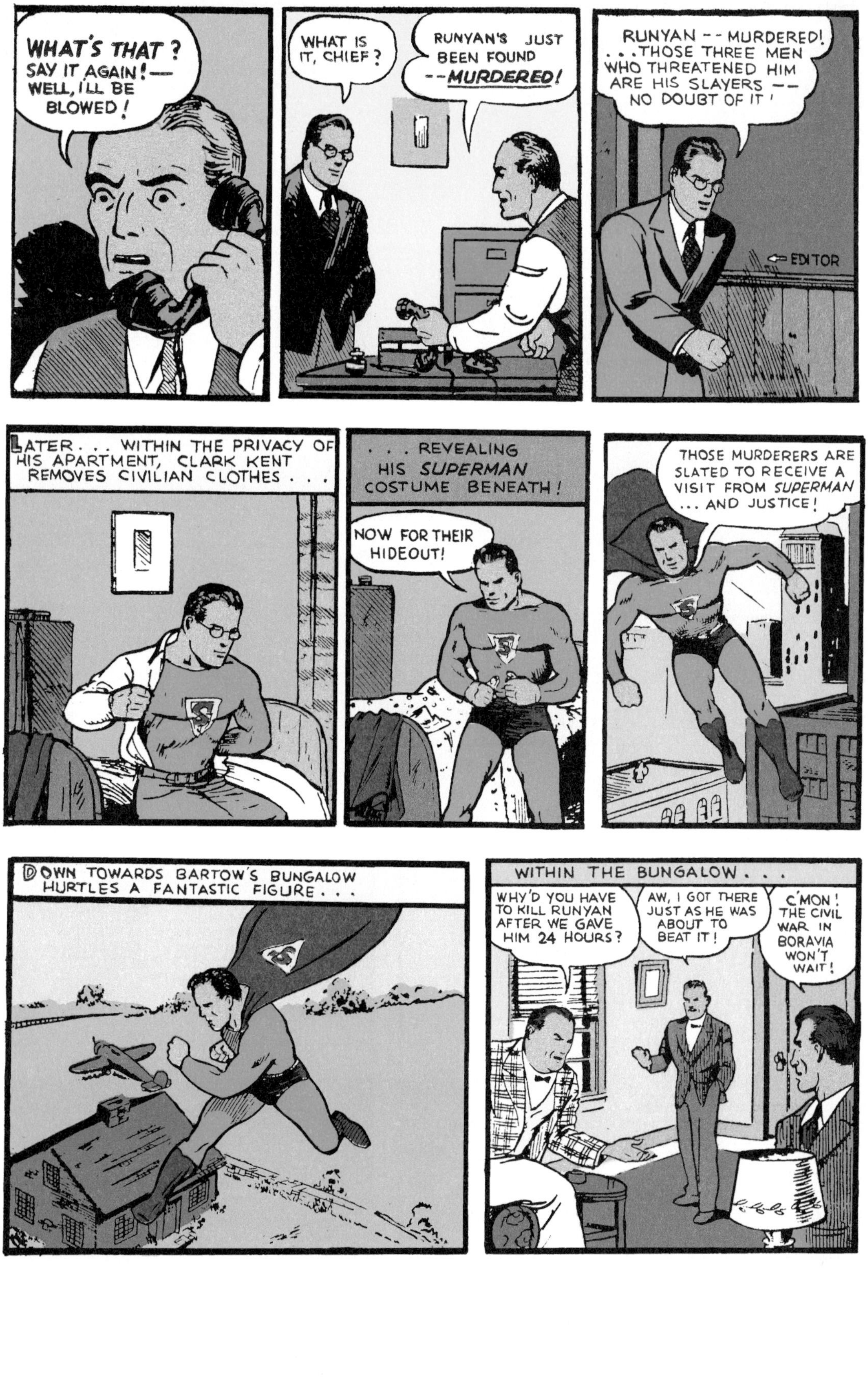
WHAT'S THAT ? SAY IT AGAIN!— WELL, I'LL BE BLOWED!
WHAT IS IT, CHIEF ?
RUNYAN'S JUST BEEN FOUND --MURDERED!
RUNYAN -- MURDERED! . . .THOSE THREE MEN WHO THREATENED HIM ARE HIS SLAYERS -- NO DOUBT OF IT!
EDITOR
LATER . . . WITHIN THE PRIVACY OF HIS APARTMENT, CLARK KENT REMOVES CIVILIAN CLOTHES . . .
. . . REVEALING HIS SUPERMAN COSTUME BENEATH!
NOW FOR THEIR HIDEOUT!
THOSE MURDERERS ARE SLATED TO RECEIVE A VISIT FROM SUPERMAN . . . AND JUSTICE!
DOWN TOWARDS BARTOW'S BUNGALOW HURTLES A FANTASTIC FIGURE . . .
WITHIN THE BUNGALOW . . .
WHY'D YOU HAVE TO KILL RUNYAN AFTER WE GAVE HIM 24 HOURS?
AW, I GOT THERE JUST AS HE WAS ABOUT TO BEAT IT!
C'MON! THE CIVIL WAR IN BORAVIA WON'T WAIT!

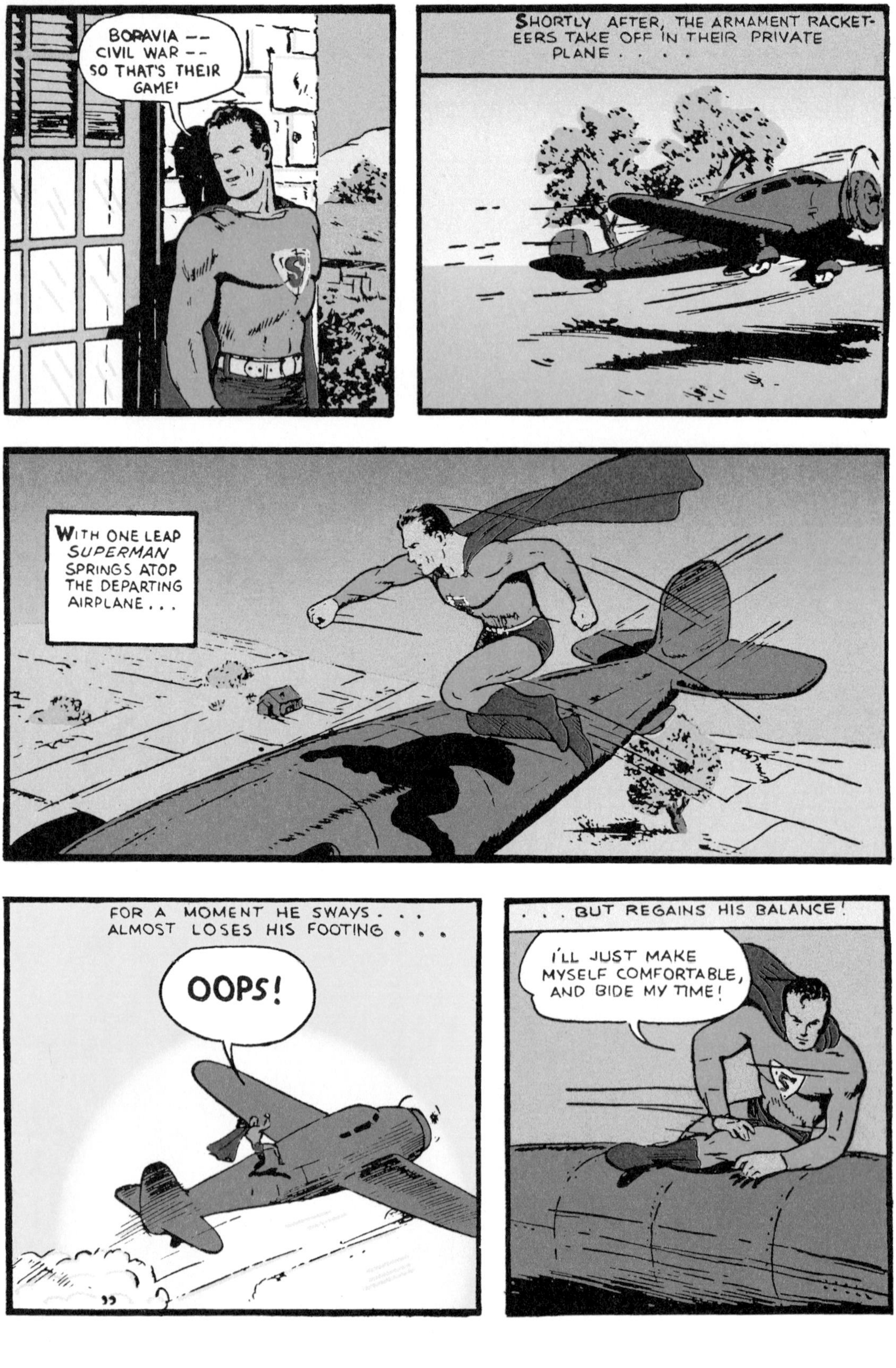
BORAVIA -- CIVIL WAR -- SO THAT'S THEIR GAME!
SHORTLY AFTER, THE ARMAMENT RACKETEERS TAKE OFF IN THEIR PRIVATE PLANE . . . .
WITH ONE LEAP SUPERMAN SPRINGS ATOP THE DEPARTING AIRPLANE . . .
FOR A MOMENT HE SWAYS . . . ALMOST LOSES HIS FOOTING . . .
OOPS!
. . . BUT REGAINS HIS BALANCE!
I'LL JUST MAKE MYSELF COMFORTABLE, AND BIDE MY TIME!

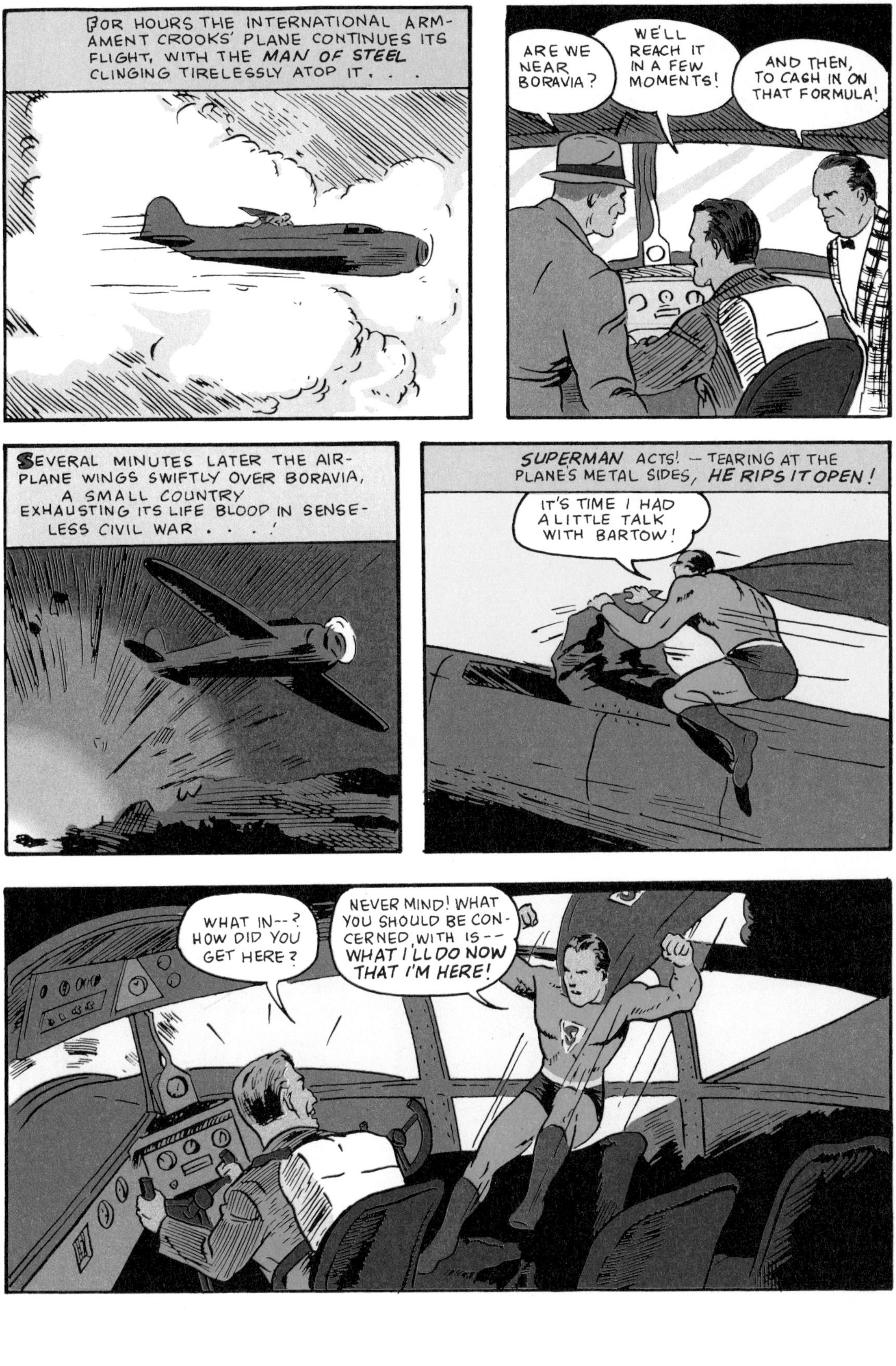
FOR HOURS THE INTERNATIONAL ARMAMENT CROOKS' PLANE CONTINUES ITS FLIGHT, WITH THE MAN OF STEEL CLINGING TIRELESSLY ATOP IT . . .
ARE WE NEAR BORAVIA?
WE'LL REACH IT IN A FEW MOMENTS!
AND THEN, TO CASH IN ON THAT FORMULA!
SEVERAL MINUTES LATER THE AIRPLANE WINGS SWIFTLY OVER BORAVIA, A SMALL COUNTRY EXHAUSTING ITS LIFE BLOOD IN SENSELESS CIVIL WAR . . . !
SUPERMAN ACTS! — TEARING AT THE PLANE'S METAL SIDES, HE RIPS IT OPEN!
IT'S TIME I HAD A LITTLE TALK WITH BARTOW!
WHAT IN--? HOW DID YOU GET HERE?
NEVER MIND! WHAT YOU SHOULD BE CONCERNED WITH IS -- WHAT I'LL DO NOW THAT I'M HERE!

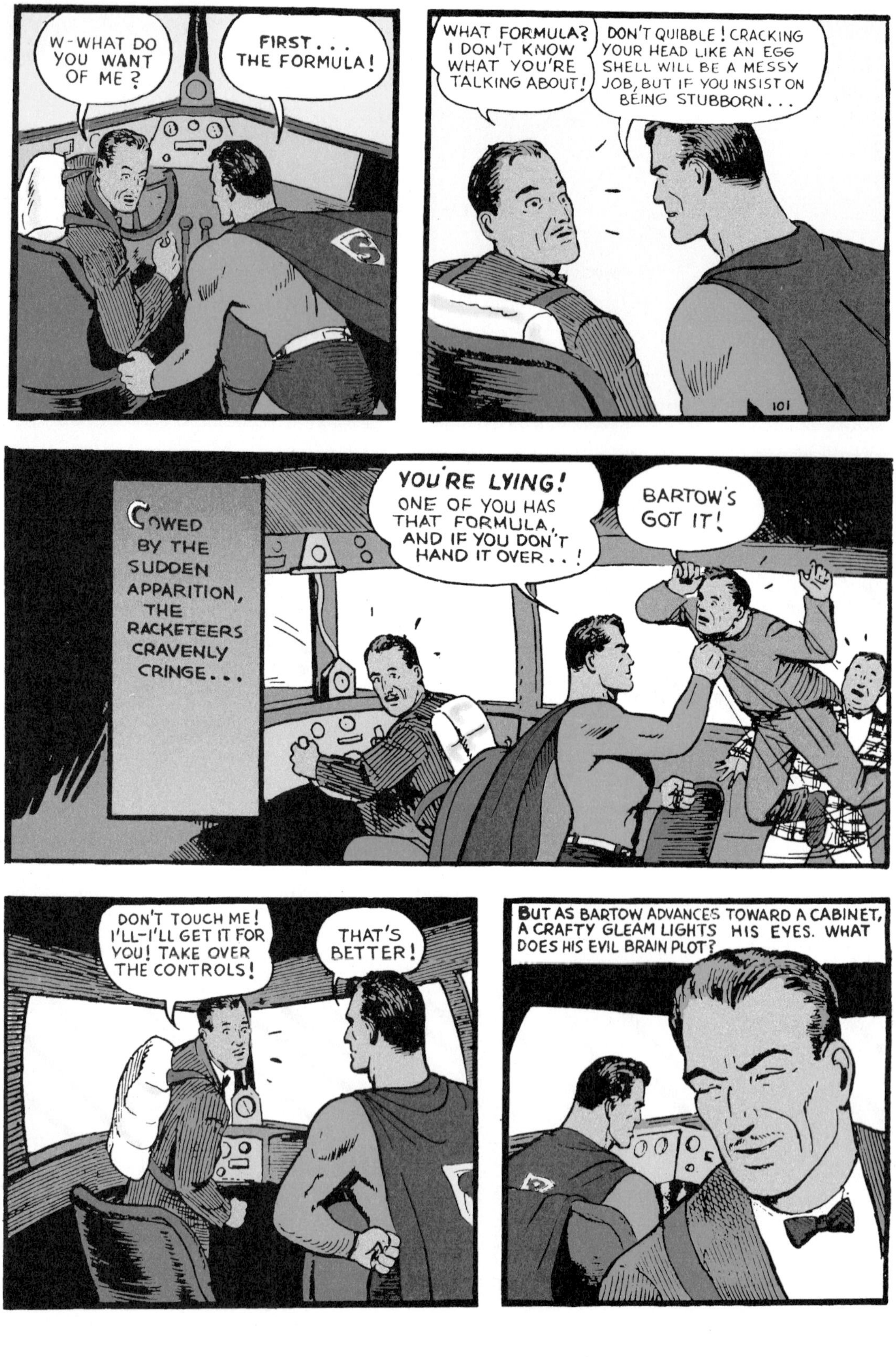
W-WHAT DO YOU WANT OF ME?
FIRST... THE FORMULA!
WHAT FORMULA? I DON'T KNOW WHAT YOU'RE TALKING ABOUT!
DON'T QUIBBLE! CRACKING YOUR HEAD LIKE AN EGG SHELL WILL BE A MESSY JOB, BUT IF YOU INSIST ON BEING STUBBORN...
101
COWED BY THE SUDDEN APPARITION, THE RACKETEERS CRAVENLY CRINGE...
YOU'RE LYING! ONE OF YOU HAS THAT FORMULA, AND IF YOU DON'T HAND IT OVER..!
BARTOW'S GOT IT!
DON'T TOUCH ME! I'LL-I'LL GET IT FOR YOU! TAKE OVER THE CONTROLS!
THAT'S BETTER!
BUT AS BARTOW ADVANCES TOWARD A CABINET, A CRAFTY GLEAM LIGHTS HIS EYES. WHAT DOES HIS EVIL BRAIN PLOT?

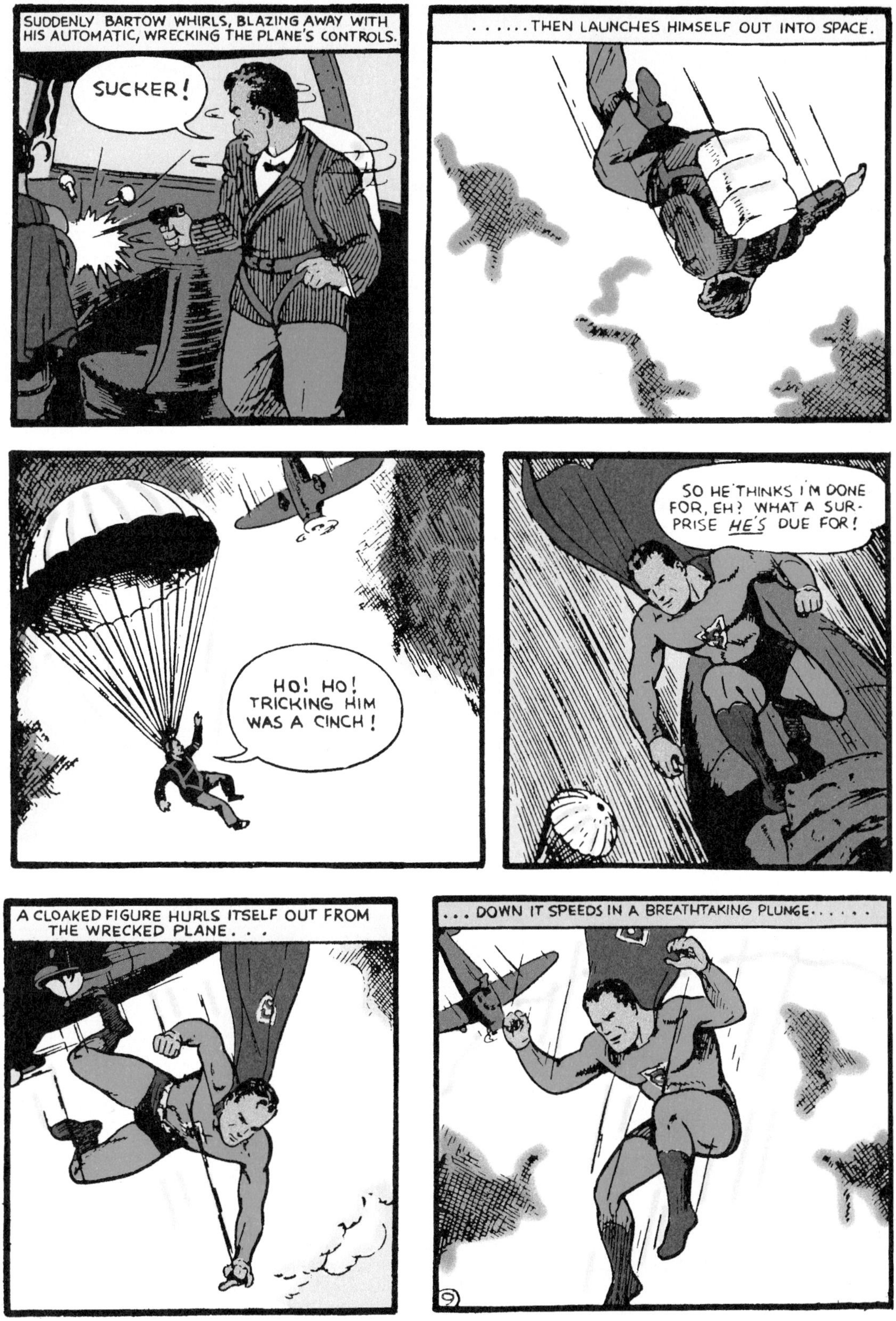
SUDDENLY BARTOW WHIRLS, BLAZING AWAY WITH HIS AUTOMATIC, WRECKING THE PLANE'S CONTROLS.
SUCKER!
......THEN LAUNCHES HIMSELF OUT INTO SPACE.
HO! HO! TRICKING HIM WAS A CINCH!
SO HE THINKS I'M DONE FOR, EH? WHAT A SURPRISE HE'S DUE FOR!
A CLOAKED FIGURE HURLS ITSELF OUT FROM THE WRECKED PLANE...
...DOWN IT SPEEDS IN A BREATHTAKING PLUNGE.....
9

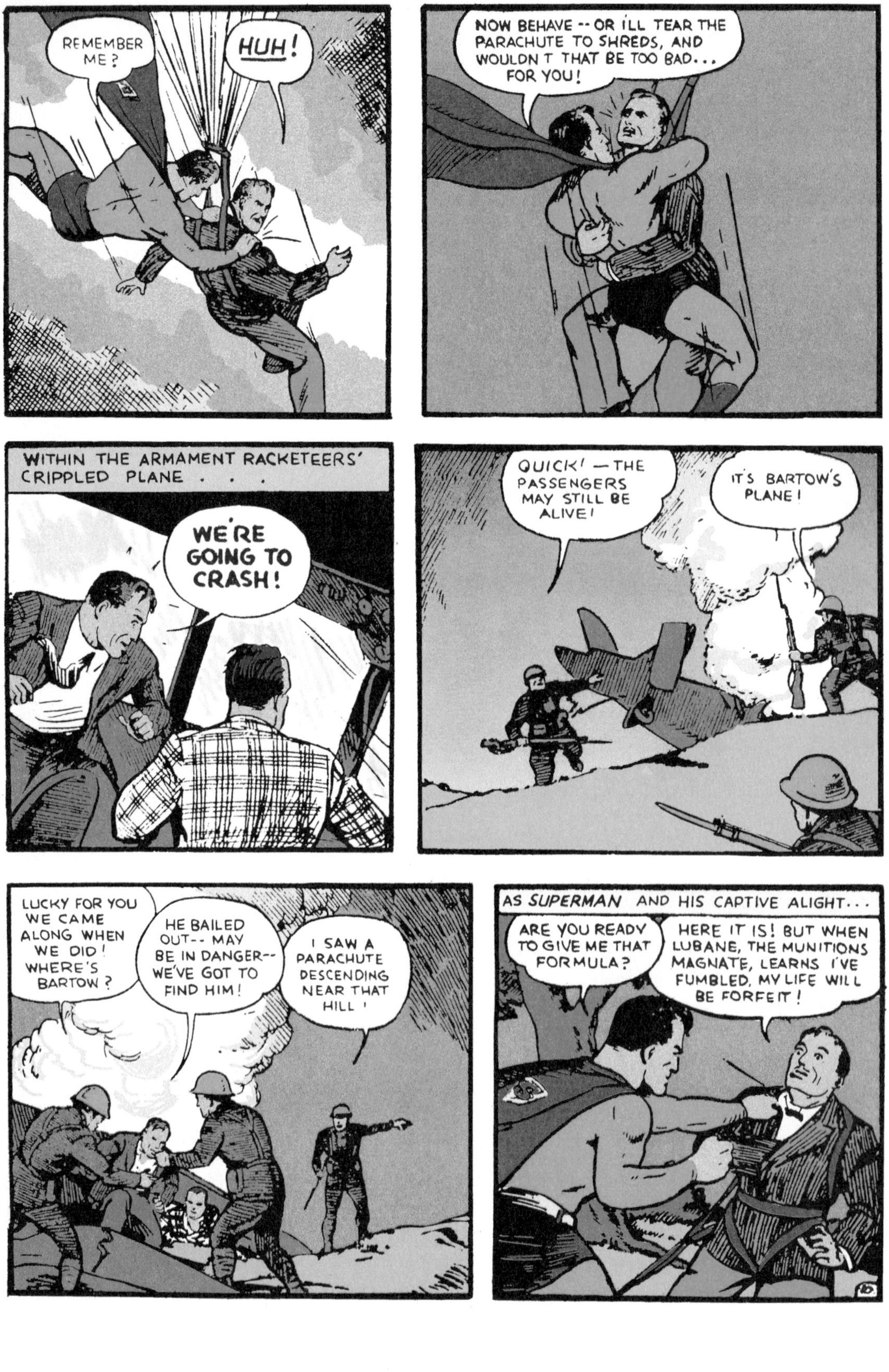
REMEMBER ME?
HUH!
NOW BEHAVE -- OR I'LL TEAR THE PARACHUTE TO SHREDS, AND WOULDN T THAT BE TOO BAD... FOR YOU!
WITHIN THE ARMAMENT RACKETEERS' CRIPPLED PLANE . . .
WE'RE GOING TO CRASH!
QUICK! —THE PASSENGERS MAY STILL BE ALIVE!
IT'S BARTOW'S PLANE!
LUCKY FOR YOU WE CAME ALONG WHEN WE DID! WHERE'S BARTOW?
HE BAILED OUT-- MAY BE IN DANGER-- WE'VE GOT TO FIND HIM!
I SAW A PARACHUTE DESCENDING NEAR THAT HILL!
AS SUPERMAN AND HIS CAPTIVE ALIGHT...
ARE YOU READY TO GIVE ME THAT FORMULA?
HERE IT IS! BUT WHEN LUBANE, THE MUNITIONS MAGNATE, LEARNS I'VE FUMBLED, MY LIFE WILL BE FORFEIT!

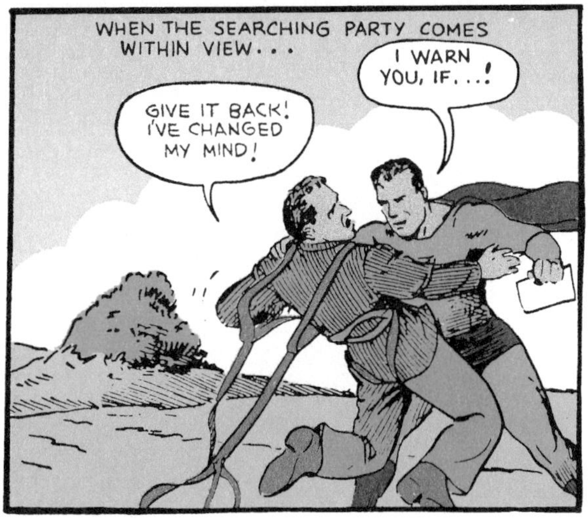
WHEN THE SEARCHING PARTY COMES WITHIN VIEW...
I WARN YOU, IF...!
GIVE IT BACK! I'VE CHANGED MY MIND!

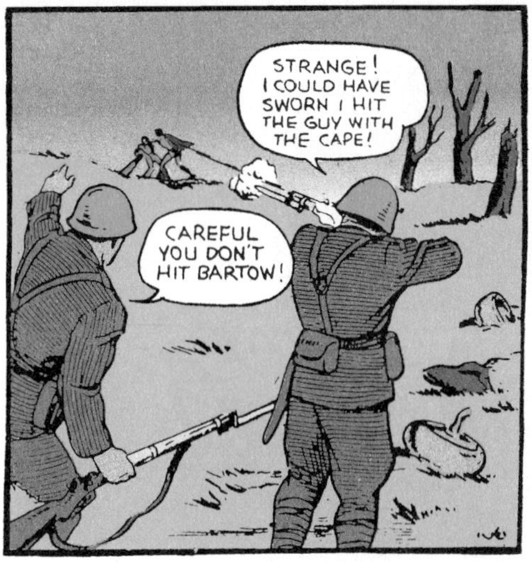
STRANGE! I COULD HAVE SWORN I HIT THE GUY WITH THE CAPE!
CAREFUL YOU DON'T HIT BARTOW!

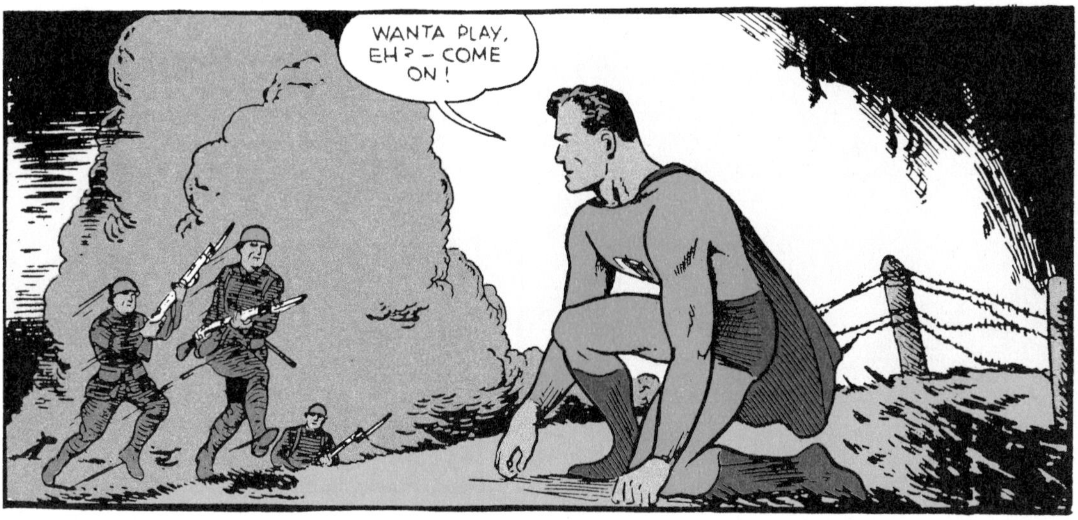
WANTA PLAY, EH? – COME ON!

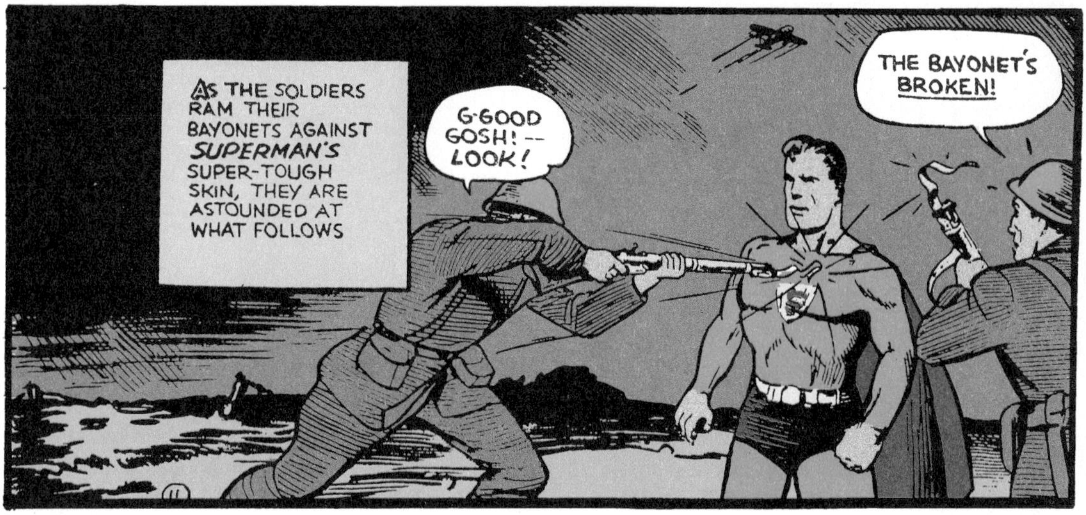
AS THE SOLDIERS RAM THEIR BAYONETS AGAINST SUPERMAN'S SUPER-TOUGH SKIN, THEY ARE ASTOUNDED AT WHAT FOLLOWS
G-GOOD GOSH! -- LOOK!
THE BAYONET'S BROKEN!

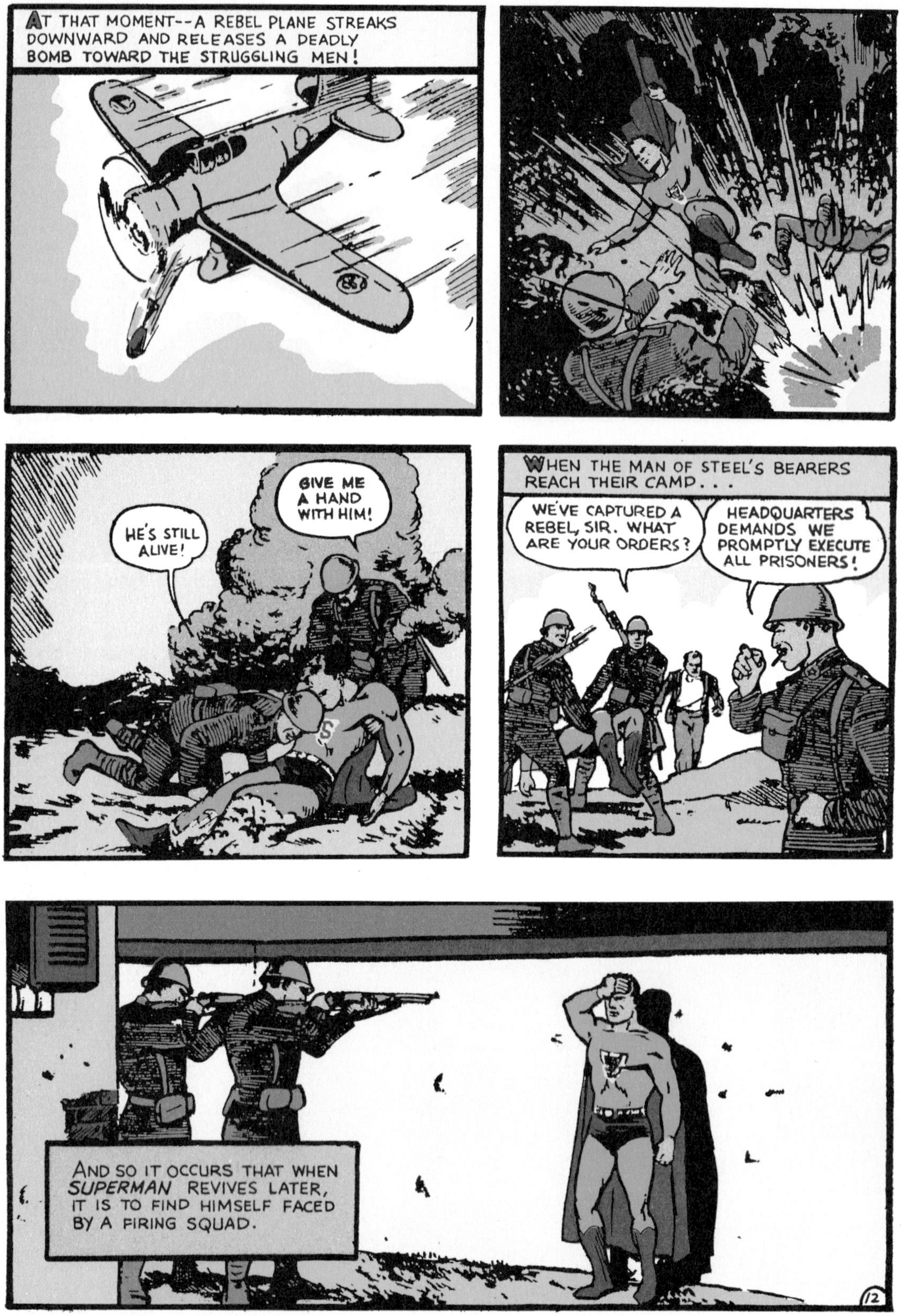
AT THAT MOMENT--A REBEL PLANE STREAKS DOWNWARD AND RELEASES A DEADLY BOMB TOWARD THE STRUGGLING MEN!
HE'S STILL ALIVE!
GIVE ME A HAND WITH HIM!
WHEN THE MAN OF STEEL'S BEARERS REACH THEIR CAMP . . .
WE'VE CAPTURED A REBEL, SIR. WHAT ARE YOUR ORDERS?
HEADQUARTERS DEMANDS WE PROMPTLY EXECUTE ALL PRISONERS!
AND SO IT OCCURS THAT WHEN SUPERMAN REVIVES LATER, IT IS TO FIND HIMSELF FACED BY A FIRING SQUAD.
12

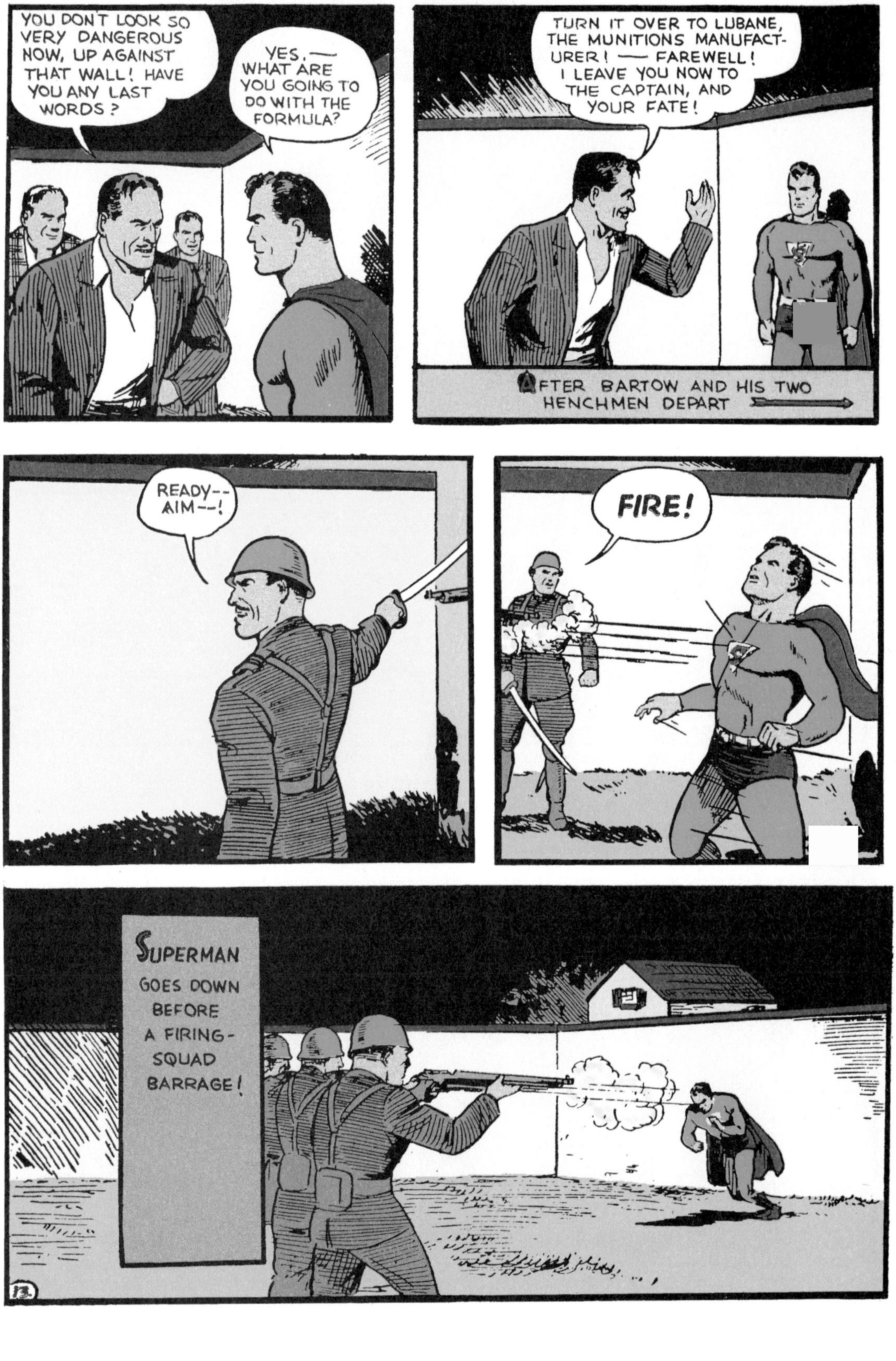
YOU DON'T LOOK SO VERY DANGEROUS NOW, UP AGAINST THAT WALL! HAVE YOU ANY LAST WORDS?
YES, — WHAT ARE YOU GOING TO DO WITH THE FORMULA?
TURN IT OVER TO LUBANE, THE MUNITIONS MANUFACT-URER! — FAREWELL! I LEAVE YOU NOW TO THE CAPTAIN, AND YOUR FATE!
AFTER BARTOW AND HIS TWO HENCHMEN DEPART
READY-- AIM--!
FIRE!
SUPERMAN GOES DOWN BEFORE A FIRING-SQUAD BARRAGE!
13.

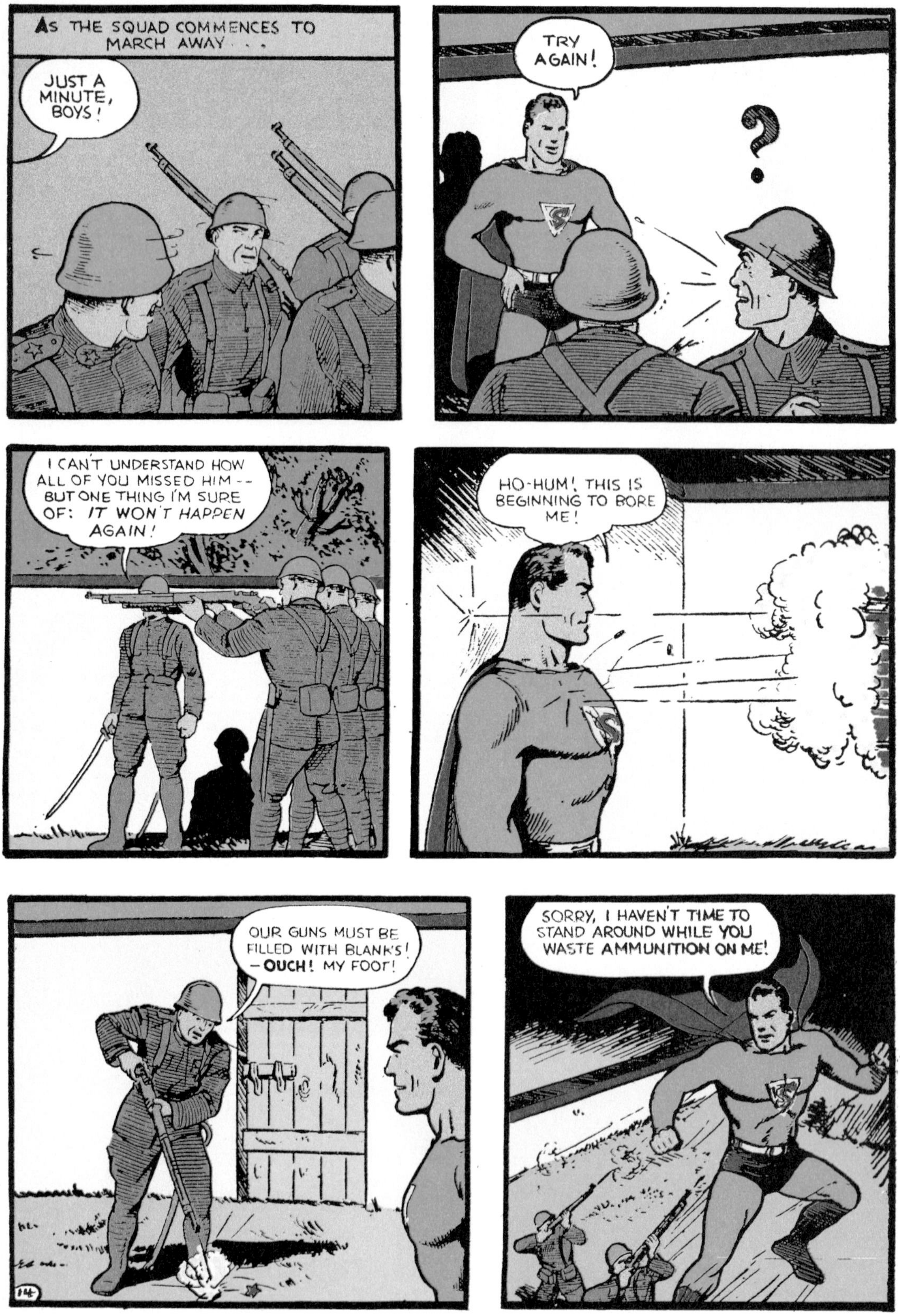
AS THE SQUAD COMMENCES TO MARCH AWAY . . .
JUST A MINUTE, BOYS!
TRY AGAIN!
?
I CAN'T UNDERSTAND HOW ALL OF YOU MISSED HIM -- BUT ONE THING I'M SURE OF: IT WON'T HAPPEN AGAIN!
HO-HUM! THIS IS BEGINNING TO BORE ME!
OUR GUNS MUST BE FILLED WITH BLANKS! --OUCH! MY FOOT!
SORRY, I HAVEN'T TIME TO STAND AROUND WHILE YOU WASTE AMMUNITION ON ME!

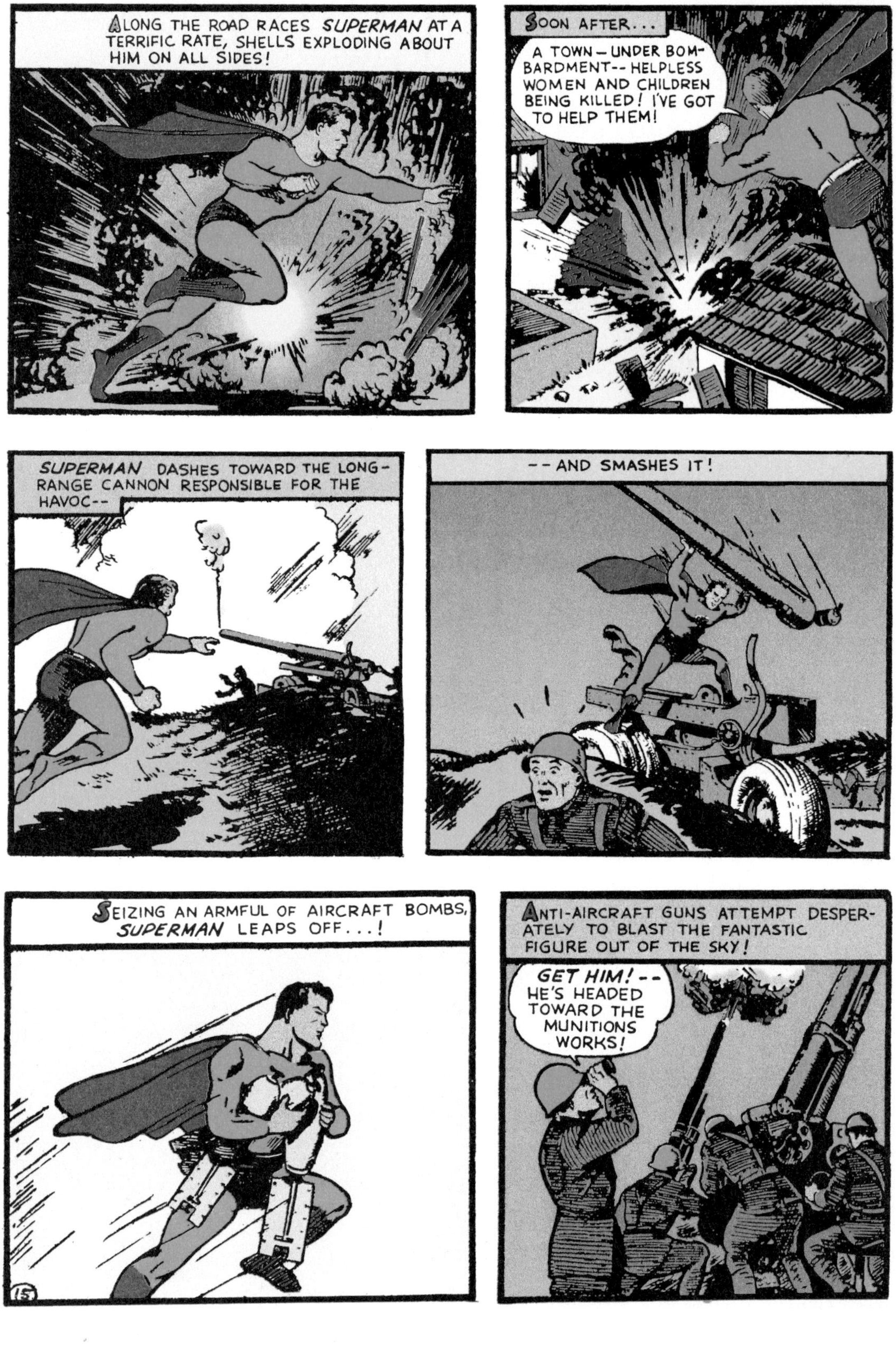
ALONG THE ROAD RACES SUPERMAN AT A TERRIFIC RATE, SHELLS EXPLODING ABOUT HIM ON ALL SIDES!
SOON AFTER...
A TOWN — UNDER BOMBARDMENT-- HELPLESS WOMEN AND CHILDREN BEING KILLED! I'VE GOT TO HELP THEM!
SUPERMAN DASHES TOWARD THE LONG-RANGE CANNON RESPONSIBLE FOR THE HAVOC--
-- AND SMASHES IT!
SEIZING AN ARMFUL OF AIRCRAFT BOMBS, SUPERMAN LEAPS OFF...!
15
ANTI-AIRCRAFT GUNS ATTEMPT DESPERATELY TO BLAST THE FANTASTIC FIGURE OUT OF THE SKY!
GET HIM! -- HE'S HEADED TOWARD THE MUNITIONS WORKS!

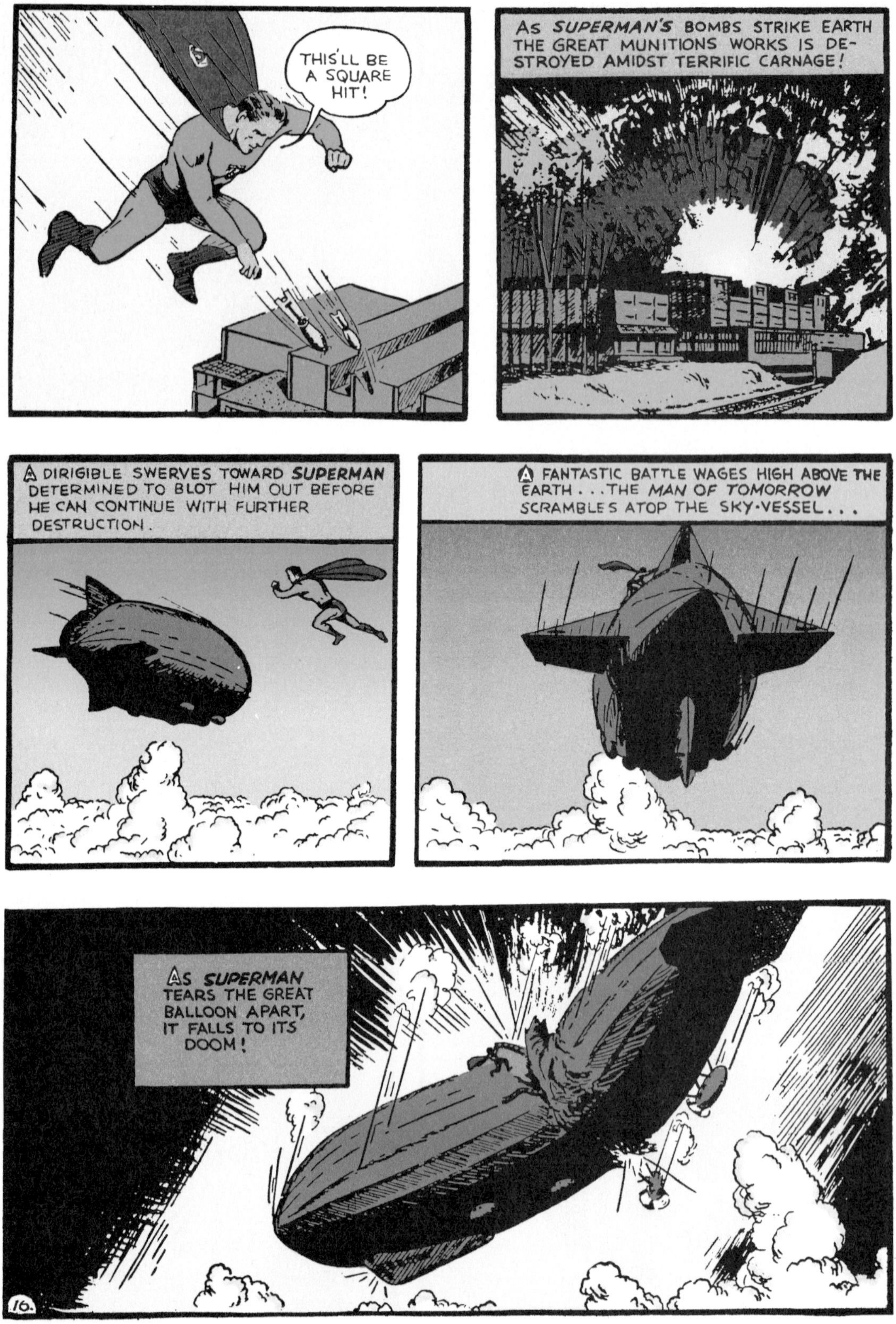
THIS'LL BE A SQUARE HIT!
AS SUPERMAN'S BOMBS STRIKE EARTH THE GREAT MUNITIONS WORKS IS DESTROYED AMIDST TERRIFIC CARNAGE!
A DIRIGIBLE SWERVES TOWARD SUPERMAN DETERMINED TO BLOT HIM OUT BEFORE HE CAN CONTINUE WITH FURTHER DESTRUCTION.
A FANTASTIC BATTLE WAGES HIGH ABOVE THE EARTH . . . THE MAN OF TOMORROW SCRAMBLES ATOP THE SKY-VESSEL . . .
AS SUPERMAN TEARS THE GREAT BALLOON APART, IT FALLS TO ITS DOOM!
16.

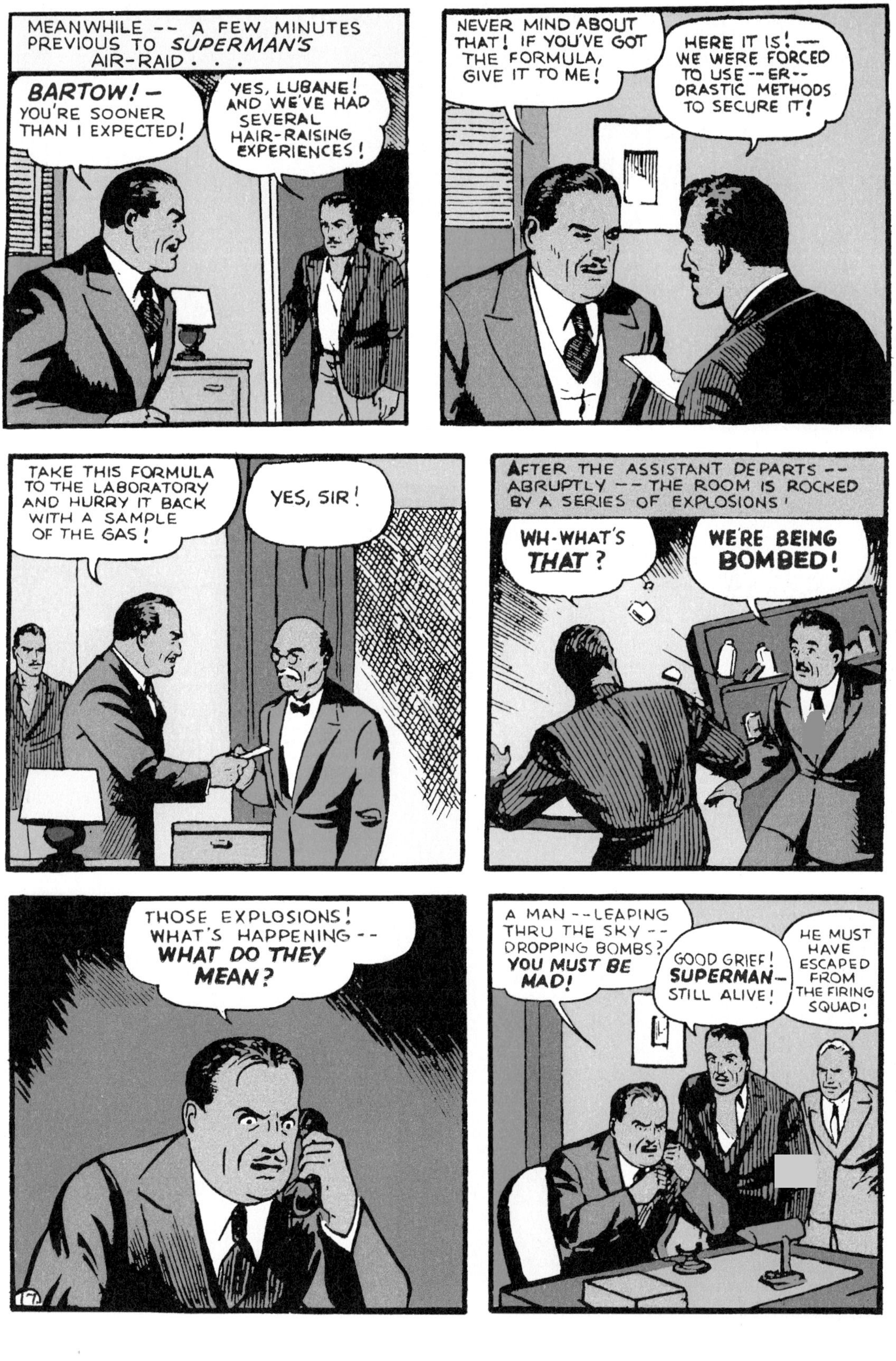
MEANWHILE -- A FEW MINUTES PREVIOUS TO SUPERMAN'S AIR-RAID . . .
BARTOW! — YOU'RE SOONER THAN I EXPECTED!
YES, LUBANE! AND WE'VE HAD SEVERAL HAIR-RAISING EXPERIENCES!
NEVER MIND ABOUT THAT! IF YOU'VE GOT THE FORMULA, GIVE IT TO ME!
HERE IT IS! — WE WERE FORCED TO USE -- ER -- DRASTIC METHODS TO SECURE IT!
TAKE THIS FORMULA TO THE LABORATORY AND HURRY IT BACK WITH A SAMPLE OF THE GAS!
YES, SIR!
AFTER THE ASSISTANT DEPARTS -- ABRUPTLY -- THE ROOM IS ROCKED BY A SERIES OF EXPLOSIONS!
WH-WHAT'S THAT?
WE'RE BEING BOMBED!
THOSE EXPLOSIONS! WHAT'S HAPPENING -- WHAT DO THEY MEAN?
A MAN -- LEAPING THRU THE SKY -- DROPPING BOMBS? YOU MUST BE MAD!
GOOD GRIEF! SUPERMAN — STILL ALIVE!
HE MUST HAVE ESCAPED FROM THE FIRING SQUAD!

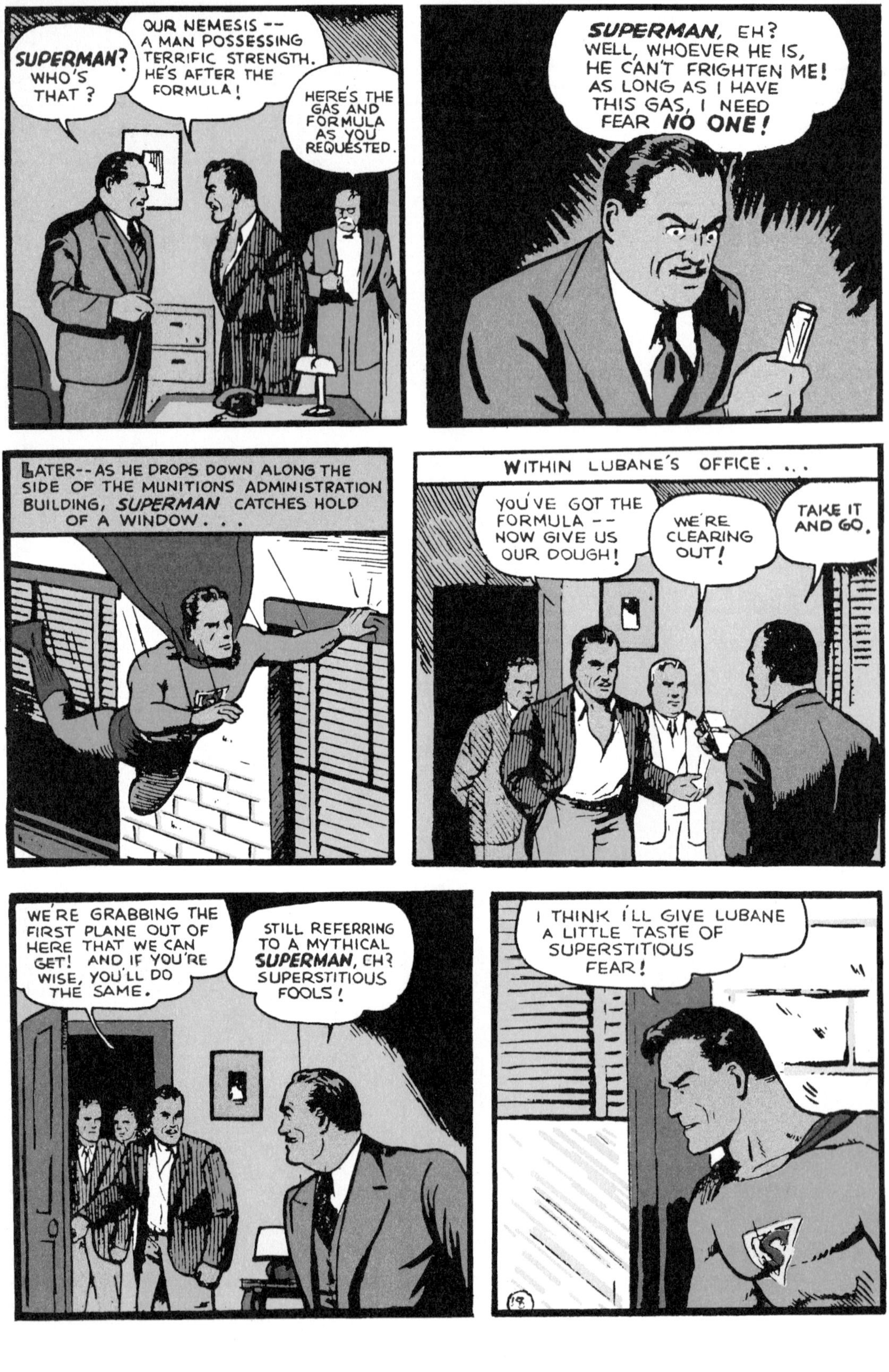
SUPERMAN? WHO'S THAT?
OUR NEMESIS -- A MAN POSSESSING TERRIFIC STRENGTH. HE'S AFTER THE FORMULA!
HERE'S THE GAS AND FORMULA AS YOU REQUESTED.
SUPERMAN, EH? WELL, WHOEVER HE IS, HE CAN'T FRIGHTEN ME! AS LONG AS I HAVE THIS GAS, I NEED FEAR NO ONE!
LATER--AS HE DROPS DOWN ALONG THE SIDE OF THE MUNITIONS ADMINISTRATION BUILDING, SUPERMAN CATCHES HOLD OF A WINDOW...
WITHIN LUBANE'S OFFICE...
YOU'VE GOT THE FORMULA -- NOW GIVE US OUR DOUGH!
WE'RE CLEARING OUT!
TAKE IT AND GO.
WE'RE GRABBING THE FIRST PLANE OUT OF HERE THAT WE CAN GET! AND IF YOU'RE WISE, YOU'LL DO THE SAME.
STILL REFERRING TO A MYTHICAL SUPERMAN, EH? SUPERSTITIOUS FOOLS!
I THINK I'LL GIVE LUBANE A LITTLE TASTE OF SUPERSTITIOUS FEAR!
18

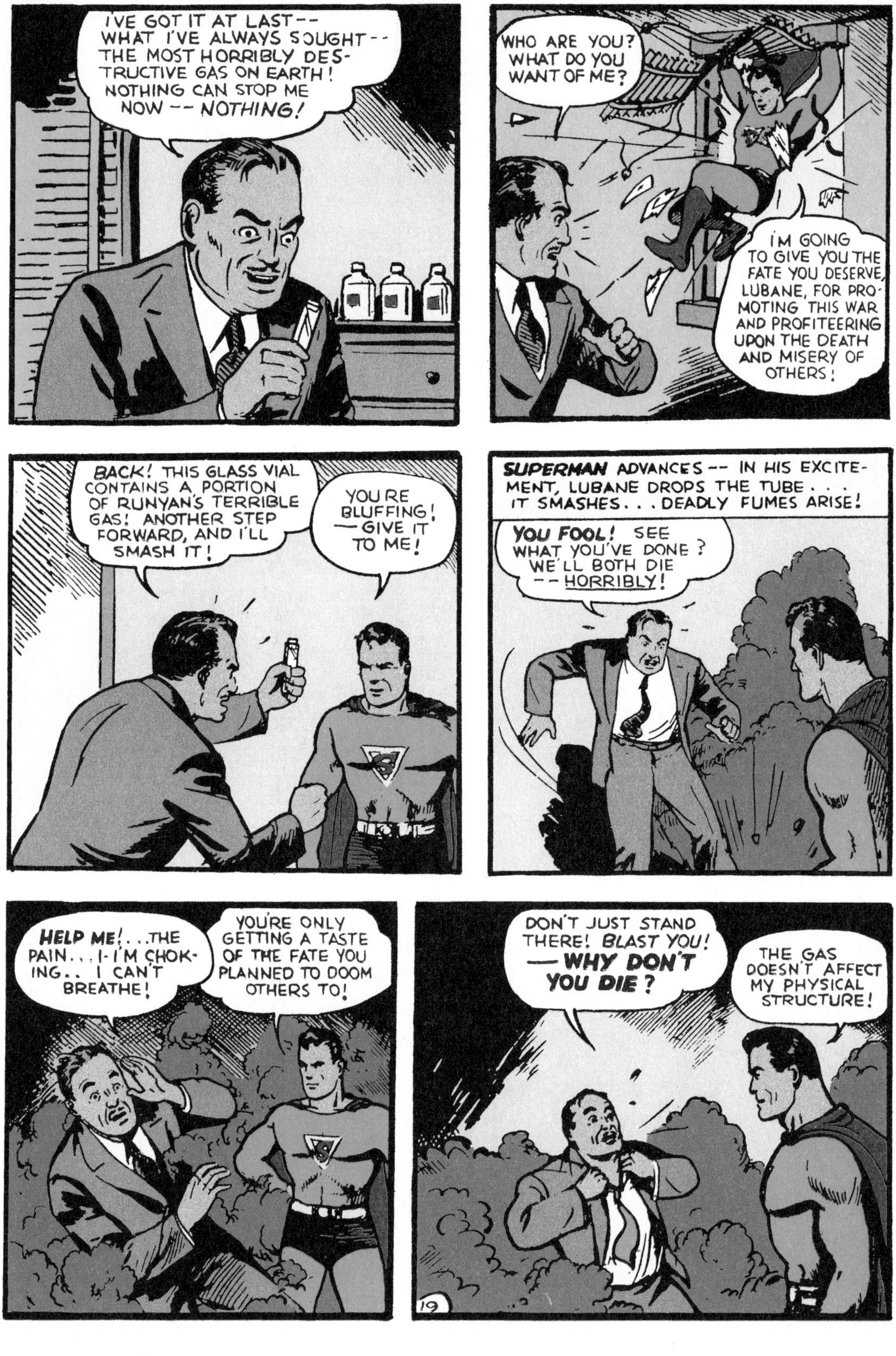
I'VE GOT IT AT LAST-- WHAT I'VE ALWAYS SOUGHT-- THE MOST HORRIBLY DES-TRUCTIVE GAS ON EARTH! NOTHING CAN STOP ME NOW -- NOTHING!
WHO ARE YOU? WHAT DO YOU WANT OF ME?
I'M GOING TO GIVE YOU THE FATE YOU DESERVE, LUBANE, FOR PRO-MOTING THIS WAR AND PROFITEERING UPON THE DEATH AND MISERY OF OTHERS!
BACK! THIS GLASS VIAL CONTAINS A PORTION OF RUNYAN'S TERRIBLE GAS! ANOTHER STEP FORWARD, AND I'LL SMASH IT!
YOU'RE BLUFFING! —GIVE IT TO ME!
SUPERMAN ADVANCES -- IN HIS EXCITE-MENT, LUBANE DROPS THE TUBE . . . IT SMASHES . . . DEADLY FUMES ARISE!
YOU FOOL! SEE WHAT YOU'VE DONE? WE'LL BOTH DIE --HORRIBLY!
HELP ME! . . .THE PAIN. . . I-I'M CHOK-ING. . I CAN'T BREATHE!
YOU'RE ONLY GETTING A TASTE OF THE FATE YOU PLANNED TO DOOM OTHERS TO!
DON'T JUST STAND THERE! BLAST YOU! —WHY DON'T YOU DIE?
THE GAS DOESN'T AFFECT MY PHYSICAL STRUCTURE!
19

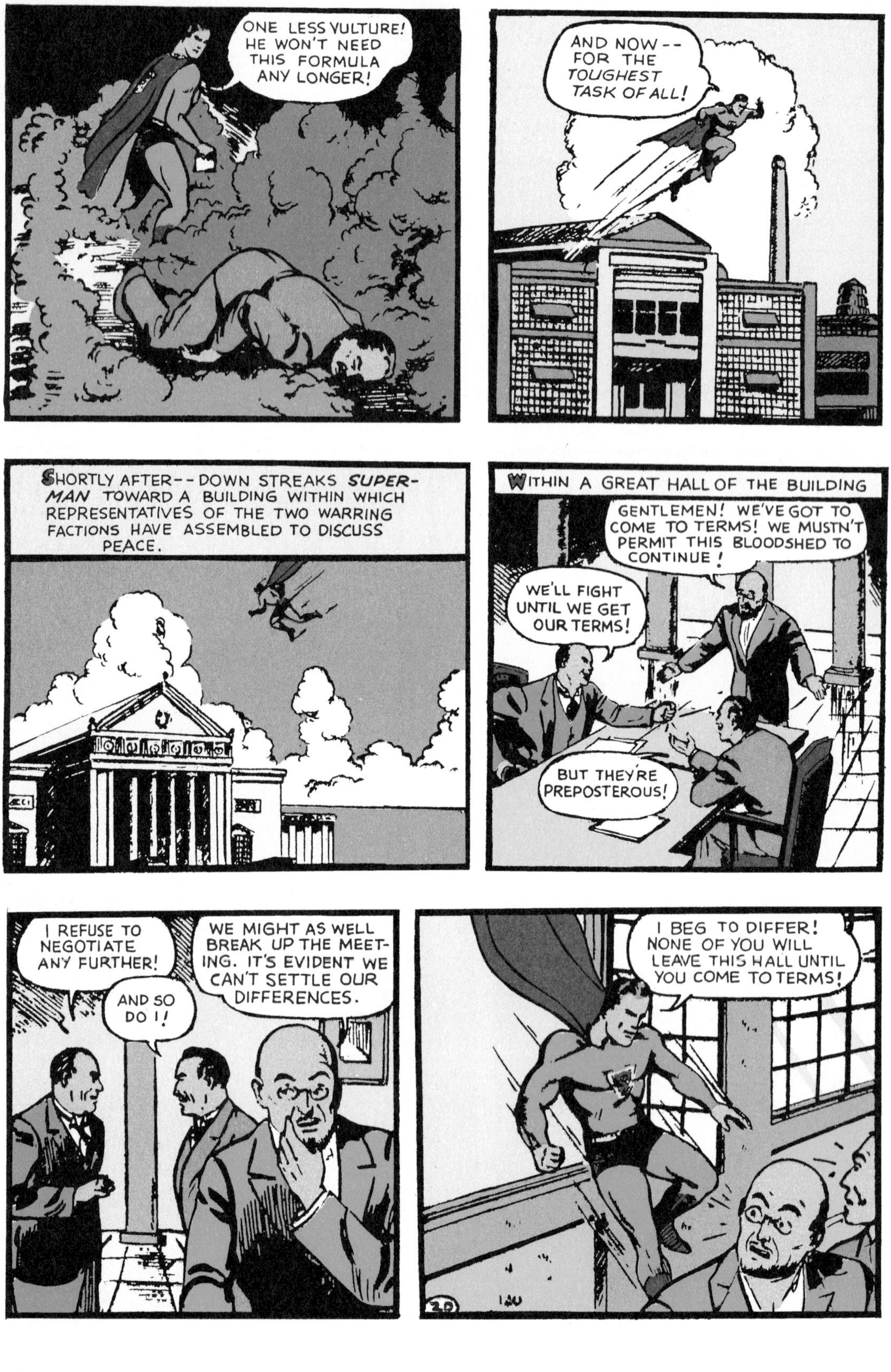
ONE LESS VULTURE! HE WON'T NEED THIS FORMULA ANY LONGER!
AND NOW -- FOR THE TOUGHEST TASK OF ALL!
SHORTLY AFTER-- DOWN STREAKS SUPERMAN TOWARD A BUILDING WITHIN WHICH REPRESENTATIVES OF THE TWO WARRING FACTIONS HAVE ASSEMBLED TO DISCUSS PEACE.
WITHIN A GREAT HALL OF THE BUILDING
GENTLEMEN! WE'VE GOT TO COME TO TERMS! WE MUSTN'T PERMIT THIS BLOODSHED TO CONTINUE!
WE'LL FIGHT UNTIL WE GET OUR TERMS!
BUT THEY'RE PREPOSTEROUS!
I REFUSE TO NEGOTIATE ANY FURTHER!
AND SO DO I!
WE MIGHT AS WELL BREAK UP THE MEETING. IT'S EVIDENT WE CAN'T SETTLE OUR DIFFERENCES.
I BEG TO DIFFER! NONE OF YOU WILL LEAVE THIS HALL UNTIL YOU COME TO TERMS!

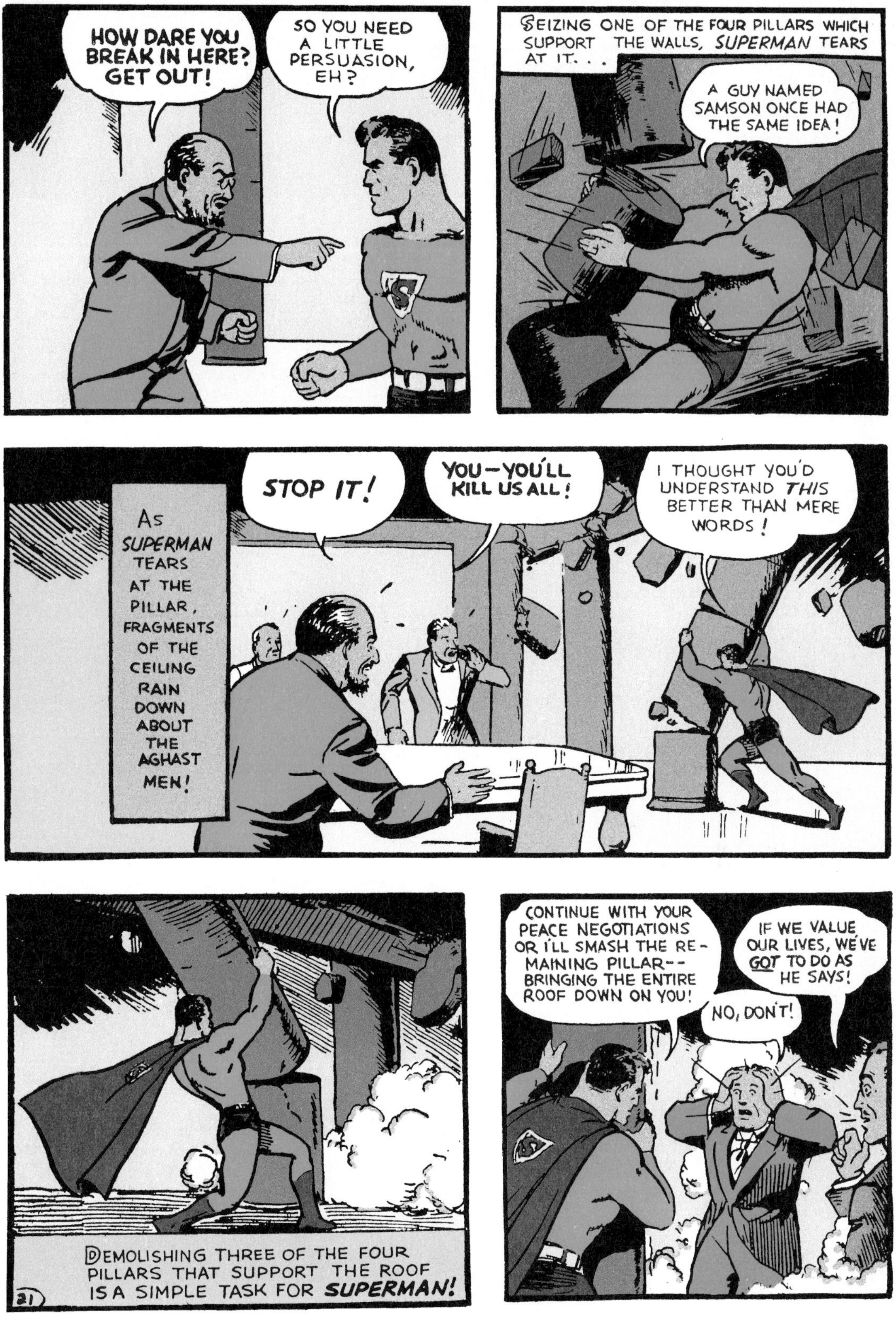
HOW DARE YOU BREAK IN HERE? GET OUT!
SO YOU NEED A LITTLE PERSUASION, EH?
SEIZING ONE OF THE FOUR PILLARS WHICH SUPPORT THE WALLS, SUPERMAN TEARS AT IT. . .
A GUY NAMED SAMSON ONCE HAD THE SAME IDEA!
AS SUPERMAN TEARS AT THE PILLAR, FRAGMENTS OF THE CEILING RAIN DOWN ABOUT THE AGHAST MEN!
STOP IT!
YOU—YOU'LL KILL US ALL!
I THOUGHT YOU'D UNDERSTAND THIS BETTER THAN MERE WORDS!
DEMOLISHING THREE OF THE FOUR PILLARS THAT SUPPORT THE ROOF IS A SIMPLE TASK FOR SUPERMAN!
21
CONTINUE WITH YOUR PEACE NEGOTIATIONS OR I'LL SMASH THE RE-MAINING PILLAR-- BRINGING THE ENTIRE ROOF DOWN ON YOU!
NO, DON'T!
IF WE VALUE OUR LIVES, WE'VE GOT TO DO AS HE SAYS!

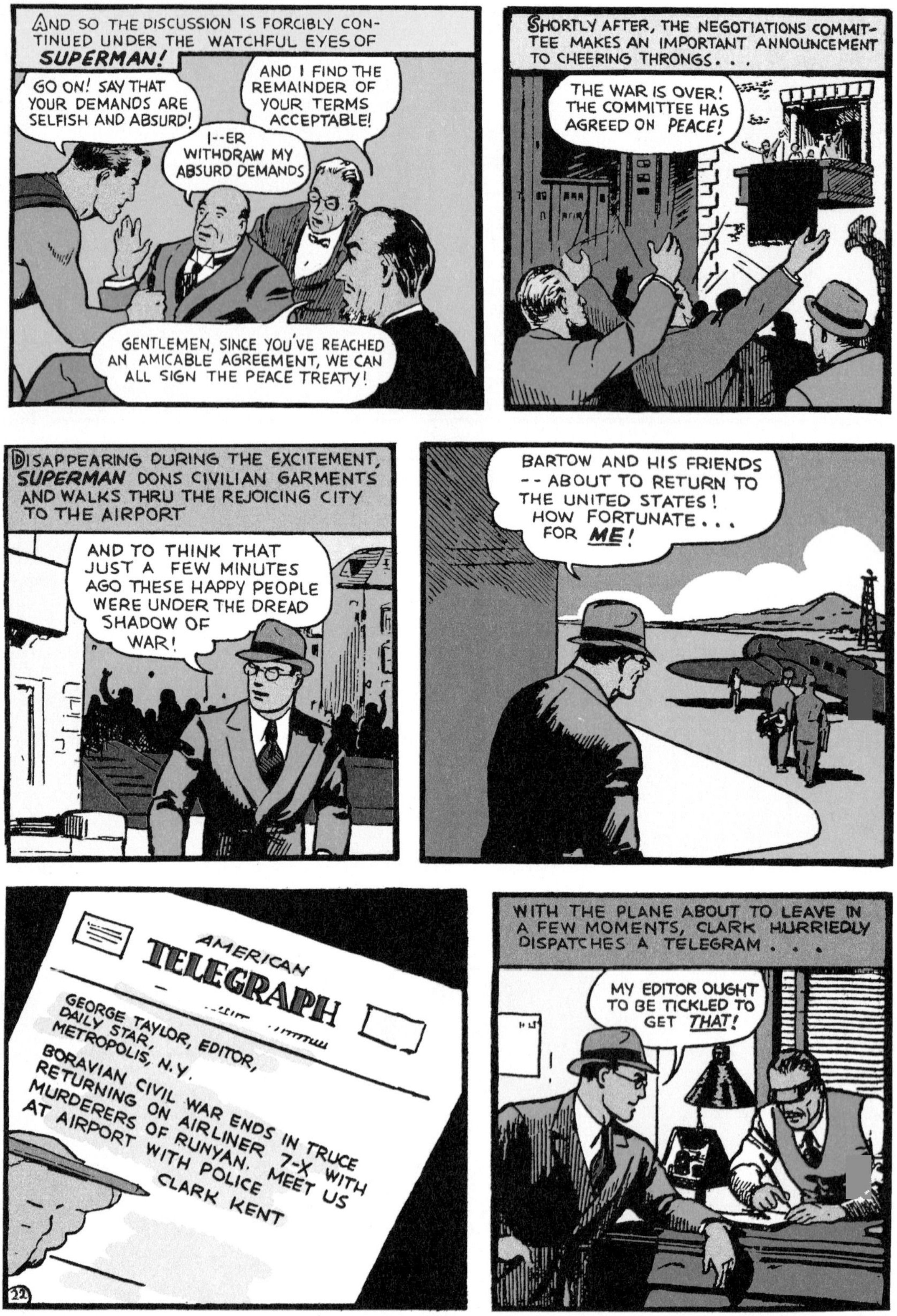
AND SO THE DISCUSSION IS FORCIBLY CONTINUED UNDER THE WATCHFUL EYES OF SUPERMAN!
GO ON! SAY THAT YOUR DEMANDS ARE SELFISH AND ABSURD!
I--ER WITHDRAW MY ABSURD DEMANDS
AND I FIND THE REMAINDER OF YOUR TERMS ACCEPTABLE!
GENTLEMEN, SINCE YOU'VE REACHED AN AMICABLE AGREEMENT, WE CAN ALL SIGN THE PEACE TREATY!
SHORTLY AFTER, THE NEGOTIATIONS COMMITTEE MAKES AN IMPORTANT ANNOUNCEMENT TO CHEERING THRONGS . . .
THE WAR IS OVER! THE COMMITTEE HAS AGREED ON PEACE!
DISAPPEARING DURING THE EXCITEMENT, SUPERMAN DONS CIVILIAN GARMENTS AND WALKS THRU THE REJOICING CITY TO THE AIRPORT
AND TO THINK THAT JUST A FEW MINUTES AGO THESE HAPPY PEOPLE WERE UNDER THE DREAD SHADOW OF WAR!
BARTOW AND HIS FRIENDS -- ABOUT TO RETURN TO THE UNITED STATES! HOW FORTUNATE . . . FOR ME!
AMERICAN TELEGRAPH
GEORGE TAYLOR, EDITOR, DAILY STAR, METROPOLIS, N.Y.
BORAVIAN CIVIL WAR ENDS IN TRUCE RETURNING ON AIRLINER 7-X WITH MURDERERS OF RUNYAN. MEET US AT AIRPORT WITH POLICE
CLARK KENT
22
WITH THE PLANE ABOUT TO LEAVE IN A FEW MOMENTS, CLARK HURRIEDLY DISPATCHES A TELEGRAM . . .
MY EDITOR OUGHT TO BE TICKLED TO GET THAT!

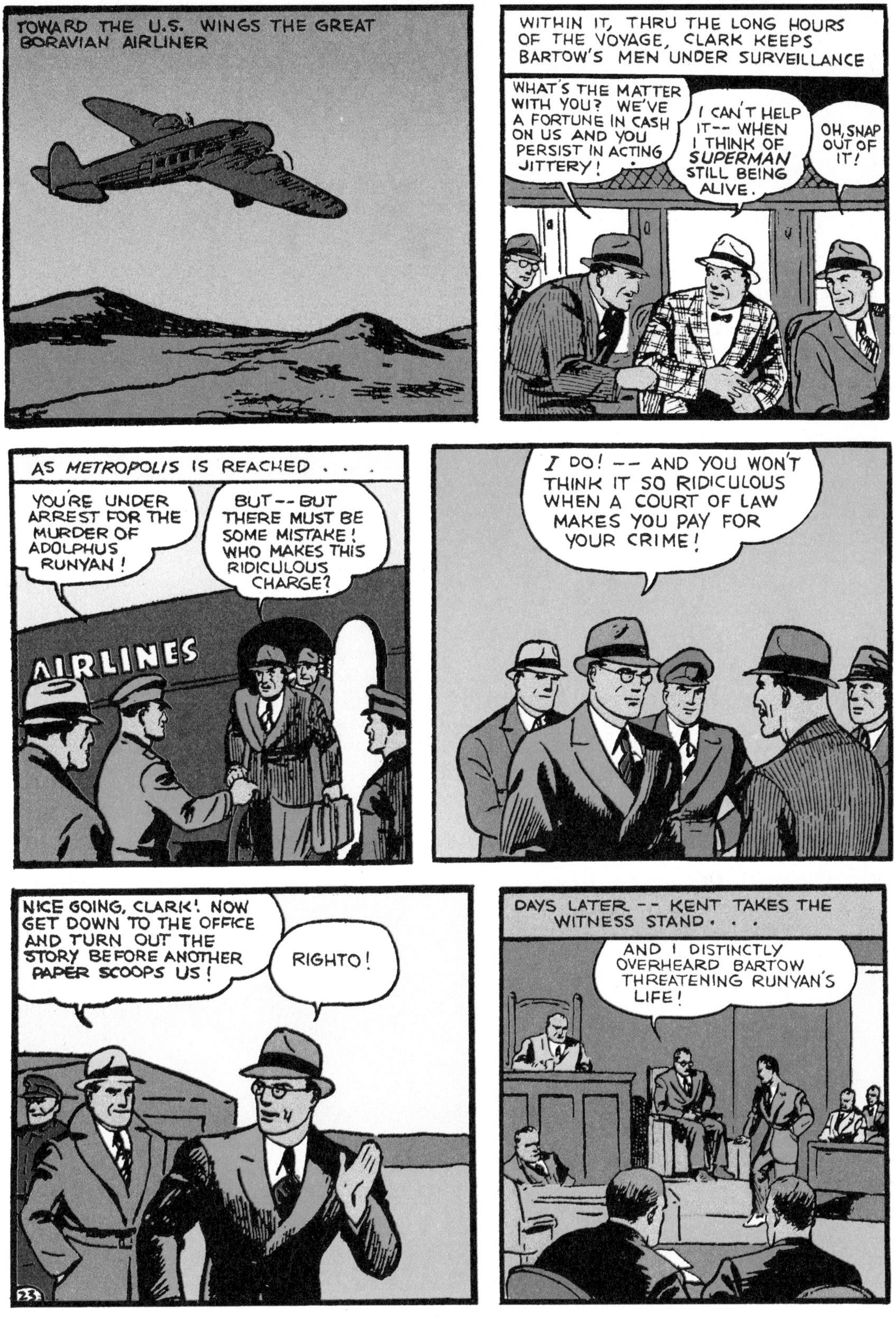
TOWARD THE U.S. WINGS THE GREAT BORAVIAN AIRLINER
WITHIN IT, THRU THE LONG HOURS OF THE VOYAGE, CLARK KEEPS BARTOW'S MEN UNDER SURVEILLANCE
WHAT'S THE MATTER WITH YOU? WE'VE A FORTUNE IN CASH ON US AND YOU PERSIST IN ACTING JITTERY!
I CAN'T HELP IT-- WHEN I THINK OF SUPERMAN STILL BEING ALIVE.
OH, SNAP OUT OF IT!
AS METROPOLIS IS REACHED . . .
YOU'RE UNDER ARREST FOR THE MURDER OF ADOLPHUS RUNYAN!
BUT--BUT THERE MUST BE SOME MISTAKE! WHO MAKES THIS RIDICULOUS CHARGE?
AIRLINES
I DO! -- AND YOU WON'T THINK IT SO RIDICULOUS WHEN A COURT OF LAW MAKES YOU PAY FOR YOUR CRIME!
NICE GOING, CLARK! NOW GET DOWN TO THE OFFICE AND TURN OUT THE STORY BEFORE ANOTHER PAPER SCOOPS US!
RIGHTO!
DAYS LATER -- KENT TAKES THE WITNESS STAND . . .
AND I DISTINCTLY OVERHEARD BARTOW THREATENING RUNYAN'S LIFE!

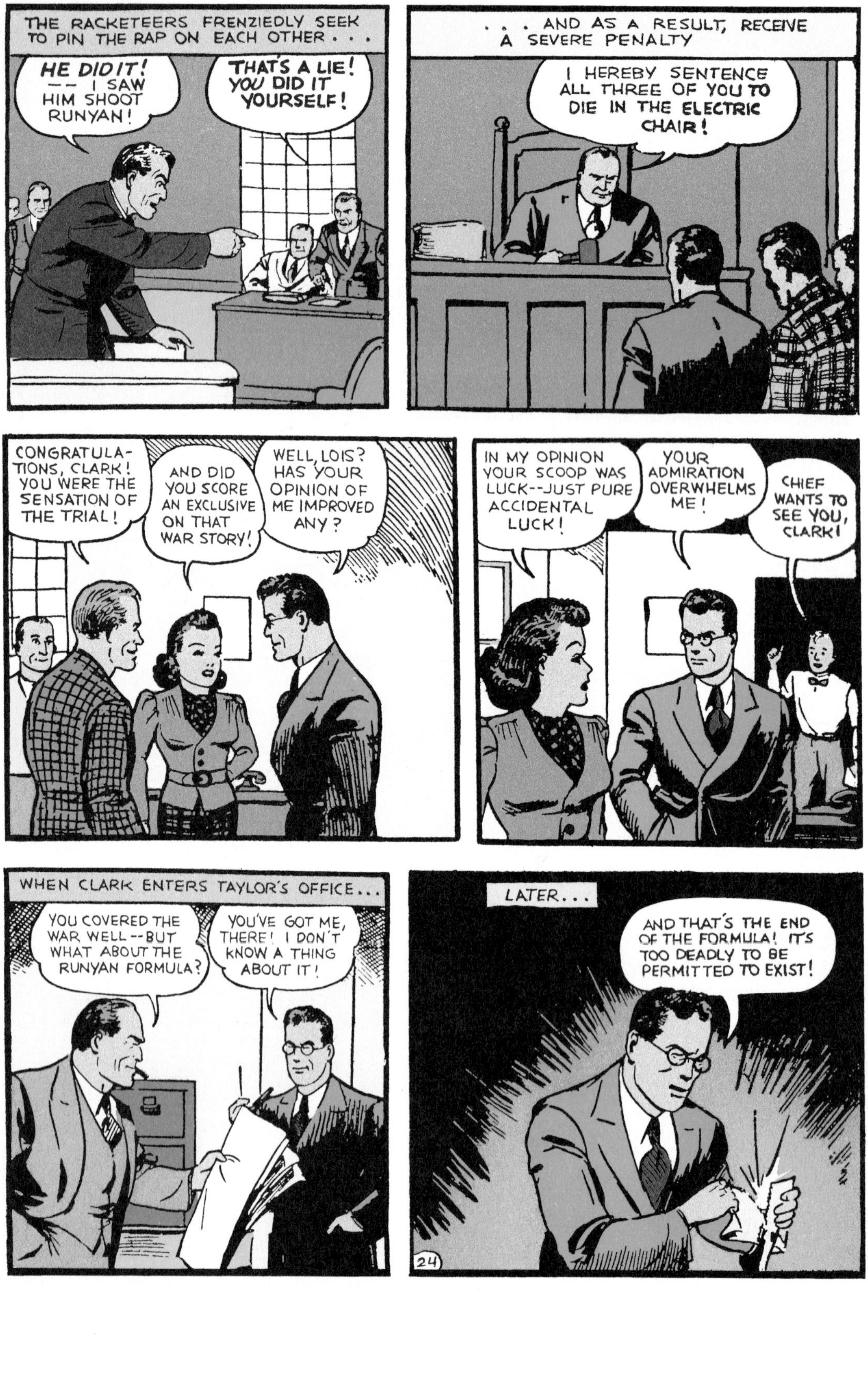
THE RACKETEERS FRENZIEDLY SEEK TO PIN THE RAP ON EACH OTHER . . .
HE DID IT! -- I SAW HIM SHOOT RUNYAN!
THAT'S A LIE! YOU DID IT YOURSELF!
. . . AND AS A RESULT, RECEIVE A SEVERE PENALTY
I HEREBY SENTENCE ALL THREE OF YOU TO DIE IN THE ELECTRIC CHAIR!
CONGRATULATIONS, CLARK! YOU WERE THE SENSATION OF THE TRIAL!
AND DID YOU SCORE AN EXCLUSIVE ON THAT WAR STORY!
WELL, LOIS? HAS YOUR OPINION OF ME IMPROVED ANY?
IN MY OPINION YOUR SCOOP WAS LUCK--JUST PURE ACCIDENTAL LUCK!
YOUR ADMIRATION OVERWHELMS ME!
CHIEF WANTS TO SEE YOU, CLARK!
WHEN CLARK ENTERS TAYLOR'S OFFICE...
YOU COVERED THE WAR WELL--BUT WHAT ABOUT THE RUNYAN FORMULA?
YOU'VE GOT ME, THERE! I DON'T KNOW A THING ABOUT IT!
LATER...
AND THAT'S THE END OF THE FORMULA! IT'S TOO DEADLY TO BE PERMITTED TO EXIST!
24

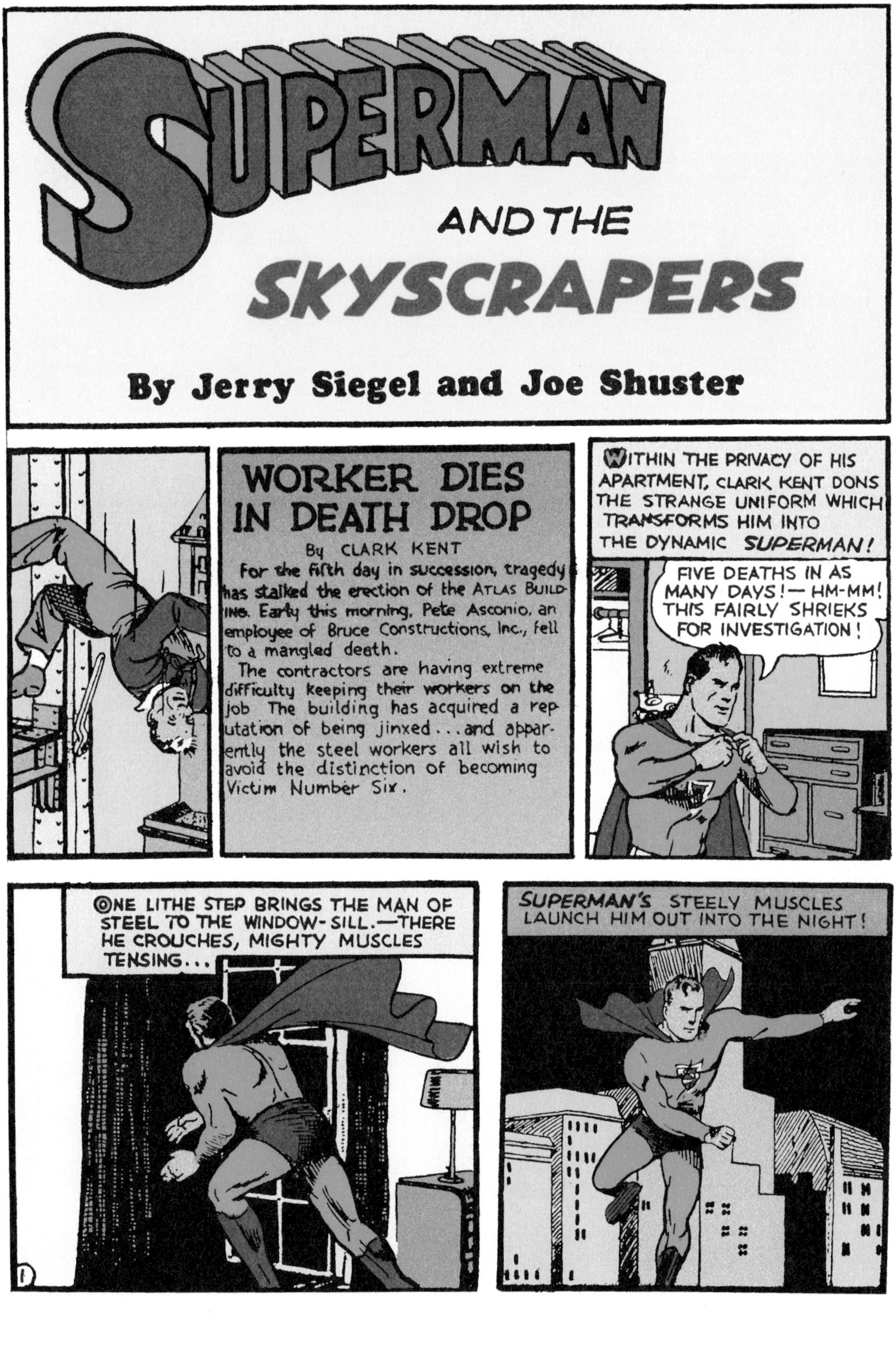
SUPERMAN
AND THE
SKYSCRAPERS
By Jerry Siegel and Joe Shuster
WORKER DIES IN DEATH DROP
By CLARK KENT
For the fifth day in succession, tragedy has stalked the erection of the ATLAS BUILDING. Early this morning, Pete Asconio, an employee of Bruce Constructions, Inc., fell to a mangled death.
The contractors are having extreme difficulty keeping their workers on the job. The building has acquired a reputation of being jinxed...and apparently the steel workers all wish to avoid the distinction of becoming Victim Number Six.
WITHIN THE PRIVACY OF HIS APARTMENT, CLARK KENT DONS THE STRANGE UNIFORM WHICH TRANSFORMS HIM INTO THE DYNAMIC SUPERMAN!
FIVE DEATHS IN AS MANY DAYS!— HM-MM! THIS FAIRLY SHRIEKS FOR INVESTIGATION!
ONE LITHE STEP BRINGS THE MAN OF STEEL TO THE WINDOW-SILL.—THERE HE CROUCHES, MIGHTY MUSCLES TENSING...
SUPERMAN'S STEELY MUSCLES LAUNCH HIM OUT INTO THE NIGHT!

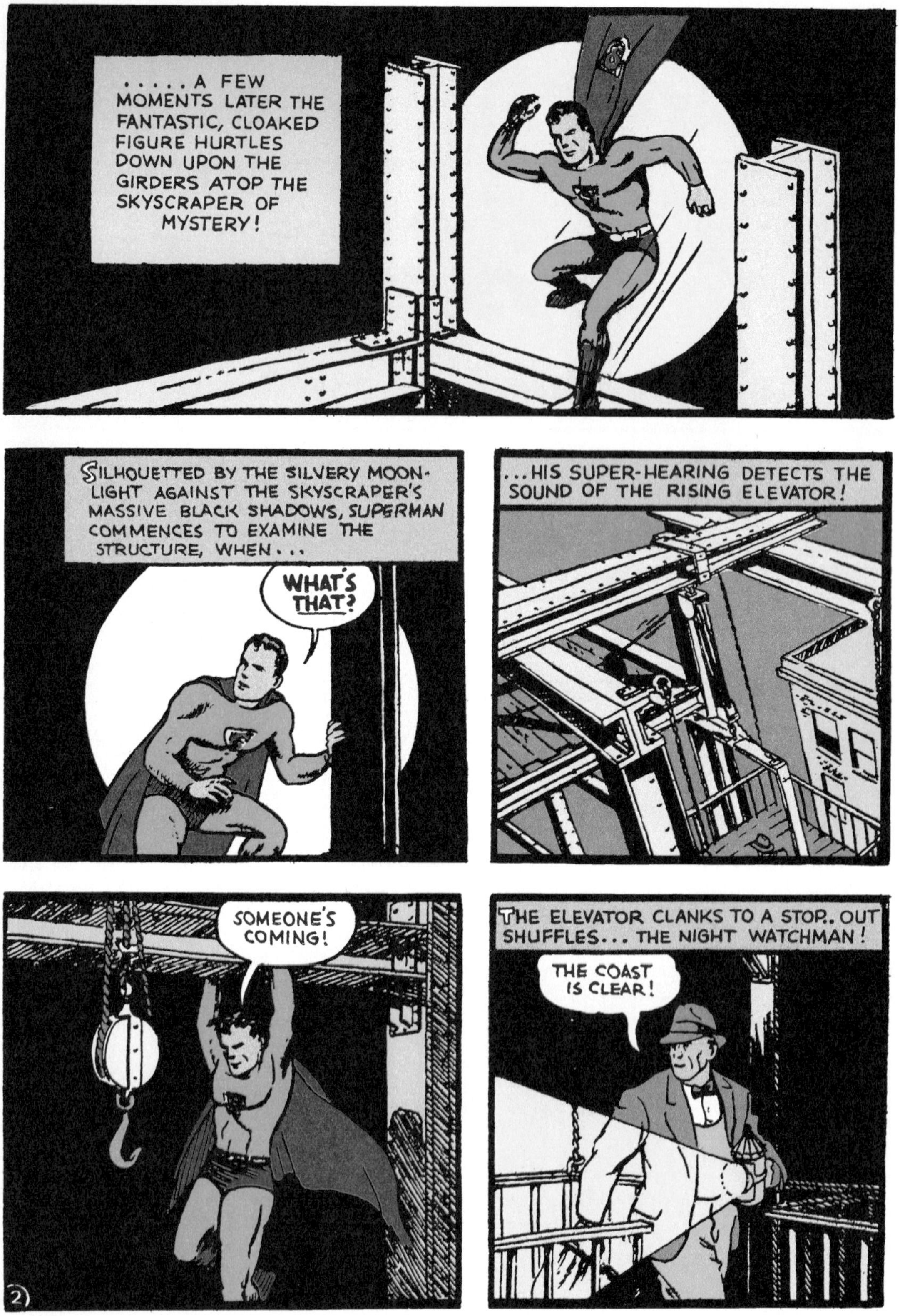
. . . . . A FEW MOMENTS LATER THE FANTASTIC, CLOAKED FIGURE HURTLES DOWN UPON THE GIRDERS ATOP THE SKYSCRAPER OF MYSTERY!
SILHOUETTED BY THE SILVERY MOON-LIGHT AGAINST THE SKYSCRAPER'S MASSIVE BLACK SHADOWS, SUPERMAN COMMENCES TO EXAMINE THE STRUCTURE, WHEN . . .
WHAT'S THAT?
. . . HIS SUPER-HEARING DETECTS THE SOUND OF THE RISING ELEVATOR!
SOMEONE'S COMING!
2
THE ELEVATOR CLANKS TO A STOP.. OUT SHUFFLES . . . THE NIGHT WATCHMAN!
THE COAST IS CLEAR!

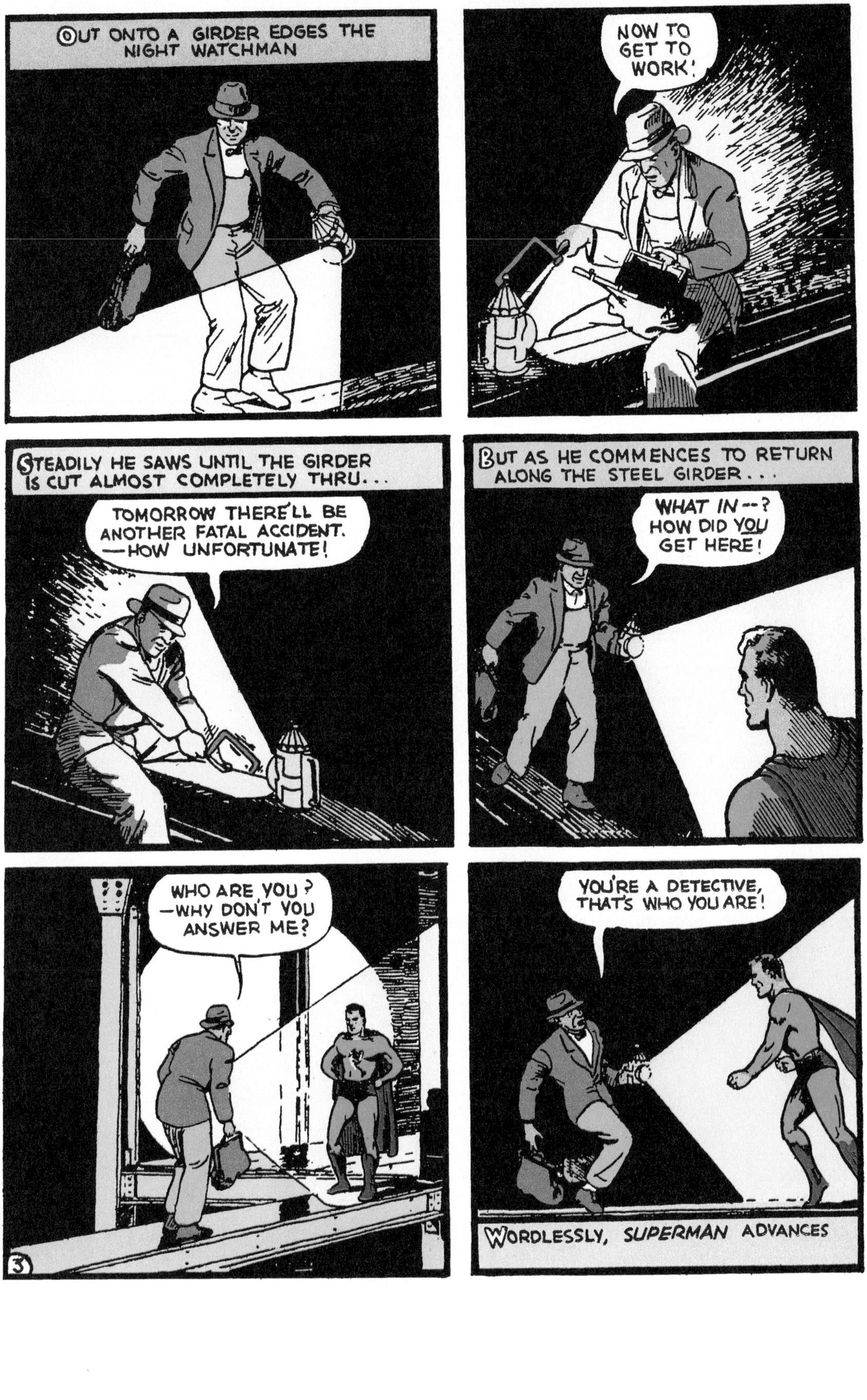
OUT ONTO A GIRDER EDGES THE NIGHT WATCHMAN
NOW TO GET TO WORK!
STEADILY HE SAWS UNTIL THE GIRDER IS CUT ALMOST COMPLETELY THRU...
TOMORROW THERE'LL BE ANOTHER FATAL ACCIDENT. —HOW UNFORTUNATE!
BUT AS HE COMMENCES TO RETURN ALONG THE STEEL GIRDER...
WHAT IN --? HOW DID YOU GET HERE!
WHO ARE YOU? —WHY DON'T YOU ANSWER ME?
3
YOU'RE A DETECTIVE, THAT'S WHO YOU ARE!
WORDLESSLY, SUPERMAN ADVANCES

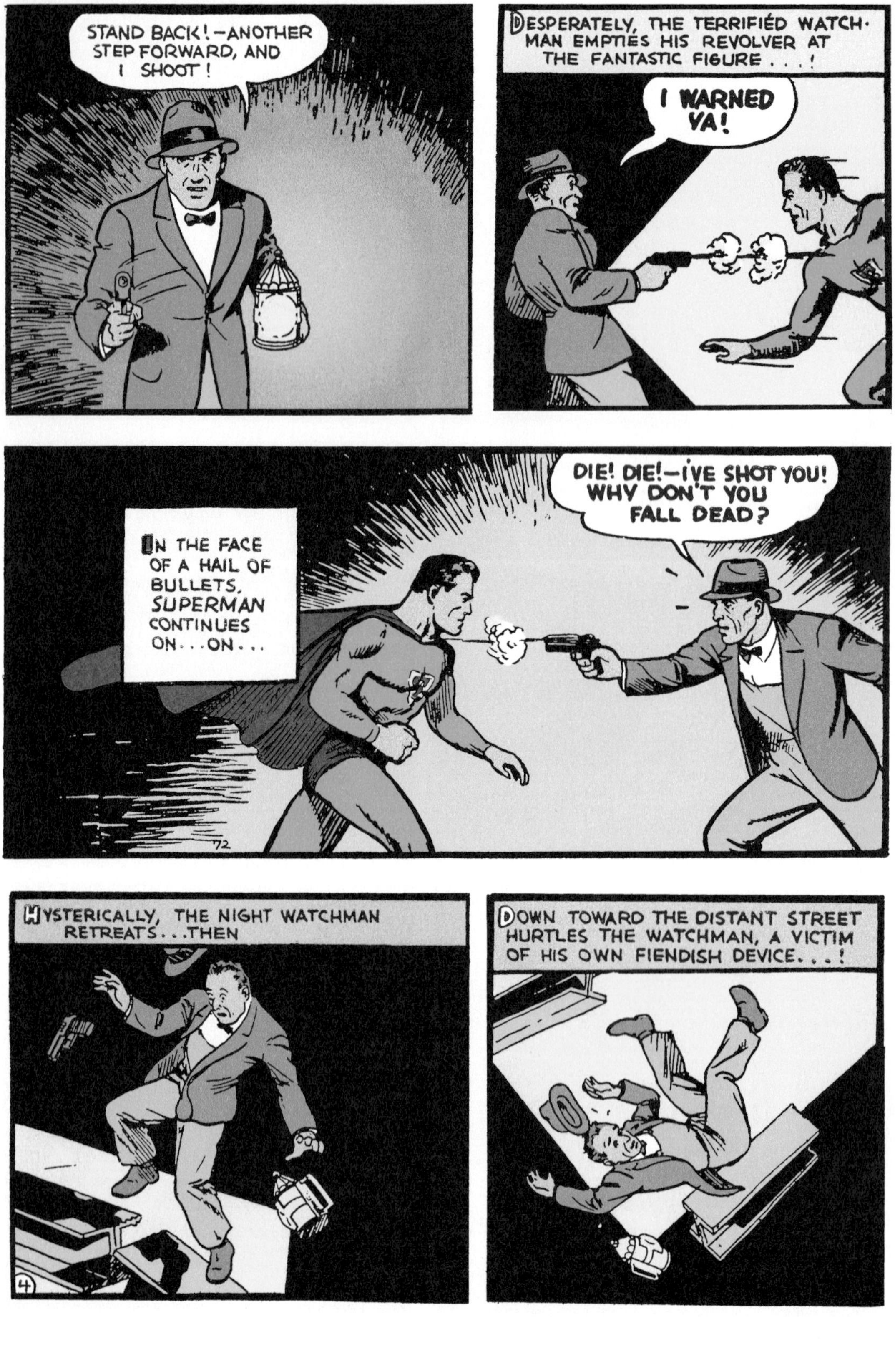
STAND BACK! —ANOTHER STEP FORWARD, AND I SHOOT!
DESPERATELY, THE TERRIFIÉD WATCH-MAN EMPTIÉS HIS REVOLVER AT THE FANTASTIC FIGURE . . . !
I WARNED YA!
IN THE FACE OF A HAIL OF BULLETS, SUPERMAN CONTINUES ON . . . ON . . .
DIE! DIE!—I'VE SHOT YOU! WHY DON'T YOU FALL DEAD?
HYSTERICALLY, THE NIGHT WATCHMAN RETREATS . . . THEN
DOWN TOWARD THE DISTANT STREET HURTLES THE WATCHMAN, A VICTIM OF HIS OWN FIENDISH DEVICE . . . !

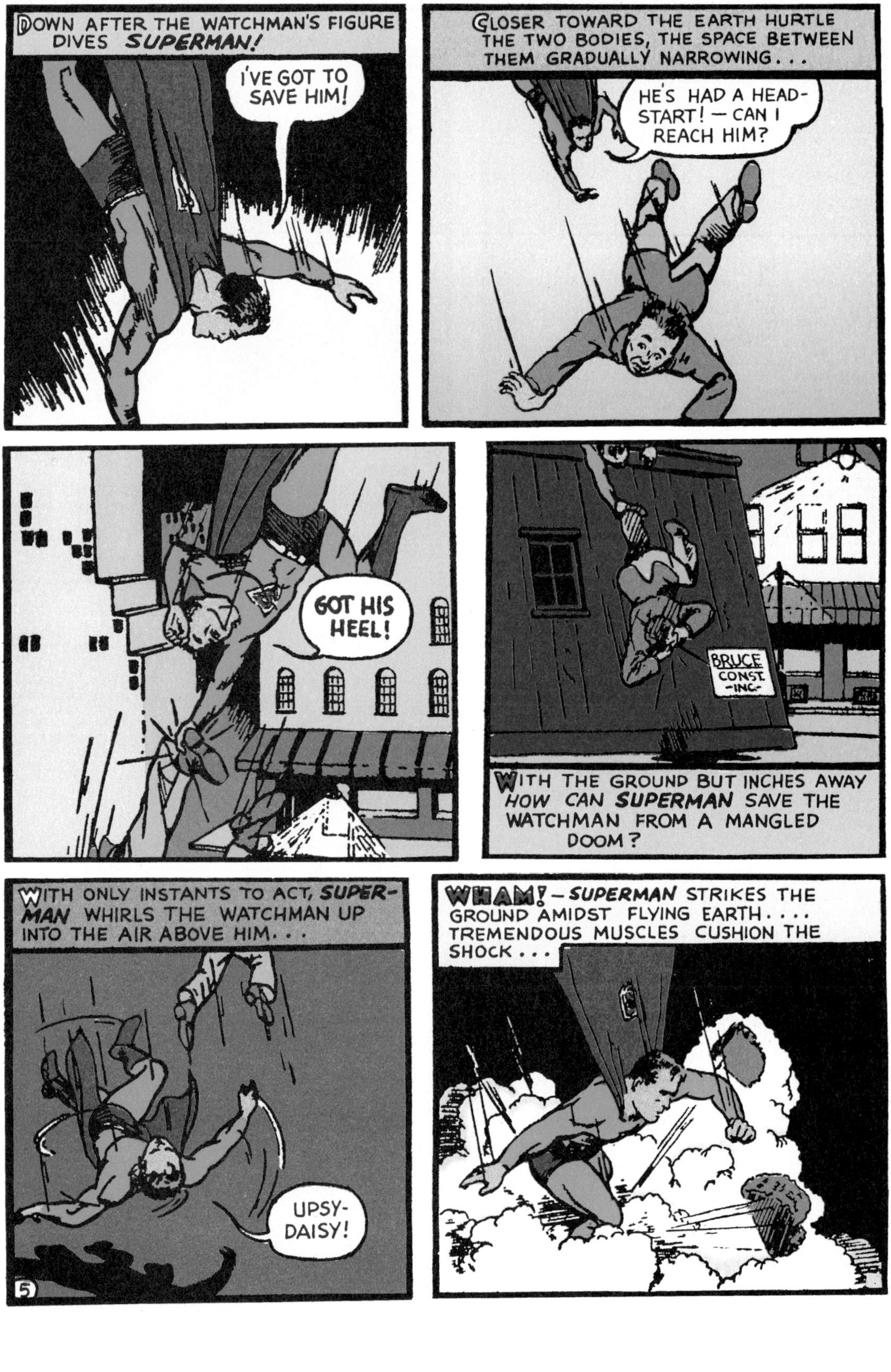
DOWN AFTER THE WATCHMAN'S FIGURE DIVES SUPERMAN!
I'VE GOT TO SAVE HIM!
CLOSER TOWARD THE EARTH HURTLE THE TWO BODIES, THE SPACE BETWEEN THEM GRADUALLY NARROWING . . .
HE'S HAD A HEAD-START! — CAN I REACH HIM?
GOT HIS HEEL!
BRUCE CONST. -INC-
WITH THE GROUND BUT INCHES AWAY HOW CAN SUPERMAN SAVE THE WATCHMAN FROM A MANGLED DOOM?
WITH ONLY INSTANTS TO ACT, SUPERMAN WHIRLS THE WATCHMAN UP INTO THE AIR ABOVE HIM . . .
UPSY-DAISY!
5
WHAM! — SUPERMAN STRIKES THE GROUND AMIDST FLYING EARTH . . . . TREMENDOUS MUSCLES CUSHION THE SHOCK . . .

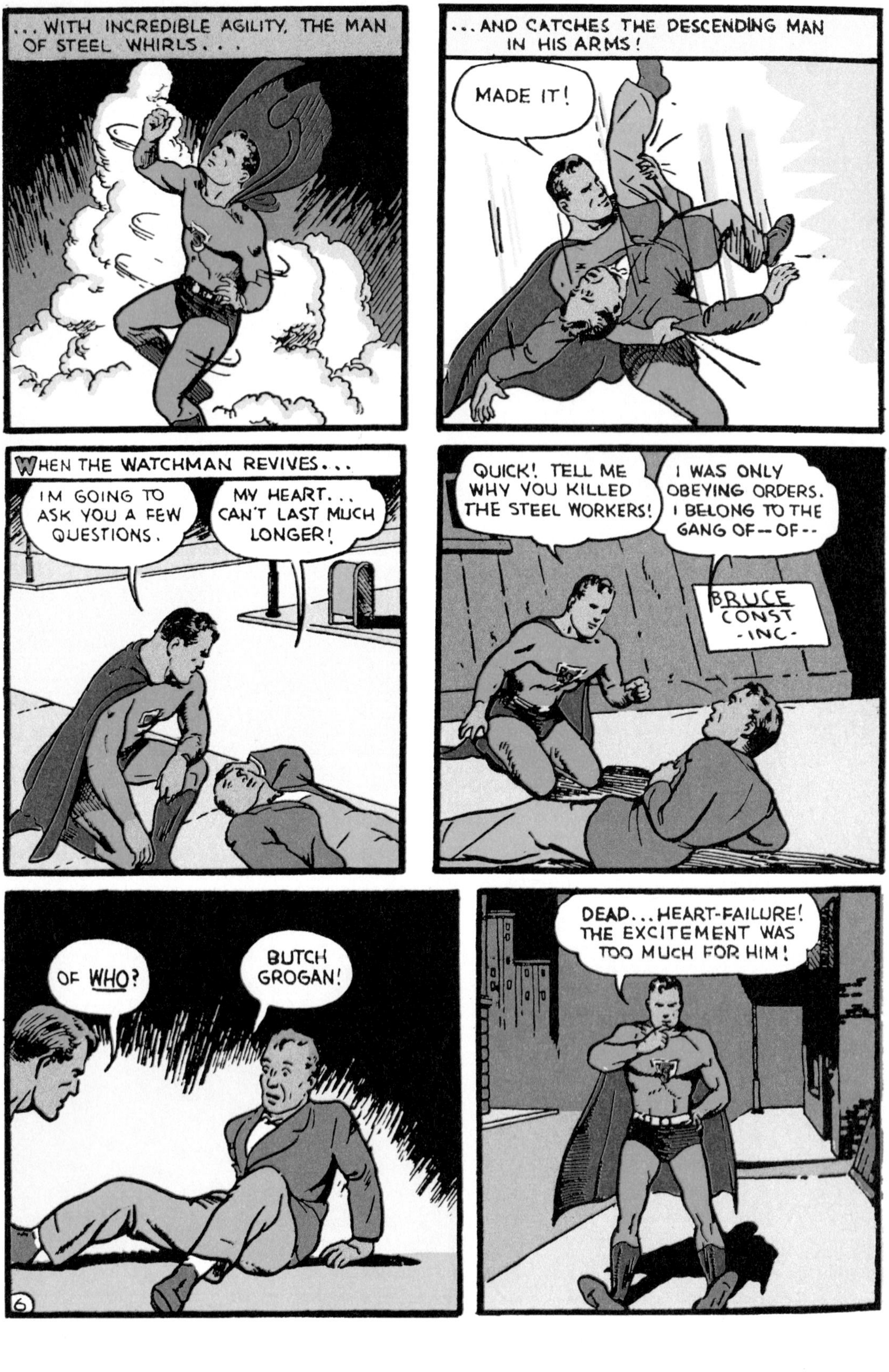
...WITH INCREDIBLE AGILITY, THE MAN OF STEEL WHIRLS...
...AND CATCHES THE DESCENDING MAN IN HIS ARMS!
MADE IT!
WHEN THE WATCHMAN REVIVES...
I'M GOING TO ASK YOU A FEW QUESTIONS.
MY HEART... CAN'T LAST MUCH LONGER!
QUICK! TELL ME WHY YOU KILLED THE STEEL WORKERS!
I WAS ONLY OBEYING ORDERS. I BELONG TO THE GANG OF--OF--
BRUCE CONST -INC-
OF WHO?
BUTCH GROGAN!
6
DEAD...HEART-FAILURE! THE EXCITEMENT WAS TOO MUCH FOR HIM!

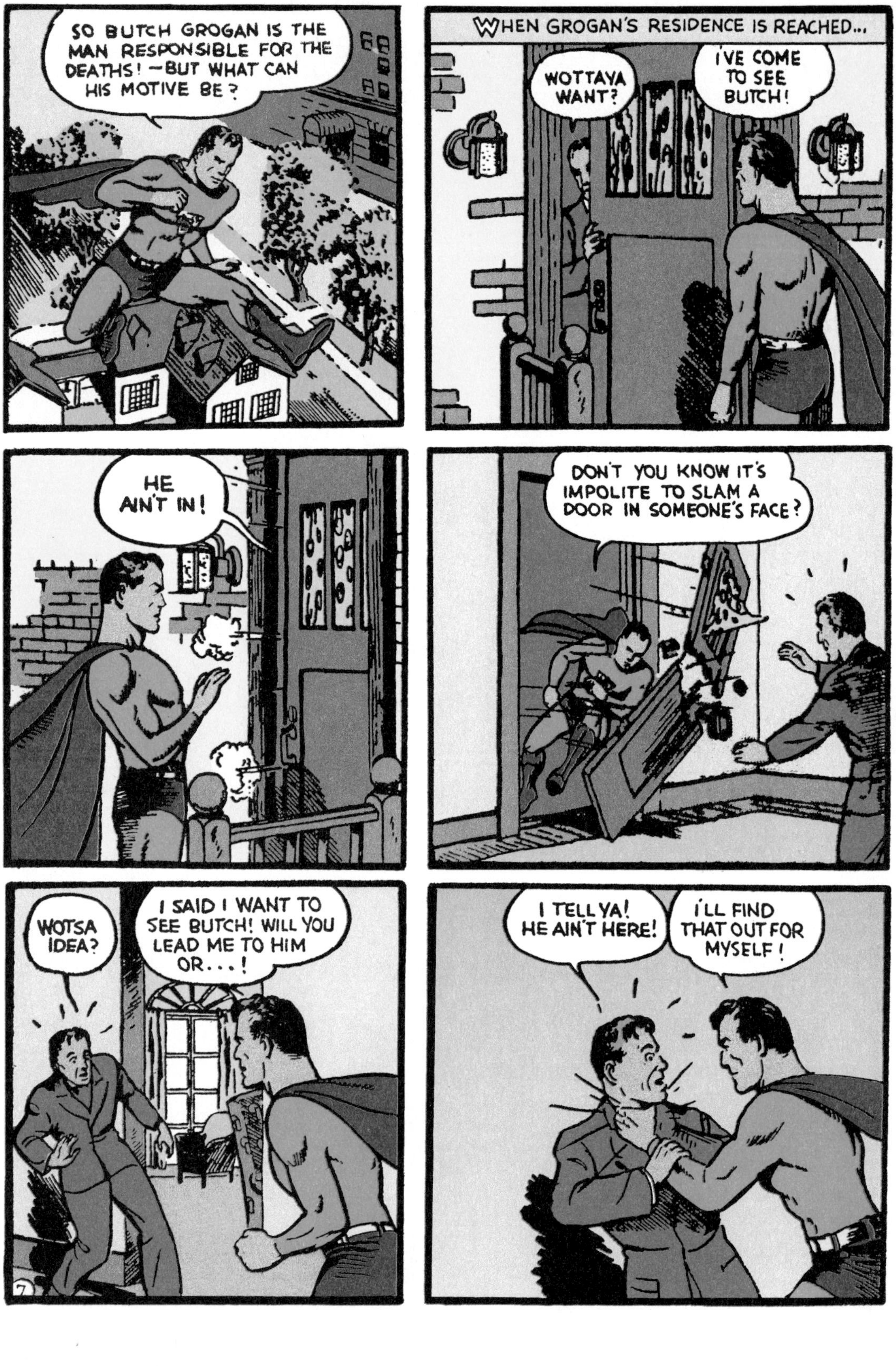
SO BUTCH GROGAN IS THE MAN RESPONSIBLE FOR THE DEATHS! —BUT WHAT CAN HIS MOTIVE BE?
WHEN GROGAN'S RESIDENCE IS REACHED...
WOTTAYA WANT?
I'VE COME TO SEE BUTCH!
HE AIN'T IN!
DON'T YOU KNOW IT'S IMPOLITE TO SLAM A DOOR IN SOMEONE'S FACE?
WOTSA IDEA?
I SAID I WANT TO SEE BUTCH! WILL YOU LEAD ME TO HIM OR...!
7
I TELL YA! HE AIN'T HERE!
I'LL FIND THAT OUT FOR MYSELF!

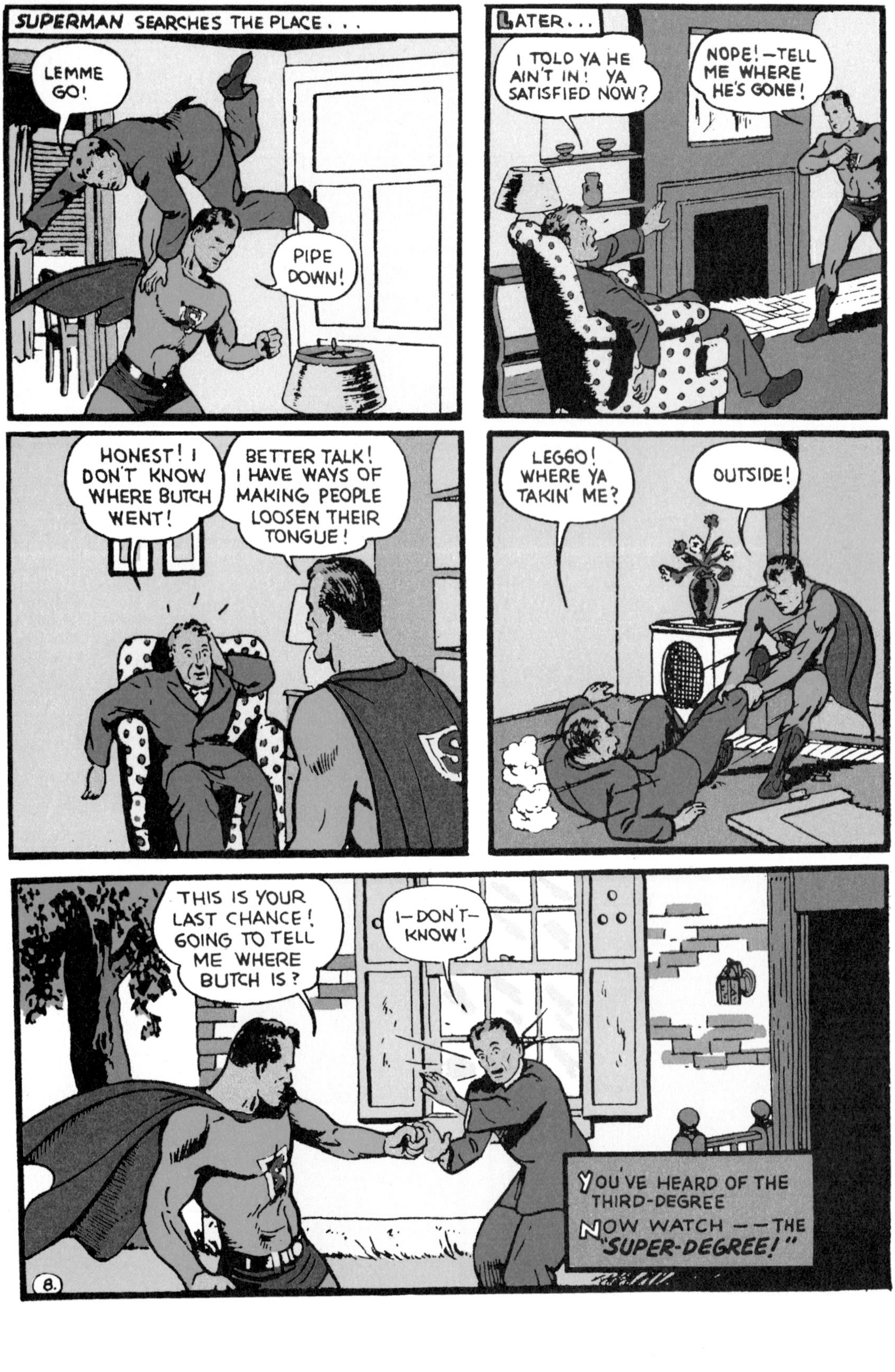
SUPERMAN SEARCHES THE PLACE . . .
LEMME GO!
PIPE DOWN!
LATER . . .
I TOLD YA HE AIN'T IN! YA SATISFIED NOW?
NOPE! —TELL ME WHERE HE'S GONE!
HONEST! I DON'T KNOW WHERE BUTCH WENT!
BETTER TALK! I HAVE WAYS OF MAKING PEOPLE LOOSEN THEIR TONGUE!
LEGGO! WHERE YA TAKIN' ME?
OUTSIDE!
THIS IS YOUR LAST CHANCE! GOING TO TELL ME WHERE BUTCH IS?
I—DON'T—KNOW!
YOU'VE HEARD OF THE THIRD-DEGREE
NOW WATCH — —THE "SUPER-DEGREE!"
8.

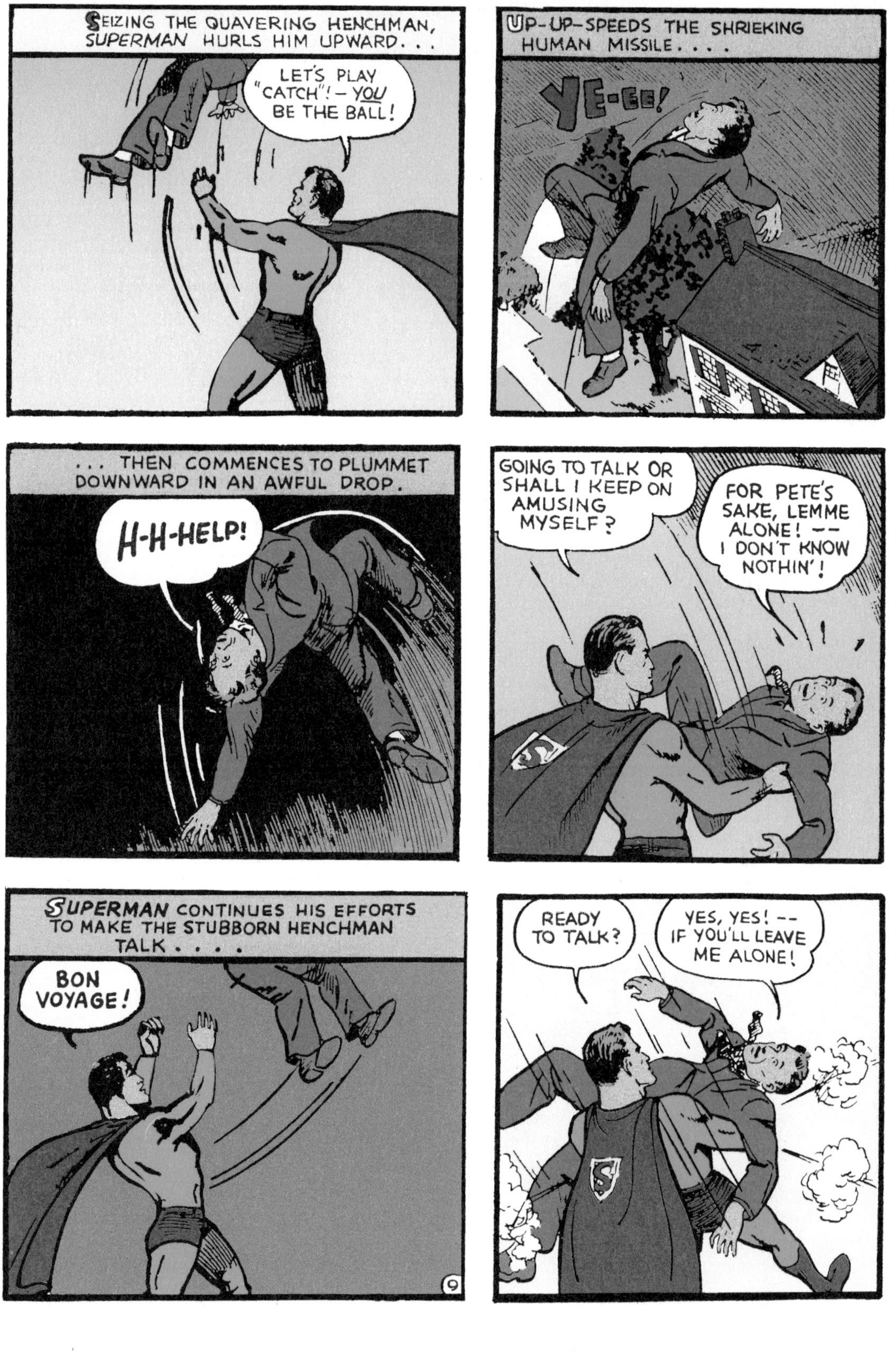
SEIZING THE QUAVERING HENCHMAN, SUPERMAN HURLS HIM UPWARD. . .
LET'S PLAY "CATCH"! – YOU BE THE BALL!
UP-UP-SPEEDS THE SHRIEKING HUMAN MISSILE. . . .
YE-EE!
. . . THEN COMMENCES TO PLUMMET DOWNWARD IN AN AWFUL DROP.
H-H-HELP!
GOING TO TALK OR SHALL I KEEP ON AMUSING MYSELF?
FOR PETE'S SAKE, LEMME ALONE! -- I DON'T KNOW NOTHIN'!
SUPERMAN CONTINUES HIS EFFORTS TO MAKE THE STUBBORN HENCHMAN TALK . . . .
BON VOYAGE!
9
READY TO TALK?
YES, YES! -- IF YOU'LL LEAVE ME ALONE!

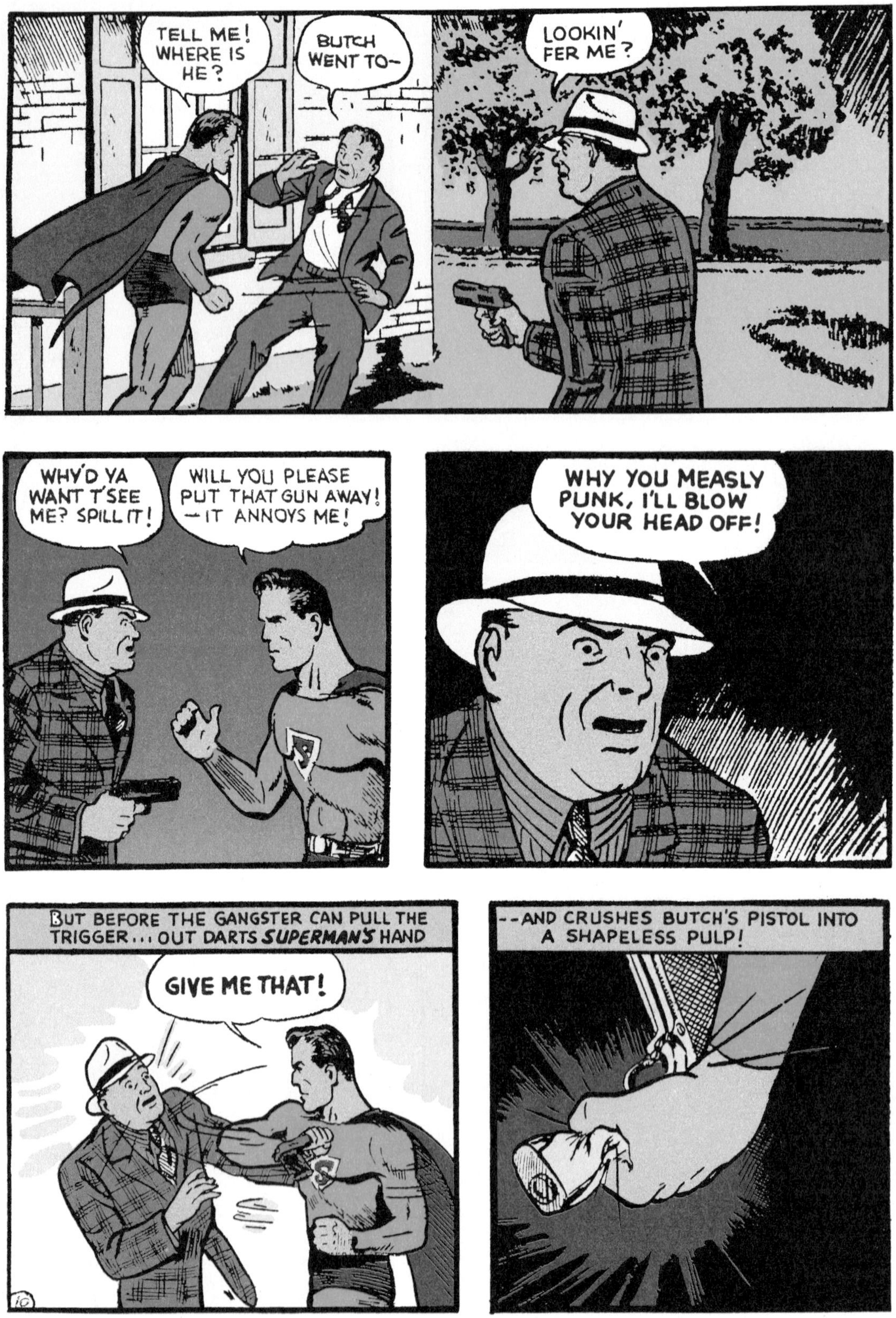
TELL ME! WHERE IS HE?
BUTCH WENT TO–
LOOKIN' FER ME?
WHY'D YA WANT T'SEE ME? SPILL IT!
WILL YOU PLEASE PUT THAT GUN AWAY! —IT ANNOYS ME!
WHY YOU MEASLY PUNK, I'LL BLOW YOUR HEAD OFF!
BUT BEFORE THE GANGSTER CAN PULL THE TRIGGER... OUT DARTS SUPERMAN'S HAND
GIVE ME THAT!
--AND CRUSHES BUTCH'S PISTOL INTO A SHAPELESS PULP!

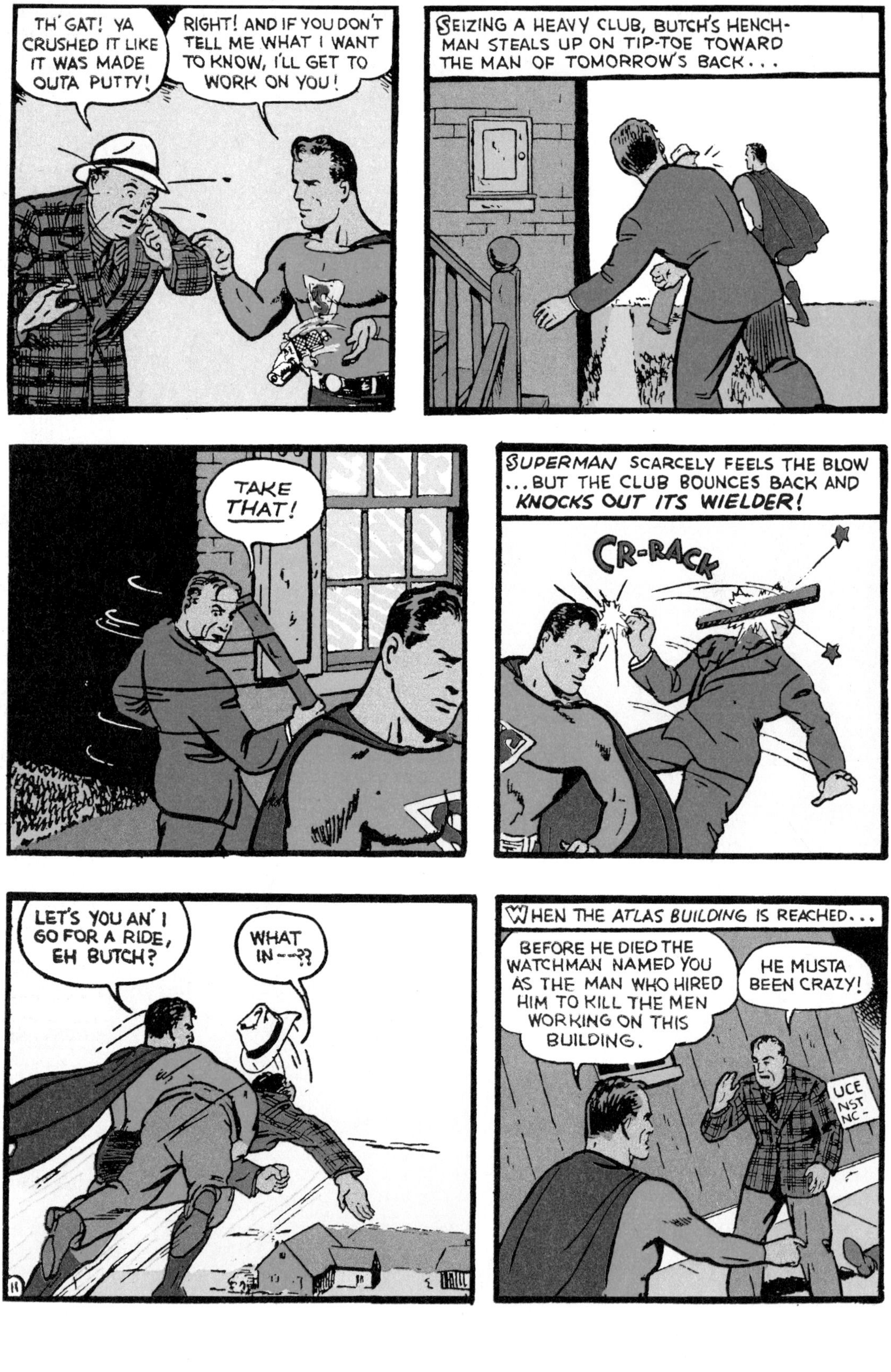
TH' GAT! YA CRUSHED IT LIKE IT WAS MADE OUTA PUTTY!
RIGHT! AND IF YOU DON'T TELL ME WHAT I WANT TO KNOW, I'LL GET TO WORK ON YOU!
SEIZING A HEAVY CLUB, BUTCH'S HENCH-MAN STEALS UP ON TIP-TOE TOWARD THE MAN OF TOMORROW'S BACK...
TAKE THAT!
SUPERMAN SCARCELY FEELS THE BLOW ...BUT THE CLUB BOUNCES BACK AND KNOCKS OUT ITS WIELDER!
CR-RACK
LET'S YOU AN' I GO FOR A RIDE, EH BUTCH?
WHAT IN--??
WHEN THE ATLAS BUILDING IS REACHED...
BEFORE HE DIED THE WATCHMAN NAMED YOU AS THE MAN WHO HIRED HIM TO KILL THE MEN WORKING ON THIS BUILDING.
HE MUSTA BEEN CRAZY!
UCE
NST
NC-

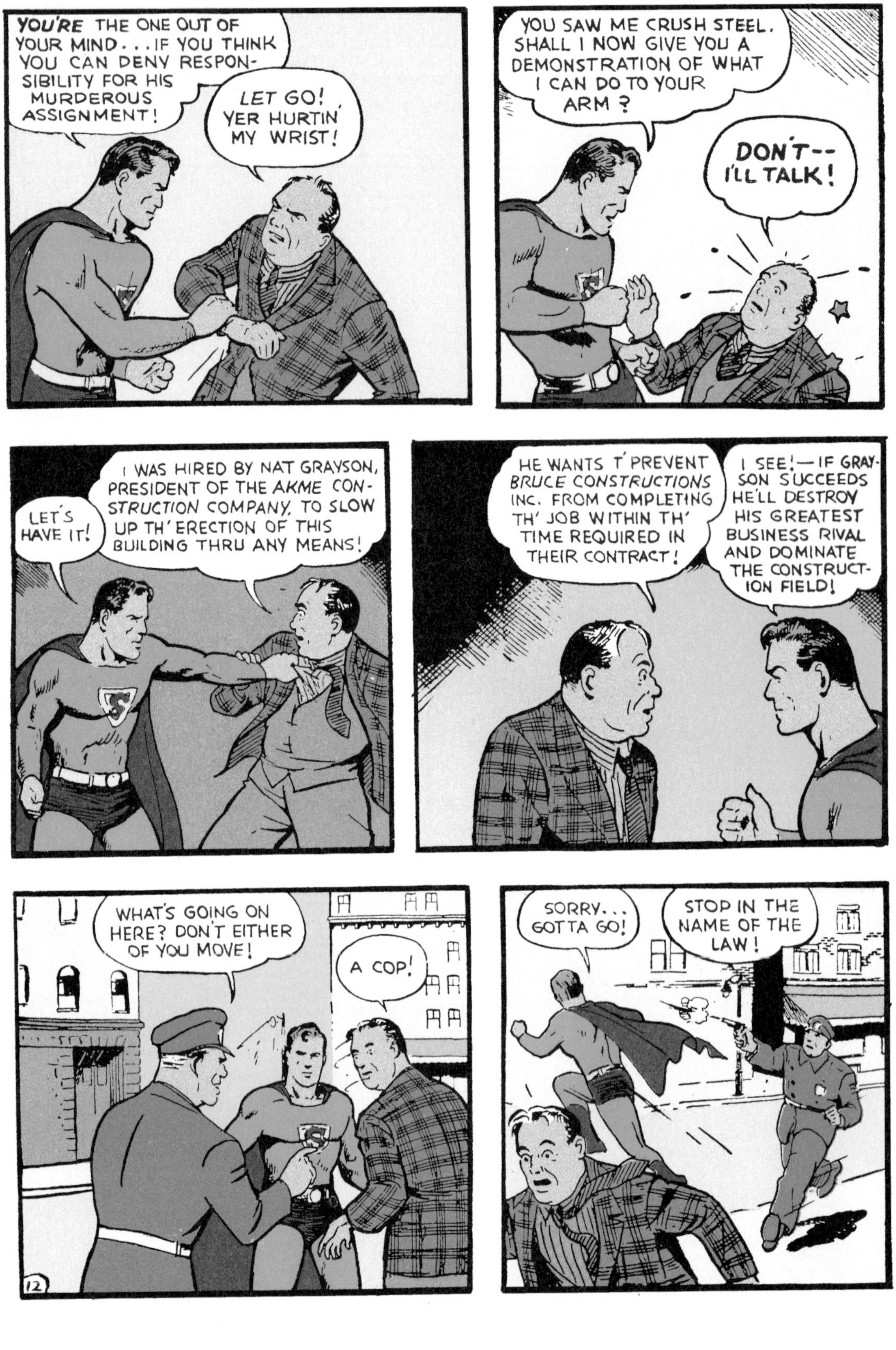
YOU'RE THE ONE OUT OF YOUR MIND... IF YOU THINK YOU CAN DENY RESPONSIBILITY FOR HIS MURDEROUS ASSIGNMENT!
LET GO! YER HURTIN' MY WRIST!
YOU SAW ME CRUSH STEEL. SHALL I NOW GIVE YOU A DEMONSTRATION OF WHAT I CAN DO TO YOUR ARM?
DON'T-- I'LL TALK!
LET'S HAVE IT!
I WAS HIRED BY NAT GRAYSON, PRESIDENT OF THE AKME CONSTRUCTION COMPANY, TO SLOW UP TH' ERECTION OF THIS BUILDING THRU ANY MEANS!
HE WANTS T' PREVENT BRUCE CONSTRUCTIONS INC. FROM COMPLETING TH' JOB WITHIN TH' TIME REQUIRED IN THEIR CONTRACT!
I SEE!—IF GRAYSON SUCCEEDS HE'LL DESTROY HIS GREATEST BUSINESS RIVAL AND DOMINATE THE CONSTRUCTION FIELD!
WHAT'S GOING ON HERE? DON'T EITHER OF YOU MOVE!
A COP!
12
SORRY... GOTTA GO!
STOP IN THE NAME OF THE LAW!

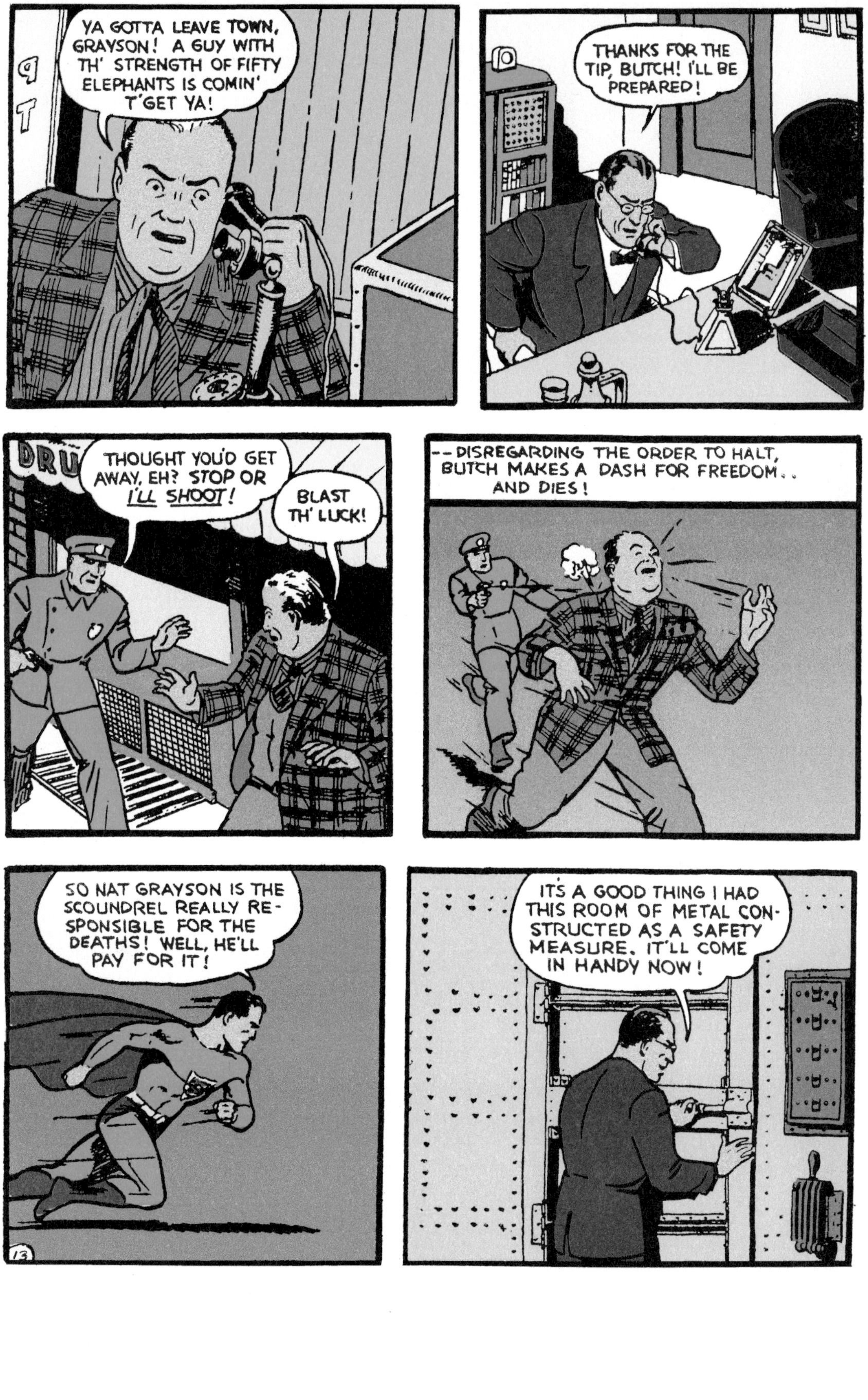
YA GOTTA LEAVE TOWN, GRAYSON! A GUY WITH TH' STRENGTH OF FIFTY ELEPHANTS IS COMIN' T'GET YA!
THANKS FOR THE TIP, BUTCH! I'LL BE PREPARED!
DRU
THOUGHT YOU'D GET AWAY, EH? STOP OR I'LL SHOOT!
BLAST TH' LUCK!
--DISREGARDING THE ORDER TO HALT, BUTCH MAKES A DASH FOR FREEDOM.. AND DIES!
SO NAT GRAYSON IS THE SCOUNDREL REALLY RE-SPONSIBLE FOR THE DEATHS! WELL, HE'LL PAY FOR IT!
IT'S A GOOD THING I HAD THIS ROOM OF METAL CON-STRUCTED AS A SAFETY MEASURE. IT'LL COME IN HANDY NOW!

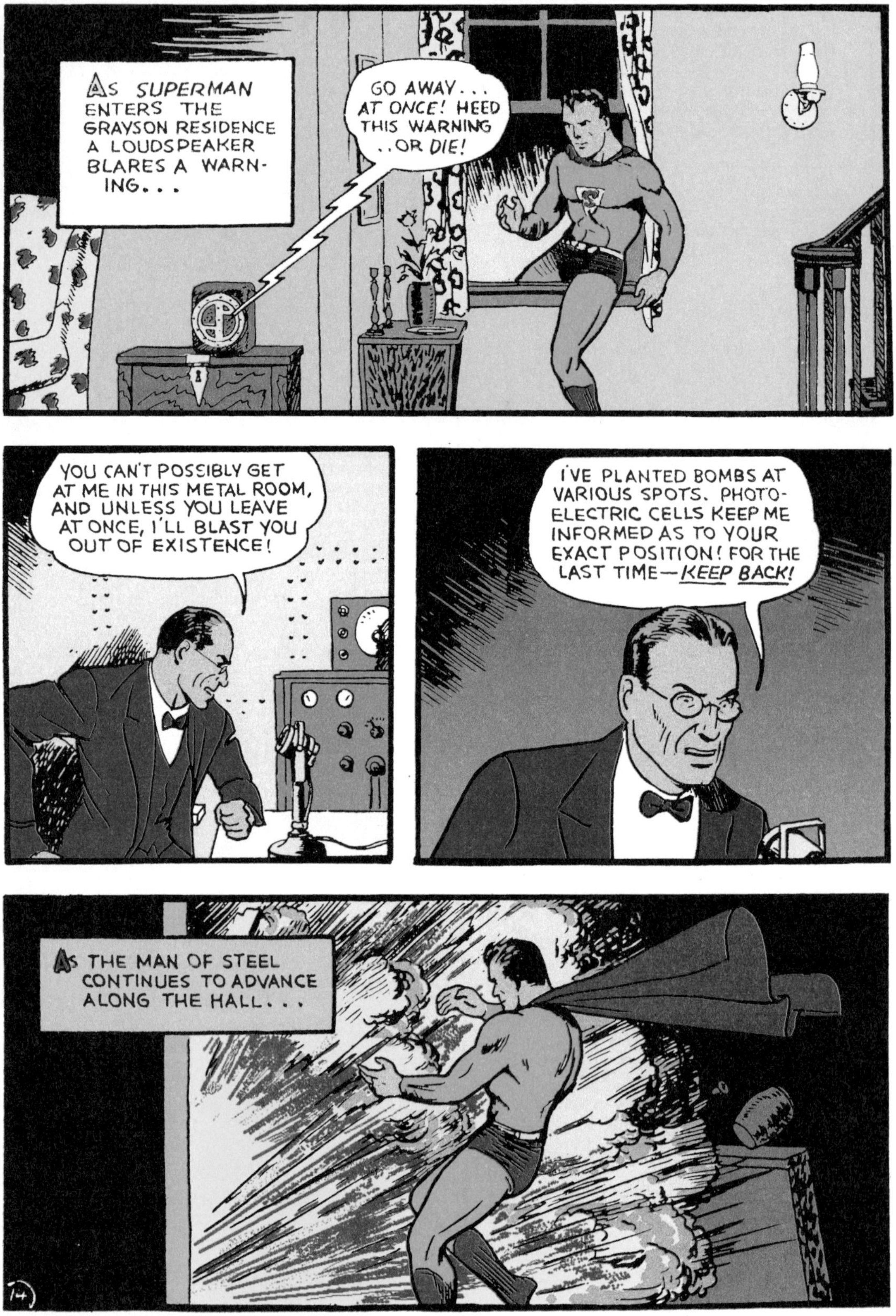

AS SUPERMAN ENTERS THE GRAYSON RESIDENCE A LOUDSPEAKER BLARES A WARNING...
GO AWAY... AT ONCE! HEED THIS WARNING ..OR DIE!
YOU CAN'T POSSIBLY GET AT ME IN THIS METAL ROOM, AND UNLESS YOU LEAVE AT ONCE, I'LL BLAST YOU OUT OF EXISTENCE!
I'VE PLANTED BOMBS AT VARIOUS SPOTS. PHOTO-ELECTRIC CELLS KEEP ME INFORMED AS TO YOUR EXACT POSITION! FOR THE LAST TIME—KEEP BACK!
AS THE MAN OF STEEL CONTINUES TO ADVANCE ALONG THE HALL...

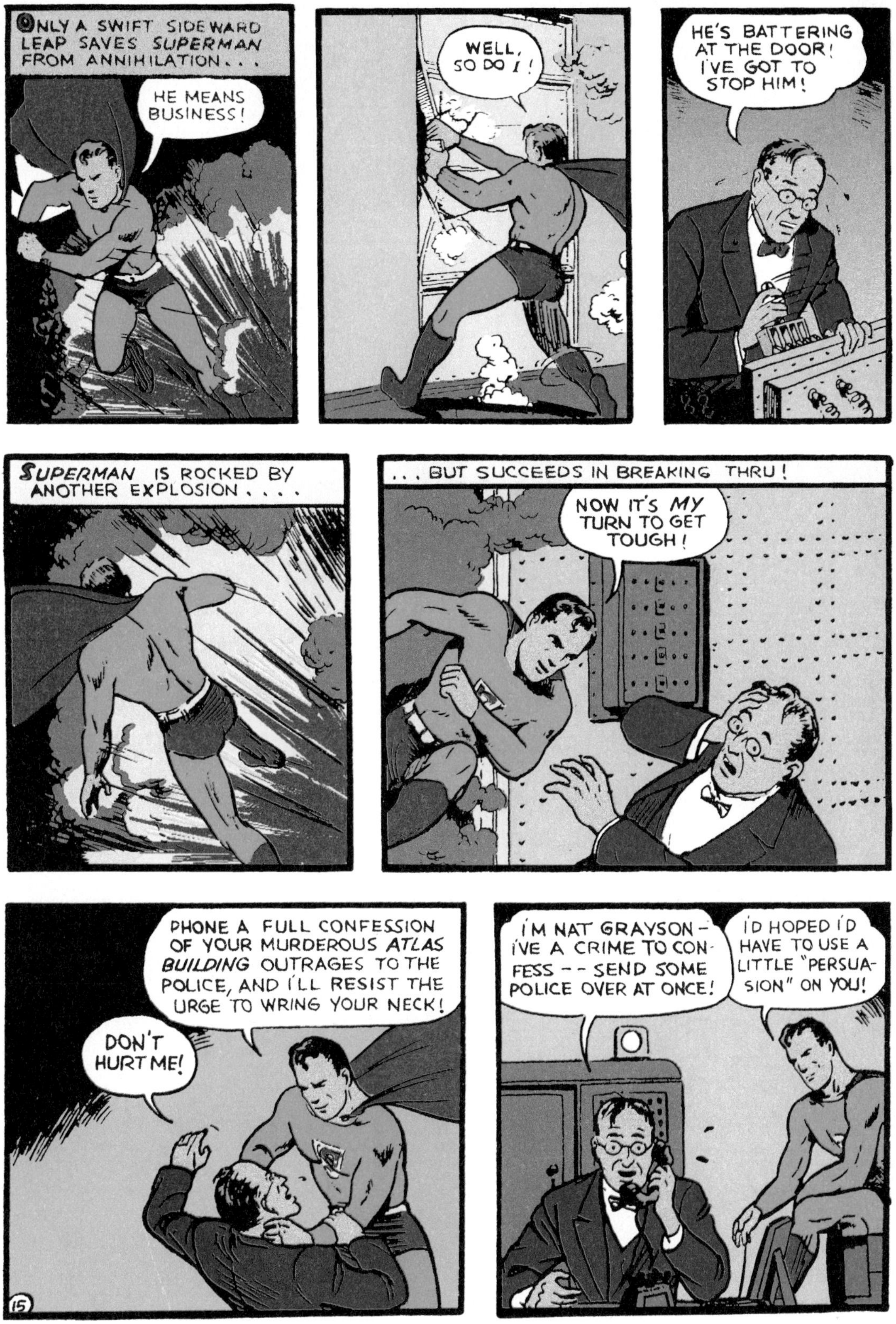
ONLY A SWIFT SIDEWARD LEAP SAVES SUPERMAN FROM ANNIHILATION . . .
HE MEANS BUSINESS!
WELL, SO DO I!
HE'S BATTERING AT THE DOOR! I'VE GOT TO STOP HIM!
SUPERMAN IS ROCKED BY ANOTHER EXPLOSION . . . .
. . . BUT SUCCEEDS IN BREAKING THRU!
NOW IT'S MY TURN TO GET TOUGH!
PHONE A FULL CONFESSION OF YOUR MURDEROUS ATLAS BUILDING OUTRAGES TO THE POLICE, AND I'LL RESIST THE URGE TO WRING YOUR NECK!
DON'T HURT ME!
15
I'M NAT GRAYSON – I'VE A CRIME TO CONFESS -- SEND SOME POLICE OVER AT ONCE!
I'D HOPED I'D HAVE TO USE A LITTLE "PERSUASION" ON YOU!

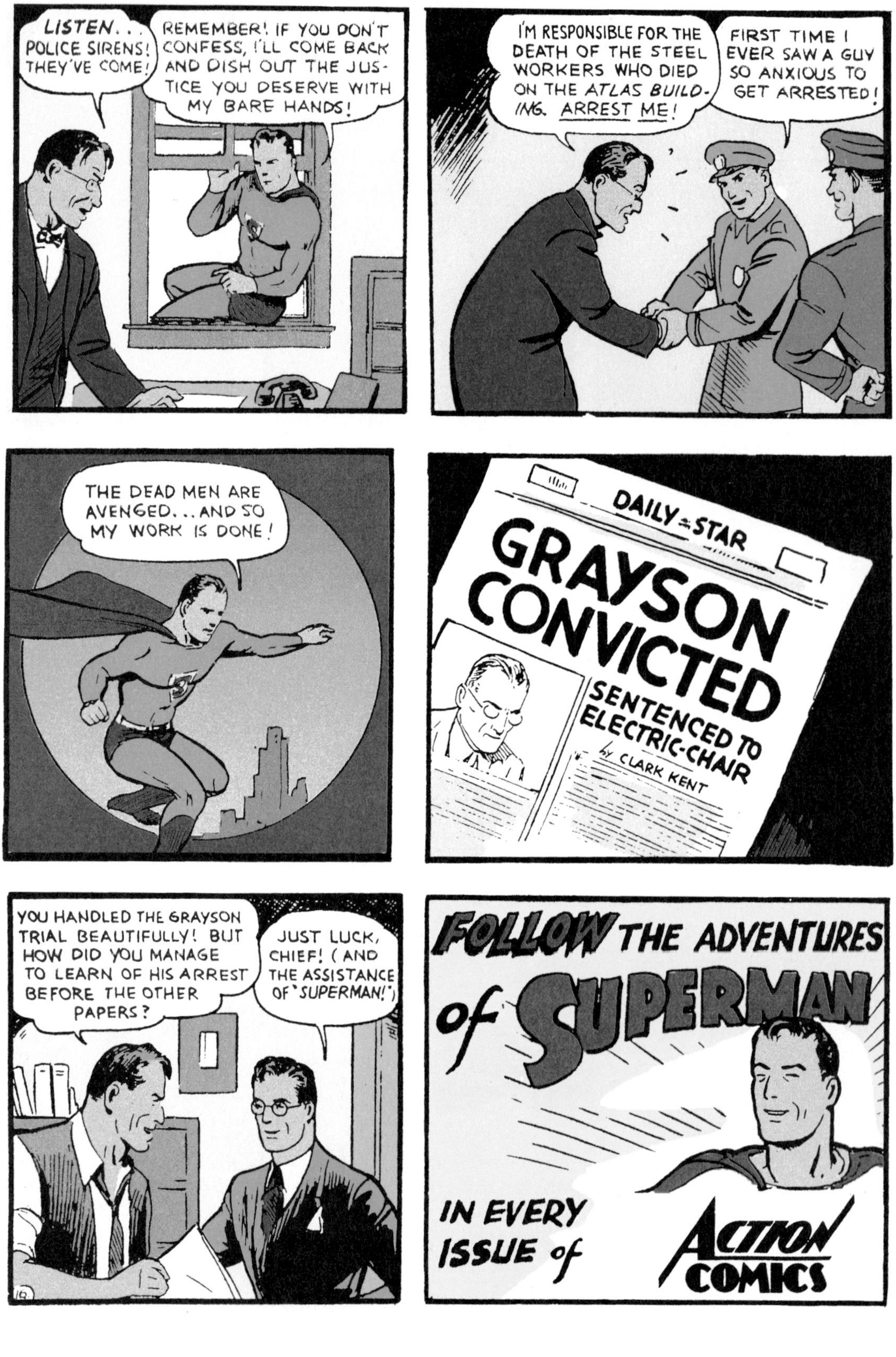
LISTEN... POLICE SIRENS! THEY'VE COME!
REMEMBER! IF YOU DON'T CONFESS, I'LL COME BACK AND DISH OUT THE JUSTICE YOU DESERVE WITH MY BARE HANDS!
I'M RESPONSIBLE FOR THE DEATH OF THE STEEL WORKERS WHO DIED ON THE ATLAS BUILDING. ARREST ME!
FIRST TIME I EVER SAW A GUY SO ANXIOUS TO GET ARRESTED!
THE DEAD MEN ARE AVENGED... AND SO MY WORK IS DONE!
DAILY STAR
GRAYSON CONVICTED
SENTENCED TO ELECTRIC-CHAIR
by CLARK KENT
YOU HANDLED THE GRAYSON TRIAL BEAUTIFULLY! BUT HOW DID YOU MANAGE TO LEARN OF HIS ARREST BEFORE THE OTHER PAPERS?
JUST LUCK, CHIEF! (AND THE ASSISTANCE OF 'SUPERMAN!')
FOLLOW THE ADVENTURES of SUPERMAN
IN EVERY ISSUE of
ACTION COMICS

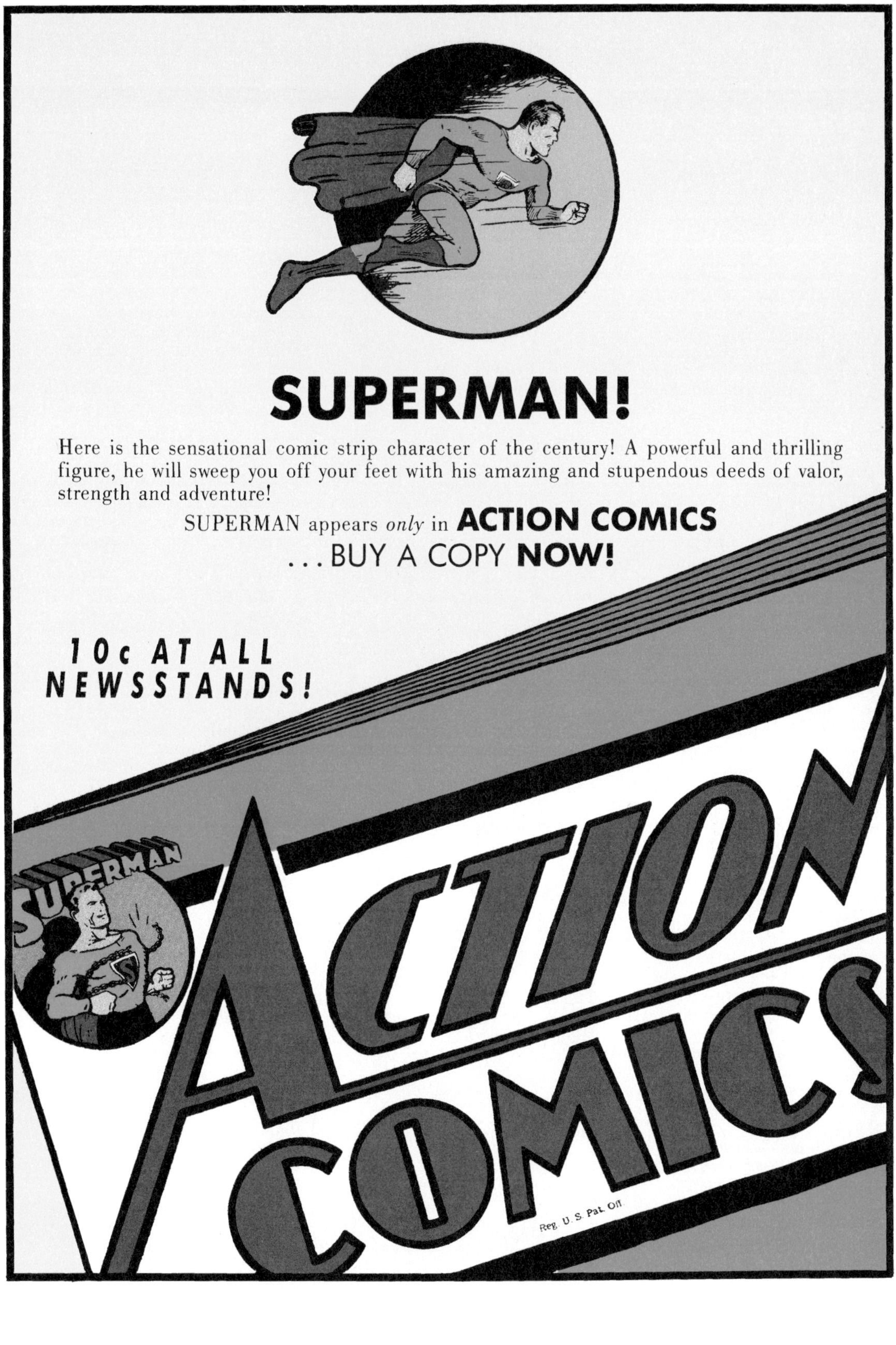

SUPERMAN!
Here is the sensational comic strip character of the century! A powerful and thrilling figure, he will sweep you off your feet with his amazing and stupendous deeds of valor, strength and adventure!
SUPERMAN appears *only* in ACTION COMICS
...BUY A COPY NOW!
10c AT ALL NEWSSTANDS!
SUPERMAN
ACTION COMICS
Reg. U. S. Pat. Off.

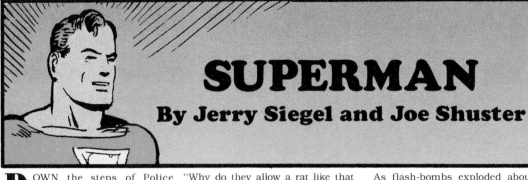

SUPERMAN

By Jerry Siegel and Joe Shuster

DOWN the steps of Police Headquarters hurried "Big Mike" Caputo, roughly shouldering aside any unfortunate figure that happened to bar his path. Huge, hulking in size, was the ruthless racketeer, and in his roughshod lumbering gait was revealed something of the brutality of the man.

A small mob of reporters hurried toward "Big Mike" as he hove into sight. "Hold it, Mike," one of them called. And then another piped up, "Let's have it. Just what went on in there between the Chief of Police and yourself?"

"Big Mike" paused in his stride, scowled, then assuming a false face of geniality, said, "Just a little friendly talk, that's all!"

Clark Kent, ace scribe on the *Daily Star*, commented: "Friendly, eh? Since when does the Police Chief of *Metropolis* get pally with a murderous hoodlum who has been kicked out of a dozen states?"

Mike's huge paw of a fist darted out, seized the luckless reporter by the shirt front. He cried: "Why, you little squirt, I'll—!"

His face ashen, the *Daily Star* reporter attempted to stutter an apology, but before he could get more than a few words out, Mike's fist smashed directly into his face. Kent went down like a sack. Caputo turned grimly toward the other waiting reporters. "Any more cracks?"

As no reply came, Mike continued on his way to the steps' bottom, crammed his great bulk into a taxi, and disappeared from view as it was driven off.

Eager hands assisted Clark Kent erect. "What hit me?" groaned Clark. "A sledge hammer?"

"No," replied one of the other reporters. "Caputo's fist! That was a pretty foolhardy thing to do: insult him to his face!"

Clark tenderly felt his jaw.

"Why do they allow a rat like that to roam the streets?"

"I can answer that," came a nearby voice.

The reporters' eyes swung to the doorway, and there stood the Chief of Police himself! "Caputo, since he was forced to leave several other cities, has been looking *Metropolis* over, and apparently thinks it's ripe for the plucking."

"And you're going to stand by and let him commit a crime," cried Clark.

"I warned him," said the Chief sternly. "I called him into my office and told him straight to his face . . . one false move, and it's into a cell he goes!"

"Nice goin', Chief!" applauded one of the reporters.

"Think so?" asked the Chief, smiling. "Then how about writing it up in your papers. And if you'd like some pictures of me to appear with the articles, well, far be it that I should argue with the Gentlemen of the Press."

As flash-bombs exploded about the Chief of Police, Clark Kent unobtrusively slipped away from the others. Amazingly enough, once he had succeeded in eluding the others, he no longer appeared like a man who had been on the receiving end of a terrific haymaker. No patting of a tender aching jaw, now . . . instead, that jaw was set firmly in an attitude of grim determination.

Shortly after, within a dark alley, Clark Kent glanced swiftly about, made certain he was unobserved, then swiftly stripped off his outer garments, revealing himself clad in the fantastic costume that was talked about from one end of the nation to the other: the uniform of SUPERMAN, Savior of the Helpless and Oppressed!

A huge leap carried the Man of Steel high into the air. One of his outflung arms seized the roof of a building and drew him safely up atop the edifice. There he poised, his great scarlet cloak whipping out behind him, glancing swiftly about in various directions. His eyes blazed with a fierce penetrating flame, as well they might, for he was surveying the surrounding vicinity with his amazing telescopic, X-ray eyesight. And in a few moments he had located the object of his search: Caputo leaving his taxi, and entering a dejected looking boarding house.

A GREAT spring carried the Man of Tomorrow out over the city, soaring high above the traffic below, and landed him near the boarding house. Several more cautious springs from building to building, and SUPERMAN found himself on a ledge outside the boarding house, staring into a window . . . and seeing within, Caputo seated at a table in conference with two hirelings.

Within the room, Caputo spoke

harshly, confidently, "It's a cinch. This town is just rolling in gravy, waiting to be plucked...and we're the men to do it! Listen, Sneer, and you too, Fink! Give me a month, and I'll have every business man paying tribute to me, 'Big Mike' Caputo—or else!"

The two remaining men in the room glanced hastily at each other, muttered under their breath, then dropped their eyes. Caputo instantly glared. "What's the matter with you guys?" he bellowed. "It's a great plan, isn't it? Then why the glum looks?"

One of the men spoke hesitantly. "It's not that we haven't got confidence in you, 'Big Mike'. It's that we happen to have been in this town longer than you, and we know..."

"The blazes with what you know..." rasped Caputo. "I say I can take over this town, and if you two weasels are getting chicken-livered...!"

"But—" interposed the other hireling, "—you're not counting on ...SUPERMAN!"

"SUPERMAN?" questioned Caputo. "And who in blazes is *he*?"

"That's just it!" whispered Sneer. "Nobody knows. He's a will-of-the-wisp...a phantom of the night. He preys on evil-doers who operate in *Metropolis*...and once that bozo's on your trail, brother, you're *sunk!*"

Caputo smashed his fist against the table, arose. "Yeah? Well, just let him watch out if he tackles me. I'm pretty tough myself!"

"You don't get it," interposed Fink. "The guy ain't human. He's got super-strength. He could take you, Caputo, and twist you into a pretzel, honest he could!"

Caputo roared, reached across the table, clutched at the helpless Fink. "He could *what*...?" he bellowed.

Fink tried to reply...but no words would come. Caputo smirked with satisfaction. They were afraid of him, these riff-raff were. Why with one smash of his fist he could ...Suddenly he paused, noting that though Fink was trembling, his eyes were fastened upon something behind Caputo's back. Abruptly dropping Fink, "Big Mike" whirled...then gasped.

For stepping thru the window, and regarding him coolly, was the strangest-attired man Caputo had ever seen. A man clad entirely in a skin-tight costume with the letter

"S" emblazoned strikingly upon his chest—and upon his back, a flaring cloak.

"What th'—? exploded Caputo. "What is this? Wh- who are you?"

"It's *him!*" cried Sneer hoarsely. "It's—it's—SUPERMAN!"

For a moment, Caputo stood stunned, then he cried, "You fools! He's no more supernatural than you or me! Come on, let's rush him!"

Sneer and Fink rushed, all right —but directly from the room.

SUPERMAN smiled amusedly, then spoke, "It looks like your 'friends' have run out on you. It's between you and me, now—'Big Mike'...are you ready to make a bargain with me?"

"A bargain...?" asked Mike, suspicious.

"Yes," said SUPERMAN. "You seem to believe that you are physically my master. Well, what say, we find out? We'll fight it out, you and I. And the winner, it's pledged, leaves town in a jiffy! A battle between us, 'Big Mike', to decide whether good or evil rules this city!—Agreed?"

"Agreed!" shouted "Big Mike", and leapt directly at the costumed figure.

With a crash the two struck! Mike swung at his adversary, groaned with pain as his fist collided with granite-like skin. "Hey!" he cried.

Next instant, Mike was whirling up thru the air! Up he flew, then with a WHAM! crashed against the ceiling amidst a deluge of raining plaster. Down he hurtled, and into a relentless, steel grip. Around

and around, he circled about SUPERMAN'S head.

"Just like on the Merry-Go-Round," grinned SUPERMAN, "Want a repeat-ride?"

"Big Mike" bellowed his protest. But in the middle of his cry, SUPERMAN loosened his grip, and Caputo went flying across the room...on...on thru the air... and OUT THE WINDOW!

Down thru space dropped Caputo, amidst a soul-tearing shriek. Down he hurtled...but a few moments later, steely arms encircled him from behind, as SUPERMAN, flashing down after him, gripped his figure. Down—smashing into earth, with SUPERMAN absorbing the fall! Then, he was dangling in the air, his collar gripped firmly in SUPERMAN's hand.

"Fergoshsakes!" wept Caputo. "Have a heart! Lemme go!"

"Done!" said SUPERMAN. "But I've your solemn word that you'll clear out of Metropolis pronto. We want none of your kind, here!"

"I'll do it!" cried "Big Mike", "I'll beat it outa here—*gladly!*"

"And just remember," SUPERMAN called after the fleeing racketeer. "If you decide to come back, I'll give you an encore of this that'll make our first match appear mild!"

* * *

That evening, the *Daily Star* carried the following headline on an inner page:
POLICE CHIEF MAKES
  RACKETEER LEAVE TOWN
  By Clark Kent

The End.

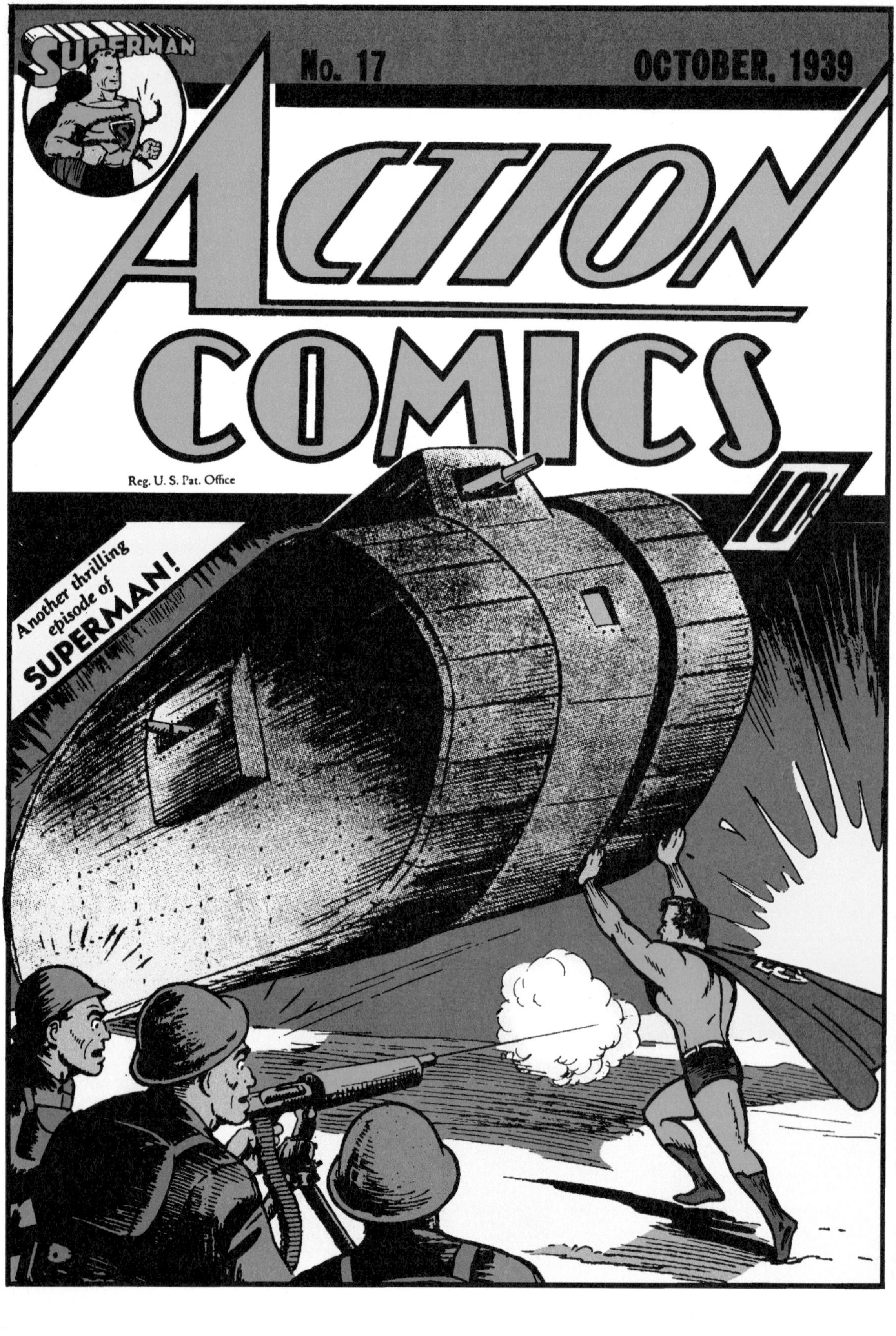
SUPERMAN
No. 17
OCTOBER, 1939
ACTION COMICS
Reg. U. S. Pat. Office
10¢
Another thrilling episode of SUPERMAN!

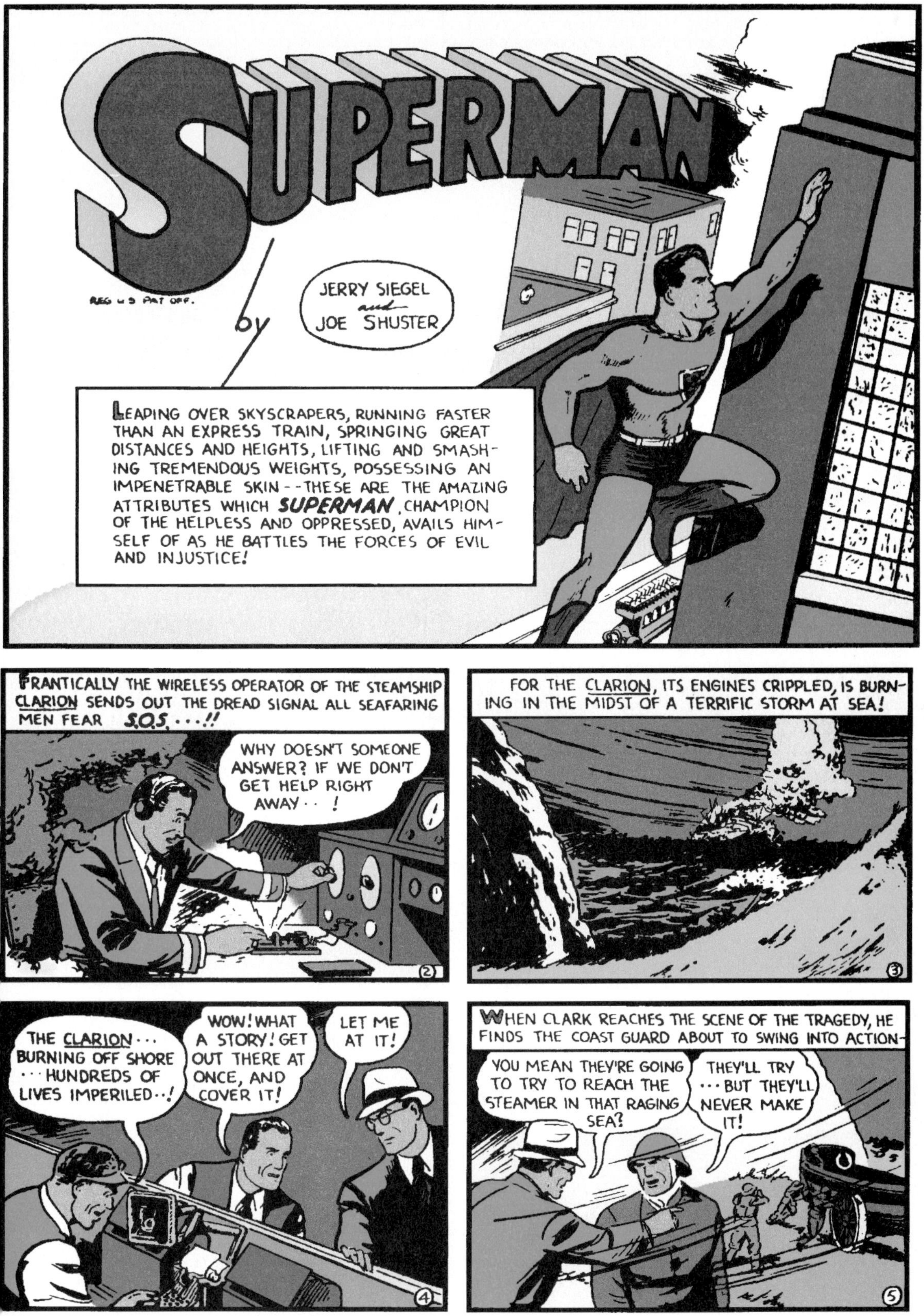
SUPERMAN
REG. U.S. PAT. OFF.
by JERRY SIEGEL and JOE SHUSTER
LEAPING OVER SKYSCRAPERS, RUNNING FASTER THAN AN EXPRESS TRAIN, SPRINGING GREAT DISTANCES AND HEIGHTS, LIFTING AND SMASHING TREMENDOUS WEIGHTS, POSSESSING AN IMPENETRABLE SKIN--THESE ARE THE AMAZING ATTRIBUTES WHICH SUPERMAN, CHAMPION OF THE HELPLESS AND OPPRESSED, AVAILS HIMSELF OF AS HE BATTLES THE FORCES OF EVIL AND INJUSTICE!
FRANTICALLY THE WIRELESS OPERATOR OF THE STEAMSHIP CLARION SENDS OUT THE DREAD SIGNAL ALL SEAFARING MEN FEAR S.O.S....!!
WHY DOESN'T SOMEONE ANSWER? IF WE DON'T GET HELP RIGHT AWAY.. !
2
FOR THE CLARION, ITS ENGINES CRIPPLED, IS BURNING IN THE MIDST OF A TERRIFIC STORM AT SEA!
3
THE CLARION... BURNING OFF SHORE ...HUNDREDS OF LIVES IMPERILED..!
WOW! WHAT A STORY! GET OUT THERE AT ONCE, AND COVER IT!
LET ME AT IT!
4
WHEN CLARK REACHES THE SCENE OF THE TRAGEDY, HE FINDS THE COAST GUARD ABOUT TO SWING INTO ACTION-
YOU MEAN THEY'RE GOING TO TRY TO REACH THE STEAMER IN THAT RAGING SEA?
THEY'LL TRY ...BUT THEY'LL NEVER MAKE IT!
5

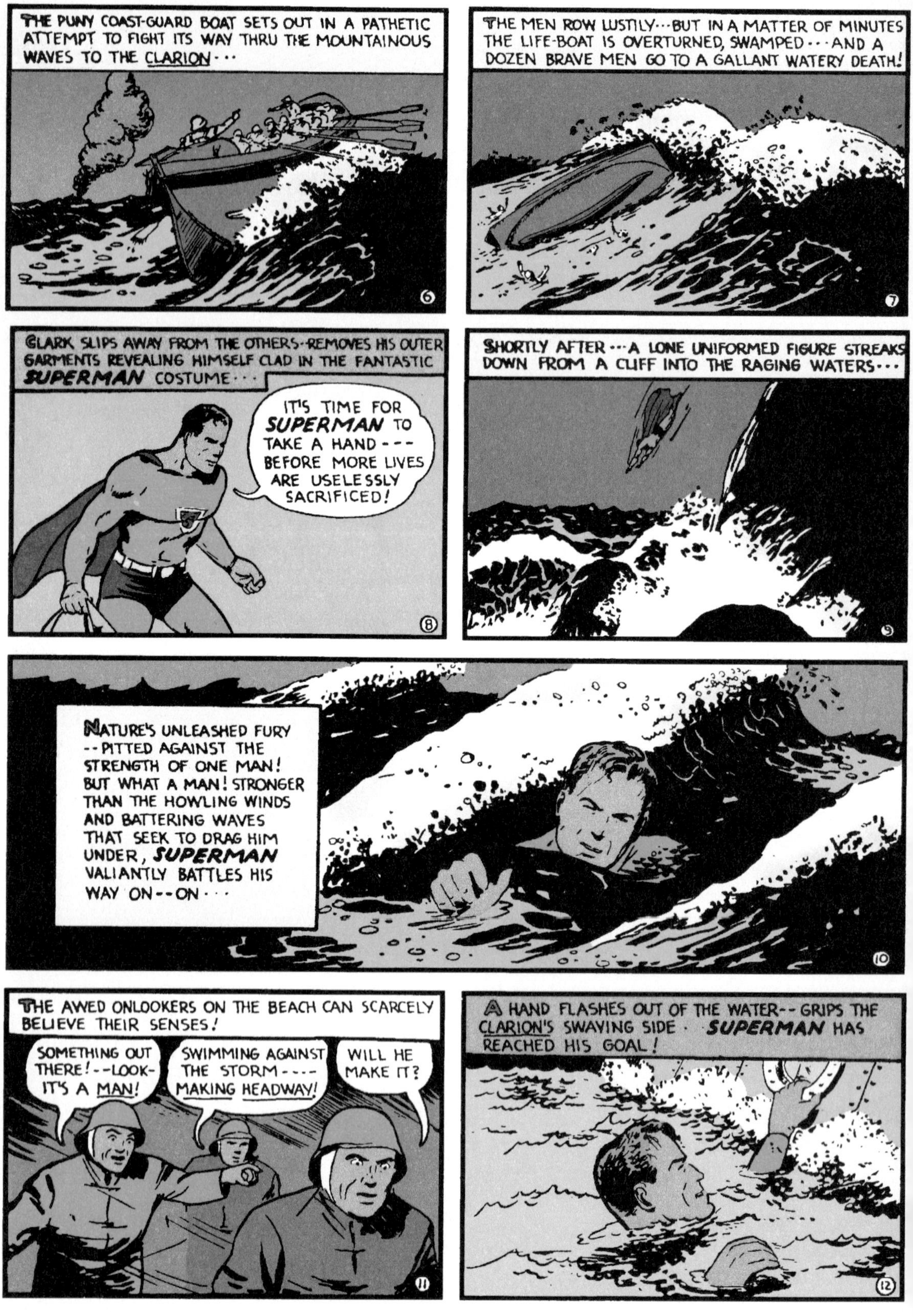
THE PUNY COAST-GUARD BOAT SETS OUT IN A PATHETIC ATTEMPT TO FIGHT ITS WAY THRU THE MOUNTAINOUS WAVES TO THE CLARION...
6
THE MEN ROW LUSTILY...BUT IN A MATTER OF MINUTES THE LIFE-BOAT IS OVERTURNED, SWAMPED...AND A DOZEN BRAVE MEN GO TO A GALLANT WATERY DEATH!
7
CLARK SLIPS AWAY FROM THE OTHERS-REMOVES HIS OUTER GARMENTS REVEALING HIMSELF CLAD IN THE FANTASTIC SUPERMAN COSTUME...
IT'S TIME FOR SUPERMAN TO TAKE A HAND--- BEFORE MORE LIVES ARE USELESSLY SACRIFICED!
8
SHORTLY AFTER---A LONE UNIFORMED FIGURE STREAKS DOWN FROM A CLIFF INTO THE RAGING WATERS...
9
NATURE'S UNLEASHED FURY --PITTED AGAINST THE STRENGTH OF ONE MAN! BUT WHAT A MAN! STRONGER THAN THE HOWLING WINDS AND BATTERING WAVES THAT SEEK TO DRAG HIM UNDER, SUPERMAN VALIANTLY BATTLES HIS WAY ON--ON...
10
THE AWED ONLOOKERS ON THE BEACH CAN SCARCELY BELIEVE THEIR SENSES!
SOMETHING OUT THERE!--LOOK- IT'S A MAN!
SWIMMING AGAINST THE STORM---- MAKING HEADWAY!
WILL HE MAKE IT?
11
A HAND FLASHES OUT OF THE WATER--GRIPS THE CLARION'S SWAYING SIDE. SUPERMAN HAS REACHED HIS GOAL!
12

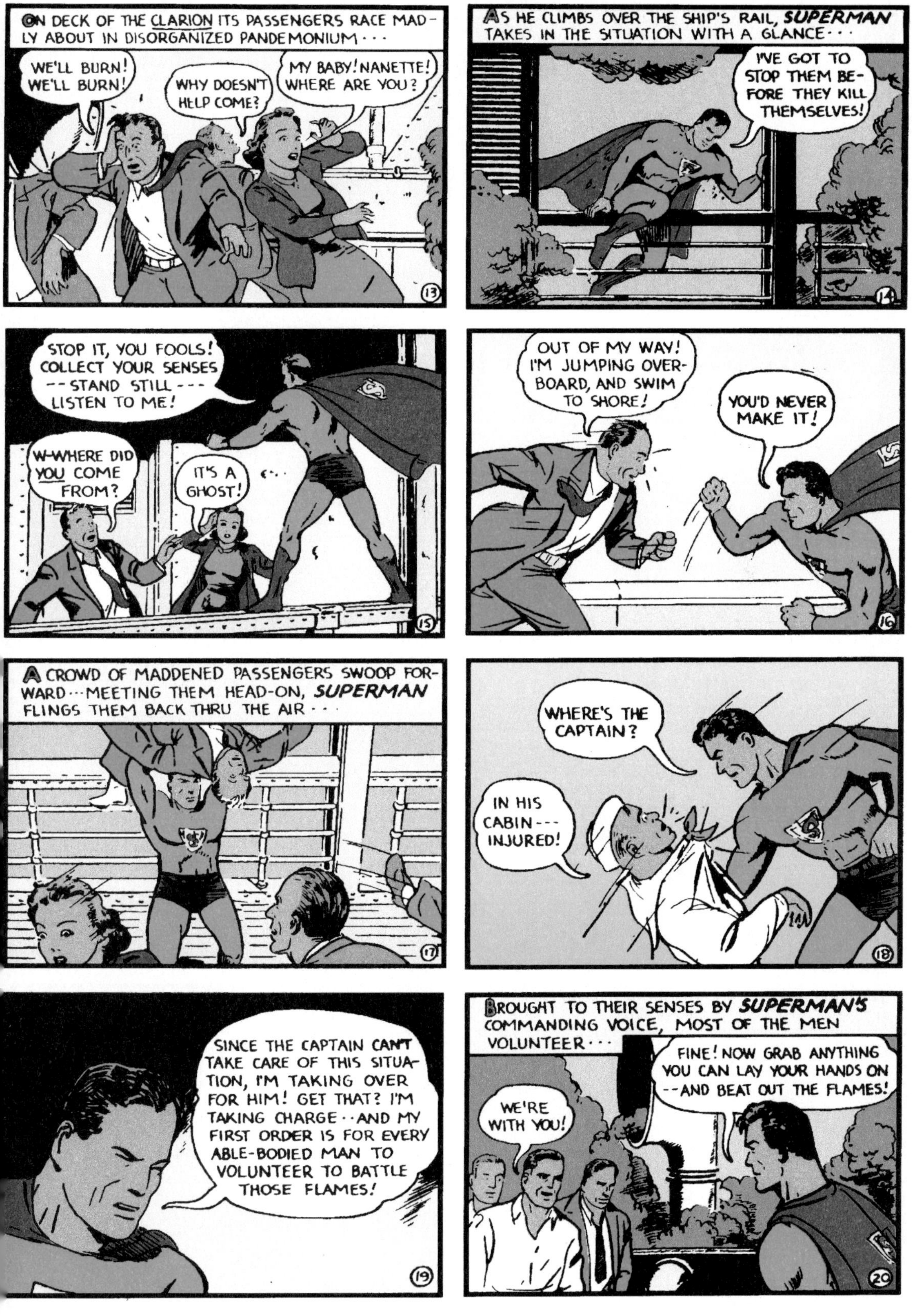
ON DECK OF THE CLARION ITS PASSENGERS RACE MADLY ABOUT IN DISORGANIZED PANDEMONIUM · · ·
WE'LL BURN! WE'LL BURN!
WHY DOESN'T HELP COME?
MY BABY! NANETTE! WHERE ARE YOU?
13
AS HE CLIMBS OVER THE SHIP'S RAIL, SUPERMAN TAKES IN THE SITUATION WITH A GLANCE · · ·
I'VE GOT TO STOP THEM BEFORE THEY KILL THEMSELVES!
14
STOP IT, YOU FOOLS! COLLECT YOUR SENSES --STAND STILL --- LISTEN TO ME!
W-WHERE DID YOU COME FROM?
IT'S A GHOST!
15
OUT OF MY WAY! I'M JUMPING OVERBOARD, AND SWIM TO SHORE!
YOU'D NEVER MAKE IT!
16
A CROWD OF MADDENED PASSENGERS SWOOP FORWARD··· MEETING THEM HEAD-ON, SUPERMAN FLINGS THEM BACK THRU THE AIR · · ·
17
WHERE'S THE CAPTAIN?
IN HIS CABIN--- INJURED!
18
SINCE THE CAPTAIN CAN'T TAKE CARE OF THIS SITUATION, I'M TAKING OVER FOR HIM! GET THAT? I'M TAKING CHARGE ·· AND MY FIRST ORDER IS FOR EVERY ABLE-BODIED MAN TO VOLUNTEER TO BATTLE THOSE FLAMES!
19
BROUGHT TO THEIR SENSES BY SUPERMAN'S COMMANDING VOICE, MOST OF THE MEN VOLUNTEER · · ·
FINE! NOW GRAB ANYTHING YOU CAN LAY YOUR HANDS ON --AND BEAT OUT THE FLAMES!
WE'RE WITH YOU!
20

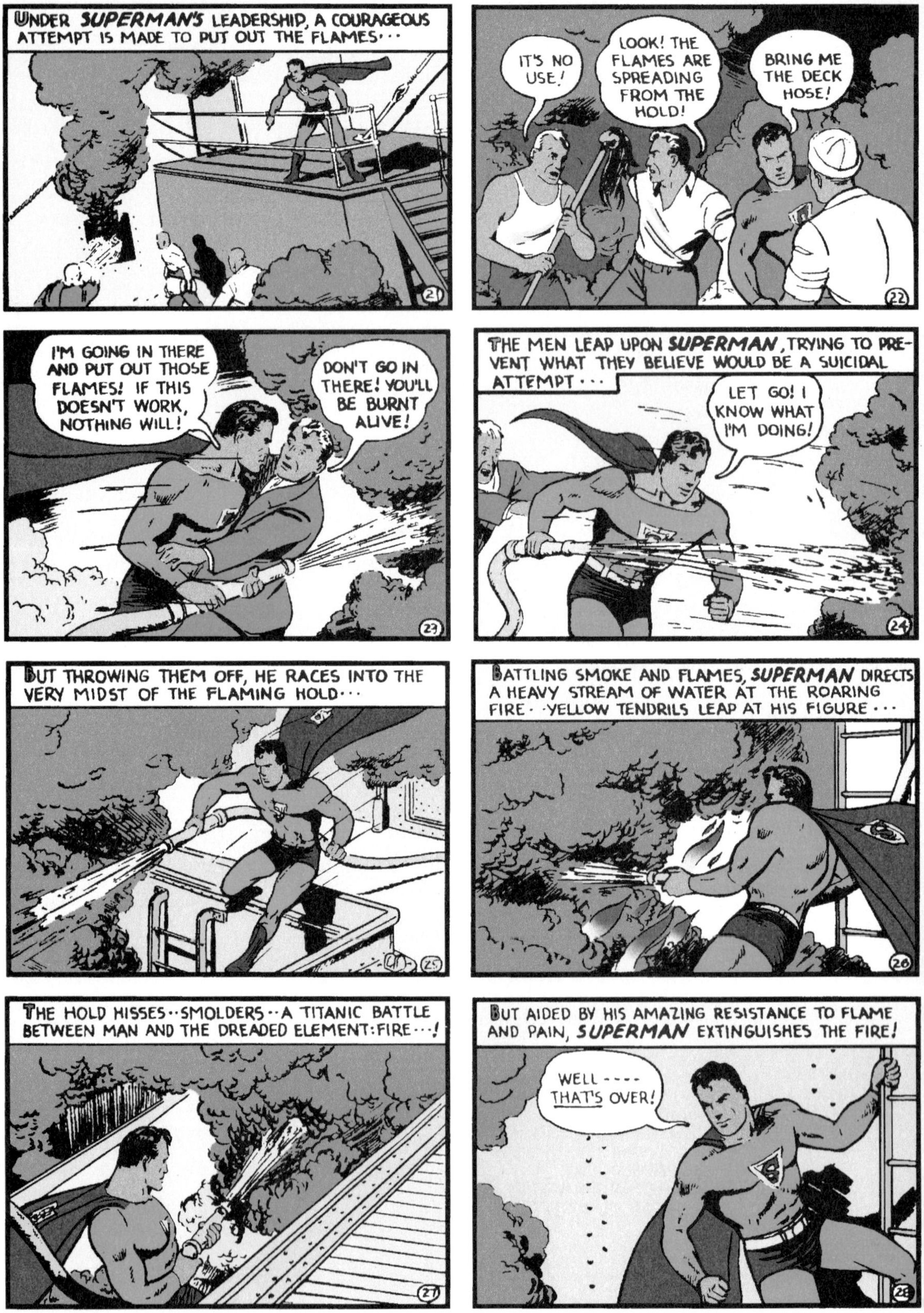
UNDER SUPERMAN'S LEADERSHIP, A COURAGEOUS ATTEMPT IS MADE TO PUT OUT THE FLAMES···
IT'S NO USE!
LOOK! THE FLAMES ARE SPREADING FROM THE HOLD!
BRING ME THE DECK HOSE!
I'M GOING IN THERE AND PUT OUT THOSE FLAMES! IF THIS DOESN'T WORK, NOTHING WILL!
DON'T GO IN THERE! YOU'LL BE BURNT ALIVE!
THE MEN LEAP UPON SUPERMAN, TRYING TO PREVENT WHAT THEY BELIEVE WOULD BE A SUICIDAL ATTEMPT···
LET GO! I KNOW WHAT I'M DOING!
BUT THROWING THEM OFF, HE RACES INTO THE VERY MIDST OF THE FLAMING HOLD···
BATTLING SMOKE AND FLAMES, SUPERMAN DIRECTS A HEAVY STREAM OF WATER AT THE ROARING FIRE· ·YELLOW TENDRILS LEAP AT HIS FIGURE···
THE HOLD HISSES··SMOLDERS··A TITANIC BATTLE BETWEEN MAN AND THE DREADED ELEMENT: FIRE···!
BUT AIDED BY HIS AMAZING RESISTANCE TO FLAME AND PAIN, SUPERMAN EXTINGUISHES THE FIRE!
WELL ---- THAT'S OVER!

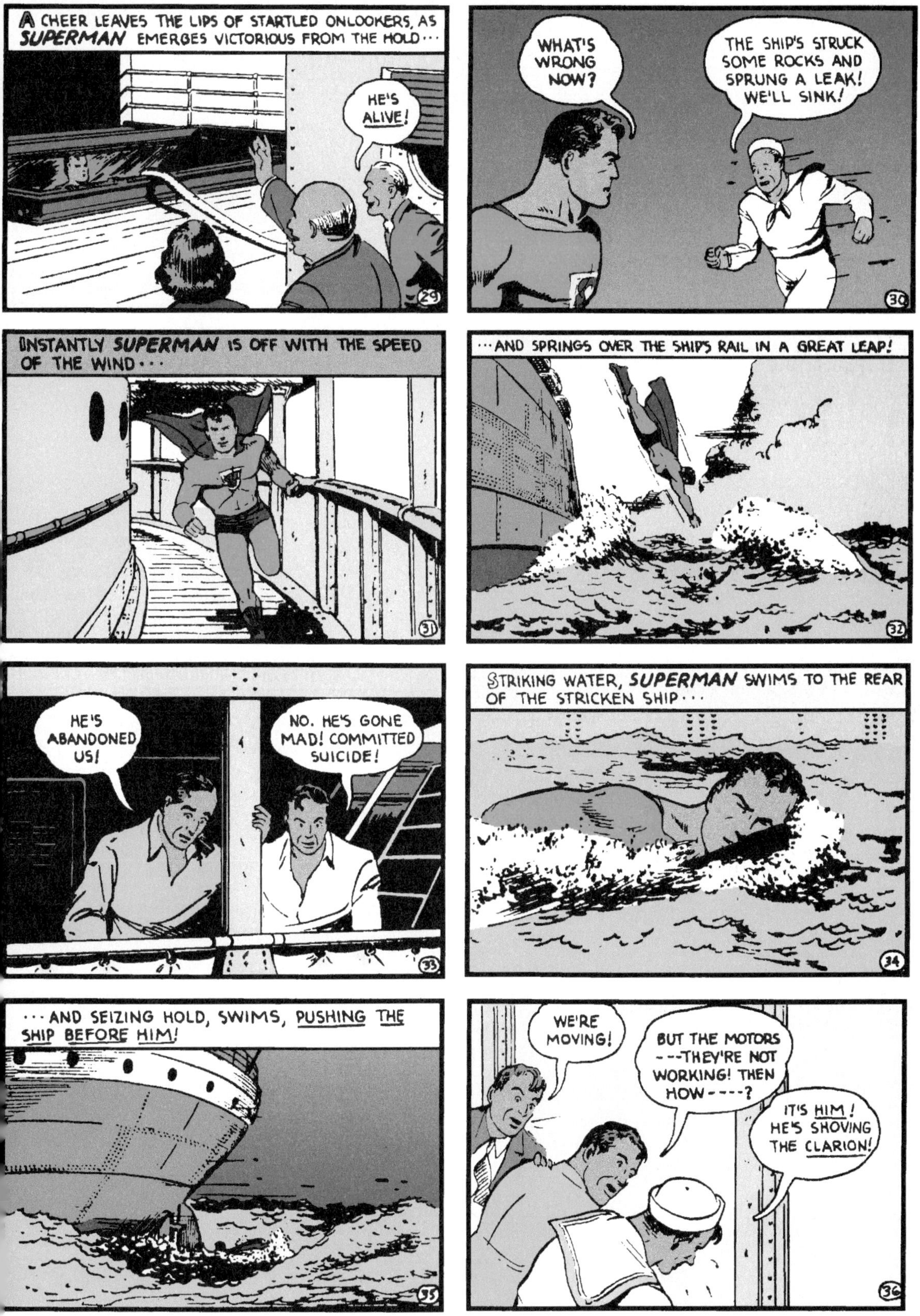
A CHEER LEAVES THE LIPS OF STARTLED ONLOOKERS, AS SUPERMAN EMERGES VICTORIOUS FROM THE HOLD...
HE'S ALIVE!
WHAT'S WRONG NOW?
THE SHIP'S STRUCK SOME ROCKS AND SPRUNG A LEAK! WE'LL SINK!
INSTANTLY SUPERMAN IS OFF WITH THE SPEED OF THE WIND...
...AND SPRINGS OVER THE SHIP'S RAIL IN A GREAT LEAP!
HE'S ABANDONED US!
NO. HE'S GONE MAD! COMMITTED SUICIDE!
STRIKING WATER, SUPERMAN SWIMS TO THE REAR OF THE STRICKEN SHIP...
...AND SEIZING HOLD, SWIMS, PUSHING THE SHIP BEFORE HIM!
WE'RE MOVING!
BUT THE MOTORS ---THEY'RE NOT WORKING! THEN HOW----?
IT'S HIM! HE'S SHOVING THE CLARION!

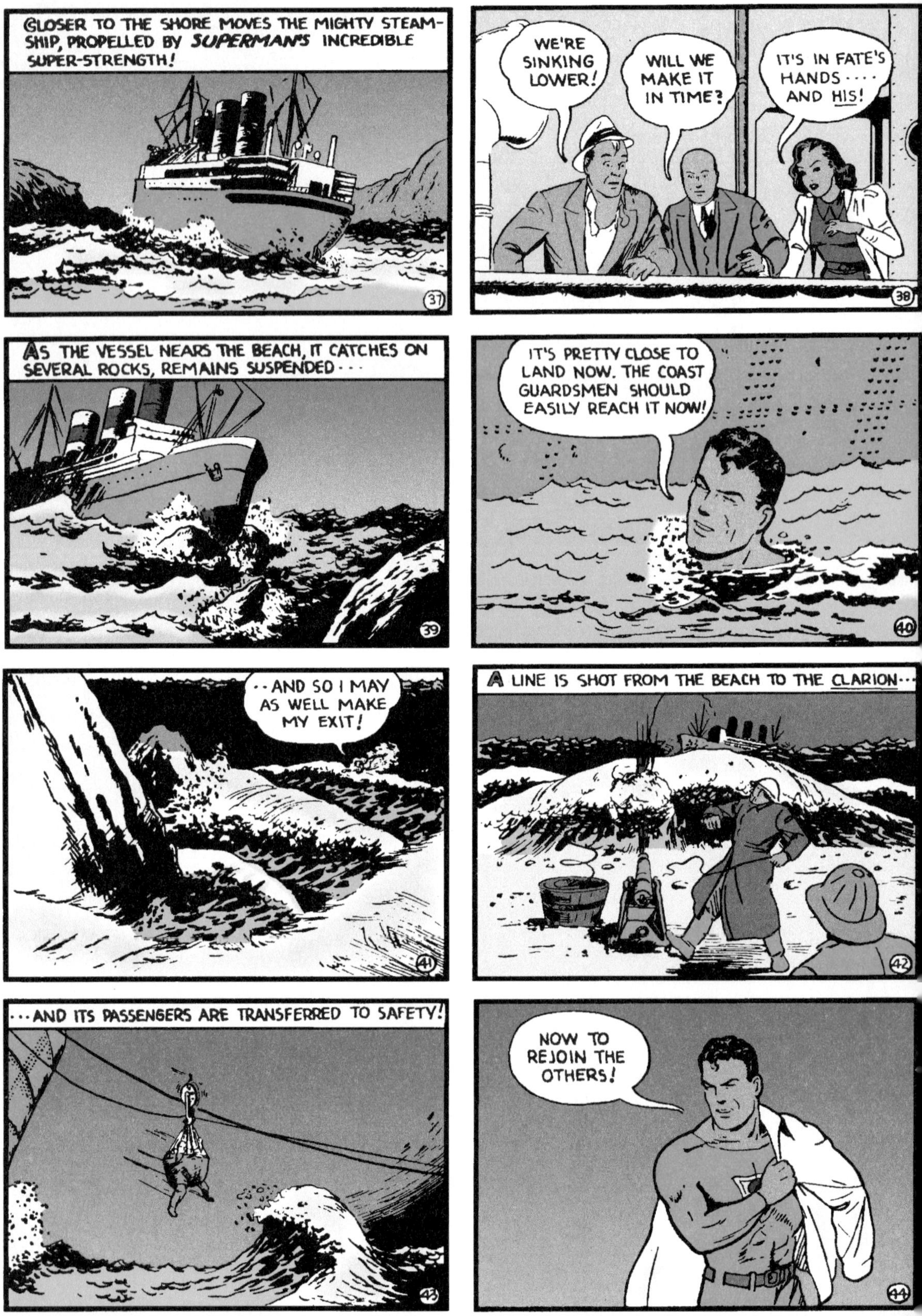
CLOSER TO THE SHORE MOVES THE MIGHTY STEAMSHIP, PROPELLED BY SUPERMAN'S INCREDIBLE SUPER-STRENGTH!
37
WE'RE SINKING LOWER!
WILL WE MAKE IT IN TIME?
IT'S IN FATE'S HANDS.... AND HIS!
38
AS THE VESSEL NEARS THE BEACH, IT CATCHES ON SEVERAL ROCKS, REMAINS SUSPENDED...
39
IT'S PRETTY CLOSE TO LAND NOW. THE COAST GUARDSMEN SHOULD EASILY REACH IT NOW!
40
..AND SO I MAY AS WELL MAKE MY EXIT!
41
A LINE IS SHOT FROM THE BEACH TO THE CLARION...
42
...AND ITS PASSENGERS ARE TRANSFERRED TO SAFETY!
43
NOW TO REJOIN THE OTHERS!
44

Next morning, Clark suggests to his city editor··

CITY EDITOR

ABOUT THAT STORY I WROTE UP LAST NIGHT ·· I'D LIKE TO VISIT THE CLARION'S WRECK THIS MORNING. THERE MAY BE A POSSIBILITY OF MORE NEWS.

GO TO IT!

When Clark reaches his destination, he finds the CLARION has settled upon its side, and investigators are about to board it···

I'M FROM THE DAILY STAR. MAY I ACCOMPANY YOU ON BOARD?

IF YOU WISH!

Together with the investigators, Clark seeks the cause of the tragedy····

IT WAS CLAIMED THAT THE FIRE SPREAD FROM ONE OF THE HOLDS.

THEN THAT'LL BE OUR FIRST STOP!

When they enter the hold··

LOOK! QUANTITIES OF INFLAMMABLES, AND BROKEN GAS-OLINE CANS!

YOU'RE RIGHT!

IT LOOKS LIKE SABOTAGE!

THIS VESSEL WAS DELIBERATELY SET AFIRE!

EXCUSE ME! I'M IN A HURRY!

Excited by his discovery, Clark hurries to the main office of the DEERING LINES, owners of the CLARION···

I TELL YOU NO ONE CAN SEE THE GENERAL MANAGER! HE'S NOT IN!

WE'LL SEE ABOUT THAT!

GENERAL MANAGER

- PRIVATE -

STOP IT! PUT ME DOWN!

FIRST WE'LL SEE IF YOU'RE LYING!

321

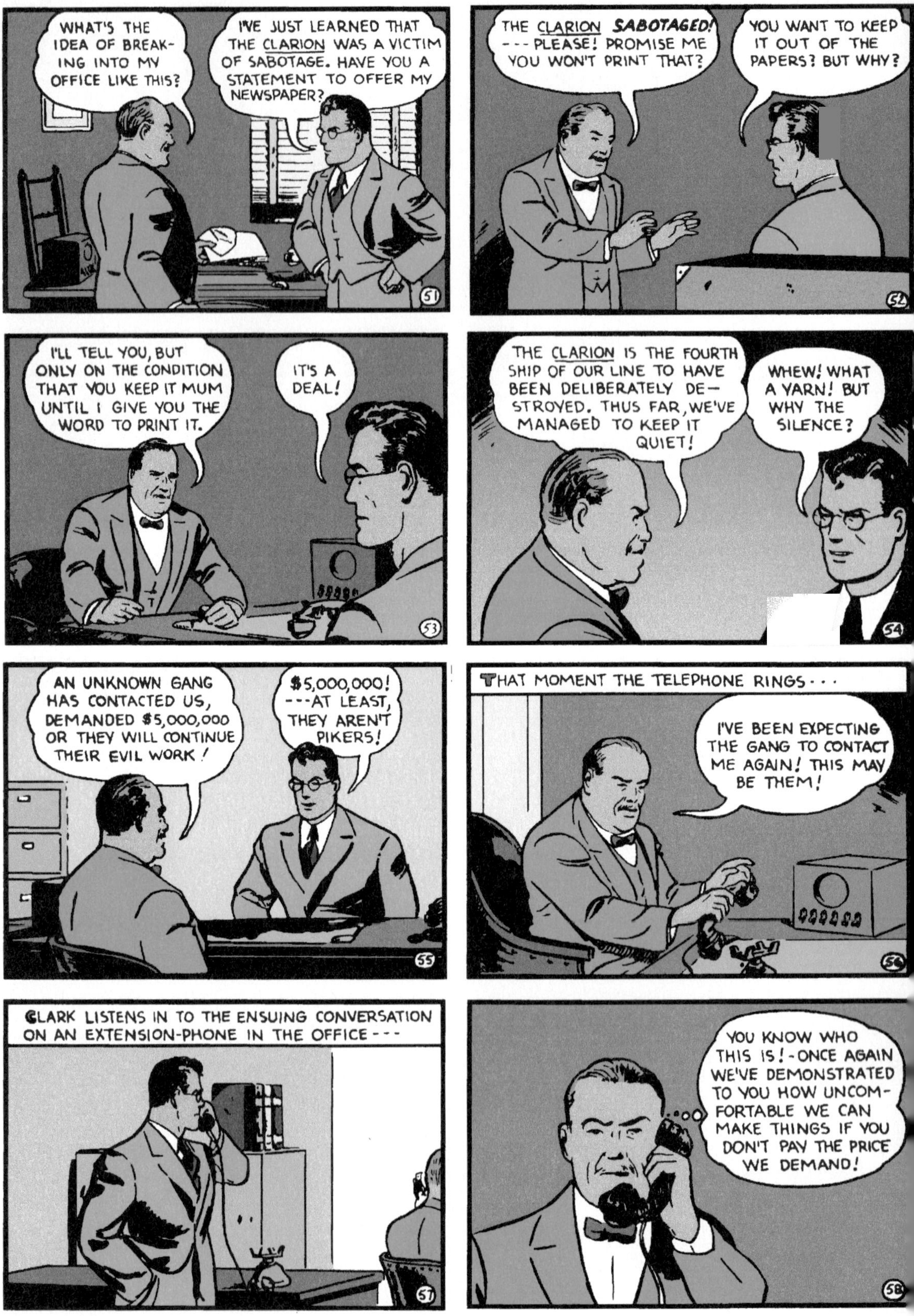
WHAT'S THE IDEA OF BREAKING INTO MY OFFICE LIKE THIS?
I'VE JUST LEARNED THAT THE CLARION WAS A VICTIM OF SABOTAGE. HAVE YOU A STATEMENT TO OFFER MY NEWSPAPER?
51
THE CLARION SABOTAGED! ---PLEASE! PROMISE ME YOU WON'T PRINT THAT?
YOU WANT TO KEEP IT OUT OF THE PAPERS? BUT WHY?
52
I'LL TELL YOU, BUT ONLY ON THE CONDITION THAT YOU KEEP IT MUM UNTIL I GIVE YOU THE WORD TO PRINT IT.
IT'S A DEAL!
53
THE CLARION IS THE FOURTH SHIP OF OUR LINE TO HAVE BEEN DELIBERATELY DESTROYED. THUS FAR, WE'VE MANAGED TO KEEP IT QUIET!
WHEW! WHAT A YARN! BUT WHY THE SILENCE?
54
AN UNKNOWN GANG HAS CONTACTED US, DEMANDED $5,000,000 OR THEY WILL CONTINUE THEIR EVIL WORK!
$5,000,000! ---AT LEAST, THEY AREN'T PIKERS!
55
THAT MOMENT THE TELEPHONE RINGS---
I'VE BEEN EXPECTING THE GANG TO CONTACT ME AGAIN! THIS MAY BE THEM!
56
CLARK LISTENS IN TO THE ENSUING CONVERSATION ON AN EXTENSION-PHONE IN THE OFFICE---
57
YOU KNOW WHO THIS IS!-ONCE AGAIN WE'VE DEMONSTRATED TO YOU HOW UNCOMFORTABLE WE CAN MAKE THINGS IF YOU DON'T PAY THE PRICE WE DEMAND!
58

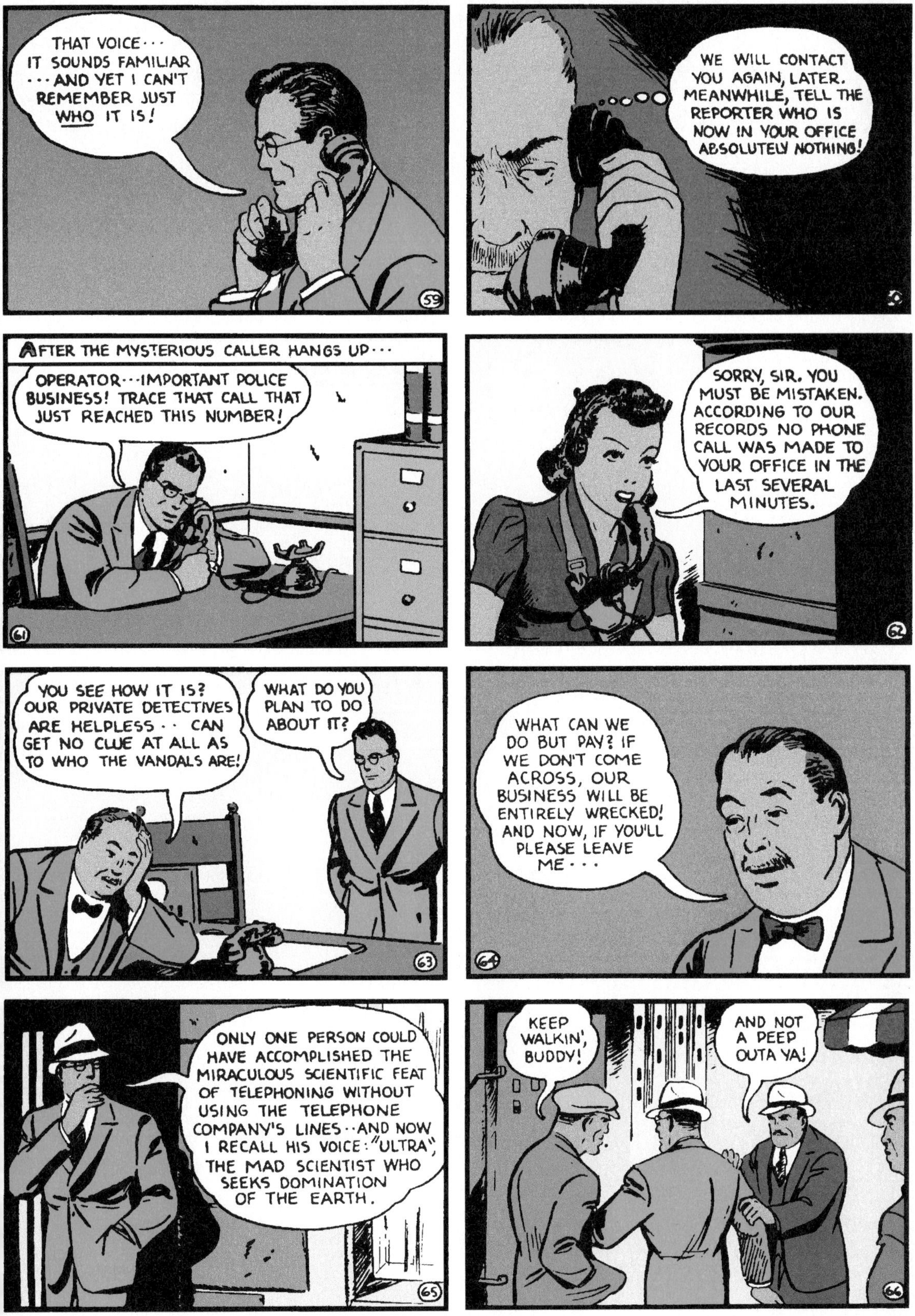
THAT VOICE··· IT SOUNDS FAMILIAR ···AND YET I CAN'T REMEMBER JUST WHO IT IS!
WE WILL CONTACT YOU AGAIN, LATER. MEANWHILE, TELL THE REPORTER WHO IS NOW IN YOUR OFFICE ABSOLUTELY NOTHING!
AFTER THE MYSTERIOUS CALLER HANGS UP···
OPERATOR···IMPORTANT POLICE BUSINESS! TRACE THAT CALL THAT JUST REACHED THIS NUMBER!
SORRY, SIR. YOU MUST BE MISTAKEN. ACCORDING TO OUR RECORDS NO PHONE CALL WAS MADE TO YOUR OFFICE IN THE LAST SEVERAL MINUTES.
YOU SEE HOW IT IS? OUR PRIVATE DETECTIVES ARE HELPLESS·· CAN GET NO CLUE AT ALL AS TO WHO THE VANDALS ARE!
WHAT DO YOU PLAN TO DO ABOUT IT?
WHAT CAN WE DO BUT PAY? IF WE DON'T COME ACROSS, OUR BUSINESS WILL BE ENTIRELY WRECKED! AND NOW, IF YOU'LL PLEASE LEAVE ME···
ONLY ONE PERSON COULD HAVE ACCOMPLISHED THE MIRACULOUS SCIENTIFIC FEAT OF TELEPHONING WITHOUT USING THE TELEPHONE COMPANY'S LINES··AND NOW I RECALL HIS VOICE: "ULTRA", THE MAD SCIENTIST WHO SEEKS DOMINATION OF THE EARTH.
KEEP WALKIN', BUDDY!
AND NOT A PEEP OUTA YA!

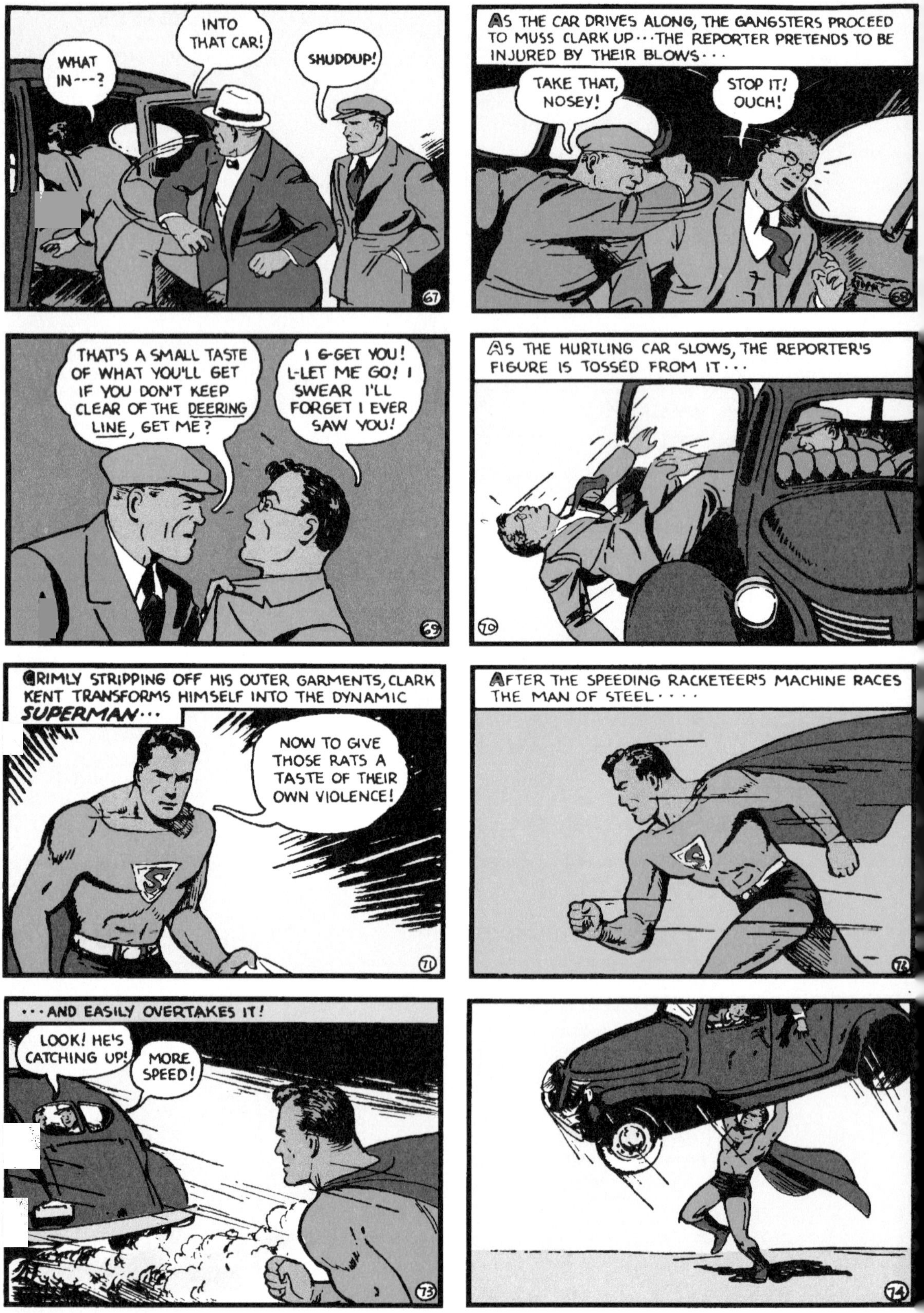
WHAT IN---?
INTO THAT CAR!
SHUDDUP!
AS THE CAR DRIVES ALONG, THE GANGSTERS PROCEED TO MUSS CLARK UP··· THE REPORTER PRETENDS TO BE INJURED BY THEIR BLOWS···
TAKE THAT, NOSEY!
STOP IT! OUCH!
THAT'S A SMALL TASTE OF WHAT YOU'LL GET IF YOU DON'T KEEP CLEAR OF THE DEERING LINE, GET ME?
I G-GET YOU! L-LET ME GO! I SWEAR I'LL FORGET I EVER SAW YOU!
AS THE HURTLING CAR SLOWS, THE REPORTER'S FIGURE IS TOSSED FROM IT···
GRIMLY STRIPPING OFF HIS OUTER GARMENTS, CLARK KENT TRANSFORMS HIMSELF INTO THE DYNAMIC SUPERMAN···
NOW TO GIVE THOSE RATS A TASTE OF THEIR OWN VIOLENCE!
AFTER THE SPEEDING RACKETEER'S MACHINE RACES THE MAN OF STEEL····
···AND EASILY OVERTAKES IT!
LOOK! HE'S CATCHING UP!
MORE SPEED!

UP--UP LEAPS *SUPERMAN* WITH HIS HUGE BURDEN··

Y-YEE-EOOW!

LEMME OUT! DON'T LET IT GET ME!

AS HE LANDS ATOP A SKYSCRAPER, *SUPERMAN* DEPOSITS THE AUTO NONE TOO GENTLY···

··· THEN LEAPS OFF!

THAT OUGHT TO THROW A LITTLE FEAR INTO THEM!

WHEN THE TERRIFIED GANGSTERS REPORT BACK TO THEIR CHIEF----

WHAT'S HAPPENED? SPEAK UP, YOU FOOLS!

IT WAS LIKE A NIGHTMARE! AN INCREDIBLY STRONG GUY SCARED US SILLY WITH HIS SUPER-STRENGTH!

SUPERMAN!- SO HE'S MIXING IN! THAT MEANS I'VE GOT TO ACT -- AND *FAST!*

"ULTRA", MAD SCIENTIFIC GENIUS, ADJUSTS THE MIRACULOUS INVENTION WITH WHICH HE CAN CUT IN ON ANY TELEPHONE LINE WITHOUT PHYSICAL CONTACT···

IF I'M GOING TO CONTINUE MY COSTLY SUBVERSIVE ACTIVITIES, I'VE GOT TO GET CAPITAL·· HUGE SUMS OF IT··· AT ONCE!

YOU AGAIN!

THE TIME HAS COME FOR YOU TO DELIVER THE $5,000,000. SEND A MESSENGER TO 211 COURT AVENUE, AT ONCE··· OR THERE WON'T BE A SINGLE STEAMER INTACT ON YOUR LINE THIS TIME TO-MORROW!

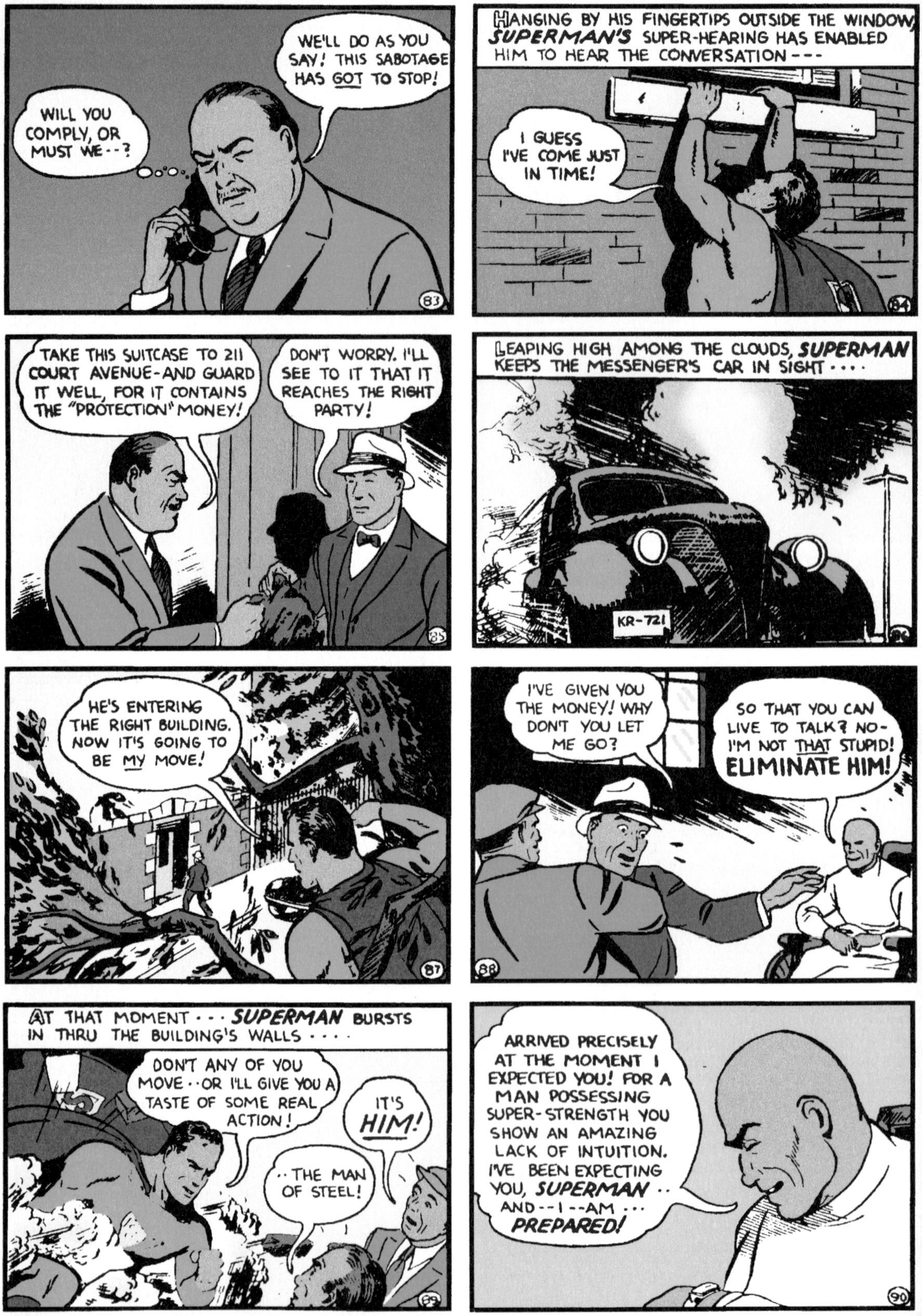
WILL YOU COMPLY, OR MUST WE--?
WE'LL DO AS YOU SAY! THIS SABOTAGE HAS GOT TO STOP!
83
HANGING BY HIS FINGERTIPS OUTSIDE THE WINDOW, SUPERMAN'S SUPER-HEARING HAS ENABLED HIM TO HEAR THE CONVERSATION---
I GUESS I'VE COME JUST IN TIME!
84
TAKE THIS SUITCASE TO 211 COURT AVENUE-AND GUARD IT WELL, FOR IT CONTAINS THE "PROTECTION" MONEY!
DON'T WORRY. I'LL SEE TO IT THAT IT REACHES THE RIGHT PARTY!
85
LEAPING HIGH AMONG THE CLOUDS, SUPERMAN KEEPS THE MESSENGER'S CAR IN SIGHT....
KR-721
86
HE'S ENTERING THE RIGHT BUILDING. NOW IT'S GOING TO BE MY MOVE!
87
I'VE GIVEN YOU THE MONEY! WHY DON'T YOU LET ME GO?
SO THAT YOU CAN LIVE TO TALK? NO-I'M NOT THAT STUPID! ELIMINATE HIM!
88
AT THAT MOMENT... SUPERMAN BURSTS IN THRU THE BUILDING'S WALLS....
DON'T ANY OF YOU MOVE..OR I'LL GIVE YOU A TASTE OF SOME REAL ACTION!
IT'S HIM!
..THE MAN OF STEEL!
89
ARRIVED PRECISELY AT THE MOMENT I EXPECTED YOU! FOR A MAN POSSESSING SUPER-STRENGTH YOU SHOW AN AMAZING LACK OF INTUITION. I'VE BEEN EXPECTING YOU, SUPERMAN.. AND--I--AM... PREPARED!
90

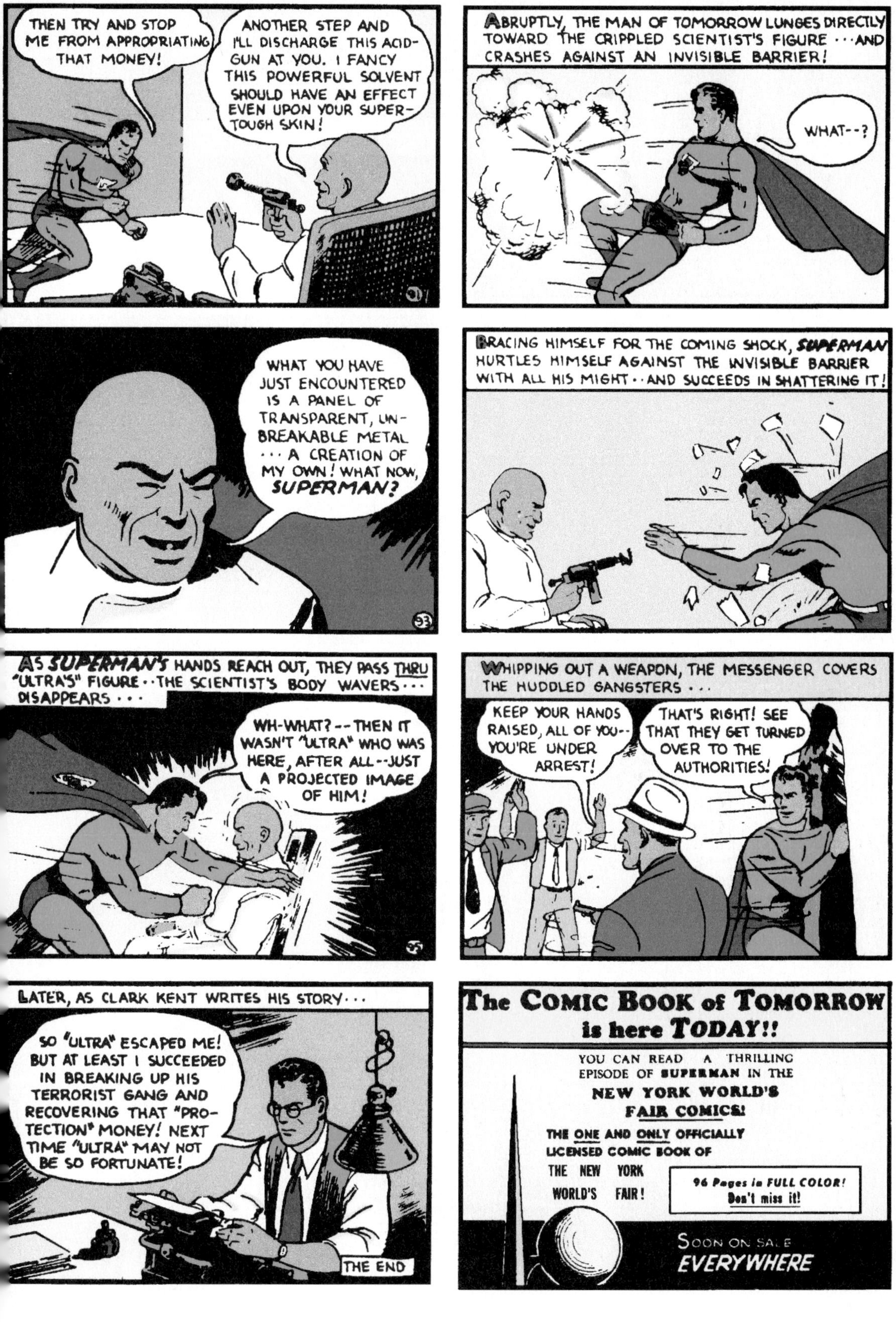
THEN TRY AND STOP ME FROM APPROPRIATING THAT MONEY!
ANOTHER STEP AND I'LL DISCHARGE THIS ACID-GUN AT YOU. I FANCY THIS POWERFUL SOLVENT SHOULD HAVE AN EFFECT EVEN UPON YOUR SUPER-TOUGH SKIN!
ABRUPTLY, THE MAN OF TOMORROW LUNGES DIRECTLY TOWARD THE CRIPPLED SCIENTIST'S FIGURE ··· AND CRASHES AGAINST AN INVISIBLE BARRIER!
WHAT--?
WHAT YOU HAVE JUST ENCOUNTERED IS A PANEL OF TRANSPARENT, UNBREAKABLE METAL ··· A CREATION OF MY OWN! WHAT NOW, SUPERMAN?
BRACING HIMSELF FOR THE COMING SHOCK, SUPERMAN HURTLES HIMSELF AGAINST THE INVISIBLE BARRIER WITH ALL HIS MIGHT·· AND SUCCEEDS IN SHATTERING IT!
AS SUPERMAN'S HANDS REACH OUT, THEY PASS THRU "ULTRA'S" FIGURE ·· THE SCIENTIST'S BODY WAVERS ··· DISAPPEARS ···
WH-WHAT? -- THEN IT WASN'T "ULTRA" WHO WAS HERE, AFTER ALL -- JUST A PROJECTED IMAGE OF HIM!
WHIPPING OUT A WEAPON, THE MESSENGER COVERS THE HUDDLED GANGSTERS ···
KEEP YOUR HANDS RAISED, ALL OF YOU -- YOU'RE UNDER ARREST!
THAT'S RIGHT! SEE THAT THEY GET TURNED OVER TO THE AUTHORITIES!
LATER, AS CLARK KENT WRITES HIS STORY ···
SO "ULTRA" ESCAPED ME! BUT AT LEAST I SUCCEEDED IN BREAKING UP HIS TERRORIST GANG AND RECOVERING THAT "PROTECTION" MONEY! NEXT TIME "ULTRA" MAY NOT BE SO FORTUNATE!
THE END
The COMIC BOOK of TOMORROW is here TODAY!!
YOU CAN READ A THRILLING EPISODE OF SUPERMAN IN THE NEW YORK WORLD'S FAIR COMICS!
THE ONE AND ONLY OFFICIALLY LICENSED COMIC BOOK OF THE NEW YORK WORLD'S FAIR!
96 Pages in FULL COLOR! Don't miss it!
SOON ON SALE EVERYWHERE

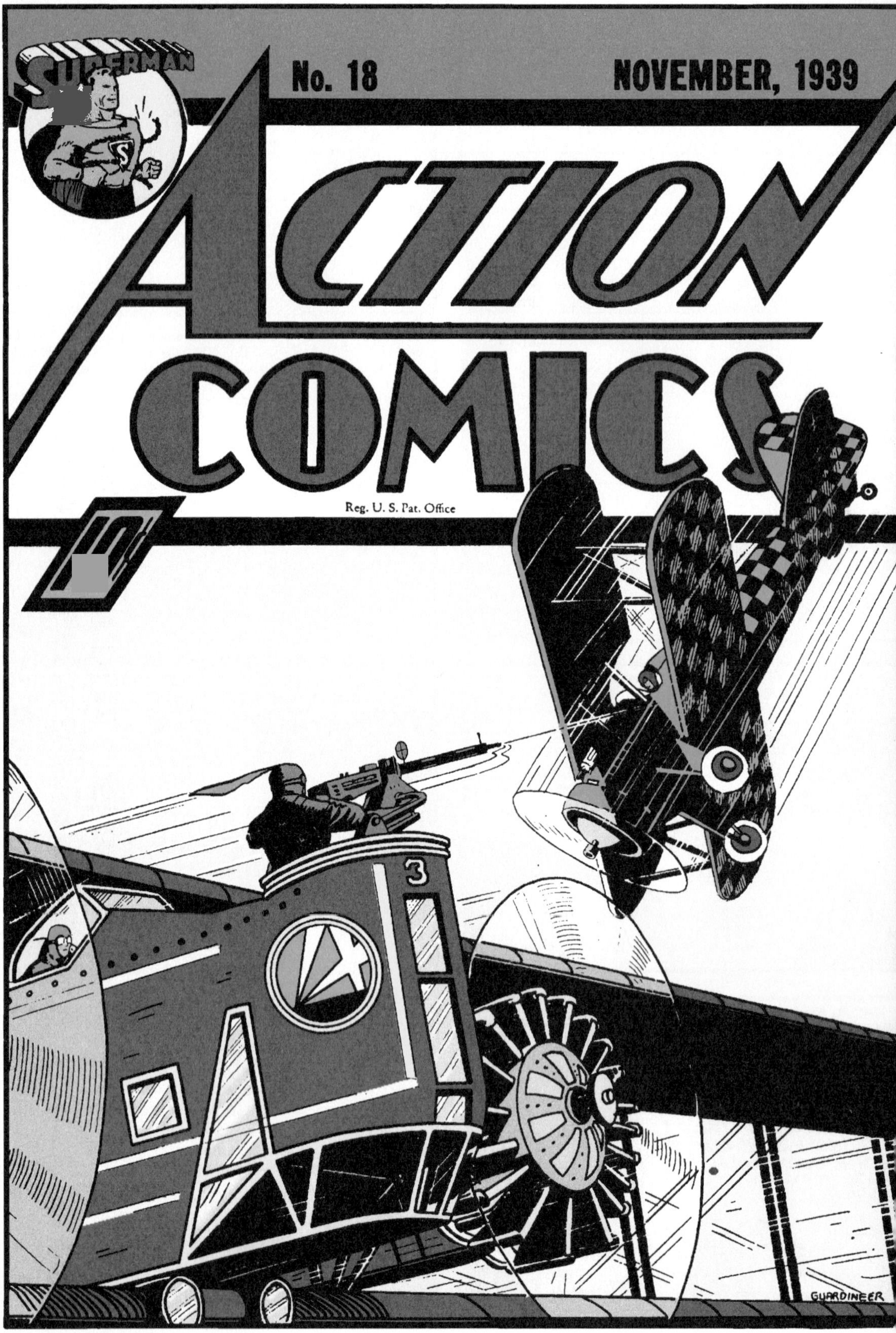
SUPERMAN
No. 18
NOVEMBER, 1939
ACTION COMICS
Reg. U. S. Pat. Office
3
GUARDINEER

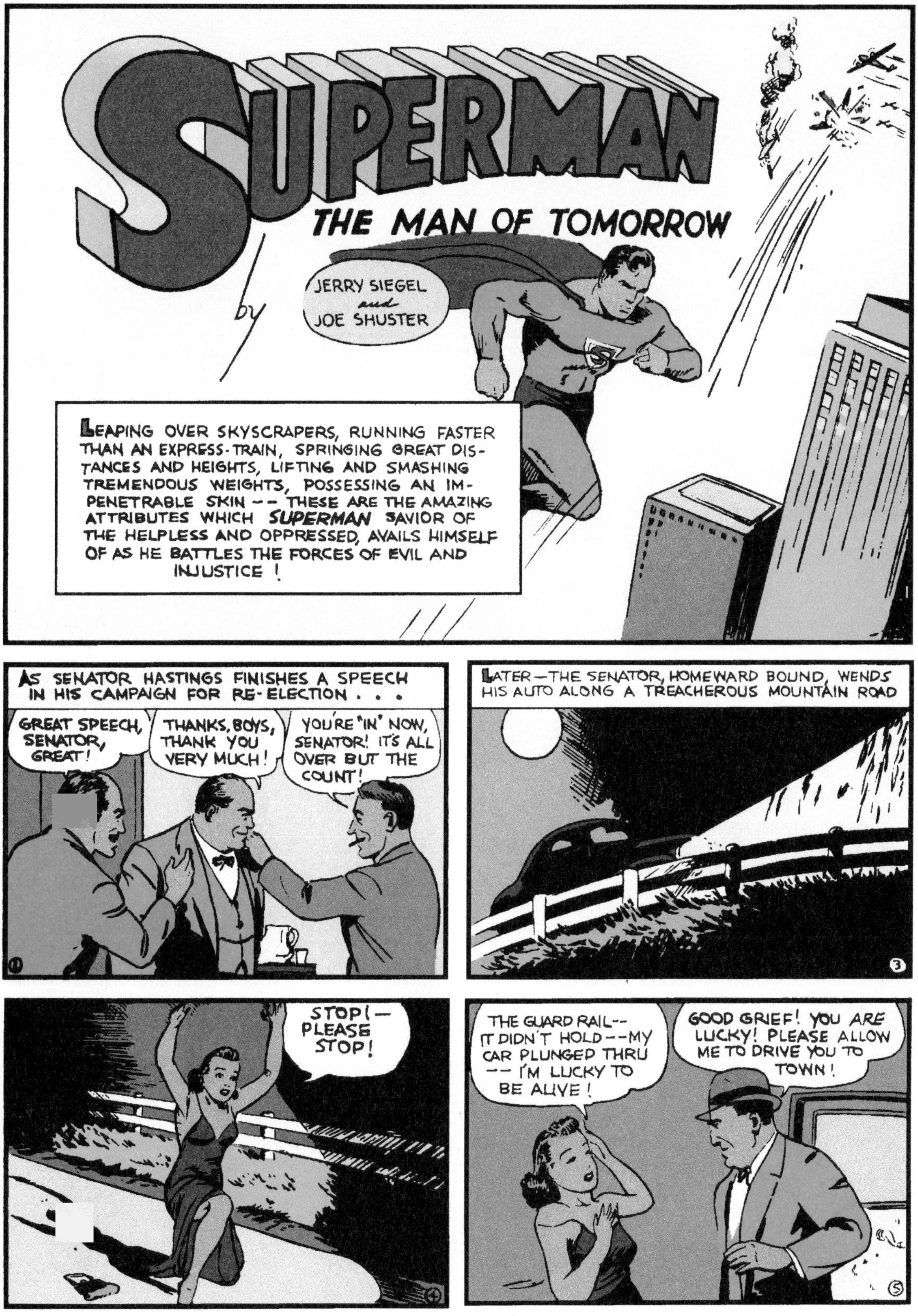
SUPERMAN
THE MAN OF TOMORROW
by
JERRY SIEGEL and JOE SHUSTER
LEAPING OVER SKYSCRAPERS, RUNNING FASTER THAN AN EXPRESS-TRAIN, SPRINGING GREAT DISTANCES AND HEIGHTS, LIFTING AND SMASHING TREMENDOUS WEIGHTS, POSSESSING AN IMPENETRABLE SKIN -- THESE ARE THE AMAZING ATTRIBUTES WHICH SUPERMAN SAVIOR OF THE HELPLESS AND OPPRESSED, AVAILS HIMSELF OF AS HE BATTLES THE FORCES OF EVIL AND INJUSTICE !
AS SENATOR HASTINGS FINISHES A SPEECH IN HIS CAMPAIGN FOR RE-ELECTION . . .
GREAT SPEECH, SENATOR, GREAT!
THANKS, BOYS, THANK YOU VERY MUCH!
YOU'RE "IN" NOW, SENATOR! IT'S ALL OVER BUT THE COUNT!
1
LATER—THE SENATOR, HOMEWARD BOUND, WENDS HIS AUTO ALONG A TREACHEROUS MOUNTAIN ROAD
3
STOP! — PLEASE STOP!
4
THE GUARD RAIL-- IT DIDN'T HOLD--MY CAR PLUNGED THRU -- I'M LUCKY TO BE ALIVE!
GOOD GRIEF! YOU ARE LUCKY! PLEASE ALLOW ME TO DRIVE YOU TO TOWN!
5

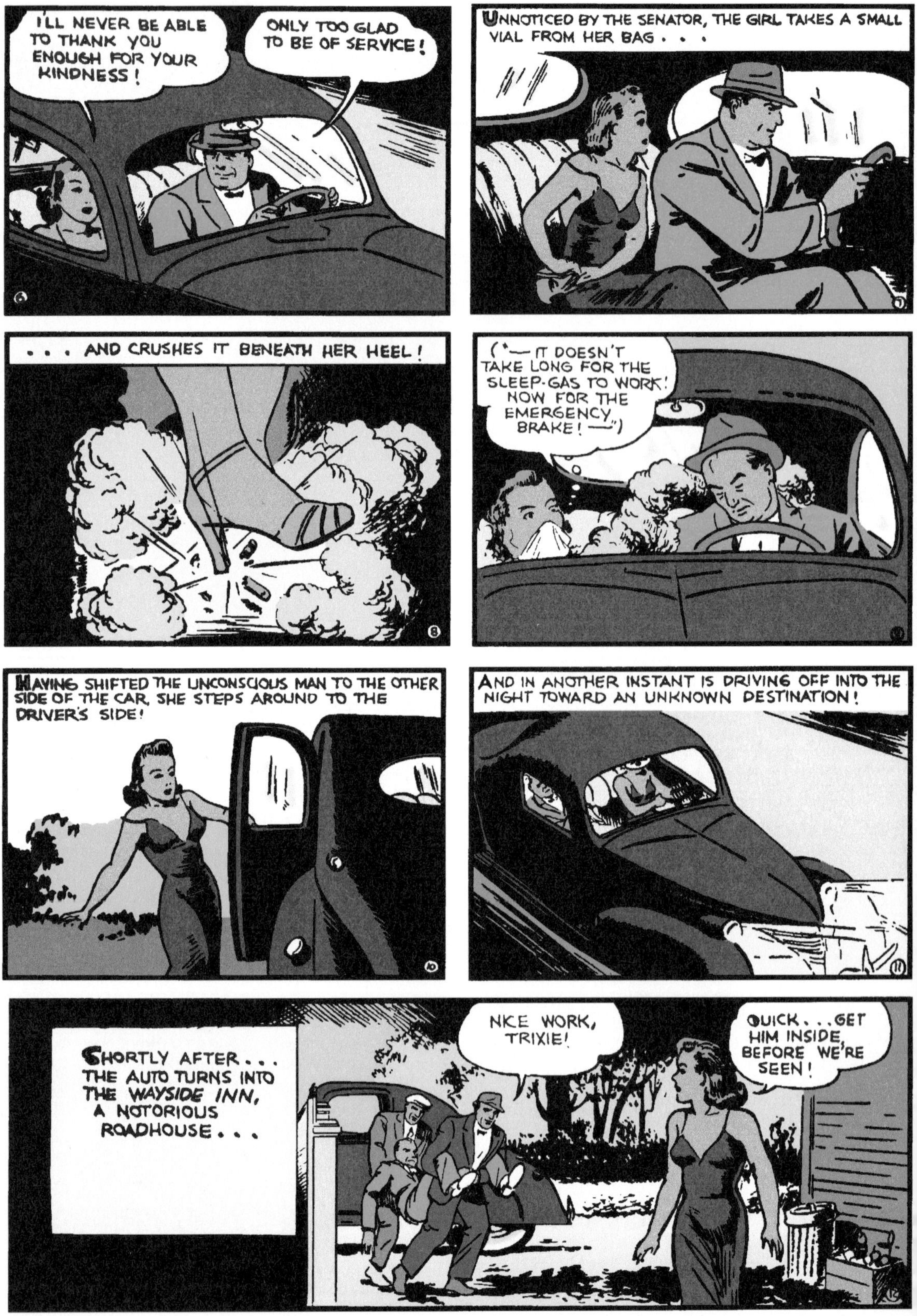
I'LL NEVER BE ABLE TO THANK YOU ENOUGH FOR YOUR KINDNESS!
ONLY TOO GLAD TO BE OF SERVICE!
UNNOTICED BY THE SENATOR, THE GIRL TAKES A SMALL VIAL FROM HER BAG . . .
. . . AND CRUSHES IT BENEATH HER HEEL!
("—IT DOESN'T TAKE LONG FOR THE SLEEP-GAS TO WORK! NOW FOR THE EMERGENCY BRAKE!—")
HAVING SHIFTED THE UNCONSCIOUS MAN TO THE OTHER SIDE OF THE CAR, SHE STEPS AROUND TO THE DRIVER'S SIDE!
AND IN ANOTHER INSTANT IS DRIVING OFF INTO THE NIGHT TOWARD AN UNKNOWN DESTINATION!
SHORTLY AFTER... THE AUTO TURNS INTO THE WAYSIDE INN, A NOTORIOUS ROADHOUSE...
NICE WORK, TRIXIE!
QUICK...GET HIM INSIDE, BEFORE WE'RE SEEN!

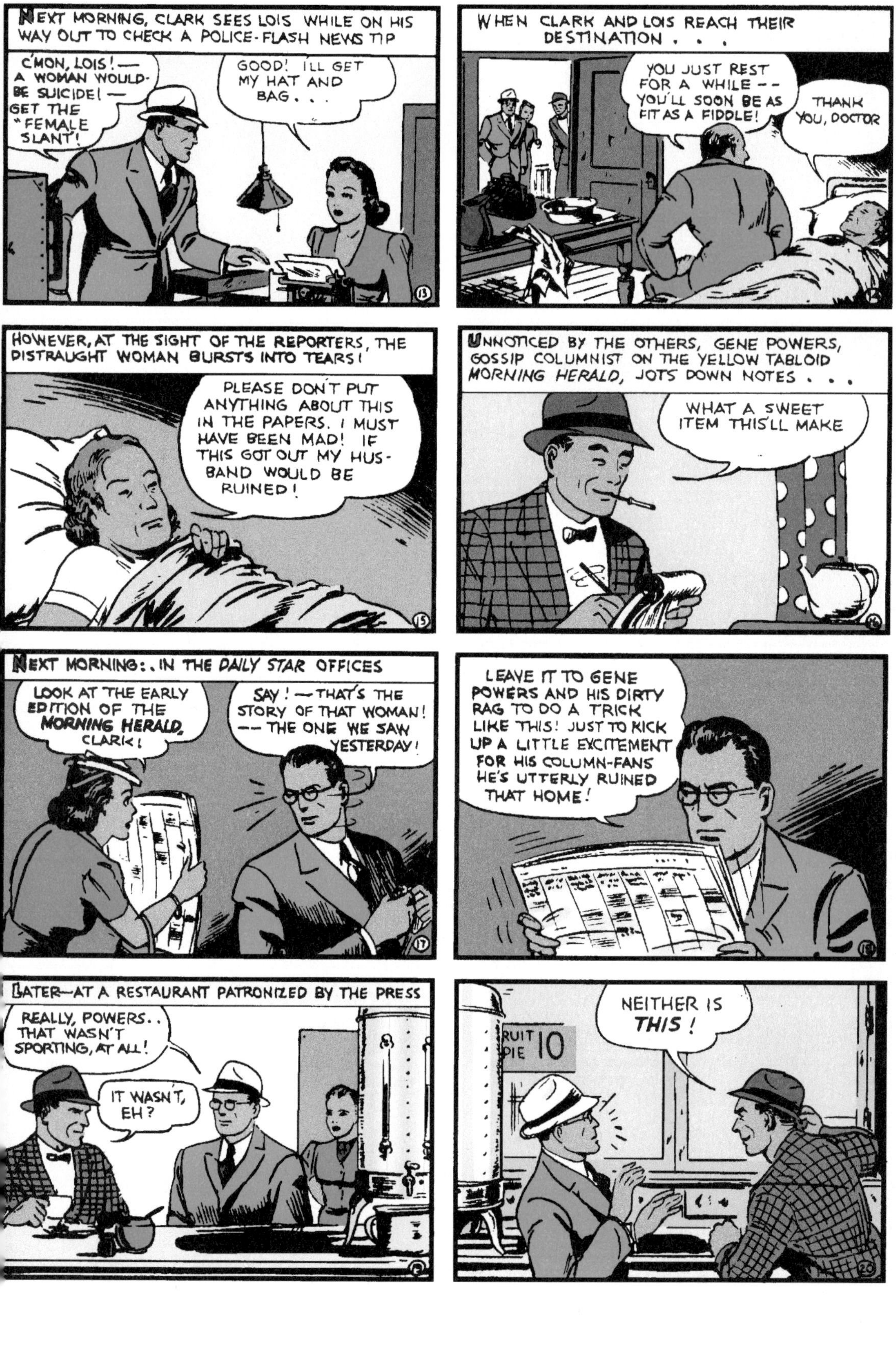
NEXT MORNING, CLARK SEES LOIS WHILE ON HIS WAY OUT TO CHECK A POLICE-FLASH NEWS TIP
C'MON, LOIS! — A WOMAN WOULD-BE SUICIDE! — GET THE "FEMALE SLANT"!
GOOD! I'LL GET MY HAT AND BAG . . .
WHEN CLARK AND LOIS REACH THEIR DESTINATION . . .
YOU JUST REST FOR A WHILE -- YOU'LL SOON BE AS FIT AS A FIDDLE!
THANK YOU, DOCTOR
HOWEVER, AT THE SIGHT OF THE REPORTERS, THE DISTRAUGHT WOMAN BURSTS INTO TEARS!
PLEASE DON'T PUT ANYTHING ABOUT THIS IN THE PAPERS. I MUST HAVE BEEN MAD! IF THIS GOT OUT MY HUS-BAND WOULD BE RUINED!
UNNOTICED BY THE OTHERS, GENE POWERS, GOSSIP COLUMNIST ON THE YELLOW TABLOID MORNING HERALD, JOTS DOWN NOTES . . .
WHAT A SWEET ITEM THIS'LL MAKE
NEXT MORNING:. IN THE DAILY STAR OFFICES
LOOK AT THE EARLY EDITION OF THE MORNING HERALD, CLARK!
SAY! — THAT'S THE STORY OF THAT WOMAN! -- THE ONE WE SAW YESTERDAY!
LEAVE IT TO GENE POWERS AND HIS DIRTY RAG TO DO A TRICK LIKE THIS! JUST TO KICK UP A LITTLE EXCITEMENT FOR HIS COLUMN-FANS HE'S UTTERLY RUINED THAT HOME!
LATER—AT A RESTAURANT PATRONIZED BY THE PRESS
REALLY, POWERS.. THAT WASN'T SPORTING, AT ALL!
IT WASN'T, EH?
FRUIT PIE 10
NEITHER IS THIS!

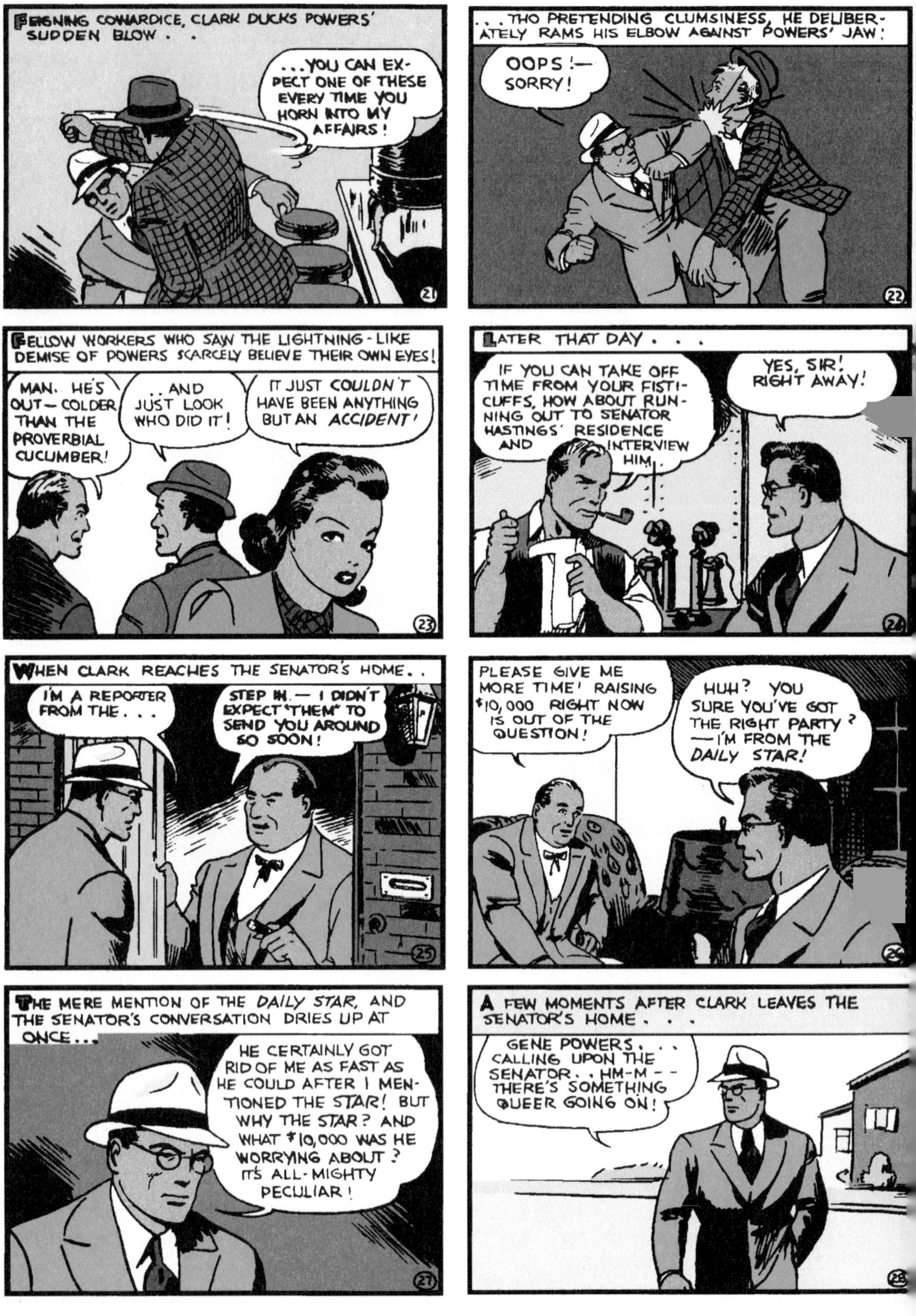
FEIGNING COWARDICE, CLARK DUCKS POWERS' SUDDEN BLOW . .
...YOU CAN EXPECT ONE OF THESE EVERY TIME YOU HORN INTO MY AFFAIRS!
. . . THO PRETENDING CLUMSINESS, HE DELIBERATELY RAMS HIS ELBOW AGAINST POWERS' JAW!
OOPS!— SORRY!
FELLOW WORKERS WHO SAW THE LIGHTNING-LIKE DEMISE OF POWERS SCARCELY BELIEVE THEIR OWN EYES!
MAN. HE'S OUT—COLDER THAN THE PROVERBIAL CUCUMBER!
..AND JUST LOOK WHO DID IT!
IT JUST COULDN'T HAVE BEEN ANYTHING BUT AN ACCIDENT!
LATER THAT DAY . . .
IF YOU CAN TAKE OFF TIME FROM YOUR FISTICUFFS, HOW ABOUT RUNNING OUT TO SENATOR HASTINGS' RESIDENCE AND INTERVIEW HIM.
YES, SIR! RIGHT AWAY!
WHEN CLARK REACHES THE SENATOR'S HOME. .
I'M A REPORTER FROM THE . . .
STEP IN.— I DIDN'T EXPECT "THEM" TO SEND YOU AROUND SO SOON!
PLEASE GIVE ME MORE TIME! RAISING $10,000 RIGHT NOW IS OUT OF THE QUESTION!
HUH? YOU SURE YOU'VE GOT THE RIGHT PARTY? —I'M FROM THE DAILY STAR!
THE MERE MENTION OF THE DAILY STAR, AND THE SENATOR'S CONVERSATION DRIES UP AT ONCE...
HE CERTAINLY GOT RID OF ME AS FAST AS HE COULD AFTER I MENTIONED THE STAR! BUT WHY THE STAR? AND WHAT $10,000 WAS HE WORRYING ABOUT? IT'S ALL-MIGHTY PECULIAR!
A FEW MOMENTS AFTER CLARK LEAVES THE SENATOR'S HOME . . .
GENE POWERS. . . CALLING UPON THE SENATOR. . HM-M - - THERE'S SOMETHING QUEER GOING ON!

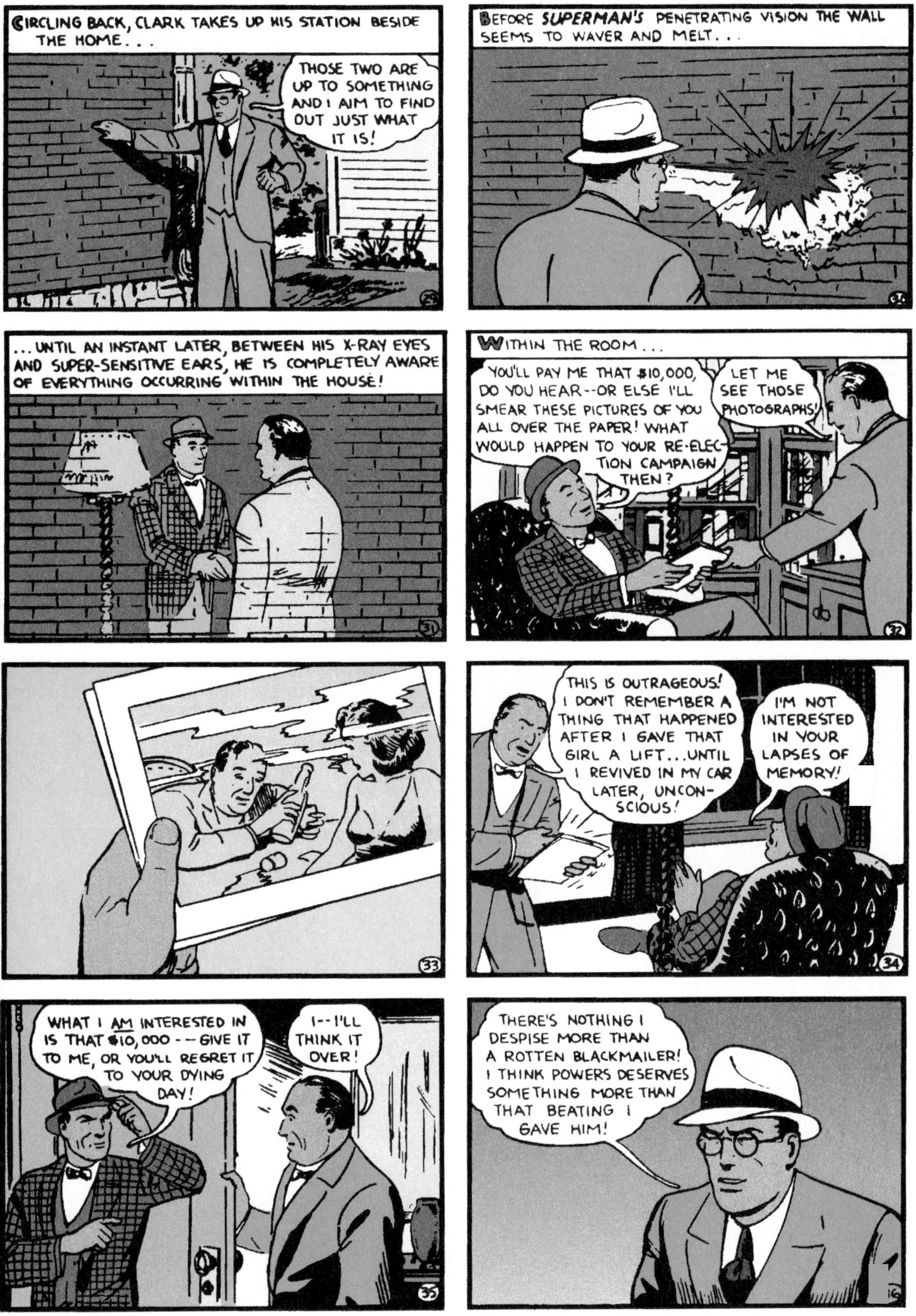
CIRCLING BACK, CLARK TAKES UP HIS STATION BESIDE THE HOME...
THOSE TWO ARE UP TO SOMETHING AND I AIM TO FIND OUT JUST WHAT IT IS!
BEFORE SUPERMAN'S PENETRATING VISION THE WALL SEEMS TO WAVER AND MELT...
...UNTIL AN INSTANT LATER, BETWEEN HIS X-RAY EYES AND SUPER-SENSITIVE EARS, HE IS COMPLETELY AWARE OF EVERYTHING OCCURRING WITHIN THE HOUSE!
WITHIN THE ROOM...
YOU'LL PAY ME THAT $10,000, DO YOU HEAR--OR ELSE I'LL SMEAR THESE PICTURES OF YOU ALL OVER THE PAPER! WHAT WOULD HAPPEN TO YOUR RE-ELECTION CAMPAIGN THEN?
LET ME SEE THOSE PHOTOGRAPHS!
THIS IS OUTRAGEOUS! I DON'T REMEMBER A THING THAT HAPPENED AFTER I GAVE THAT GIRL A LIFT...UNTIL I REVIVED IN MY CAR LATER, UNCONSCIOUS!
I'M NOT INTERESTED IN YOUR LAPSES OF MEMORY!
WHAT I AM INTERESTED IN IS THAT $10,000--GIVE IT TO ME, OR YOU'LL REGRET IT TO YOUR DYING DAY!
I--I'LL THINK IT OVER!
THERE'S NOTHING I DESPISE MORE THAN A ROTTEN BLACKMAILER! I THINK POWERS DESERVES SOMETHING MORE THAN THAT BEATING I GAVE HIM!

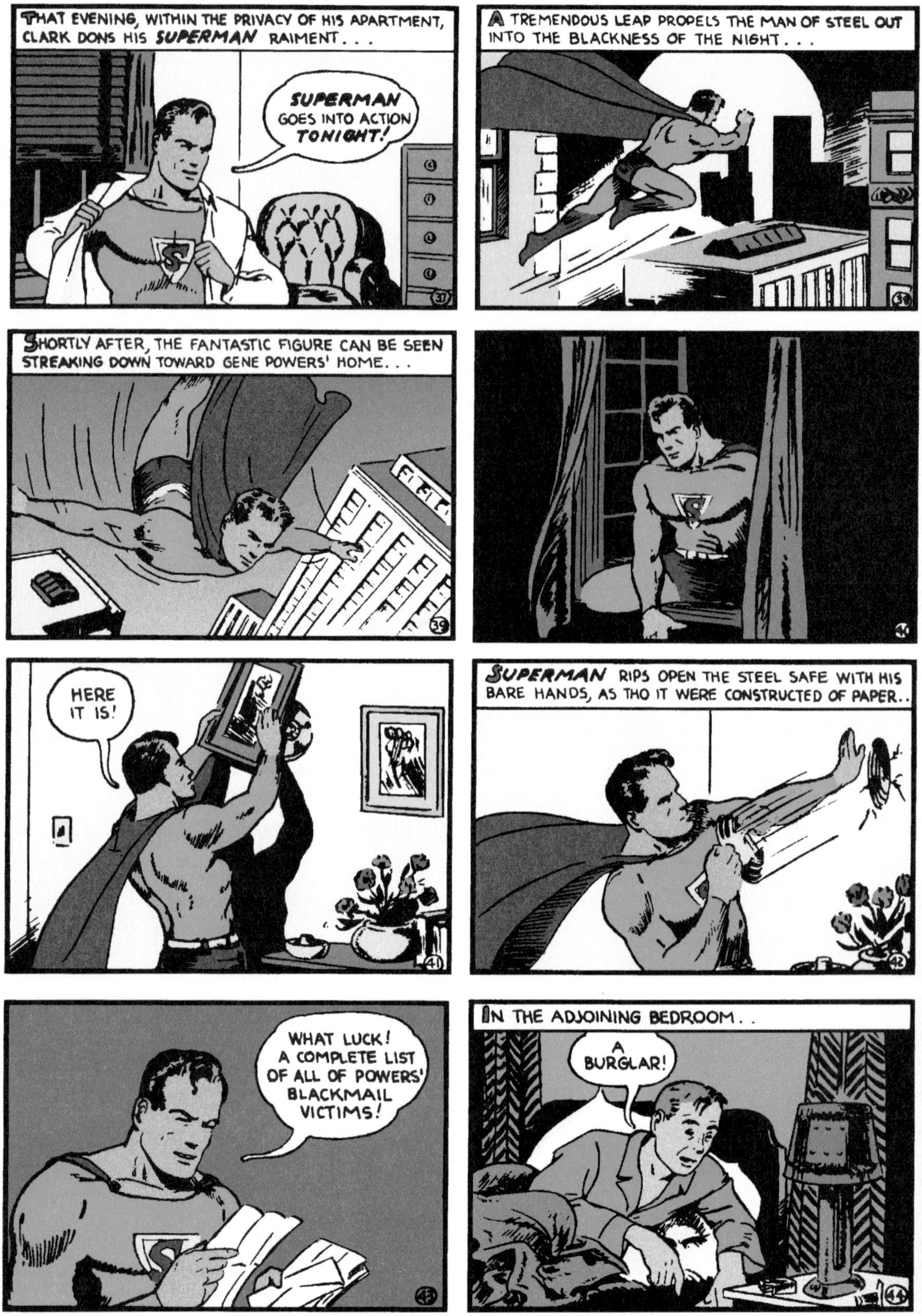
THAT EVENING, WITHIN THE PRIVACY OF HIS APARTMENT, CLARK DONS HIS SUPERMAN RAIMENT . . .
SUPERMAN GOES INTO ACTION TONIGHT!
37
A TREMENDOUS LEAP PROPELS THE MAN OF STEEL OUT INTO THE BLACKNESS OF THE NIGHT . . .
38
SHORTLY AFTER, THE FANTASTIC FIGURE CAN BE SEEN STREAKING DOWN TOWARD GENE POWERS' HOME. . .
39
40
HERE IT IS!
41
SUPERMAN RIPS OPEN THE STEEL SAFE WITH HIS BARE HANDS, AS THO IT WERE CONSTRUCTED OF PAPER. .
42
WHAT LUCK! A COMPLETE LIST OF ALL OF POWERS' BLACKMAIL VICTIMS!
43
IN THE ADJOINING BEDROOM. .
A BURGLAR!
44

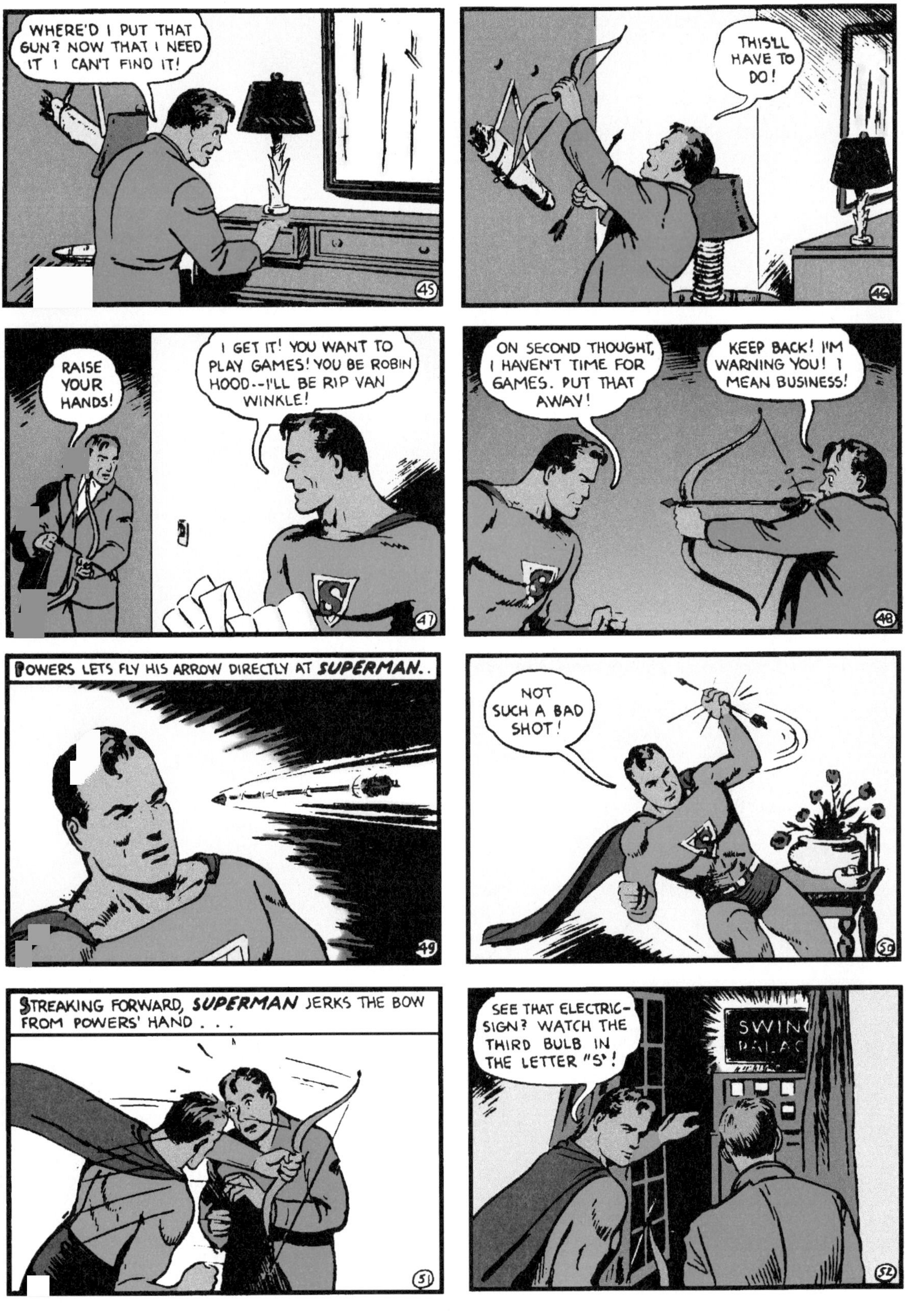
WHERE'D I PUT THAT GUN? NOW THAT I NEED IT I CAN'T FIND IT!
THIS'LL HAVE TO DO!
RAISE YOUR HANDS!
I GET IT! YOU WANT TO PLAY GAMES! YOU BE ROBIN HOOD--I'LL BE RIP VAN WINKLE!
ON SECOND THOUGHT, I HAVEN'T TIME FOR GAMES. PUT THAT AWAY!
KEEP BACK! I'M WARNING YOU! I MEAN BUSINESS!
POWERS LETS FLY HIS ARROW DIRECTLY AT SUPERMAN..
NOT SUCH A BAD SHOT!
STREAKING FORWARD, SUPERMAN JERKS THE BOW FROM POWERS' HAND . . .
SEE THAT ELECTRIC-SIGN? WATCH THE THIRD BULB IN THE LETTER "S"!

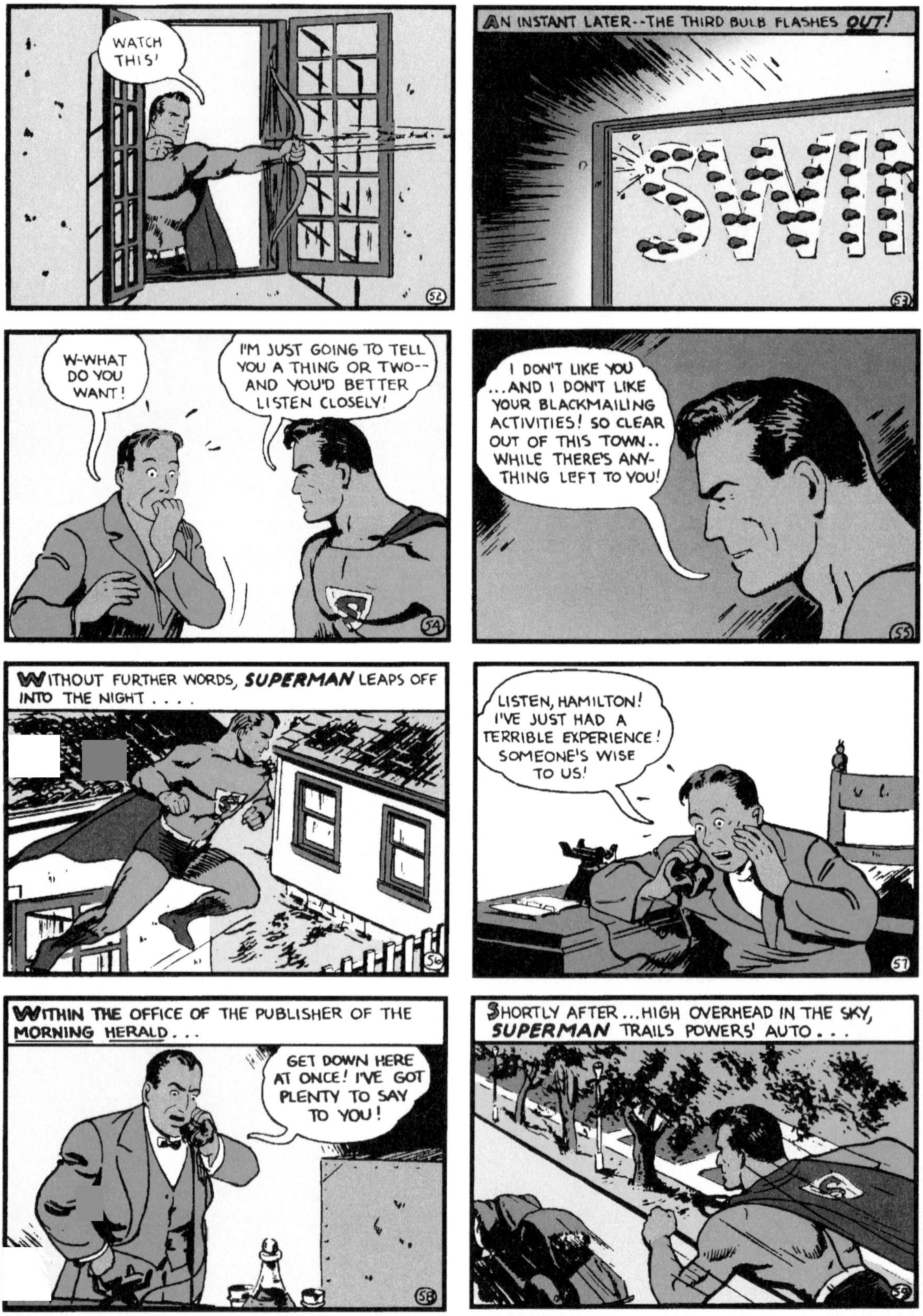
WATCH THIS!
AN INSTANT LATER--THE THIRD BULB FLASHES OUT!
W-WHAT DO YOU WANT!
I'M JUST GOING TO TELL YOU A THING OR TWO--AND YOU'D BETTER LISTEN CLOSELY!
I DON'T LIKE YOU ...AND I DON'T LIKE YOUR BLACKMAILING ACTIVITIES! SO CLEAR OUT OF THIS TOWN.. WHILE THERE'S ANYTHING LEFT TO YOU!
WITHOUT FURTHER WORDS, SUPERMAN LEAPS OFF INTO THE NIGHT . . . .
LISTEN, HAMILTON! I'VE JUST HAD A TERRIBLE EXPERIENCE! SOMEONE'S WISE TO US!
WITHIN THE OFFICE OF THE PUBLISHER OF THE MORNING HERALD . . .
GET DOWN HERE AT ONCE! I'VE GOT PLENTY TO SAY TO YOU!
SHORTLY AFTER ... HIGH OVERHEAD IN THE SKY, SUPERMAN TRAILS POWERS' AUTO . . .

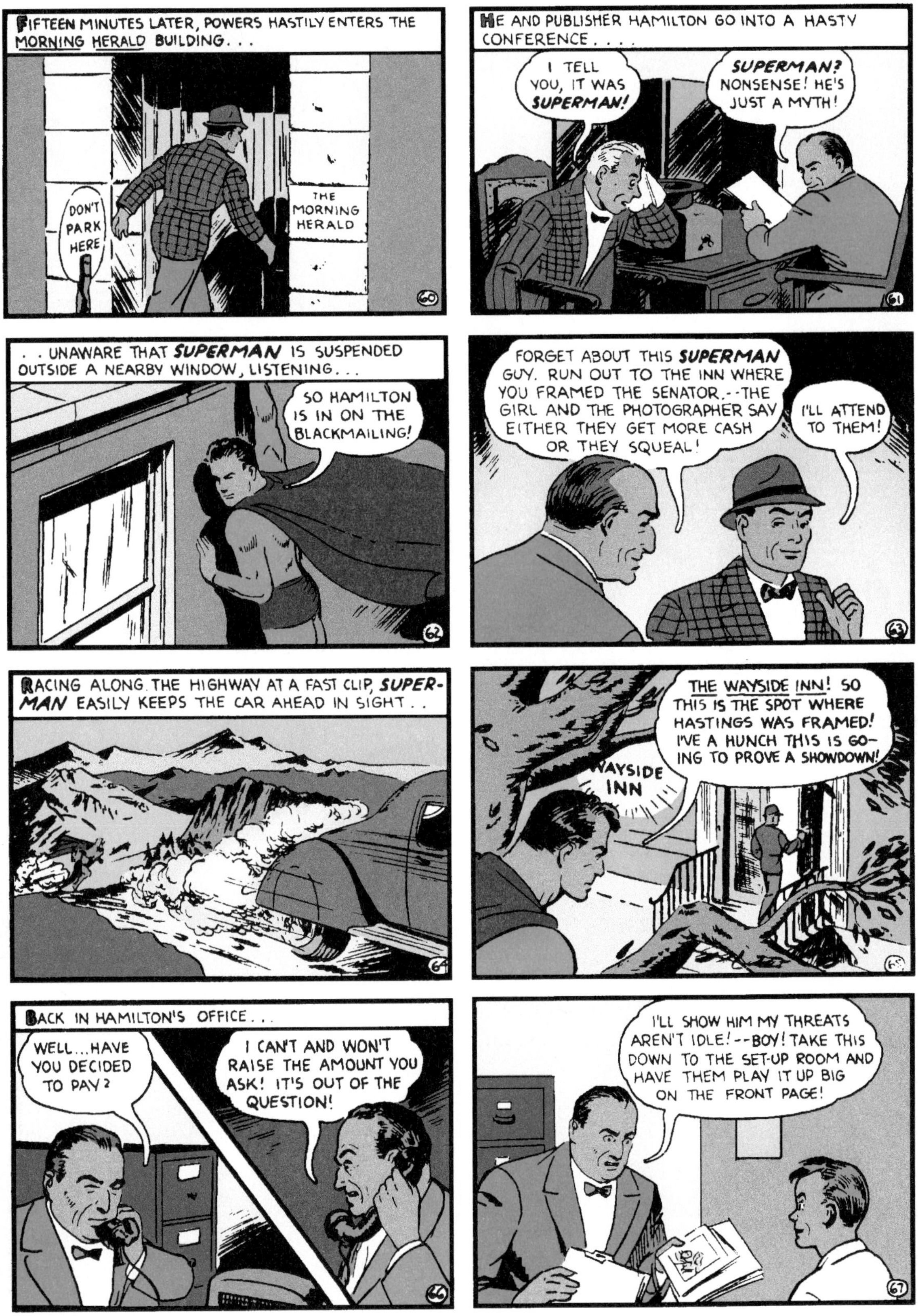
FIFTEEN MINUTES LATER, POWERS HASTILY ENTERS THE MORNING HERALD BUILDING. . .
DON'T PARK HERE
THE MORNING HERALD
HE AND PUBLISHER HAMILTON GO INTO A HASTY CONFERENCE. . . .
I TELL YOU, IT WAS SUPERMAN!
SUPERMAN? NONSENSE! HE'S JUST A MYTH!
. . UNAWARE THAT SUPERMAN IS SUSPENDED OUTSIDE A NEARBY WINDOW, LISTENING. . .
SO HAMILTON IS IN ON THE BLACKMAILING!
FORGET ABOUT THIS SUPERMAN GUY. RUN OUT TO THE INN WHERE YOU FRAMED THE SENATOR.--THE GIRL AND THE PHOTOGRAPHER SAY EITHER THEY GET MORE CASH OR THEY SQUEAL!
I'LL ATTEND TO THEM!
RACING ALONG THE HIGHWAY AT A FAST CLIP, SUPERMAN EASILY KEEPS THE CAR AHEAD IN SIGHT. .
THE WAYSIDE INN! SO THIS IS THE SPOT WHERE HASTINGS WAS FRAMED! I'VE A HUNCH THIS IS GOING TO PROVE A SHOWDOWN!
WAYSIDE INN
BACK IN HAMILTON'S OFFICE. . .
WELL...HAVE YOU DECIDED TO PAY?
I CAN'T AND WON'T RAISE THE AMOUNT YOU ASK! IT'S OUT OF THE QUESTION!
I'LL SHOW HIM MY THREATS AREN'T IDLE!--BOY! TAKE THIS DOWN TO THE SET-UP ROOM AND HAVE THEM PLAY IT UP BIG ON THE FRONT PAGE!

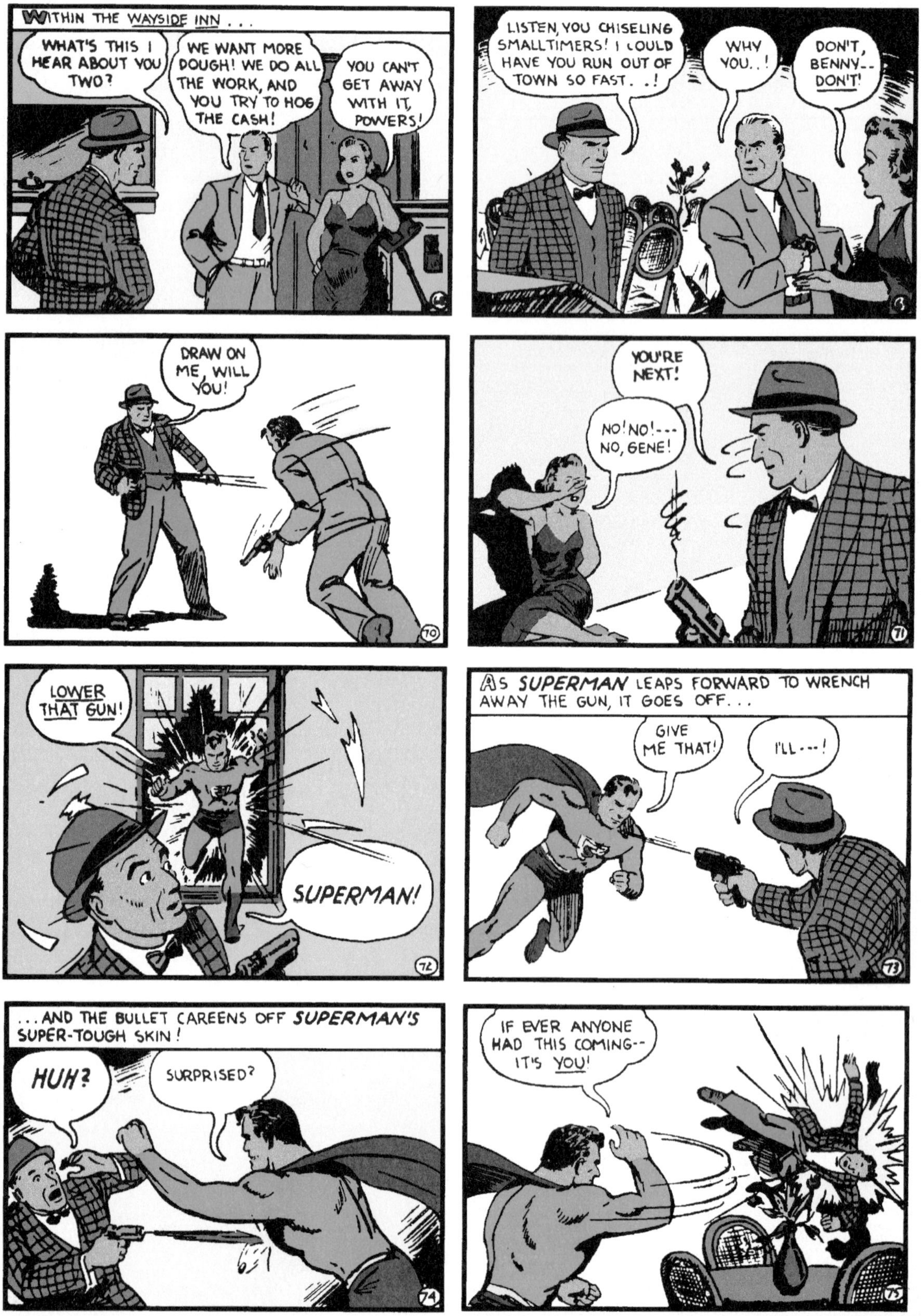
WITHIN THE WAYSIDE INN . . .
WHAT'S THIS I HEAR ABOUT YOU TWO?
WE WANT MORE DOUGH! WE DO ALL THE WORK, AND YOU TRY TO HOG THE CASH!
YOU CAN'T GET AWAY WITH IT, POWERS!
LISTEN, YOU CHISELING SMALLTIMERS! I COULD HAVE YOU RUN OUT OF TOWN SO FAST. .!
WHY YOU. .!
DON'T, BENNY-- DON'T!
DRAW ON ME, WILL YOU!
YOU'RE NEXT!
NO! NO!--- NO, GENE!
LOWER THAT GUN!
SUPERMAN!
AS SUPERMAN LEAPS FORWARD TO WRENCH AWAY THE GUN, IT GOES OFF. . .
GIVE ME THAT!
I'LL---!
. . . AND THE BULLET CAREENS OFF SUPERMAN'S SUPER-TOUGH SKIN!
HUH?
SURPRISED?
IF EVER ANYONE HAD THIS COMING-- IT'S YOU!

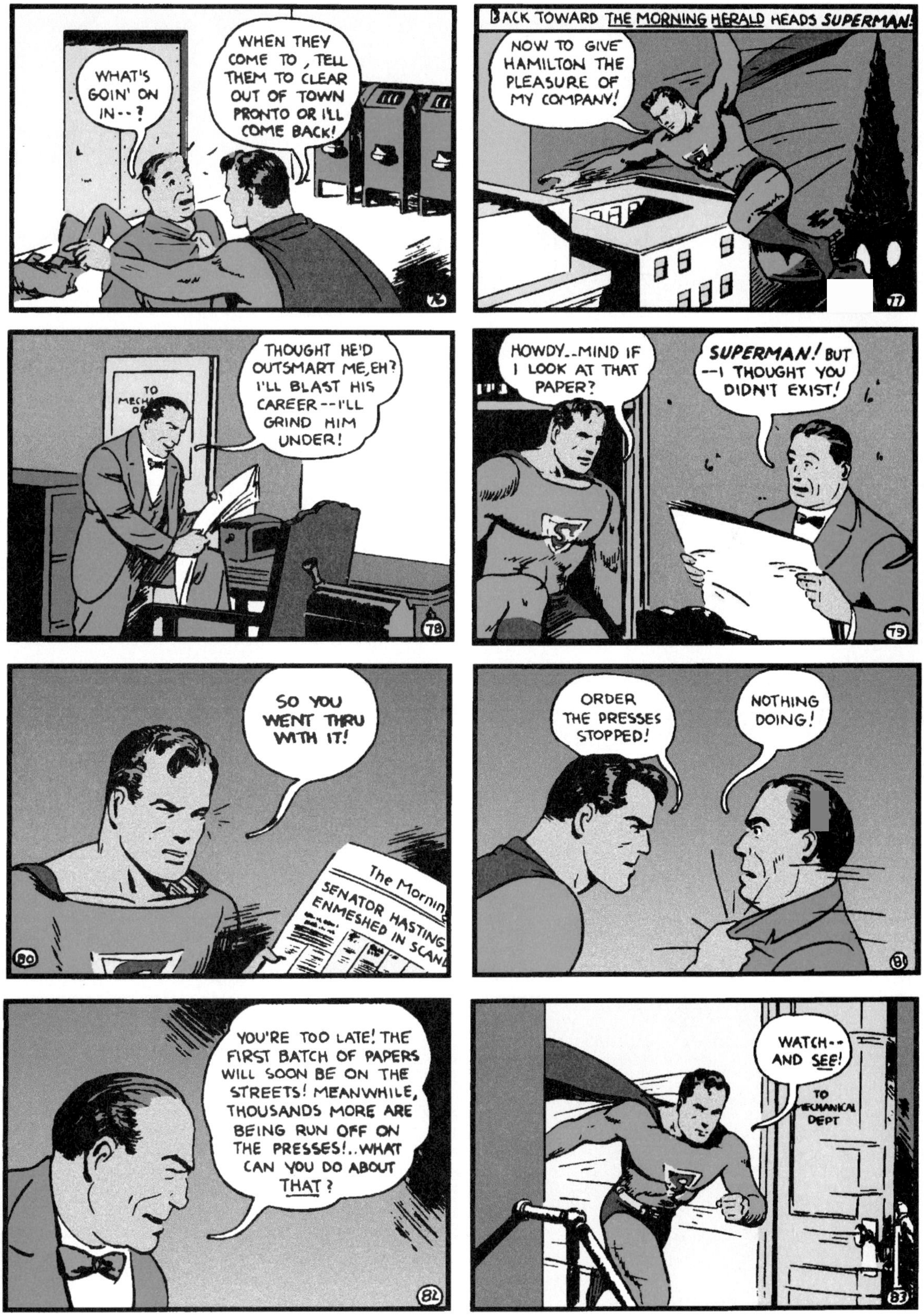
WHAT'S GOIN' ON IN--?
WHEN THEY COME TO, TELL THEM TO CLEAR OUT OF TOWN PRONTO OR I'LL COME BACK!
BACK TOWARD THE MORNING HERALD HEADS SUPERMAN!
NOW TO GIVE HAMILTON THE PLEASURE OF MY COMPANY!
THOUGHT HE'D OUTSMART ME, EH? I'LL BLAST HIS CAREER--I'LL GRIND HIM UNDER!
HOWDY..MIND IF I LOOK AT THAT PAPER?
SUPERMAN! BUT --I THOUGHT YOU DIDN'T EXIST!
SO YOU WENT THRU WITH IT!
ORDER THE PRESSES STOPPED!
NOTHING DOING!
YOU'RE TOO LATE! THE FIRST BATCH OF PAPERS WILL SOON BE ON THE STREETS! MEANWHILE, THOUSANDS MORE ARE BEING RUN OFF ON THE PRESSES!..WHAT CAN YOU DO ABOUT THAT?
WATCH--AND SEE!

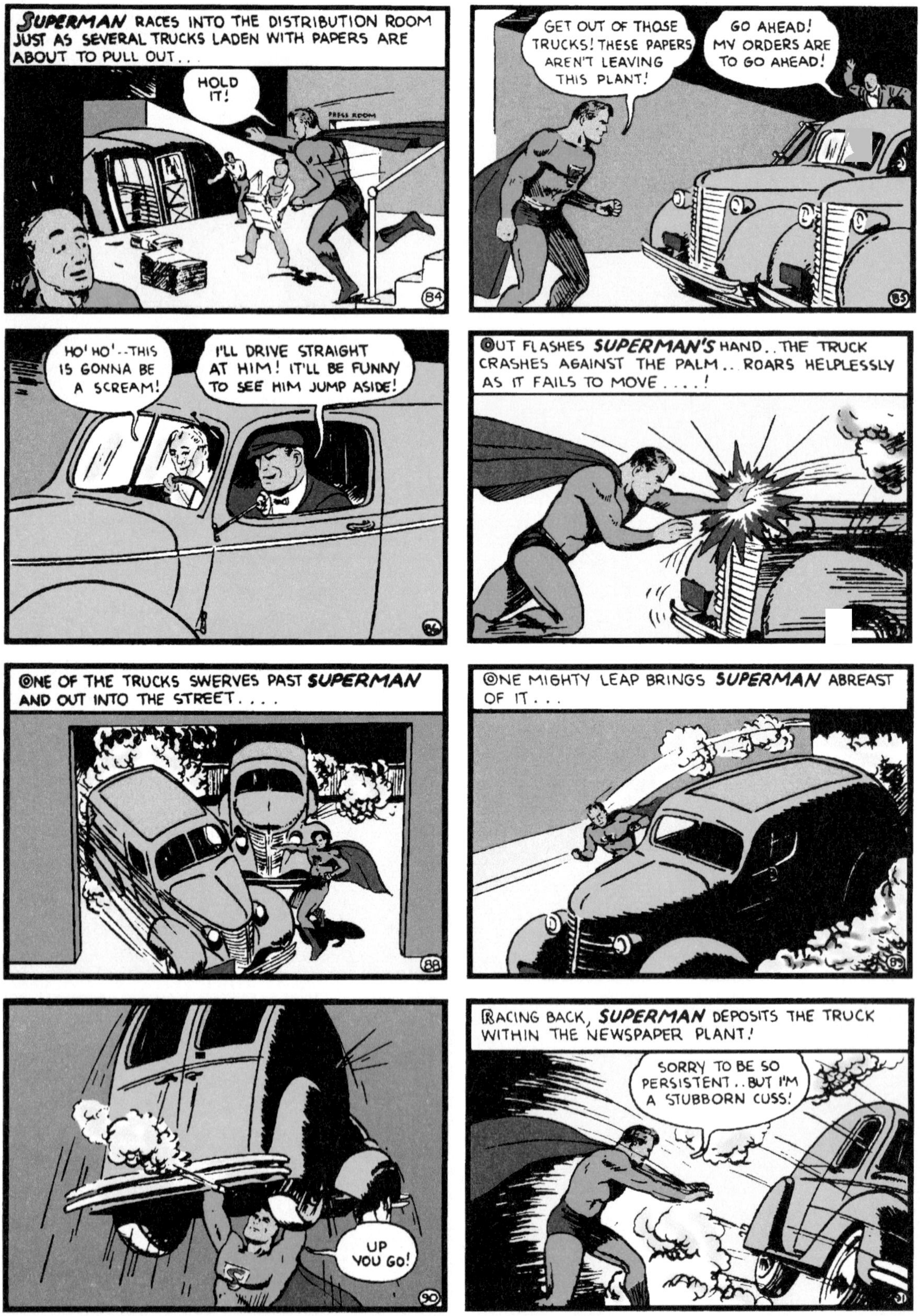
SUPERMAN RACES INTO THE DISTRIBUTION ROOM JUST AS SEVERAL TRUCKS LADEN WITH PAPERS ARE ABOUT TO PULL OUT. .
HOLD IT!
PRESS ROOM
GET OUT OF THOSE TRUCKS! THESE PAPERS AREN'T LEAVING THIS PLANT!
GO AHEAD! MY ORDERS ARE TO GO AHEAD!
HO' HO'--THIS IS GONNA BE A SCREAM!
I'LL DRIVE STRAIGHT AT HIM! IT'LL BE FUNNY TO SEE HIM JUMP ASIDE!
OUT FLASHES SUPERMAN'S HAND. . THE TRUCK CRASHES AGAINST THE PALM. . ROARS HELPLESSLY AS IT FAILS TO MOVE . . . . !
ONE OF THE TRUCKS SWERVES PAST SUPERMAN AND OUT INTO THE STREET . . . .
ONE MIGHTY LEAP BRINGS SUPERMAN ABREAST OF IT . . .
UP YOU GO!
RACING BACK, SUPERMAN DEPOSITS THE TRUCK WITHIN THE NEWSPAPER PLANT!
SORRY TO BE SO PERSISTENT. . BUT I'M A STUBBORN CUSS!

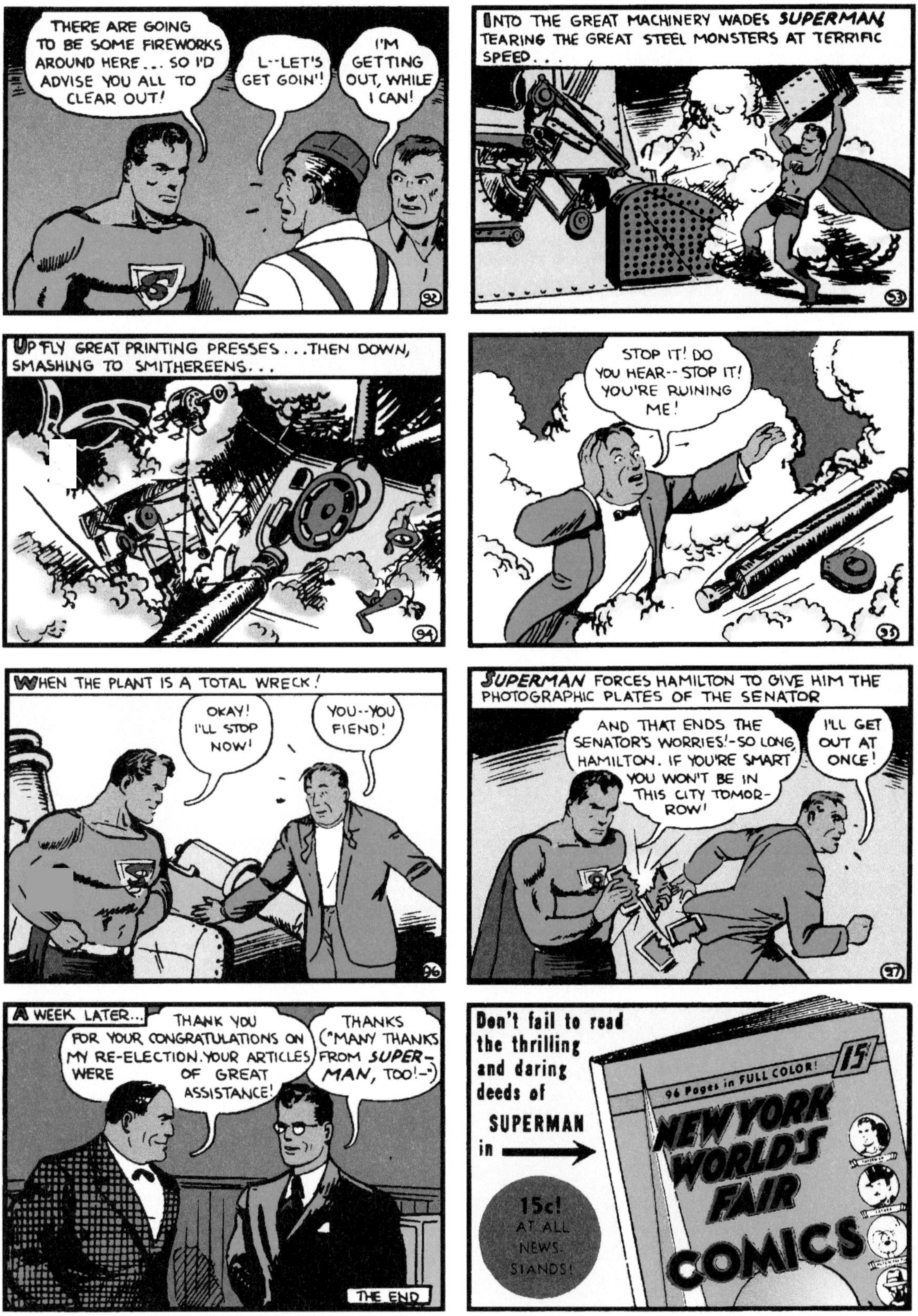

THERE ARE GOING TO BE SOME FIREWORKS AROUND HERE... SO I'D ADVISE YOU ALL TO CLEAR OUT!
L--LET'S GET GOIN'!
I'M GETTING OUT, WHILE I CAN!
INTO THE GREAT MACHINERY WADES SUPERMAN TEARING THE GREAT STEEL MONSTERS AT TERRIFIC SPEED...
UP FLY GREAT PRINTING PRESSES...THEN DOWN, SMASHING TO SMITHEREENS...
STOP IT! DO YOU HEAR-- STOP IT! YOU'RE RUINING ME!
WHEN THE PLANT IS A TOTAL WRECK!
OKAY! I'LL STOP NOW!
YOU--YOU FIEND!
SUPERMAN FORCES HAMILTON TO GIVE HIM THE PHOTOGRAPHIC PLATES OF THE SENATOR
AND THAT ENDS THE SENATOR'S WORRIES!-SO LONG, HAMILTON. IF YOU'RE SMART YOU WON'T BE IN THIS CITY TOMORROW!
I'LL GET OUT AT ONCE!
A WEEK LATER...
THANK YOU FOR YOUR CONGRATULATIONS ON MY RE-ELECTION. YOUR ARTICLES WERE OF GREAT ASSISTANCE!
THANKS ("MANY THANKS FROM SUPERMAN, TOO!-")
THE END
Don't fail to read the thrilling and daring deeds of
SUPERMAN
in
15c! AT ALL NEWS-STANDS!
96 Pages in FULL COLOR!
15¢
NEW YORK WORLD'S FAIR COMICS

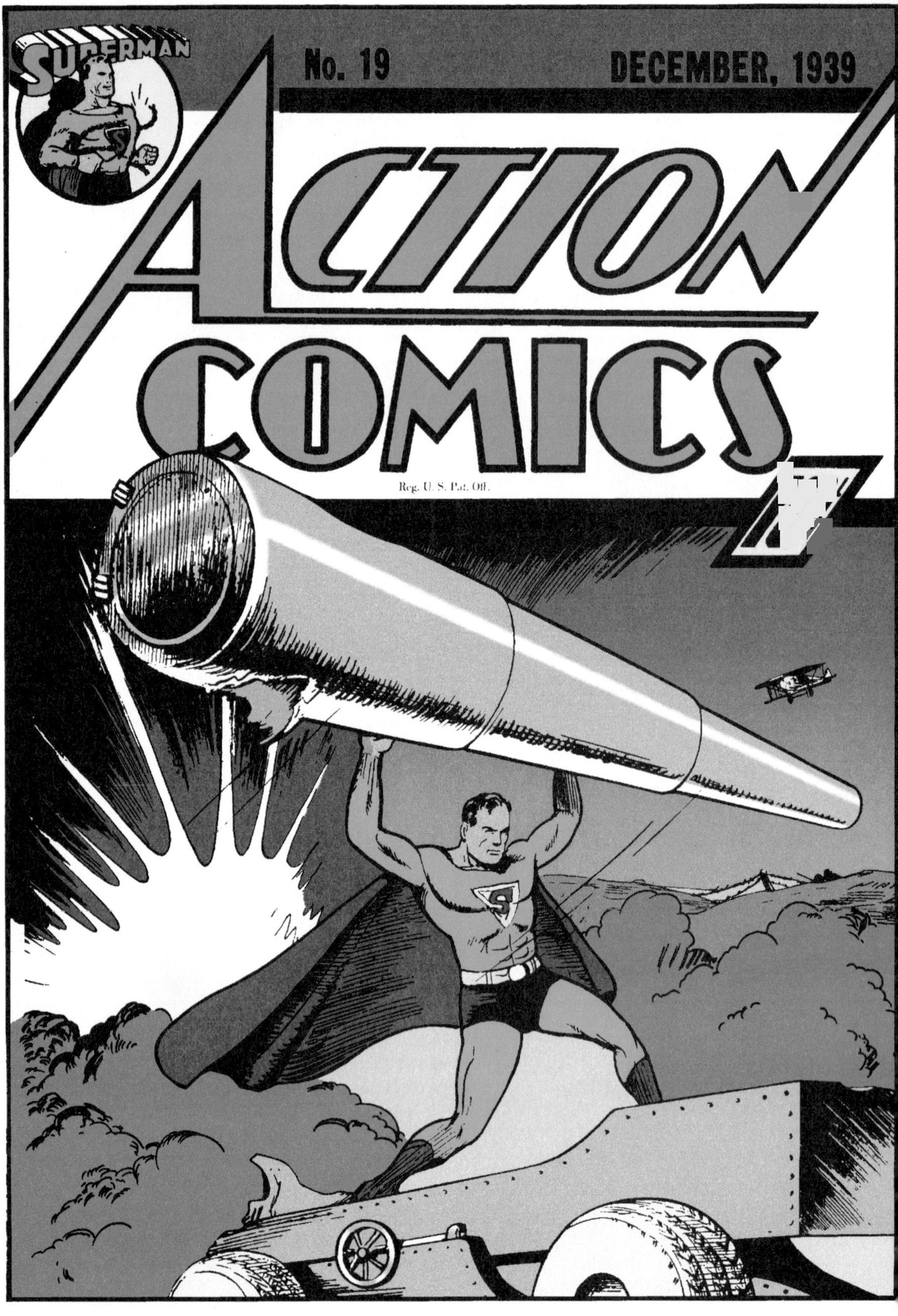
SUPERMAN
No. 19
DECEMBER, 1939
ACTION
COMICS
Reg. U. S. Pat. Off.

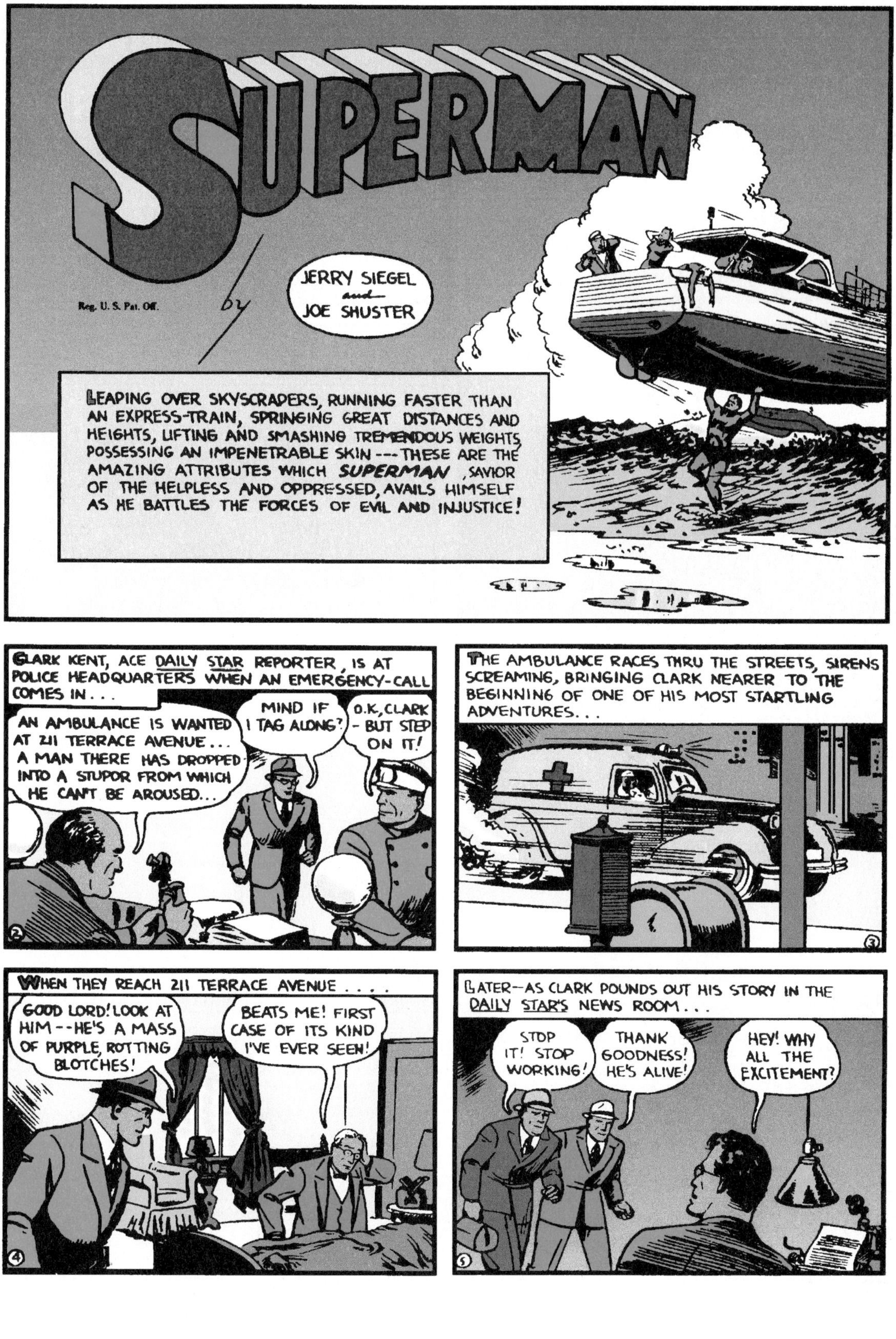
SUPERMAN
Reg. U. S. Pat. Off.
by
JERRY SIEGEL and JOE SHUSTER
LEAPING OVER SKYSCRAPERS, RUNNING FASTER THAN AN EXPRESS-TRAIN, SPRINGING GREAT DISTANCES AND HEIGHTS, LIFTING AND SMASHING TREMENDOUS WEIGHTS, POSSESSING AN IMPENETRABLE SKIN --- THESE ARE THE AMAZING ATTRIBUTES WHICH SUPERMAN , SAVIOR OF THE HELPLESS AND OPPRESSED, AVAILS HIMSELF AS HE BATTLES THE FORCES OF EVIL AND INJUSTICE!
CLARK KENT, ACE DAILY STAR REPORTER , IS AT POLICE HEADQUARTERS WHEN AN EMERGENCY-CALL COMES IN . . .
AN AMBULANCE IS WANTED AT 211 TERRACE AVENUE . . . A MAN THERE HAS DROPPED INTO A STUPOR FROM WHICH HE CAN'T BE AROUSED . . .
MIND IF I TAG ALONG?
O.K., CLARK - BUT STEP ON IT!
2
THE AMBULANCE RACES THRU THE STREETS, SIRENS SCREAMING, BRINGING CLARK NEARER TO THE BEGINNING OF ONE OF HIS MOST STARTLING ADVENTURES . . .
3
WHEN THEY REACH 211 TERRACE AVENUE . . . .
GOOD LORD! LOOK AT HIM --HE'S A MASS OF PURPLE, ROTTING BLOTCHES!
BEATS ME! FIRST CASE OF ITS KIND I'VE EVER SEEN!
4
LATER--AS CLARK POUNDS OUT HIS STORY IN THE DAILY STAR'S NEWS ROOM . . .
STOP IT! STOP WORKING!
THANK GOODNESS! HE'S ALIVE!
HEY! WHY ALL THE EXCITEMENT?
5

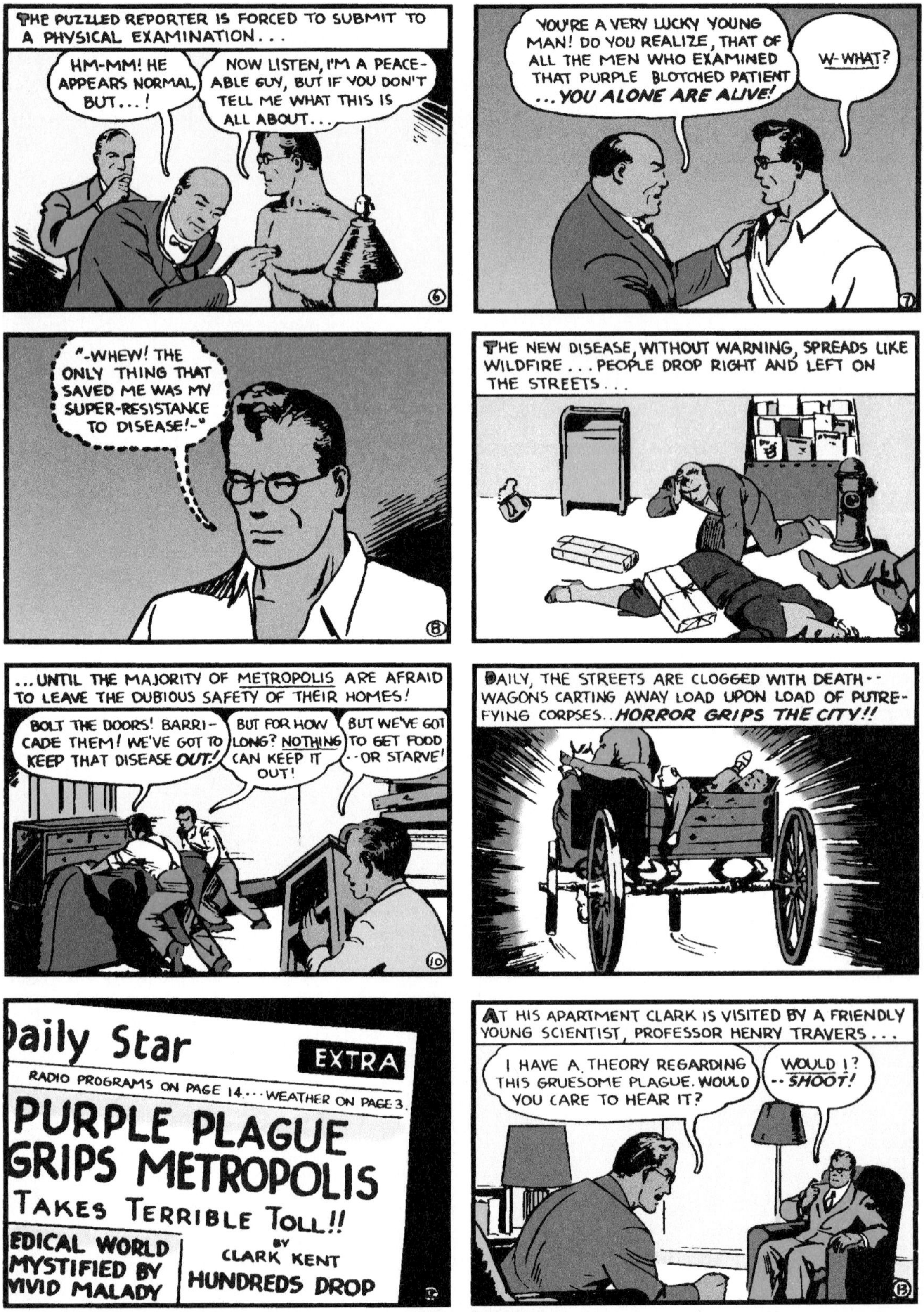
THE PUZZLED REPORTER IS FORCED TO SUBMIT TO A PHYSICAL EXAMINATION . . .
HM-MM! HE APPEARS NORMAL, BUT . . . !
NOW LISTEN, I'M A PEACE-ABLE GUY, BUT IF YOU DON'T TELL ME WHAT THIS IS ALL ABOUT . . .
YOU'RE A VERY LUCKY YOUNG MAN! DO YOU REALIZE, THAT OF ALL THE MEN WHO EXAMINED THAT PURPLE BLOTCHED PATIENT . . . YOU ALONE ARE ALIVE!
W-WHAT?
"-WHEW! THE ONLY THING THAT SAVED ME WAS MY SUPER-RESISTANCE TO DISEASE!-"
THE NEW DISEASE, WITHOUT WARNING, SPREADS LIKE WILDFIRE . . . PEOPLE DROP RIGHT AND LEFT ON THE STREETS . . .
. . . UNTIL THE MAJORITY OF METROPOLIS ARE AFRAID TO LEAVE THE DUBIOUS SAFETY OF THEIR HOMES!
BOLT THE DOORS! BARRI-CADE THEM! WE'VE GOT TO KEEP THAT DISEASE OUT!
BUT FOR HOW LONG? NOTHING CAN KEEP IT OUT!
BUT WE'VE GOT TO GET FOOD . . OR STARVE!
DAILY, THE STREETS ARE CLOGGED WITH DEATH-- WAGONS CARTING AWAY LOAD UPON LOAD OF PUTRE-FYING CORPSES.. HORROR GRIPS THE CITY!!
Daily Star
EXTRA
RADIO PROGRAMS ON PAGE 14 . . . WEATHER ON PAGE 3.
PURPLE PLAGUE GRIPS METROPOLIS
TAKES TERRIBLE TOLL!!
EDICAL WORLD MYSTIFIED BY VIVID MALADY
BY CLARK KENT
HUNDREDS DROP
AT HIS APARTMENT CLARK IS VISITED BY A FRIENDLY YOUNG SCIENTIST, PROFESSOR HENRY TRAVERS . . .
I HAVE A THEORY REGARDING THIS GRUESOME PLAGUE. WOULD YOU CARE TO HEAR IT?
WOULD I? --SHOOT!

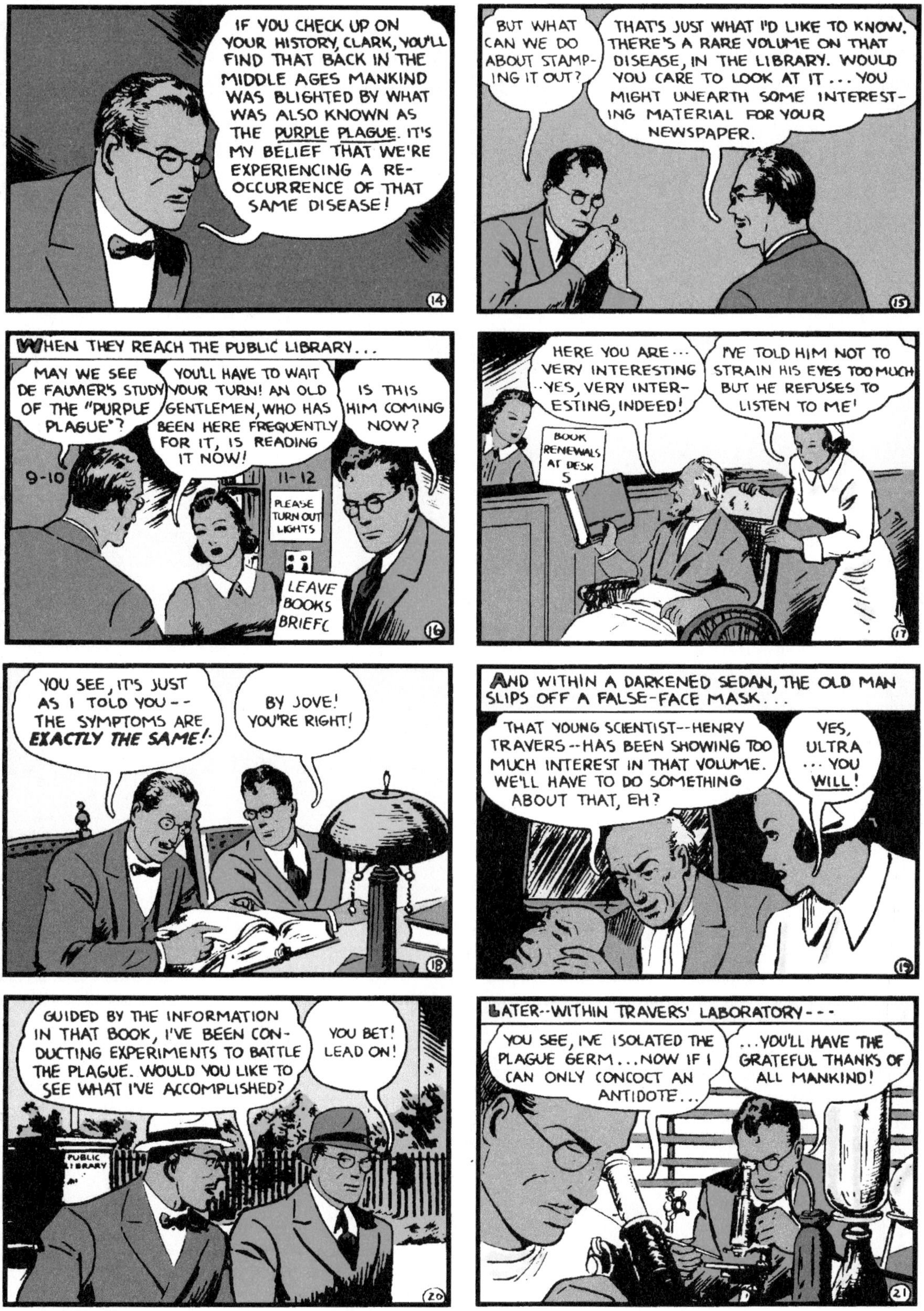
IF YOU CHECK UP ON YOUR HISTORY, CLARK, YOU'LL FIND THAT BACK IN THE MIDDLE AGES MANKIND WAS BLIGHTED BY WHAT WAS ALSO KNOWN AS THE PURPLE PLAGUE. IT'S MY BELIEF THAT WE'RE EXPERIENCING A RE-OCCURRENCE OF THAT SAME DISEASE!
14
BUT WHAT CAN WE DO ABOUT STAMPING IT OUT?
THAT'S JUST WHAT I'D LIKE TO KNOW. THERE'S A RARE VOLUME ON THAT DISEASE, IN THE LIBRARY. WOULD YOU CARE TO LOOK AT IT... YOU MIGHT UNEARTH SOME INTERESTING MATERIAL FOR YOUR NEWSPAPER.
15
WHEN THEY REACH THE PUBLIC LIBRARY...
MAY WE SEE DE FAUVIER'S STUDY OF THE "PURPLE PLAGUE"?
YOU'LL HAVE TO WAIT YOUR TURN! AN OLD GENTLEMEN, WHO HAS BEEN HERE FREQUENTLY FOR IT, IS READING IT NOW!
IS THIS HIM COMING NOW?
9-10
11-12
PLEASE TURN OUT LIGHTS
LEAVE BOOKS BRIEFC
16
HERE YOU ARE... VERY INTERESTING ..YES, VERY INTERESTING, INDEED!
I'VE TOLD HIM NOT TO STRAIN HIS EYES TOO MUCH BUT HE REFUSES TO LISTEN TO ME!
BOOK RENEWALS AT DESK 5
17
YOU SEE, IT'S JUST AS I TOLD YOU-- THE SYMPTOMS ARE EXACTLY THE SAME!
BY JOVE! YOU'RE RIGHT!
18
AND WITHIN A DARKENED SEDAN, THE OLD MAN SLIPS OFF A FALSE-FACE MASK...
THAT YOUNG SCIENTIST--HENRY TRAVERS--HAS BEEN SHOWING TOO MUCH INTEREST IN THAT VOLUME. WE'LL HAVE TO DO SOMETHING ABOUT THAT, EH?
YES, ULTRA ... YOU WILL!
19
GUIDED BY THE INFORMATION IN THAT BOOK, I'VE BEEN CONDUCTING EXPERIMENTS TO BATTLE THE PLAGUE. WOULD YOU LIKE TO SEE WHAT I'VE ACCOMPLISHED?
YOU BET! LEAD ON!
PUBLIC LIBRARY
20
LATER--WITHIN TRAVERS' LABORATORY---
YOU SEE, I'VE ISOLATED THE PLAGUE GERM...NOW IF I CAN ONLY CONCOCT AN ANTIDOTE...
...YOU'LL HAVE THE GRATEFUL THANKS OF ALL MANKIND!
21

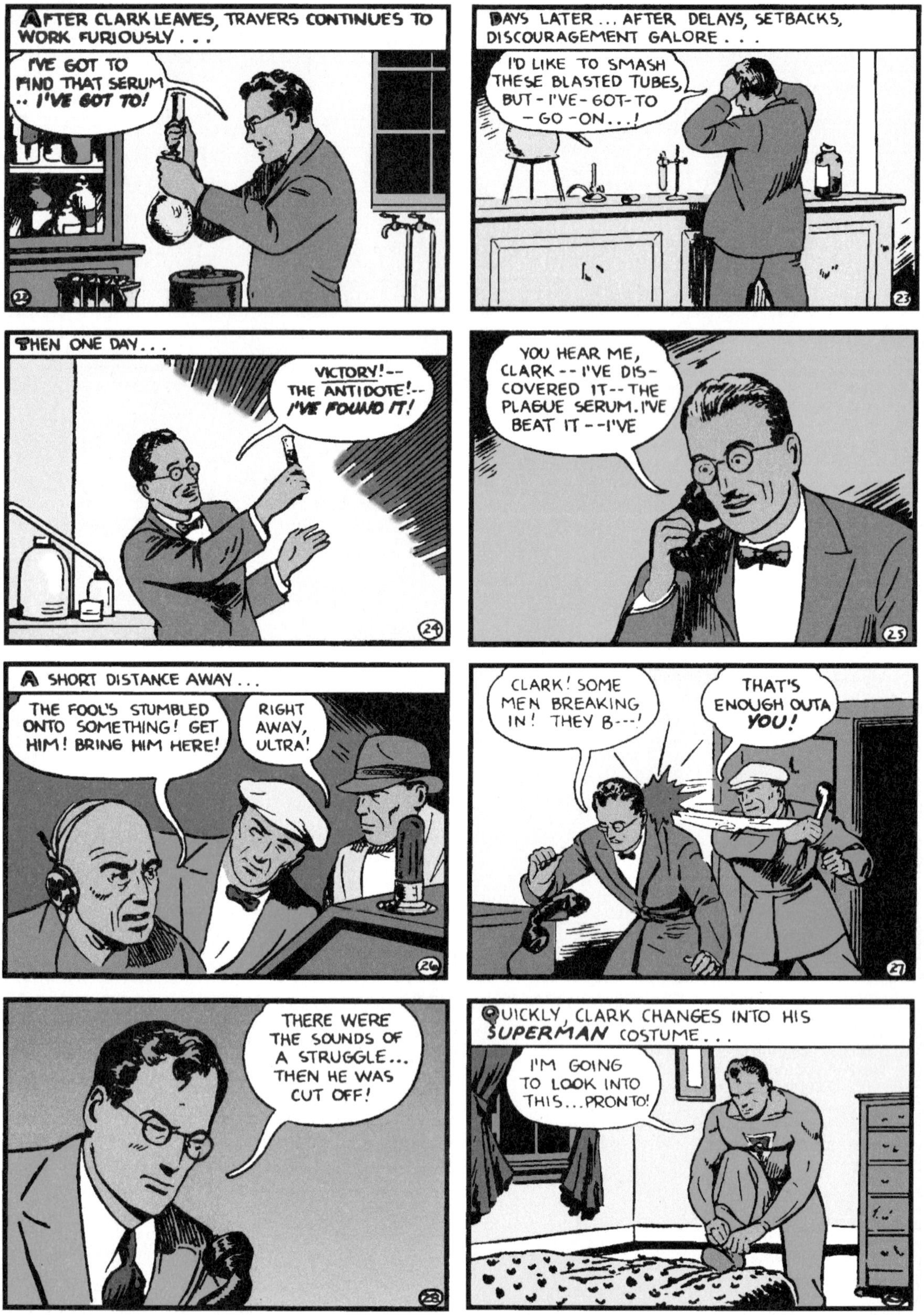
AFTER CLARK LEAVES, TRAVERS CONTINUES TO WORK FURIOUSLY . . .
I'VE GOT TO FIND THAT SERUM .. I'VE GOT TO!
DAYS LATER ... AFTER DELAYS, SETBACKS, DISCOURAGEMENT GALORE . . .
I'D LIKE TO SMASH THESE BLASTED TUBES, BUT - I'VE - GOT-TO - GO - ON...!
THEN ONE DAY . . .
VICTORY!-- THE ANTIDOTE!-- I'VE FOUND IT!
YOU HEAR ME, CLARK -- I'VE DIS-COVERED IT -- THE PLAGUE SERUM. I'VE BEAT IT --I'VE
A SHORT DISTANCE AWAY . . .
THE FOOL'S STUMBLED ONTO SOMETHING! GET HIM! BRING HIM HERE!
RIGHT AWAY, ULTRA!
CLARK! SOME MEN BREAKING IN! THEY B---!
THAT'S ENOUGH OUTA YOU!
THERE WERE THE SOUNDS OF A STRUGGLE... THEN HE WAS CUT OFF!
QUICKLY, CLARK CHANGES INTO HIS SUPERMAN COSTUME . . .
I'M GOING TO LOOK INTO THIS...PRONTO!

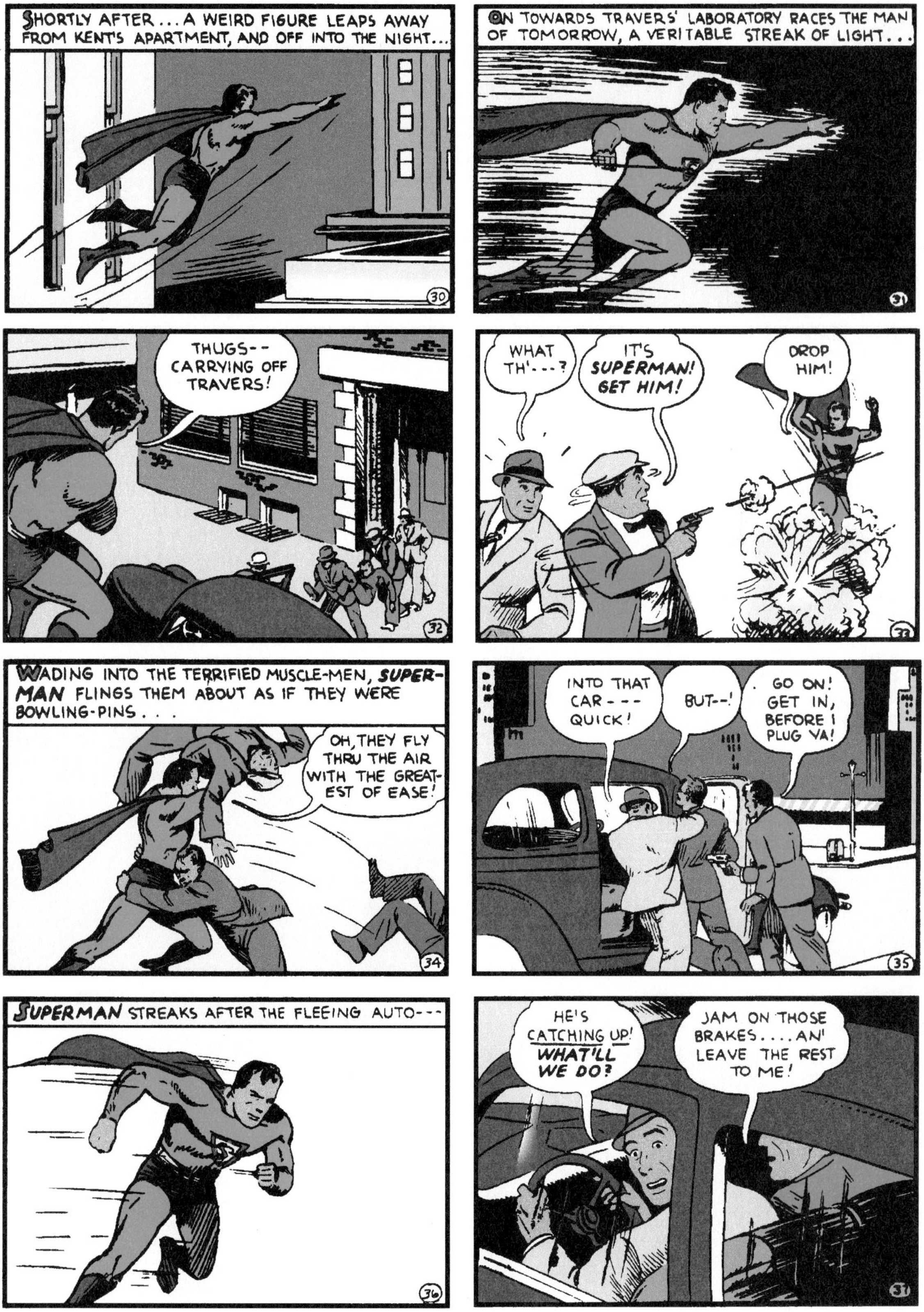
SHORTLY AFTER... A WEIRD FIGURE LEAPS AWAY FROM KENT'S APARTMENT, AND OFF INTO THE NIGHT...
30
ON TOWARDS TRAVERS' LABORATORY RACES THE MAN OF TOMORROW, A VERITABLE STREAK OF LIGHT...
31
THUGS-- CARRYING OFF TRAVERS!
32
WHAT TH'---?
IT'S SUPERMAN! GET HIM!
DROP HIM!
WADING INTO THE TERRIFIED MUSCLE-MEN, SUPERMAN FLINGS THEM ABOUT AS IF THEY WERE BOWLING-PINS...
OH, THEY FLY THRU THE AIR WITH THE GREATEST OF EASE!
34
INTO THAT CAR--- QUICK!
BUT--!
GO ON! GET IN, BEFORE I PLUG YA!
35
SUPERMAN STREAKS AFTER THE FLEEING AUTO---
36
HE'S CATCHING UP! WHAT'LL WE DO?
JAM ON THOSE BRAKES....AN' LEAVE THE REST TO ME!

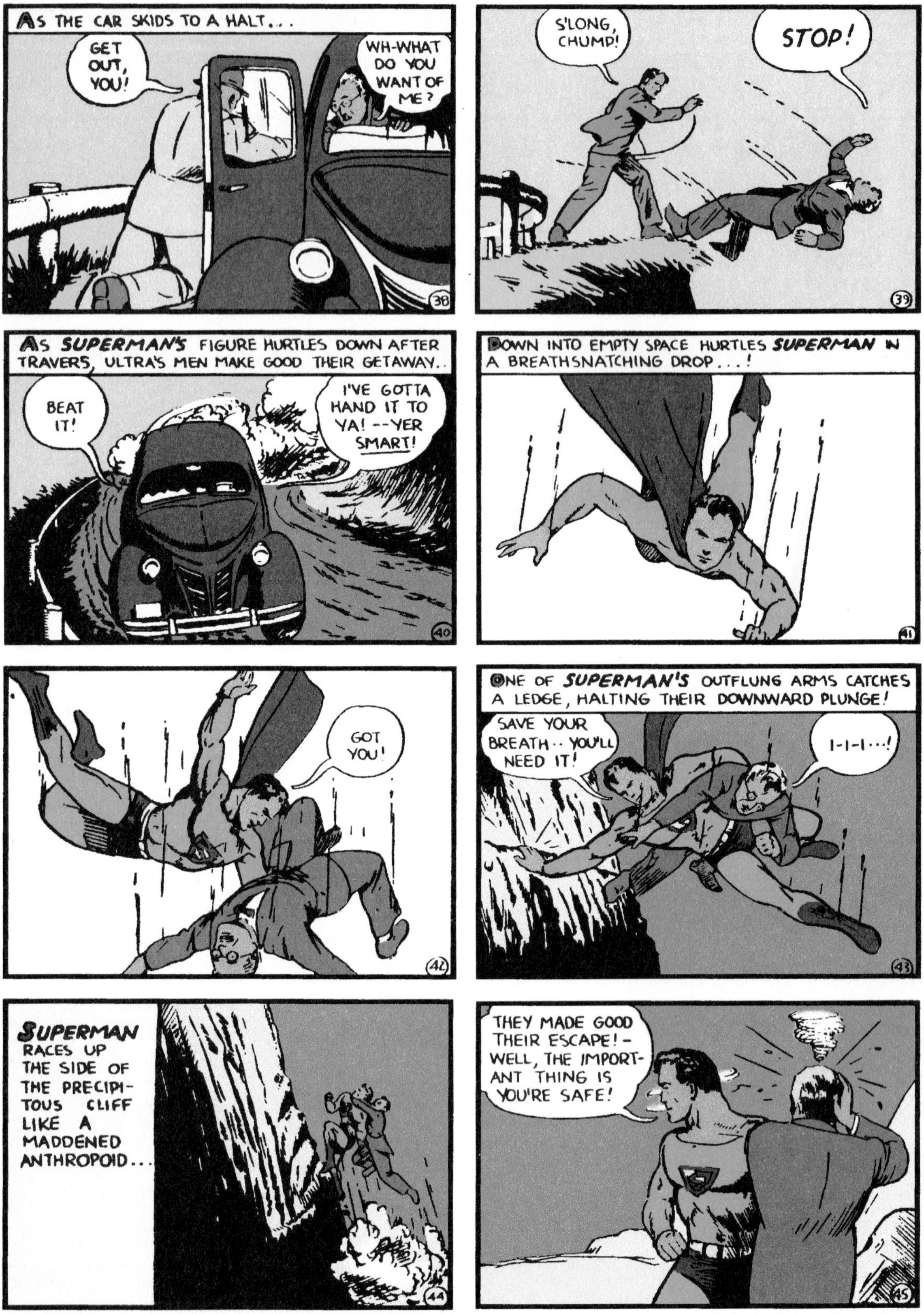
AS THE CAR SKIDS TO A HALT...
GET OUT, YOU!
WH-WHAT DO YOU WANT OF ME?
S'LONG, CHUMP!
STOP!
AS SUPERMAN'S FIGURE HURTLES DOWN AFTER TRAVERS, ULTRA'S MEN MAKE GOOD THEIR GETAWAY..
BEAT IT!
I'VE GOTTA HAND IT TO YA! --YER SMART!
DOWN INTO EMPTY SPACE HURTLES SUPERMAN IN A BREATHSNATCHING DROP...!
GOT YOU!
ONE OF SUPERMAN'S OUTFLUNG ARMS CATCHES A LEDGE, HALTING THEIR DOWNWARD PLUNGE!
SAVE YOUR BREATH.. YOU'LL NEED IT!
I-I-I...!
SUPERMAN RACES UP THE SIDE OF THE PRECIPI-TOUS CLIFF LIKE A MADDENED ANTHROPOID...
THEY MADE GOOD THEIR ESCAPE! - WELL, THE IMPORT-ANT THING IS YOU'RE SAFE!

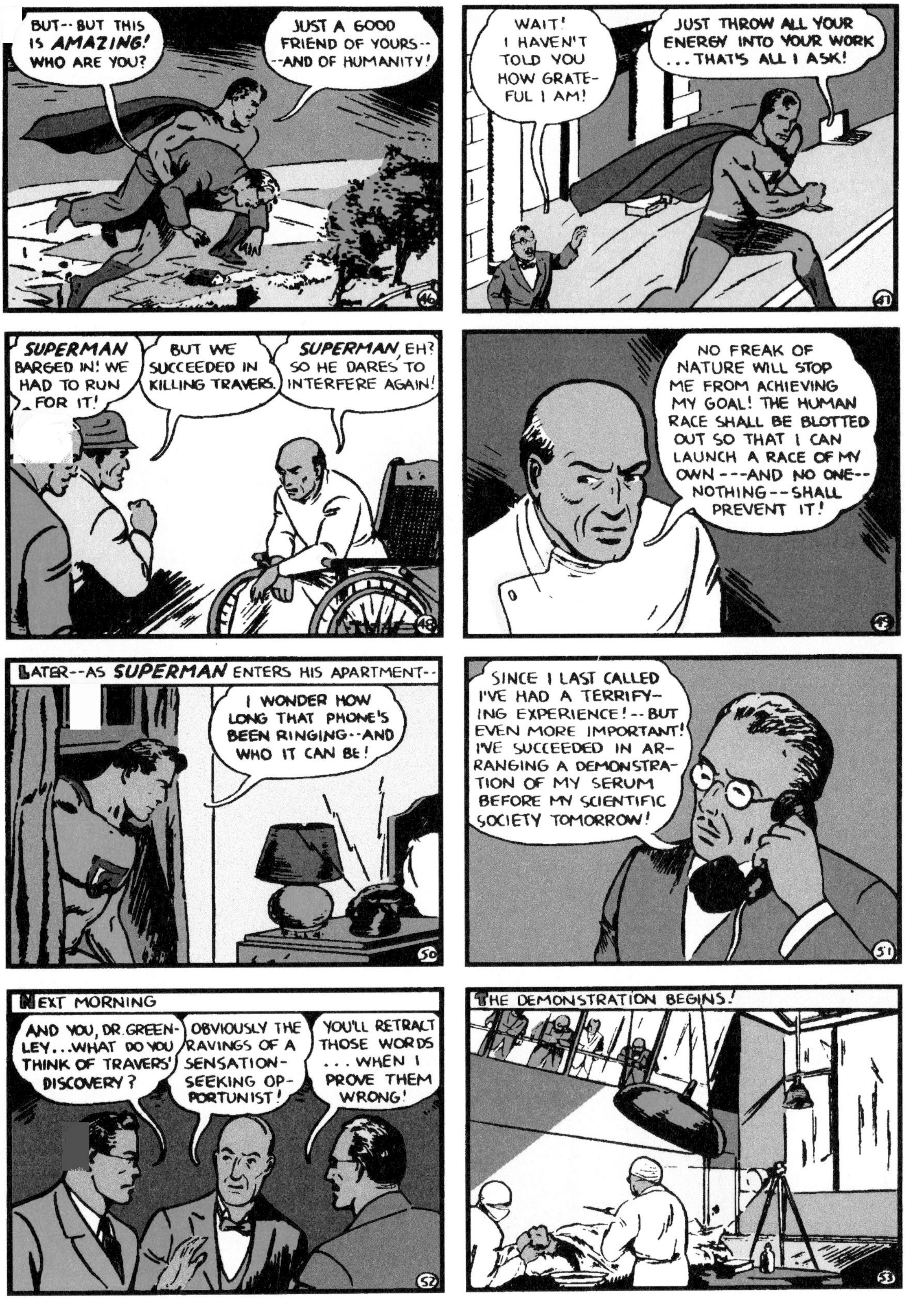
BUT--BUT THIS IS AMAZING! WHO ARE YOU?
JUST A GOOD FRIEND OF YOURS-- --AND OF HUMANITY!
WAIT! I HAVEN'T TOLD YOU HOW GRATEFUL I AM!
JUST THROW ALL YOUR ENERGY INTO YOUR WORK ... THAT'S ALL I ASK!
SUPERMAN BARGED IN! WE HAD TO RUN FOR IT!
BUT WE SUCCEEDED IN KILLING TRAVERS.
SUPERMAN, EH? SO HE DARES TO INTERFERE AGAIN!
NO FREAK OF NATURE WILL STOP ME FROM ACHIEVING MY GOAL! THE HUMAN RACE SHALL BE BLOTTED OUT SO THAT I CAN LAUNCH A RACE OF MY OWN---AND NO ONE-- NOTHING--SHALL PREVENT IT!
LATER--AS SUPERMAN ENTERS HIS APARTMENT--
I WONDER HOW LONG THAT PHONE'S BEEN RINGING--AND WHO IT CAN BE!
SINCE I LAST CALLED I'VE HAD A TERRIFYING EXPERIENCE!--BUT EVEN MORE IMPORTANT! I'VE SUCCEEDED IN ARRANGING A DEMONSTRATION OF MY SERUM BEFORE MY SCIENTIFIC SOCIETY TOMORROW!
NEXT MORNING
AND YOU, DR. GREENLEY...WHAT DO YOU THINK OF TRAVERS' DISCOVERY?
OBVIOUSLY THE RAVINGS OF A SENSATION-SEEKING OPPORTUNIST!
YOU'LL RETRACT THOSE WORDS ... WHEN I PROVE THEM WRONG!
THE DEMONSTRATION BEGINS!

THE ASSEMBLED SCIENTISTS WATCH TENSELY AS PROFESSOR TRAVERS INJECTS HIS SERUM INTO A VICTIM OF THE PURPLE PLAGUE...

SEVERAL MINUTES LATER...

WELL, WHERE ARE THE GOOD RESULTS YOU SO LOUDLY PREDICTED?

I-I CAN'T UNDERSTAND IT! THERE DOESN'T APPEAR TO BE ANY IMPROVEMENT IN THE PATIENT!

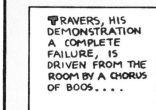

TRAVERS, HIS DEMONSTRATION A COMPLETE FAILURE, IS DRIVEN FROM THE ROOM BY A CHORUS OF BOOS....

FAKER!

THROW HIM OUT!

BOO!

I'M RUINED-- DISGRACED!

TOUGH LUCK! AND YOU WERE SO CERTAIN THAT YOU'D DISCOVERED A SATISFACTORY SERUM!

THAT EVENING

TRAVERS IS BADLY IN NEED OF ENCOURAGE-MENT--AND HERE'S WHERE HE GETS IT!

AS THE MAN OF STEEL LANDS OUTSIDE TRAVERS' LABORATORY, HE HEARS SMASHING SOUNDS FROM WITHIN....

YOU!--DESTROYING YOUR INSTRUMENTS YOURSELF ...WHAT'S THE IDEA?

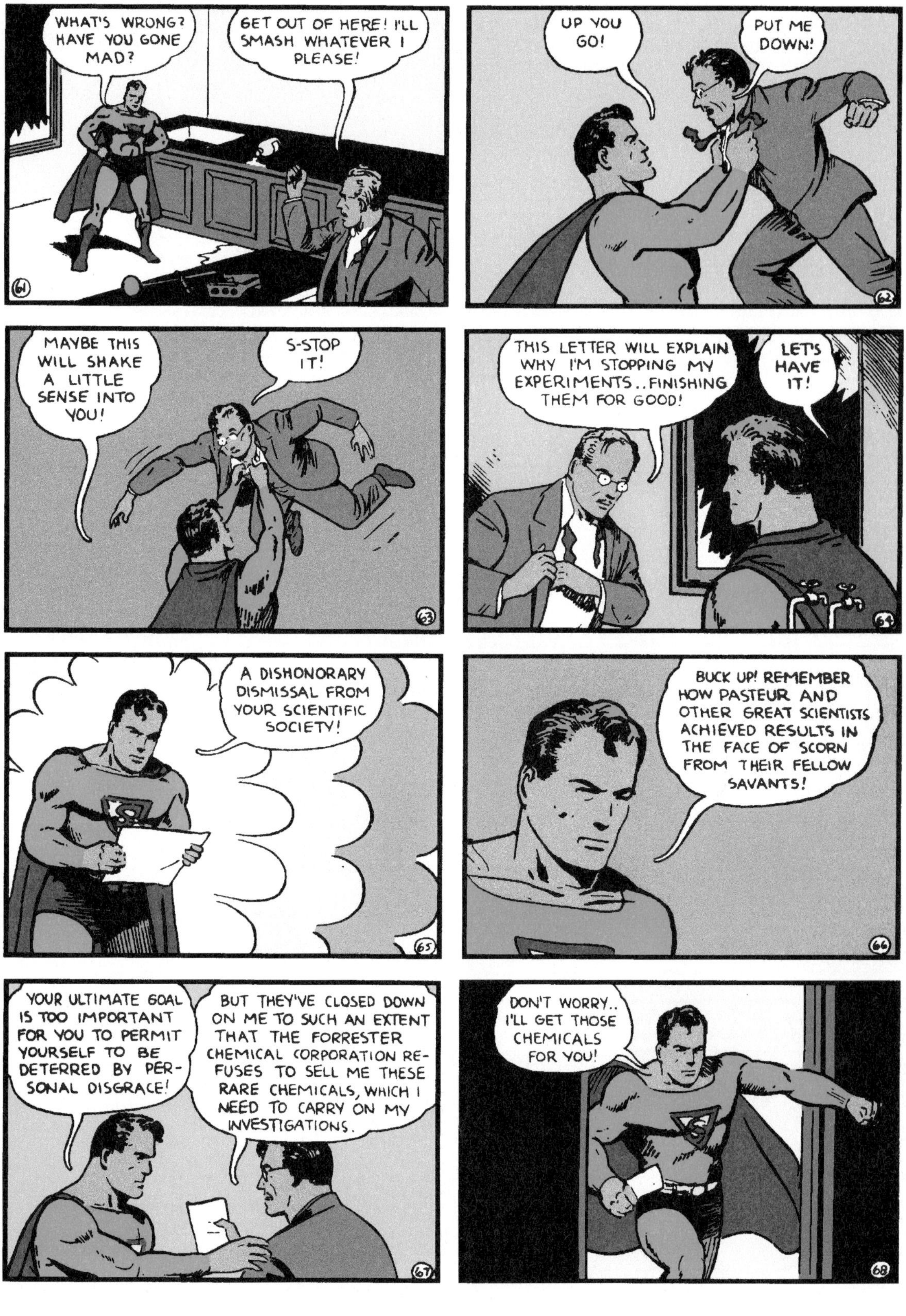

WHAT'S WRONG? HAVE YOU GONE MAD?
GET OUT OF HERE! I'LL SMASH WHATEVER I PLEASE!
61
UP YOU GO!
PUT ME DOWN!
62
MAYBE THIS WILL SHAKE A LITTLE SENSE INTO YOU!
S-STOP IT!
63
THIS LETTER WILL EXPLAIN WHY I'M STOPPING MY EXPERIMENTS..FINISHING THEM FOR GOOD!
LET'S HAVE IT!
64
A DISHONORARY DISMISSAL FROM YOUR SCIENTIFIC SOCIETY!
65
BUCK UP! REMEMBER HOW PASTEUR AND OTHER GREAT SCIENTISTS ACHIEVED RESULTS IN THE FACE OF SCORN FROM THEIR FELLOW SAVANTS!
66
YOUR ULTIMATE GOAL IS TOO IMPORTANT FOR YOU TO PERMIT YOURSELF TO BE DETERRED BY PERSONAL DISGRACE!
BUT THEY'VE CLOSED DOWN ON ME TO SUCH AN EXTENT THAT THE FORRESTER CHEMICAL CORPORATION REFUSES TO SELL ME THESE RARE CHEMICALS, WHICH I NEED TO CARRY ON MY INVESTIGATIONS.
67
DON'T WORRY.. I'LL GET THOSE CHEMICALS FOR YOU!
68

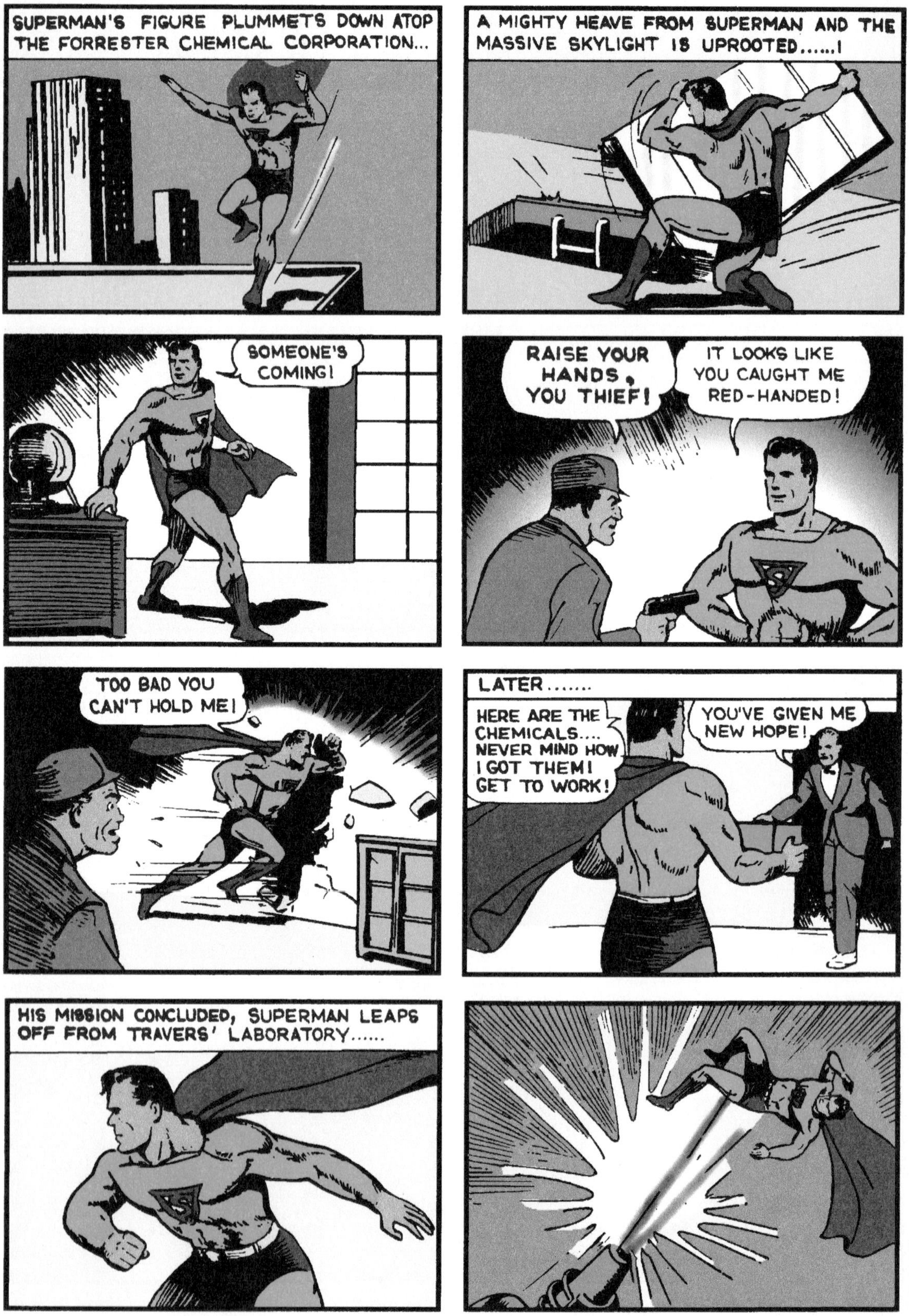
SUPERMAN'S FIGURE PLUMMETS DOWN ATOP THE FORRESTER CHEMICAL CORPORATION...
A MIGHTY HEAVE FROM SUPERMAN AND THE MASSIVE SKYLIGHT IS UPROOTED......!
SOMEONE'S COMING!
RAISE YOUR HANDS, YOU THIEF!
IT LOOKS LIKE YOU CAUGHT ME RED-HANDED!
TOO BAD YOU CAN'T HOLD ME!
LATER.......
HERE ARE THE CHEMICALS.... NEVER MIND HOW I GOT THEM! GET TO WORK!
YOU'VE GIVEN ME NEW HOPE!
HIS MISSION CONCLUDED, SUPERMAN LEAPS OFF FROM TRAVERS' LABORATORY......

LATER....
HERE'S YOUR SUPERMAN... UNCONSCIOUS!
I THOUGHT THAT ELECTRIC-GUN WOULD BE SUFFICIENT!
YOU ARE LOSING ALL WILL-POWER OF YOUR OWN! YOU CAN ONLY DO AS I DIRECT!
BEHOLD HOW MEEKLY HE STANDS! SUPERMAN IS MY SLAVE, SUBJECT TO MY EVERY MENTAL WHIM!
YOU WILL ASSIST MY MEN SPREAD THE PURPLE PLAGUE!
YES...MASTER!
A FANTASTIC AIRSHIP OF ULTRA'S CREATION WINGS OUT OVER THE CITY, TO SPREAD ITS CARGO OF PURPLE DEATH...!
NOW!—SEIZE THOSE GERM-LADEN TUBES! TOSS THEM OUT!
I-WILL-OBEY!
BUT WHIRLING SUDDENLY, SUPERMAN DARTS FORWARD AND WRECKS THE FANTASTIC SHIP'S CONTROLS....!
NEXT STOP FOR THIS PLANE-ETERNITY!
DOWN TOWARD EARTH PLUNGES THE CRIPPLED VESSEL.... AND TOTAL DESTRUCTION....
GOOD RIDDANCE!
THE SHIP IS DESTROYED ...AND SUPERMAN MADE GOOD HIS ESCAPE!
BLAST HIM! I WAS TRICKED — HE ONLY PRETENDED TO BE UNDER MY HYPNOTIC SUGGESTION!

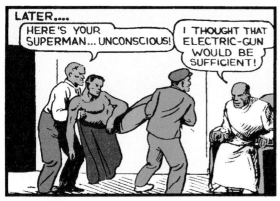

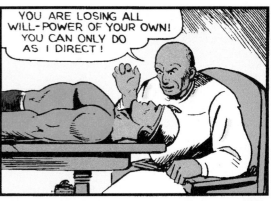

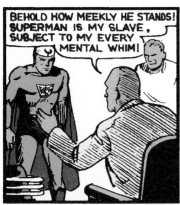

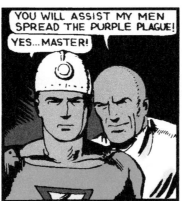

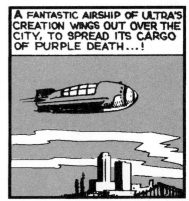

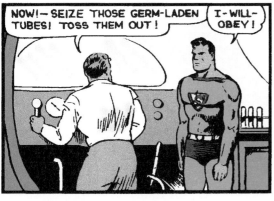

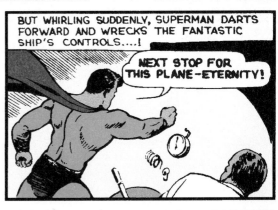

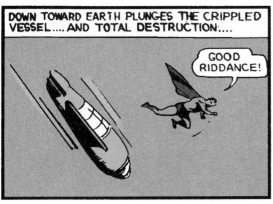

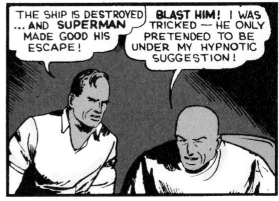

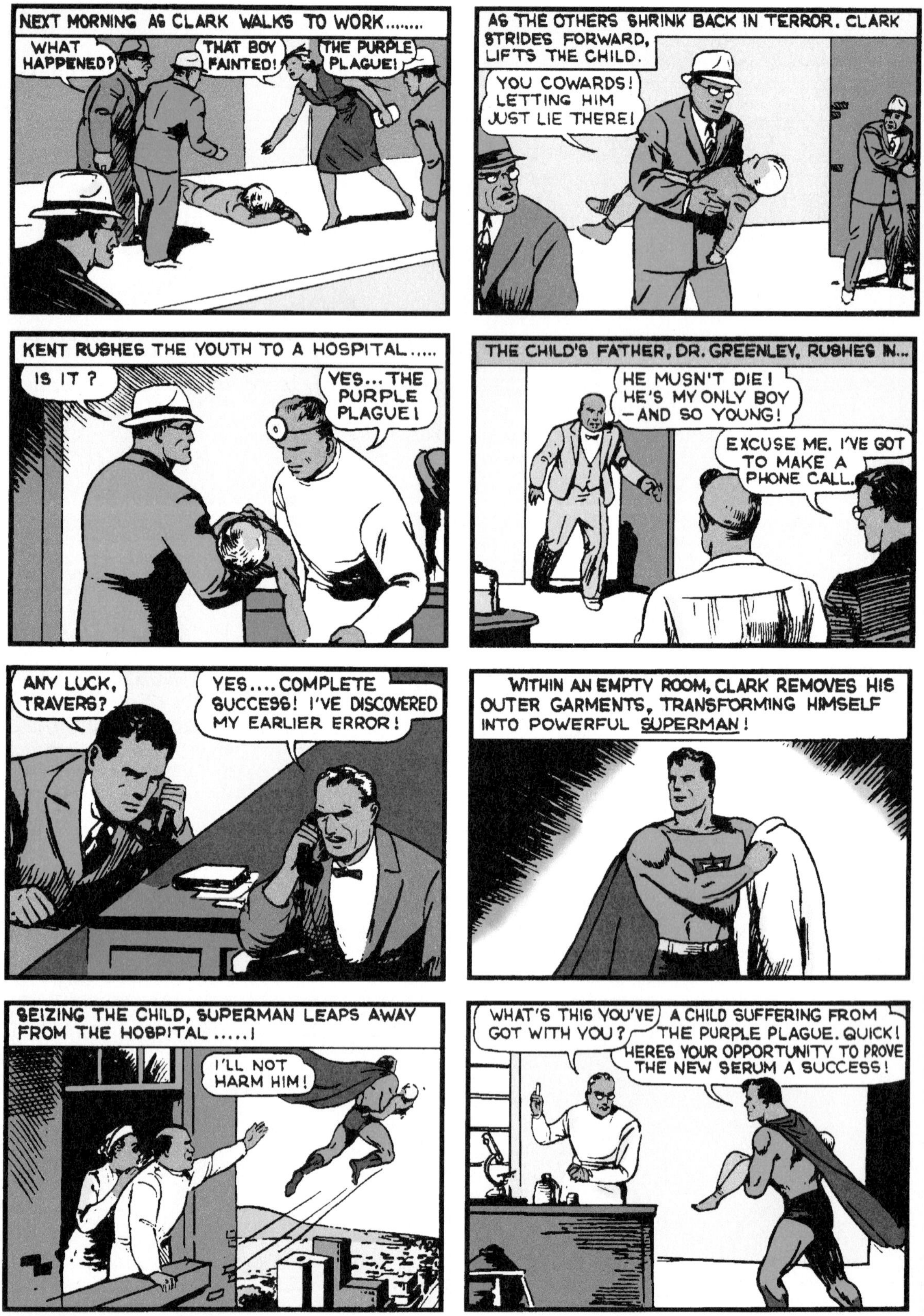
NEXT MORNING AS CLARK WALKS TO WORK........
WHAT HAPPENED?
THAT BOY FAINTED!
THE PURPLE PLAGUE!
AS THE OTHERS SHRINK BACK IN TERROR, CLARK STRIDES FORWARD, LIFTS THE CHILD.
YOU COWARDS! LETTING HIM JUST LIE THERE!
KENT RUSHES THE YOUTH TO A HOSPITAL.....
IS IT ?
YES...THE PURPLE PLAGUE!
THE CHILD'S FATHER, DR. GREENLEY, RUSHES IN...
HE MUSN'T DIE! HE'S MY ONLY BOY —AND SO YOUNG!
EXCUSE ME. I'VE GOT TO MAKE A PHONE CALL.
ANY LUCK, TRAVERS?
YES....COMPLETE SUCCESS! I'VE DISCOVERED MY EARLIER ERROR!
WITHIN AN EMPTY ROOM, CLARK REMOVES HIS OUTER GARMENTS, TRANSFORMING HIMSELF INTO POWERFUL SUPERMAN!
SEIZING THE CHILD, SUPERMAN LEAPS AWAY FROM THE HOSPITAL.....!
I'LL NOT HARM HIM!
WHAT'S THIS YOU'VE GOT WITH YOU?
A CHILD SUFFERING FROM THE PURPLE PLAGUE. QUICK! HERES YOUR OPPORTUNITY TO PROVE THE NEW SERUM A SUCCESS!

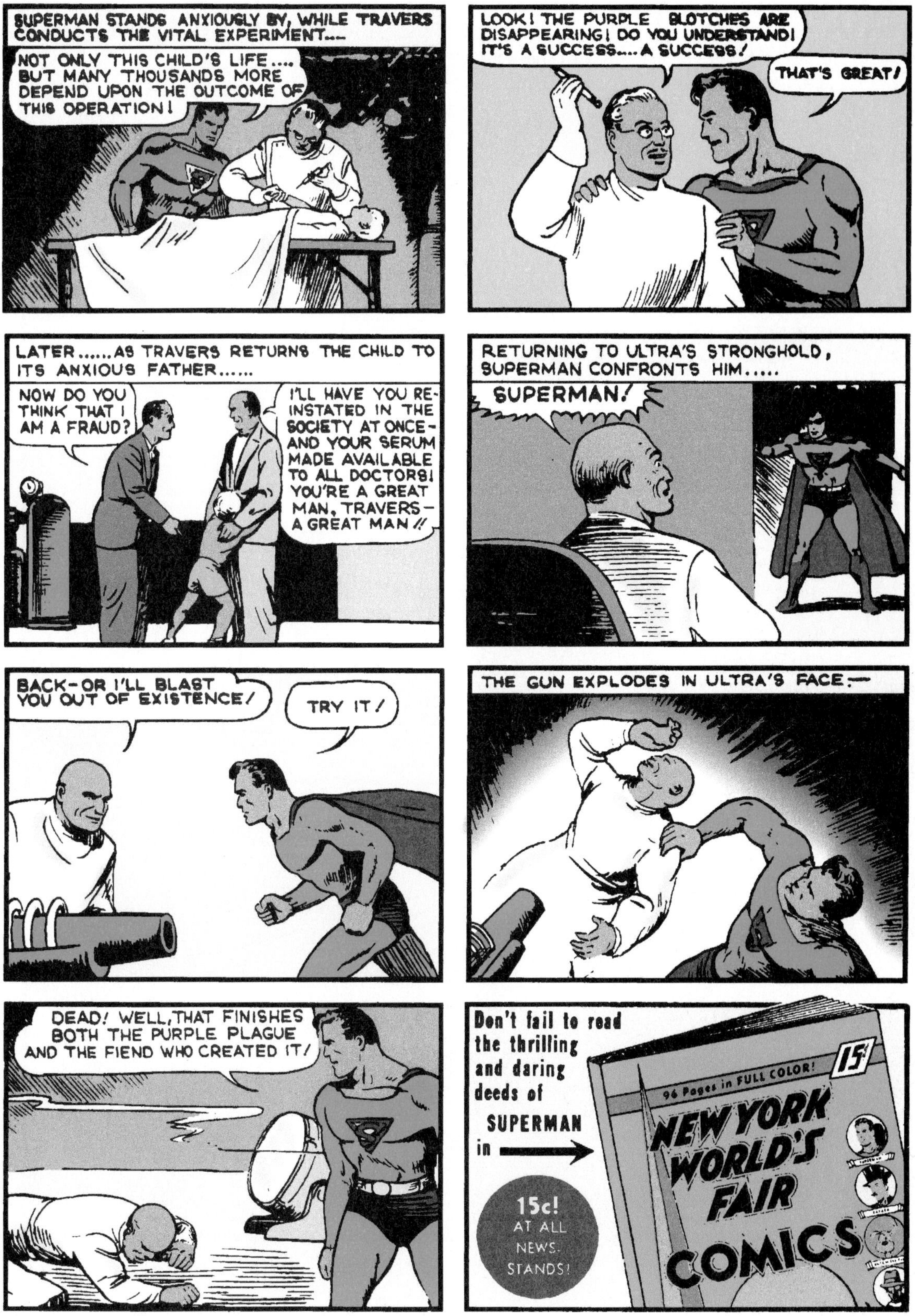
SUPERMAN STANDS ANXIOUSLY BY, WHILE TRAVERS CONDUCTS THE VITAL EXPERIMENT....
NOT ONLY THIS CHILD'S LIFE.... BUT MANY THOUSANDS MORE DEPEND UPON THE OUTCOME OF THIS OPERATION!
LOOK! THE PURPLE BLOTCHES ARE DISAPPEARING! DO YOU UNDERSTAND! IT'S A SUCCESS....A SUCCESS!
THAT'S GREAT!
LATER......AS TRAVERS RETURNS THE CHILD TO ITS ANXIOUS FATHER......
NOW DO YOU THINK THAT I AM A FRAUD?
I'LL HAVE YOU RE-INSTATED IN THE SOCIETY AT ONCE- AND YOUR SERUM MADE AVAILABLE TO ALL DOCTORS! YOU'RE A GREAT MAN, TRAVERS- A GREAT MAN!!
RETURNING TO ULTRA'S STRONGHOLD, SUPERMAN CONFRONTS HIM.....
SUPERMAN!
BACK-OR I'LL BLAST YOU OUT OF EXISTENCE!
TRY IT!
THE GUN EXPLODES IN ULTRA'S FACE—
DEAD! WELL, THAT FINISHES BOTH THE PURPLE PLAGUE AND THE FIEND WHO CREATED IT!
Don't fail to read the thrilling and daring deeds of
SUPERMAN
in
15c! AT ALL NEWS. STANDS!
15¢
96 Pages in FULL COLOR!
NEW YORK WORLD'S FAIR
COMICS

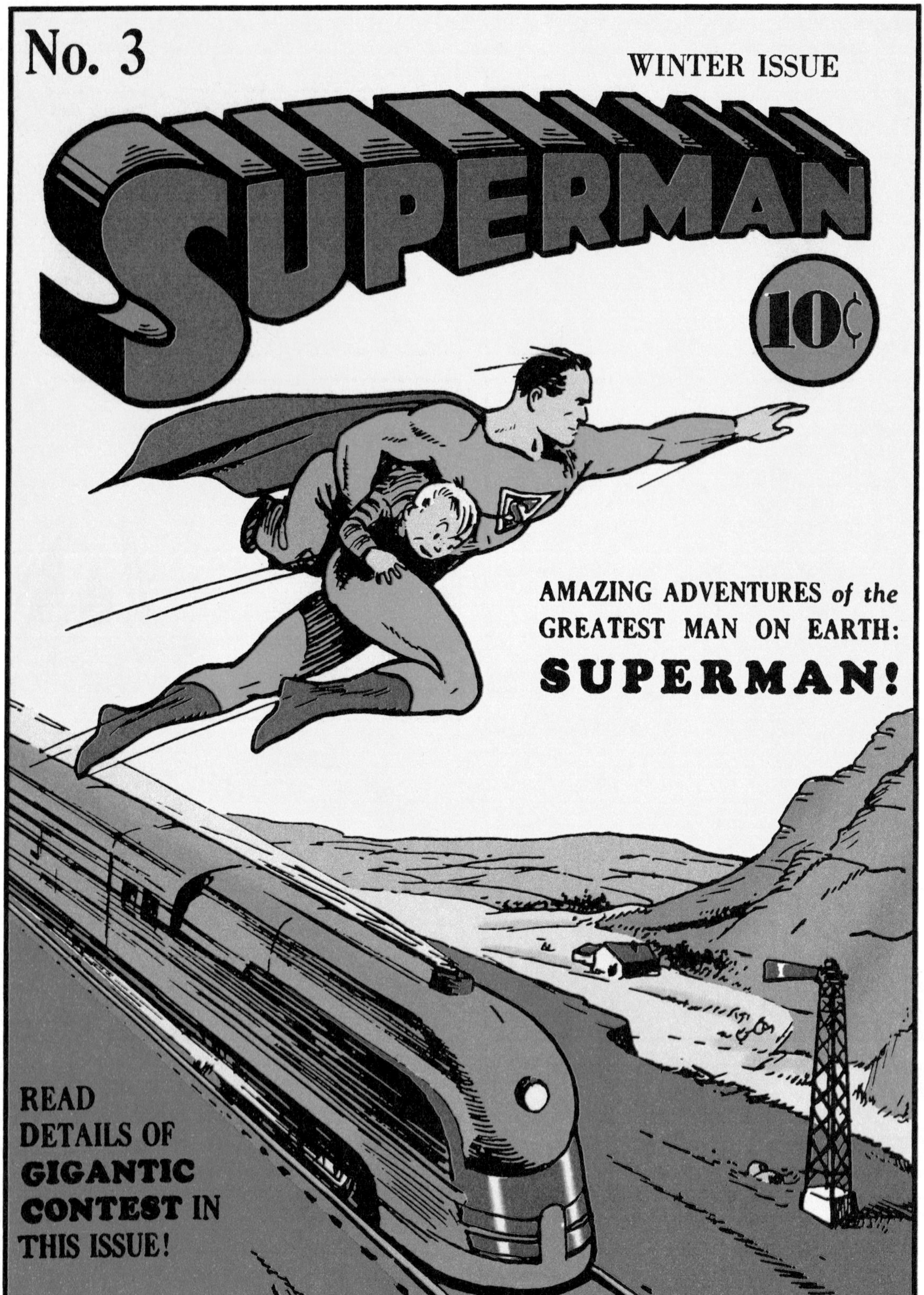
No. 3
WINTER ISSUE
SUPERMAN
10¢
AMAZING ADVENTURES of the GREATEST MAN ON EARTH:
SUPERMAN!
READ DETAILS OF GIGANTIC CONTEST IN THIS ISSUE!

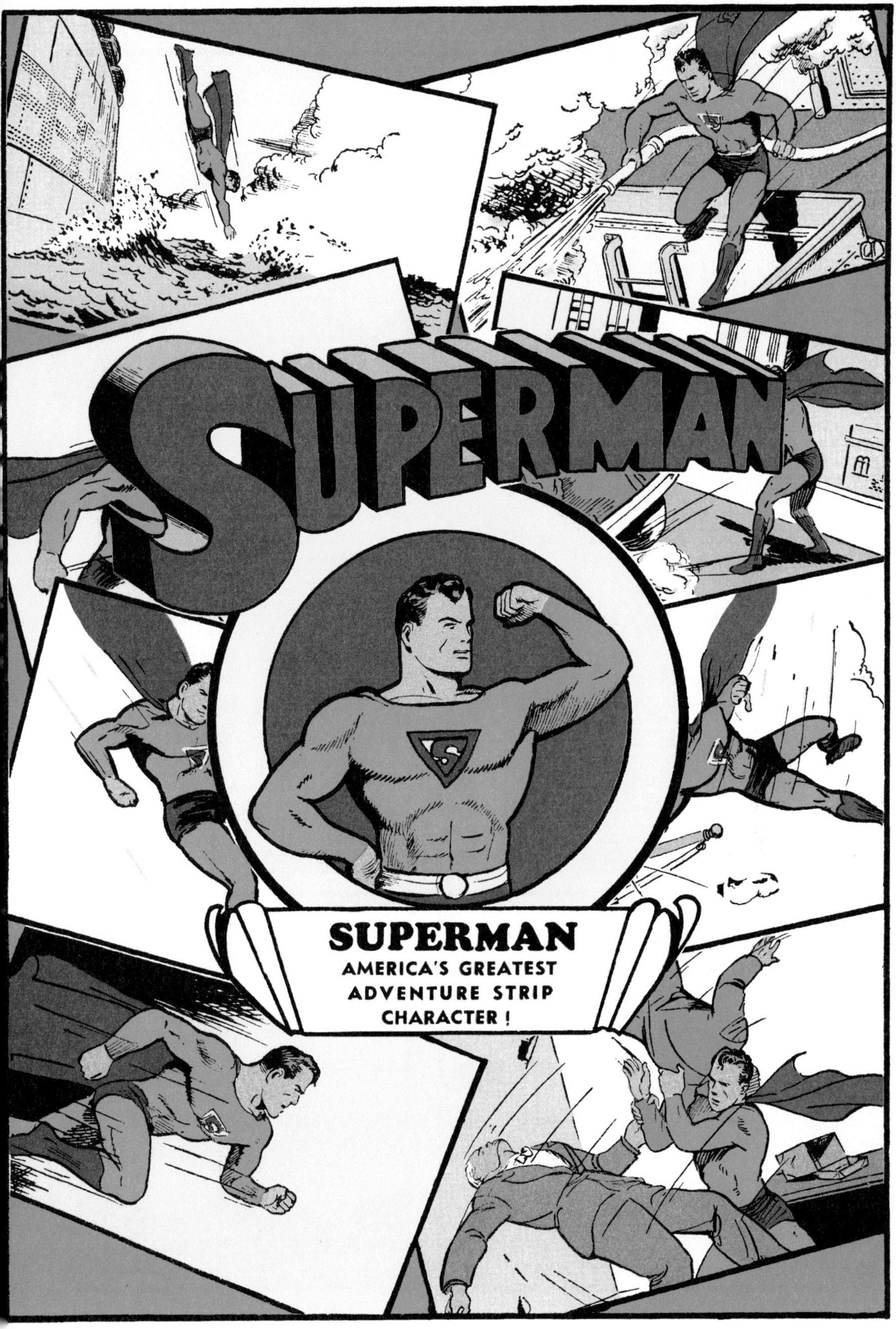
SUPERMAN
SUPERMAN
AMERICA'S GREATEST
ADVENTURE STRIP
CHARACTER !

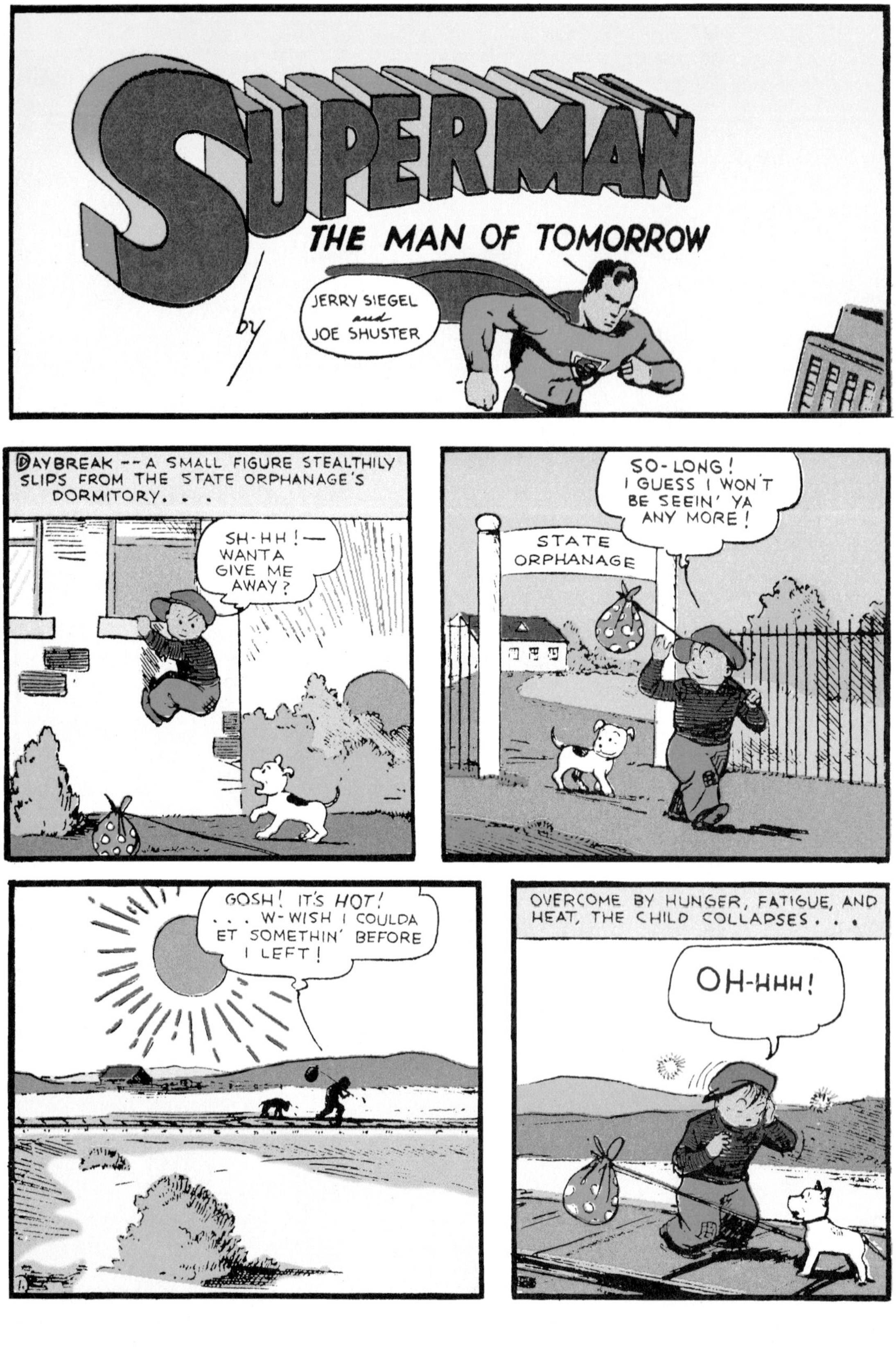
SUPERMAN
THE MAN OF TOMORROW
by
JERRY SIEGEL and JOE SHUSTER
DAYBREAK -- A SMALL FIGURE STEALTHILY SLIPS FROM THE STATE ORPHANAGE'S DORMITORY. . .
SH-HH! — WANTA GIVE ME AWAY?
STATE ORPHANAGE
SO-LONG! I GUESS I WON'T BE SEEIN' YA ANY MORE!
GOSH! IT'S HOT! . . . W-WISH I COULDA ET SOMETHIN' BEFORE I LEFT!
OVERCOME BY HUNGER, FATIGUE, AND HEAT, THE CHILD COLLAPSES. . .
OH-HHH!

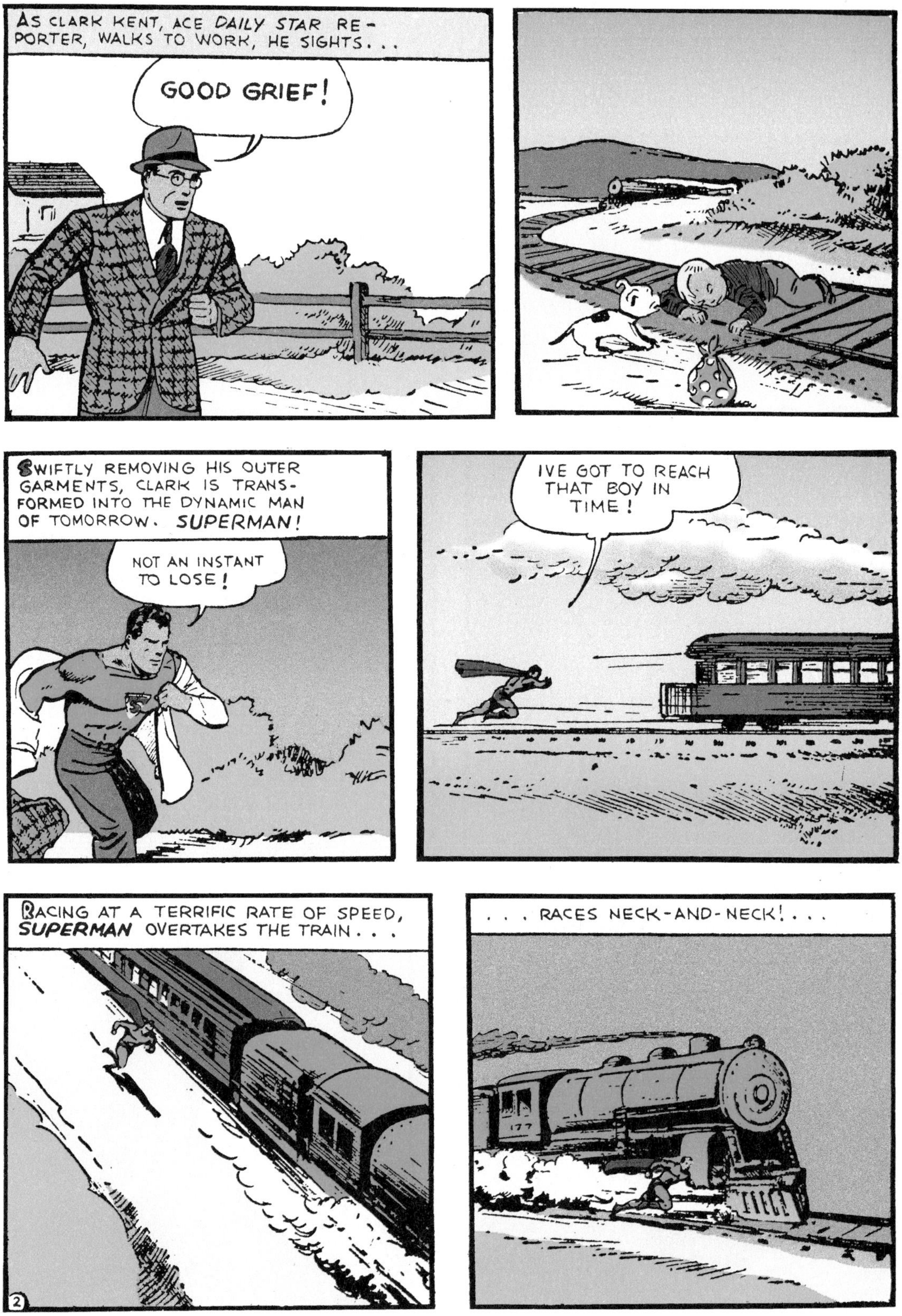
AS CLARK KENT, ACE DAILY STAR REPORTER, WALKS TO WORK, HE SIGHTS . . .
GOOD GRIEF!
SWIFTLY REMOVING HIS OUTER GARMENTS, CLARK IS TRANSFORMED INTO THE DYNAMIC MAN OF TOMORROW. SUPERMAN!
NOT AN INSTANT TO LOSE!
IVE GOT TO REACH THAT BOY IN TIME!
RACING AT A TERRIFIC RATE OF SPEED, SUPERMAN OVERTAKES THE TRAIN . . .
2
. . . RACES NECK-AND-NECK! . . .

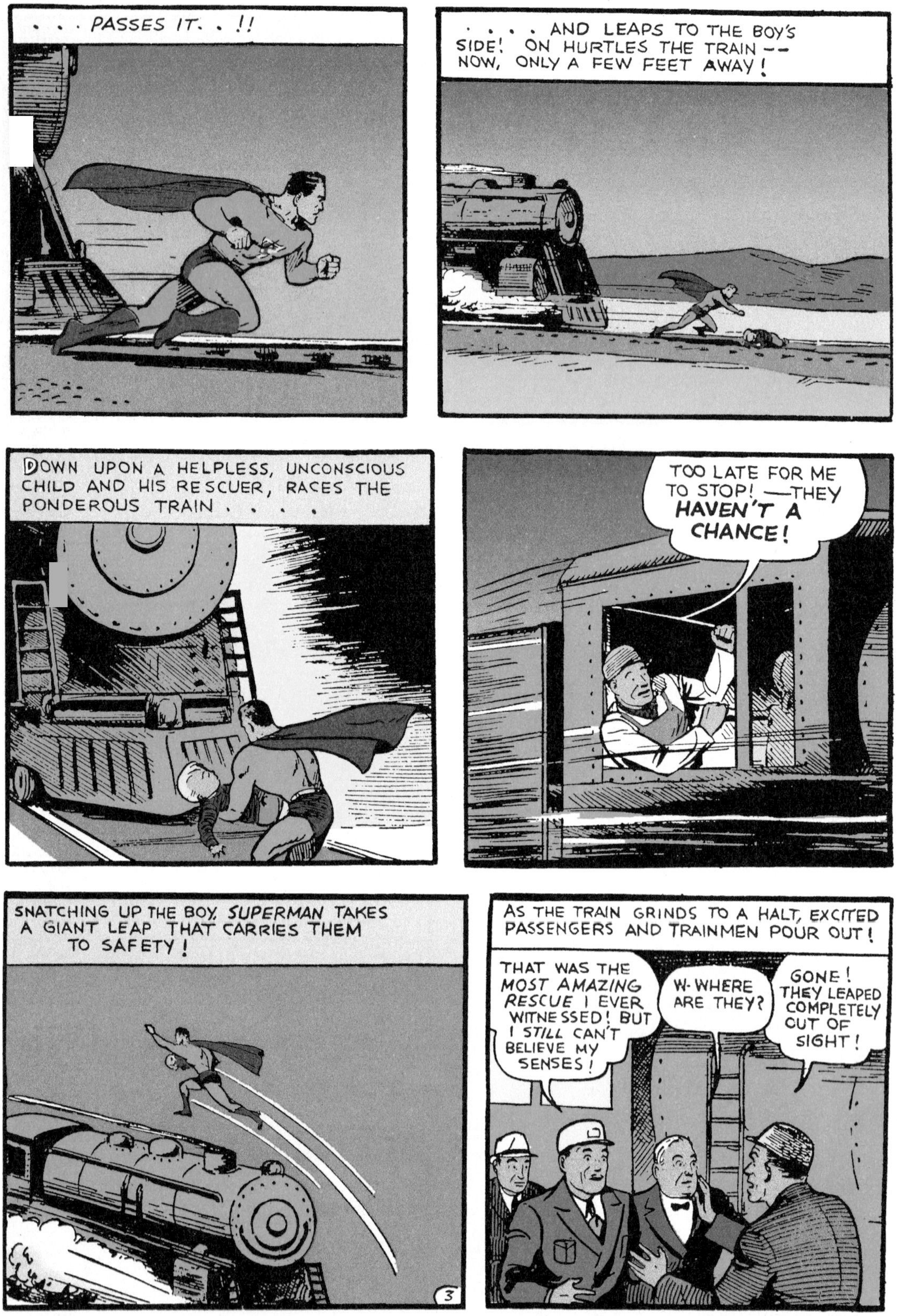

. . . PASSES IT. . !!
. . . . AND LEAPS TO THE BOY'S SIDE! ON HURTLES THE TRAIN -- NOW, ONLY A FEW FEET AWAY!
DOWN UPON A HELPLESS, UNCONSCIOUS CHILD AND HIS RESCUER, RACES THE PONDEROUS TRAIN . . . .
TOO LATE FOR ME TO STOP! —THEY HAVEN'T A CHANCE!
SNATCHING UP THE BOY, SUPERMAN TAKES A GIANT LEAP THAT CARRIES THEM TO SAFETY!
3
AS THE TRAIN GRINDS TO A HALT, EXCITED PASSENGERS AND TRAINMEN POUR OUT!
THAT WAS THE MOST AMAZING RESCUE I EVER WITNESSED! BUT I STILL CAN'T BELIEVE MY SENSES!
W-WHERE ARE THEY?
GONE! THEY LEAPED COMPLETELY OUT OF SIGHT!

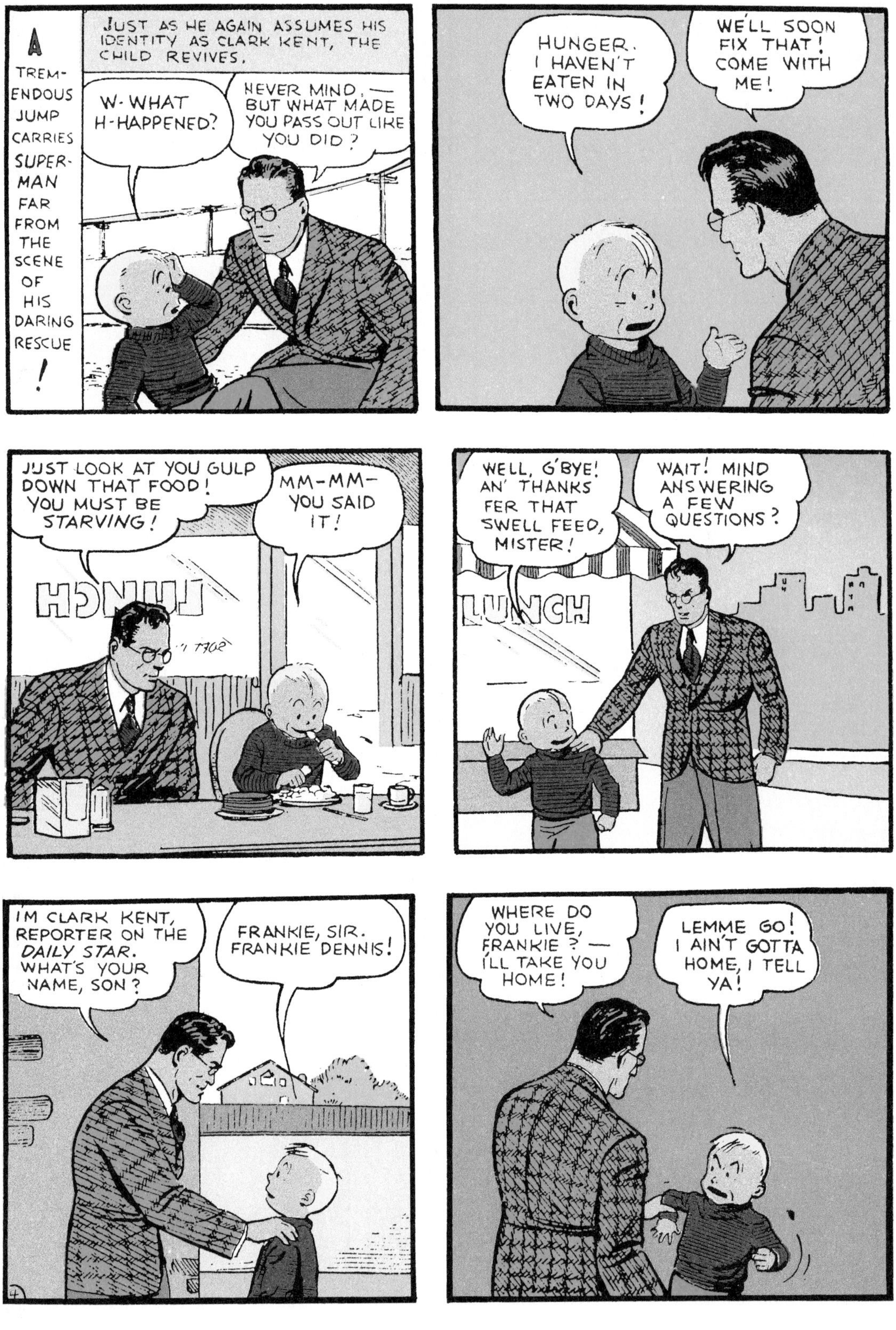
A TREMENDOUS JUMP CARRIES SUPERMAN FAR FROM THE SCENE OF HIS DARING RESCUE!
JUST AS HE AGAIN ASSUMES HIS IDENTITY AS CLARK KENT, THE CHILD REVIVES.
W-WHAT H-HAPPENED?
NEVER MIND,— BUT WHAT MADE YOU PASS OUT LIKE YOU DID?
HUNGER. I HAVEN'T EATEN IN TWO DAYS!
WE'LL SOON FIX THAT! COME WITH ME!
JUST LOOK AT YOU GULP DOWN THAT FOOD! YOU MUST BE STARVING!
MM-MM- YOU SAID IT!
WELL, G'BYE! AN' THANKS FER THAT SWELL FEED, MISTER!
WAIT! MIND ANSWERING A FEW QUESTIONS?
LUNCH
I'M CLARK KENT, REPORTER ON THE DAILY STAR. WHAT'S YOUR NAME, SON?
FRANKIE, SIR. FRANKIE DENNIS!
WHERE DO YOU LIVE, FRANKIE?— I'LL TAKE YOU HOME!
LEMME GO! I AIN'T GOTTA HOME, I TELL YA!

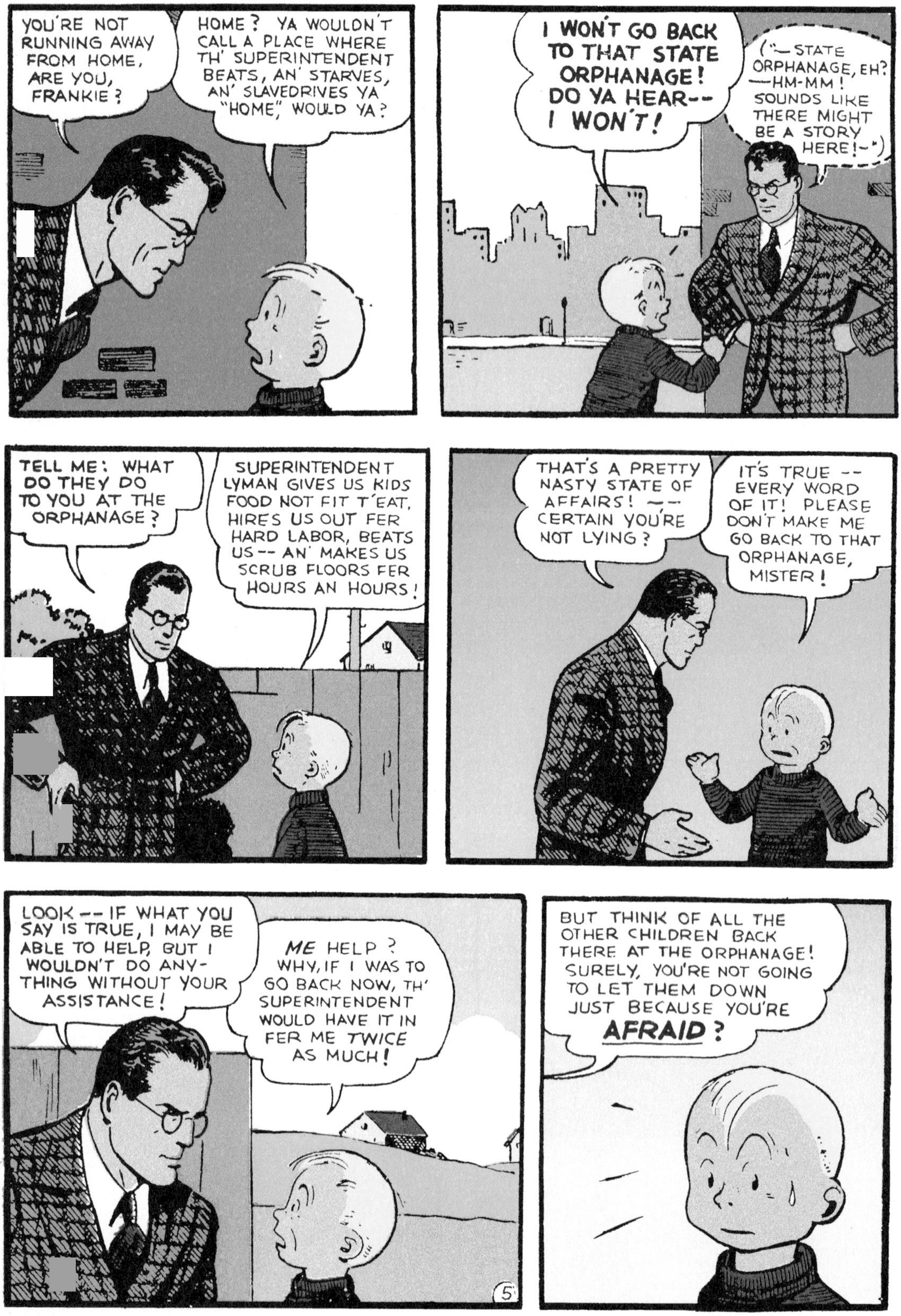
YOU'RE NOT RUNNING AWAY FROM HOME, ARE YOU, FRANKIE?
HOME? YA WOULDN'T CALL A PLACE WHERE TH' SUPERINTENDENT BEATS, AN' STARVES, AN' SLAVEDRIVES YA "HOME," WOULD YA?
I WON'T GO BACK TO THAT STATE ORPHANAGE! DO YA HEAR-- I WON'T!
("—STATE ORPHANAGE, EH? —HM-MM! SOUNDS LIKE THERE MIGHT BE A STORY HERE!-")
TELL ME: WHAT DO THEY DO TO YOU AT THE ORPHANAGE?
SUPERINTENDENT LYMAN GIVES US KIDS FOOD NOT FIT T'EAT, HIRES US OUT FER HARD LABOR, BEATS US-- AN' MAKES US SCRUB FLOORS FER HOURS AN HOURS!
THAT'S A PRETTY NASTY STATE OF AFFAIRS! —— CERTAIN YOU'RE NOT LYING?
IT'S TRUE -- EVERY WORD OF IT! PLEASE DON'T MAKE ME GO BACK TO THAT ORPHANAGE, MISTER!
LOOK -- IF WHAT YOU SAY IS TRUE, I MAY BE ABLE TO HELP, BUT I WOULDN'T DO ANY-THING WITHOUT YOUR ASSISTANCE!
ME HELP? WHY, IF I WAS TO GO BACK NOW, TH' SUPERINTENDENT WOULD HAVE IT IN FER ME TWICE AS MUCH!
5
BUT THINK OF ALL THE OTHER CHILDREN BACK THERE AT THE ORPHANAGE! SURELY, YOU'RE NOT GOING TO LET THEM DOWN JUST BECAUSE YOU'RE AFRAID?

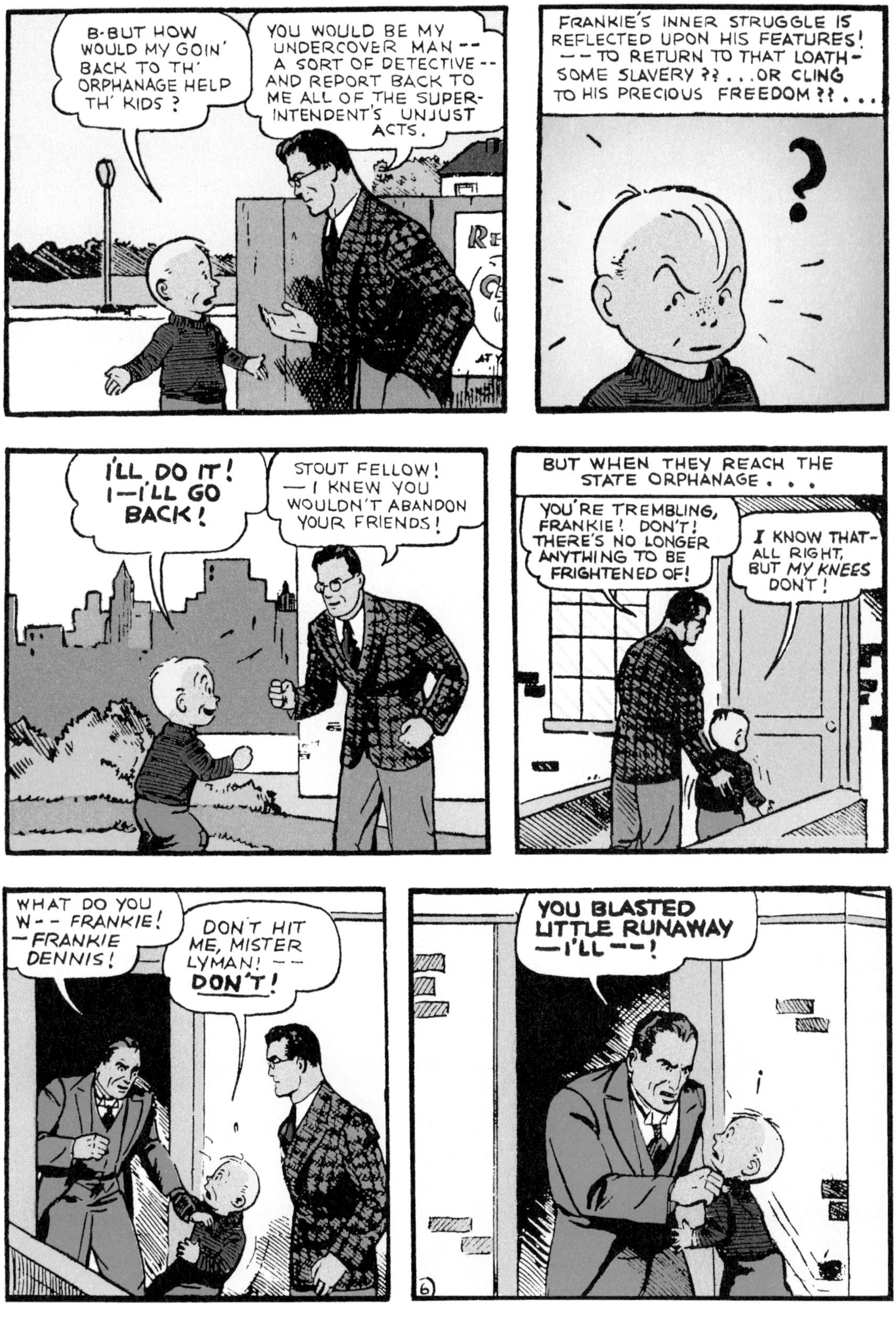
B-BUT HOW WOULD MY GOIN' BACK TO TH' ORPHANAGE HELP TH' KIDS ?
YOU WOULD BE MY UNDERCOVER MAN -- A SORT OF DETECTIVE -- AND REPORT BACK TO ME ALL OF THE SUPER-INTENDENT'S UNJUST ACTS.
FRANKIE'S INNER STRUGGLE IS REFLECTED UPON HIS FEATURES! -- TO RETURN TO THAT LOATH-SOME SLAVERY ?? . . . OR CLING TO HIS PRECIOUS FREEDOM ?? . . .
?
I'LL DO IT! I--I'LL GO BACK!
STOUT FELLOW! -- I KNEW YOU WOULDN'T ABANDON YOUR FRIENDS!
BUT WHEN THEY REACH THE STATE ORPHANAGE . . .
YOU'RE TREMBLING, FRANKIE! DON'T! THERE'S NO LONGER ANYTHING TO BE FRIGHTENED OF!
I KNOW THAT-ALL RIGHT, BUT MY KNEES DON'T!
WHAT DO YOU W-- FRANKIE! -- FRANKIE DENNIS!
DON'T HIT ME, MISTER LYMAN! -- DON'T!
YOU BLASTED LITTLE RUNAWAY -- I'LL --!
6

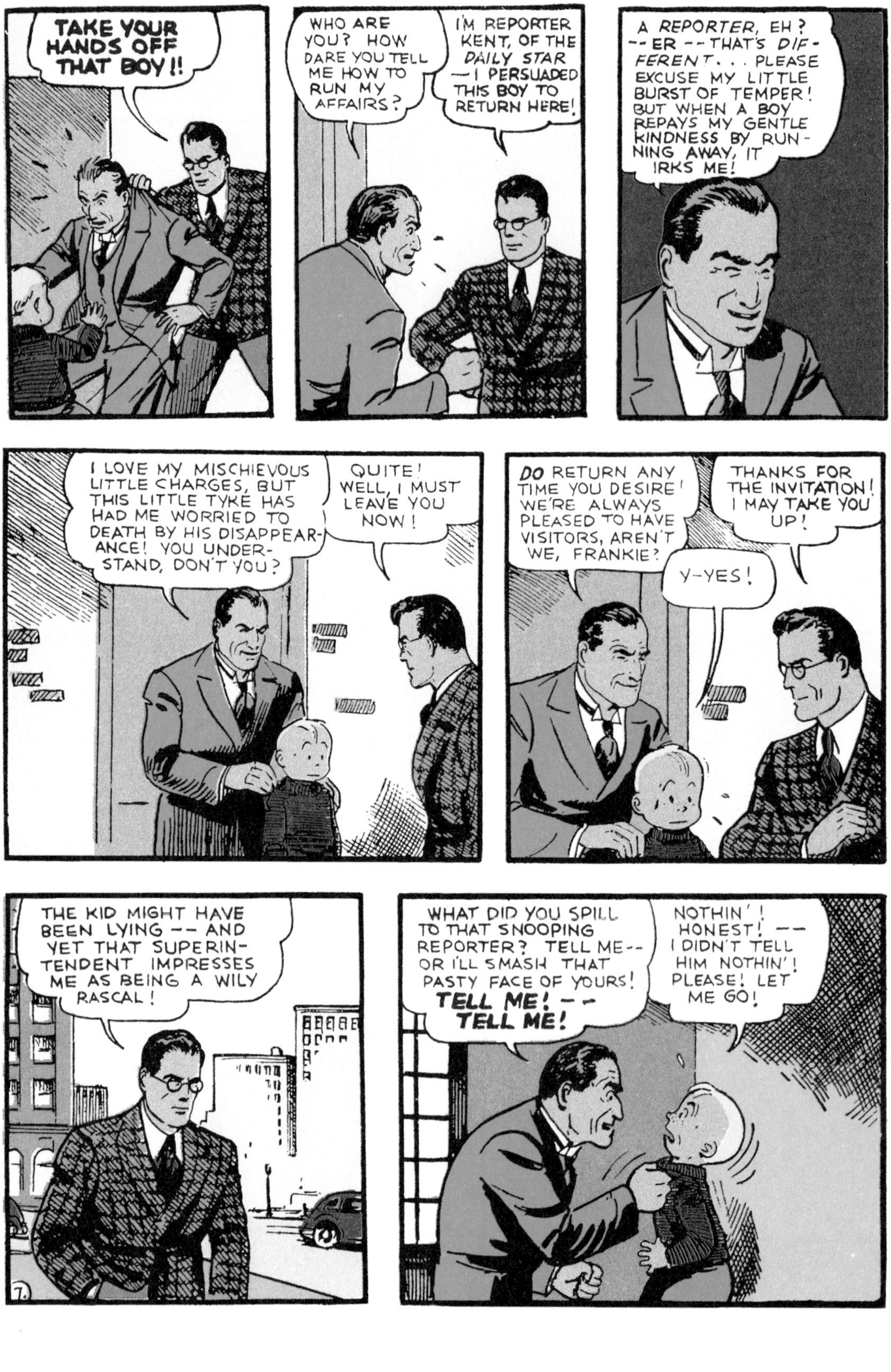
TAKE YOUR HANDS OFF THAT BOY!!
WHO ARE YOU? HOW DARE YOU TELL ME HOW TO RUN MY AFFAIRS?
I'M REPORTER KENT, OF THE DAILY STAR — I PERSUADED THIS BOY TO RETURN HERE!
A REPORTER, EH? --ER --THAT'S DIF-FERENT... PLEASE EXCUSE MY LITTLE BURST OF TEMPER! BUT WHEN A BOY REPAYS MY GENTLE KINDNESS BY RUN-NING AWAY, IT IRKS ME!
I LOVE MY MISCHIEVOUS LITTLE CHARGES, BUT THIS LITTLE TYKE HAS HAD ME WORRIED TO DEATH BY HIS DISAPPEAR-ANCE! YOU UNDER-STAND, DON'T YOU?
QUITE! WELL, I MUST LEAVE YOU NOW!
DO RETURN ANY TIME YOU DESIRE! WE'RE ALWAYS PLEASED TO HAVE VISITORS, AREN'T WE, FRANKIE?
Y-YES!
THANKS FOR THE INVITATION! I MAY TAKE YOU UP!
THE KID MIGHT HAVE BEEN LYING -- AND YET THAT SUPERIN-TENDENT IMPRESSES ME AS BEING A WILY RASCAL!
7.
WHAT DID YOU SPILL TO THAT SNOOPING REPORTER? TELL ME-- OR I'LL SMASH THAT PASTY FACE OF YOURS! TELL ME! -- TELL ME!
NOTHIN'! HONEST! -- I DIDN'T TELL HIM NOTHIN'! PLEASE! LET ME GO!

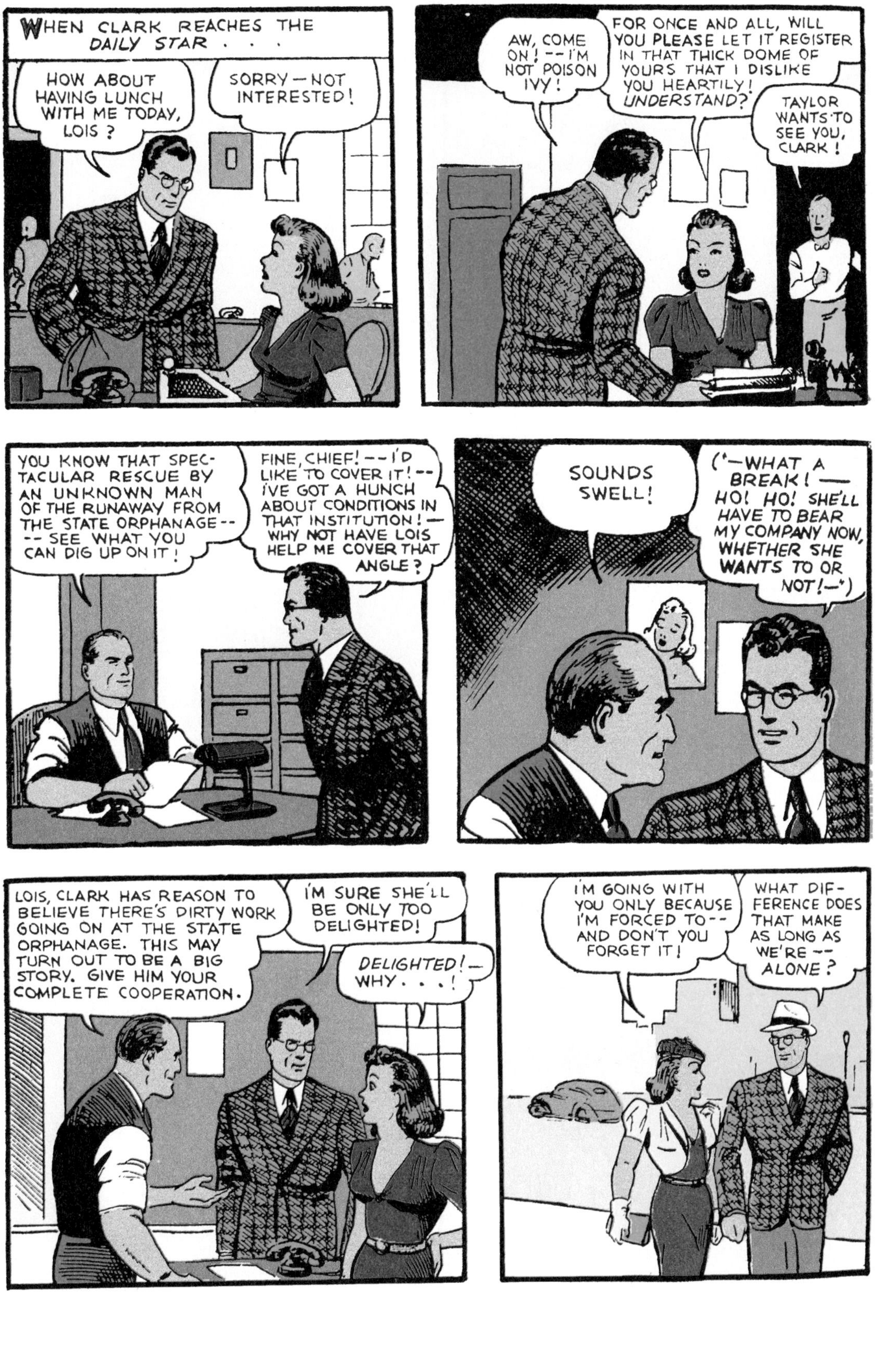

WHEN CLARK REACHES THE DAILY STAR . . .
HOW ABOUT HAVING LUNCH WITH ME TODAY, LOIS ?
SORRY — NOT INTERESTED!
AW, COME ON! -- I'M NOT POISON IVY!
FOR ONCE AND ALL, WILL YOU PLEASE LET IT REGISTER IN THAT THICK DOME OF YOURS THAT I DISLIKE YOU HEARTILY! UNDERSTAND?
TAYLOR WANTS TO SEE YOU, CLARK!
YOU KNOW THAT SPECTACULAR RESCUE BY AN UNKNOWN MAN OF THE RUNAWAY FROM THE STATE ORPHANAGE -- -- SEE WHAT YOU CAN DIG UP ON IT!
FINE, CHIEF! -- I'D LIKE TO COVER IT! -- I'VE GOT A HUNCH ABOUT CONDITIONS IN THAT INSTITUTION! — WHY NOT HAVE LOIS HELP ME COVER THAT ANGLE?
SOUNDS SWELL!
('—WHAT A BREAK! — HO! HO! SHE'LL HAVE TO BEAR MY COMPANY NOW, WHETHER SHE WANTS TO OR NOT!—')
LOIS, CLARK HAS REASON TO BELIEVE THERE'S DIRTY WORK GOING ON AT THE STATE ORPHANAGE. THIS MAY TURN OUT TO BE A BIG STORY. GIVE HIM YOUR COMPLETE COOPERATION.
I'M SURE SHE'LL BE ONLY TOO DELIGHTED!
DELIGHTED! — WHY . . . !
I'M GOING WITH YOU ONLY BECAUSE I'M FORCED TO -- AND DON'T YOU FORGET IT!
WHAT DIFFERENCE DOES THAT MAKE AS LONG AS WE'RE -- ALONE?

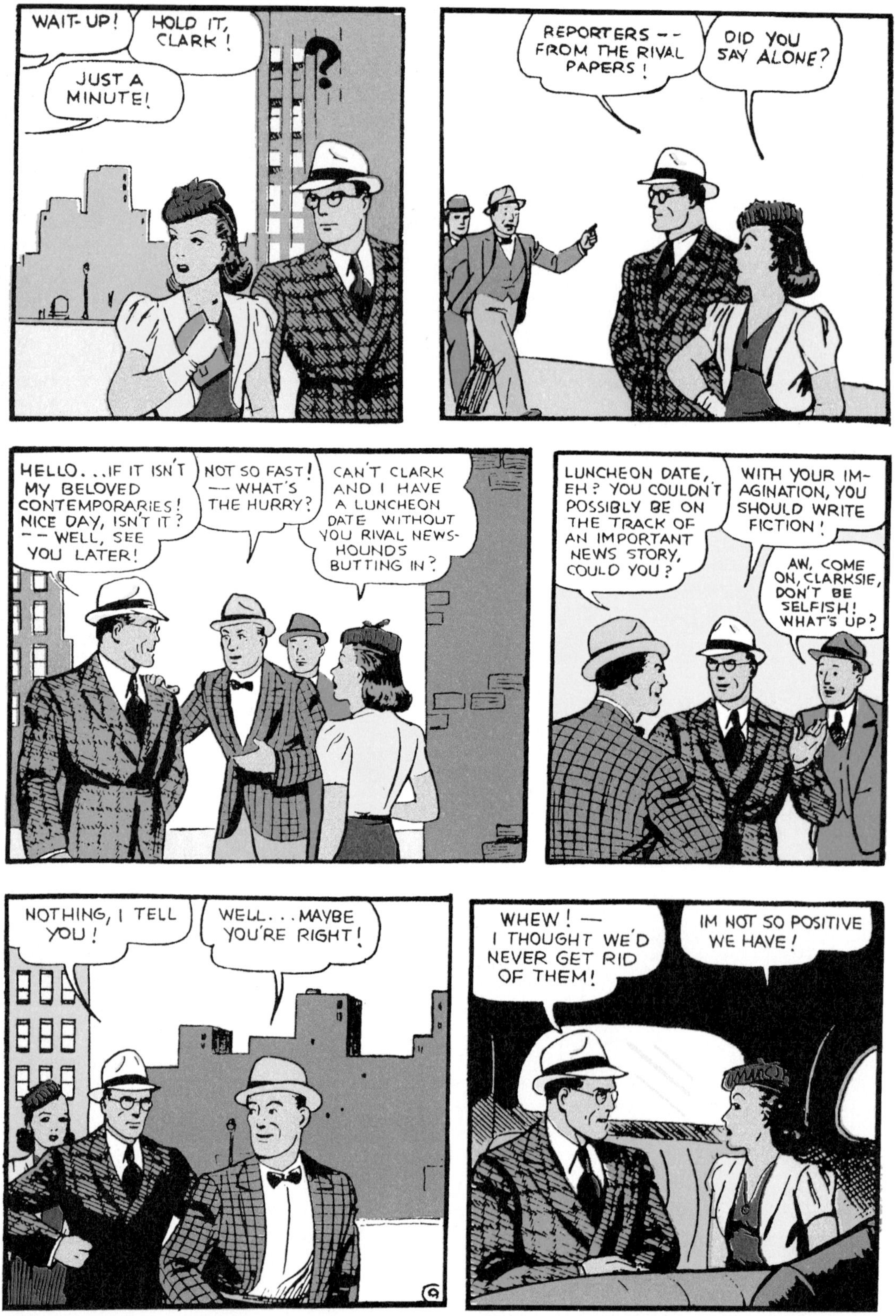
WAIT-UP!
HOLD IT, CLARK!
JUST A MINUTE!
REPORTERS -- FROM THE RIVAL PAPERS!
DID YOU SAY ALONE?
HELLO...IF IT ISN'T MY BELOVED CONTEMPORARIES! NICE DAY, ISN'T IT? -- WELL, SEE YOU LATER!
NOT SO FAST! — WHAT'S THE HURRY?
CAN'T CLARK AND I HAVE A LUNCHEON DATE WITHOUT YOU RIVAL NEWS-HOUNDS BUTTING IN?
LUNCHEON DATE, EH? YOU COULDN'T POSSIBLY BE ON THE TRACK OF AN IMPORTANT NEWS STORY, COULD YOU?
WITH YOUR IM-AGINATION, YOU SHOULD WRITE FICTION!
AW, COME ON, CLARKSIE, DON'T BE SELFISH! WHAT'S UP?
NOTHING, I TELL YOU!
WELL...MAYBE YOU'RE RIGHT!
9
WHEW! — I THOUGHT WE'D NEVER GET RID OF THEM!
IM NOT SO POSITIVE WE HAVE!

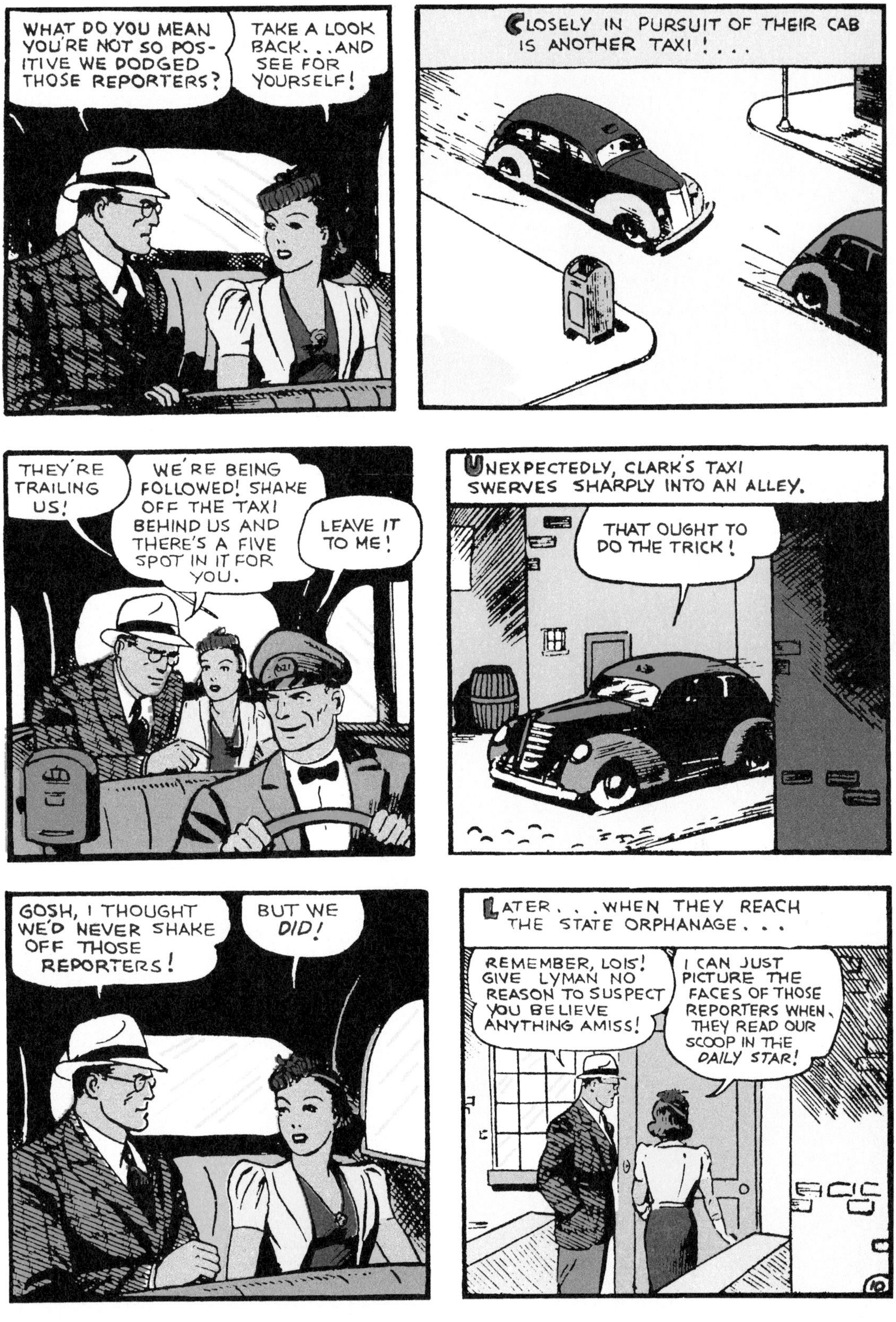
WHAT DO YOU MEAN YOU'RE NOT SO POSITIVE WE DODGED THOSE REPORTERS?
TAKE A LOOK BACK. . .AND SEE FOR YOURSELF!
CLOSELY IN PURSUIT OF THEIR CAB IS ANOTHER TAXI! . . .
THEY'RE TRAILING US!
WE'RE BEING FOLLOWED! SHAKE OFF THE TAXI BEHIND US AND THERE'S A FIVE SPOT IN IT FOR YOU.
LEAVE IT TO ME!
UNEXPECTEDLY, CLARK'S TAXI SWERVES SHARPLY INTO AN ALLEY.
THAT OUGHT TO DO THE TRICK!
GOSH, I THOUGHT WE'D NEVER SHAKE OFF THOSE REPORTERS!
BUT WE DID!
LATER. . .WHEN THEY REACH THE STATE ORPHANAGE . . .
REMEMBER, LOIS! GIVE LYMAN NO REASON TO SUSPECT YOU BELIEVE ANYTHING AMISS!
I CAN JUST PICTURE THE FACES OF THOSE REPORTERS WHEN THEY READ OUR SCOOP IN THE DAILY STAR!
10

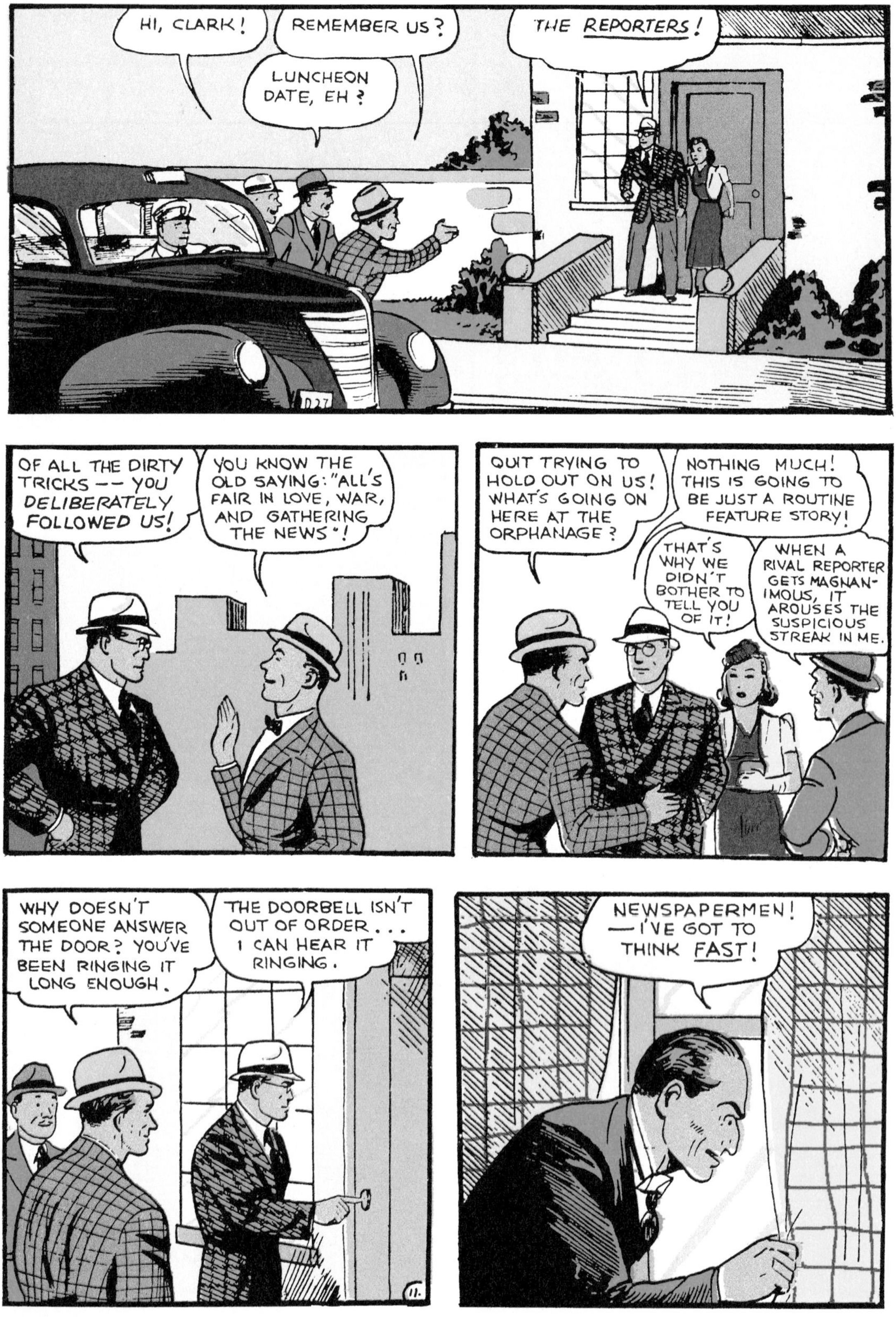
HI, CLARK!
REMEMBER US?
LUNCHEON DATE, EH?
THE REPORTERS!
OF ALL THE DIRTY TRICKS -- YOU DELIBERATELY FOLLOWED US!
YOU KNOW THE OLD SAYING: "ALL'S FAIR IN LOVE, WAR, AND GATHERING THE NEWS"!
QUIT TRYING TO HOLD OUT ON US! WHAT'S GOING ON HERE AT THE ORPHANAGE?
NOTHING MUCH! THIS IS GOING TO BE JUST A ROUTINE FEATURE STORY!
THAT'S WHY WE DIDN'T BOTHER TO TELL YOU OF IT!
WHEN A RIVAL REPORTER GETS MAGNANIMOUS, IT AROUSES THE SUSPICIOUS STREAK IN ME.
WHY DOESN'T SOMEONE ANSWER THE DOOR? YOU'VE BEEN RINGING IT LONG ENOUGH.
THE DOORBELL ISN'T OUT OF ORDER . . . I CAN HEAR IT RINGING.
11.
NEWSPAPERMEN! —I'VE GOT TO THINK FAST!

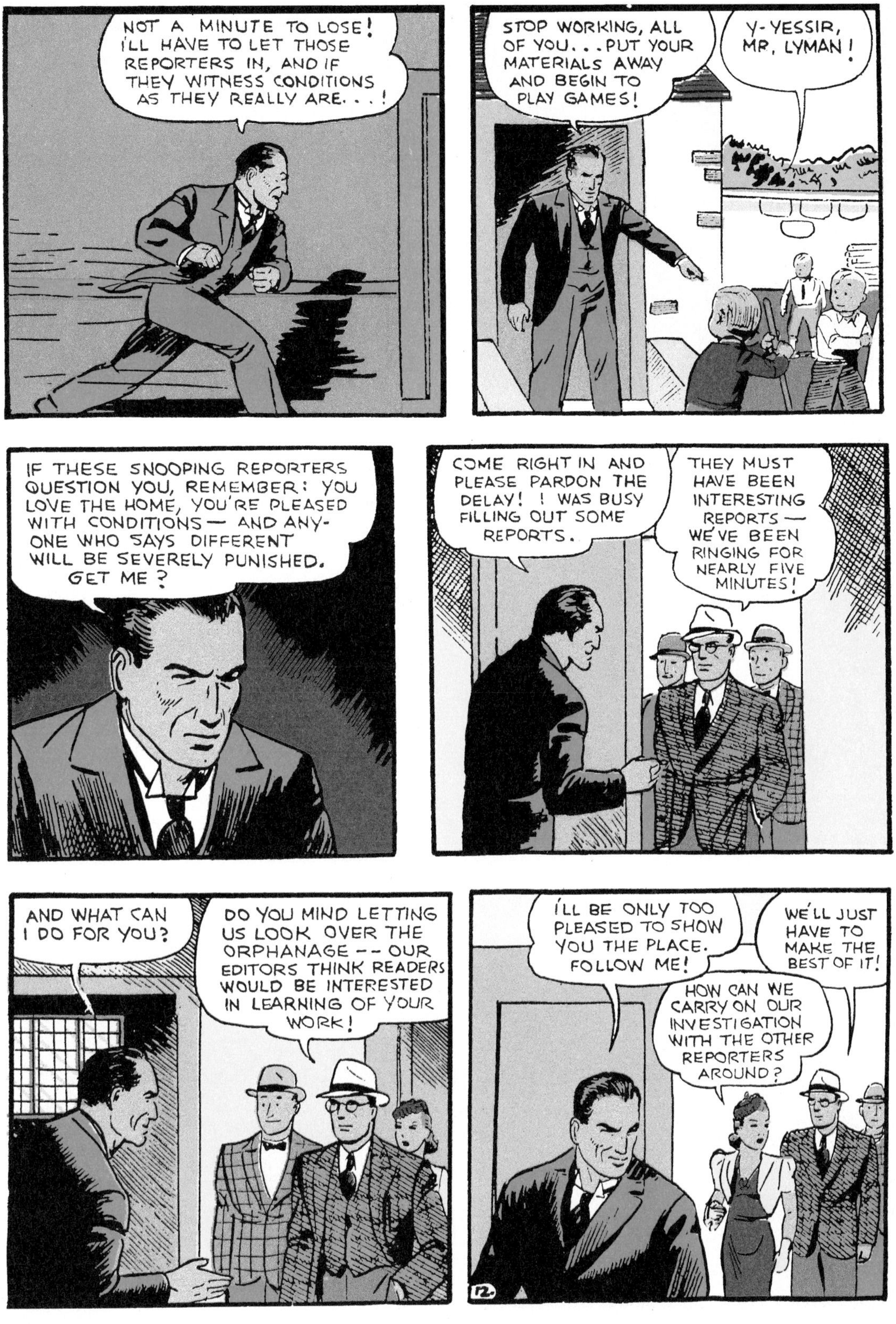
NOT A MINUTE TO LOSE! I'LL HAVE TO LET THOSE REPORTERS IN, AND IF THEY WITNESS CONDITIONS AS THEY REALLY ARE. . . !
STOP WORKING, ALL OF YOU. . . PUT YOUR MATERIALS AWAY AND BEGIN TO PLAY GAMES!
Y-YESSIR, MR. LYMAN!
IF THESE SNOOPING REPORTERS QUESTION YOU, REMEMBER: YOU LOVE THE HOME, YOU'RE PLEASED WITH CONDITIONS — AND ANYONE WHO SAYS DIFFERENT WILL BE SEVERELY PUNISHED. GET ME?
COME RIGHT IN AND PLEASE PARDON THE DELAY! I WAS BUSY FILLING OUT SOME REPORTS.
THEY MUST HAVE BEEN INTERESTING REPORTS — WE'VE BEEN RINGING FOR NEARLY FIVE MINUTES!
AND WHAT CAN I DO FOR YOU?
DO YOU MIND LETTING US LOOK OVER THE ORPHANAGE -- OUR EDITORS THINK READERS WOULD BE INTERESTED IN LEARNING OF YOUR WORK!
I'LL BE ONLY TOO PLEASED TO SHOW YOU THE PLACE. FOLLOW ME!
HOW CAN WE CARRY ON OUR INVESTIGATION WITH THE OTHER REPORTERS AROUND?
WE'LL JUST HAVE TO MAKE THE BEST OF IT!
12.

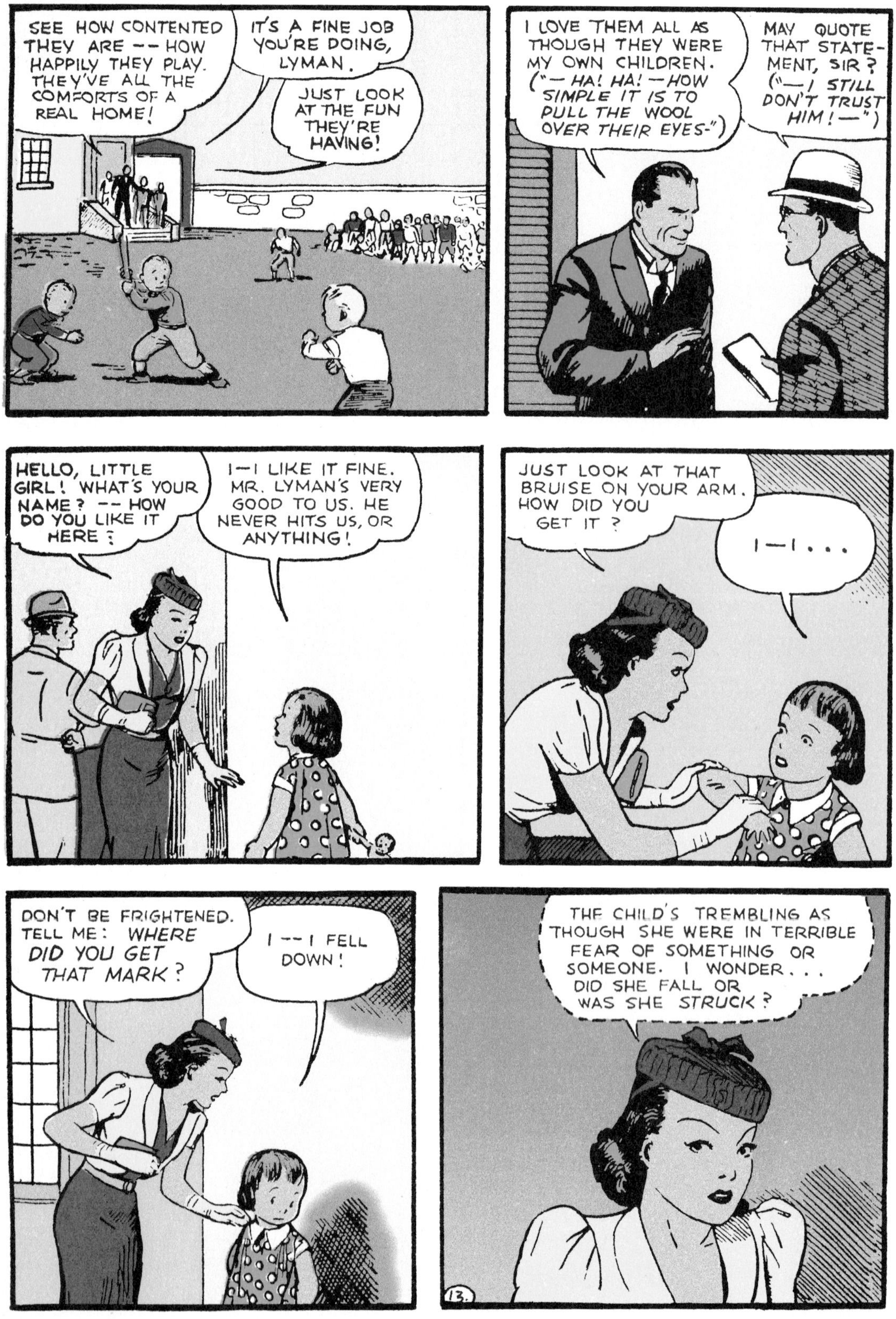
SEE HOW CONTENTED THEY ARE -- HOW HAPPILY THEY PLAY. THEY'VE ALL THE COMFORTS OF A REAL HOME!
IT'S A FINE JOB YOU'RE DOING, LYMAN.
JUST LOOK AT THE FUN THEY'RE HAVING!
I LOVE THEM ALL AS THOUGH THEY WERE MY OWN CHILDREN. ("— HA! HA! — HOW SIMPLE IT IS TO PULL THE WOOL OVER THEIR EYES-")
MAY QUOTE THAT STATEMENT, SIR? ("— I STILL DON'T TRUST HIM! —")
HELLO, LITTLE GIRL! WHAT'S YOUR NAME? -- HOW DO YOU LIKE IT HERE?
I—I LIKE IT FINE. MR. LYMAN'S VERY GOOD TO US. HE NEVER HITS US, OR ANYTHING!
JUST LOOK AT THAT BRUISE ON YOUR ARM. HOW DID YOU GET IT?
I—I . . .
DON'T BE FRIGHTENED. TELL ME: WHERE DID YOU GET THAT MARK?
I -- I FELL DOWN!
THE CHILD'S TREMBLING AS THOUGH SHE WERE IN TERRIBLE FEAR OF SOMETHING OR SOMEONE. I WONDER. . . DID SHE FALL OR WAS SHE STRUCK?
13.

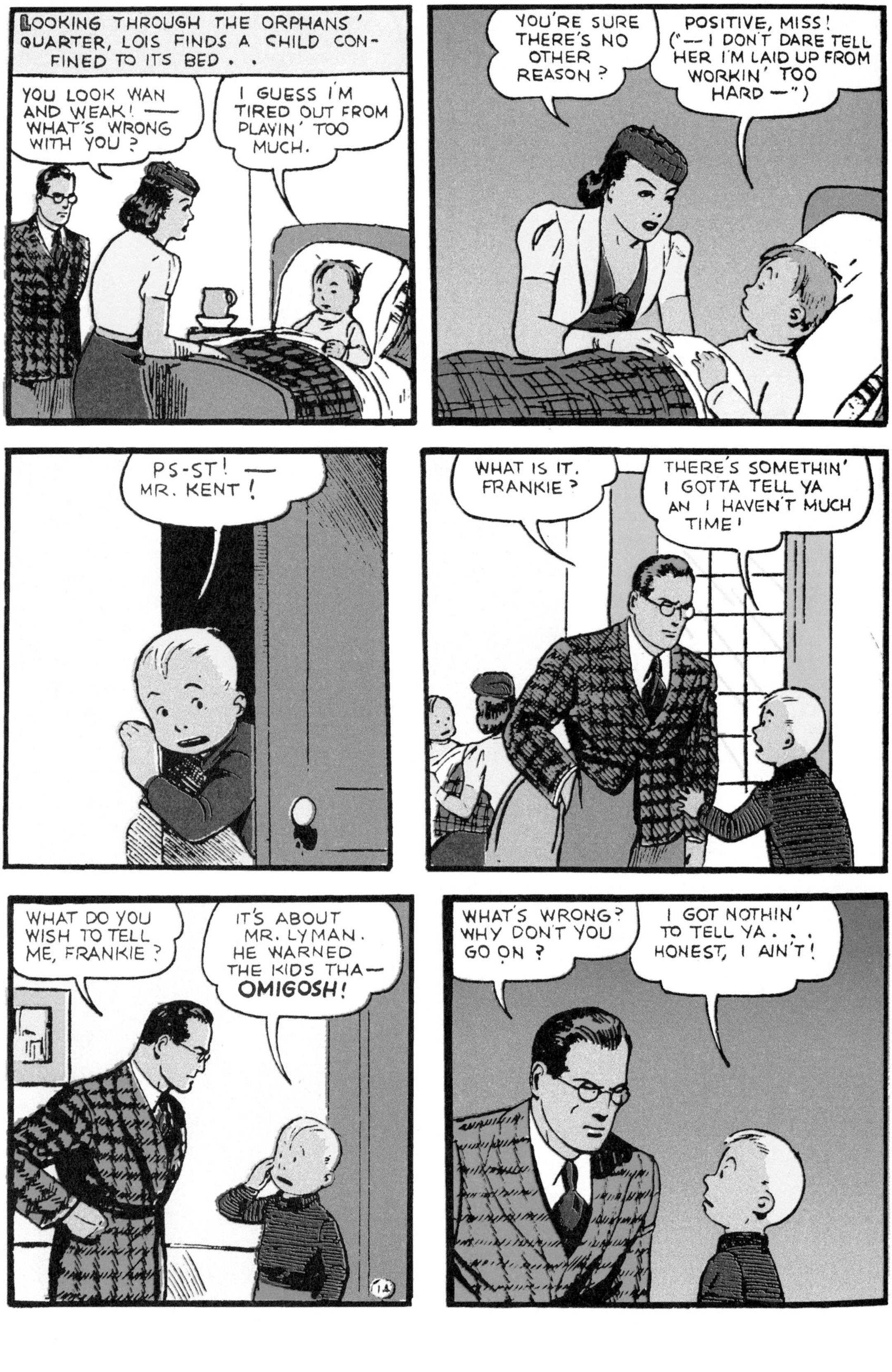
LOOKING THROUGH THE ORPHANS' QUARTER, LOIS FINDS A CHILD CONFINED TO ITS BED . .
YOU LOOK WAN AND WEAK! — WHAT'S WRONG WITH YOU ?
I GUESS I'M TIRED OUT FROM PLAYIN' TOO MUCH.
YOU'RE SURE THERE'S NO OTHER REASON ?
POSITIVE, MISS! ("— I DON'T DARE TELL HER I'M LAID UP FROM WORKIN' TOO HARD —")
PS-ST! — MR. KENT !
WHAT IS IT, FRANKIE ?
THERE'S SOMETHIN' I GOTTA TELL YA AN I HAVEN'T MUCH TIME!
WHAT DO YOU WISH TO TELL ME, FRANKIE ?
IT'S ABOUT MR. LYMAN. HE WARNED THE KIDS THA— OMIGOSH!
WHAT'S WRONG? WHY DON'T YOU GO ON ?
I GOT NOTHIN' TO TELL YA . . . HONEST, I AIN'T!

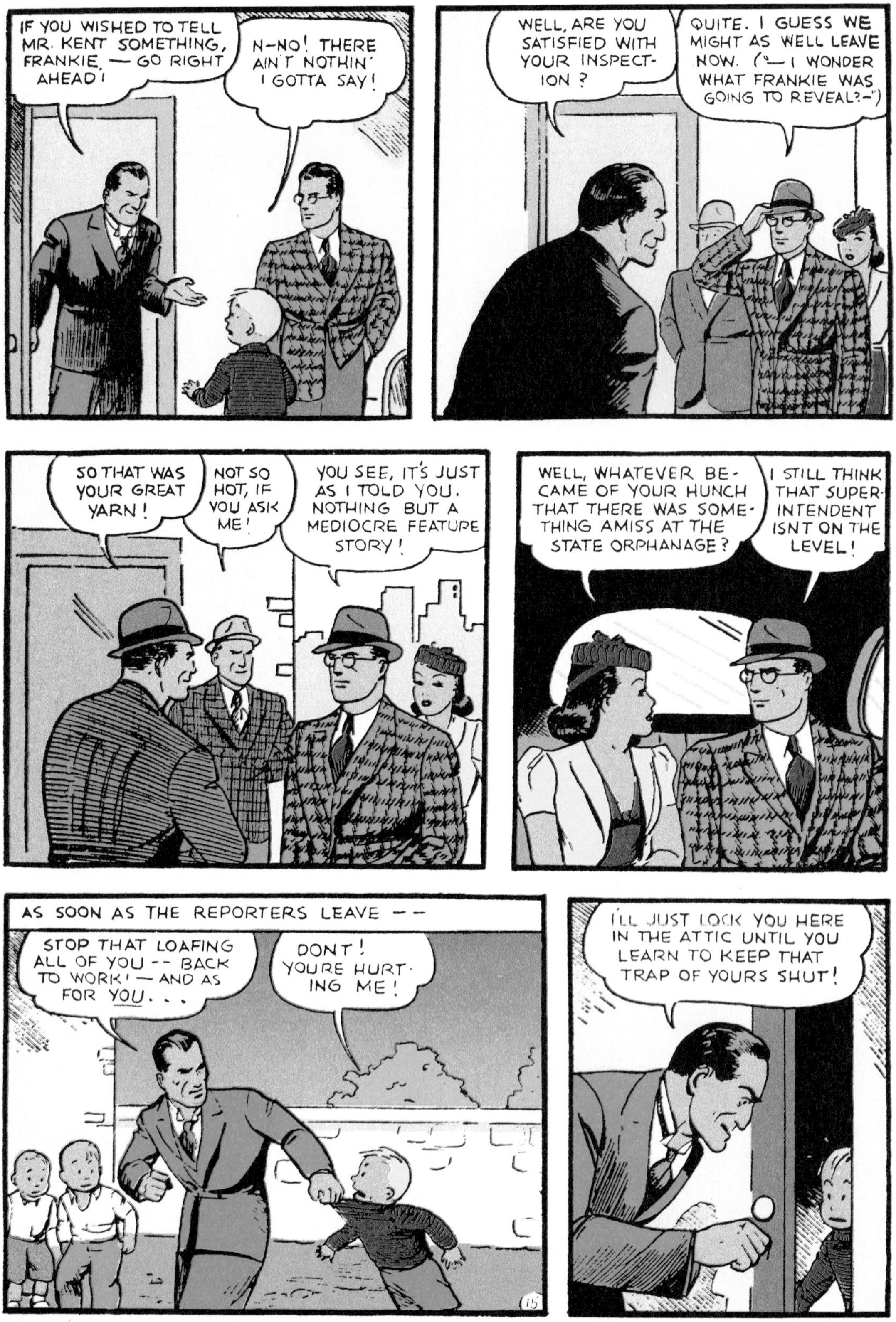
IF YOU WISHED TO TELL MR. KENT SOMETHING, FRANKIE, — GO RIGHT AHEAD!
N-NO! THERE AIN'T NOTHIN' I GOTTA SAY!
WELL, ARE YOU SATISFIED WITH YOUR INSPECTION ?
QUITE. I GUESS WE MIGHT AS WELL LEAVE NOW. ("— I WONDER WHAT FRANKIE WAS GOING TO REVEAL?—")
SO THAT WAS YOUR GREAT YARN!
NOT SO HOT, IF YOU ASK ME!
YOU SEE, IT'S JUST AS I TOLD YOU. NOTHING BUT A MEDIOCRE FEATURE STORY!
WELL, WHATEVER BECAME OF YOUR HUNCH THAT THERE WAS SOMETHING AMISS AT THE STATE ORPHANAGE?
I STILL THINK THAT SUPERINTENDENT ISNT ON THE LEVEL!
AS SOON AS THE REPORTERS LEAVE --
STOP THAT LOAFING ALL OF YOU -- BACK TO WORK! — AND AS FOR YOU. . .
DONT! YOU'RE HURTING ME!
15
I'LL JUST LOCK YOU HERE IN THE ATTIC UNTIL YOU LEARN TO KEEP THAT TRAP OF YOURS SHUT!

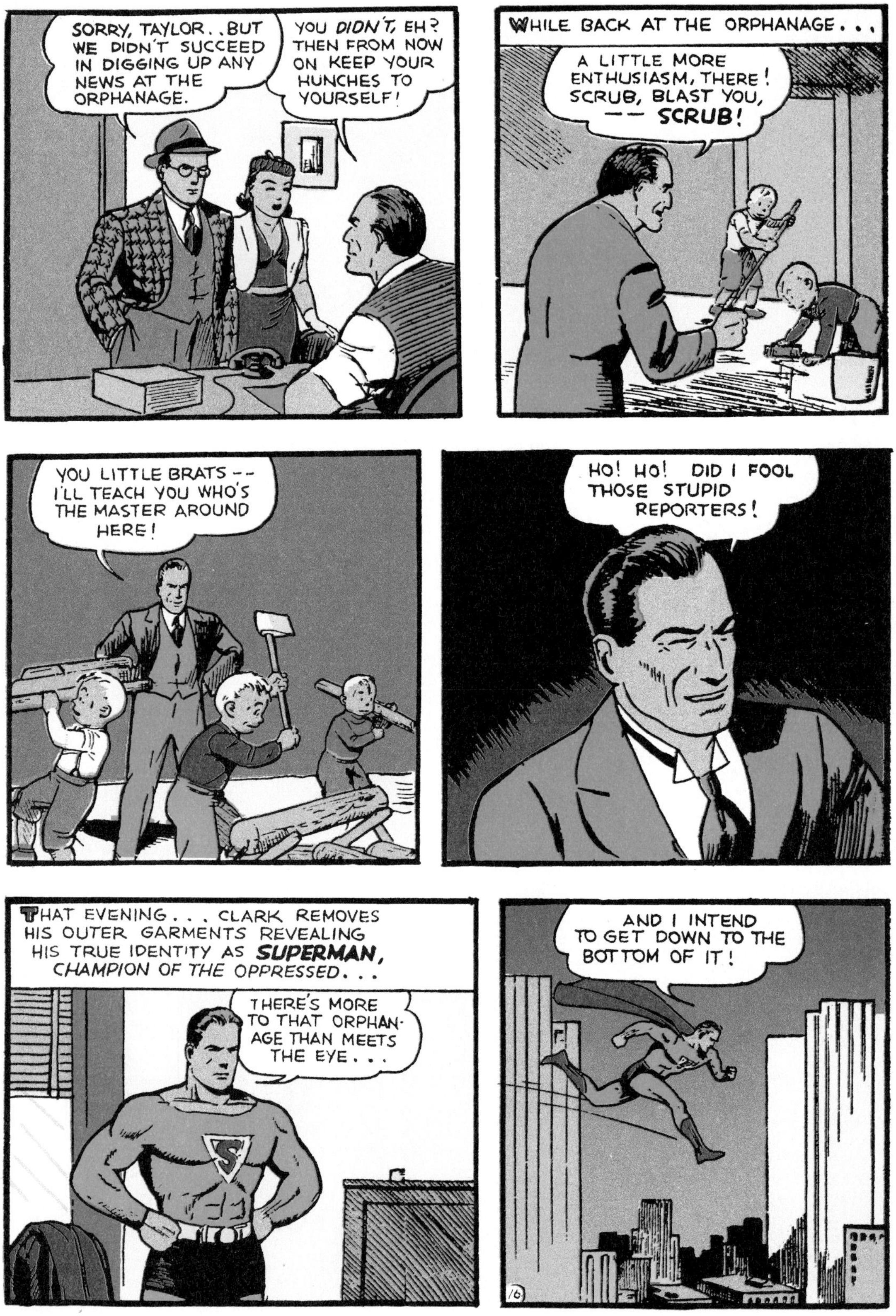
SORRY, TAYLOR..BUT WE DIDN'T SUCCEED IN DIGGING UP ANY NEWS AT THE ORPHANAGE.
YOU *DIDN'T*, EH? THEN FROM NOW ON KEEP YOUR HUNCHES TO YOURSELF!
WHILE BACK AT THE ORPHANAGE...
A LITTLE MORE ENTHUSIASM, THERE! SCRUB, BLAST YOU, -- **SCRUB!**
YOU LITTLE BRATS -- I'LL TEACH YOU WHO'S THE MASTER AROUND HERE!
HO! HO! DID I FOOL THOSE STUPID REPORTERS!
THAT EVENING... CLARK REMOVES HIS OUTER GARMENTS REVEALING HIS TRUE IDENTITY AS **SUPERMAN,** CHAMPION OF THE OPPRESSED...
THERE'S MORE TO THAT ORPHANAGE THAN MEETS THE EYE...
AND I INTEND TO GET DOWN TO THE BOTTOM OF IT!

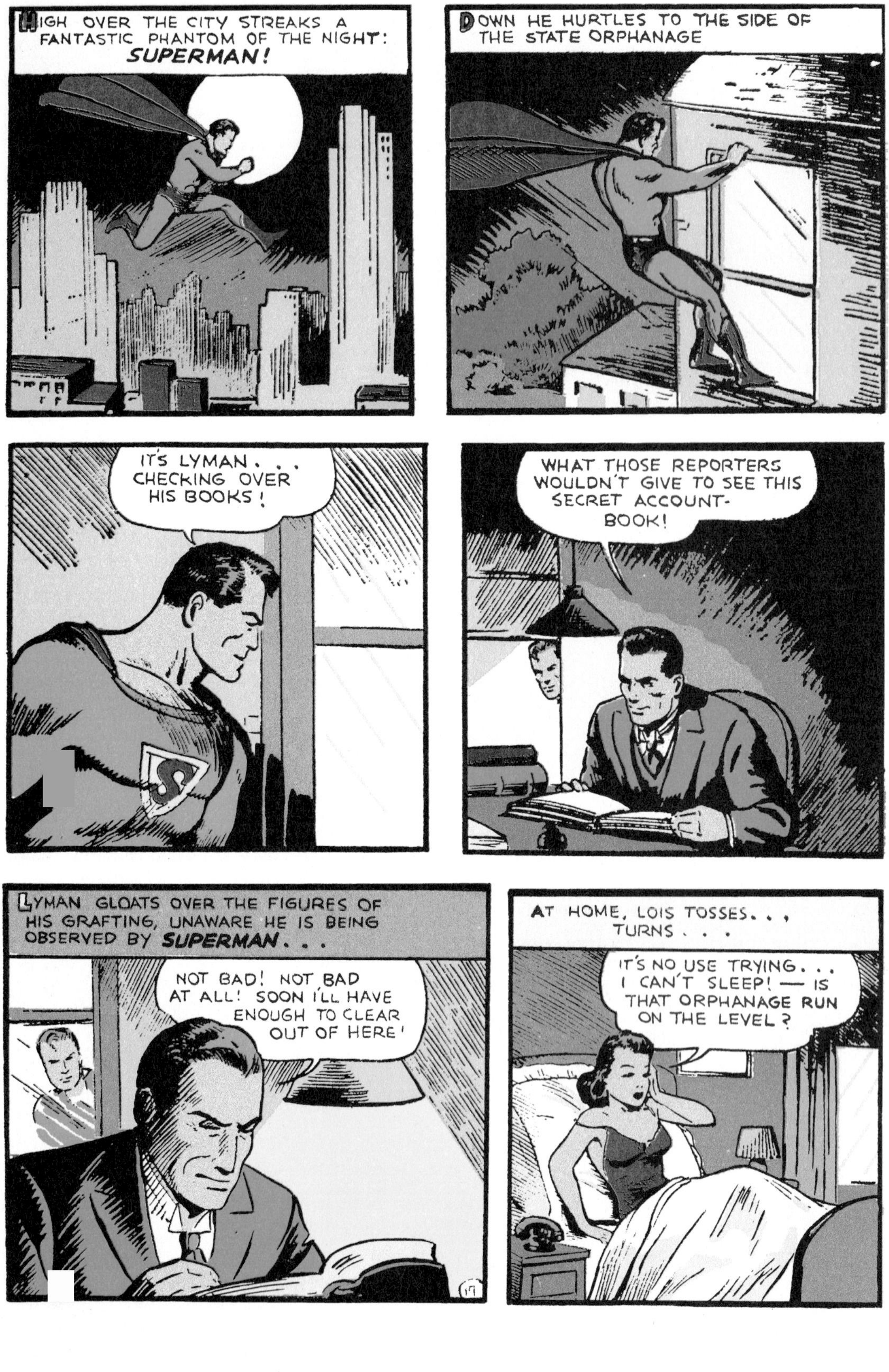
HIGH OVER THE CITY STREAKS A FANTASTIC PHANTOM OF THE NIGHT: SUPERMAN!
DOWN HE HURTLES TO THE SIDE OF THE STATE ORPHANAGE
IT'S LYMAN. . . CHECKING OVER HIS BOOKS!
WHAT THOSE REPORTERS WOULDN'T GIVE TO SEE THIS SECRET ACCOUNT-BOOK!
LYMAN GLOATS OVER THE FIGURES OF HIS GRAFTING, UNAWARE HE IS BEING OBSERVED BY SUPERMAN. . .
NOT BAD! NOT BAD AT ALL! SOON I'LL HAVE ENOUGH TO CLEAR OUT OF HERE!
AT HOME, LOIS TOSSES. . , TURNS . . .
IT'S NO USE TRYING. . . I CAN'T SLEEP! — IS THAT ORPHANAGE RUN ON THE LEVEL?

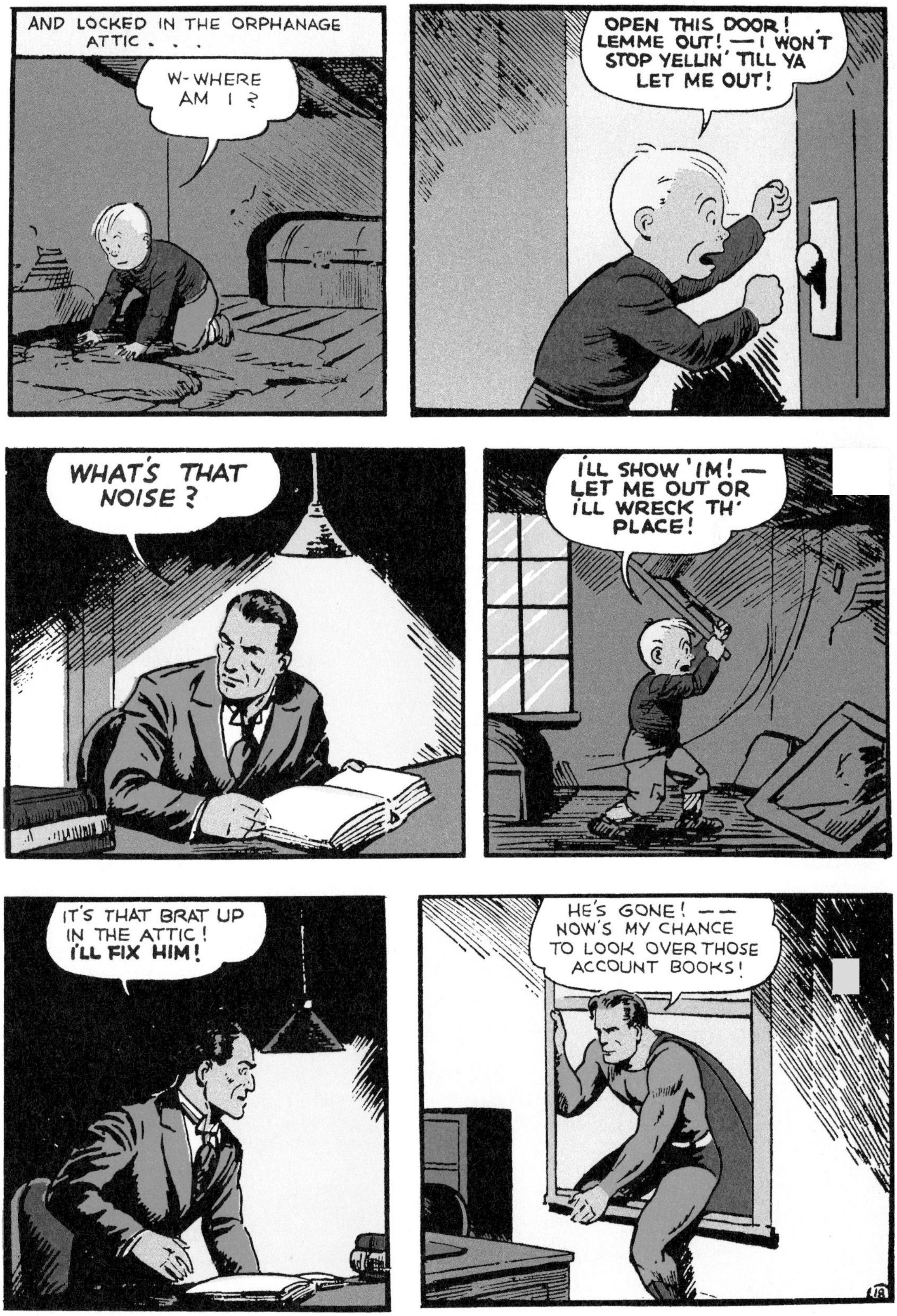
AND LOCKED IN THE ORPHANAGE ATTIC . . .
W-WHERE AM I ?
OPEN THIS DOOR! LEMME OUT! — I WON'T STOP YELLIN' TILL YA LET ME OUT!
WHAT'S THAT NOISE?
I'LL SHOW 'IM! — LET ME OUT OR I'LL WRECK TH' PLACE!
IT'S THAT BRAT UP IN THE ATTIC! I'LL FIX HIM!
HE'S GONE! — — NOW'S MY CHANCE TO LOOK OVER THOSE ACCOUNT BOOKS!
18

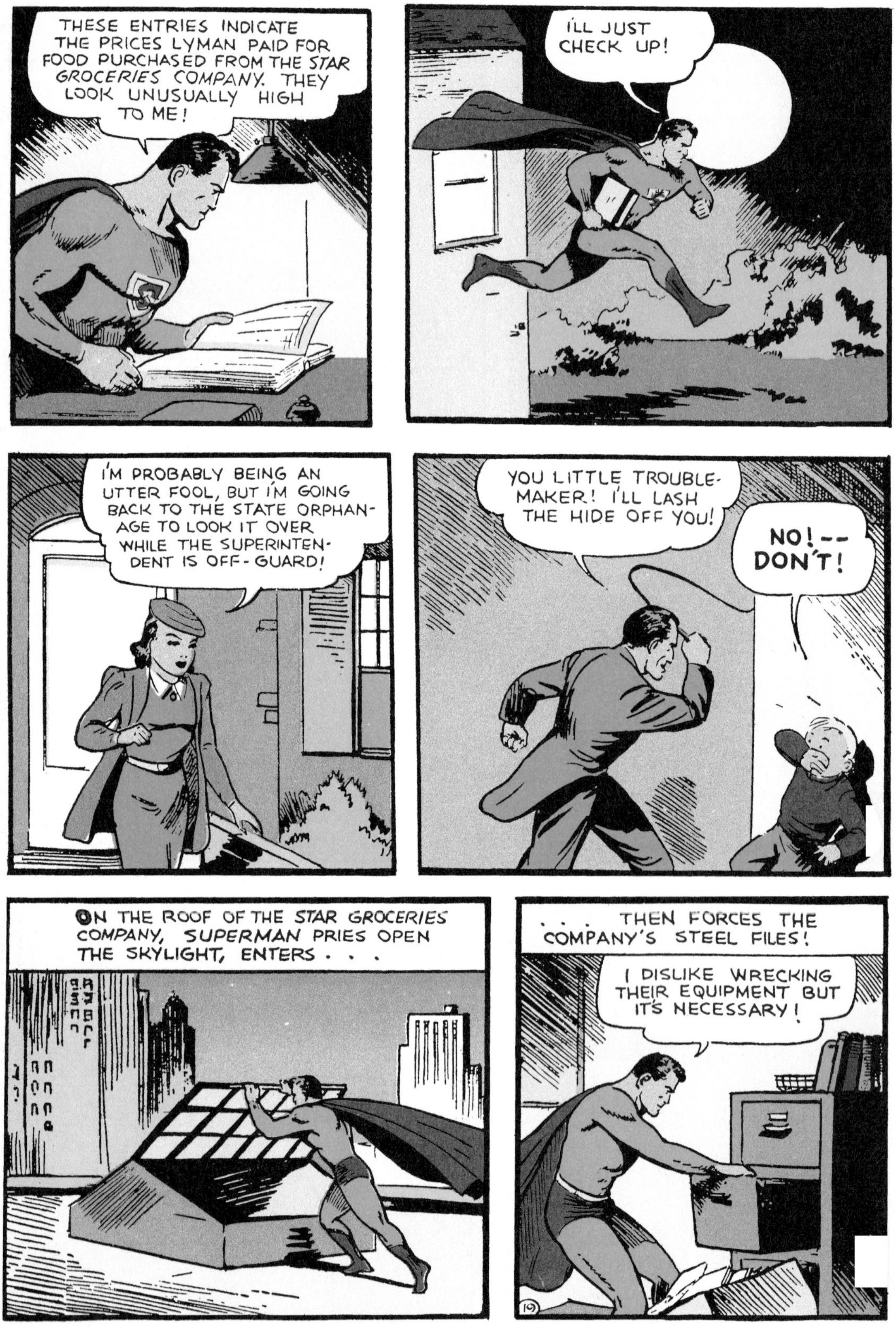
THESE ENTRIES INDICATE THE PRICES LYMAN PAID FOR FOOD PURCHASED FROM THE STAR GROCERIES COMPANY. THEY LOOK UNUSUALLY HIGH TO ME!
I'LL JUST CHECK UP!
I'M PROBABLY BEING AN UTTER FOOL, BUT I'M GOING BACK TO THE STATE ORPHANAGE TO LOOK IT OVER WHILE THE SUPERINTENDENT IS OFF-GUARD!
YOU LITTLE TROUBLE-MAKER! I'LL LASH THE HIDE OFF YOU!
NO!-- DON'T!
ON THE ROOF OF THE STAR GROCERIES COMPANY, SUPERMAN PRIES OPEN THE SKYLIGHT, ENTERS . . .
. . . THEN FORCES THE COMPANY'S STEEL FILES!
I DISLIKE WRECKING THEIR EQUIPMENT BUT IT'S NECESSARY!
19

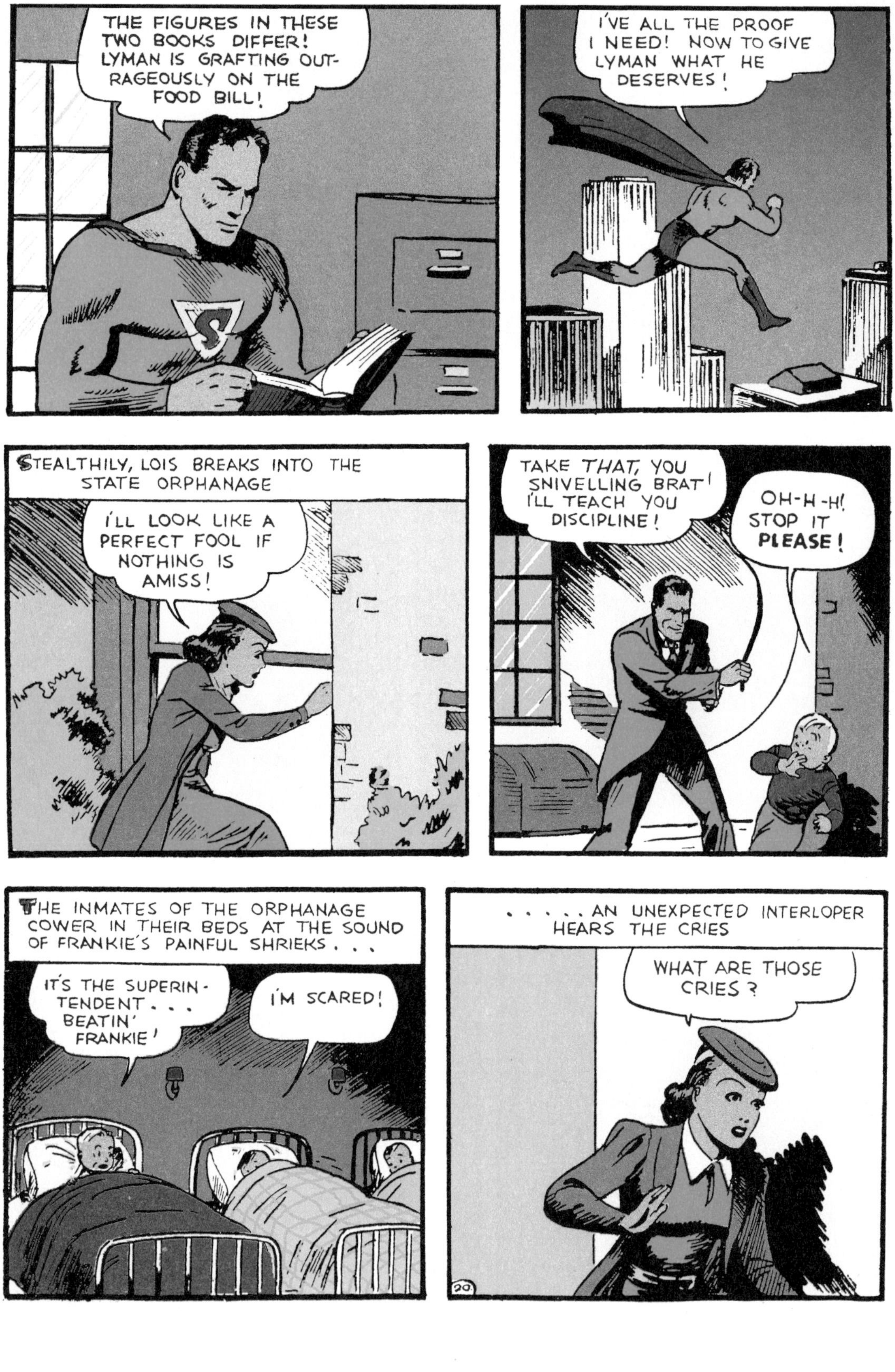
THE FIGURES IN THESE TWO BOOKS DIFFER! LYMAN IS GRAFTING OUT-RAGEOUSLY ON THE FOOD BILL!
I'VE ALL THE PROOF I NEED! NOW TO GIVE LYMAN WHAT HE DESERVES!
STEALTHILY, LOIS BREAKS INTO THE STATE ORPHANAGE
I'LL LOOK LIKE A PERFECT FOOL IF NOTHING IS AMISS!
TAKE THAT, YOU SNIVELLING BRAT! I'LL TEACH YOU DISCIPLINE!
OH-H-H! STOP IT PLEASE!
THE INMATES OF THE ORPHANAGE COWER IN THEIR BEDS AT THE SOUND OF FRANKIE'S PAINFUL SHRIEKS . . .
IT'S THE SUPERIN-TENDENT . . . BEATIN' FRANKIE'
I'M SCARED!
. . . . . AN UNEXPECTED INTERLOPER HEARS THE CRIES
WHAT ARE THOSE CRIES?
20

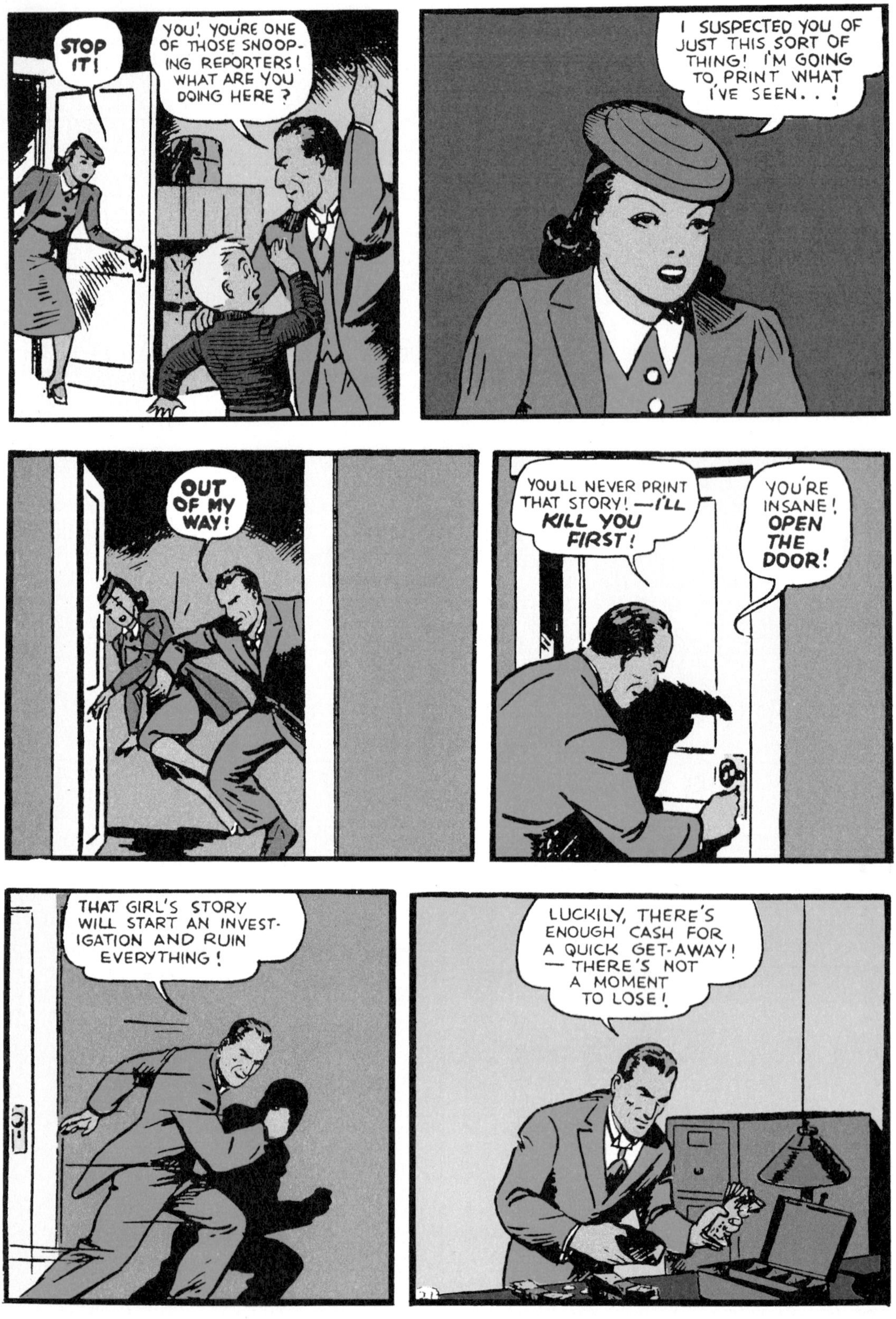
STOP IT!
YOU! YOU'RE ONE OF THOSE SNOOPING REPORTERS! WHAT ARE YOU DOING HERE?
I SUSPECTED YOU OF JUST THIS SORT OF THING! I'M GOING TO PRINT WHAT I'VE SEEN..!
OUT OF MY WAY!
YOU'LL NEVER PRINT THAT STORY! —I'LL KILL YOU FIRST!
YOU'RE INSANE! OPEN THE DOOR!
THAT GIRL'S STORY WILL START AN INVESTIGATION AND RUIN EVERYTHING!
LUCKILY, THERE'S ENOUGH CASH FOR A QUICK GET-AWAY! —THERE'S NOT A MOMENT TO LOSE!

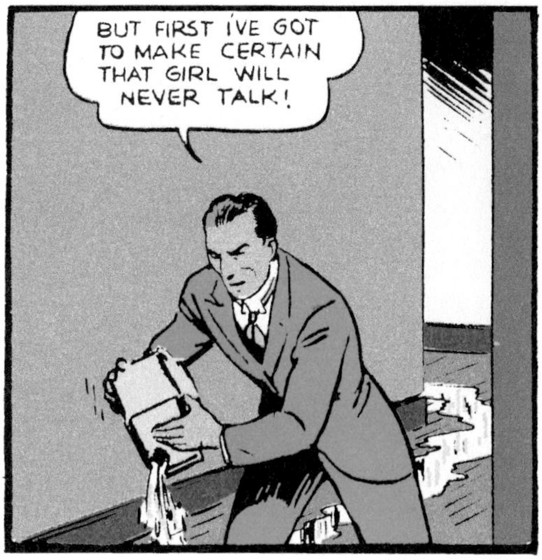
BUT FIRST I'VE GOT TO MAKE CERTAIN THAT GIRL WILL NEVER TALK!

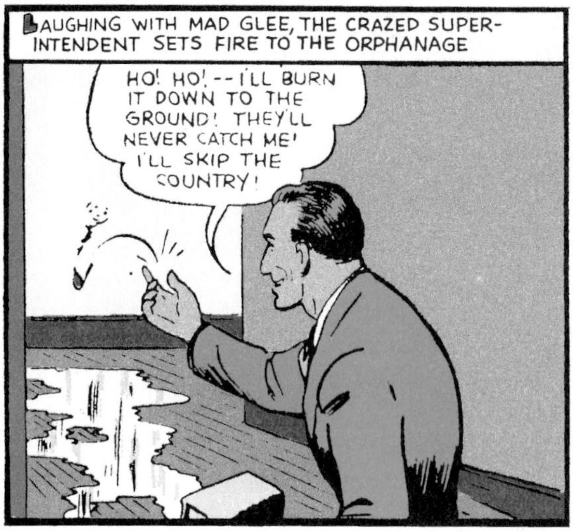
LAUGHING WITH MAD GLEE, THE CRAZED SUPER-INTENDENT SETS FIRE TO THE ORPHANAGE
HO! HO! -- I'LL BURN IT DOWN TO THE GROUND! THEY'LL NEVER CATCH ME! I'LL SKIP THE COUNTRY!

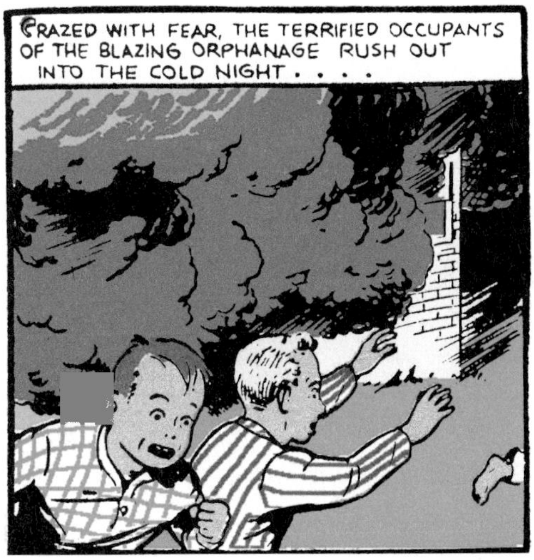
CRAZED WITH FEAR, THE TERRIFIED OCCUPANTS OF THE BLAZING ORPHANAGE RUSH OUT INTO THE COLD NIGHT . . . .

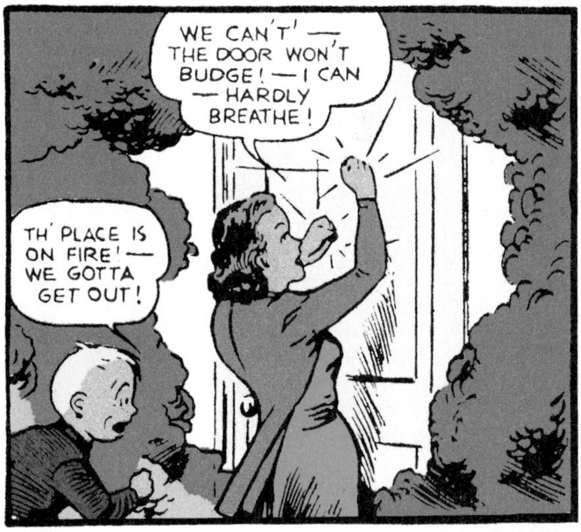
WE CAN'T! — THE DOOR WON'T BUDGE! — I CAN — HARDLY BREATHE!
TH' PLACE IS ON FIRE! — WE GOTTA GET OUT!

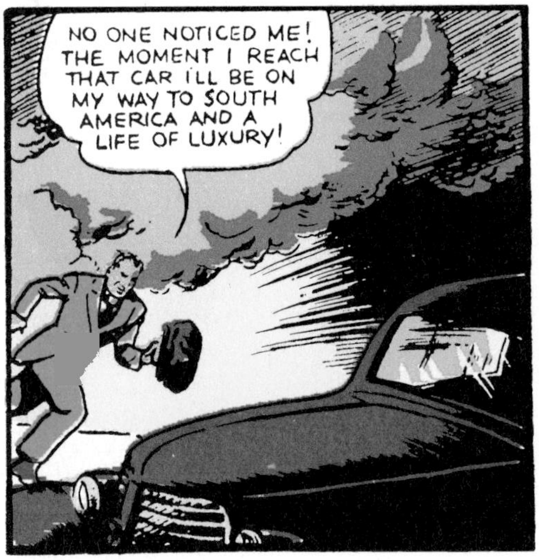
NO ONE NOTICED ME! THE MOMENT I REACH THAT CAR I'LL BE ON MY WAY TO SOUTH AMERICA AND A LIFE OF LUXURY!

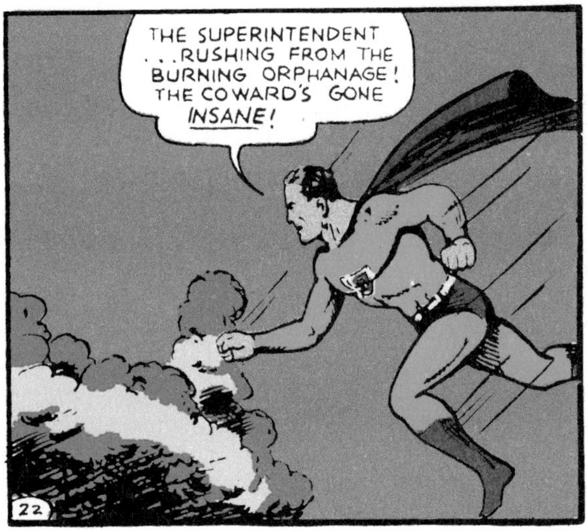
THE SUPERINTENDENT . . . RUSHING FROM THE BURNING ORPHANAGE! THE COWARD'S GONE INSANE!
22

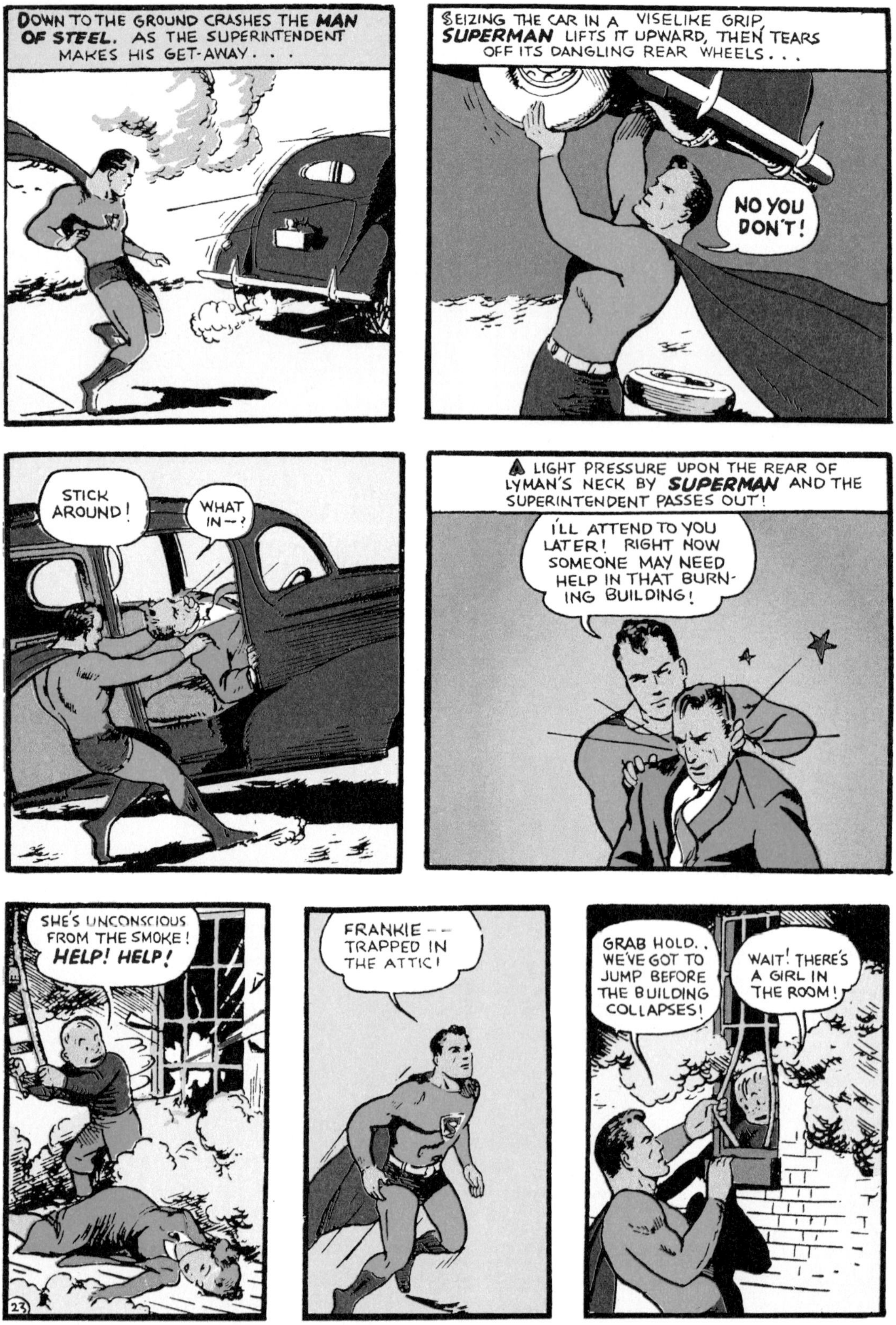
DOWN TO THE GROUND CRASHES THE MAN OF STEEL. AS THE SUPERINTENDENT MAKES HIS GET-AWAY . . .
SEIZING THE CAR IN A VISELIKE GRIP, SUPERMAN LIFTS IT UPWARD, THEN TEARS OFF ITS DANGLING REAR WHEELS . . .
NO YOU DON'T!
STICK AROUND!
WHAT IN--?
A LIGHT PRESSURE UPON THE REAR OF LYMAN'S NECK BY SUPERMAN AND THE SUPERINTENDENT PASSES OUT!
I'LL ATTEND TO YOU LATER! RIGHT NOW SOMEONE MAY NEED HELP IN THAT BURNING BUILDING!
SHE'S UNCONSCIOUS FROM THE SMOKE! HELP! HELP!
23
FRANKIE -- TRAPPED IN THE ATTIC!
GRAB HOLD. . WE'VE GOT TO JUMP BEFORE THE BUILDING COLLAPSES!
WAIT! THERE'S A GIRL IN THE ROOM!

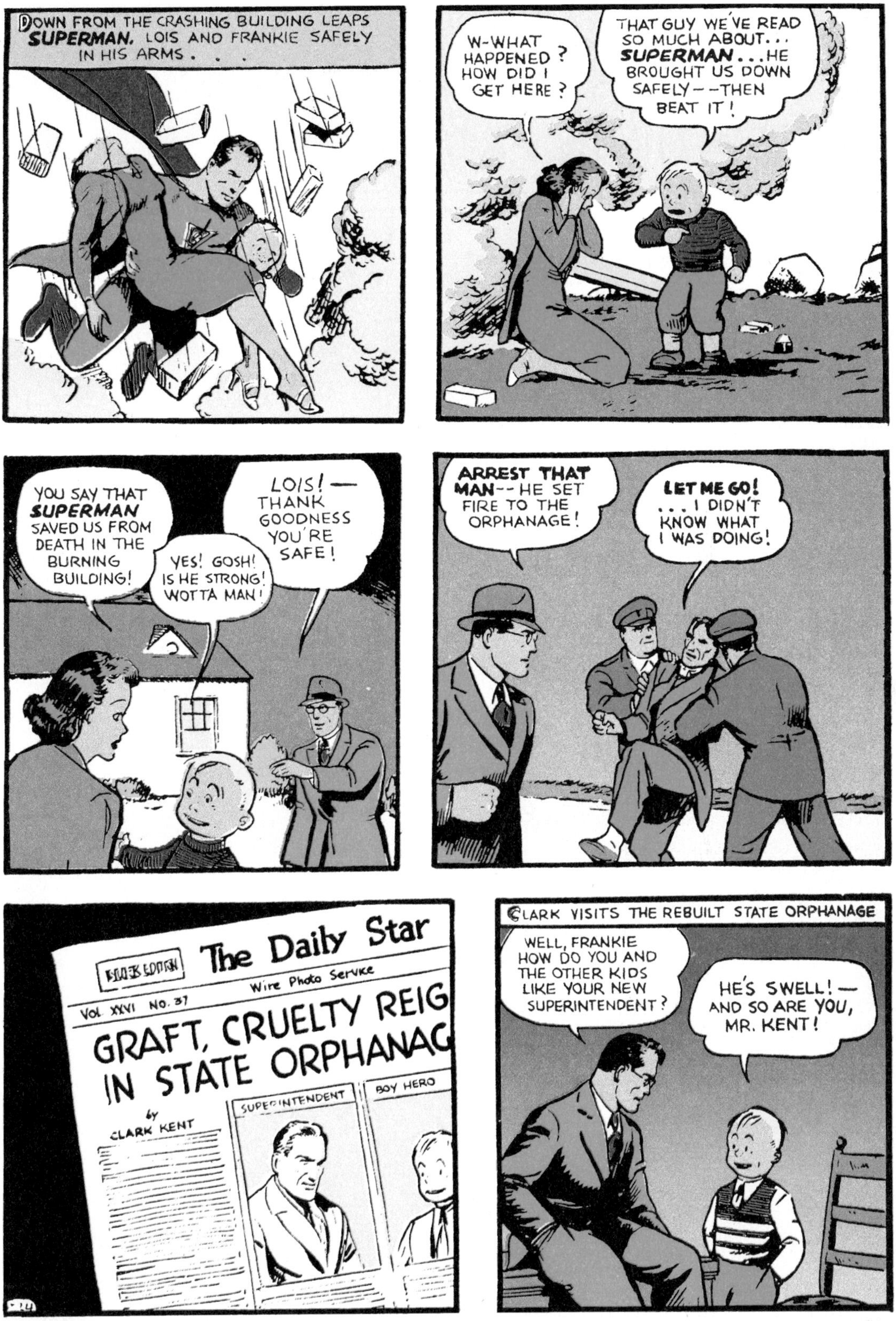
DOWN FROM THE CRASHING BUILDING LEAPS SUPERMAN, LOIS AND FRANKIE SAFELY IN HIS ARMS . . .
W-WHAT HAPPENED? HOW DID I GET HERE?
THAT GUY WE'VE READ SO MUCH ABOUT... SUPERMAN...HE BROUGHT US DOWN SAFELY--THEN BEAT IT!
YOU SAY THAT SUPERMAN SAVED US FROM DEATH IN THE BURNING BUILDING!
YES! GOSH! IS HE STRONG! WOTTA MAN!
LOIS!— THANK GOODNESS YOU'RE SAFE!
ARREST THAT MAN--HE SET FIRE TO THE ORPHANAGE!
LET ME GO! ...I DIDN'T KNOW WHAT I WAS DOING!
The Daily Star
Wire Photo Service
Vol. XXVI No. 37
GRAFT, CRUELTY REIG
IN STATE ORPHANAG
by CLARK KENT
SUPERINTENDENT
BOY HERO
CLARK VISITS THE REBUILT STATE ORPHANAGE
WELL, FRANKIE HOW DO YOU AND THE OTHER KIDS LIKE YOUR NEW SUPERINTENDENT?
HE'S SWELL!— AND SO ARE YOU, MR. KENT!

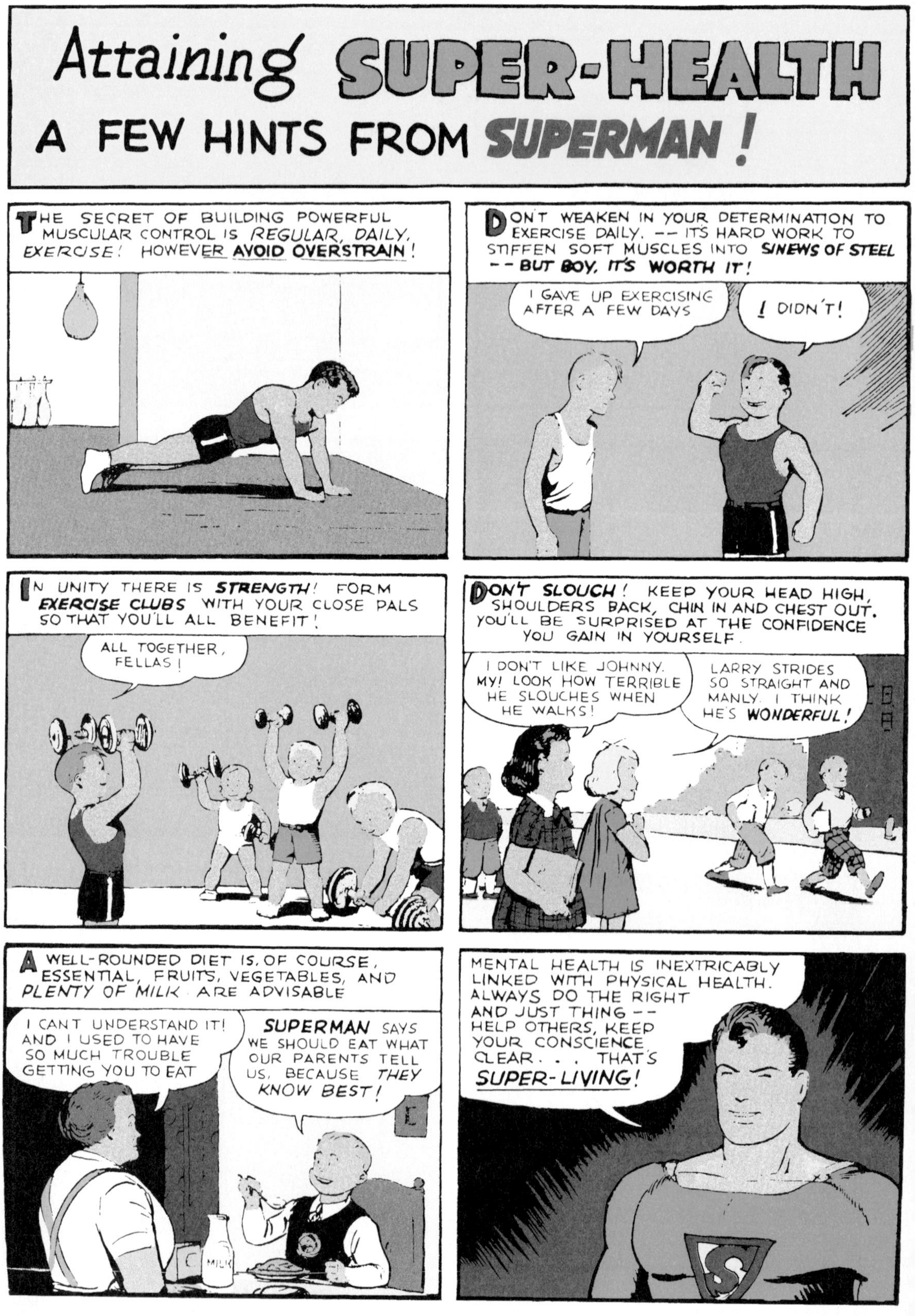
Attaining SUPER-HEALTH
A FEW HINTS FROM SUPERMAN!
THE SECRET OF BUILDING POWERFUL MUSCULAR CONTROL IS REGULAR, DAILY, EXERCISE! HOWEVER AVOID OVERSTRAIN!
DON'T WEAKEN IN YOUR DETERMINATION TO EXERCISE DAILY. -- IT'S HARD WORK TO STIFFEN SOFT MUSCLES INTO SINEWS OF STEEL -- BUT BOY, IT'S WORTH IT!
I GAVE UP EXERCISING AFTER A FEW DAYS
I DIDN'T!
IN UNITY THERE IS STRENGTH! FORM EXERCISE CLUBS WITH YOUR CLOSE PALS SO THAT YOU'LL ALL BENEFIT!
ALL TOGETHER, FELLAS!
DON'T SLOUCH! KEEP YOUR HEAD HIGH, SHOULDERS BACK, CHIN IN AND CHEST OUT. YOU'LL BE SURPRISED AT THE CONFIDENCE YOU GAIN IN YOURSELF.
I DON'T LIKE JOHNNY. MY! LOOK HOW TERRIBLE HE SLOUCHES WHEN HE WALKS!
LARRY STRIDES SO STRAIGHT AND MANLY. I THINK HE'S WONDERFUL!
A WELL-ROUNDED DIET IS, OF COURSE, ESSENTIAL, FRUITS, VEGETABLES, AND PLENTY OF MILK ARE ADVISABLE
I CANT UNDERSTAND IT! AND I USED TO HAVE SO MUCH TROUBLE GETTING YOU TO EAT
SUPERMAN SAYS WE SHOULD EAT WHAT OUR PARENTS TELL US, BECAUSE THEY KNOW BEST!
MILK
MENTAL HEALTH IS INEXTRICABLY LINKED WITH PHYSICAL HEALTH. ALWAYS DO THE RIGHT AND JUST THING -- HELP OTHERS, KEEP YOUR CONSCIENCE CLEAR. . . THAT'S SUPER-LIVING!

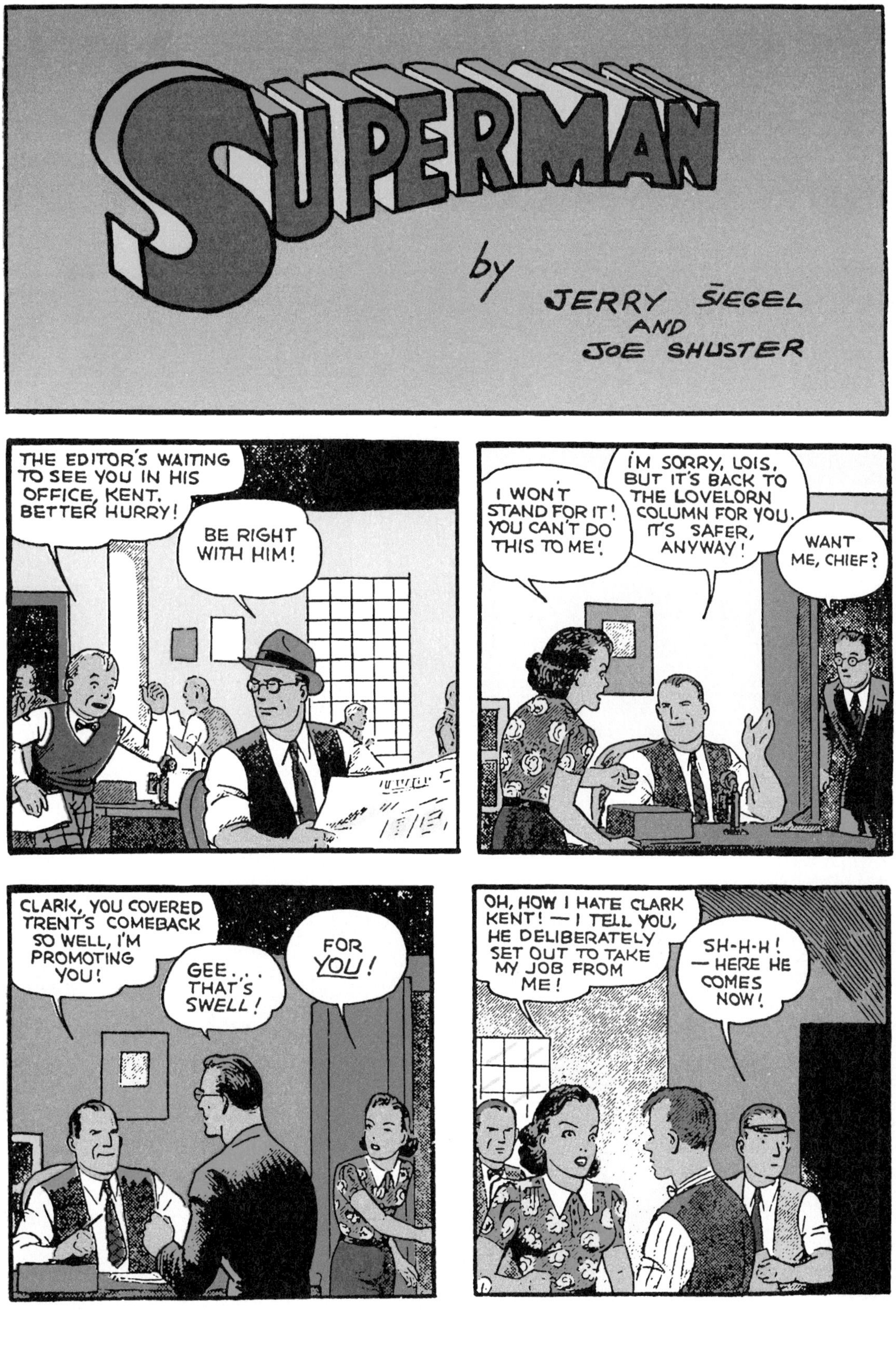
SUPERMAN
by
JERRY SIEGEL
AND
JOE SHUSTER
THE EDITOR'S WAITING TO SEE YOU IN HIS OFFICE, KENT. BETTER HURRY!
BE RIGHT WITH HIM!
I WON'T STAND FOR IT! YOU CAN'T DO THIS TO ME!
I'M SORRY, LOIS, BUT IT'S BACK TO THE LOVELORN COLUMN FOR YOU. IT'S SAFER, ANYWAY!
WANT ME, CHIEF?
CLARK, YOU COVERED TRENT'S COMEBACK SO WELL, I'M PROMOTING YOU!
GEE... THAT'S SWELL!
FOR YOU!
OH, HOW I HATE CLARK KENT! — I TELL YOU, HE DELIBERATELY SET OUT TO TAKE MY JOB FROM ME!
SH-H-H! — HERE HE COMES NOW!

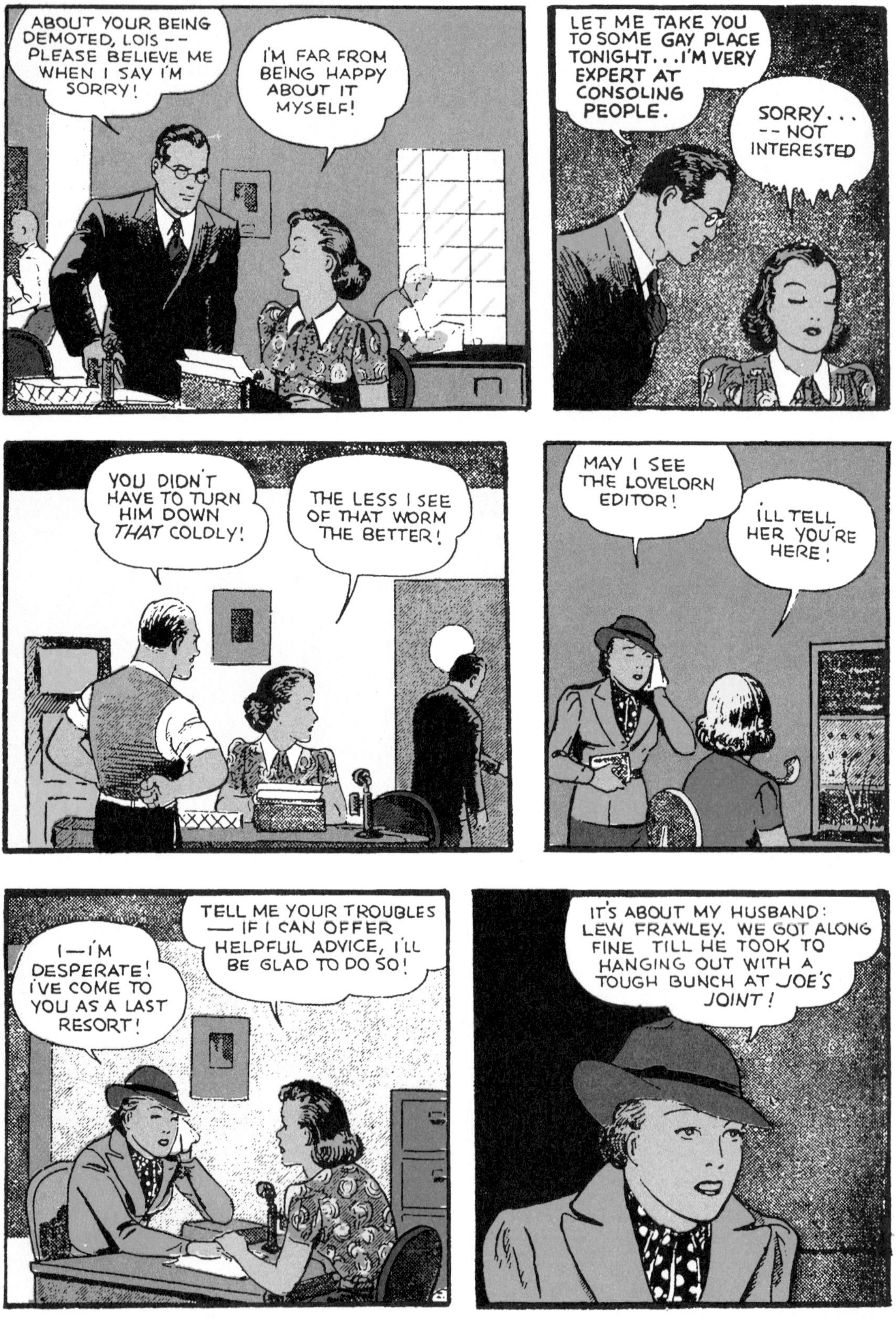
ABOUT YOUR BEING DEMOTED, LOIS -- PLEASE BELIEVE ME WHEN I SAY I'M SORRY!
I'M FAR FROM BEING HAPPY ABOUT IT MYSELF!
LET ME TAKE YOU TO SOME GAY PLACE TONIGHT...I'M VERY EXPERT AT CONSOLING PEOPLE.
SORRY... -- NOT INTERESTED
YOU DIDN'T HAVE TO TURN HIM DOWN *THAT* COLDLY!
THE LESS I SEE OF THAT WORM THE BETTER!
MAY I SEE THE LOVELORN EDITOR!
I'LL TELL HER YOU'RE HERE!
I—I'M DESPERATE! I'VE COME TO YOU AS A LAST RESORT!
TELL ME YOUR TROUBLES — IF I CAN OFFER HELPFUL ADVICE, I'LL BE GLAD TO DO SO!
IT'S ABOUT MY HUSBAND: LEW FRAWLEY. WE GOT ALONG FINE TILL HE TOOK TO HANGING OUT WITH A TOUGH BUNCH AT *JOE'S JOINT*!

NOW HE RARELY COMES HOME . . . WHEN HE DOES, HE BEATS ME! -- THIS IS A PHOTO OF HIM.
AND WORSE -- I THINK HE'S JOINED A GANG OF SMUGGLERS!
GIVE ME A FEW DAYS.— PERHAPS I'LL BE ABLE TO HELP YOU GET YOUR HUSBAND BACK. -- ("— GOLLY! THIS SOUNDS LIKE THE TIP TO A GREAT STORY THAT MAY WIN ME BACK MY NEWS REPORTER JOB!—")
BR-RR! — DID LOIS TURN ME DOWN COLD WHEN I ASKED FOR THAT DATE!
I'VE CHANGED MY MIND, CLARK. I'D BE DELIGHTED TO ACCOMPANY YOU TONIGHT!
YOU WHAT-? G-GOSH! -- THAT'S GREAT!
THAT EVENING
MIND IF I INSTRUCT THE CAB DRIVER WHERE TO GO?
NOT AT ALL!
JOE'S JOINT! —WHY, THIS IS ONE OF THE TOUGHEST JOINTS ON THE WATERFRONT!
I KNOW IT! S'MATTER? AFRAID TO ENTER?
JOE'S JOINT

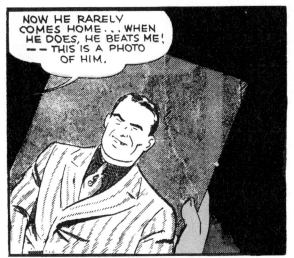

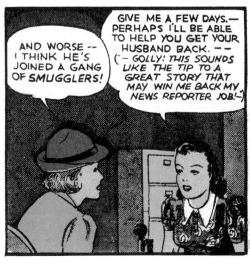

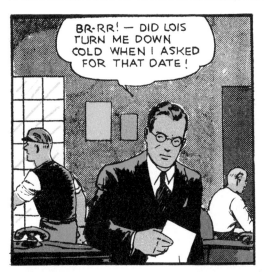

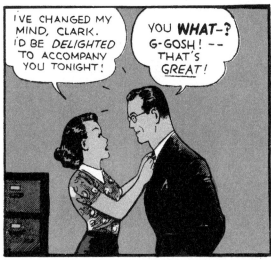

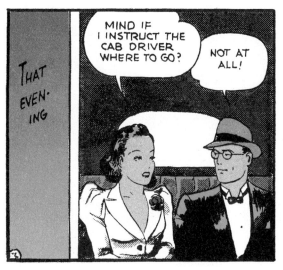

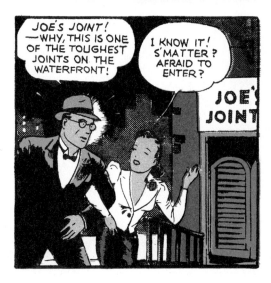

IT WAS STUBBORN AND DANGEROUS FOR YOU TO INSIST WE COME HERE!
NOT SCARED, ARE YOU? — A LITTLE SLUMMING WILL DO YOU GOOD!
("—THE MAN AT THAT TABLE... HE'S LEW FRAWLEY! —I'VE GOT TO CATCH HIS ATTENTION!—")
DELIBERATELY, LOIS WINKS.. !
UM-MM! — IS THAT GOOD-LOOKER GIVIN' YOU TH' EYE!
WATCH ME GIVE 'ER A BREAK AN' CUT IN!
GO TO IT, LEW!
HI-YA, BABE! — HOW'S ABOUT YOU AN' ME DANCIN'?
HOLD ON! THIS ISN'T A "CUT-IN" DANCE!
DON'T GET FLIP WID ME! —BEAT IT, PUNK!
ULP-!

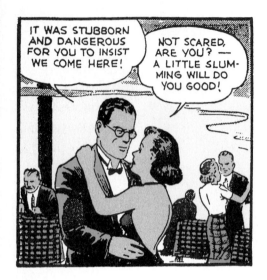

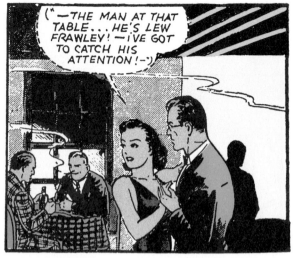

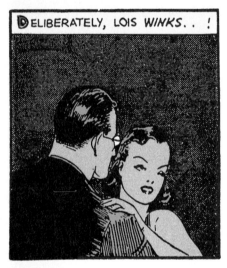

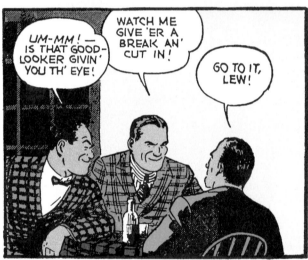

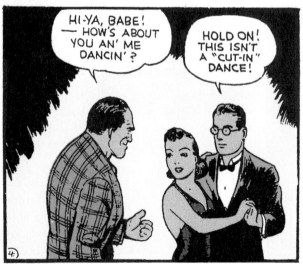

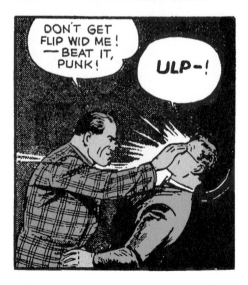

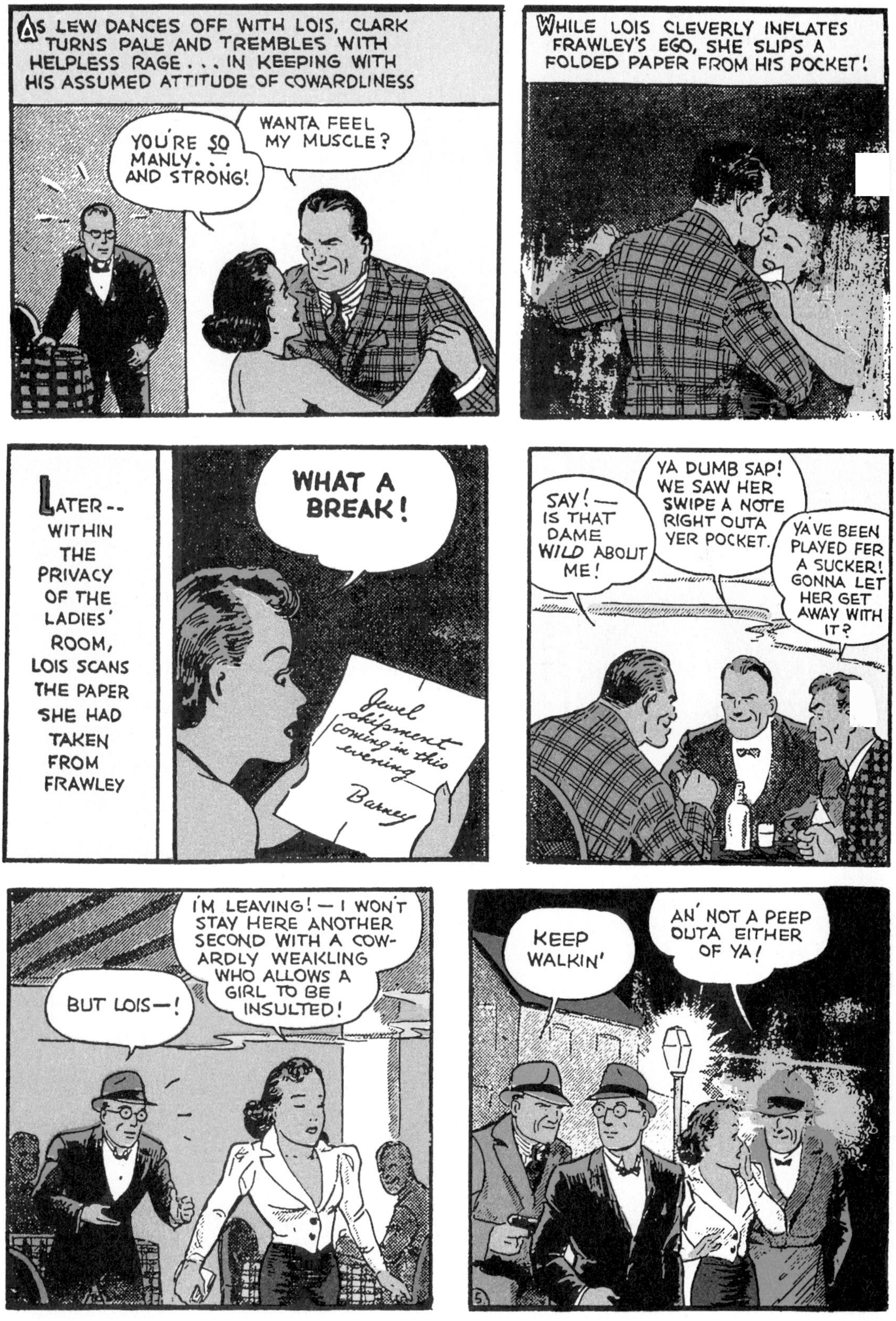
AS LEW DANCES OFF WITH LOIS, CLARK TURNS PALE AND TREMBLES WITH HELPLESS RAGE . . . IN KEEPING WITH HIS ASSUMED ATTITUDE OF COWARDLINESS
WANTA FEEL MY MUSCLE?
YOU'RE SO MANLY. . . AND STRONG!
WHILE LOIS CLEVERLY INFLATES FRAWLEY'S EGO, SHE SLIPS A FOLDED PAPER FROM HIS POCKET!
LATER -- WITHIN THE PRIVACY OF THE LADIES' ROOM, LOIS SCANS THE PAPER SHE HAD TAKEN FROM FRAWLEY
WHAT A BREAK!
Jewel shipment coming in this evening — Barney
SAY! — IS THAT DAME WILD ABOUT ME!
YA DUMB SAP! WE SAW HER SWIPE A NOTE RIGHT OUTA YER POCKET.
YA'VE BEEN PLAYED FER A SUCKER! GONNA LET HER GET AWAY WITH IT?
I'M LEAVING! — I WON'T STAY HERE ANOTHER SECOND WITH A COWARDLY WEAKLING WHO ALLOWS A GIRL TO BE INSULTED!
BUT LOIS—!
KEEP WALKIN'
AN' NOT A PEEP OUTA EITHER OF YA!

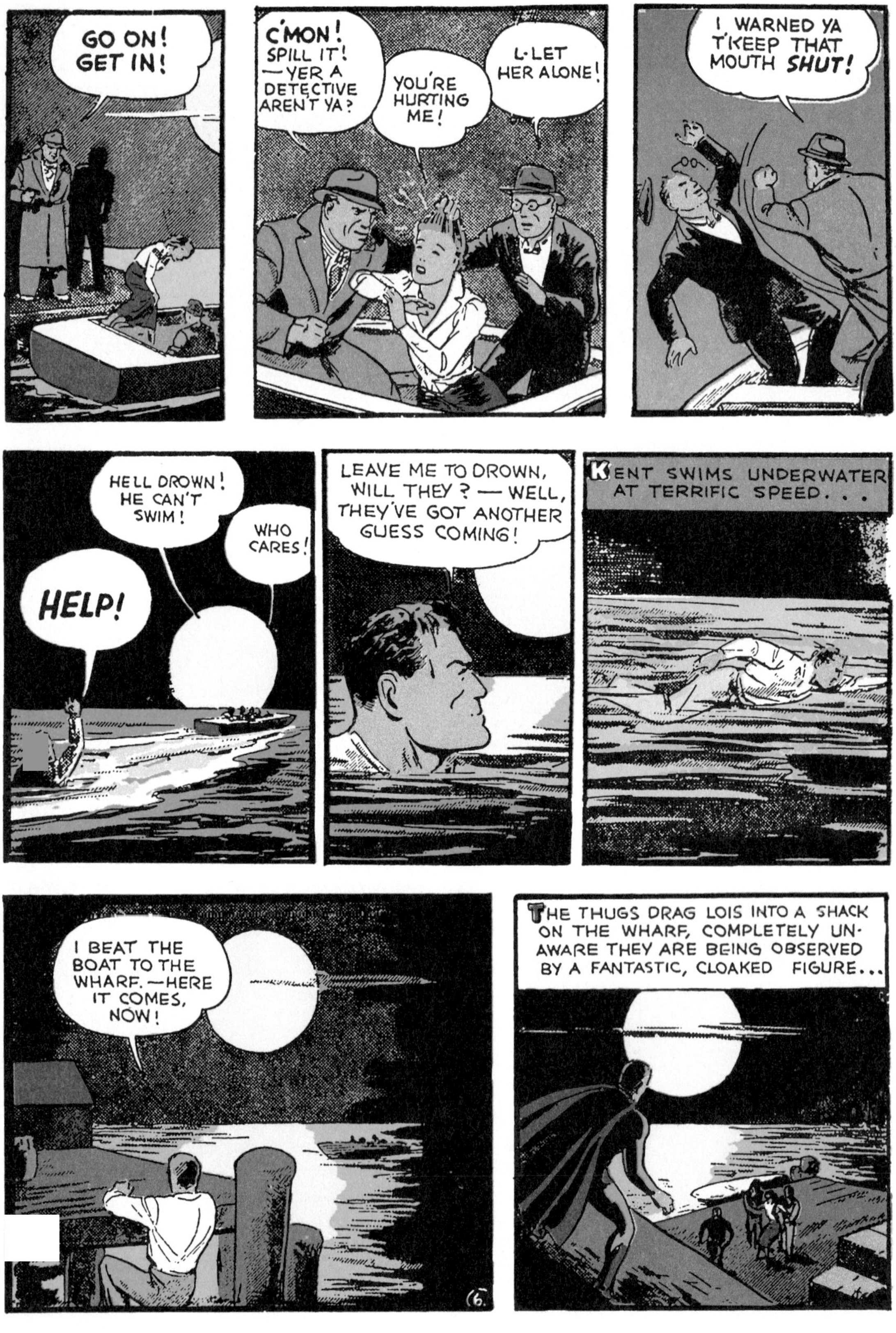
GO ON! GET IN!
C'MON! SPILL IT! —YER A DETECTIVE AREN'T YA?
YOU'RE HURTING ME!
L-LET HER ALONE!
I WARNED YA T'KEEP THAT MOUTH SHUT!
HE'LL DROWN! HE CAN'T SWIM!
WHO CARES!
HELP!
LEAVE ME TO DROWN, WILL THEY? — WELL, THEY'VE GOT ANOTHER GUESS COMING!
KENT SWIMS UNDERWATER AT TERRIFIC SPEED. . .
I BEAT THE BOAT TO THE WHARF. —HERE IT COMES, NOW!
THE THUGS DRAG LOIS INTO A SHACK ON THE WHARF, COMPLETELY UN-AWARE THEY ARE BEING OBSERVED BY A FANTASTIC, CLOAKED FIGURE...

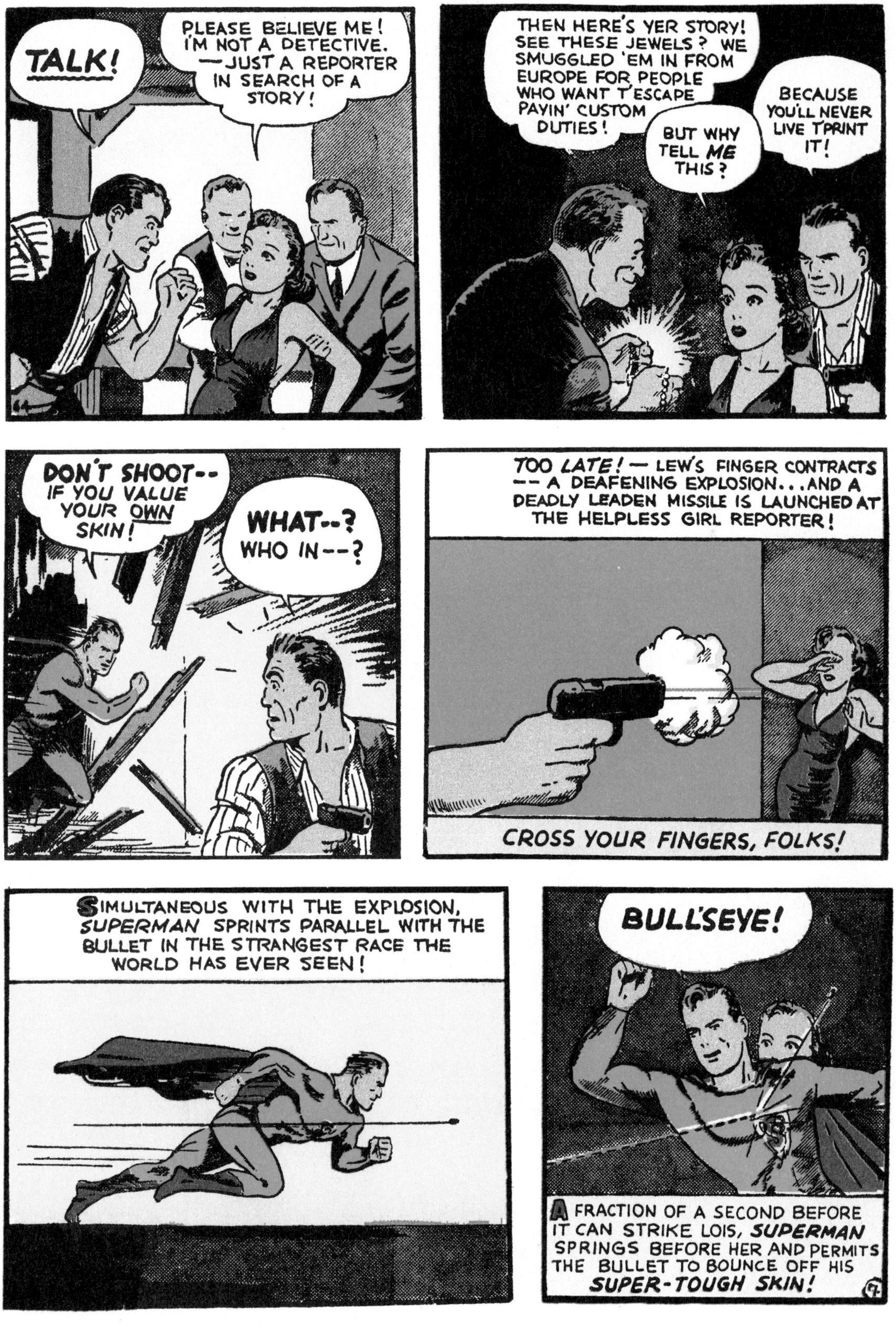
TALK!
PLEASE BELIEVE ME! I'M NOT A DETECTIVE. —JUST A REPORTER IN SEARCH OF A STORY!
THEN HERE'S YER STORY! SEE THESE JEWELS? WE SMUGGLED 'EM IN FROM EUROPE FOR PEOPLE WHO WANT T'ESCAPE PAYIN' CUSTOM DUTIES!
BUT WHY TELL ME THIS?
BECAUSE YOU'LL NEVER LIVE T'PRINT IT!
DON'T SHOOT-- IF YOU VALUE YOUR OWN SKIN!
WHAT--? WHO IN--?
TOO LATE! — LEW'S FINGER CONTRACTS -- A DEAFENING EXPLOSION... AND A DEADLY LEADEN MISSILE IS LAUNCHED AT THE HELPLESS GIRL REPORTER!
CROSS YOUR FINGERS, FOLKS!
SIMULTANEOUS WITH THE EXPLOSION, SUPERMAN SPRINTS PARALLEL WITH THE BULLET IN THE STRANGEST RACE THE WORLD HAS EVER SEEN!
BULL'SEYE!
A FRACTION OF A SECOND BEFORE IT CAN STRIKE LOIS, SUPERMAN SPRINGS BEFORE HER AND PERMITS THE BULLET TO BOUNCE OFF HIS SUPER-TOUGH SKIN!
7

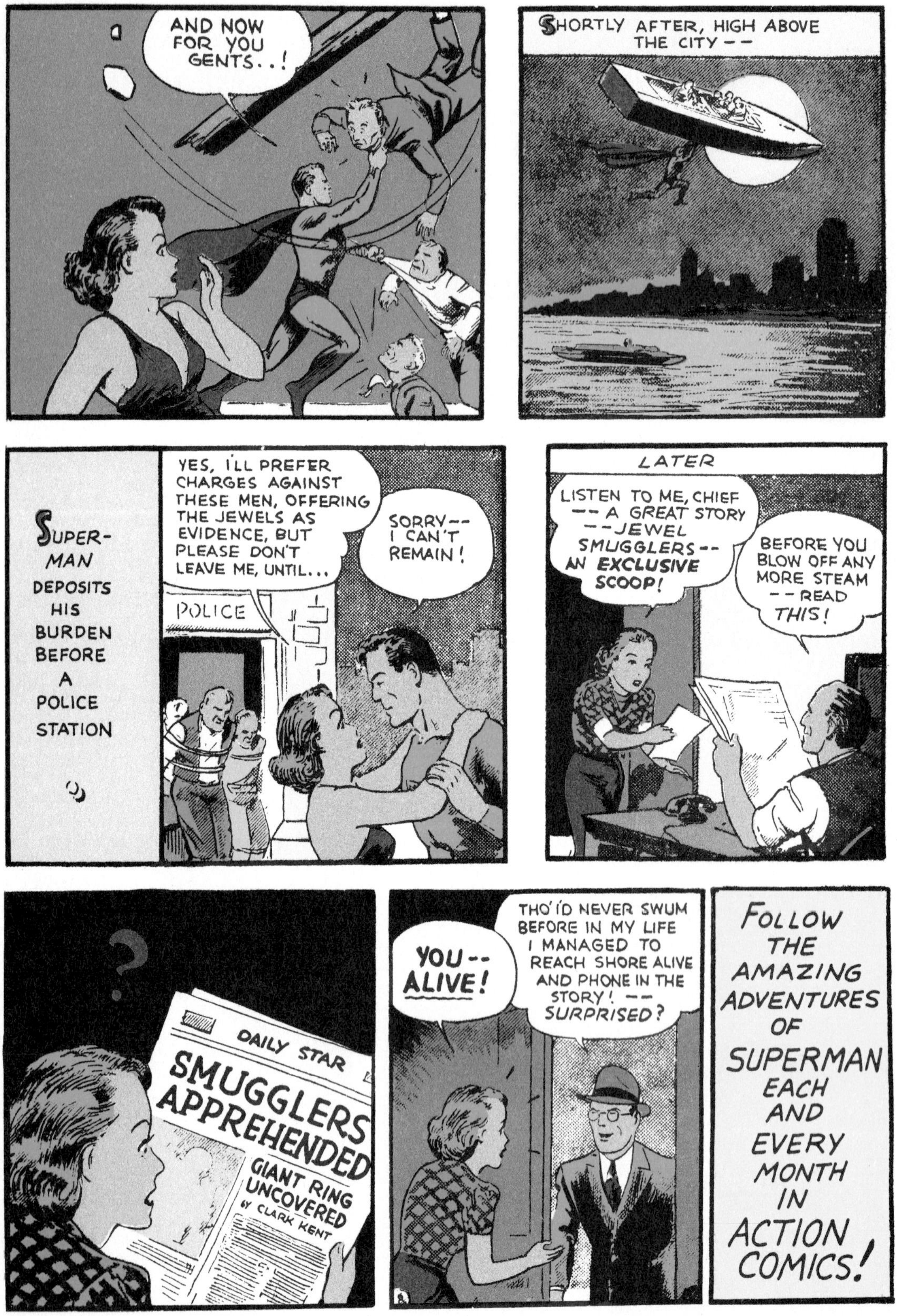
AND NOW FOR YOU GENTS..!
SHORTLY AFTER, HIGH ABOVE THE CITY --
SUPERMAN DEPOSITS HIS BURDEN BEFORE A POLICE STATION
YES, I'LL PREFER CHARGES AGAINST THESE MEN, OFFERING THE JEWELS AS EVIDENCE, BUT PLEASE DON'T LEAVE ME, UNTIL...
SORRY-- I CAN'T REMAIN!
POLICE
LATER
LISTEN TO ME, CHIEF -- A GREAT STORY --JEWEL SMUGGLERS -- AN EXCLUSIVE SCOOP!
BEFORE YOU BLOW OFF ANY MORE STEAM -- READ THIS!
?
DAILY STAR
SMUGGLERS APPREHENDED
GIANT RING UNCOVERED
BY CLARK KENT
YOU-- ALIVE!
THO' I'D NEVER SWUM BEFORE IN MY LIFE I MANAGED TO REACH SHORE ALIVE AND PHONE IN THE STORY! -- SURPRISED?
FOLLOW THE AMAZING ADVENTURES OF SUPERMAN EACH AND EVERY MONTH IN ACTION COMICS!

BIOGRAPHIES

JERRY SIEGEL

Born in 1914 in Cleveland, Ohio, Jerome Siegel was, as a teenager, a fan of the emerging literary genre that came to be known as science fiction. Together with schoolmate Joe Shuster, Siegel published several science-fiction fan magazines, and in 1933 they came up with their own science-fiction hero – Superman. Siegel scripted and Shuster drew several weeks' worth of newspaper strips featuring their new creation, but garnered no interest from publishers or newspaper syndicates. It wasn't until the two established themselves as reliable adventure-strip creators at DC Comics that the editors at DC offered to take a chance on the Superman material – provided it was re-pasted into comic-book format for DC's new magazine, ACTION COMICS.

Siegel wrote the adventures of Superman (as well as other DC heroes) through 1948 and then again from 1959-1966, in the interim scripting several newspaper strips including *Funnyman* and *Ken Winston*. Jerry Siegel died in January, 1996.

JOE SHUSTER

Joseph Shuster was born in 1914 in Toronto, Canada. When he was nine, his family moved to Cleveland, Ohio, where Shuster met Jerry Siegel. The two became fast friends and collaborators; together, they published the earliest science-fiction fan magazines, where Shuster honed his fledgling art skills. In 1936, he and Siegel began providing DC Comics with such new features as DR. OCCULT, SLAM BRADLEY and RADIO SQUAD before selling Superman to DC in 1938.

Influenced by such comic-strip greats as *Wash Tubbs'* Roy Crane, Joe Shuster drew Superman through 1947, after which he left comic books to create the comic strip *Funnyman*, again with Siegel. Failing eyesight cut short his career, but not before his place in the history of American culture was assured. Shuster died of heart failure on July 30, 1992.

THE GOLDEN AGE

SUPERMAN

VOLUME ONE